NOR : RA

D0301627

WITHDRAWN
FROM STOCK

NORLINK ITEM

3 0129 022 695 218

THE VICTORIA HISTORY
OF THE
COUNTIES OF ENGLAND

———

A HISTORY OF
WILTSHIRE

VOLUME XI

THE VICTORIA HISTORY
OF THE
COUNTIES OF ENGLAND

EDITED BY C. R. ELRINGTON

THE UNIVERSITY OF LONDON
INSTITUTE OF
HISTORICAL RESEARCH

Oxford University Press, Walton Street, Oxford OX2 6DP

OXFORD LONDON GLASGOW
NEW YORK TORONTO MELBOURNE WELLINGTON
KUALA LUMPUR SINGAPORE HONG KONG TOKYO
DELHI BOMBAY CALCUTTA MADRAS KARACHI
NAIROBI DAR ES SALAAM CAPE TOWN

© *University of London 1980*

ISBN 0 19 722751 1

NOR·RA

NORTH TYNESIDE LIBRARIES

NORFOLK LIBRARY AND INFORMATION SERVICE	
SUPPLIER	NTC
INVOICE No.	13
ORDER DATE	10-4-95
COPY No.	

R942·31

*Printed in Great Britain
at the University Press, Oxford
by Eric Buckley
Printer to the University*

INSCRIBED TO THE
MEMORY OF HER LATE MAJESTY

QUEEN VICTORIA

WHO GRACIOUSLY GAVE THE TITLE TO

AND ACCEPTED THE DEDICATION

OF THIS HISTORY

STOCKTON HOUSE: THE DRAWING-ROOM

A HISTORY OF
WILTSHIRE

EDITED BY D. A. CROWLEY

VOLUME XI

DOWNTON HUNDRED

ELSTUB AND EVERLEIGH HUNDRED

PUBLISHED FOR

THE INSTITUTE OF HISTORICAL RESEARCH

BY

OXFORD UNIVERSITY PRESS

1980

Distributed by Oxford University Press until 1 January 1983
thereafter by Dawsons of Pall Mall

CONTENTS OF VOLUME ELEVEN

LIST OF ILLUSTRATIONS

Thanks are rendered to the following for permission to reproduce material and for the loan of photographs: B. T. Batsford Ltd., his grace the Duke of Beaufort, P.C., K.G., G.C.V.O., the Trustees of the British Museum, Brig. Sir Richard Anstruther-Gough-Calthorpe, Bt., C.B.E., LL.D., D.L., the Cambridge University Committee for Aerial Photography, *Country Life*, the Courtauld Institute of Art (for photographs of the Buckler paintings), Downton Tanning Co. Ltd., Mr. George Jeffreys, the National Monuments Record, Capt. D. A. P. O'Reilly, R.N., Mrs. Ralph Partridge, the Salisbury and South Wiltshire Museum, the Wiltshire Archaeological Society, and the Wiltshire Record Office. Photographs dated 1977 and 1978 are by A. P. Baggs.

b 2

LIST OF ILLUSTRATIONS

LIST OF MAPS

All the maps were drawn by K. J. Wass, of the Department of Geography, University College, London, from drafts prepared by D. A. Crowley and Janet H. Stevenson. The parish, tithing, and township boundaries on the hundred and parish maps are taken from inclosure maps and from the tithe maps of the earlier 19th century.

EDITORIAL NOTE

THE present volume, the twelfth in the Wiltshire series to be published, has been prepared like its predecessors under the superintendence of the Wiltshire Victoria County History Committee. The origin and early constitution of the Committee were described in the Editorial Note to the *Victoria History of Wiltshire*, Volume VII. In 1975 the Committee adopted a new constitution and a new system of management, under which it provides the funds for the Institute of Historical Research of the University of London to employ the Wiltshire Editor and Assistant Editors and to meet other necessary expenses. The District Councils of Kennet, Salisbury, North Wiltshire, and West Wiltshire were invited to join the Wiltshire County Council and Thamesdown District Council in contributing to the funds and in sending representatives to the Committee. Each of them has done so, and the University has pleasure in expressing its gratitude to all those Local Authorities and to the Committee for their generous co-operation in enabling it to continue publication of the Wiltshire *History*.

Group Captain F. A. Willan, C.B.E., D.F.C., D.L., Chairman of the Wiltshire County Council, has continued as Chairman of the Committee. Miss Elizabeth Crittall, Assistant Editor from 1948 when full-time work on the Wiltshire *History* began and Editor from 1955, retired at the end of July 1977. Dr. D. A. Crowley, formerly Assistant Editor, succeeded her, and in May 1978 Miss Jane Freeman became Assistant Editor.

Thanks are rendered to many people who have helped in the compilation of the volume by granting access to documents and buildings in their care or ownership, by giving information, or by offering advice. Many are named in the footnotes or in the preamble to the List of Illustrations. The death in 1978 of Mr. R. E. Sandell, Honorary Librarian of the Wiltshire Archaeological and Natural History Society and a long-standing member of the Wiltshire Victoria County History Committee, to whose knowledge and friendly assistance this volume, like earlier ones, owes very much, is recorded with great regret. Special mention must also be made of the help given in many ways by the Wiltshire County Archivist and his staff both at Trowbridge and in Salisbury, by the Hampshire County Archivist and her staff, by the Librarian of Winchester cathedral (the Revd. Canon F. Bussby), and by the Archivist of Winchester College (Mr. Peter Gwyn).

An outline of the structure and aims of the series as a whole, as also of its origins and progress, is included in the *General Introduction* to the *Victoria History* (1970).

WILTSHIRE
VICTORIA COUNTY HISTORY COMMITTEE

As at 1 January 1979

GROUP CAPT. F. A. WILLAN, C.B.E., D.F.C., D.L., *Chairman* ⎞ *Representing the Wiltshire County Council*
MR. N. J. M. ANDERSON, M.C., D.L. ⎠

COUNCILLOR A. J. MASTERS ⎞ *Representing the Thamesdown Borough*
COUNCILLOR L. M. SMITH ⎠ *Council*

COUNCILLOR D. G. WADDILOVE — *Representing the Kennet District Council*

COUNCILLOR MRS. S. E. STRATTON — *Representing the Salisbury District Council*

COUNCILLOR MRS. A. M. C. BRAKSPEAR — *Representing the North Wiltshire District Council*

COUNCILLOR MRS. A. M. CASE — *Representing the West Wiltshire District Council*

MR. C. R. ELRINGTON — *Representing the Central Committee of the Victoria County History*

Co-opted Members

DR. R. F. HUNNISETT   DR. G. D. RAMSAY
DR. J. H. P. PAFFORD, D.LIT.   DR. C. F. SLADE

MR. D. M. KENT, *Hon. Secretary*
MR. E. J. P. THORNTON, *Hon. Treasurer*

LIST OF CLASSES OF DOCUMENTS
IN THE PUBLIC RECORD OFFICE
USED IN THIS VOLUME
WITH THEIR CLASS NUMBERS

Air Ministry
    Air 2   General Correspondence
    Air 28   Stations Operation Record Books

Chancery
        Proceedings
    C 1   Early
    C 2   Series I
    C 3   Series II
    C 54   Close Rolls
    C 66   Patent Rolls
    C 78   Decree Rolls
    C 115   Masters' Exhibits, Duchess of Norfolk Deeds
        Inquisitions post mortem
    C 134   Series I, Edw. II
    C 136   Ric. II
    C 137   Hen. IV
    C 138   Hen. V
    C 139   Hen. VI
    C 140   Edw. IV and V
    C 142   Series II
    C 143   Inquisitions ad quod damnum
    C 145   Miscellaneous Inquisitions
    C 146   Ancient Deeds, Series C

Court of Common Pleas
        Feet of Fines
    C.P. 25 (1)   Series I
    C.P. 25 (2)   Series II
    C.P. 40   Plea Rolls
    C.P. 43   Recovery Rolls

Duchy of Lancaster
    D.L. 1   Equity Proceedings, Pleadings
    D.L. 3   Depositions and Examinations, Series I
    D.L. 29   Ministers' Accounts
    D.L. 30   Court Rolls
    D.L. 41   Miscellanea
    D.L. 42   Miscellaneous Books
    D.L. 43   Rentals and Surveys
    D.L. 44   Special Commissions and Returns

Exchequer, King's Remembrancer
    E 106   Extents of Alien Priories, etc.
    E 126   Entry Books of Decrees and Orders, Series IV
    E 134   Depositions taken by Commission
    E 149   Inquisitions post mortem, Series I
    E 159   Memoranda Rolls
    E 178   Special Commissions of Inquiry
    E 179   Subsidy Rolls etc.

Exchequer, Augmentation Office
    E 301   Certificates of Colleges and Chantries
    E 317   Parliamentary Surveys

    E 318   Particulars for Grants of Crown Lands

Exchequer, Lord Treasurer's Remembrancer's and Pipe Offices
    E 372   Pipe Rolls

Exchequer, Exchequer of Receipt
    E 407   Miscellanea

Home Office
        Census Papers
    H.O. 107   Population Returns
    H.O. 129   Ecclesiastical Returns

Inland Revenue
    I.R. 29   Tithe Apportionments
    I.R. 30   Tithe Maps

Supreme Court of Judicature
    J 4   Affidavits, Series I
    J 15   Entry Books of Decrees and Orders (Chancery Division)

Justices Itinerant, Assize and Gaol Delivery Justices, etc.
    J.I. 1   Eyre Rolls, Assize Rolls, etc.

Court of King's Bench (Crown Side)
    K.B. 26   Curia Regis Rolls

Ministry of Health
    M.H. 12   Poor-Law Union Papers

Maps and Plans
    M.R.   Maps, plans, or pictures taken from various classes

Privy Council Office
    P.C. 1   Papers, mainly unbound

Probate
    Prob. 11   Registered Copies of Wills proved in Prerogative Court of Canterbury

Court of Requests
    Req. 2   Proceedings

Special Collections
    S.C. 2   Court Rolls
    S.C. 6   Ministers' and Receivers' Accounts
    S.C. 12   Rentals and Surveys (Portfolios)

Court of Star Chamber
    Sta. Cha. 8   Proceedings, Jas. I

Court of Wards and Liveries
    Wards 2   Deeds and Evidences
    Wards 7   Inquisitions post mortem

NOTE ON ABBREVIATIONS

Among the abbreviations and short titles used are the following, in addition to those listed in the Victoria History's *Handbook for Editors and Authors*.

Acct. of Wilts. Schs.	*An Account of Schools for the Children of the Labouring Classes in the County of Wiltshire*, H.C. 27 (1859 Sess. 1), xxi (2)
Aubrey, *Nat. Hist. Wilts.* ed. Britton	John Aubrey, *Natural History of Wiltshire*, ed. John Britton (London, 1847)
Aubrey, *Topog. Coll.* ed. Jackson	*The Topographical Collections of John Aubrey*, ed. J. E. Jackson (Devizes, 1862)
C.C.C., Oxf.	Corpus Christi College, Oxford
Cal. Feet of F. Wilts. 1195–1272, ed. Fry	*A Calendar of the Feet of Fines relating to Wiltshire, 1195–1272*, ed. E. A. Fry (Devizes, 1930)
Ch. Commrs.	Church Commissioners
Char. Com.	Charity Commission
Colvin, *Brit. Architects*	H. M. Colvin, *Biographical Dictionary of British Architects, 1600–1840* (London, 1978)
D. & C. Winton.	Dean and Chapter of Winchester
Dors. R.O.	Dorset Record Office
Educ. Enquiry Abstract	*Abstract of Returns relative to the State of Education in England*, H.C. 62 (1835), xliii
Educ. of Poor Digest	*Digest of Returns to the Select Committee on the Education of the Poor*, H.C. 224 (1819), ix (2)
Endowed Char. Wilts.	*Endowed Charities of Wiltshire*, H.C. 273 (1908), lxxx (northern division); H.C. 273–i (1908), lxxxi (southern division)
Finberg, *Early Wessex Chart.*	H. P. R. Finberg, *Early Charters of Wessex* (Leicester, 1964)
Fry, *Land Utilisation Wilts.*	A. H. Fry, *Wiltshire* (Report of the Land Utilisation Survey of Britain, lxxxvii)
Glos. R.O.	Gloucestershire Record Office
H.R.O.	Hampshire Record Office
Hoare, *Mod. Wilts.*	Sir Richard Colt Hoare and others, *History of Modern Wiltshire* (London, 1822–43)
N.M.R.	National Monuments Record
N.R.A.	National Register of Archives
Nightingale, *Wilts. Plate*	J. E. Nightingale, *Church Plate of Wiltshire* (Salisbury, 1891)
P.N. Wilts. (E.P.N.S.)	J. E. B. Gover, Allen Mawer, and F. M. Stenton, *Place-Names of Wiltshire* (English Place-Name Society, xvi)
Pevsner, *Wilts.* (2nd edn.)	Nikolaus Pevsner, *Buildings of England: Wiltshire*, revised by Bridget Cherry (London, 1975)
Phillipps, *Wilts. Inst.*	*Institutiones Clericorum in Comitatu Wiltoniae*, ed. Sir Thomas Phillipps (priv. print. 1825)
Poor Law Com. 2nd Rep.	*Second Annual Report of the Poor Law Commissioners for England and Wales*, H.C. 595 (1836), xxix (1)
Rep. Com. Eccl. Revenues	*Report of the Commissioners appointed to Inquire into the Ecclesiastical Revenues of England and Wales* [67], H.C. (1835), xxii
Returns relating to Elem. Educ.	*Returns relating to Elementary Education*, H.C. 201 (1871), lv
Return of Non-Provided Schs.	*Return of Schools Recognised as Voluntary Public Elementary Schools*, H.C. 178–xxxi (1906), lxxxviii
S.R.O.	Somerset Record Office
Sar. Dioc. R.O.	Salisbury Diocesan Record Office
Sar. Dioc. Regy.	Salisbury Diocesan Registry
W.A.M.	*Wiltshire Archaeological and Natural History Magazine*
W.A.S.	Wiltshire Archaeological and Natural History Society
W.A.S. Libr.	Library of W.A.S. in the Museum, Long Street, Devizes
W.N. & Q.	*Wiltshire Notes and Queries* (8 vols. 1893–1916)
W.R.O.	Wiltshire Record Office

NOTE ON ABBREVIATIONS

W.R.S.	Wiltshire Record Society (*formerly* Records Branch of W.A.S.)
Walters, *Wilts. Bells*	H. B. Walters, *Church Bells of Wiltshire* (Devizes, 1927)
Wilts. Cuttings	Volumes of newspaper and other cuttings in W.A.S. Libr.
Wilts. Inq. p.m. 1242–1326 (Index Libr.)	*Abstracts of Wiltshire Inquisitiones post mortem in the reigns of Henry III, Edward I, and Edward II, 1242–1326*, ed. E. A. Fry (Index Library, xxxvii)
Wilts. Inq. p.m. 1327–77 (Index Libr.)	*Abstracts of Wiltshire Inquisitiones post mortem in the reign of Edward III, 1327–77*, ed. Ethel Stokes (Index Library, xlviii)
Wilts. Inq. p.m. 1625–49 (Index Libr.)	*Abstracts of Wiltshire Inquisitiones post mortem in the reign of Charles I, 1625–49*, ed. G. S. and E. A. Fry (Index Library, xxiii)
Wilts. Q. Sess. Rec. ed. Cunnington	*Extracts from the Quarter Sessions Great Rolls of the 17th Century*, ed. B. H. Cunnington (Devizes, 1932)
Wilts. Tracts	Collections of tracts in W.A.S. Libr.
Winch. Coll.	Winchester College

DOWNTON HUNDRED

THE hundred of Downton in 1831 was an aggregate of the hundred of Downton and the hundred or liberty of East Knoyle. It consisted of four physically separate pre-Reformation parishes, Downton and Bishopstone in the south-east of the county and East Knoyle and Fonthill Bishop in the south-west.[1] All the parishes except Fonthill were large, and the hundred contained some 25 villages and was divided into 13 administrative tithings. There were 4 medieval chapelries, and in the 19th century 6 additional civil parishes were recognized and 4 new ecclesiastical districts were created.

Downton hundred originated in grants of immunity for lands assessed at 100 hides, or of the land with its immunity, by Anglo-Saxon kings to bishops of Winchester.[2] The private hundred thus established, and the wide range of administrative and judicial liberties later held in respect of it, passed with the see.[3] The 100 hides was the assessment of a possibly unbroken tract of land extending from Downton in the Christchurch Avon valley perhaps far up the Ebble valley. Tenth-century alienations reduced the lands to the estates, later parishes, of Downton and Bishopstone but not the assessment or the bishops' liberties. The composition of the hundred was thereafter unaltered, and within it no lord inferior to the bishop withdrew his men from it. The rector of Downton and later the impropriators of the rectory held the only separate view of frankpledge. At least from the early 13th century the bishops held no court for the whole hundred but the tourns held for both Downton and Bishopstone, each attended by the tithingmen of several tithings, were like those of hundreds.[4]

About 1084 East Knoyle was in Mere hundred and Fonthill Bishop was in Dunworth hundred.[5] In the 13th century the bishops of Winchester, lords in both places, succeeded in withdrawing their men from those hundreds.[6] They took liberties similar to those enjoyed for Downton hundred and for both places exercised them in a tourn held for what by 1249 was called the hundred of East Knoyle.[7] Neither the lordship nor the composition of that hundred, which included Hindon, was changed. For purposes of privately exercised jurisdiction the hundred or liberty of Knoyle continued into the 19th century, but for other purposes its constituents had been added to Downton hundred by the 18th century.[8]

[1] *V.C.H. Wilts.* iv. 328.
[2] Eric John, *Orbis Britanniae*, 108–11; Helen M. Cam, *Law-Finders and Law-Makers*, 28, 62–3.
[3] See pp. 43–4.
[4] See pp. 15–16, 43–4. Rights of jurisdiction were alienated from the see in the mid 16th cent. by lease and royal grant.
[5] *V.C.H. Wilts.* ii, pp. 180–1, 208–9.
[6] *Rot. Hund.* (Rec. Com.), ii (1), 234.
[7] *Crown Pleas, 1249* (W.R.S. xvi), p. 187.
[8] e.g. *Q. Sess. 1736* (W.R.S. xi), p. 137.

DOWNTON HUNDRED c.1840

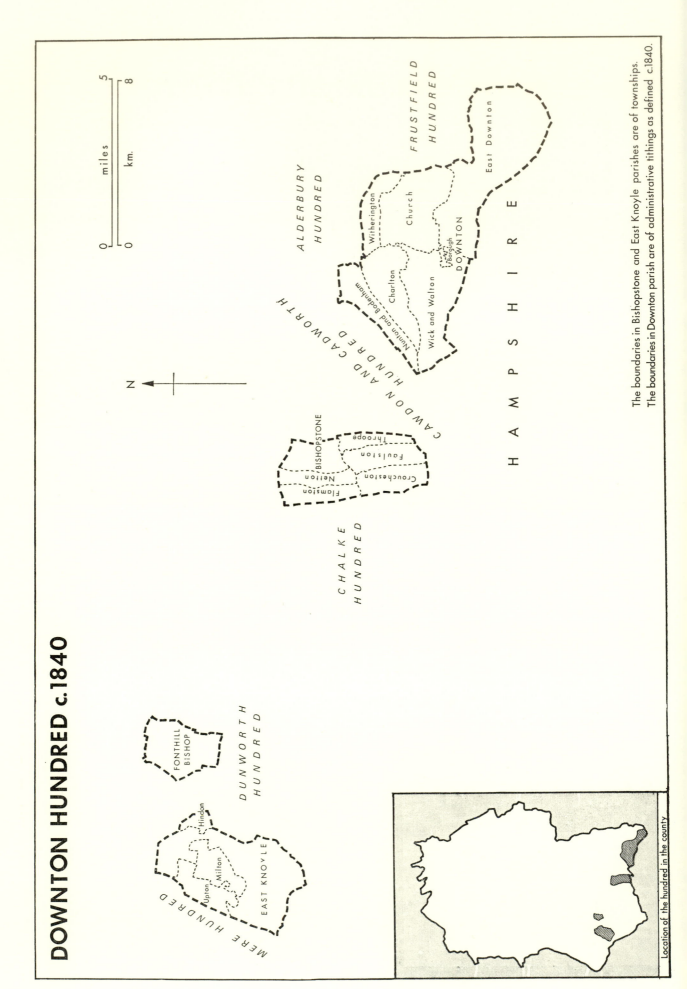

miles 0 — 5

km. 0 — 8

N

ALDERBURY HUNDRED

FRUSTFIELD HUNDRED

Witherington

Church

East Downton

Charlton

Nunton and Bodenham

Wick and Walton

Borough

DOWNTON

HAMPSHIRE

CAWDON AND CADWORTH HUNDRED

BISHOPSTONE

Netton

Throope

Flamston

Faulston

Croucheston

CHALKE HUNDRED

FONTHILL BISHOP

DUNWORTH HUNDRED

Hindon

Upton

Milton

EAST KNOYLE

MERE HUNDRED

The boundaries in Bishopstone and East Knoyle parishes are of townships.
The boundaries in Downton parish are of administrative tithings as defined c.1840.

Location of the hundred in the county

2

BISHOPSTONE

THE parish of Bishopstone, 1,882 ha. (4,649 a.), is 8 km. south-west of Salisbury.[1] Measuring 6 km. by 3 km. it forms a rectangle, lies north and south across the Ebble valley between Broad Chalke to the west and Stratford Tony to the east, and is bisected by the Ebble which flows west to east across it. On the downs to the north it marches with Wilton and Burcombe Without and on those to the south with Martin (Hants). The parish contains six ancient townships, each running back from a village by the river and reaching up to the down as a long narrow strip. Bishopstone, c. 905 a., Netton, c. 555 a., and Flamston, c. 670 a., lie north of the river, Throope, c. 468 a., Faulston, c. 940 a., and Croucheston, c. 910 a., lie opposite them south of the river.[2]

Before the 10th century the land of the modern parish almost certainly, and the land to the east of it probably, were part of a single estate called Downton.[3] In the later 10th century the whole of the Ebble valley between the Chalkes and the Avon valley lands of Downton was apparently called 'Ebbesborne', and land in that region was then separated from Downton to its east and Bishopstone to its west under royal charters.[4] Bishopstone, thus physically severed from Downton, established itself as a parish between 1086 and 1208, presumably when its church was built.[5] The parish at first retained the name 'Ebbesborne'. In the early Middle Ages the epithet 'Bishop's' was often used to distinguish it from Ebbesborne Wake further up the valley, and only in the later Middle Ages did 'Bishopston' become the parish's usual name.[6]

Bishopstone's western boundary was defined in a charter of Stoke Farthing in Broad Chalke of 955, and its eastern boundary in a charter of Stratford Tony of 986.[7] Both boundaries were essentially straight and possibly approximate to those of the modern parish, except that what is north of the Roman road in the modern parish of Stratford Tony remained in Bishopstone in 986. In 997 the bounds of Bishopstone were themselves given.[8] Prominent features on them included to the south Grim's ditch, which still marked the boundary in 1976, and to the north the ridge way on the watershed of the Ebble and Nadder. Afterwards the parish gained an area of down north of that ridge way but lost the northern part of what is now Stratford Tony.

The parish is characterized by the very simple geological formation of the Ebble valley.[9] Chalk outcrops over the whole of it. Across its middle, except between Flamston and Croucheston where the stream is wide and shallow, the river has deposited a strip of alluvium, broader in the east than in the west. To the north and south of that, except where the land slopes steeply to the river between Throope and Faulston, are bands of valley gravel, much broader in the west than in the east. On the downs the chalk is overlain by deposits of clay-with-flints, in the north extensive on Bishopstone, Netton, and especially Flamston downs. In the later 17th century John Aubrey mentioned that on Flamston down there was a quarry for spar from which glass could be made.[10] The relief is sharper in the southern half of the parish. Ragland's hill and the higher ground west of it overhang the river between Throope and Faulston, and there are several steep sided coombs between Throope hill, 154 m., the summit of Faulston down, 171 m., and Croucheston down, 156 m. In the northern half the land rises steadily from river to watershed where Lyons barrow, 181 m., is on the parish boundary.

Land-use was typical of such geologically simple parishes: there was meadow land on the alluvium, arable on the valley gravel and the lower slopes of the chalk, and rough pasture on the downs.[11] Sheep-and-corn husbandry prevailed in all six townships.[12] Although not extensively wooded the whole parish lay within the outer bounds of Cranborne chase, and in the 13th century suffered from the activities of the foresters.[13] The downs in the southern half were part of Verditch chase but it is unlikely that by the later 18th century there was much woodland there.[14] From the later 18th century, and especially between 1792 and 1838, it seems that large areas of the downs in both halves of the parish were ploughed, and in the 18th and early 19th century farm buildings were erected on all the downs except that of Netton.[15] Those in the south later became the farmsteads of downland farms.[16] In the 19th century trees were planted on the clay-with-flints of the northern downs, especially at Foxholes on Flamston down and in a coomb on Netton down.[17] Bishopstone down north of the ridge way was detached from the farms of the parish and, part of the Wilton estate of the earls of Pembroke, also planted with trees.[18]

[1] This article was written in 1976. Maps used include O.S. Maps 1″, sheet 15 (1811 edn.); 1/50,000, sheet 184 (1974 edn.); 1/25,000, SU 02 (1958 edn.); 6″, Wilts. LXX (1889 edn.), LXXI (1888 edn.).

[2] For the areas see W.R.O., Tithe Award.

[3] For the early hist. of Downton see pp. 27–8.

[4] Finberg, Early Wessex Chart. pp. 92, 94, 101; Arch. Jnl. lxxvii. 56–7, 65–8, 96–7. Earlier 'Ebbesborne' seems to have been a regional name for the whole Ebble valley which was broken up and allotted under royal grants in the 10th cent.: Finberg, Early Wessex Chart. pp. 88–9, 91.

[5] Bishopstone was itself a man. only after 1086. For its ch. see below.

[6] Early refs. to 'Bishopston' in P.N. Wilts. (E.P.N.S.), 392 seem likely to be to Bishopstone in Ramsbury hund.

[7] Arch. Jnl. lxxvii. 40, 96–7.

[8] Ibid. lxxvi. 146–8. The boundaries appear in fabricated charters ascribed to earlier times but cannot be said with certainty to be earlier than 997.

[9] Geol. Surv. Map 1″, drift, sheets 298 (1950 edn.), 314 (1948 edn.).

[10] Aubrey, Nat. Hist. Wilts. ed. Britton, 41.

[11] e.g. W.R.O., Inclosure Award.   [12] See below.

[13] V.C.H. Wilts. iv. 458–9; Rot. Hund. (Rec. Com.), ii (1), 257.

[14] Andrews and Dury, Map (W.R.S. viii), pl. 2.

[15] Ibid.; W.R.O., Inclosure Award; Tithe Award.

[16] See below.

[17] O.S. Maps 6″, Wilts. LXV (1890 edn.), LXX (1889 edn.).

[18] B.L. Map Libr., 'Outlying Portion of the Wilton Estate', sale cat.

BISHOPSTONE c.1792

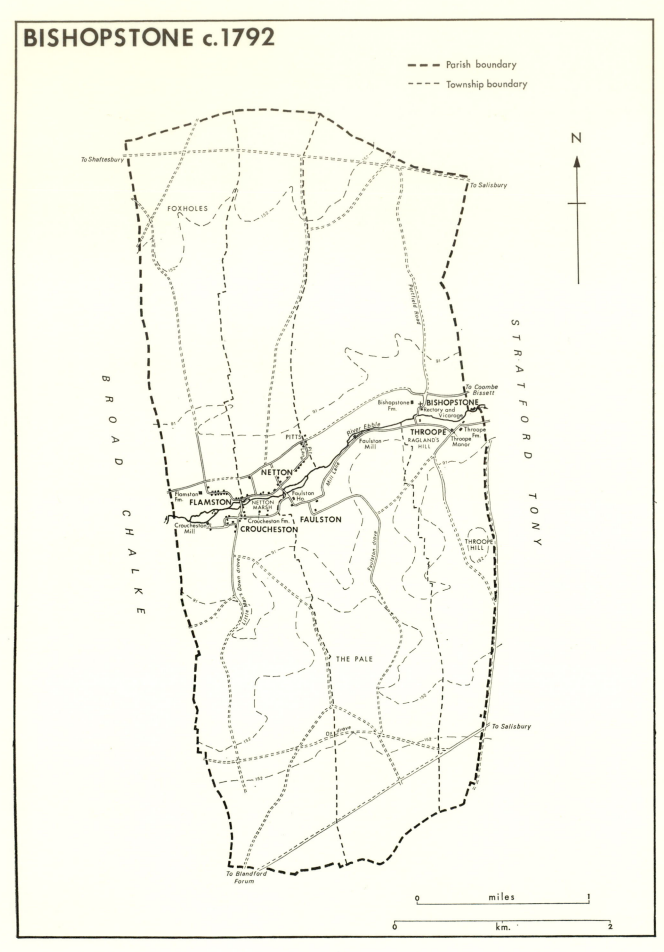

Parish boundary
Township boundary

N

To Shaftesbury

FOXHOLES

BROAD

CHALKE

152

91

Portfield Road

155

To Salisbury

91

STRATFORD TONY

To Coombe Bissett

Bishopstone Fm.

BISHOPSTONE
Rectory and Vicarage

River Ebble

THROOPE
RAGLAND'S HILL

Throope Fm.
Throope Manor

PITTS

Faulston Mill

River Ebble

NETTON

91

91

Mill Lane

Flamston Fm.

FLAMSTON

NETTON MARSH

Faulston Ho.

FAULSTON

Croucheston Mill

Croucheston Fm.

CROUCHESTON

Little Man's Down droves

91

91

152

THROOPE HILL

152

Faulston drove

THE PALE

152

152

91

152

Ox drove

152

To Salisbury

152

To Blandford Forum

0   miles   1

0   km.   2

4

The Roman road from old Salisbury to Dorchester (Dors.) crosses the parish, making a diversion from its otherwise straight course to circumvent the coombs of Faulston and Croucheston.[19] The ridge way from Salisbury to Shaftesbury (Dors.), which crosses the downs at the north end of the parish, was the main road between those towns and was turnpiked under an Act of 1762. The turnpike trust was allowed to lapse in the 1780s, however, and the road was superseded by the newly turnpiked road along the Nadder valley.[20] The old road fell into disuse. In 1976, when it was called the old Shaftesbury drove, it remained a passable track across the parish. The main road from Salisbury to Blandford Forum (Dors.), turnpiked under an Act of 1756,[21] crosses the downs at the south end of the parish. On Throope down a ridge way called Ox drove diverges from it and leads westwards across the downs towards Shaftesbury. Between those ancient and prominent downland routes the road through Coombe Bissett and Broad Chalke, which links the Ebble valley villages from Bodenham in Downton to Alvediston, passes north of the river through Bishopstone parish where there is also a parallel road south of the river. From those roads droves lead up to the downs but only one of them, Bishopstone drove (now Portfield Road) leading northwards to Wilton, has been metalled and tarred.

Artefacts of the Mesolithic Period and later indicate prehistoric activity in the parish, but Bishopstone has not been rich in archaeological discoveries.[22] Nine bowl-barrows and slight traces of a field system on Bishopstone down have been found.[23] Their names and their sites on the valley gravel, where there were adequate water supply and drainage, indicate the probably Saxon origin of the six riverside villages of the parish.[24] The pattern of settlement changed little until the 19th century. A small community then grew beside the road from Coombe Bissett to Broad Chalke between Netton and Bishopstone and the downland farmsteads were established. The roadside settlement was called the Pitts in 1841.[25] Early-14th-century taxation assessments show the six villages to have been small but the total population of the parish, in which there were 325 poll-tax payers in 1377, was probably greater than those of most of its neighbours.[26] A similar situation is indicated by 16th-century assessments.[27] In 1801 the population was 535 and by 1831 it had reached 663.[28] By 1841 it had fallen to 569, partly because in 1838 57 people emigrated to Australia and houses were demolished.[29] Out of that total 298 lived north of the river, almost certainly more than half of them in Netton and the Pitts, 164 in Croucheston, 76 in Faulston, and 31 in Throope.[30] The population rose again to stand at 685 in 1861 but thereafter declined steadily until 1931 when it was 411. New housing built after the Second World War led to a rise in the population to 540 in 1971.[31]

The small nucleated villages of Bishopstone and Throope at the east end of the parish were different in character from the villages at the west end. Bishopstone, as its name suggests,[32] contained the bishop of Winchester's demesne farmstead,[33] and the parish church was built there. In the early Middle Ages the village seems to have contained a number of small farmsteads, presumably grouped around the church, but by at least the early 16th century they had been deserted,[34] and Bishopstone (now Manor) Farm, the church, and the rectory-house stood isolated from the more populous part of the parish to the west. The road leading southwards across the river from the road from Coombe Bissett to Broad Chalke ran east of the church between it and the old rectory- and vicarage-house. It was closed when the new Rectory was built in 1815 and a new road was made west of the church.[35] In 1976 the village still consisted only of Manor Farm, formerly called Bishopstone House,[36] the church, the new Rectory (then called Bishopstone House) and its lodge, a small house on the site of the old rectory- and vicarage-house, and some cottages. Manor Farm is an early-19th-century brick house surrounded by extensive 19th-century farm buildings.

Throope was the smallest of the six villages[37] and, as its name implies,[38] was isolated from the other settlements. From at least the 16th century it seems to have contained no more than a single farmstead.[39] In 1976 the farm buildings included two large barns probably of the later 18th century. Below Ragland's hill near the river a pair of cottages of 17th-century or earlier origin possibly marked the site of another farmstead. In 1927 a house called Raglands with extensive outbuildings was built on that hill.[40]

At least three of the four villages clustered at the west end of the parish were street villages. Netton street ran not quite straight from Netton marsh to Pit Lane. Farmsteads and cottages stood along it mainly on the north side.[41] The eastern end of the street has never been made up and in 1976 the eastern and western ends were no longer joined. The line of the whole street was still marked by some cottages and small farm-houses of the 17th and 18th centuries. The Three Horse Shoes was built at the western end in the 19th century. The White Hart beside the road from Coombe Bissett to Broad Chalke, at the top of the road leading from Netton marsh, was a public house in 1792,[42] but the present building is of the 19th century. In the early 19th century Netton Farm was built further along the main road near the Pitts and Netton House, later extended, near the White Hart. In 1885 the parish hall was built beside the road leading from Netton marsh and in 1921 was extended as a war memorial. In 1970 it was reopened after repairs.[43] Council

[19] V.C.H. Wilts. i (1), 43; W.A.M. xxxiii. 325.
[20] V.C.H. Wilts. iv. 262.   [21] Ibid. 259.
[22] Ibid. i (1), 42–3.   [23] Ibid. 159, 273.
[24] P.N. Wilts. (E.P.N.S.), 392–3.
[25] H.O. 107/1174.
[26] V.C.H. Wilts. iv. 299, 308.
[27] Taxation Lists (W.R.S. x), 116.
[28] V.C.H. Wilts. iv. 341.
[29] Ibid. 319; Wilts. Cuttings, xxi. 137–8.
[30] H.O. 107/1174; cf. W.R.O., Tithe Award map.
[31] V.C.H. Wilts. iv. 341; Census, 1971.
[32] P.N. Wilts. (E.P.N.S.), 392.
[33] See below.   [34] See below.
[35] W.R.O., Inclosure Award map; Tithe Award map.
[36] Ibid. Inclosure Award map.
[37] e.g. V.C.H. Wilts. iv. 299, 308.
[38] E. Ekwall, Dict. Eng. P.N. 468.
[39] See p. 14.
[40] Bishopstone Scrap Bk. penes Miss M. Freya Watkinson, Faulston Ho.
[41] W.R.O., Inclosure Award map.
[42] Ibid.
[43] Bishopstone Scrap Bk. penes Miss Watkinson; Char. Com. file 246932; Wilts. Cuttings, xiv. 349.

houses were built to the north of it *c.* 1955, and in the 1960s a private housing estate was built east of Netton House between Netton street and the main road. In 1976 the Pitts was a group of 19th-century cottages south of the road with the school, some mid-20th-century council houses, and a small council housing estate of the 1970s north of the road.

Flamston street, with Flamston Farm at its west end, was a street of small farmsteads until the earlier 19th century.[44] In the earlier 20th century the street was still lined with thatched cottages[45] of which two remain. Several modern houses and bungalows have replaced the others. Flamston Farm is a 19th-century farm-house, formerly of three storeys, reduced in height and remodelled in the 1970s. East of it are extensive ranges of barns and farm buildings.

In the late 18th century Croucheston village stretched from Croucheston mill eastwards to Little Man's Down (later Croucheston) drove and along a street to Croucheston Farm.[46] There has since been little settlement in the street from which egress to the east was cut off in the mid 19th century.[47] In 1976 there were a few cottages and houses of the 17th century and later at the street's west end. At its east end Croucheston Farm, now almost square, has a north-east corner of late-17th-century origin which was part of a house largely demolished *c.* 1800. New ranges were then built to the west and south and the remainder of the older building was refaced. In 1976 there were two small houses probably of 17th-century origin in Croucheston drove, and west of the drove the buildings included an 18th-century farm-house with 19th-century additions, a small 17th-century house, the nonconformist chapel attached to a late-18th-century house, and a number of 19th-century cottages.

It seems likely that in the Middle Ages there was a street of tenant farmsteads east of Faulston manor-house. The farmsteads were later abandoned and Faulston thereafter consisted of no more than the manor-house and its farm buildings until the mid 17th century. New farmsteads were then built south-east of the manor-house between Mill Lane and the north end of Faulston drove.[48] In 1976 the farm buildings beside the manor-house included a stable court of the later 19th century. The large estate farmstead south-east of the house is also of the 19th century. In 1976 no cottage at Faulston appeared older than the 19th century.

In the 19th century there were erected throughout the parish many cottages and farm buildings in the characteristic style of the Wilton estate. Many survive, and the use of alternate bands of flint and red brick for their walls is a feature of the parish. Two avenues of trees, predominantly beeches, beside Portfield Road on Bishopstone down are similarly

characteristic of the Wilton estate. In the 20th century some buildings including a riding-stable and a garage have been erected beside the road from Salisbury to Blandford Forum.

MANORS AND OTHER ESTATES. The land which became the parish of Bishopstone was almost certainly included in the estate called 'Downton' given to the church of Winchester as an early endowment.[49] In 902 Bishop Denewulf granted to Beornwulf 15 hides, presumably of that estate, at 'Ebbesborne'.[50] The remainder of the estate passed to King Edward the Elder in 909. In 947 King Edred granted an estate of 5 *mansae* at 'Ebbesborne' to Alfsige, and in 957 King Edwy granted the same land to Alfric.[51] Further grants of 5 *cassati* at 'Ebbesborne' were made in 956 by King Edwy to Wulfric and in 961 by King Edgar to Byrnsige, and a grant of 5 *manentes* in 986 by King Ethelred to Alfgar.[52] The effect of the grants of land at 'Ebbesborne' was clearly to leave the land at Bishopstone isolated from the main part of the estate at Downton,[53] and, when it was restored to the Old Minster in 997, Downton and Bishopstone were thus detached portions of the estate.[54] The creation of free tenures between 1066 and 1086 probably led to the emergence of Faulston, Flamston, Throope, and Croucheston manors in the Bishopstone portion, which in 1086 was still considered part of the bishop of Winchester's Downton estate.[55]

In the early 13th century *BISHOPSTONE* was itself a manor.[56] Like Downton manor it passed with the see of Winchester until 1551 when, following the deprivation of Bishop Gardiner, Bishop Ponet granted it to Edward VI.[57] The king immediately granted it to Sir William Herbert, created earl of Pembroke in that year.[58] In 1553, after the accession of Queen Mary, Pembroke was expelled by the restored Gardiner. Ponet's grant to Edward VI was cancelled under royal warrant,[59] and in 1558 the manor was regranted to Gardiner's successor White.[60] The first parliament of Elizabeth I's reign returned it to Pembroke,[61] and the manor afterwards passed with the Pembroke title. From the later Middle Ages, as at Downton, the copyholds, which were held under the manor for fixed payments, began to assume the importance of freeholds, and the descents of the principal ones, in Croucheston and Netton, are traced below. In 1947 the demesne land, Bishopstone farm, was sold with Flamston and Netton farms (see below) to Guy Temple Montacute Larnach-Nevill, marquess of Abergavenny (d. 1954).[62] In 1956 those lands were bought for Henry Edward Hugh Pelham-Clinton-Hope, duke of Newcastle, and they belonged to Newcastle Estates in 1976.[63]

44 W.R.O., Inclosure Award map; Tithe Award map.
45 Photograph in Bishopstone Scrap Bk. *penes* Miss Watkinson.
46 W.R.O., Inclosure Award map.
47 Cf. ibid. Tithe Award map; O.S. Map 6″, Wilts. LXX (1889 edn.).   48 See pp. 13–14.
49 Cf. Finberg, *Early Wessex Chart.* p. 235 and n. 2; for Downton see below, pp. 27–8.
50 Finberg, *Early Wessex Chart.* p. 79.
51 Ibid. pp. 88–9, 93.   52 Ibid. pp. 92, 94, 101.
53 Cf. bounds recited in *Arch. Jnl.* lxxvi. 296–8, 298–9; lxxvii. 55–7, 65–8, 96–7.
54 Finberg, *Early Wessex Chart.* pp. 102–3.

55 *V.C.H. Wilts.* ii, pp. 79, 119.
56 B.L. Eg. MS. 2418, f. 64v.
57 *Cal. Pat.* 1550–3, 178; cf. Downton below, p. 28.
58 E 318/Box 30/1688 rot. 2; *Cal. Pat.* 1550–3, 197.
59 Act for the Assurance of Certain Lands to Patentees of Edw. VI, 1 Eliz. I, 36 (Original Act).
60 *Cal. Pat.* 1557–8, 146–7.
61 Act for the Assurance of Certain Lands to Patentees of Edw. VI, 1 Eliz. I, 36 (Original Act).
62 B.L. Map Libr., 'Outlying Portion of the Wilton Estate', sale cat.; Wilton Ho. Mun., sale file.
63 Ex inf. Estate Accountant, Newcastle Estates, Warminster.

The manor of *FLAMSTON* probably emerged from one of the estates, held of the bishop of Winchester, which became heritable between 1066 and 1086,[64] but it is not clear from which. In the 12th century Flamston belonged to members of the Flambard family and passed, presumably by inheritance, to Geoffrey de Stawell, grandson of Geoffrey Flambard.[65] In 1202 Geoffrey de Stawell defended his title against his relative Walter Flambard who apparently claimed the right of his brother Robert (d. *c.* 1200).[66] Geoffrey was succeeded by his son Adam to whom Walter son of Robert Flambard gave up all claim to Flamston in 1227.[67] Adam de Stawell was succeeded in 1231–2 by Sir Henry de Stawell,[68] presumably his son, who was in turn succeeded, apparently in the 1260s, by another Geoffrey de Stawell,[69] possibly his own son. In 1304 Geoffrey settled the manor on himself for life with remainder to Gunnore, widow of his son Matthew,[70] but in the same year conveyed it for life to John Uppehull,[71] possibly Gunnore's husband, who held until at least 1345.[72] After Uppehull's death the manor reverted to Sir Geoffrey de Stawell, probably the man of that name who was lord of Cothelstone (Som.)[73] and presumably the heir of Geoffrey de Stawell (fl. 1304). Sir Geoffrey (d. 1362)[74] held it in 1358.[75] He conveyed it to be held by his son William of another son Matthew.[76] In 1368 Matthew conveyed the reversion to John Lye as security for a loan,[77] and in 1374, presumably after William's death, the manor was conveyed to Lye in fee.[78]

After the death of John Lye in 1390[79] the manor was held by his widow Agnes, apparently wife of John Pokerwell in 1395[80] but again called Agnes Lye at her death in 1421.[81] She was succeeded by her grandson John Lye who died *c.* 1452 leaving as heir his son John, a minor.[82] John Lye (later Leigh)[83] entered in 1464,[84] was knighted in 1501, and held until his death *c.* 1523.[85] Sir John was predeceased by his son Henry and settled Flamston on Henry's daughter Mary, in 1524 the widow of William Long.[86] By 1525 Mary had married George de la Lynde, later knighted.[87] Mary died between 1545 and 1547,[88] and Sir George in 1556 when the manor passed to Edward, his son by his second wife Anne.[89] Edward died in 1556 and the manor was divided among Sir George's sisters Avice, wife of Sir Thomas Trenchard (d. 1557) and afterwards of Gilbert Wells, Warborough, wife of Thomas Morton,

and Anne, wife of Robert Williams.[90] In 1565 Avice's son Henry Trenchard conveyed his third to Robert Williams.[91] Robert and Anne (both d. 1569) were succeeded by their son John (later knighted),[92] to whom Thomas Morton conveyed his third in 1576.[93] Sir John Williams (d. 1617) was succeeded by his grandson John Williams[94] whose trustees sold the manor of Flamston to William Herbert, earl of Pembroke, in 1627.[95] The manor afterwards passed with the Pembroke title until 1947 when Flamston farm was sold with Bishopstone farm.[96] The Lyes had a manor-house at Flamston but nothing is known of its size and architectural style.[97]

Between 1066 and 1086 14 hides of the bishop of Winchester's estate, including the later manor of *FAULSTON*, were acquired by William de Braose (later Brewes), lord of Bramber (Suss.).[98] The overlordship of Faulston, held of the bishops,[99] passed with the barony of Bramber to William's son Philip (d. between 1134 and 1155), grandson William (d. *c.* 1192), and great-grandson William (d. 1211) whose lands were confiscated in 1208. The lands were restored to that William's younger son Reynold in 1216 but *c.* 1220 passed to John de Brewes, son of William's son William (d. 1210).[1] John (d. 1232) was succeeded by his son William (d. 1290–1) and grandson William de Brewes (d. 1326), Lord Brewes, whose daughter Aline (d. 1331), wife of John de Mowbray (d. 1322), Lord Mowbray, succeeded to the barony of Bramber.[2] Aline's son John, Lord Mowbray (d. 1361), was said to be overlord of Faulston in the year of his death.[3] He was succeeded by his son John, Lord Mowbray (d. 1368), and grandson John de Mowbray, earl of Nottingham (d. unmarried 1382–3),[4] but nothing further is heard of the Mowbrays as overlords, and in 1412 the heir of their tenants was said to hold Faulston immediately of the bishop of Winchester.[5]

The manor of Faulston was held in the early 13th century by Ralph le Tablier[6] who was succeeded in 1238 by his son Thomas,[7] knighted before 1249.[8] In the 1280s a Thomas le Tablier, perhaps Sir Thomas's son, held the manor[9] which passed to Guy le Tablier, possibly Thomas's son.[10] Guy's heir was his daughter Edith, wife of Richard of Grimstead.[11] In 1289 the manor was in the hands of trustees,[12] but in 1309 was settled on Richard and Edith.[13] Their heir was their son Thomas (d. 1328) whose son

[64] See above.   [65] *Cur. Reg. R.* v. 244.
[66] Ibid. ii. 101.
[67] Ibid. 197–8; C.P. 25(1)/250/6 no. 70.
[68] H.R.O. Eccl. 2/159282, rot. 12.
[69] Cf. *Reg. Pontoise* (Cant. & York Soc.), ii. 390; J.I. 1/998 rot. 26d.
[70] W.R.O. 492/68–9.   [71] Ibid. 492/70.
[72] Ibid. 492/71.   [73] J. Collinson, *Som.* iii. 250.
[74] *V.C.H. Wilts.* viii. 83.   [75] W.R.O. 492/76–81.
[76] Ibid. 492/84.   [77] Ibid. 492/84–8.
[78] Ibid. 492/89.   [79] Cf. ibid. 492/90; 492/91.
[80] Ibid. 492/92.   [81] C 138/55 no. 21.
[82] Ibid.; *Cal. Fine R.* 1452–61, 18.
[83] Cf. *V.C.H. Hants*, v. 171.
[84] C 140/11 no. 35.   [85] *W.N. & Q.* v. 77.
[86] C 1/538/16; W.R.O. 492/95.
[87] J. Hutchins, *Dors.* iv. 479; C.P. 25(2)/51/364/ 17 Hen. VIII Mich. no. 23.
[88] Hutchins, *Dors.* iv. 479; C.P. 25(2)/66/545/1 Edw. VI East. no. 1.
[89] Hutchins, *Dors.* iv. 479; W.R.O. 492/96.
[90] Hutchins, *Dors.* iv. 479; W.R.O. 492/96. Cf. C.P. 25(2)/51/364/17 Hen. VIII Mich. no. 23; C.P. 25(2)/51/366/

20 Hen. VIII Mich. no. 23.
[91] W.R.O. 492/96–7.   [92] Hutchins, *Dors.* ii. 524.
[93] W.R.O. 492/96.   [94] C 142/652 no. 183.
[95] W.R.O. 492/96; 492/101–2.
[96] B.L. Map Libr., 'Outlying Portion of the Wilton Estate', sale cat.; see above.   [97] W.R.O. 492/93–5.
[98] *V.C.H. Wilts.* ii, p. 119. The form of the name is discussed in *Complete Peerage*, i. 21 n.
[99] e.g. B.L. Eg. MS. 2418, f. 61.
[1] Sanders, *Eng. Baronies*, 108.
[2] Ibid.; *Complete Peerage*, s.v. Brewes, Mowbray.
[3] *Cal. Inq. p.m.* xi, p. 176.
[4] *Complete Peerage*, s.v. Mowbray.
[5] C 137/85 no. 13.
[6] H.R.O. Eccl. 2/159282, rot. 12.
[7] *Close R.* 1237–42, 76–7.
[8] *Crown Pleas, 1249* (W.R.S. xvi), p. 113.
[9] *Reg. Pontoise* (Cant. & York Soc.), ii. 388.
[10] Hoare, *Mod. Wilts.* Downton, 6.
[11] Ibid. Alderbury, 202.
[12] *Feet of F.* 1272–1327 (W.R.S. i), p. 32; Hoare, *Mod. Wilts.* Downton, 6.
[13] *Feet of F.* 1272–1327 (W.R.S. i), p. 73.

Thomas died a minor in 1328 leaving as coheirs his father's sisters Margaret, wife of Thomas Benton, and Catherine, wife of Ralph Buckland.[14] Faulston was allotted to Margaret (d. 1340) and Thomas (d. 1358) except for the third assigned in dower to the elder Thomas Grimstead's widow Joan (d. 1361).[15]

The Bentons, whose family name came to be rendered Baynton, were succeeded by their son Nicholas (d. 1412)[16] and grandson Sir Nicholas Baynton (d. 1422)[17] whose widow Joan held until 1429. She then conveyed Faulston to her son Sir John Baynton on her marriage with William Whaplode.[18] Sir John died in 1465 leaving a widow Catherine who held until her death in 1473.[19] In 1475 their son Sir Robert was attainted for having supported Henry VI at the battle of Tewkesbury in 1471[20] and the manor was granted to John Cheyne.[21] In 1484 Cheyne was himself attainted following Buckingham's rebellion against Richard III[22] who in 1485 granted Faulston to George Nevill.[23] After the battle of Bosworth the manor was restored to Cheyne (knighted 1485, created Lord Cheyne 1487, d.s.p. 1499).[24] It apparently passed to Anne, daughter and heir of Sir Edward Trussel and a minor in 1500,[25] but in 1503 the attainder of Sir Robert Baynton was reversed and Faulston restored to his son John.[26] In 1516 John Baynton was succeeded by his son Sir Edward[27] and the manor was settled for their lives on Sir Edward and his second wife Isabel.[28] Sir Edward died in 1545[29] and Isabel, afterwards wife of Sir James Stumpe (d. 1563) and Thomas Stafford,[30] held until her death in 1573, when she was succeeded by her son Henry Baynton.[31] Before Isabel's death an interest in the manor had apparently been conveyed to Anthony White and his wife Mary,[32] but in 1577 Charles Vaughan bought the interests of both Henry Baynton and the Whites.[33]

Vaughan (d. 1597) was succeeded by his grand-nephew Walter Vaughan (knighted 1603).[34] After Sir Walter's death in 1639 the manor passed to Dorothy, widow of his eldest son Sir Charles, and afterwards to his son George (knighted 1643).[35] Sir George, an active supporter of Charles I, was wounded at the battle of Lansdowne in 1643 but fought again in 1644 and 1645.[36] In 1645 Faulston House and the manor were occupied by the parliamentary committee for Wiltshire.[37] In 1649 Vaughan sold the manor to Philip, earl of Pembroke and Montgomery (d. 1650).[38] It passed with the Pembroke title until in 1919 Faulston farm was sold to

the tenant W. H. Brown.[39] In 1932 Brown sold to George Watkinson (d. 1972) whose daughter Miss M. Freya Watkinson owned the land in 1976.[40]

Faulston was the home of the Bayntons probably from the earlier 14th century to the early 16th.[41] Traces of a moat can be seen on the north, east, and south sides of the present house, and in the south-east angle of the enclosure there is a tall circular tower with evidence of high abutting walls on two sides.[42] The tower, which is of alternate bands of stone and faced flint, may date from the licence to crenellate granted to Nicholas Baynton in 1376,[43] but its only architectural feature is a late-medieval doorway to the southern wall-walk. The house may have lain within the walled enclosure or have formed one side of it with a walled court to the south. It passed with the manor and was occupied by the Vaughans.[44] It was 'slighted' in 1645.[45] Aubrey described Faulston House as 'noble old-fashioned'. He mentioned its moat, embattled walls, and two south-facing towers.[46] A short stretch of walling forming part of the south-west corner of the present house is of similar character to the tower, and the main east wall of the house has in it four doorways of late-15th- or 16th-century character which suggest that it may have been part of a screens passage or entrance hall. The double pile plan of the house, however, dates from a mid-17th-century reconstruction, presumably after the manor changed hands in 1649, and there are mullioned windows of that period in the north and west walls. The house was remodelled in the early 19th century when the south entrance front was refenestrated and the present staircase was inserted, and again later in that century when the kitchen was partly rebuilt, and perhaps reduced in size, and the interior was refitted.

In the early 13th century land in the parish, later called the manor of *THROOPE*, was held with land in Kilmeston (Hants) by William Gimmings. Before 1224 William's brother Thomas succeeded him although his widow Alice, wife of John de la Bere, held a third in dower.[47] Before 1250 Thomas gave the land in exchange for land in Farlington (Hants) to Roger de Merlay on the marriage of his son Nicholas to Roger's daughter Agnes, but later the exchange seems to have been reversed.[48] Thomas held until at least 1275.[49] Nicholas (d. 1282) left as heir a son John[50] who held in 1290.[51] It is not clear how the Gimmingses' land descended in the 14th

[14] Hoare, *Mod. Wilts.* Alderbury, 202; *Cal. Inq. p.m.* vii, pp. 111–13.
[15] *Cal. Inq. p.m.* vii, pp. 130–1; *Cal. Fine R. 1327–77*, 105–6.
[16] *Cal. Inq. p.m.* x, pp. 349–50; xi, pp. 10–11; C 137/85 no. 13. [17] C 138/59 no. 48.
[18] C.P. 25(1)/257/61 no. 45; *V.C.H. Hants*, iv. 185.
[19] C 140/17 no. 30; C 145/327 no. 43.
[20] *Rot. Parl.* (Rec. Com.), vi. 145.
[21] *Cal Pat. 1467–77*, 533–4.
[22] *Rot. Parl.* (Rec. Com.), vi. 246.
[23] *Cal. Pat. 1476–85*, 549–50.
[24] *Rot. Parl.* (Rec. Com.), vi. 273; *Complete Peerage*, s.v. Cheyne.
[25] *Cal. Pat. 1494–1509*, 188.
[26] *Rot. Parl.* (Rec. Com.), vi. 526; *Cal. Pat. 1494–1509*, 374.
[27] Burke, *Ext. & Dorm. Baronetcies* (1844), 452–3.
[28] *L. & P. Hen. VIII*, xv, p. 218.
[29] C 142/72 no. 109.
[30] *W.N. & Q.* viii. 474–5.
[31] C 142/167 no. 115.

[32] *Extents for Debts* (W.R.S. xxviii), pp. 79–80.
[33] C.P. 25(2)/240/19 Eliz. I Trin.; E 159/375 rot. 223; C.P. 25(2)/240/25 Eliz. I East.; Req. 2/281/36.
[34] C 142/249 no. 64.
[35] *Wilts. Inq. p.m. 1625–49* (Index Libr.), 427–31.
[36] *V.C.H. Wilts.* v. 139.
[37] *W.A.M.* xxvi. 344, 388.
[38] Wilton Ho. Mun., bk. containing scheds. of deeds, 119. [39] W.A.S. Libr., sale cat. xv, nos. 3, 4.
[40] Ex inf. Miss Watkinson, Faulston Ho.
[41] E 179/196/8; Leland, *Itin.* ed. Toulmin Smith, i. 258. Cf. *W.N. & Q.* iii. 131. [42] See plate facing p. 209.
[43] *Cal. Pat. 1374–7*, 353.
[44] *Wilts. Inq. p.m. 1625–49* (Index Libr.), 431.
[45] Edmund Ludlow, *Memoirs*, ed. C. H. Firth, i. 124.
[46] Aubrey, *Nat. Hist. Wilts.* ed. Britton, 101–2.
[47] *Cur. Reg. R.* xi, pp. 273, 347–8; xii, pp. 486–7; C.P. 25(1)/250/4 no. 32.
[48] *Cal. Inq. p.m.* i, pp. 55–6; *Close R. 1247–51*, 393.
[49] *Rot. Hund.* (Rec. Com.), ii (1), 257.
[50] *Cal. Inq. p.m.* ii, p. 263.
[51] *Abbrev. Plac.* (Rec. Com.), 222.

century. In 1307 John's land in Kilmeston was alienated in mortmain,[52] but that at Throope possibly passed like Chessell manor in Shalfleet (I.W.) to Nicholas Gimmings (d. 1349) and John de Lisle (d. 1349).[53] John de Lisle's widow Joan possibly married Geoffrey Rookley, lord of the manor of Arreton (I.W.).[54] In 1417 John Rookley, perhaps their son, granted the Throope land to Dominic Uppehull and his wife Alice for their lives with successive remainders to William and Lewis Meux, sons of Richard Meux.[55]

In 1428 Lewis Meux held the land.[56] He was succeeded by his son Thomas (d. before 1472), grandson Sir William Meux (fl. 1507), and great-grandson John Meux (d.s.p. 1568) whose heir was apparently his grand-nephew John Meux (knighted 1605, d. 1629).[57] Sir John married Cecily, daughter of William Button of Alton Priors in Overton, a relative of whom seems to have farmed the land in the early 17th century.[58] He was succeeded by his son Sir John (d. 1657) and grandson Sir William Meux (d. 1697)[59] who held in 1670.[60] The elder Sir John's granddaughter Eleanor Compton (d.s.p. c. 1707) married Sir Robert Button (d. 1678).[61] In a way that is not clear Throope passed from the Meuxes to Buttons, but apparently to a member of that branch of the Button family which had been farming it since the early 17th century.[62] It was held by John Button (d. 1730) who was succeeded by his sons John (d. 1738) and George (d. 1763).[63] George's heir was his sister Mary (d. 1768), wife of Henry Rooke (d. c. 1794) of Breamore (Hants). Throope passed to Mary's son John Rooke who succeeded c. 1812 by his nephew Henry Rooke (d. 1850). Henry left as heir his daughter Maria, wife of Walter Young (d. 1894).[64] In 1899 the land was sold by Young's trustees to the Wilton estate.[65] In 1919 Throope farm was sold to Josiah Antell[66] whose sons Percy and Thomas sold it c. 1930 to Lt.-Cdr. L. C. Ansdell. In 1933 it was sold to Algernon George de Vere Capell, earl of Essex, and in 1955 to Antony Henry Head, Viscount Head, the owner in 1976.[67]

The main east front of Throope Manor is of five bays. It was arranged symmetrically in the mid or later 18th century, but in its two southern bays incorporates the end of an earlier range which was probably built in the 17th century. Inside is much reset early-17th-century panelling. The 18th-century house, which was almost square, was greatly enlarged to the south and west in the 1930s by Lord Essex.[68]

Land in Throope was held freely by John Martin (d. 1461) of Gillingham (Dors.). He is said to have granted it in 1458–9 for the saying of a mass in St. James's aisle in Gillingham parish church.[69] The land was held by the Fraternity of Jesus in Gillingham until the dissolution of the chantries.[70] In 1557 it was granted by the Crown to John Eliott and Alexander Chesenall.[71] They immediately conveyed it to Thomas St. Barbe who sold it to John Newman. In 1566–7 Newman's title was challenged by Christopher Withers and his wife Joan, a descendant of John Martin.[72] The descent of the land thereafter is not clear. Newman's title was apparently proved[73] but later the land was merged with Throope manor.[74]

Holdings in Throope were parts of both Bishopstone and Faulston manors. A substantial holding was part of Faulston manor in 1328.[75] It passed with the manor to the earls of Pembroke and Montgomery.[76] From the mid 17th century to the 19th members of the Button and Rooke families held it by copies,[77] and the land was merged with Throope farm when it was bought by the Wilton estate in 1899.[78] The holding attached to Bishopstone manor was similarly held from the early 18th century by different members of the Button and Rooke families and was also merged with Throope farm.[79]

In the early 13th century William Daundely held an estate of the bishop of Winchester in the parish.[80] It later passed to Walter Daundely, lord of the manor of Chilton Candover (Hants),[81] and in 1275 was held by Robert Daundely.[82] The Daundelys' estate, of which nothing further is heard, cannot be identified with certainty, but was possibly the overlordship of land in Croucheston which passed in the Bramshott family. The Daundelys' heirs were the Bayntons and in the 17th century and later Croucheston manor was said to be held of Faulston manor.[83]

In 1227 William de Lusteshull quitclaimed land to William Bramshott.[84] The land seems to have passed like the manor of Bramshott (Hants) through the Bramshott family.[85] A William Bramshott held it in the early 14th century,[86] and in 1406 William Bramshott (d. between 1432 and 1444) held it.[87] That last William's heir was his son John (d. 1468) who in 1455 made a settlement of the land, then called *CROUCHESTON* manor.[88] John's heirs were his daughters Elizabeth, wife of John Dudley, and Margaret, wife of Sir John Pakenham,[89] but it is not clear how Croucheston descended until in 1516 it was conveyed by trustees to Ivychurch

[52] *V.C.H. Hants*, iii. 323.   [53] Ibid. v. 273.
[54] Ibid. n. 39; *Suss. Arch. Coll.* lxxiii. 107.
[55] C.P. 25(1)/256/60 no. 19.
[56] *Feud. Aids*, v. 232.
[57] *V.C.H. Hants*, v. 250; *Genealogist*, N.S. xii. 167.
[58] *Wilts. Pedigrees* (Harl. Soc. cv, cvi), 33; *D.N.B.* s.v. Ralph Button.   [59] *V.C.H. Hants*, v. 250.
[60] Wilton Ho. Mun., ct. roll.
[61] G.E.C. *Baronetage*, i. 193.
[62] For those Buttons see Wilton Ho. Mun., surveys of Faulston, 1672, 1705.
[63] Ibid. survey of Bishopstone, c. 1740.
[64] Ibid. surveys of Bishopstone, c. 1740, and Faulston, 1705; W.R.O., Land Tax.
[65] W.A.S. Libr., sale cat. xxi, no. 10; Wilton Ho. Mun., 'Property Purchased and Sold', 40.
[66] W.A.S. Libr., sale cat. xv, nos. 3, 4.
[67] Ex inf. Viscount Head, Throope Man.
[68] Ibid.   [69] Req. 2/26/34.
[70] E 318/Box 40/2148 rot. 2.
[71] *Cal. Pat.* 1557–8, 204.   [72] Req. 2/26/34.
[73] *Survey of Lands of Wm., First Earl of Pembroke*, ed. C. R. Straton (Roxburghe Club, 1909), i. 299.
[74] e.g. W.R.O., Inclosure Award.
[75] *Cal. Inq. p.m.* vii, p. 111; see above.
[76] Wilton Ho. Mun., survey, 1672.
[77] Ibid.; survey, 1705.
[78] Ibid. quit-rent bk. 1889–1905, f. 160.
[79] Ibid. surveys, 1632, c. 1740; quit-rent bk. 1889–1905, f. 160.
[80] B.L. Eg. MS. 2418, f. 61. The fam. name was formerly rendered 'de Andely': *V.C.H. Hants*, iv. 185.
[81] *Reg. Pontoise* (Cant. & York Soc.), ii. 387; *V.C.H. Hants*, iv. 185.
[82] *Rot. Hund.* (Rec. Com.), ii (1), 256.
[83] *V.C.H. Hants*, iv. 185; Wilton Ho. Mun., surveys, 1672, 1705.   [84] C.P. 25(1)/250/5 no. 17.
[85] *V.C.H. Hants*, ii. 492.
[86] *Wilts. Inq. p.m.* 1327–77 (Index Libr.), 30; E 179/196/8.
[87] C.P. 25(1)/256/59 no. 4; *V.C.H. Hants*, v. 247.
[88] C.P. 25(1)/257/64 no. 34.
[89] *V.C.H. Hants*, v. 247.

Priory.[90] The priory retained it until the Dissolution when it passed to the Crown.[91]

The manor was granted to Ellis Wynne in 1563[92] and was apparently sold by him soon afterwards. It possibly belonged to Edward Hayward in 1576[93] and it descended through the Hayward family. Another Edward Hayward probably held it *c.* 1628.[94] He was succeeded by his son Edward and grandson George Hayward who in 1678 sold the manor to Richard Kitson.[95] In 1691 Kitson sold it to John Ballard, a doctor of medicine, who was succeeded by his son the Revd. John Ballard, and grandson John Ballard, a Fellow of Winchester College.[96] In 1767 that last John sold the manor to Edward Hewett (d. 1796) who devised it to his nephew John Hewett (d. 1805).[97] About 1816 John Hewett's widow Sarah, then Sarah Chamberlain, sold it to James Swayne (d. 1866).[98] About 1885 the land was acquired by the Wilton estate from James's son Henry, apparently by exchange, and was added to Croucheston farm (see below).[99]

In 1189 Waverley Abbey was confirmed in an estate in Croucheston which had possibly been an early grant by the abbey's founder William Giffard (d. 1129), bishop of Winchester, or his successor Bishop Blois.[1] The land remained with the abbey until it passed to the Crown at the Dissolution.[2] In 1536 it was granted to Sir William Fitzwilliam[3] and in 1538 apparently conveyed to Thomas Chaffin (will proved 1559) of Salisbury, whose son Thomas died holding it in 1619.[4] The younger Thomas left a son Thomas and grandson Thomas Chaffin, one of whom sold the land to Edward Hewett (will dated 1662).[5] Hewett devised it to his son Nicholas, and it passed to Nicholas's son Nicholas and grandson Richard Panton Hewett who in 1728 sold to the Revd. John Ballard.[6] The estate afterwards passed with the manor of Croucheston.[7]

A substantial holding in Croucheston was part of Faulston manor in 1328.[8] It passed with the manor to the earls of Pembroke and Montgomery,[9] and in the 19th century was the basis of Croucheston farm to which Croucheston manor (see above) and Alfred Morrison's land (see below) were added.[10] In 1919 the farm was sold to C. M. Wort and it later passed to his son George and grandson Mr. J. H. Wort who owned it in 1976.[11]

A substantial copyhold of inheritance in Croucheston, held of Bishopstone manor, was entered in 1543 by Hugh King who held it until at least 1576.[12] John

King entered it in 1610 and held it until at least 1632.[13] In 1672 Edward King held it and in 1729 Edward King, presumably another, was succeeded by his brother John (d. *c.* 1746), whose heir was another brother Thomas. In 1746 Thomas settled the land on himself for life with remainder to William Clarke, and in 1750 Clarke died holding it. His heir was his brother John (d. 1764) who was succeeded by his son William, a minor, admitted in 1778. William (d. 1792) was succeeded by his brother Edward (d. 1795) whose widow Elizabeth, wife of Thomas Harding, held the land until 1821 when Maria, daughter of Edward Clarke and wife of Joseph Nowlson, was admitted. In 1824 the Nowlsons sold it to Elizabeth Snook (d. 1845).[14] She devised the land to trustees to pay certain annuities and afterwards to the children of Ann, wife of John Stevens.[15] In 1881 the children, John Henry Stevens, Anna Maria Stevens, and William Snook Stevens (d. 1883) were admitted.[16] The land, which was the only substantial estate in the parish never part of the Wilton estate, was enfranchised in 1895.[17] In 1933 it belonged to John Stevens,[18] and in 1976 partly to Mr. J. H. Wort and partly to Mr. Richard Lamb.[19]

Another substantial copyhold of inheritance in Croucheston was entered by John Gyett in 1514–15, and a John Gyett held until at least 1576.[20] In 1605 Thomas Hewett entered it. He held it until at least 1632,[21] and afterwards the land descended in the Hewett family. In 1709 Thomas, son of another Thomas Hewett, was admitted.[22] His widow Tabitha held the land from Thomas's death in 1739 until her own in 1777 when she was succeeded by her grandson Thomas Hewett (d. 1805). That Thomas's widow Sarah held it until her death in 1829 and was succeeded by her son John Hewett, who in 1840 sold it to James Swayne.[23] The land passed with Swayne's manor of Croucheston until 1860 when the copyhold of inheritance was sold to Alfred Morrison of Fonthill House in Fonthill Gifford.[24] About 1890 the land passed, presumably by sale, to the Wilton estate and became part of Croucheston farm (see above).[25]

A substantial copyhold of inheritance in Netton, held of Bishopstone manor, was entered in 1530–1 by Christopher Whitmarsh who held it until at least 1567.[26] In 1576 William Whitmarsh probably held it.[27] Jasper Shergall entered it in 1615 and held it

90 C 142/31 no. 95.
91 *Valor Eccl.* (Rec. Com.), ii. 96.
92 *Cal. Pat.* 1560–3, 586.
93 *Taxation Lists* (W.R.S. x), 116.   94 E 179/199/398.
95 W.R.O. 130/9, covenant, Hayward with Eyre; Kitson's mortgage.
96 Ibid. bargain and sale, Eyre to Ballard. For the Ballards see Hoare, *Mod. Wilts.* Downton, 3.
97 Hoare, *Mod. Wilts.* Downton, 3; W.R.O. 577/4, par. reg.
98 Hoare, *Mod. Wilts.* Downton, 3; W.R.O., Land Tax.
99 Wilton Ho. Mun., quit-rent bk. 1879–88; rent bk. 1889.
1 *Cart. Antiq.* (Pipe R. Soc. xxxiii), p. 162; *V.C.H. Surr.* ii. 77.   2 *Valor Eccl.* (Rec. Com.), ii. 35.
3 *L. & P. Hen. VIII*, xi, p. 88.
4 C.P. 25(2)/46/321/29 Hen. VIII East. no. 32; *Wilts. Inq. p.m.* 1625–49 (Index Libr.), 196–7.
5 *Wilts. Pedigrees* (Harl. Soc. cv, cvi), 36–7; W.R.O. 130/9, will of Edw. Hewett.
6 W.R.O. 130/9, will of Edw. Hewett; bargain and sale, Hewett to Ballard.   7 See above.

8 *Cal. Inq. p.m.* vii, p. 111; see above.
9 Wilton Ho. Mun., survey, 1672.
10 Cf. W.R.O., Tithe Award; Wilton Ho. Mun., rent bks. 1883–91.
11 W.A.S. Libr., sale cat. xv, no. 3; Wilton Ho. Mun., sale file; local information.
12 *First Pembroke Survey*, ed. Straton, i. 303; *Taxation Lists* (W.R.S. x), 116.
13 *Pembroke Man.* (W.R.S. ix), pp. 113–14.
14 Wilton Ho. Mun., surveys, 1632, *c.* 1740.
15 Ibid. ct. bk. 1820–50, 174.   16 Ibid. 254–65.
17 Ibid. 335–7.   18 Ibid. unnumbered pp. at end.
19 Local information.
20 *First Pembroke Survey*, ed. Straton, i. 303; *Taxation Lists* (W.R.S. x), 116.
21 *Pembroke Man.* (W.R.S. ix), p. 114.
22 Wilton Ho. Mun., survey, 1632.
23 Ibid. survey, *c.* 1740.
24 Ibid. ct. bk. 1820–50, 193–5.
25 Ibid. rent bk. 1891.
26 *First Pembroke Survey*, ed. Straton, i. 300.
27 *Taxation Lists* (W.R.S. x), 116.

until at least 1632.[28] The land passed to his son John whose daughter and heir Hannah married William Whitehart.[29] In 1718 Whitehart died holding the land which passed to his son William and grandson William Whitehart, who in 1773 sold it to Thomas Bevis (d. 1778). Bevis's widow Anne held it until her death in 1803 when it passed to Sarah, niece of Thomas Bevis and wife of James Wilton. At Sarah's death in 1826 Thomas Browning was admitted under Thomas Bevis's will. In 1827 he sold the land to William Rowden (d. 1855).[30] After his death Rowden's land was held by his trustees until 1865, when they sold it to George, earl of Pembroke and Montgomery.[31] It was added to Flamston farm and passed with the manor of Bishopstone.[32] A small manor-house called Netton Old Farmhouse in 1947 passed with the estate. It is a symmetrical house dated 1637 with walls of chequered stone and flint rising two full storeys with attics and with a thatched roof.

Another substantial copyhold of inheritance in Netton was entered by Giles King in 1558.[33] Another Giles King entered it in 1614 and held it until at least 1632.[34] The land passed to his son Giles (d. 1711) and great-grandson Giles King who in 1723 sold it to John Barber. In 1731 Barber was succeeded by his son John who in 1777 sold the land to John Baker (d. 1789). In 1795 Baker's executors sold it to John Johnson (d. 1799), who was succeeded by his son John (d. 1807) and grandson William Johnson. In 1810 William sold the estate to Christopher Crouch who in 1825 sold it to Elizabeth Snook.[35] The land thereafter passed with Elizabeth's land in Croucheston[36] until the Stevenses sold it to Alfred Morrison in 1882.[37] In 1885 it passed, apparently by exchange, to the Wilton estate and was added to Netton farm (see below).[38]

A copyhold of inheritance of some 50 a. in Netton had been acquired by an earl of Pembroke and Montgomery by 1792.[39] Another of similar size was bought in 1855[40] and a third of similar size was also bought.[41] Those three holdings formed the basis of Netton farm to which Morrison's land (see above) was added. Netton farm passed with the manor of Bishopstone.[42]

ECONOMIC HISTORY. In 997 Bishopstone accounted for 45 of the 100 *mansae* of the bishop of Winchester's Downton estate. In Domesday Book

it was included in the assessment of Downton.[43] The bishops' manor of Bishopstone, of which the other manors in the parish were held,[44] and which included customary tenants in Bishopstone, Netton, and Croucheston but demesne land in apparently no other part of the parish but Bishopstone tithing,[45] was at farm in the period 1208–11 but in hand from 1211.[46]

The land of Bishopstone tithing, including Netton, was shared in the Middle Ages by the bishop in demesne and by his customary tenants of Bishopstone and Netton. The arable was cultivated as two fields, as three from c. 1300.[47] The amount sown for the bishop was usually above 250 a. until c. 1280, declined gradually c. 1280–1350, and from 1350 to 1450 averaged c. 150 a. The number of sheep kept for him varied considerably in the 13th century and on only a few occasions exceeded 600. In the 14th century his sheep farming increased in importance, and in the earlier 15th century the sheep in his flock consistently numbered over 800.[48] If used, tenants' labour services were probably sufficient for most demesne husbandry.[49] In the early 13th century the bishop apparently had nine 2-virgaters at Netton and eighteen ½-virgaters at Bishopstone.[50] In 1456 the demesne land, but not the sheep and pasture for 600 wethers, was leased;[51] in 1475 the sheep pasture was leased with the land;[52] and in 1532 the whole manor other than the rights of lordship was leased.[53] On one of those occasions, possibly in 1456, the lands of the eighteen ½-virgaters in Bishopstone were added to the demesne lands which were separated from the lands of the customary tenants of Netton, concentrated in Middle and East fields in the east part of the tithing, and inclosed.

In 1567 the demesne farm, later called Bishopstone farm, included some 800 a.[54] Leases of the land and fixed rents of the customary tenants of Netton and Croucheston were held for lives at a fixed rent, but were paid for by large fines.[55] They passed from Thomas ApRice, lessee in 1532,[56] to his relative George Penruddock (knighted 1568) of Compton Chamberlayne,[57] to Penruddock's relative Thomas Smith, and to Smith's son Thomas (will proved 1647).[58] Members of the Trotman family and their trustees held from 1648 to 1786 when Henry, earl of Pembroke and Montgomery, took the estate in hand.[59] Bishopstone farm, 892 a. in 1838 but later reduced to 845 a. south of the old Shaftesbury drove,[60] was afterwards let at rack-rent.[61] Farm

[28] *Pembroke Man.* (W.R.S. ix), p. 110.
[29] Wilton Ho. Mun., ct. roll, 1670; survey, 1632.
[30] Ibid. surveys, 1632, c. 1740.
[31] Ibid. ct. bk. 1820–50, 204–15.
[32] See above.
[33] *First Pembroke Survey*, ed. Straton, i. 301.
[34] *Pembroke Man.* (W.R.S. ix), pp. 111–12.
[35] Wilton Ho. Mun., surveys, 1632, c. 1740.
[36] See above.
[37] Wilton Ho. Mun., ct. bk. 1820–50, 265–7.
[38] Ibid. rent bk. 1886.
[39] W.R.O., Inclosure Award.
[40] Wilton Ho. Mun., ct. bk. 1820–50, 187–90.
[41] Cf. W.R.O., Tithe Award; Wilton Ho. Mun., rent bk. 1883.
[42] See above.
[43] See p. 35.
[44] B.L. Eg. MS. 2418, f. 61.
[45] See below.
[46] J. Z. Titow, 'Land and Population on the Bishop of Winchester's Estates 1209–1350' (Camb. Univ. Ph.D. thesis, 1962), 7; *Pipe R. 1210* (P.R.S. N.S. xxvi), 82; *Pipe R. 1211* (P.R.S. N.S. xxviii), 170.
[47] e.g. H.R.O. Eccl. 2/159305, rot. 6d. (1282–3); Eccl.

2/159337, rot. 5d. (1324–5).
[48] Titow, 'Land and Pop.', Table I; H.R.O. Eccl. 2/159384, rot. 7 (1376–7); Eccl. 2/159422, rot. 3 (1420–1); Eccl. 2/159443, rot. 3 and d. (1452–3).
[49] B.L. Eg. MS. 2418, ff. 64v.–66; H.R.O. Eccl. 2/159384, rot. 7 and d.
[50] B.L. Eg. MS. 2418, ff. 64v.–66.
[51] H.R.O. Eccl. 2/155827.
[52] Ibid. Eccl. 2/155840.
[53] *First Pembroke Survey*, ed. Straton, i. 299–300.
[54] Ibid.; cf. New Court farm in Wick tithing in Downton: below, p. 74.
[55] e.g. Wilton Ho. Mun., survey, 1632.
[56] H.R.O. Eccl. 2/155882. For the relationships see *Wilts. Pedigrees* (Harl. Soc. cv, cvi), 149.
[57] *First Pembroke Survey*, ed. Straton, i. 299.
[58] *Pembroke Man.* (W.R.S. ix), p. 109; *W.N. & Q.* viii. 69.
[59] Wilton Ho. Mun., surveys, 1632, c. 1740.
[60] W.R.O., Tithe Award; B.L. Map Libr., 'Outlying Portion of the Wilton Estate', sale cat.
[61] Wilton Ho. Mun., survey, c. 1740.

buildings were erected on the down, and presumably much of the pasture there ploughed, between 1792 and 1838.[62] In 1976 the farm, then called Manor farm, was worked primarily from Bishopstone and devoted to mixed farming.

The nine 2-virgaters apparently in Netton in the early 13th century held virgates nominally of 16 a.[63] After the lands of Netton and Bishopstone were separated, the customary tenants of Netton cultivated the lands of their township alone and in common. In 1567 the 18 yardlands were shared among eight copyholders whose rents and fines were fixed, but a few of whose formerly onerous labour services were still recorded.[64] In 1632 there were ten copyholders with holdings varying from those of Jasper Shergall, whose 4 yardlands consisted of 70 a. and feeding for 168 sheep and 14 beasts, and Giles King, 3 yardlands with 55 a. and feeding for 126 sheep and 10 beasts, to two of fewer than 15 a. The arable land of Netton, presumably the former West field of Bishopstone tithing, was cultivated in three fields, some 275 a. north of the road from Coombe Bissett to Broad Chalke.[65] North of it there were downs, probably totalling some 220 a.,[66] with pasture for cattle and 736 sheep,[67] abated to c. 700 in 1667.[68] Some 52 a. of inclosed lands lay in small closes of meadow between Netton street and the river, and in long narrow closes of arable between the farmsteads on the north side of the street and the road from Coombe Bissett to Broad Chalke.[69]

About 1750 there were roughly the same number of farms as in 1632, and indeed as there had been since the Middle Ages,[70] but in 1792, when the common fields and downs were inclosed, there were half as many.[71] After inclosure Thomas Bevis's farm measured 213 a., John Baker's executors' 157 a., and there were three farms of c. 50 a.[72] Netton marsh, 6 a., remained a common feeding- and watering-place and in 1838 was deemed parochial land.[73] In 1827 Bevis's farm, the westernmost strip of Netton land, was acquired by the tenant of Flamston farm which adjoined it.[74] The land has since remained part of Flamston farm although the buildings in Netton street were not given up until 1947.[75] In the later 19th century the three farms of c. 50 a. were amalgamated to form Netton farm, to which the farm formerly Baker's, with its extensive early-19th-century buildings beside the road from Coombe Bissett to Broad Chalke, was added in 1885. Netton farm then measured 295 a.[76] It was halved c. 1914 and the eastern half afterwards merged with Bishopstone farm.[77] In 1976 Netton remained a

mixed farm sandwiched between Bishopstone and Flamston farms.[78]

From the mid 13th century to the mid 14th part of Flamston manor was possibly held by lease.[79] In 1358, presumably on entering the manor,[80] Sir Geoffrey de Stawell regranted several smallholdings, some formerly held in bondage, freely for lives,[81] and there were then other smallholdings in Flamston township held freely.[82] The demesne was possibly in hand in the later 14th century, when the demesne and tenantry arable lands were intermingled in two common fields,[83] and in the early 15th century, but in 1413 Agnes Lye leased it to her son Nicholas and, with all the buildings except the living accommodation in the manor-house, it was leased again in 1432.[84] For most of the 16th century members of the Atwater family were lessees.[85]

In 1632 the township contained some 60 a. of inclosed lands, 420 a. of arable then in three common fields, and common pasture for some 1,000 sheep and 160 other animals. The lands were reckoned 20 yardlands and were shared among the demesne farm and two smaller holdings, presumably former copyholds, all held by lease, eight copyholds, and the glebe farm.[86] The accounting of the demesne at 9 yardlands, the glebe at 1, and the small leaseholds and copyholds at a total of 10 possibly reflected an early and equal division of the township between demesne, from which the glebe was later taken, and tenantry land, and was an accurate measure of the division in 1632. The inclosed lands included, in the south-west corner of the township, 22 a. of demesne arable south of the road from Coombe Bissett to Broad Chalke and 15 a. of arable in crofts north of the road held by the other tenants.[87]

The number of farms seems to have changed little before the later 18th century.[88] In 1771 the demesne, which from 1622 or earlier had been leased for years on lives and sub-let, was let at rackrent by Henry, earl of Pembroke and Montgomery.[89] Between then and 1792 several of the smaller holdings were added to it.[90] The common lands were inclosed in 1792. The western and northern parts of the arable land and the whole of the down were allotted to the demesne farm which then measured c. 550 a., had buildings at the west end of Flamston street, and was later called Flamston farm. There remained five small copyholds, none above 25 a., with land in the south-east corner of the township near their farmsteads along the street. The church's land in Flamston was exchanged for land in Faulston.[91] By 1838 Flamston farm had absorbed virtually

[62] W.R.O., Inclosure Award map; Tithe Award map.
[63] B.L. Eg. MS. 2418, ff. 64v.–65; H.R.O. Eccl. 2/159384, rot. 7.
[64] *First Pembroke Survey*, ed. Straton, i. 300–2.
[65] *Pembroke Man.* (W.R.S. ix), pp. 110–12.
[66] W.R.O., Inclosure Award.
[67] *Pembroke Man.* (W.R.S. ix), pp. 110–12.
[68] Wilton Ho. Mun., ct. rolls.
[69] Cf. W.R.O., Inclosure Award; *Pembroke Man.* (W.R.S. ix), pp. 110–12.
[70] Wilton Ho. Mun., survey, c. 1740; W.A.S. Libr., 'Terrae Pembrochianae', 72–3.
[71] W.R.O., Inclosure Award.   [72] Ibid. Tithe Award.
[73] Ibid.; Inclosure Award. For its later use see below.
[74] W.R.O., Land Tax; see above, p. 11.
[75] B.L. Map Libr., 'Outlying Portion of the Wilton Estate', sale cat.
[76] See p. 11; Wilton Ho. Mun., rent bk. 1886.

[77] Wilton Ho. Mun., audit bk.; B.L. Map Libr., 'Outlying Portion of the Wilton Estate', sale cat.
[78] Local information.
[79] C.P. 25(1)/251/12 no. 3; *Feet of F. 1327–77* (W.R.S. xxix), p. 88.   [80] See p. 7.
[81] W.R.O. 492/76–81.   [82] Ibid. 492/71–5.
[83] Ibid. 492/82–3.   [84] Ibid. 492/93–4.
[85] Ibid. 492/95; *Taxation Lists* (W.R.S. x), 116; *Poverty in Salisbury* (W.R.S. xxxi), p. 33.
[86] *Pembroke Man.* (W.R.S. ix), pp. 126–9; Sar. Dioc. R.O., Glebe Terrier.
[87] Cf. *Pembroke Man.* (W.R.S. ix), pp. 126–9; W.R.O., Inclosure Award map.
[88] Cf. *Pembroke Man.* (W.R.S. ix), pp. 126–9; Wilton Ho. Mun., survey, 1705.
[89] *Pembroke Man.* (W.R.S. ix), p. 126; Wilton Ho. Mun., surveys, 1631, 1705.
[90] W.R.O., Inclosure Award.   [91] Ibid.

the whole township. Much of the down had presumably been ploughed, and new buildings had been erected on the southern edge of the down and further north beside an extensive new covert at Foxholes.[92] From 1827 some 213 a. of Netton were held with the farm,[93] which measured 875 a. in 1883.[94] Edwin Dibben, then the tenant, was a noted breeder of Hampshire Down sheep.[95] By 1947 the downland north of the old Shaftesbury drove and the meadow land south of the farmstead had been detached from the farm, 774 a. The buildings at Foxholes were then used as a piggery.[96] In 1976 Flamston remained a large mixed farm.

In the Middle Ages the lands of Croucheston township were cultivated in common[97] and shared among the bishop of Winchester's customary tenants, Waverley Abbey, and the holders of Croucheston and Faulston manors. Waverley Abbey's land, which in the late 13th century was held by a tenant for 20s. a year, was assessed at 1 hide,[98] Croucheston manor at 3 hides.[99] In the earlier 13th century the bishop's land was reckoned 17 virgates, 12 held each for 4s. a year and numerous labour services and 5 for 10s. a year each without labour service. The 5 virgates had all been held by Nicholas of Coombe, and their terms of tenure were possibly the result of a commutation arranged between Nicholas and a bishop.[1] In 1328 the lord of Faulston held in Croucheston more than half of an estate consisting of 1 carucate of land, 4 a. of meadow, and 56s. a year rent.[2]

In the mid 16th century the arable land of the township was cultivated in three common fields, East, West, and to the north of them Middle, in all some 450 a., and there were separate downs for sheep and cattle, some 400 a., of which Cow down was the southernmost.[3] In the mid 17th century there were some eight farms. The largest, 130 a. with feeding for 260 sheep and 26 beasts, was that of Faulston manor, which from 1667 or earlier earls of Pembroke and Montgomery leased for years on lives for heavy fines.[4] Croucheston manor consisted of 120 a. and feeding rights.[5] The lands formerly of Waverley Abbey apparently consisted of no more than 20 a. with feeding for 40 sheep and 3 beasts, and was later added to Croucheston manor.[6] There were five copyhold of inheritance tenants of Bishopstone manor in Croucheston. In all they held some 180 a. and disproportionately large stints of 600 sheep and 31 beasts.[7]

The common fields and downs were inclosed in 1792. After inclosure there were four farms of more than 100 a., three of fewer than 100 a. The larger farms were allotted lands in long narrow strips running back to the downs from the farmsteads in Croucheston street.[8] The easternmost, Faulston manor land, 221 a., became the base for Croucheston farm. It was let at rack-rent from 1811.[9] In 1838 its tenant James Swayne owned the next farm to the west, Croucheston manor, then 245 a., and in 1840 bought John Hewett's, the next farm to the west of that, 140 a.[10] Elizabeth Snook's farm, 171 a., lay along the western boundary of the parish.[11] Although not in single ownership until c. 1890,[12] Croucheston farm apparently remained intact. In 1919, when there were probably other farms of 171 a. and 93 a. in the township,[13] Croucheston was a mixed farm of 632 a. with buildings in Croucheston and on the down.[14] Croucheston Down farm was afterwards detached from it, but other land was added and in 1976 Croucheston was still a large mixed farm worked from Croucheston street. Croucheston Down remained a separate mainly arable farm.[15]

The land in Faulston was all part of Faulston manor. In 1328 the demesne land of the manor was said to be 250 a. of arable, 6 a. of meadow, and a pasture called Ox down; and near the manor-house were a sheepfold and a rabbit warren. In 1340 there were said to be only 160 a. of arable. In 1328 there were five bond tenants and eleven cottars, in 1340 five bond tenants and three cottars. In the township's open field demesne and tenantry strips were apparently intermingled, and the upland pastures were used in common.[16] In 1387 the bondmen and bond tenants rebelled against their lord Nicholas Baynton by withdrawing their customary services and, it seems, by resisting attempts to enforce them.[17] The cause of the rebellion, which a commission of oyer and terminer was issued to suppress, is nowhere recited but possibly lay in a desire of Baynton, who by then may have rebuilt and fortified the manor-house,[18] to inclose the flat summit of Faulston down, later called the Pale. That inclosure was effective in 1618, when the Pale was marked on a map as a park,[19] and the late 14th century seems the most likely date for it. Later, probably in the 15th century as at Bishopstone,[20] the customary holdings were given up and merged in the demesne as a single farm, which in the late 15th century and the 16th members of the Aynoll family apparently held.[21] In 1647 the Faulston House committee leased it for £170.[22]

After Philip, earl of Pembroke and Montgomery, acquired the manor, the farm was divided into an inclosed home farm, Faulston, and the remaining lands of the township, the 'outlands' around the east and south sides of the farm.[23] Faulston farm was held by leases for years on lives under heavy fines

[92] Ibid. Tithe Award.
[93] See above.
[94] Wilton Ho. Mun., rent bk.
[95] W.A.M. xlv. 339.
[96] B.L. Map Libr., 'Outlying Portion of the Wilton Estate', sale cat.
[97] Wilts. Inq. p.m. 1327–77 (Index Libr.), 29; S.C. 6/1119/7.
[98] Feet of F. 1272–1327 (W.R.S. i), p. 30.
[99] C.P. 25(1)/250/5 no. 17.
[1] B.L. Eg. MS. 2418, f. 65 and v.
[2] Cf. Cal. Inq. p.m. vii, p. 111; Wilts. Inq. p.m. 1327–77 (Index Libr.), 29–30.
[3] E 318/Box 48/2570 rot. 5; First Pembroke Survey, ed. Straton, i. 302–4. Cf. W.R.O., Inclosure Award.
[4] Wilton Ho. Mun., surveys of Faulston, 1672, 1705.
[5] W.R.O. 130/9, covenant, Hayward with Eyre (1678).

[6] Ibid. 130/9, bargain and sale, Hewett to Ballard (1728); see above.
[7] Pembroke Man. (W.R.S. ix), pp. 113–14.
[8] W.R.O., Inclosure Award.
[9] Wilton Ho. Mun., survey of Faulston, 1705.
[10] W.R.O., Tithe Award; see above.
[11] W.R.O., Tithe Award.
[12] See above.
[13] Cf. W.R.O., Tithe Award; Wilts. Cuttings, v. 109.
[14] W.A.S. Libr., sale cat. xv, no. 3.
[15] Local information.
[16] Wilts. Inq. p.m. 1327–77 (Index Libr.), 24, 27–9, 274.
[17] Cal. Pat. 1385–9, 319.   [18] See above.
[19] M.R. 260.   [20] See above.
[21] e.g. C 1/65/85; C 1/716/26–31; E 179/197/199.
[22] W.A.M. xxvi. 388.
[23] Wilton Ho. Mun., survey, 1672.

until 1809.[24] It consisted of some 288 a. including 112 a. of arable land and the Pale, 80 a. of rough grazing in which the earls of Pembroke and Montgomery reserved feeding for deer. The rent included twelve trout for the fishing but the tenant was entitled to the second best acre of underwood cut each year at Verndich in Broad Chalke.[25] The 'outland', none of it held customarily, was divided equally into six. New farmsteads were built on 6 a. of dry meadow taken from Faulston farm between Faulston drove and Mill Lane and in 1650–1 the six farms were leased, two together and four separately, for years on lives under fines totalling £2,200. Common husbandry was practised in two meadows each of 6 a., three arable fields and a close totalling some 180 a., and the down, 426 a., on which 840 sheep could be kept. That 'outdown' was also open to the lord's deer.[26] From 1767 the tenures on lives began to be eliminated.[27] The 'outlands' were inclosed in 1792.[28] Four of the farms, in single occupancy at rack-rent, were allotted some 410 a.; the remaining two farms, also in single occupancy, were allotted some 178 a.; the rector and vicar was allotted 29 a. to replace his lands in Flamston. In 1803 the 'outlands' were united as a single farm, and the common feeding of 13 a. of the steeper slopes of the down perpetuated by the inclosure award was thus eliminated.[29]

In 1838 the township contained Faulston farm, 301 a. with buildings on the opposite side of the road to the west side of the manor-house, and the 'outland' farm, 610 a. with buildings on the site of the six farmsteads but also with buildings and presumably ploughed land on the down.[30] Apart from 210 a., which in the later 19th century were leased to Edwin Dibben, tenant of Flamston farm, the two farms were later merged as Faulston farm.[31] In the 19th century extensive new buildings were erected for it on the site of the six farmsteads. In 1919 Faulston farm measured 707 a.[32] The remaining land in the township, some 200 a. in the north-east corner, was part of Throope farm and remained so in 1976.[33] In 1932 Faulston Down farm was detached, and in 1976 Faulston farm was an arable and beef farm of 480 a. Faulston Down remained a separate farm.[34]

In the Middle Ages the lands of Throope were used in common by the holders of Throope manor and the estate which passed to the Fraternity of Jesus in Gillingham, and by the tenants of Faulston and Bishopstone manors who held land in Throope. Throope manor consisted of a demesne farm reckoned 1 carucate and, in the early 15th century,

of five small tenant holdings totalling some 35 a.[35] Tenants were not subsequently mentioned, and in the 16th century all the lands of the manor were apparently leased to members of the Ragland family.[36] The fraternity's lands, leased for 50s. a year in the mid 16th century, were presumably not extensive.[37] The copyholds in Throope which were part of Faulston manor were moderately sized,[38] but the copyholder of Bishopstone manor who held there had a cottage and only some 6–8 a.[39]

In the 17th century the arable, some 300 a., was cultivated in three common fields and there was a down for sheep and feeding in common for cattle.[40] From 1702 the copyhold of inheritance land of Bishopstone manor in Throope passed with Throope manor as Throope farm, with which the land of the Fraternity of Jesus had probably been merged.[41] From 1708 the three copyholds of Faulston manor, together amounting to 88 a. and feeding for 200 sheep and 14 other animals, were held by members of the Button and Rooke families, but not by those who owned Throope farm.[42] It is likely, however, that the whole of Throope was worked as a single farm from 1708, and that cultivation in common was thus effectively eliminated.[43] To resolve uncertainties about which lands belonged to Throope farm, and which to Faulston manor, an award was made in 1762 under an agreement of 1758 to separate the lands.[44] The eastern side of the arable land and the whole of the down were allotted as the freehold and copyhold of inheritance land of Throope farm, 351 a., which was inclosed.[45] Barns had been erected on the down, much of which had presumably been ploughed, by 1773.[46] The western side of the arable land was allotted to the three copyholds for lives of Faulston manor, 115 a., which theoretically remained under common cultivation until at inclosure in 1792 allotments were made in respect of each copyhold.[47] All remained part of Throope farm, 468 a. in 1838,[48] although held by the owner of that farm from only 1850.[49]

In the later 19th century a separate sheep-and-corn farm of 152 a., Throope Down farm, was established on the down and centred on the old barns near the road from Salisbury to Blandford Forum.[50] It had been reunited with Throope farm by 1919 and some 200 a. of Faulston added to make Throope farm then 689 a.[51] Throope Down farm was again separate in 1939,[52] but in 1976 its land was worked from outside the parish and its buildings, apart from a 20th-century house, had been taken down. Throope farm, which was worked with land in Stratford Tony, was in 1976 devoted mainly to arable and beef production.[53] The buildings at

[24] Wilton. Ho. Mun., surveys, 1672, 1705.
[25] Ibid. survey, 1672.
[26] Ibid.   [27] Ibid. survey, 1705.
[28] W.R.O., Inclosure Award.
[29] Wilton Ho. Mun., survey, 1705.
[30] W.R.O., Tithe Award.
[31] Wilton Ho. Mun., rent bks.
[32] W.A.S. Libr., sale cat. xv, no. 3.
[33] Ibid.; ex inf. Viscount Head, Throope Man.
[34] Ex inf. Miss M. Freya Watkinson, Faulston Ho.
[35] Abbrev. Plac. (Rec. Com.), 222; C.P. 25(1)/256/60 no. 19.
[36] e.g. Taxation Lists (W.R.S. x), 44; C 2/Jas. I/H 12/34.
[37] E 318/Box 40/2148 rot. 2.   [38] See below.
[39] W.R.O. 492/4, ct. held 14 Jan. 1493; First Pembroke Survey, ed. Straton, i. 303.
[40] Pembroke Man. (W.R.S. ix), p. 115; Wilton Ho. Mun.,

survey of Faulston, 1672.
[41] Wilton Ho. Mun., survey of Bishopstone, 1632; see above.
[42] Wilton Ho. Mun., survey of Faulston, 1705.
[43] About 1760 the 3 copyholds were said to be 'roofless': ibid.
[44] Ibid. bk. containing scheds. of deeds, 120.
[45] W.R.O., Inclosure Award.
[46] Andrews and Dury, Map (W.R.S. viii), pl. 2.
[47] W.R.O., Inclosure Award.
[48] Ibid. Tithe Award.
[49] Wilton Ho. Mun., survey of Faulston, 1705.
[50] Cf. W.R.O., Tithe Award; W.A.S. Libr., sale cat. xxi, no. 10.
[51] Ibid. sale cat. xv, no. 3.
[52] Kelly's Dir. Wilts. (1939).
[53] Ex inf. Viscount Head.

Raglands were used before the Second World War for dog-breeding,[54] and after that war for the breeding of turkeys and silver foxes. Turkey farming increased in the 1950s but ceased c. 1960.[55]

In 1890 Netton marsh,[56] through which the Ebble flowed as a broad and shallow stream, was used by Isaac Barter to make a watercress bed of c. 1 a. south of Netton street.[57] By the mid 20th century a new bed had been built on the opposite side of the Netton–Croucheston lane. After the Second World War the first bed was enlarged to the east, a small new bed was made near the site of Croucheston mill, and a large bed was made on a meadow south of Flamston Farm.[58] That last bed was given up c. 1960 and later converted into a pond for trout farming. The cress beds, which have remained in the Barter family, are fed with pure water springing from artesian wells at a constant 51 °F. The cress, cut and packed at Netton, has long been sent nightly to London, and in 1976 was also sent to Bristol and Plymouth. Mr. H. S. Barter then had c. 3 a. of beds at Netton and c. 5 a. at Coombe Bissett, and employed a total of some sixteen men and women which was increased by some casual labour in the summer.[59]

MILLS. One or more of the seven mills on the bishop of Winchester's Downton estate in 1086 was possibly at Bishopstone.[60] A mill, presumably that on the Ebble at Croucheston, was held customarily of Bishopstone manor in the early 13th century.[61] Croucheston mill remained a customary holding of the manor and became a copyhold of inheritance.[62] In the early 17th century it was held by the lessee of Bishopstone manor, but afterwards seems to have belonged to millers except in the period 1832–60, when James Swayne owned it, and in the 20th century, when it passed in the Barter family.[63] The mill and mill-house were rebuilt in 1475–6.[64] In the earlier 16th century the tenants of Bishopstone manor were still being ordered to take their grain to it.[65] Possibly in the earlier 18th century it was used to mill malt and in 1753 a near-by malt-house was mentioned.[66] By then, however, the mill was again used only for corn. In 1944, when its buildings were apparently of the 18th century, it was burned down.[67] From c. 1900 the mill had been worked by members of the Kent family.[68] After the Second World War the firm of Kent & Brogan, from c. 1956 Kent & Fleet, began to produce animal foodstuffs on the site. New ranges of buildings have been erected to house modern milling and mixing equipment and for storage. Kent & Fleet produces high quality feed for all farm livestock and does business throughout the county and beyond.[69]

There was probably a mill at Faulston in the early 14th century,[70] and millers were mentioned in the later 15th century.[71] The mill passed with Faulston manor,[72] and with Bishopstone manor to Newcastle Estates.[73] From 1666 to 1809 it was leased with Faulston farm.[74] In 1666 the mill was said to house both corn- and malt-mills.[75] In 1709 it was agreed that the farmer of Bishopstone might water his western meadows from the mill hatches, and that in return he would take his corn to Faulston mill for grinding.[76] The mill, called Lower mill in 1919,[77] continued to grind until the Second World War.[78] It is partly weatherboarded and probably of the 18th century. It retains its wheel and much 19th-century machinery. The mill-house adjoins it to the north and forms a range at right angles to it. The house is of brick and stone and 18th-century or earlier in origin. It has been modernized and extended in recent years.

LOCAL GOVERNMENT. The liberties of the bishops of Winchester in respect of Downton hundred, acquired before the Conquest and defined in the later 13th century, gave them rights of jurisdiction over Bishopstone as well as over Downton.[79] Separate courts for Bishopstone were apparently being held in the early 13th century.[80] The bishops exercised jurisdiction over the whole parish which was then already divided into three tithings, Bishopstone, Faulston, and Flamston.[81] In the 13th century the king's justices reckoned the townships of Croucheston and Netton to be tithings,[82] and in the late 18th century Croucheston, Netton, and Throope were all called tithings,[83] but none was ever represented by a tithingman in a court of a bishop of Winchester or of an earl of Pembroke. Those courts reckoned Bishopstone tithing to include Netton, Faulston tithing to include Croucheston, and, although they were in opposite corners of the parish, Flamston tithing to include Throope.[84] For other purposes, however, Croucheston and Throope were often considered parts of Bishopstone tithing.[85]

As at Downton the bishops exercised leet jurisdiction twice a year in tourns held by the steward near Hock-tide and Martinmas.[86] In the later 15th

[54] Kelly's Dir. Wilts. (1939).
[55] Bishopstone Scrap Bk. penes Miss Watkinson; ex inf. Viscount Head.   [56] See above.
[57] Bishopstone Scrap Bk. penes Miss Watkinson; O.S. Map 6″, Wilts. LXX. NE. (1901 edn.); see plate facing p. 49.
[58] O.S. Maps 1/25,000, 41/02 (1949 edn.); 1″, sheet 167 (1960 edn.).   [59] Ex inf. Mr. H. S. Barter.
[60] V.C.H. Wilts. ii, p. 119.
[61] B.L. Eg. MS. 2418, f. 65.
[62] First Pembroke Survey, ed. Straton, i. 302.
[63] Pembroke Man. (W.R.S. ix), p. 113; Wilton Ho. Mun., surveys, 1632, c. 1740; ct. bk. 1820–50, pp. 190–1; ex inf. Mr. Barter.
[64] H.R.O. Eccl. 2/155840.   [65] W.R.O. 492/6.
[66] Wilton Ho. Mun., ct. bk. 1724–68, ct. of 1753.
[67] Bishopstone Scrap Bk. penes Miss Watkinson.
[68] Wilton Ho. Mun., ct. bk. 1820–50, pp. 337–9; Kelly's Dir. Wilts. (1907).
[69] Ex inf. Mr. K. D. Pratt, Kent & Fleet.

[70] Wilts. Inq. p.m. 1327–77 (Index Libr.), 29.
[71] W.R.O. 492/9.
[72] C.P. 25(2)/240/25 Eliz. I East.
[73] B.L. Map Libr., 'Outlying Portion of the Wilton Estate', sale cat.; local information.
[74] Wilton Ho. Mun., surveys, 1672, 1705.
[75] Ibid. survey, 1672.   [76] W.R.O. 212B/5922.
[77] W.A.S. Libr., sale cat. xv, no. 3.
[78] Kelly's Dir. Wilts. (1939); local information.
[79] See p. 43.
[80] H.R.O. Eccl. 2/159282, rot. 12.   [81] Ibid.
[82] Crown Pleas, 1249 (W.R.S. xvi), p. 183.
[83] W.R.O., Inclosure Award.
[84] e.g. ibid. 492/4.
[85] e.g. H.R.O. Eccl. 1/85/5; E 179/199/398.
[86] This para. is based on late-15th- and early-16th-cent. ct. rolls in W.R.O. 492/4; 492/9; 893/1–2; 893/5–7 and in H.R.O. Eccl. 1/79/16–25; Eccl. 1/85/1–6; Wilton Ho. Mun., late-17th-cent. ct. rolls, and ct. bks. 1690–1723; 1724–68; 1742–1819; 1820–50.

century the Bishopstone tourn was held on the day following that for Downton. It proceeded on the presentments of the three tithingmen in turn. Cert-money, which had been commuted by the early 13th century, was paid. Offences presented by the tithingmen included breaches of the peace, poaching, public nuisances, and breaches of the assize of ale and millers' malpractices, but were not annually numerous. The presentments were affirmed by a jury of twelve freemen who sometimes reported additional offences. Brewers were occasionally presented by the ale-taster himself. The business of the tourn had become stereotyped by the later 17th century when only one, called a view of frankpledge, was held each year in September. From then until the mid 19th century, when the view ceased, nuisances were sometimes presented by the jurors but usually nothing was done but to record the annual elections of the constable and three tithing-men.

In the 14th and 15th centuries two bailiff's courts for Bishopstone manor were held between the tourns although, as in the later 15th century, manorial business could presumably be done also in the tourn.[87] In the later 15th century and the early 16th four manor courts were held each year in addition to the tourns to deal with matters such as admittances to holdings, tenements needing repair, stray animals, and pleas between tenants. The assize of ale was also enforced. In the later 17th century manor courts were held annually on the same day as the views and sometimes at other times, proceeding on present-ments of the homage. The most important business was the recording of conveyances and settlements of copyholds of inheritance and, until inclosure, of changes in the rules for common husbandry. In the early 19th century, when the copyholds were fewer, larger, and more often held by absentee landlords, the convening of the homage became more difficult and conveyancing out of court more desirable. In 1850 a tenant's widow was said to hold by favour and not by right because her husband had not been admitted 'through want of customary tenants to form a manor court'. No court was held after c. 1850. Admittances were thereafter always made out of court, sometimes in solicitors' offices in London.

No court record for Faulston manor survives. Separate courts were held by the earls of Pembroke and Montgomery for Flamston manor.[88] In the later 17th century and the early 18th they were held annually in April or May and, proceeding on the presentments of the homage, dealt with copyhold and agrarian business, but never with much in any one year. From the early 18th century the frequency of the courts declined with the number of copyholds

in Flamston, and none was apparently held after 1817.

No record of parochial government is known. The poor were relieved partly in a workhouse near the Three Horse Shoes.[89] The average annual expenditure on the poor in the period 1833–5 was £906, a high figure for a parish of Bishopstone's size. The parish joined the Wilton poor-law union in 1836.[90]

CHURCH. Bishopstone was probably served from Downton in 1086.[91] It is likely that a parish church was built soon afterwards and Bishopstone detached from Downton, but the first evidence of Bishopstone church is from its 12th-century masonry.[92] In 1264 the church supported a rector and a vicar,[93] but the precise date, circumstances, and provisions of the ordination of the vicarage are unknown. Vicars and sinecure rectors continued to be instituted until 1815 when the two benefices were united in a rectory by Act.[94] Apparently from 1584, however, it was the custom to appoint the same man to both rectory and vicarage.[95] In 1925 the benefice was united with the rectory of Stratford Tony.[96] Since 1972 those parishes have been part of the Chalke Valley group ministry with a curate-in-charge resident at Bishop-stone.[97]

The advowson of the rectory was held with the bishopric of Winchester until in the mid 16th century it passed with the manor to the earls of Pembroke.[98] In 1244, 1261, 1262, 1349, and 1531 the king presented sede vacante.[99] At least from 1302 the advowson of the vicarage belonged to the rectors. Except in 1513 and 1574, when their grantees presented, rectors presented vicars until 1575.[1] The earls of Pembroke thereafter presented to both benefices, except in 1662 when the king's prerogative right to present was exercised because the rector and vicar was promoted to a bishopric.[2] From 1925 the patronage of the united benefice was shared by the earls of Pembroke and Montgomery and Corpus Christi College, Oxford.[3] In 1972 the Pembroke and Montgomery share was transferred to the bishop of Salisbury with whom the college has since shared the right to nominate the curate-in-charge.[4]

In 1291 the rectory was assessed at £21 6s. 8d. and in 1535 at £20, on both occasions at more than the average for a Wiltshire parish church.[5] The vicarage, assessed at £4 6s. 8d., was poor in 1291 but, at £12 in 1535, was later more highly valued.[6] Taken together from the late 16th century the rectory and vicarage made a valuable living, worth £400 a year in 1650[7] and some £350 c. 1740.[8] The rector's

[87] e.g. H.R.O. Eccl. 2/159384, rot. 7; Eccl. 2/159443, rot. 3. The remainder of this para. is based on ct. rec. cited above, n. 86.
[88] Wilton Ho. Mun., late-17th-cent. ct. rolls; ct. bks. 1690–1723; 1724–1817.
[89] Endowed Char. Wilts. (S. Div.), 46; Bishopstone Scrap Bk. penes Miss Watkinson.
[90] Poor Law Com. 2nd Rep. 560.
[91] See p. 46.
[92] See below.
[93] H.R.O. Eccl. 2/159295, rot. 4d.
[94] L. J. 1. 323–4, 387.
[95] Phillipps, Wilts. Inst. i. 232; ii. 7.
[96] Lond. Gaz. 30 June 1925, pp. 4361–3.
[97] Ibid. 26 Oct. 1972, p. 12603.
[98] Cal. Pat. 1232–47, 414; Phillipps, Wilts. Inst. i. 31,

63, 105, 108, 113, 132, 144, 149, 197.
[99] Cal. Pat. 1232–47, 414, 416; 1258–66, 136; 1266–72, 730; 1348–50, 376; L. & P. Hen. VIII, v, p. 130.
[1] Phillipps, Wilts. Inst. i. 4, 10, 15, 20, 75, 76, 80, 85, 123, 128, 136, 154, 173, 185, 190, 193, 203, 204, 210, 227.
[2] Ibid. 232; ii. 7, 19–20, 25–6, 27, 32, 42, 61, 72, 91.
[3] Lond. Gaz. 30 June 1925, pp. 4361–3; Crockford (1935).
[4] Lond. Gaz. 30 June 1972, p. 7865; Crockford (1975–6).
[5] Tax. Eccl. (Rec. Com.), 181; Valor Eccl. (Rec. Com.), ii. 108.
[6] Tax. Eccl. (Rec. Com.), 181; Valor Eccl. (Rec. Com.), ii. 108.
[7] W.A.M. xl. 304.
[8] W.A.S. Libr., 'Terrae Pembrochianae', 69.

average yearly income was £806 from 1829 to 1831, which shows that the living was still rich.[9]

It is not clear how the tithes and glebe were shared between the rector and vicar in the Middle Ages. In the 17th century the rector and vicar was entitled to all the tithes of the whole parish[10] which in 1838 were valued at £969 and commuted to a rent-charge.[11]

In 1677 the rector and vicar had some 2 a. west of the church, a nominal 21½ a. with pasture rights in common at Flamston, and 11 a. of inclosed land at Faulston apparently replacing some 2 a. and pasture rights formerly held in common.[12] The lands in Flamston and Faulston were replaced by an allotment of 28 a. at Faulston at inclosure in 1792.[13] In 1815 some 2 a. east of the church were acquired for a new house.[14] In 1838 the rector held some 32 a.,[15] some 25 a. of which were sold in 1947.[16] In 1545 the rector endowed the vicarage, until then lacking a house, with the living quarters on the first floor of the gate-house of the Rectory.[17] In 1677 there were two glebe-houses near the church, presumably the rectory-house and its gate-house,[18] but in 1792 only one.[19] In 1815 a new Rectory north-east of the church was built to designs ascribed to John Lowder of Bath.[20] It is of brick with a slated roof and has a square main block of two storeys with a service wing to the north. A five-sided conservatory was added to the east garden front in 1828.[21] In 1951, when it was called Bishopstone House, it was sold to Cdr. H. F. P. Grenfell, R.N. (Rtd.), who brought the wrought iron balustrading from Paultons in Eling (Hants).[22] The small house on the site of the old rectory- and vicarage-house is of the late 18th century. The Rectory built in 1951 stands on the north side of the road from Broad Chalke to Coombe Bissett c. 400 m. west of the church.

St. Andrew's chapel at Faulston is recorded in 1328 when it apparently stood very close to the manor-house.[23] Vicars regularly served it in the 14th century, and in 1389 the inhabitants' rights to burial, marriage, and baptism there were acknowledged.[24] The chapel was still in use in 1406[25] but was not afterwards mentioned. Flamston chapel is recorded in 1390 when the vicar acknowledged his duty to find a chaplain to serve it. Only burials were reserved for the mother church.[26] The chapel was still in use in 1406, when a light to St. Anne burned in it, and in 1443.[27] It did not survive the Reformation.

In 1310 the rector Ralph de Buckland, who by dispensation had been ordained priest while under

age, was licensed to be absent to study for two years.[28] Afterwards some notable clerics held the church. Richard Thormerton, the king's proctor at Rome and a pluralist, was rector from 1335 until he resigned in 1346 on receiving a canonry of Wells.[29] Nicholas Bildeston, at the same time archdeacon of Winchester and dean of Salisbury, was rector from 1423 to 1441.[30] John Earle, presented to the rectory and vicarage in 1639,[31] was deprived in the Civil War and went into exile as chaplain to Charles II.[32] His livings were given to a chaplain of Philip, earl of Pembroke and Montgomery, Ranulph Caldecot, who preached every Sunday.[33] Earle was restored in 1660 but resigned in 1662 on his promotion to the bishopric of Worcester, and in 1663 he was translated to Salisbury.[34] In 1671 Caldecot was again presented and he held the livings until 1688.[35] His successor John Younger, rector and vicar until 1728, held several canonries, was keeper of the Bodleian Library, Oxford, and became dean of Salisbury in 1705.[36] Francis Lear, curate from 1847 and rector 1850–1914, was archdeacon of Salisbury from 1875 to 1913.[37] In 1864, when a curate was employed, services were held twice on Sundays, with sermons, and on holy days. The Sacrament was administered at the great festivals and on the first Sunday in every month. There were some 120 communicants.[38] At least from 1899 to 1921 an additional Sunday service was held in the parish room.[39]

The church of *ST. JOHN THE BAPTIST* is built of rubble and ashlar and has a chancel with north-east stair turret and north vestry, central tower with north and south transepts, and nave with south porch.[40] A small round-headed window above the south crossing arch and the rubble walls of the nave are evidence of a 12th-century building which had become cruciform by the later 13th century, the date of the crossing arches. In the mid 14th century the church was extensively rebuilt or altered so that, at least from the outside, little of the earlier work could be seen. The chancel, vestry, and south transept were rebuilt in ashlar and given vaulted ceilings. The north transept is less elaborate than the south but has similar flowing tracery. It appears that both transepts were built as chapels since there is a large double tomb recess in the north wall and an external tomb with canopied shelter on the south wall. The remodelling of the nave was probably slightly later and was also less elaborate: the walls were heightened and new windows and buttresses added. The short upper stage of the tower, probably built soon after 1406,[41] carried the wooden spire

---

[9] *Rep. Com. Eccl. Revenues*, 824–5.
[10] Sar. Dioc. R.O., Glebe Terrier.
[11] W.R.O., Tithe Award.
[12] Sar. Dioc. R.O., Glebe Terrier; see above, p. 14.
[13] W.R.O., Inclosure Award.
[14] Sar. Dioc. R.O., Pet. for Faculties, bdle. 2, no. 32.
[15] W.R.O., Tithe Award.
[16] Ch. Commrs., benefice file.
[17] Mun. D. & C. Winton., ledger bk. IV, ff. 46v.–47.
[18] Sar. Dioc. R.O., Glebe Terrier.
[19] W.R.O., Inclosure Award map.
[20] Sar. Dioc. R.O., Pet. for Faculties, bdle. 2, no. 32; *Country Life*, 12 Nov. 1959.
[21] *Country Life*, 12 Nov. 1959.
[22] Ibid.; Wilts. Cuttings, xxi. 137–8.
[23] *Cal. Inq. p.m.* vii, pp. 130–1.
[24] Copy of a letter of 1891 from H. J. M. Swayne to the rector: *penes* Miss M. Freya Watkinson, Faulston Ho.
[25] *Tropenell Cart.* ed. J. S. Davies, i, p. 222.

[26] W.R.O. 492/263.
[27] *Tropenell Cart.* ed. Davies, i, p. 222; C 140/11 no. 35.
[28] *Cal. Papal Reg.* ii. 51; *Reg. Ghent* (Cant. & York Soc.), ii. 896.
[29] Phillipps, *Wilts. Inst.* i. 31; *Cal. Papal Reg.* iii. 77–8; *Cal. Papal Pets.* i. 4, 10, 17, 122.
[30] Phillipps, *Wilts. Inst.* i. 113, 132; Le Neve, *Fasti, 1300–1541, Salisbury*, 4; Le Neve, *Fasti, 1300–1541, Mon. Cathedrals*, 51.   [31] Phillipps, *Wilts. Inst.* ii. 19–20.
[32] *Walker Revised*, ed. A. G. Matthews, 372; *D.N.B.*
[33] *W.A.M.* xl. 304; xlvi. 396.
[34] *Walker Revised*, ed. Matthews, 372; *D.N.B.*
[35] Phillipps, *Wilts. Inst.* ii. 32, 42.
[36] Ibid. 42, 61; *Naish's Diary* (W.R.S. xx), 54 and n.
[37] *W.A.M.* xxxviii. 536; *The Times*, 20 Feb. 1914.
[38] Sar. Dioc. R.O., Vis. Queries.
[39] W.R.O. 577/11; Ch. Commrs., benefice file.
[40] See plate facing p. 81.
[41] *Tropenell Cart.* ed. Davies, i, p. 221.

that was extant in 1567.[42] The final structural addition was the 15th-century porch of two storeys.[43] The church was restored in the period 1836–9 under the supervision of the rector, George Augustus Montgomery, and much continental woodwork was introduced. After Montgomery's accidental death in 1842 his canopied tomb-chest, designed by A. W. N. Pugin, was placed in the south transept.[44] The porch was rebuilt in 1884 and the east window renewed in 1899.[45]

A bell was given to the church in 1406.[46] There were three bells in 1553. They were replaced successively in 1583, 1587, and 1652 by the three bells which hung in the church in 1976.[47]

In 1553 12 oz. of plate were taken for the king and a chalice weighing 6 oz. was left.[48] In 1663 Bishop Earle gave the parish a set of silver-gilt plate consisting of two chalices, two patens, and a dish, all made in Cologne.[49] That plate belonged to the church in 1976.[50]

By will proved 1843 G. A. Montgomery gave £1,000 after the death of his widow Cecilia (d. 1879) to restore the church. The money was intended for works of beautification and was not to be used for repairs. The new porch and east window were bought with it.[51] In 1971 the fund stood at £180.[52]

The registers of baptisms, beginning in 1636, and of marriages and burials, from 1639, are complete.[53]

NONCONFORMITY. Roger Vaughan and his wife Anne, sister of Henry Arundell, Baron Arundell of Wardour, were presented as popish recusants at Bishopstone in 1670,[54] but in 1676 there was said to be no papist in the parish.[55] There were then two Protestant dissenters,[56] William Aynoll of Flamston and his wife, who were frequently reported nonconformists until the 1680s.[57] A dissenters' meeting-house was certified in 1705,[58] and in the early 19th century there were possibly several houses in the parish certified for dissenters' meetings.[59] In 1833 the Primitive Methodists opened a chapel at Croucheston.[60] In 1864 it was said that there were some 40 dissenters but that many more people attended services in the chapel, which was in a more populous part of the parish than the church.[61] Services were still held in the chapel in 1976.

EDUCATION. In 1818 the poor of Bishopstone had no means of having their children educated.[62]

Two day-schools were started before 1833,[63] but neither had a special building. A new school was built at the Pitts in 1843,[64] and in 1854 a teacher's house was provided with help from the committee of the Privy Council.[65] In 1864 the boys left when they were eight or nine, the girls at ten or eleven, but a winter evening-school was held for boys.[66] By 1886 the school had been extended by the addition of an infants' schoolroom to the west.[67] In 1909 the average attendance at the school was 99,[68] in 1914 93, but by 1938 had fallen to 37.[69] In 1976 there were some twenty children on the roll and in 1977 the school was closed.[70] By a deed of 1843 Cecilia, relict of G. A. Montgomery, the rector, endowed the school with £395, the income from which, £12 in 1859, was at least until 1906 spent on general maintenance.[71] The school stands on rising ground above the road from Coombe Bissett to Broad Chalke. Reset in the gable are fragments of carved medieval stonework and a cartouche of royal arms.

CHARITIES FOR THE POOR. By will proved 1650 Dame Dorothy Gorges, formerly wife of Sir Charles Vaughan of Faulston,[72] gave £500 to the poor, £200 of which was to be invested for binding apprentices and relieving the impotent. By 1833 all trace of the charity had been lost.[73]

A gift of £100 to help the poor was apparently invested in the Hindon turnpike by an unknown donor. In 1812 the investment, called the Poor's Money, was transferred to the parish workhouse at five per cent and £10 was thereafter distributed in sums of 1s. and 1s. 6d. every other year. In 1830 and 1831 the money was spent on coal given or sold cheaply to the poor. When the workhouse was closed the £100 was not repaid and payments ceased.[74] The charity was apparently replaced, however, by G. A. Montgomery's Coal Charity. By will proved 1843 Montgomery gave the interest on £300 after the death of his widow Cecilia (d. 1879) to buy coal for sale cheaply to the poor, if as much money could be raised from subscriptions as from the charity. In 1906, when the income was £7 from the charity and £5 from subscription, coal was bought and sold.[75] In 1966 2 cwt. of coal was given to each of nine families. The endowment was increased in 1966 (see below), and in 1972 £85 was spent on providing 2 cwt. of coal for each of 35 parishoners.[76]

[42] First Pembroke Survey, ed. Straton, i. 299.
[43] J. Buckler, water-colour in W.A.S. Libr., vol. ii. 6 (1805).
[44] W.R.O. 577/13; W.A.M. xxvi. 205.
[45] Endowed Char. Wilts. (S. Div.), 51–2.
[46] Tropenell Cart. ed. Davies, i, p. 222.
[47] Walters, Wilts. Bells, 27; ex inf. the curate-in-charge, the Revd. P. R. Lewis, Bishopstone Rectory.
[48] Nightingale, Wilts. Plate, 46.
[49] Ibid. 46–7, where the date of the donation is misprinted; Pevsner, Wilts. (2nd edn.), 117.
[50] Ex inf. the Revd. P. R. Lewis.
[51] Endowed Char. Wilts. (S. Div.), 51–2.
[52] Char. Com. file 201494.
[53] W.R.O. 577/1–10. Transcripts for 1601 and 1622–37 are in Sar. Dioc. R.O.
[54] J. A. Williams, Cath. Recusancy in Wilts. (Cath. Rec. Soc.), p. 344.
[55] W.N. & Q. iii. 538.   [56] Ibid.
[57] Williams, Cath. Recusancy (Cath. Rec. Soc.), p. 276.
[58] W.R.O., Certs. Dissenters' Meeting-Houses.

[59] Sar. Dioc. R.O., Certs. Dissenters' Meeting-Houses. Some of the certs. for 'Bishopstone' are possibly for Bishopstone in Ramsbury hund.
[60] Sar. Dioc. R.O., Certs. Dissenters' Meeting-Houses.
[61] Ibid. Vis. Queries.
[62] Educ. of Poor Digest, 1019.
[63] Educ. Enquiry Abstract, 1028.
[64] Endowed Char. Wilts. (S. Div.), 48–50.
[65] W.R.O. 782/9; 577/13.
[66] Sar. Dioc. R.O., Vis. Queries.
[67] O.S. Map 6", Wilts. LXX (1889 edn.); W.R.O. 782/9.
[68] Return of Non-Provided Schs. 19.
[69] Bd. of Educ., List 21, 1914–38 (H.M.S.O.).
[70] Ex inf. Chief Education Officer, County Hall, Trowbridge.
[71] Endowed Char. Wilts. (S. Div.), 48–50; Acct. of Wilts. Schs. 6.
[72] Hutchins, Dors. iii. 343.
[73] Endowed Char. Wilts. (S. Div.), 46.
[74] Ibid.   [75] Ibid. 50–1.
[76] Char. Com. file 201494.

The rights of poor people to cut furze on the downs were confined at inclosure in 1792 to the allotments of land, totalling some 15 a. on Flamston, Croucheston, and Netton downs, made to the poor for the purpose. The cutting of furze had declined by 1906. In 1966 the Poor's Lands were sold for £850, which was invested to augment Montgomery's Coal Charity.[77]

DOWNTON

Downton, including Redlynch, Morgan's Vale and Woodfalls, and No Man's Land, pp. 19–52; Barford, pp. 52–5; Charlton, pp. 55–9; Hamptworth, pp. 59–62; Nunton and Bodenham, pp. 62–8; Standlynch, pp. 68–72; Wick pp. 72–5; Witherington, pp. 75 7.

THIS article[78] deals with the entire ancient parish of Downton whose lands, which now make up Downton, Redlynch, and nearly half of Odstock parishes, 14,466 a. (5,709 ha.), formed a rough triangle, with the apex 3 km. SSE. of Salisbury cathedral, and the base along some 13 km. of the Wiltshire–Hampshire border.[79] Downton was part of a great estate granted early to Winchester cathedral. It was separated from that part of the estate west of it in the 10th century, and from Bishopstone after 1086.[80] Thereafter the church built at Downton before 1086 served, and received tithes from, the entire episcopal estate at Downton which, notwithstanding great extent, geological variety, and the growth of many villages and hamlets, remained a single parish until the 19th century. Two extraparochial places bordered it, Langley Wood and No Man's Land.[81] Langley Wood had long been thought part of Whiteparish, which embraced it on three sides, and was deemed so in 1841.[82] Although it was later part of Downton civil parish, its history is therefore reserved for treatment with that of Whiteparish. In 1841 No Man's Land was counted with that part of Bramshaw parish in Cawdon and Cadworth hundred but, embraced on three sides by Downton parish and later being part of Redlynch civil parish,[83] its history is treated here. The article deals first with the parish as a whole and then with Downton proper, including the civil parishes of Redlynch, Morgan's Vale and Woodfalls, and No Man's Land. Certain aspects of the histories of other ancient settlements in the parish, Barford, Charlton, Hamptworth, Nunton and Bodenham, Standlynch, Wick, and Witherington, are dealt with afterwards under headings bearing the names of those places.

The bounds of the estate which became Downton parish were related in 997.[84] They cannot be represented in detail on a modern map but, since certain points in them, notably Bramshaw Wood in Bramshaw (Hants) and the confluence of the Christchurch Avon and the Ebble, remained boundary points, it seems likely that those early bounds and the parish boundary of 1841 were roughly the same. In places they followed natural or topographical features. The northern side of a ridge, the watershed of the Avon and Test, marks the south-eastern boundary with Hampshire; the river Blackwater

and for short distances the Avon and Ebble were boundaries; and Grim's ditch and Witherington ring are on the bounds. Elsewhere, drawn straight, the boundaries disregarded relief. That between Hamptworth and Landford commons was probably drawn during 19th-century inclosure.

The lands thus defined fall naturally into two parts, the Upper Cretaceous rocks of the Avon valley and the younger Eocene rocks south-east of a line drawn roughly from Downton Brickworks to Templeman's Farm.[85] On both sides of the Avon valley Upper Chalk outcrops, overlain by a strip of valley gravel and alluvium 1·5 km. wide beside the river, and by small areas of clay-with-flints on Nunton down and of plateau gravel near Standlynch, Barford, and Downton. On both sides of the valley the bottom of the chalk outcrops is roughly marked by the 46 m. contour. The deposits of alluvium and gravel extend from the river further on the west side than on the east. West of them the land rises sharply as a bluff and then to a series of peaks, from Clearbury ring (142 m.) to Gallows hill (114 m.), separated by steep-sided dry valleys, before rolling back to Whitsbury down (Hants). The corresponding bluff is closer to the river on the east side. The hills are as high, 154 m. between Witherington and Standlynch downs and 109 m. on Barford down, but the dry valleys less deeply incised and the relief gentler. The whole area is of the type with which sheep-and-corn husbandry is normally associated. Some of the downs were ploughed in the Romano-British Period,[86] but from Saxon times to the 19th century the use of the alluvium for meadow land, valley gravel for pasture and arable, and Upper Chalk for arable and sheep pasture seems to have remained largely unchanged. Shortage of arable land at times of rising population, however, led to the ploughing of some of the chalk lands on the east side of the valley, especially around Downton and Pensworth, in the early Middle Ages, and of much upland pasture in the 18th and 19th centuries. The frequency of large timber-framed and weatherboarded granaries on staddle-stones throughout the parish is presumably a result of that later ploughing. The later growth of dairy farming led to the grassing down of former arable land on the valley gravel. There were woodlands on the downs on the east

[77] Endowed Char. Wilts. (S. Div.), 47–8; Char. Com. file 201494.
[78] Written 1975–6.
[79] Maps used include: O.S. Maps 1/50,000, sheet 184 (1974 edn.); 1/25,000, SU 11 (1961 edn.), SU 12 (1958 edn.), SU 21 (1961 edn.), SU 22 (1958 edn.); 6″, Wilts. LXXI (1886 edn.), LXXII (1885 edn.), LXXVI (1880 edn.), LXXVII (1881 edn.).
[80] See p. 3.

[81] V.C.H. Wilts. iv. 351, 354.
[82] E 134/11 Jas. I Mich./13; H.O. 107/114.
[83] H.O. 107/104; V.C.H. Wilts. iv. 356 n. Bramshaw, but not No Man's Land, is treated in V.C.H. Hants, iv. 623–6.
[84] W.A.M. xxxvi. 51–5. For the date see above, p. 3 n.
[85] Geol. Surv. Maps 1″, drift, sheets 298 (1950 edn.), 314 (1948 edn.), 315 (1948 edn.).
[86] V.C.H. Wilts. i (1), 275, 277.

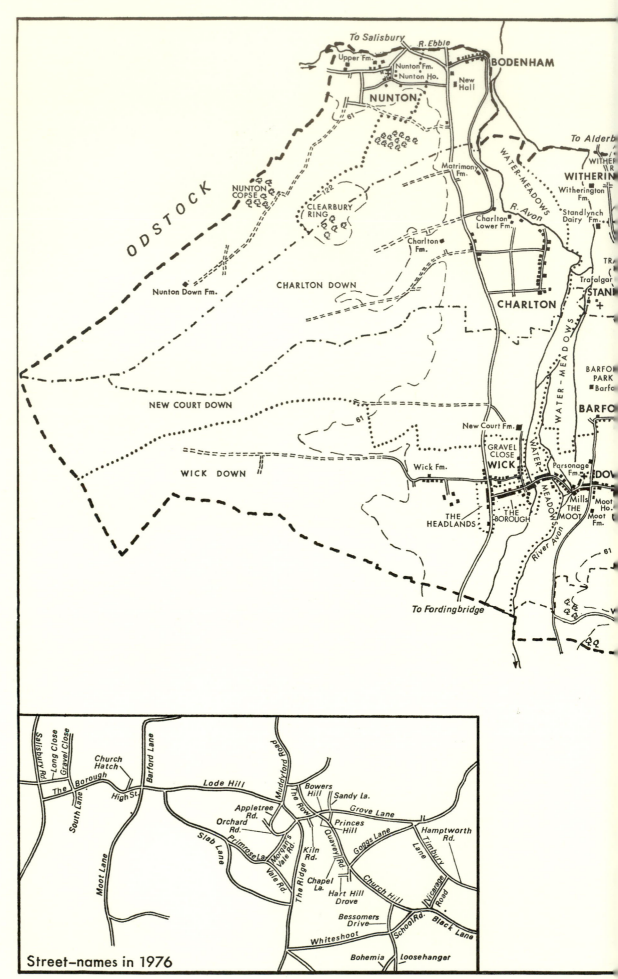

To Salisbury   R. Ebble

BODENHAM

Upper Fm.

Nunton Fm.
Nunton Ho.

New
Hall

To Alderb

NUNTON

61

WITHER
R

WITHERIN

Witherington

WATER-MEADOWS

Matrimon
Fm.

Standlynch
Dairy Fm.

NUNTON
COPSE

122

Charlton
Lower Fm.

R. Avon

TRA

CLEARBURY
RING

Charlton
Fm.

Trafalgar

STAN

R. Avon

ODSTOCK

CHARLTON DOWN

Nunton Down Fm.

CHARLTON

BARFO
PARK
Barfo

WATER-MEADOWS

BARFO

NEW COURT DOWN

61

New Court Fm.

WATER-MEADOWS

GRAVEL
CLOSE
WICK

DO

WICK DOWN

Wick Fm.

Parsonage
Fm.

Mills
THE
MOOT

Moot
Ho.

Moot
Fm.

THE
HEADLANDS

THE
BOROUGH

WATER-MEADOWS

61

River Avon

To Fordingbridge

Street–names in 1976

Salisbury Rd.

Long Close

Gravel Close

Church
Hatch

Barford Lane

Muddyford Road

Long Close

The   Borough

South Lane

High St.

Lode Hill

Bowers
Hill

Sandy La.

Grove Lane

The Row

Appletree
Rd.

Princes
Hill

Hamptworth
Rd.

Orchard
Rd.

Moot Lane

Slab Lane

Primrose La.

Morgan's Vale Rd.

Kiln
Rd.

Quaveri Rd.

Goggs Lane

Timbury Lane

The Ridge

Vale Rd.

Chapel
La.

Hart Hill
Drove

Church Hill

Vicarage   Road

Bessomers
Drive

School Rd.

Black Lane

Whiteshoot

Bohemia   Loosehanger

20

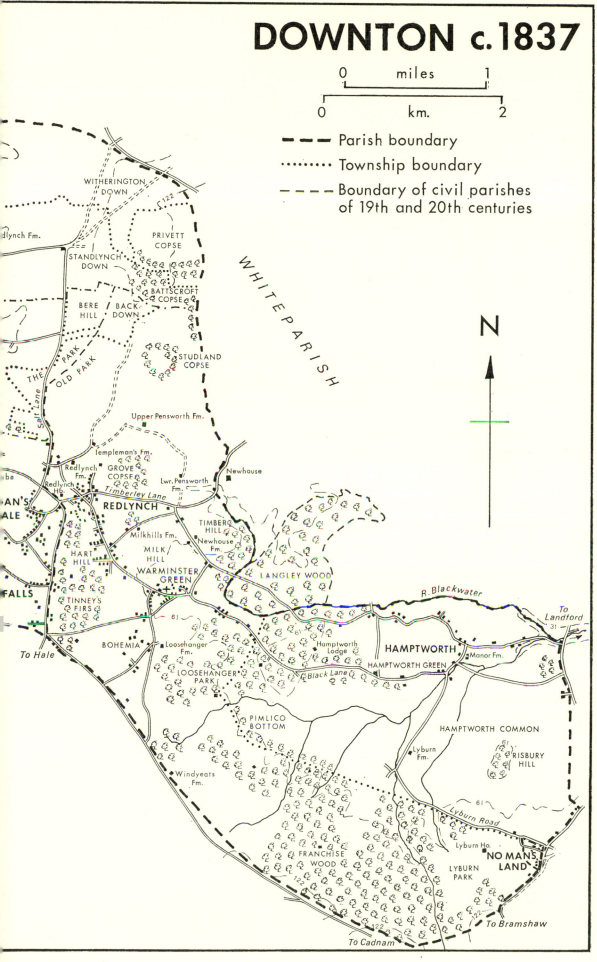

DOWNTON c.1837

0 miles 1
0 km. 2

--- Parish boundary
········· Township boundary
– – – Boundary of civil parishes
of 19th and 20th centuries

N

WITHERINGTON DOWN
Standlynch Fm.
122
PRIVETT COPSE
STANDLYNCH DOWN
BATTSCROFT COPSE
BERE HILL
BACK DOWN
WHITEPARISH
THE
PARK
OLD PARK
STUDLAND COPSE
Salt Lane
Upper Pensworth Fm.
Templeman's Fm.
Redlynch Fm.
GROVE COPSE
Lwr. Pensworth Fm.
Newhouse
Redlynch Ho.
Redlynch
Timberley Lane
AN'S
ALE
REDLYNCH
TIMBER HILL
Milkhills Fm.
Newhouse Fm.
ba
HART HILL
MILK HILL
WARMINSTER GREEN
LANGLEY WOOD
R. Blackwater
FALLS
TINNEY'S FIRS
61
To Landford
31
BOHEMIA
Loosehanger Fm.
Hamptworth Lodge
HAMPTWORTH
Manor Fm.
To Hale
LOOSEHANGER PARK
Black Lane
HAMPTWORTH GREEN
PIMLICO BOTTOM
HAMPTWORTH COMMON
Lyburn Fm.
RISBURY HILL
61
Windyeats Fm.
Lyburn Road
FRANCHISE WOOD
Lyburn Ho.
LYBURN PARK
NO MANS LAND
122
To Bramshaw
To Cadnam

21

side which, apart from that on Standlynch down, have been largely cleared.

The south-east part of the parish is geologically more complex, the use of the land less closely related to the outcrops. An irregular band of Reading Beds outcrops across the parish from the brickworks to Templeman's Farm, covered in several small areas by plateau gravel. South-east of it is an area of London Clay around Warminster Green (now called Lover) and Bohemia, which runs north-east to Newhouse in Whiteparish and in a narrow strip along the Blackwater valley to Hamptworth. Along the southern parish boundary Bracklesham Beds outcrop in an arc from No Man's Land to Pound bottom. Between them and the clay is a large area of Bagshot Sands, covered by plateau gravel around Woodfalls and on Risbury hill and by valley gravel beside the streams flowing through Hamptworth to the Blackwater. The road from Morgan's Vale church to North Charford (Hants) marks a north–south ridge, 114 m. at Woodfalls, from which the land slopes steeply west to the Avon and east to Redlynch and Warminster Green. At North Charford the ridge turns to the south-east and is followed by the parish boundary. From it the land slopes, steeply at first, in ridges and valleys north to the Blackwater. Ridges are marked by the hill south-west of Hamptworth Lodge, over 76 m., and by Risbury hill, over 61 m. The valleys contain a number of small streams flowing to the Blackwater and thence to the Test. There was woodland on the clay and on parts of the Bracklesham Beds. That on the clay was cleared at Hamptworth and around Warminster Green in the early Middle Ages, but woodland remains near Bohemia and at Timber hill near Newhouse. On most of the Reading Beds there was pasture, and on most of the Bagshot Sands and Bracklesham Beds, a large open area which was called the Franchise, there were extensive rough pastures. Both areas could support woodland and in some places were ploughed. In the 19th century there was much arable land on the Reading Beds and London Clay, most of which has reverted to pasture, and afforestation, continued into the 20th century, on the Bagshot Sands and Bracklesham Beds.

The road from Salisbury west of the Avon to Fordingbridge and Ringwood (both Hants) is the main means of communication with the parish from outside, but was not turnpiked. The routes that ran down the Avon valley from Salisbury closer to the river, and which linked the villages of the parish, were perhaps older. The evidence of direct roads from Bodenham through Charlton to Downton, and from Witherington through Standlynch and Barford to Downton, could be seen in 1975, but the western road, in places unsuitable for wheeled vehicles, had been superseded by more circuitous routes, and the eastern road had been much diverted in the 17th and 18th centuries. Although not previously prominent as a route,[87] the road from Downton to Cadnam (Hants) along the ridge between the Avon and Test valleys was turnpiked with other New Forest roads under an Act of 1832.[88] From the highest point of the ridge at Redlynch three apparently ancient lanes lead to the north-east and east ends of the parish.[89] Salt Lane, so called in 1539[90] but now Muddyford Road, runs northwards across the downs to Pepperbox hill in Whiteparish and to Dean Hill. Timberley Lane leads to Hamptworth. It was called Timbrell Lane in 1585,[91] once probably Timber Hill Lane, and is now Bowers Hill, Timbury Lane, and Hamptworth Road. Black Lane, so called in 1681,[92] runs to the parish boundary at Landford but not beyond. From the 13th century to the 19th it separated the cultivated land to the north of it from the common pasture to the south of it. In places it is now called Princes Hill, Quavey Road, Church Hill, and Black Lane. In 1866 the Salisbury & Dorset Junction Railway was made from the Salisbury–Romsey line at Alderbury to West Moors near Wimborne (Dors.).[93] It ran across the parish east of the Avon, through Downton station half-way up Lode Hill, and crossed the river as it left the parish. The line was closed in 1964.[94]

In the later 17th century there were attempts to make the Avon navigable through Downton to Salisbury.[95] They failed, perhaps partly because in the late 17th century the river was much used for watering meadows.[96] The construction of new carriages on both sides of the river, and of weirs and hatches for the drowning, and the ridging of the meadow land has had a lasting effect on the valley's scenery. The construction of several mansions with extensive gardens and parks in the late 17th century and the 18th had a similarly lasting effect there. In the east part of the parish the most significant topographical change was the afforestation that followed inclosure in the 19th century.

Although some of the eastern part of Downton parish was within the bounds of Melchet forest until formally excluded in 1377, the exemption of the bishop of Winchester's own woods from the regard in the early 13th century freed most of that part from the foresters' jurisdiction.[97] West of the Avon the parish was within the outer boundaries of Cranborne chase and was so marked on a map of 1618.[98] The foresters' activities caused resentment even after the grant of free warren to the bishop in the early 13th century had invalidated title to the Downton portion of the outer bounds.[99]

A succession of prehistoric settlers occupied sites in the parish. Castle meadow at Downton, excavated 1956–7, was the site of the only large Mesolithic settlement known in Wiltshire, possibly occupied in the 4th or 3rd millenium B.C. The site was also occupied in the late Neolithic Period and the early Bronze Age, but no occupation is thought to have been intensive or prolonged.[1] Archaeological discoveries, barrows, and other earthworks including Clearbury ring, an Iron-Age hill-fort, indicate

[87] Andrews and Dury, Map (W.R.S. viii), pl. 3.
[88] V.C.H. Wilts. iv. 263.
[89] Cf. Andrews and Dury, Map (W.R.S. viii), pl. 3; W.R.O., Inclosure Award map.
[90] Sar. Dioc. R.O., misc. papers, survey of Barford.
[91] Ibid. Detecta Bk.
[92] W.R.O. 490/1063.
[93] V.C.H. Wilts. iv. 286.

[94] Ex. inf. P.R. Dept., British Rail, S.R.
[95] V.C.H. Wilts. iv. 272; W.A.M. lxv. 172–6.
[96] W.R.O. 490/898.   [97] V.C.H. Wilts. iv. 427–9.
[98] Ibid. 458; M.R. 260.
[99] Rot. Hund. (Rec. Com.), ii (1), 257; V.C.H. Wilts. iv. 459.
[1] V.C.H. Wilts. i (2), 282–3; W.A.M. lxiv. 18; lviii. 116–42.

prehistoric activity in other parts of the parish.[2] A Roman villa, excavated 1955–7, was built at Downton in the late 3rd or early 4th century,[3] and there was another Romano-British settlement on Witherington down.[4]

The evidence of names containing Saxon elements and of sites on the gravel terraces above the Avon suggest that the villages of Nunton, Bodenham, Charlton, Walton, and Wick west of the river, and of Witherington, Standlynch, Barford, and Downton east of it were establishing themselves or growing in Saxon times.[5] All had attached to them long narrow strips of land reaching from the river to the downs. Bodenham and Charlton, street villages, were possibly planned settlements dependent on Downton, and Charlton's name perhaps increases that possibility.[6] Its name and its site close to Downton suggest that Walton was an early settlement greatly dependent on Downton manor.[7] The remaining villages, tightly clustered, possibly grew later out of outlying farms, in the cases of at least Nunton, Wick, and Witherington probably subsidiary centres of Downton manor. The early-medieval centuries were a period of growth in those villages. In the early 13th century Downton borough was established and some of the villages were as populous as at any time in their histories.[8] Away from the Avon valley where only Pensworth and Hamptworth were villages, both probably rather straggly, settlement was lighter and more dispersed.

In 1334 the taxation assessments for the villages in the parish, £35 7s. when taken together, were apparently higher than those for any other non-urban parish in the county.[9] There were 733 poll-tax payers in 1377, some 500 of them in the Avon valley villages.[10] The evidence of shrunken and deserted villages shows the population of the whole parish to have been lower in the later Middle Ages than before,[11] but its distribution remained roughly constant until the 20th century. In 1801 the parish population was 2,688, and, including No Man's Land, 4,144 in 1841 when about two-thirds of the inhabitants were living in the Avon valley. In 1901 it was 3,846, still similarly distributed. In the early 20th century, however, the Avon valley villages became less, the east side of the parish more, populous. In 1931 the parish population, 3,921, was divided equally between the two parts and in 1971, when it totalled 5,620 after a rapid post-war rise, the populations of the civil parishes of Redlynch and Downton were still virtually equal.[12]

Nunton and Bodenham and Standlynch were in the 19th century deemed civil parishes.[13] In 1894 the civil parish, formerly extra-parochial place, of Langley Wood, then in the same ownership as Hamptworth, was added to Downton civil parish.[14]

Thereafter the increased population, the establishment of new ecclesiastical parishes,[15] and the growth of new institutions led the civil parish of Downton to be dismembered. In 1896 Redlynch parish was created from the eastern part, in 1897 Charlton and Witherington were united with Standlynch to make the civil parish of Standlynch with Charlton All Saints, and in 1923 Morgan's Vale and Woodfalls were taken to form a new civil parish.[16] The residual civil parish of Downton measured 4,103 a. (1,661 ha.).[17] In 1934 Standlynch with Charlton All Saints civil parish was reunited with Downton, and Morgan's Vale and Woodfalls transferred with the civil parish, formerly extra-parochial place, of No Man's Land to Redlynch.[18] In 1971 Downton parish, 2,942 ha. (7,270 a.), housed 2,816 people.[19]

The moderately luxurious villa at Downton was the centre of a typical Roman farmstead.[20] It was superseded by Saxon settlement on sites perhaps nearer the river and was deserted. Downton was probably the principal village in the locality in the 7th and 8th centuries and acquired an even greater local importance as the centre of the bishop of Winchester's manor. The manor was one of the earliest endowments and richest manors of the see,[21] and by the late 11th century, when William I visited Downton,[22] it is likely that a manor-house had been built on the riverside site later occupied by Old Court.[23]

Downton village is divided topographically into three sections.[24] The church was built east of and overlooking the river on higher ground than the bishop's house and settlement grew up in the street between them. The diversion of the Avon to drive the mills at Old Court[25] left a rectangular island and settlement grew along the road across it. Another, probably later, diversion made an island of Old Court.[26] In the early 13th century Bishop Roches planned a borough settlement along a wide street west of the Avon. Plots were offered with free burgage tenure, with which the right to vote in parliamentary elections later passed, and by the 1230s some 120 had been taken and presumably built on.[27] There were later reckoned to be 127 burgages.[28] The borough, extending settlement across the river along the road through the bishop's meadows, was planted on an obvious site.[29] It was successfully founded, but part of its purpose was possibly to help Downton to develop into a market town and in that it failed, probably because of the proximity of Salisbury.

The three sections were linked by bridges. The borough was joined to the island by Catherine bridge, so called possibly in the early 15th century and certainly in the 16th,[30] presumably the 'fair

[2] V.C.H. Wilts. i (1), 64, 93, 99, 140, 170, 186, 188, 210, 252, 265, 275, 277.
[3] Ibid. i (2), 448–9; W.A.M. lviii. 303–41.
[4] W.A.M. lxii. 81.
[5] P.N. Wilts. (E.P.N.S.), 393–8; E. Ekwall, Dict. Eng. P.N.
[6] Cf. Ekwall, op. cit. 96; H. P. R. Finberg, 'Charltons and Carltons', Lucerna, 144–60, especially pp. 157–8. Finberg's explanation seems very unlikely for this Charlton.   [7] V.C.H. Wilts. i (2), 482–3.
[8] B.L. Eg. MS. 2418, ff. 61–64v.
[9] V.C.H. Wilts. iv. 296, 299.
[10] Ibid. 308.   [11] See pp. 25, 52, 76.
[12] V.C.H. Wilts. iv. 347, 354–7; Census, 1971.

[13] V.C.H. Wilts. iv. 355.
[14] Ibid. 347 n.   [15] See pp. 49, 58.
[16] V.C.H. Wilts. iv. 347 nn.   [17] Census, 1931.
[18] V.C.H. Wilts. iv. 347 n., 355 n., 356 n.
[19] Census, 1971.   [20] V.C.H. Wilts. i (2), 448–9.
[21] See below.   [22] Reg. Regum Anglo-Norm. i, no. 147.
[23] See p. 29.   [24] See plate facing p. 49.
[25] See below.   [26] See below.
[27] M. W. Beresford, New Towns of the Middle Ages, 505; M. W. Beresford, 'Six New Towns of the Bishops of Winchester, 1200–55', Medieval Arch. iii. 193–5.
[28] W.R.O. 490/851 (1630).
[29] Cf. Beresford, 'New Towns', Medieval Arch. iii. 194–5.
[30] Winch. Coll. Mun. 5038.

bridge of stone' mentioned by Leland c. 1538.[31] It was rebuilt in 1735–6,[32] and again in 1820 as a three-arched bridge of red brick,[33] the iron rails and balustrading of which survive. The island was joined to High Street by Mill bridge. In the later 17th century a new carriage for watering meadows bisected the borough.[34] It was crossed by Kingston bridge.[35]

In the mid 13th century Downton probably consisted of a continuous line of settlement from the church to the Salisbury–Fordingbridge road. Apart from Old Court and the rectory-house it contained no great wealth. Although it was assessed for taxation as highly as Calne and Cricklade in 1334 the borough clearly failed to grow, and the assessment of the remainder was only a little higher than Wick's, lower than Pensworth's, and a quarter of Charlton's. The 214 poll-tax payers of 'Downton' in 1377 were probably inhabitants of the whole settlement, which in 1841 housed 743 people.[36]

By the later 15th century prosperity at the east end had apparently increased. Settlement had developed in High Street, so called in 1452,[37] off the direct path from Old Court to the church. From the mid 15th century the area was called the east borough and by then had apparently assumed characteristics more urban than the nominally burghal west end.[38] Trade and industry were concentrated around the mills and later the tannery, and housing in High Street and Church Hatch. By the later 18th century housing extended into Barford Lane, so called in 1539,[39] and Moot Lane, up Lode Hill, called Node Hill in 1539,[40] and into Slab Lane.[41] The pattern changed little until the 1950s and 1960s when council and private housing estates were built in Moot Lane.

The island was reckoned part of the west borough in the later 15th century,[42] and votes were later attached to properties on it. Buildings stood along both sides of the borough street in 1618,[43] but the borough was not prosperous. When their houses were flooded in 1636 the islanders complained of their poverty,[44] and in 1628 and 1642 taxation assessments of the borough were low.[45] Along the main road at the western end, called the Headlands, prosperity and settlement grew, however, and by the early 18th century that area had been built up and was then deemed part of the borough.[46] In 1773 there was building in the middle, but none on the north side, of the street at the west end.[47] Buildings in the borough, the island, and the headlands to which votes were attached were numbered with small stone tablets to correspond with the numbers marked on a map and survey of 1784.[48] Many of the tablets, some reset, remained in 1975. Like that in the east borough the pattern of settlement in the west borough changed little in the 19th century

despite much building and rebuilding. In the 20th century a scatter of housing has developed on the west side of Salisbury Road and several workshops and small warehouses have been built on the east side. The area between the Headlands and Wick was built up with estates of bungalows and houses, mainly in the 1960s.

There was a 'hostel' in Downton in 1503.[49] In the 16th century innkeeping was possibly a growing occupation although in 1576 the justices, while allowing one inn to continue, forbade others to accommodate travellers and tried to control lodging.[50] The White Horse in the middle of the borough, perhaps the 'hostel' and the sanctioned inn, was open in 1599.[51] It was possibly already the centre of activities concerned with parliamentary elections but its importance as a social centre was further increased in the later 17th century, from which time manorial courts and probably elections were held in the school built behind it, and fairs were held near by.[52] The school and fairs were founded by Sir Joseph Ashe, Bt., lord farmer of Downton, who was then constructing the near-by carriage under Kingston bridge and rebuilding at New Court.[53] The White Horse was rebuilt in the early 18th century, possibly with materials and busts from Old Court. The borough cross at which the members of parliament were returned stood outside.[54] It was repaired in 1797,[55] restored in 1897, when a crocketed finial replaced a lamp on it, and in 1953, but was damaged in 1964.[56] In 1975 the medieval base stood on a later stepped plinth which bore inscriptions commemorating the restorations of 1797 and 1897. In the east borough the King's Arms at the junction of Church Hatch and High Street, a public house in 1628[57] and rebuilt in the late 18th century, seems to have prospered most; in the Headlands the Bull, an early-18th-century building with various later extensions, open as a public house in 1726,[58] catered for travellers along the main road, and continued to do so in 1975. In 1889, when there were at least five public houses in Downton,[59] the inhabitants ballotted to decide the future of two whose leases had fallen in. As a result one was closed.[60] In 1975 there were five public houses in Downton.

In 1975 Downton borough remained a wide street with a verge on the south side. From the Headlands to Catherine bridge it was characterized by a number of thatched cottages of the 17th century and later, interspersed by larger and mostly later buildings which on the south side include a former corn merchant's facing down the street from Catherine bridge, the former workhouse beside it, the White Horse, and a supermarket beside that. An early-18th-century brick and thatch house stands behind thatched cottages at the west end. Between

[31] Leland, *Itin.* ed. Toulmin Smith, i. 262.
[32] W.R.O. 490/948.
[33] Ibid. 1306, par. rec., Bridge Cttee. min.
[34] See p. 75.
[35] *Andrews and Dury, Map* (W.R.S. viii), pl. 3.
[36] *V.C.H. Wilts.* iv. 296, 299, 308, 347.
[37] Winch. Coll. Mun. 5091.
[38] W.R.O. 490/1169.
[39] Ibid. 893/2, p. 15.   [40] Ibid.
[41] *Andrews and Dury, Map* (W.R.S. viii), pl. 3.
[42] Winch. Coll. Mun. 5042.   [43] M.R. 260.
[44] *Wilts. Q. Sess. Rec.* ed. Cunnington, 121–2.
[45] W.R.O. 490/782; E 179/259/22.   [46] W.R.O. 490/830.

[47] *Andrews and Dury, Map* (W.R.S. viii), pl. 3.
[48] W.R.O. 490/780a.
[49] *Cal. Inq. p.m. Hen. VII*, ii, pp. 460–1.
[50] *Sess. Mins.* (W.R.S. iv), 19.   [51] C 2/Jas. I/I 9/4.
[52] W.R.O. 490/535, surrender by Ivie, 1701; 490/780a; Wilts. Cuttings, xii. 354.   [53] See below and pp. 73, 75.
[54] *Univ. Brit. Dir.* ii (1793 edn.), 845; W.R.O. 490/780a.
[55] The cross as then restored was drawn by J. Buckler, water-colour in W.A.S. Libr., vol. i. 22.
[56] Wilts. Cuttings, xiv. 294; xxii. 257.
[57] W.R.O. 490/783.   [58] E 134/12 Geo. I Mich./27.
[59] *Kelly's Dir. Wilts.* (1890).
[60] Wilts. Cuttings, xii. 348.

the White Horse and Fairfield House, an early-18th-century house greatly enlarged *c.* 1875,[61] South Lane contains a chapel and Borough House, a small brick and stone house dated 1673. Opposite, Gravel Close, in Wick tithing, containing a school, houses, and a former chapel, has become topographically part of Downton. In the Headlands a brick house of *c.* 1700 was the oldest building. The Bull, a pair of timber-framed and thatched cottages, and, set back from the road, a brick residence with a principal front of three bays to the west were of the 18th century. The 20th-century housing along Salisbury Road included a detached Edwardian villa called Scotts House.

At the east end of the borough the street narrows and turns across the island where the houses are mostly 19th-century. At Mill bridge the road bends sharply over the two still prominent mill-streams where the mills and the large tannery stand opposite each other. High Street and Church Hatch mostly contain 18th- and 19th-century brick houses but there are timber-framed and thatched cottages cased in brick at the top of High Street. There is a late-18th-century terrace of six brick houses on the south side of High Street. Tannery House opposite the tannery is of the early 20th century. The cottages at Waterside (formerly Watershoot Lane),[62] beside the mill-stream, are of the 19th and early 20th centuries. Barford Lane has at the south end a school, the old and new Vicarages, Hamilton House, built in the late 18th century, a 17th-century timber-framed and thatched cottage, and two 18th-century houses of brick and thatch. Further along the lane is housing of the 18th century and later, and behind it the modern telephone exchange. Moot Lane opposite contains two late-19th-century houses, Moot House, Moot Farm, and modern housing. From the top of High Street, Lode Hill rises steeply through a cutting past the site of the station to the saw-mill at the top. The buildings in it, and those in the northern part of Slab Lane, are, apart from one 18th-century timber-framed and thatched cottage, mostly 19th-century brick houses and cottages, none of much substance. A feature of the houses in Downton generally is that many contain high quality 18th-century brickwork. The recent building behind the Headlands and in Moot Lane has meant that the traditional line of settlement is no longer the most populous. In 1971 almost certainly over 2,000 of the inhabitants of Downton civil parish[63] lived in Downton. Many of the new residents travel daily to work in Salisbury, but because of the larger local community shops in the borough and High Street dealing in many kinds of goods have remained in business and possibly increased in number.

The Downton Society, established in 1788, was incorporated as a Friendly Society in 1794.[64] It remained active in the 1920s but has since been wound up.[65] Attempts were made to start a cottage

hospital in 1869–70.[66] A hospital was possibly established but nothing is known of it now. The parish hall in the borough, formerly a school, became the Memorial Hall after the First World War.[67] In 1768 its M.P.s gave Downton a new fire engine made by Nuttall & Co., Long Acre, London. It was used until at least 1891,[68] and in 1975 was in Salisbury Museum. Street lighting by oil was provided by subscription from 1890.[69] From 1931 Downton was supplied with electricity from the mills.[70] A sewage works was built to the south of the village after the Second World War.

Downton was the birthplace of the soldier, writer, and ecclesiastic Nicholas Upton (d. 1457).[71] Admiral Sir Roger Curtis, who defended Gibraltar in 1781–2,[72] was born in the Parsonage where a portrait of Sir Walter Raleigh hung until it was sold to the National Portrait Gallery *c.* 1858.[73]

REDLYNCH. The ecclesiastical and, from 1896, civil parish of Redlynch included all the lands east of the Ridge and Salt Lane, 5,452 a. (2,205 ha.).[74] The landscape and history of the north part of that area is different from that of the south part. The lands of a village called Pensworth on the inclosed chalklands north of Grove copse were first mentioned in 1227.[75] Pensworth's origin apparently lay in the inclosure, ploughing, and tenanting of the downland by the rector of Downton, probably in the 12th century.[76] The rector did not add to his burden of service by building a church, and the village, apparently consisting of farms strung out along the road round the north and east sides of the copse, was less nucleated than those of the Avon valley. In 1327 and 1332, when the Bucklands' house and farmstead of Redlynch manor were included,[77] its higher assessment for taxation shows it to have been wealthier and probably more populous than most of those villages.[78] There were 53 poll-tax payers in 1377, more than for each of the other villages of the parish except Downton and Charlton.[79] By the mid 15th century the village had apparently declined.[80] By the 16th century, when it was no longer separately assessed for taxation,[81] the amalgamation of holdings resulting in fewer and more distant farmsteads had caused the village to lose its identity. A few farmsteads remained and in 1773 a small settlement was mapped,[82] but in 1837 Upper and Lower Pensworth were the only farmsteads.[83] Upper Pensworth Farm, marking the site of the 1773 settlement, was demolished between 1957 and 1968.[84]

South of Grove copse the land remained open pasture and heath until 1822, apart from Timber and Milk hills and Loosehanger park which were inclosed in the 13th and 17th centuries respectively.[85] Settlement was dispersed and of the poor squatter type. Redlynch was given as an address in 1612.[86]

[61] W.A.S. Libr., sale cat. xxvi, no. 20.
[62] H.R.O. Eccl. 2/155642, pp. 33–7 (1586).
[63] *Census*, 1971.   [64] W.R.O. 1306, par. rec.
[65] Local information.   [66] W.R.O. 1306, par. rec.
[57] *Kelly's Dir. Wilts.* (1939).
[68] Wilts. Cuttings, i. 105.   [69] Ibid. xiii. 71.
[70] 'Downton Electricity Special Order, 1929', *Electricity (Supply) Acts, Special Orders* (Min. of Transport); Wilts. Cuttings, xxvii. 80.
[71] Cf. *D.N.B.*; A. B. Emden, *Biog. Reg. Univ. Oxf. to 1500*, iii. 1933–4.
[72] *D.N.B.*   [73] *W.N. & Q.* vi. 88, 97–8.

[74] O.S. Map 6″, Wilts. LXXVII. NW. (1902 edn.).
[75] C.P.25(1)/250/5 no. 10.
[76] See p. 38.   [77] See pp. 31–2.
[78] E 179/196/7–8.   [79] *V.C.H. Wilts.* iv. 308.
[80] Winch. Coll. Mun. 4955.
[81] e.g. *Taxation Lists* (W.R.S. x), 44, 115–17.
[82] *Andrews and Dury, Map* (W.R.S. viii), pl. 3.
[83] W.R.O., Tithe Award.
[84] O.S. Maps 1″, sheet 167 (1960 edn.); 1/50,000, sheet 184 (1974 edn.).
[85] W.R.O., Inclosure Award; see below, pp. 35, 37.
[86] W.R.O. 914/1.

In 1773 settlement was along the roads and the edges of the commons, especially along Black Lane at Redlynch and Warminster Green, and there was a pocket of settlement at Bohemia.[87] Population and housing were probably increasing in the later 18th century, perhaps in connexion with local trade and industry.[88] Recent growth was indicated in 1780 by a surveyor's complaint that the commons were being 'daily' encroached on for the building of cottages and houses.[89] After the commons were inclosed in 1822[90] the land between the Row, Salt Lane, the Ridge, and Bowers Hill was imparked,[91] but much land, divided into small allotments, was freed for building.[92] In Redlynch parish there was, however, no immediate haste to build. The 19th and 20th centuries have been a period of rebuilding and gradual expansion. Of the buildings standing in 1822 only a few cottages survived in 1975. Their replacements and the new buildings, however, fitted into the pattern of settlement laid down before inclosure. Two focal points developed, at Redlynch around the road junction at the top of Princes Hill, and at Warminster Green where Redlynch church and school were built. The southern part of the road between them, dividing two farms, has never been built up. At Redlynch settlement spread out from the road junction, where the King's Head was open by 1848.[93] Rollington House, a substantial red-brick residence with a large contemporary stable block, was built in Princes Hill in 1894–5.[94] A house and reading room were built in Bowers Hill at the bottom of Sandy Lane in 1899.[95] Housing increased down Princes Hill to Chapel Lane and Hart Hill Drove. There was more 19th-century building around the triangle of roads at Warminster Green. In 1872 the Foresters Arms was built at the corner of Church Hill and Vicarage Lane,[96] and Redlynch Vicarage was built at the corner of Black Lane and Vicarage Lane in 1881.[97] A church hall was built at the bottom of Church Hill in 1912.[98] By 1876 Warminster Green had assumed the name Lover.[99] Settlement extended into Loosehanger and Whiteshoot where a substantial brick house with a symmetrical front decorated with pronounced stone dressings was built in 1885.[1] There was also 19th-century settlement at Bohemia, the name applied to the area between Whiteshoot and the road called Bohemia, and a few cottages and houses were built in the Franchise. In the 20th century housing has increased in all those areas, still concentrated largely on the former commons. The population was 1,279 in 1901, 1,191 in 1931.[2] There has been no rapid mid-20th-century expansion as at Downton, Morgan's Vale, and Woodfalls, and the old pattern of settlement remained in 1975. The clay lands of Timber and Milk hills were largely unaffected by the gradual 19th- and 20th-century increase in housing. In 1975 there were two 18th-century farm-

houses, a cottage of 17th- or 18th-century origin, and a 19th-century house in Timbury Lane, and 19th- and 20th-century buildings in Goggs Lane, including Milk Hills Farm built in 1880,[3] and Vicarage Lane. None of the farm land, however, has been broken up for building. The civil parish of Redlynch, 2,531 ha. (6,252 a.), to which Morgan's Vale and Woodfalls parish had been added in 1934, housed 2,804 people in 1971.[4]

MORGAN'S VALE AND WOODFALLS. The ecclesiastical and, from 1923 to 1934, civil parish of Morgan's Vale and Woodfalls, west of the Ridge, was roughly triangular, 787 a. (318 ha.) in 1931.[5] It included the Upper and Lower Woodfalls estates and its western boundary was drawn to include Paccombe farm but to exclude Moot farm at Downton.[6] From the Middle Ages the chalkland in the west part of the triangle was inclosed, but that in the north part, Paccombe common, remained open until 1822. The pasture lands in the east part at Morgan's hill, Morgan's vale, and Woodfalls also remained open until 1822.[7] Between those pastures and the chalk there were farmsteads on the two Woodfalls estates,[8] but nowhere was there a medieval village, and neither Morgan's Vale nor Woodfalls was assessed separately for taxation or otherwise recognized as a village before the 19th century.

Morgan's Vale took its name from the triangular area of common between the Ridge and Vale and Morgan's Vale Roads.[9] Early settlement there was in the lower part of Morgan's Vale Road where there were cottages in 1773.[10] After the commons were inclosed in 1822,[11] settlement grew on the inclosures at Morgan's vale and Morgan's hill until by 1841 Morgan's Vale had identity as a village with concentrations of housing in Morgan's Vale and Orchard Roads.[12] It continued to grow in the later 19th century and places of worship and education were built. Tower House, a brick house chiefly remarkable for its clock-tower, was built in the 1890s at the junction of Morgan's Vale and Vale Roads.[13] The Appletree public house at the bottom of Appletree Road was opened in the early 20th century, and a church hall was built in the Ridge in 1920.[14] The character of the area has been changed more, however, by the mid-20th-century council housing between Orchard Road and the Ridge and by several small private estates at the bottom of Appletree Road and off the Ridge. That new building has meant that by 1975 the former commons at Morgan's vale and Morgan's hill had been almost completely built up. By contrast there was little post-inclosure building on the many small allotments at Paccombe common. On the northern part of it, by the chalk pit in Salt Lane, the Grange, later Down House, a substantial brick house with formal gardens, was built in the earlier 20th century.

[87] *Andrews and Dury, Map* (W.R.S. viii), pl. 3.
[88] See below.   [89] W.R.O. 490/793, Wapshare's val.
[90] Ibid. Inclosure Award.
[91] Ibid. Tithe Award.
[92] *Rep. Com. on Employment in Agric.* [4202–i], p. 246, H.C. (1868–9), xiii.
[93] *Kelly's Dir. Wilts.* (1848).
[94] W.A.S. Libr., sale cat. xxvii, no. 18.
[95] Date on bldg.   [96] Date on bldg.
[97] See below.   [98] *Kelly's Dir. Wilts.* (1939).
[99] O.S. Map 6″, Wilts. LXXVII (1881 edn.).
[1] Date on bldg.

[2] *V.C.H. Wilts.* iv. 356.   [3] Date on bldg.
[4] *Census*, 1971.   [5] Ibid. 1931.
[6] Cf. W.R.O., Tithe Award; O.S. Map 6″, Wilts. LXXVII. NW. (1927 edn.). For the estates and farms see below.
[7] W.R.O., Inclosure Award.   [8] See below.
[9] W.R.O., Inclosure Award.
[10] *Andrews and Dury, Map* (W.R.S. viii), pl. 3.
[11] W.R.O., Inclosure Award.
[12] H.O. 107/1174; W.R.O., Tithe Award.
[13] O.S. Map 6″, Wilts. LXXVII. NW. (1902 edn.).
[14] *Kelly's Dir. Wilts.* (1939).

In 1773 there was a line of cottages at Woodfalls up Slab Lane from Woodfalls Farm to the New Inn on the Ridge.[15] At inclosure small allotments suitable for building were made on both sides of the Ridge at Woodfalls.[16] They were not immediately built on and the pattern of settlement changed slowly. In the 19th century the buildings in Slab Lane were nearly all replaced and near the top a substantial villa, Elmfield, was built in the earlier 20th century for J. G. S. Mitchell.[17] The main development of Woodfalls as a village was in the later 19th century when houses were built on inclosure allotments on both sides of the Ridge and in Vale Road. The New Inn was refronted and renamed the Old Inn,[18] and places of worship were built. They included in 1882 the Mission Hall,[19] used in 1975 by the Woodfalls band.[20] Building has continued in the 20th century especially on the Ridge, where the Bat and Ball public house has opened, and in Vale Road, but also in Slab and Primrose Lanes. In 1975 Woodfalls remained a loose settlement of generally small houses and cottages of the 19th and 20th centuries. In 1831 an Admiralty semaphore station was built on the Ridge opposite the junction with Slab Lane, part of an uncompleted line to the west of England.[21]

In 1921 the population of Morgan's Vale and Woodfalls was 572. It had risen to 630 by 1931[22] and, although not demonstrated in separate returns, a much greater rise had taken place by 1971.

No Man's Land. About 1807 No Man's Land was a group of cottages standing on common land in Downton parish beside the Wiltshire–Hampshire border near Bramshaw Wood.[23] The hamlet was counted with Downton parish in censuses until 1831,[24] but the relief of so poor and remote a community as No Man's Land evidently was can hardly have appealed to the Downton overseers and by 1841 it had been excluded from the parish. The use of the common on which the unlicensed cottages stood, so isolated from the villages with rights over it, was in practice denied by the cottagers. Its omission from the East Downton and Hamptworth inclosure award of 1822[25] implicitly allowed title to the land to pass to the squatters. It is likely that tithes had never been demanded from so small and recent a settlement, since to do so would probably have been to incur an obligation to relieve its poor, and No Man's Land was omitted from Downton tithe award in 1837, thereby establishing that it was outside the ancient parish.[26] Thus disowned by Downton, No Man's Land was returned as an extra-parochial place in the 1841 census.[27] It was deemed a civil parish under the Extra-parochial

Places Act, 1857, and joined Alderbury poor-law union in 1869.[28] In 1934 it was annexed to Redlynch civil parish.[29]

The boundaries of No Man's Land, defined by the East Downton and Hamptworth inclosure award, enclosed a roughly square piece of land, 14 a. (5.7 ha.).[30] North Lane, extended at inclosure by Lyburn Road, separated No Man's Land from Hamptworth,[31] and a road which was extended across Landford common to Plaitford at inclosure in 1861[32] separated it from Bramshaw (Hants). Settlement probably began in the later 18th century. It grew between the parallel North and South Lanes and spilled over the parish boundary southwards into a third parallel lane, Chapel Lane, and northwards into York Drove and School Road in Hamptworth. The population was 133 in 1831, reached a peak of 173 in 1851, and declined to 125 in 1931.[33] No figure is available but by 1975 it had certainly risen again. No Man's Land was then a village of poor cottages of the early 19th century and later and of 20th-century houses. From the Lamb, open as a public house in 1881,[34] it looked eastwards to Bramshaw Wood across a clearing on which the parish erected a Gothic well-house as a war memorial in 1921.[35] Behind the Lamb the village still formed a square with offshoots into Hamptworth common down York Drove and School Road where most of the buildings were 20th-century. A village hall with a reading room and library was built in North Lane in 1910.[36] In 1975 it was a private house.

MANORS AND OTHER ESTATES. Tradition and a charter falsified by the monks of Winchester[37] assert that DOWNTON was one of the three manors with which the church of Winchester, built c. 650 and from 676 the cathedral church,[38] was originally endowed by King Cenwalh (d. 674).[39] There is no firm evidence that the endowment was made so early but the gift of a substantial place with a large area of fertile land surrounding it to a newly founded see is likely at that early stage of Christianity in England, and Cenwalh may well have made such a gift of Downton to Winchester.[40] The late 8th century is the earliest time from which the cathedral church can be said with certainty to have been endowed with Downton. Between 793 and 796 King Offa granted to that church, or perhaps simply confirmed its right to, 100 *mansae* there.[41] That estate, probably an unbroken tract of land extending from the Avon valley perhaps all the way up the Ebble valley, passed with the church until in 909 King Edward the Elder obtained a life-lease of it

[15] *Andrews and Dury, Map* (W.R.S. viii), pl. 3.
[16] W.R.O., Inclosure Award.
[17] Local information.
[18] *Kelly's Dir. Wilts.* (1890).
[19] Wilts. Cuttings, xii. 348.   [20] Local information.
[21] W.R.O., Tithe Award; ex inf. Mr. Geoffrey Wilson, 34 Melrose Road, London, S.W. 19.
[22] *V.C.H. Wilts.* iv. 354 and n.
[23] O.S. Map 1″, sheet 15 (1811 edn.). Traditions about the settlement are recounted in H. M. Livens, *No Man's Land* (priv. print. 1910).
[24] *V.C.H. Wilts.* iv. 347.
[25] W.R.O., Inclosure Award.
[26] Ibid. Tithe Award.   [27] H.O. 107/1174.
[28] *V.C.H. Wilts.* iv. 354; *Names of Unions and Poor Law*

Pars. [C. 5191], p. 5, H.C. (1887), lxx.
[29] *V.C.H. Wilts.* iv. 356.
[30] O.S. Map 6″, Wilts. LXXVII (1881 edn.).
[31] W.R.O., Inclosure Award.
[32] *Inclosure Awards* (W.R.S. xxv), p. 90.
[33] *V.C.H. Wilts.* iv. 347, 354.
[34] O.S. Map 6″, Wilts. LXXVII (1881 edn.).
[35] Wilts. Cuttings, xv. 286.
[36] *Kelly's Dir. Wilts.* (1939).
[37] For the early Winchester chart. and their falsification see Finberg, *Early Wessex Chart.* pp. 214–48.
[38] *V.C.H. Hants.* ii. 2.
[39] *Reg. Pontoise* (Cant. & York Soc.), ii. 609.
[40] *V.C.H. Wilts.* ii, p. 84.
[41] Finberg, *Early Wessex Chart.* pp. 71–2.

from Bishop Frithustan, possibly for the support of some of his thegns.[42] Although restitution was promised then and again in the will of King Edred (d. 955) it seems that the estate remained in the kings' hands.[43] While they held it in the 10th century kings alienated, without a corresponding reduction in hidation, lands between Nunton and Bishopstone and to the west of Bishopstone, some of which they granted to thegns.[44] In 997, when King Ethelred restored it to the Old Minster, the Downton estate was thus in detached portions, the land at Downton assessed at 55 *mansae*, that at Bishopstone at 45 *mansae*.[45]

In the time of King Cnut, 1016–35, lands in the Downton portion of the estate at Witherington, assessed at 3 hides, and at Standlynch, at 2 hides, were alienated.[46] The remainder belonged to the minster in 1066.[47] In the division of estates between the bishop and the monks of the cathedral monastery, which probably took place before 1070, it was allotted to the bishop. Between 1066 and 1086 four free tenures in lands assessed at 27½ hides were created from it.[48] Domesday Book does not tell where the lands lay, but from them emerged the manors and estates of Redlynch, Hamptworth, Woodfalls, and Charlton around Downton and several manors around Bishopstone. Between 1066 and 1086 land assessed at 4 hides was taken from the bishop's estate for the king's forest, probably from the Downton portion, and another estate of 4 hides was taken for Downton church, probably in the same period and almost certainly from the Downton portion.[49] In 1086 the bishop was left with an estate assessed at 59½ hides, probably more than half of it at Downton,[50] which continued to pass with the see. Bishopstone was afterwards itself a manor.

In 1551 Bishop Gardiner was deprived and his successor Ponet was compelled to surrender many of his lands, including Downton, to Edward VI who in the same year leased the entire manor including the lordship.[51] From 1553 Gardiner, restored by Queen Mary, probably received the income.[52] The lease was cancelled under a royal warrant and in 1558 Bishop White was formally regranted the episcopal lands. In 1558–9, however, the lease was re-activated by Act.[53] The events of the Reformation apparently had a far-reaching effect at Downton. In the 15th century, presumably to stabilize the income from the manor after a period of falling profits, bishops had granted leases of the demesne lands at fixed rents renewable apparently without fine, and rents for and fines for admission to copyholds became fixed.[54] It seems to have been in the Reformation

period that such fixed rents and fines established themselves as invariable. In the later 18th century and in the 19th leases of some of the demesne lands were paid for by substantial fines,[55] but there is no earlier evidence of such payments. Having thus had a variable income compounded into a largely fixed income the manor was of progressively less value to the bishops. Even in the later 18th century and the 19th it was comparatively of much less value than it had been before the Reformation. On the other hand the leaseholds and copyholds, called copyholds of inheritance, held by tenures so favourable in the long term, gradually assumed the importance of freeholds and their descents are traced under the headings of the villages in which they lay. From the later 16th century what passed with the see were the fixed rents of the leases of the lordship and the demesne lands, some £150 a year, the right to receive 'knowledge money' on the succession of each bishop, £33 13s. 4d. in 1630 and commuted to that sum in 1806,[56] and various woodlands in the eastern part of the parish.[57] That estate was confiscated during the Civil War but the trustees for the sale of bishops' lands were ordered to delay selling it because of the possible value of the trees to the Navy, and it was restored.[58] In the later 19th century the rents and fines were extinguished when the freeholds of the lordship and the demesne lands were sold to the leaseholders.[59]

Woodlands on the downs on the east side of the Avon valley remained part of the bishops' manor until 1592 when they were disparked and allotted in strips to those with rights to repair their leasehold and copyhold tenements with the bishops' wood.[60] Old Park, on the top of Barford down, was divided among New Court farm, Witherington farm, and Old Court and Downton mills.[61] The allotments in respect of the two farms passed with the farms to the Longford estate. The remainder was acquired by the Longford estate in the mid 20th century.[62] Privett copse, south of Witherington down, and Farthingley copse were allotted respectively to the copyholders of East Downton, Bodenham, Charlton, and Wick and of Nunton.[63] By the late 18th century most of Privett copse had become part of the Trafalgar estate.[64] As Privett farm it passed with that estate and in 1953, as part of Standlynch farm, became part of the Longford estate.[65] At least from the early 17th century the bishops' woods at Loosehanger belonged to the farmers in fee of New Court farm.[66] They were imparked,[67] and the park passed with the farm until the 19th century when it became part of Newhouse estate.[68] Loosehanger Park is a small early-17th-century stone lodge of a single

[42] Finberg, *Early Wessex Chart.* pp. 80–1, 224, 244.
[43] Ibid. pp. 80–1, 236.
[44] Ibid. pp. 88–9, 91–2, 94, 101; see above, p. 6 and n. 53.
[45] Finberg, *Early Wessex Chart.* pp. 102–3.
[46] *V.C.H. Wilts.* ii, p. 119. The location of the 5 hides may be inferred from Dom. Bk.: ibid. pp. 150, 151, 161, 163.   [47] Ibid. p. 119.
[48] Ibid. pp. 79, 85, 119.   [49] Ibid. p. 119.
[50] Ibid. pp. 119, 150, 151, 161, 163.
[51] *Cal. Pat.* 1550–3, 178; H.R.O. Eccl. 2/155897.
[52] e.g. H.R.O. Eccl. 2/155895.
[53] *Cal. Pat.* 1557–8, 146–7; Act for the Assurance of Certain Lands to Patentees of Edw. VI, 1 Eliz. I, 36 (Original Act).
[54] W.R.O. 490/784.   [55] H.R.O. Eccl. 2/248947.

[56] Ibid. Eccl. 2/155642, pp. 33–7, 159–61; Eccl. 2/155643, pp. 95–7; Eccl. 2/155644, pp. 57–8; Eccl. 2/155504, pp. 69–77.
[57] See below.
[58] *Cal. S.P. Dom.* 1649–50, pp. 50, 53; 1655–6, pp. 291, 305.
[59] See below; and below, pp. 54, 76.
[60] W.R.O. 893/4, p. 125; 490/1187.
[61] Longford Castle Mun., map of Old Park, 1734; see pp. 29, 40, 73, 76.
[62] Ex inf. Mr. D. Newton, Longford Estate Office.
[63] W.R.O. 490/802, rental, 1737.
[64] B.L. Map Libr., 'Surveys and Maps of Several Estates . . . in the Property of Hen. Dawkins'; see below, p. 70.   [65] W.R.O. 1008/27.
[66] Ibid. 490/783; see p. 73.   [67] See p. 37.
[68] Ex inf. Mr. G. Jeffreys, Newhouse; see below.

storey with cellars and attics enlarged in the 19th century. The bishops' wood in the Franchise, Franchise wood, 181 a. between Pound bottom and Franchises wood,[69] was sold in 1874 to George Morrison and became part of Hamptworth Lodge estate.[70]

The lordship of Downton manor was leased in 1551 to Sir William Herbert, created earl of Pembroke that year, and again under the Act of 1558-9. Leases passed with the Pembroke title until 1662 when Philip, earl of Pembroke and Montgomery, was replaced as lord farmer by Sir Joseph Ashe, Bt.[71] The lease passed in 1686 to Sir Joseph's son Sir James, in 1734 to Sir James's nephew Joseph Ashe Wyndham (otherwise Wyndham Ashe), and in 1741 was bought by Anthony Duncombe (created Lord Feversham in 1747).[72] At his death in 1763 Lord Feversham left a widow Anne (d. 1795), from 1765 wife of William Bouverie, Viscount Folkestone (created earl of Radnor in that year), a daughter Anne (d. 1829), from 1777 wife of Jacob, earl of Radnor (d. 1828), and a daughter Frances, wife of John Bowater. For the benefit of his daughters he devised his lease of the lordship in trust for sale. The successors to his freehold and copyhold property, Thomas Duncombe and the Shaftos,[73] had first refusal.[74] Presumably because of that the lease was not sold and the trust not executed. Lord Feversham's executors remained lessees until a Chancery decree permitted an open sale in 1806.[75] The lease was bought by Jacob, earl of Radnor (d. 1828),[76] and was held in trust for successive earls of Radnor until in 1875 the Ecclesiastical Commissioners conveyed the reversion in fee to Jacob, earl of Radnor (d. 1889).[77] The lordship has since passed with the Radnor title.

In 1138 Downton was among the manors on which Bishop Blois is said to have built castles[78] and the earthwork called the Moot, of a type used for motte-and-bailey castles of that date, was probably thrown up then. Because 18th-century landscape gardening gave it terraces the Moot has excited theories, now discredited, that it was made before the Conquest as a meeting-place and, within a pre-Roman earthwork, it is plausible that meetings could have been held there.[79] Archaeological inspection has yielded no trace of masonry on the motte (the 'Moot'),[80] and it therefore seems that the castle planned in 1138 was never built. The bishops retained the house which had probably

been there since at least the late 11th century, however, and instead of building a new castle possibly replaced the existing house with, or converted it into, a fortified palace comparable to that at Bishop's Waltham (Hants).[81] It stood on the east bank of the Avon below the Moot, from which it was later cut off by a mill-stream.[82] It was used regularly by bishops and visited by kings.[83] As a result of several visits by King John local tradition gave it the name 'King John's Palace'.[84] Bishops were still living at Downton in the later 14th century,[85] but possibly not for long thereafter. In 1415 the house was called 'vetus curia'.[86] About that time it was replaced by a new manorial centre called New Court west of the Avon and, as it fell out of use, assumed the name Old Court.[87] It still stood in 1647 but the fact that the trustees of bishops' lands valued, at £80, only the house's materials suggests that it had long been uninhabited and perhaps that it was derelict.[88] In the early 18th century part of what remained was taken down and some of the materials, including two carved wooden busts purported to be of King John and Queen Isabel of Angoulême, were re-used in the White Horse inn.[89] The remainder was marked on a map of 1734 as 'the ruins'.[90] In 1801, when presumably nothing of the house remained above ground, walling was said to have stood within living memory.[91] Foundations and other stonework have since been discovered by excavation,[92] but neither allow a precise date or exact dimensions to be given for the house.

The site of Old Court seems to have been first leased in the later 16th century, its value apparently that of the pasture within its bounds.[93] In 1647 it was granted with Downton mills to William Eyre,[94] in 1661 leased to Henry Eyre, apparently as trustee for his nephew William, and afterwards passed with the mills.[95]

In the Middle Ages the bishops' manor included extensive lands east of Downton from which three substantial copyhold of inheritance estates emerged in the 16th and 17th centuries. By the late 1520s Richard Matthew (d. 1557)[96] had accumulated a large holding.[97] In 1566 his son Tristram conveyed a large part of it, including lands east of Barford down and land at Paccombe, to John Stockman.[98] The Barford portion was merged with Barford farm and its subsequent history is treated with that of Barford.[99] The Paccombe land, *PACCOMBE* farm,

[69] W.R.O., Tithe Award.
[70] H.R.O. Eccl. 2/170400; see below, p. 60.
[71] H.R.O. Eccl. 2/159493; Eccl. 2/155642-3; Eccl. 2/159475/35.
[72] W.R.O. 490/793; for the Ashes see Burke, *Ext. & Dorm. Baronetcies* (1838), 16; F. Blomefield, *Norf.* viii. 115; for Feversham and his descendants see *Complete Peerage*, s.vv. Feversham, Radnor.
[73] See p. 54.
[74] *Univ. Brit. Dir.* ii (1793 edn.), 846.
[75] H.R.O. Eccl. 2/155498-504; W.R.O. 490/779.
[76] W.R.O. 490/234.
[77] H.R.O. Eccl. 2/155505-15; Eccl. 2/172546.
[78] *Annales Monastici* (Rolls Ser.), ii. 51.
[79] *W.A.M.* xxi. 351-4; xxiv. 30; xxxviii. 513; xl. 352; xli. 97; xliii. 379-80; lvi. 249-50; lviii. 124-9; *V.C.H. Wilts.* i (1), 265; *Arch. Jnl.* xxxii. 305-9; civ. 166.
[80] *Arch. Jnl.* xxxii. 308.
[81] Cf. *V.C.H. Hants*, iii. 277-8 and plate facing p. 278.
[82] e.g. H.R.O. Eccl. 2/155510, pp. 563-70.
[83] e.g. *Close R.* 1227-31, 483; 1268-72, 447, 539; *Reg.*

Pontoise (Cant. & York Soc.), i. 36-7; *Reg. Woodlock* (Cant. & York Soc.), i, *passim*.
[84] 'Itin. King John', *Descr. Pat. R.* (Rec. Com.); Hoare, *Mod. Wilts.* Downton, 18.
[85] *Reg. Wykeham* (Hants Rec. Soc.), ii. 621-4.
[86] H.R.O. Eccl. 2/159417, rott. 3d.-4d.
[87] Ibid. Eccl. 2/159444, rott. 2-3.
[88] C 54/3369 no. 3.
[89] *Gent. Mag.* lvii (2), 951-2.
[90] Longford Castle Mun., map of Downton mill.
[91] *W.A.M.* xxix. 102-3; *Univ. Brit. Dir.* ii (1793 edn.), 845.
[92] *W.A.M.* lix. 125; lxi. 98-9.
[93] H.R.O. Eccl. 2/159475/1 (1593).
[94] C 54/3369 no. 3.
[95] H.R.O. Eccl. 2/155643, pp. 95-7; *Ho. of Lords MSS.* N.S. vii, pp. 12-13.
[96] Prob. 11/39 (P.C.C. 52 Wrastley).
[97] W.R.O. 490/800; cf. E 179/197/50.
[98] Sar. Dioc. R.O., misc. papers, copies of ct. rec.
[99] See pp. 53-4.

passed with Barford farm until the sale of 1806,[1] when it was bought by Jacob, earl of Radnor.[2] In 1822 allotments totalling 55 a. in the Franchise were made in respect of Paccombe farm.[3] In the later 19th century or early 20th the farm was sold to Jonathan Taunton.[4] It passed to his son J. W. Taunton after whose death it was sold to J. G. S. Mitchell (d. 1964), whose executors owned it in 1975.[5] The land in the Franchise, Radnor firs and other land, was part of Newhouse estate in 1975.[6] Paccombe Farmhouse is a substantial brick house of two dates in the early 19th century with contemporary and later farm buildings. Paccombe House is a large gentleman's residence of the early 20th century.

By the late 16th century a large holding had been accumulated by John Studley.[7] It passed to Griffin Studley who held it in 1628 and to John Studley who held it in the 1640s when the holding apparently included Tristram Matthew's land nearest Downton.[8] A Mrs. White held it in 1659.[9] By 1676 the land had passed to James Lynch and c. 1700 part of it was sold to Francis Coles who already held a farmstead near the Moot,[10] possibly that held by William Thring c. 1500.[11] Coles added further lands to his farm which in the 18th century was called *THRINGS*, afterwards *MOOT*.[12] He was succeeded after 1724 by his younger brother Jonathan (d. 1742)[13] whose son William (d. 1784) devised the estate for life to John Greene (fl. 1800) with remainder to Diana (d. 1788), widow of John Shuckburgh (d. 1782).[14] The land passed to Diana's son the Revd. Charles William Shuckburgh (d. 1833) whose widow Henrietta held it in 1837.[15] Allotments totalling 65 a. near Bohemia were added to the estate at inclosure in 1822.[16] The lands passed to Charles's and Henrietta's son William Pigott Shuckburgh (d. 1860). In the later 19th century Moot farm was bought by E. J. Hall and descended through the Hall family. In the mid 20th century it was bought by J. G. S. Mitchell and belonged to his executors in 1975,[17] when some of the allotments near Bohemia were part of Newhouse estate.[18] A house called Downton House in 1773,[19] later Moot House, was built on the estate. It passed with the land until the later 19th century. From 1873 to 1911 it belonged to E. P. Squarey, joint founder of the firm of estate agents Rawlence & Squarey.[20] The house, of red brick with stone dressings, has a square plan with a principal west elevation of five bays and two storeys with basement and attics. Its construction has been variously ascribed to c. 1650 with alterations of 1720,[21] to c. 1685,[22] and to 1700,[23] but if any part of the existing house is much

earlier than 1700 it has been obscured by the house's later alteration. The exterior appears to be of one build in the early 18th century. Inside the house only the back stair seems contemporary with the exterior and that, like the apparently 18th-century interior decoration, may be largely a product of skilled restoration after the house was damaged by fire in 1923.[24] Across Moot Lane the gardens of the house are approached through gates set in early-20th-century balustrading. The landscaping, which in its present form is probably of the mid or late 18th century, makes use of the Moot earthwork and the slope down to the river and is notable for its strong relief. The slope is terraced and above it on the motte is a fine 18th-century octagonal summer-house which, like a contemporary gazebo, was derelict in 1976. Moot Farm is a 17th-century farm-house.

In 1619 William Stockman sold an estate of freehold land in Whiteparish, on which Newhouse was built, and copyhold of inheritance land in East Downton tithing to Sir Edward Gorges, Bt. (later Baron Gorges). In 1633 Lord Gorges sold it to Giles Eyre (d. 1655) who settled it on his son Ambrose. In 1660 Ambrose's son William sold it to his cousin Sir Samuel Eyre (d. 1698) who already held copyhold of inheritance land in East Downton.[25] *NEWHOUSE* estate, consisting of imparked freehold land in Whiteparish and copyhold of inheritance land and land held customarily of Winchester College in Downton parish, passed to Sir Samuel's son Sir Robert (d. 1735) and grandson Robert Eyre (d. 1752) whose widow Mary held it until her death in 1762. It passed to Robert's cousin Samuel Eyre and in 1795 to Samuel's son-in-law William Purvis Eyre. William's widow Susannah held it until her death in 1833 when it passed to her son-in-law George Matcham (d. 1877).[26] At inclosure in 1822 allotments of 18 a. near Bohemia and 57 a. in the Franchise were added to the estate which in 1837 measured some 270 a. in Downton parish.[27] Matcham was succeeded by his son William Eyre Eyre-Matcham (d. 1906), grandson George Henry Eyre Eyre-Matcham (d. 1939), and great-grandson John St. Leger Eyre-Matcham (d. 1975).[28] In 1975 the estate measured some 1,000 a., of which a small proportion was in Whiteparish.[29] In 1619 Newhouse was said to be newly built.[30] Its similarity in some respects to Longford Castle in Britford and the fact that Edward, Lord Gorges (d. c. 1650), owned both houses have led to the suggestion that it was built as a hunting lodge for Lord Gorges.[31] It appears, however, to have been bought by Gorges and, with Hamptworth Lodge,[32]

[1] W.R.O. 490/793; 490/779.
[2] Hoare, *Mod. Wilts.* Downton, 56; W.R.O. 490/234.
[3] W.R.O., Inclosure Award.
[4] Longford Castle Mun., survey, 1854.
[5] Ex inf. Mrs. T. W. Warren, 41 Gravel Close, Downton; Mr. A. S. Mitchell, Charles Mitchell & Sons Ltd., Lode Hill, Downton.   [6] Ex inf. Mr. Jeffreys.
[7] Sar. Dioc. R.O., misc. papers, copies of ct. rec.; cf. E 179/270/18.   [8] W.R.O. 490/783–4.
[9] Ibid. 490/1174, rent roll.
[10] Ibid.; 2/2.   [11] Ibid. 490/1171.
[12] Ibid. 490/1174, rent roll.   [13] See p. 56.
[14] Ibid.; Hoare, *Mod. Wilts.* Downton, 53–5.
[15] W.R.O., Inclosure Award; Tithe Award.
[16] Ibid. Inclosure Award.
[17] Local information.   [18] Ex inf. Mr. Jeffreys.

[19] *Andrews and Dury, Map* (W.R.S. viii), pl. 3.
[20] *W.A.M.* xxxvii. 169.
[21] J. Belcher and M. E. Macartney, *Later Renaissance Archit. in Eng.* i. 59–60.
[22] *Country Life,* 9 Jan. 1909.
[23] Pevsner, *Wilts.* (2nd edn.), 224.
[24] Wilts. Cuttings, xiv. 205.
[25] Hoare, *Mod. Wilts.* Frustfield, 51–2; W.R.O. 490/1174, rent roll.
[26] Hoare, *Mod. Wilts.* Frustfield, pedigree 1 at pp. 56–7.
[27] W.R.O., Inclosure Award; Tithe Award.
[28] Burke, *Land. Gent.* (1952), 1732.
[29] Ex inf. Mr. Jeffreys.
[30] Hoare, *Mod. Wilts.* Frustfield, 51–2.
[31] Pevsner, *Wilts.* (2nd edn.), 572.
[32] See p. 60.

was possibly one of a pair of hunting lodges built for William Stockman of Barford. Newhouse is notable for its unusual plan which is formed from a hexagon with sides of *c.* 18 ft. (5 m.) as a Y with a square projection to each alternate side.[33] The walls are of red brick and rise three storeys to triangular gables above each face. The trinitarian pattern suggests that the design was symbolic, as has been claimed for Longford, but nothing is known of Stockman's religious inclination. The original plan of the interior has not survived later alterations and only one upper room has a full range of early-17th-century panelling. The northern arm probably contained the kitchen. A staircase was inserted next to the kitchen in the time of Sir Robert Eyre, and in 1742 the north wing was extended when a dining-room of one lofty storey was added. There may already have been a small addition, since demolished, to the south wing when *c.* 1760 a drawing-room of comparable size to the dining-room was added to complete the symmetry of the west front. About the same time further alterations, including the insertion of a new central staircase, were made to the house. Extensive service quarters were added on the north-east side in the 19th century, and *c.* 1907 the drawing-room was redecorated in early-Georgian style by Maple & Co. The 19th-century additions were demolished in 1975 and a restoration of the house begun. Newhouse was built in imparked land surrounded by woodland. It stands at the top of a steep rise with falling ground to the south where in the early 18th century some 70 a. of landscaped park was laid out.[34] That was in decay in the early 19th century and in 1975 all that remained was a drive, flanked in part by canals, along part of the line of the western avenue.

In 1604 the executors of John Stileman sold to Giles Eyre (d. 1655), then of Redlynch, copyhold of inheritance land in East Downton tithing with the land in Whiteparish on which he built Brickworth House.[35] It was afterwards merged in Redlynch manor with which its later history is recorded.

In 1380 William of Wykeham, bishop of Winchester, was licensed to appropriate Downton church, the advowson of which belonged to his see, for the foundation of a school in Winchester.[36] Winchester College was founded in 1382.[37] The church was its earliest endowment and in 1385 Wykeham was licensed to alienate the advowson to the college.[38] The manor of *DOWNTON RECTORY*, consisting of land, great tithes, and the advowson, remained among the college's estates. In the 19th and 20th centuries the land was alienated, the tithes have been redeemed, but the advowson belonged to the college in 1975.[39]

The oldest part of the rectory-house, called Downton Manor in 1975, is the northern end of the main range which contains elements of a substantial hall-house of the early 14th century. The walls of that house were partly of stone and partly timber-framed. Its roof was arch-braced. Fragments of an open truss remain at its southern end next to the present entrance. Against the northern end of its east wall there is a stone building, also of the early 14th century, which has a moulded doorway and cusped lancet windows. Its small size, orientation, and decoration suggest that it was built as a chapel. In the 17th century the house was refenestrated and the floor levels altered to provide accommodation on two floors above reduced cellars. It was also extended southwards in similar style. About 1680 there was said to be 'a very good house and garden fit for any gentleman to live in'.[40] The chapel was ceiled and panelled in the early 18th century and more internal alterations were made in the 19th century. Restoration, with the exposure of some early features, has taken place in recent years. The house was lived in by Sir Thomas Wilkes and the Raleighs while lessees.[41]

The college's demesne land, Parsonage farm, was sold in 1921 to W. J. Barrow whose son-in-law B. L. Bishop owned it in 1975.[42] The woodland, Grove copse at Pensworth, had become part of Newhouse estate by 1900.[43]

Of the college's copyhold lands those forming part of the Trafalgar estate of Horatio, Earl Nelson,[44] were enfranchised in 1867.[45] Except for Lord Nelson's allotments in the Franchise, 69 a., which became part of Hamptworth Lodge estate,[46] they passed with the estate until 1953. As Upper Pensworth farm and Studlands, merged with Redlynch and Templeman's farms, they were then sold as part of Templeman's farm.[47] Upper Pensworth Farm, demolished after 1953, was a moderately sized farm-house apparently built in the 18th or 19th century.[48]

The copyhold lands part of the Newhouse estate of George Matcham, Lower Pensworth farm,[49] were enfranchised in 1871.[50] That farm passed with Newhouse estate like Matcham's copyhold of inheritance land in East Downton. Lower Pensworth Farm is a 19th-century house of brick with a slated roof.

Between 1066 and 1086 free tenures were apparently created in lands east of Downton held of the bishop of Winchester by William de Braose, Waleran the huntsman, Ralf, and Ansgot, but none in particular of those grants can be identified with the 2 hides at 'Pensworth Barford' held in the earlier 13th century by Robert son of Baldwin and later called the manor of *REDLYNCH*.[51] By 1288 those hides may have passed to Ralph de Buckland, possibly the son of Hugh son of Hugh de Buckland.[52] In 1332, the year of his death, Ralph settled 2 carucates at Redlynch on his son Sir John for life with remainder to Sir John's sons John, Thomas,

[33] See plate facing p. 33.
[34] Hoare, *Mod. Wilts.* Frustfield, 52; *Andrews and Dury, Map* (W.R.S. viii), pl. 3.
[35] C 2/Jas. I/E 5/20; Hoare, *Mod. Wilts.* Frustfield, 34.
[36] *Cal. Pat.* 1377–81, 483.
[37] *V.C.H. Hants,* ii. 262–3.
[38] Ibid. 288; *Cal. Pat.* 1381–5, 574–5.
[39] See below.   [40] Winch. Coll. Mun. 5122.
[41] *W.A.M.* lxi. 49, 61 n.; xlii. 307–12; see below.
[42] W.A.S. Libr., sale cat. xxiv, no. 18; local information.
[43] Ex inf. Mr. Jeffreys.
[44] See below and p. 70.
[45] Winch. Coll. Mun. 21328.
[46] Ex inf. Mr. N. J. M. Anderson, Hamptworth Lodge.
[47] W.R.O. 1008/27; see below and p. 70.
[48] W.R.O. 1008/27.
[49] See below.   [50] Winch. Coll. Mun. 21328.
[51] *V.C.H. Wilts.* ii, pp. 79, 119; see above; B.L. Eg. MS. 2418, f. 61.
[52] Ralph was the bp. of Winchester's bailiff at Downton 1288–9: H.R.O. Eccl. 2/159311, rot. 4d.; for his ancestors see *V.C.H. Hants,* iv. 526.

and Nicholas.[53] The manor passed to the eldest of them, Sir John (d. 1362),[54] and to his brother Sir Thomas (d. 1379).[55] It was held after Sir Thomas's death by his widow Maud[56] with remainder to their daughter Margaret and her husband John Wroth.[57] Maud was presumably living in 1396,[58] but the manor afterwards passed like that of Puckshipton in Beechingstoke to Edward Tiptoft, earl of Worcester (d. 1485).[59] At the partition of Lord Worcester's estates it was possibly allotted to Philippe (fl. 1487), relict of Thomas de Ros, Lord Ros, and then wife of Edward Grimston. Philippe's son Edmund, Lord Ros (d. 1508), whose heir was his sister Isabel, was from 1492 in the custody of Isabel's husband Sir Thomas Lovel.[60] Edward, Lord Dudley, one of Lord Worcester's heirs, may have taken the profits of the manor for a time, but in 1490 he conveyed it to Lovel (d. 1524)[61] who devised it to his nephew Sir Francis Lovel (d. 1550).[62] It passed to Sir Francis's son Sir Thomas who in 1554 settled it on John Farley for 22 years.[63] In 1566–7, however, presumably after Farley's death, it was sold with land in Barford to John Stockman.[64] In 1567 the manor was split. Stockman then sold the larger part, later called Redlynch farm, to the lessee Robert Snelgar or Snelgrove (d. 1593).[65] Snelgar was succeeded by his son Ambrose (fl. 1628),[66] whose heir was his daughter Jane, wife of Giles Eyre (d. 1655). The farm, which was held with a copyhold of inheritance estate in East Downton tithing, thereafter passed from father to son in the Eyre family of Brickworth to Giles (d. 1685), Sir Giles (d. 1695), Giles (d. 1734), and Giles (d.s.p. 1750).[67] The last Giles was succeeded by his nephew Henry Eyre (d.s.p. 1799). Henry's heir was his nephew John Maurice Eyre (d. 1815) and his heir was his daughter Frances, wife of Thomas Bolton. In 1835 Bolton succeeded his father as Earl Nelson and he held the farm in Frances's right until his death in 1835. At inclosure in 1822 10 a. and 4 a. in Paccombe common were allotted for respectively Redlynch farm and the copyhold land.[68] Frances held both estates, 173 a. and 45 a. in 1837,[69] until her death in 1878 when they passed to her son Horatio, Earl Nelson. They afterwards descended with the Trafalgar estate.[70] In 1948 the land was sold, as Redlynch farm, with Templeman's and

Upper Pensworth farms, and in 1953, with the addition of Studlands, as part of Templeman's farm, 448 a., to Jacob, earl of Radnor.[71] It remained part of the Longford estate in 1975.[72] Redlynch Farm is a small brick house of the early 19th century.

In 1567 John Stockman sold the smaller part of Redlynch manor, later called Templeman's farm, to William Juniper (d. 1569).[73] William had a son William but by 1580 the land belonged to John Chaffyn, the son-in-law of Robert Snelgar who bought Redlynch farm.[74] John Chaffyn of Everleigh, probably the same man, apparently held it at his death c. 1627.[75] In 1598 John's daughter Joyce married his tenant George Reynolds,[76] and the land passed to John Reynolds, presumably a child of that marriage. Apparently in the 1650s John was succeeded by George Reynolds (fl. 1720), presumably his son. George was succeeded by John Reynolds of Everleigh, presumably his own son,[77] who by 1736 had sold the land to William Kervill (d. 1791).[78] William was succeeded by his brother John (d. c. 1808). In 1808 the land was sold to Peter Templeman.[79] At inclosure in 1822 9 a. in Paccombe common was allotted for the farm which measured some 113 a. in 1837.[80] William, Earl Nelson, bought it c. 1823.[81] His executors held it in 1837[82] and it passed with the Trafalgar estate to the Longford estate.[83] Templeman's Farm seems an early-19th-century house greatly enlarged later in the century.

One of the estates, held of the bishop of Winchester, which became heritable between 1066 and 1086 was possibly the land on which settlements called Woodfalls were established, but it is impossible to say which one.[84] In the earlier 13th century Gilbert of Milford held land at Woodfalls assessed at 1½ hide,[85] later called the manor of *UPPER WOODFALLS* or Woodfalls farm. He was apparently succeeded by Sir Stephen of Milford, a county coroner, who died c. 1260 holding land at Woodfalls assessed at 1½ hide and who in 1261, after his death, was called Stephen of Woodfalls.[86] Stephen's heir was his son William, a minor c. 1260.[87] William of Milford apparently settled at Woodfalls and came to be called Sir William of Woodfalls.[88] In 1307 he settled the land on himself and his wife Margaret (fl. 1342) and their issue.[89]

[53] *Feet of F.* 1327–77 (W.R.S. xxix), p. 36; for John's (? eldest) son Ralph see ibid. pp. 15–16.
[54] *Cal. Inq. p.m.* xi, p. 230.
[55] Ibid. xv, p. 38.
[56] Ibid.; C.P. 25 (1)/289/52 no. 4; *Cal. Close*, 1377–81, 194.
[57] *Cal. Inq. p.m.* xv, p. 38.
[58] C 136/95 no. 53.
[59] *V.C.H. Wilts.* x. 15; for Edw.'s heirs see below, p. 53.
[60] *Complete Peerage*, s.v. Ros.
[61] C.P. 25(1)/294/79 no. 21. In Lovel's accts. of 1523 Redlynch man. was described as 'recovered against Dudley': *L. & P. Hen. VIII*, iv (1), p. 155.
[62] Prob. 11/23 (P.C.C. 27 Jankyn). For the Lovels see Blomefield, *Norf.* i. 323.
[63] C.P. 25(2)/81/693 no. 33.
[64] Hoare, *Mod. Wilts.* Downton, 52; C.P. 25(2)/239/9 Eliz. I Hil.
[65] W.R.O. 490/801; Hoare, *Mod. Wilts.* Downton, 52; Sar. Dioc. R.O., misc. papers, copy of ancient doc.
[66] W.R.O. 490/783.
[67] For the Eyres see Hoare, *Mod. Wilts.* Frustfield, pedigree 2 at pp. 56–7; Burke, *Land. Gent.* (1952), 785–6.
[68] W.R.O., Inclosure Award.
[69] Ibid. Tithe Award.

[70] See p. 70.
[71] W.R.O. 1008/27; see below.
[72] Ex inf. Mr. D. Newton, Longford Estate Office.
[73] C.P. 25(2)/239/9 & 10 Eliz. I Mich.; C 142/152 no. 168.
[74] W.R.O. 490/801; *Wilts. Pedigrees* (Harl. Soc. cv, cvi), 182.
[75] Prob. 11/151 (35 Skinner). He held it in 1614: W.R.O. 464/44.
[76] W.R.O. 464/44.
[77] Ibid. 490/783; 192/24b; 490/802; 464/44; Hoare, *Mod. Wilts.* Downton, 52.
[78] Hoare, *Mod. Wilts.* Downton, 52; W.R.O. 490/802.
[79] Hoare, *Mod. Wilts.* Downton, 52; W.R.O. 464/44; Land Tax.
[80] W.R.O., Inclosure Award; Tithe Award.
[81] Hoare, *Mod. Wilts.* Downton, 52; W.R.O., Land Tax.
[82] W.R.O., Tithe Award.
[83] Ibid. 1008/27; see p. 70.
[84] *V.C.H. Wilts.* ii, p. 119; see above, p. 26.
[85] B.L. Eg. MS. 2418, f. 61.
[86] *Cal. Inq. p.m.* i, p. 305; *Close R.* 1259–61, 439.
[87] *Cal. Inq. p.m.* i, p. 305.
[88] Cf. Winch. Coll. Mun. 5066, 5076.
[89] *Feet of F.* 1272–1327 (W.R.S. i), p. 58; Winch. Coll. Mun. 5084.

WESTWOOD MANOR, BUILT FROM THE LATE 15TH CENTURY

KNOYL HOUSE, REBUILT 1880

HAMPTWORTH LODGE, BUILT 1912

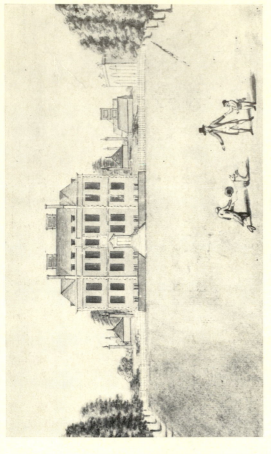

BARFORD HOUSE

DOWNTON: NEWHOUSE (in Whiteparish)

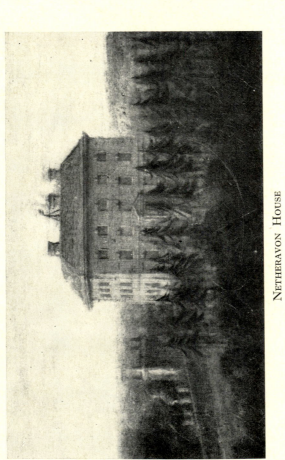

NETHERAVON HOUSE

BODENHAM: NEW HALL

Sir William was dead in 1323.[90] The land was settled *c.* 1361 on the marriage of Joan of Woodfalls, possibly a granddaughter of Sir William of Woodfalls, and Hugh Cheyne (later knighted).[91] After Sir Hugh's death without issue in 1390,[92] Joan married Sir Thomas Blount (executed 1400) and Thomas Linford (d. 1423) who held the land in her right in 1401.[93] Joan's heirs are not known. In 1412 Edmund Dauntsey, who held other lands formerly Joan's, was said to hold it,[94] but its subsequent descent is not clear.

Francis Palmer of Lindley (Yorks. W.R.) held the manor in 1566.[95] He sold it in 1580 to Ralph Coles (d. 1595) who devised it to his son Barnabas (d. 1653).[96] Barnabas's heir was his son William (d. 1697)[97] whose heir was his grandson Barnaby.[98] After Barnaby died in 1737 the manor was held by Thomas Cooper, a Salisbury grocer.[99] It passed *c.* 1745 to Henry Archer of Warwick (d. 1768) and thence to his widow Lady Elizabeth Archer (d. 1789).[1] It descended with the manor of Hale (Hants) and was sold after Elizabeth's death to Joseph May.[2] Joseph's widow Mary held it *c.* 1798–1824. In 1822 83 a. in the Franchise and 16 a. at Woodfalls were allotted at inclosure.[3] The land descended to Mary's son Joseph but by 1837 had passed, presumably by sale, to Joseph Goff (d. 1875). Goff was succeeded by his grandsons J. G. S. Goff (d. 1881) and A. H. S. Goff (d. 1936), who sold the land to Capt. T. V. Booth Jones in 1920.[4] Woodfalls farm was later sold to J. G. S. Mitchell whose executors owned it in 1975.[5] The land in the Franchise, with that allotted in respect of Lower Woodfalls (see below), from Golden Cross to Pound bottom, became part of Hamptworth Lodge estate.[6]

Woodfalls Farm is an early-17th-century house of brick with stone dressings. Many original features were removed or replaced, especially in the 19th century.

In the earlier 13th century Alan of Woodfalls held land at Woodfalls assessed at 1 hide,[7] later called the manor of *LOWER WOODFALLS* or Lower Lodge (later Lodge) farm. It is likely that John of Woodfalls held it in 1249.[8] John died *c.* 1288. His widow Agnes held the land during the minority of his heir,[9] apparently a son John who held it in 1323.[10] The descent thereafter is not clear but the land later passed to Sir Thomas de Buckland who in 1377 settled it on himself for life.[11] He

died holding it in 1379.[12] It passed to John Wroth and descended like the manor of Puckshipton in Beechingstoke until the death of Lady (Joan) Ingoldisthorpe in 1494.[13] In 1502 the manor was allotted to Joan's granddaughter and coheir Lucy, wife of Sir Anthony Brown.[14] In 1516 she sold it to Richard Fox, bishop of Winchester and founder of Corpus Christi College, Oxford, who endowed the college with it in 1519.[15] At inclosure in 1822 an allotment of 73 a. in the Franchise was added to the land.[16] The college sold it all in 1864 to Joseph Goff and it has since passed with the manor of Upper Woodfalls.[17]

The Woodfalls family seem to have occupied a manor-house on the land, at least until 1323 when John of Woodfalls's 'court' was mentioned.[18] Nothing of the house is known to survive. Lodge Farm is a T-shaped 18th-century house of brick and tile with a symmetrical front of five bays and a short rear wing. It was extended in the 19th and 20th centuries.

In 1279 Simon de la Bere and his wife Euphemia conveyed 1 carucate in Downton to Roger de Stepesham and his wife Joan in exchange for other land.[19] It was possibly the carucate with meadow and rent in Downton and Whiteparish settled on Thomas and Isabel Gerberd in 1341.[20] Thomas was apparently lord of Odstock manor.[21] The land seems to have passed with that manor through the Gerberd family to the Webbs.[22] John Webb (d. 1680) held it in 1628[23] and it passed with his manor of Hamptworth.[24] At inclosure in 1822 some 4 a. at Bohemia was added to the estate, called Timberleys farm,[25] which measured *c.* 49 a. in 1837.[26] That farm was sold to George Matcham in 1858 and passed with the Newhouse estate.[27] Timbury Lane Farm, as it was called in 1975, is a small timber-framed house of the 17th or 18th century.

In 1376 Thomas Snel settled an estate of some 40 a. in East Downton tithing on himself and his wife Eustacia.[28] Thomas apparently held another small estate at Downton, formerly William Cove's.[29] Between 1388 and 1392 he conveyed some of the land and life interests in more of it to Robert Boset, and in 1395 and 1396 quitclaimed all his rights in the lands to Robert.[30] In 1411 Robert (d. before 1419) granted the reversion to Winchester College[31] and the lands were added to the rectorial estate.

[90] Winch. Coll. Mun. 5076.
[91] *Cal. Fine R.* 1356–68, 181; cf. *Feet of F.* 1272–1327 (W.R.S. i), p. 58; 1327–77 (W.R.S. xxix), p. 134.
[92] C 136/58 no. 8.
[93] *Cal. Close,* 1399–1402, 440; for Thomas Linford's d. see C 139/26 no. 45.
[94] *Feud. Aids,* vi. 457.   [95] W.R.O. 490/1170.
[96] C 142/313 no. 24; C 142/663 no. 160; Hoare, *Mod. Wilts.* Downton, 31.
[97] *W.N. & Q.* iii. 428; C 78/1778 no. 13.
[98] C 78/1778 no. 13.
[99] Hoare, *Mod. Wilts.* Downton, 31; W.R.O. 490/802; 212B/2821.   [1] W.R.O. 490/802; cf. below, p. 39.
[2] *V.C.H. Hants,* iv. 578; W.R.O. 490/802; Land Tax.
[3] W.R.O., Land Tax; Inclosure Award.
[4] Ibid. Land Tax; Tithe Award; Burke, *Land. Gent.* (1952), 998–9.
[5] Ex inf. Mr. A. S. Mitchell, Charles Mitchell & Sons Ltd., Lode Hill.
[6] Ex inf. Mr. N. J. M. Anderson, Hamptworth Lodge; see p. 60.
[7] B.L. Eg. MS. 2418, f. 61.

[8] C.P. 25(1)/251/16 no. 79.
[9] H.R.O. Eccl. 2/159311, rott. 4d.–6.
[10] Winch. Coll. Mun. 5076.
[11] C 138/5 no. 53.   [12] *Cal. Inq. p.m.* xv, p. 38.
[13] *V.C.H. Wilts.* x. 15–16.
[14] C.C.C., Oxf., Mun., deeds LA 29, pp. 376 sqq.
[15] Ibid. pp. 332 sqq.
[16] W.R.O., Inclosure Award.
[17] C.C.C., Oxf., Mun., lease bk. 1859–68, p. 301.
[18] Winch. Coll. Mun. 5076.
[19] *Feet of F.* 1272–1327 (W.R.S. i), p. 63.
[20] Ibid. 1327–77 (W.R.S. xxix), p. 68.
[21] Hoare, *Mod. Wilts.* Cawden, 19–20.
[22] A fuller acct. of the descent of Odstock man. is reserved for a later vol.   [23] W.R.O. 490/783.
[24] See p. 60.   [25] W.R.O. 490/802.
[26] Ibid. Inclosure Award; Tithe Award.
[27] Ibid. 490/1012; see above.
[28] *Feet of F.* 1327–77 (W.R.S. xxix), p. 146.
[29] Winch. Coll. Mun. 4983.
[30] Ibid. 4982; 4984–5; 4987–91; 4993.
[31] Ibid. 5000–6; 5012–13.

In the early 19th century John Bailey (d. before 1822), who farmed a large area in the parish,[32] held an estate at Redlynch made up of various freehold, leasehold, and copyhold of inheritance lands, some 50 a., on which he built Redlynch House.[33] A sale allotment of 50 a. in Paccombe common was added in 1822 but sold by 1837.[34] Redlynch House and park, 25 a., was bought before 1833 by William, Earl Nelson, and used by his son-in-law Samuel Hood, Baron Bridport.[35] It had been sold by 1837 to Thomas William Coventry.[36] It belonged to R. A. Ferryman in the later 19th century, was the seat of Octavius Robinson (d. 1904),[37] and in 1922 was again sold, presumably to Lt.-Col. Francis R. Tarleton (d. 1950), the occupant in 1939.[38] In 1975 the house belonged to Mr. Adrian Farquhar. It is a substantial square house of c. 1822 partly remodelled later in the 19th century.

The commons in East Downton tithing were inclosed in 1822.[39] Extensive areas of land, especially in the Franchise, were added to existing estates and new estates were created.[40] Jacob, earl of Radnor, was allotted 195 a. in respect of New Court and Witherington farms,[41] of which Cloven hill plantation, 125 a., later became part of Hamptworth Lodge estate and Quar hill plantation, 70 a., later became part of Newhouse estate.[42] Robert Eden Duncombe Shafto was allotted 75 a., 81 a., and 50 a. for respectively the freehold, leasehold, and copyhold parts of the Barford estate.[43] The leasehold land, Franchises common and Franchises common wood, descended to Shafto's son Robert Duncombe Shafto, who bought the reversion in fee in 1865,[44] and passed with the manor of Hamptworth.[45] At inclosure John Pern Tinney of Salisbury, who previously held no land in the parish, bought and afforested allotments of 52 a. at Paccombe common, Tinney's firs, and 132 a. in the Franchise, Tinney's plantation, Burnt Tree copse, Firs Hill copse, and Ashens Hat.[46] By 1837 Shafto's neighbouring freehold and copyhold of inheritance allotments, Franchises wood, had been added.[47] In 1837, with those allotments and another in Paccombe common bought from the representatives of John Bailey, Tinney's successor William Henry Tinney held 375 a.[48] The Tinneys' land in the Franchise was subsequently divided between the Lyburn House estate (see below) and Hamptworth Lodge estate which encompassed Franchises wood. Tinney's firs became part of Newhouse estate.[49] At inclosure James Wapshare bought an

allotment of 278 a. in the westernmost part of the Franchise.[50] He converted some 100 a. to arable, some of it near No Man's Land tenanted, and established a farm at Lyburn House.[51] The Lyburn House estate belonged to Frederick Bradburn in 1858,[52] passed to his son Frederick Ashe Bradburn, and in the early 20th century to R. C. Leigh.[53] The estate, 450 a. including much of the Tinneys' land, was later bought by J. G. S. Mitchell and belonged to his executors in 1975.[54] Lyburn House was built c. 1822 with farm buildings to which others were added later.

The establishment of over 100 freely alienable burgage tenements in the early 13th century[55] was the origin of several freehold estates which became important, though not territorially great, by encompassing a number of such holdings, to which votes in parliamentary elections were attached.[56] John Uffenham alias Lawrence seems to have held such an estate in the mid 15th century.[57] In 1495 his son John settled it on himself and his wife Alice. The younger John died in 1503 holding a 'hostel', 31 burgages, and some 25 a. of land in Downton which passed, apart from the 'hostel', to his relative Richard Uffenham.[58] In 1528–9 Richard held 39 burgages[59] but the later descent of the estate is not clear.

In 1528–9 Sir Francis Lovel held sixteen burgages.[60] They apparently passed with the manor of Barford through the Stockman family to Sir Francis Chaplin and to Sir Charles Duncombe.[61] Between 1698 and 1708 Duncombe bought a number of other burgages[62] and in 1709 held some thirty.[63]

An estate including fifteen burgages was conveyed by John Stockman (d. 1605) to William Juniper (d. 1569) in 1567.[64] William's son William sold it c. 1594 to Thomas Elliott, a Salisbury wool-draper, who in 1622 settled the estate on himself for life with remainder to his younger son Nicholas.[65] Thomas died in 1625 holding nine burgages and in 1647 the estate belonged to Nicholas.[66] In 1721 John Elliott sold it to Anthony Duncombe (d. 1763) who bought a number of other burgages.[67] The burgages inherited by Lord Feversham from Sir Charles Duncombe passed at his death like Barford manor to Thomas Duncombe and the Shaftos. Those he bought passed to his executors.[68]

Giles Eyre of Brickworth in Whiteparish held some eleven burgages c. 1700.[69] In 1709 John Eyre, presumably his brother, held more than twenty which Giles Eyre (d.s.p. 1750) held c. 1740.[70] In

[32] e.g. W.R.O. 490/779.
[33] Ibid. Inclosure Award; Hoare, Mod. Wilts. Downton, 52.
[34] W.R.O., Inclosure Award; Tithe Award.
[35] Hoare, Mod. Wilts. Downton, 52.
[36] Ibid. 71; W.R.O., Tithe Award.
[37] Wilts. Cuttings, i. 32; W.A.M. xxxiii. 416.
[38] Kelly's Dir. Wilts. (1939).
[39] W.R.O., Inclosure Award.
[40] Allotments in respect of estates in E. Downton tithing are mentioned above with the estates in question.
[41] W.R.O., Inclosure Award.
[42] Ex inf. Mr. Anderson; Mr. G. Jeffreys, Newhouse.
[43] W.R.O., Inclosure Award.
[44] Ibid. Tithe Award; H.R.O. Eccl. 2/155515, pp. 25–9.
[45] See p. 60.
[46] W.R.O., Inclosure Award.
[47] Ibid. Tithe Award.
[48] Ibid.
[49] Ex inf. Mr. Anderson; Mr. Jeffreys.
[50] W.R.O., Inclosure Award.
[51] Ibid. Tithe Award.
[52] Ibid. 490/1012.
[53] Livens, No Man's Land (priv. print. 1910); Kelly's Dir. Wilts. (1899, 1911).
[54] Ex inf. Mr. A. S. Mitchell.
[55] See above.
[56] See below.
[57] B.L. Add. Ch. 7583; V.C.H. Wilts. v. 35.
[58] V.C.H. Wilts. v. 35; Cal. Inq. p.m. Hen. VII, ii, pp. 460–1.
[59] W.R.O. 490/800.
[60] Ibid.
[61] See pp. 53–4.
[62] W.R.O. 490/261.
[63] Ibid. 490/802.
[64] C.P. 25(2)/239/9 & 10 Eliz. I Mich.; C 142/152 no. 168.
[65] C 2/Eliz. I/E 4/21; Wilts. Inq. p.m. 1625–49 (Index Libr.), 365–8.
[66] Wilts. Inq. p.m. 1625–49 (Index Libr.), 365–8; Hoare, Mod. Wilts. Downton, 19.
[67] W.R.O. 490/260.
[68] Univ. Brit. Dir. ii (1793 edn.), 846.
[69] W.R.O. 490/830.
[70] Ibid. 490/802; 490/830.

1773 John Eyre of Landford sold them to Thomas Duncombe.[71]

In 1780 about a third of the tenements in the borough belonged to Robert Shafto, about a third to Lord Feversham's executors, and about a third to other owners.[72] Under an estate Act of 1801 Robert Eden Duncombe Shafto sold his burgages c. 1805 to Jacob, earl of Radnor, who in 1806 also bought those held by the executors.[73] Many properties in the borough have since passed with the Radnor title.

AGRICULTURE. The Romano-British villa at Downton was part of a sizeable farmstead whose occupants grew corn and pulse crops.[74] Contemporary field systems on New Court and Charlton downs (129 ha.), on Nunton down (at least 12 ha.), and on Standlynch and Witherington downs (36 ha.) indicate that large areas of the chalk uplands were cultivated.[75] The bishop of Winchester's estate was assessed at 100 mansae in the 790s.[76] The 997 assessment of Downton at 55 mansae and Bishopstone at 45 mansae is, since so much of Downton was then woodland and heath, possibly a rough measure of the relative values of those places.[77] The grant of Downton potentially brought all the agrarian life of the area under the bishop's control and in 1086 much of his estate was organized as a manor. Downton and Bishopstone were then treated as a single very large estate. The bishop had on it demesne assessed at 30 hides with 13 ploughs and 40 serfs, and 64 villeins and 27 bordars with a total of 17 ploughs held land assessed at some 29½ hides. There were 60 a. of meadow, pasture 2 leagues by 1, and woodland 1½ by ½ league.[78] Although the overall values of Downton and Bishopstone possibly bore the same relationship to each other as in 997, since the various types of land were not necessarily in the same proportion to each other at both places, that part of the Domesday assessment relating only to Downton cannot be gauged.

DOWNTON MANOR. In the early 13th century the bishops' manor encompassed lands in all parts of the parish except Standlynch and Hamptworth.[79] Sheep-and-corn husbandry predominated.[80] The principal area of demesne arable land was in Wick tithing, then worked from the manorial centre at Old Court.[81] There were also demesne lands and farm buildings at Nunton and Witherington and formerly perhaps at Barford. In addition customary holdings in all the tithings had apparently been drawn in when the demesne was expanding.[82] West of the Avon there were extensive demesne meadows in Wick tithing and some in Nunton. East of the Avon there were demesne meadows at Witherington; the meadows between Barford and Downton were used in common by the bishop and the rector until 1311 when common rights were extinguished.[83] Large areas of the chalk downs on both sides of the river were demesne pastures,[84] and in the east and south-east parts of the parish the extensive areas of woodland and heath were theoretically demesne.[85]

Direct cultivation of the demesne was at a high point in 1208–9 with 838 a. sown, and at Michaelmas 1209 there were 91 oxen and 2,233 sheep.[86] In the early and mid 13th century additional arable land was assarted from woodland in East Downton tithing, between 1225 and 1247 at Timber hill, where 76 a. were sown in 1232, and in 1251–2 at Loosehanger, where 47 a. were sown in 1252 and 158½ a. in 1266. The arable in both places was inclosed.[87] Most demesne arable, however, remained in the open field.[88] Over 900 a. were sown for the bishop in 1225 and 1254,[89] but from the late 1260s the area of demesne arable declined, sometimes rapidly. It never rose above 700 a. after 1268, above 600 a. after 1282, above 500 a. after 1308, above 400 a. after 1319, above 300 a. after 1347, above 200 a. in the 15th century.[90] That decline can be explained only by a steady transfer of land to the tenants. The small pieces of demesne arable among the tenants' lands were appended to customary holdings and translated to customary tenure. Such land was called 'bourdland' and permanently distinguished from 'bondland'.[91] By 1349 some was attached to most holdings in all the villages on the manor.[92] By contrast the main demesne arable lands were leased, those at Nunton before 1376 and those at Witherington later.[93] The land at Timber hill and Loosehanger probably reverted to pasture.[94] In 1376–7 there was demesne arable land only in the tithing of Wick,[95] and as part of New Court farm that was leased in 1418.[96] Neither cattle nor sheep rearing on the demesne declined so rapidly as arable cultivation.[97] There were often more than 2,000 sheep on the demesne in the 13th century, never more than 2,000 after 1312, but totals below 1,000 were rare.[98] Upland pasture on the chalk on the east side of the Avon valley and pasture in the former woodlands in East Downton tithing were absorbed as bourdland into customary holdings,[99] meadows and pastures at Nunton and Witherington were leased,[1] but most of the Avon valley

[71] Ibid. 490/249/2.   [72] Ibid. Land Tax.
[73] Ibid. 490/249/1; Land Tax; 490/779; 490/234.
[74] V.C.H. Wilts. i (2), 447, 448–9, 450, 458, 466.
[75] Ibid. i (1), 275, 277.
[76] Finberg, Early Wessex Chart. pp. 71–2.
[77] Ibid. pp. 102–3.
[78] V.C.H. Wilts. ii, p. 119.
[79] B.L. Eg. MS. 2418, ff. 61–64v. References to villages in this para. should be followed up in the econ. hist. sections of their own hists.
[80] J. Z. Titow, Eng. Rural Soc. 1200–1350, 106–14.
[81] e.g. H.R.O. Eccl. 2/159457, rott. 8–9.
[82] e.g. Charlton: p. 57.
[83] Winch. Coll. Mun. 4976.
[84] Titow, Eng. Rural Soc. 106.
[85] See below.
[86] Titow, Eng. Rural Soc. 106–14.
[87] J. Z. Titow, 'Land and Population on the Bishop of

Winchester's Estates 1209–1350' (Camb. Univ. Ph.D. thesis, 1962), 81–2; Titow, Eng. Rural Soc. 198–201.
[88] H.R.O. Eccl. 2/159457, rott. 8–9.
[89] Titow, 'Land and Pop.', Table I.
[90] Ibid.; for 1350–1453 see e.g. A. Elizabeth Levett, Black Death on the Estates of the See of Winchester, 132; H.R.O. Eccl. 2/159417, rott. 3d.–4d. (1414–15).
[91] This is not the accepted view of 'bourdland': Levett, Black Death, 70 n. 2; V.C.H. Wilts. iv. 10; but cf. V.C.H. Wilts. vi. 93.
[92] H.R.O. Eccl. 2/159385, rot. 3d.
[93] See pp. 65, 76.   [94] See below.
[95] H.R.O. Eccl. 2/159385, rot. 4d.
[96] Ibid. Eccl. 2/159420, rot. 4. For the later hist. of New Ct. farm see pp. 74–5.
[97] Titow, 'Land and Pop.', Tables III, IV.
[98] Ibid. Table IV.
[99] See below.   [1] See pp. 65, 76.

meadows and a great sheep walk were still part of the demesne when it was leased.[2]

The bishop had some 175 customary tenants in the earlier 13th century, including some 57 virgaters, 40 ½-virgaters, and 30 ¼-virgaters ('ferlingers').[3] In 1208–9 their rents totalled £35 2s. 2d.[4] Their labour services were probably sufficient for most demesne cultivation even at its height and there is no reason to doubt that the demesne was largely cultivated by the tenants,[5] who probably held nearly twice as much as arable as the lord when the demesne was at its most extensive.[6] In the 14th and 15th centuries the number of tenants declined. That can be ascribed partly to the plagues of 1349 and 1361–2 which left a number of holdings vacant.[7] In 1377 there were some 150 tenants.[8] In the mid 15th century a smaller number is implied.[9] The transfer of agricultural resources from the lord to the tenantry was, however, reflected by the payment of more rent. The total paid rose steadily until it was over £70 in 1332.[10] Later evidence shows the tenants to have held by Borough English.[11]

Between 1418, when the last demesne lands were leased, and 1551, when the lordship of the manor was leased, the bishops' income from the manor came primarily from rents and other payments. Most had become fixed by 1551.[12] In 1737 the lord farmer was entitled to customary, freehold, and wood rents from the several villages, knighthamhold rents from Charlton,[13] the old burgage rents, fishing rents, lawday silver paid by the various tithings, and various other rents.[14] In addition he took the profits of courts, mostly small entry fines and commuted heriots for copyhold of inheritance lands.[15] The total annual income of some £123 was held from the bishops for a net rent of some £86.[16]

EAST DOWNTON AND CHURCH TITHINGS. This sub-section deals with agriculture in the whole of East Downton tithing except Hamptworth and of Church tithing except Barford and Standlynch.[17] In 1086 the only substantial area of tillage seems to have been that of the bishop's tenants, probably south-east of Old Court. The 4-hide estate of the church and some of the knights' estates alienated after 1066 lay in the area but no plough or tenant on them was mentioned.[18] The chalklands above Downton and beyond the downs of Barford, Standlynch, and Witherington were probably open pastures and woodlands, and the Hampshire basin soils south-east of them were covered almost entirely by heath and woodland. The 4 hides taken from the bishop's estate by William I for his forest, from 2 hides of which the inhabitants were driven,[19] were possibly taken from land south-east of where

No Man's Land now is to include Bramshaw Wood, and never returned. It is more likely, however, that they were taken from what became the Franchise, regarded topographically but not legally as part of the New Forest until inclosure in 1822.[20] If so the early-13th-century declaration that the bishop's woods were free from the regard, though the deer remained the king's, was equivalent to restoration to the bishop and disafforestation.[21]

In the two centuries after the Conquest there was clearly a substantial increase of cultivated land in the tithings. Possibly in the 12th century the rector and the lords of Redlynch manor seem to have inclosed and ploughed on the chalk, particularly around Pensworth;[22] in the early 13th century the episcopal assarting at Timber hill and Loosehanger, between Timberley Lane and the old Black Lane, brought the clay into cultivation for the first time;[23] and the lords of the Woodfalls manors may have assarted west of Woodfalls at the same time. There remained, however, substantial areas of uninclosed grassland and woodland. If, as may be supposed, they included all those lands inclosed in 1822, there were some 550 a. of grassland among the areas of arable at Paccombe common, 102 a., Morgan's hill and Morgan's vale, 14 a. and 35 a., and Redlynch, 131 a., and between the arable lands and the woodland and heath at Woodfalls, 104 a., Warminster Green, 35 a., and Bohemia, 129 a.[24] The arable and pasture lands extended eastwards roughly to a line from the south-west corner of Langley wood to where the road now called Bohemia crosses the county boundary. East of that was woodland and heath, some 1,100 a. The lands in the tithings were shared among five major estates, part of the bishop's manor, the rector's manor, Redlynch manor, and the two Woodfalls manors. Common husbandry was never widely practised and, although their lands were in places intermingled and pasture was used in common, the economic histories of those estates are treated separately.

At the height of demesne cultivation in the early 13th century the bishop of Winchester had sheep folds at the Park, Bere hill, some of which was sometimes ploughed,[25] and Paccombe,[26] and at times 150 a. sown on the assarted land.[27] From the mid 13th century, however, the level of demesne farming east of the Avon fell, and in the 15th century the diminished demesne farm apparently had no land there.[28] The bishops retained woods on the chalk at Old Park, Privett, and Farthingley, at Timber hill and Loosehanger, and in the Franchise where Franchise wood was an ancient oak forest[29] surrounded by heath. The bishops had free warren from the early 13th century.[30] The king confirmed

[2] See p. 74.   [3] B.L. Eg. MS. 2418, ff. 61–64v.
[4] Titow, Eng. Rural Soc. 106.
[5] B.L. Eg. MS. 2418, ff. 61–64v.; Titow, Eng. Rural Soc. 133–6; Levett, Black Death, 115; A. Ballard, 'Downton', in Levett, Black Death, 215.
[6] Winch. Coll. Mun. 4957.
[7] Ballard, 'Downton', in Levett, Black Death, 213–14.
[8] Ibid. 212.   [9] See pp. 52, 76.
[10] Titow, 'Land and Pop.', Table V.
[11] W.R.O. 490/1187 (1672).
[12] e.g. H.R.O. Eccl. 2/159500/3 (1488); Eccl. 2/155893 (1555).   [13] See p. 56.
[14] W.R.O. 490/802.   [15] Ibid. 490/779.
[16] e.g. H.R.O. Eccl. 2/155642, pp. 33–7.
[17] Agric. in the excepted areas is dealt with in the econ.

hist. sections of the articles bearing the names of those places as titles.
[18] V.C.H. Wilts. ii, p. 119.
[19] Ibid. pp. 119, 208.
[20] Andrews and Dury, Map (W.R.S. viii), pl. 3; Hoare, Mod. Wilts. Downton, 13.
[21] V.C.H. Wilts. iv. 428.
[22] See below.   [23] See above.
[24] W.R.O., Inclosure Award.
[25] Titow, 'Land and Pop.', 81–2.
[26] H.R.O. Eccl. 2/159500/3.
[27] Ibid. Eccl. 2/159457, rott. 8–9.
[28] e.g. ibid. Eccl. 2/159417, rott. 3d.–4d. (1414–15).
[29] Ex inf. Mr. N. J. M. Anderson, Hamptworth Lodge.
[30] Rot. Hund. (Rec. Com.), ii (1), 257.

liberty of the chase *c.* 1284.[31] The woods were excluded from leases of the lordship of the manor,[32] but the right to hunt was included. In the early 17th century, when it was said that deer had always been in the chase, the right was vigorously defended by the lord farmer.[33] About 1650, however, there were no longer deer in the Franchise.[34] In 1592 Old Park, Privett, and Farthingley were disparked and allotted to those with rights to the bishop's wood.[35] The copyholders of the several villages paid 1*s.* an acre for some 130 a. of wood in 1737.[36] By the early 19th century most of those woods had been converted to arable.[37] Probably in the mid 17th century the woods at Loosehanger were inclosed by bank and ditch, still to be seen, and in the later 17th century, when they were used for the production of barrel timber, Loosehanger was described as a park.[38] It was leased as a farm only *c.* 1740 when it consisted of 73 a. and the herbage of 137 a. of woodland.[39] It measured 109 a. in 1837[40] and remained a separate farm until *c.* 1969.[41] The woods at Timber hill passed by copy with Newhouse.[42] The remaining woods were surveyed by parliamentary commissioners 1647–50. Those with rights in them were said to be the lessee of Witherington farm (10 trees), the lessee of Downton mills (2 trees or 2 tons of timber, 10,000 turfs, and wood to repair the great weir of the mills), and the woodreeve (2 trees). The copyholders had established by custom the right to pay only 5*s.* a tree for wood to repair their tenements. The lord farmer was entitled to wood to repair the west end of the mill bridge, Catherine bridge, and Long bridge in Nunton, and to maintain the pounds at Downton and Charlton.[43] Franchise wood, 180 a. in 1822,[44] was restored after the Interregnum.[45] In 1975 it was still forest.

In the earlier 13th century the bishop had some 31 tenants at Downton: seventeen shared 8 virgates; the remainder were cottagers.[46] Their arable land south-east of Old Court was later called the south field of Downton.[47] At least from the late 13th century extensive areas of inclosed demesne lands east of Downton were attached to the small customary holdings.[48] In the early 16th century the customary tenants held some 665 a. there, some 509 a. of former demesne, bourdland, and 156 a. of customary land, bondland, all by copy.[49] Some of the bondland was cultivated in common but over 100 a. were inclosed. The bourdland included the woods at Timber hill and Loosehanger and 433 a. of land in closes including Bere hill, the Park, the Moot (10 a.), Milk hill, and Paccombe. All those lands were shared among twenty tenants. Richard Matthew held 176 a., and much other land was attached to Barford, Redlynch, and later Parsonage

farms.[50] In 1628 Griffin Studley's farm, later Moot farm, probably comprised most of the bondland near Downton.[51] By 1709 Paccombe farm, some 78 a., had been established on the chalk above Downton.[52] Some of the Newhouse estate was imparked,[53] but two small farms were established at Milk hill and Timber hill. In the early 19th century some 800 a., excluding lands allotted at inclosure in 1822, were apparently held by copy of Downton manor east of the Avon. Some 155 a. were part of Barford farm, 30 a. part of Loosehanger farm, 76 a. part of Parsonage farm, 87 a. made up Paccombe farm, 170 a. Moot farm, 40 a. were part of Redlynch farm, 79 a. at Privett were part of the Standlynch estate, and 159 a. part of Newhouse estate. In 1837 Paccombe farm was a compact largely arable farm of 73 a. between Slab Lane and the farm-house beside Lode Hill, and Moot farm was a compact farm of 155 a. between the northern part of Slab Lane and the Avon.[54] Both remained separate farms until the mid 20th century when they were added to Woodfalls farm.[55] Lands on both sides of Moot Lane were built upon in the mid 20th century. In 1837 Milk Hills farm measured 87 a.[56] In 1975 it was a solely dairy farm of 70 a. The farm at Timber hill was a dairy farm of 83 a. in 1975 when it was called Newhouse farm. Opposite Milkhills Farm in Goggs Lane there was in 1975 a market garden of some 10 a. belonging to T. G. Ings & Sons, fruiterers and greengrocers of Salisbury.

In 1305 the rector's estate consisted of the spiritualities of the church, a demesne farm, and customary holdings.[57] The spiritualities were the most valuable. Until 1383 they included nearly all tithes and oblations from the whole parish and were possibly worth £150 a year.[58] In 1368–9 some 550 qr. of corn, mostly from tithes but including the produce of the demesne, were threshed and winnowed, and 260 lambs and 41 piglets were received in tithes.[59] About the time that Winchester College was endowed with the church[60] the great tithes were assessed at £111 10*s.*[61] From 1390 the tithes were usually leased with the demesne.[62] In 1551 the college leased them both on favourable terms to Sir Thomas White of South Wanborough (Hants) and his son Thomas in gratitude for service,[63] and leases were afterwards granted to John Stockman of Barford and to William, earl of Pembroke.[64] In 1582 a lease for 40 years from 1585 was granted to Elizabeth I for Sir Thomas Wilkes (d. 1598), a clerk of the Privy Council.[65] By 1601 it had apparently passed to Sir Carew Raleigh (d. 1626), elder brother of Sir Walter, who was succeeded by his son Gilbert (d. 1628), grandson Gilbert (d. 1675), great-grandson Sir Charles (d. 1698), and great-great-

[31] *Reg. Pontoise* (Cant. & York Soc.), ii. 417–19.
[32] e.g. H.R.O. Eccl. 2/155642, pp. 33–7.
[33] Sta. Cha. 8/183/39.   [34] W.R.O. 490/784.
[35] Ibid. 893/4, p. 125; see above.
[36] W.R.O. 490/802.   [37] Ibid. Tithe Award.
[38] E 134/18 Chas. II Mich./6.
[39] W.R.O. 490/791.   [40] Ibid. Tithe Award.
[41] Ex inf. Mr. G. Jeffreys, Newhouse.
[42] See below.
[43] W.R.O. 490/784.
[44] Ibid. Inclosure Award.   [45] See above.
[46] B.L. Eg. MS. 2418, f. 61 and v.
[47] Winch. Coll. Mun. 5064.
[48] H.R.O. Eccl. 2/159500/3.
[49] W.R.O. 490/800.   [50] See below and p. 54.

[51] W.R.O. 490/783.
[52] Ibid. 490/802; 490/793, survey.
[53] Hoare, *Mod. Wilts.* Downton, 56.
[54] W.R.O., Inclosure Award; Tithe Award.
[55] Ex inf. Mr. A. S. Mitchell, Chas. Mitchell & Sons Ltd., Lode Hill.
[56] W.R.O., Tithe Award.
[57] Winch. Coll. Mun. 4953.
[58] Ibid. 4957; see below.
[59] Winch. Coll. Mun. 5362.   [60] See above.
[61] Winch. Coll. Mun. 4957.
[62] Ibid. 5368–75; 5409–12; 5431–52; 5454–5541.
[63] Ibid. 22993, ff. 145v.–146.
[64] Ibid. 22996, index.
[65] Ibid. 4970.

grandson Carew Raleigh.[66] Leases were held by the Raleighs or their trustees until in 1713, after Carew's death, a Chancery decree forced a sale.[67] A lease was assigned to Anthony Duncombe in 1717. The leasehold passed like Duncombe's leasehold of the lordship of Downton manor and was bought by Lord Radnor in 1806.[68] In the 17th and 18th centuries leases were renewed every three or four years under fines roughly equal to a year's value of the tithes and demesne [69] which were sub-let.[70] The tithes were valued at some £1,628 in 1837, commuted in 1840,[71] and taken back in hand by the college.

The location of the land, known from later evidence,[72] shows the bishop of Winchester to have granted the rector a narrow strip running back from Downton and a detached area of down at Pensworth, probably 500 a. in all. The land near Downton, divided between demesne and tenantry land, was presumably assarted soon after 1086 and was cultivated in common.[73] The demesne farm was small, 39 a. sown in 1368–9 for example,[74] and sheep were not usually kept.[75] In 1698 the farm, Parsonage, was organized for dairying.[76] Afterwards other land, including copyhold of inheritance land of Downton manor in East Downton tithing, was added to the farm which in 1806 was an arable and dairy farm of 192 a.[77] From the time that the college resumed the rectory estate until the land was sold in 1921 the demesne, apart from Grove copse, was leased as a small dairy farm.[78] Parsonage farm was still that in 1975. In 1305 the rector had three tenants holding some 33 a. and eighteen cottagers at Downton.[79] In 1521 all Winchester College's customary lands at Downton were leased together as a small farm with some 45 a. and a new tenement, in 1724 said to be on the corner of Barford Lane and High Street.[80] By 1837 the farm had been broken up.[81]

The rector's land at Pensworth lay mainly north of Grove copse. It had possibly been intended as a sheep-run for the rector but, presumably in the 12th century and the early 13th, was colonized, inclosed, and much of it tilled. In 1305 some twenty tenants at Pensworth shared 4½ virgates and some 30 a. Their annual rents totalled £5 13s. together with customary payments and labour services.[82] In the mid 16th century there were only five copyholds and, together some 350 a., they remained separate in the mid 17th century.[83] In the mid 18th century the college's principal copyholder was Mary Eyre, relict of Robert Eyre of Newhouse.[84] Her holding, Lower Pensworth farm, 165 a. in 1797, passed with Newhouse.[85] The farm was compact, adjoining Newhouse, and became the home farm of the estate.[86]

In 1975 it was a dairy farm of 132 a. In 1780 copyhold farms of 59 a. and 45 a. were held by Henry Dawkins of Standlynch. They passed with Standlynch manor to the Nelsons.[87] The larger, with land adjoining Studlands copse, was sub-let with Titchborne farm in Whiteparish, the smaller was Upper Pensworth farm.[88] By 1797 Upper Pensworth farm had been increased to 92 a.[89] and a further copyhold of 49 a. was added c. 1830.[90] In 1948 Upper Pensworth farm was part of Redlynch farm. In 1953 those three former copyholds were all part of Templeman's farm and remained so in 1975.[91]

The land of Redlynch manor, assessed at 2 hides,[92] lay mainly north of Redlynch on inclosed downland.[93] How much of it was demesne and how much customary is not clear. It is possible, however, that the division of the estate in 1567 followed the division between demesne and customary land since the smaller portion was described as six copyholds.[94] If so the demesne passed as Redlynch farm, the copyholds became the farm later called Templeman's. In 1628 Redlynch farm was reckoned to be some 100 a.[95] At least from the mid 17th century 40 a. of copyhold of inheritance land of Downton manor between Slab Lane and Lode Hill were permanently attached to it,[96] and 14 a. at Paccombe were added at inclosure in 1822.[97] In 1837, when it was held with Templeman's, Redlynch was a predominantly arable farm.[98] It continued to be held with Templeman's farm. The six copyholds were said to include some 80 a. in 1628,[99] and as Templeman's farm measured 114 a. in 1837.[1] New farm buildings were erected in 1838,[2] and at least from then Templeman's was the principal farm centre. With Redlynch and Upper Pensworth farms it measured 382 a. in 1948. By 1953 Barford Down farm, 169 a., had also been added. The enlarged Templeman's was then a mixed farm of 612 a.[3] In 1975 it was held by lease under the Longford estate.[4]

In the earlier 13th century both the Woodfalls estates, Upper (Woodfalls farm) and Lower (Lodge farm), were composite holdings. Upper Woodfalls was assessed at 1½ hide and ½ virgate, Lower Woodfalls at 1½ hide and 2 virgates. Both holdings of 1½ hide were apparently free. The ½ virgate, said to have been formerly villein land, and the 2 virgates, the rent of one having been commuted to 8s. for all services and of the other acquitted for service as forester, were clearly former customary lands held freely.[5] The virgates were presumably the lands near the Avon, the hides, probably uncultivated when granted, the lands further east. In 1628 Woodfalls

[66] Hist. MSS. Com. 9, Salisbury, xi, p. 14; for the Raleighs see Hoare, Mod. Wilts. Downton, 37.
[67] Winch. Coll. Mun. 22993–23005; C 78/1410 no. 14.
[68] W.R.O. 490/233; see above.
[69] Winch. Coll. Mun. 23005–13; 5133–44.
[70] e.g. ibid. 5134; W.R.O. 490/807.
[71] W.R.O., Tithe Award.
[72] e.g. ibid.; Winch. Coll. Mun. 21326.
[73] Winch. Coll. Mun. 4976; 5016; 5408.
[74] Ibid. 5362.
[75] Ibid. 5430.
[76] W.A.M. xlii. 307–12.
[77] W.R.O. 490/779; 490/807.
[78] W.A.S. Libr., sale cat. xxiv, no. 18.
[79] Winch. Coll. Mun. 4953.
[80] Ibid. 22993, f. 1 and v.; 5132.
[81] W.R.O., Tithe Award.
[82] e.g. Winch. Coll. Mun. 4953.
[83] Ibid. 4956; 5216.
[84] Ibid. 5154.

[85] Ibid. 5151; 21326.
[86] W.R.O., Tithe Award; ex inf. Mr. Jeffreys.
[87] Winch. Coll. Mun. 5357; see below, p. 70.
[88] B.L. Map Libr., 'Surveys and Maps of Several Estates . . . in the Property of Hen. Dawkins'.
[89] Winch. Coll. Mun. 21326.
[90] Ibid.
[91] W.R.O. 1008/27; ex inf. Mr. D. Newton, Longford Estate Office; see below.
[92] B.L. Eg. MS. 2418, f. 61.
[93] Winch. Coll. Mun. 4957.
[94] Sar. Dioc. R.O., misc. papers, copies of ancient doc
[95] W.R.O. 490/783.
[96] See above; W.R.O., Tithe Award.
[97] W.R.O., Inclosure Award.
[98] Ibid. Tithe Award.
[99] Ibid. 490/783.
[1] Ibid. Tithe Award.
[2] Ibid. 464/78.
[3] Ibid. 1008/27.
[4] Ex inf. Mr. Newton.
[5] B.L. Eg. MS. 2418, f. 61.

farm was said to measure 276 a.[6] At least after it left the Coles family in 1737[7] it was leased and was sometimes held with Lodge and Moot farms.[8] In 1837 it was a mainly arable farm of 290 a., mostly between the farm-house and Lodge farm and reaching from Woodfalls almost to Moot Lane.[9] The land between Slab and Primrose Lanes was afterwards detached to make Days farm, a small dairy farm in 1975, and at Woodfalls lands were detached to make two small pasture farms, one of which continued in 1975. Much of the remaining land was later laid to grass. Lodge farm and later Paccombe and Moot farms were added and in 1975 Woodfalls was an extensive mixed farm.[10] Lodge farm was probably leased in the later Middle Ages. Corpus Christi College at first leased to farmers but from the mid 16th century usually to gentry who sub-let.[11] Leases under heavy fines were for years and after 1739 were granted to the owners of Upper Woodfalls manor.[12] In 1610 Lodge farm consisted of the farmstead, c. 100 a. east of the Downton–Hale road, 40 a. west of it, and rights of common pasturage in the New Forest.[13] In 1837 the farm, some 135 a. reaching along the southern parish boundary nearly to Woodfalls, was held separately.[14] It afterwards became part of Woodfalls farm,[15] and most of its land, except that on the chalk, was converted to pasture.

The freeholding which passed with Hamptworth manor, called Timberleys in 1796,[16] was in 1837 a primarily arable farm of 35½ a. with a farmstead on the south side of Timberley Lane.[17] By 1858 it had become a small dairy farm without arable land.[18] It was a dairy farm of some 40 a. in 1975.

The 550 a. of open pastures west of Loosehanger park were of obvious value to the farmers: for example, feeding on the common and forest was reckoned to add ten per cent to the value of Templeman's farm in 1788.[19] They were inclosed, divided, and allotted in 1822.[20] Since the allottees included a number of smallholders many of the new fields, especially at Paccombe, measured less than 1 a. Between 1822 and 1837 many were ploughed.[21] Several small arable farms were established on the inclosures including Whiteshoot on allotments near Bohemia, Backs (later Locks) between Redlynch and Warminster Green, and Muddyford on Paccombe common.[22] By 1975 much of the former common had been built on, especially at Morgan's hill, Morgan's vale, and Woodfalls. The remainder was again mainly pasture.

In the 13th and 14th centuries tenants had to pay the bishop for pannage, herbage, and pasture in the 900 a. of heath in the Franchise.[23] In the later Middle Ages no one would buy the pasture[24] and the heath was presumably left open and used occasionally without payment or challenge. By the early 16th century, when all the tenants of Downton claimed common feeding in the Franchise, right of common had apparently been established, although the men of Landford continued to pay for it.[25] The Franchise was inclosed in 1822. The cost of the inclosure award was met by the sale of much of the land to be inclosed and rights of turbary, wood, and feeding were extinguished by allotment of the remainder.[26] New farms were established and there was much afforestation. The largest new farm, Lyburn Park, was in the easternmost allotment. In 1837 it included 60 a. of arable, 97 a. of pasture, and 98 a. of woodland.[27] The arable later went out of cultivation and in 1975 the Lyburn House estate, enlarged to some 400 a., specialized in cattle rearing at Lyburn Park farm and some forestry. By 1837 trees had been planted on most of the remaining lands of the Franchise, presumably for commercial exploitation.[28] In 1975 the woods in the eastern part, forming part of Lyburn House estate, and those in the central part, on the Hamptworth Lodge estate, were still exploited commercially. Those mainly in the western part, on the Newhouse estate, were used partly for sport. The remaining heath, especially Golden Cross, was used for cattle rearing.

The men of Downton had pasture rights in the New Forest. They were accustomed to feed their animals in the Godshill bailiwick and in 1291 successfully claimed the right to pay their corn-rent for it at Downton.[29] All the tenants of Downton manor claimed common in the forest in the early 16th century;[30] and in 1670 the warden of Winchester College claimed for his tenants at Downton common pasturage for all cattle at all times 'according to the assize of the forest', hunting and close warren, and the right to keep dogs unexpedited.[31] It seems that feeding rights continued to be enjoyed. In 1788 6d. and 7½ bu. of barley were paid to the warden of the forest for feeding there for Templeman's farm.[32]

MILLS. In 1086 the bishop of Winchester had on his Downton estate, but not necessarily all at Downton, seven mills paying 60s.[33] The corn-mill at Downton was leased, presumably in the late 12th century, but in 1208 was in hand.[34] The site of that mill was almost certainly that between Old Court and the church still occupied by Downton mills. Water was taken from the Avon c. 400 m. north of Downton. The weir built to raise the water-level was later called Wild weir,[35] said in 1647 to be some 200 yd. long.[36] The mill-leet ran east of the river. After passing through the mill the water rejoined the Avon north of Old Court. An additional corn-mill and mill-house and a new weir were built c. 1247.[37] Possibly when that mill was built, but also

[6] W.R.O. 490/783.   [7] See above.
[8] W.R.O. 490/793, Wapshare's val.; 490/807.
[9] Ibid. Tithe Award.   [10] Ex inf. Mr. Mitchell.
[11] C.C.C., Oxf., Mun., lease bks. 1517–51, ff. 37, 105; 1551–68, f. 107v.
[12] Ibid. lease bks.; W.R.O. 212B/2821; see above.
[13] C.C.C., Oxf., Mun., Kb 3, survey.
[14] W.R.O., Tithe Award.   [15] Ex inf. Mr. Mitchell.
[16] W.R.O. 490/802.   [17] Ibid. Tithe Award.
[18] Ibid. 490/1012.   [19] Ibid. 490/1064.
[20] Ibid. Inclosure Award.
[21] Ibid.; Tithe Award.
[22] Ibid. Tithe Award; local information.
[23] Titow, Eng. Rural Soc. 106, 117–18; cf. Andrews and

Dury, Map (W.R.S. viii), pl. 3; W.R.O., Inclosure Award.
[24] H.R.O. Eccl. 2/159500/3.
[25] W.R.O. 490/800.
[26] Ibid. Inclosure Award.
[27] Ibid. Tithe Award.   [28] Ibid.
[29] J.I. 1/1014 rot. 11d.   [30] W.R.O. 490/800.
[31] Winch. Coll. Mun. 6184.   [32] W.R.O. 490/1064.
[33] V.C.H. Wilts. ii, p. 119; for Bodenham, Nunton, Standlynch, and Witherington mills see below.
[34] B.L. Eg. MS. 2418, f. 61v.; Titow, Eng. Rural Soc. 107.
[35] H.R.O. Eccl. 2/155642, pp. 33–7.
[36] W.R.O. 490/784.
[37] H.R.O. Eccl. 2/159457, rott. 8–9.

possibly later and perhaps after Old Court had been deserted, a second channel was made taking water east of Old Court and thus making an island of it.[38] The two mills remained in the bishops' hands until *c.* 1400.[39] In the early 16th century, when they were said to be under one roof,[40] they were leased with the fulling-mill (see below), suit of tenants to and customary works on the mills, and fishing from Wild weir to the mills' trash pool.[41] No tithe had been paid in respect of the mills before 1245 when the bishop granted 20*s.* in place of tithes to the rector, a payment assigned to the chaplain of Burnell's chantry in 1298.[42] When the chantry was dissolved payment was made to the vicar, but lessees were in addition charged with paying a further 20*s.* to the Crown if demanded.[43]

From the 16th century Downton mills, including the mills described below, passed as a single property, the two corn-mills under one roof, a third mill adjoining them, and a mill-house. The rent became fixed by custom; from the later 18th century leases, like those of Old Court, were renewed under substantial fines.[44] Sir Thomas Wilkes was lessee in 1593.[45] The mills passed like his lease of Downton rectory to Sir Carew Raleigh,[46] but by 1622 belonged to Giles Eyre (d. 1655) of Brickworth.[47] In 1647 they were granted with Old Court to William Eyre of Odstock, probably Giles's son,[48] and in 1677 were leased by the bishop of Winchester to William Eyre, then late of Newhouse, William's nephew.[49] In 1707 William was a lunatic and his estate was sold.[50] In 1775 the lease belonged to John Gibbs (d. 1788) and it passed like his estate in Wick until at least 1845, but probably not after 1851.[51] In 1845 and 1880 the property consisted of flour-, grist-, and paper-mills, an edge-tool grinding shed on the east side of the mills, the meadow between the mills and the weir, the fishing rights, allotments at Old Park and Redlynch, 25 a., in place of the rights to wood, and payments from landowners taking water from the leet.[52] In 1881 the mills and Old Court were sold by the Ecclesiastical Commissioners to the Revd. Daniel James Eyre.[53] The corn-mills probably continued to grind until they were bought in the early 20th century by the Southern Tanning Company. In 1929 that company converted them into an electricity generating station, presumably to supply their tannery opposite but also to supply most of Downton.[54] A special company, Downton Electric

Light Company Ltd., was formed to operate the station which was taken over by the Central Electricity Generating Board following nationalization in 1948. The station was closed in 1973.[55] In 1975 the mills were empty. The surviving buildings date from the 18th and 19th centuries.

At least from the early 13th century malt was ground in the bishops' mill,[56] possibly in a separate mill under the same roof since *c.* 1240 the 'malt-mill' was repaired,[57] and malt continued to come from the mill until it was leased.[58] The malt-mill was possibly converted to grind corn and was perhaps one of the two corn-mills under one roof in 1510.[59] Downton mills were said in 1647 to include a malt-mill[60] but, although there were malt-houses at Downton,[61] there is no further evidence of malt grinding.

The fulling-mill at Downton, first mentioned in 1215, was one of the earliest in Wiltshire.[62] Later evidence suggests that it was separate from, but adjacent to, the corn-mills, apparently on their west side.[63] By at least *c.* 1240 it had been farmed.[64] In order to find a tenant in the later 13th century the rent had to be reduced[65] and in the earlier 14th century the mill was apparently unoccupied. In 1349 it was derelict. It was then leased for life on condition that the tenant should rebuild it.[66] It was presumably rebuilt but was later taken in hand again for lack of a tenant, converted to grind corn, and in the early 15th century leased with the other Downton mills.[67] The order by which it was converted was frequently repeated on the bishops' account rolls but the mill had possibly been reconverted to fulling by 1453 when, with the eel fishery, it was leased separately.[68] About 1485 it was leased to Nicholas Potter,[69] and later there was a William Potter (d. 1523), fuller, of Downton.[70] The fulling-mill, again leased with the corn-mills, was frequently mentioned thereafter,[71] but there is no firm evidence that it was used for fulling. In the late 1830s it was empty, one of the range of buildings standing in 1975.[72]

About 1710 there was a paper-mill at Downton,[73] part of Downton mills in 1769[74] and described as 'good' in 1791.[75] It stood at the western end of the mill buildings, was driven by a single wheel, incorporated a drying-shed,[76] and apparently remained in use until the First World War.[77] Like the corn-mills, in 1929 it became part of the generating station.

[38] e.g. Longford Castle Mun., map of Downton mills (1734).
[39] Cf. H.R.O. Eccl. 2/159385, rott. 3–5 (1376–7); Eccl. 2/159417, rott. 3d.–4d. (1414–15).
[40] Ibid. Eccl. 2/155858.
[41] Ibid. Eccl. 2/155642, pp. 159–61.
[42] Winch. Coll. Mun. 5020.
[43] H.R.O. Eccl. 2/155642, pp. 159–61.
[44] Ibid. Eccl. 2/248947.
[45] Ibid. Eccl. 2/159475/1.
[46] Ibid. Eccl. 2/159475/16; see above.
[47] H.R.O. Eccl. 2/159475/21.
[48] C 54/3369. For the Eyres see Hoare, *Mod. Wilts.* Frustfield, pedigrees at pp. 56–7.
[49] H.R.O. Eccl. 2/155644, pp. 111–14.
[50] *Ho. of Lords MSS.* [N.S.], vii, pp. 12–13.
[51] H.R.O. Eccl. 2/155500, pp. 91–7; see below, p. 74.
[52] H.R.O. Eccl. 2/155510, pp. 570–8; W.R.O., Inclosure Award; Ch. Commrs. file 60855.
[53] Ch. Commrs. file 60353.
[54] 'Downton Electricity Special Order, 1929', *Electricity (Supply) Acts, Special Orders* (Min. of Transport).
[55] Wilts. Cuttings, xxvii. 80; ex inf. Mr. D. A. E. Cross, Salisbury Tech. Coll.
[56] Titow, *Eng. Rural Soc.* 107.
[57] E 407/Box 5/6.
[58] e.g. H.R.O. Eccl. 2/159385 (1376–7).
[59] Ibid. Eccl. 2/155858. [60] W.R.O. 490/784.
[61] Ibid. 490/249/2. [62] *V.C.H. Wilts.* iv. 119.
[63] H.R.O. Eccl. 2/155510, pp. 570–8 (1845); W.R.O., Tithe Award. [64] E 407/Box 5/6.
[65] H.R.O. Eccl. 2/159311, rott. 4d.–6 (1288–9).
[66] Levett, *Black Death*, 46.
[67] H.R.O. Eccl. 2/159417, rott. 3d.–4d.
[68] Ibid. Eccl. 2/159444, rott. 2–3.
[69] Ibid. Eccl. 2/159500/3.
[70] *L. & P. Hen. VIII*, iii, p. 1263.
[71] e.g. H.R.O. Eccl. 2/155642, pp. 33–7 (1586).
[72] W.R.O., Tithe Award. [73] Ibid. 490/783.
[74] A. H. Shorter, *Paper Mills and Paper Makers in Eng. 1495–1800* (Paper Publications Soc.), 246; cf. H.R.O. Eccl. 2/155500, pp. 91–7.
[75] *V.C.H. Wilts.* iv. 245.
[76] W.R.O., Tithe Award; H.R.O. Eccl. 2/155510, pp. 570–8.
[77] *Kelly's Dir. Wilts.* (1907, 1923).

FISHING. The right of fishing the Avon through the parish from Bodenham apparently belonged wholly to the lord of Downton manor and was part of his demesne.[78] By c. 1383 part of the fishery, presumably that south of Old Court and later said to be copyhold,[79] had been detached from the demesne.[80] Fishing in the waters from Bodenham bridge to Standlynch bridge and from Standlynch bridge to Wild weir was at farm in 1510.[81] From 1575, when John Stockman, then lord of Barford manor, secured the lease, fishing from Wild weir to Standlynch bridge passed with that manor.[82] By 1586 fishing in the mill river from Wild weir to the mills' trash pool had been leased with the mills, and that in the Avon from Wild weir as far south as, and in the waters around, Old Court had been leased with Old Court.[83] At least from the mid 17th century the fishing from Bodenham to Standlynch was held by the lord of Standlynch manor and passed with that manor.[84] By the early 18th century the copyhold fishery south of Old Court had been annexed to Barford manor.[85]

Coarse fish predominated but trout could be caught in the gravel shallows.[86] Umbers were found c. 1650–1850.[87] In 1916 salmon were said to spawn each year and after fish passes were made in the 1950s salmon were taken in spring and summer.[88] After nearly all the fishing had passed to the Longford estate in the mid 20th century commercial fish farming began with breeding tanks in the shallows at Standlynch and Charlton.

The bishops of Winchester had established an eel fishery at Downton by the early 13th century. It was apparently sold annually in the early 14th century.[89] By 1414 it had been leased with the mills,[90] and from the later 15th century was at farm with the fulling-mill.[91] In 1782 it was said that 5 cwt. of eels, sold at 2d. a pound, were sometimes caught in a night.[92]

In the early 14th century the bishop kept swans on the river.[93] They were reckoned part of the manorial stock and 203 remained on the manor in 1377.[94] None remained in 1453.[95]

MARKETS AND FAIRS. Downton borough was first called the 'new market',[96] and in 1289 the bishop of Winchester claimed a Thursday market, apparently still held in the late 14th century.[97] There were trades in Downton usually associated with markets,[98] but the market was presumably discontinued long before 1703 when Sir Charles Duncombe petitioned for a Thursday market.[99] The petition was apparently successful and c. 1720 a Thursday market was again held.[1] It failed to re-establish itself, however, and by 1792 none was held.[2]

Fairs were held at Downton in 1249.[3] In 1289 the bishop claimed a fair on the eve, day, and morrow of St. Laurence (9–11 August),[4] but such fairs seem to have died out. In 1676 two yearly fairs at Downton, on 12 April and 21 September, were granted to Giles Eyre, the trustee of Sir Joseph Ashe and Henry Eyre.[5] They were held along the western part of the borough street.[6] About 1791 they were held on 23 April and 2 October, the first for cattle and pedlars, the other for sheep and horses.[7] In 1679 the tolls were granted to endow Downton free school. In 1831 they were worth £9 3s. net, an average of £22 17s. gross 1897–1900.[8] Fairs were held in the early 20th century but were discontinued c. 1914.[9]

TRADES AND INDUSTRIES. There was a tanner in Downton in 1606 and tanning continued through the 17th century.[10] In 1717 the tan-yard, formerly Peter Coles's, was acquired by Joseph Davies.[11] It stood on a site opposite Downton mills.[12] In the later 18th century and the early 19th John Gibbs and his son John were tanners there,[13] and in 1830 George Hooper was.[14] Nobes & Hunt Ltd. were tanners in 1903.[15] In 1919 the Southern Tanning Company Ltd. was formed and built a substantial new tannery on the site. That company failed c. 1930 and was replaced by the Downton Tanning Company Ltd.[16] which has since specialized in sole leather for shoes and leather for riding equipment, belts, and cases. The tannery houses some traditional machinery, including a water-wheel to provide motive power for the tanning vats,[17] but since the Second World War additions to the buildings have been made to house several new processes in the production of leather. In 1976 some 50 people were employed at the tannery.[18]

Shoemaking and other leather trades seem to have flourished at Downton alongside the tanning industry. There were shoemakers there at least from

---

[78] H.R.O. Eccl. 2/159457, rott. 8–9.
[79] W.R.O. 490/779.
[80] Winch. Coll. Mun. 4957.
[81] H.R.O. Eccl. 2/155858.
[82] Sar. Dioc. R.O., misc. papers, copies of ct. rec.; W.R.O. 490/802, surveys, 1653, 1737; see pp. 53–4.
[83] H.R.O. Eccl. 2/155642, pp. 33–7, 159–61; Eccl. 2/155643, pp. 95–7.
[84] See p. 70.
[85] W.R.O. 490/802, surveys, 1653, 1737.
[86] V.C.H. Wilts. iv. 367.
[87] Aubrey, Nat. Hist. Wilts. ed. Britton, 62.
[88] W.A.M. xxxix. 261.
[89] Titow, Eng. Rural Soc. 114, 122.
[90] H.R.O. Eccl. 2/159417, rott. 3d.–4d.
[91] Ibid. Eccl. 2/159500/3.
[92] Ibid. Eccl. 2/248947.
[93] Titow, Eng. Rural Soc. 132.
[94] H.R.O. Eccl. 2/159385, rott. 3–5.
[95] Ibid. Eccl. 2/159444, rott. 2–3.
[96] Titow, Eng. Rural Soc. 106.
[97] J.I. 1/1011 rot. 58d.; V.C.H. Wilts. iv. 16.
[98] e.g. Early-Stuart Tradesmen (W.R.S. xv), pp. 11, 14, 15.
[99] Cal. S.P. Dom. 1703–4, 379.

[1] Britannia Depicta (1970 edn.), 136.
[2] Rep. Com. Mkt. Rights [C. 5550], p. 214, H.C. (1888), liii.
[3] Crown Pleas, 1249 (W.R.S. xvi), p. 171.
[4] J.I. 1/1011 rot. 58d.
[5] Cal. S.P. Dom. 1675–6, pp. 389, 527; Hoare, Mod. Wilts. Downton, 22.
[6] W.R.O. 490/780a.
[7] Univ. Brit. Dir. ii (1793 edn.), 845.
[8] Endowed Char. Wilts. (S. Div.), 146–7, 150–1.
[9] Char. Com. file 309440.
[10] Sta. Cha. 8/145/2; Wilts. Inq. p.m. 1625–49 (Index Libr.), 366; J. A. Williams, Catholic Recusancy in Wilts. (Cath. Rec. Soc.), p. 292.
[11] W.R.O. 490/289, indenture, Adams to Davies.
[12] Ibid. 490/780a.
[13] H.R.O. Eccl. 2/155499, pp. 105–7; Eccl. 2/155503, pp. 492–5.
[14] Pigot, Nat. Com. Dir. (1830), 800.
[15] Kelly's Dir. Wilts. (1903).
[16] V.C.H. Wilts. iv. 236.
[17] Ex inf. Mr. D. A. E. Cross, Salisbury Tech. Coll.
[18] Ex inf. Mr. G. A. Lunt, Director, Downton Tanning Co. Ltd.; see plate facing p. 48.

the 16th century,[19] and at various times collarmakers and glovers.[20] About 1791, for example, there were six shoemakers, a glover, and a tawer and breeches-maker.[21] There were still four shoemakers in 1907 but in 1923 there was none.[22]

In the early 13th century at least two weavers settled in the new borough.[23] Weaving of linen and, presumably, of wool was practised in the early 17th century.[24] Linen-weaving continued in the 18th century and a ticking factory, working in 1801, was established.[25] It is not certain how long it survived. There was said to be 'some weaving' in 1907,[26] but commercial weaving has ceased since then. At least from the 15th century there were tailors at Down-ton.[27] In 1830, for example, there were four,[28] but the trade apparently died out in the early 20th century. A branch factory of the Wilton Royal Carpet Factory was established in the workhouse on the south side of Downton borough after 1904. By 1927 it had been closed.[29]

A vintner was operating in Downton in the later 13th century.[30] At least from the 18th century there were several maltsters.[31] The four in business c. 1791 produced some 2,000 qr. of malt a year.[32] About 1810 malting was pre-eminent in Downton and said to be 'carried on to a very considerable extent'.[33] It died out in the later 19th century. There was a firm of bacon curers at Downton in 1923.[34] In 1929 the South Wilts. Bacon Curing Company Ltd. con-verted the workhouse into a bacon-curing factory with a capacity of up to 100 pigs a week. In 1934 I. Beer & Sons Ltd. took over that firm and enlarged the factory to take 500 pigs a week. In 1953 the factory was again enlarged and in 1956 had a staff of c. 100 and a capacity of 1,600 pigs. Bacon, sausages, hams, and cooked meats were produced until the factory was closed in 1968. The company I. Beer & Sons Ltd. belonged to Fitch Lovell Ltd. which transferred bacon retailing to the new pro-visions warehouse in Salisbury Road.[35] In 1975 that warehouse was used by the associated company Lovell & Christmas (Southern) Ltd.

There was a clock-maker at Downton in 1722.[36] At least from 1714 to 1845 edge-tools were ground in the workshop adjoining Downton mills.[37] Shortly before the Second World War the Downton Engineering Works Ltd. opened in Long Close.[38] In the early 1950s that firm established a national reputation for tuning motor-car engines and it

expanded into Salisbury Road. In 1976 the works was closed.

Paper was made at the Downton mill at least from 1710 to 1914, in the later 19th century by Messrs. Wiggins, Teape, Carter, & Barlow and in the early 20th century by Mark Palmer & Son. The mill specialized in hand-made writing-paper and account book paper.[39]

In the 17th and 18th centuries members of the Road or Rhodes family were basket-makers in Downton.[40] Basket and wicker chair making per-sisted until the Second World War.[41]

In 1972 the workhouse factory was taken over by the Chemical Pipe & Vessel Co. Ltd., manufac-turers of thermoplastic pipes and fittings. In 1976 the company employed some twenty people.[42] In 1975 there was a colour film processing laboratory which belonged to United Photo and was in Salis-bury Road.

REDLYNCH. In the late 18th century and the early 19th several trades were prominent at Redlynch. On the common land where clay was available there were two brick-kilns, on the west side of Kiln Road and south of that at Hart hill.[43] In 1757 that in Kiln Road was apparently long established,[44] and it perhaps made the high quality bricks for which 18th-century buildings in Downton are notable. In 1780 a surveyor complained about the great quantity of clay and chalk taken for the brick- and lime-kilns.[45] Both brick-kilns were apparently working in the early 20th century[46] but have since been closed.

Lace-making had possibly become a cottage in-dustry at Redlynch by c. 1700.[47] It was perhaps at its height in the late 18th century since in 1833 it was said to have declined.[48] In 1841, however, when there were some 74 lace-makers, most the wives and daughters of cottagers, the trade was still widely practised.[49] It declined rapidly thereafter and in 1867 was said to have stopped.[50] Attempts were later made to revive the craft and traditional designs were collected.[51] Small quantities of lace continued to be made and sold locally until the mid 20th century.[52]

Redlynch was a local centre for metal-working. In 1837 there were several smithies and a foundry, that of James Shelley in which a bell for Downton church was cast.[53] That trade too declined

[19] Sess. Mins. (W.R.S. iv.), 109.
[20] e.g. Wilts. Apprentices (W.R.S. xvii), pp. 15, 26, 48, 53, 56, 69, 74, 78, 94, 107, 109, 110, 124, 176.
[21] Univ. Brit. Dir. ii (1793 edn.), 847–8.
[22] Kelly's Dir. Wilts. (1907, 1923).
[23] Beresford, New Towns of the Middle Ages, 505.
[24] Early-Stuart Tradesmen (W.R.S. xv), pp. 11, 14.
[25] V.C.H. Wilts. iv. 178.
[26] Kelly's Dir. Wilts. (1907).
[27] Winch. Coll. Mun. 5016 (1411).
[28] Pigot, Nat. Com. Dir. (1830), 800.
[29] V.C.H. Wilts. iv. 182; O.S. Map 6″, Wilts. LXXVII. NW. (1927 edn.).
[30] Crown Pleas, 1249 (W.R.S. xvi), p. 41; J.I. 1/1005 rot. 121.
[31] e.g. Wilts. Apprentices (W.R.S. xvii), p. 56.
[32] Univ. Brit. Dir. ii (1793 edn.), 846.
[33] Potts Gaz. of Eng. and Wales (1810).
[34] Kelly's Dir. Wilts. (1923).
[35] V.C.H. Wilts. iv. 223; ex inf. Mr. L. A. Bailey, The Ridge, Redlynch.
[36] Wilts. Apprentices (W.R.S. xvii), p. 125.

[37] W.R.O. 906/W 55, mortgage, Penny to Davies; H.R.O. Eccl. 2/155510, pp. 570–8.
[38] Kelly's Dir. Wilts. (1939).
[39] W.R.O. 490/783; V.C.H. Wilts. iv. 245.
[40] Williams, Cath. Recusancy (Cath. Rec. Soc.), p. 334; Wilts. Apprentices (W.R.S. xvii), pp. 55, 125.
[41] Kelly's Dir. Wilts. (1939).
[42] Ex inf. Mr. M. Heathcote, Works Manager.
[43] W.R.O., Tithe Award.
[44] Ibid. 906/W 65.
[45] Ibid. 490/793, Wapshare's val.
[46] O.S. Map 6″, Wilts. LXXVII. NW. (1902 edn.).
[47] V.C.H. Wilts. iv. 180.
[48] Hoare, Mod. Wilts. Downton, 36–7.
[49] H.O. 107/1174.
[50] Rep. Com. on Employment in Agric. [4202-i], p. 247, H.C. (1868–9), xiii.
[51] Wilts. Cuttings, vii. 359; Downton Lace Ind. (anon. pamphlet, Salisbury, 1961). A sample of lace is in Salis-bury Museum.
[52] W.R.O. 850/1–6.
[53] Ibid. Tithe Award.

in the later 19th century although the small forge at Redlynch in 1975 was a vestige of it.

Broom-making was a traditional trade at Redlynch carried on by thirteen people in 1841.[54] There were broom-squires in the parish until the Second World War.[55]

MORGAN'S VALE AND WOODFALLS. There were two brickyards in Morgan's Vale in 1837 at the south end of Morgan's Vale Road.[56] They were later closed but a brickworks further up Morgan's Vale Road, on land between that road and the Ridge, was established and continued to make bricks until c. 1953 when the near-by clay ran out.[57] All that remained of that brickworks in 1975 were the chimneys of a kiln and of a 19th-century house. The works belonged to the firm of Charles Mitchell & Sons Ltd., started at Woodfalls c. 1900 by Charles Mitchell and greatly expanded between the World Wars by his son J. G. S. Mitchell. It began as a firm of builders and later of builders merchants, brick-makers, and sawyers.[58] In 1936 the Weymouth Brick & Tile Company opened Downton Brickworks beside Moot Lane at the parish boundary. It had two coal-fired kilns. Charles Mitchell & Sons Ltd. bought the brickworks in 1955 and added two new oil-fired kilns.[59] Sand and clay were taken from pits behind the works in Hampshire and made into small quantities of special purpose red and white bricks. In 1975 some 40,000 bricks were made weekly.[60] Between the World Wars Charles Mitchell & Sons Ltd. built new premises at the top of Lode Hill in Downton parish for their trade as builders merchants and sawyers. In 1975 the firm also made wooden pallets and packaging.[61]

There was iron-founding at Woodfalls in 1855 and by 1875 the firm of Herbert Smith & Sons had established the New Forest Ironworks on the Ridge between Morgan's Vale and Appletree Roads. The works incorporated a foundry and the firm manufactured agricultural implements until the 1920s.[62] By 1939 the foundry had been closed and the business had become general, especially motor, engineering.[63] A garage belonging to August Motors Ltd. was on the site in 1975.

The presence of five shoemakers in Morgan's Vale in 1841 suggests that at that time the trade there was locally prominent. There were also several lace-makers at Morgan's Vale and Woodfalls.[64]

LOCAL GOVERNMENT. The late-7th or late-8th-century grant of Downton to the bishopric of Winchester seems to have carried with it immunity from most royal dues.[65] An increasing number of rights came to be bound up with that immunity, so that on the basis of those early grants the bishops had absorbed complete hundredal powers for the Downton estates by 1086.[66] The liberty to punish minor breaches of the peace was exercised in the early 13th century,[67] and in the later 13th century the bishop's privileges were defined as return of writs, estreats, pleas of vee de naam, infangthief and outfangthief, felons' chattels, gallows, pillory, tumbril, and the enforcement of the assizes of bread and of ale.[68] The bishops' right to exercise for the whole of Downton parish the jurisdiction of the sheriff in his tourn was afterwards unchallenged. The rector of Downton church stood to the bishop as the bishop stood to the king. His liberties, which were distrained by the king in 1281, were view of frankpledge, felons' chattels, and the enforcement of the two assizes. The rector claimed them to safeguard his right to amercements of his men arising from the bishops' exercise of jurisdiction.[69] Later rectors claimed by prescription,[70] and after appropriation Winchester College exercised its right in its own court.

Administration in the Downton part of the private hundred of Downton was itself hundredal in form. By 1208 the parish had been divided into six tithings, Downton, Church, Wick, Charlton, Bodenham, and Witherington.[71] Downton tithing encompassed the settlements at Woodfalls, Redlynch, Warminster Green, Bohemia, and Hamptworth.[72] After the borough was established the tithing was sometimes called Downton foreign,[73] and from the 16th century always East Downton tithing.[74] Church tithing encompassed Downton church, the rectors' lands and tenants at Pensworth, Redlynch manor, Barford, and Standlynch.[75] Wick tithing, which included Walton and New Court farm, was sometimes called Wick and Walton tithing and in the 18th century sometimes Wick and New Court.[76] Bodenham tithing included Nunton. It was as frequently called Nunton as Bodenham and sometimes Nunton and Bodenham tithing.[77] Possibly from 1215–16, when it was given a separate heading in the bishop's accounts,[78] the new borough was a seventh administrative unit and by the later 13th century it apparently included old Downton village.[79]

Most of the royal government within the parish was carried out by three courts, those of the lord for the manor and borough and that of the rector for his men. Leet jurisdiction over the six tithings of the manor was exercised in tourns held near Hocktide and Martinmas by the bishop's steward and, after the lordship of the manor was leased, by the

[54] H.O. 107/1174.   [55] W.A.M. l. 30–1.
[56] W.R.O., Tithe Award.
[57] Local information.
[58] Kelly's Dir. Wilts. (1903 and later edns.); local information.
[59] Ex inf. Mr. Cross.
[60] Local information; see plate facing p. 48.
[61] Ex inf. Mr. A. S. Mitchell, Chas. Mitchell & Sons Ltd., Lode Hill.
[62] Kelly's Dir. Wilts. (1855 and later edns.); local information.
[63] Kelly's Dir. Wilts. (1939).   [64] H.O. 107/1174.
[65] Finberg, Early Wessex Chart. pp. 71–2.
[66] Eric John, Orbis Britanniae, 108–11; Helen M. Cam, Law-Finders and Law-Makers, 28, 62–3.
[67] Titow, Eng. Rural Soc. 108–9.

[68] Rot. Hund. (Rec. Com.), ii (1), 235, 257; J.I. 1/1005 rot. 121; J.I. 1/1011 rot. 58d.
[69] J.I. 1/1005 rot. 122.   [70] J.I. 1/1011 rot. 57.
[71] Titow, Eng. Rural Soc. 108–9.
[72] W.R.O., Tithe Award map. For the bishops' jurisdiction over Hamptworth see H.R.O. Eccl. 2/159311, rott. 4d.–6; Hoare, Mod. Wilts. Downton, 56.
[73] J.I. 1/1011 rot. 58d.
[74] W.R.O. 490/1169.
[75] Ibid. Tithe Award map. For Standlynch see e.g. Public Works in Medieval Law (Selden Soc. xl), pp. 233–4; Taxation Lists (W.R.S. x), 117; W.R.O. 490/1169.
[76] W.R.O. 490/1172–7; 893/5–13; 893/17–23.
[77] Ibid. 490/1169–71; 893/1–4.
[78] H.R.O. Eccl. 2/159273, rot. 4.
[79] J.I. 1/1005 rot. 121; J.I. 1/1011 rot. 59.

lord farmer's steward.[80] In the 17th and 18th centuries the court was called a hundred tourn and in the 18th century the name court leet became usual. At the tourns each tithingman paid the commuted fine called tithing-penny or cert-money, possibly to free his tithing from universal attendance,[81] and presented offences committed in his tithing. The tithingmen's presentments were verified and complemented by those of a jury of twelve freemen who sometimes indicted felons. By the 17th century that procedure had become a system of double presentment, the tithingmen passing information by bill to the jurors who presented all offenders. Affrays and public nuisances had been punished as was normal in such courts since the early 13th century, and the assizes of bread and ale enforced since c. 1240.[82] In the early 16th century taverners and moral offenders and in the 17th century recusants were also dealt with. From the later 17th century, however, the tourn was apparently less important for the punishment of offenders than for the election and swearing of officers. From the early 17th century a constable was elected annually. He acted for the whole parish and from the later 17th century was often called the hundred constable. He was assisted as a peace officer by the tithingmen, who were similarly elected annually and took the same oath as the constable, but who also had to furnish lists of the inhabitants, divided by classes, of their respective tithings. Only after those constables and tithingmen were superseded as peace officers by parish constables appointed under the 1842 Act did the tourns lose all value.

Similar Martinmas and Hock-tide tourns or courts leet were held for the borough on the same days as those for the six tithings.[83] From the later 13th century the borough was divided into two aldermanries, areas corresponding to the new borough and the old village, for each of which an alderman fulfilled the functions of the tithingman of a manor tithing.[84] Procedure in the borough tourn was similar to that in the manor tourn, separate presentment by each alderman backed by a jury of freemen, later becoming double presentment. Business in the late 15th century and the 16th was what might be expected in a small town: brewers, bakers, and butchers were amerced, assaults and immorality punished, and orders to amend public nuisances made. In the 17th century it became restricted to public nuisances, sometimes dealt with by orders called by-laws. In the 18th century the tourn continued to investigate the condition of the roads and bridges in the borough but, as in the manor tourn, the principal business seems to have been the election and swearing of officers. In the later 15th century aldermen for the east and west boroughs were elected and other officers, called the borough reeve and the serjeant in 1495 when they possibly

had functions corresponding to those of the rent collector and the constable of the manor, were mentioned. In the 16th century a constable was regularly chosen. About 1600 the east and west boroughs, which had remained separate administrative districts until then, were merged. The two aldermen were replaced by an alderman and a tithingman. The new alderman's function seems to have been largely ceremonial.[85] In the later 17th century he came to be called the mayor and from 1714 carried the mace given by the borough M.P.s.[86] The constable had probably assumed most of the old aldermen's police duties and the new office of tithingman was probably similar to those of the six tithingmen of the manor. From the late 17th century a searcher, sealer, and registrar of leather was also chosen, an office which was often left unfilled in the 18th century. Those officers, all annually elected and sworn, apparently remained the agents of royal government in the borough until the early 19th century.

Public jurisdiction exercised by Winchester College for the manor of Downton Rectory was limited to the enforcement of the assizes of bread and of ale.[87] Courts were usually held twice a year in the late 14th century and the early 15th, when they were called 'courts of law' or sometimes 'views', usually once thereafter. They were attended by the tithingman of Church tithing but brewers, taverners, tapsters, and occasionally bakers were presented by the ale-taster. In the early 16th century the tithingman seems to have stopped attending and the office of ale-taster disappeared. Amercement of taverners, butchers, and brewers was thereafter occasional.

In the 18th century manorial and parochial government overlapped in some matters, particularly the maintenance of roads and bridges. Parish highway surveyors, presumably responsible for regular maintenance, were apparently appointed, but no account survives. The bad state of roads and bridges, especially Catherine bridge, continued to be presented in both manor and borough tourns and the surveyors were sometimes ordered to amend particular nuisances.[88] Poor-relief, however, was solely parochial. There were overseers in 1614,[89] but it is not clear how the poor-rates raised in the 17th century were used. By 1731 the parish had set up a workhouse under Knatchbull's Act. It stood in the borough and was run directly by the four overseers. Outdoor relief continued on a small scale.[90] The workhouse was said to be well regulated c. 1791,[91] and in 1804 it housed 32 men and 60 women.[92] It was closed when a new union workhouse was opened and in 1837 was empty.[93] In the 20th century the building has had various industrial uses.[94]

Downton parish was divided into six tithings and the borough only for the purposes of public jurisdiction exercised by the lord and lord farmer. In the

[80] Except where stated this para. is based on ct. rec. at W.R.O.: 490/1168–79; 490/1188–1212; 492/9; 893/1–23; H.R.O. Eccl. 1/79/16–25; Eccl. 1/85/1–6.
[81] 'Pro occasione relaxando': Crown Pleas, 1249 (W.R.S. xvi), p. 113. The fines were unchanged from the mid 13th cent.: H.R.O. Eccl. 2/159457, rott. 8–9.
[82] A. N. May, 'Franchise in 13th Cent. Eng.' (Camb. Univ. Ph.D. thesis, 1970), table F.
[83] Except where stated this para. is based on the doc. cited in n. 80.
[84] J.I. 1/1005 rot. 121; J.I. 1/1011 rot. 59.

[85] Hoare, Mod. Wilts. Downton, 66.
[86] W.A.M. xlvi. 108. The mace is preserved in Salisbury Museum.
[87] This para. is based on the ct. rec. at Winch. Coll.: Winch. Coll. Mun. 5104–20.
[88] e.g. W.R.O. 893/15.
[89] Ibid. 490/1198.
[90] Ibid. 1306, overseers' and workhouse accts.
[91] Univ. Brit. Dir. ii (1793 edn.), 847.
[92] W.R.O. 1306, overseers' accts.
[93] Ibid. Tithe Award map.   [94] See above.

Middle Ages, for example, attendance at coroners' inquests was required of each village and royal amercements were of villages rather than tithings.[95] In the 17th century poor-relief was administered for the whole parish and the proportion of the rate to be borne by each constituent part carefully assessed,[96] but later Nunton and Bodenham and Standlynch relieved their own poor.[97] The parish became part of Alderbury poor-law union in 1835.[98]

The private administration of Downton manor was performed through courts which, unlike the tourns, were held by the lord's bailiff. In the year 1324–5 nine were held, in 1376–7 three each for the manor and borough.[99] In the later 15th century courts were held with the tourns and, for the manor only, on about four other occasions each year, but in the 17th century the number of courts held separately declined. The courts dealt with admittances to, and conveyances of, copyholds of inheritance, pleas between tenants, and the enforcement of agrarian custom, and, since so much copyhold of inheritance and commonable land was held of the manor, they remained important. From the later 16th century intricate conveyancing procedures seem to have been carefully observed and the importance of enrolling agrarian agreements to have grown.[1] Until c. 1700 the division between such manorial business, on presentments of the tithingmen and homage, and the Crown pleas, on presentments of the tithingmen and jurors and more properly reserved for the tourns, was not strictly observed. About 1700, however, the lord farmer's jurisdictions were defined and a separate court held for each.[2] The tourn was restricted to Crown pleas. Between c. 1700 and c. 1770 a 'court baron' was held every three weeks to try actions where damage claimed was under 40s. Transfers of copyholds and matters concerning agrarian custom were confined to 'manor courts'. During the 18th century it became normal to hold such 'manor courts' only on the tourn days. In 1843 the business connected with the conveyancing of copyholds of inheritance was 'the only practically useful business connected with any of the courts' held at Downton.[3] Courts to transact it were still held in the early 20th century.[4]

The courts of the rectory manor, in which business normally associated with customary tenure was done, declined in frequency from some four a year in the late 14th century to usually one a year in the early 16th century. Procedure on matters such as dilapidated tenements and deaths of tenants was at first on presentments of the tithingman of Church tithing, in the 15th century sometimes by the bailiff or homage instead, and from the 16th century by the homage. Courts to record copyhold business continued until the 19th century.[5]

PARLIAMENTARY REPRESENTATION.
Downton was represented in parliaments sporadically between 1275, when it was first summoned, and 1437, but regularly by two members from 1441 until it was disfranchised in 1832.[6] The franchise was restricted to freeholders in the borough but probably took in more than the plots in the street demised 1200–30. In the Middle Ages the returning officer was probably a representative of the bishop of Winchester,[7] and most of the elected members may have been inhabitants of the borough.[8]

In the early 16th century the influence of the Crown, in 1529, and of the bishops was paramount,[9] but from the mid 16th century, when the lordship of the manor was leased,[10] new influences were at work on the constituency. The returning officer was apparently the bailiff of the bishop's liberty,[11] and the bailiwick passed through the Stockman family with Barford manor.[12] The lord farmer, however, retained influence in the borough through his courts which governed it.[13] Elections from 1584 to 1640, although usually returning local men, apparently reflect that combination of gentry and noble interest.[14] Those interests clashed in 1641 in a by-election to the Long Parliament disputed between Anthony Ashley Cooper, created earl of Shaftesbury in 1672, and Richard Gorges, son of Edward, Lord Gorges.[15] The local gentry interest prevailed in 1659 and 1660 when the lease of the manor was passing to Sir Joseph Ashe, Bt., but from 1661 to 1690 that same duality of interest continued, perhaps harmoniously, to be reflected in the results of elections.[16] Control over the bailiwick apparently passed with Barford manor c. 1690 to Sir Charles Duncombe who shared the constituency with the Ashes as lords farmer.[17] Stockman's charity for poor craftsmen and labourers and Sir Joseph Ashe's Free school were both perhaps started partly to increase their founders' popularity in the borough,[18] but there was no attempt to influence elections by acquiring property there until the early 18th century when the Duncombes began to buy up the freeholds.[19] When in 1741 Anthony Duncombe (later Lord Feversham) bought the lease of the manor Downton became truly a pocket borough.

Influence over the constituency was again divided after Lord Feversham's death in 1763. The bailiwick of the liberty and the borough freeholds bought by Sir Charles Duncombe passed to the Duncombes and Shaftos of Barford. The lease of the manor and the freeholds bought by Lord Feversham passed to Lord Feversham's executors who by marriage connexions represented the interests of the Pleydell-Bouveries, earls of Radnor.[20] The opposition of the Duncombes and Shaftos to the Pleydell-Bouveries led to a succession of contested elections from 1775

---

[95] J.I. 1/1005 rott. 121–2; H.R.O. Eccl. 2/159311, rott. 4d.–6.
[96] W.R.O. 490/782.
[97] See pp. 66, 68.
[98] *Poor Law Com. 2nd Rep.* 558.
[99] Titow, *Eng. Rural Soc.* 124; H.R.O. Eccl. 2/159385, rot. 5. The remainder of this para. is based on ct. rec. in W.R.O.: see above, n. 80.
[1] W.R.O. 490/1206; e.g. Bodenham inclosure agreement: 893/4, p. 62.
[2] Ibid. 490/1207.
[3] Ibid. 490/1212.   [4] Ibid. 464/15.
[5] Winch. Coll. Mun. ct. rolls and bks.

[6] *V.C.H. Wilts.* v. 72; *W.A.M.* xlvii. 177–264.
[7] *V.C.H. Wilts.* v. 157.
[8] *W.A.M.* xlvii. 177–208.
[9] *V.C.H. Wilts.* v. 117–18.
[10] See above.   [11] *V.C.H. Wilts.* v. 117.
[12] e.g. S.C. 6/Jas. I/372; see below, p. 53.
[13] See above.
[14] *W.A.M.* xlvii. 213–19.
[15] K. H. D. Haley, *First Earl of Shaftesbury*, 36–7, 123.
[16] *W.A.M.* xlvii. 221–7; *V.C.H. Wilts.* v. 163 and n.
[17] *W.A.M.* xlvii. 227–36.
[18] See below.   [19] See p. 34.
[20] See p. 54 for the settlement.

to 1790.[21] The right to act as returning officer was disputed, the Shaftos claiming it for their deputy as bailiff and the executors for their steward, the two offices having been united 1741–63.[22] The question who could rightfully vote also had to be examined, apparently for the first time. There were said to be over 100 voters in the later 17th century but in the later 18th about 20 votes usually split into about 80. The Commons favoured the Radnor interest. The steward became returning officer, the electorate was defined, and Downton again became a pocket borough.[23] In 1826, however, William, earl of Radnor, a Liberal, offered the seats on condition that those elected voted for the constituency's disfranchisement.[24]

CHURCHES. In 1086 there was a church at Downton which, serving several villages and possibly served by more than one priest, had the characteristics of a minster.[25] It was called 'the church of the . . . manor', at Downton a fact not inconsistent with minster status, and on so rich an episcopal manor its foundation may have been early. Between 1066 and 1086 a substantial estate was assigned to it.[26] Although that could mean that the church was only then being founded, it seems more likely that a rector, with an estate set aside by the bishop to support him, was then appointed to replace a college. A parson, however, was first expressly mentioned only in 1147.[27] The living remained a rectory until 1382 when, under royal licence, the church was appropriated by Bishop Wykeham for the endowment of Winchester College.[28] A vicarage was ordained in 1383.[29]

Downton church continued to serve and receive tithes from the whole manor of Downton, even though it remained the only church on the manor for less than a century after the Conquest. The early-medieval development of the Avon valley villages led to the building of three new churches, at Witherington, Standlynch, and Nunton, and the 19th-century population increase, especially in the south-east part of the parish, led to the building of another three churches, at Redlynch, Charlton, and Morgan's Vale. The extensive ecclesiastical parish was undiminished by the establishment of the three medieval churches, but ecclesiastical districts were assigned to the later ones and the chapelry of Nunton and Bodenham was transferred to another parish.

The bishop of Winchester's patronage of the church in 1147 is implied,[30] and the advowson, although first expressly mentioned only in 1281

when it was in the king's hands *sede vacante*,[31] had presumably belonged to the bishop since the first rector was appointed. The king presented again in 1282,[32] but the advowson was among the possessions confirmed to the bishop in 1284 and it passed with the see until the church was appropriated.[33] The king, however, presented in 1327 and 1346, again *sede vacante*.[34]

The estate assigned to the church between 1066 and 1086 was assessed at 4 hides.[35] The church was assessed at 100 marks in 1291,[36] one of the highest valuations in the diocese. The bishop of Winchester valued it even higher at 250 marks *c.* 1296,[37] and when the profits of the church were taken into the king's hands in 1346 they were leased for a year for 230 marks.[38]

All the tithes of the parish except those of the bishops' demesne mills, which were tithe free until 1245,[39] were owed to the rector.[40] By 1305 the glebe consisted of a demesne farm and customarily held land.[41]

In 1281 the king presented William de Hamilton who from 1286 was the king's vice-chancellor,[42] but it is not certain that he was instituted because in 1282 the king presented the Burgundian John de Montibus.[43] In 1290 the pope licensed William Burnell, the nephew of Edward I's chancellor Robert Burnell (d. 1292), to accept Downton church while he retained other benefices. The indult, which contained inexactitudes, was contested, apparently by the bishop of Salisbury, but was confirmed by the pope in 1291.[44] Burnell was provost of Wells, held prebends in Lichfield, Salisbury, and York, and was licensed to live away from Downton in order to study.[45] He was 21 and had not been ordained priest.[46] In 1292 he was elected dean of Wells.[47] By dispensation of his uncle, then bishop of Bath and Wells, he retained the provostry and Downton church. In 1295, however, the election and dispensation were found to be contrary to canon law and he resigned the deanery. Deeming Downton vacant by Burnell's acceptance of the deanery, however, the bishop of Winchester had presented his clerk Robert of Maidstone. The church was disputed between Burnell and Maidstone until in 1303 Burnell was collated.[48] Presumably because of the church's wealth Downton attracted a number of distinguished rectors in the 14th century. Burnell's successor Robert de Harwedon, presented in 1304, was a royal justice and a keeper of the bishopric of Winchester in 1304.[49] Harwedon was succeeded in 1318 by Thomas de Charlton who was consecrated bishop of Hereford in 1327 and made *custos* of

21 T. H. B. Oldfield, *Hist. of the Boroughs*, iii. 130–6.
22 In 1741 it was wrongly thought that the farmer was returning officer by virtue of his lease: W.R.O. 490/791.
23 Oldfield, *Hist. of the Boroughs*, iii. 130–6; *Borough Rec.* (W.R.S. v), 21–3.   24 *D.N.B.*
25 *V.C.H. Wilts.* ii, pp. 33, 119.   26 Ibid. p. 119.
27 Sar. Dioc. Regy., Reg. Mitford, ff. 153–4.
28 Winch. Coll. Mun. 4932–3.
29 Ibid. 4934.
30 Sar. Dioc. Regy., Reg. Mitford, ff. 153–4.
31 *Cal. Pat.* 1272–81, 427.   32 Ibid. 1281–92, 30.
33 *Cal. Chart. R.* 1257–1300, 274; Phillipps, *Wilts. Inst.* i. 5, 16, 53.
34 *Cal. Pat.* 1327–30, 193; 1345–8, 212.
35 *V.C.H. Wilts.* ii, p. 119.
36 *Tax. Eccl.* (Rec. Com.), 180.
37 *Reg. Pontoise* (Cant. & York Soc.), ii. 797. The ch.

was unaccountably valued at only 25 marks in 1330: *Cal. Papal Reg.* ii. 304.
38 *Cal. Close*, 1346–9, 181, 186. For more details see pp. 37–8.
39 See below.
40 Winch. Coll. Mun. 4934.
41 Ibid. 4953. For the details see above, p. 38.
42 *Cal. Pat.* 1272–81, 427; *D.N.B.*
43 *Cal. Pat.* 1281–92, 30; *Reg. Pontoise* (Cant. & York Soc.), i. 185.
44 *Cal. Papal Reg.* i. 517–18; for the Burnells see R. W. Eyton, *Salop.* vi. 134.
45 *Cal. Papal Reg.* i. 517–18, 525.
46 Ibid. 517–18, 530.
47 Le Neve, *Fasti Eccl. Angl.* i. 150.
48 *Cal. Papal Reg.* i. 570, 609.
49 Phillipps, *Wilts. Inst.* i. 5; *W.A.M.* xli. 461.

Ireland in 1338.[50] In 1328 John de Columpna, cardinal of St. Angelo's, was provided to the rectory,[51] but other men seem to have retained it until 1336.[52] The cardinal was incumbent by 1337[53] but in 1346, when the fruits of benefices held by non-resident aliens were confiscated, the king took the profits of the church and presented a new rector.[54] Thomas of Edington (d. before 1383),[55] nephew of his patron, presented in 1361, was the last rector.[56] The church was apparently served by curates in 1147 and 1382. In the intervening period it is likely that most rectors were non-resident although the rectory-house, built in the early 14th century,[57] was possibly for a resident rector.

Bishop Wykeham presented the first vicar in 1383[58] but in 1385, under royal licence, granted the advowson of the vicarage to Winchester College.[59] Except in 1412, when for reasons that are not clear the Crown presented following an exchange of benefices,[60] and in 1799, when the bishop collated by lapse (see below), subsequent presentations have been made by the college, patron in 1975.[61]

The vicarage was endowed with a small proportion of the church's tithes and glebe,[62] and the living was sometimes thought to be a poor one. It was worth some £17 10s. a year soon after it was ordained.[63] That figure perhaps compares not unfavourably with other livings but the vicar had to serve not only the church but also three chapels. The cost of doing so had possibly not represented a great charge to the rector but, without the income from the great tithes, was clearly a great burden on the vicar. In 1413 a vicar complained to Winchester College that his income was not sufficient to maintain him.[64] Nicholas Young, vicar from 1420 to 1428, failed to provide chaplains, presumably because of the cost. That failure led to the sequestration of the great tithes of Witherington by the ordinary. There followed an agreement between the college and the vicar under which the vicar declared himself content with the endowment of 1383 and agreed to serve the chapels, and the college settled a debt of 100 marks for him.[65] The problem, however, remained.[66] In 1535 the net value of the vicarage was assessed at £20 and in 1584 at £26 13s. 4d., figures still comparing well with those of many other parishes.[67] In 1650 the parliamentary commissioners valued the living at £48 10s.[68] In 1649 the vicar had received a parliamentary augmentation of £25 for the six months to Michaelmas,[69] and in 1655 the living was again augmented by £30.[70] Its value was again

increased from 1781 when the college, while trying to maintain the total receipts from the rectory, made a favourable lease of the great tithes of Nunton and Bodenham to the vicar,[71] and the average annual income of £571 in the years 1829–31 indicates that the living was then of above average wealth.[72] The establishment of the ecclesiastical districts of Redlynch and Charlton reduced the vicar's net income by the £75 a year with which he endowed the perpetual curacies.[73] By lessening the need to employ assistant curates, however, it reduced the costs of his ministry and so further enhanced the value of the living.

In 1383 the vicar was allotted the tithes of hay, some already commuted, and the small tithes of the parish except those arising from the manorial mills.[74] Those from Standlynch were commuted in 1549.[75] Except for some tithes of hay which had been commuted to payments of 4d. a yardland at Charlton and 4d. an acre at Nunton and Bodenham those remaining were said in 1677 to be paid in kind.[76] In 1837 they were valued at £550 and commuted to a rent-charge.[77]

In 1383 the vicarage was endowed with a new house and a garden taken from the rector's garden to the north of the church and with 1 virgate in Witherington afterwards lost.[78] A house and garden in Nunton were later added.[79] In 1975 a new Vicarage was built in the garden of the old. The greater part of the old Vicarage is the result of rebuilding c. 1783[80] which incorporated a fragment of an earlier building bearing a reset date-stone of 1640. A wing which may also have been earlier than the 18th century was demolished in the 20th century. The house retained some 18th-century stables and 19th-century outbuildings and servants' quarters.

In 1245 the bishop of Winchester granted tithes arising from the manorial mills of Downton, commuted to the yearly payment of £1, for a daily mass not afterwards mentioned.[81] About 1411 Robert Boset granted an annual rent in Whiteparish for two lights in the church.[82] In 1513 an obit for Roger Maple's soul was endowed for ten years.[83] In 1584 the vicar, Thomas Huddles, was said to be 'no preacher',[84] but his successor William Wilkes, vicar from 1587 to 1637, was made court preacher to Elizabeth I and James I, probably through the influence of his cousin Sir Thomas Wilkes, sub-lessee of the rectory.[85] Samuel Cox, vicar during the Interregnum, subscribed to the *Concurrent Testimony* of 1648 and in 1650 was said to preach every

[50] *Reg. Sandale* (Hants Rec. Soc.), 277–8 and n.; *D.N.B.*
[51] *Cal. Papal Reg.* ii. 273.
[52] Ibid. 304; *Cal. Pat.* 1334–8, 225.
[53] *Cal. Pat.* 1334–8, 488.
[54] *Cal. Fine R.* v. 484, 487; *Cal. Pat.* 1345–8, 212.
[55] Winch. Coll. Mun. 4936.
[56] Phillipps, *Wilts. Inst.* i. 53; *Cal. Papal Pets.* i. 412.
[57] See p. 31.
[58] Phillipps, *Wilts. Inst.* i. 67.
[59] Winch. Coll. Mun. 4937–8.
[60] Phillipps, *Wilts. Inst.* i. 101; *Cal. Pat.* 1408–13, 400.
[61] Phillipps, *Wilts. Inst.* (index in *W.A.M.* xxviii).
[62] See below.
[63] Winch. Coll. Mun. 4957.
[64] Ibid. 4977.   [65] Ibid. 4950–2.
[66] See pp. 67, 77.
[67] *Valor Eccl.* (Rec. Com.), ii. 100; Sar. Dioc. R.O., Detecta Bk.
[68] *W.A.M.* xl. 303–4.

[69] W. A. Shaw, *Hist. Eng. Ch.* ii. 547.
[70] *Cal. S.P. Dom.* 1655–6, 72.
[71] See p. 67. The coll. hoped to shift some of the burden of the augmentation onto its lessee by trying to prevent a proportionate decrease in the fine and rent for the rectory estate. Leases to vicars are not recorded in the coll. lease bks.
[72] *Rep. Com. Eccl. Revenues*, 832–3.
[73] See below and p. 58.
[74] Winch. Coll. Mun. 4934; 4957; see below.
[75] Winch. Coll. Mun. 4949; see below, p. 72.
[76] Sar. Dioc. R.O., Glebe Terrier.
[77] W.R.O., Tithe Award.
[78] Winch. Coll. Mun. 4934; see below, p. 77.
[79] See p. 67.
[80] *Vis. Queries, 1783* (W.R.S. xxvii), p. 92.
[81] Winch. Coll. Mun. 22993, f. 230v.
[82] Ibid. 5016.   [83] Ibid. 5098.
[84] Sar. Dioc. R.O., Detecta Bk.
[85] *W.A.M.* lxi. 49–52.

Sunday.[86] William Gale, vicar 1661–1715,[87] for a time lived away from Downton but in 1662 the churchwardens enthusiastically praised his curate.[88] Another of his curates, George Gifford, was so highly thought of by the parishioners that in 1708 they petitioned Winchester College that he might succeed Gale, and in 1715 the college presented him.[89] The increased wealth of the living from the 18th century seems to have attracted some notable incumbents. Nicholas Webb, vicar from 1721 to 1775,[90] held prebends in Lincoln, St. Paul's, and Salisbury cathedrals.[91] His successor Thomas Lear at first lived away from the parish. In 1783 his curate held morning and afternoon services on Sundays, except that once a month Nunton was served in the afternoon instead. Some ten week-day services were held in the year. There were some 150 communicants. The Sacrament was administered at the four great festivals and, because the communicants were so numerous, additionally on the two following Sundays. Children were usually catechized every Wednesday in Lent.[92] In circumstances that are not clear Lear resigned the living but was collated to it by the bishop in 1799.[93] In 1812 he was resident.[94] His successor Liscombe Clarke, archdeacon of Salisbury from 1827 to 1836,[95] employed two curates at Downton.[96] In 1864, when two curates were still employed, Sunday morning and afternoon services were held, except that in summer prayers were read in the afternoon and an evening service held. Prayers were also said on two week-days, on Holy Days, and daily in Lent. Communion was celebrated at the great festivals and on the first Sunday in each month. Some 120 communicants received the Sacrament in numbers ranging from 8 at Ascension to 57 at Easter.[97]

Under the ordination vicars had to provide for services in Downton church and all its chapels,[98] a charge clearly not scrupulously observed (see above). The reiteration of the charge in 1426 probably made little difference and arrangements for services often failed to satisfy the residents of the chapelries.[99] The vicars' ministry in other parts of the parish, especially the south-east, was hindered by distance, and in 1553 it was reported that many residents of Hamptworth failed to attend church.[1] In 1650 the parliamentary commissioners proposed to reduce the size of the parish,[2] but no action was taken until the 19th-century creation of the new ecclesiastical districts reduced it.[3] Even in 1864, though by then perhaps a little unjustly, the vicar considered 'a large scattered parish at all times a . . . hindrance'.[4]

In 1295 William Burnell founded a chantry in the church with a chaplain to celebrate mass for his soul.[5] Chaplains, who bound themselves to assist the parish clergy at times of need, were appointed by the rectors and, after the church was appropriated, by Winchester College.[6] The chantry was worth £4 6s. 2d. net in 1535, £4 0s. 4d. at the Dissolution.[7] Its portion consisted of tithes and land. In 1295 Burnell assigned to it the commuted tithes of the bishop of Winchester's Downton mills, until then paid to support the daily mass.[8] Later, perhaps after the church was appropriated, a house and 4 a. of land were given.[9] At the Dissolution the chantry-house, 15–20 a. of land, and a house in Salisbury were attached to the chantry.[10] The last chaplain lived in the chantry-house, in 1548 was said to be 'very honest' but too ill to hold a cure, and had no other living but the chantry.[11] A chantry chapel possibly stood a little to the north of the chancel and may have been connected to it by a passage leading from the blocked doorway in the north wall of the chancel. By 1344 it was dedicated to the Virgin.[12]

The church of *ST. LAURENCE*, so dedicated by 1147,[13] has a chancel, central tower with transepts, and aisled nave with south porch. It is built of rubble and brick with ashlar dressings. The three western bays of the arcade, which are of the later 12th century, probably represent the full extent of the nave at that time. They are the earliest surviving features in the building, but its considerable width suggests that, before they were built, the nave may have been unaisled. Early in the 13th century, when Downton borough was founded, the church was greatly enlarged by the addition of two eastern bays to the nave, the central tower and transepts, and the long and probably vaulted chancel. What survives of the work shows it to have been of high quality, as might be expected from the patronage. About a century later the chancel and transepts were heightened and remodelled to take on their modern form. The aisles may also have been rebuilt in the 14th century. In the 15th century a west doorway was inserted in the nave and at least some of the nave windows were renewed, but the extent of other work is obscured by later alterations. Much work on the church seems to have been done in the earlier 17th century when the upper part of the tower was reconstructed, the tracery of many windows was replaced by mullions, and, in 1648, the porch was added or rebuilt.[14] The brick parapet over the south aisle could also be of that date. In 1791 the tower was raised and given a cornice, battlements, and pinnacles.[15] The church was restored in 1859.[16]

[86] *Calamy Revised*, ed. A. G. Matthews, 557; *W.A.M.* xl. 303.
[87] Phillipps, *Wilts. Inst.* ii. 24, 53.
[88] Sar. Dioc. R.O., Chwdns.' Pres.
[89] Winch. Coll. Mun. 5131; Phillipps, *Wilts. Inst.* ii. 53.
[90] Phillipps, *Wilts. Inst.* ii. 56, 88.
[91] Le Neve, *Fasti Eccl. Angl.* ii. 146, 409, 670.
[92] *Vis. Queries, 1783* (W.R.S. xxvii), pp. 90–2.
[93] Phillipps, *Wilts. Inst.* ii. 100.
[94] Sar. Dioc. R.O., Returns to Rural Deans.
[95] Le Neve, *Fasti Eccl. Angl.* ii. 627.
[96] *Rep. Com. Eccl. Revenues*, 832–3.
[97] Sar. Dioc. R.O., Vis. Queries.
[98] Winch. Coll. Mun. 4934.
[99] See pp. 67, 71–2, 77.
[1] Sar. Dioc. R.O., Detecta Bk.
[2] *W.A.M.* xl. 303–4.

[3] See below and p. 58.
[4] Sar. Dioc. R.O., Vis. Queries.
[5] Winch. Coll. Mun. 5020.
[6] An example of the coll.'s letters of inst. and of the chaplain's oath are ibid. 5017.
[7] *Valor Eccl.* (Rec. Com.), ii. 100; E 301/59 no. 11.
[8] Winch. Coll. Mun. 5020.
[9] Ibid. 4955.
[10] E 301/59 no. 11; E 301/58 no. 41.
[11] E 301/58 no. 41.
[12] Winch. Coll. Mun. 5085a.
[13] Sar. Dioc. Regy., Reg. Mitford, ff. 153–4.
[14] J. Buckler, water-colour in W.A.S. Libr., vol. i. 21 (1801); *W.A.M.* xvii. 241.
[15] *W.A.M.* xvii. 238 n.
[16] Sar. Dioc. R.O., Pet. for Faculties, bdle. 7, no. 8; bdle. 8, no. 17.

A kiln at Downton Brickworks

Tanning in 1947

DOWNTON

BISHOPSTONE: WATERCRESS BED

EAST KNOYLE

Knoyle common, inclosed in the early 17th century, from Windmill hill

DOWNTON

View of the borough from the west, 1957. The church and the tannery are in the centre background

Work was most extensive in the chancel where the sedilia were rebuilt and new tracery inserted in the windows. The tower was restored to its former height but left with its decoration. A west gallery erected in 1734 was removed.[17] The nave retains many 17th- and 18th-century features but the west window was retraceried and a vestry was removed from the angle between the north transept and aisle. A medieval cross on a raised base stands to the south-east of the porch. By will proved 1881 John Woodlands gave £1,000 for investment to maintain the church and churchyard. In 1901 the interest, £25, was added to general church funds.[18] In 1975 it was spent on maintenance.[19]

There were four bells in 1553. Two, probably those at the bottom of the scale, were replaced in 1604. A new treble, founded by Samuel Knight of Reading and dated 1692, and a new tenor, by Clement Tosier and dated 1731, were added later. One of them, probably the treble, was a replacement, the other increased the ring to five bells. In 1856 the lower of the two 1604 bells (then iv) was replaced and the ring increased to six by a new treble, both new bells founded by C. & G. Mears of London.[20] The tenor was recast by Mears & Stainbank of Whitechapel and rehung in 1932. The medieval bell (iii) was then thought to be of the mid 14th century.[21] The ring was increased to eight after the Second World War.[22] A clock bell, founded by James Shelley of Redlynch in 1828, was hung on the tower roof.[23]

In 1553 9½ oz. of silver were taken for the king; a chalice of 5½ oz. was left. New plate was given in the 1620s.[24] In 1975 the church possessed a chalice, a paten, and a flagon, hall-marked 1620, 1628, and 1624 respectively, and two salvers hall-marked 1778.[25] The registers date from 1601 and are complete.[26]

The church of *ST. MARY* at Redlynch was built in 1837.[27] A perpetual curacy in the gift of the vicar of Downton was established and in 1841 an ecclesiastical district was assigned to the church.[28] In 1955 No Man's Land and other land were transferred from Redlynch to the parish of Bramshaw (Hants).[29] The incumbent was curate in charge of Morgan's Vale from 1950, and from 1953 to 1968 the two benefices were held in plurality.[30] They were united in 1968.[31] The living became a vicarage in the gift of the vicar of Downton and the Diocesan Board of Finance.[32]

The curate received the income from £400 given by Queen Anne's Bounty.[33] The curacy was also endowed with an annual income of £50 from the impropriators of Downton rectory, Winchester College, and £50 from the vicar.[34] A stipend of £177 was granted by the Ecclesiastical Commissioners in 1880.[35] A house was provided for the curacy by Queen Anne's Bounty, presumably *c.* 1839.[36] In 1881 a new house was built.[37]

On Census Sunday in 1851 morning and afternoon services were attended by congregations of 143 and 165.[38] In 1864 evening services replaced afternoon services in summer; prayers were said in the church on Wednesdays and Fridays and daily in Easter week; and the Sacrament was administered monthly and at Easter, Whitsun, and Christmas to some 25 communicants.[39]

The church is of grey brick. It has chancel and nave with a south porch and is in late-Gothic style. A west gallery was removed in 1919.[40] By will proved 1881 John Woodlands gave the income from £500, £12 10s. in 1901, for repairs to the church. In 1901 it was used for repairs and heating.[41] The church has one bell.[42] The chalice, paten, and flagon given in 1837 belonged to the church in 1975.[43]

The church of *ST. BIRINUS* at Morgan's Vale was built as a chapel of Downton church 1894–6.[44] In 1915 a perpetual curacy in the gift of the bishop of Salisbury, the vicar of Downton, and the owner of Redlynch House was established and an ecclesiastical district assigned to the church.[45] The perpetual curate of Redlynch was curate in charge from 1950 and the two benefices were held in plurality from 1953 to 1968 when they were united.[46] A house in Morgan's Vale Road was attached to the living.

The church, of red brick with stone dressings, has a chancel with north vestry and organ chamber, nave, and western baptistry with south porch and north vestry. It was designed by C. E. Ponting, allegedly in the style of W. D. Caröe.[47] There is one bell.[48]

ROMAN CATHOLICISM. There were several papists in Timberley Lane in the 1660s.[49] They were probably connected with the Webbs of Odstock, a prominent papist family,[50] whose farm was beside Timberley Lane. There were several papists

---

[17] Sar. Dioc. R.O., Faculties, ii, pp. 64–5; Pet. for Faculties, bdle. 7, no. 8.
[18] *Endowed Char. Wilts.* (S. Div.), 152.
[19] Ex inf. the Revd. D. J. Letcher, Downton Vicarage.
[20] Walters, *Wilts. Bells*, 77–9.
[21] Sar. Dioc. R.O., Pet. for Faculties, bdle. 70, no. 44.
[22] Ex inf. the Revd. D. J. Letcher.
[23] Walters, *Wilts. Bells*, 77.
[24] Nightingale, *Wilts. Plate*, 24.
[25] Ex inf. the Revd. D. J. Letcher.
[26] W.R.O. 914/1–29.
[27] C. Hodgson, *Queen Anne's Bounty* (1845 edn.), pp. ccxxiv, ccxxvi.
[28] Sar. Dioc. R.O., Vis. Queries, 1864; *Lond. Gaz.* 14 Sept. 1841, pp. 2299–2301.
[29] *Lond. Gaz.* 4 Feb. 1955, p. 702.
[30] *Crockford* (1951–2); *Lond. Gaz.* 24 Apr. 1953, p. 2268. [31] *Lond. Gaz.* 11 June 1968, p. 6553.
[32] *Crockford* (1973–4).
[33] Hodgson, op. cit. p. cccxxxvi; Sar. Dioc. R.O., Vis. Queries, 1864. [34] H.O. 129/263/2/1/1.

[35] *Lond. Gaz.* 9 July 1880, p. 3884.
[36] Hodgson, op. cit. pp. ccxxiv, ccxxvi, cccxxxvi; Sar. Dioc. R.O., Vis. Queries, 1864.
[37] *Lond. Gaz.* 11 Feb. 1881, p. 611.
[38] H.O. 129/263/2/1/1.
[39] Sar. Dioc. R.O., Vis. Queries.
[40] Ibid. Pet. for Faculties, bdle. 53, no. 42.
[41] *Endowed Char. Wilts.* (S. Div.), 155.
[42] Walters, *Wilts. Bells*, 163.
[43] Nightingale, *Wilts. Plate*, 27; ex inf. the Revd. R. Sharpe, Morgan's Vale Vicarage.
[44] W.R.O. 1306, par. rec.; date on ch.
[45] *Lond. Gaz.* 9 Feb. 1915, pp. 1311–13; *Kelly's Dir. Wilts.* (1939); *Crockford* (1926).
[46] *Crockford* (1951–2); *Lond. Gaz.* 24 Apr. 1953, p. 2268; 11 June 1968, p. 6553.
[47] Pevsner, *Wilts.* (2nd edn.), 381.
[48] Walters, *Wilts. Bells*, 142.
[49] Williams, *Cath. Recusancy* (Cath. Rec. Soc.), pp. 290–1.
[50] *V.C.H. Wilts.* iii. 88.

in Downton in the later 18th century. In 1914 a chapel of ease served from Salisbury was founded in Barford Lane where services were still held in 1975.[51]

PROTESTANT NONCONFORMITY. Several tradesmen were among the small group of Baptists in Downton in 1662,[52] led by Peter Coles, the tanner. A church, dated 1666 by tradition, was founded in Gravel Close and became a centre for local Baptist groups. Unusually for the time it adopted General Baptist principles and by 1701 was in touch with the General Baptist Assembly. In 1703 the church's leader, Benjamin Miller, published the only General Baptist catechism known. The church followed the trend towards Unitarianism, causing a group of Particular Baptists to secede in 1734.[53] The General Baptist church continued, without a regular teacher,[54] and joined the New Connexion in 1804.[55] In 1835 a new church was built in Gravel Close, apparently replacing one built c. 1715.[56] On Census Sunday in 1851 the three services were attended by a total of 222 people.[57] In 1894, however, three years after the New Connexion fused with the Particular Baptists, the congregation was reunited with the 1734 secessionists.[58] The Gravel Close church remained open until c. 1939. In 1975 it was used by a local band.[59]

The Particular Baptists who seceded in 1734 founded a church in South Lane c. 1738.[60] It flourished and had a regular minister. In 1851 three services were held on Sundays with average congregations of over 100.[61] In 1857 a new church with accommodation for some 350 people was built on the same site[62] and the minister's house beside it was extended. A resident minister still served the church in 1975.

In 1845 a group of Strict Baptists founded the Rehoboth chapel in Lode Hill. It had a pastor from its foundation until 1858 but not thereafter.[63] In 1851 there were average congregations of 70 at the morning services.[64] The chapel was closed in the late 1950s,[65] and in 1975 was a private house.

In 1815 a Wesleyan Methodist chapel was built in Lode Hill east of its junction with Slab Lane.[66] The two services on Census Sunday in 1851 attracted congregations totalling 278.[67] Between 1851 and 1864 the New Wesleyan Reformed chapel was opened near the mills at the bottom of High Street.[68] It was

open c. 1900,[69] but in 1975 was part of a private house. In 1896 a new Methodist chapel in High Street was built, apparently replacing the Lode Hill chapel. That chapel, with accommodation for 130, remained open in 1975.[70]

REDLYNCH. A Baptist meeting-house in Redlynch, presumably an offshoot of the Downton Baptist chapels, was licensed in 1796.[71] In 1824 a Particular Baptist chapel was built in Hart Hill Drove.[72] In 1851, when congregations averaging 80 attended afternoon services, it was served by the minister of the Rehoboth chapel, Downton.[73] It remained open in 1864 but had probably been closed by 1882.[74] A very small Baptist chapel was built in the late 19th century in Bowers Hill, to which, in 1899, the reading room was added.[75] It remained in use in 1975.

In 1810 a meeting-house for Methodists was licensed and in 1812 a small chapel was opened for Wesleyans at Warminster Green.[76] Attendances at services possibly declined after Redlynch church was built near by and in 1851 afternoon and evening services were held with average congregations of only 40–45 people.[77] In 1872 a new chapel was built in Chapel Lane, Redlynch.[78] It was still open in 1975.

MORGAN'S VALE AND WOODFALLS. In 1810 a house at Woodfalls was licensed for Methodists' meetings, and in 1833 a Primitive Methodist chapel accommodating some 200 was built at the junction of the Ridge and Vale Road. Congregations at the three services held on Census Sunday in 1851 averaged over 100.[79] The chapel was rebuilt in 1932 and had a resident minister.[80] It remained open in 1975. In 1877 a small Primitive Methodist chapel, the Ebenezer chapel, was built in Morgan's Vale Road,[81] apparently replacing an earlier chapel near the top of Slab Lane.[82] The Ebenezer chapel was closed in the mid 20th century.[83]

NO MAN'S LAND. In 1816 a dissenters' meeting-house was licensed in No Man's Land. In 1846 a mud-walled chapel for Primitive Methodists was built[84] just outside the extra-parochial place, north of Chapel Lane.[85] It was replaced by a brick building c. 1880.[86] A new Primitive Methodist chapel was built near the Lamb in 1901,[87] and remained open in 1975.

[51] V.C.H. Wilts. iii. 96–7.
[52] Sar. Dioc. R.O., Chwdns.' Pres.; Williams, Cath. Recusancy (Cath. Rec. Soc.), pp. 292, 308, 332, 334.
[53] V.C.H. Wilts. iii. 113–14, 126.
[54] Vis. Queries, 1783 (W.R.S. xxvii), p. 91.
[55] V.C.H. Wilts. iii. 136 n.
[56] W.R.O., Certs. Dissenters' Meeting-Houses.
[57] H.O. 129/263/2/1/12.   [58] V.C.H. Wilts. iii. 136.
[59] Local information.
[60] V.C.H. Wilts. iii. 126; R.G. 4/2013.
[61] H.O. 129/263/2/1/11.
[62] Kelly's Dir. Wilts. (1907).
[63] R. W. Oliver, Strict Bapt. Chapels Eng. (Strict Bapt. Hist. Soc.), v. 25.
[64] H.O. 129/263/2/1/10.
[65] R. W. Oliver, op. cit. 25.
[66] H.O. 129/263/2/1/9; W.R.O., Tithe Award map.
[67] H.O. 129/263/2/1/9.
[68] Sar. Dioc. R.O., Vis. Queries, 1864; O.S. Map 6″, Wilts. LXXVII (1881 edn.).
[69] O.S. Map 6″, Wilts. LXXVII. NW. (1902 edn.).
[70] Statistical Returns (Dept. for Chapel Affairs), ii. 75.

[71] Sar. Dioc. R.O., Return of Cert. Places; V.C.H. Wilts. iii. 137 n.
[72] Sar. Dioc. R.O., Return of Cert. Places; W.R.O., Tithe Award map.
[73] H.O. 129/263/2/1/7.
[74] Sar. Dioc. R.O., Vis. Queries, 1864; Return of Chs., Chaps., Bldgs. reg. for Religious Worship, H.C. 401, p. 6 (1882), l.
[75] Local information; see p. 26.
[76] Sar. Dioc. R.O., Return of Cert. Places.
[77] H.O. 129/263/2/1/6.   [78] Date on bldg.
[79] Sar. Dioc. R.O., Return of Cert. Places; H.O. 129/263/2/1/8.
[80] Date on bldg.; Kelly's Dir. Wilts. (1939).
[81] Date on bldg.
[82] O.S. Map 6″, Wilts. LXXVII (1881 edn.).
[83] Local information.
[84] Sar. Dioc. R.O., Return of Cert. Places; Livens, No Man's Land, 31.
[85] Cf. O.S. Maps 6″, Wilts. LXXVII (1881 edn.), LXXVII. SE. (1902 edn.).
[86] Livens, No Man's Land, 31.   [87] Date on bldg.

EDUCATION. From 1381 to 1400 parishioners of Downton were among those whose sons were given preference for entry to Winchester College.[88] There was a schoolmaster at Downton from 1645 to 1648.[89] Until the early 19th century the only school in the parish was in Downton borough,[90] but there was then a remarkable increase in the number of schools. In 1819 there were four, two of them devoted to the teaching of lace-making, and in 1833 there were 36 day- and 3 boarding-schools, most with between ten and twenty pupils.[91] They were presumably in all parts of the parish and gradually declined as the number of specially equipped schools increased.

Downton County Secondary School built off the Salisbury–Fordingbridge road in 1964 was attended by children from all parts of the parish and beyond. In 1975 it had 468 pupils.[92]

In 1679 Sir Joseph Ashe, Bt., endowed a school and school-house, called Borough House in 1975, in South Lane.[93] He endowed it with £100 and the profits of the two fairs for upkeep and a salaried master. It was for twelve boys of the borough, each to be taught no longer than three years. The invested capital was sold in 1806 and rent-charges totalling £3 18s. 7d. were bought. The school suffered from the smallness of its endowment, the fairs producing a net annual income of only some £9. In 1829 the school-house was dilapidated and in 1833 the school was elementary. It was enlarged by twenty boys sent at the vicar's expense, but in 1857 there were no more than twenty pupils in all. By will proved 1871 Mary Clarke, the widow of a former vicar, gave £100 to enlarge the school, but the buildings remained inadequate despite that, and by a Scheme of the Charity Commissioners the school was closed in 1890 and the buildings were sold in 1891.[94] The endowment, but not the bequest, was merged with the charitable funds of the British school by a Scheme of 1914.[95]

In 1841 a British boys' school was built in the borough.[96] In 1857 it had 88 pupils and was 'a model of good management and of efficiency'.[97] It was closed in 1894. Its buildings remained in use while a new school was built and by a Scheme of 1899 became a parish hall, the income from which was used for exhibitions for scholars and student teachers.[98] Downton Educational Foundation was created by the Scheme of 1914 merging the incomes from the British school building and the Free school endowment. The income was used for exhibitions or to supply special educational facilities.[99] At least part of the school building is incorporated in the Memorial Hall.

The Free school and the British school, both for boys, were replaced by the school built in Gravel Close in 1895,[1] which could accommodate 74 infants and 264 older children. A total of 225 children were taught in 1914, 192 in 1927, and 143 in 1938.[2] Until the new secondary school was opened Gravel Close school was a secondary school but afterwards it was for juniors and infants. In 1975 it had 269 pupils.[3]

By will proved 1786 Emma Noyes bequeathed £200 to endow schools in Charlton and East Downton tithings. A small girls' school managed by the vicar was apparently started in Downton.[4] That was probably the origin of the National girls' school built in 1830 in Barford Lane near the Vicarage, attended by 47 girls in 1833.[5] By will proved 1841 Liscombe Clarke, the vicar, gave the interest on £500 to pay a schoolmistress after the death of his wife. The school was superintended by his widow.[6] She enlarged it in 1850[7] and in 1857, when its efficiency was praised, it had 90–100 pupils.[8] The Noyes bequest, some £3 2s. 6d., was lost to Morgan's Vale school, probably in 1879.[9] In 1900 the Clarke bequest yielded £11 5s. which was added to the school's general fund.[10] In 1914 the school, which could accommodate 47 infants and 129 older children, was mixed. The average attendance, 96, remained roughly constant until 1938.[11] Afterwards the school was mainly for juniors and infants. They were transferred to the Gravel Close school when the new secondary school was opened and the Barford Lane school was closed. In 1975 the buildings were being converted into a church hall.[12]

A British girls' school was built in 1847 but by 1857, when it had 56 pupils, it had become an infants' school.[13] It was presumably the school at the west end of the borough which had been closed by the earlier 20th century.[14]

REDLYNCH. A National school was opened at Warminster Green c. 1839.[15] In 1856 62 children, including 12 infants, attended it.[16] In 1864 the children left when they were aged about eleven but there was an evening-school for boys.[17] The school was rebuilt, apparently completely, in 1878,[18] and in 1906, when the average attendance was 97, could accommodate 156 children.[19] Average attendance declined steadily to 30 in 1938.[20] In 1975 the school was an infant and junior school with some 91 children on the roll.[21] The school was aided by the charity of Liscombe Clarke, vicar of Downton, who by will proved 1841 gave the interest on £500 to the master and mistress. In 1901 the income was £11 5s.,[22] in 1975 £14.[23]

[88] Reg. Wykeham (Hants Rec. Soc.), ii. 408 and n.
[89] Wilts. Cuttings, iv. 266.
[90] Vis. Queries, 1783 (W.R.S. xxvii), pp. 91–2.
[91] Educ. of Poor Digest, 1025; Educ. Enquiry Abstract, 1036.
[92] Ex inf. Chief Education Officer, County Hall, Trowbridge.   [93] See p. 25.
[94] Endowed Char. Wilts. (S. Div.), 146–7, 150–1; Acct. of Wilts. Schs. 21.   [95] Char. Com. file 309440.
[96] Endowed Char. Wilts. (S. Div.), 153.
[97] Acct. of Wilts. Schs. 21.
[98] Endowed Char. Wilts. (S. Div.), 153–5.
[99] Char. Com. file 309440.
[1] Endowed Char. Wilts. (S. Div.), 153; date on bldg.
[2] Bd. of Educ., List 21, 1914–38 (H.M.S.O.).
[3] Ex inf. Chief Education Officer.
[4] Endowed Char. Wilts. (S. Div.), 148.

[5] Educ. Enquiry Abstract, 1036.
[6] Endowed Char. Wilts. 152–3.
[7] Ibid.   [8] Acct. of Wilts. Schs. 21.
[9] Endowed Char. Wilts. (S. Div.), 151.
[10] Ibid. 152–3.
[11] Bd. of Educ., List 21, 1914–38 (H.M.S.O.).
[12] Local information.   [13] Acct. of Wilts. Schs. 21.
[14] Local information.
[15] Return of Non-Provided Schs. 27.
[16] Acct. of Wilts. Schs. 21.
[17] Sar. Dioc. R.O., Vis. Queries.   [18] Date on bldg.
[19] Return of Non-Provided Schs. 27.
[20] Bd. of Educ., List 21, 1914–38 (H.M.S.O.).
[21] Ex inf. Chief Education Officer.
[22] Endowed Char. Wilts. (S. Div.), 155.
[23] Ex inf. the Revd. R. Sharpe, Morgan's Vale Vicarage.

MORGAN'S VALE AND WOODFALLS. In 1869 a National school for infants was built near the top of Morgan's Vale Road.[24] About 1905 it could accommodate some 132 children but in 1906 the average attendance was only 46.[25] From c. 1920 the school was for juniors as well as infants.[26] The average attendance in 1938 was 57,[27] and in 1975 the school had 121 infants and juniors on the roll.[28] Presumably from 1869 the school benefited from the Emma Noyes bequest, the income from which, £3 15s. in 1901, was added to its general funds.[29] Nothing was paid to the school from the charity in 1975.[30]

CHARITIES FOR THE POOR. In 1627 William Stockman gave six cottages and 60 a. in Whiteparish in trust to relieve poor craftsmen and labourers in Downton parish with large families. The income was to be distributed in addition to normal poor-relief. About 1780 the trustees decided that only those with more than two children under ten should benefit, at the rate of 2s. or 2s. 6d. for each child. Those already relieved by the parish were excluded. In 1794 some accumulated income and profit from the sale of timber were used to buy £300 stock which yielded £7 10s. a year. In the early 19th

century about £40 was distributed annually. In 1833 the land in Whiteparish was a farm, Chadwell, said to be 40 a., leased for £40 a year. It was sold after 1901 and in 1970 the charity had an income of £176. In the 1960s annual payments averaged c. £150. In 1970 the charity was merged by a Scheme with John Woodlands's charities (see below) and devoted to the general relief of the needy in Downton and Redlynch parishes. In 1973 the income of the two charities was £280 of which £235 was spent on emergency relief.[31]

By will proved 1881 John Woodlands gave to the trustees of Stockman's charity £1,000 to benefit old men and £500 for widows and spinsters. The interest, £25 and £12 10s., was paid yearly in sums of 5s. 6d. to men over 65 and 5s. to women over 60. In 1901 77 men and 87 women benefited. In 1960 £39 was spent. The charities were united with Stockman's by Scheme in 1970.[32]

In 1894 George Wing established the Harriett Woodyear charity in memory of his aunt by giving the income from £294 stock for biannual distribution to six single women of Redlynch ecclesiastical parish, preferably those living at Morgan's Vale.[33] In 1972 the income of £8 was distributed as directed.[34]

BARFORD

STANDING on the valley gravel above the alluvium on the east bank of the Avon Barford was probably a pre-Conquest village like its northern neighbours Standlynch and Witherington, but it was not expressly mentioned before 1194.[35] The village was small and close to Downton and in the early Middle Ages the demesne and customary land of Downton manor probably embraced all its lands.[36] It therefore seems that the village was founded and the lands colonized early from Downton. Barford was one of the smallest of the villages near Downton in the earlier 13th century.[37] Its taxation assessment shows it to have been as wealthy and perhaps as populous as most of those villages in 1334,[38] but in the later 14th century and the 15th it clearly declined. In 1377 it had only 23 poll-tax payers, fewer than all the other villages of the parish except Standlynch and Walton.[39] About 1500 the village consisted of only two farmsteads and from the mid 16th century of only one.[40] That was badly damaged by fire c. 1590.[41] From then until the mid 19th century a manor-house, a farmstead, and probably a few labourers' cottages made a small settlement,[42] but one which was never assessed separately for taxation nor returned separately in censuses. Since the mid 19th century there has been a single farmstead on the site of the old village and another on the downs.

The lands of Barford were a strip running back from the village by the Avon and an almost detached area of down, called Redlynch down in 1539,[43] later Back down.[44] In the mid 16th century more of the downs on the east side of the Avon valley, formerly some of the bishop of Winchester's demesne lands, Bishopsdean and Huntingdean north of Paccombe common and the Park and Bere hill,[45] were united with them.[46] In 1837 all of Barford's lands, c. 825 a., were considered part of Church tithing.[47] All except Back down, which was placed in Redlynch parish, have remained in Downton parish.

Barford stood beside the direct road from Downton to Standlynch, Witherington, and Salisbury marked in 1975 by a farm road and a footpath. A manor-house stood there at least from the 14th century. Probably c. 1700 some 180 a. of land around a new mansion was imparked and traffic diverted to a road skirting it. The park was bounded on the west by a carriage taking water to Barford meadows probably made about the same time.[48] In the 19th century cottages were built on the east side of the park and on the south side where the new road diverged from the old road to Standlynch. In the early 20th century there was a golf course on the downs.[49]

[24] W.R.O. 1306, par. rec.; Kelly's Dir. Wilts. (1907).
[25] Return of Non-Provided Schs. 22.
[26] Bd. of Educ., List 21, 1919 (H.M.S.O.), 361; 1922, 360.   [27] Ibid. 1938, 425.
[28] Ex inf. Chief Education Officer.
[29] Endowed Char. Wilts. (S. Div.), 148, 151.
[30] Ex inf. the Revd. R. Sharpe.
[31] Endowed Char. Wilts. (S. Div.), 145–6, 149–50; Char. Com. file 202233.
[32] Endowed Char. Wilts. (S. Div.), 152; Char. Com. file 204633.
[33] Endowed Char. Wilts. (S. Div.), 155–6.

[34] Char. Com. file 241006.
[35] Rot. Cur. Reg. (Pipe R. Soc. xiv), 70.
[36] See below.   [37] B.L. Eg. MS. 2418, ff. 61–64v.
[38] V.C.H. Wilts. iv. 299.   [39] Ibid. 308.
[40] See below.   [41] W.R.O. 893/4, p. 84.
[42] e.g. Andrews and Dury, Map (W.R.S. viii), pl. 3.
[43] Sar. Dioc. R.O., misc. papers, survey, 1539.
[44] W.R.O. 490/781.
[45] Ibid.; 490/793, Wapshare's val.; cf. 464/22; and see below.
[46] W.R.O. 490/797.   [47] Ibid. Tithe Award.
[48] See below.   [49] W.R.O. 1008/27.

MANOR. In 1066 land assessed at ½ hide at 'Bereford', but not reckoned part of Downton hundred in 1084, was held by Bolle. In 1086 'Engenold' held it of Waleran the huntsman.[50] There is room for doubt where the land lay. Since the 2 hides at Standlynch were part of the hundred and the 3 hides at Witherington had almost certainly been so before 1016, it seems very doubtful that land at Barford by Downton assessed at only ½ hide could have been excluded from the grants to the bishops of Winchester of 100 *mansae*.[51] If Waleran's land was at Barford by Downton and not Barford St. Martin the assessment of lands around Downton totalled 100½ hides in 1086 when a total 100 hides might be expected.[52] The fact that 'Engenulf' held more of Bolle's land of Waleran in near-by Whaddon in Alderbury[53] does suggest that 'Bereford' was Barford by Downton, and in that case the Barford estate of 1086 had possibly been alienated from the bishop early and without a corresponding change in the hidation of his estate. On the other hand, Waleran's lands, including Hamptworth, passed to the Ingham family[54] and, since Sir Oliver Ingham, Lord Ingham (d. 1344), held ¼ knight's fee expressly stated to be in Barford St. Martin and other lands, including Whaddon, formerly Waleran's,[55] Bolle's and Waleran's land in 'Bereford' may be taken to be in Barford St. Martin.

Tenure in fee of 1 hide and ½ virgate in Barford was claimed in 1194 by Ralph of Barford, William son of Arthur, and Robert Pettit, the nephews and heirs of William son of Gerard who, they claimed, died holding the land after 1154.[56] Their claims were successfully resisted by the bishop of Winchester but the land, possibly the bishop's demesne in Barford,[57] seems afterwards to have been granted freely although not subinfeudated.[58] In 1227, following an assize of *mort d'ancestor*, it was conveyed to William son of Gilbert by Auger Luggere and his wife Elisanta.[59] William still held it in 1249[60] and his son William held it c. 1266.[61] In a way that is not clear the land had passed by 1288 to Thomas de Haddon.[62] In 1289 it was conveyed by Thomas and his wife Joan to Roger del Gardin and his wife Joan for an annual rent.[63] Roger and Joan extinguished the rent by purchase in 1295,[64] and Roger died c. 1300 holding the land.[65] In 1309 it was conveyed by Roger's son John and Geoffrey Scurlag and his wife Joan, presumably Roger's relict, to Ralph of Barford.[66] In 1327, probably the year of his death, Ralph settled the estate on himself and on

John of Barford, possibly his son, and his wife Isabel, with remainder to John de Buckland, his son Ralph, and Ralph's heirs.[67] John of Barford apparently held it 1378–9,[68] but afterwards the land seems to have passed to the Bucklands, lords of Redlynch manor, or their heirs. In 1407 Sir John Wroth died holding *BARFORD* manor and the manors of Redlynch and Lower Woodfalls.[69]

Those manors passed like Puckshipton manor in Beechingstoke to John Tiptoft, earl of Worcester (executed 1470), and to his son Edward, earl of Worcester (d.s.p. 1485).[70] Lord Worcester's estates were partitioned among his heirs, his father's sisters Philippe, widow of Thomas de Ros, Lord Ros (executed 1464), Joan (d. 1494), widow of Sir Edmund Ingoldisthorpe, and Edward Sutton (or Dudley, d. 1532, from 1487 Lord Dudley), the son of the third sister Joyce who married Sir Edmund Dudley (d. 1483).[71] Barford was allotted to Joan but in 1489 Lord Dudley, perhaps her trustee, settled it on Geoffrey Downes, an associate of Joan, for life.[72] In 1502, presumably after Geoffrey's death, Joan's lands were partitioned among her granddaughters and heirs. Barford was allotted to Margaret, wife of Sir John Mortimer,[73] but by 1522 it had passed by purchase to Philippe Lady Ros's son-in-law and heir Sir Thomas Lovel (d.s.p. 1524)[74] who had recovered Redlynch manor from Lord Dudley in 1490.[75] Barford manor then passed as part of Redlynch manor to Sir Thomas Lovel (d. 1567) who in 1566–7 sold both manors to John Stockman.[76] Stockman sold Redlynch[77] but retained and resided at Barford.[78]

From the later 15th century all the bishop of Winchester's customary land in Barford, Barford farm, was leased,[79] and from 1564 to Stockman.[80] In 1566 Stockman also acquired copyhold of inheritance land of Downton manor adjoining his Barford lands to the south and east.[81] The leasehold and copyhold estates, both by then very favourable tenures,[82] passed to his son William with his freehold estate as one manor. John died in 1605 but his lands had been held since c. 1594 by William, who in 1598 and 1599 received royal grants of them,[83] and who bought one of the Hamptworth manors.[84] William was succeeded in 1635 by his son William who died in 1650 leaving as heir his brother Joseph (d. after 1670).[85] Joseph had sons William, John, and Joseph and left a widow Constance but between 1673 and 1677 his lands at Barford were sold to Sir Francis Chaplin (d. 1680), an alderman of London.[86]

[50] *V.C.H. Wilts.* ii, p. 151.   [51] See pp. 27–8.
[52] *V.C.H. Wilts.* ii, cf. pp. 119, 150, 151, 161, 163, 208.
[53] Ibid. p. 151.
[54] Hoare, *Mod. Wilts.* Heytesbury, 229–30.
[55] *Cal. Inq. p.m.* viii, p. 376.
[56] *Rot. Cur. Reg.* (Pipe R. Soc. xiv), 70.
[57] See below.   [58] B.L. Eg. MS. 2418, f. 61v.
[59] C.P. 25(1)/250/5 no. 10.
[60] *Civil Pleas, 1249* (W.R.S. xxvi), pp. 87, 122.
[61] *Reg. Pontoise* (Cant. & York Soc.), ii. 389.
[62] H.R.O. Eccl. 2/159311, rott. 4d.–6.
[63] *Feet of F.* 1272–1327 (W.R.S. i), p. 35.
[64] Ibid. p. 40.   [65] *Cal. Inq. p.m.* iii, p. 437.
[66] *Feet of F.* 1272–1327 (W.R.S. i), p. 73.
[67] Ibid. 1327–77 (W.R.S. xxix), pp. 15–16; E 179/196/7.
[68] E 179/239/193.   [69] C 137/58 no. 23.
[70] *V.C.H. Wilts.* x. 15.
[71] Hoare, *Mod. Wilts.* Downton, 44; *Complete Peerage*, s.v. Ros, Dudley; *Cal. Inq. p.m. Hen. VII*, i, p. 466.
[72] *Cal. Inq. p.m. Hen. VII*, i, pp. 466–7; W. G. Searle,

Hist. of Queens' Coll. (Camb. Antiq. Soc. 8vo. ser. ix), 119–20.
[73] C.C.C., Oxf., Mun., deeds LA 29, pp. 376 sqq.
[74] *L. & P. Hen. VIII*, iv (1), p. 155; Prob. 11/23 (P.C.C. 27 Jankyn, will of Sir Thomas Lovel); *Complete Peerage*, xi. 106–7.
[75] See p. 32.   [76] Ibid.; W.R.O. 490/1198.
[77] Hoare, *Mod. Wilts.* Downton, 52.
[78] *Taxation Lists* (W.R.S. x), 117.
[79] See below.   [80] W.R.O. 490/781.
[81] Sar. Dioc. R.O., misc. papers, copies of ct. rec.
[82] See p. 28.
[83] Hoare, *Mod. Wilts.* Downton, 30; W.R.O. 490/784; *Cal. S.P. Dom.* 1598–1601, pp. 79, 218.   [84] See p. 60.
[85] *Wilts. Inq. p.m.* 1625–49 (Index Libr.), 217; Hoare, *Mod. Wilts.* Downton, 39; H.R.O. Eccl. 2/155644, p. 82; W.R.O. 490/1174, rent roll.
[86] Hoare, *Mod. Wilts.* Downton, 39; W.R.O. 130/16, lease, Errington to Chaplin; 490/1174, rent roll; 490/892; 490/802; H.R.O. Eccl. 2/155644, pp. 82–4.

Sir Francis had sons John, to whom the freehold and leasehold passed, and Robert, to whom the copyhold passed.[87] The whole estate was sold c. 1690 to the wealthy banker and politician Sir Charles Duncombe (d. 1711) who devised it to his nephew Anthony Duncombe, later Lord Feversham.[88]

At Lord Feversham's death in 1763 the freehold and copyhold estates passed to Sir Charles Duncombe's grand-nephew Thomas Duncombe (d. 1779) whose heir was his daughter Anne, wife of Robert Shafto (d. 1797).[89] Anne and Robert's eldest son John died unmarried in 1802 and those estates passed to their son Robert Eden Duncombe Shafto (d. 1848).[90] Under the Feversham settlement the copyholds were offered for sale in 1806 and were bought by Shafto.[91] In 1763 the leasehold estate passed, like his lease of Downton manor, to Lord Feversham's executors, though sub-let to Thomas Duncombe and the Shaftos.[92] At the sale of 1806 the lease was bought by Shafto and that too passed with the freehold estate.[93] In the 19th century leases were renewed under heavy fines.[94] At inclosure in 1822 substantial allotments of land in the Franchise were made in respect of the Barford estate which, except for the allotments,[95] was sold c. 1835 to Thomas, Earl Nelson.[96] In 1865 Horatio, Earl Nelson, bought the reversion in fee of the leasehold portion.[97] The Barford estate passed with the Trafalgar estate and in 1953 became part of the Longford estate.[98]

A 'court', presumably a manor-house, stood at Barford c. 1300.[99] A manor-house, possibly the same building, stood on the freehold estate in 1539.[1] John Stockman, said to be of Wade (Hants) in 1564-5, of Barford in 1568-9,[2] was building a new house to replace it in 1569.[3] His son William possibly built Newhouse and Hamptworth Lodge as its hunting lodges.[4] Barford House was rebuilt c. 1700 by Sir Charles Duncombe. The new house was symmetrical, of red brick with stone dressings. The west front was of nine bays, the central five slightly recessed, and of two storeys with attics and a basement.[5] Lord Feversham was said to have lived there with 'considerable splendour'. The house was taken down in 1815.[6] In 1975 the site of its basement was marked by a tree-filled depression flanked by a terrace. South of the site there remains a large farmyard with brick buildings of the 17th and 18th centuries, including an aisled barn of six bays. Barford farm-house is in the south-west corner of the yard. It was enlarged in the 19th century, possibly when Barford House was taken down. Between the house and the river are walled gardens probably of 18th-century origin. An avenue, the only survivor of a larger formal layout, runs in the opposite direction.

ECONOMIC HISTORY. In the early 13th century all the land at Barford was held of the bishop of Winchester but no episcopal demesne lay there. The free tenement was reckoned 1 hide and ½ virgate and there were twelve customary holdings, some 5 virgates, whose tenants owed labour service and rents totalling some 46s. Unlike the other lands held freely of Downton manor the free tenement at Barford was not held for military service.[7] That and its rough equality in area with the customary lands[8] suggest that it may earlier have been the bishops' demesne in Barford. If so it may have been demised freely after 1209 when the bishop had a shepherd there.[9] In the Middle Ages the almost detached down was several for the freeholder but the remaining down, the arable, east of the old road to Standlynch, and the meadow land were commonable and in most places the free and customary lands were intermingled.[10]

In the later 15th century, when there was little demand for the land,[11] the customary holdings were amalgamated to form a single farm, the tenure was converted to leasehold, the annual rent doubled, and the farm, Barford, leased for £4 13s. 4d. a year.[12] It passed to a succession of farmers including Roger Maple (1510), Maurice Maple (1533), and Richard Abarrow (1555).[13] The rent was never changed and until much later leases were renewed apparently without fine.[14] About 1567 that farm and the freehold farm were united.[15] In 1569 the leasehold measured some 315 a., more in the northern half than in the southern half of the township, and the freehold some 343 a., mostly in the southern half. The copyhold of inheritance land added to the farm measured some 171 a. in 1569.[16] It had formerly been episcopal demesne pasture and had been converted to copyhold tenure, probably in the 15th century.[17] Bishopsdean and Huntingdean were arable, 50 a., and the Park and Bere hill remained pasture, 121 a. The merging of all those lands in a single farm eliminated cultivation in common. In 1569, when Barford was a compact farm of some 829 a., most of the fields had been inclosed and Horden field, 118 a. of arable on the east side of the old road to Standlynch, was about to be inclosed.[18]

While in the hands of the Stockmans in the 16th and 17th centuries Barford farm was probably not leased. The extensive system of watered meadows

[87] H.R.O. Eccl. 2/155644, pp. 82-4; W.R.O. 893/13, pp. 394-5.
[88] W.R.O. 893/13, pp. 394-5; for the Duncombes see Hoare, Mod. Wilts. Downton, 39, 45; D.N.B.; Complete Peerage, s.v. Feversham.
[89] Hoare, Mod. Wilts. Downton, 39, 45; W.R.O. 490/793, Wapshare's val.
[90] Burke, Peerage (1959), 853; W.R.O. 490/792.
[91] W.R.O. 490/779; 610/27; 464/1.
[92] H.R.O. Eccl. 2/153321/10-15; W.R.O. 490/793, Wapshare's val.
[93] H.R.O. Eccl. 2/153325.
[94] Ibid. Eccl. 2/248947.
[95] See p. 34.
[96] W.R.O. 464/48, admittance of Nelson.
[97] H.R.O. Eccl. 2/155515, pp. 119-23.
[98] W.R.O. 1008/27; ex inf. Mr. D. Newton, Longford Estate Office.

[99] Cal. Inq. p.m. iii, p. 437.
[1] Sar. Dioc. R.O., misc. papers, survey.
[2] Winch. Coll. Mun. 22996.
[3] W.R.O. 490/781.
[4] See pp. 30-1, 60.
[5] J. Sigrist, water-colour in Salisbury Museum; see plate facing p. 33.
[6] Hoare, Mod. Wilts. Downton, 39.
[7] B.L. Eg. MS. 2418, ff. 61v.-62.
[8] e.g. W.R.O. 490/781 (1569).
[9] Titow, Eng. Rural Soc. 106.
[10] Sar. Dioc. R.O., misc. papers, survey, 1539.
[11] H.R.O. Eccl. 2/159500/3.
[12] Ibid. Eccl. 2/155858.
[13] Ibid.; Eccl. 2/155877; Eccl. 2/155893.
[14] e.g. ibid. Eccl. 2/155644, pp. 82-4.
[15] See above.
[16] W.R.O. 490/781.
[17] See p. 37.
[18] W.R.O. 490/781.

was possibly laid down *c.* 1698 when Standlynch mill was moved and the meadows of Witherington and New Court were being drowned.[19] In the early 18th century the making of Barford park caused the conversion of some arable to pasture.[20] By 1806, however, Bere hill and other downland had been ploughed.[21] At least in the later 18th century the farm was leased; one farmer was Moses Boorn who invented a drill for corn patented in 1789.[22] The land in Downton Franchise allotted at inclosure in 1822 in respect of feeding for 300 sheep was not added to the farm.[23]

In 1830 Barford farm measured 775 a. The remaining land of Barford, between Barford farm and the demesne land of Downton rectory and Paccombe common, was part of Parsonage farm.[24] Barford Down farm was established in the mid 19th century as an arable and pasture farm with some 170 a. of down taken from Barford farm.[25] The land formerly part of Parsonage farm was restored to Barford (afterwards Barford Park) farm.[26] In 1953 Barford Park was a mixed farm of 685 a.; Barford Down farm was part of Templeman's farm.[27] In 1975 Barford Park and Barford Down farms were worked under licence from the Longford estate as mixed farms but with much arable land.[28]

CHARLTON

THE regular and often straight boundaries of Charlton tithing enclosed some 1,700 a.[29] In its eastern part, where some 2–3 km. of the Avon was in the tithing, there is little alluvial land west of the river and some 100 a. of alluvium between the Avon and the meadows of Witherington were in Charlton.[30] In 1851 an ecclesiastical parish was formed from Charlton and Witherington tithings.[31] Those tithings were united with Standlynch in the civil parish of Standlynch with Charlton All Saints in 1897. That new parish was absorbed by Downton parish in 1934,[32] but Charlton All Saints remained an ecclesiastical parish in 1975.

Charlton is a street village, a form of settlement not typical in the valleys of south Wiltshire, in a tithing containing no substantial area of manorial demesne.[33] It is possible that the village was a planned settlement, built for tenants of Downton manor to whom the land of the tithing was assigned for cultivation in exchange for labour on the demesne between Charlton and Wick. It was a large village with an apparently even distribution of wealth among the husbandmen. In the Middle Ages the tenants were as numerous there as in the other villages dependent on Downton and the holdings, each a complete virgate, larger.[34] The tithing was, therefore, with Church the most highly rated of the parish for cert-money and in the early 14th century the village was apparently the wealthiest and most populous.[35] Although its 1334 assessment at 200s., the twelfth highest in the county, was inexplicably high,[36] Charlton was consistently highly assessed for taxation. The village contained no particularly wealthy farmer and total assessments were high because it was more populous and because many personal assessments were above average.[37] There were 114 poll-tax payers in 1377.[38] In the 16th century it was apparently less wealthy than Downton,[39] but the impression of Charlton in the 16th, 17th, and 18th centuries remains one of a village focused on a group of substantial farmers of roughly equal resources.[40] In 1628 its rateable value was about an eighth of the parish.[41]

Charlton street was almost certainly once part of a direct road from Bodenham to Walton and Downton. In the 1770s the south end was almost solidly built up.[42] Settlement at the north end was less dense, but a line of farmsteads took the street settlement as far as the farmstead later called Charlton Dairy Farm. It closely followed the curve of the river which, wider, shallower, and with several islands in it, was there called Charlton broads. In the early 19th century, however, the number of farms in the tithing and of farmsteads in the street both declined. Charlton Manor and Matrimony Farm were built away from the village and the farmsteads in the north of the street, and the path of the street itself, disappeared and left Charlton Dairy Farm isolated.[43] In the south of the street, however, one or two farmsteads and several farm-houses survived.[44]

Already by the 1770s there had been settlement by the Salisbury–Fordingbridge road,[45] and the Stag public house had been opened by 1848.[46] That settlement did not grow and since the mid 19th century new building in the village has mostly been south of the church in the shortened street, where a public house called the Vine was open in the late 19th century.[47] In the 20th century, however, some council houses and a block of estate cottages dated 1949 have been built beside the road from the Stag to the church. In 1841 Charlton housed 300 people.[48] The population was probably *c.* 300 in 1901–31[49] and has remained roughly constant since then.

[19] See pp. 71, 75, 77.
[20] Cf. Sar. Dioc. R.O., misc. papers, survey, 1569; W.R.O. 464/22.   [21] W.R.O. 490/779.
[22] Ibid. 490/807; *V.C.H. Wilts.* iv. 85.
[23] W.R.O., Inclosure Award; Sar. Dioc. R.O., misc. papers, copies of ct. rec.   [24] W.R.O. 490/797.
[25] Cf. Ibid. Tithe Award; O.S. Map 6″, Wilts. LXXII (1885 edn.).
[26] W.R.O. 464/2.   [27] Ibid. 1008/27.
[28] Ex inf. Mr. Newton.   [29] W.R.O., Tithe Award.
[30] B.L. Map Libr., 'Surveys and Maps of Several Estates . . . the Property of Hen. Dawkins' (1779).
[31] *Lond. Gaz.* 1 Aug. 1851, pp. 1971–2.
[32] *V.C.H. Wilts.* iv. 347 n., 357 n.
[33] See below.   [34] B.L. Eg. MS. 2418, ff. 61–64v.
[35] H.R.O. Eccl. 2/159457, rott. 8–9.
[36] *V.C.H. Wilts.* iv. 299, 303.

[37] e.g. ibid. 299; E 179/196/7–8.
[38] *V.C.H. Wilts.* iv. 308.
[39] e.g. E 179/197/50; *Taxation Lists* (W.R.S. x), 116–17.
[40] e.g. *Taxation Lists* (W.R.S. x), 117; W.R.O. 490/783, survey, 1628; 490/802, rentals.
[41] W.R.O. 490/782.
[42] *Andrews and Dury, Map* (W.R.S. viii), pl. 3; B.L. Map Libr., 'Surveys of Estates of Hen. Dawkins'.
[43] Cf. B.L. Map Libr., 'Surveys of Estates of Hen. Dawkins'; W.R.O., Inclosure Award map; Tithe Award map; O.S. Map 6″, Wilts. LXXI (1886 edn.).
[44] W.R.O., Tithe Award.
[45] *Andrews and Dury, Map* (W.R.S. viii), pl. 3; B.L. Map Libr., 'Surveys of Estates of Hen. Dawkins'.
[46] *Kelly's Dir. Wilts.* (1848).
[47] O.S. Map 6″, Wilts. LXXI (1886 edn.).
[48] *V.C.H. Wilts.* iv. 347.   [49] Ibid. 357.

Matrimony Farm was built in the north of the tithing between 1807 and 1837 with an octagonal red-brick farm-house east of the road from Bodenham overlooking the Avon and with farm buildings mostly west of the road.[50] The house was enlarged to the south soon after it was built, but a new house was built west of the road c. 1900. After inclosure in 1807 Charlton Manor, a large brick farm-house five bays by three bays, was built below the scarp west of the Salisbury–Fordingbridge road.[51] The houses formerly near the site of Charlton Dairy Farm had all been demolished by 1975.

An 18th-century farm-house enlarged at various dates and recently modernized stood at the south end of Charlton street in 1975, and east of it were a pair of 19th-century cottages and an 18th-century brick farm-house formerly thatched and recently extensively renovated. The street contained several timber-framed and thatched cottages, mostly cased in brick, and a symmetrical brick house dated 1692, but most of the buildings were houses of the 19th and 20th centuries. The Stag has apparently been rebuilt in the 20th century but the other buildings beside the main road showed their 18th-century origins.

ESTATES. Free tenure of an estate at Charlton was probably acquired by Waleran the huntsman between 1066 and 1086.[52] The estate descended with his land at Hamptworth to John of St. Quentin,[53] but afterwards passed to Joan Neville's son William de St. Martin who was overlord in 1275.[54] William (d. 1290–1) was succeeded by his son Reynold but by c. 1286 his land at Charlton had been re-united with Hamptworth in the Ingham family and again passed with Hamptworth.[55] In 1376, however, a panel of jurors declared that they did not know whether the overlord was Sir Miles de Stapleton, Lord Ingham, lord of Hamptworth manor, or the bishop of Winchester, lord of Downton manor,[56] and lords of Hamptworth were not subsequently named as overlords of land in Charlton.

William de St. Martin's land was held by the heirs of William of Grimstead,[57] presumably his son John (d. c. 1314) who apparently held it in 1310.[58] It passed to John's son John (d. between 1344 and 1348)[59] and grandson Sir John whose heir was his daughter Joan (d. before 1375), wife of Thomas Rivers. Joan and Thomas had no issue and after Thomas's death in 1375 it was first said that the land should revert to John FitzEllis of Whiteparish, but afterwards that it should revert to Thomas of Grimstead in fee tail.[60] Thomas possibly died without issue and the estate escheated to the bishop of Winchester.[61] The see's tenure of it was confirmed by a conveyance of 1393.[62] To distinguish it from the bondland and bourdland held like the other customary lands of Downton manor by Borough English the tenure of the holdings of Rivers's land, to which normal rules of inheritance applied, was called knighthamhold.[63]

From 1375 all the land of Charlton was held immediately of the bishops by customary, knighthamhold, or free tenure. The rents for, and fines for admission to, customary and knighthamhold lands, all conveyed through Downton manor court, were fixed by custom in the Middle Ages and in the 17th century such copyholds of inheritance were as important as freeholds. By that time, however, bondland, bourdland, knighthamhold land, and freehold land had become intermingled in the principal estates in Charlton.[64]

A substantial farm, which in the 16th century had passed in the Eastman family,[65] was held in 1623 by Henry White (d. 1626).[66] It passed to his younger son Henry,[67] and at least from 1662 to 1680 was held by Henry's son Thomas.[68] It was bought in 1690 by Francis Coles (d. c. 1691), brother of William Coles (d. 1697) who held Upper Woodfalls manor,[69] passed to his younger son Jonathan (d. 1742),[70] and descended like Moot farm in Downton[71] until in 1798 Jacob, earl of Radnor, bought the reversion from the Revd. Charles Shuckburgh and in 1800 bought the land from the life tenant, John Greene.[72]

The family of Newman was prominent in Charlton in the 15th and 16th centuries,[73] and in 1628 several Newmans held substantial farms.[74] John Newman's had passed by 1641 to Rowland Newman who in 1677 conveyed it to his son John.[75] It was probably held by a John Newman until at least 1736.[76] In 1742 Joan, widow of George Newman, conveyed the farm to her daughter Cecilia and her husband George Button of Throope in Bishopstone. It descended to Button's sister and heir Mary, wife of Henry Rooke (d. c. 1794) of Breamore (Hants), who conveyed it to Henry in 1763.[77] It passed to Henry's son Peter (d. c. 1805), of Witherington, whose son Henry sold that and the Rookes' other land in Charlton to Jacob, earl of Radnor, in 1811.[78]

The estate held by Lewis Newman in 1628[79] passed to his son Robert after 1657.[80] Robert held in 1665, but in 1677 the land apparently belonged to John Fox (d. 1691) of Avebury whose heir was his brother Sir Stephen Fox (d. 1716).[81] By 1709 the land had passed, presumably by sale, to Maurice Buckland,[82] and it descended with Standlynch manor until Dame Frances and Sir George Vandeput

---

[50] Cf. W.R.O., Inclosure Award map; Tithe Award map.
[51] Ibid. Inclosure Award; O.S. Map 1", sheet 15 (1811 edn.).
[52] V.C.H. Wilts. ii, pp. 79, 119.
[53] Reg. Pontoise (Cant. & York Soc.), ii. 390; see below, pp. 59–60.
[54] Rot. Hund. (Rec. Com.), ii (1), 257.
[55] Reg. Pontoise (Cant. & York Soc.), ii. 595.
[56] Cal. Inq. p.m. xiv, p. 113.
[57] Rot. Hund. (Rec. Com.), ii (1), 257.
[58] Cal. Inq. p.m. v, p. 124.
[59] Ibid. viii, p. 376.   [60] Ibid. xiv, pp. 112–13.
[61] H.R.O. Eccl. 2/159417, rott. 3d.–4d.
[62] Cal. Close, 1392–6, 112.   [63] W.R.O. 490/1187.
[64] For the areas of the estates in 1779 see below.
[65] W.R.O., Inclosure Award.

[66] Wilts. Pedigrees (Harl. Soc. cv, cvi), 214; Wilts. Inq. p.m. 1625–49 (Index Libr.), 438–40.
[67] W.R.O. 490/783; E 179/259/22.
[68] W.R.O. 490/1174; 490/1181, mortgage by White.
[69] C 78/1778 no. 13.   [70] W.R.O. 490/762; 490/1217.
[71] See p. 30.   [72] W.R.O. 490/165.
[73] e.g. Cal. Close, 1422–9, 131; Taxation Lists (W.R.S. x), 44, 117.
[74] W.R.O. 490/783.
[75] E 179/259/22; W.R.O. 490/1217.
[76] W.R.O. 490/802; 490/1174; Q. Sess. 1736 (W.R.S. xi), 136.
[77] W.R.O. 490/166.   [78] Ibid.; 490/170; 490/172–3.
[79] Ibid. 490/783.   [80] Ibid. 490/181, surrender.
[81] Ibid. 490/802; Hoare, Mod. Wilts. Alderbury, 37.
[82] W.R.O. 490/802.

sold it to Thomas Lydiatt (d. 1761), rector of Kimbolton (Hunts.).[83] Lydiatt was succeeded by his son the Revd. Thomas Troughton Lydiatt who sold the land to Peter Rooke in 1789.[84]

In the 16th and 17th centuries the Noyes family was prominent in Charlton.[85] In 1628 Richard Noyes held a small estate which was probably that held by John Noyes in 1641 and by a younger Richard Noyes in 1653.[86] Between 1665 and 1677 it passed to the younger Richard's widow Eleanor,[87] and afterwards to Jasper Bampton who held it in 1698.[88] Bampton already held an estate in Charlton which John Bampton had held in 1662. Both estates passed with the Bamptons' land in Nunton[89] until 1720 when Anthony Duncombe was admitted to them.[90] The Charlton land afterwards passed with the lease of the lordship of Downton manor to the earls of Radnor.[91]

In 1628 a substantial farm was held by a widow Noyes and in 1662 a widow Noyes still held it.[92] Henry Noyes held it in 1678[93] and it passed to another Henry Noyes, possibly his son, who added to it a farm which had belonged to Henry Barnes in 1628 and to Charles Barnes in 1662.[94] The lands apparently passed to successive Henry Noyeses until the later 18th century.[95] In 1775 Henry Dawkins was admitted to them and they thereafter passed with Standlynch manor.[96]

Land in Charlton had long been part of Standlynch manor.[97] William le Dun (d. c. 1311) held some in the right of his wife Christine la Bays.[98] John Dun (d. 1374) later held it.[99] In 1428 it was said to be held by William le Dun's heirs and was presumably among the lands of John Hugyn, then lord of Standlynch, who was also said to hold land formerly John Grimstead's, presumably knighthamhold lands.[1] In 1628 Walter Buckland held Witherington mead, 29 a., and 6 a. of other meadow.[2] The Bucklands increased their holding in the 17th century principally, it seems, by buying the meadow land of several holdings east of the river.[3] In the later 17th century Maurice Buckland acquired Fox's farm (see above). That was sold apart from Standlynch manor in 1754 but, after he acquired Standlynch in 1766, Henry Dawkins bought several estates in Charlton besides Noyes's and they all passed with Standlynch manor.[4]

A small portion of the Newmans' lands, most of which passed to George Button in 1742 (see above), passed under a settlement of 1726 to a John Newman who held it in 1750.[5] Another John Newman held it until his death in 1822 and bought various other lands. He devised his lands to his brother George whose heirs, his grand-nephews Gay Thomas

Attwater and George Henry Attwater, sold the estate to Jacob, Viscount Folkestone, in 1859.[6] It afterwards passed with the Longford estate.

Thomas Ringwood (fl. 1427) conveyed some freely held land to Richard Ludlow. Richard sold it to William Ludlow (d. 1478), of Hill Deverill, and it passed to William's son John (d. 1487) who was succeeded by his son John, grandson William Ludlow, and great-grandson George Ludlow.[7] In 1599 George's son Sir Edmund disposed of it by lease, but it afterwards passed to William Fursbye who held it in 1645.[8] He sold it to John Sadler who held it in 1676,[9] but the holding was afterwards broken up.

In the mid 19th century Charlton lands were divided between the Longford and Trafalgar estates, some 1,150 a. and 513 a. respectively.[10] The Longford estate bought out the Trafalgar estate in the mid 20th century.

ECONOMIC HISTORY. In the Middle Ages the arable land of Charlton, extending westwards from the village across the valley gravel to the Salisbury–Fordingbridge road and west of that road on the Upper Chalk, was probably all cultivated in common. There was a common pasture for sheep beyond the arable land west of a line running south from Clearbury ring.[11] The tithing contained some 150 a. of alluvial land but that east of the river, about two-thirds, was possibly not well enough drained to be cultivated intensively. The narrow strip of meadow west of the river was roughly bounded as far south as Charlton street by the Bodenham–Charlton road. On the valley gravel around the village and between the street and the meadows there were probably small inclosed pastures. In the earlier 13th century the bishop of Winchester had 28 tenants, 27 of whom each held 1 virgate.[12] A typical virgate included 1½ a. of meadow, presumably several, and an inclosed pasture,[13] but the tenants also had a small meadow in common.[14] There was no great area of episcopal demesne, but the existence of at least 50 a. of bourdland in the later Middle Ages suggests that holdings had at some time been drawn into demesne.[15] In 1314 John of Grimstead's land was held freely by twelve tenants for rents totalling £5 a year.[16] There is no reason to doubt that in the Middle Ages the land was cultivated in many farms of roughly equal size. In the 15th century, however, larger holdings emerged,[17] and in the 16th century there were apparently several large farms.[18]

By 1628 the arable land on the valley gravel east of

[83] Ibid. 490/171; for the Lydiatts see J. and J. A. Venn, *Alumni Cantab.* i (3), 120; ii (4), 243.
[84] W.R.O. 490/168.   [85] e.g. E 179/270/18.
[86] W.R.O. 490/783; 490/802; E 179/259/22.
[87] W.R.O. 490/802.
[88] Ibid. Inclosure Award; 490/1174.
[89] Ibid. 490/1174; see below, p. 64.
[90] W.R.O., Inclosure Award.   [91] Ibid. 490/779.
[92] Ibid. 490/802; 490/1174.
[93] Ibid. 490/181, mortgage.
[94] Ibid. 490/802, rental, 1709; 490/783; 490/1174.
[95] Ibid. 490/802.
[96] Ibid. Inclosure Award; see below, p. 70.
[97] See pp. 68–70.   [98] *Cal. Inq. p.m.* v, p. 186.
[99] H.R.O. Eccl. 2/159385, rot. 3.
[1] *Feud. Aids*, v. 232.
[2] W.R.O. 490/783; *Wilts. Inq. p.m.* 1625–49 (Index Libr.), 352.

[3] W.R.O. 490/802, rental, 1709; 490/1217.
[4] Ibid. 490/802, rental, 1796; Inclosure Award.
[5] Hoare, *Mod. Wilts.* Downton, 60; W.R.O. 490/802.
[6] W.R.O. 490/175.
[7] C 1/57/99–100; *Cal. Inq. p.m. Hen. VII*, i, p. 369; Burke, *Land. Gent.* (1906), i. 213.
[8] W.A.S. Libr., Story-Maskelyne MSS. file K.
[9] W.R.O. 490/759.
[10] Ibid. Tithe Award.
[11] Cf. B.L. Map Libr., 'Surveys of Estates of Hen. Dawkins' (1779).
[12] B.L. Eg. MS. 2418, f. 63 and v.
[13] e.g. H.R.O. Eccl. 2/159500/3.
[14] B.L. Eg. MS. 2418, f. 63v.
[15] e.g. H.R.O. Eccl. 2/159500/3.
[16] *Wilts. Inq. p.m.* 1242–1326 (Index Libr.), 396.
[17] H.R.O. Eccl. 2/159500/3.
[18] e.g. E 179/197/50.

the Salisbury–Fordingbridge road, some 235 a., had been inclosed. It seems that the small common meadow had also been inclosed. The arable land on the chalk, 593 a., was still cultivated in three common fields. There were 3 farms of more than 100 a., 4 of 50–100 a., 6 of 25–50 a., and 6 smaller farms. The downs could support a total of 1,800 sheep.[19] Rents for bondland and bourdland totalled some £13 a year, for knighthamhold lands £7 14s.[20] Most of the farms presumably had land east of the river but in the 17th century an increasing amount of it was attached to Standlynch farm.[21] In 1665 the main carriage from Alderbury to Standlynch to water Witherington meadows also watered and drained the meadows of Charlton east of the river, of which a large portion belonged to the lord of Standlynch manor. The southernmost of Charlton's meadows west of the Avon could be watered from the main carriage to New Court meadows.[22] In the early 18th century there was apparently a plan to inclose the common down but it was not carried out.[23] Common husbandry on the chalk continued in the 17th and 18th centuries. The farms, characteristically of 15–100 a. with feeding rights for sheep, belonged to, and were usually occupied by, apparently prosperous yeomen.[24] No very large farm seems to have emerged before the later 18th century.

In 1779 the down, 569 a., could support 1,851 sheep. Between the down and the Salisbury–Fordingbridge road the three arable fields, 528 a. in all, were still cultivated in strips averaging c. 1 a. Some 262 a. of inclosed arable land lay on the valley gravel east of the road and there were some 83 a. of meadow and pasture west of the river and 99 a. of meadow east of it. There were some eleven farms. Henry Dawkins's land, 253 a., was worked as two farms and some 60 a. of meadow land was part of Standlynch farm, Peter Rooke held 213 a., the Revd. Thomas Troughton Lydiatt 159 a., William Coles 113 a., and Lord Feversham's executors 84 a. All had feeding rights on the down equivalent to 92, 430, 95, 70, and 55 a. respectively. There were 4 farms over 100 a., 3 of 50–100 a., and 4 below 50 a. They included land in the three common fields in roughly equal proportions.[25]

The common fields and down of Charlton were inclosed in 1807 under an Act of 1801.[26] The lands were redistributed among the farms by allotments and exchanges and at the same time, as more lands were acquired by the Longford and Standlynch (Trafalgar) estates, the number of farms decreased. In 1837 the earl of Radnor owned some 966 a., the north part of the tithing, worked as two long and narrow farms running back from the river, Charlton (later Charlton Manor) farm, 675 a. including Charlton Lower (later Charlton Dairy) farm, and Matrimony farm, 270 a. in Charlton and 61 a., later more, in Bodenham.[27] Both had newly built farmsteads. In 1837 Earl Nelson's land was worked as a long and narrow farm, 312 a., in the south part of the tithing, and some 100 a. of meadow land was part of Standlynch farm. George Newman's farm, 191 a., lay in the middle part of the tithing between the lands of the Longford and Trafalgar estates.[28] It was added to Charlton Manor farm after 1859. In the 1930s most of the land east of the Salisbury–Fordingbridge road and some near Charlton Manor west of it was pasture and meadow. Most of the chalk was ploughed; only Clearbury ring and a strip of land near the western boundary remained rough pasture.[29] Those land-uses had changed little by 1975 when all the land was held in hand by the Longford estate.[30]

CHURCH. A church was built at Charlton in 1851,[31] partly at the expense of Horatio, Earl Nelson.[32] A perpetual curacy in the gift of the vicar of Downton was established and the tithings of Charlton and Witherington were assigned to the church as an ecclesiastical district.[33] In 1969 Witherington was transferred to Alderbury parish.[34]

The curacy was endowed with an annual income of £25 from Winchester College, impropriators of Downton church, £25 from the vicar of Downton, and £33 from Queen Anne's Bounty.[35] In 1862 a house was built on the east side of Charlton street.[36] The curate's stipend was raised by donations of £100 in 1868 and of £500 in 1878,[37] and in 1880 the Ecclesiastical Commissioners gave an annual stipend of £86.[38]

Lord Nelson's private chaplain was the first perpetual curate.[39] In 1864 morning and evening Sunday services were held. Morning services were held on Wednesdays and Fridays and Holy Days although the average attendance was only six; evening services were held during Lent and Advent. There were some 55 communicants of whom an average of 18–25 received the Sacrament once a month and at the main festivals.[40]

The church of *ALL SAINTS*, of red and purple brick, has a chancel and a nave with north transept and south porch. It was built in Early English style from designs of T. H. Wyatt.[41] The transept was added in 1891.[42] Two bells of 1850 were hung in the church. The smaller was replaced in 1898.[43] The vicar of Downton gave a chalice, paten, and dish bearing hall-marks of 1848, and a flagon was given when the church was dedicated.[44]

[19] W.R.O. 490/759; 490/783.
[20] Ibid. 490/802, rental, 1653; 490/1174, rent rolls.
[21] Ibid. 490/802, rental, 1709.
[22] Ibid. 490/897.   [23] Ibid. 490/1068.
[24] Cf. ibid. 490/783 (1628); 17th- and 18th-cent. rentals in 490/802; 490/1174; E 179/259/22 (1641–2).
[25] B.L. Map Libr., 'Surveys of Estates of Hen. Dawkins'.
[26] W.R.O., Inclosure Award.
[27] Ibid. Tithe Award; see below, p. 66.
[28] W.R.O., Tithe Award.
[29] [1st] Land Util. Surv. Map, sheets 122, 131.
[30] Ex inf. Mr. D. Newton, Longford Estate Office.
[31] H.O. 129/263/2/2/3.
[32] C. Hodgson, *Queen Anne's Bounty* (Suppl. 1864), pp. xxvi, lxxiv.

[33] *Lond. Gaz.* 1 Aug. 1851, pp. 1971–2; *Clergy List* (1859).
[34] *Lond. Gaz.* 14 Feb. 1969, p. 1707.
[35] Sar. Dioc. R.O., Vis. Queries, 1864.
[36] Hodgson, op. cit. pp. liii, lxxiv; O.S. Map 6″, Wilts. LXXI (1886 edn.).
[37] *Lond. Gaz.* 5 June 1868, p. 3173; 10 May 1878, p. 2998.
[38] Ibid. 9 July 1880, p. 3889.
[39] H.O. 129/263/2/2/3; and see below, p. 72.
[40] Sar. Dioc. R.O., Vis. Queries.
[41] Pevsner, *Wilts.* (2nd edn.), 161.
[42] *Kelly's Dir. Wilts.* (1903).
[43] Walters, *Wilts. Bells*, 50.
[44] Nightingale, *Wilts. Plate*, 23–4.

NONCONFORMITY. A Baptist meeting-place in Charlton was licensed in 1796 and several more nonconformist meeting-places in the period 1815–30.[45] In the earlier 19th century there was a small congregation of Primitive Methodists.[46] A small Wesleyan Methodist chapel on a site opposite the church given by Jacob, Viscount Folkestone, was built in 1864.[47] It was closed c. 1970.[48]

EDUCATION. By will proved 1786 Emma Noyes gave the interest on £100 to pay for the teaching of six or eight children at Charlton. A small school was established for girls, of whom no more than one from a family was allowed to attend.[49] In 1858 40–50 children were taught in temporary buildings while, at the expense of Horatio, Earl Nelson, a new National school was being built behind the street on the east side opposite the church.[50] The Noyes endowment, then £3 10s. a year, was transferred to the new school.[51] In 1864 it was said that children attended until they were thirteen or fourteen and that a winter night-school flourished.[52] The school could accommodate 99. In 1906 the average attendance was 56.[53] It fell to 43 in 1919, 17 in 1938,[54] and in 1968 the school was closed.[55] In 1975, when nothing was known of the endowment, the school was a private house.

HAMPTWORTH

THE village of Hamptworth, some 7 km. away, is isolated from Downton by the woods at Loosehanger and by Langley wood. Its lands were bounded to the west by those woods and to the north by the Blackwater. At inclosure in 1822 the bounds of Hamptworth common in the south part of the township were defined by straight lines and that with Downton marked by a new road.[56] The township, some 1,780 a. in 1837,[57] was part of East Downton tithing,[58] and reckoned a tithing itself only in 19th-century censuses.[59]

Hamptworth was first mentioned in the early 13th century.[60] Edward I passed through it in 1306.[61] In 1334 its assessment for taxation at 40s. shows it to have been as wealthy as most of the Avon valley villages in the parish and in 1377 the number of poll-tax payers, 36, was average for the parish.[62] At least from the 17th century Hamptworth village consisted of farmsteads strung out along the road from Langley wood to Landford, and that remained the pattern until the later 19th century.[63] In 1841 there were 202 people living in the township.[64]

The focus of settlement began to change in the later 19th century. There were already a few houses at Hamptworth Green in 1773.[65] At inclosure a new road, Lyburn Road, was made across Hamptworth common and extended to No Man's Land.[66] By 1876 settlement at Hamptworth Green at the top of it had increased and a few cottages had been built beside it near No Man's Land. Several small farmsteads had also been built on the allotment of common bisected by York Drove and by the verge of the road from No Man's Land to Plaitford.[67] At the same time the old village along Hamptworth Road had begun to decline as farms were amalgamated[68] and new housing was built elsewhere. In the 20th century settlement has grown in York Drove and particularly in School Road.

In 1975 the pattern of the old Hamptworth village could still be seen. Along the road were several 17th-century houses, including Cuckoo and Smallbrook Farms, some formerly associated with small farms. They were mostly timber-framed with thatched roofs. In some much walling had been replaced by brick. The Cuckoo inn is a building of c. 1800. At the west end of Hamptworth Road there were several early-19th-century lodges and a pair of estate cottages dated 1934. Manor Farm is probably of medieval origin but the remaining buildings at Hamptworth Green were 19th- or 20th-century and not of high quality. Most of those living on the land of the old township occupied the modern houses in piecemeal developments near No Man's Land.

MANORS. Between 1066 and 1086 free tenure of an estate in Hamptworth and Charlton, held of the bishop of Winchester, was acquired by Waleran the huntsman.[69] Waleran was succeeded by his son William, grandson Waleran (fl. 1130–1), great-grandson Walter Waleran, and great-great-grandson Walter Waleran (d. 1200–1) who left daughters Cecily, Isabel, and Aubrey as coheirs.[70] The estate at Hamptworth and Charlton was held in the earlier 13th century by William Neville, Isabel's husband.[71] The Nevilles left a daughter Joan,[72] but by 1247 it apparently belonged to Aubrey, formerly wife of Robert de Pole and John of Ingham, and then wife of William de Botreaux.[73] In the 1260s John of

[45] Sar. Dioc. R.O., Return of Cert. Places.
[46] Church Bells, 29 Apr. 1898.
[47] Sar. Dioc. R.O., Vis. Queries, 1864; date on bldg.
[48] Local information.
[49] Endowed Char. Wilts. (S. Div.), 148.
[50] Acct. of Wilts. Schs. 21.
[51] Ibid.; Endowed Char. Wilts. (S. Div.), 148.
[52] Sar. Dioc. R.O., Vis. Queries.
[53] Return of Non-Provided Schs. 28.
[54] Bd. of Educ., List 21, 1919, 1938 (H.M.S.O.).
[55] Ex inf. Chief Education Officer, County Hall, Trowbridge.   [56] W.R.O., Inclosure Award.
[57] Ibid. Tithe Award.
[58] e.g. Hoare, Mod. Wilts. Downton, 56.
[59] H.O. 107/1174.
[60] P.N. Wilts. (E.P.N.S.), 395.

[61] Cal. Pat. 1301–7, 418.
[62] V.C.H. Wilts. iv. 299, 308.
[63] B.L. Map Libr., copy of 'Plott of the Man. of Hamptworth . . . belonging to John Webb Esq. taken in . . . 1638'; O.S. Maps 1″, sheet 15 (1811 edn.); 6″, Wilts. LXXVII (1881 edn.).   [64] V.C.H. Wilts. iv. 347.
[65] Andrews and Dury, Map (W.R.S. viii), pl. 3.
[66] W.R.O., Inclosure Award.
[67] O.S. Map 6″, Wilts. LXXVII (1881 edn.).
[68] See below.
[69] V.C.H. Wilts. ii, p. 119; and cf. B.L. Eg. MS. 2418, f. 61.   [70] Hoare, Mod. Wilts. Cawden, 73.
[71] B.L. Eg. MS. 2418, f. 61.
[72] V.C.H. Hants, iv. 521.
[73] H.R.O. Eccl. 2/159457, rot. 8d.; Cal. Inq. p.m. i, p. 232.

St. Quentin held it of the heir of his wife, perhaps Aubrey,[74] but at her death c. 1270 Aubrey de Botreaux again held Hamptworth.[75]

The manor of *HAMPTWORTH* passed to Aubrey's son Oliver Ingham (d. c. 1282),[76] grandson Sir John Ingham (d. c. 1310)[77] who in 1294 devised it for life to Ralph de Brightwell, precentor of Salisbury cathedral,[78] and great-grandson Sir Oliver Ingham, Lord Ingham (d. 1344).[79] It was held by Lord Ingham's widow Elizabeth until her death in 1350[80] when it reverted to his daughter Joan (*suo jure* Baroness Ingham), widow of Sir Roger Lestrange, Lord Strange (d. 1349), and afterwards wife of Sir Miles de Stapleton (d. 1364).[81] She died in 1365. The manor passed with the Ingham title through the Stapleton family until the death of Sir Miles de Stapleton in 1466 when a partition of Sir Miles's land between his heirs Elizabeth, wife of Sir William Calthorpe, and Joan, wife of Christopher Harcourt (later knighted), was ordered.[82] There is no evidence that any of the manor passed to the Calthorpes. Joan and Sir Christopher were succeeded by their son Sir Simon (d. 1547), grandson Sir John Harcourt (d. 1565), and great-grandson Sir Simon Harcourt.[83] In 1579 the manor was sold with land in West Dean to Henry Giffard (d. 1592).[84] It passed to his sons William (d. c. 1597)[85] and Sir Richard who sold it to William Stockman of Barford in 1603–4.[86] It thereafter passed with the freehold part of Barford manor to Robert Eden Duncombe Shafto (d. 1848) and to his son Robert Duncombe Shafto (d. 1889) who sold it c. 1870 to George Morrison (d. 1884).[87] After the death of George's widow Barbara in 1907 it passed to his nephew H. C. Moffatt (d. 1945), of Goodrich (Herefs.), who settled it on his nephew H. C. Cumberbatch. After Cumberbatch's death in 1957 it passed as the Hamptworth Lodge estate to Moffatt's grandson Mr. N. J. M. Anderson, the owner in 1975.[88]

About 1601 and 1609 some 22 a. of Hamptworth common near Langley wood were inclosed by William Stockman.[89] That was possibly the site of Hamptworth Lodge which, with Newhouse in Whiteparish,[90] may therefore have been built for Stockman as one of a pair of hunting lodges. A picture of the house reveals its 17th-century origin and its considerable size.[91] It was substantially altered in the late 19th century by George Morrison who renewed most of the windows and gables.[92] Apart from a few rooms in the north servants' wing the

house was completely demolished c. 1910. In 1912 a large house in the vernacular style to designs of Sir Guy Dawber was built for H. C. Moffatt on its site and incorporated the surviving rooms of the old house.[93] The new house is timber-framed with brick nogging; it contains a large hall, and much of the interior is panelled with woods from the estate. It housed Moffatt's collection of early furniture as well as many reproduction pieces and other works in wood by his own hand.[94] The house stands in woodland with formal gardens on the south and west fronts. Around the estate are several red-brick cottages with cast iron window-frames, all in a characteristic style.

At least from the early 16th century there was a second estate in Hamptworth.[95] Between 1533 and 1544 Edmund son of Thomas Estcourt claimed that land there had descended to him from his ancestors but that Robert Kellaway was depriving him of it.[96] Robert had a son John and by 1566 he and Edmund Estcourt had apparently settled the disputes between the two families. John then conveyed the land in Hamptworth to Edmund.[97] Edmund had a son Thomas and a grandson Thomas Estcourt and in 1596 the two Thomases conveyed their manor of *HAMPTWORTH* to John Webb (d. 1625), the nephew of Edmund's son Giles.[98] The manor thereafter passed from father to son in the Webb family of Odstock to Sir John (d. 1680), Sir John (d. 1700), Sir John (d. 1745), Sir Thomas (d. 1763), and Sir John (d. 1797) who devised it to Frederick Webb.[99] Between 1822 and 1837 some 245 a. passed to Robert Eden Duncombe Shafto,[1] presumably by sale. The remainder was sold in 1858,[2] and later passed with the Hamptworth Lodge estate.

ECONOMIC HISTORY. In the Middle Ages Hamptworth was held with part of Charlton as a 5-hide estate.[3] The respective hidations of the two parts of the estate are not known but it is unlikely that Hamptworth, with its poorer soils, was valued more highly than the part of Charlton. In 1282 Hamptworth manor was reckoned at only 1 messuage, 40 a. of arable, and 40s. rent,[4] but late-13th- and early-14th-century taxation assessments apparently show Hamptworth to have been an average village of peasant farmers.[5] Sheep-and-corn husbandry was practised.[6]

Cultivation at Hamptworth before inclosure was confined to the rectangle defined on the north side

---

[74] *Reg. Pontoise* (Cant. & York Soc.), ii. 390.
[75] *Cal. Inq. p.m.* i, p. 232.
[76] Ibid. ii, p. 242.   [77] Ibid. v, p. 124.
[78] *Cal. Pat.* 1292–1301, 79.
[79] *Cal. Inq. p.m.* viii, pp. 374–81.
[80] *Cal. Close*, 1343–6, 306–7; *Cal. Inq. p.m.* ix, p. 395.
[81] *Cal. Close*, 1349–54, 260.
[82] *Complete Peerage*, s.v. Ingham; *Cal. Fine R.* 1461–71, 193–4.
[83] Burke, *Land. Gent.* (1906), i. 771.
[84] C.P. 25(2)/260/21 Eliz. I Trin.; C 142/234 no. 73. For W. Dean see *V.C.H. Hants.* iv. 521.
[85] C 142/248 no. 13.
[86] W.R.O. 492/103; C.P. 25(2)/369/1 Jas. I Mich.
[87] Cf. pp. 53–4; *Harrod's Dir. Wilts.* (1865); Mercer & Crocker, *Dir.* (1872).
[88] Burke, *Land. Gent.* (1952), 1830, 2535; ex inf. Mr. Anderson, Hamptworth Lodge.
[89] E 134/11 Jas. I Mich./13.   [90] See pp. 30–1.
[91] In Hamptworth Lodge in 1975.
[92] Photograph in Hamptworth Lodge in 1975.
[93] *Building News*, 13 June 1913; see plate facing p. 32.
[94] H. C. Moffatt, *Illustrated Description of some of the Furniture at Goodrich Court, Herefs., and Hamptworth Lodge, Wilts.* (Oxf. priv. print. 1928).
[95] For the division see below.
[96] C 1/785/20; C 1/981/73–8.
[97] *W.N. & Q.* v. 320; cf. *V.C.H. Wilts.* viii. 39.
[98] *Glos. Pedigrees* (Harl. Soc. xxi), 55–7; C.P. 25(2)/242/38 Eliz. I Hil.
[99] Burke, *Land. Gent.* (1952), 2667–8; Hoare, *Mod. Wilts.* Downton, 57.
[1] W.R.O., Inclosure Award; Tithe Award.
[2] Ibid. 490/1012.
[3] *V.C.H. Wilts.* ii, p. 119; B.L. Eg. MS. 2418, f. 61.
[4] *Cal. Inq. p.m.* ii, p. 242.
[5] H.R.O. Eccl. 2/159311, rott. 4d.–6; E 179/196/7–8.
[6] Winch. Coll. Mun. 4957; 5362; 5387–8.

by the Blackwater, on the south by Black Lane, on the east by Landford, and on the west by the road north from the present Home Farm.[7] Outside that rectangle to the west, between Black Lane and the Blackwater, is ancient oak forest continuing Langley wood; south of Black Lane was predominantly rough pasture.[8] The division into two estates made by the late 16th century cut the rectangle north–south into almost equal squares. The land west of Hamptworth Green belonged to the manor which passed to the Shaftos, east of it was the Webbs' land.[9] The regularity of the division and the general lack of evidence of more than a single estate in the Middle Ages suggest a 16th-century partition. In the late 16th century and the 17th both estates consisted of small or moderately sized farms.[10] The farmsteads, certainly those on the Webbs' estate, lay along Hamptworth Road which bisected the 500 a. of cultivated land. All that land was apparently several. It lay in arable crofts, characteristically of 3–8 a., and small meadows.[11] Despite later references to 'Middle field' and 'West field'[12] it is unlikely that it had ever been otherwise cultivated. The tenants of both manors did, however, enjoy substantial common rights. Near New Court Farm, some 7·5 km. away, the first cut of Hamptworth mead, but nothing thereafter, was reserved for the men of Hamptworth in common.[13] A total triennial rent of 4s. was paid to the lord of Downton manor and in addition 2s. was paid for the right to cut weeds at New Court.[14] The origin of those rights is unknown. Hamptworth inclosure award ignores them and rights in the meadow were still claimed in 1837.[15] More valuable perhaps were the common pastures at Hamptworth itself. The forest north of Black Lane was apparently reserved for the lord of Hamptworth manor, but there was common pasture between the two estates at Hamptworth Green and, south of Black Lane, Hamptworth common lay open for the feeding of animals and the taking of wood and trees.[16] The men of Hamptworth strove to preserve their exclusive rights to their commons which were possibly being over exploited in the mid 18th century. In 1758 the tenants of the Duncombes' manor petitioned unsuccessfully for the resumption of manorial courts, which had been discontinued, so that rights of common feeding and turbary could be defended.[17] While seeking to keep outsiders from their own commons, however, the men of Hamptworth claimed common rights for themselves outside Hamptworth. They claimed feeding in Langley wood,[18] and at least the Webbs' tenants had rights in some 83 a. of common land in the detached part of Whiteparish later annexed to Landford.[19]

The western of the two manors was valued at £5 11s. 2d. c. 1593.[20] In 1738 there were eight copyholders and twelve leaseholders.[21] Rents totalled

some £15 10s. None of the farms was large, most probably smaller than 50 a.,[22] although by 1783 a larger farm had grown from an accumulation of smaller holdings.[23] In 1638 the eastern of the two manors consisted of six holdings varying in size from 67 a. to 21 a., some 250 a. of land of which some 20 a. was in Whiteparish.[24]

Some small piecemeal inclosure had taken place in the 17th century[25] but Hamptworth Green and Hamptworth common, all the land south of Black Lane and north of Black Lane between the cultivated land and Hamptworth Lodge, were inclosed in 1822 under the East Downton award.[26] Robert Eden Duncombe Shafto and his tenants were allotted some 565 a. in the west part of the township, Frederick Webb 672 a., including a sale allotment of 264 a., in the east part, some 255 a. of which had passed to Shafto by 1837. Some of that 255 a. was ploughed and a new farm, Lyburn, established. It encompassed a smaller farm and in 1837 measured 270 a. including some 200 a. of arable and pasture east of Lyburn Road. A principally arable farm of 55 a. around Hamptworth Road was the only other farm on Shafto's manor. The remainder of his land, some 648 a., was woodland and rough pasture mainly south of Hamptworth Lodge. On Webb's manor in the eastern part of the township Hamptworth Manor farm, some 372 a. in 1837, included most of the old land in the north-east corner of the township and some 220 a. of pasture between Black Lane and Risbury hill. South of Risbury hill the land was held by smallholders and farmers from other parishes in parcels, some of which were converted to arable.[27]

As part of the Hamptworth Lodge estate a new farm, Home, was established near Hamptworth Lodge.[28] That, 227 a., and Hamptworth Manor farm, 126 a., were in hand in 1954. The remaining farms including Lyburn were taken in hand between 1954 and 1960. In 1975 cattle, sheep, and pigs were reared on the estate and some corn and vegetables grown. The area of woodland on the estate, which specialized in commercial forestry, was increased by plantations of coniferous trees at Pine hill and Pimlico bottom in the later 19th century and on Hamptworth common around Risbury hill c. 1953. A saw-mill south of Lyburn Farm was driven by water until c. 1900. In 1975 an electrically powered mill operated near Home Farm. The land east and south-east of Risbury hill was then predominantly pasture used from smallholdings at No Man's Land and from outside the parish.[29]

CHURCH. A church at Hamptworth was possibly planned in the mid 15th century. In 1466 the lord of the manor was said to hold 'the advowson of the church of Hamptworth'. Its valuation at only 1d.,

---

[7] Cf. W.R.O., Inclosure Award; B.L. Map Libr., copy of 'Plott of the Man. of Hamptworth . . . belonging to John Webb Esq. taken in . . . 1638'.
[8] *Andrews and Dury, Map* (W.R.S. viii), pl. 3; ex inf. Mr. Anderson.
[9] B.L. Map Libr., 'Plott of Hamptworth'.
[10] Ibid.; Req. 2/238/57.
[11] B.L. Map Libr., 'Plott of Hamptworth'.
[12] W.R.O. 490/1011.
[13] Ibid. 490/788; Tithe Award.
[14] Ibid. 490/779.
[15] Ibid. Tithe Award.
[16] Ibid. Inclosure Award.
[17] Ibid. 490/1016.

[18] E 134/11 Jas. I Mich./13.
[19] B.L. Map Libr., 'Plott of Hamptworth'; *V.C.H. Wilts.* iv. 351.
[20] C 142/234 no. 73.   [21] W.R.O. 490/811.
[22] Cf. ibid.; Req. 2/238/57.
[23] W.R.O. 490/1014.
[24] B.L. Map Libr., 'Plott of Hamptworth'.
[25] E 134/11 Jas. I Mich./13.
[26] W.R.O., Inclosure Award.
[27] Ibid. Tithe Award.
[28] O.S. Map 6″, Wilts. LXXVII (1881 edn.).
[29] Ex inf. Mr. Anderson.

however, suggests that no church was standing and, since no more is heard of advowson or church, it is likely that none was ever built.[30] In 1650 it was thought that Hamptworth should be annexed to Landford parish,[31] but it remained in Downton parish until becoming part of Redlynch ecclesiastical parish in 1841. In the later 19th century Hamptworth and No Man's Land school was licensed for worship and services were held there by the vicar of Redlynch.[32]

NONCONFORMITY. A meeting-house for Methodists was licensed in 1812 and in 1825 a Primitive Methodist chapel was built, possibly beside the Landford–Bramshaw road.[33] It was said to have been attended at the three services on Census Sunday in 1851 by congregations averaging 80, as many probably drawn from Landford as from Hampt-

worth.[34] A new chapel was built beside that road in 1866[35] and remained open in 1975. In 1876 a Wesleyan Methodist chapel was built in Hamptworth village at the top of Lyburn Road with accommodation for 80. Services were still held in it in 1973 but by 1975 it had been closed.[36]

EDUCATION. In 1867 a small National school to designs of Sir Gilbert Scott was built on Hamptworth common for the children of Hamptworth and No Man's Land.[37] Its accommodation was doubled to 80 by new building in 1894 when a master's house was added.[38] In 1906 the average attendance was 41,[39] 37 in 1938.[40] In 1975, by which time the school had been embraced by the village of No Man's Land and had come to be called No Man's Land school, some 71 children attended.[41]

NUNTON AND BODENHAM

THE villages of Nunton and Bodenham with their lands together constituted a tithing and chapelry. The inhabitants' attempts to make Nunton church independent of Downton church in the 16th and 17th centuries failed.[42] Relieving its own poor, however, the chapelry was deemed an ancient parish in the 19th century.[43] In 1934 it was transferred to Odstock parish.[44] The tithing was reckoned to contain 28–30 households c. 1577[45] and a tenth of the rateable wealth of Downton parish in 1628.[46] The population of the parish, 1,215 a. (492 ha.),[47] was 221 in 1801.[48] It stood above 300 for much of the 19th century but had declined to 259 in 1931.[49]

Nunton and Bodenham, so long united administratively, remained separate villages, each with its own lands. Nunton's were more extensive, reaching back from the Ebble some 6 km. to a point on the Wiltshire–Hampshire border beyond Grim's ditch. Nunton copse, which lies partly on the clay-with-flints overlying the chalk, was possibly planted in the 18th century.[50] Probably because at some time it had all belonged to the bishop of Winchester's demesne farm at Nunton[51] the down south-west of Clearbury ring and Nunton copse was all Nunton land. North-east of the down the tithing was divided almost equally into two narrow strips, that of Nunton lying in the north-west half.[52] Bodenham's land, the least extensive of any ancient village in Downton parish, some 325 a. (132 ha.), enclosed the north-west half of the hill topped by Clearbury ring.[53]

In the earlier 13th century Nunton village consisted of a demesne and small tenant farmsteads, probably grouped around the church, and a mill.[54] Early-14th-century taxation assessments show it to have been of average prosperity among the villages of the parish, wealthier than Bodenham but less so than Wick.[55] There were 43 poll-tax payers in 1377, again an average number.[56] In the 17th and 18th centuries the population of Nunton was probably smaller than that of Bodenham.[57] In 1773 Nunton was a very small settlement around the church and Nunton House and on the north side of the road to Odstock.[58] By 1837 settlement along the north side of that road had grown between the church and Upper Farm.[59] In the 19th century, when the Salisbury–Fordingbridge road was remade west of its old course through Longford park, a new bridge, New (later Nunton) bridge, was made over the Ebble near Nunton and a new road made to it from the church.[60] West of the church the Gables (later Nunton Cottage) was built in red brick with gables and tall chimneys c. 1880.[61] In the 19th and 20th centuries houses and bungalows have been built in the road running south from the road to Odstock and along that from Nunton church to Bodenham. Presses House was built in Georgian style on high ground south of the church in 1936.[62] Old people's homes were built beside the road to Odstock in the 1970s.

In 1975 Nunton, more populous than Bodenham, stretched as a continuous but well spaced line of

---

[30] C 140/19 no. 19. [31] *W.A.M.* xl. 303.
[32] *Kelly's Dir. Wilts.* (1899).
[33] Sar. Dioc. R.O., Return of Cert. Places.
[34] H.O. 129/263/2/1/5. [35] Date on bldg.
[36] *Statistical Returns* (Dept. for Chapel Affairs), ii. 75; date on bldg.
[37] Plans among Downton par. rec. in W.R.O. 1306.
[38] *Return of Non-Provided Schs.* 27; *Kelly's Dir. Wilts.* (1907). [39] *Return of Non-Provided Schs.* 27.
[40] *Bd. of Educ., List 21, 1938* (H.M.S.O.), 425.
[41] Ex inf. Chief Education Officer, County Hall, Trowbridge. [42] See below.
[43] See below; *V.C.H. Wilts.* iv. 355.
[44] *V.C.H. Wilts.* iv. 355 n.
[45] Winch. Coll. Mun. 4965. [46] W.R.O. 490/782.
[47] O.S. Map 6″, Wilts. LXXI (1886 edn.).

[48] *V.C.H. Wilts.* iv. 355. [49] Ibid.
[50] It was not mentioned at inclosure in 1720: W.R.O. 893/15, pp. 10–12; but was mapped in 1773: *Andrews and Dury, Map* (W.R.S. viii), pl. 2. [51] See below.
[52] Cf. W.R.O. 893/15, pp. 10–12; 490/743; Tithe Award.
[53] Cf. ibid. 490/746; Tithe Award.
[54] B.L. Eg. MS. 2418, f. 64 and v.
[55] E 179/196/8; *V.C.H. Wilts.* iv. 299.
[56] *V.C.H. Wilts.* iv. 308. [57] See below.
[58] *Andrews and Dury, Map* (W.R.S. viii), pls. 2–3.
[59] W.R.O., Tithe Award.
[60] Cf. O.S. Maps 1″, sheet 15 (1811 edn.); 6″, Wilts. LXXI (1886 edn.), LXXI. NE. (1900 edn.).
[61] W.R.O. 490/445; O.S. Maps 6″, Wilts. LXXI. NE. (1900 edn.), LXXI. NE. (1924 edn.).
[62] Wilts. Cuttings, xxiii. 140.

settlement from Bodenham to Odstock. Only Nunton House and Lower Nunton Farm were houses older than the 19th century. At the west end of the village near Nunton (formerly Upper) Farm, which has been rebuilt in the 20th century, were some 19th-century cottages, one of them thatched and plastered. The Radnor Arms, opened as a public house by 1920,[63] is a small 19th-century house extended on its east and west sides. Settlement on the down at Yews Farm has been continuous since before 1773,[64] but no building earlier in date than a disused 19th-century house remains.

Shortly after it had crossed the Ebble the old Salisbury–Fordingbridge road was left at right angles by a lower road which, linking several villages in Downton parish, followed the courses of the Ebble and Avon to Downton.[65] Bodenham occupies the east–west part of that road from its junction with the old main road to where it turns southwards to follow the course of the Ebble which makes a right angle before joining the Avon. Like Charlton it was a street village, and with Charlton it shared a lack of manorial demesne among its lands and, in the Middle Ages, holdings more uniform and highly rated than those of the other villages.[66] It was possibly a settlement dependent on Downton and planned to house tenants to cultivate virgin land and work on the demesne at Nunton. The compact and very regular appearance of the village even in the 19th and 20th centuries still conveyed an impression of early planning.[67] In the earlier 13th century there were a mill and some dozen farmsteads there.[68] Its low early-14th-century taxation assessments show the village to have been, with Walton and Standlynch, one of the smallest in the parish.[69] In 1377, when there were 44 poll-tax payers, it was probably as populous as Nunton,[70] and in the 17th and 18th centuries, when there were more cottages than in Nunton,[71] was probably more so. New Hall was built near the village in the early 18th century and the land around it imparked.[72] In 1773 Bodenham street contained a string of buildings, more on the north side than the south.[73] From the mid 19th century there has been no farmstead in the village,[74] and in the 19th and 20th centuries little new building.

The old Salisbury–Fordingbridge road, running from north to south, crossed the Ebble near Bodenham.[75] Its bridge was presumably that called Long bridge which the inhabitants of the tithing, allowed wood from Downton Franchise,[76] were frequently ordered to repair.[77] In 1794 a section of it was diverted to the west away from New Hall.[78] Later, after it was diverted out of Longford park, the road approached Bodenham south-eastwards from the new Nunton bridge.[79] Radnor Hall, with a caretaker's house attached, was built beside it in 1893 for men working on the Longford estate.[80] A new dual carriageway road commissioned in 1962[81] diverted the road away from the village, and as a result Radnor Hall was left standing on a triangular island between the roads.

In 1975 the village street, sloping gently eastwards towards the rivers, had at the west end near the gateway to Longford park a pair of brick cottages with a gabled addition to the south. Near the top of the street was a 19th-century house with a cob garden wall and Bodenham House. Further down the street were mostly poor cottages. A number, timber-framed and thatched, were of the 17th century, several having been cased in brick in the 1770s. In 1975 many were empty but in 1976 some were being renovated.

ESTATES. In the earlier 13th century William Gimmings, who held Throope in Bishopstone,[82] held land at Bodenham assessed at 1 hide.[83] In 1427 Richard and Agnes Holbeche conveyed a small estate to Thomas Ringwood.[84] Thomas sold some land, possibly in Charlton, to Richard Ludlow.[85] His Bodenham estate, perhaps that formerly Gimmings's, passed in the Ringwood family like the reputed manor of Cridlestyle in Fordingbridge (Hants) until the time of John Ringwood (d. 1544–5),[86] but, since it was not listed among his lands at his death,[87] probably not thereafter. It was presumably the land bought by Thomas Carpenter alias Wheeler from John Gifford in 1565.[88] It passed to Thomas's son Thomas (d. c. 1668) whose nephew Thomas Carpenter alias Wheeler held it in 1677.[89] In ways that are not clear it passed to William Bailey who held it in 1709, John Barrow (dead in 1737) and his widow who held it until at least 1740,[90] and, presumably before 1745, to Thomas Attwater who in 1750 held that freehold estate and copyhold of inheritance land.[91] Thomas was succeeded by his son Gay Thomas (d. c. 1792), grandson Philemon Attwater (d. 1832), and great-grandson Thomas Gay Attwater who in 1851 sold the estate, consisting of freehold and copyhold of inheritance lands which could not then be distinguished, to Jacob, Viscount Folkestone.[92] It has since passed with the Longford estate. Bodenham House, on the north side of the street, was built for Thomas Attwater in 1745[93] and passed with the land. It is a brick house with a symmetrical front of five bays, stone keystones, and a bracketed porch. It was extended to the north in the 19th century. From c. 1900 to 1904 it was

[63] *Kelly's Dir. Wilts.* (1920).
[64] *Andrews and Dury, Map* (W.R.S. viii), pl. 2.
[65] Ibid. pl. 3.   [66] See below.
[67] e.g. W.R.O., Tithe Award map.
[68] B.L. Eg. MS. 2418, ff. 63v.–64.
[69] E 179/196/8; *V.C.H. Wilts.* iv. 299.
[70] *V.C.H. Wilts.* iv. 308.
[71] e.g. W.R.O. 490/802, rentals, 1709, 1724.
[72] See below.
[73] *Andrews and Dury, Map* (W.R.S. viii), pl. 3.
[74] See below.
[75] *Andrews and Dury, Map* (W.R.S. viii), pl. 3.
[76] W.R.O. 490/802.   [77] e.g. ibid. 490/1198.
[78] Ibid. Q. Sess. enrolments, diversion of highways, no. 18.

[79] Ibid. Britford Tithe Award map; O.S. Map 6″, Wilts. LXXI (1886 edn.).
[80] *Kelly's Dir. Wilts.* (1939).
[81] *Wilts. Times*, 27 Apr. 1962.
[82] See p. 8.
[83] B.L. Eg. MS. 2418, f. 61.
[84] C.P. 25(1)/257/61 no. 32.
[85] See p. 57.
[86] *V.C.H. Hants*, iv. 571.
[87] C 142/71 no. 113.
[88] *W.N. & Q.* v. 318; W.R.O. 2/2.
[89] W.R.O. 2/2.
[90] Ibid. 490/802.   [91] Ibid.
[92] Ibid. 490/440, Attwater deed; 490/145, Attwater deed.
[93] Date-stone on bldg.

occupied by Eglantine Pleydell-Bouverie and her husband Sir Augustus Keppel Stephenson, Director of Public Prosecutions 1884–94.[94]

All the remaining lands of Nunton and Bodenham were demesne and customary lands of the bishops of Winchester. From the later Middle Ages both types of land were merged in copyholds which, like those elsewhere on the bishops' manor of Downton, came to assume the importance of freeholds.

In the early 16th century a substantial copyhold of inheritance in Nunton belonged to William Bampton.[95] It had passed by 1560 to John Bampton who was succeeded in 1599 by his son John.[96] The land was held until 1668 by, presumably another, John Bampton,[97] and passed to his nephew Richard Bampton who was succeeded in 1672 by his son Jasper (d. 1737).[98] Jasper's heir was his son John (d. 1751), a canon of Salisbury, who devised the land, after the death or re-marriage of his wife Catherine, to the university of Oxford to endow an annual series of eight sermons. The university held the lands until an Act passed in 1805 enabled it to exchange them with Jacob, earl of Radnor, for lands at Wing (Bucks.).[99] The exchange was completed in 1807,[1] and the land at Nunton has since passed with the Radnor title.

A substantial copyhold of inheritance in Nunton, in the Eastman family in 1502,[2] was held by John Eastman in the period 1523–60 and by Walter Eastman, possibly his son, in 1571.[3] Walter's widow Alice was admitted in 1575, and in 1592 his son Walter surrendered in favour of another son John[4] who held until at least 1628.[5] In 1641 the land was probably held by Cecily Eastman,[6] but later had apparently passed to John Clarke who, probably c. 1650, had acquired a copyhold of inheritance in Bodenham.[7] Clarke's lands in both townships were held by his widow Elizabeth in 1658,[8] and afterwards by his son John (d. 1669)[9] whose heir was probably a son John.[10] That John apparently died in the 1670s. His widow Elizabeth held until 1693 when she settled the land on her son Jonathan Clarke (d. 1701) whose heir was his daughter Martha.[11] In 1715 Martha married William Batt (d. 1772) who considerably enlarged the estate, mainly by buying land at Nunton.[12] Their heir was their eldest son William. He died in 1792 and was succeeded by his nephew John Thomas Batt (d. 1831) whose widow Susan held the land until her death in 1843.[13] The estate passed to the younger William's grand-nephew Gen. Edward Pery Buckley (d. 1873) who

was succeeded by his son Alfred (d. 1900) and grandson Maj. Edward Duncombe Henry Buckley (d. 1931).[14] In 1921 part of the estate, Lower Nunton farm, was sold to Jacob, earl of Radnor, and has since passed with the Longford estate.[15] The remainder descended to Maj. Buckley's son Maj. Edward Geoffrey Mildmay Buckley (d. 1941) whose widow Gladys sold it to William, earl of Radnor, in 1958.[16] Nunton House was built on the estate, probably by William Batt about the time of his marriage to Martha Clarke. The house forms the southern end of a continuous range which includes Lower Nunton farm-house but appears to have always been a self-contained house. It was built on a simple plan of a central stair hall with a principal room to each side. The walls are of brick and the main front to the south is a distinguished composition of seven bays. The central three bays project slightly and are pedimented, all the angles being accentuated by giant pilasters of ashlar. Inside, the woodwork of the staircase and the panelling and moulded plaster ceiling of the drawing-room are of similarly high quality. A short back wing, apparently of the early 19th century but probably replacing an earlier building, joins the house to the farm-house which is probably 18th-century but much modernized. Nunton House passed with the estate until 1921 but in the earlier 18th century was replaced as the principal residence by New Hall in Bodenham. New Hall was a red-brick house with a west front of five bays, the central three framed by pilasters supporting a pediment.[17] By 1791 it had been extended by balanced wings to the north and south and the east front had canted bays of mid-18th-century character.[18] In 1792 the house was enlarged into, or replaced by, one whose design has been attributed to James Wyatt.[19] It had a main front of eleven bays, the central five recessed and fronted by an Ionic portico in antis.[20] That house was burned down in 1881,[21] and replaced by a smaller, but still substantial, house of red brick with stone dressings. The new house was built in a mid-Georgian style with symmetrical fronts to the south, east, and west and pedimented porches to the east and west. It passed with the estate until 1958 when it was sold to the crime novelist John Creasy (d. 1973), author of some 560 books.[22] The stable block, called Clock House in 1975, was built in the 18th century of red brick round three sides of a courtyard. It was converted into flats c. 1960. New Hall and Clock House are approached past a late-19th-century lodge.

[94] W.A.M. xliii. 357; Who Was Who, 1897–1916, 674.
[95] E 179/197/50; Taxation Lists (W.R.S. x), 44.
[96] E 179/198/275; Prob. 11/94 (P.C.C. 72 Kydd).
[97] W.R.O. 490/1217.
[98] Ibid.; Hoare, Mod. Wilts. Downton, 65.
[99] J. Foster, Alumni Oxon. 1500–1714, i. 65; D.N.B.; Oxf. Univ. and Radnor Exch. Act, 45 Geo. III, c. 82 (Local and Personal). The sermons were first delivered in 1779. From 1895 they were given biennially: Hist. Reg. Univ. Oxf., 120 n.
[1] W.R.O. 490/154, surrender by Scott.
[2] Ibid. 490/1217.
[3] E 179/197/50; E 179/198/275; E 179/198/284.
[4] W.R.O. 490/1217.
[5] Ibid. 490/783.
[6] E 179/259/22.
[7] W.R.O. 490/148, admittance of Clarke, 1655, surrender by Clarke, 1659; 490/1174, rent roll.
[8] Ibid. 490/1174, rent roll.
[9] Ibid. 490/148, admittance of Clarke, 1655; Hoare,

Mod. Wilts. Downton, 65.
[10] Cf. Hoare, Mod. Wilts. Downton, 61, 64; W.R.O. 490/1174, rent roll; 490/148, surrender by Clarke, 1693.
[11] W.R.O. 490/148, surrender by Clarke; 490/1174, rent roll; Hoare, Mod. Wilts. Downton, 61, 64.
[12] Hoare, Mod. Wilts. Downton, 64; see below.
[13] Hoare, Mod. Wilts. Downton, 61; W.R.O., Tithe Award; memorials in Nunton ch.
[14] Burke, Land. Gent. (1952), 298.
[15] Country Life, 23 Apr. 1921; ex inf. Mr. D. Newton, Longford Estate Office.
[16] Ex inf. Mr. Newton.
[17] Oil painting in Salisbury Museum attributed to Peter Tillemans (1684–1734); see plate facing p. 33.
[18] J. Sigrist, water-colour in Salisbury Museum.
[19] Hoare, Mod. Wilts. Downton, 61; J. Britton, Beauties of Wilts. i. 114.
[20] Photograph in N.M.R.
[21] W.A.M. xlv. 509.
[22] Ex inf. Mr. Newton; Who's Who, 1973, 735.

The largest copyhold of inheritance in Nunton in the later 16th century was apparently the Figges's. Matthew Figge was succeeded in 1576 by his son Ambrose who, with his sons Matthew and Ambrose, sold the estate to William Stockman of Barford in 1622.[23] The land passed with Barford but before 1668 was split into three farms and sold. One farm passed to Richard Bampton and descended with the Bampton estate.[24] Another passed to Thomas Wheeler (d. 1679) whose son James sold it to Jonathan Clarke in 1690.[25] The third passed to Thomas Eastman (d. c. 1670)[26] and his son Moses (d. c. 1698)[27] whose widow Mary apparently sold it to William Batt between 1709 and 1720.[28]

A copyhold of inheritance farm in Nunton descended in a family called Carpenter in the 15th century, frequently Wheeler alias Carpenter in the 16th century, and usually Wheeler in the 17th and 18th centuries. In 1492 William Carpenter was admitted to it on the death of his father William and in 1541 Thomas Wheeler alias Carpenter was admitted to it on the surrender of his father, another William. Thomas was succeeded c. 1586 by his son Anthony who settled the land on his son Thomas 1624-6.[29] A succession of Thomas Wheeler alias Carpenters held it until at least 1724,[30] but much of the estate afterwards passed to the Batts.[31]

A similar holding in Nunton passed in the Chubb family at least from the early 16th century until, between 1720 and 1724, Thomas Chubb sold it to William Batt.[32] A small copyhold of inheritance farm belonged to William Pinhorne in 1628.[33] It passed to Abraham Pinhorne who in 1661 sold it to Edward Froud (d. c. 1680).[34] Froud's heir was his daughter Anne, wife of Franklin Newham who held until at least 1724.[35] At least some of the land subsequently passed to the Batts.[36]

A small area of copyhold of inheritance land in Bodenham was acquired by Sir Edward des Bouverie with Longford Castle in 1717.[37] It passed with the Longford estate and earls of Radnor increased their estate in Bodenham by purchases of small holdings and much cottage property in the late 18th and early 19th centuries, and by the acquisition in 1805–7 of Bampton's Nunton estate which included land there.[38] After the Attwater and New Hall estates had been bought, the Longford estate encompassed nearly the whole of Bodenham.

ECONOMIC HISTORY. Nunton's arable land reaching from the valley gravel of the village across the chalk to between Nunton copse and Clearbury ring was probably all cultivated in common in the Middle Ages. South-west of it was a narrow sheep run some 3 km. long and north of it some 35 a. of meadow land beside the Ebble.[39] In the Middle Ages the land was shared between the bishop of Winchester's demesne and his customary tenants. Most of the meadow land was in demesne and large demesne flocks were probably kept on the down.[40] In 1247–8 some 66 a. were sown for the bishop and a demesne farmstead stood at Nunton.[41] The customary holdings were small. In the earlier 13th century some fifteen tenants held 7 virgates and some 60 a., most of which had at some time been in demesne.[42] By the early 14th century demesne farming had further declined,[43] and in 1376 the demesne arable, meadows, and pastures, but apparently not the sheep folds on the down, were at farm.[44] Those lands, however, were not leased as a single farm. The meadows were leased to 'the men of Nunton' and in the 15th and 16th centuries the arable and pasture, presumably held in parcels by the tenants, and the down, used in common by them, became parts of the copyholds, from which rents totalled £13 11s. 1d.[45]

By 1628 some 106 a. of arable land, presumably near the village, had been inclosed. Some 278 a. were then cultivated in three common fields. The down, c. 450 a., could support 1,200 sheep. Stockman's farm measured 130 a., Bampton's 79 a., Wheeler's 61 a., and Eastman's 53 a., and there were three smaller farms.[46] In 1676 an agreement between Elizabeth Clarke, Edward Froud, and Henry Hare, Baron Coleraine, then owner of Longford Castle, led to the meadows east of Nunton mill being watered. Ambiguity in the agreement later caused disputes between William Batt (d. 1772) and William, Viscount Folkestone, over the use of the water.[47]

The common fields and downs of Nunton were inclosed by agreement in 1720.[48] There were then two very large farms, Batts, allotted 287 a., and Bampton's, allotted 192 a. Wheeler's and Chubb's were the other farms over 50 a. and most of both was soon after embraced by Batt's.[49] Downland of both Batt's (later Nunton) and Bampton's (later Upper) farms was ploughed and a farm, Nunton Down (later Yews) established before 1773 on the down of Batt's.[50] By 1780 the down of Bampton's had reverted to pasture.[51] In the 1830s Nunton and Nunton Down farms, 469 a., and Upper farm, 335 a., were leased together.[52] All were long and narrow but, since no general exchange of lands had been made to make the farms compact, the fields of Upper and Nunton farms and of Upper and Nunton Down farms were intermingled.[53]

In 1921 the farmstead of Nunton farm and 61½ a.

[23] W.R.O. 490/1217.
[24] Ibid.; 490/154, surrender by Scott, 1807.
[25] Ibid. 490/1217.   [26] Ibid.
[27] Ibid. 490/1174, rent roll.
[28] Ibid. 490/802; 893/15, pp. 10-12.
[29] Ibid. 490/1217.
[30] Ibid. 490/1174, rent roll; 490/802.
[31] Ibid. 490/154, draft surrender by Buckley, 1884.
[32] e.g. E 179/197/50; W.R.O. 490/1217; 490/1174, rent roll; 893/15, pp. 10-12; 490/802.
[33] W.R.O. 490/783.
[34] Ibid. 490/1217.   [35] Ibid.; 490/802.
[36] Ibid. 490/154, draft surrender by Buckley, 1884.
[37] Ibid. 490/802, rent rolls, 1709, 1724; Hoare, Mod. Wilts. Cawden, 34.
[38] e.g. W.R.O. 490/152; Land Tax; 490/154, surrender

by Scott, 1807.
[39] For the location and areas cf. ibid. 490/783 (1628); 893/15, pp. 10-12 (1720); Tithe Award (1837).
[40] Titow, Eng. Rural Soc. 106, 110.
[41] H.R.O. Eccl. 2/159457, rott. 8-9.
[42] B.L. Eg. MS. 2418, f. 64 and v.
[43] Titow, Eng. Rural Soc. 116-18, 128-9.
[44] H.R.O. Eccl. 2/159385, rot. 3d.
[45] W.R.O. 490/800.
[46] Ibid. 490/783; 490/1217.
[47] Ibid. 490/894.
[48] Ibid. 893/15, pp. 10-12.   [49] See above.
[50] Andrews and Dury, Map (W.R.S. viii), pl. 2.
[51] W.R.O. 490/441, letter, Home to Radnor, 1780; survey, c. 1780.
[52] Ibid. 490/443-4.   [53] Ibid. Tithe Award

of meadow and pasture north and west of it were sold as Lower farm. The chalkland of Nunton farm became part of Yews farm. As part of the Longford estate in 1975 Yews farm was worked in hand as part of Odstock farm and Upper and Lower farms were farmed under licence.[54] Most of the chalk was arable land and the alluvium and valley gravel were permanent grassland.

The land of Bodenham included no substantial portion of episcopal demesne. In the earlier 13th century eleven customary tenants shared 12 virgates and 1 hide was held freely.[55] The alluvium east of the present Nunton bridge was apparently Bodenham land and the acre of meadow land attached to each virgate was possibly there. A marsh common to the men of Bodenham was presumably the low-lying land east of the lower Bodenham–Charlton road south of the point where the road is on the very bank of the river.[56] South-west of the village the arable was cultivated in common, and there was a common sheep down, presumably on the hill topped by Clearbury ring. The common fields and down were inclosed by agreement in 1588,[57] but a survey of 1628 indicates pre-inclosure arrangements.[58] There were 81 a. of down and 132 a. of arable on the chalk above the Salisbury–Fordingbridge road and the road to Nunton, together called Odstock way. Below Odstock way were 60 a. of arable on the valley gravel and 33½ a. of meadow and pasture around the village. No farm had grown large by 1628. Two exceeded 50 a. and there were four of between 20 a. and 50 a., but even they were small for farms after inclosure. Customary rents had become fixed at £5 17s.[59]

In the 17th and 18th centuries an increasing amount of Bodenham land was detached from farms based in the village. The Bamptons' and Batts' lands were probably worked from Nunton,[60] the Avon meadow land was attached to, though not always sub-let with, New Court farm,[61] and in the later 18th century some 75 a. around New Hall were imparked.[62] In the later 18th century and the early 19th the lands of the Attwaters, Batts, and earls of Radnor were consolidated by purchases and exchanges.[63] Attwater's, with buildings behind Bodenham House and at the bottom of the street on the north side and 142 a. lying principally in a strip above the Salisbury–Fordingbridge road adjoining Charlton land, was then the only farm based in Bodenham. The Batts' land was nearly all within New Hall park. Lord Radnor's estate consisted of property in the village, meadow and woodland in hand, 43 a. including the new plantation on Bodenham hill, and the former Bodenham down, 61 a. then tilled, which was leased with Matrimony farm in Charlton.[64] After Lord Folkestone bought it in 1851 Attwater's farm was

apparently merged with Matrimony farm. In 1975 much of the agricultural land of Bodenham, still mainly arable on the chalk, remained part of Matrimony farm.[65]

MILLS. A mill at Nunton was held customarily from at least the earlier 13th century.[66] It was presumably a corn-mill then, but in the 17th century was being used to make paper.[67] In 1676 the copyhold of the mill and its lands were acquired by Lord Coleraine, probably for reasons connected with the watering of Nunton and Longford meadows, and it passed with the Longford estate.[68] The mill was referred to in later conveyances of the land,[69] but it is not clear how long paper-milling continued. The terms of references made to the paper-mill in 1762 suggest that it had long been demolished.[70] Its site was presumably on the meadow land called Mill meads in 1837;[71] if so, the mill stood on the Ebble NNW. of the church.

A mill at Bodenham was similarly held customarily in the early 13th century.[72] In 1488 the mill lay empty for much of the year while a new weir and new flood-gates were made.[73] From 1693 it passed like Nunton mill with the Longford estate. It remained a corn-mill.[74] A diversion of the Avon at its confluence with the Ebble seems to mark the site of the mill which had been demolished by 1773.[75]

LOCAL GOVERNMENT. The tithingman of Nunton and Bodenham attended Downton manorial courts where public nuisances in the tithing were often presented.[76] In the early 18th century, however, the churchwardens rather than the tithingman saw to their amendment,[77] and surveyors of the roads were later appointed.[78] Overseers' accounts exist for the chapelry from 1701.[79] There were always two overseers. In 1701 expenditure was £7 14s. In the early 18th century relief was mostly in the form of necessary goods given to the poor but by 1741, when expenditure was £33 10s., regular doles were usual. Early-19th-century accounts show annual expenditure of sometimes over £300.

CHURCH. As parts of its masonry show a church was standing at Nunton c. 1200. It was annexed to Downton church as a chapel, probably from its foundation but, unlike the probably earlier chapels at Standlynch and Witherington, was not served under a special arrangement. In 1915 the chapelry of Nunton and Bodenham was detached from Downton and annexed to Odstock parish.[80]

All the tithes of Nunton and Bodenham belonged to Downton church. The great tithes were granted

[54] Ex inf. Mr. Newton.
[55] B.L. Eg. MS. 2418, ff. 63v.–64.
[56] Cf. ibid.; Geol. Surv. Map 1″, drift, sheet 298 (1950 edn.).
[57] W.R.O. 893/4, p. 62.
[58] Ibid. 490/746; for the date cf. 490/783.
[59] Ibid. 490/788.   [60] See above.
[61] W.R.O. 490/788; 490/807.
[62] Andrews and Dury, Map (W.R.S. viii), pl. 3.
[63] e.g. W.R.O. 490/154, surrender by J. T. Batt, 1800.
[64] Ibid. Tithe Award.   [65] Ex inf. Mr. Newton.
[66] B.L. Eg. MS. 2418, f. 64v.
[67] V.C.H. Wilts. iv. 245; W.R.O. 490/894, agreement, Clarke, Froud, Coleraine.
[68] W.R.O. 490/147, surrender, Gardiner to Coleraine; Coleraine to Bouverie, 1722.
[69] e.g. ibid. admittance of Bouverie, 1736.
[70] Ibid. 490/894, Batt–Folkestone correspondence.
[71] Ibid. Tithe Award.
[72] B.L. Eg. MS. 2418, f. 63v.
[73] H.R.O. Eccl. 2/159500/3.
[74] W.R.O. 490/1217; 490/147.
[75] Andrews and Dury, Map (W.R.S. viii), pl. 3.
[76] e.g. W.R.O. 893/13, p. 22.
[77] Ibid. 783/33.
[78] The accts. for 1808–45 are ibid. 783/30–1.
[79] Ibid. 783/33–5.
[80] Lond. Gaz. 10 Aug. 1915, pp. 7885–91.

to Winchester College. To maintain divine service in Nunton church the college paid the vicar of Downton a pension, said in 1580 to be 40s., and gave a gown or 10s. for the use of the curate at Nunton.[81] The payments ceased c. 1540 but were resumed c. 1580.[82] In 1781, when the college leased the great tithes of the chapelry to the vicar for £15 a year,[83] it was possibly intended that at least part of the vicar's additional income derived from them should be devoted to the service of Nunton. In 1837, when the lease was still held for £15 a year, the tithes were valued at £150. Leases continued until withdrawn by the college in 1882.[84]

The vicar of Downton was entitled to the small tithes but held no glebe in Nunton and Bodenham.[85] In 1577 there was a house in which a curate might live, but then and in 1585 it was said to be in decay.[86] It still stood in the 17th century.[87] A new house was built in the early 19th century near the south side of the church. A schoolroom was added at the back c. 1830.[88] In 1864 there was said to be a cottage, presumably that house, thought unfit for a curate.[89] A rectory-house for the parish of Odstock with Nunton and Bodenham was built on the south side of the Nunton–Bodenham road in 1914.[90]

A chapel was erected in the angle between the chancel and the south aisle, probably in the earlier 13th century, but nothing is known of its dedication, purpose, or possible endowment. In 1382–3 the church was served by chaplains.[91] When the vicarage of Downton was ordained in 1383 services became the responsibility of vicars but, to judge from the proceedings of 1425, it is unlikely that the church was well served.[92] In 1550 the vicar employed a curate apparently living at Nunton,[93] but his parishioners were not satisfied. In 1577 they tried to prove that the church should be detached from Downton.[94] Failing in that, in 1580 they persuaded Winchester College to resume the pension paid to benefit Nunton,[95] and in 1617 renewed their efforts to prove the chapelry a parish.[96] In 1650 the parliamentary commissioners accepted that Nunton should be severed from Downton.[97] They recommended vainly that instead it be united with Odstock. The curate charged with immorality in 1646[98] had presumably left and not been replaced by 1650 when the commissioners remarked that the parishioners desired preaching at the church every Sunday.[99] In 1662 the inhabitants of Nunton, petitioning Winchester College for a resident minister, complained that there had not been one for nearly two

years and in that time the curate of Downton had preached at Nunton only twice.[1] In the early 18th century there was a resident curate[2] but, even after the college leased the great tithes to the vicar, there was not always one. In 1783 the church was served only once a month and the Sacrament administered four times a year.[3] By 1829, however, a resident curate had been appointed.[4] In 1864 two services were held on Sundays in the winter and three in summer; Communion was celebrated at the usual festivals and on the first Sunday of every month to some 20–25 communicants.[5] In 1975 the church was served every Sunday.

The church of *ST. ANDREW* is of rubble with ashlar dressings. It has an aisled chancel and a nave with south aisle and porch. The chancel arch is of c. 1200 and suggests that there was a small church of that date to which a south aisle and south chapel were added in the earlier 13th century, when the chancel may also have been lengthened. A south porch and a low timber tower, which apparently rose above the western bay of the nave, had been added by the early 19th century.[6] The church was restored 1854–5 under the direction of T. H. Wyatt.[7] All the external walls were apparently rebuilt using some early features. In 1933 the south chapel was extended eastwards to the same line as the chancel and a balancing aisle to the north.[8]

There were three bells in 1553. The treble bears no inscription and may not have been replaced; the tenor was replaced by a bell founded by William Purdue in 1641; the other bell was replaced by one founded by Clement Tosier in 1701.[9] Those three bells hung in the church in 1975.[10]

There were 22½ oz. of plate in 1553 when 14 oz. were taken for the king. A new chalice and paten cover were given in 1677 and a paten similar to those of Downton hall-marked 1778 was given later.[11] Those items and some 20th-century plate belonged to the church in 1975.[12]

The registers are complete from 1672.[13]

NONCONFORMITY. There were dissenters, probably Baptists, in Nunton and Bodenham in the 1660s,[14] and Elizabeth Clarke's house was licensed for Presbyterian meetings in 1672.[15] In 1776 and 1780 Baptist meeting-places in Bodenham were licensed and in 1839 a chapel was built there.[16] It was served from the Brown Street Particular Baptist church, Salisbury.[17] On Census Sunday in

---

[81] Winch. Coll. Mun. 4966. The dates of the first payment and of the gift are unknown.
[82] Winch. Coll. Mun. 4966–7.
[83] W.R.O. 1306, Downton par. rec.
[84] Ibid.; Tithe Award.
[85] Sar. Dioc. R.O., Glebe Terrier, 17th cent.
[86] Ibid. Detecta Bks.
[87] Ibid. Glebe Terrier, 17th cent.
[88] *Return of Non-Provided Schs.* 40.
[89] Sar. Dioc. R.O., Vis. Queries.
[90] W.R.O. 783/17.
[91] Winch. Coll. Mun. 5363.
[92] See pp. 48, 77.
[93] Sar. Dioc. R.O., Detecta Bk.
[94] Winch. Coll. Mun. 4965. It was possibly an attempt to deprive Winch. Coll. of the great tithes of Nunton: 5020.
[95] Ibid. 4967.   [96] Ibid. 5124–5.
[97] *W.A.M.* xl. 303–4.
[98] *Walker Revised*, ed. Matthews, 377.
[99] *W.A.M.* xl. 303–4.

[1] Winch. Coll. Mun. 5127.
[2] Sar. Dioc. R.O., Clergy Bk. 1698–1714, f. 132.
[3] *Vis. Queries, 1783* (W.R.S. xxvii), p. 91.
[4] *Rep. Com. Eccl. Revenues*, 832–3.
[5] Sar. Dioc. R.O., Vis. Queries.
[6] J. Buckler, water-colour in W.A.S. Libr., vol. i. 22 (1801).
[7] Sar. Dioc. R.O., Pet. for Faculties, bdle. 5, no. 10.
[8] Ibid. bdle. 72, no. 24; bdle. 73, no. 4.
[9] Walters, *Wilts. Bells*, 149.
[10] Ex inf. the Revd. D. V. Evening, Nunton Rectory.
[11] Nightingale, *Wilts. Plate*, 24.
[12] Ex inf. the Revd. D. V. Evening.
[13] W.R.O. 783/1–7. Transcripts for the periods 1623–38 and 1670–2 are in Sar. Dioc. R.O.
[14] Williams, *Cath. Recusancy* (Cath. Rec. Soc.), pp. 328, 330, 331.
[15] *Cal. S.P. Dom.* 1672, 238.
[16] Sar. Dioc. R.O., Return of Cert. Places.
[17] *V.C.H. Wilts.* vi. 158.

1851 a congregation of 81 attended the evening service.[18] A new chapel, restored in 1964,[19] was said to have been built in 1860.[20] The chapel stands on the south side of Bodenham street. In 1975 services were regularly held.

EDUCATION. There were two day-schools in the parish in 1833: one, started in 1826, was attended by 26 children and supported by the parents; the other, attended by 32 children, was supported by

the generosity of a lady.[21] Neither occupied a special building.[22] The Sunday school, however, was held in the glebe-house at Nunton converted for the purpose.[23] In 1846 its schoolroom was adapted for use by an elementary school which in 1860 received money from the state. The average attendance was 49 in 1863 but had fallen to 36 by 1903. In 1922 the school was closed and the children transferred to Odstock.[24] The schoolroom was a private house in 1975.

STANDLYNCH

A VILLAGE of Standlynch was first mentioned in 1086.[25] It was possibly developing and the lands around it coming under cultivation in the early 11th century when a bishop of Winchester granted land there.[26] The effect of the grant was perhaps to license the settlement and give rough definition to its lands which made a narrow rectangle, 713 a. in 1879.[27] In the south-west part of the township, where the land falls steeply to the river and the Avon has deposited no alluvium on its east bank, alluvial land west of the river was in Standlynch.[28] In the east part the land narrowed to enclose a tongue of woodland, Battscroft copse.

Standlynch was in the Church tithing of Downton parish. From the 16th century it contained a single estate,[29] and at some time its lord, presumably to avoid relieving the poor of Downton, made Standlynch responsible for the relief of its own poor. That action could be defended on the grounds that the tithes of Standlynch had been commuted, that its church, when open, was supported by its lord, and that it was therefore outside Downton parish.[30] Standlynch was returned as an ancient parish in the 1801 census.[31] It joined Alderbury poor-law union in 1835.[32] From 1897 to 1934 it was part of the civil parish of Standlynch with Charlton All Saints,[33] and afterwards again part of Downton parish.[34]

The village of Standlynch stood in the south-west corner of its lands and was linked with Witherington, Barford, and Downton by a direct path.[35] Like the other Avon valley villages of the parish it stood on the shelf of valley gravel but, unlike them, close to the Avon where there was no alluvium. The village was not wealthy compared with the others. In 1334 its taxation assessment was, with Walton's and Bodenham's, the lowest for the parish and in 1377 there were eighteen poll-tax payers.[36] Like Witherington and Barford it apparently became even less populous in the 15th century.[37] In the 16th and 17th centuries it consisted of the closely grouped manor-house, church, farmstead, and mill. In the 18th century even that small settlement died and its population was scattered. A new farmstead was

built near the water-meadows to the north of Standlynch, probably when the land was watered in the late 17th century. In 1733 Standlynch House, called Trafalgar House from 1815,[38] was built on the rising ground to the north-east of the village and the land around it imparked. The adjoining land of Barford had earlier been imparked and a road skirting both parks superseded the direct road north from Downton.[39] Sandwiched between the two parks and cut off from the road and agricultural land the village was deserted. New farmsteads were built east of the road and in the park and the old manor-house and farmstead were demolished.[40] The population of Standlynch, presumably consisting mostly of servants in Standlynch (Trafalgar) House and agricultural labourers and their families, was 41 in 1801, had risen to 107 by 1871, and declined to 72 by 1891 and 67 by 1931.[41] No figure is available but Standlynch almost certainly housed fewer people than that in 1975. The church, the mill, and a few other buildings stood on the site of the old village. The planned wilderness of the old manor-house, 3 a. cut into rectangles by walks,[42] was turned into a kitchen garden for Trafalgar House and in the early 19th century surrounded by the high wall still standing. The river there showed signs of several diversions and had in it several low-lying islands. Standlynch Farm, a T-shaped red-brick house of c. 1733, was extended westwards in the late 19th century. The original stables were standing in 1975 and outbuildings of the 18th century remained among the extensive farm buildings of later date. Standlynch Dairy Farm, said to be old in 1814,[43] in 1975 consisted of only a cattleyard and disused sheds. Trafalgar Farm consisted of 19th-century buildings.

MANOR. Land at Standlynch assessed at 2 hides was alienated from the bishop of Winchester's Downton estate in the time of King Cnut (1016–35).[44] By 1086 it had been divided into three small estates.[45]

[18] H.O. 129/263/2/3/13.   [19] Wilts. Cuttings, xxii. 239.
[20] Kelly's Dir. Wilts. (1907).
[21] Educ. Enquiry Abstract, 1029.
[22] W.R.O., Tithe Award.
[23] Educ. Enquiry Abstract, 1029; W.R.O. 783/29; Return of Non-Provided Schs. 40.   [24] W.R.O. 783/28–9.
[25] V.C.H. Wilts. ii, pp. 150, 151, 161.
[26] Ibid. p. 119.
[27] O.S. Map 6″, Wilts. LXXII (1885 edn.).
[28] W.R.O., Tithe Award.   [29] See below.
[30] See below.   [31] V.C.H. Wilts. iv. 357.
[32] Poor Law Com. 2nd Rep. 558.

[33] V.C.H. Wilts. iv. 357 and n.
[34] Ibid. 347 and n.
[35] O.S. Map 6″, Wilts. LXXII (1885 edn.).
[36] V.C.H. Wilts. iv. 299, 308.
[37] See below.   [38] See below.
[39] See p. 52.   [40] See below.
[41] V.C.H. Wilts. iv. 357; Kelly's Dir. Wilts. (1939).
[42] W.R.O. 490/1068; Andrews and Dury, Map (W.R.S. viii), pl. 3.
[43] B.L. Add. MS. 42777, ff. 143–4.
[44] V.C.H. Wilts. ii, pp. 119, 208.
[45] Ibid. pp. 150, 151, 161.

In 1066 one estate was held by Colo. It had passed by 1084 to Waleran the huntsman, whose extensive estates included Hamptworth and land at Charlton, and in 1086 was assessed at 1 hide.[46] Like Hamptworth it passed to Waleran's descendants,[47] and then, like Charlton, to William de St. Martin who was overlord of land in Standlynch in 1275.[48] It was held of William by the heirs of John de Campeny but no more is heard of land in Standlynch held by either.

In 1373 Sir Thomas de Buckland (d. 1379) disposed of a life interest in land at Standlynch which could possibly have been that formerly Waleran's.[49] It was reckoned Sir Thomas's land in 1376.[50] The later descent of the land is not clear. The land was perhaps that which Richard Beauchamp (d. 1481), bishop of Salisbury, held at Standlynch in 1476,[51] but where it lay and how Beauchamp acquired it is not known. Bishop Beauchamp devised it to his nephew Sir Richard Beauchamp (d. 1508), Lord St. Amand,[52] after whose attainder 1483–4[53] the Crown granted it to Nicholas Rigby.[54] It was possibly restored to St. Amand after 1485 but it is not clear how it passed. Since remainder after a seven-year lease of 1465 was granted to Henry Hugyn (fl. 1475), and he or his heirs were apparently lessees in 1485, it is likely that the land passed to him or his heirs (see below).[55]

Another Standlynch estate, assessed at ½ hide, was held by Alwi son of Turber in 1086.[56] Alwi's heirs are not known but his land at Standlynch seems to have passed, as did a moiety of his manor of West Tytherley (Hants),[57] to Richard de Cardeville who was overlord of land in Standlynch in 1198 and until his death c. 1247.[58] The overlordship of Cardeville's descendants was not afterwards mentioned.

In 1198 Richard de Cardeville's land was held by Philip Lingiur.[59] Philip left a daughter Alice, wife of William de la Falaise (fl. 1231),[60] but there is no evidence that the Falaises held the land. In 1232 Robert of Witherington seems to have held ½ hide at Standlynch,[61] possibly the same land; but by 1249 it had apparently passed to Laurence Aygnel, 'of Standlynch',[62] mesne tenant of Richard de Cardeville in South Midgham in Fordingbridge (Hants),[63] and 2 virgates of it, disputed in 1249,[64] were acknowledged by William son of Robert of Witherington to be Laurence Aygnel's in 1268.[65] Laurence was

dead in 1270.[66] The land remained in the Aygnel family, presumably passing to John Aygnel, who held Laurence's land at South Midgham in 1316, and to another John Aygnel (fl. 1364).[67] The second John's heir seems to have been his daughter Catherine, wife of John Shaw, to both of whom a trustee quitclaimed the land in 1381.[68] Afterwards, however, the land passed, possibly by purchase, to a Meriet (see below). In 1418 Thomas and Eleanor Meriet conveyed it with their other land in Standlynch to John Hugyn (see below).[69]

The third Standlynch estate, assessed at ½ hide, was held by Leofing in 1066, and by William de Falaise in 1086. It was held of William by Alward.[70] Its later descent is uncertain. It was possibly the land in Standlynch held by Robert Boiaceus in 1147.[71] Robert's land had passed to Simon de Brewes by the early 13th century when at 2 hides it was the most highly assessed estate there.[72] It was held by John son of Robert de Bamse in the 1260s.[73] Its later descent is again uncertain but it seems to have passed to William le Dun who held land in Standlynch in 1275 and died holding it c. 1311.[74]

William le Dun's heir was his son John, an idiot,[75] His land seems to have passed to another of his sons, William, said in 1336 to be 'of Standlynch',[76] and to John Dun, perhaps the elder William's grandson, said to be 'of Standlynch' in 1374.[77] John then settled the land on his wife Eleanor for life and apparently died in the same year.[78] Eleanor afterwards married Thomas Meriet.[79] John apparently left daughters Agnes, wife of Henry Not, and Elizabeth, wife of John Park. In 1399 Agnes and Henry conveyed their reversionary interest in a third of the land to William Woodhay,[80] Agnes's 'cousin',[81] and in 1402 William conveyed his interests to John and Elizabeth Park.[82] In 1406 John and Elizabeth conveyed their reversionary interests to John Hugyn,[83] and in 1418 Thomas and Eleanor Meriet conveyed the land to Hugyn with their land formerly held by John Aygnel.[84] Hugyn was apparently succeeded by a Richard Hugyn (fl. 1451),[85] perhaps his son, and a Henry Hugyn (fl. 1465),[86] perhaps his grandson, who seems to have united all the Standlynch lands in his ownership (see above).

Henry Hugyn left a widow Elizabeth (fl. 1505) and daughters Dorothy and Grace.[87] Dorothy married Henry Gaynesford and had a son Thomas. Between 1533 and 1544, after her death, Thomas claimed

[46] Ibid. pp. 151, 208.
[47] B.L. Eg. MS. 2418, f. 61.
[48] Rot. Hund. (Rec. Com.), ii (1), 257.
[49] W. H. Turner and H. O. Coxe, Cal. Chart. Bodl. 586; and see above, p. 32.
[50] H.R.O. Eccl. 2/159385, rot. 3.
[51] Sar. Dioc. Regy., Reg. Beauchamp, ii, f. 2.
[52] Prob. 11/7 (P.C.C. 4 Logge).
[53] Complete Peerage, xi. 303.
[54] B.L. Harl. MS. 433, f. 32.
[55] Hist. MSS. Com. 12, Wells, ii, p. 189.
[56] V.C.H. Wilts. ii, p. 161.
[57] V.C.H. Hants, iv. 519–20.
[58] Ibid. 520; Bk. of Fees, i. 12; B.L. Eg. MS. 2418, f. 61.
[59] Bk. of Fees, i. 12.   [60] V.C.H. Hants, iv. 568.
[61] Cur. Reg. R. xiv, p. 428.
[62] Civil Pleas, 1249 (W.R.S. xxvi), pp. 95, 108, 125, 151; K.B. 26/135 rot. 11; K.B. 26/138 rot. 16.
[63] V.C.H. Hants, iv. 573.
[64] Civil Pleas, 1249 (W.R.S. xxvi), pp. 95, 108; K.B. 26/135 rot. 11; K.B. 26/138 rot. 16.
[65] C.P. 25(1)/251/21 no. 4.
[66] Ex. e Rot. Fin. (Rec. Com.), ii. 503.
[67] V.C.H. Hants, iv. 573 and n. 188.
[68] Turner and Coxe, Cal. Chart. Bodl. 587.
[69] Ibid.   [70] V.C.H. Wilts. ii, p. 150.
[71] Sar. Dioc. Regy., Reg. Mitford, ff. 153–4.
[72] B.L. Eg. MS. 2418, f. 61.
[73] Reg. Pontoise (Cant. & York Soc.), ii. 390.
[74] Rot. Hund. (Rec. Com), ii (1), 257; Cal. Inq. p.m. v, p. 140.
[75] Cal. Inq. p.m. v, p. 140.
[76] Turner and Coxe, Cal. Chart. Bodl. 586.
[77] Hoare, Mod. Wilts. Cawden, 46. It is assumed that 'Guyn' is a misprint of 'Duyn'.
[78] Turner and Coxe, Cal. Chart. Bodl. 586–7.
[79] The Eleanor, wife of Thomas Meriet, whose life interest is mentioned in 1394 is presumed to have been John's widow: C.P. 25(1)/256/57 no. 7.
[80] C.P. 25(1)/256/58 no. 1.
[81] Turner and Coxe, Cal. Chart. Bodl. 584.
[82] Ibid.   [83] C.P. 25(1)/256/58 no. 44.
[84] Turner and Coxe, Cal. Chart. Bodl. 587.
[85] Ibid. 585.
[86] Hist. MSS. Com. 12, Wells, ii, p. 189.
[87] Ibid.; C 1/993/13.

Grace's moiety, but the claim of Thomas Woodshaw to be the legitimate son of Grace and Thomas Woodshaw was apparently substantiated.[88] In 1543 Gaynesford and Woodshaw conveyed their moieties of the manor of *STANDLYNCH* to William Green, Woodshaw for an annual rent-charge of £5 which Green extinguished by purchase in 1551.[89] Green (will proved 1555) had a son Francis who sold the reversion to Walter Buckland in 1573.[90] William's widow Elizabeth held until at least 1576, but by 1587 the manor was Buckland's.[91] Walter (d. 1600) settled it on his wife Barbara.[92] She was a recusant and two-thirds of her lands were granted to Sir John Rodney in 1611.[93] The whole manor passed, however, to Walter's second son Maurice (d. 1615)[94] and to Maurice's son Walter (d. 1638) whose widow held a third as dower until at least 1649.[95] Walter's son Walter, who fought for the king in the first Civil War, was also accused of popery.[96] His lands were sequestered in 1645 but he compounded for his two-thirds of the manor in 1649.[97] Walter (d. before 1677)[98] was succeeded by his son Maurice (d. 1710) and grandson Philip (d. 1724).[99]

Philip Buckland's heir was his brother Maurice who in 1726 sold the manor to Sir Peter Vandeput, Bt. (d. 1748), who left a widow Frances and a son Sir George.[1] In 1752 they sold the manor to William Young (created a baronet 1769, d. 1788).[2] In 1766 Standlynch was sold to Henry Dawkins (d. 1814) who devised it for sale.[3] In 1815 it was bought by the Crown and settled on the heirs of Vice-Admiral Horatio Nelson, Viscount Nelson.[4] The manor, much enlarged and called the Trafalgar estate, passed with the Nelson title until the Trafalgar Estates Act, 1947, permitted its sale.[5] Edward, Earl Nelson, sold it in 1948 to John Francis Godolphin, duke of Leeds, who in 1953 sold the estate, 3,390 a., to Jacob Pleydell-Bouverie, Viscount Folkestone.[6] Lord Folkestone succeeded to the earldom of Radnor in 1968 and the land was part of the Longford estate in 1975.

In the early 13th century the abbess of Romsey was said to hold ½ hide in Standlynch of the king.[7] That reference is the only one to a Romsey holding and is perhaps mistaken.

Laurence Aygnel, lord of one of the Standlynch estates in 1249, apparently occupied a house on it.[8] The Duns also lived at Standlynch in the 14th century, and it seems that the Hugyns did so in the 15th.[9] The manor-house which stood there in the early 18th century was possibly medieval with extensions, apparently of the late 16th century and presumably built by the Bucklands. It lay close to the river near the church[10] on the north side of a complex of walled gardens and outbuildings[11] some of which remain. It was ranged round three sides of a courtyard which was open to the north and there was a small park with an axial avenue on that side. A plan to rebuild the house on the same site was apparently considered and rejected.[12] The house was described as 'ruinous' in 1748.[13] A new house bearing the date 1733 on the rainwater heads was built on higher ground further east for Sir Peter Vandeput, Bt., to designs attributed to his relative Roger Morris.[14] Standlynch (later Trafalgar) House has the usual Palladian plan with two larger rooms at the centre and smaller rooms at each corner and has main fronts of seven bays. The walls are of brick with stone dressings, the principal windows having 'Gibbs' surrounds. Some of the original interior decoration, including the staircase and richly stuccoed cube hall, survives. The house was greatly enlarged for Henry Dawkins, a member of the Society of Dilletanti, in 1766. Wings, each nine bays by three, were added to the north and south and attached to the house by corridors. The architect was the younger John Wood but Nicholas Revett appears to have been responsible for the interior decoration. Revett also designed the porch in the Delian Doric order added to the east front of the central block and probably new fittings for some of the rooms including the library.[15] At the same time Cipriani was employed to decorate the parlour at the south-east corner. He covered the walls with a continuous landscape in which there are foreground scenes with figures including those of Venus and Shakespeare.[16] The interior of the north wing appears to have been replanned in the earlier 19th century, perhaps at the time the house was acquired for the Nelson family, and that of the south wing was remodelled after a fire in 1866. The house is on a spur overlooking the Avon and the ground, level to the east, falls steeply on the other three sides. On the west side there are terraced gardens with formal ponds apparently of the late 19th century but possibly adapted from features of the original landscape garden which was designed by Charles Bridgeman.[17] The house passed with the Trafalgar estate to the Longford estate until it was sold to Associated Electrical Industries Ltd. in 1958. In 1961 the company sold it to its chairman Oliver Lyttelton, Viscount Chandos. In 1971 Lord Chandos sold it to Mr. J. G. Pinckney.[18]

[88] C 1/993/13.
[89] C.P. 25(2)/46/323 nos. 3, 20; C.P. 25(2)/65/532 no. 69.
[90] Prob. 11/37 (P.C.C. 28 More); C.P. 25(2)/239/15 Eliz. I Hil.
[91] *Taxation Lists* (W.R.S. x), 117; E 179/270/18.
[92] C 142/260 no. 132.
[93] Turner and Coxe, *Cal. Chart. Bodl.* 587.
[94] C 142/260 no. 132; Prob. 11/126 (P.C.C. 86 Rudd, will of Maur. Buckland).
[95] *Wilts. Inq. p.m.* 1625–49 (Index Libr.), 351–2; *W.A.M.* xxiii. 331.
[96] *W.A.M.* xxiii. 331.
[97] *Cal. Cttee. for Compounding*, i. 78; iii. 1739; *W.A.M.* xxiii. 331.   [98] Mon. on ch.
[99] Hoare, *Mod. Wilts.* Downton, at pp. 50–1, where Phil.'s date of d. is misprinted.
[1] Ibid.; ibid. 48; W.R.O. 490/171, deed, Young to Vandeput and Lydiatt, 1754.
[2] C.P. 25(2)/1234/25 Geo. III East.

[3] Hoare, *Mod. Wilts.* Downton, 48.
[4] Trafalgar Estates Acts, 55 Geo. III, c. 96 and 10 & 11 Geo. VI, c. 34.
[5] *Complete Peerage*; 10 & 11 Geo. VI, c. 34.
[6] *The Times*, 18 July 1953.
[7] B.L. Eg. MS. 2418, f. 61.
[8] *Civil Pleas, 1249* (W.R.S. xxvi), p. 95.
[9] Hist. MSS. Com. 12, *Wells*, ii, p. 189.
[10] Hoare, *Mod. Wilts.* Downton, 48.
[11] Bodl. MS. Gough Drawings, a. 3, ff. 24, 36.
[12] Ibid. f. 25, drawing attributed to Chas. Bridgeman.
[13] *Country Life*, 13 July 1945.
[14] See plate facing p. 144.
[15] Pevsner, *Wilts.* (2nd edn.), 529; Colvin, *Brit. Architects*, 684, 912.
[16] Hoare, *Mod. Wilts.* Downton, 48.
[17] Pevsner, *Wilts.* (2nd edn.), 530.
[18] Wilts. Cuttings, xxii. 9; *The Times*, 18 July 1953; 14 May 1971; *Daily Telegraph*, 17 Aug. 1971.

ECONOMIC HISTORY. In 1086 the three estates of Standlynch, assessed at a total of 2 hides and worth 25s., had land for 1½ plough and 14 a. of meadow.[19] In the Middle Ages each estate probably consisted of demesne and customary land. In 1311 William le Dun had a farm of some 110 a., six ½-virgaters owing labour services and 5s. rent each, and two cottagers.[20] The practice of sheep-and-corn husbandry[21] on such small farms was almost certainly in common but it is not known how it was organized.

In the early 15th century two of the manors were united by ownership and by the later 15th century the third had been linked with them by lease.[22] The tenant farms were probably taken into the demesnes, the demesnes merged to make a single farm, and common cultivation and customary tenure thus eliminated. That had apparently happened by the 1540s[23] and had possibly accompanied similar 15th-century developments at Standlynch's neighbours Barford and Witherington. Standlynch farm's principal buildings stood in the village near the manor-house, mill, and church. From the 1640s the farm was leased and may not have been in hand again until the later 18th century.[24]

In the late 17th century works for watering the meadows of Charlton, Witherington, and Standlynch were carried out east of the Avon,[25] and it seems likely that Standlynch Dairy farm was established then beside the newly watered meadow land to the north of the village. The building of Standlynch House in 1733,[26] and the imparking of some 150 a. of land, presumably deprived Standlynch farm of most of its lowland pasture, some arable land, and access to its remaining lands on the chalk. A new farmstead was built on the eastern side of the park.[27] In 1779 all the lands were in hand as a mixed farm of 804 a. There were 58 a. of meadow on both sides of the river in Standlynch and 59 a. of meadow adjoining it to the north on the east side of the river in Charlton and Witherington, all used from Standlynch Dairy. East of the road round the park 268 a. of arable land and 143 a. of down pasture in Standlynch and 79 a. of land formerly Privett copse[28] were worked from Standlynch Farm. Standlynch park measured some 158 a. and Battscroft copse beyond the down some 58 a.[29]

As part of the Trafalgar estate Standlynch farm and Standlynch Dairy farm were leased, sometimes together.[30] In 1948 Standlynch Dairy farm, 146 a., and Standlynch farm, 294 a., were held together. Privett farm, 104 a., was leased separately. In 1953, with other lands, they were all leased together as a single mixed farm, 654 a.[31] As part of the Longford estate Trafalgar farm, then including all but 10 a. of the park, was in hand in 1975. Standlynch farm, including Privett farm, was leased.[32]

MILL. There was a water-mill on the manor of William le Dun in 1311.[33] A mill at Standlynch was mentioned in 1383,[34] but not again until 1575–6 when a new mill and weir were built.[35] The mill passed with Standlynch manor. Its site is not known. In the later 17th century and the early 18th its weir was used as a lock for barges navigating the Avon. The mill was moved to facilitate the watering of meadows, possibly Barford's,[36] and a new mill was built in 1697–8.[37] It stands near the site of the manor-house, farmstead, and church, presumably very near but perhaps a little to the south of the site of the old mill. The eastwards diversion of the river to it was achieved by a weir some 200 yd. to the north.[38] The water passed through the mill into the carriage taking it to Barford meadows. In 1884 the mill housed an engine to pump water to Trafalgar House.[39] The mill remained in use in 1907.[40] In 1948 it housed electricity generating plant and machinery to pump water to the Trafalgar estate.[41] It was converted to a salmon hatchery in 1963.[42]

CHURCH. In 1147 a provision, intended to be permanent, was made for the service of a church at Standlynch, presumably then newly founded. The rector of Downton, with the approval of the archbishop of Canterbury and the bishops of Salisbury and Winchester, assigned the tithes arising from the fee of Robert Boiaceus, the 4 a. of land previously granted by Robert to the rector in exchange for the promise of a graveyard at Standlynch, and a house in Standlynch to support a priest. The chaplaincy did not become a benefice. Rectors appointed priests in consultation with Robert and his heirs. Rights of baptism and burial were also granted but the church remained a daughter church of Downton. To mark that fact the chaplain of Standlynch was each year to place ¼ mark on the altar of Downton church and Robert Boiaceus, when at Standlynch, was to attend Downton church twice a year.[43]

Those arrangements probably lasted until Downton church was appropriated.[44] When the vicarage was ordained the vicar was assigned all the small tithes of Standlynch and the duty of serving its church.[45] The great tithes of the land, then held by Thomas Meriet, were apparently reclaimed by the appropriators and the chaplain's land was resumed by Meriet.[46] The offering presumably lapsed. From 1383 residents of Standlynch therefore relied for services in their church on the vicar of Downton. At first the vicar appointed a stipendiary chaplain who was required to celebrate mass on Sundays, Wednesdays, and Fridays. In 1399, however, the chaplain was withdrawn.[47] Meriet complained to the bishop but, despite later charges to the vicar to provide services in his chapels,[48] it seems likely that

[19] V.C.H. Wilts. ii, pp. 150, 151, 161.
[20] C 134/20 no. 10.   [21] Winch. Coll. Mun. 4957.
[22] See above.   [23] C 1/1170/59.
[24] W.A.M. xxvi. 356; W.R.O. 924/1.
[25] See p. 58.   [26] See above.
[27] W.R.O. 924/1.   [28] See pp. 36–7.
[29] B.L. Map Libr., 'Surveys and Maps of Several Estates . . . in the Property of Hen. Dawkins'.
[30] W.R.O., Tithe Award.   [31] Ibid. 1008/27.
[32] Ex inf. Mr. D. Newton, Longford Estate Office.
[33] Turner and Coxe, Cal. Chart. Bodl. 586.
[34] Winch. Coll. Mun. 4934.

[35] W.R.O. 490/1198.   [36] See pp. 54–5, 77.
[37] W.R.O. 490/927; Country Life, 13 July 1945.
[38] O.S. Map 6", Wilts. LXXII (1885 edn.).
[39] B.L. Add. MS. 42777, ff. 143–4.
[40] Kelly's Dir. Wilts. (1907).
[41] W.R.O. 1008/27.
[42] Wilts. Cuttings, xxii. 183.
[43] Sar. Dioc. Regy., Reg. Mitford, ff. 153–4.
[44] There was no stipendiary chaplain 1382–3: Winch. Coll. Mun. 5363.
[45] Ibid. 4934.   [46] Ibid. 4957; 4953.
[47] Ibid. 4948.   [48] See p. 47.

services at Standlynch were subsequently neglected. The lack of them was probably why William Green, then lord of the manor, in 1543 challenged the impropriators, Winchester College, by withholding tithes.[49] The dispute which followed ended in a composition in 1549.[50] The tithes of Standlynch were commuted, the great tithes for an annual payment to the impropriators of £3 6s. 8d., converted to a statutory rent-charge in 1840,[51] the small tithes for an annual payment to the vicar of £1, a payment which had lapsed by 1839.[52] In exchange the vicar was freed from the duty of serving the church. The inhabitants of Standlynch were free to attend Downton church and Standlynch church was presumably closed.

In the early 17th century the lords of Standlynch manor were recusants,[53] and perhaps used the church for masses. In 1650 the parliamentary commissioners recommended that it be 'taken away and united' to Downton.[54] In 1677 Maurice Buckland, then lord of the manor, largely rebuilt the church,[55] but no provision was made to perpetuate services in it and it remained a private chapel for the lords of the manor. In the 19th century services were held in it by the private chaplain of Horatio, Earl Nelson (d. 1913), and residents of Charlton were admitted to public worship until Charlton church was built in 1851.[56] From 1913 to 1947 Thomas, Earl Nelson, used it as a private Roman Catholic chapel.[57] Since then it has remained closed.

The church is built of flint and ashlar, much of it set chequerwise, and has chancel, nave with north vestry, and south porch. In 1147 its dedication was to St. Mary,[58] but later, probably in 1914, it became the church of *MARY QUEEN OF ANGELS AND ST. MICHAEL AND ALL THE ANGELS*. Parts of the chancel and niches on each side of the chancel arch survive from the later Middle Ages. The nave appears to have been completely rebuilt in 1677 when it was given mullion and transom windows and a central doorway in a symmetrical north elevation and a bell-gable.[59] In the period 1859–66 it was again rebuilt in early-Gothic style to designs of William Butterfield,[60] and the chancel was remodelled to conform to it. The nave contains a standing monument to Thomas, Earl Nelson (d. 1835), designed in Gothic style by William Osmond.[61] There is a single bell cast in 1726.[62]

ROMAN CATHOLICISM. The Bucklands, lords of Standlynch manor from the late 16th century, were papists. Their lands were sequestered and the whole family and its servants were named as recusants c. 1629.[63] Walter Buckland (d. before 1677) received the Sacrament in 1641 but suspicion of his popery remained while he opposed Parliament in the Civil War, and in 1646 he was obliged to receive the Sacrament again.[64] His wife and his tenant at Standlynch remained papists.[65] Standlynch church was possibly used for masses but Walter's son Maurice seems to have conformed and in 1677 rebuilt the church.[66] Horatio, Earl Nelson (d. 1913), was a leader among the Church of England laity in 19th-century Wiltshire but in 1896 his wife became a Roman Catholic.[67] Their son Thomas was of his mother's faith and on his succession to the earldom in 1913 turned Standlynch church into a private Roman Catholic chapel served by a resident priest.[68]

WICK

THE regular boundaries of Wick tithing enclosed some 2,750 a.[69] In the early 13th century land was taken from the tithing for the creation of Downton borough.[70] The tithing contained a large area of the bishop of Winchester's demesne on which New Court was built probably c. 1418,[71] and the lands of Wick and Walton villages.[72] It was often called Wick and Walton tithing and from the later Middle Ages sometimes Wick and New Court tithing.[73]

The villages of Wick and Walton were established across the river from Downton. Their names, suggesting origins as respectively a centre of demesne dairy farming and a settlement for those working on the demesne,[74] imply that they were established from, and dependent on, Downton. They stood on twin sites on the valley gravel. Downton borough was built close to them,[75] and their sites have been used by buildings serving it. Long Close contains the old village of Wick and was called Wick in the early 19th century.[76] Long Close road was formerly Wick street.[77] The name Walton has been lost but the site of the village was almost certainly at Gravel Close where Walton close was mentioned in the later 17th century.[78] Although taken together for many manorial purposes, and linked with West Downton in 1408–9,[79] the villages remained distinct.

Walton was smaller than Wick. In 1334 its taxation assessment, although the lowest in the parish, equalled those of Bodenham and Standlynch. It declined in the later 14th century and in 1377 had only five poll-tax payers, the second lowest total in the county.[80] It afterwards lost its identity as a

[49] C 1/1170/59.   [50] Winch. Coll. Mun. 4949.
[51] W.R.O., Tithe Award.
[52] Ibid.   [53] See below.
[54] W.A.M. xl. 303.   [55] See below.
[56] Hoare, *Mod. Wilts.* Downton, 50; H.O. 129/263/2/2/3; *Church Bells*, 29 Apr. 1898.   [57] See below.
[58] Sar. Dioc. Regy., Reg. Mitford, ff. 153–4.
[59] J. Buckler, water-colour in W.A.S. Libr., vol. ii. 34 (1805); date on bldg.
[60] Pevsner, *Wilts.* (2nd edn.), 531.
[61] Ibid.   [62] Walters, *Wilts. Bells*, 203.
[63] W.N. & Q. viii. 344.   [64] W.A.M. xxiii. 331.
[65] Williams, *Cath. Recusancy* (Cath. Rec. Soc.), pp. 320–1.

[66] See above.
[67] V.C.H. Wilts. iii. 79; *Complete Peerage*, ix. 465–6.
[68] *Daily Mail*, 22 Nov. 1913; *Kelly's Dir. Wilts.* (1939).
[69] W.R.O., Tithe Award.
[70] B.L. Eg. MS. 2418, f. 63.
[71] See pp. 29, 35.   [72] See below.
[73] e.g. W.R.O. 490/779.
[74] P.N. Wilts. (E.P.N.S.), 25, 395; V.C.H. Wilts. i (2), 482.
[75] B.L. Eg. MS. 2418, ff. 62v.–63.
[76] W.R.O., Inclosure Award; Tithe Award.
[77] Ibid. 490/1083.   [78] Ibid. 490/897
[79] Winch. Coll. Mun. 5387.
[80] V.C.H. Wilts. iv. 299, 305, 308, 312.

village. Its name continued to be linked with that of Wick in the tithing name but was no longer applied to the settlement which survived at Gravel Close. Meadowside, a substantial house extended *c.* 1902[81] and linked with the Downton General Baptist chapel, was built there in the 18th century. Several cottages were there in the early 19th century including two of the 17th and 18th centuries, timber-framed and thatched, still standing. Two terraces of cottages were built in the 19th century and estate cottages built in 1952[82] took the settlement nearer to New Court.

Wick was more prosperous and populous. Its taxation assessment of 1334 and its 43 poll-tax payers in 1377 show it to have been of average size among the villages of the parish.[83] In the 18th century, following an inclosure of arable lands and changes in land-use,[84] new farmsteads were built below the scarp of the downs away from the borough and west of the Salisbury–Fordingbridge road, and that area was called Wick village in 1773.[85] The older settlement in Long Close declined. In the early 19th century there were cottages and two farm-steads there and at the crossing of the road from Long Close to Wick with the Salisbury–Fording-bridge road.[86] The house called Long Close was greatly enlarged in the late 19th century. Little besides that house and a few cottages of the 18th century and later remained in 1975. A 17th-century timber-framed and thatched cottage still stands in Wick Lane but the new Wick village apparently began with Wick (later Lower Wick) Farm built in 1732.[87] Middle Wick Farm and possibly a few smaller farmsteads and some cottages were there in 1773,[88] and a malt-house stood there in 1837.[89] The settlement grew in the 19th century and a farmstead, Upper Wick (later Botley's), was built on the downs before 1875.[90] Wick House, a substantial residence of red brick in mixed 17th- and 18th-century styles, was built in 1890 at the south end of the settlement.[91] In the 20th century Middle Wick Farm was replaced by a new farm-house, Wick Meadow Farm. Council houses were built at the Downton end of the village in the mid 20th century, and in the 1960s the gardens of Wick House, which reached to the Headlands of the borough, were built on.

Wick was a village of copyhold farmsteads[92] which, with New Court, made the tithing compara-tively wealthy in the 16th century and afterwards.[93] In 1841 the tithing housed 285 people.[94] In 1975 a line of east–west settlement, parallel to and north of Downton borough, could still be traced from Gravel Close through Long Close to Wick. Gravel Close and Long Close, however, had been absorbed topographically into Downton, and Wick, although a separate village, was hard pressed by the modern housing of Downton.

ESTATES. Wick tithing consisted of demesne and customary land of Downton manor. The demesne, *NEW COURT* farm, was leased by the bishop of Winchester in 1418.[95] It was held by a succession of farmers, but in 1581 the Crown secured a 61-year lease to run from 1594 and in 1592 the bishop granted the farm to the Crown at fee farm. Eliza-beth I granted it to Sir Thomas Gorges of Longford in Britford in 1592.[96] Sir Thomas was succeeded in 1610 by his son Sir Edward (created Baron Gorges of Dundalk in 1620) who was granted free warren and free fishing in 1618.[97] Gorges sold the farm *c.* 1651 to Sir Joseph Ashe (created a baronet in 1660),[98] who became lord farmer of Downton manor in 1662, and it passed with the lease of the lordship of the manor to the earls of Radnor.[99] A substantial allot-ment of land in Downton Franchise was made in respect of the farm in 1822.[1] In 1916 New Court farm was sold to R. G. Read but in 1928 bought back by Jacob, earl of Radnor. It remained part of the Longford estate in 1975.[2]

New Court Farm was built, probably *c.* 1680 by Sir Joseph Ashe, Bt., as a large T-shaped brick and stone house. Soon afterwards it was doubled to an H-plan.[3] The 17th-century aisled barn of nine bays is probably contemporary. Another farm building incorporates walls of an early-17th-century house.

The customary holdings, for which the rents and fines for admission were fixed by custom in the Middle Ages, were easily conveyed through the manor court. Such copyholds of inheritance were as valuable as freeholds. In the mid 16th century two substantial holdings belonged to William and Maurice Fursbye, probably father and son,[4] and in the 1580s passed to Maurice's son Thomas.[5] Between 1607 and 1628[6] the larger holding passed to Henry Johnson and he and his son Henry held it with other land until at least 1698.[7] It belonged to Francis Coles in 1709,[8] and afterwards passed like Moot farm in Downton[9] until in the early 19th century the Revd. C. W. Shuckburgh sold it to Jacob, earl of Radnor (d. 1828).[10] Wick (later Lower Wick and now Wick) farm has, except for a short period in the earlier 20th century, since passed with the Radnor title.[11]

Some of the Fursbyes' land was conveyed by Thomas Fursbye to John Ivie in 1621. In 1643 Ivie settled it on the marriage of John son of Hugh Ivie and Eleanor Pitman.[12] In 1672 Eleanor held it. In 1683 it passed to her youngest son George whose widow Elizabeth later held it.[13] In 1700 it belonged

[81] W.A.S. Libr., sale cat. xxvi, no. 19.
[82] Date on bldg.
[83] *V.C.H. Wilts.* iv. 299, 308.
[84] See below.
[85] *Andrews and Dury, Map* (W.R.S. viii), pl. 3.
[86] W.R.O., Inclosure Award; Tithe Award.
[87] Date on bldg.
[88] *Andrews and Dury, Map* (W.R.S. viii), pl. 3.
[89] W.R.O., Tithe Award.   [90] Ibid. 490/532.
[91] W.A.S. Libr., sale cat. xxiv, no. 14.
[92] See below.   [93] e.g. E 179/197/50.
[94] *V.C.H. Wilts.* iv. 347.
[95] H.R.O. Eccl. 2/159420, rot. 4d.
[96] C 66/1392 mm. 9–11.
[97] C 142/318 no. 180; C 66/2173 no. 6.

[98] W.R.O. 166/1, deed of Ashe.
[99] See p. 29.   [1] See p. 34.
[2] Ex inf. Mr. D. S. Chichester, Longford Estate Office.
[3] W.R.O. 490/936.
[4] Ibid. 490/800; *Taxation Lists* (W.R.S. x), 115.
[5] W.R.O. 490/535, copy.
[6] *Early-Stuart Tradesmen* (W.R.S. xv), p. 9; W.R.O. 490/783.
[7] W.R.O. 490/1174, rent roll.
[8] Ibid. 490/802.
[9] See p. 30.
[10] Hoare, *Mod. Wilts.* Downton, 58.
[11] Ex inf. Mr. D. Newton, Longford Estate Office.
[12] W.R.O. 490/535, copy.
[13] Ibid. 490/895.

to George's brother Thomas with reversion to their nephew James, son of James Ivie, rector of Ashmore (Dors.).[14] By 1709, however, it had passed to Francis Coles and was merged with his other land in Wick.[15]

In the mid 16th century substantial copyholds of inheritance belonged to John and Richard Overy, probably father and son.[16] They apparently passed to Alexander Overy (d. c. 1597), possibly Richard's son.[17] The Overys' lands were probably those held in 1628 by Edward, Baron Gorges,[18] which were probably, like New Court farm, sold c. 1651. At least some of them passed to Henry Johnson and were merged with his other land in Wick.[19]

In the later 16th century a fair-sized copyhold of inheritance belonged to Henry Gauntlett,[20] and in 1628 to Maurice Gauntlett, presumably his son.[21] Maurice (d. c. 1632) was succeeded by his son John[22] whose own son John was admitted to the holding in 1663.[23] The younger John (d. c. 1687) left a widow Mary,[24] who held until at least 1698,[25] and a son Henry.[26] In 1727 Henry's son Maurice was granted reversion,[27] but in 1747 the land apparently belonged to Henry's son John, of Whiteparish.[28] It passed to another Henry Gauntlett whose heir was his brother William. William devised it to his daughter Frances, wife of Christopher Hill Harris.[29] In 1778 the Harrises sold it to Christopher Lewis of New Court whose daughter Anne sold the land, Middle Wick farm, to trustees of William Eyre of Newhouse in 1810.[30] The farm passed with the Newhouse estate until c. 1920, since when it has been part of the Longford estate.[31] At various dates other copyholds were added to the Gauntletts' lands, in particular John Hayter's in 1723.[32]

A substantial copyhold of inheritance belonging to Thomas Randall in the mid 16th century was possibly the basis of the estate held c. 1780 by John Gibbs (d. 1788),[33] but several other copyholds of inheritance were also among its lands.[34] Gibbs's widow held them until c. 1793, another John Gibbs, presumably his son, from c. 1794 to c. 1804, James Bailey, possibly the younger Gibbs's son-in-law, from c. 1804 to c. 1822, and Bailey's widow Elizabeth from c. 1822 to c. 1831.[35] The Baileys' heir was their son John Gibbs Bailey,[36] who in 1851 sold to William Botley.[37] Upper Wick (later Botley's) farm was sold by Botley in 1875. Part was bought by Jacob, earl of Radnor, and added to the Longford estate. The house and most of the land, however, were bought by John Taunton (d. 1896).[38] Botley's farm was sold by the trustees of Taunton's will in 1911.[39] In 1975 it belonged to Brig. V. O. Lonsdale.

ECONOMIC HISTORY. Wick tithing included more than 3 km. of meadow land beside the Avon, a broad strip of valley gravel between the alluvium and the chalk escarpment, and some 7–8 sq. km. of down.[40] In the Middle Ages the valley gravel was divided between pasture, mostly east of the Salisbury–Fordingbridge road, and arable, mostly west of the road. Behind the escarpment some of the chalk was ploughed, leaving some 3 km. of sheep-runs. Those lands were shared between the demesne of Downton manor and customary holdings in Wick and Walton. In 1247–8 some 340 a. and in 1288–9 over 400 a. of demesne land were sown.[41] The area sown fell rapidly, to 254 a. in 1324–5 and to 170 a. in 1416–17.[42] In the 13th century the tenants of Wick and Walton apparently held less land than their lord. In 1211 the bishop paid them £5 15s. because their lands had been ravaged (gwarata), presumably by the bishop himself.[43] In the earlier 13th century some 16 virgates were shared among 33 tenants and there were twelve lesser tenants. Their rents totalled £6 7s. 6d.[44] The holdings and rents were increased in the 14th century[45] when probably some 100 a. of bourdland[46] were appended to them, and in 1383 the tenants apparently ploughed twice as much land as the lord.[47]

In 1418 the demesne was leased with the buildings at New Court presumably newly built.[48] Probably about that time the lands of the tithing were divided between the customary holdings of Wick, which were allotted the southern half, and New Court farm, which was allotted the northern half apparently including the customary holdings of Walton. Although expressly said to be so only in 1741[49] New Court farm was, apart from Hamptworth mead,[50] almost certainly several from then. Compared to the arable acreage of the farm, the meadows and lowland and upland pastures were unusually extensive. The meadow land extended from between Charlton and Standlynch villages to south of Downton borough on the opposite bank of the river to Old Court.[51] The remaining land lay north and west of New Court. The long and narrow farm, some 1,250 a.,[52] was ideally suited to sheep-and-corn husbandry. It was held of the bishop for £50 a year by a succession of farmers including, in the later 15th century and the early 16th, John Maple and William and John Irish and, in the early and mid 16th century, Vincent and William Juniper.[53] After 1592, however, the fee-farmers, who held from the bishops for £50,[54] sublet at much higher rents.[55]

14 W.R.O. 490/1082. 15 Ibid. 490/802.
16 Ibid. 490/800.
17 E 179/270/18; W.N. & Q. viii. 326.
18 W.R.O. 490/783.
19 Ibid. Inclosure Award.
20 e.g. Taxation Lists (W.R.S. x), 115; E 179/270/18.
21 W.R.O. 490/783. 22 Ibid. 166/1, copy.
23 Ibid. 906/W 45. 24 Ibid. 166/1, copies, 1686, 1688.
25 Ibid. 490/1174, rent rolls.
26 Ibid. 166/1, copy, 1705.
27 Ibid. 490/535, copy. 28 Ibid. 1030/5.
29 Ibid. 906/W 71; 130/16, will of Wm. Gauntlett.
30 Hoare, Mod. Wilts. Downton, 58.
31 Local information. 32 W.R.O. 906/W 59.
33 Ibid. 490/800; Land Tax.
34 Ibid. Inclosure Award.
35 Ibid. Land Tax; 490/531.
36 Ibid. 490/531. 37 Ibid. 490/531–2.
38 Ibid. 490/532.

39 W.A.S. Libr., sale cat. xxiv, no. 12.
40 W.R.O., Tithe Award.
41 H.R.O. Eccl. 2/159457, rott. 8–9; Eccl. 2/159311, rott. 4d.–6.
42 Titow, Eng. Rural Soc. 128–9; H.R.O. Eccl. 2/159419, rot. 4.
43 Pipe R. of the Bishopric of Winch. 1210–11, ed. N. R. Holt, 34.
44 B.L. Eg. MS. 2418, ff. 62v.–63.
45 H.R.O. Eccl. 2/159385, rot. 3d.; for rents see above, p. 36. 46 W.R.O. 490/800.
47 Winch. Coll. Mun. 4957.
48 H.R.O. Eccl. 2/159419, rot. 4.
49 W.R.O. 490/791. 50 See p. 61.
51 See below. 52 W.R.O., Tithe Award.
53 H.R.O. Eccl. 2/159444, rott. 2–3; Eccl. 2/159500/3; Eccl. 2/155648, ff. 30v.–35; Eccl. 2/155893; C 78/45 no. 1.
54 C 66/1392 mm. 9–11.
55 e.g. W.R.O. 490/793, Wapshare's val.

In 1665 Sir Joseph Ashe, Bt., secured acceptance of a scheme to drown the meadows in the northern part of the farm. A carriage was built to take water from the Avon at Charlton above Standlynch weir.[56] For their land crossed by the carriage the farmers of Charlton agreed to accept the use of the water on their own meadows or a rent calculated at £4 an acre.[57] In 1672 the water-meadow system was extended southwards. A new carriage was made c. 1 km. above Wild weir, joined the old carriage above New Court, and took water under Downton borough through the meadows of Wick to Landshire ditch on the parish boundary.[58] Some 150 a. of New Court meadows between the river and the carriages were improved. Some 74 a., from Charlton to New Court, remained part of the farm. The remainder, from New Court to the meadows of Wick south of the borough, were detached.[59]

In 1689 New Court farm, which formerly included a rabbit warren of 10 a.,[60] consisted of 76 a. of meadow, 129 a. of lowland pasture, mostly between the carriages and the Salisbury–Fordingbridge road, 346 a. of arable land, and 610 a. of down. About 1716 some 50 a. of lowland pasture and 40 a. of down were ploughed.[61] In 1741 the farm was said to carry 1,600 sheep and 50 cows.[62] In 1822 rights of feeding on Downton commons were replaced by an allotment of 125 a. but that was not added to the farm which in 1837 measured 1,183 a.[63] In the 19th and 20th centuries it has been worked as a mixed farm.

By 1712 the improved meadows south of New Court had been leased as Green farm with buildings south of Catherine bridge. Although totally dependent on an adequate water supply and at the end of a long water-meadow system the farm commanded a high rent. In 1780 it measured 83 a.[64] but by 1806 had been reduced to 49 a. south of the borough.[65] Its lands, the last in Downton to be watered, were flooded until the 1960s. In 1975 they were part of Wick Meadow farm.[66]

At least from 1418 the lands of Wick and Walton villages, some 1,500 a., all belonged to copyholds. Common cultivation prevailed. In the mid 16th century there were reckoned to be some 430 a. of arable in three fields.[67] There were some 27 a. of meadow land and 136 a. of inclosed lands, north and south of the borough and mostly east of the Salisbury–Fordingbridge road, including at least 18 a. then lately inclosed from the arable. The

farmers could feed 100 sheep to a yardland on the down, had rights of feeding and turbary in the New Forest, and shared a marsh, 40 a., in Wick.[68]

Before 1628, possibly c. 1600, most of the arable between the road and the escarpment, some 150 a., was inclosed.[69] A small area of the marsh, called the Moor, remained common,[70] and there remained three common fields on the chalk.[71] In 1628 there were some 27 tenants holding 4 farms of more than 50 a., 3 of 25–50 a., and 20 of fewer than 25 a. of which several were very small. Feeding rights for a total of 1,740 sheep on some 600 a. of down added much to the holdings.[72] In the 18th century farmsteads were built on the newly inclosed land and two of the three large farms which developed in the 17th and 18th centuries were based there.[73] The extension of the main water carriage from New Court to Landshire ditch in 1672 enabled Wick meadows to be watered. Before 1723,[74] perhaps c. 1700, some 200–300 a. of down were ploughed, in the northern half of Wick's land in New field adjoining New Court down, and in the southern half in Stanbury and Scotland fields as far west as the later site of Botley's Farm.[75] The newly tilled land was held by the tenants in pieces averaging 5 a., compared to 2–3 a. in the older fields,[76] and apparently remained commonable.[77] Some 372 a. of down pasture remained.[78]

Although the award was not enrolled until 1847[79] the lands of Wick had been inclosed by 1819 under an Act of 1816.[80] By that time most of the copyholds had been merged into three large farms, Lower and Middle Wick with farmsteads in the new village, and James Bailey's with buildings in the old village.[81] Under the award they were concentrated respectively in the north, south, and middle parts of the lands of Wick. After inclosure Lower Wick measured 784 a., Middle Wick 288 a., and Bailey's 232 a.[82] Between 1851 and 1875 a new farmstead, Upper Wick Farm (later Botley's) was built on the down. In 1875 85 a. of Botley's farm became part of Lower Wick farm.[83] In the 20th century much of the meadow and pasture lands of Lower and Middle Wick farms has been merged to make Wick Meadow farm; the arable lands of Middle Wick farm have been added to Lower Wick farm.[84] In 1975 Wick Meadow, partly worked from Long Close, was a solely pasture farm, and Wick (formerly Lower Wick), 540 a., was a primarily arable farm.[85] Botley's was an upland arable farm.

WITHERINGTON

THE early history of Witherington ran parallel with that of Standlynch.[86] Its lands, the subject of an early-11th-century grant by a bishop of Winchester,[87]

were possibly then coming into cultivation and being defined. At their eastern end the ridge running north-east from the summit of Standlynch and

[56] Ibid. 490/897.   [57] Ibid. 490/792, indenture.
[58] Ibid. 490/897; 490/903.
[59] Ibid. 490/787.   [60] Sta. Cha. 8/221/33.
[61] W.R.O. 490/788 (cf. 1689, 1709, 1716 surveys).
[62] Ibid. 490/791.
[63] Ibid. Inclosure Award; Tithe Award.
[64] Ibid. 490/793, Wapshare's val.
[65] Ibid. 490/779.   [66] Ex inf. Mr. Chichester.
[67] W.R.O. 490/800; 490/535, Fursbyes' copies.
[68] Ibid. 490/800.
[69] Cf. ibid.; 490/783; 490/535, Fursbyes' copies.
[70] Ibid. Inclosure Award.

[71] Ibid. 490/1079.   [72] Ibid. 490/783.
[73] Ibid. Tithe Award.   [74] Ibid. 906/W 59.
[75] Ibid. Inclosure Award; Tithe Award.
[76] Ibid. 490/1080.
[77] Ibid. 906/W 59; Inclosure Award.
[78] Ibid. 490/796.   [79] Ibid. Inclosure Award.
[80] Ibid. 490/796.   [81] Ibid. Tithe Award.
[82] Ibid. 490/796.   [83] Ibid. 490/531–2.
[84] Local information.
[85] Ex inf. Mr. Newton; local information.
[86] See p. 68.
[87] V.C.H. Wilts. ii, pp. 119, 163, 208.

Witherington downs divided Witherington from Privett copse. The village, first mentioned in 1086,[88] may have been developing at the time of the early-11th-century grant. Its site cannot be precisely located but Witherington Farm, standing on a narrow strip of valley gravel, presumably marks it. If so the belt of alluvium between the village and the river was c. 1 km. wide in places. Much of it, however, was granted with an estate in Charlton[89] where, west of the river, there is little alluvium, and from the later 14th century or the 15th was reckoned part of Charlton tithing.[90] The lands of Witherington were thus separated from the river and in the late 17th century marked off from those of Charlton to their west by a new water carriage laid straight between Alderbury and Standlynch.[91] Witherington Farm stood beside the road from Downton to Salisbury through Barford and Standlynch until 1685 when the road was diverted to higher ground to the east.[92] The old road through Witherington remains visible. The tithing was coincident with Witherington farm, some 628 a. in 1782.[93]

Witherington was the smallest and least populous tithing of Downton. In the 16th century it was sometimes counted with Church tithing,[94] and in 1837 with Charlton tithing.[95] It became part of Standlynch with Charlton All Saints parish in 1897.[96] In the 13th and 14th centuries the village, with less land than others in the Avon valley, was, like Standlynch, of below average population and wealth among the villages of the parish. Its taxation assessment was low in 1334 and there were 34 poll-tax payers in 1377.[97] In the 15th century the village was deserted. The people were said to have died or left,[98] and afterwards the tithing was rarely mentioned by name in taxation assessments. Witherington Farm remained and, apart from a pair of 19th-century cottages, those of the farm have since been the only domestic buildings in the tithing. The population was 14 in 1841.[99]

ESTATES. Land at Witherington assessed at 3 hides was alienated from the bishop of Winchester's Downton lands in the time of King Cnut, 1016–35.[1] In 1086 it was held by Edward whose father had held it in 1066.[2] By the 13th century, however, it had been reunited with Downton manor.[3]

From at least the later 15th century the demesne and customary lands, virtually the whole tithing, were leased by the bishops as a single farm, Witherington.[4] In 1533 the lease was held by Ivy-church Priory,[5] in 1638 by Philip, earl of Pembroke and Montgomery.[6] It passed with the Pembroke title and from 1662, when at the old rent it was a very favourable tenure for the lessee,[7] with the lease of the lordship of Downton manor.[8] In the 19th century leases were renewed under heavy fines.[9] In 1822 a substantial allotment of land in Downton Franchise was made in respect of the farm.[10] The reversion in fee was sold to Jacob, earl of Radnor, with the reversion in fee of the lordship of the manor in 1875.[11] Witherington farm passed with the Radnor title until 1944 when it was sold to E. S. Fleetwood. In 1975 it belonged to Mr. B. W. Gibbon.[12] Witherington Farm is a substantial brick farm-house of the 18th century.

A mill and a small estate in Witherington were held with their Charlton land by the Grimsteads in the 14th century,[13] and were conveyed with that land to William of Wykeham, bishop of Winchester, in 1393.[14] The estate apparently consisted mostly of meadow land by the Avon and was afterwards deemed part of Charlton tithing.[15]

ECONOMIC HISTORY. In 1086 there was 1 plough on the demesne and another was shared by 4 villeins, 5 *coscez*, and 3 bordars, but the land at Witherington was sufficient for 3 ploughs. There were 20 a. of meadow and 3 furlongs of woodland. The estate had been worth £3 and was then worth £4.[16]

As part of Downton manor Witherington may have been divided about equally between demesne and tenantry land when demesne farming was at its height in the early 13th century. There were demesne buildings and servants, and in 1247–8 some 84 a. of demesne land were sown.[17] There were seventeen tenants sharing 12 virgates and nine cottagers.[18] Demesne farming afterwards declined although in 1324–5, when 12 a. were sown, a shepherd kept the bishop's wethers at Witherington and there were still demesne buildings.[19] In the 15th century the number of tenants also fell and by 1453 the demesne and tenantry land, apart from the down, had been merged into a single farm and leased. The bishops seem to have retained the down for the demesne longer than the other lands, but by 1453 that too was sold annually and in 1487 was included in the lease of the remaining lands.[20] Witherington farm was then leased for 8½ marks and in the early 16th century for £9.[21] The rent paid to the bishop for the farm was not subsequently changed.[22] Ivychurch

[88] *P.N. Wilts.* (E.P.N.S.), 397.
[89] See below.
[90] B.L. Map Libr., 'Surveys and Maps of Several Estates . . . in the Property of Hen. Dawkins', map of Charlton (1779).
[91] See below.   [92] W.R.O. 490/1069.
[93] H.R.O. Eccl. 2/248947.
[94] *Taxation Lists* (W.R.S. x), 115–17; E 179/198/284.
[95] W.R.O., Tithe Award.
[96] *Kelly's Dir. Wilts.* (1907).
[97] *V.C.H. Wilts.* iv. 299, 308.
[98] H.R.O. Eccl. 2/159500/3.
[99] *V.C.H. Wilts.* iv. 347.
[1] Ibid. ii, pp. 119, 163, 208.
[2] Ibid. p. 163.
[3] Titow, *Eng. Rural Soc.* 106; B.L. Eg. MS. 2418, f. 62 and v.   [4] See below.
[5] H.R.O. Eccl. 2/155877.

[6] W.R.O. 490/232, lease, Pembroke to Goldstone.
[7] See p. 28.
[8] H.R.O. Eccl. 2/155643, pp. 242–6; see above, p. 29.
[9] H.R.O. Eccl. 2/248947.
[10] See p. 34.
[11] H.R.O. Eccl. 2/172546.
[12] Ex inf. Mr. D. Newton, Longford Estate Office.
[13] *Feet of F.* 1327–77 (W.R.S. xxix), p. 90; *Cal. Inq. p.m.* xiv, pp. 112–13.
[14] *Cal. Close*, 1392–6, 112.
[15] See above.
[16] *V.C.H. Wilts.* ii, p. 163.
[17] H.R.O. Eccl. 2/159457, rott. 8–9.
[18] B.L. Eg. MS. 2418, f. 62 and v.
[19] Titow, *Eng. Rural Soc.* 115–36.
[20] H.R.O. Eccl. 2/159444, rott. 2–3; Eccl. 2/159500/3.
[21] Ibid. Eccl. 2/159500/3; Eccl. 2/155858.
[22] e.g. ibid. Eccl. 2/248947 (1782).

Priory probably sub-let the farm,[23] but later some lessees, including John Gawen from at least 1555 to 1576,[24] seem to have occupied. From the later 16th century sub-leasing was usual.[25]

Sir Joseph Ashe, Bt., then lessee, matched his scheme for watering the meadows of New Court farm[26] with another for watering those of Witherington by taking water from the Avon in Alderbury. Agreements with other landowners were reached *c.* 1665 and the works completed by 1691.[27] A carriage took water from the river near Bodenham south-eastwards through Alderbury, eastwards along the Alderbury–Witherington boundary, southwards through Witherington, and back to the Avon at Standlynch. The meadows of Witherington were watered between that carriage and the carriage branching from it which marked the Witherington–Charlton boundary. In 1782 Witherington farm, some 628 a., included 39 a. of watered meadow, 26 a. of meadow and pasture, 328 a. of arable, and 223 a. of down pasture. It was held with its tithes from the lords farmer of Downton by Peter Rooke for rents totalling £368 a year.[28] The water-meadow lay between the two carriages, the lowland pasture between the farmstead and the new Downton–Alderbury road, and the arable between the road and the steeper slopes of the down, roughly delineated by the 76 m. contour.[29] Some 70 a. of land in the Franchise replaced feeding rights on Downton commons in 1822 but were not added to the farm.[30] Some 75 a. of the down were tilled in 1837.[31] In 1975 Witherington was a mixed farm.

MILLS. There was a mill paying 10s. at Withering-ton in 1086.[32] Later the bishop of Winchester had two mills there. In the early 13th century both seem to have been held freely.[33] One was mentioned again in 1383[34] but not thereafter. The other became part of the Charlton lands of the Grimsteads. It was presumably working in 1348 but was no longer standing in 1376.[35]

CHURCH. A church at Witherington was presumably standing and dependent on Downton church in 1147 when a priest of Witherington witnessed deeds providing for services at Standlynch church.[36] To support the priest serving it 1 virgate in Witherington was attached to the church, but it is not known who gave the land and when.[37] In 1382 the chaplain received a stipend, apparently in addition to the income from the land.[38] When Downton vicarage was ordained in 1383 the land was assigned to the vicar and services became his charge.[39] At least in the early 15th century no chaplain was maintained although the chapel was kept in repair.[40] In 1425 the bishop of Salisbury sequestrated the tithes of the chapelry and provided a stipendiary chaplain.[41] By 1426, however, the sequestration had been ended.[42] The vicar accepted his obligation to serve the church but, since no more is heard of it, he probably did not do so. Especially since the population of Witherington was much smaller in the 15th century than it had been in the 13th and 14th centuries[43] it seems likely that the church decayed and was abandoned, perhaps in the mid 15th century. The virgate was lost by the vicar.[44]

FONTHILL BISHOP

FONTHILL BISHOP is 22 km. east of Salisbury, one in a line of villages on the northern slopes of the Nadder valley.[45] The parish, 727 ha. (1,797 a.), is a rough oblong, 2.5 km. east to west and 3.5 km. north to south. At its south end the Nadder divides it from Fonthill Gifford and a well defined ridge is its boundary with Tisbury and Chilmark. Elsewhere the boundaries ignore relief. In the early 19th century that to the west with Berwick St. Leonard was straightened by exchanges confirmed in the Berwick St. Leonard inclosure award of 1840.[46]

Apart from an outcrop of Upper Greensand across the southern part in the form of the boundary ridge the parish lies wholly on chalk.[47] Its three highest points are at its north-west, north-east, and south-east corners, 213 m., 198 m., and 189 m.

respectively. The village is in the south-west corner on the young Nadder at 107 m., and from the other three corners the land slopes towards it in a series of ridges and dry valleys. Both the greensand ridge in the extreme south of the parish and clay-with-flints which overlies the chalk in the extreme north support woodland; Little Ridge wood in the south and Fonthill Bushes in the north are probably ancient woodland.[48] There was a warren in the north-west corner of the parish on land which was planted with trees between 1800 and 1838. South of the church land was taken in the early 19th century for part of Fonthill lake, the island in which is in Fonthill Bishop.[49] Land in that southern part of the parish was increasingly drawn into Fonthill park in Fonthill Gifford, Tisbury, and Chilmark and woods were

[23] *L. & P. Hen. VIII*, vi, p. 415.
[24] H.R.O. Eccl. 2/155893; *Taxation Lists* (W.R.S. x), 117.
[25] W.R.O. 490/232.   [26] See p. 75.
[27] W.R.O. 490/893; 490/897.
[28] H.R.O. Eccl. 2/248947; W.R.O. 490/793, Wapshare's val.   [29] W.R.O., Tithe Award.
[30] Ibid. Inclosure Award.
[31] Ibid. Tithe Award.
[32] *V.C.H. Wilts.* ii, p. 163.
[33] B.L. Eg. MS. 2418, f. 62.
[34] Winch. Coll. Mun. 4934.
[35] *Feet of F.* 1327–77 (W.R.S. xxix), p. 90; *Cal. Inq. p.m.* xiv, p. 113.
[36] Sar. Dioc. Regy., Reg. Mitford, ff. 153–4.

[37] Winch. Coll. Mun. 4934.
[38] Ibid. 5363.   [39] Ibid. 4934.
[40] See p. 47; Winch. Coll. Mun. 5407.
[41] Winch. Coll. Mun. 4952.
[42] Ibid. 4951.   [43] See above.
[44] Cf. Sar. Dioc. R.O., Glebe Terrier, 1677.
[45] This article was written in 1977. Maps used include O.S. Maps 1″, sheet 14 (1817 edn.), sheet 167 (1960 edn.); 1/50,000, sheet 184 (1974 edn.); 1/25,000 ST 93 (1958 edn.); 6″, Wilts. LXIV (1889 edn.).
[46] W.R.O. 135/32; Inclosure Award.
[47] Geol. Surv. Maps 1″, drift, sheet 298 (1950 edn.); 1/50,000, solid and drift, sheet 297 (1972 edn.).
[48] *Andrews and Dury, Map* (W.R.S. viii), pls. 4, 5.
[49] W.R.O. 135/32; Tithe Award.

grown in Fonthill clump and on other lands.[50] Meadow and pasture land lay near the river and the village, and the arable lands and upland pastures of the village lay on the chalk east and north of it between the parish's two wooded extremities.[51]

Early-14th-century taxation assessments indicate that Fonthill Bishop was of average wealth among its neighbours,[52] and there were 77 poll-tax payers in 1377.[53] The village was possibly relatively smaller in the later 16th century.[54] In 1801 the population was 194. It rose to 228 in 1821 but afterwards, and especially in the period 1881–1921, declined until it stood at 117 in 1931.[55] There were 123 inhabitants in 1971.[56]

Building throughout the parish has been predominantly in stone. Until the 19th century Fonthill Bishop was essentially a village of small farmsteads strung north to south along its street which was bisected near the church by the road from Willoughby Hedge in West Knoyle through Hindon to Barford St. Martin, Wilton, and Salisbury, turnpiked under an Act of 1761.[57] By 1800, when the line of the street remained well defined, there had been some cottage building west of the church.[58] In 1837 there was a malt-house in the street.[59] Later the form of the village changed. In the period 1881–1921 many of the buildings west of the church and in the street south of the road from Willoughby Hedge to Barford St. Martin were demolished,[60] and since then the growing importance of that road has encouraged settlement beside it. In 1977 no building earlier than 1800 stood south of the road although the line of the street was visible. The older buildings stand on the west side of the northern part of the street. They include two early-18th-century houses, one near the church and one later enlarged, a remodelled 17th-century house, and Baker's Farm. The focus of the village remained the crossing of street and road where the church, the old school, the old rectory-house, and principal farm-houses stand, but the buildings are not closely gathered. Behind the church is an early-19th-century farm-house enlarged in the later 19th century and on the south side of the road is a late-19th-century farm-house, a range of later-19th-century cottages of which the south end is dated 1864, and farm buildings dated 1887. The King's Arms, open as a public house in 1794,[61] and some 20th-century estate cottages and council houses stand by the road east of the crossing.

There has been little settlement in the parish away from the village. The New Inn in Chicklade Bottom beside the main London–Exeter road, turnpiked

under an Act of 1762,[62] was so called in 1773.[63] The building, which is of the later 18th century, afterwards became a farm-house.[64] Fonthill Lodge, a house on the downs used for inoculating and boarding sufferers from smallpox, was apparently in the parish. It was open from at least 1766 to 1773.[65]

MANOR AND OTHER ESTATES. Athelwulf's morning-gift to his wife Athelthryth was a 5-hide estate at Fonthill which in the late 9th century she sold to Oswulf. Helmstan later acquired it but, when accused of the theft of a belt, his right was disputed by Athelhelm. Helmstan proved his right but for help in doing so and for a life-lease granted the land to Ordlaf. In exchange for land elsewhere Ordlaf in 900 granted Fonthill, then said to be 10 hides, to Denewulf, bishop of Winchester.[66] The manor of FONTHILL passed with the see and was apparently not surrendered at the Reformation. There is similarly no evidence of sale by the parliamentary trustees in the Interregnum. The lordship of the manor was retained by the Ecclesiastical Commissioners after the land was sold.[67]

The demesne lands of the manor were leased to farmers from the early 15th century,[68] including in the 16th century Robert and Edward Mayo.[69] Edward's heir was his daughter Thomasine, wife of William Grove (d. 1582) who was lord of Ferne manor in Donhead St. Andrew.[70] The Groves were succeeded by their son William (d. 1622). About 1610 the lease was acquired like that of the demesne lands of East Knoyle manor by Henry Mervyn (knighted 1619), lord of the manor of Fonthill Gifford from 1611.[71] The lease was apparently sold with Fonthill Gifford to Mervyn's brother-in-law Mervyn Tuchet, earl of Castlehaven,[72] to whom a new lease was made in 1629.[73] Leases afterwards passed with the manor of Fonthill Gifford, in the earldom of Castlehaven until the 1630s, in the Cottington family until c. 1744, and in the Beckford family.[74] In 1822 a lease was sold with Fonthill Gifford by William Beckford (d. 1844) to John Farquhar to whom a new lease was made in 1825.[75]

About two-thirds of the parish were in freeholds and in copyholds[76] which, held under fines and for rents which were both fixed, from the 16th century began to assume the importance of freeholds.[77] In 1662 5 free and 24 customary tenants were named[78] and no estate grew large until the 18th century.[79] In 1459 Robert Hungerford, Lord Hungerford, died seised of a freehold which passed with the manor of

[50] Cf. W.R.O. 135/32; Tithe Award; O.S. Map 6", Wilts. LXIV (1889 edn.).
[51] W.R.O. 135/32.
[52] E 179/196/8; V.C.H. Wilts. iv. 300.
[53] V.C.H. Wilts. iv. 309.
[54] Taxation Lists (W.R.S. x), 159.
[55] V.C.H. Wilts. iv. 348.
[56] Census, 1971.
[57] W.R.O. 135/32; V.C.H. Wilts. iv. 270.
[58] W.R.O. 135/32.
[59] Ibid. Tithe Award.
[60] O.S. Maps 6", Wilts. LXIV (1889 edn.), LXIV. NE., NW. (1926 edn.); V.C.H. Wilts. iv. 348.
[61] H.R.O. Eccl. 2/159622.
[62] V.C.H. Wilts. iv. 270.
[63] Andrews and Dury, Map (W.R.S. viii), pl. 4.
[64] W.R.O., Tithe Award.
[65] V.C.H. Wilts. v. 322; Andrews and Dury, Map (W.R.S. viii), pl. 4.
[66] Eng. Hist. Doc. c. 500–1042, ed. Dorothy Whitelock, pp. 501–3; V.C.H. Wilts. ii, pp. 7–8; Finberg, Early Wessex Chart. pp. 33–4, 77, 81.
[67] Kelly's Dir. Wilts. (1907); see below.
[68] See below.
[69] H.R.O. Eccl. 2/155869; Eccl. 2/155892.
[70] Hoare, Mod. Wilts. Dunworth, pedigree facing p. 58.
[71] H.R.O. Eccl. 2/159475; Misc. Gen. et Her. n.s. i. 359; see below, p. 86.
[72] Misc. Gen. et Her. n.s. i. 359; H.R.O. Eccl. 2/159475.
[73] H.R.O. Eccl. 2/155642, pp. 54–5, 70–2.
[74] Ibid. Eccl. 2/153284; Hoare, Mod. Wilts. Dunworth, 15, 20–2.
[75] Hoare, Mod. Wilts. Dunworth, 26–7; H.R.O. Eccl. 2/155507, pp. 35–40.
[76] W.R.O., Tithe Award.
[77] e.g. ibid. Q. Sess. enrolled deeds, loose deed 8 (1796).
[78] H.R.O. Eccl. 1/100/4, ct. held 24 Sept.
[79] e.g. W.R.O., Land Tax add. (1740).

Fonthill Gifford to members of the Mervyn family,[80] and from 1611 with the lease of the demesne land of Fonthill Bishop.[81] The lords of Fonthill Gifford increased their holdings in Fonthill Bishop by purchases from George Barber and Joseph Bate, probably in the earlier 17th century.[82] From c. 1750 the Beckfords steadily bought up the remaining freeholds and copyholds.[83] In 1800 William Beckford's leasehold, freehold, and copyhold estate included nearly the whole parish and it was all sold to Farquhar.[84]

In 1826 Farquhar sold the lands north of the road from Willoughby Hedge to Barford St. Martin, Fonthill farm, to Henry King (d. 1844) of Chilmark and assigned the lands south of the road with Font-hill Abbey to his nephew George Mortimer.[85] Fonthill farm passed to King's son Frederick (d. 1893) who in 1860 bought from Bishop Sumner the freehold of the land held by lease.[86] The farm was sold by Frederick's son, the Revd. Frederick King, to Alfred Morrison in 1897 when the copyhold land was enfranchised.[87] Mortimer sold his land in 1829–30 to James Morrison (d. 1857) whose son Alfred (d. 1897) bought the freehold of the leased lands from the bishop in 1859.[88] From 1897 virtually the whole parish has passed in the Morrison family with Fonthill House in Fonthill Gifford and later with Little Ridge (Fonthill House) in Chilmark to Alfred's son Hugh (d. 1931) and grandson John Granville Morrison (created Baron Margadale 1964). It belonged to the Morrison estate in 1977.[89]

In 1744 the lands bought from Barber and Bate were sold by Francis Cottington to the tenant William Baker who already held copyhold of inheritance land.[90] Baker's substantial freehold and copyhold estate apparently passed to his son William (d. 1789),[91] and was the last in Fonthill Bishop to pass to the lord of Fonthill Gifford manor when in 1796 his grandson William Baker sold to William Beckford.[92] Baker's Farm is of the early 18th century.

ECONOMIC HISTORY. A field system of some 230 a. north of the London–Exeter road on Fonthill down indicates extensive prehistoric ploughing.[93] About 900 Fonthill was described both as 5 hides and 10 *manentes*.[94] In 1066 there were 10 hides. In 1086 there was land for 7 ploughs: 5 hides were in the bishop of Winchester's demesne on which there

were 2 ploughs and 5 serfs; 8 villeins and 5 bordars shared 3 ploughs. There were 8 a. of meadow, and pasture and woodland were each ½ league long and 3 furlongs broad. The estate was worth £14 having formerly been worth £10.[95]

In the Middle Ages the sheep-and-corn husbandry on the chalkland of the parish was in common. At least in the 13th and 14th centuries the arable lands of the bishops of Winchester's demesne farm and of the free and customary tenants were apparently intermingled in the common fields. The bishops' land, however, was possibly in complete furlongs and included the coomb below Little Ridge which was apparently several.[96] The bishops' and tenants' flocks possibly shared the same downs and at least in the 14th century there was a shepherd for the tenantry besides one for the demesne flock.[97] The bishops' demesne land was leased for a period ending in 1217. It was in hand in the periods 1217–19 and 1225–7 but otherwise leased for £28 a year until c. 1235.[98] When in hand in the 13th century over 200 a. were sometimes sown on the demesne and only in the 1290s were fewer than 150 a. sown.[99] In the early 14th century over 200 a. were still occasionally sown, but from the 1320s the area sown for the bishops gradually declined and from the 1340s fewer than 100 a. were normally sown.[1] Especially because the bishops' sheep farming at Fonthill was integrated with that of their other Wiltshire manors[2] the number of sheep kept varied greatly each year: for example, the number kept averaged nearly 400 in the 1270s, some 40 in the 1280s.[3] In the later 14th century the yearly average was c. 400.[4] In the early 13th century ewes were kept, later wethers.[5] In 1417 the demesne lands were leased with the tenants' rents and services for £20 a year.[6] In the 13th century the bishops, their customary tenants, and their free tenants possibly held equal proportions of the agricultural land. In the later Middle Ages the customary holdings probably grew. In 1376 they were 5 virgates, 21 ½-virgates, 1 ¼-virgate, and 4 smaller holdings.[7] There were probably c. 25 tenants then as later.[8] They held by Borough English for rents then totalling £5 3s. 8d. and labour services; clearly none had a very large holding.[9] Later evidence shows that some 10 virgates were held freely.[10]

In the 15th, 16th, and 17th centuries cultivation continued largely in common and regulations for it

[80] C 139/172 no. 17; Hoare, *Mod. Wilts.* Dunworth, 14–15, pedigree facing p. 20; H.R.O. Eccl. 2/415808.
[81] e.g. H.R.O. Eccl. 1/100/4, ct. held 24 Sept. 1662.
[82] W.R.O. 383/529, Cottington's deed of trust (1646).
[83] Ibid. Land Tax and add.
[84] Ibid. 135/32; Land Tax.
[85] Hoare, *Mod. Wilts.* Dunworth, 23–4; W.A.S. Libr., Benett–Stanford papers, draft hist.; W.R.O., Tithe Award.
[86] H.R.O. Eccl. 2/155513, pp. 410–15.
[87] Ex inf. Mr. A. B. Hayne, Fonthill Estate Office, Fonthill Bishop; Ch. Commrs., survey bk. DD 5, p. 617.
[88] W.A.S. Libr., Benett–Stanford papers, draft hist.; W.R.O., Land Tax; H.R.O. Eccl. 2/155513, pp. 399–405; Burke, *Land. Gent.* (1952), 1830.
[89] Ex inf. Mr. Hayne.
[90] W.R.O., Q. Sess. enrolled deeds, 79; Land Tax add.
[91] H.R.O. Eccl. 2/159622.
[92] W.R.O., Q. Sess. enrolled deeds, loose deed 8.
[93] *V.C.H. Wilts.* i (1), 276.
[94] Ibid. ii, p. 86.
[95] Ibid. pp. 119–20.
[96] e.g. H.R.O. Eccl. 2/159290, rot. 1 (1248–9); Eccl.

2/159327, rot. 4 and d. (1312–13); for the coomb cf. W.R.O., Tithe Award.
[97] e.g. H.R.O. Eccl. 2/159354, rot. 6d. (1343–4); Eccl. 2/159384, rott. 8d.–9 (1376–7).
[98] Ibid. Eccl. 2/159274, rot. 9d.; Eccl. 2/159278, rot. 5d.; J. Z. Titow, 'Land and Population on the Bishop of Winchester's Estates 1209–1350' (Camb. Univ. Ph.D. thesis, 1962), Table V.
[99] Titow, 'Land and Pop.', Table I.
[1] Ibid.; e.g. H.R.O. Eccl. 2/159384, rott. 8d.–9 (1376–7); Eccl. 2/159402, rott. 6d.–7 (1395–6).
[2] *V.C.H. Wilts.* iv. 19.
[3] Titow, 'Land and Pop.', Table IV.
[4] H.R.O. Eccl. 2/159384, rott. 8d.–9 (1376–7); Eccl. 2/159402, rott. 6d.–7 (1395–6).
[5] Ibid. Eccl. 2/159281, rot. 2 (1226–7); Eccl. 2/159290, rot. 1 (1248–9).
[6] Ibid. Eccl. 2/159421 (1419–20).
[7] Ibid. Eccl. 2/159384, rott. 8d.–9.
[8] Ibid.; Eccl. 1/100/4 (1662).
[9] Ibid. Eccl. 2/415808; Req. 2/397/100.
[10] H.R.O. Eccl. 2/415808.

were often recorded in the manor courts and tourns.[11] The stint of sheep at 60 to a virgate fixed in 1539 was generous.[12] The demesne apparently remained the only large farm. It included half the cut of two meadows totalling 8 a. in Stockton which was usually sub-let.[13] Fonthill farm, then held of the bishop for £22 12s. a year on leases paid for by substantial fines, was being sub-let for £126 a year in 1724.[14] None of the free or customary holdings seems to have been much enlarged and in the early 18th century the c. 26 tenanted virgates still seem to have been held by some fifteen tenants with farmsteads along the street.[15] The freehold which passed with the manor of Fonthill Gifford was possibly partly merged with the land of that manor since in 1539 John Mervyn, in drowning some of his holding, obscured the parish boundary.[16] In 1603–4 Sir James Mervyn was said to have unlawfully fished the Nadder in Fonthill Bishop and in 1722 Francis Cottington was denied the right to keep swans there.[17]

In the 18th century most cultivation in common and nearly all the smaller holdings were eliminated. There had been some inclosure near the village by 1744.[18] Thereafter the decrease in the number of farms, as Baker's farm grew and more of the freeholds and copyholds passed to the Beckfords,[19] made possible a larger inclosure. By an agreement which may have been c. 1760[20] the arable lands around the village were inclosed. Fonthill farm's land was concentrated north of the village in a single piece adjoining Berwick St. Leonard and extending nearly to the London–Exeter road, and east of the village between the road from Willoughby Hedge to Barford St. Martin and the northern ridge of the coomb. An area of land north of the village also extending to the London–Exeter road was allotted to freeholders and copyholders for several use.[21] At least from then but perhaps from before 1716[22] the upland pasture was divided between a westerly farm down and an easterly tenantry down. Fonthill farm was thus several, and a small farm was established on the northernmost of the new inclosures near the London–Exeter road.[23] For the remaining farms, of which there were perhaps seven or eight in 1780,[24] cultivation continued in common on the down and in four arable fields in the east part of the parish.[25] Common husbandry ceased after William Beckford bought Baker's farm in 1796, and after all the tenantry lands were merged in that farm and a small exchange was made with the rector.[26] By 1837, when there were 871 a. of arable in the parish, some 70 a. of downland pasture had been ploughed. The agricultural land south of the road from Willoughby Hedge to Barford St. Martin then made a farm of 266 a. with buildings in the southern part of the street. North of that road were Fonthill farm with buildings near the church and 502 a. of land in a strip beside the western parish boundary, Baker's farm with buildings at the north end of the street and 801 a. in the eastern half of the parish, and the upland farm of c. 55 a. beside the London–Exeter road. There were 231 a. of woodland.[27] Fonthill Bushes, in the north-east corner of the parish, had apparently been divided and allotted with the arable c. 1760.[28] Little Ridge wood, at the south end, was part of Fonthill park. After 1876 Baker's farm was merged in Fonthill farm, called Kingstead in 1886, and Baker's farm buildings were given up.[29] In 1977 about half the parish was in Kingstead farm and half in hand.[30]

MILL. There was a mill worth 5s. at Fonthill in 1086[31] and a customarily held mill in the Middle Ages,[32] both presumably driven by the Nadder. The mill was said to be ruined in 1539.[33] It was possibly restored and may have continued to work until the early 18th century.[34]

LOCAL GOVERNMENT. From the 13th century Fonthill Bishop was within the public jurisdiction exercised by the bishops of Winchester for their hundred or liberty of East Knoyle. Fonthill was a tithing of the hundred[35] and, although the bishops' profits of the tourn relating only to Fonthill were separately accounted for,[36] there is no reason to doubt that the Fonthill tithingman made presentments at the East Knoyle tourn long before 1464, the date of its first surviving separately enrolled record.[37] The bishops' liberties and the timing and procedure of the tourns are discussed elsewhere.[38] In the later 15th century and the 16th the tithingman of Fonthill presented offences similar to those presented by the tithingmen of Knoyle and Milton, mainly those of brewers and millers and sometimes affrays. From the late 17th to the mid 19th century public nuisances in Fonthill were presented in the annual tourns by the 'jury for the king', and manorial matters by the homage in the same way as those for the other places in the hundred.[39] Until a parish constable was appointed Fonthill was within the precinct of the single constable of Knoyle hundred.[40]

Separate manor courts for Fonthill were held by the bishops' bailiffs. In 1312–13 six were held, in 1343–4 nine, and in the later 14th century and the

---

[11] e.g. H.R.O. Eccl. 1/100/4.
[12] Ibid. Eccl. 1/79/23, ct. held 2 June.
[13] *Survey of Lands of Wm., First Earl of Pembroke*, ed. C. R. Straton (Roxburghe Club, 1909), i. 208; E 134/4 Anne Trin./5; E 134/5 & 6 Anne Hil./5.
[14] e.g. H.R.O. Eccl. 2/153284, nos. 3, 4 (1758); Eccl. 2/248953, p. 37.
[15] W.R.O., Land Tax add.
[16] H.R.O. Eccl. 1/79/23, ct. held 2 June.
[17] Ibid. Eccl. 1/144/1; Eccl. 2/159619.
[18] W.R.O., Q. Sess. enrolled deeds, 79.
[19] Ibid. Land Tax and add.
[20] Ibid. add.; in 1823 it was said to have been 'many years ago': H.R.O. Eccl. 2/248947.
[21] W.R.O. 135/32.
[22] H.R.O. Eccl. 2/159619.
[23] W.R.O. 135/32.
[24] Ibid. Land Tax.
[25] Ibid. 135/32.
[26] Ibid.
[27] Ibid. Tithe Award.
[28] Ibid. Land Tax add.
[29] Ibid.; O.S. Map 6″, Wilts. LXIV (1889 edn.).
[30] Ex inf. Mr. Hayne.
[31] *V.C.H. Wilts.* ii, p. 119.
[32] H.R.O. Eccl. 2/159274, rot. 9d. (1217–18); Eccl. 2/159384, rott. 8d.–9 (1376–7).
[33] Ibid. Eccl. 1/79/23, ct. held 24 Aug.
[34] W.R.O., Land Tax add.
[35] Cf. H.R.O. Eccl. 2/159290, rot. 1; J.I. 1/998 rot. 38.
[36] H.R.O. Eccl. 2/159290, rot. 1.
[37] Ibid. Eccl. 1/79/16.
[38] See pp. 93–4.
[39] Ct. rec. and presentment bks. in H.R.O. and W.R.O. 492/9; 492/33; 893/1–2.
[40] H.R.O. Eccl. 1/92/1–12.

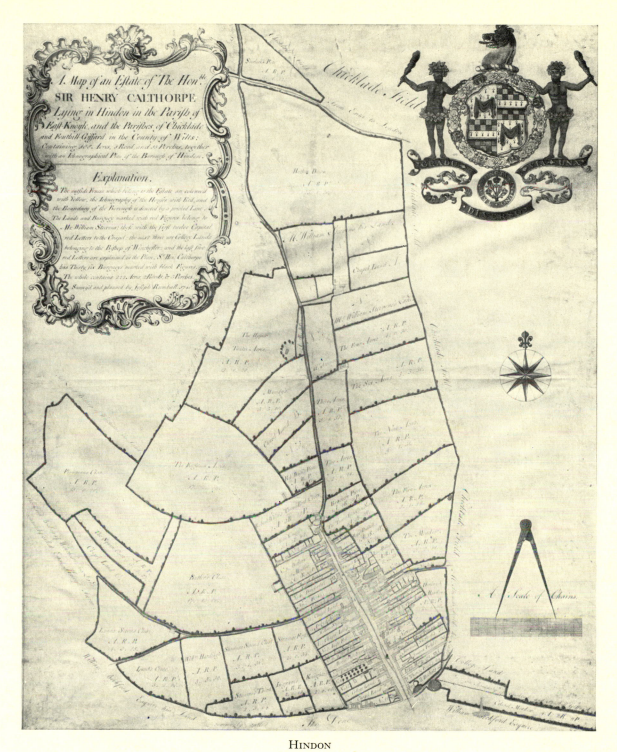

HINDON

Map of the borough and chapelry in 1748

BISHOPSTONE
The church of St. John the Baptist in 1805

HINDON
The church of St. John the Baptist in 1804

early 15th there were two a year.[41] In the early 16th century courts were again more numerous, and offences such as the keeping of unringed pigs, unlawful gaming, and harbouring of suspects, elsewhere normally presented at views of frankpledge, were sometimes dealt with in addition to the usual business of recording deaths of tenants, surrenders and admittances, the arrival of stray animals, and breaches of manorial custom. The Fonthill tithingman was elected at the courts at that time.[42] Fewer courts were held later and as at Knoyle manorial business was in the 17th century transferred to the annual tourn.

No record survives to illuminate parish government at Fonthill Bishop before the parish joined Tisbury poor-law union in 1835.[43]

CHURCH. A church was mentioned in 1242.[44] From 1914 to 1916 the rectory was held in plurality with the rectory of Berwick St. Leonard and in 1916 the benefices were united.[45] In 1966 the two parishes were united as the parish of Berwick St. Leonard with Fonthill Bishop.[46] From 1939 the benefice has been held by the rectors of Fonthill Gifford.[47]

The advowson of the rectory passed like the lordship of the manor with the see of Winchester.[48] Presentations were made by the king *sede vacante* in 1242 and 1243 and for reasons that are not clear in 1332.[49] The bishops' grantees presented in 1447 and 1566.[50] In 1852 the advowson was transferred to the bishop of Oxford, and in 1965 to the bishop of Salisbury.[51]

The living was valued at 10 marks in 1291, an average assessment for a Wiltshire parish.[52] Its true value was given as 25 marks.[53] In 1535 its net value was £10, in 1650 £60, and c. 1830 £246 net, values indicating a living of average wealth.[54] The rector was entitled to all tithes from the whole parish. They were valued at £259 in 1837 and commuted in 1839.[55] The glebe land in the arable fields was exchanged at inclosure for a field near the village.[56] In 1837 the glebe measured 4 a.[57] Part of the old house was incorporated in the east side of the new Rectory which was built in 1819[58] with a principal front of three wide bays to the south. The house was sold in 1961–2.[59]

In 1304 Richard Trenchefoil was presented to the church while an acolyte. He was licensed to study

for three years and was ordained priest in 1307.[60] Another acolyte, John de Madele, was presented in 1326.[61] In 1553 the homilies were given instead of sermons and there were still no sermons in 1585.[62] From 1620 to 1639 Christopher Wren, from 1623 rector of East Knoyle and later dean of Windsor, was rector.[63] At least in 1634 he employed a curate.[64] Robert Olding, presented in 1644, preached twice every Sunday. He subscribed to the *Concurrent Testimony* of 1648 but, suspected of royalism, had been deprived by 1655.[65] He was afterwards restored.[66] In 1783 the church was served by a curate who also served Fonthill Gifford and Berwick St. Leonard and lived at Chicklade. A single Sunday service and Communion services four times a year were held at Fonthill Bishop.[67] The curate served for at least 35 years.[68] In 1851 the church was served by a curate living in the Rectory,[69] but from 1858 to 1960 rectors were apparently resident.[70] In 1864 services with sermons were held twice every Sunday with congregations averaging c. 70 and the Sacrament was administered to some 33 communicants about ten times a year.[71]

The church of *ALL SAINTS* is built of rubble with ashlar dressings and has a chancel, central tower with transepts, and nave with south porch. There is no feature which can be ascribed with certainty to a period earlier than the 13th century, but the walls of the nave appear to be older than the crossing arch which may have been made into its eastern end. The chancel, although much rebuilt, retains a mid-13th-century character and the transepts were built later in that century. The only later addition is the 15th-century porch which was built when both doorways and the west window were renewed. The chancel was rebuilt in 1871[72] and the remainder of the fabric was extensively restored in 1879 under the direction of T. H. Wyatt.[73]

In 1553 there were two bells,[74] one of which, thought to date from c. 1320, remains in the church. In 1879 the second was replaced by a bell founded by Mears and Stainbank of Whitechapel and both were rehung.[75]

In 1553 a chalice weighing 6 oz. was left for the parish and 1 oz. of silver taken for the king. The old plate was replaced by chalice, paten, and flagon given in 1858. That set of plate and an additional paten belonged to the church in 1977.[76]

The registers of marriages date from 1754, of baptisms from 1769, and of burials from 1796.[77]

[41] H.R.O. Eccl. 2/159327, rot. 4 and d.; Eccl. 2/159354, rot. 6d.; Eccl. 2/159384, rott. 8d.–9; Eccl. 2/159436, rot. 3d.
[42] Ibid. Eccl. 1/79/23; W.R.O. 893/1.
[43] *Poor Law Com. 2nd Rep.* 560.
[44] *Cal. Pat. 1266–72*, 718.
[45] *Clergy List* (1915); *Crockford* (1926).
[46] *Lond. Gaz.* 25 Nov. 1966, p. 12829.   [47] *Crockford.*
[48] Phillipps, *Wilts. Inst.* (index in *W.A.M.* xxviii. 220).
[49] *Cal. Pat. 1266–72*, 718; *1232–47*, 358; *1330–4*, 256.
[50] Phillipps, *Wilts. Inst.* i. 138, 222.
[51] *Lond. Gaz.* 4 June 1852, p. 1580; 3 Dec. 1965, p. 11309.
[52] *Tax. Eccl.* (Rec. Com.), 181.
[53] *Reg. Pontoise* (Cant. & York Soc.), ii. 796.
[54] *Valor Eccl.* (Rec. Com.), ii. 106; *W.A.M.* xl. 303; *Rep. Com. Eccl. Revenues*, 834–5.
[55] W.R.O., Tithe Award.
[56] Ibid. 135/32.   [57] Ibid. Tithe Award.
[58] Sar. Dioc. R.O., Mortgages, no. 36.
[59] Ex inf. the rector, the Revd. J. Ellis, Fonthill Gifford Rectory.

[60] *Reg. Ghent* (Cant. & York Soc.), ii. 635, 870; *Reg. Woodlock* (Cant. & York Soc.), ii. 791.
[61] *Reg. Martival* (Cant. & York Soc.), i. 359.
[62] Sar. Dioc. R.O., Detecta Bks.
[63] Phillipps, *Wilts. Inst.* ii. 10, 19; see below, p. 95.
[64] *Subscription Bk. 1620–40* (W.R.S. xxxii), p. 53.
[65] *W.A.M.* xix. 190; xxxiv. 183; *Walker Revised*, ed. A. G. Matthews, 378.
[66] Phillipps, *Wilts. Inst.* ii. 36.
[67] *Vis. Queries, 1783* (W.R.S. xxvii), pp. 108–9.
[68] Ibid.; *Educ. of Poor Digest*, 1027.
[69] H.O. 129/266/3/4/6.
[70] Sar. Dioc. R.O., Vis. Queries, 1864; *Crockford.*
[71] Sar. Dioc. R.O., Vis Queries.
[72] *W.A.M.* xl. 166.
[73] Sar. Dioc. R.O., Pet. for Faculties, bdle. 27, no. 3.
[74] *W.A.M.* xii. 370.
[75] Walters, *Wilts. Bells*, 88.
[76] Nightingale, *Wilts. Plate*, 59; ex inf. the Revd. J. Ellis.
[77] Ex inf. the Revd. J. Ellis. Transcripts for several earlier periods are in Sar. Dioc. R.O.

The old register was said to have been accidentally burnt in 1759.[78]

NONCONFORMITY. There was no nonconformist in Fonthill Bishop in 1676.[79] There were a few papists in the later 18th century.[80] A house was registered for dissenters' meetings in 1819[81] but no chapel has been built.

EDUCATION. By a deed of 1787 Samuel Gattrell gave £350 for the teaching of sixteen poor children of the parish. The interest, £10 a year, was given to a schoolmistress who lived and taught in a house in the village.[82] In 1808 those taught were aged between four and eight,[83] and in 1833 the sixteen charity pupils were augmented by a few who paid.[84] An elementary school was built near the east end of the church probably in 1841 and the charity funds were used for its general expenses.[85] In 1858 from fifteen to twenty children were taught but older children went to school in Hindon.[86] A Scheme of 1905 required that the income from Gattrell's charity should be spent on bursaries for Fonthill Bishop children pursuing further education, or to buy books for the school library.[87] The school could hold 78 children but in 1906 the average attendance was only 33.[88] The average attendance reached 42 in 1927 but thereafter declined and in 1971 the school was closed.[89] In 1977 the income from Gattrell's foundation was being allowed to accumulate.[90]

CHARITY FOR THE POOR. In his lifetime Henry Spencer (d. 1811) gave 15s. at Christmas in sums of 1s. to the oldest parishioners. In 1832 Spencer's heirs gave £25 to perpetuate his practice. It is unlikely that distribution was frequent since by 1869 a sum of £47 had been accumulated. In 1906 the endowment was £46, the income from which was distributed to poor parishioners once in three years. In 1905 £3 3s. was given.[91] In the 1970s the charity fund was used occasionally to help aged parishioners in need.[92]

EAST KNOYLE

THE ancient parish of East Knoyle, c. 5,786 a. (2,341 ha.), included the chapelry of Hindon, 228 a. (92 ha.).[93] The parish, on a north-east to south-west axis some 27 km. west of Salisbury and 6 km. ESE. of Mere, was rectangular, some 6 km. long and 4 km. wide. In the 19th century Hindon was a civil parish.[94] Its history is related below under its own heading. In 1885 the southern portion of Pertwood parish was added to East Knoyle which was thus enlarged to 2,398 ha. (5,926 a.).[95]

In two places the parish boundaries were straight. The western boundary with West Knoyle, described in a mid-10th-century charter, was made along a stream and an ancient ditch,[96] and the northern with Pertwood ran along the top of a ridge. At the south end of the parish the boundaries with Sedgehill and Tisbury followed streams. The southeastern boundary across the grassland between Knoyle and Tisbury had been fixed by 984.[97] The boundaries enclose three types of classic Wiltshire scenery.[98] In the northern half of the parish chalk outcrops and there is the usual bare downland of ridges and dry valleys. The land slopes from west to east with the highest land over 213 m. near Willoughby Hedge in West Knoyle and over 205 m. on the north-western boundary with Kingston Deverill. An Upper Greensand ridge runs from north-east to south-west across the middle of the parish to include Cleeve hill, the twin peaks of Haddon hill, and Knoyle ridge, all over 213 m., and broadens to include Barn's (formerly Baldwin's)[99] and Windmill hills. The greensand is much eroded and the relief consequently hilly and complicated. Below it in the southern part of the parish Kimmeridge clay outcrops and the land is by comparison flat. Shaftesbury Lane marks a low watershed between the rivers Sem, flowing eastwards to the Nadder, and Lodden, flowing westwards to the Christchurch Stour. The spring line is at the junction of the greensand and clay and several small streams springing there drain the land which slopes gently southwards and to east and west, to 114 m. at Kinghay in the south-east corner of the parish and to below 91 m. in the south-west corner. Since its inclosure was completed in the mid 17th century[1] the land has been a patchwork of fields divided by hedges and ditches.[2]

Land-use in the Middle Ages was normal for such a parish lying across the geological outcrops: the arable was on the southern slopes of the chalk; the clay was predominantly pasture and, although no alluvium, there was presumably meadow land beside the streams; much of the greensand was pasture; and the northern chalk downs were extensive sheep pastures. Arable cultivation increased in the 17th and 18th centuries,[3] and by 1838 much of the down-

[78] Vis. Queries, 1783 (W.R.S. xxvii), p. 109.
[79] W.N. & Q. iii. 538.
[80] V.C.H. Wilts. iii. 96.
[81] Sar. Dioc. R.O., Return of Cert. Places.
[82] Endowed Char. Wilts. (S. Div.), 177–8.
[83] Lambeth MS. 1732.
[84] Endowed Char. Wilts. (S. Div.), 178.
[85] Acct. of Wilts. Schs. 24; Return of Non-Provided Schs. 18.   [86] Acct. of Wilts. Schs. 24.
[87] Endowed Char. Wilts. (S. Div.), 179–80.
[88] Return of Non-Provided Schs. 18.
[89] Bd. of Educ., List 21 (H.M.S.O.); ex inf. Chief Education Officer, County Hall, Trowbridge.
[90] Ex inf. the Revd. J. Ellis.
[91] Endowed Char. Wilts. (S. Div.), 177–9.

[92] Ex inf. the Revd. J. Ellis.
[93] This article was written in 1977. Maps used include O.S. Maps 1", sheet 15 (1811 edn.), sheet 166 (1959 edn.); 1/50,000, sheet 183 (1974 edn.), sheet 184 (1974 edn.); 1/25,000, ST 82 (1960 edn.), ST 83 (1957 edn.), ST 93 (1958 edn.); 6", Wilts. LVII (1889 edn.), LVIII (1889 edn.), LXIII (1890 edn.), LXIV (1889 edn.).
[94] See below.
[95] V.C.H. Wilts. viii. 58; Census, 1971.
[96] Arch. Jnl. lxxvii. 19–22.
[97] Ibid. 94.
[98] Geol. Surv. Map 1/50,000, solid and drift, sheet 297 (1972 edn.).
[99] W.R.O. 364/12 (1715).   [1] See pp. 92–3.
[2] See plate facing p. 49.   [3] See pp. 90, 93.

land and some of the clay had been tilled.[4] The chalk has remained under the plough but in 1977 the greensand and clay were predominantly pasture lands. There is no early record of extensive woodland in the parish. Knoyle answered at late-12th-century forest eyres and in 1228 the land west of Shaftesbury Lane was defined as part of Selwood forest. It was disafforested in 1330.[5] There was a 'Westwood' in the parish in the Middle Ages but its location is not certain.[6] In 1773 only Knoyle ridge and an area south of the church were wooded,[7] both part of the demesne land of East Knoyle manor.[8] Woods were planted in Summerleaze in the 19th century, and by 1838 a number of small woods had been grown, presumably for sport, in the south part of the parish.[9] More trees were planted in Clouds House park in the late 19th century and the centre of the parish had a well-wooded appearance in 1977.

The Roman road from Badbury (Dors.) towards Bath may have crossed the parish but its course is not clear.[10] The main road from Warminster to Shaftesbury (Dors.) runs from north to south across the parish. The southern part was laid straight at the mid-17th-century inclosure when on each side of it many paths, some of which have become roads, were defined and confirmed.[11] That southern section, Shaftesbury Lane, was turnpiked under an Act of 1753.[12] The northern section leading to Warminster was turnpiked under an Act of 1765.[13] The downs in the northern part of the parish are crossed by two east–west roads which converge a little beyond the parish boundary at Willoughby Hedge, the southern from Barford St. Martin, Wilton, and Salisbury, the northern from Amesbury. It is unlikely that before the 18th century either had more than local prominence. They were turnpiked under Acts of 1761 and 1762.[14] The southern was afterwards well used by coaches at least as far as Hindon, but in the 20th century, especially since 1936, has been surpassed in importance by the northern which, more direct and passing through fewer villages than the road through Salisbury and Shaftesbury, has been made part of the main London–Exeter road and improved.[15]

Few archaeological discoveries have been made in the parish but a hill-fort on Two Mile down indicates prehistoric settlement.[16] Later settlement was nucleated in valleys on the greensand at East Knoyle, Upton, and Milton, and further south dispersed on the clay. Knoyle, near the junction of the greensand and clay, was so called in the 10th century.[17] Upton, called 'Childecnoel' in 1201[18] and Upton in the mid 13th century,[19] and Milton (Middleton), so called in the mid 13th century,[20] presumably originated as hamlets dependent on Knoyle and in 1285 Upton was thus described.[21] There had been settlement on the clay east of Shaftesbury Lane by the mid 13th century and there

was more west of it after the mid-17th-century inclosure.[22] Only three farmsteads have been established on the chalk, two probably in the 18th century and the third in the mid 20th century.[23] Stone has been the predominant building material of the parish but from the late 18th century soft red bricks have been used, presumably those made at the brickyard which lay below Windmill hill near outcrops of both greensand and clay.[24] Taxation assessments of the early 14th century show the population of the parish to have been above average but not unusually dense.[25] There were 183 poll-tax payers in 1377, 146 in Knoyle and presumably Milton, and 37 in Upton.[26] The parish was apparently still of above average wealth in the 16th century, and in 1576 the second highest personal assessment in the county for the subsidy was of an East Knoyle man.[27] In 1801 the population was 853. It was over 1,000 from 1831 to 1871 but afterwards fell steadily. In 1841 East Knoyle had 541 inhabitants, Milton 358, and Upton 139. The population of the whole parish was 660 in 1931, 700 in 1971.[28]

East Knoyle has always been the largest village in the parish. It originated on higher ground west of the Warminster–Shaftesbury road where the chief messuage and demesne farmstead of East Knoyle manor and the church and rectory-house were built. The village did not develop on that site since most tenant farmsteads were established in the dependent villages. It grew in areas east of the church along the Warminster–Shaftesbury road, and west of the church at Holloway which was a settlement largely of customarily held cottages dependent on the rectory manor.[29] By the late 18th century the Warminster–Shaftesbury road had been built up on both sides for c. 800 m. from north of Knoyle House, around which it was forced to make a very sharp bend, past the Black Horse inn as far as the Benett (later Seymour) Arms, a 17th- or 18th-century building extended in the 19th century.[30] In the 19th and 20th centuries there has been ribbon development southwards along the road, especially on the east side. Holloway and the roadside settlement were not directly linked. A road led westwards from the Warminster–Shaftesbury road to the demesne farmstead which, west of the church, formed a rough square in which the road ended. Holloway was approached up a steep hill by a road leading northwards from the Warminster–Shaftesbury road and passing round the north of the church and farmstead.[31] That road was diverted to the south in 1804 when the rector enlarged the garden of his new house.[32] The demesne farmstead went out of use in the mid 19th century and in 1856 the road leading westwards from the Warminster–Shaftesbury road was extended through the farmstead to meet the southwards bulge of the diversion and thus lead to Holloway.[33] The tithe-barn near the church was

4 W.R.O., Tithe Award.
5 V.C.H. Wilts. iv. 414–15.
6 H.R.O. Eccl. 2/159343, rott. 5d.–7.
7 Andrews and Dury, Map (W.R.S. viii), pl. 4.
8 H.R.O. Eccl. 2/155514, pp. 11–39.
9 W.R.O., Tithe Award.   10 V.C.H. Wilts. i (1), 67.
11 H.R.O. Eccl. 2/159512/8.   12 V.C.H. Wilts. iv. 259.
13 Ibid. 257, 267.   14 Ibid. 262.
15 Ibid. 265.   16 Ibid. i (1), 67, 265.
17 Arch. Jnl. lxxvii. 94.   18 See p. 87.
19 B.L. Eg. MS. 2418, f. 67v.
20 Crown Pleas, 1249 (W.R.S. xvi), p. 114.

21 Cal. Chart. R. 1257–1300, 289.
22 See below.   23 See below; local information.
24 W.R.O., Tithe Award.
25 E 179/196/8; V.C.H. Wilts. iv. 300.
26 V.C.H. Wilts. iv. 309.
27 Taxation Lists (W.R.S. x), 44, 158–9.
28 V.C.H. Wilts. iv. 351; Census, 1971.
29 W.R.O., Tithe Award.
30 Ibid.; Andrews and Dury, Map (W.R.S. viii), pl. 4.
31 Andrews and Dury, Map (W.R.S. viii), pl. 4.
32 W.R.O. 536/13.
33 Wilts. Cuttings, xi. 24; see below, p. 90.

– – – Parish boundary

------ Township boundary

PERTWOOD

To the Deverills

To Warminster

Knoyle Down Fm.

To London via Amesbury

183

183

WILLOUGHBY HEDGE

To Exeter

TWO MILE DOWN

Hawking Down Fm.

To Chicklade

MILTON AND

UPTON DOWN

HINDON

183

CLEEVE HILL

Chapel Fm.

WEST KNOYLE

UPTON

Upton Fm.

Upton Knoyle Fm.

HADDON HILL

FONTHILL GIFFORD

MILTON

183

Sheephouse Fm.

THE GREEN

BARN'S HILL

Milton Fm.

183

183

WINDMILL HILL

Windmill

Clouds Ho.

CLOUDS PARK

Workhouse

KNOYLE RIDGE

UNDERHILL

KNOYLE HILL

Slades Ho.

N

Vernhill Fm.

Brickyard Fm.

Rectory

EAST KNOYLE

Knoyle Ho.

To Mere

122

Lugmarsh Fm.

Manor Fm.

HOLLOWAY

SUMMERLEAZE

Moor's Fm.

Little Leigh Fm.

Summerleaze Fm.

Friar's Hayes Fm.

122

New Leaze Fm.

Upper Leigh Fm.

Shaftesbury Lane

Blackhouse Fm.

KINGHAY

SEDGEHILL

Redhouse Fm.

Coleman's Fm.

Lower Leigh Fm.

TISBURY

To Shaftesbury

122

0   miles   1

0   km.   2

demolished in 1868 and a barn opposite the church on the south side of the road was burned down in 1961.[34] A farm building possibly of the 17th century, also on the south side of the road, has been converted to a dwelling-house. The hall of the 14th-century demesne farm-house,[35] on the north side of the road, was restored and became the parish room to which a larger room was added at the west end in 1908.[36] There are several 17th-century cottages near the centre of the village and at Holloway, and a few 18th-century cottages in various places. Slades House was built between Knoyle House and Clouds House before 1773[37] and was rebuilt in the later 19th century. Knoyle House, so prominent in the middle of the village, was demolished in 1954[38] leaving the village centre open. Few houses of architectural pretension remain in the village where in 1977 the buildings, most concentrated at the north end of Shaftesbury Lane, were mainly cottages, houses, and bungalows of the 19th and 20th centuries. By the late 18th century small settlements had established themselves north and south of Windmill hill at the Green, where there are two 17th-century cottages, and at Bath, later called Underhill.[39] That at the Green grew in the 19th century when the Fox and Hounds public house and a nonconformist chapel were opened,[40] and especially in the mid 20th century when some 25 council houses were built. That at Underhill has also grown in the 20th century and in 1977 the 20th-century houses outnumbered the 19th-century cottages, many of which have been enlarged in the 20th century.

The farmsteads on the clay in the southern part of the parish include buildings which range in date from the 14th century to the 20th century. Settlement was apparently earlier east than it was west of Shaftesbury Lane. At least some of the eastern farmsteads, but except in one case not their present buildings, originated in the Middle Ages.[41] Between Blackhouse Farm and Coleman's Farm a number of cottages was built on the verge in the early 19th century. Settlement began west of the road after the mid-17th-century inclosure,[42] but Redhouse Farm is the only house built then to have survived. Most of the buildings on the farms were erected or replaced at various times in the 19th century. Little Leigh is a substantial farm-house west of Holloway on the borders of the greensand and clay. It was built on a three-room plan probably in the period 1600–25 and retains many of its original fittings. Since 1945 there have been additions at the north end.

Milton was a village of tenant farmsteads in a street running in an arc down the valley between Haddon and Barn's hills. The street makes an elbow below Clouds House. Its lower north-east end is more thickly populated than its north-west end. There are 17th-century stone farm-houses at

both ends, and along the whole length of the street are many houses clearly of earlier origin than their earliest datable features which are generally derived from 18th- and 19th-century remodellings. The village includes a small stone house bearing the date 1734 and a mid-18th-century house of five bays at the north-east end, and an extensive range of now disused 19th-century farm buildings at the elbow of the street.

The smaller farmsteads of Upton village were strung along nearly 800 m. of a street between Upton Knoyle manor-house at the south end and Chapel Farm between Cleeve and Haddon hills at the north end. There were ponds in the street at the south end, where the road splits into two, and in the middle. Two wells are said to have been used for medicinal purposes.[43] The population of the village has never been great.[44] Since the late 19th century several buildings have been demolished and not replaced, and the population has presumably shrunk still further. Of the present buildings the two principal houses and between them Upton Farm, a 17th-century stone farm-house on a traditional three-room plan, were built before 1700. There is an 18th-century cottage towards the south end of the street but nearly every other building is of the 19th century.

MANORS AND OTHER ESTATES. In 1066 Aileva held East Knoyle. Later it was held by William FitzOsbern, earl of Hereford, and was presumably among the many English lands which William I granted to William for his part in the Conquest.[45] William FitzOsbern was succeeded by his son Roger de Breteuil in 1071. In 1075 Roger rebelled against William I and his lands were confiscated.[46] In 1086 East Knoyle was therefore the king's.[47] It was not afterwards mentioned among the lands of Roger's descendants,[48] and was possibly given by William II to Henry de Beaumont (d. 1119) after he was created earl of Warwick in 1088. The earldom passed to Henry's son Roger (d. 1153) and to Roger's son William (d. 1184).[49] Between 1174 and 1184 William sold the manor of *KNOYLE* to the see of Winchester.[50] After his death, however, his widow Maud claimed it from Bishop Ilchester as dower and at the will of Henry II it was assigned to her. To prevent it from passing at Maud's death to William's brother and heir Waleran, earl of Warwick, Bishop Lucy in 1200 claimed it from Waleran in the king's court.[51] In that year the bishop bought the reversion from the earl,[52] and by 1204 Maud had died.[53] The manor subsequently passed with the see and was not among the lands which Bishop Ponet was compelled to surrender to Edward VI in 1551.[54] In 1650 the trustees for the sale of bishops' lands sold it to the regicide Edmund Ludlow.[55] It had been restored by 1661 and again

[34] W.R.O. 536/10; pencil drawing in village hall.
[35] See below.   [36] Date on bldg.
[37] *Andrews and Dury, Map* (W.R.S. viii), pl. 4.
[38] See below.
[39] *Andrews and Dury, Map* (W.R.S. viii), pl. 4.
[40] O.S. Map 6″, Wilts. LXIII (1890 edn.).
[41] See pp. 89, 92.   [42] See pp. 92–3.
[43] *W.A.M.* lvi. 389.
[44] e.g. *V.C.H. Wilts.* iv. 309, 351.
[45] Ibid. ii, pp. 118–19; *Complete Peerage.*

[46] *Complete Peerage.*
[47] *V.C.H. Wilts.* ii, p. 118.
[48] For whom see *Complete Peerage*, s.v. Hereford, Leicester, Norfolk.
[49] *Complete Peerage*, s.v. Warwick.
[50] *Cur. Reg. R.* i. 240–1.   [51] Ibid.
[52] Ibid.; *Reg. Pontoise* (Cant. & York Soc.), ii. 739–40.
[53] *Complete Peerage*, s.v. Warwick.
[54] *Cal. Pat.* 1550–3, 178.
[55] C 54/3508 no. 32.

passed with the see.[56] Even after the land was sold[57] the lordship of the manor was retained by the Ecclesiastical Commissioners.[58]

From the 16th century copyholds of Knoyle manor, held under fines and for rents which were both fixed, began to assume the importance of freeholds.[59] Some were in Knoyle but most were in Milton.[60] None seems to have exceeded 100 a.[61] and their descents are not traced. In the 19th century most of such copyholds of inheritance were acquired by the Seymours.[62] The demesne lands of Knoyle manor and the right to receive the copyholders' rents, but not the right to hold courts, were leased to farmers until 1567 when Bishop Horne granted a 79-year lease from 1592 to Elizabeth I.[63] Before 1592 the queen assigned the lease to Thomas Mompesson of Corton who in 1604 assigned it to Sir Edward Bellingham.[64] About 1610 it was acquired like the lease of the demesne lands of Fonthill Bishop manor by Henry Mervyn (knighted 1619).[65] It passed with that lease and the manor of Fonthill Gifford to the earls of Castlehaven and by sale to Francis Cottington, Lord Cottington, who went into exile in 1646.[66] The lease was sequestered and from 1647 held by Sir Roger Palmer who in 1650 assigned it to Edmund Ludlow.[67] In 1661 Charles II assigned the remainder of the lease of Elizabeth I to Henry Hyde (styled Viscount Cornbury from that year)[68] who surrendered and obtained a new lease for lives from Bishop Duppa.[69] Cornbury was lessee until 1673 when Bishop Morley leased to Francis Morley, possibly his son.[70] Leases for lives, renewed for substantial fines, passed in the Morley family of Droxford (Hants),[71] and after 1782 to a relative Charles Ingoldsby Paulet (d. 1843), marquess of Winchester.[72] After 1843 the lease was acquired by the sub-lessee Henry Seymour (d. 1849) and his wife Jane and in 1852 a new lease was made to Jane and her son Alfred Seymour.[73] In 1862 Seymour bought the reversion in fee of those leased demesne lands, c. 2,023 a. comprising mainly Manor (then part of Park), Sheephouse, Knoyle Down, Friar's Hayes, and Summerleaze farms.[74] In 1877 he sold, with his other lands in Knoyle west of the Hindon–Shaftesbury road,[75] all but Sheephouse and Summerleaze farms which after his death in 1888 passed with Knoyle House and other lands east of that road to his daughter Jane Margaret (d. 1943).[76] They were sold in 1948.[77] In 1977 Summerleaze farm

belonged to the Clouds estate trustees.[78] The old farm-house lies at the northern edge of a group of 19th- and 20th-century farm buildings. It was replaced c. 1900 by a large house standing a short distance to the west. In 1948 Sheephouse farm was bought by Maj. F. H. Crawshay Bailey and in 1977 belonged to Mr. Neil Rimmington as part of the Fonthill Abbey estate.[79] Friar's Hayes farm passed with the Clouds estate[80] until 1919.[81] In 1977 it belonged to Mr. R. E. Drake.[82] Park and Knoyle Down farms also passed with the Clouds estate and were sold in 1936 to John Granville Morrison (created Baron Margadale 1964) of Fonthill House.[83] In 1977 Knoyle Down farm still belonged to the Morrison estate.[84] Knoyle Down Farm is of the early 19th century and has 20th-century additions. Near it are early-19th-century farm buildings of brick. Park farm was sold in 1971 to the Clouds estate trustees, the owners in 1977.[85] Park Farm occupies the site of the former parish workhouse.[86] The farm-house was apparently built in the mid 19th century.

In the 14th century the bishop of Winchester's chief messuage in Knoyle had a chapel within its confines.[87] The house was presumably occupied by the farmers of the demesne and from 1592 by the sub-lessees. The hall of a 14th-century house survives as a parish room. A photograph of the house before 1908 and before its restoration shows it to have had an upper floor entered through the present window. In 1740 a house, presumably substantial, beside the Warminster–Shaftesbury road was held freely by William Seymour, son of Sir Edward Seymour (d. 1741).[88] After William's death in 1747 the house, later called Knoyle House, passed to his brother Francis (d. 1761) and to Francis's son Henry (d. 1805) and grandson Henry Seymour (d. 1849) who built up the Seymour estate in the parish.[89] It was the manor-house occupied by Alfred Seymour and belonged to his daughter Jane until 1943.[90] After 1888 its lessees included Richard de Aquila Grosvenor, Lord Stalbridge, in 1889[91] and Beatrix, dowager countess of Pembroke (d. 1944), from 1914.[92] After the Second World War it was a home for elderly women.[93] It was demolished in 1954.[94] Photographs of the house show it to have been of various dates from the 17th to the 19th centuries.[95] In the later 19th century Alfred Seymour apparently planned to replace it by a new house on

56 H.R.O. Eccl. 2/159475.　57 See below.
58 H.R.O. Eccl. 2/155514, pp. 11–39.
59 Cf. Bishopstone, Downton: pp. 6, 28.
60 See below.　61 e.g. W.R.O., Tithe Award.
62 See below. Cf. W.R.O., Tithe Award; B.L. Map Libr., 'Partic. of Freehold at E. Knoyle', sale cat.
63 C 2/Jas. I/G 8/42.
64 Ibid.; C 2/Jas. I/G 5/2.
65 H.R.O. Eccl. 2/159475.
66 Ibid.; see above, p. 78; Complete Peerage.
67 E 134/13 Chas. II Mich./10.
68 Cal. S.P. Dom. 1660–1, p. 496; Complete Peerage, s.v. Clarendon.
69 H.R.O. Eccl. 2/155643, pp. 23–4.
70 Ibid. pp. 419–21; J. Foster, Alumni Oxon. 1500–1714, iii. 1033.
71 H.R.O. Eccl. 2/153287.
72 Ibid. Eccl. 2/155498, pp. 225–9; Complete Peerage.
73 H.R.O. Eccl. 2/155511, pp. 538–49; W.R.O., Tithe Award.
74 H.R.O. Eccl. 2/155514, pp. 11–39.
75 B.L. Map Libr., 'Partic. of Freehold', sale cat.; and see below.
76 Burke, Land. Gent. (1906), ii. 1509; see below.
77 Local information.
78 Ex inf. Mr. S. E. Scammell, Clouds Estate Office; see below.
79 Local information.　80 See below.
81 W.A.S. Libr., sale cat. xv, no. 6.
82 Local information.
83 W.A.S. Libr., Benett–Stanford papers, draft hist.; ex inf. Mr. A. B. Hayne, Estate Office, Fonthill Bishop.
84 Ex inf. Mr. Hayne.
85 Ex inf. Mr. Scammell; see below.
86 See below.
87 H.R.O. Eccl. 2/159343, rott. 5d.–7.
88 W.R.O., Land Tax add.; Burke, Peerage (1959), 2099.
89 W.A.M. xlix. 258; Andrews and Dury, Map (W.R.S. viii), pl. 4; Burke, Peerage (1959), 2099.
90 W.R.O. 186, game bk.; see above.
91 Wilts. Cuttings, i. 219.
92 W.R.O. 1265/51.
93 Local information.
94 Personal observation by Dr. R. B. Pugh and Miss Elizabeth Crittall.
95 Photographs in E. Knoyle par. room.

the site of the old Clouds House,[96] and drawings of a new house were made for him by Edward Blore.[97] The plan was abandoned presumably because of the financial difficulties which caused Seymour to sell the Clouds estate,[98] but the sale of the Clouds estate in 1877 made possible the reconstruction of Knoyle House in 1880. As rebuilt to designs of R. H. Carpenter and Benjamin Ingelow[99] the house extended some 60 m. along the south side of the Warminster–Shaftesbury road and had a garden front overlooking terraces to the south. It was raised a storey, a central hall and picture gallery were built on the site of an open courtyard, and a new staircase and a circular drawing-room were added. The style was mixed and the roof-line was broken by numerous gables and ornamental chimneys.[1]

Two other farms, New Leaze and Blackhouse, were part of the demesne of Knoyle manor and were held by leases from the bishops.[2] Blackhouse was sold to the tenant John Lambert in 1871.[3] At least from 1910 to 1947 it was like Lower Leigh farm part of the Pythouse estate.[4] Blackhouse Farm is an 18th-century stone house. In 1892 the Ecclesiastical Commissioners sold New Leaze to James Lush.[5] In the 20th century it has had a succession of different owners.[6]

In the 19th century Milton farm, consisting largely of copyhold of inheritance land in Milton,[7] grew substantially. It passed with the Seymour estate until 1877 and with the Clouds estate until 1936 but by then had been broken up.[8]

In 1086 Gilbert of Breteuil held 1 hide in Knoyle.[9] Other of Gilbert's lands passed to a Robert of Breteuil,[10] but it is not clear what happened to his estate at Knoyle. In 1201 Stanley Abbey bought lands at 'Childecnoel' from Michael son of Reynold of Knoyle, possibly Gilbert's Domesday estate.[11] In 1204 the abbey sold to Godfrey de Lucy, bishop of Winchester.[12] In the same year Bishop Lucy gave the land, later called the manor of UPTON or Chapel farm, to the prior and convent of St. Swithun for his anniversary.[13] The Old Minster held the manor until 1284 when, as part of the composition of that year between the prior and the bishop, it was returned to the bishop.[14] Together with but separate from[15] Knoyle manor it subsequently passed with the see and, as in the case of Knoyle, the Ecclesiastical Commissioners retained the lordship of the manor after the land was sold.[16]

Like those of Knoyle manor the copyholds of inheritance of Upton manor, none of which had grown to considerable size by 1800,[17] were bought up by the Seymours in the 19th century.[18] The demesne lands of Upton manor, Chapel farm, and the right to receive the copyholders' rents were leased to farmers.[19] In the earlier 17th century they were leased to George Mervyn, and a George Mervyn held them until 1669.[20] Leases for lives for substantial fines were made to Robert Compton of Mere (from 1669),[21] Elizabeth Buck, the sister of Sir James Howe, Bt., of Berwick St. Leonard (from 1698), and Robert Lock (fl. c. 1730) and his widow Susanna (from 1738).[22] In 1754 a lease was made to Edmund Ashby who was succeeded by his son George (d. 1808), president of St. John's College, Cambridge, and by George's amanuensis Thomas Lyas.[23] In 1832 the lease was acquired by Henry Seymour whose son Alfred in 1862 bought the reversion in fee of the lands held by it.[24] Chapel farm thereafter passed like Park farm.[25] The oldest part of Chapel Farm is the short range three storeys high at its southern end which is probably of the later 16th century. It was extended to the west in the 17th century and to the north in the 18th century, when kitchens were built at ground level to replace those in the basement of the old house. A chapel, possibly built close to the house for a Mervyn, was mentioned in 1610.[26] It gave its name to the farm but no later reference to it is known.

In the early 13th century Osbert Baldwin held land assessed at 2 hides.[27] It was presumably the land in Upton which Thomas Baldwin held in the later 13th century and in 1306 sold to Walter Scudamore.[28] That land, later called the manor of UPTON KNOYLE, seems to have passed in the Scudamore family like the manor of Upton Scudamore.[29] In the later 14th century and the early 15th John Chitterne was apparently buying land in various places, possibly to settle on the marriage of his sister Agnes and William Milbourne,[30] and his purchases probably included Upton Knoyle of which he died seised.[31] The manor passed to the Milbournes and to their son Richard, grandson Simon, great-grandson Sir Thomas (d. c. 1492),[32] and great-great-grandson Henry (d. 1519) whose son Richard Milbourne died without issue in 1532.[33] The Milbournes' lands were then disputed by Henry's widow Margaret, formerly wife of Anthony Ernle and then wife of Roger Yorke, William Fauconer, grandson of Sir Thomas's sister Agnes, and Joan Brooke and Margaret Halswell,

---

[96] See below.
[97] B.L. Add. MS. 42028, ff. 19–21.
[98] See below.   [99] See plate facing p. 32.
[1] Bernard Falk, *Naughty Seymours*, 253 n.; photographs in E. Knoyle par. room.
[2] H.R.O. Eccl. 2/155642–4; Eccl. 2/155498–515; see below, pp. 92–3.   [3] Ch. Commrs. file 44170.
[4] W.R.O. 636/11; see below.
[5] Ch. Commrs., survey bk. DD 5, p. 634.
[6] Local information.
[7] W.R.O., Tithe Award.
[8] B.L. Map Libr., 'Partic. of Freehold', sale cat.; sale cat. 1936 *penes* Mr. Scammell.
[9] *V.C.H. Wilts.* ii, pp. 118–19, 210.
[10] *V.C.H. Berks.* iv. 461.
[11] *Pipe R.* 1201 (P.R.S. n.s. xiv), 83–4.
[12] C.P. 25(1)/250/3 no. 1.
[13] *Chartulary Winch. Cath.* ed. A. W. Goodman, pp. 7, 45–6. For the identification cf. C.P. 25(1)/250/10 no. 53; B.L. Eg. MS. 2418, f. 68; H.R.O. Eccl. 2/155643, pp. 94–5.
[14] *Reg. Pontoise* (Cant. & York Soc.), ii. 430–1.

[15] e.g. H.R.O. Eccl. 2/155648 (1503).
[16] Ibid. Eccl. 2/155514, pp. 11–39; see below.
[17] W.R.O., Inclosure Award.
[18] Cf. ibid.; Tithe Award; B.L. Map Libr., 'Partic. of Freehold', sale cat.
[19] See below.
[20] C 54/3508 no. 32; H.R.O. Eccl. 2/155933; Eccl. 2/155643, pp. 94–5, 447–8. His or their relationship to the Mervyns who owned Upton Knoyle (see below) is not clear.
[21] H.R.O. Eccl. 2/155643, pp. 447–8.
[22] Ibid. Eccl. 2/153308; Eccl. 2/248954.
[23] Ibid. Eccl. 2/153308–12; *D.N.B.*
[24] H.R.O. Eccl. 2/153313–14; Eccl. 2/155514, pp. 11–39.
[25] See above.   [26] H.R.O. Eccl. 1/92/12.
[27] B.L. Eg. MS. 2418, f. 66v.
[28] *Feet of F.* 1272–1327 (W.R.S. i), pp. 22, 57.
[29] *V.C.H. Wilts.* viii. 81; e.g. E 179/196/8 (1332).
[30] *V.C.H. Hants.* iv. 327; *V.C.H. Wilts.* vii. 201.
[31] C 1/748/50.
[32] C 1/797/20–4; *Cal. Inq. p.m. Hen. VII*, i, p. 356.
[33] C 142/34 no. 58; C 142/57 no. 6.

descendants of John Chitterne's sister Christine.[34] A Chancery decree of 1538 settled them on Margaret Yorke for life with remainder to Fauconer.[35] In 1539, however, those two settled Upton Knoyle on Richard Milbourne's widow Edith, wife of Edward Twinyhoe, for her life.[36] In 1544 Fauconer conveyed his interest to Robert Titherley,[37] husband of Margaret Yorke's daughter Elizabeth Ernle,[38] who apparently occupied the manor,[39] and in 1556 the Twinyhoes conveyed their interest to Robert.[40] In 1576 Robert's son William sold to John Mervyn of Pertwood.[41] The manor passed in the Mervyn family, apparently with Pertwood manor, to Thomas (d.s.p. 1622–3) and George, the sons of John Mervyn (d. 1601), and to George's son John (fl. 1670) who sold to his brother Richard (d. 1669), chancellor of Exeter cathedral.[42] Richard was succeeded by his sons George (d. c. 1680) and John of Bratton Clovelly (Devon), on whose marriage the manor was settled in 1690. John (d. 1729) had a son John (d. unmarried) but his heir was probably his grand-nephew John who was presumably the John Mervyn who in 1750 sold the manor to Nicholas Williams.[43] The manor passed to Charles Williams (d. 1806) and to Charles's son William Mead alias Williams (d. c. 1814) and grandson Charles William Mead (d. 1826). Mead's heir was his son Charles who died a minor in 1829 leaving as heir his uncle James Charles Williams who immediately sold to Henry Seymour.[44] The land subsequently passed with Seymour's manor of Upton and became part of Chapel farm.[45] A substantial manor-house was built in the late 16th century, presumably for a Mervyn. It had a main range of two rooms with a short cross-wing at its north end and another, possibly service, range abutting the centre of the east side. The house, called Upton Manor, has been added to only in the mid 20th century when kitchens and bathrooms were built in the north-east angle.

In the early 13th century 14 virgates of Knoyle manor in East Knoyle and Milton were held freely.[46] Their descents cannot be traced but it was presumably from those lands that five freeholds which became substantial had emerged by the 16th century.

An estate in Milton occupied by John Cloud and later called the manor of *CLOUDS* was sold by John Stephens of Portsmouth in 1551, apparently to a trustee of Robert Goldsborough (d. 1581).[47] In 1577 Robert settled it on his son John (d. c. 1585).[48] John was succeeded by his son Robert (fl. 1610) and Robert's son Augustin who compounded in 1648.[49] In 1658 Augustin sold the estate to William Coker

of Frampton (Dors.) who in 1672 sold it to Nathaniel Still (d. 1701).[50] It was gradually increased as it descended in the Still family to Nathaniel's son Robert (d. 1728), grandson James (d. 1803), and great-grandson James Charles Still (d. 1828), whose executors sold it to Henry Seymour.[51] The estate passed with Seymour's land in East Knoyle and his two manors in Upton to his son Alfred.[52] When in 1876 the western part of the Seymour estate was offered for sale without Knoyle House prospective purchasers were invited to regard the land of Clouds, on which Seymour had apparently intended to build a new house for himself, as a new focus.[53] Seymour's lands mainly west of the Hindon–Shaftesbury road were bought in 1877 by the Hon. Percy Scawen Wyndham (d. 1911).[54] They included Park (formerly Manor), Knoyle Down, and Friar's Hayes farms, the manors of Upton and Upton Knoyle,[55] and the manor of Clouds, and were afterwards called the Clouds estate. They passed to Wyndham's son the Rt. Hon. George Wyndham (d. 1913) and to his grandsons Percy Lyulph Wyndham (d. 1914) and Guy Richard Charles Wyndham, who in 1919 and 1936 sold the estate which was largely broken up.[56] By 1977 a new Clouds estate, consisting of Clouds House and several farms in the parish, had been built up by Mr. S. E. Scammell and placed in the hands of trustees.[57] A new house was built on his estate by Robert Goldsborough (d. 1581). That was apparently replaced in the 18th or early 19th century by the small house with a garden front of three bays which was demolished in 1881.[58] A new Clouds House was designed for Percy Wyndham by Philip Webb, built near the site of its predecessor by the Gloucester firm of Estcourt, and completed in 1883 at a cost of £100,000. In 1889 a serious fire caused damage which cost £40,000 to repair.[59] Webb's design was in a distinctive style which incorporated elements from the 14th century to the 18th.[60] The main block, mostly of stone, was arranged round a central covered courtyard which acted as a hall and gave access by closed first-floor galleries to the bedrooms. The south elevation of six bays beneath three gables was symmetrical but the east and west elevations had irregularly placed square and canted bays. To the north a service range extended eastwards to meet lower brick outbuildings. North-west of the house near the Green an extensive walled kitchen-garden was laid out. In the early 20th century Arthur Balfour was a frequent visitor to the house.[61] In 1936 the house was sold to speculators who resold to Percy Houghton-Brown.[62] In 1938 it

[34] C 1/748/50; C 1/786/50–3; C 1/797/18–24; C 1/900/3.
[35] C 1/797/21.
[36] C.P. 25(2)/52/374/31 Hen. VIII Trin. no. 13; *V.C.H. Wilts.* vii. 202.
[37] C.P. 25(2)/46/323/36 Hen. VIII Mich. no. 52.
[38] W. Berry, *Hants Pedigrees*, 273.
[39] Sar. Dioc. R.O., Detecta Bk. 1550.
[40] C.P. 25(2)/81/694/2 & 3 Ph. & M. Trin. no. 19.
[41] C.P. 25(2)/239/18 & 19 Eliz. I Mich.; H.R.O. Eccl. 1/87/9.
[42] *V.C.H. Wilts.* viii. 59; Hoare, *Mod. Wilts.* Mere, 180; W. R. Drake, *Fasciculus Mervinensis* (Lond. priv. print. 1873), 47, app. iii.
[43] W.R.O. 1126/12, sched. of deeds; W. R. Drake, *Devonshire Notes and Notelets* (Lond. priv. print. 1888), 21.   [44] W.R.O. 1126/12, abstr. of title.
[45] Ibid. Tithe Award; see above.
[46] B.L. Eg. MS. 2418, f. 66v.
[47] W.R.O. 212B/3623–5; *W.A.M.* li. 391.

[48] W.R.O. 212B/3625; *W.A.M.* li. 390, 391.
[49] H.R.O. Eccl. 1/92/12; *W.A.M.* li. 391; *Cal. Cttee. for Compounding*, i, p. 78.
[50] W.R.O. 212B/3638–9.
[51] *W.A.M.* li. 393; W.R.O., Land Tax.
[52] See above.
[53] B.L. Map Libr., 'Partic. of Freehold', sale cat.; see above.
[54] Letter dated 2 June 1908 from P. S. Wyndham *penes* General Ed. *V.C.H.*   [55] See above.
[56] *W.A.M.* xxxvii. 167; xxxviii. 123, 647; W.A.S. Libr., sale cat. xv, no. 6; Benett–Stanford papers, draft hist.; ex inf. Mr. A. B. Hayne, Estate Office, Fonthill Bishop.
[57] Ex inf. Mr. Scammell, Clouds Estate Office.
[58] W.R.O. 212B/3625; B.L. Map Libr., 'Partic. of Freehold', sale cat.; W.A.S. Libr., Benett–Stanford papers, photographs.   [59] Wilts. Cuttings, i. 219.
[60] See plate facing p. 144.   [61] *W.A.M.* xli. 73–4.
[62] W.A.S. Libr., Benett–Stanford papers, draft hist.

was 'georgianized' and greatly reduced in size by the removal of all but the basement of the service range, most of the bays on the east and west fronts, and the gables and tall chimneys of the roof.[63] A mezzanine floor was inserted into the northern part of the main block and the hall was partly filled in and redecorated in the Italian quattrocento style. The house was later used as a home by the Church of England Children's Society. In 1963 it was sold to the Clouds estate trustees,[64] and in 1977 was used as a school for some 50 maladjusted boys with a staff of eight teachers.[65]

From at least the early 13th century a freehold passed in the Sturge family.[66] Richard Sturge (d. 1504–5) presumably held it. His heir was his daughter Elizabeth, wife of John Horsey (d. 1531).[67] The Horseys held it in 1525.[68] They apparently settled their land in East Knoyle, *LEIGH* or Upper Leigh farm, on their younger son Jasper and in 1544 their elder son Sir John quitclaimed to Jasper.[69] In 1554–5 Jasper's son George sold the farm and his lands in Milton and Upton to Corpus Christi College, Oxford, whose president was then rector of East Knoyle.[70] In 1875 the college sold the estate to Alfred Seymour.[71] The lands in Milton and Upton were among Seymour's lands sold in 1877.[72] They passed with the Clouds estate and in 1977 most were parts respectively of Holden's and Chapel farms.[73] Upper Leigh farm passed with Knoyle House[74] and was sold in 1948 to W. H. Burton. In 1977 it belonged to Mr. E. H. Burton.[75] Upper Leigh Farm contains a long range probably built in two stages in the 17th century. A stair turret was built in the second stage during which some of the upper rooms were heightened. A new parlour wing was added beyond the stairs in 1891.[76] North-west of the house the farm buildings include a timber-framed granary on staddle-stones and a medieval barn with buttressed stone walls and a cruck-framed roof of five bays.[77]

A freehold in the south-east corner of the parish later called *LOWER LEIGH* farm belonged in 1535 to the chantry of Compton Pauncefoot (Som.).[78] It passed to the Crown at the Dissolution and in 1545 was granted to John Whitehorn and John Bailey who immediately granted it to William Hunton (d. c. 1581).[79] The land passed to Hunton's son Thomas (d. 1631) and to Thomas's son James (fl. 1639).[80] Its later descent is not clear. It was possibly the land, sequestered from Francis Toope in 1645, which was bought from the Treason Trustees by Matthew Davies in 1653. That land was being claimed in 1653

by Toope, Davies, and Robert Moore who claimed to be Toope's mortgagee.[81] The result of those claims and the subsequent descent of Lower Leigh are unknown. In 1750 the farm belonged to Richard Jackson, rector of Donhead St. Mary, after whose death in 1796 it passed to his successor at Donhead Gilbert Jackson (d. 1816).[82] It was held by Gilbert's widow until c. 1822 and then passed, presumably by sale, to George Fort of Alderbury.[83] About 1870 Vere Fane-Benett-Stanford of Pythouse in Tisbury acquired the land which passed like Pythouse to his son John Montagu Fane-Benett-Stanford (d. 1947).[84] In 1977 Lower Leigh farm belonged to Cdr. J. M. Child.[85] Lower Leigh Farm, formerly the farm-house of an adjacent copyhold,[86] is a house of 18th-century origin with additions, including a new west front of c. 1840, of several dates in the 19th century.

In the early 13th century John Coleman held 2 virgates freely.[87] In 1412 his land belonged to Sir Walter Hungerford.[88] It passed like the manor of Rushall until 1474 when *COLEMAN'S* was settled on Margaret, Baroness Botreaux (d. 1478).[89] The descent of the land is afterwards obscure. It belonged to Nicholas Bacon (fl. 1591) and was held by his widow Elizabeth until her death c. 1609. Elizabeth's heir was her daughter Joan, wife of William Noyes.[90] She died seised in 1622 when the land passed to her son William who presumably sold it.[91] In 1636 Christopher Benett died seised.[92] He had a son Thomas but the descent of Coleman's is again not clear. In the mid 18th century it belonged to William Coles (d. 1784) and passed with Moot farm in Downton until 1796 when Henry Spencer bought out the interests of John Greene and the Revd. Charles William Shuckburgh.[93] About 1810 the land passed, presumably by sale, to Peter, brother of James Still of Clouds.[94] It was acquired by Henry Seymour c. 1828,[95] and passed with Knoyle House to his son Alfred who in 1876 conveyed it to Vere Fane-Benett-Stanford in an exchange of lands.[96] It was added to and until 1947 remained part of Lower Leigh farm.[97]

In 1734 *REDHOUSE* farm was bought from a Mr. Coward by Wilton Free School. The school held it until 1880 when it was sold,[98] apparently to Alfred Seymour. It passed with Knoyle House until 1948.[99] By 1977 it had been broken up.[1] Redhouse Farm is a 17th-century house.

ECONOMIC HISTORY. The existence of field systems on Two Mile down and near Hindon

[63] Pevsner, *Wilts.* (2nd edn.), 232.
[64] Wilts. Cuttings, xxii. 223; ex inf. Mr. Scammell.
[65] Ex inf. Mr. A. S. Newbegin, Acting Headmaster.
[66] B.L. Eg. MS. 2418, f. 66v.
[67] J. Hutchins, *Dors.* iv. 367, 427.
[68] C.C.C., Oxf., Mun., deeds, LA 29, p. 104.
[69] C.P. 40/1123 Carte rot. 17d.
[70] C.C.C., Oxf., Mun., deeds, LA 29, pp. 108–90.
[71] Ibid. lease bk. 1874–84, pp. 100–3.
[72] B.L. Map Libr., 'Partic. of Freehold', sale cat.
[73] Local information; see p. 91.   [74] See above.
[75] Ex inf. Mr. Burton, Upper Leigh Farm.
[76] Date on bldg.   [77] See plate facing p. 209.
[78] *Valor Eccl.* (Rec. Com.), i. 152.
[79] *Cal. Pat.* 1547–8, 278, 287–8.
[80] *Wilts. Pedigrees* (Harl. Soc. cv, cvi), 95–6; E 159/478 Communia Trin. rot. 12.
[81] *Cal. Cttee. for Compounding*, i, p. 77; iv. 3111–12.
[82] C.C.C., Oxf., Mun., 533, maps 23–4; Hoare, *Mod.*

Wilts. Dunworth, 198.
[83] W.R.O., Land Tax.
[84] Ibid. add.; Burke, *Land. Gent.* (1906), ii. 1569.
[85] Ex inf. Cdr. Child, Lower Leigh Farm.
[86] W.R.O., Tithe Award.
[87] B.L. Eg. MS. 2418, f. 66v.
[88] *Feud. Aids*, vi. 530; cf. *Cal. Close*, 1454–61, 441.
[89] *V.C.H. Wilts.* x. 139; C.P. 25(1)/257/65 no. 31.
[90] H.R.O. Eccl. 1/92/11, ct. held Martinmas 7 Jas. I.
[91] *Wilts. Inq. p.m.* 1625–49 (Index Libr.), 124–6; cf. *V.C.H. Wilts.* x. 165.
[92] *Wilts. Inq. p.m.* 1625–49 (Index Libr.), 349–50.
[93] W.R.O., Land Tax add.; Q. Sess. enrolled deeds, loose deed 7; see above, p. 30.
[94] W.R.O., Land Tax.   [95] Ibid.
[96] Ibid. 186, newspaper cutting.
[97] Ibid. 636/11; see above.
[98] *Endowed Char. Wilts.* (S. Div.), 851, 871–2.
[99] W.R.O. 1265/54.   [1] Local information.

indicates early ploughing on the downs.[2] The northern half of East Knoyle, however, was part of the Wiltshire chalk country where sheep-and-corn husbandry predominated from at least the Middle Ages until the 19th century. In that period the northernmost of the downs in the parish were mainly pasture, and the arable lay on the chalk nearer the villages. The southern part of the parish, Knoyle common, was part of the small Wiltshire butter country. It was apparently pasture in 984 and has since remained largely so.[3]

In 1086 Knoyle was assessed at 30 hides. The king's demesne, on which there were 5 ploughs and 10 serfs, was reckoned 17½ hides; Gilbert of Breteuil's hide was worth 7s. 6d. and had on it 3 bordars; and the remaining hides were held by 16 villeins, 10 bordars, and 18 *coscez* who shared 10 ploughs. Those figures possibly show a large demesne farm already relying on the tenants for its cultivation. The whole estate had been worth £28 and was then worth £30. There were 15 a. of meadow, pasture 1 league long and ½ league wide, and woodland ½ league square.[4] The Domesday figures presumably refer to the whole ancient parish in which in the early 13th century there were the bishop of Winchester's demesne lands, 2 hides, 14 virgates, and some smallholdings held freely, 16 virgates, 16 ½-virgates, and various smallholdings held customarily, and the manor of Upton.[5]

In the 12th century, when cultivation at East Knoyle was presumably expanding, the manor was passing from royal to episcopal through noble possession and the hand of lordship was possibly light.[6] That may have resulted in the three significant features of the parish's agrarian history. There emerged in the parish before 1300 four separate systems of common fields and pastures, those of Knoyle, Hindon, Upton, and Milton.[7] Hindon is dealt with elsewhere.[8] The several agrarian units, each with its own rules of common husbandry, presumably developed as more land was used and boundaries between the villages' lands were defined. Its large amount of land held freely also made Knoyle remarkable among the bishop of Winchester's manors.[9] The 12th century is a likely time for the freeholds to have been created and may also have been the time when a few farms established themselves on Knoyle common. The farms, later called Upper Leigh, Lower Leigh, and Coleman's, were apparently there before 1250.[10] Their tenure of Knoyle manor was perhaps no more than a mark of dependence made for licence to inclose and build on the common. The definition of each village's lands which took place in the northern half of the parish was, however, not mirrored in the southern half, and Knoyle was remarkable thirdly for the fact that intercommoning among the men of the three villages continued on the common until the mid 17th century. The remainder of this section deals in turn with agriculture in each of the three townships and afterwards with the common.

The township of Knoyle contained the bishop of Winchester's demesne lands and some free and customary holdings. In 1208–9 some 360 a. were sown for the bishop. That was an average figure for the period 1209–80 when the area sown was only occasionally over 500 a. or under 300 a.[11] From those figures it is clear that most of the chalkland on the east side of the parish was then episcopal demesne. Less land was sown for the bishops after 1280 but never fewer than 200 a. before 1349;[12] in 1377–8 196 a. were sown.[13] If fully used labour services from the sixteen virgaters and seventeen ½-virgaters, who all held by Borough English, were almost certainly sufficient for the entire cultivation of the demesne.[14] The downs in the northern part made East Knoyle one of the bishops' most important sheep farms. The men of Upton and Milton had correspondingly small sheep pastures.[15] More than 1,000 sheep were kept in 1208 and numbers over 2,000 were not uncommon in the 13th and occasional in the 14th century, totals well above average for the episcopal estate.[16] At the same time dairy farming on the lowland was also important.[17]

In 1405 the demesne, including large areas of upland and lowland pasture and some 200 a. of arable land, was leased with the rents, but not the fines, of the tenants for £80 a year.[18] It had been taken back in hand by 1438 but leased again by 1451.[19] There is no evidence for the Middle Ages or later that the demesne lands on the chalk were commonable. From at least 1512 to 1581 Richard and William Hunton were farmers.[20] In the early 17th century the demesne was sub-let to Robert Toope.[21] By 1650 it had been split into four main farms:[22] the principal farmstead with c. 90 a. of pasture, 200 a. of arable land, and a large area of down, all later called Manor farm, Friar's Hayes and Summerleaze farms,[23] and the down, at the north end of the parish, which had been for wethers and was later called Knoyle Down farm. Later Sheephouse farm was established on the down of Manor farm. In 1782 Manor farm measured 170 a., including 88 a. of woodland, Sheephouse 761 a., half arable and half pasture, and Knoyle Down 467 a., presumably partly arable.[24] In the early 19th century Manor farm, which until then had been worked from buildings beside the church, was merged with Clouds farm (see below) and worked from the buildings near Clouds and Slades Houses.[25] The buildings near the church were afterwards given up.[26]

[2] V.C.H. Wilts. i (1), pp. 265, 275.
[3] Arch. Jnl. lxxvii. 94.
[4] V.C.H. Wilts. ii, pp. 118–19.
[5] B.L. Eg. MS. 2418, ff. 66–8.
[6] See above.
[7] The separation of Upton is implied in B.L. Eg. MS. 2418, ff. 67v.–68; of Milton in Tropenell Cart. ed. J. S. Davies, ii, p. 1.
[8] See p. 100.
[9] B.L. Eg. MS. 2418.
[10] See above.
[11] J. Z. Titow, 'Land and Population on the Bishop of Winchester's Estates 1209–1350' (Camb. Univ. Ph.D. thesis, 1962), Table I.
[12] Ibid.
[13] H.R.O. Eccl. 2/159385, rot. 5d.

[14] B.L. Eg. MS. 2418, ff. 66–8; H.R.O. Eccl. 2/159384, rott. 7d.–8d.; Eccl. 2/415808.
[15] See below.
[16] Titow, 'Land and Pop.', 48–9, Table IV.
[17] e.g. H.R.O. Eccl. 2/159275, rot. 7d. (1218–19).
[18] Ibid. Eccl. 2/159417, rot. 5.
[19] Ibid. Eccl. 2/159435, rott. 3d.–4d.; Eccl. 2/159444, rot. 3.
[20] Ibid. Eccl. 2/155860; Eccl. 2/155915.
[21] W.R.O. 753/1, ff. 189–92.
[22] C 54/3508 no. 32.   [23] See below.
[24] H.R.O. Eccl. 2/248947.   [25] W.R.O., Tithe Award.
[26] B.L. Map Libr., 'Partic. of Freehold at E. Knoyle', sale cat.

After 1838 Sheephouse farm was split between Manor and Knoyle Down farms, respectively 448 a. and 834 a. in 1852.[27] By 1876 a new farmstead on the workhouse site had been erected for Manor farm which was renamed Park.[28] After 1876 Sheephouse again became a farm, 139 a. in 1940.[29] In 1977 Park was a mixed farm of c. 450 a., Knoyle Down a largely arable farm of c. 700 a., and Sheephouse a farm of c. 150 a.[30]

It is not clear how many of the bishop's free and customary tenants held in Knoyle township in the early 13th century. Several holdings had been taken into demesne,[31] but some presumably passed back to tenants in the later Middle Ages. In 1513 rents from customary tenants in Knoyle were £19 18s. 9d., from free tenants £5 17s.,[32] and in the early 17th century there were eleven freeholders and thirteen copyholders in the tithing.[33] All those totals included holdings on Knoyle common.[34] Holdings on the chalk and greensand near the village seem to have been very small. In 1662 and 1736 the east, north, and west fields of Knoyle were mentioned.[35] Their location is not certain but they probably lay near East Knoyle village on the chalk west of the road to Hindon.[36] In 1780, when Henry Seymour apparently held most among seven tenants, they were inclosed by private agreement.[37] The land was part of several small farms in 1838,[38] and has since been taken mainly into Park farm. The tenants' common pastures for sheep and cattle, Windmill hill, Knoyle hill, and Shaftesbury Lane, were not inclosed in 1780.[39] The wide verge formerly on the east side of Shaftesbury Lane was built on in the 19th century, but Knoyle hill, 8 a., and Windmill hill, 34 a., remained common. In 1955 the Church Commissioners conveyed the lord of the manor's rights in the lands to the parish council.[40]

The township of Milton contained the lands of the rector and of customary and free tenants of Knoyle manor. Its fields were clearly worked in common in the later 13th century.[41] Later evidence shows them to have been on the chalk north and north-east of the village, over 400 a.[42] In 1671 there were three fields.[43] The common pastures were on Haddon hill and on downland near the road from Willoughby Hedge to Barford St. Martin. There was probably no boundary between those pastures and those of the men of Upton in the same places.[44] In the 16th century and later the rector and two of the principal freeholders had several downs,[45] but it is not clear when those downs were separated from the down of the customary tenants and small freeholders which remained common. The lands around

Barn's hill were inclosed pastures.[46] In 1705 the rector held 73 a. in the fields and 30 a. of down,[47] in 1750 Corpus Christi College held 50 a. in the fields, 10 a. of inclosed pasture, and 18 a. of down.[48] In 1513 rents from customary tenants totalled £8 9s., those from free tenants 1 mark;[49] there were five freeholders and thirteen copyholders in the early 17th century when the amount of land held by each class probably corresponded roughly to their numbers.[50] In 1558 those tenants assigned their common down, 30 a., to the farmer of the demesne of East Knoyle manor who exchanged it with the lessee of the parsonage for the rector's down. Despite requests to the farmer and rector and legal action they had not recovered it by 1594 but presumably did so later.[51]

In 1799 the common fields were inclosed by Act under a joint award with Upton.[52] Only four farms, including the rector's and Corpus Christi's, were allotted more than 50 a. of arable. The Clouds estate then seems to have consisted of inclosed pastures on Barn's hill, arable allotments totalling some 47 a., and feeding for 148 sheep. The remaining land was shared among some twelve smaller farms presumably with farmsteads in Milton street. The pastures on Haddon hill, 28 a., and the down, 21 a., were distinguished from those of Upton but remained commonable. They and the Upton part of Haddon hill were for a total of 1,145 sheep of the freeholders and copyholders of Milton and of the small farmers of Upton. On Haddon those sheep could be joined by 523 sheep of the rector, Corpus Christi College, and the other Milton freeholder who had a several down.

By 1838 Clouds farm had been merged with Manor farm in East Knoyle;[53] much freehold and copyhold of inheritance land in Milton had been merged by Henry Seymour into Milton farm, 155 a. with buildings at the north end of the street; and there were still small farms based in the street.[54] In 1876 Milton farm measured 270 a.[55] That holding was broken up in the 20th century but in 1977 Milton, c. 70 a., was still the only farm worked from the street.[56] The remaining lands in the south part of the township were then mainly parts of Park farm, and those in the north part, including 85 a. of former glebe land, were mainly parts of Holden's farm which was established after the Second World War as a mixed upland farm of c. 500 a. with lands from Milton, Park, and Chapel farms.[57] Haddon hill was never inclosed and has become a common for the whole parish. The Church Commissioners conveyed the lord of the manor's rights in it to the parish council with their rights in Knoyle and Windmill hills.[58] Their rights in the common down were conveyed to John Granville Morrison in 1948.[59]

[27] H.R.O. Eccl. 2/155511, pp. 538–49.
[28] B.L. Map Libr., 'Partic. of Freehold', sale cat.
[29] W.R.O. 1265/50.
[30] Ex inf. Mr. S. E. Scammell, Clouds Estate Office; Mr. A. B. Hayne, Estate Office, Fonthill Bishop; local information.
[31] E 407/Box 5/6.
[32] H.R.O. Eccl. 2/155860.
[33] W.R.O. 536/41.
[34] See below.
[35] H.R.O. Eccl. 1/100/4; W.R.O. 212B/3657.
[36] Cf. W.R.O. 328/1; Land Tax; Tithe Award.
[37] Ibid. 328/1.
[38] Ibid. Tithe Award.
[39] Ibid. 328/1.
[40] Ch. Commrs., survey bk. DD 5, p. 616.
[41] Tropenell Cart. ed. Davies, ii, p. 1.
[42] Cf. W.R.O., Inclosure Award; Land Tax; Tithe Award.
[43] Sar. Dioc. R.O., Glebe Terrier.
[44] W.R.O., Inclosure Award; Tithe Award map.
[45] C.C.C., Oxf., Mun., deeds, LA 29, p. 193; C 3/238/29; Sar. Dioc. R.O., Glebe Terrier, 1671.
[46] W.R.O. 364/11.
[47] Sar. Dioc. R.O., Glebe Terrier.
[48] C.C.C., Oxf., Mun., 533, maps 23–4.
[49] H.R.O. Eccl. 2/155860.
[50] W.R.O. 536/41.
[51] C 3/238/29.
[52] W.R.O., Inclosure Award.
[53] See above.
[54] W.R.O., Tithe Award.
[55] B.L. Map Libr., 'Partic. of Freehold', sale cat.
[56] Sale cat. 1936 penes Mr. Scammell; local information.
[57] Ex inf. Mr. Hayne.
[58] Ex inf. Mr. Scammell; Ch. Commrs., survey bk. DD 5, p. 616.
[59] Ch. Commrs., survey bk. DD 5, p. 616.

The township of Upton contained the demesne and tenanted lands of Upton manor and the manor of Upton Knoyle which never had customary tenants. The arable land was on the chalk north of the village.[60] It was used in common presumably in the 13th century when east and west fields were named,[61] and certainly in the 18th century when there were three fields divided into small strips in the usual way.[62] A several down, c. 46 a. in 1790,[63] was part of the demesne of Upton manor but the tenants of that manor and the lord of Upton Knoyle manor fed their sheep in common, and effectively in common with the copyholders and small freeholders of Milton.[64] In the early 13th century a pasture called the Frith, possibly near the village, was common to all the villagers.[65]

In 1288–9 90 a. were sown for the bishop of Winchester on the demesne of Upton manor, 73 a. in 1330–1, and 68 a. in 1377–8.[66] In the later 13th century and the early 14th sheep were not kept. In the later 14th century, however, there was a wether flock which numbered over 500 in 1395.[67] Like that of East Knoyle the demesne farm was leased in 1405 with the rents and services of the tenants[68] but, unlike Knoyle, was never taken back in hand. The annual rent was £11 in 1405, £12 6s. 8d. in 1482, and not afterwards changed.[69] The farm, called Chapel by 1650,[70] had buildings at the north end of the street. In 1790 it measured 236 a., including 149 a. in the common fields, with additional land at Lugmarsh.[71]

In the early 13th century 2 virgates and 7 ½-virgates were held of Upton manor for rents and onerous labour services.[72] In 1288–9 rents totalled 23s. 3d.;[73] in the early 17th century there were eight copyholders.[74] The manor of Upton Knoyle was held of Knoyle manor for 15s. and a few labour services in the early 13th century.[75] In 1283 it was reckoned 1 carucate.[76] Later evidence shows it to have been smaller than Chapel farm, but by the late 18th century the addition of copyhold of inheritance land of Upton manor had made it roughly equal in size to that farm.[77] It had buildings at the southern end of Upton street.[78] There were five small freeholds c. 1638[79] some of which, including that of Corpus Christi College, were apparently held of Upton Knoyle manor.[80]

The arable fields of Upton, c. 400 a., were inclosed with those of Milton in 1799.[81] Chapel farm was allotted the easternmost lands, 144 a., Upton Knoyle farm was allotted 121 a., and the remainder was divided among several free and customary small farms. The common pastures were not inclosed but their use was regulated by the award. That on the down, 19 a., was common to Chapel and Upton Knoyle farms, 102 sheep. That on Haddon hill, 15 a., was fed on by the same flocks as the Milton part of Haddon.

Upton Knoyle farm, including a large area of copyhold of inheritance land, measured c. 395 a. in 1807 and Chapel farm measured 285 a. in 1808 when there were also some five small farms and several smallholdings in Upton.[82] By 1838 the two large farms had been merged as Chapel farm and Henry Seymour had amalgamated most of the copyholds into Upton farm with buildings in the middle of Upton street on the west side.[83] In 1876 Chapel farm measured 703 a. mainly on the chalk north of the village, Upton farm 117 a. mainly below Cleeve hill west of Upton street.[84] In 1977 Chapel was a primarily arable farm of some 500 a. and Upton, then called Upton Dairy, a mixed farm of some 100 a.[85] The Upton part of Haddon hill was part of the parish common. The lord of the manor's rights in the formerly common down were conveyed with those in Milton down in 1948.[86]

The great lowland common of Knoyle on the clay of the Vale of Wardour extended over at least 1,500 a. The north-eastern part of it called Summerleaze, c. 350 a., was part of the bishop of Winchester's demesne farm although common rights over it were enjoyed by others.[87] The remainder included some lands which were inclosed in the Middle Ages but otherwise was open to the animals of all parishioners.[88] The inclosures were east of Shaftesbury Lane and were possibly complete in the early 13th century, by which time probably fewer than 400 a. had been inclosed.[89] They resulted in the establishment of three farms. Upper Leigh, possibly the largest, included 83 a. of inclosed lands in 1555;[90] Lower Leigh was leased for £5 11s. a year in 1548;[91] and Coleman's was c. 55 a. in 1622.[92] There were in addition inclosed meadows in the south-east corner of the parish including Jaghay which was apparently part of the Pythouse estate in the early 17th century;[93] and on some of the bishop of Winchester's demesne meadows, which had presumably been inclosed out of the common, Blackhouse farm had been established by 1635.[94]

Knoyle common west of Shaftesbury Lane was until 1330 within Selwood forest and could not lawfully have been inclosed without royal licence.[95] Its inclosure began under articles drawn up by

---

[60] Cf. W.R.O., Inclosure Award; Tithe Award.
[61] H.R.O. Eccl. 2/159311, rott. 3–4.
[62] Ibid. Eccl. 2/248947.
[63] Ibid.
[64] W.R.O., Inclosure Award; see above.
[65] C.P. 25(1)/250/10 no. 3; B.L. Eg. MS. 2418, f. 68.
[66] H.R.O. Eccl. 2/159311, rott. 3–4; Eccl. 2/159343, rott. 5d.–7; Eccl. 2/159385, rot. 7.
[67] Ibid. Eccl. 2/159385, rot. 7; V.C.H. Wilts. iv. 25.
[68] H.R.O. Eccl. 2/159417, rot. 5.
[69] Ibid.; Eccl. 2/155844; e.g. Eccl. 2/248954 (1727).
[70] C 54/3508 no. 32.
[71] H.R.O. Eccl. 2/248947; see below.
[72] B.L. Eg. MS. 2418, ff. 67d.–68.
[73] H.R.O. Eccl. 2/159311, rott. 3–4.
[74] W.R.O. 536/41.
[75] B.L. Eg. MS. 2418, f. 66v.
[76] Feet of F. 1272–1327 (W.R.S. i), p. 22.
[77] W.R.O., Inclosure Award.

[78] Ibid. Tithe Award.
[79] Ibid. 536/41.
[80] C.C.C., Oxf., Mun., deeds, LA 29, p. 193.
[81] W.R.O., Inclosure Award.
[82] Ibid. 1126/12, partic. of farm; H.R.O. Eccl. 2/248947.
[83] W.R.O., Tithe Award.
[84] B.L. Map Libr., 'Partic. of Freehold', sale cat.
[85] Ex inf. Mr. Scammell.
[86] See above.
[87] See below.
[88] E 159/478 Communia Trin. rot. 12 mm. i–ix; W.R.O. 536/41.
[89] A new inclosure at Lushley was mentioned in the early 13th cent. (E 407/Box 5/6) but no new inclosure after that. For descents of the farms see above.
[90] C.C.C., Oxf., Mun., deeds, LA 29, p. 192.
[91] E 318/2075.
[92] Wilts. Inq. p.m. 1625–49 (Index Libr.), 124.
[93] Ibid. 194.
[94] H.R.O. Eccl. 2/155642, pp. 153–4.
[95] V.C.H. Wilts. iv. 417.

agreement in 1636. It was agreed that of perhaps 750 a. to be disposed of there should be allotments of 100 a. to the bishop of Winchester, 100 a. to his lessee, 12 a. a yardland to the farmers, and 4 a. or 3 a. each to the cottagers. The inclosure was stopped by a dispute over whether the allotments of 100 a. should be fragmented, as the bishop and his lessee wished, or intact. The Exchequer decreed in 1638 that they should be intact and that, despite the agreement, the amounts of other allotments should be at the allotters' discretion.[96] In 1641 it was agreed to proceed under the terms of the decree.[97] In 1651 there were still disputes over how the land had been inclosed and in 1657 the parties appointed a commission which reported in 1658. The commissioners' findings were disputed and they resigned.[98] Later evidence shows the inclosure to have stood on roughly the terms of the 1636 agreement.[99] Allotments were made in respect of the farms on the common already inclosed.[1] The bishop's allotment, New Leaze, was in the extreme south-west corner of the parish. Buildings were erected on it and an arable and pasture farm, New Leaze, c. 100 a., was established.[2] The allotment to the bishop's lessee was at Friar's Hayes where Friar's Hayes farm, 110 a., had been established by 1650.[3] Other new farms were set up on the inclosures including Redhouse by 1773[4] and Moor's and Brickyard by 1838.[5] A barn and 42 a. at Lugmarsh were then part of Chapel farm, and Vernhill farm, 35 a., had been established on the allotment to Corpus Christi College.[6] The rector received an allotment of 13 a. north of Friar's Hayes: seventeen of his nineteen cottagers, most of them at Holloway and Knoyle, received allotments of 3 a. or 4 a.[7]

In 1838 the common on both sides of Shaftesbury Lane was still a patchwork of small fields, none more extensive than c. 20 a., held of Knoyle manor freely, by lease, or by copy. There were still many owners but some of the farms had grown, presumably at the expense of smallholders based in the three villages. East of Shaftesbury Lane were the older farms, Upper Leigh, 147 a., Lower Leigh, 150 a., Blackhouse, 28 a., Coleman's, 72 a., and Kinghay, 43 a.; west of it were New Leaze, 100 a., Friar's Hayes, 211 a., Redhouse, 102 a., Moor's, 56 a., and a few farms of less than 50 a.[8] All were then arable and pasture farms but later dairy farming predominated.[9] East of the lane Lower Leigh, Kinghay, and Coleman's, all parts of the Pythouse estate, were merged into a farm measuring 318 a. in 1910.[10] In 1977 Lower Leigh, 216 a., and Coleman's were again

separate farms.[11] Upper Leigh, c. 100 a., and Blackhouse remained similarly separate farms.[12] West of the lane Lugmarsh, Moor's, and Friar's Hayes were in 1919 pasture farms of respectively 142 a., 145 a., and 188 a.[13] They and New Leaze remained farms in 1977 but Redhouse was broken up.[14] On both sides of the lane pasture farming still predominated but there was again some tillage.

Certain free tenants claimed feeding for a total of 30 oxen with the bishop of Winchester's oxen, presumably in Summerleaze, in the earlier 13th century.[15] Summerleaze, said in 1782 to be 'a large piece of greensward ground much in the nature of a common',[16] remained part of the bishops' demesne and was used by the lessees for cattle and sheep. In 1600 Thomas Mompesson sub-let it to Sir Richard Grobham and there followed a dispute in which each impounded the other's animals.[17] It was later sub-let as a farm, 360 a. in 1782, and buildings were erected on it.[18] The commoners had feeding from 3 May to 30 November.[19] In 1782 they numbered four, including the rector and Corpus Christi College, and had rights for 37 beasts.[20] Summerleaze was inclosed by Act in 1867. The commoners' rights were replaced by allotments which they exchanged with Alfred Seymour for lands in other parts of the parish.[21] In 1977 Summerleaze was a mixed farm of c. 360 a.[22]

MILLS. The first mill in East Knoyle was apparently built in the earlier 13th century.[23] It was in the south-west corner of the parish at a place called Lushley near the confluence of the several south-flowing streams.[24] There is no evidence that it survived the Middle Ages. A windmill was part of the manor of Knoyle in 1377–8 when two new sail-yards were bought.[25] Its site is unknown but was possibly on Windmill hill. It seems to have worked until replaced by a new windmill built there c. 1536.[26] There was still a miller in 1855 but the mill had ceased working by 1886.[27] The circular stone post standing in 1977 had no datable feature. The weatherboarded cap and two sails shown in photographs of c. 1930 and earlier[28] have been removed.

LOCAL GOVERNMENT. In the Middle Ages only the bishops of Winchester exercised public jurisdiction from within East Knoyle. The bishops assumed for Knoyle many of the liberties which they had in the manor of Downton.[29] In 1255 they were defined as return of writs, vee de naam, and

[96] E 159/478 Communia Trin. rot. 12 mm. i–ix.
[97] Hist. MSS. Com. 3, *4th Rep., Ho. of Lords*, p. 88.
[98] E 178/5711.   [99] See plate facing p. 49.
[1] e.g. W.R.O. 212B/3639.
[2] H.R.O. Eccl. 2/153291, nos. 5, 7, 9–11, 13, 15, 21–2, 24, leases, 1660–1780.   [3] C 54/3508 no. 32.
[4] *Andrews and Dury, Map* (W.R.S. viii), pl. 4.
[5] W.R.O., Tithe Award.
[6] *Andrews and Dury, Map* (W.R.S. viii), pl. 4; H.R.O. Eccl. 2/248947; W.R.O., Tithe Award.
[7] Sar. Dioc. R.O., Glebe Terrier, 1671; W.R.O., Tithe Award.   [8] W.R.O., Tithe Award.
[9] W.A.S. Libr., sale cat. xv, no. 6.
[10] W.R.O. 636/11.
[11] Ex inf. Cdr. J. M. Child, Lower Leigh Farm.
[12] Local information.
[13] W.A.S. Libr., sale cat. xv, no 6.
[14] Local information.
[15] B.L. Eg. MS. 2418, f. 66v.

[16] H.R.O. Eccl. 2/248947.
[17] C 2/Jas. I/G 8/42.
[18] H.R.O. Eccl. 2/248947; W.R.O., Tithe Award.
[19] W.R.O. 364/10 (1613).
[20] H.R.O. Eccl. 2/248947; Sar. Dioc. R.O., Glebe Terrier, 1705; C.C.C., Oxf., Mun., Kd. 1, terrier, 1786.
[21] W.R.O., Inclosure Award.
[22] Ex inf. Mr. Scammell.
[23] Cf. H.R.O. Eccl. 2/159275, rot. 7d.; E 407/Box 5/6.
[24] B.L. Eg. MS. 2418, f. 66v.; E 407/Box 5/6.
[25] H.R.O. Eccl. 2/159385, rot. 6d.
[26] Mun. D. & C. Winton., ledger bk. III, f. 66; Albert Goldsbrough, *Memorials of the Goldesborough Fam.* (Cheltenham and Lond. priv. print. 1930), 166.
[27] *Kelly's Dir. Wilts.* (1855); O.S. Map 6", Wilts. LXIII (1890 edn.).
[28] Goldsbrough, op. cit. facing p. 166; W.A.S. Libr., Benett–Stanford papers, photographs.
[29] See p. 43.

view of frankpledge.[30] In 1275 the bishop also claimed gallows and the assize of bread and ale,[31] and in 1289 felons' chattels, pillory, and tumbril.[32] Although part of the bailiwick of Downton, East Knoyle was for the purposes of the bishops' jurisdiction under those liberties never merged with the hundred of Downton. It remained separate and, including Hindon and Fonthill Bishop, was called a hundred and sometimes a liberty.[33] In the Middle Ages the hundred contained three tithings, Knoyle, Milton, and Fonthill Bishop.[34] Upton, which was then in Milton tithing although separately represented at royal inquests and in tax lists,[35] established itself as an additional tithing in the 17th century although its 'foreman' was never called a tithing-man.[36] The tithings of East Knoyle and Fonthill were, however, united in a single constablewick.[37]

In the early 13th century bishops held Hock-tide and Martinmas tourns for the hundred as they did elsewhere.[38] The assize of ale was enforced from the mid 13th century.[39] The first separately enrolled records of the tourn known to survive are for 1464.[40] Procedure was similar to that of contemporary Downton tourns. The tithingmen of Fonthill, Knoyle, and Milton and the bailiff of Hindon presented and a jury of twelve freemen affirmed and added to the presentments. In the later 15th century and the 16th the presentments of the Knoyle and Milton tithingmen were not numerous and, apart from recording that cert-money was paid, were mainly of brewers, butchers, and millers. Occasionally, however, affrays and breaches of agrarian custom were dealt with and further offences, including public nuisances, were presented by the jurors. From the mid 16th century elections of constables of the hundred were recorded. In the 17th century the constable and the tithingmen made formal presentments at each tourn but rarely of an offence beyond failing to attend the tourn. The jurors, however, regularly presented offenders and were particularly concerned with the condition of roads and bridges, sometimes ordering the parish to repair. From the later 17th century tourns were held annually in September. The tithingmen presented nothing but the payment of cert-money, and the courts proceeded on the presentments of two juries. The 'jury for the king' continued to present public nuisances and the homage presented manorial business formerly transacted in separate courts.[41] Tourns continued thus until the mid 19th century and ostensibly serious presentments of nuisances were still made. They included the presentment in 1829 of the trustees of the Shaftesbury turnpike for encroaching on the waste by building on it a turnpike gate and house. By 1800, however, the main work of the jurors was to present the choice of constables,

tithingmen, and foremen of Upton and of the homage to present the customs of the manor.

Overseers and waywardens were being appointed for East Knoyle in the early 17th century:[42] Hindon and Fonthill Bishop apparently had their own officers. Later there were surveyors of roads for each of the three Knoyle tithings.[43] Outdoor relief under the Elizabethan poor law totalled £8 in 1607.[44] More money was being spent in the 1630s but the most rapid increase in spending, to over £50 a year in the period 1665–7, was after the Restoration.[45] In the late 17th century more than half the annual expenditure was on monthly doles.[46] In 1733 the parish repaired a house in Milton tithing to receive the poor who in 1749 were required to be badged.[47] A surgeon and apothecary was regularly appointed.[48] Indoor relief certainly increased in the 18th century,[49] and in 1750 a condition of outdoor relief was that those owning a dwelling-house convey reversion of it to the parish. A determination to insist on that condition was marked by the vestry's resolution, repeated in 1794, to appeal against an order of any justice to relieve unconditionally.[50] In 1776–7 £245 was spent.[51] By the mid 18th century the office of overseer had been attached to farms and rotated, and from 1794 was held for two years.[52] In 1796 a salaried deputy overseer was appointed.[53] In 1811 the parish agreed to provide a new workhouse which was built a little north of East Knoyle village beside the road to Hindon.[54] The parish nominated a visitor to inspect it each year and from 1825 paid a full-time governor and governess.[55] Its inhabitants were uniformed.[56] In 1835 East Knoyle joined Mere poor-law union,[57] and in 1841 sold its workhouse and five tenements.[58] The site of the workhouse is that of Park Farm.[59]

Private jurisdiction through manorial courts was exercised by the bishops of Winchester and by the rectors. The bishop's courts for the manor of East Knoyle were held several times a year by his bailiff.[60] In the Middle Ages the courts enforced customary obligations to the lord, heard pleas between tenants, and presentments by the homage that, for example, tenants had died and agrarian customs had been breached, and witnessed surrenders and admittances.[61] In the 16th century the tithingmen of East Knoyle and Milton, the foreman of Upton, and the homage all presented. From c. 1515 separate courts were held for the manor of Upton.[62] Manor courts apparently ceased in the later 17th century. The business, by then principally the recording of conveyances of copyholds of inheritance, was transferred to the annual tourns where in 1702 and 1720 the bishop was presented for not keeping three-weekly courts for the liberty.[63] No record, beyond copies,[64] survives of rectors' courts which were presumably

30 *Rot. Hund.* (Rec. Com.), ii (1), 234.
31 Ibid. 251. 32 J.I. 1/1011 rot. 54.
33 e.g. H.R.O. Eccl. 1/79/16; E 179/196/8; *Taxation Lists* (W.R.S. x), 158.
34 W.R.O. 492/9 (1464). For Hindon see p. 101.
35 e.g. J.I. 1/998A rot. 38; E 179/196/8.
36 H.R.O. Eccl. 1/92/1–12. 37 Ibid.
38 e.g. H.R.O. Eccl. 2/159287, rot. 20 and d. (1244–5).
39 e.g. ibid.
40 W.R.O. 492/9. Except where stated the remainder of this para. is based on ct. rec. and presentment bks. in H.R.O. and W.R.O. 492/9; 492/32–4; 893/1–2.
41 See below. 42 W.R.O. 536/26.
43 Ibid. 536/23, min. of 1828.
44 Ibid. 536/26. 45 Ibid.
46 Ibid. 47 Ibid.; 536/16.
48 Ibid. 536/23. 49 Ibid. 536/27–9.
50 Ibid. 536/23. 51 Ibid. 536/29.
52 Ibid. 536/16; 536/23. 53 Ibid. 536/23.
54 Ibid. Q. Sess. enrolled deeds, loose deed 17; Tithe Award.
55 Ibid. 536/23. 56 Ibid. min. of 1834.
57 *Poor Law Com. 2nd Rep.* 559. 58 W.R.O. 536/23.
59 W.A.S. Libr., Benett–Stanford papers.
60 e.g. H.R.O. Eccl. 2/159384, rott. 7d.–8d. (1376–7).
61 W.R.O. 492/32. 62 Ibid. 893/1.
63 H.R.O. Eccl. 2/159619.
64 e.g. W.R.O. 212B/3666.

held solely for surrenders of and admittances to copyholds.

CHURCH. A church was standing at Knoyle before the Conquest.[65] In the early 13th century a chapel of ease was built at Hindon which became a separate ecclesiastical parish in 1869.[66] In 1914 318 a. of East Knoyle, New Leaze and Friar's Hayes farms, were made part of the new ecclesiastical parish of Sedgehill.[67] From 1952 the rectory was held in plurality with the living of Sedgehill.[68] In 1976 it was united with the vicarage of Hindon with Chicklade and Pertwood.[69]

The advowson of the rectory passed with the lordship of Knoyle manor. From 1199 to 1201 it was disputed between Godfrey de Lucy, bishop of Winchester, and Maud de Beaumont, countess of Warwick, who claimed it as part of her dower,[70] but after her death it passed with the see of Winchester.[71] The only recorded presentations not by a bishop were in 1559 and 1570,[72] in the Civil War and Interregnum,[73] and in 1660 when the Crown presented after the ejection of the incumbent.[74] In 1865 the advowson was transferred to the see of Oxford[75] and in 1953 to the see of Salisbury.[76] The bishop of Salisbury was patron in 1977.

Medieval and modern valuations, including those of 1291 at £20 and 1296 at 60 marks,[77] of 1650 at £230 excluding Hindon's tithes,[78] and of 1829–31 at £850,[79] show the living to have always been rich. The rector was entitled to all the tithes from the whole parish including Hindon.[80] Those of East Knoyle were valued at £925 in 1837 and commuted in 1841, those of Hindon valued at £70 in 1843 and commuted in 1844.[81] The glebe, consisting of a demesne farm and land held customarily, some 170 a. in all, was considered a manor.[82] The copyholds were enfranchised in the late 19th century,[83] and 85 a. of upland demesne were sold in 1947 to John Granville Morrison (Lord Margadale).[84] Some 13 a. of land on Knoyle common were part of the living in 1977.[85] Parts of the medieval glebe-house can be seen in a low range abutting the west side of the later Rectory, now called Knoyle Place, in which there are some old walls containing parts of two 15th-

century doorways apparently at the opposite ends of a cross-passage. The remainder was presumably demolished when in 1799[86] the large almost square new house was built with an eastern entrance front of three bays and a southern garden front of five bays. In 1935 the Rectory was sold to Sir Francis Geoffrey Fison,[87] and from 1965 has belonged to Sir John Eden.[88] The new Rectory at Holloway, formerly Holloway Farm, is a late-17th-century house with a symmetrical front to the west and a rear service wing.[89] It was sold in 1977 when the incumbent lived at Hindon.[90]

In the 14th century several of the rectors are known to have been pluralists.[91] Stephen Morpeth, rector 1405–68, already a pluralist, was in 1409 licensed to study for three years.[92] He became a chaplain of Henry V and held among other livings the deanery of the free chapel of St. Nicholas in Wallingford castle.[93] Robert Morwent, rector 1523–58, was president of Corpus Christi College, Oxford, from 1537 and in 1550 a curate served the church.[94] After Morwent's death, presumably when the living was in Elizabeth I's gift after the Marian Bishop White was deprived in 1559, John Haytor, the lessee of the tithes and glebe,[95] was licensed to present. His nominee was his son Thomas who was later found to have been under age and not in holy orders. In 1570 Bishop Horne granted the advowson for one turn to James Mervyn who presented John Mervyn. After contests between Thomas Haytor and John Mervyn in the spiritual and secular courts and twice by force at the rectory-house Mervyn retained the living, but the church was served by a curate.[96] The rector from 1623 was Christopher Wren, dean of Windsor from 1635.[97] Wren was registrar of the Order of the Garter, a position which he used to invoke the king's intervention when his pigeon-house was undermined by the saltpetre commissioner in 1636.[98] He held other parish livings and was the father of Sir Christopher Wren, who was born at East Knoyle in 1631 or 1632.[99] Sir Christopher kept a link with the parish until 1662 when he surrendered a small copyhold of inheritance.[1] Dean Wren compounded for the rectory in 1645, but in 1646 it was sequestered for his support of the king and given to William Clifford who was later said to preach twice

[65] See below. [66] See pp. 101–2.
[67] Lond. Gaz. 18 Aug. 1914, pp. 6488–92.
[68] Ibid. 8 Feb. 1952, p. 792; Crockford (1975–6).
[69] Lond. Gaz. 21 May 1976, p. 7542.
[70] Rot. Cur. Reg. (Rec. Com.), i. 304; ii. 61, 67, 211, 266; Cur. Reg. R. i. 283, 329, 400, 402, 454–5; ii. 27, 121.
[71] Reg. Pontoise (Cant. & York Soc.), ii. 739–40; cf. Cal. Chart. R. 1257–1300, 273–4; Phillipps, Wilts. Inst. (index in W.A.M. xxviii. 223).
[72] For the circumstances see below.
[73] See below.
[74] Calamy Revised, ed. A. G. Matthews, 232.
[75] Lond. Gaz. 4 June 1852, p. 1580; Sar. Dioc. R.O., Vis. Queries, 1864; Clergy List (1892).
[76] Lond. Gaz. 30 Oct. 1953, p. 5775.
[77] Tax. Eccl. (Rec. Com.), 181; Reg. Pontoise (Cant. & York Soc.), ii. 796.
[78] W.A.M. xl. 308.
[79] Rep. Com. Eccl. Revenues, 838–9.
[80] Sar. Dioc. R.O., Glebe Terrier, 1705.
[81] W.R.O., Tithe Awards.
[82] Cf. Sar. Dioc. R.O., Glebe Terriers, 1671, 1705; W.R.O., Tithe Award. For the details see above.
[83] B.L. Map Libr., 'Partic. of Freehold', sale cat.
[84] Ch. Commrs., benefice file.
[85] Ex inf. the rector, the Revd. L. W. Daffurn, Hindon

Vicarage.
[86] Sar. Dioc. R.O., Mortgages, no. 1e.
[87] Ch. Commrs., benefice file.
[88] Wilts. Cuttings, xxii. 290.
[89] Ibid. xxvii. 176.
[90] Ex inf. the Revd. L. W. Daffurn.
[91] Reg. Martival (Cant. & York Soc.), i. 29; Cal. Papal Reg. iii. 543; Cal. Papal Pets. i. 514.
[92] Phillipps, Wilts. Inst. i. 93, 158; Cal. Pat. 1405–8, 247; 'Reg. Hallum', ed. Joyce M. Wilkinson (Oxf. Univ. B.Litt. thesis, 1959), 388.
[93] Cal. Papal Reg. ix. 33–4; V.C.H. Berks. ii. 104.
[94] Phillipps, Wilts. Inst. i. 197; V.C.H. Oxon. iii. 225; Sar. Dioc. R.O., Detecta Bk. 1550.
[95] C 3/238/29.
[96] Sta. Cha. 7/12/30; Phillipps, Wilts. Inst. i. 225; Sar. Dioc. R.O., Detecta Bk. 1585.
[97] Phillipps, Wilts. Inst. ii. 12; D.N.B. s.v. Sir Chris. Wren; see plate facing p. 97.
[98] Cal. S.P. Dom. 1637, 61, 187, 259, 531; 1637–8, 37, 143, 232.
[99] D.N.B. s.v. Sir Chris. Wren. The date of Sir Chris.'s birth is given as 20 Oct. 1632 in Chris. Wren, Parentalia (Lond. 1750), 181, his christening as 20 Nov. 1631 in the transcribed par. reg.: W.R.O. 536/2, and photocopy in ch.
[1] H.R.O. Eccl. 1/100/4, ct. held 24 Sept.

every Sunday.[2] Clifford's son Samuel succeeded him in 1655 and was ejected in 1660.[3] His successor Enoch Gray was also ejected for nonconformity and both remained in the parish.[4] Samuel Rolleston, archdeacon of Salisbury 1732–66, was rector 1745-6.[5] His successor Charles Wake, whose assistant curate was a local landowner and who held other livings, in 1783 held services twice on Sundays and administered the Sacrament at the great festivals. His curate catechized.[6] In 1864 the rector held services with sermons thrice on winter and twice on summer Sundays with an average congregation of 220. Communion was once a month for the 80–100 communicants.[7] In 1977 services were held every Sunday.

The church of *ST. MARY* is built mostly of coursed rubble, which was formerly rendered,[8] and has a chancel with south organ chamber, a nave with short aisles, north-western vestry, and south porch, and a west tower. Parts of the walls of the nave and of the western part of the chancel remain from a pre-Conquest church. Early features which survive are an exposed length of double plinth and cut back blind arcading on the north wall of the chancel, and possibly the north doorway. Early in the 13th century the chancel was extended and refenestrated. Later in that century north and south transeptal chapels were added to the nave. The porch was built in the 14th century and the tower in the 15th when the south doorway and east window were also inserted. The arrangement of the interior is shown in a plan of 1632.[9] About 1639 the chancel was decorated with plasterwork, designed by Dean Wren and executed by Robert Brockway, depicting scenes from the Old and New Testaments.[10] In 1714 a west gallery was erected,[11] and in 1756 the lead was removed from the roof and replaced by stone tiles.[12] The first of several 19th-century enlargements was the extension of the north transept into an aisle in 1829, perhaps by John Peniston of Salisbury who is known to have built a gallery about then.[13] In 1845 the south aisle and the vestry were added, the chancel arch was widened, the gallery enlarged, and there was general restoration under Wyatt and Brandon.[14] The organ chamber was added, the gallery removed, and the church refitted under Sir Arthur Blomfield in 1875-6.[15] A new burial ground opened in 1899[16] contains Wyndham corner, a partly walled enclosure by Detmar Blow with ground and wall monuments and a central monolith.

There were four bells in 1553.[17] The treble was recast in 1627.[18] In the 18th century the ring was increased to six: bells (i)–(iii) were founded by William Cockey of Frome (Som.) in 1726, (iv) came from the same foundry in 1748, and (v) and (vi) were probably also by Cockey.[19] Bell (v) was recast by Robert and James Wells of Aldbourne in 1794 and the tenor by Mears and Stainbank of Whitechapel in 1839 when all the bells were rehung. The bells were restored and rehung in 1933[20] and were still in the church in 1977.[21]

In 1553 the king's commissioners took 4 oz. of plate from the parish and left 11 oz. Augustus Mervyn (d. 1637) gave a new paten and Richard Hill, rector 1662–95, gave two chalices and a paten in 1677 and a flagon in 1681.[22] Those pieces still belonged to the church in 1977.[23]

The registers date from 1538. Entries before 1636 are transcriptions. Richard Dew was appointed parish registrar in 1654 and from 1653 the registers are complete.[24]

NONCONFORMITY. An East Knoyle man was suspected of recusancy in 1584,[25] in 1586 a Roman Catholic priest ordained abroad was arrested in Knoyle,[26] and it is possible that in the early 17th century several papists lived at Knoyle.[27] Between 1662 and 1706 several papist families were named but never more than six people at once.[28]

After their ejection from the rectory Samuel Clifford and Enoch Gray apparently led an Independent congregation at Knoyle and in 1662 there were also some Baptists.[29] In 1676 there were 45 nonconformists, an unusually high number for a place outside the cloth-working areas of the county.[30] The Baptist congregation, whose leader John Williams attended the London General Assemblies of 1689 and 1692, was possibly linked with Baptists in neighbouring villages. It continued until 1743 but afterwards died out and in 1783 there was no nonconformist at Knoyle.[31]

In 1797 and 1805 dwelling-houses were certified as meeting-houses for Independents.[32] In 1827 the Independents, under the patronage of Charles Jupe, a silk manufacturer of Mere, opened a cottage for worship and a chapel was built to adjoin it.[33] In 1849 the chapel was bought by the rector and closed. The congregation converted a cottage into a meeting-

[2] *W.A.M.* xxxiv. 173; *Walker Revised*, ed. A. G. Matthews, 382; *W.A.M.* xl. 308.
[3] *Calamy Revised*, ed. Matthews, 122.
[4] Ibid. 232; Sar. Dioc. R.O., Chwdns.' Pres. 1662.
[5] Phillipps, *Wilts. Inst.* ii. 71; Le Neve, *Fasti Eccl. Angl.* ii. 627.
[6] *Vis. Queries, 1783* (W.R.S. xxvii), pp. 103, 131-3.
[7] Sar. Dioc. R.O., Vis. Queries.
[8] J. Buckler, water-colour in W.A.S. Libr., vol. ii. 18 (1804).
[9] W.R.O. 536/18; see plate facing this p.
[10] *W.A.M.* iii. 117–18; see plate facing p. 97.
[11] W.R.O. 536/16.
[12] Sar. Dioc. R.O., Pet. for Faculties, bdle. 1, no. 23.
[13] W.R.O. 536/19; Colvin, *Brit. Architects*, 630.
[14] W.R.O. 536/18.
[15] Sar. Dioc. R.O., Pet. for Faculties, bdle. 23, no. 16; W.R.O. 536/18–19.
[16] W.R.O. 536/14.
[17] Walters, *Wilts. Bells*, 114.
[18] W.R.O. 536/15, bond of Lott.
[19] Walters, *Wilts. Bells*, 113–14. The order of the bells

given by Walters is corrected in a letter of 1941 from Mears and Stainbank to Col. J. M. Fane-Benett-Stanford: W.A.S. Libr., Benett–Stanford papers.
[20] Walters, *Wilts. Bells*, 113; Sar. Dioc. R.O., Pet. for Faculties, bdle. 72, no. 45.
[21] Ex inf. the Revd. L. W. Daffurn.
[22] Nightingale, *Wilts. Plate*, 60–1.
[23] Ex inf. the Revd. L. W. Daffurn.
[24] W.R.O. 536/2–8. The marriage reg. has been printed: *Wilts. Par. Reg.* (Mar.), ed. W. P. W. Phillimore and J. Sadler, iii. 1–37.
[25] *V.C.H. Wilts.* iii. 36.
[26] Ibid. 87.
[27] Ibid. 89 and n.
[28] J. A. Williams, *Catholic Recusancy in Wilts.* (Cath. Rec. Soc.), pp. 196, 205, 206, 255, 259, 327, 333, 348.
[29] Sar. Dioc. R.O., Chwdns.' Pres. 1662.
[30] *V.C.H. Wilts.* iii. 119.
[31] Ibid. 112; *Vis. Queries, 1783* (W.R.S. xxvii), p. 132.
[32] Sar. Dioc. R.O., Return of Cert. Places.
[33] Ibid.; S. B. Stribling, *Hist. of Wilts. & E. Som. Cong. Union 1797–1897* (1897), 58–9.

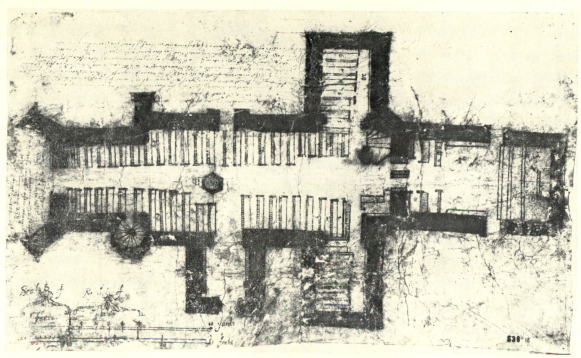

EAST KNOYLE

A plan of the church of St. Mary made in 1632

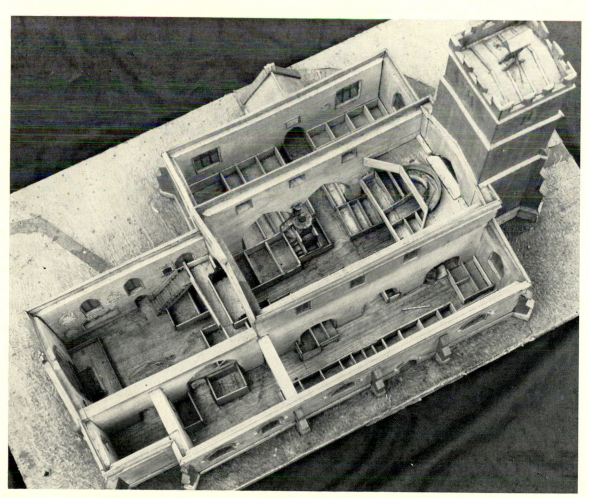

WROUGHTON

A model of the church of St. John the Baptist and St. Helen made in 1839

Plasterwork of *c.* 1639 in the church of St. Mary

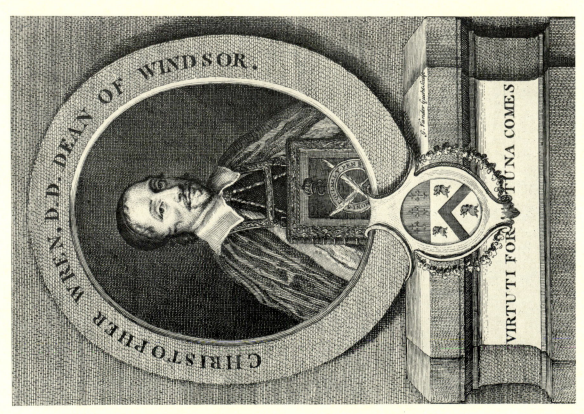

Christopher Wren, rector 1623–46

EAST KNOYLE

house and on Census Sunday in 1851 36 and 35 people attended the morning and evening services.[34] Jupe built a new Congregational chapel and school-room in the village at the top end of Shaftesbury Lane in 1854.[35] It was served by ministers of the Wiltshire and East Somerset Congregational Union and a manse had been added by 1906.[36] The church remained open and had a resident pastor in 1977.[37]

A chapel, later called the Ebenezer chapel, was built at the Green for Primitive Methodists in 1843.[38] In 1851 congregations of 90 and 79 attended after-noon and evening services.[39] The church, which is dated 1857, had been closed by 1977.

The East Knoyle and Semley Baptist chapel had a schoolroom in Knoyle which in 1821 was licensed for meetings.[40] It flourished for a time but the room had apparently been closed by 1851.[41]

EDUCATION. In 1683 a school was being held by an unlicensed nonconformist.[42] By will proved 1707 the rector Charles Trippett gave £100 to be invested for a school for poor children. The capital was invested in 1765 and the interest, £5 a year, was given to the mistress of the Sunday school. Before 1783 Mary Shaw, widow of the rector John Shaw (d. 1745), gave by will £100 to assist the teaching of poor children and the interest, £6, was applied with Trippett's money.[43]

In 1808 the two charities provided for the teaching of 26 children; another school had recently been started; and there were some smaller schools.[44] In 1818 the charity money was given to a mistress who taught 27 children and there were four other day-schools for a total of 65 children.[45] Those schools possibly included the Baptist school, which in 1821 is the first known to have had a special room but in 1833 was apparently a Sunday school.[46] The school partly supported by the charities was in 1833 attended by 54 children but was still held in the mistress's house, leased to her by the rector. At two other schools there were 31 and 15 pupils.[47] By 1839 a new schoolroom near Knoyle House had been built for the charity school,[48] but other schools continued and in 1858 there were three in the parish, the National school supported partly by the charities, a private school for some twenty children of farmers and tradesmen, and for the Congregationalists a British school adjoining the chapel.[49] A new National school was built between the church and the Rectory in 1872–3. It is of stone with details in a Moorish style to designs of G. Aitchison.[50] The British school, which had an average attendance of

38 in 1870,[51] had been closed by 1881[52] and from then the National school was the only one in the parish. In 1906 the average attendance was 135.[53] It had fallen to 89 by 1922 and to 74 by 1936.[54] In 1977 there were 29 pupils.[55]

Trippett's and Mary Shaw's charities, managed by the trustees of Robert Compton's charity (see below), were merged with Compton's by a Scheme of 1897. In 1903 their joint income, £8, was paid to the school.[56] In 1975 they were united as the East Knoyle Educational Charity and in 1976 the income of £7 was given to the school.[57]

CHARITIES FOR THE POOR. By will proved 1687 Robert Compton gave £300 to invest in land for the purposes of binding orphan children apprentice and relieving the old and feeble poor not otherwise relieved. In 1692 the trustees were mortgagees of an estate of 27 a. in Upton and Milton and from 1717 owned it. To augment the charity the trustees were given £20 by Francis Morley in 1693 and £40 by Edward Sanger in 1713, and in 1766 £50 from those gifts was invested. In 1833 the total income was £38: £5 was placed annually in an apprenticing fund, the remainder distributed at Whitsun among some 30 unrelieved poor over 60 who received between 10s. and £3 15s. each. In 1867 the income was £62 of which £42 was distributed.[58] The trustees administered several other East Knoyle charities[59] of which by a Scheme of 1897 they became trustees.[60] The charities thus merged were united by a Scheme of 1975 as the East Knoyle Welfare Trust and the East Knoyle Educational Charity. In 1976 the trust had an income of £327 of which £60 was spent on apprenticing, £261 on winter fuel for 24 pensioners.[61]

In 1690 Robert Compton's widow Susannah gave 11 a. to benefit unrelieved poor of the parish. The rent from it, £18 in 1833, was received by the trustees of Robert Compton's charity who distri-buted money in November, in 1833 in sums of between 1s. 6d. and 16s. The charity was merged with Robert Compton's in 1897.[62] In 1962 the land was apparently sold and £990 invested. Income that year was £47 of which most was spent on coal.[63] In 1975 the charity was united with Robert Compton's.[64]

John Shaw (d. 1745), the rector,[65] gave by will £50 to benefit the poor of East Knoyle. In 1766 that sum with interest, £74, was given to trustees who, when the capital reached £80, distributed £4 a year. In 1829 the capital was invested. In 1832 the trustees

[34] Stribling, op. cit. 58–9; H.O. 129/267/1/1/3.
[35] Stribling, op. cit. 58–9; V.C.H. Wilts. iii. 146 n. 42.
[36] Endowed Char. Wilts. (S. Div.), 273.
[37] Local information.
[38] Sar. Dioc. R.O., Certs. Dissenters' Meeting-Houses.
[39] H.O. 129/267/1/1/2.
[40] Sar. Dioc. R.O., Certs. Dissenters' Meeting-Houses.
[41] W.A.M. xxviii. 151. It is not mentioned in H.O. 129/267.
[42] Sar. Dioc. R.O., Chwdns.' Pres.
[43] Endowed Char. Wilts. (S. Div.), 265–6; Vis. Queries, 1783 (W.R.S. xxvii), p. 132.
[44] Lambeth MS. 1732.
[45] Educ. of Poor Digest, 1030.
[46] Sar. Dioc. R.O., Certs. Dissenters' Meeting-Houses; Educ. Enquiry Abstract, 1040.
[47] Educ. Enquiry Abstract, 1040.
[48] W.R.O., Tithe Award.

[49] Acct. of Wilts. Schs. 29.
[50] W.R.O. 536/22; see plate facing p. 145.
[51] W.R.O. 536/22.
[52] Rep. of Educ. Cttee. of Council, 1881–2 [C 3312–I], p. 285, H.C. (1882), xxiii.
[53] Return of Non-Provided Schs. 22.
[54] Bd. of Educ., List 21 (H.M.S.O.).
[55] Ex inf. Chief Education Officer, County Hall, Trow-bridge.
[56] Endowed Char. Wilts. (S. Div.), 268–71.
[57] Char. Com. file 202028; see below.
[58] Endowed Char. Wilts. (S. Div.), 262–4, 267.
[59] See below.
[60] Endowed Char. Wilts. (S. Div.), 268.
[61] Char. Com. file 202028. For the charity see above.
[62] Endowed Char. Wilts. (S. Div.), 264, 268.
[63] Char. Com. file 202028.
[64] See above.   [65] Phillipps, Wilts. Inst. ii. 71.

of Robert Compton's charity distributed the income, £2 14s., in sums of 1s. at Christmas and in 1897 the charity was merged with Compton's. In 1904 the beneficiaries were the 21 parishioners receiving poor-relief who were each given 2s. 4½d.[66] Under a Scheme of 1950 the income was devoted to emergency relief in money or goods.[67] In 1962 £3 15s. was spent. The charity was united with the Comptons' charities in 1975.[68]

Anthony Burbidge (d. 1823) gave by will £100 to benefit poor widows and widowers over 50 at Christmas. Benefit was confined to practising Anglicans. The money was invested in 1833 and £5 distributed among ten widows and five widowers. In 1906 6s. was paid to each of seven or eight poor widows and widowers.[69] The charity, whose subsequent history is not clear, has possibly been merged with Robert Compton's.

HINDON

HINDON is a settlement planned by a bishop of Winchester and founded in the early 13th century. The tenements were built on both sides of a street and behind them were narrow burgage plots, vestiges of which remain visible.[70] The main period of building seems to have been 1218–20.[71] Like other contemporary new towns Hindon was presumably conceived as a centre for artisans and of trade in their and other wares.[72] It was established on chalk downland in the north-east corner of the manor and parish of East Knoyle nearer to Chicklade, Berwick St. Leonard, and the Fonthills than to East Knoyle. The street ran north-west to south-east down a steep hill and ended abruptly at the parish boundary.[73] It was part of a road which was possibly ancient but apparently without prominence,[74] and the straightness of the street is a mark of the bishop's planning rather than the road's original course. If, as may be assumed, it was previously unoccupied Hindon's site on remote downland in a far corner of the parish calls for an explanation. The most likely one is perhaps that Hindon was built as far as possible from the rival centres of Mere and Shaftesbury (Dors.), and as near as possible to the villages of the upper Nadder valley and to those lying along the Wylye between the market towns of Warminster and Wilton.

It was possibly intended that the burgesses should have no land beyond the burgage plots. Soon after foundation, however, at least 75 a. of land in plots of 1–10 a. were conveyed for 6d. an acre to inhabitants, presumably to ensure the survival of so young and remote a community,[75] and c. 1231 the bishop sold a coomb of his down to the burgesses for an annual payment of 15s.[76] Those lands, whose boundaries were the straight boundaries of East Knoyle, were presumably the lands around Hindon which with the village became the chapelry, 228 a. (92 ha.).[77] Hindon remained a chapelry of East Knoyle until 1869 but, relieving its own poor, was considered a civil parish.[78] In 1934 parts of Chicklade, Berwick

St. Leonard, and Fonthill Gifford parishes were transferred to Hindon[79] whose bounds were thus extended southwards and eastwards to enclose a roughly square parish, 417 ha. (1,031 a.).[80]

Hindon survived as a settlement and c. 1250, when there were some 150 houses,[81] its population was apparently above that of an average village. There were no more than 77 poll-tax payers in 1377[82] and Hindon was clearly not a large settlement in the 17th century.[83] In 1801 the population was 793. It reached a peak of 921 in 1831 when there were some 190 houses.[84] What prosperity Hindon had was due more to its market and fairs,[85] and to its position on and near main roads, than to its industry. From the later Middle Ages Hindon's status as a parliamentary borough[86] may have attracted investment and occasional trade, and its central position in south-west Wiltshire made it a centre of local government. Between 1530 and 1660 it was sometimes a venue for quarter sessions and in 1786 was made the centre of a petty sessional division.[87] In 1688 Clarendon met William of Orange there.[88] The road from Barford St. Martin, Wilton, and Salisbury to Willoughby Hedge in West Knoyle crossed Hindon street. Especially after that and the main London–Exeter road across the downs were turnpiked in the 18th century,[89] Hindon attracted much coach traffic, providing for which was probably its principal industry.[90] There were fourteen inns and public houses in 1754,[91] and in the early 19th century the inns were still numerous.[92] In 1830 London coaches from Exeter left daily from the Swan and from Barnstaple (Devon) nightly from the Lamb, and there were corresponding services westwards.[93] Such was the vitality of Hindon in the 18th century that it quickly recovered after a serious fire which spread along the street and did much damage 2–3 July 1754.[94] In the 19th century, however, after the peak of 1831, Hindon declined. The population had fallen to 603 by 1871 and the decline continued until 1931 when there were 376 inhabitants.[95] By then

66 Endowed Char. Wilts. (S. Div.), 264, 268, 271.
67 Char. Com. Scheme.   68 Ibid. file 202028.
69 Endowed Char. Wilts. (S. Div.), 265, 272.
70 M. W. Beresford, 'Six New Towns of the Bishops of Winchester, 1200–55', Medieval Arch. iii. 200–2.
71 Ibid. 200, 202; H.R.O. Eccl. 2/159275, rot. 7d.
72 M. W. Beresford, New Towns of the Middle Ages, 55–60.
73 O.S. Map 6″, Wilts. LXIV (1889 edn.); cf. V.C.H. Wilts. iv, pl. facing p. 368.
74 e.g. Andrews and Dury, Map (W.R.S. viii), pl. 4.
75 H.R.O. Eccl. 2/159278, rot. 5 and d.; Eccl. 2/159280, rot. 4d.
76 Ibid. Eccl. 2/159282, rot. 6 and d.
77 O.S. Map 6″, Wilts. LXIV (1889 edn.); see plate facing p. 80.

78 V.C.H. Wilts. iv. 350; see below.
79 V.C.H. Wilts. iv. 350 n.
80 Census, 1971.
81 Beresford, 'New Towns', Medieval Arch. iii. 202.
82 V.C.H. Wilts. iv. 309.
83 e.g. W.A.M. xxxviii. 605.
84 V.C.H. Wilts. iv. 350; H.R.O. 26M62, box 22, poll bk. 1826.   85 See below.
86 See below.   87 V.C.H. Wilts. v. 88, 177.
88 Ibid. 168.   89 See p. 83.
90 J. Britton, Beauties of Eng. and Wales, xv. 262.
91 Wilts. Cuttings, i. 19.
92 Hoare, Mod. Wilts. Mere, 194.
93 Pigot, Nat. Com. Dir. (1830), 802.
94 Wilts. Cuttings, i. 19; B.L. Ch. Briefs, A. i. 4.
95 V.C.H. Wilts. iv. 350.

market and fairs had ceased and there were only two public houses, the Lamb and the Grosvenor Arms which both remained open in 1977.[96] The magistrates' court was moved to Tisbury in 1887.[97] Hindon's decline coincided with and has been attributed to its disfranchisement in 1832,[98] but probably as important was the railway connexion of London to Taunton and Exeter in the early 1840s[99] and a decline in road traffic through the borough. Some of the population decline in Hindon after 1831 was compensated by the growth of settlement around the bottom of the street. That settlement, including a school and a nonconformist chapel,[1] was part of Hindon although situated in the three neighbouring parishes. In 1934 it was transferred to Hindon with its population of some 110.[2] In 1971 Hindon's population was 534.[3]

In 1748 there were unbroken lines of buildings on both sides of the whole length of the street and behind them many cottages, some of them in rows endways on in the narrow burgage plots, and other buildings had by then been erected on those plots.[4] The market was presumably held along the whole street and a market building then stood in the street between the points at which the road from Barford St. Martin to Willoughby Hedge entered and left it. The survival of a number of houses which are of the early 18th century or earlier, particularly on the west side of the street, suggests that the fire of 1754 did not seriously affect every building and belies the contemporary claim that little of Hindon survived.[5] Damage was clearly extensive, however, in the centre of the street on the east side, where on both sides of the road from Barford St. Martin the buildings behind the street were most numerous. Part of that area was not rebuilt and in 1977 remained an empty square around the south and west sides of which the road from Barford St. Martin to Willoughby Hedge passed. On the east side of the street south of that road, however, is a group of houses which seem to have been built soon after 1754. Hindon is still characterized by its long straight street which was lined with trees in 1863.[6] It contains a mixture of houses dating from the later 17th century to the 19th. Stone predominated until the later 18th century; red brick afterwards became more common. A notable feature of the centre of the street on the west side is a group of substantial buildings whose frontages are pierced by carriage entrances and which were presumably inns. Mid-20th-century council houses have been built behind the church at the north-west end of the street. The settlement at the south-east end is on a north-east to south-west line at right angles to the street.

There were a few houses on the downs in 1748.[7] One of them, Hawking Down House, was replaced by a small house in Tudor style which was described as new in 1838. The new house was said to have been built for the valet of William Beckford (d. 1844), possibly c. 1822 when Beckford left Fonthill Gifford.[8]

MANOR. The land on which Hindon was built and the land which became the chapelry were part of the bishop of Winchester's manor of East Knoyle. The lands were held freely and the bishops remained overlords.[9] The freeholds were at first small but in the 14th century the Mussel family, including Walter (fl. 1297), his son John (fl. 1332), and grandson Philip Mussel (fl. 1380), apparently accumulated a substantial estate.[10] Philip's heir was his sister Joan, wife of John Brit (fl. 1430) who bought more land, probably including the 94 a. held by Thomas Mussel in 1348.[11] The Brits' heirs were Joan's cousins Joan, wife of Richard Herdell, and Catherine, wife of Richard Coof.[12] Their land in Hindon was allotted to the Herdells whose son Robert mortgaged it to Thomas Tropenell in 1452. Tropenell (d. 1488) entered in 1456 and, despite disputes before and after then, retained his manor of HINDON.[13] The manor passed to his son Christopher (d. 1503), Christopher's son Thomas (d. 1547), and Thomas's son Giles (d. 1553) whose heirs were his four sisters.[14] Hindon was allotted to his sister Eleanor, wife of Andrew Blackman who held the manor until his death in 1588.[15] Blackman's successor was the one of his three daughters who married Richard Mompesson, whose brother and heir Drew held the manor in 1600.[16] Drew Mompesson was succeeded by his son Jasper who, a debtor, conveyed it to William and Robert Toope as trustees for the payment of debts and legacies.[17] Despite Mompesson's attempts to stop them the Toopes sold the manor c. 1620, possibly to Edward Perry (d. 1648), a Hindon innkeeper, who held it c. 1641.[18] In 1670 it was conveyed by James Perry, possibly Edward's son, and others to Thomas Thynne,[19] whose executors sold it to Sir Matthew Andrews of Mere, presumably c. 1683.[20] In 1701 Sir Matthew sold it to Thomas Jervoise.[21] About 1738 the manor was acquired, presumably by purchase from Jervoise, by Henry Calthorpe (knighted 1744, d. 1788) whose heir was his nephew Sir Henry Gough-Calthorpe, Bt. (created Baron Calthorpe 1796, d. 1798).[22] The manor, in 1820 consisting of 179 a. and some 89 houses,[23] passed with the Calthorpe title to Sir Henry's sons Charles (d. 1807), George (d. 1851), and Frederick Gough, Lord Calthorpe,

[96] Kelly's Dir. Wilts. (1923).
[97] V.C.H. Wilts. v. 260 n. 5.
[98] Beresford, 'New Towns', Medieval Arch. iii. 202.
[99] V.C.H. Wilts. iv. 283.   [1] See below.
[2] V.C.H. Wilts. iv. 350.   [3] Census, 1971.
[4] Map penes Sir Richard Anstruther-Gough-Calthorpe, Bt., Elvetham Farm Ho., Hartley Wintney, Hants; see plate facing p. 80.
[5] Gent. Mag. xxiv. 337.
[6] Kelly's Dir. Wilts. (1907).
[7] Map penes Sir Richard Anstruther-Gough-Calthorpe, Bt.
[8] MSS. penes the Hon. J. I. Morrison, Hawking Down Ho.   [9] e.g. Feud. Aids, v. 227.
[10] Tropenell Cart. ed. Davies, ii, pp. vii, 1–20.

[11] Ibid. pp. vii, 12–15, 20.
[12] Ibid. pp. vii, 15–16.
[13] Ibid. pp. vii, 15–16, 27–82.
[14] Cal. Inq. p.m. Hen. VII, ii, p. 438; C 142/87 no. 93; C 142/101 no. 116; pedigree in Tropenell Cart. ed. Davies, ii.   [15] Prob. 11/72 (P.C.C. 26 Rutland).
[16] Ibid.; Hoare, Mod. Wilts. Heytesbury, 219; Dunworth, 8.   [17] C 2/Jas. I/M 15/75.
[18] W.A.M. xxxviii. 605; Early-Stuart Tradesmen (W.R.S. xv), p. 19; H.R.O. Eccl. 2/159619.
[19] C.P. 25(2)/745/22 Chas. II Mich.
[20] Cal. S.P. Dom. 1683, Jan.–June, 314; C 54/4937 no. 8; W.A.M. xviii. 371.   [21] C 54/4937 no. 8.
[22] C.P. 43/621 rot. 217; Burke, Peerage (1959), 377 and n.
[23] H.R.O. 26M62, box 22, partic. of property.

who apparently in the 1850s sold it to Richard Grosvenor, marquess of Westminster.[24] The manor passed with Fonthill Abbey to Westminster's widow Elizabeth Mary (d. 1891) who sold her life interest to Sir Michael Robert Shaw-Stewart, Bt. (d. 1903), the husband of her daughter Octavia.[25] At Octavia's death in 1921 the manor passed to her son Walter Richard Shaw-Stewart who sold it in 1922.[26] The manor was broken up.[27]

ECONOMIC HISTORY. AGRICULTURE. There is evidence of prehistoric ploughing on the downs near Hindon,[28] but when it was demised to the burgesses c. 1231 the coomb was a pasture for the bishop of Winchester's sheep.[29] By the later 13th century the burgesses had ploughed it. The east and west fields of Hindon were mentioned then and in the early 14th century in terms which indicate that they were divided into small strips and cultivated in common in the manner normal in older established field systems.[30] The plots of 1–10 a. conveyed to individual burgesses, however, were presumably several and inclosed.[31] References to a north field in 1332 and later suggest cultivation in three fields.[32] There was common feeding, presumably on the summit called Hocken (later Hawking) down in the north end of the chapelry.[33] Strip cultivation still prevailed in 1431,[34] but there is no evidence of it later. The land had possibly been inclosed by the mid 16th century when many small closes were mentioned.[35] Hocken down, which in the mid 18th century lay divided among several farms,[36] had presumably been inclosed with it. In 1741 there were several small farms in Hindon.[37] In 1843 there were three of 30–45 a. and three of 10–20 a. All had farmsteads in the street except Hawking Down farm, 18 a., which, however, then had no land on the old Hocken down. Nearly all the land was ploughed.[38] In 1923 there were still several farms in Hindon, some apparently including land in other parishes.[39] In 1977 most of the land of the parish, more arable in the northern half, pasture in the southern half, was shared among smallholders.[40]

MARKETS AND FAIRS. A market-place and a building for merchants were provided and a cross raised in 1218–19, and in 1219 the bishop of Winchester was granted a Thursday market.[41] The weekly market seems to have begun immediately.

Frequent references to stallage and shambles suggest that it continued without interruption,[42] and a claim that many were attracted to it was implied in 1405.[43] Hindon was noted for its market in the mid and later 16th century when clerks of the market had opportunities to be corrupt which might not have existed had the market been less popular.[44] In the 17th century it clearly flourished as a corn market: Aubrey, rather surprisingly, rated it second only to Warminster c. 1650,[45] and c. 1707 it was coupled with Chippenham as a great Wiltshire market.[46] The market was still held in the early 19th century[47] but then its prominence may have been less marked, and in the later 19th century it seems to have declined rapidly. It ceased in the early 1880s.[48]

A Michaelmas fair was granted with the market in 1219 and seems to have been annually held.[49] In 1332, however, it was replaced by two yearly three-day fairs at Ascension and St. Luke's (18 October) which were then granted to the bishop.[50] Like the market the fairs seem to have flourished but by the 1790s, when dealing in cattle and cheese was mentioned, they had been restricted to single days, the Monday before Whitsun and 29 October.[51] In the later 19th century they were held on 27 May and 29 October. In the early 20th century only the autumn fair was held and after the First World War none was held.[52]

TRADE AND INDUSTRY. From its foundation most of the inhabitants of Hindon presumably supported themselves through trade.[53] In 1558 the town was said to abound in artisans,[54] but it has never contained a great concentration of any one trade. While the market and fairs flourished many were engaged in baking, brewing, and innkeeping,[55] and in the later 18th century the support of travellers was said to be the chief trade.[56] That trade was reduced in the 19th century when the market and fairs and coach travel declined, but revived somewhat when motor traffic increased in the mid 20th century.

In the 15th and 16th centuries there were weavers in Hindon.[57] In the late 18th century the town had a small share in the linen, dowlas, and tick-weaving industry based at Mere, but had almost lost it by 1820. Similarly the making of silk twist was in decline in 1820.[58] About 1700 there were three clock-makers and the Gerard and Stephens families continued clock-making until the late 18th century.[59] Gunpowder was apparently made at Hindon until

[24] Complete Peerage; Acct. of Wilts. Schs. 27; cf. Norah Sheard, Hist. of Hindon (priv. print.), 29.
[25] Wilts. Cuttings, xvi. 283; Burke, Peerage (1959), 2360; Kelly's Dir. Wilts. (1907).
[26] Wilts. Tracts, 166, no. 6, sale cat.
[27] Local information.
[28] V.C.H. Wilts. i (1), 275.
[29] H.R.O. Eccl. 2/159282, rot. 6 and d.
[30] Tropenell Cart. ed. Davies, ii, pp. 1–8.
[31] H.R.O. Eccl. 2/159278, rot. 5 and d.
[32] Tropenell Cart. ed. Davies, ii, pp. 8, 12, 75.
[33] Ibid. p. 17.   [34] Ibid. p. 75.
[35] C.P. 40/1161 Carte rott. 12 and d., 14 and d.; E 301/58 f. 25; C 2/Eliz. I/E 2/52.
[36] W.R.O., Land Tax add.
[37] Ibid.   [38] Ibid. Tithe Award.
[39] Wilts. Tracts, 166, no. 6, sale cat.; Kelly's Dir. Wilts. (1923).   [40] Local information.
[41] H.R.O. Eccl. 2/159275, rot. 7d.; Rot. Litt. Claus. (Rec. Com.), i. 389.
[42] Beresford, New Towns, 506 (1235–6); H.R.O. Eccl.

2/159297, rot. 4 (1265–6); Tropenell Cart. ed. Davies, ii, p. 62 (1460).   [43] Cal. Papal Reg. vi. 51.
[44] W.A.M. xii. 379–80; xxxv. 31; V.C.H. Wilts. v. 100.
[45] Aubrey, Nat. Hist. Wilts. ed. Britton, 115.
[46] W.N. & Q. iii. 377.
[47] Pigot, Nat. Com. Dir. (1844), 18.
[48] Kelly's Dir. Wilts. (1880, 1885).
[49] Rot. Litt. Claus. (Rec. Com.), i. 389; Beresford, 'New Towns', Medieval Arch. iii. 214.
[50] Cal. Chart. R. 1327–41, 258.
[51] Univ. Brit. Dir. iii (1794 edn.), 269.
[52] Kelly's Dir. Wilts. (1885 and later edns.).
[53] See above.   [54] Cal. Pat. 1557–8, 375.
[55] e.g. W.R.O. 492/9 (1464).
[56] Britton, Beauties of Eng. and Wales, xv. 262.
[57] Tropenell Cart. ed. Davies, ii, p. 44; Sess. Mins. (W.R.S. iv), 12, 55.
[58] V.C.H. Wilts. iv. 176 and n. 59, 178.
[59] W.A.M. xlviii. 313, 315, 316; Wilts. Apprentices (W.R.S. xvii), p. 104; Sar. Dioc. R.O., Papists Returns, 1767; Univ. Brit. Dir. iii (1794 edn.), 274.

the making was transferred to Salisbury *c.* 1636.[60] Trades and industries in Hindon were otherwise what might have been expected to meet the needs of the agrarian economies of the surrounding villages: craftsmen working in wood, metal, and leather were frequently mentioned,[61] as were other tradesmen such as chandlers and surgeons,[62] but no business has ever grown to a substantial size. In 1977 most of the working population was employed outside the parish.

LOCAL GOVERNMENT. In the Middle Ages Hindon was governed through the bishop of Winchester's tourns held for the liberty of East Knoyle.[63] Hindon was part of no tithing. Its bailiff fulfilled the functions of the tithingmen in East Knoyle and Fonthill Bishop, and Hindon had its own constable.[64] The bailiff presented more breaches of the assizes of bread and ale than did the tithingmen, presumably because of Hindon's market and fairs. In 1464, for example, 2 brewers, 9 taverners, 2 innkeepers, 3 bakers, and 1 butcher were amerced.[65] Other offenders were less frequently presented although in the late 15th century and the 16th affrays, unlawful gaming, and moral offences were sometimes dealt with.[66] In the 17th and 18th centuries public nuisances were the main Hindon matters presented, and both before and after the fire of 1754 the dangerous condition of chimneys was frequently reported. In 1732 and 1754 the stocks, blindhouse, pillory, and cross were said to need repair.[67]

Hindon was responsible for relieving its own poor but no record of its doing so survives. In 1812 the inhabitants agreed to provide a new workhouse and by the 1820s a house and malt-house in the street had been converted.[68] In 1835 Hindon joined Tisbury poor-law union.[69]

PARLIAMENTARY REPRESENTATION. Hindon was summoned to parliament first in 1378 and continually until 1385 but returned no member.[70] From 1448–9 until it was disfranchised in 1832 it was regularly summoned and represented by two members.[71] The returning officer was the bailiff appointed by the bishop of Winchester.[72] The franchise was possibly in the burgage holders but in the mid 17th century was apparently broadened: in 1646 and perhaps in 1660 there were double returns, of elections both by the burgesses and by the inhabitants at large.[73] In 1688 there were some 120 electors,[74] presumably the occupiers of all houses in the borough, and in 1701 and 1728 the franchise was formally vested in the householders.[75]

The influence of bishops of Winchester has been detected in 16th-century elections of members, few

of whom had local connexions.[76] From the late 16th century, however, episcopal influence waned and members of prominent south-west Wiltshire families began to be elected. The families included those of Mervyn, Thynne, Hyde, and Ludlow in the earlier 17th century and those of Hyde, Thynne, Howe, and Benett in the later 17th century.[77] The borough, open and corrupt, was the stage on which fierce local rivalries were enacted.[78] The Morley family, members of which were lessees of the demesne of Knoyle manor, enjoyed a period of influence from 1695 to 1710 but afterwards the pattern of representation changed.[79]

Hindon was reckoned an exceptionally corrupt borough by even 18th-century standards.[80] In 1702 a bill to widen the franchise to include freeholders in Downton hundred qualified to vote in county elections was passed by the Commons but went no further, and in 1774, when an election was declared void after reciprocal accusations of bribery by all four candidates, a disfranchisement bill was unsuccessfully introduced.[81] Because seats could be bought Hindon attracted a variety of candidates without local connexion. Its M.P.s included from 1735 to 1741 Henry Fox, afterwards created Baron Holland, and from 1761 to 1768 the legal writer and judge Sir William Blackstone.[82] In the 18th century, however, the influence of the Calthorpe and Beckford families grew as each acquired property in Hindon. Calthorpes appeared among the members in the earlier 18th and earlier 19th centuries and William Beckford from 1790 to 1818.[83] From the later 18th century until disfranchisement the influence on elections of the lords of Hindon and Fonthill Gifford manors was paramount.[84]

CHURCH. A chapel was built when Hindon was founded.[85] It was presumably poorly served by the rector and at least in the later 14th century, when the inhabitants had to attend their parish church, almost certainly closed. About 1405 it was refounded and apparently partly rebuilt. The inhabitants were granted rights of burial and baptism in it but not of marriage, and the church remained dependent on East Knoyle as a chapel. Under the terms of a papal licence it was served by a chaplain nominated by the rector or, if he failed to appoint, by the inhabitants of Hindon themselves.[86] The chapel was not endowed at foundation but it seems that in the 15th century the congregation, as permitted by the papal licence and it is said with royal licence, endowed it with buildings in Hindon and with land. In return the inhabitants secured sole right of appointment from the rector[87] who nevertheless retained the tithes of the chapelry.[88] The church's endowment was

[60] *Cal. S.P. Dom.* 1636–7, 53.
[61] e.g. *Wilts. Apprentices* (W.R.S. xvii); Pigot, *Nat. Com. Dir.* (1830), 802.
[62] e.g. Williams, *Cath. Recusancy* (Cath. Rec. Soc.), pp. 317, 347 (1664–5).   [63] See above.
[64] Ct. rec. in H.R.O. and W.R.O. 492/9; 492/33; 893/1–2.
[65] W.R.O. 492/9.
[66] e.g. H.R.O. Eccl. 1/79/16; Eccl. 1/79/21.
[67] Ibid. Eccl. 2/159619–22.
[68] W.R.O., Q. Sess. enrolled deeds, loose deed 18; H.R.O. 26M62, box 22, partic. of property.
[69] *Poor Law Com. 2nd Rep.* 560.
[70] *V.C.H. Wilts.* v. 73.   [71] *W.A.M.* xlvii. 205–57.
[72] T. H. B. Oldfield, *Hist. of the Boroughs,* iii. 157.

[73] *V.C.H. Wilts.* v. 145, 157 and n. 16.
[74] *W.A.M.* xviii. 371.
[75] Oldfield, *Hist. of the Boroughs,* iii. 156, 157.
[76] *V.C.H. Wilts.* v. 117–18.
[77] *W.A.M.* xlvii. 213–27.
[78] e.g. *V.C.H. Wilts.* v. 145, 157.
[79] *W.A.M.* xlvii. 227–31.
[80] *V.C.H. Wilts.* v. 224.
[81] Ibid. 225.   [82] *D.N.B.*
[83] *V.C.H. Wilts.* v. 225.   [84] Ibid.
[85] H.R.O. Eccl. 2/159278, rot. 5 and d.
[86] *Cal. Papal Reg.* vi. 51.
[87] Ibid.; *W.A.M.* xii. 379–80.
[88] *Cal. Pat.* 1557–8, 375.

confiscated at the dissolution of the chantries and in 1549 part of it was sold by the Crown.[89] The inhabitants, stating that the church could not be maintained without an endowment, petitioned for its restoration and in 1558 the Crown restored the unsold portion. A corporation of governors was established to hold and manage it for the maintenance of the chaplain and chapel, and the word 'free' was subsequently prefixed to the church's name. Although not expressly stated it is clear that from then the right of appointment passed to the Crown.[90] About 1650 the parliamentary commissioners recommended that Hindon should become a parish,[91] but it remained a chapelry and in 1783 there was still no right of marriage.[92] The corporation of governors was reconstituted in 1779 and in 1868 the real property in the chapel's endowment was sold.[93] After commutation in 1844[94] the rent-charge in respect of the great tithes of Hindon was received by the chaplain and by 1864 marriages were being performed in the church. The perpetual curacy was therefore sometimes styled a rectory[95] until in 1869 Hindon became a district chapelry and the living became a vicarage.[96] In 1922 the benefice was united with the benefice of the united parishes of Chicklade and Pertwood.[97] From then until 1960 the Crown presented alternately and since 1960 has been sole patron.[98] In 1972 the parish was united with the parish of Chicklade and Pertwood as the parish of Hindon with Chicklade and Pertwood, the benefice of which was in 1976 united with the benefice of East Knoyle.[99]

The living has never been rich. At the Dissolution the endowment consisted of 20 a. with pasture rights in Milton and East Knoyle and land and tenements in Hindon, all valued at £3 14s. 3d.[1] The premises in Hindon were restored in 1558[2] and in 1636 the chaplain's stipend was only £16.[3] In the Interregnum the tithes of Hindon as well as the rents from those premises, £49 in all, were paid to the curate.[4] In 1808 the endowment produced some £60.[5] In 1821 it was augmented by lot with £400 from Queen Anne's Bounty[6] but, with a net annual value averaging £75 1829–31, the living remained poor.[7] It was augmented by the great tithes of Hindon which at least from 1844 to 1869 the rectors of East Knoyle seem to have allowed the chaplains to receive.[8] The proceeds of the sale of premises in 1868 were invested for the incumbents by the Charity Commissioners.[9]

In 1636 the chaplain was said to have a house in the churchyard later called the Parsonage, presumably a glebe-house.[10] In 1680 it was said to need repair.[11] In 1783 the chaplain lived in Hindon but not in the Parsonage which in 1833 was said to be unfit for residence.[12] In 1864 there was said to be no glebe-house.[13] West of the church on land formerly in Chicklade a new house was built in 1950 and enlarged in 1960.[14]

In 1636 a dispute between the chaplain, Samuel Yarworth, and the governors over his stipend and behaviour led to Yarworth's forcible removal from his house and to a suit in the court of High Commission.[15] George Jenkins, chaplain during the Civil War, conformed and in 1648 subscribed to the *Concurrent Testimony*.[16] In 1662 the church lacked much that was thought necessary for divine worship.[17] In 1783 it was served by the chaplain John Evans who with his brother James held Sunday services in four local churches. Those at Hindon were held in the morning and afternoon. Prayers were said on two weekdays and the Sacrament was administered at the great festivals to some twenty communicants.[18] On Census Sunday in 1851 there were congregations of 160 and 240 at the morning and evening services.[19] In 1864 two Sunday services were still being held but Holy Communion was less frequent than in many parishes.[20]

In 1553 the dedication was to St. Luke,[21] but was later to *ST. JOHN THE BAPTIST*. About 1804 the church consisted of apparently undivided nave and chancel, a south tower the lower stage of which served as a porch, and a small south transeptal chapel against the tower to the west. The tower appears to have been that built at foundation and parts of the nave and chancel may also have survived from that time. The west doorway and window and a south window of the nave were later-medieval, and the south window of the chapel was 18th-century.[22] In 1836 the church was enlarged to designs of William Gover.[23] A north aisle was added and a round-headed window placed in the south wall of the nave at the west end.[24] In 1870–1 the church was taken down and rebuilt in Early English style to designs of T. H. Wyatt and at the expense of Richard, marquess of Westminster (d. 1869).[25] The new church has chancel with south vestry, an aisled and clerestoried nave, and a south tower which serves as a porch.

In 1553 there were two bells. Later there were

[89] E 301/58 ff. 24v.–25; *Cal. Pat.* 1548–9, 286; see below.
[90] *Cal. Pat.* 1557–8, 375.   [91] *W.A.M.* xl. 308.
[92] *Vis. Queries, 1783* (W.R.S. xxvii), p. 120.
[93] *Endowed Char. Wilts.* (S. Div.), 232–7.
[94] See p. 95.
[95] H.O. 129/266/3/7/8; Sar. Dioc. R.O., Vis. Queries, 1864.
[96] *Lond. Gaz.* 22 June 1869, pp. 3544–5.
[97] Ibid. 18 Aug. 1922, pp. 6077–8.
[98] Ibid.; 5 Aug. 1960, p. 5370.
[99] Ibid. 30 May 1972, p. 6506; 21 May 1976, p. 7542.
[1] E 301/58 ff. 24v.–25.
[2] *Cal. Pat.* 1557–8, 375–6.
[3] *Cal. S.P. Dom.* 1635–6, 217.
[4] *W.A.M.* xl. 308.   [5] B.L. Ch. Briefs, B. xlviii. 9.
[6] C. Hodgson, *Queen Anne's Bounty* (1845 edn.), p. cccxxxv.
[7] *Rep. Com. Eccl. Revenues*, 836–7; *V.C.H. Wilts.* iii. 53.
[8] H.O. 129/266/3/7/8; Sar. Dioc. R.O., Vis. Queries, 1864.
[9] *Endowed Char. Wilts.* (S. Div.), 236–7.
[10] *Cal. S.P. Dom.* 1635–6, 217; *Vis. Queries, 1783* (W.R.S. xxvii), p. 120.
[11] Sar. Dioc. R.O., Diocese Bk.
[12] *Vis. Queries, 1783* (W.R.S. xxvii), p. 120; *Rep. Com. Eccl. Revenues*, 836–7.
[13] Sar. Dioc. R.O., Vis. Queries.
[14] Ex inf. the Revd. L. W. Daffurn, Hindon Vicarage.
[15] *Cal. S.P. Dom.* 1635–6, 217, 434, 502, 506, 515; *Wilts. Q. Sess. Rec.* ed. Cunnington, 117.
[16] *W.A.M.* xxxiv. 182; *Calamy Revised*, ed. Matthews, 557.   [17] Sar. Dioc. R.O., Chwdns.' Pres.
[18] *Vis. Queries, 1783* (W.R.S. xxvii), pp. 9, 119–20.
[19] H.O. 129/266/3/7/8.
[20] Sar. Dioc. R.O., Vis. Queries.
[21] *W.A.M.* xii. 370.
[22] J. Buckler, water-colour in W.A.S. Libr., vol. ii. 3 (1804); see plate facing p. 81.
[23] Colvin, *Brit. Architects*, 355.
[24] *W.A.M.* xlii. 200.
[25] Sar. Dioc. R.O., Pet. for Faculties, bdle. 18, no. 12.

five which with additional metal Abel Rudhall cast into six in 1754.[26] They were rehung in 1934[27] and remained in the church in 1977.[28]

In 1553 a chalice of 9 oz. was left when the king's commissioners took 2½ oz. of plate. New plate consisting of chalice, paten, and flagon was given under his will by James Ames (d. 1828), a Hindon surgeon.[29] It belonged to the church in 1977.[30]

The registers date from 1599.[31]

NONCONFORMITY. The Roman Catholic martyr John Story was chosen M.P. for Hindon in 1547.[32] In the late 17th century Hindon was probably under the strong Catholic influence emanating from Fonthill Gifford and it housed a small papist community. Papists remained there throughout the 18th century. In the later 18th century, when their leader was Henry Lambert, a surgeon, they were said to be part of the Wardour congregation.[33]

There were four Protestant nonconformists in Hindon in 1676.[34] In 1787 a dwelling-house was certified for Independents,[35] and in 1810 a Congregational church was built near Hindon on land in Fonthill Gifford, claimed as an offshoot by both Warminster and Trowbridge.[36] On Census Sunday in 1851 there were congregations of 95 and 64 at the two services.[37] The church was possibly served from East Knoyle in the later 19th century.[38] By 1977 it had been closed.

A room was certified for Primitive Methodists in 1836 and in 1841 the Providence chapel was built for them behind the south side of the street. A total of 80 attended the two services on Census Sunday in

1851.[39] In 1896 that chapel was replaced by one, on the north side of the street,[40] in which services were still held in 1977.

EDUCATION. In 1783 poor children were taught at a school supported by William Beckford of Fonthill Gifford.[41] In 1818 there were also a school supported by George, Baron Calthorpe, presumably that near Hindon on Chicklade land, and three schools for very young children.[42] In 1822 Lord Calthorpe seems to have enlarged his school to make separate boys and girls schools. In 1833 those schools were attended by some 136 children and there were then three small day- and boarding-schools for 36–40 pupils.[43] In 1858 there was still another school in the parish,[44] but in 1864 only Lord Calthorpe's, then a single school at which children stayed until they were twelve or thirteen.[45] In 1881 it was attended by children from Chicklade and possibly from other parishes.[46] In 1906 the average attendance was 133.[47] It had fallen to 74 by 1936.[48] In 1977 there were seventeen children on the roll.[49]

CHARITY FOR THE POOR. By will proved 1828 James Ames gave an annuity of £10 to the overseers for distribution in bread and clothing to the relieved poor. In 1833 it was distributed in coal. In 1860 the charity's capital was £333. The annual income of £8 6s. 8d. was spent on bread and calico given out on Christmas eve.[50] The charity was regulated by Schemes of 1913 and 1957. In 1965 twenty people each received 8s. 6d.[51]

[26] Walters, *Wilts. Bells*, 104.
[27] Sar. Dioc. R.O., Pet. for Faculties, bdle. 75, no. 20.
[28] Ex inf. the Revd. L. W. Daffurn.
[29] Nightingale, *Wilts. Plate*, 60.
[30] Ex inf. the Revd. L. W. Daffurn.
[31] Ibid.   [32] *D.N.B.*
[33] Williams, *Cath. Recusancy* (Cath. Rec. Soc.), pp. 8, 78, 90 n. 123, 190–1, 255, 259, 285, 287, 315, 316, 317, 347.   [34] *W.N. & Q.* iii. 538.
[35] *V.C.H. Wilts.* iii. 134 n. 2.
[36] Ibid. 133; Stribling, *Wilts. & E. Som. Cong. Union*, 51.   [37] H.O. 129/266/3/8/11.
[38] Stribling, op. cit. 51.
[39] Sar. Dioc. R.O., Certs. Dissenters' Meeting-Houses; H.O. 129/266/3/7/9.

[40] O.S. Maps 6″, Wilts. LXIV (1889 edn.), LXIV. NW. (1901 edn.); date on bldg.
[41] *Vis. Queries, 1783* (W.R.S. xxvii), p. 120.
[42] *Educ. of Poor Digest*, 1028.
[43] *Educ. Enquiry Abstract*, 1039.
[44] *Acct. of Wilts. Schs.* 27.
[45] Sar. Dioc. R.O., Vis. Queries.
[46] *Rep. of Educ. Cttee. of Council, 1881–2* [C 3312–I], p. 285, H.C. (1882), xxiii.
[47] *Return of Non-Provided Schs.* 39.
[48] Bd. of Educ., List 21, 1936 (H.M.S.O.), 424.
[49] Ex inf. Chief Education Officer, County Hall, Trowbridge.
[50] *Endowed Char. Wilts.* (S. Div.), 235, 237.
[51] Char. Com. file 202800.

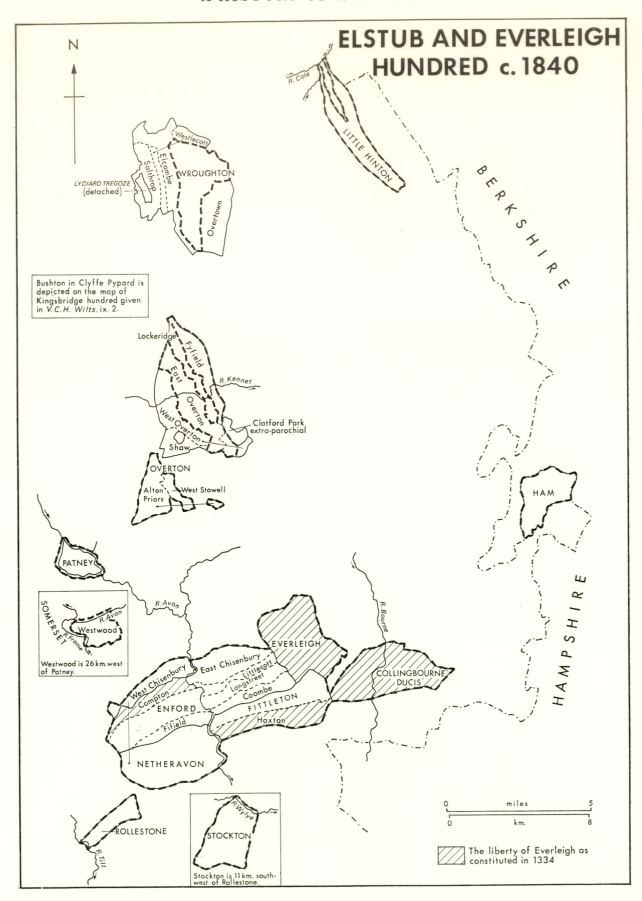

ELSTUB AND EVERLEIGH HUNDRED c. 1840

N

R. Cole

LITTLE HINTON

BERKSHIRE

Westlecott

Elcombe

Salthrop

WROUGHTON

LYDIARD TREGOZE (detached)

Overtown

Bushton in Clyffe Pypard is depicted on the map of Kingsbridge hundred given in *V.C.H. Wilts.* ix. 2.

Lockeridge

Fyfield

East

R. Kennet

Overton

West Overton

Clatford Park extra-parochial

Shaw

OVERTON

Alton Priors — West Stowell

HAM

PATNEY

R. Avon

SOMERSET

R. Avon

Westwood

R. Frome

Westwood is 26 km. west of Patney.

EVERLEIGH

R. Bourne

HAMPSHIRE

West Chisenbury — East Chisenbury

Littlecott

Longstreet

Compton

Coombe

COLLINGBOURNE DUCIS

ENFORD

FITTLETON

Fifield

Haxton

NETHERAVON

miles 0 ——— 5

km. 0 ——— 8

ROLLESTONE

R. Wylye

STOCKTON

R. Till

Stockton is 11 km. south-west of Rollestone.

The liberty of Everleigh as constituted in 1334

ELSTUB AND EVERLEIGH HUNDRED

THE HUNDRED of Elstub and Everleigh as constituted in 1841 was an amalgamation of the medieval hundred of Elstub and the liberty of Everleigh. It comprised the whole of ten ancient parishes and in addition three chapelries which had become civil parishes and three tithings.[1] The ancient parishes were Collingbourne Ducis, Enford (including the tithings of Enford, East Chisenbury, Compton, Coombe, Fifield, Littlecott, and Longstreet), Everleigh, Fittleton (including Haxton tithing), Ham, Little Hinton, Netheravon (with its detached tithing of West Chisenbury), Patney, Rollestone, and Stockton. The chapelries and civil parishes were Alton Priors (including West Stowell tithing), Fyfield, and Westwood. The tithings were those of Bushton in Clyffe Pypard, East Overton in Overton, and Wroughton in Wroughton. Westwood was a chapelry of Bradford on Avon but, when the history of that parish was related,[2] was reserved for treatment under Elstub and Everleigh hundred. Overton parish, which included Alton Priors, Fyfield, and East Overton, also included West Overton, Shaw, and Lockeridge in Selkley hundred, and Wroughton parish included Elcombe, Salthrop, Westlecott, and Overtown which with Uffcott in Broad Hinton formed a group called 'the five tithings' attached to Blackgrove (later Kingsbridge) hundred,[3] but, because the parish church of Overton was in East Overton tithing and Wroughton parish church was in Wroughton tithing, the histories of the whole of both parishes are given below. The history of Bushton, however, was given with that of the parish in which it lay.[4]

In 1086 the hundred of Elstub comprised Enford, in which the tithings of East Chisenbury and Fifield were included, Netheravon with West Chisenbury, and Fittleton which probably included Haxton.[5] The compact block of land so formed was situated on the eastern edge of Salisbury Plain. It extended across two chalk bluffs divided by the valley of the Christchurch Avon through which ran one of the roads linking Devizes, Pewsey, and the vale between them with Salisbury. The hundred took its name from Elstub, a riverside meadow in Enford tithing, where much elder could still be seen in 1978.[6] When and how the prior of St. Swithun, Winchester, owner in 1255, acquired the hundred is unknown but in 1086 he already held the estate in which the hundred meeting-place lay.[7] The priors much enlarged Elstub hundred in the 13th century by adding to it their other estates scattered widely over the county in other hundreds. The 'ragged' hundred so created lacked geographical unity, its members being linked only by a common ownership. Little Hinton in the north of the county was withdrawn from Thornhill hundred in the earlier 13th century,[8] Patney in mid Wiltshire from Studfold c. 1248,[9] Stockton in the south from Branch before 1249,[10] East Overton tithing and Fyfield chapelry from Selkley in the early 13th century,[11] Alton Priors from Swanborough by 1281,[12] Wroughton tithing from Blackgrove by 1316,[13] and Ham from Kinwardstone by 1334. Although Westwood on the Somerset

[1] Census, 1841.
[2] V.C.H. Wilts. vii. 24 n.
[3] Ibid. ix. 4.
[4] Ibid. 3, 23 sqq.
[5] Ibid. ii, p. 184.
[6] P.N. Wilts. (E.P.N.S.), 327.
[7] Rot. Hund. (Rec. Com.), ii (1), 230.
[8] Ibid. 233.
[9] Ibid. 235.
[10] Ibid. 233; Crown Pleas, 1249 (W.R.S. xvi), pp. 187, 252.
[11] Rot. Hund. (Rec. Com.), ii (1), 270.
[12] Ibid. 234; Plac. de Quo Warr. (Rec. Com.), 806.
[13] Rot. Hund. (Rec. Com.), ii (1), 243; Feud. Aids, v. 202.

border was included in Elstub for taxation purposes in 1334, it was not finally transferred from Bradford hundred until the mid 16th century.[14] Rollestone on Salisbury Plain was transferred from Dole between 1428 and 1524 although it had no known connexion with St. Swithun's.[15] Bushton in Clyffe Pypard, another property belonging to St. Swithun's, was transferred to Elstub in the mid 16th century.[16] At the Dissolution the hundred passed to the Crown. Although it was not expressly mentioned in the grant of 1541[17] which transferred much of the property of St. Swithun's to the new cathedral chapter of Winchester, Elstub hundred was apparently included in the endowment.

The townships of West Chisenbury, in Netheravon, and Fittleton claimed to answer at the sheriff's tourn in both 1255 and 1275, and in 1275 East Chisenbury in Enford claimed franchises associated with view of frankpledge.[18] Lords who held estates within Elstub, as constituted in 1275, either denied or encroached upon the liberties enjoyed by the prior there. In the 15th century Margaret Dyneley and William Darell, successively lords of Fittleton and of Coombe in Enford, apparently held the view within both manors, a right unsuccessfully challenged by the prior of St. Swithun.[19] Franchisal jurisdiction associated with the view of frankpledge within the capital manor of Enford, to which the priors of St. Swithun had been entitled, was included in a grant of the manor made by the Crown to Thomas Culpeper in 1541.[20] In 1597 the Crown expressly granted to those living in Netheravon all the liberties and franchises to which tenants of the duchy of Lancaster, of which Netheravon was then a part, were entitled.[21] Separate franchisal courts were held there in the 16th century by duchy officials and in 1652 the courts were still entitled to try all actions under 40s. between duchy tenants. Fishing rights in the Avon also belonged to the Sovereign as duke of Lancaster.[22]

The liberties, including return of writs, taken by the earls of Leicester within Everleigh manor, where they had a prison in the mid 13th century, had by 1334 been extended over their other Wiltshire estates except Netheravon, Ablington in Figheldean, and Chitterne. Thus by 1334 Everleigh and Collingbourne Ducis had been withdrawn from Kinwardstone hundred, Compton tithing in Enford from Amesbury hundred, and Haxton tithing in Fittleton from Elstub hundred, to form the liberty of Everleigh.[23] No record exists to illustrate the administration of the liberty or the business of its courts. After the estates of the liberty became part of the duchy of Lancaster in the later 14th century and the earlier 15th the duchy seems, at least in the mid 16th century, to have exercised franchisal rights in Everleigh, to the court of which Haxton and Compton then still owed suit, and in Collingbourne Ducis where separate courts were held.[24] Although Compton had reverted to Amesbury hundred for certain administrative purposes by the end of the 14th century, it apparently continued to be considered part of the liberty. In the 17th century, however, it owed suit at the Amesbury hundred courts. Not until 1841 was it finally reckoned part of Elstub and Everleigh hundred.[25] In the 15th century the liberty, wrongly referred to in 1428 as a hundred, was generally treated as part of Elstub hundred for the purposes of central government but c. 1540 was still recognized as a separate entity.[26] Hundred and

[14] V.C.H. Wilts. iv. 299; Feud. Aids, v. 246; E 179/197/155; Taxation Lists (W.R.S. x), 4.
[15] Rot. Hund. (Rec. Com.), ii (1), 254; Feud. Aids, v. 243; E 179/197/152.
[16] V.C.H. Wilts. ix. 3.
[17] L. & P. Hen. VIII, xvi, p. 417.
[18] Rot. Hund. (Rec. Com.), ii (1), 230, 258.
[19] B.L. Harl. Roll CC. 23; V.C.H. Hants, ii. 115.
[20] C 66/708 m. 5.   [21] D.L. 41/3/10.
[22] D.L. 30/127/1902 ff. 1–3, 35; D.L. 30/127/1903 m. 2d.; E 317/Wilts. 37 m. 3.

[23] Crown Pleas, 1249 (W.R.S. xvi), p. 197; Wilts. Inq. p.m. 1327–77 (Index Libr.), 15; V.C.H. Wilts. iv. 299; Levi Fox, 'Honor of Leic. 1066–1399', E.H.R. liv. 402. The earl of Leicester attempted to withdraw Compton from Amesbury as early as 1256: Close R. 1254–6, 439–40.
[24] D.L. 30/127/1902 ff. 26, 31, 32v., 39; D.L. 30/127/1904.
[25] E 179/196/51; Feud. Aids, v. 240; W.R.O. 192/24A; Land Tax; Census, 1841.
[26] Feud. Aids, v. 233; L. & P. Hen. VIII, xiv (1), p. 301; W.R.O. 130/71, Ayer's quietus, c. 1540.

liberty were deemed to be merged by 1545,[27] and thereafter formed the hundred of Elstub and Everleigh.

The extensive liberties to which the prior of St. Swithun was entitled in Elstub were granted by royal charters of 1208 and 1232. They included freedom from suit of shire and hundred and return of writs, which meant that the prior could exclude the sheriff from the hundred.[28] Because of the difficulty of administering a disjointed hundred, Elstub until the Dissolution was divided into two units, one in the Avon valley centred on Enford where the prior had a prison in 1249,[29] and the other on Alton Priors. The courts for the Enford portion, entitled hundred courts and later hundred courts with views of frankpledge, were held in Elstub meadow by the prior's steward at Hock-tide and Martinmas on the same days as the Enford manor courts. To them the tithings of Netheravon, West Chisenbury, East Chisenbury, Littlecott and Fifield (later Littlecott and Longstreet), Coombe, Fifield, and Fittleton with Haxton owed suit.[30] The tithings of East Overton, Alton Priors, West Stowell, and Patney attended the courts held twice yearly at Alton Priors.[31] The prior did not apparently expect the outlying tithings of Bushton, Westwood, Wroughton, Little Hinton, Ham, and Stockton to attend and exercised his franchisal jurisdiction at their own courts. After the Dissolution, however, courts, usually called views of frankpledge and courts of the hundred, for Elstub and Everleigh in its entirety, of which records for 1580 and a few years in the 17th century survive, were held in Elstub meadow by the deputy of the steward of Winchester chapter. In 1580 all the tithings, including Compton, which comprised the 19th-century hundred attended.[32] In the 17th century the suitors were Enford and its tithings including Compton, Netheravon with West Chisenbury, Fittleton with Haxton, Everleigh, Collingbourne Ducis, Stockton, Rollestone, Patney, East Overton, Fyfield, Alton Priors, West Stowell, and Bushton. Westwood attended in 1685 but the other outliers Ham, Little Hinton, and Wroughton did not.[33] The scantiness of the hundred court rolls, both before and after the Dissolution, suggests that both the priors of St. Swithun and Winchester chapter may have exercised their franchisal rights at the manorial courts, and that from an early date the hundred courts were formal occasions at which decisions made, judgements given, and elections of tithingmen made locally were merely confirmed.[34]

[27] *Taxation Lists* (W.R.S. x), 3.
[28] *Rot. Chart.* (Rec. Com.), 183; *Cal. Chart. R. 1226–57*, 145; *Rot. Hund.* (Rec. Com.), ii (1), 230; *V.C.H. Wilts.* v. 56–8.   [29] *Crown Pleas, 1249* (W.R.S. xvi), p. 197.
[30] Mun. D. & C. Winton., 13th- and 14th-cent. hund. ct. rolls; B.L. Harl. Rolls W. 3–31; V. 20–33; CC. 23.
[31] Mun. D. & C. Winton., 13th- and 14th-cent. ct. rolls.
[32] B.L. Harl. Roll V. 34.

[33] Mun. D. & C. Winton., box 84, 17th-cent. hund. ct. rolls; Florence R. Goodman, *Revd. Landlords and their Tenants* (Winch. priv. print. 1930), 398. In 1651, however, W. Chisenbury, inexplicably, was reckoned part of Swanborough hund.: *V.C.H. Wilts.* x. 4.
[34] B.L. Harl. Rolls W. 3–31; V. 20–33; Mun. D. & C. Winton., 13th- and 14th-cent. hund. ct. rolls and ct. rolls for Alton Priors; box 84, 17th-cent. hund. ct. rolls.

COLLINGBOURNE DUCIS

COLLINGBOURNE DUCIS is the smaller and more southerly of the two adjoining parishes called Collingbourne.[1] Originally the name, meaning stream of Cola's people, may have applied to the whole of the upper part of the Bourne valley.[2] As the element *inga* implies, it was settled comparatively early.[3]

A distinction between the two Collingbournes existed in 903 when 50 hides and the church at what was later called Collingbourne Kingston were granted to the New Minster at Winchester.[4] Its neighbour on the south had been given a distinguishing name of Earl's (*Comitis*) by 1256 when the earl of Leicester was lord of the manor.[5] The name Duke's (*Ducis*) supplanted Earl's after the Wiltshire lands of the honor of Leicester became part of the duchy of Lancaster,[6] and was fairly regularly used from the early 15th century. The parish has also frequently been called Lower Collingbourne.

The parish lies on the Upper Chalk of Salisbury Plain and is bisected by the Bourne which rises a few miles north of the village, flows southwards through it, and is compounded with the village name.[7] For much of its course through Collingbourne Ducis the Bourne is a small stream, dry in summer; but in the past it was liable to flood in wet weather. Early meetings of the parish council were much concerned with flooding in the village street. Refuse frequently blocked the stream's course under the bridges.[8]

The gravels of the river's shallow valley provide the site of the village, and those of a now virtually dry eastern tributary that of the hamlet of Cadley, the only other settlement in the parish. Three western tributaries of the Bourne, now likewise dry, have scored narrow gravel covered valleys through the chalk. South of the village the Bourne is flanked on either side by water-meadows and beyond them the land rises to heights of over 150 m. on the chalk, climbing rather more steeply on the eastern side. Much of that side was occupied by the southern end of Collingbourne woods, part of Chute forest until the 14th century.[9] There was some felling in the 19th century, particularly near Wick down,[10] but in 1929 the woods covered over 300 a.,[11] roughly the same area as in 1975. South of the woods and in the extreme south-east corner of the parish is Crawlboys farm, with a farm-house and some of its buildings dating from the late 17th century or early 18th. The remoteness of the farm from the village and church, and its connexion with the woods, of which some of its early owners were guardians, made it a virtually detached part of the parish.[12]

Until 1934 the parish covered 3,431 a. (1,388 ha.), and was roughly crescent shaped. The eastern end of its southern boundary is formed by a bank and ditch, following a line, the curve of which suggests that it may represent the northern boundary of the park of Ludgershall Castle. In 1934 Collingbourne Sunton, a hamlet which is beside a continuation of Collingbourne Ducis village street, and the northern part of the hamlet of Cadley, both of which until then were in Collingbourne Kingston, were brought into Collingbourne Ducis parish. A narrow projection was thereby added on the north,[13] giving a total area of 1,469 ha. (3,629 a.).

Collingbourne Ducis adjoins Ludgershall, an early market centre, on the south-east. It is 17 km. south of Marlborough and 24 km. north of Salisbury. Before 1831 the two principal routes leading southwards towards Salisbury bypassed the village. That from Hungerford (Berks.) entered the parish by the Shears inn and in 1772 was turnpiked as far as Southly bridge.[14] The stretch beyond that towards Salisbury was later abandoned. The road from Marlborough to Salisbury, had it kept its original course, would have missed the parish altogether. That road, however, fell out of use beyond Everleigh, and in 1831 a sort of link road was formed by turnpiking the road running from Southgrove copse in Burbage, through the two Collingbourne villages, and up Shaw hill in Collingbourne Ducis to join the Hungerford–Salisbury road.[15] Its course as the main road was almost immediately changed. At the south end of the village, instead of climbing Shaw hill, it took a more westerly route, called in 1777 Small Way, and followed the Bourne towards Salisbury.[16] The Andover–Devizes road, crossing the parish from east to west, and the Bourne by Leckford bridge, was turnpiked under an Act of 1762.[17] The Swindon, Marlborough & Andover Railway, opened in 1882, ran through the parish with a station at Cadley.[18] The line was closed in 1961.[19]

Prehistoric finds and sites, particularly the barrow cemeteries on Snail and Cow downs, indicate the congregation of men in the region from late Neolithic times.[20] There is also evidence of farming activity on the downs in the late Bronze Age and the Romano-British Period.[21] Short stretches of prehistoric ditch occur along the southern and western boundaries and there is an early enclosure on Wick down. The great Iron-Age fort on Sidbury hill in North Tidworth, a focus for many tracks and ditches, is near the southern parish boundary.[22]

In 1334 Collingbourne Ducis was taxed rather

[1] This article was written in 1975.
[2] *P.N. Wilts.* (E.P.N.S.), 342.
[3] *V.C.H. Wilts.* i (2), 479.
[4] Finberg, *Early Wessex Chart.* p. 80.
[5] *Close R.* 1254–6, 410.   [6] See p. 137.
[7] Maps used include: O.S. Maps 1/50,000, sheet 184 (1974 edn.); 1/25,000, SU 25 (1958 edn.); 6″, Wilts. XLVIII (1883 and later edns.), XLIX (1883 and later edns.); 1/2,500, Wilts. XLVIII (1880 and later edns.), XLIX (1880 and later edns.); Geol. Surv. Map 1″, drift, sheet 282 (1967 edn.), sheet 283 (1959 edn.).

[8] W.R.O. 426/1.   [9] *V.C.H. Wilts.* iv. 425.
[10] W.R.O. 9, acct. bks.
[11] *Wilts. Gaz.* 19 Sept. 1929.   [12] See pp. 110–11.
[13] *Census*, 1931 (pt. II, 1934).
[14] *V.C.H. Wilts.* iv. 262.
[15] Ibid.; *Cary's Improved Eng.* (1832), map 18.
[16] W.R.O. 451/97.
[17] *V.C.H. Wilts.* iv. 260.   [18] Ibid. 281.
[19] Ex inf. P.R. Dept., British Rail, W.R.
[20] *W.A.M.* lvi. 127–48; x. 85–105.
[21] Ibid. lvi. 130.   [22] *V.C.H. Wilts.* i (1), 255, 264.

lower than Everleigh, the only other entire parish in the liberty of Everleigh, to which they both belonged. In 1377, however, it had 127 poll-tax payers to Everleigh's 99.[23] To the benevolence of 1545 it contributed £7, Everleigh £4. To the subsidy of 1576 it paid £8, a little less than Everleigh.[24] In 1801 the population was 457. In 1861 it was 564 but thereafter declined. The boundary change of 1934 added 166 inhabitants and in 1951 the population was 544.[25] In 1971 it was 590.[26]

The village of Collingbourne Ducis is strung out for nearly 1 km. along the main road to Marlborough. The church, manor farm-house (now called Court Farm), and the old and new rectory-houses stand towards the southern end of the street which there widens and is called Church Street. The farm buildings of Collingbourne farm stood north of the rectory-house until the 19th century. At that end of the village, until filled in c. 1960, there was a large pond called Great Mere formed by a widening of the Bourne. It could be crossed by a ford.[27] North-west of Great Mere was another large pond in 1777 which had disappeared by the 1880s.[28] East of Great Mere, along Mill Lane, stood the windmill in 1773.[29]

The early manor farm-house was probably represented in 1975 by the house called the Hermitage. That house dates mainly from the 18th century but possibly incorporates part of an earlier building. The present Court Farm, which adjoins it, was built for a marquess of Ailesbury in the 1850s. Spaced out along both sides of the street are a number of small timber-framed houses, their walls chiefly infilled with flint, rubble, and brick. Some are thatched. Most appear to be of 17th- or 18th-century origin. Linden Cottage is dated 1694. Houses on the west side are reached by small bridges spanning the Bourne which runs down that side of the road.

The hamlet of Cadley lies north-east of Collingbourne Ducis village along Cadley Road, which formerly continued eastwards beyond the Shears inn.[30] In the 18th century the main settlement at Cadley seems to have been concentrated about the crossing of Cadley Road and the Hungerford–Salisbury road.[31] In 1777 there were at least fourteen houses in the hamlet.[32] The railway station and a small nonconformist chapel were built along Cadley Road in the 1880s. In 1975 almost nothing remained of the settlement at the cross-road and 19th- and 20th-century development has been concentrated at the western end of Cadley Road.

In 1604 the rector and eighteen parishioners petitioned for a licence for Robert Fay to keep a victualling house. A reason given was that many travellers lost on the downs sought shelter in the village.[33] The Shears inn at Cadley was in existence at least in 1773.[34] The present building is of the early

19th century. A New Inn is mentioned in 1844;[35] the Blue Lion was in the village street in 1863[36] and probably much earlier. After the coming of the railway it was called the Blue Lion and Railway Hotel. The present building, which is of vitreous brick with red-brick dressings, dates from the early 18th century.

William Batt (1744–1812), physician and scientist, was born in Collingbourne Ducis where his family held land. He practised for many years in Genoa.[37]

MANORS. At the time of Domesday Collingbourne Ducis was held by the king, having been held by Harold before the Conquest.[38] It may, with Everleigh, have been granted to Robert de Beaumont (d. 1118), said to have been created earl of Leicester, for like Everleigh it belonged to Robert's grandson to whom the earldom of Leicester passed.[39] Thereafter COLLINGBOURNE DUCIS passed with the earldom in the same way as Everleigh to become part of the duchy of Lancaster's Wiltshire estate. In 1536 Collingbourne was granted, like Everleigh, to Edward Seymour, Viscount Beauchamp (from 1537 earl of Hertford, from 1546 duke of Somerset, the Lord Protector).[40]

After the Protector's execution in 1552 Collingbourne passed to his son Edward Seymour, then a minor.[41] It was confirmed to Edward, by then created earl of Hertford, in 1581.[42] Edward was succeeded in 1621 by his grandson William, who was restored as duke of Somerset in 1660, a month before he died without surviving issue.[43] His grandson and heir, William, duke of Somerset, died a minor and unmarried in 1671. That William's Wiltshire estates then devolved upon his sister Elizabeth, wife of Thomas Bruce, who succeeded as earl of Ailesbury in 1685 and died in 1741.[44]

Collingbourne passed to Charles, son of Thomas and Elizabeth, on whose death in 1747 the earldom of Ailesbury became extinct. Charles's lands and the barony of Bruce of Tottenham passed to the son of his sister Elizabeth, wife of George Brudenell, earl of Cardigan (d. 1732). That son, Thomas Brudenell-Bruce, was created earl of Ailesbury in 1776 and died in 1814. His younger son Charles was created marquess of Ailesbury in 1821 and died in 1856.[45] Collingbourne continued to descend with the Ailesbury title until 1929 when with other parts of the Savernake estate it was broken up and sold in lots.[46] Two of the principal farms, Court and Hougomont,[47] were sold respectively to A. J. Bridgman and J. P. Wiltshire. Both farms were bought by the War Department in 1939.[48]

An estate including 10 virgates of land was conveyed in 1326 by Henry of Hanydon, a chaplain, and John Tourand to Walter Douce and Emmeline his wife.[49] That may be an early reference to the estate

[23] Ibid. iv. 299, 308.
[24] Taxation Lists (W.R.S. x), 3, 124.
[25] V.C.H. Wilts. iv. 345.   [26] Census, 1971.
[27] W.R.O. 9, map, 1777; local information.
[28] W.R.O. 9, map, 1777; O.S. Map 1/2,500, Wilts. XLVIII. 3 (1880 edn.); local information.
[29] Andrews and Dury, Map (W.R.S. viii), pl. 9.
[30] W.R.O. 9, map, 1777.
[31] Andrews and Dury, Map (W.R.S. viii), pl. 9.
[32] W.R.O. 9, survey.
[33] Hist. MSS. Com. 55, Var. Coll. i, p. 77.
[34] W.R.O. 9, survey.   [35] Ibid. Tithe Award.
[36] Ibid. 665/22, par. jnl.   [37] D.N.B.
[38] V.C.H. Wilts. ii, p. 118.   [39] See p. 136.
[40] D.L. 42/22 f. 146v.   [41] Cal. Pat. 1553, 4.
[42] C 66/1218 m. 33; Complete Peerage, s.v. Hertford.
[43] Complete Peerage, s.v. Somerset.
[44] Ibid. s.v. Ailesbury.   [45] Ibid.
[46] W.A.S. Libr., sale cat. xxviii, no. 29.   [47] See below.
[48] W.A.S. Libr., sale cat. xxviii, no. 29; ex inf. Defence Land Agent, Durrington.
[49] Feet of F. 1272–1327 (W.R.S. i), p. 122.

called *COLLINGBOURNE FARM* which John Dowse (d. 1535 or 1536) held of the duchy of Lancaster.[50] John was succeeded by his son Richard, perhaps the free tenant of that name present at the court of Collingbourne Ducis manor in 1572.[51]

A Richard Dowse died in 1611 or 1612 having settled an estate of some 390 a., then called a manor, upon his son Thomas.[52] In 1615–16 Thomas settled it on his son Richard, and in 1640–1 Richard settled it on his son Walter. Richard and Walter conveyed it in 1656 to William Long.[53] William Long conveyed it to Richard Long, and Richard to his son Henry.[54] In 1724 Henry Long of Melksham conveyed the manor, or 'reputed manor called Collingbourne Farm', to the Revd. Thomas Cheney. It then included rather more than 200 a. and paid a quit-rent to the lord of Collingbourne Ducis manor. Cheney was followed soon after 1724 by his son Thomas. The younger Thomas died in 1764; the farm passed to Robert Lowth, soon to become bishop of Oxford and later bishop of London,[55] whose wife Mary was a cousin of the younger Thomas.

The bishop died in 1787 having left the farm to his wife for life. In 1794 she conveyed it to their son Robert who sold it in 1805 to Thomas Bruce, earl of Ailesbury (d. 1814). Thenceforth it was merged in the manor of Collingbourne Ducis.

About 1400 an estate called the manor of *CRAWLBOYS*, of which John Skilling was tenant, was granted by John Croilboys and his wife Agnes to Sir Thomas de Skelton and his wife Joan.[56] In 1464 Crawlboys was among the estates conveyed by John Wynnard and his wife Elizabeth to John Wydeslade in fee.[57] By then the custody of the chase of Collingbourne Ducis went with the grant of Crawlboys.[58] In 1482 Thomas Wayte died seised of Crawlboys and the keepership of the woods in the right of his wife Elizabeth, perhaps the daughter of John Wydeslade. His heir was his brother William.[59] In 1552 Peter Merkat held Crawlboys as a free tenant of Collingbourne Ducis manor.[60]

By 1575 Crawlboys and the custody of the Collingbourne woods had passed to Thomas Philpot (d. 1586) who also held the manor of Chute and the wardenship of Chute forest.[61] Thomas's son and heir, Sir George Philpot, died in 1624 seised of Crawlboys and the custody of the woods.[62] His heir was his son, Sir John (d. c. 1634), who was compensated by the king for the loss of the wardenship.[63] The connexion between Crawlboys and the custody of the Collingbourne woods was apparently then severed.[64] Sir John's son, Sir Henry, succeeded him[65] but was probably the last Philpot to hold Crawlboys.

The later descent of Crawlboys farm can be traced only intermittently. In 1703 George Parry held it as a free tenant of the capital manor.[66] In the later 18th century it was held by William Garrard.[67] In 1844 Joseph Hague Everett owned it[68] and a Mr. Everett still owned it in 1863.[69] In 1935 it was acquired by the Hon. Bryan Guinness, later Lord Moyne, who owned it in 1975.[70]

ECONOMIC HISTORY. Collingbourne Ducis increased in value from £40 to £60 between King Harold's time and the Domesday survey.[71] In 1086 there was land for 45 ploughs. On the 5 demesne hides there were 12 serfs with 5 ploughs. There were also elsewhere on the estate 49 villeins and 26 bordars with 15 ploughs. There was pasture 2 leagues long by 1 league broad.

In 1212 the manor was valued at £20, or, with its stock, at £34. Included in the stock were over 1,000 sheep.[72] In 1361 there were reckoned to be 500 a. of arable, half of which was sown every year, leaving the other half fallow.[73] Among the customary tenants was a class known as Mondaymen employed chiefly for work with the demesne flocks.[74] From the 13th century to the 15th those flocks contained over 1,000 sheep.[75]

A close connexion existed between Collingbourne Ducis and Everleigh during the time that both formed part of the duchy of Lancaster's Wiltshire estate. Produce was exchanged between the two, and the comparatively sparsely wooded Everleigh depended largely on Collingbourne for timber.[76] In the later 15th century the office of hayward for both manors was apparently used to reward a royal servant.[77] In 1444–5 the demesne farms of both manors were leased together to John Stamford of Rushall, the duchy's stock-keeper.[78]

At Collingbourne in the 15th century the demesne lands were leased out in lots. There were usually seven parcels in addition to the manor farm.[79] In 1461–2 Richard Batt, who for several years had been bailiff of the manor, leased the farm in partnership with William Dyper.[80] Dyper continued alone as lessee and was followed after 1524 by William Button. By 1552 Button had been succeeded by Thomas Dowse, perhaps a son of the Richard Dowse who held Collingbourne farm at that date.[81] Thomas had been succeeded by Sir Francis Dowse by 1608.[82]

In 1552 the manor farm had three small inclosed arable fields, and the common arable was in East, Middle, and West fields which lay together on the west side of the later main Marlborough–Salisbury

[50] *Cal. Pat.* 1553, 386.
[51] Ibid.; W.R.O. 192/6, ct. roll.
[52] C 142/323 no. 89.
[53] W.R.O. 9/9/71, papers about Lowth's estate.
[54] This and further inf. from ibid. 9/9/70, abstr. of title.
[55] *D.N.B.*
[56] *Cal. Close*, 1402–5, 273–4.
[57] *W.N. & Q.* ii. 14–15.
[58] Ibid.
[59] Ibid. 16.
[60] D.L. 42/108 f. 51v.
[61] C.P. 25(2)/260/18 & 19 Eliz. I Mich. For the Philpot fam. see *V.C.H. Hants*, iii. 407.
[62] C 142/402 no. 129.
[63] *Cal. S.P. Dom.* 1660–1, 410.
[64] The custody of the woods was probably merged in that of Chute forest and descended with Chute man.
[65] W.R.O. 9, survey, 1635; *Cal. S.P. Dom.* 1660–1, 410.
[66] W.R.O. 9, survey, 1703.
[67] Ibid. 9, surveys, 1745, n.d.
[68] Ibid. Tithe Award.
[69] Ibid. 665/22.
[70] Ex inf. Lord Moyne, Biddesden Ho., Ludgershall.
[71] *V.C.H. Wilts.* ii, p. 118.
[72] *Rot. Litt. Claus.* (Rec. Com.), 117–18, 130.
[73] *Wilts. Inq. p.m.* 1327–77 (Index Libr.), 287–8.
[74] Ibid.; see below, p. 138.
[75] e.g. D.L. 29/628/11058; D.L. 29/683/11072.
[76] e.g. D.L. 29/685/11089.
[77] D.L. 29/690/11189.
[78] D.L. 29/685/11089.
[79] e.g. D.L. 29/683/11070; D.L. 29/685/11089; D.L. 29/687/11134.
[80] D.L. 29/687/11134.
[81] D.L. 42/108 ff. 51v.–56v.; and see above.
[82] W.R.O. 9, Liber A.

road. An outfield had been created along the southern end of the three.[83] In the 18th century a rotation of three corn crops succeeded by one year fallow was followed in the three fields, and alternate years corn crop and fallow in the outfield.[84] Most of the 16th-century copyholders held 1 virgate of arable with other scattered small parcels of land. Among the smaller holdings was the workland, measuring 10 a. In 1552 there were 5 Mondaylands, the original holding of the Mondayman, but then held with other pieces of land. A ½-reeveland, measuring 15 a., occurs at the same date.[85]

A string of small inclosed water-meadows, known at least in 1651 as ropes, followed the curve of the Bourne south of the village.[86] The size of a single rope varied, ¼ a. being about average. In the 18th century some tenants held as many as six ropes.[87]

In the mid 16th century there were about 250 a. of down for the demesne farm, including 100 a. on Cow down. The tenantry had 100 a. on Snail down and 40 a. elsewhere. Wick heath in the north-east part of the parish provided 30 a. of common land and there was another common of 10 a. Stinting allowed for 70 sheep for every yardland, 15 sheep for a workland, and 10 sheep for a Mondayland.[88]

A complaint in the manor court in 1590 about the ploughing of Widgerly down presages the changes in the pattern of farming then beginning and carried through in the 18th century.[89] In the 1730s downland belonging to the manor farm in the south part of the parish was first burnt and then ploughed. More land on Cow and Snail downs was similarly treated soon afterwards when tenants surrendered their common rights in return for permission to plough and inclose for themselves in the same region. As a result the manor farm acquired an inclosed farm on Cow down called in 1745 New farm.[90]

The breaking up of the downs for arable was accompanied from the late 17th century by a long series of agreements between the lord of the manor, freeholders, and tenants for inclosure and exchanges of the common land.[91] Awards by specially appointed commissioners were made in 1738 and 1775.[92] That of 1775 provided for the continued cultivation of the three common fields and the outfield, for feeding the downs in common, and for the allotment of sheep leazes.[93] The last agreement for exchanges, divisions, and inclosure was made in 1815, and although an award was intended, none has been found.[94]

By the mid 18th century the ploughing of the downs had reduced the number of sheep kept on the manor farm from 1,300 to about half that number. Reductions were agreed for all the farms in the parish. On Collingbourne farm the number fell from 385 to 330; on the glebe farm from 140 to 120.

Husbandry throughout the 18th century was strictly regulated. The new agrarian arrangements, and in particular the rights of way along droves leading to and from the new inclosures, were recorded in the manor courts.[95]

There were two freehold farms within Collingbourne. Crawlboys farm, in its isolated situation, had no share in the common fields and was farmed in severalty.[96] In 1608 it was said to be totally inclosed with banks and ditches.[97] It was, therefore, not included in any of the agreements for exchanges of land in the 18th century and was independent of the regulations laid down for the rest of the parish.

Collingbourne farm, known as either Cheney's or Lowth's in the 18th century, was included in many of the inclosure agreements,[98] so that by 1777 much of the farm lay consolidated and inclosed in the north-east part of the parish.[99] When bought by Lord Ailesbury in 1810 it measured 387 a. Thereafter it was merged with the adjoining land of Church Street farm (see below). Its buildings were in disrepair in 1763.[1] A new farm-house was built c. 1845 and the farm became known as Mount Orleans.[2] When sold in 1929 it had 592 a. and was farmed by H. C. Pullen.[3]

Church Street farm grew from an accumulation of copyholds acquired c. 1751 by Robert Shepherd and Robert Croome, a wheelwright, both of Collingbourne Ducis.[4] Its farm-house lay east of and close to Court Farm.[5] In 1777, farmed by Robert Croome, the farm measured 706 a. and included some of the new arable on Cow down and two ropes of water-meadow.[6] Croome was succeeded before 1810 by Harry Pike, and he before 1844 by George Pike.[7] By 1929 most of the farm had been merged with Mount Orleans farm.[8]

In 1745 the manor farm was known as Court farm, and farm and farm-house were divided between two tenants, Hester Callow and William Maton.[9] In 1773 Edward Andrews, then tenant of both parts, was given leave to plough part of Tatshanger down for the cultivation of sainfoin. The farm's arable then included part of the land on Cow down, ploughed for the first time in 1738, and was arranged in five fields.[10] In 1777 the farm measured 759 a.[11] Andrews was followed as tenant before 1810 by William Blatch and in 1844 Leonard Pitt Maton was tenant.[12] In 1867 John Russ was farmer and a new farm-house had recently been built.[13] At the sale of 1929 the farm was estimated at 859 a.[14] In 1975 it was farmed by Mr. P. J. Gordon.[15]

Another substantial farm originated in the accumulation of a number of leaseholds and copyholds held in the 17th and 18th centuries by members of the Batt family.[16] In 1774 Elizabeth Batt and her son William Batt, the physician, surrendered their

[83] D.L. 42/108 ff. 51v.–56v.
[84] W.R.O. 665/12, survey, 1745.
[85] D.L. 42/108 ff. 51v.–56v.
[86] W.R.O. 192/24b.
[87] Ibid. 665/12, survey, 1745.
[88] D.L. 42/108 ff. 51v.–56v.
[89] W.R.O. 9, ct. bk. 1590–1606.
[90] Ibid. 665/12, survey, 1745.
[91] Ibid. 9/9/4–6.
[92] Ibid. 9/9/14–15.
[93] Ibid. 9/9/15.
[94] Ibid. 426/38.
[95] Ibid. 9, ct. rolls, 1732–41, ct. bk. 1759–1821.
[96] D.L. 42/108 ff. 51v.–56v.
[97] W.R.O. 9, Liber A.
[98] Ibid. 9/9/20.
[99] Ibid. 9, map, 1777.
[1] Ibid. 9, partic. of Cheney's estate.

[2] Ibid. 9, acct. bks.
[3] W.A.S. Libr., sale cat. xxviii, no. 29.
[4] W.R.O. 9/9/170.
[5] Ibid. 9, survey, 1745.
[6] Ibid. 9, survey, 1777.
[7] Ibid. 9, acct. bks.; Tithe Award.
[8] W.A.S. Libr., sale cat. xxviii, no. 29.
[9] W.R.O. 9, survey, 1745.
[10] Ibid. 9, survey, 1773.
[11] Ibid. 9, survey, 1777.
[12] Ibid. 9, acct. bk.; Tithe Award.
[13] Ibid. 9, estate rep. and val.
[14] W.A.S. Libr., sale cat. xxviii, no. 29.
[15] Ex inf. Defence Land Agent, Durrington.
[16] W.R.O. 9/9, TS. cal.

holdings to Lord Bruce.[17] The farm so formed was held by John Bailey in 1777 and measured 162 a. Land in the south-west part of the parish was added to it, including part of New farm on Cow down created in 1738.[18] William Bailey was the tenant in 1810 and soon after the farm-house, called Hougomont, was built.[19] In 1844 John Bailey farmed the 778 a. of Hougomont farm.[20] In 1867 the farmer was Charles Petar.[21] When sold in 1929 the farm measured 832 a.[22] In 1975 it was farmed by Mr. F. J. Wallis.[23]

A report on Lord Ailesbury's Collingbourne farms in 1867 found that in spite of the advantages of suitable soils and good communications, Court, Hougomont, and Mount Orleans farms were not well farmed. An inefficient rotation of crops, it was alleged, was followed, and too many breeding ewes kept at the expense of sheep for fattening and cattle. The report was also critical of the labour upon the farms.[24]

After the break-up of the Ailesbury estate in 1929 the farms continued as mixed farms. After 1939, however, when the War Office acquired the western half of the parish, restrictions were imposed upon Hougomont and Court farms, and crops could not be grown in tank-training areas.[25]

A small foundry, known as the Bourne Iron Works, was established on the east side of the village street by James Rawlings in the 1860s. The Rawlings family manufactured agricultural implements there until the outbreak of the Second World War.[26] A group of local farmers acquired the premises in 1958 and a company, later called Hosier Farming Systems, was formed to manufacture milking machines and some other farming equipment. In 1973 it became a subsidiary of the Hillspan Group of Eastleigh (Hants). In 1975 it employed 110 people.[27]

In 1086 a third of Chute forest belonged to the king's manor of Collingbourne which also had woodland measuring 1 league square.[28] The third of Chute probably refers to Collingbourne woods, the southern part of which occupied much of the eastern half of Collingbourne Ducis. By 1330 the woods had been disafforested[29] and thenceforth remained in the hands of the lord of the manor until 1929.

By 1464 the southern part of the woods had been made a chase known as Collingbourne Ducis chase. From then until the mid 17th century its keepership belonged to the holders of Crawlboys farm.[30]

In 1540 the woods covered about 265 a. and included 14 coppices and 2,338 trees.[31] They remained unsold at the sale of the Savernake estate in 1929, but soon after were acquired by the Forestry Commission, which still owned them in 1975.[32]

The timber was valued among the assets of the manor at 60s. a year in 1297.[33] In 1540 the farmer of the manor farm was allowed ten loads of wood a year, and tenants on some other duchy manors had allowances of wood from Collingbourne.[34] Curtailment of those allowances after Collingbourne passed to the duke of Somerset produced complaints in the manor court in 1552.[35] When sold c. 1929 the woods were highly valued for the shooting which was let for £99 a year.[36]

There was a windmill on the manor in 1361.[37] There was a mill leased for about 10s. a year in the 15th century.[38] A mill leased by one of the Dowse family in 1552 was described as a horse-mill.[39] The windmill stood south-east of the village in 1773.[40]

MARKET AND FAIRS. A weekly market and two annual fairs were granted to the duke of Lancaster (d. 1361) in 1353. The market was to be held on Mondays and the fairs on the eve, feast, and morrow of St. Barnabas (11 June) and of St. Andrew (30 Nov.).[41] Nothing more is heard of the Monday market and in the mid 16th century a combined fair and market was held annually and called St. Andrew's fair. The duke of Somerset's bailiff bought eight halters and whipcord there c. 1548.[42] Measuring and weighing beams were in use in the early 17th century.[43]

In the later 16th century the fair was leased by the lord of the manor to Francis Vincent.[44] In 1608 a Francis Vincent, then the lessee, was described as a gentleman, and in 1612 as the servant of the earl of Hertford (d. 1621).[45] In 1617 Francis Vincent and his son John were lessees,[46] and the Vincent family continued as lessees until the mid 18th century and possibly longer.[47] It is not known precisely when the fair was last held. It was recorded in a list of fairs of 1792 as being held on 11 December, but does not appear in one of 1888.[48]

The fair was held at Hill field, otherwise Fair close, apparently at the southern end of the village where the ground was liable to flooding.[49] Stands and booths were damaged by water c. 1590.[50]

LOCAL GOVERNMENT. It has been suggested that Collingbourne Ducis, as it was later called, did not belong to any hundred in the 11th century. In

17 W.R.O. 9/9/204.
18 Ibid. 9, survey, 1777; see above.
19 W.R.O. 9, acct. bks.   20 Ibid. Tithe Award.
21 Ibid. 9, estate rep. and val.
22 W.A.S. Libr., sale cat. xxviii, no. 29.
23 Ex inf. Defence Land Agent, Durrington.
24 W.R.O. 9, estate rep. and val.
25 Ex inf. Defence Land Agent, Durrington; Wilts. Gaz. 5 July 1973.
26 Kelly's Dir. Wilts. (1939 and earlier edns.).
27 Information about Hosiers from Mr. E. W. Hughes, former managing director. See also V.C.H. Wilts. iv. 111.
28 V.C.H. Wilts. ii, p. 59.
29 Ibid. iv. 425, where 'Collingbourne Abbatis' is wrongly identified as Collingbourne Ducis.
30 See p. 110.   31 D.L. 3/36 S3 ff. 55–8.
32 Wilts. Gaz. 19 Sept. 1929; ex inf. Mr. W. E. Cave, Everleigh.

33 Wilts. Inq. p.m. 1242–1326 (Index Libr.), 217–18.
34 D.L. 30/127/1904.   35 Ibid.
36 Wilts. Gaz. 19 Sept. 1929.
37 Wilts. Inq. p.m. 1327–77 (Index Libr.), 287–8.
38 e.g. D.L. 29/685/11089; D.L. 29/687/11137; D.L. 29/690/11189.
39 D.L. 42/108 ff. 51v.–56v.
40 Andrews and Dury, Map (W.R.S. viii), pl. 9.
41 Cal. Chart. R. 1341–1417, 132.
42 Hist. MSS. Com. 58, Bath, iv. p. 335.
43 W.R.O. 9, Liber A.
44 Ibid. ct. bk. 1590–1606; survey, 1599.
45 Ibid. Liber A; 9/9/120.   46 Ibid. 9/9/121.
47 Ibid. 665/12, survey, 1745; 9/9, TS. cal.
48 Rep. Com. Mkt. Rights [C. 5550], App. p. 214, H.C. (1888), liii.
49 W.R.O. 665/12, survey, 1745.
50 Ibid. 9, ct. bk. 1590–1606.

the geld rolls it was not returned as part of any hundred, but was placed as if it were a small hundred on its own.[51]

Court books and rolls survive from the later 16th century until 1821 when the court met for the last time.[52] They show a view of frankpledge and manor court to have been held together twice a year. From the late 16th century, and particularly in the 18th century, the court was much concerned to record and regulate the agrarian changes taking place.[53]

The vestry, made up of the more substantial ratepayers, met, occasionally at least, in the earlier 19th century at the New Inn.[54] In 1833 it agreed to provide vaccination for the infant poor and 73 children were vaccinated. In 1835 it appointed a doctor to tend the poor. The vestry decided upon the distribution of wood given every year to the parish by Lord Ailesbury. In 1843 it made arrangements and certain payments for sixteen people emigrating to Australia.[55] Records of overseers' disbursements and some receipts survive from 1770 to 1912.[56] Collingbourne became part of Pewsey poor-law union in 1836.[57]

CHURCH. By 1086 the tithes of Collingbourne Ducis had been granted to Gerald of Wilton, a priest, and the church, presumably as a consequence, was reputed to be impoverished and ruinous.[58] Before 1228 it was granted to Wherwell Abbey.[59] Although the abbey did not appropriate the revenues, the abbesses drew a pension of £8 from the church.[60] The benefice was united with that of Collingbourne Kingston in 1963. The rectory of Everleigh was added to the united benefice, thereafter called the Collingbournes and Everleigh, in 1975.[61] Collingbourne Ducis and Everleigh were united to create a new ecclesiastical parish called Collingbourne Ducis and Everleigh in 1977.[62]

The abbesses of Wherwell presented rectors until the dissolution of their house in 1539, but apparently shortly before then the next turn was granted away, for in 1545 John Salmon presented by consent of the abbess.[63] The advowson had, however, been included in the grant of the manor to Edward Seymour (the Lord Protector, d. 1552) in 1536[64] and on the death of the rector presented by Salmon, Seymour, by then earl of Hertford, presented.[65] His widow Anne, duchess of Somerset (d. 1587), presented in 1554,[66] but the advowson, unlike the manor, apparently did not pass to Seymour's son, and in 1581 the patron was Sir Richard Kingsmill.[67]

In 1614 and 1633 the king exercised the patronage, but on the first occasion merely confirmed Kingsmill's presentation.[68] By 1650 the patronage had been restored to Seymour's great-grandson William, marquess of Hertford, later duke of Somerset (d. 1660).[69] From him it passed to his grandson and heir as duke of Somerset (d. 1671) who presented in 1662.[70] After the duke's death the advowson did not pass like the manor and in 1700 Merton College, Oxford, presented one of their Fellows to the living.[71] The king exercised the patronage in the following year, but only to confirm Merton's presentation.[72] In 1735 the advowson returned, after over 70 years, to the hands of the lord of the manor when Charles, Lord Bruce of Whorlton, later earl of Ailesbury (d. 1746), presented.[73] Lord Ailesbury presented again in 1743 and thereafter the advowson descended like the Ailesbury title[74] until 1957 when it was transferred to the bishop.[75] When the Collingbournes and Everleigh were united in 1975 the bishop of Salisbury as patron of Collingbourne Ducis was allotted the first and fourth of five turns.[76]

In 1291 the church was valued at £6 13s. 4d.,[77] in 1535 at £16 net.[78] At both dates £8 was deducted for the pension due to the abbess of Wherwell. The pension passed to the Crown at the Dissolution, and was still payable in 1783.[79] In 1650 the rectory with glebe was said to be worth £300.[80] From 1829 to 1831 the average net income was £585.[81]

In 1086 ½ hide belonged to the church.[82] In 1671 there were 60½ a. of arable glebe lying scattered in the west and east fields.[83] Right of common for 140 sheep went with the glebe in 1783 and there was a large parsonage-house with a farmyard and meadow land adjoining.[84] The glebe, measuring some 55 a., still belonged to the benefice in 1975 and was farmed with Hougomont farm.[85] A new rectory-house, designed by Benjamin Ingelow, was built on roughly the same site as the old in 1863.[86] In 1964 a smaller house was built in the grounds for the incumbent of the united benefice of the Collingbournes.[87] All tithes were due to the rector and were commuted in 1846 for a rent-charge of £636.[88]

Possibly as at Trowbridge, the lord of the manor exercised archidiaconal jurisdiction within the parish from at least the late 13th century.[89] After 1544, when Edward Seymour, by then Lord Hertford (d. 1552), was granted the former prebend of Bedwyn,[90] Collingbourne Ducis and Great and Little Bedwyn formed a peculiar, known as the peculiar of the Lord Warden of Savernake Forest, the hereditary office held by the Seymours and their successors the

[51] V.C.H. Wilts. ii, p. 213; Crown Pleas, 1249 (W.R.S. xvi), p. 218.
[52] The earliest is 1552: D.L. 30/127/1904. There are two for the 17th cent. in W.R.O. 192/24b, and many ibid. 9.
[53] See above.   [54] W.R.O. 665/22, par. jnl.
[55] Ibid.   [56] Ibid. 426/30–1.
[57] Ibid. 426/30.   [58] V.C.H. Wilts. ii, pp. 34, 118.
[59] Dugdale, Mon. ii. 638.   [60] See below.
[61] Lond. Gaz. 29 Mar. 1963, p. 2824; ex inf. Dioc. Registrar.
[62] Ex inf. Dioc. Registrar.
[63] Phillipps, Wilts. Inst. (index in W.A.M. xxviii. 217).
[64] D.L. 42/22 f. 146v.
[65] Phillipps, Wilts. Inst. i. 212.
[66] Ibid. 216.   [67] Ibid. 230.
[68] Ibid. ii. 8, 16.   [69] W.A.M. xl. 298.
[70] Phillipps, Wilts. Inst. ii. 25.   [71] Ibid. 45.
[72] Ibid.   [73] Ibid. 66.

[74] Complete Peerage, s.v. Ailesbury; see above.
[75] Phillipps, Wilts. Inst. ii; board in ch.
[76] Ex inf. Dioc. Registrar.
[77] Tax. Eccl. (Rec. Com.), 189.
[78] Valor Eccl. (Rec. Com.), ii. 151.
[79] Sar. Dioc. R.O., Glebe Terrier.
[80] W.A.M. xl. 298.
[81] Rep. Com. Eccl. Revenues, 831.
[82] V.C.H. Wilts. ii, p. 118.
[83] Sar. Dioc. R.O., Glebe Terrier.
[84] Ibid.
[85] Ex inf. the Revd. P. D. C. Amor, Collingbourne Ducis Rectory.
[86] A. Savidge, Parsonage in Eng. (S.P.C.K.), 144.
[87] Ex inf. the Revd. P. D. C. Amor; Dioc. Registrar.
[88] W.R.O., Tithe Award.
[89] V.C.H. Wilts. vii. 149.
[90] L. & P. Hen. VIII, xix (1), p. 14.

Bruces.[91] In 1663 the duke of Somerset appointed the rector of Collingbourne Ducis as his official for the peculiar,[92] and later lords of the manor frequently, but not invariably, made like appointments. The Collingbourne churchwardens presented faults to the official twice a year at visitation courts held either in Collingbourne Ducis or Great Bedwyn church. At Collingbourne presentations were usually either for non-attendance at church or for failure to maintain pews which were the personal responsibility of their owners.[93] As everywhere else the peculiar jurisdiction was abolished in 1847.[94]

In 1536 Robert Richardson, rector 1506–44, had licence to absent himself from the parish, perhaps one of many such dispensations as until 1522 he was also vicar of St. Mary's, Marlborough, and between 1510 and 1535 master of St. John's Hospital there.[95] Between 1633 and 1662 three active presbyterians held the living. Henry Scudder (1633–c. 1650) was a member of the Westminster Assembly and the author of several treatises. Adoniram Byfield (c. 1650–60) was one of the scribes to the assembly and an assistant commissioner for Wiltshire under the ordinance for ejecting 'scandalous' ministers.[96] Daniel Burgess (1660–2), in spite of appeals from his patron, the duke of Somerset (d. 1671), to conform, was ejected from the living for his nonconformity and retired to Marlborough.[97]

In the 18th century there were rectors with commitments outside the parish. William Sherwin (1700–35), a Fellow of Merton College, Oxford, spent the last fifteen years of his incumbency in Chichester, where he was a residentiary canon.[98] A curate served the church meanwhile, and probably continued to do so during the incumbency of the following rector, the Hon. Thomas Bruce (1735–8), who never resided.[99] William Tomblins (1756–88) lived in Collingbourne although he also held the rectory of Upham (Hants).[1] Thomas Talbot (1743–58) had a detailed survey made of the parish at his own expense.[2]

Among later incumbents Charles Francis (1788–1821) employed a curate and only occasionally resided, as he also served the church of Mildenhall.[3] W. C. Lukis (1855–62) published the first record of English bell inscriptions in 1857 and was a local antiquary.[4]

In 1650 it was proposed that the residents of Crawlboys Farm should attend Ludgershall church which was much closer than their parish church. At the same time the inhabitants of Collingbourne Sunton, then in Collingbourne Kingston, except those on Dr. Hyde's farm, were to be brought into the parish of Collingbourne Ducis.[5] In 1676 the rector reported 170 conformists in the parish.[6] In 1783, although there was no dissenter, the incumbent considered church attendances to be rather poor.

Services were held twice on Sundays and Holy Communion celebrated four times a year, when there were never more than twenty communicants.[7] On Census Sunday in 1851 it was estimated that 100 were in church in the morning and 90 in the afternoon.[8] In 1864 there were reckoned to be more than 80 communicants, of whom on average 29 attended at the great festivals. The congregation then averaged about 50, and would have been larger but for the bad accommodation in the church.[9]

The early dedication of the church was to St. Mary but by 1786 had been changed to *ST. ANDREW*.[10] The building of flint and rubble with stone dressings stands on high ground at the southern end of the village. It consists of chancel with north vestry and organ chamber, an aisled nave with south porch, and a west tower.

In the early 13th century there was an aisled nave, with arcades of three bays in transitional style, and presumably a chancel. The chancel was enlarged or rebuilt later in the century and new windows were put into the aisles early in the 14th century, the south aisle probably being rebuilt at that time. The tower arch may be late-14th-century and the oblong plan of the tower suggests an earlier date than the 15th century, at which time it was rebuilt. Within the middle stage of the tower is a large dovecot with nesting-boxes lining all four walls. A square aperture to the outside has an alighting and taking-off platform. The south doorway of the church and the window to its east were renewed in the 16th century.

The chancel was rebuilt on a narrower plan in 1856 by Lukis when he became rector.[11] The north vestry was added at the same time. The architect was G. E. Street. In 1877, with Sir Arthur Blomfield as architect,[12] the nave and aisles were thoroughly restored and re-roofed and a new porch was built to replace one of brick dated 1791. The chancel arch was renewed and an organ-chamber added. The tower was restored in 1902 with money from Charles Francis's charity. The west window by Ward and Hughes was inserted c. 1887 by John Mackrell to commemorate his ancestors.[13]

Charles Francis (d. 1821) bequeathed £100 to provide a fund for church repairs. The money has since been used for that purpose. John Mackrell gave £200 to maintain the window in the west wall of the tower. Some of the interest has been used to pay insurance premiums and the rest, in accordance with Mackrell's wishes, on benefits for the poor.[14]

A brass on the south wall of the chancel commemorates Edward (d. 1631 aged 11 months), son of William Seymour, duke of Somerset (d. 1660).[15] In 1553 the church kept its silver chalice, but 17 oz. of silver were taken for the king.[16] In 1783, besides the chalice, the church had some pewter vessels.[17]

---

[91] *Guide to Rec. Offices* (Wilts. C.C.), iv. 105–6.
[92] W.R.O. 9, appointment by Somerset of Charlott.
[93] Sar. Dioc. R.O., ct. and vis. papers.
[94] *Fasti Eccl. Sar.* ed. W. H. Jones, ii. 362.
[95] *V.C.H. Wilts.* iii. 342.   [96] *D.N.B.*
[97] *Calamy Revised*, ed. A. G. Matthews, 88.
[98] *W.A.M.* xxvi. 320.   [99] Ibid. 326.
[1] *W.N. & Q.* ii. 19; *Vis. Queries, 1783* (W.R.S. xxvii), p. 75.
[2] W.R.O. 665/12.   [3] *W.A.M.* xli. 132–3.
[4] W.R.O. 665/12, survey, 1745; *V.C.H. Wilts.* iii. 79.
[5] *W.A.M.* xl. 298.   [6] *W.N. & Q.* iii. 537.

[7] *Vis. Queries, 1783* (W.R.S. xxvii), p. 75.
[8] H.O. 129/261/2/7.
[9] Sar. Dioc. R.O., Vis. Queries.
[10] Dugdale, *Mon.* ii. 638; J. Bacon, *Thesaurus*, 890.
[11] For detailed acct. of ch. see *W.A.M.* xlii. 568–73. A water-colour by J. Buckler is in W.A.S. Libr., vol. iv. 6 (1806).   [12] W.R.O. 665/12, survey, 1745.
[13] *Endowed Char. Wilts.* (S. Div.), 112.
[14] Ibid. 108, 112.
[15] E. Kite, *Wilts. Brasses*, 87–8; *W.N. & Q.* ii. 588.
[16] Nightingale, *Wilts. Plate*, 166.
[17] Sar. Dioc. R.O., Glebe Terrier.

New plate was acquired in the 19th century. It included a chalice, given at the time of the restoration of 1877, and a small cup with handle, a paten, and an alms-dish given by Charles Francis.[18] Two small items were added in the 20th century.[19] In 1783 there were four bells,[20] later six: (ii), by Robert Wells of Aldbourne, and (vi), by James Borough of Devizes, were recast in 1902. Bells (iii) and (iv) are 17th-century and (v) early-16th-century. The treble was added in 1927.[21] The registers begin in 1653, and, except for a gap for marriages between 1727 and 1730, are complete.[22]

NONCONFORMITY. There was no dissenter in the parish in 1676.[23] Some houses in the village were used for nonconformist worship in the earlier 19th century. That of John Hillier was registered in 1812, that of John Lansley or Lousley in 1828 and 1844, and that of Joseph Butcher in 1840. At Cadley the house of Joseph Allen was registered in 1834.[24] In 1838 there were thought to be 22 Baptists and 36 Primitive Methodists meeting in houses in the neighbourhood.[25] A chapel was built by the Primitive Methodists in 1849 and on Census Sunday in 1851 it was reckoned that 195 people attended there in the morning, 194 in the afternoon, and 210 in the evening.[26]

In 1864 there were thought to be some 200 nonconformists. The Wesleyan Methodists and Baptists attended chapels outside the parish.[27] A new Primitive Methodist chapel was built at Cadley in 1880 and in 1975 was still in use.[28]

EDUCATION. In 1819 there were two schools for about 35 children, most of whom were paid for by the rector. About twelve children came from neighbouring parishes. A strong desire for education prevailed,[29] but in 1833 there was no school.[30]

In 1858 between 20 and 30 children were taught in a dame school and others went to the school in Collingbourne Kingston. In 1859, however, a school, supported by the National Society, was opened with a certificated master in charge.[31] The architect of the new building was Samuel Overton.[32] Average attendance throughout the later 19th century was around 80.[33] School pence were abolished in 1891, and a penny bank opened in the school to which parents could subscribe.[34] The school had 85 children in 1975.[35] In 1864 there was an evening-school during the winter for about twenty young men and boys.[36]

CHARITIES FOR THE POOR. George John Hooper by his will proved 1862 left £100 for investment to provide coal for poor widows in the parish. Marianna Hooper by her will proved 1867 left £100 similarly to buy flannel or blankets for poor working women. In 1904 the income from G. J. Hooper's bequest was £2 10s. and eight widows received 9 cwt. of coal each. Marianna Hooper's charity by that date had been extended to needy children as well as poor women and that year nine recipients received vouchers worth about 5s. each. Elizabeth Piper by her will proved 1890 bequeathed £200 for investment to provide coals and blankets for the elderly. In 1904 the income was about £5 and there were thirteen beneficiaries.[37]

The poor also sometimes benefited from John Mackrell's charity which was primarily intended to maintain the west window in the church.[38] In 1904 nearly £5 was distributed.[39]

In 1975 the two Hooper charities yielded £2.50 each. That of Elizabeth Piper brought in about £5. All three were spent on vouchers for groceries at Christmas.[40]

ENFORD

THE parish of Enford lies in the north-east corner of Salisbury Plain some 22 km. north of Salisbury.[41] In its ancient form it was oval and slanted north-east to south-west. No natural feature, except the Christchurch Avon which formed the north-western boundary with West Chisenbury, a detached tithing of Netheravon, defined its limits.[42] The area of the ancient parish was increased to 3,314 ha. (8,190 a.) when West Chisenbury was added in 1885.[43] The modern parish measures over 11 km. at its widest point from Enford down at the west end to Coombe hill at the east end and in length about 4 km. from the northern boundary near Chisenbury camp to Coombe hamlet on the southern boundary. On either side of the Avon, which flows through the middle of the parish, the six tithings of Enford extended finger-like to east and west.[44] Their hamlets face each other across the Avon. Those on the west bank, Compton, Enford, and Fifield, cluster in the wide loops formed by the meandering

[18] Nightingale, *Wilts. Plate*, 166.
[19] Ex inf. the Revd. P. D. C. Amor.
[20] Sar. Dioc. R.O., Glebe Terrier.
[21] Walters, *Wilts. Bells*, 61; ex inf. the Revd. P. D. C. Amor.
[22] W.R.O. 665. The marriage reg. has been printed: *Wilts. Par. Reg.* (Mar.), ed. W. P. W. Phillimore and J. Sadler, xii. 133–47.
[23] *W.N. & Q.* iii. 537.
[24] W.R.O., Return of Regns.
[25] W.R.O. 665/22, par. jnl.   [26] H.O. 129/261/2/7.
[27] Sar. Dioc. R.O., Vis. Queries.
[28] Date on bldg.   [29] *Educ. of Poor Digest*, 1024.
[30] *Educ. Enquiry Abstract*, 1034.
[31] *Acct. of Wilts. Schs.* 16.   [32] W.R.O. 782/32.
[33] *Acct. of Wilts. Schs.* 16; W.R.O. 665/18, sch. accts.

[34] W.R.O. 665/18, sch. accts.
[35] Local information.
[36] Sar. Dioc. R.O., Vis. Queries.
[37] *Endowed Char. Wilts.* (S. Div.), 108–12.
[38] See above.
[39] *Endowed Char. Wilts.* (S. Div.), 112.
[40] Ex inf. the Revd. P. D. C. Amor.
[41] This article was written in 1975.
[42] Maps used include: O.S. Maps 1/50,000, sheet 184 (1974 edn.); 1/25,000, SU 04 (1958 edn.), SU 05 (1958 edn.), SU 14 (1958 edn.), SU 15 (1958 edn.); 6″, Wilts. XLVII (1889 edn.), SU 04 NE. (1961 edn.), SU 05 SE. (1961 edn.), SU 14 NW. (1961 edn.), SU 15 SE. (1961 edn.), SU 15 SW. (1961 edn.).
[43] *Census*, 1881, 1891.
[44] W.R.O., Inclosure Award maps.

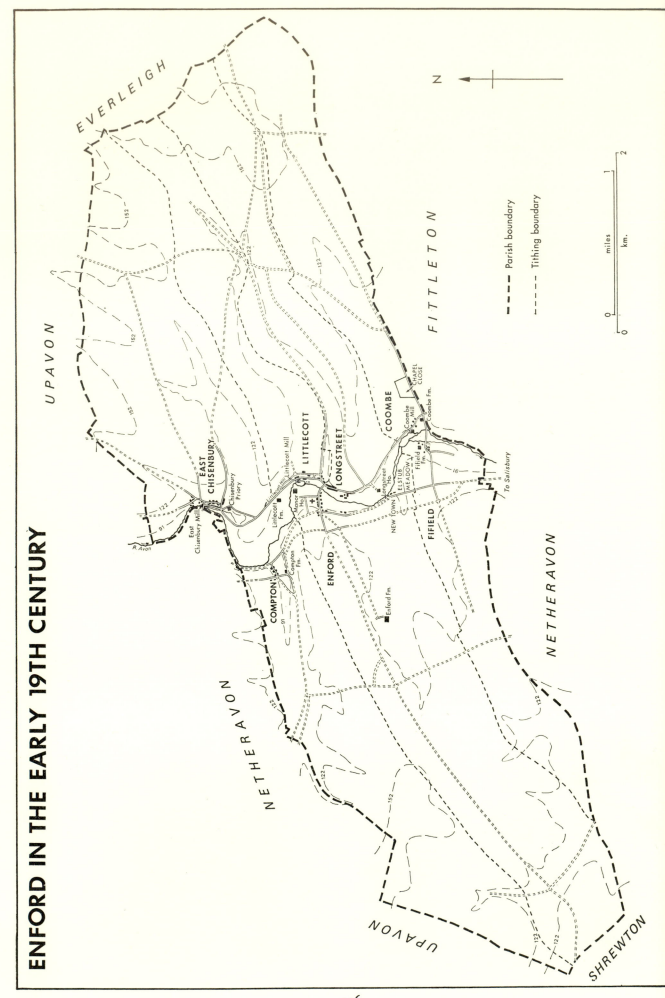

ENFORD IN THE EARLY 19TH CENTURY

EVERLEIGH

UPAVON

FITTLETON

152

152

152

122

122

122

EAST
CHISENBURY

Chisenbury
Priory

LITTLECOTT

Littlecott Mill

LONGSTREET

COOMBE

CHAPEL
CLOSE

Coombe Fm.

Coombe
Mill

16

To Salisbury

East
Chisenbury Mill

R. Avon

91

122

Littlecott
Fm.

Manor
Ho.

COMPTON

Compton
Fm.

ENFORD

Longstreet
Ho.

ELSTUB
MEADOW

NEW TOWN

Fifield
Fm.

FIFIELD

122

91

122

122

Enford Fm.

NETHERAVON

NETHERAVON

122

122

152

UPAVON

122

122

SHREWTON

N

miles

km.

0   1   2

---- Parish boundary

---- Tithing boundary

river. The eastern hamlets of East Chisenbury, Littlecott, Longstreet, and Coombe, stand directly opposite. Compton alone has no eastern twin. New Town, consisting of a scatter of cottages south of Enford village, was considered part of Enford tithing.[45] Longstreet, known as 'Fyfhyde' or 'Lange-fyfyde' in the Middle Ages, and Littlecott probably formed the medieval tithing of Littlecott and Fifield.[46] They appear to have emerged as separate tithings by the 18th century.[47] All the other tithings seem to have existed in the 13th century.[48] East Chisenbury, so designated in the 13th century to distinguish it from the Chisenbury in Netheravon, was called alternatively Chisenbury Priors, or, later, Priory from its connexion with Ogbourne Priory.[49]

The valley carved from north to south through Enford by the Avon divides the parish into two geologically identical halves.[50] Both contain massive bluffs of Upper Chalk which rise from heights of over 107 m. to over 152 m. on either side of the valley. The higher slopes once provided grazing for large flocks of sheep. The lower reaches were formerly occupied by open fields, and were, although mostly in Ministry of Defence ownership, largely under arable cultivation in 1976. North-east of East Chisenbury clay-with-flints deposits are found in two places, in one of which a height of 172 m. is reached. On the north-western boundary with West Chisenbury an eastwards flowing tributary of the Avon gouged out a valley, now mostly dry, called Water Dean Bottom on whose floor the Middle Chalk is exposed. The hamlet of Compton grew up on the gravel deposits left by the stream near its confluence with the Avon. The Middle Chalk is also exposed east of the hamlets of East Chisenbury and Littlecott. Narrow strips of gravel, nowhere over 500 m. wide, which have been deposited on either side of the river, provide the relatively dry terraces on which Enford's village and hamlets developed. East of Coombe another of the Avon's tributary streams, also now dry, cut a valley through the chalk. It is indicated by the gravel deposits which extend along the south-eastern parish boundary for about 2.5 km. Between the gravel terraces and the Avon the river banks are covered with rich alluvial soils. Once the site of common meadows, the area was still lush grassland in 1976.

The plentiful archaeological evidence found in the parish indicates human activity there from the Neolithic Period. Remains include barrows of various types and numerous ditches.[51] In the Iron Age there may have been a fairly settled community in the area later covered by East Chisenbury tithing. Of the two hill-forts there, Chisenbury camp or trendle and Lidbury camp, Lidbury has an as-sociated field system (350 a.) on Littlecott down.[52] Slag found in Lidbury camp's ditch may suggest iron-working there at that time.[53] Enford down and Rainbow bottom both show extensive field systems, and others extend into the parish from Everleigh, Fittleton, and Upavon.[54] Settlement on the downs, particularly at East Chisenbury, may have continued unbroken into Romano-British times. A street village of that period existed at Chisenbury warren in the extreme north-east corner of the parish.[55] Remains of a domestic building of similar date found between the Avon and the Salisbury Upavon road near Compton indicate settlement there.[56]

For medieval taxation purposes Chisenbury was always assessed separately, and Coombe included in the neighbouring manor of Fittleton. Compton was often dealt with separately since it was usually considered part of the liberty of Everleigh. Sometimes it was included in Amesbury hundred. Little-cott and Fifield tithing was sometimes assessed with Enford and sometimes separately.[57] In 1377 Chisenbury had 96 poll-tax payers, Littlecott and Fifield 49, and Enford, probably then including Fifield tithing, 32.[58] In the 16th century the parish, then assessed as an entity, made the highest taxation contributions in Elstub hundred.[59] In 1576 Compton tithing was assessed with Alton, in Figheldean, as part of Amesbury hundred.[60] It has been calculated that 616 people lived in the parish in 1676.[61] When systematic enumerations began in 1801 814 people lived there.[62] Fifield, the only tithing for which separate figures were then given, had 140 inhabitants. Numbers in Enford as a whole had fallen slightly by 1811 but thereafter rose and in 1831 reached 961. By 1841 the population had fallen to 797, of whom 187 lived at Enford, 149 at Chisenbury, 73 at Compton, 79 in Coombe, 98 in Fifield, 52 in Littlecott, 81 in Longstreet, and 78 in New Town. The total increased to 911 in 1851 and remained fairly steady for the next 20 years. During the 1860s Fifield's population decreased because young men were apparently leaving the hamlet to seek work elsewhere.[63] The later 19th century saw a steady decline in population, despite the addition of 47 people when West Chisenbury was transferred to Enford in 1885.[64] In 1921 652 people lived in Enford. Figures rose to 716 in 1931 but in general the 20th century witnessed a slow decline. In 1971 656 people lived in the civil parish.

The Avon, zigzagging southwards across the plain, has determined the pattern of Enford's communications with the surrounding area. The roads and lanes which link the parish to near-by settlements constitute a ladder-like network along its valley. Of those which served Enford and its hamlets

---

[45] W.R.O., Inclosure Award map of Enford.
[46] *Feet of F.* 1327–77 (W.R.S. xxix), p. 120; C 136/95 no. 53; Mun. D. & C. Winton., 13th- and 14th-cent. Elstub hund. ct. rolls.
[47] W.R.O. 772/19, poor-rate assessment, 1763.
[48] Mun. D. & C. Winton., 13th-cent. Elstub hund. ct. rolls; 13th-cent. Enford ct. rolls.
[49] *P.N. Wilts.* (E.P.N.S.), 328; W.R.O. 865/332, 17th- and 18th-cent. Chisenbury ct. papers; C 3/121/6; *Andrews and Dury, Map* (W.R.S. viii), pl. 8. In the 19th cent. it was the man.-ho. which was usually referred to as Chisenbury Priory: see below. The hist. of Netheravon par. is treated below.
[50] This para. is based on Geol. Surv. Map 1″, drift, sheet 282 (1959 edn.).

[51] *V.C.H. Wilts.* i (1), 69, 209, 214, 254, 256.
[52] Ibid. 69, 265, 275; i (2), 410.
[53] Ibid. iv. 250.   [54] Ibid. i (1), 275–6.
[55] Ibid. 69; i (2), 445.   [56] *W.A.M.* lxii. 126.
[57] *V.C.H. Wilts.* iv. 297, 299, 306, 308; land at Compton seems to have been considered part of an estate in Amesbury: W.R.O. 283/59, deeds, 1382–1664.
[58] *V.C.H. Wilts.* iv. 308.
[59] *Taxation Lists* (W.R.S. x), 3, 121.
[60] Ibid. 131; and see above, n. 57.
[61] *W.N. & Q.* iii. 539.
[62] All population figures from *V.C.H. Wilts.* iv. 348; *Census,* 1961, 1971.
[63] *V.C.H. Wilts.* iv. 323.
[64] *Census,* 1891.

in the later 18th century, ones not still in use could usually be traced in 1976 as footpaths.[65] On either side of the Avon roads, probably of considerable antiquity, wind parallel to it, mostly clinging to the gravel terrace directly below the scrub-fringed lee of the plain but occasionally forsaking it for an exposed course over the chalk, as at the northern end of Chisenbury tithing and west of Enford village. The road west of the river was turnpiked in 1840.[66] A toll-house and associated gate still stood in the village street near the church in 1876.[67] Most roads leading east and west across the plain fell out of general use after much downland in Enford was bought by the War Department in the late 19th century and the early 20th.[68] In 1956 the Crown successfully prosecuted the Wiltshire county council, as the representatives of the parishioners of Enford, for failing to keep a stretch of Water Lane in repair.[69]

From at least the later 18th century the roads running along the valley sides were linked by lanes carried across the river by numerous bridges.[70] Of the bridges linking East Chisenbury with West Chisenbury the wooden footbridge at the northern end of East Chisenbury was replaced by a suspension footbridge made by James Dredge in 1848. After its demolition in 1960 it was replaced by a concrete structure.[71] The bridge which carried the lane over the Avon from Enford to Longstreet was replaced in 1844 by a three-span cast iron beam bridge made by Tasker & Fowle of Andover. A new bridge, supported on the original piers, was built in 1971.[72] A concrete footbridge linked Coombe and Fifield in 1976.

The village of Enford lies among meadows on the Avon's west bank between the river and the main Salisbury road. It flanks the lane, known in the earlier 20th century as Enford Hill, which runs eastwards across the river to Longstreet.[73] The only surviving buildings of any age are the church and the former Vicarage, in 1976 called Enford House.[74] The manor-house, reputedly destroyed by fire, stood north-east of the church by the Avon.[75] Until recently Enford Hill was fairly closely built up with cottages. Most were apparently of 19th-century date and all displayed the combination of thatched roofs, timber-framing, and the use of bricks and chalk blocks typical of the area.[76] Only one or two remained in 1976. Manor Cottage, which stands some distance north-east of the church, was originally a small 18th-century house. It was partly reconstructed at first floor level in the 19th century. A symmetrical range of three cottages with a central pediment was built on its east side c. 1800 and demolished c. 1950.[77] A few houses, their sites cut into the chalk, stand along Chapel Lane west of the Upavon–Salisbury road. Some 1.5 km. south-west of that lane Enford Farm, from which the manorial demesne was worked in the 19th century, stands exposed on open downland.[78] Originally a narrow mid-18th-century house five bays wide, its size was doubled, and many alterations made both inside and out, in the 19th century. New Town, mentioned in the later 17th century, lies 500 m. south of Enford and comprises a few brick cottages of the 19th century and later scattered along the east side of the main Salisbury road.[79] The Elstub hundred courts were probably formerly held in Elstub meadow, which borders the Avon to the south-east.

Longstreet, which extends southwards from Lower Farm at the east end of Enford bridge and for 500 m. along either side of the lane running south to Coombe, is mentioned in the 13th century.[80] The lane, which contains the one or two shops in the parish, is closely built up with large cottages giving directly upon it. Although nothing of 17th-century date remains visible, a house on the west side bears evidence of 18th-century refronting. Opposite it stands the Swan inn, which from the early 18th century to the later 19th was part of the Longstreet farm estate.[81] The building the inn occupied in 1976 was of later-18th-century date and much enlarged in the 19th century. Its sign spans the road at roof level. Most houses in the hamlet date from the 18th and 19th centuries and are built of various mixtures of brick, flint, and chalk. A few are timber-framed and have thatched roofs. At the southern end of the hamlet a broad shelf somewhat above road level is all that remains of a road which once ran parallel on the east.

The hamlet of Littlecott comprises, besides Littlecott Farm and mill, a few houses of various dates from the 17th century scattered along the lane running north on the Avon's east bank from Longstreet to East Chisenbury. Littlecott House, essentially a substantial brick building of the later 19th century, has been the official residence of the Station Commander, and later of the A.O.C., R.A.F. Upavon, since 1928.[82] A council housing estate of the earlier 20th century stands north of Water Lane.

Coombe lies on the same side of the Avon near the southern parish boundary. The extensive outbuildings of Coombe Farm and a few houses of more recent construction stand along the east side of the hamlet's lane, known in the early 19th century as Coombe street.[83] Coombe Cottage, which stands north of the farm-house on the west side, is a small 17th-century timber-framed and gabled house almost completely encased with walls of brick, flint, and chalk. The scarred landscape east of Coombe shows chalk to have been extensively quarried there at some date.

Fifield, opposite Coombe west of the Avon, is approached from the main Salisbury road by a long lane, on either side of which the hamlet huddles near the river. On the lane's north side the former

[65] Andrews and Dury, Map (W.R.S. viii), pl. 8.
[66] V.C.H. Wilts. iv. 264.
[67] Sar. Dioc. R.O., Pet. for Faculties, bdle. 24, no. 2.
[68] See below.
[69] The Crown sought to establish the county council's obligation to maintain the road: The Times, 6–7 Jan. 1956; 29 Mar. 1956.
[70] Andrews and Dury, Map (W.R.S. viii), pl. 8.
[71] N. A. H. Lawrance, 'Notes for a hist. of Enford' (MS. penes Sir Ric. Harvey, Bt., Chisenbury Priory, in 1975), 115.   [72] Ibid.

[73] Photograph c. 1932 penes Sir Ric. Harvey.
[74] See p. 131.
[75] Local information; see below.
[76] Photograph c. 1932 penes Sir Ric. Harvey.
[77] Local information.   [78] See p. 126.
[79] Sar. Dioc. R.O., Chwdns.' Pres. 1683.
[80] P.N. Wilts. (E.P.N.S.), 329.
[81] W.R.O. 212B/3022; 212B/3030; 212B/3061; Alehouse-keepers' Reg. 1822; W.A.S. Libr., sale cat. vii, no. 56.
[82] Ex inf. Defence Land Agent, Durrington.
[83] W.R.O., Inclosure Award map.

Fifield Farm, in 1976 called Fifield Avon, stands enclosed to the east by a cob wall. Its main north–south 17th-century range, which once had lateral gables, is timber-framed with brick nogging and some replacement in brick. The south end was heightened to two full storeys c. 1800 and the south front extended to the east by one room and given a central doorway. After having been divided into cottages, the house was brought back into single occupation in the 20th century and remodelled in 1972 when a stone fire-place was introduced into the principal room.[84] Opposite that house a cluster of three small thatched and timber-framed houses, probably of 17th-century date, have been partly encased with brick, flint, or chalk walls.

The small hamlet of East Chisenbury lies north of Chisenbury Priory on the former western boundary of the ancient parish. It is ranged east of the Avon on either side of the lane leading north to Upavon. Another lane, still used as a footpath in 1976, once ran parallel to it along the river bank.[85] Four of the most substantial cottages are timber-framed with thatched roofs. Although added to and partly rebuilt in brick at various dates, they appear to be of 17th-century origin. They were perhaps formerly attached to copyholds in Chisenbury tithing. There are also some 18th- and 19th-century cottages, and an inn, the Red Lion, of 19th-century date. At various dates in the earlier 20th century council housing, including blocks of flats, has been built on the east of the lane at the hamlet's northern end.

In the later 18th century and the earlier 19th Compton hamlet comprised a few dwellings which clustered in Water Dean Bottom between Compton Farm and the main Salisbury road.[86] By the 1880s, however, the farm-house stood solitary, as it did in 1976.[87]

MANORS AND OTHER ESTATES. In 934 King Athelstan expressly granted an estate of 30 hides at Enford to support the cathedral clergy of Winchester.[88] Of those 30 hides 5 were held of the monks in 1086 by William, 2 by Harold, 3 by an unnamed Englishman, and 1 by the priest at Enford.[89] Except the priest's hide none may be certainly identified with any of the estates traced below. The monks of the Old Minster, later St. Swithun's Priory, held the manor of *ENFORD* until the Dissolution.[90] They were granted free warren within the manorial demesne in 1300.[91]

The Crown granted the manor to Thomas Culpeper in 1541.[92] After Culpeper's attainder and execution later the same year Enford was forfeited to the Crown, which in 1543 granted the estate to Winchester College.[93] In 1551 Culpeper's elder brother Thomas successfully established his title to the manor under the terms of the grant made to his brother in 1541.[94] He was succeeded c. 1558 by his son Sir Alexander (d. 1600), and grandson Sir Anthony Culpeper.[95] During 1614 and 1615 the manor was apparently sold to members of the Petre family. In 1614 John Petre received a Crown grant of the estate and the following year Sir Anthony Culpeper conveyed the same property to John's brother Thomas.[96] In 1621 John and Thomas, with Thomas Forster, sold to William Rolfe, who sold in 1635 to Sir Henry Clarke.[97]

At Sir Henry's death c. 1654 the manor passed to his second son Henry (d. 1681), M.P. for Great Bedwyn in 1661, under the terms of a settlement made in 1639.[98] In 1673 the younger Henry settled the estate on his son Henry and daughter-in-law Hester. Thus the third Henry, M.P. for Ludgershall in 1685, was succeeded at his death in 1689 by his widow Hester (fl. 1715).[99] From Hester the manor passed to her son George Clarke, who in 1747 sold it to Sir Hildebrand Jacob, Bt. (d. 1790).[1] Jacob sold it in 1748 to Paulet St. John (d. 1780), who in 1763 settled the manor on his son Sir Henry Paulet St. John.[2] Sir Henry sold it c. 1769 to Thomas Benett (d. 1797).[3]

Thomas's son John Benett (d. 1852) sold the estate, which then extended over most of Enford and Fifield tithings, in 1836 to Sir Edmund Antrobus, Bt. (d. 1870). Sir Edmund's son and namesake, the third baronet, sold Enford manor (then reckoned at 2,384 a.) in 1899 to the War Department, whose successor, the Ministry of Defence, was owner in 1975.[4]

The capital messuage of Enford, then described as a 'mansion-house', stood north-east of the church in a loop of the Avon opposite Littlecott mill in the earlier 19th century.[5] It was no longer standing c. 1886.[6]

The 5 hides at Enford held in 1086 by William[7] were in 1275 held by John of Fifield.[8] Presumably after 1275 what is probably the same estate was held by Simon of Fifield, who arranged that after his death it should remain to St. Swithun's Priory.[9] It apparently thereafter merged in the convent's manor of Enford.

In 1066 Harding held land later called the manor

---

[84] Ex inf. the occupier.
[85] *Andrews and Dury, Map* (W.R.S. viii), pl. 8; W.R.O., Inclosure Award map.
[86] *Andrews and Dury, Map* (W.R.S. viii), pl. 8; O.S. Map 1″, sheet 14 (1817 edn.).
[87] O.S. Map 6″, Wilts. XLVII (1889 edn.).
[88] Finberg, *Early Wessex Chart.* p. 83.
[89] *V.C.H. Wilts.* ii, p. 120.
[90] Ibid.; *Bk. of Fees*, ii. 737; *Valor Eccl.* (Rec. Com.), vi, App. p. vii. [91] *Cal. Chart. R.* 1300–26, 1.
[92] *L. & P. Hen. VIII*, xvi, p. 382.
[93] J. D. Mackie, *Earlier Tudors*, 418; C 66/729 m. 6.
[94] *Cal. Pat.* 1550–3, 159; Winch. Coll. Mun. 8188.
[95] Prob. 11/41 (P.C.C. 60 Noodes); C 142/123 no. 96; B.L. Harl. Ch. III. E. 58; C 142/262 no. 108.
[96] C 66/2032 m. 12; C.P. 25(2)/370/12 Jas. I Hil.; *Complete Peerage*, x. 506.
[97] C.P. 25(2)/372/18 Jas. I Hil.; C.P. 25(2)/510/11 Chas. I Mich.

[98] *Cal. S.P. Dom.* 1671–2, 53; *V.C.H. Wilts.* v. 148–9, 159 n.; *Cal. Treas. Bks.* 1681–5, 207; except where stated this para. is based on W.R.O. 413/151, abstr. of title.
[99] *W.A.M.* xlvii. 225; *Cal. Treas. Bks.* 1689–92, 153, 452; W.R.O. 7/13, ct. bk., ct. held Nov. 1689; 772/1, par. reg.
[1] *Q. Sess. 1736* (W.R.S. xi), 138; Burke, *Ext. & Dorm. Baronetcies* (1844), 280.
[2] G.E.C. *Baronetage*, i. 157.
[3] Burke, *Commoners*, i. 248–9.
[4] Burke, *Land. Gent.* (1871), i. 84; W.R.O. 772/21, rate bk. 1836–45; Inclosure Award and maps; Tithe Award; Burke, *Peerage* (1959), 80; *Salisbury Plain (Property Purchased)*, H.C. 14, pp. 2–3 (1900), xlix.
[5] W.R.O., Inclosure Award and map.
[6] O.S. Map 6″, Wilts. XLVII (1889 edn.).
[7] *V.C.H. Wilts.* ii, p. 120.
[8] *Rot. Hund.* (Rec. Com.), ii (1), 258.
[9] *Chartulary Winch. Cath.* ed. A. W. Goodman, p. 97.

of *COMPTON*.[10] At the Conquest the estate was granted to Aubrey de Couci but he forfeited it *c.* 1080.[11] In 1086 the king held Compton.[12] The estate seems to have been granted, like Aubrey's Leicestershire possessions, to Hugh de Grentmesnil (d. 1093).[13] After the death on crusade of Hugh's son Ives, the Grentmesnil lands in England were appropriated by Robert, count of Meulan (later earl of Leicester, d. 1118), to whom they had been entrusted during Ives's absence.[14] Compton thus became part of the honor of Leicester. Its overlordship passed like the capital manor of Netheravon and was partitioned with the honor in 1206–7 after the death in 1204 of Robert, earl of Leicester.[15] The overlordship of that moiety allotted to the earl of Winchester is last mentioned *c.* 1264.[16] The overlordship of the other moiety descended like the Leicester moiety of the capital manor of Netheravon and eventually became part of the duchy of Lancaster.[17]

In 1248 Walter the clerk, of 'Tydewyk', and his wife Agnes held a moiety of Compton of Simon, earl of Leicester.[18] What may be the same estate was held by the Breamore family as mesne tenants in 1298 and in the 15th century was called the manor of *COMPTON BREAMORE*.[19] John Breamore, who held the estate in 1348, was succeeded by his son, another John.[20] The younger John was succeeded at his death in 1361 by his daughter Avice.[21] The estate then passed like the manor of West Chisenbury in Netheravon to Richard Browning (d. 1573).[22] Richard's son Francis in 1577 sold it to John Ranger,[23] who, with his son Robert, sold it in 1595 to George Duke (d. 1610).[24] Compton Breamore then passed in the Duke family to George's descendant Robert (d. 1793), who sold in 1761 to William Hussey.[25]

The earl of Winchester's moiety, held *c.* 1264 by William Burdet, may be identifiable with the estate, known from the 17th century as the manor of *COMPTON COOMBE*, held in 1293 by the Coombe family.[26] Then and in 1329 the Coombes were said to hold under the Breamores,[27] but in 1298 under Edmund, late earl of Lancaster. Richard of Coombe died *c.* 1293 seised with his son Richard

of 6 bovates of land at Compton.[28] The younger Richard settled the estate in 1313 on himself and his wife Anstice.[29] By 1325 the land had passed, according to the 1313 settlement, to Richard's nephew Richard who that year settled it on himself, his wife Maud, and their son, another Richard.[30] The nephew Richard died seised *c.* 1329 of 5 virgates in Compton.[31] The lands presumably passed to his widow Maud and eventually to his son Richard, who, as Sir Richard of Coombe (d. 1361), exchanged his Compton lands in 1358 with Adam Kingsmill for others elsewhere.[32] What is evidently the same estate was, however, the property of Walter of Coombe before 1361.[33] It passed to Walter's son Robert who was in possession by 1412.[34] Robert was succeeded by his son John and grandson Richard of Coombe. Richard was dead by *c.* 1456–60, when his brother John claimed the Compton estate.[35]

The manor of Compton Coombe was held by the Dauntsey family in the earlier 16th century.[36] From William Dauntsey (d. 1543) it passed to his brother Ambrose (d. 1555), and to Ambrose's son John (d. 1559).[37] John was succeeded by his sons Ambrose (d. 1562) and John.[38] In 1628 Sir John Dauntsey sold it to James Ley, earl of Marlborough (d. 1629), whose son Henry, earl of Marlborough, sold it *c.* 1630 to Thomas Bower (d. 1635).[39] Thomas's son Henry sold the manor to the Revd. John Straight in 1658.[40] On Straight's death in 1680 Compton Coombe passed to his son John.[41] The younger John was dead by 1703 and his son William in possession.[42] William Straight's successor at his death *c.* 1724 was his kinsman the Revd. John Straight (d. 1736).[43] In 1750 Mary, John's widow, and her son William Straight sold the estate to Edward Marchant. He in 1761 sold to William Hussey, who bought Compton Breamore in the same year.[44]

Thus reunited the moieties passed successively, under the terms of the will of William Hussey (d. 1813), to his grand-nephew John D. Hussey (d. 1817), and then to John's nephew Ambrose Hussey.[45] Ambrose was succeeded in 1849 by his son Ambrose D. Hussey (Hussey-Freke from 1863), who in 1897 sold the Compton estate (922 a.) to the War

---

[10] *V.C.H. Wilts.* ii, p. 134.
[11] Ibid.; F. M. Stenton, *Anglo-Saxon Eng.* 614.
[12] *V.C.H. Wilts.* ii, pp. 134–5.
[13] Stenton, op. cit. 614 n.; *V.C.H. Leics.* i. 290–1.
[14] *V.C.H. Leics.* i. 290–1; Levi Fox, 'Honor of Leic. 1066–1399', *E.H.R.* liv. 390; *Complete Peerage*, vii. 520.
[15] See p. 168.
[16] Hist. MSS. Com. 78, *Hastings*, i, p. 331.
[17] *Pipe R.* 1218 (P.R.S. N.S. xxxix), 10; *Bk. of Fees*, ii. 746, 1421; *Close R.* 1254–6, 439–40; *Wilts. Inq. p.m.* 1242–1326 (Index Libr.), 218–19; 1327–77 (Index Libr.), 399–400; *Cal. Close*, 1360–4, 208; D.L. 43/23/7.
[18] *Bk. of Fees*, ii. 1421.
[19] *Wilts. Inq. p.m.* 1242–1326 (Index Libr.), 218–19; *Feud. Aids*, vi. 627.
[20] *Feet of F.* 1327–77 (W.R.S. xxix), p. 90; *Cal. Close*, 1360–4, 208.
[21] *Wilts. Inq. p.m.* 1327–77 (Index Libr.), 276; see below, p. 173.
[22] *Wilts. Inq. p.m.* 1327–77 (Index Libr.), 399–400; *Feud. Aids*, v. 240; vi. 541, 627; W.R.O. 7/31, deeds, 14 May 1554, 20 July 1572; *Herald and Gen.* iii. 519.
[23] *Herald and Gen.* iii. 519; W.R.O. 7/31, deed, 10 Nov. 1576; C.P. 25(2)/240/19 Eliz. I Hil.
[24] W.R.O. 7/31, deeds, 20 Oct., 26 May 1594; C.P. 25(2)/242/37 & 38 Eliz. I Mich. For a descent of the Duke fam. see Burke, *Commoners* (1833–8), i. 285–6.
[25] W.R.O. 7/31, deeds, 28 Sept. 1623, 13 Feb. 1728, 2 Sept. 1761.
[26] *Wilts. Inq. p.m.* 1242–1326 (Index Libr.), 197; C.P. 25(2)/369/8 Jas. I Mich.
[27] *Wilts. Inq. p.m.* 1327–77 (Index Libr.), 44–5.
[28] Ibid. 1242–1326 (Index Libr.), 197, 218–19.
[29] *Feet of F.* 1272–1327 (W.R.S. i), p. 84; *W.N. & Q.* vii. 500.
[30] *Feet of F.* 1272–1327 (W.R.S. i), p. 120; *Wilts. Inq. p.m.* 1242–1326 (Index Libr.), 197, 277.
[31] *Wilts. Inq. p.m.* 1327–77 (Index Libr.), 44–5.
[32] B.L. Harl. MS. 1623, f. 22.
[33] *W.N. & Q.* vii. 502; Walter of Coombe and John Breamore (d. 1361) are together described as lords of Compton before 1375: Hist. MSS. Com. 55, *Var. Coll.* iv, p. 160.
[34] *Feud. Aids*, vi. 539; *W.N. & Q.* vii. 502.
[35] *W.N. & Q.* vii. 503–5; C 1/26/453.
[36] C.P. 25(2)/46/322 no. 39.
[37] Prob. 11/29 (P.C.C. 28 Spert); *Wilts. Pedigrees* (Harl. Soc. cv, cvi), 43–5; C 142/114 no. 76; C 142/119 no. 186.
[38] C 142/119 no. 186; C 142/132 no. 23.
[39] C.P. 25(2)/508/4 Chas. I Mich.; *Complete Peerage*, viii. 488–90; C 142/518 no. 73.
[40] C 142/518 no. 73; C.P. 25(2)/609/1658 Hil.
[41] W.R.O. 7/28, will of John Straight.
[42] Ibid. abstr. of title.
[43] Ibid.; J. Foster, *Alumni Oxon. 1500–1714*, iv. 1433.
[44] W.R.O. 7/28, abstr. of title.
[45] Ibid. 7/33, abstr. of title (with pedigree of Hussey fam.); *V.C.H. Wilts.* vi. 121.

Department, whose successor, the Ministry of Defence, was owner in 1975.[46]

Compton Farm, from which the reunited estate was worked from at least the later 18th century, is set back west of the Salisbury–Upavon road in Water Dean Bottom.[47] The original small 18th-century brick farm-house was much enlarged in the 19th century.

In 1275 the bishop of Winchester held 1 knight's fee in Coombe subinfeudated in moieties.[48] He is last expressly mentioned in 1282 as overlord of the moiety then held by Adam de Grindham and in the mid 14th century as overlord of that held by the Coombe family.[49] By the 16th century the reunited estate was considered to be part of the duchy of Lancaster.[50]

Richard of Coombe held in 1275 the moiety later called the manor of COOMBE.[51] A Simon of Fittleton held what is clearly the same estate c. 1282.[52] He may have been the father of Richard of Coombe who died seised c. 1293 of 1 carucate of land at Coombe.[53] Richard's son Simon died c. 1300 seised of 100 a. there.[54] The estate passed to Simon's posthumous son Richard (d. c. 1329), who in turn was succeeded by his widow Maud, with whom he was jointly enfeoffed.[55] Maud, who married secondly Robert of Ramsbury, died c. 1352 when Coombe passed to her son Sir Richard of Coombe (d. 1361).[56] Sir Richard conveyed the manor to William Holbeach and his wife Maud.[57] William died in 1367 and, under the terms of a settlement of 1364, Maud succeeded her husband at Coombe.[58] Maud apparently sold the estate c. 1385 to Robert Dyneley and his wife Margaret. She, then the widow of Sir Percival Sowdan, in 1427 sold it to William Darell.[59] On William's death the manor passed to his widow Elizabeth (d. 1464), with whom he had evidently been seised jointly.[60] Elizabeth was succeeded by her son Sir George Darell (d. 1474) and grandson Sir Edward Darell (d. 1530).[61] Sir Edward's heir was his grandson Sir Edward Darell (d. 1549)[62] who settled Coombe on himself and his second wife Mary for lives in 1548.[63] On the death in 1598 of Mary, who married secondly Philip Maunsell and thirdly Henry Fortescue, the manor passed to John Darell, the grandson of Sir

Edward (d. 1549).[64] He sold the manor in 1612 to Thomas Jeay.[65]

Jeay was succeeded at his death in 1623 by his son, another Thomas, who sold in 1626 to Sir Richard Grobham.[66] The property thereafter descended like St. Amand's manor in Netheravon to John Howe, Lord Chedworth (d. 1804).[67] Chedworth's trustees sold the estate, which then comprised two farms, to John Montagu Poore in 1807.[68] Poore was succeeded by his son Robert Montagu Poore in 1808.[69] On Robert's death c. 1837 Coombe passed to his widow Anna Maria, who married secondly Mark Anthony Saurin.[70] On her death in 1865 she was succeeded by her son Robert Poore (d. 1918).[71] The Poores apparently retained the farm in the earlier 20th century.[72] In 1975 it was owned by Mr. S. Crook.

Coombe Farm stands immediately north of the southern parish boundary on the west side of the lane from Fittleton to East Chisenbury.[73] The old range, running east–west, is now rendered. In 1778 that wing was partly encased and extended in brick, and a new east front built to produce an L-shaped house.[74]

The other moiety of Coombe was held by Philip de Grindham in 1275.[75] Adam de Grindham held the same estate c. 1282.[76] From Adam the estate passed successively to his son and grandson, both named John, and to his great-grandson Adam. Adam's heir was his son John de Grindham who was succeeded by his daughter Margaret.[77] She may perhaps be identified as the Margaret who, with her husband Robert Turny, was owner in 1387.[78] In 1428 the moiety was held by another Robert Turny, who, with his wife Christine, before 1431 sold it to William Darell, already owner of the other moiety.[79]

The estate known from the 16th century as the manor of ENFORD LITTLECOTT, LITTLE-COTT FIFIELD, or LITTLECOTT, may perhaps be identifiable with the 8 virgates held at Littlecott by Simon of Littlecott in the early 14th century.[80] A Simon of Littlecott, perhaps the same, was a free tenant of the capital manor of Enford in 1333.[81] Another Simon of Littlecott apparently owed suit there in 1360.[82] What may be the same estate at Littlecott was held by Ralph Littlecott in

[46] W.R.O. 7/33, abstr. of title; *Salisbury Plain (Property Purchased)*, H.C. 14, pp. 2–3 (1900), xlix.
[47] *Andrews and Dury, Map* (W.R.S. viii), pl. 8; O.S. Map 6", Wilts. XLVII (1889 edn.).
[48] *Rot. Hund.* (Rec. Com.), ii (1), 258.
[49] *Wilts. Inq. p.m. 1327–77* (Index Libr.), 228.
[50] C 142/51 no. 2; C 142/230 no. 63.
[51] *Rot. Hund.* (Rec. Com.), ii (1), 258.
[52] *Reg. Pontoise* (Cant. & York Soc.), ii. 389.
[53] *Wilts. Inq. p.m. 1242–1326* (Index Libr.), 197; B.L. Harl. MS. 1623, f. 22.
[54] *Wilts. Inq. p.m. 1242–1326* (Index Libr.), 277.
[55] Ibid.; *1327–77* (Index Libr.), 44–5; *Feet of F. 1272–1327* (W.R.S. i), p. 120.
[56] B.L. Harl. MS. 1623, ff. 21v., 22; *W.N. & Q.* vii. 437–8; *Cat. Anct. D.* iii, C 3073; i, C 248; *Wilts. Inq. p.m. 1327–77* (Index Libr.), 228.
[57] B.L. Harl. MS. 1623, f. 21v.
[58] *Wilts. Inq. p.m. 1327–77* (Index Libr.), 342–3; *Feet of F. 1327–77* (W.R.S. xxix), p. 125; *Cat. Anct. D.* iii, C 2975, C 2962; *Cal. Close, 1377–81*, 381, 464.
[59] *Cat. Anct. D.* i, C 495; ii, C 2677.
[60] C 140/12 no. 13.
[61] Ibid.; C 140/48 no. 14; C 142/51 no. 2.
[62] C 142/51 no. 2; *W.A.M.* iv, pedigree facing p. 226.
[63] C.P. 25(2)/66/546 no. 12; *W.A.M.* iv, pedigree facing

p. 226.
[64] *W.A.M.* iv, pedigree facing p. 226.
[65] C.P. 25(2)/370/10 Jas. I Mich.
[66] *Wilts. Inq. p.m. 1625–49* (Index Libr.), 3–4; C.P. 25(2)/508/1 Chas. I Hil.
[67] See p. 170; W.R.O. 530, abstr. of title.
[68] W.R.O. 530, sale cat.; 998, Poore deeds, decree, 1810.
[69] Burke, *Land. Gent.* (1937), 1829; W.R.O., Enford Inclosure Award.
[70] W.R.O. 998, Poore deeds, mar. settlements, 16 May 1833, 1839; will of R. M. Poore pr. 1837; I.R. 29/38/85.
[71] Burke, *Land. Gent.* (1937), 1829; W.R.O. 998, Poore deeds, letters of admin. 10 June 1865.
[72] *Kelly's Dir. Wilts.* (1903 and later edns.).
[73] I.R. 29/38/85; I.R. 30/38/85.
[74] Bricks for the alterations were then bought from Lydeway in Urchfont: W.R.O. 415/89, acct. bk.
[75] *Rot. Hund.* (Rec. Com.), ii (1), 258.
[76] *Reg. Pontoise* (Cant. & York Soc.), ii. 388.
[77] B.L. Royal MS. App. 89, f. 153.
[78] C.P. 25(1)/256/55 no. 35.
[79] *Feud. Aids*, v. 233; C 146/10403; see above.
[80] Katharine A. Hanna, 'Winch. Cath. Custumal' (Southampton Univ. Coll. M.A. thesis, 1954), 441 and nn. 3–4; Req. 2/8/293; C 1/995/13.
[81] B.L. Harl. Roll W. 8.
[82] Ibid. W. 13.

1484.[83] Ralph's lands passed to Simon Littlecott, whose daughter and heir Alice married Robert Thornborough (d. 1522).[84] Robert held the estate for life after Alice's death, and was succeeded by his son William (d. 1535), and grandson John.[85] John's son Edward seems to have been in possession in 1599.[86] The manor was afterwards owned by Sir George Kingsmill (d. 1606), who in 1605 settled it for life on his wife Sarah (d. 1629).[87]

Thereafter the descent of the property is obscure. The manor may perhaps be identified with the estate which Robert Hunt held at Littlecott in 1656.[88] What may be the same lands were held in 1727 by Charles Gresley and Joan, widow of Thomas Gresley.[89] The Gresleys remained owners until the end of the 18th century.[90] By 1804 John Moore owned Littlecott and in 1841 the estate was held by his trustees.[91] The farm was bought in the 1860s by Welbore Ellis Agar, earl of Normanton (d. 1868), and descended with that title until 1898. At that date the estate, then enlarged by the addition of another farm at Littlecott and reckoned at 565 a., was offered for sale. As the property of A. E. B. Maton it was bought in 1912 by the War Department, whose successor, the Ministry of Defence, was owner in 1976.[92]

Littlecott Farm, which stands on the west side of the lane running along the east bank of the Avon from Longstreet to East Chisenbury, is a T-shaped chalk and flint house of the 18th century much altered in the 19th century.[93] It was occupied as two dwellings in 1976.

In 1360 Henry Tidworth held an estate of the lord of the capital manor of Enford.[94] It may be identified with what became known variously as the manor of *FIFIELD, LONG FIFIELD,* or *LONGSTREET.*[95] The estate had passed by 1361 to John Wroth, who was succeeded in 1396 by his son John (d. 1407).[96] The estate passed like the manor of Puckshipton in Beechingstoke to Joan, Lady Ingoldisthorpe (d. 1494).[97] She was succeeded at Fifield by her granddaughter and coheir Elizabeth, widow of Thomas le Scrope, Lord Scrope (d. 1493).[98] Elizabeth in 1511 conveyed the estate to Richard Fox, bishop of Winchester, who afterwards gave it to St. Swithun's Priory.[99] By 1535 the profits of the manor, then usually called Long Fifield, had been allotted to the priory's hoarder

and kitchener.[1] At the Dissolution the manor passed to the Crown, which in 1541 granted it to the newly formed cathedral chapter at Winchester.[2]

The reversion of the estate, then leased by Thomas Dreweatt, was sold in 1857 by Winchester chapter, with the Ecclesiastical Commissioners' consent, to D. H. Dreweatt, R. Goddard, and J. Tanner, perhaps Dreweatt's trustees.[3] In 1861 Dreweatt offered Longstreet farm (390 a.) for sale.[4] Mr. T. Crook was owner in 1976.

Longstreet House stands on the Avon's east bank between the river and the lane leading north to Longstreet hamlet.[5] Its driveway was once flanked by an avenue of elms.[6] The house, of earlier-17th-century origin, is built of flint and chalk, in 1976 rendered and colour-washed on the east, and has stone framed windows and doorways and a slated roof.[7] In the 18th century the interior, especially on the first floor, was remodelled extensively. Externally the house was given a more symmetrical appearance by extensions made to north and south in the 19th century. The east entrance front was aggrandized by the addition of semi-octagonal bays at ground floor level on either side of its original gabled two-storeyed porch, and ornamented with cut barge-boards at the same date.

In 1367 a John de Buttesthorn held an estate at Enford of the prior of St. Swithun.[8] The priory's overlordship is last mentioned in 1494.[9]

John de Buttesthorn, perhaps another, died seised in 1399 of 1 carucate and some meadow land in Enford which may be identified with the estate called *LONGSTREET* farm in the 17th century.[10] John was succeeded by his daughter Elizabeth, wife of Sir John Berkeley.[11] Sir John held the estate in 1412 and at his death in 1427 it passed, like the manor of Chamberlain's, Grimstead's, or Compton's Bemerton, to Sir Maurice Berkeley (d. 1474), his son by Elizabeth.[12] Sir Maurice's son and successor William (d. 1485) was succeeded by his sister Katharine, who married first John Stourton, Lord Stourton (d. 1485), and second Sir John Brereton.[13] At Katharine's death in 1494 her Enford estate passed to her second husband, who was succeeded by his daughter by Katharine, Werburgh (d. 1525).[14] Werburgh's second husband Sir William Compton held the lands until his death in 1528 when they passed to Peter, his son by Werburgh.[15] At Peter's

[83] B.L. Harl. Roll V. 22.
[84] W. Berry, *Hants Genealogies*, 86–7; C 142/39 no. 109.
[85] C 142/39 no. 109; C 142/58 no. 2; C.P. 25(2)/239/15 Eliz. I Trin. no. 727.
[86] B.L. Harl. Roll W. 33.
[87] C 142/374 no. 89; *Complete Peerage*, xii (2), 949 sqq.
[88] E 178/6121.
[89] W.R.O. 212B/3051.
[90] Ibid. Land Tax.
[91] Ibid.; Inclosure Award; I.R. 29/38/173.
[92] W.A.S. Libr., sale cat. ii, no. 15; Burke, *Peerage* (1959), 1684; ex inf. Defence Land Agent, Durrington; see below.
[93] W.R.O., Inclosure Award and map; I.R. 29/38/173; I.R. 30/38/173.
[94] B.L. Harl. Roll W. 13; W.R.O. 7/13, Enford survey, p. 13.
[95] *Feud. Aids*, vi. 538; C 54/379 no. 9; C 3/439/130.
[96] *Feet of F.* 1327–77 (W.R.S. xxix), p. 120; C 136/95 no. 53; C 137/58 no. 23.
[97] *Feud. Aids*, vi. 538; *V.C.H. Wilts*. x. 15; *Cal. Inq. p.m. Hen. VII*, i, pp. 464, 466–7.
[98] *Cal. Inq. p.m. Hen. VII*, i, pp. 464, 466–7; *Complete Peerage*, xi. 569–70.

[99] C 54/379 no. 9; *Valor Eccl.* (Rec. Com.), vi, App. p. viii.
[1] *Valor Eccl.* (Rec. Com.), vi, App. p. viii.
[2] C 66/709 mm. 5 sqq.
[3] Ex inf. Ch. Commrs.; I.R. 29/38/175; I.R. 30/38/175.
[4] W.R.O. 374/129, sale cat.
[5] I.R. 29/38/175; I.R. 30/38/175.
[6] W.R.O. 374/129, sale cat. (1861).
[7] Mun. D. & C. Winton., survey of chap. man. 1649, f. 158.
[8] B.L. Harl. Roll W. 16.
[9] *Cal. Inq. p.m. Hen. VII*, i, pp. 478–9.
[10] C 136/102 no. 6; W.R.O. 212B/2997.
[11] C 136/102 no. 6.
[12] *Feud. Aids*, vi. 530; T. D. Fosbrooke, *Glos.* i. 411; *Complete Peerage*, xii (1), 303–4; *V.C.H. Wilts*. vi. 42 and n.
[13] The following descent corrects that given in *V.C.H. Wilts*. vi. 42 on certain points. *Cal. Inq. p.m. Hen. VII*, iii, p. 546; i, pp. 478–9; *Complete Peerage*, xii (1), 303–4.
[14] *Cal. Inq. p.m. Hen. VII*, i, pp. 478–9; *Cal. Close, 1485–1500*, 299–300; C 142/43 no. 71.
[15] C 142/43 no. 71; Hoare, *Mod. Wilts*. Frustfield, 49; *Complete Peerage*, iii. 390–1; C 142/48 no. 158.

death in 1544 the estate came to his son Henry Compton, later Lord Compton.[16]

Henry, Lord Compton, sold the estate to Simon Hunt in 1575.[17] Simon was succeeded at his death in 1591 by his son Thomas.[18] Thomas (will proved 1622) was succeeded by his son Thomas (d. by Apr. 1656) and grandson, also Thomas.[19] Thomas the grandson c. 1656 sold Longstreet farm to William (later Sir William) Constantine.[20] On Sir William's death in 1670, the farm passed successively, according to the terms of his will, to his widow Anne (d. 1684) and daughter Anne.[21] In 1698 Anne, then the wife of Richard Hosier, sold to Thomas Hunt (d. 1711).[22] In 1713 it was decreed in Chancery that the farm should be sold to pay Hunt's debts when his daughter and heir Anne reached 21 years.[23] In 1720 Longstreet was sold to John Baden.[24]

Baden (d. 1726) was succeeded by his son Robert (d. 1730), who devised Longstreet to his cousin William.[25] In 1759 William Baden sold the farm to his nephew Robert Baden (d. 1806), who devised it to Andrew Baden (d. 1819), son of Edmund Smith Baden of Day House in Chiseldon.[26] Longstreet apparently remained in the Baden family throughout the 19th century. In 1826 Miriam, widow of Andrew Baden, farmed there and in 1844 another Andrew Baden, presumably her son, was owner.[27] The Badens apparently still owned the property in the earlier 20th century.[28] The Ministry of Defence acquired that part of the farm nearest the hamlet of Longstreet from H. T. and H. Young in 1968 and two years later bought the remainder, further east on the downs, from L. E. Bull and R. J. Combes.[29]

Two houses, in 1976 known as Baden Farm and the Grange, were attached to the estate.[30] Baden Farm, from which the land was still worked in 1976, stands at right angles to the lane which curves southwards to Coombe. It is a partly timber-framed and partly brick and flint thatched house dating from the 17th century. The Grange, of flint and brick with a hipped roof, stands west of it beside the Avon. A small house was built, perhaps by one of the Badens, in the earlier 18th century. It was probably Robert Baden (d. 1806) who converted it to a double pile plan by adding a block on the east, and who extended it to the south by building a low kitchen range. In the mid 20th century the house was enlarged on the north-west and replanned internally, and a water-garden was constructed to the west beside the Avon. In 1976 the Grange, then detached

from the farm, was the home of Lt.-Col. J. R. Merton, a portrait painter. The late-18th-century stables and coach-house east of the house have been converted as a studio.

In 1320 Peter de la Folye conveyed a small estate in Enford and Littlecott to Henry de la Folye.[31] Five years later Henry acquired more land there from Philip de la Hulle.[32] A Henry de la Folye, perhaps the same, in 1337 settled the estate on himself for life with successive remainders to his son Adam and daughter Joan.[33] The estate then passed like the manor of West Chisenbury in Netheravon to Joan Ringwood and Clemence Devereux in 1416.[34]

In 1540 Robert Richards sold to his brother Edward a small estate in Littlecott and Enford.[35] Edward Richards still held 1 hide in 1553.[36] It seems probable that the estate passed to Sir Richard Grobham (d. 1629) and descended like the manor of Coombe to John, Lord Chedworth (d. 1804), who died seised of a farm of 136 a. at Littlecott.[37] It was offered for sale in 1807 and may then have been bought by the tenant Henry Hunt, whose family had apparently been lessees since the earlier 17th century.[38] In 1814 Hunt sold to William Akerman, owner in 1817.[39] George Taylor owned the farm, then reckoned at 217 a., in 1840.[40] Like the manor of Littlecott, the land was bought in the 1860s by the earl of Normanton and thereafter merged in that estate.[41]

Lower Farm, from which the land was worked from at least the earlier 19th century, stands on the east side of Longstreet at its junction with the road carried across the Avon by Enford bridge.[42] It is an L-shaped brick house of the early 19th century and the garden retains a cob wall to the south.

In 1571 Robert Richards owned a farm at Longstreet, then tenanted by John Miles.[43] Miles seems to have acquired the freehold by 1579.[44] The farm was apparently the property of John Barnaby c. 1582.[45] A John Barnaby, probably the same, held the estate in 1602.[46] It was afterwards bought by Sir Richard Grobham, who in 1627 settled the lands on his wife Margaret for life as jointure.[47] The lands seem to have merged in Grobham's other estates in Enford.

An estate of 5 virgates at Compton was held in 1627 by Henry Buckerfield, a lunatic.[48] The estate seems to have belonged in 1650 to Henry's younger son Bartholomew who in that year sold it to John Rolfe. It was then said to be in Compton Breamore.[49]

---

[16] C 142/72 no. 105; *Complete Peerage*, iii. 390–1, where Henry's date of d. is given as 1539. It is clear, however, that he died in 1544: C 142/72 no. 105.

[17] W.R.O. 212B/2994.   [18] C 142/232 no. 31.

[19] W.R.O. 212B/2995–6; 212B/2999–3000; 212B/3002–3; Prob. 11/139 (P.C.C. 34 Savile).

[20] W.R.O. 212B/3003; J. Hutchins, *Dors.* iii. 304.

[21] W.R.O. 212B/3108; Prob. 11/334 (P.C.C. 145 Penn, will of Wm. Constantine); Prob. 11/376 (P.C.C. 70 Hare, will of Anne Constantine).

[22] W.R.O. 212B/3108.   [23] Ibid.

[24] Ibid.; 212B/3040–1.

[25] Ibid. 212B/3054; 212B/3108; 772/2, par. reg.

[26] Ibid. 212B/3108.   [27] Ibid.; I.R. 29/38/175.

[28] *Kelly's Dir. Wilts.* (1848 and later edns.).

[29] Ex inf. Defence Land Agent, Durrington.

[30] I.R. 29/38/175; I.R. 30/38/175.

[31] *Feet of F.* 1272–1327 (W.R.S. i), p. 103.

[32] Ibid. p. 122.

[33] Ibid. 1327–77 (W.R.S. xxix), p. 50.

[34] See p. 173; *Wilts. Inq. p.m.* 1327–77 (Index Libr.), 276, 399–400; *Cal. Fine R.* 1413–22, 140.

[35] B.L. Add Ch. 15126.

[36] W.R.O. 7/13, Enford survey, p. 17.

[37] See p. 121; B.L. Add. Ch. 15138; W.R.O. 530, sale cat.

[38] W.R.O. 530, sale cat.; Land Tax; B.L. Add. Ch. 15138. Hunt is probably identifiable with the radical orator Henry Hunt: *V.C.H. Wilts.* x. 162.

[39] W.R.O. 101/165/5, deed, Akerman, Hunt, 1814; 7/13, Enford survey, p. 17; Inclosure Award.

[40] I.R. 29/38/173; I.R. 30/38/173.

[41] W.A.S. Libr., sale cat. ii, no. 15.

[42] W.R.O., Inclosure Award map; I.R. 29/38/173; I.R. 30/38/173.

[43] B.L. Add. Ch. 15127.   [44] Ibid. 15128.

[45] Ibid. 15131.   [46] Ibid. Harl. Roll X. 1.

[47] *Wilts. Inq. p.m.* 1625–49 (Index Libr.), 103–7.

[48] Ibid. 44.

[49] Ibid.; W.R.O. 7/31, deed, 17 Jan. 1650.

Rolfe sold it in 1698 to the executors of Robert Hillman, who in 1702 sold it to George Duke, of Sarson, in Amport (Hants).[50] In 1743 George's son John sold to Frances Offley, who was to hold the estate as security until John's kinsman Robert Duke (d. 1749) of Lake, in Wilsford, should repay the money that she had lent him to buy the lands.[51] Robert's son Robert discharged the debt and in 1751 Frances conveyed the estate to him.[52] Thenceforth it became part of the manor of Compton Breamore.[53]

William of East Dean in 1301 gave a rent of 1 mark yearly from John of Littlecott's lands in Coombe and Littlecott to Amesbury Priory for the soul of Eleanor of Provence (d. 1291), widow of Henry III, who had entered the convent in 1285.[54] The rent is last mentioned in 1541.[55]

The profits of Enford church were appropriated in 1291 by the convent of St. Swithun, Winchester.[56] The appropriated rectory passed to the Crown at the Dissolution and was granted in 1541 to Thomas Culpeper the younger.[57] Thereafter it descended with the capital manor to Anthony Culpeper who sold it in 1602 to Sir Richard Grobham (d. 1629).[58] The property passed in the same way as the manor of Netheravon St. Amand to John Howe, Lord Chedworth (d. 1804).[59]

Of the hide of land to which the priest at Enford was entitled in 1086 some was allotted to the vicar in 1270 and 1292.[60] Besides the great tithes, in 1341 the appropriators had a house and 1 carucate and 2 virgates of land at Enford. No more is heard of that house and land, which may eventually have been merged in the capital manor, also held by St. Swithun's. The tithes arising from Compton tithing were replaced by a payment of £55 in 1772.[61] By 1807 the great tithes from the estate at East Chisenbury belonging to St. Katharine's Hospital, London, had been commuted to a modus of £8 10s.[62] In 1807 Lord Chedworth's trustees offered the money payments and the remaining tithes for sale in lots.[63] Those tithes arising from Enford and Fifield tithings were apparently bought by John Benett who held nearly all the land there.[64] The Littlecott tithes were bought, with an estate in the tithing, by Henry Hunt.[65] The impropriated tithes arising from the vicarial glebe in the tithing were ceded to the vicar at Littlecott inclosure in 1817.[66] After 1830 George Taylor, who then owned Hunt's Littlecott estate, sold all the great tithes not arising from his own lands. In 1840 he was allotted a rent-charge of £55

in place of both great and small tithes from his farm, and Elizabeth Godden, who then owned the remainder of the great tithes of Littlecott, received a rent-charge of £85 to replace both great and small tithes.[67] The impropriated tithes of Coombe tithing were evidently sold with Coombe farm in 1807 to John M. Poore. Those arising from the farm were afterwards merged, while to replace the remainder Anna M. Saurin, widow of Robert M. Poore, was allotted a rent-charge of £50 in 1843.[68] The great tithes of Longstreet were owned in 1844 by Thomas Dreweatt, who in that year received a rent-charge of £182 in lieu.[69] In 1857 Thomas and Edward Gaby, who then owned the modus paid from the estate of St. Katharine's Hospital at Chisenbury, received a rent-charge of £135 in lieu. The Ecclesiastical Commissioners, owners of the impropriated tithes arising from the former prebendal estate at Chisenbury, were then allotted a rent-charge of £28 to replace them.[70]

In 1066 Spirtes the priest held an estate at Chisenbury.[71] Niel the physician held the manor of *CHISENBURY*, later called *CHISENBURY PRIORS* or *PRIORY*, in 1086. It then belonged to the church of Netheravon.[72] The manor was afterwards held by Robert, count of Meulan (d. 1118).[73] The overlordship of the estate passed with a moiety of the honor of Leicester to Edmund, earl of Lancaster, and is last mentioned in 1275.[74]

In 1112 the count of Meulan gave the manor to the abbey of Bec-Hellouin (Eure), and the income from it was apparently set aside for the support of the monks' kitchen.[75] In 1254, however, the profits were assigned for life to William de Guineville (d. 1258) when he retired as the abbot of Bec's proctor-general in England.[76] Chisenbury was administered, from at least the 13th century, from Bec's Ogbourne estate.[77] In 1404, ten years before the formal suppression of the non-conventual alien priories, Chisenbury was granted at farm to William of St. Vaast (d. 1404), prior of Ogbourne, and John, later duke of Bedford, for lives or while the war with France continued.[78] On the duke of Bedford's death in 1435 the Crown granted the profits of Chisenbury to his brother Humphrey, duke of Gloucester (d. 1447), who apparently soon surrendered them.[79]

The Crown granted the manor in 1441 to the hospital of St. Katharine by the Tower, London.[80] Although a Crown grant of Chisenbury was made in 1451 to Eton College it does not seem to have

[50] W.R.O. 7/31, deeds, 6 Mar. 1698, 1–2 May 1702; Burke, *Commoners* (1833–8), i. 285–6.
[51] W.R.O. 7/31, deed, 28–9 Sept. 1743; Burke, *Commoners* (1833–8), i. 285–6.
[52] Burke, *Commoners* (1833–8), i. 285–6; W.R.O. 7/31, deed, 13–14 May 1751.   [53] See above.
[54] *Wilts. Inq. p.m.* 1242–1326 (Index Libr.), 284–5; *Cal. Pat.* 1292–1301, 596; *V.C.H. Wilts.* iii. 247, where Coombe and Littlecott are said incorrectly to be in Figheldean.
[55] *V.C.H. Wilts.* iii. 255.   [56] See p. 130.
[57] *L. & P. Hen. VIII*, xvi, p. 382.
[58] See above; *L. & P. Hen. VIII*, xviii, pp. 533–4; *Cal. Pat.* 1550–3, 159; B.L. Harl. Ch. 111. E. 58; C 142/262 no. 108; B.L. Harl. Ch. 77. C. 32; *Wilts. Inq. p.m.* 1625–49 (Index Libr.), 103–7.
[59] See p. 170; W.R.O. 530, abstr. of title.
[60] *V.C.H. Wilts.* ii, p. 120; Winch. Coll. Mun. 8182; see below, p. 131.
[61] W.R.O., Inclosure Award.   [62] Ibid. 530, sale cat.
[63] Ibid.   [64] I.R. 29/38/113; see above.

[65] W.R.O. 530, sale cat.; see above.
[66] W.R.O. 772/45, memo. Feb. 1814.
[67] Ibid. 212A/36/43, deed, Taylor, Scriven, 1830; I.R. 29/38/173; see above.
[68] I.R. 29/38/85; see above.   [69] I.R. 29/38/175.
[70] I.R. 29/38/67.   [71] *V.C.H. Wilts.* ii, pp. 157–8.
[72] Ibid.; 'Priory' is first added in the 16th cent.: C 3/121/6. 'Priors' was also used alternatively from the 13th cent. to the 18th: *Rot. Hund.* (Rec. Com.), ii (1), 258; W.R.O. 865/332, 17th- and 18th-cent. ct. papers.
[73] *Reg. Regum Anglo-Norm.* ii, no. 1004; *Complete Peerage*, vii. 523 sqq.
[74] See p. 169; *Rot. Hund.* (Rec. Com.), ii (1), 258.
[75] *Reg. Regum Anglo-Norm.* ii, no. 1004; *Sel. Doc. Eng. Lands of Abbey of Bec* (Camd. 3rd ser. lxxiii), 9.
[76] Marjorie Morgan, *Eng. Lands of Abbey of Bec*, 43.
[77] Ibid. 41; S.C. 6/1127/11.
[78] Morgan, op. cit. 128, 131.
[79] C 139/77 no. 36; *Cal. Pat.* 1436–41, 188–9; *Complete Peerage*, v. 730–7.
[80] *Cal. Pat.* 1436–41, 529, 562.

been permanent and the estate was restored to St. Katharine's in 1462.[81] The hospital remained owner until the 20th century. The copyhold lands of the manor, in the north part of Chisenbury, were sold at an unknown date. The greater part was included in the estate sold by A. E. B. Maton to the War Department in 1912. The following year St. Katharine's sold 308 a. to the War Department.[82] In 1921 the remainder of the estate, 74 a., except the manorial rights, was sold to A. J. Phillips, Robert Dixon, and M. L. Mason. They in turn sold to F. V. Lister in 1923.[83] The property afterwards changed hands several times, and in 1964 half of it was bought by Sir Richard Harvey, Bt., owner in 1975.[84]

St. Katharine's Hospital leased the estate for lives from at least the 16th century. The Maton family were lessees until 1587 when Leonard Maton assigned the remainder of his term to his son-in-law Matthew Grove.[85] Thereafter the Groves established themselves at Chisenbury as virtual lords.[86] In 1613 Chisenbury Priory manor was leased to Hugh Grove (fl. 1650), Matthew's nephew.[87] Hugh died after 1650 and it is uncertain whether his son Hugh, who was executed in 1655 for his part in Penruddock's rising, predeceased him.[88] By 1658, however, the younger Hugh's son, also called Hugh, was lessee, and on his death that year devised his interest in Chisenbury to his widow Anne for life.[89] A new lease was made to Anne in 1660 and in 1682 she assigned her interest to her brother-in-law John Grove (d. 1699).[90] In 1708 the manor was leased to Thomas Chafin of Zeals.[91] When Chafin's lease was surrendered in 1724, Hugh Grove, son of John (d. 1699), obtained an interest.[92] After Hugh's death in 1765, a lease was granted in 1768 to his nephew William Chafin Grove (d.s.p. 1793) of Zeals.[93] After William Chafin Grove's death his trustees held the property on behalf of his widow Elizabeth (d. 1832), and nephew Chafin Grove (d. 1851).[94] Chafin Grove was succeeded by his cousin William Chafin Grove (d. 1859).[95] On the death without issue in 1865 of William's son and successor, another William, the Chisenbury estate passed to his sister Julia (d. 1891), on whose death the family's connexion with the manor ended.[96]

The house attached to the estate has been known as Chisenbury Priory since at least the later 19th century.[97] It is set among walled gardens east of the Avon and is approached from the lane running northwards from Littlecott by a long tree-lined drive.[98] It may perhaps have been Hugh Grove (fl. 1650) who constructed the original L-shaped house of rubble with stone dressings which had two storeys and attics. Later in the 17th century the addition of a back wing on the north-east resulted in an open-sided court being formed on the north of the house. It may have been at about that time that a water-garden, fed by a leat constructed from the river along the valley side west of the hamlet of East Chisenbury, was laid out west of the house.[99] The present water-garden was designed and planted by Sir Richard Harvey, Bt., and Lady Harvey. In the early 18th century the north-east rear wing was fitted with panelling. Building operations in the later 18th century both enlarged and modernized the house. About 1767 the south entrance front was given a fashionable brick façade with stone dressings.[1] The architraves of the ground floor windows on that elevation were then surrounded by alternating segmental and triangular pediments. At the same time the interior of the main block was refitted with panelling and moulded plaster ceilings were inserted in the principal rooms. A little later a long kitchen wing of flint, chalk, and brick was added on the west.[2] The thorough restoration which the house underwent after 1923 included the introduction of a 17th-century panelled interior in the north-west wing, the repair of the garden walls, and the addition of formal entrance gates with brick piers to the southern forecourt.

Some time before 1462 John Stourton, Lord Stourton, held an estate at Chisenbury which descended like the manor of Poulshot.[3] John was succeeded there by his son William, who in 1468 settled the lands on his son John and daughter-in-law Katharine.[4] Thus Katharine (d. 1494) succeeded her husband at his death in 1485.[5] When Katharine died, the estate reverted to her husband's brother William, Lord Stourton (d. 1524).[6] The land passed with the Stourton title to William, Lord Stourton, who sold it to Thomas Long in 1544 and confirmed the sale four years later.[7] From Thomas, who died

[81] Ibid. 1446–52, 423; 1461–7, 140; *Cal. Fine R.* 1461–71, 55.
[82] W.R.O., Inclosure Award; ex inf. Defence Land Agent, Durrington.
[83] Copy of deed, 1921, endorsed with note of 1923 sale, *penes* Sir Ric. Harvey, Bt., Chisenbury Priory.
[84] Ex inf. Sir Ric. Harvey.
[85] Guildhall MS. 9760/30/1; C 3/121/6; C 2/Eliz. I/G 9/16; *Extents for Debts* (W.R.S. xxviii), pp. 116–17.
[86] W.R.O. 865/332, 17th- and 18th-cent. ct. papers.
[87] B.L. Harl. MS. 5097, ff. 24v., 25; Hutchins, *Dors.* iii. 568.
[88] *Reg. Adm. Middle Temple*, comp. H. A. C. Sturgess, i. 69, 119; Foster, *Alumni Oxon. 1500–1714*, ii. 615; C 54/3504 no. 29; *V.C.H. Wilts.* v. 148–9. The younger Hugh was living at Chisenbury in 1641: E 179/239/207.
[89] C 54/3504 no. 29; Prob. 11/277 (P.C.C. 295 Wootton); W.R.O. 865/48, abstr. of title.
[90] Guildhall MS. 9760/30/3; W.R.O. 865/56, deed, 8 Mar. 1682; Foster, *Alumni Oxon. 1500–1714*, ii. 615.
[91] Guildhall MS. 9760/30/4.
[92] Ibid. 9760/30/5; J. and J. A. Venn, *Alumni Cantab.* i (2), 271.
[93] Venn, op. cit. 271; Guildhall MS. 9760/30/8; Burke, *Land. Gent.* (1952), 304.
[94] Guildhall MSS. 9760/30/11–12; Burke, *Land. Gent.*

(1952), 304.
[95] Burke, *Land. Gent.* (1952), 304; W.R.O., Inclosure Award; Venn, *Alumni Cantab.* ii (3), 165.
[96] Burke, *Land. Gent.* (1952), 304; Guildhall MS. 9760/30/18.
[97] *Kelly's Dir. Wilts.* (1855 and later edns.); O.S. Map 6″, Wilts. XLVII (1889 edn.).
[98] W.R.O., Inclosure Award map; O.S. Map 6″, Wilts. XLVII (1889 edn.).
[99] The leat is clearly shown by 1773: *Andrews and Dury, Map* (W.R.S. viii), pl. 8.
[1] That date and the initials 'W.G.' appear on the rainwater heads of the south front. 'W.G.' may perhaps be William Grove (d. 1768), a younger brother of the lessee Hugh Grove (d. 1765): Burke, *Land. Gent.* (1952), 304. Hugh appears to have assigned his term to William.
[2] The date 1772 and indecipherable initials appear there.
[3] *V.C.H. Wilts.* vii. 122; *Cal. Close,* 1461–8, 122.
[4] *Cal. Close,* 1461–8, 122; *Cal. Inq. p.m. Hen. VII,* i, pp. 60–1; *Complete Peerage,* xii (1), 301 sqq.
[5] *Cal. Inq. p.m. Hen. VII,* i, pp. 60–1, 478–9.
[6] *Cal. Fine R.* 1485–1509, pp. 217–18; *Complete Peerage,* xii (1), 301 sqq.
[7] *Complete Peerage,* xii (1), 301 sqq.; C.P. 25(2)/46/323/36 Hen. VIII Mich. no. 54; C.P. 25(2)/65/531/2 Edw. VI East. no. 38.

c. 1562, the estate passed to his widow Joan (d. 1583), and nephew Edward Long (d. 1622).[8] Edward's son and successor Gifford died seised in 1635.[9] The estate has not been traced further. It seems likely, however, that it was later acquired by the Grove (sometimes Chafin Grove) family, and is probably identifiable with the 193 a. of freehold land owned at East Chisenbury by William Chafin Grove in 1856.[10]

In 1874 Julia Chafin Grove and her trustees sold the estate to the Ecclesiastical Commissioners.[11] It thereafter merged with the lands of the prebend of Chute and Chisenbury at East Chisenbury.[12]

An estate at Chisenbury was apparently held by the earls of Leicester.[13] Its overlordship passed like a moiety of the honor of Leicester to Edmund, earl of Lancaster, and is last mentioned in 1275.[14]

The estate was granted to Salisbury chapter and its profits formed part of the endowment of a prebend within the cathedral.[15] The manor of *CHISENBURY*, or *CHISENBURY PREBEND* as it became known, remained the property of the prebendaries of Chisenbury (later called Chute and Chisenbury) until the 19th century.[16] Their tenure was interrupted when in 1650 the estate passed to parliamentary trustees.[17] Under the provisions of the Cathedrals and Ecclesiastical Commissioners Act of 1840 the lands became vested the same year in the Ecclesiastical Commissioners on the voidance of the prebend.[18] The estate was augmented in 1874 by the purchase of another 200 a. in East Chisenbury. The enlarged estate, 621 a., was sold in 1912 by the Ecclesiastical Commissioners to the War Department, whose successor, the Ministry of Defence, was owner in 1976.[19]

In 1595 Matthew Grove was tenant. From him the leasehold apparently passed like that of the manor of Chisenbury Priory until the 19th century.[20]

ECONOMIC HISTORY. In 1066 the parish contained, besides the estate of the monks of Winchester cathedral at Enford, independent estates at East Chisenbury and Compton. The Enford estate then included four smaller ones and numerous lesser estates had emerged at Enford and East Chisenbury by the 13th century.

The estate at Enford had been worth £34 when the bishop of Winchester first received it. It was assessed for geld at 30 hides in 1066. In 1086 it contained land enough for 24 ploughs. The 10 demesne hides, worth £20 and perhaps to be identified with the later manor of Enford, supported 3 ploughs and 6 serfs. Elsewhere on the estate 12 villeins and 15 bordars had 10 ploughs. The estate's meadow land covered 17 a. and there was pasture 2½ leagues long and 1½ league broad. In 1086 the four smaller estates attached to it between them contained land for 10 ploughs and together were worth £19.[21]

The demesne mentioned in 1086 apparently remained in hand until the earlier 15th century, when the work force comprised the usual manorial officials, 5 ploughmen, 2 carters, and a dairywoman.[22] A farmer is first mentioned in 1433.[23] Thereafter the demesne was farmed at £40 yearly until the later 15th century when the rent was £46, a sum which remained constant in the 16th century.[24] The increase may perhaps be accounted for by the fact that from at least 1485 until the end of the 16th century the manorial mill mentioned below was leased with the demesne.[25] The Maton family were farmers throughout the 16th century.[26] Enford farm, the lands of which were situated west of the Avon and were conterminous with Enford tithing, represented the demesne in the earlier 19th century.[27]

The tenantry lands of the manor were situated mainly in Fifield tithing. Some time before 1248 the holder of ½-hide and seventeen virgaters held land there and paid rents totalling £13. Besides the usual agricultural duties they were bound to cart wood from Stockton and Savernake. Each could pasture 30 second-year sheep, 1 wether, oxen, and other beasts at the lord's pleasure on his hill pasture for 6*d.* yearly or certain ploughing services. In Enford tithing, besides the demesne, there were then five virgaters and two ½-virgaters owing similar duties to those of the Fifield tenants. The Enford tenants, however, were allowed to use the demesne fold and pasture unconditionally. The dairywoman, her assistants, and the shepherd then received special allowances of cheese.[28] In 1543 fourteen copyholds paid a total of £8 in Enford tithing, in which the tithing of Littlecott and Fifield (the later Littlecott and Longstreet tithings) was then apparently included. The most substantial was a composite holding of 2½ yardlands held for 35*s.* yearly. Only two tenants then held at will. In Fifield tithing the copyholds, of which there were eleven, were larger, there being six of 2 yardlands or more. Copyhold rents then totalled £9, and at least five holdings appear to have been formed by the amalgamation of smaller holdings.[29] Ten years later 26 copyhold estates within the manor paid a total of £19.[30]

During the Middle Ages the manorial economy was closely linked with that of the other Wiltshire

[8] Burke, *Commoners* (1833–8), iv. 65 sqq.; *Cal. Pat. 1560–3*, 599–600.
[9] Burke, *Commoners* (1833–8), iv. 65 sqq.; *Wilts. Inq. p.m. 1625–49* (Index Libr.), 207 sqq.
[10] W.R.O., Inclosure Award.
[11] Ex inf. Ch. Commrs.   [12] See below.
[13] *Rot. Hund.* (Rec. Com.), ii (1), 258.
[14] Ibid.; see below, p. 169.
[15] *V.C.H. Wilts.* iii. 160; *Interdict Doc.* (Pipe R. Soc. N.S. xxxiv), 16.
[16] C 54/3504 no. 29; Sta. Cha. 8/211/15; C 3/214/4; *V.C.H. Wilts.* iii. 160; *Fasti Eccl. Sar.* ed. W. H. Jones, ii. 373–5.   [17] C 54/3504 no. 29.
[18] 3 & 4 Vic. c. 113; *Fasti Eccl. Sar.* ed. Jones, ii. 375; Foster, *Alumni Oxon. 1715–1886*, iii. 916.
[19] Ex inf. Ch. Commrs.; see above.
[20] C 2/Eliz. I/G 2/55; C 54/3504 no. 29; Hutchins, *Dors.*

iii. 568; Sar. Dioc. R.O., prebendal ct. papers, licence to Anne Grove, 1674; I.R. 29/38/67; W.R.O., Inclosure Award.
[21] *V.C.H. Wilts.* ii, p. 120.
[22] B.L. Harl. Roll X. 7.   [23] Ibid. X. 8.
[24] Ibid.; X. 12; X. 14; W. 7; W.R.O. 7/13, survey, 1552–3, p. 3.
[25] B.L. Harl. Roll X. 14; W.R.O. 7/13, survey, 1552–3; Req. 2/244/36.
[26] B.L. Harl. Rolls X. 18–22; W. 7; W.R.O. 7/13, survey, 1552–3; Req. 2/244/36.
[27] W.R.O., Inclosure Award.
[28] Katharine A. Hanna, 'Winch. Cath. Custumal' (Southampton Univ. Coll. M.A. thesis, 1954), 440–1, 444–51, 455–6.
[29] Winch. Coll. Mun., lease bk. G, ff. 98v.–100v.
[30] W.R.O. 7/13, survey, 1552–3, pp. 4–12.

estates of St. Swithun's Priory. The manor, with its wide expanse of arable and grazing downland stretching westwards from Enford village, was able to support large flocks and as a result to maintain a considerable arable acreage. Worth £40 c. 1210, there were 650 ewes and 275 lambs on the estate.[31] Flocks remained large in the Middle Ages.[32] In 1335 12 weys of wool were sent to Winchester.[33] It was apparently Enford's duty, in the considerable exchanges of stock and grain made between the manors of St. Swithun's, to supply hoggasters to other Wiltshire manors in the 15th century.[34] After the demesne was leased in the early 15th century fixed amounts of wheat, barley, oats, and poultry were sent to St. Swithun's from Enford.[35] In 1403 524 a. of arable, one of the higher acreages among the Winchester estates, were cultivated at Enford. Of that total 234 a. were worked by customary tenants, 258 a. by hired labourers, and 32 a. by manorial servants.[36] In the summer of 1403 110 cheeses were produced.[37] Corn and sheep stocks continued high in the 16th century but thereafter the estate's economy is obscure until the 19th century.[38]

In the earlier 13th century, perhaps to augment that produced by the meadow land of Enford and Fifield which was in a narrow strip along the Avon's west bank, hay from 10 a. at Patney, another estate of St. Swithun's, was carted to Enford by the virgaters of the manor.[39] Most customary tenants in Enford, and all those in Fifield, in 1543 made payments, presumably for pasture rights there, for Patney 'woodfare'. Patney mead and its hay were then included in the farm of the capital manor.[40] Most meadow land in Enford and Fifield had been inclosed by 1809. That year John Benett, as lord of the capital manor, was allotted 2 a. in Enford and 1 a. in Fifield tithings.[41]

An open field system may have prevailed at Enford in 1066.[42] A south field is mentioned before 1248.[43] In the earlier 19th century the open fields of Enford and Fifield tithings were on the chalk west of the Upavon–Salisbury road and were separated from the downland pastures of the capital manor by the track running north-westwards across the plain towards Devizes. The Enford fields comprised Town fields near the village and North, Middle North, South, and Middle South fields beyond to the west,[44] but very little land in the tithing then remained uninclosed. When what did remain was inclosed in 1809 John Benett was allotted 2 a. of arable and Enford cow down, 245 a. In Fifield tithing he was allotted 189 a. of arable and 212 a. of downland. His four copyhold tenants in Fifield then received a total of 119 a. of arable.[45] A few years later all had been merged to form Fifield farm.[46]

In 1066 the manor of East Chisenbury was estimated at 8 hides and was worth £13. In 1086 the estate had land enough for 5 ploughs. There were 2 serfs with 2½ ploughs on the 4½ hides then in demesne. Elsewhere within the manor 8 villeins and 12 bordars had 2 ploughs. The meadow land extended over 20 a. and the pasture was 1 league long and 5 furlongs broad.[47]

About 1210 the manor was worth £15 and had a flock of 150 sheep.[48] In 1294 the demesne, reckoned to contain 253 a. of arable, 8 a. of meadow, and pasture for 300 sheep and 20 oxen, maintained a flock of 398 sheep. Its total value was then £9, and that of the entire estate £18.[49] By the earlier 15th century the demesne had been farmed at £16 yearly.[50] It is to be identified with Chisenbury farm, 751 a. in 1792, which then occupied the southerly half of East Chisenbury tithing.[51]

The tenantry lands of Chisenbury were in the northern half of the tithing.[52] In the earlier 13th century twelve virgaters each paid 5s. and owed the usual agricultural duties. From the six cottars, who each held 5 a., were drawn the ploughman and the shepherds. The ploughmen's wives milked the ewes and made cheese. In addition two crofters paid small money rents and owed certain duties. At the same date another estate of 6 virgates, which paid 23s. yearly, also formed part of the estate.[53] It was considered a freehold in 1294.[54] There were then 7 virgaters each paying 5s., 4 tenants who held 1½ virgate each, 4 ½-virgaters, and 5 cottars. All, except the ½-virgaters who owed works only and the cottars who held for rent, owed both rents and works.[55] In 1792 there were within the manor 6 copyholders who held a total of 130 a. in the north part of the tithing, 8 cottagers, and 1 free tenant whose farm extended to 106 a.[56]

The sheep-and-corn husbandry of the estate persisted into the 19th century. The manor's meadow land, called Tenanting mead, was situated north-west of the hamlet between the Avon and the lane to Enford. In 1792 Chisenbury farm had its own fields, named as the fields above Appleton, the Ride, Middle, Bottom, and Larkball fields, in the south-western quarter of the tithing. The tenants' open arable was situated immediately north of them and included the Broak, Hangman's, Summer, and Lyden fields. Beyond to the east of the arable lay the demesne and tenantry down pastures.[57] In 1809, when the tenantry lands were inclosed, the devisees of William Chafin Grove, as tenants of St. Katharine's Hospital, were allotted 133 a., including 105 a. of downland, which adjoined Chisenbury farm to the south. The remaining land, chiefly arable, was redistributed among the six copyholders in allotments totalling 103 a. Some 177 a. were then

[31] *Interdict Doc.* (Pipe R. Soc. N.S. xxxiv), 17, 23.
[32] Mun. D. & C. Winton., acct. rolls, 1248, 1280, 1299, 1309, 1316; B.L. Harl. Roll X. 7; X. 12.
[33] *Obedientiaries' R. St. Swithun's*, ed. G. W. Kitchin (Hants Rec. Soc.), 226.
[34] Joan G. Greatrex, 'Admin. Winch. Cath. Priory temp. Beaufort' (Ottawa Univ. Ph.D. thesis, 1972), 169–70.
[35] Ibid. 156.   [36] Ibid. App. B. 2, v.
[37] B.L. Harl. Roll X. 7.   [38] Req. 2/244/36.
[39] Hanna, 'Winch. Cath. Custumal', 444–51.
[40] Winch. Coll. Mun., lease bk. G, ff. 98v.–100v.
[41] W.R.O., Inclosure Award.
[42] *V.C.H. Wilts.* ii, p. 13 n.

[43] Hanna, 'Winch. Cath. Custumal', 444; Mun. D. & C. Winton., acct. roll, 1280.
[44] W.R.O. 413/111, early-19th-cent. map.
[45] Ibid. Inclosure Award.
[46] W.R.O. 413/43, earlier-19th-cent. map.
[47] *V.C.H. Wilts.* ii, p. 157.
[48] *Interdict Doc.* (Pipe R. Soc. N.S. xxxiv), 27.
[49] E 106/2/2 m. 5; E 106/2/3 m. 2.   [50] S.C. 6/1116/13.
[51] Guildhall MS. 9715; 9776.
[52] W.R.O., Inclosure Award; Guildhall MS. 9715; 9776.
[53] *Sel. Doc. Eng. Lands of Abbey of Bec* (Camd. 3rd ser. lxxiii), 54 sqq.   [54] E 106/2/2 m. 5.   [55] Ibid.
[56] Guildhall MS. 9715; 9776.   [57] Ibid. 9715; 9776.

allotted to replace the lands in the commons and open fields of the farm of the free tenant.[58]

In 1066 Compton was assessed for geld at 7 hides and valued at £10. It was worth the same in 1086 when the estate had enough land for 6 ploughs. The 3 hides and 1 virgate in demesne were worked by 6 serfs with 1 plough. Elsewhere at Compton there were 5 villeins and 5 *coscez* with 3 ploughs. There were 5 a. of meadow and pasture 3 furlongs long and 1 furlong broad.[59]

In 1765 the demesne was represented by Compton farm, then assessed at some 24 yardlands, which by that date had been enlarged by the addition of various smaller estates. The only substantial estate then held of the manor was a leasehold of 27 a. The open arable lay in North, South, Near, and Barrow fields, all of which were subdivided. Of the 894 a. of the manor 596 a. were arable and 294 a. pasture. There was a waste of 60 a. on which the farmer of Compton could pasture 1,120 sheep.[60] At inclosure in 1772 William Hussey as lord received 867 a. and his leasehold tenant 27 a.[61]

Details of the economy of the other estates in the parish are scanty. About 1210 the prebendal estate at Chisenbury was worth £4.[62] No more is known of it until 1700 when it was worth £64 and comprised in demesne 120 a. of arable, 4 a. of pasture, and Long mead, 4 a. It also included four copyhold estates.[63] When the open fields of East Chisenbury were inclosed in 1809, two tenants of the prebendary there were together allotted 37 a. The four copyholders received a total of 17 a. including a little meadow land.[64]

Longstreet tithing was divided into two estates. Of the more northerly, known in 1976 as Baden farm, practically nothing is known until the 19th century. That to the south, Longstreet farm, was the estate of Winchester chapter.[65] Its demesne was farmed at £9 3s. 4d. during the 16th and 17th centuries.[66] The estate was let on leases for lives and held in the later 16th century by the Rolfe family, and by a branch of the Poore family in the 18th century and the early 19th.[67] In 1649 the farm, worth £120, comprised 184 a. of arable in High field, 84 a. in Lower field, 5 a. of water-meadows west of the farm-house, 6 a. of pasture near by, a meadow of 2 a., and feeding for 600 sheep on Longstreet down.[68] The farm had 21 a. of pasture, including a water-meadow of 5 a., in 1805. Its 240 a. of arable were then in Pooklanch, Middle, South, Hanging, Pintail, and High fields.[69] When the open fields and commons of Longstreet were inclosed in 1809 the assignee of Winchester chapter's tenant John Poore was allotted 372 a. of which 187 a. were downland. Andrew Baden was allotted 309 a. including a down of 164 a. for Baden farm.[70]

Littlecott tithing, like that of Longstreet, included two fairly large farms. Of their economy nothing is known before the 19th century. The open arable was then apparently situated in Upper field adjoining Chisenbury, and in Middle and Lower fields. Beyond it to the east were downland pastures. The meadows lay between the Avon and the lane along which Littlecott hamlet stood. In 1817 719 a. of arable, meadow, and pasture were inclosed. The lord of Littlecott received 332 a. including a down of 181 a., and for his farm in the southern half of Littlecott William Akerman was allotted 222 a. including 99 a. of downland.[71]

The old sheep-and-corn husbandry predominated in the parish throughout the 19th century. Cobbett remarked on the many wheat ricks he saw in 1826 at Chisenbury farm.[72] On Enford farm, however, arable gave way to dairy farming when S. W. Farmer (d. 1926), the partner of Frank Stratton, rented the land in the later 19th century.[73] Other farms in the parish probably continued to maintain sheep.[74] In the 1880s F. R. Moore of Littlecott was a noted breeder of Wiltshire Down rams.[75]

After the acquisition by the War Department in the later 19th century and the earlier 20th of most large farms in the parish, the agricultural use of much land on either side of the Avon became limited. West of the river the downs were included in the firing ranges of Salisbury Plain. Some 200 a. east of the Avon at East Chisenbury were later included in the airfield of the Central Flying School established in the adjoining parish of Upavon in 1912.[76] Land at Littlecott bought by the Wiltshire county council in 1911 was afterwards equipped as smallholdings.[77] In 1976 all farms in Enford were given over to mixed farming. Those of Coombe and Longstreet, the only privately owned farms in the parish and together reckoned at c. 1,200 a., were worked by Crook Bros.[78] All the farms in Ministry of Defence ownership were then administered by the Department of the Environment and farmed subject to certain restrictions. East of the Avon Mr. H. Young tenanted Baden farm, 142 ha. (351 a.), and Mr. C. B. Wookey held most land at Littlecott and East Chisenbury. West of the river 625 ha. (1,545 a.) at Enford, Fifield, and Compton were leased by Mr. E. V. Sargent and Mr. J. Waight.[79]

MILLS. In 1086 two mills on the monks' estate at Enford paid 25s.[80] One was perhaps either the mill at Littlecott or that at Fifield mentioned in the 13th and 15th centuries, or it may have been at either Compton or Coombe.[81] The other was attached to the demesne of the capital manor and tenanted yearly at 15s. in the earlier 13th century.[82] In 1726

[58] W.R.O., Inclosure Award.
[59] *V.C.H. Wilts.* ii, p. 134.
[60] W.R.O. 7/37, survey.
[61] Ibid. Inclosure Award.
[62] *Interdict Doc.* (Pipe R. Soc. N.S. xxxiv), 20.
[63] W.R.O. 865/332, 17th- and 18th-cent. ct. papers, f. 18.
[64] Ibid. Inclosure Award.   [65] See p. 122.
[66] Mun. D. & C. Winton., N.R.A. box 87, 16th-cent. acct. rolls; ibid. N.R.A. box 84, survey of chap. man. 1670–3.
[67] Ibid. N.R.A. box 87, 16th-cent. acct. rolls; W.R.O. 415/87, 18th-cent. acct. bk.
[68] Mun. D. & C. Winton., survey of chap. man. 1649, ff. 158–61.
[69] H.R.O., Eccl. Commrs. 59608, survey, ff. 1–7.
[70] W.R.O., Inclosure Award.   [71] Ibid.

[72] W. Cobbett, *Rural Rides*, ed. G. D. H. and Margaret Cole, ii. 364.
[73] *W.A.M.* xliii. 494; xlv. 340; *Kelly's Dir. Wilts.* (1898 and later edns.).
[74] e.g. Compton: Wilts. Cuttings, i. 200.
[75] Ibid. xix. 117–18.
[76] *V.C.H. Wilts.* x. 161, 169; ex inf. Chief Surveyor of Defence Lands, Tolworth Tower, Surbiton.
[77] See p. 131; *V.C.H. Wilts.* v. 281.
[78] Ex inf. Mr. T. Crook, Longstreet Farm.
[79] Ex inf. Defence Land Agent, Durrington.
[80] *V.C.H. Wilts.* ii, p. 120.
[81] Hanna, 'Winch. Cath. Custumal', 450; B.L. Harl. Roll X. 7; see below.
[82] Hanna, 'Winch. Cath. Custumal', 441.

the inhabitants of Coombe, who had their own mill,[83] and those of Compton, as well as the Enford tenants, were ordered to grind their corn there.[84] In 1840 the mill, which straddled the Avon north-east of the church, was considered to lie in Littlecott tithing.[85] It continued to descend with the capital manor and in 1899 passed with it to the War Department.[86] Known from at least the mid 19th century as Littlecott mill, it remained in use until the early 20th century.[87] The 19th-century mill-house and buildings were sold by the War Department in 1960 and were occupied as a private dwelling in 1976.[88]

There was a mill worth 10s. within the manor of Compton in 1086.[89] At least from the 13th century the estate descended in moieties and its mill may have been shared by the tenants of Compton Breamore and Compton Coombe. The moiety attached to the Breamore estate is last mentioned in 1348.[90] The Coombe moiety, with some land, was conveyed by feoffees to Walter, son of Richard Coombe of North Tidworth, and his wife Edith in 1337.[91] By 1356 Walter had been succeeded by his son Walter.[92] The younger Walter is probably the Walter of Coombe who in 1379 held not only a moiety of the mill, but the entire Compton Combe estate.[93] No more is known of the Coombe moiety.

A mill attached to Coombe manor was let for some £4 in the 15th century.[94] It passed with the manor until 1811 when the trustees of Lord Chedworth sold it to Christopher Crouch, who sold it in 1819 to Sir John Methuen Poore, Bt.[95] The mill was reunited with the manor when Sir John (d. 1820) devised it to his nephew Robert Montagu Poore, lord of Coombe.[96] Thereafter it appears to have again descended like the manor of Coombe.[97] Its ownership, however, has not been traced further. The mill remained in use until the early 20th century.[98] In 1976 the mill-house, apparently of 19th-century date, was a private dwelling and stood beside the Avon west of the Coombe–Littlecott lane. The mill buildings retain an iron water-wheel made in the later 19th century by Tasker & Sons of Andover (Hants).[99]

In 1086 the estate later called the manor of Chisenbury contained a mill which paid 7s. 6d.[1] In the early 13th century the proctor of Ogbourne, as representative of Chisenbury's lord the abbot of Bec, was bound to pay 2d. yearly to Roger de la

Folye, probably lord of West Chisenbury, for the mill sluice.[2] The mill remained part of the estate until at least 1923, when it was sold with what remained of the manor to F. V. Lister.[3] Mill and mill-house, no longer standing in 1976, were formerly situated on the marshy river bank north-east of the footbridge leading across the Avon to West Chisenbury.[4]

LOCAL GOVERNMENT. The franchisal jurisdiction of the prior and convent of St. Swithun, Winchester, as lords of Enford, extended to varying degrees over the entire parish except Compton manor which in 1334 was deemed part of the liberty of Everleigh.[5] The prior's prison at Enford, mentioned in 1249, perhaps served not only the parish but also that part of his hundred of Elstub situated in the valley of the Christchurch Avon.[6] In 1255 St. Swithun's had return of writs within the manor, a right confirmed in 1285.[7]

The priory's manorial rights, however, were limited to the capital manor, which then apparently comprised the tithings of Enford and Fifield.[8] Separate manorial courts were held by the lords of East Chisenbury and Coombe, who also claimed certain franchisal jurisdiction.[9] It is not clear where the tithing of Littlecott and Fifield, mentioned from the 13th to the 16th centuries and to be identified with the later tithings of Littlecott and Longstreet, owed suit.

Records of courts at which both Enford and Fifield homages presented survive for 1281, and thereafter continue spasmodically until the 18th century.[10] The courts were generally held twice yearly and in the Middle Ages on the same day as the hundred court of Elstub which was held in a meadow south of New Town between the Upavon–Salisbury road and the river.[11] They dealt with the usual copyhold business and small administrative matters. In 1483, however, the homage of Enford reported that all the manorial buildings were in need of thorough repair.[12] Although Fifield homage frequently presented all well, in the early 16th century it accused the inhabitants of Netheravon of encroaching on land in Fifield and ploughing it.[13] In 1506 tenants of the capital manor in Fifield were ordered to grind their corn at Enford mill.[14] Certain

[83] See below.
[84] E 134/12 Geo. I. Hil./19; E 126/23 f. 431.
[85] I.R. 29/38/173; I.R. 30/38/173.
[86] Mun. D. & C. Winton., acct. rolls, 1280, 1299, 1316; B.L. Harl. Roll X. 7; X. 14–15; Winch. Coll. Mun., lease bk. G, f. 100 and v.; C.P. 25(2)/372/18 Jas. I Hil.; W.R.O. 212B/3010; *Salisbury Plain (Property Purchased)*, H.C. 14, pp. 2–3 (1900), xlix.
[87] *Kelly's Dir. Wilts.* (1848 and later edns.).
[88] Ex inf. Defence Land Agent, Durrington.
[89] *V.C.H. Wilts.* ii, p. 134.
[90] *Feet of F.* 1327–77 (W.R.S. xxix), p. 90.
[91] *W.N. & Q.* vii. 501.
[92] *Wilts. Inq. p.m.* 1327–77 (Index Libr.), 333–4.
[93] *W.N. & Q.* vii. 502.
[94] B.L. Royal MS. App. 89, f. 153.
[95] Winch. Coll. Mun., lease bk. G, f. 99; W.R.O. 998, Poore deeds, 6 Apr. 1819; see above, p. 121.
[96] W.R.O. 998, Poore deeds, copy will of J. M. Poore; G.E.C. *Baronetage*, v. 306.
[97] W.R.O. 998, Poore deeds, copy will of R. M. Poore, pr. 1837.   [98] *Kelly's Dir. Wilts.* (1848 and later edns.).
[99] L. T. C. Rolt, *Waterloo Ironworks*, 51, 60 n., 65.

[1] *V.C.H. Wilts.* ii, p. 157.
[2] *Sel. Doc. Eng. Lands of Abbey of Bec* (Camd. 3rd ser. lxxiii), 57.
[3] E 106/2/2; Guildhall MS. 9715; 9776; I.R. 29/38/67; I.R. 30/38/67; deed, Phillips, Dixon, Mason to Lister, 1923, *penes* Sir Ric. Harvey, Bt., Chisenbury Priory.
[4] Guildhall MS. 9715; 9776; I.R. 29/38/67; I.R. 30/38/67. Part of the machinery is preserved in the tithe-barn at Bradford on Avon: Lawrance, 'Notes for a hist. of Enford' (MS. *penes* Sir Ric. Harvey), 116.
[5] *V.C.H. Wilts.* iv. 299; see above, pp. 105–7.
[6] *Crown Pleas, 1249* (W.R.S. xvi), p. 197.
[7] *Rot. Hund.* (Rec. Com.), ii (1), 230; *Cal. Chart. R.* 1257–1300, 322.
[8] Mun. D. & C. Winton., Elstub hund. roll, 1281; *L. & P. Hen. VIII*, xiv (1), p. 301.   [9] See below.
[10] Unless expressly stated, this para. is based on Mun. D. & C. Winton., ct. rolls, 1281–2, 1290–3, 1296–9, 1306–9, 1322–3, 1326, 1330–1; B.L. Harl. Rolls W. 3–17; W. 19–26; W. 28–31; V. 20–32; X. 1; X. 3–6; W.R.O. 7/13, ct. bk. 1599–1723.   [11] W.R.O., Inclosure Award.
[12] B.L. Harl. Roll V. 33d.
[13] Ibid. V. 29; V. 30d.   [14] Ibid. V. 29d.

franchisal jurisdiction within the capital manor to which St. Swithun's had been entitled until the Dissolution was granted with Enford in 1541 to Thomas Culpeper.[15] Although courts were thenceforth called views of frankpledge and courts baron, the only additional business dealt with was the election of tithingmen for Enford and Fifield tithings.

Inhabitants of Coombe tithing, who from at least the 13th century shared a common lordship with the neighbouring manor of Fittleton, owed suit at the court of that manor.[16] At the biannual courts, which surviving 15th-century records show to have been designated views of frankpledge and manorial courts, presentments included those made by the tithingman and homage of Coombe.[17]

In 1275 the prior of Ogbourne, as proctor of Bec Abbey in England, claimed the right to have gallows and to hold the assize of bread and of ale within Bec's manor of Chisenbury.[18] Medieval courts, records of which survive for some years in the 13th and 14th centuries, were called courts in the 13th century and in the 14th courts and views of frankpledge. Two tithingmen presented at the courts and views, which, like the earlier courts, were generally held twice yearly.[19] Those of the 17th and 18th centuries for which records survive were called either views of frankpledge and courts baron or courts leet and baron. They were generally held once yearly in autumn by the Groves and their successors the Chafin Groves as tenants of St. Katharine's Hospital, London. The only vestige of franchisal jurisdiction then to survive was presentment by the tithingman. Otherwise the court's functions were limited to purely manorial affairs such as the regulation of small agricultural matters and copyhold business.[20]

Numerous papers of the overseers of the poor survive.[21] They include poor-rate assessments and disbursements covering various years in the 18th and 19th centuries for all Enford's tithings. Henry ('Orator') Hunt's claim in 1815 that half the agricultural labourers in the parish were paupers may not perhaps have been unfounded.[22] After 1835, when Enford became part of Pewsey poor-law union, and throughout the 1840s an average of some £50, one of the larger totals for Pewsey union, was spent on out-relief in the parish.[23] In 1858 £97 was so spent.[24]

Summary accounts of the surveyors of highways for Fifield tithing run from 1803 to 1817.[25] There are also 19th-century highway account and rate books for Littlecott and Longstreet tithings, which then appear to have been administered together for all local government purposes.[26]

CHURCH. There was probably a church on the estate of the cathedral monks of Winchester at Enford in 1086. It was possibly served by the priest who then held land, presumably for his support, within that estate.[27] The advowson of the rectory apparently belonged to the bishops of Winchester; in 1280 the Crown presented during a vacancy.[28] In the 12th and 13th centuries, however, the bishop's patronage was disputed by the convent of St. Swithun.[29] The quarrel was resolved in 1284 when St. Swithun's finally acknowledged the bishop's right.[30] The rectors presented by the bishops appointed vicars to serve the cure and for their support allowed them the altarage, mortuary fees, and small tithes from the parish in return for a yearly payment of 40s. and 1 lb. of cheese.[31] A vicarage was ordained in 1270 and augmented in 1292.[32] In 1290 the bishop granted the advowson of the rectory to the convent of St. Swithun, lords of the capital manor, who appropriated the church the following year.[33] Thereafter the priors presented vicars until the Dissolution, except in 1494 when the right was delegated to Thomas Jame.[34]

In 1539 the advowson passed to the Crown, which in 1541 granted it to Thomas Culpeper the younger.[35] It thereafter passed like the capital manor to William Rolfe,[36] and, while it did, the lords of Enford frequently delegated their right to present. Thus in 1572 Hugh Powell presented, in 1592 Philip Powell, and in 1623 Henry Crispe and John Thorpe.[37] In 1636 William Rolfe settled the advowson on himself and his wife Sarah, who survived him and who, as Sarah Methwold, sold the advowson to the governors of Christ's Hospital, then in London, in 1676.[38] In 1973 the vicarage was added to the united benefice of Netheravon with Fittleton, thereafter called Netheravon with Fittleton and Enford. The first turn of presentation was then allotted to the patrons of Enford, Christ's Hospital.[39]

In 1291 the vicarage was assessed for taxation at £5.[40] It was worth £20 in 1535.[41] In the later 1640s the vicarage was worth £120.[42] From 1829 to 1831 the net average yearly income of the benefice was £350.[43]

By the 13th century the small tithes had been assigned for the vicar's support.[44] When the vicarage was augmented in 1292 the vicar was apparently

15 C 66/708 m. 5, where the date of the grant is given as Apr. 1542. Since Culpeper was executed in 1541 the date Apr. 1541 given in L. & P. Hen. VIII, xvi, p. 382 appears to be the correct one.
16 See p. 147.   17 S.C. 2/208/59.
18 Rot. Hund. (Rec. Com.), ii (1), 258.
19 King's Coll., Camb., Mun. C. 2; C. 4–10; C. 12–13; C. 15; C. 19.   20 W.R.O. 865/332, ct. papers.
21 Ibid. 772/17–42.
22 Wilts. Cuttings, xvi. 96.
23 Poor Law Com. 2nd Rep. 560; W.R.O. 772/36, Pewsey union quarterly abstr. 1836–46.
24 W.R.O. 772/37, list of paupers relieved, 1858.
25 Ibid. 772/14.   26 Ibid. 772/15–16; Land Tax.
27 V.C.H. Wilts. ii, pp. 33, 120.
28 Cal. Pat. 1272–81, 403.
29 Chartulary Winch. Cath. ed. Goodman, pp. 2–3.
30 Ibid. p. 189 n.; Reg. Pontoise (Cant. & York Soc.), ii. 419–20, 431–3.

31 Winch. Coll. Mun. 8182.   32 Ibid.
33 Cal. Chart. R. 1257–1300, 363; Sar. Chart. and Doc. (Rolls Ser.), 366.
34 Phillipps, Wilts. Inst. (index in W.A.M. xxviii. 219).
35 Winch. Chap. Doc. 1541–7, ed. G. W. Kitchin and F. T. Madge (Hants Rec. Soc.), 1; L. & P. Hen. VIII, xvi, p. 382.
36 L. & P. Hen. VIII, xviii, pp. 533–4; Cal. Pat. 1550–3, 159; B.L. Harl. Ch. 111. E. 58; C.P. 25(2)/372/18 Jas. I Hil.
37 Phillipps, Wilts. Inst. i. 226, 233; ii. 12.
38 Abstr. of title of Christ's Hosp. penes the incumbent, the Revd. J. E. Jackson, Netheravon Vicarage.
39 Ex inf. Dioc. Registrar.
40 Tax. Eccl. (Rec. Com.), 180.
41 Valor Eccl. (Rec. Com.), ii. 145.
42 W.A.M. xix. 189.
43 Rep. Com. Eccl. Revenues, 832–3.
44 Winch. Coll. Mun. 8182.

also allowed the great tithes from the glebe then allotted to him in Compton tithing.[45] By 1705 the vicar received a payment of £1 6s. 8d. in place of vicarial tithes from the Chisenbury estate of St. Katharine's Hospital. The prebendary of Chute and Chisenbury similarly took vicarial tithes from his lands at Chisenbury, and he made no payment for those from his demesne. For those arising from his tenantry lands, however, he gave the vicar 26 lb. of wool and 3s. 4d. each year.[46] At an unknown date the vicar's right to tithes in kind from Coombe and Littlecott mills was replaced by moduses of 11s. for each.[47] During the later 18th century and the earlier 19th the vicar's right to all remaining tithes in kind from the parish was gradually replaced by allotments of land. Thus in 1772 when the open fields of Compton were inclosed the vicar received 60 a. to replace his tithes and glebe there.[48] In 1809 the vicar was allotted 171 a. in Enford, Coombe, Longstreet, and East Chisenbury tithings in place of those tithes not already replaced by money payments.[49] When the fields of Littlecott were inclosed in 1817 the vicar exchanged his tithes there with William Akerman, owner of a farm in the tithing, for 14 a.[50] The vicar may afterwards have purchased those arising from his own Littlecott lands, mentioned below, because in 1840 they were expressly merged in his freehold. The rest of the vicarial tithes of Littlecott, which by that time had been sold off, were then extinguished by the rent-charges allotted in place of the great tithes.[51] In 1840 and 1843 the moduses of 11s. paid in respect of Littlecott and Coombe mills were converted into rent-charges.[52] The payments from East Chisenbury were replaced by a rent-charge of £3 9s. in 1844.[53]

At the ordination of the vicarage the vicar was assigned 7 a. from the rectorial glebe in Enford and Fifield (later Longstreet) fields and a meadow in Broad mead, and absolved from the 40s. that he paid to the rector yearly.[54] At the augmentation of the vicarage in 1292 the vicar was excused his yearly gift of cheese to St. Swithun's, as rector, and given 2 virgates of land in Compton and another meadow.[55] The vicars retained that estate until the later 18th century.[56] The Compton lands were probably replaced in 1772 by the allotment then made in place of tithes there.[57] In 1809 6 a. in Enford tithing were allotted to replace vicarial glebe in Enford and Longstreet tithings.[58] The vicar then also exchanged with the lord of the capital manor certain lands to which he was entitled in Enford and Fifield tithings for some 60 a. in Littlecott and 14 a. in Compton.[59] The Littlecott lands were replaced by an allotment

of 111 a. when that tithing's open fields were inclosed in 1817.[60] Thus, with the lands acquired to replace tithes, the vicar had an estate of c. 354 a. in the 19th century.[61] Some 62 a. were sold to the War Department in 1898.[62] In 1911 another 136 a. were sold in lots to local landowners. The largest parcels, 54 a. in Coombe and 42 a. in Chisenbury, were sold to Robert Poore and E. B. Maton respectively.[63] The same year another 152 a. were sold to the Wiltshire county council.[64] Most of the remaining few acres of glebe were sold off in the 1960s and 1970s.[65]

A vicarage-house is first mentioned in 1588.[66] That which existed in the 17th century survived as the north-west wing of the house which stood south-west of the church behind a thatched cob wall in 1976.[67] In 1783 the Vicarage was reported to be much dilapidated and was restored by James Boyer, vicar 1782–93, who also enlarged and refronted it in 1784 by adding a new brick block on the east containing a staircase and principal rooms.[68] Service quarters and out-buildings were added in the 19th century. In the earlier 20th century the coach-house was converted for use as a music-room and there and in other rooms reproduction fittings in 18th-century style were introduced.[69] In 1976 Enford House, as it was then called, was occupied as two dwellings. About 1876 a site for a new house on the east side of the Upavon–Salisbury road was acquired.[70] A small 19th-century brick house there was afterwards converted and extended as a Vicarage.[71] That was sold as a private dwelling and replaced by a new Vicarage north of it in 1965.[72] When Enford was combined with the united benefice of Netheravon with Fittleton in 1973 that house was in turn sold for private use, and in 1976 the incumbent of the united benefice lived at Netheravon.[73]

John Westley, vicar 1472–94, gave a flock of 1,000 sheep to support a chaplain to celebrate mass in Enford church.[74] The chaplains appointed in the earlier 16th century had a house near the church.[75] More sheep were later given to replenish the flock, then apparently depleted.[76] The flock was let at £7 14s. 6d. in 1548.[77] The chantry property then included 30¼ oz. of plate and some vestments.[78] The chantry-house afterwards probably became part of the capital manor and was burnt down in the later 16th century.[79]

Thomas Jeay, vicar 1592–1623, bequeathed £10 for investment to pay for the preaching of a sermon each Easter Monday in Enford church. The charity is not heard of after 1783.[80]

John Enford, instituted in 1419, served the church

[45] Ibid.   [46] Sar. Dioc. R.O., Glebe Terrier.
[47] I.R. 29/38/173; I.R. 29/38/85.
[48] W.R.O., Inclosure Award.   [49] Ibid.
[50] Ibid.   [51] I.R. 29/38/173; and see above, p. 124.
[52] I.R. 29/38/173; I.R. 29/38/85.   [53] I.R. 29/38/67.
[54] Winch. Coll. Mun. 8182.   [55] Ibid.
[56] Sar. Dioc. R.O., Glebe Terriers.
[57] W.R.O., Inclosure Award.   [58] Ibid.
[59] Ibid.; 772/45, letter and memo., Trumper to vicar, 1807.   [60] Ibid. Inclosure Award.
[61] Return of Glebe, H.C. 307, p. 164 (1887), lxiv.
[62] Salisbury Plain (Property Purchased), H.C. 14, pp. 4–5 (1900), xlix.   [63] Wilts. Cuttings, xvi. 162.
[64] Ex inf. Ch. Commrs.
[65] Ibid.; Lawrance, 'Notes for a hist. of Enford' (MS. penes Sir Ric. Harvey), 85.
[66] Sar. Dioc. R.O., Glebe Terrier.

[67] Ibid. Glebe Terrier, 1678; W.R.O., Inclosure Award map.
[68] Sar. Dioc. R.O., Glebe Terrier, 1783; Phillipps, Wilts. Inst. ii. 92, 97; Boyer is suggested by Lawrance, op. cit. 99. The date 1784 appears on the N. elevation of the E. wing.   [69] Ex inf. Mrs. D. Campbell, Enford Ho.
[70] Sar. Dioc. R.O., Pet. for Faculties, bdle. 24, no. 2.
[71] Ibid.   [72] Lawrance, op. cit. 99.
[73] Wilts. Gaz. 8 Nov. 1973.
[74] Phillipps, Wilts. Inst. i. 161, 176; E 301/58/26.
[75] B.L. Harl. Roll X. 18; E 301/58/26; Winch. Coll. Mun., lease bk. G, ff. 98v., 99.
[76] E 301/58/26.   [77] Ibid.
[78] Ibid.; W.A.M. xxii. 329.
[79] Sar. Dioc. R.O., Glebe Terrier, 1588; Req. 2/159/105.
[80] Phillipps, Wilts. Inst. i. 233; ii. 12; Sar. Dioc. R.O., Glebe Terrier, 1783.

for most of the earlier 15th century.[81] William Fauntleroy, vicar 1511–35, was a noted pluralist among whose many preferments was a canonry in Lincoln cathedral.[82] Thomas Jeay was also rector of Fittleton.[83] The incumbencies of Henry Culpeper, vicar 1623–70, and Thomas Jacob, vicar 1670–1725, together spanned over a century.[84] Culpeper, a younger son of Sir Anthony, the last Culpeper to hold the capital manor, subscribed to the Wiltshire *Concurrent Testimony* of 1648 and was reported to preach regularly.[85] William Cooke, vicar 1733–80, was also rector of Didmarton with Oldbury (Glos.) and chaplain to the earl of Suffolk. Among the works he published on numismatic and antiquarian subjects were *An Inquiry into Patriarchal and Druidical Religion, Temples, etc. . . . (1754)* and *A Medallic History of Imperial Rome . . . (1781)*.[86] James Boyer, vicar 1782–93, did not reside since from 1776 to 1799 he was headmaster of Christ's Hospital.[87]

Curates assisted the incumbents in the later 18th century and in the 19th.[88] Two Sunday services, one with a sermon, were held in 1783, but very few weekday ones. The eight communion services held over the past year had been attended, in a parish reported to have its share of 'practical atheists', by an average of twenty communicants.[89] Average attendances on Sundays over the past year were reckoned in 1851 as 135 at morning and 120 at afternoon services.[90] Congregations averaged 160 on Sundays in 1864. Weekday services were then held during Lent and Holy Week. The Sacrament was administered at the great festivals, again to an average of some twenty communicants. Fewer attended the monthly celebrations of Holy Communion.[91]

The church of *ALL SAINTS*[92] stands between the west bank of the Avon and the Upavon–Salisbury road.[93] Of flint rubble and ashlar, in places rendered, it comprises chancel with octagonal north chapel, aisled and clerestoried nave with south porch, and west tower. A church probably stood there by the later 11th century.[94] It was perhaps into the nave walls of that building that the arches of the present four-bay arcades were cut in the mid 12th century.[95] The south doorway is of later-12th-century date. The chancel arch appears to have been reconstructed at about the same time. The chancel, the internal north wall of which retains its original arcading, was probably rebuilt some time after 1223

when 60 bent timbers were allotted by the Crown for the purpose.[96] The octagonal building, north of the chancel and joined to it by a short passage, is of the same date. It was probably intended as a chapel since it retains aumbries and a piscena, and either it or the north aisle may perhaps be identifiable with the chapel of St. Audrey at Enford mentioned in 1391.[97] Lead was bequeathed to roof a porch in 1267.[98] The south aisle was widened *c.* 1300, its original doorway being reset and a new porch added. The north aisle was much enlarged and its east end fitted as a chapel in the earlier 14th century. The fact that the north aisle extended westwards beyond the nave suggests the existence of a west tower by that time. In the earlier 14th century, too, a four-light east window was inserted in the chancel and diagonal buttresses added externally at its east end. The roof of the nave was raised and a clerestory, blind to the north but with four two-light windows to the south, was added in the 15th century. The west tower was then rebuilt and a slender spire added. The tower stands somewhat higher than the nave, from which it is approached by steps, to accommodate the westwards rise in the ground. At the same date a rood-screen with a newel stair at the south-east corner of the nave was inserted. A partial reconstruction of the chancel was begun in 1779.[99] The south chancel wall was then rebuilt in brick and the roof renewed.

By 1807 the churchyard had been enclosed, at least to the north, south, and west, by a thatched cob wall, a part of which remained to the south in 1976. The spire fell in 1817.[1] The considerable damage to nave, aisles, and tower was apparently made good in the later 1820s and the church was reopened in 1831.[2] Repairs were partly financed by the sale for £345 of the lead with which nave and aisles had formerly been roofed.[3] The thorough restoration and refitting of the church undertaken by C. E. Ponting in 1893 included the provision of a new nave ceiling, the rendering of most of the internal walls, and the blocking of the doorway in the north aisle.[4]

Two monuments are noteworthy. In the north aisle Jennifer Baskerville (d. 1616), the mother-in-law of Thomas Petre who with his brother John held the capital manor in the early 17th century, is represented by a small free-standing stone effigy of a kneeling woman.[5] On the south wall of the chancel a wall tablet by Thomas King of Bath (d. 1804)

[81] Phillipps, *Wilts. Inst.* i. 108, 146.
[82] A. B. Emden, *Biog. Reg. Univ. Oxf. to 1500*, ii. 671.
[83] See p. 148.
[84] Phillipps, *Wilts. Inst.* ii. 12, 31, 59.
[85] *Kent Pedigrees* (Harl. Soc. xlii), 62–3; *Calamy Revised*, ed. A. G. Matthews, 557; *W.A.M.* xix. 189.
[86] *D.N.B.*
[87] W. Trollope, *Hist. Christ's Hosp.* 136–7.
[88] *Vis. Queries, 1783* (W.R.S. xxvii), pp. 98–9; *Rep. Com. Eccl. Revenues*, 832–3; Sar. Dioc. R.O., Vis. Queries, 1864.
[89] *Vis. Queries, 1783* (W.R.S. xxvii), pp. 98–9.
[90] H.O. 129/261/1/5.
[91] Sar. Dioc. R.O., Vis. Queries.
[92] An additional dedication to St. Margaret occurs in the 1890s: Lawrance, 'Notes for a hist. of Enford' (MS. *penes* Sir Ric. Harvey), 40. A mistake arose because Hoare, *Mod. Wilts.* Elstub and Everley, 29 mis-identified Enford ch. with that of Poughley Priory in Chaddleworth (Berks.) which was dedicated to St. Margaret and stood on a site called 'Ellenfordemere': *V.C.H. Berks.* ii. 85; *P.N. Berks.*

(E.P.N.S.), 289–92. The dedication of Enford is clear: J. Ecton, *Thesaurus*, 394; *W.A.M.* xv. 102; *Crockford* (1896 and later edns.).
[93] See plate facing p. 160.
[94] *V.C.H. Wilts.* ii, p. 120.
[95] Suggested by Pevsner, *Wilts.* (2nd edn.), 239.
[96] *Rot. Litt. Claus.* (Rec. Com.), i. 540.
[97] *Ely Dioc. Remembrancer*, clxxiv. 213.
[98] *Sar. Chart. and Doc.* (Rolls Ser.), 344–5.
[99] Bricks for the purpose were brought that year from Lydeway in Urchfont: W.R.O. 415/89; *V.C.H. Wilts.* x. 184.
[1] Both wall and spire are depicted by J. Buckler in water-colours of 1807: W.A.S. Libr., vol. v. 4, 5.
[2] Both clerestory and nave are dated 1825: *W.A.M.* xxxi. 71, 74; Wilts. Cuttings, xix. 159.
[3] Lawrance, 'Notes for a hist. of Enford' (MS. *penes* Sir Ric. Harvey), 103.
[4] Sar. Dioc. R.O., Pet. for Faculties, bdle. 33, no. 9; *W.A.M.* xxvii. 4; Lawrance, op. cit. 41; Wilts. Cuttings, i. 374.   [5] Inscription beneath effigy.

commemorates the Poore family of Longstreet.[6] The royal arms dated 1831, placed above the chancel arch after the completion of the repairs of the 1820s, were restored in 1970.[7] The church clock of *c.* 1700 apparently had no external face in the early 19th century. One on the tower's south wall was provided in 1846.[8] The stump of a churchyard cross, already dilapidated in 1807, stands beside the south porch.[9] Several later-18th-century tomb-chests stand south of the church.

The king's commissioners took 23½ oz. of plate in 1553 but left a chalice for the parish. In 1976 the church possessed, besides several pieces of 19th- and 20th-century date, a later-16th-century chalice, a paten hall-marked 1716 and inscribed as the gift of Thomas Jacob, vicar 1670–1725, and an alms-dish given by William Scrachly in 1753.[10] In 1553 Enford church had four bells and a sanctus bell. There was a ring of six in 1975. Of those (ii), 1619, is by Roger Purdue (d. 1640), (iv), 1629, and (v), 1658, by John Lott, (vi), 1791, by Robert Wells, and (iii), 1813, by James Wells. The peal was rehung in 1912 when (i), by Taylor of Loughborough, was added.[11]

Registrations of baptisms begin in 1631, marriages and burials in 1633. All are deficient for the period 1643–53, although a few births and baptisms are recorded. Marriages are lacking for the period 1665–71. Otherwise the registers appear complete.[12]

A chapel at Compton, possibly dedicated to St. Nicholas, was given by Geoffrey de Brionne some time before 1118 to the abbey of Bec-Hellouin. The gift was confirmed by Robert, count of Meulan (later earl of Leicester, d. 1118).[13] In the later 12th century the abbey apparently gave up its right to the chapel in favour of the rector of Enford in return for a yearly payment of 13*s.* 4*d.* on 6 December.[14] The chapel, like Enford church, was probably appropriated in 1291 by St. Swithun's, Winchester.[15] Between 1358 and 1361 the convent agreed to keep the chancel in repair, while dwellers in Compton were to supply the chapel's furnishings.[16] In 1365 the inhabitants of Compton established that they, and not the vicar of Enford, were entitled to appoint and maintain the chaplain.[17] The chapel is last mentioned in 1395 when an altar in honour of St. Nicholas was dedicated there.[18]

A chapel, served by a chaplain, probably existed at Coombe *c.* 1194.[19] It stood east of the lane running through the hamlet towards Fittleton. A field called Chapel close marked its site in the early 19th century.[20] Chaplains were appointed and largely supported, probably in consultation with the chief inhabitants of the tithing, by the lords of that moiety of Coombe manor held by the Coombe family and their successors.[21] They also received whatever offerings were made at the chapel.[22] In 1387 the vicar of Enford challenged the right of the lord of Coombe to appoint and complained that, because mass was celebrated earlier at the chapel on Sundays and festivals, inhabitants of Enford attended there rather than at the parish church.[23] In 1391 the inhabitants of Coombe accused the vicar of keeping the chapel and the house attached to it in his own hands, of demanding 13*s.* 4*d.* yearly from the chaplain, and of preventing the chaplain from celebrating mass there.[24] Later in 1391 the lord of Coombe's right to appoint chaplains acceptable to the vicar received episcopal confirmation. The chaplains, however, were ordered thenceforth to say mass at the mother-church on Sundays and festivals.[25] An altar, dedicated to St. Nicholas like that in the chapel at Compton, was consecrated at Coombe chapel in 1395.[26] The lords of Coombe are last mentioned as patrons in 1464.[27]

There may have been a chapel dedicated to St. Audrey within the parish church in the 14th century.[28] It was probably then served by the parochial chaplain mentioned in 1387 and 1391.[29]

NONCONFORMITY. Only one person did not conform in Enford in 1676.[30] Certain parishioners who refused to attend church in the 1680s may have been nonconformists.[31] A house to be used by dissenters was certified at Enford in 1710.[32] Independency flourished in the parish in the late 18th century, and houses were registered by Independents at Compton in 1798 and at Fifield and Enford in 1797.[33]

Baptists were licensed to worship at Enford in 1799.[34] A chapel for Particular Baptists was built *c.* 1819 on the west side of the lane running south-westwards to Enford Farm.[35] On Census Sunday in 1851 101 people attended in the morning, 112 in the afternoon, and 120 in the evening.[36] The chapel became War Department property in 1899 and was destroyed by fire in 1959. Services were held *c.* 1968 in a private house.[37]

In 1821 a house at East Chisenbury was certified

[6] R. Gunnis, *Brit. Sculptors,* 229.
[7] Lawrance, op. cit. 55.
[8] SE. view of ch. in 1807 by J. Buckler: W.A.S. Libr., vol. v. 4; Lawrance, op. cit. 106.
[9] So depicted by Buckler in 1807: W.A.S. Libr., vol. v. 4.
[10] Nightingale, *Wilts. Plate,* 113–14; Lawrance, op. cit. 63.
[11] Walters, *Wilts. Bells,* 82, 288, 304, 314–15; *W.A.M.* xxxviii. 133.
[12] W.R.O. 772/1–6; transcripts exist for 1605, 1623–9, and 1663–79 in Sar. Dioc. R.O.
[13] Morgan, *Eng. Lands of Abbey of Bec,* 140; *Complete Peerage,* vii. 523–6.
[14] Mun. St. Geo.'s Chap., Windsor, XI. G. 13; for evidence of date see Le Neve, *Fasti, 1066–1300, Mon. Cath.* 4, 94; Morgan, op. cit. 140; *Sel. Doc. Eng. Lands of Abbey of Bec* (Camd. 3rd ser. lxxiii), 57.
[15] Morgan, op. cit. 140.
[16] Hist. MSS. Com. 55, *Var. Coll.* iv, p. 160; for dating evidence, see Le Neve, *Fasti, 1300–1541, Salisbury,* 1.
[17] Hist. MSS. Com. 55, *Var. Coll.* iv, p. 159.
[18] Ibid.
[19] *Sar. Chart. and Doc.* (Rolls Ser.), 54.
[20] W.R.O., Inclosure Award map.
[21] Hist. MSS. Com. 55, *Var. Coll.* iv, p. 159; B.L. Harl. MS. 1623, ff. 17, 24.
[22] Hist. MSS. Com. 55, *Var. Coll.* iv, p. 159.
[23] Ibid.
[24] B.L. Harl. MS. 1623, f. 24.
[25] Ibid. f. 17.
[26] Hist. MSS. Com. 55, *Var. Coll.* iv, p. 159.
[27] C 140/12 no. 13; *Cal. Fine R. 1461–71,* 141–2.
[28] See above.
[29] Hist. MSS. Com. 55, *Var. Coll.* iv, p. 159.
[30] *W.N. & Q.* iii. 536.
[31] Sar. Dioc. R.O., Chwdns.' Pres. 1683, 1686.
[32] W.R.O., Certs. Dissenters' Meeting-Houses.
[33] *W.A.M.* lxi. 65.
[34] *V.C.H. Wilts.* iii. 137 and n. 37.
[35] H.O. 129/261/1/7; *Kelly's Dir. Wilts.* (1875); O.S. Map 6", Wilts. XLVII (1889 edn.).
[36] H.O. 129/261/1/7.
[37] R. W. Oliver, *Strict Bapt. Chapels Eng.* (Bapt. Hist. Soc.), v. 22; *Salisbury Plain (Property Purchased),* H.C. 14, pp. 2–3 (1900), xlix.

for worship by 'independent' Methodists.[38] The same denomination certified a house at Enford in 1823 but no more is heard of that.[39] The Chisenbury group may have flourished and is probably to be identified with the Primitive Methodists who built a chapel there *c.* 1845.[40] On Census Sunday in 1851 fourteen people attended chapel in the morning, 48 in the afternoon, and 51 in the evening.[41] A new chapel was built on the east side of the lane from Littlecott to Upavon in 1896.[42] Sunday services were still held in 1976.

EDUCATION. In 1548 the chaplain who served Westley's chantry in Enford church was reported to have taught children in the parish.[43] John Adams alias Coleman, although not licensed to do so, taught at Enford in 1686.[44] The parish had no school in 1783.[45] The north aisle of the church was, however, used as a school in the early 19th century.[46] A day-school in the parish was attended in 1818 by 23 children, and two 'elementary' schools were each attended by seven pupils.[47] In 1833 twelve boys and fifteen girls were taught in a day-school at Enford supported by subscription.[48]

In 1842 a sum raised by subscription under the auspices of John Prince, vicar 1793–1833, was used to buy £670 stock, the annual interest to be administered by the incumbent and used to support a church school at Enford.[49] About 1845 such a school with house adjoining was provided by Sir Edmund Antrobus, Bt., lord of the capital manor of Enford, on the west side of the Upavon–Salisbury road.[50] In 1858 it was supported partly by Sir Edmund and partly by £15 income from the endowment. It was then attended, albeit irregularly, by 20–30 pupils taught by a mistress who had received some training at Salisbury.[51] On return day in 1871 22 boys and 39 girls were present at the school, which by then was affiliated to the National Society.[52] In 1899 the school buildings were sold with the manor of Enford to the War Department, which transferred the freehold to the school managers.[53] The school received £18 from Prince's charity in 1901.[54] In 1906 it had been attended by an average of 124 pupils over the past year.[55] Average attendance figures remained fairly steady until 1912 and then slowly declined until in 1938 an average of 91 children was taught there.[56]

In 1966 the school was closed and replaced by two classrooms constructed next to the village hall at Longstreet.[57] The income from Prince's charity was transferred to the new school, where in 1976 57 children from Enford and its hamlets were taught by three teachers.[58] The charity income given to the school in 1977 was some £10 yearly.[59]

A boarding-school at Enford was kept by Robert Tucker in the 1840s and 1850s.[60] Ann Pearce kept a day-school at Longstreet in 1855.[61] What is apparently the same school was run by Jane Dear from at least 1867 to 1880.[62] Dissenters, whether the Enford Baptists or Chisenbury Methodists is unknown, supported a school in the parish where 40 children were taught in 1858.[63]

CHARITIES FOR THE POOR. Robert Baden of Littlecott, probably the Robert who died seised of Longstreet farm in 1730, bequeathed £20, the interest to be given each Easter to the poor of Enford.[64] An unknown benefactor may have augmented that sum *c.* 1738. In 1783 the overseers were apparently accustomed to distribute £13 10s. each Easter to the unrelieved poor.[65] They continued payment of yearly doles in the early 19th century. Part of the capital of Baden's gift was later deemed lost. That deficiency was made good, and the capital much increased, by subscription. In 1815 a total of £70 was invested and the annual income of £3 3s. 6d. thereafter used to buy bread which was given out in January or February to those who did not receive parish relief. In 1901 the yearly income of £2 7s. 4d. was allowed to accumulate over three years and the total then used to buy bread.

William Munday by will proved 1810 bequeathed £20, the interest to be spent on bread for the poor of Coombe tithing each Christmas. In 1901 the annual income of 15s. 4d. was spent trienially according to Munday's wishes.[66]

J. H. Alt, vicar 1834–75, at an unknown date gave money, the interest to be used to provide coal for widows in Enford. The sum seems to have been represented by stock worth £80.[67]

By a Scheme of 1967 the Baden, Munday, and Alt charities were amalgamated and the joint income, then under £5 yearly, was distributed to needy parishioners either as money grants or as gifts in kind.[68]

38 Sar. Dioc. R.O., Certs. Dissenters' Meeting-Houses.
39 Ibid.   40 H.O. 129/261/1/6.
41 Ibid.
42 Date on chapel; O.S. Map 6", Wilts. XLVII (1889 edn.).
43 E 301/58/26.
44 Sar. Dioc. R.O., Chwdns.' Pres.
45 *Vis. Queries, 1783* (W.R.S. xxvii), pp. 98–9.
46 Lawrance, 'Notes for a hist. of Enford' (MS. *penes* Sir Ric. Harvey), 97.
47 *Educ. of Poor Digest,* 1026.
48 *Educ. Enquiry Abstract,* 1037.
49 Lawrance, op. cit. 72, 96; *Endowed Char. Wilts.* (S. Div.), 169.
50 *Return of Non-Provided Schs.* 22; O.S. Map 6", Wilts. XLVII (1889 edn.).
51 *Acct. of Wilts. Schs.* 22.
52 *Returns relating to Elem. Educ.* 424–5.
53 *Return of Non-Provided Schs.* 22, where the Antrobus property is said to have been sold in 1897. It is clear that

it was sold in 1899: *Salisbury Plain (Property Purchased),* H.C. 14, pp. 2–3 (1900), xlix.
54 *Endowed Char. Wilts.* (S. Div.), 169.
55 *Return of Non-Provided Schs.* 22.
56 *Bd. of Educ., List 21* (H.M.S.O.).
57 Lawrance, op. cit. 98.
58 Ex inf. the Revd. J. E. Jackson, Netheravon Vicarage.
59 Ex inf. Sar. Dioc. Council of Educ.
60 *Kelly's Dir. Wilts.* (1848, 1855).
61 Ibid. (1855).
62 Ibid. (1867, 1875, 1880).
63 *Acct. of Wilts. Schs.* 22.
64 All inf. unless otherwise stated from *Endowed Char. Wilts.* (S. Div.), 168–9; for Baden, see W.R.O. 212B/3054; 212B/3108.
65 *Vis. Queries, 1783* (W.R.S. xxvii), pp. 98–9.
66 *Endowed Char. Wilts.* (S. Div.), 168–9.
67 Lawrance, 'Notes for a hist. of Enford' (MS. *penes* Sir Ric. Harvey), 72–3, 95.
68 Ibid. 96; Char. Com. file 245166.

EVERLEIGH

EVERLEIGH lies mostly at heights of between 150 m. and 180 m. towards the north-eastern edge of Salisbury Plain.[69] High on the plain the village occupies an isolated site about half-way between the villages of the Bourne valley to the east and those of the Avon valley to the west.[70] The parish is roughly rectangular, nearly 5 km. long and about 3 km. wide, and covers 1,330 ha. (3,286 a.). The nearest town is Pewsey some 8 km. away. The entire parish lies on the Upper Chalk of Salisbury Plain. On the south-west and east sides the heads of three dry valleys with their floorings of gravel have cut into the chalk plateau for short stretches.

The name Everleigh comes from the Old English *eofor*, a wild boar, and *leah*, a clearing,[71] a reminder that the parish lay within the old natural forest of Chute.[72] The parish came within the bounds of the royal forest of Chute when at their broadest. It was, however, outside the forest in 1300.[73] There are important Romano-British settlement sites a little to the west of the parish, and barrows, or groups of barrows, serve as marks on the parish boundary.[74] A commission was appointed in 1290 to determine the course of that boundary in the north-west where it ran between Everleigh and Pewsey.[75] In 1591 the prominent landmark of Sidbury hill was taken as marking the southernmost point of the parish,[76] but in 1975 it was south of the boundary in North Tidworth. Within Everleigh there are comparatively few prehistoric sites, another indication of original forest cover. Traces of field systems remain in the south-west corner of the parish, probably connected with the Romano-British settlement at Coombe down in Enford.[77]

In the Middle Ages there was a scarcity of wood in the parish, for timber to inclose the lord's park was habitually obtained from the neighbouring parish of Collingbourne Ducis.[78] Early in the 19th century the surrounding landscape struck Cobbett as barren. 'Here you see miles and miles square without a tree, or hedge, or bush. It is a country of greensward', he wrote.[79] Aubrey in the 17th century, however, remarked upon a large oak coppice, although he added that it grew very poorly, not liking the chalky soil.[80] In 1975 the parish was by no means treeless. There was considerable woodland in the north-east corner, some of which at Old Hat copse was replanted with firs and beeches by the Army in 1959 and 1960.[81] Belts of trees have also been planted as windbreaks and coverts, and more recently in the southern half of the parish by the Army as shelter for manœuvres. The sycamores in a row noticed by Cobbett in 1826, to the south of the garden of the Crown inn, may have been the successors to those planted by the vicar in 1660.[82]

Several important routes have crossed the parish. The village lay on the old Salisbury–Marlborough road across the plain, which perhaps followed the course of a Roman road from Old Salisbury.[83] The stretch between Marlborough and Everleigh was turnpiked in 1762. The continuation from Everleigh to Salisbury, however, was never turnpiked and was eventually abandoned.[84] It is thought that the course through Everleigh may have formed part of the route taken by the first Saxon invaders coming up from Southampton Water.[85] The Saxon *herepath* leading from the Bourne valley to Old Salisbury crossed the parish,[86] and the road from Andover, via Ludgershall, to Devizes, now a main road, crossed the old Salisbury–Marlborough road in the village.

A charter of King Ine of 704 was dated at Everleigh,[87] perhaps implying that the place was of importance. If so, that might be the reason why Everleigh became the head of, and gave its name to, a small liberty in the 13th century.[88] In 1334 it was taxed at 110s., 20s. more than any of the other four places then composing the liberty.[89] In 1377, when only three places were included in the liberty for taxation purposes, Everleigh had far fewer poll-tax payers than Collingbourne Ducis.[90] To the benevolence of 1545 Everleigh made the fifth smallest contribution of the thirteen places taxed in the hundred of Elstub in which it was then merged.[91] To the subsidy of 1576 its contribution was the third highest of the fifteen places taxed in the hundred.[92]

There have been two main settlements in Everleigh known as West or Lower Everleigh and East Everleigh. In the 18th century West Everleigh, standing at a point where many tracks converged upon the Andover–Devizes road, had several cottages along a road, now disused, running south-east from the present main road.[93] East Everleigh, which now forms the village of Everleigh, lay to the south of the manor-house. Until 1811 the parish church and some other village buildings stood a little to the south-east of the house. In that year Francis Dugdale Astley, finding them too close to his home, had them pulled down and forthwith built a new church roughly midway between East and West Everleigh.[94] The ground in front of the manor-house was then inclosed as a park and the road diverted round it.[95] A cluster of cottages, possibly

---

[69] This article was written in 1974–5.
[70] Maps used include O.S. Maps 1″, sheet 167 (1960 edn.); 1/25,000, 41/25 (1948 edn.), 41/15 (1951 edn.); 6″, Wilts. XLII. SW. (1926 edn.), XLVIII. NW. (1926 edn.); 1/2,500, Wilts. XLII (1st and later edns.), XLVIII (1st and later edns.).
[71] *P.N. Wilts.* (E.P.N.S.), 329.
[72] *W.A.M.* xlviii. 54.
[73] *V.C.H. Wilts.* iv. 424–5, 453.
[74] Ibid. i (1), 70, 174, 209, 255, 275.
[75] *Cal. Pat.* 1281–92, 400.   [76] *W.A.M.* ii. 186.
[77] *V.C.H. Wilts.* i (1), 69.   [78] See p. 110.
[79] W. Cobbett, *Rural Rides*, ed. G. D. H. and Margaret Cole, i. 356.
[80] Aubrey, *Topog. Coll.* ed. Jackson, 365.

[81] Wilts. Cuttings, xxii. 266.
[82] Cobbett, op. cit. 52; W.R.O. 651/21, notes on par. reg.
[83] *Andrews and Dury, Map* (W.R.S. viii), pl. 9; *W.A.M.* xxxiv. 131–2.
[84] *V.C.H. Wilts.* iv. 299.
[85] *W.A.M.* xxxiv. 131–2.   [86] Ibid. xlii. 94.
[87] Finberg, *Early Wessex Chart.* p. 112.
[88] See p. 106.   [89] *V.C.H. Wilts.* iv. 299.
[90] Ibid. 308.   [91] *Taxation Lists* (W.R.S. x), 3.
[92] Ibid. 123.
[93] *Andrews and Dury, Map* (W.R.S. viii), pl. 9.
[94] Wilts. Cuttings, xviii. 52.
[95] An early-19th-cent. map in W.R.O. 1392 shows the proposed diversions.

dating from the 17th century, stood until the 1930s, when they were pulled down, to the south-west of Lower Everleigh Farm and suggest the existence of a third settlement site.[96]

In 1801 the population was 321.[97] In 1815 there were said to be seventeen cottages in the village, three with shops in them, and four houses, two of which had shops.[98] This, however, gives a false impression of the size of the village, for the population was dwindling. In 1951 it was 264; in 1971 210.[99]

Everleigh's isolated situation at a fairly important road junction called for at least one inn. The Rose and Crown is mentioned in 1713[1] and an inn of that name was part of the property acquired by Sir John Astley, Bt., in 1736 and intended by him to serve as a hunting lodge.[2] It is thought to have stood close to the manor-house and to have been cleared away with the church and other buildings early in the 19th century.[3] There was a White Hart in 1815 and a Swan in 1847,[4] but the best known inn is the Crown, still in business in the centre of the village.[5] It has been suggested that the Crown was built as a dower-house,[6] and in 1748 the building was the home of Alicia, wife of Charles Bennet, Lord Ossulston (later earl of Tankerville), a daughter of Sir John Astley (d. 1771).[7] In 1792 the Crown was functioning as an inn.[8] Sir Richard Colt Hoare, Bt., approved of it when he stayed there while excavating in the neighbourhood in the early 1800s,[9] and Cobbett praised it highly in 1826.[10] It was the meeting-place of several sporting clubs.[11] The oldest part of the house, which is of the early 18th century, is the south wing. It was formerly symmetrical and had a brick front of seven bays with a short service wing on the north-east. The wing was extended to make a nearly symmetrical east front with recessed centre in the later 18th century and more additions were made in the early 19th century.

With Pewsey Everleigh gave its name to a petty sessional division and consequently after 1863 to a highway district.[12] Petty sessions were held once a month at the Crown until c. 1907 when the court was transferred to Ludgershall.[13]

In 1975 the older part of Everleigh (formerly East Everleigh) village lay behind the Crown along a side road which once continued as a way to West Everleigh.[14] One cottage is dated 1732 with the initials 'AMH'. Since the Army acquired most of the land c. 1937 a few houses have been built for service families. There has also been a little council and some private building. Apart from the manor-house, the Crown, and West Everleigh Farm, the only house of any size in the parish is Lower House Farm, which stands away from the village to the east. The oldest part of the house, which is probably 17th-century, is a range running east–west and having a three-roomed plan. The parlour end was extended to form a wing with a brick front facing south in the 18th century and then was again enlarged early in the 19th century. A chimney stack bears the date 1715 and the initials 'TAK', and a rainwater head the date 1828 and the initials 'WP'. The house shows signs of having been refurbished in the 18th century and may have been occupied by Sir John Astley after he acquired it in 1736. Further improvements were probably made by William Pinkney who was tenant from c. 1805 until 1845.

The downs to the south of the village with their gentle incline southwards have been extensively used for sport, particularly hunting and falconry.[15] A great hare warren lay there in the 16th century and was still marked on a map of 1773.[16] Aubrey mentions a racecourse and the race-post formed a boundary mark in 1669.[17] Cricket was played on the downs in the 18th century.[18] Alma clump, a mound once planted with trees to commemorate the return of Sir John Astley (d. 1894) from the Crimean War, stands on the edge of the downland just south of the Crown.[19] In 1975 it was overgrown with scrub. Since the 1930s all the downland has been devoted to military training. Much of it is enclosed with wire; firs have been planted for shelter and the ground is scarred with tank tracks. The road through it from Fittleton to Everleigh was built by the Army.[20]

MANOR AND OTHER ESTATES. Everleigh is not named in Domesday Book but it may have been among the lands granted to Robert de Beaumont (d. 1118), said to have been created earl of Leicester, who accompanied the Conqueror to England.[21] It was held by his grandson Robert (d. 1190) to whom the earldom of Leicester descended.[22] Robert's son Robert, earl of Leicester, died childless in 1204 and his lands were partitioned between his sisters Amice, wife of William des Barres and relict of Simon de Montfort (d. c. 1188), and Margaret, wife of Saier de Quency (created earl of Winchester in 1207).[23]

The partition was complicated by the assignment of dower to Robert's widow Loretta (d. 1266) and the claims of his mother Parnel, heir to the Norman honor of Grandmesnil (d. 1212).[24] Everleigh was granted in 1212 to the earl of Winchester, Margaret's husband, for the performance of Parnel's will.[25] In

[96] Ex inf. Mr. W. E. Cave, Everleigh.
[97] V.C.H. Wilts. iv. 348.
[98] W.R.O. 651/10, terrier.
[99] V.C.H. Wilts. iv. 348; Census, 1971.
[1] W.R.O. 651/3, par. reg.
[2] Act for Exchanging Lands, 9 Geo. II, c. 9 (Priv. Act); Camb. Univ. Libr., Queens' Coll. Mun. 17/16/5.
[3] W. A. Edwards, Everleigh (priv. print. 1967), 16.
[4] W.R.O. 651/10, terrier; 772/13, transfer of licence.
[5] See plate facing p. 225.
[6] Edwards, op. cit. 18.
[7] W.R.O. 651/21, notes from par. reg.
[8] Edwards, op. cit. 19.   [9] Ibid.
[10] Cobbett, Rural Rides, ed. G. D. H. and Margaret Cole, i. 356–7.   [11] Edwards, op. cit. 19.
[12] V.C.H. Wilts. v. 250, 260.

[13] Edwards, op. cit. 27.
[14] Andrews and Dury, Map (W.R.S. viii), pl. 9.
[15] V.C.H. Wilts. iv. 362, 378, 382–3.
[16] See p 139.
[17] Aubrey, Nat. Hist. Wilts. ed. Britton, 117; W.R.O. 651/2, terrier.
[18] V.C.H. Wilts. iv. 378.
[19] Edwards, op. cit. 27.
[20] V.C.H. Wilts. iv. 266.
[21] Complete Peerage, vii. 523; Levi Fox, 'Honor of Leic. 1066–1399', E.H.R. liv. 386–7.
[22] Complete Peerage, s.v. Leicester; Pipe R. 1172–3 (P.R.S. xix), 102.
[23] Complete Peerage, s.v. Leicester.
[24] Fox, 'Honor of Leic.', E.H.R. liv. 392–3.
[25] Rot. Litt. Claus. (Rec. Com.), i. 130.

1244, however, it was in the hands of Simon de Montfort, the grandson of Amice by her first husband,[26] who succeeded to his father's English lands and the earldom of Leicester in 1239.[27]

Shortly before de Montfort's death at Evesham in 1265 Everleigh seems to have been exchanged with the king for other lands.[28] After de Montfort's death it passed with the rest of the honor of Leicester to Edmund (d. 1296), fourth son of Henry III, created earl of Lancaster in 1267.[29] It then passed with the Lancaster title until the death of Henry, duke of Lancaster, in 1361.[30]

On the partition of the duke's lands between his two daughters Everleigh, with most of the lands of the honor of Leicester, went to the elder daughter Maud, wife of William, duke of Bavaria.[31] Maud died in 1362 and was succeeded by her sister Blanche, wife of John of Gaunt (d. 1399), earl (later duke) of Lancaster.[32] When Henry, son of John and Blanche, became King Henry IV the lands of the duchy of Lancaster, which included Everleigh, were attached to the Crown.[33]

Except for a short time in the 16th century Everleigh remained part of the duchy until the mid 17th century. With other lands it was granted as dower to Alice, countess of Lincoln, widow of Thomas, earl of Lancaster (executed in 1322).[34] It was among the lands conveyed to trustees for the performance of the wills of Henry V and Henry VI.[35]

In 1547 Everleigh was granted to Edward Seymour, duke of Somerset, but on the duke's attainder and execution in 1552 it reverted to the duchy of Lancaster.[36] Several officers of the duchy were among the lessees of the manor. Sir Edward Hungerford (d. 1522), lessee in 1496, was steward of the duchy lands in Wiltshire.[37] Richard Baker, lessee between 1535 and 1552, may also have been an officer.[38] In 1581 the lessee was Henry Sadler, another steward of the duchy lands and third son of Sir Ralph Sadler, chancellor of the duchy from 1568 to 1587. It is believed that Ralph was himself lessee at some time.[39] Both Sadlers were renowned as falconers and Everleigh afforded outstanding opportunities for sport.[40] Henry was succeeded by Francis Sadler, who had a daughter baptized at Everleigh in 1620, and Francis by George Sadler who had daughters baptized there in 1630 and 1631.[41]

In 1625 Everleigh was among the duchy estates conveyed to trustees for the City of London in payment of a loan to the Crown.[42] By 1636 it had passed to George Evelyn, one of the six clerks in

Chancery, who died at Everleigh in that year.[43] He was followed by his son Sir John Evelyn, who styled himself 'of Everleigh' in 1640,[44] and was still there in 1648.[45] That year, however, a series of conveyances resulted in the sale in 1649 of the manor by Henry Andrews and his wife Mary to William Barker, alderman of London.[46] From William it went to a grandson Robert Barker (d. 1722), and from Robert, after a contested will, to his nephew Robert Barker.[47] That Robert, in financial difficulties, sold Everleigh in 1765 to Sir John Astley, Bt., of Patshull (Staffs.).[48]

Sir John had already acquired a small estate in Everleigh in 1736 from which he hunted.[49] He died in 1771 and Everleigh passed to his cousin Francis Dugdale Astley.[50] F. D. Astley was succeeded in 1818 by his son John, created a baronet in 1821. John was followed in 1842 by his son Francis. Sir Francis died in 1873 but in 1856 the family had left Everleigh and after some years returned to their seat at Elsham (Lincs.).[51] Sir Francis was succeeded by his son John (d. 1894) whose son and heir F. E. G. Astley assumed the name Astley-Corbett in 1889 and died in 1939. Between 1917 and 1919, however, the manor-house and Everleigh estate were sold.[52] The manor-house and 1,100 a. were sold in 1917 to a timber merchant. In 1919 they were bought by the National Deposit Friendly Society which in 1954 sold them to the War Department.[53] Lower House farm and West Everleigh farm were bought c. 1918 by J. G. Hossack who sold them forthwith to Joseph Nicholls and William Francis Hazell.[54] In 1937 the War Department bought the whole of West Everleigh farm, 1,361 a., and 957 a. of Lower House farm.[55]

Between 1856 and 1917 the Astleys leased the manor-house to various tenants. Henry Fitzroy, a member of Palmerston's government in 1856–7, was the first and Francis Alexander (d. 1914) the last. It was bought by the National Deposit Friendly Society as a convalescent home. It was requisitioned in 1939 as a military hospital and after 1945 became an army research laboratory, named after 1951 the David Bruce Laboratory.[56]

According to tradition the house was built by Sir Ralph Sadler and in the mid 19th century some of the interior was thought to date from his time. The drawing-room was then wainscoted in oak and there was an elaborate carved and gilded ceiling.[57] In it hung a portrait of Sir Ralph, perhaps by Mare Gerhardt (1580–1635), dressed as a falconer with a hawk on his arm. The picture was removed to the

[26] Close R. 1242–7, 268.
[27] Complete Peerage, vii. 543–7.
[28] Cal. Pat. 1258–66, 424.
[29] Rot. Hund. (Rec. Com.), ii (1), 259; Complete Peerage, vii. 379.
[30] Complete Peerage, vii. 378–410.
[31] Cal. Fine R. 1356–68, 165.
[32] Wilts. Inq. p.m. 1327–77 (Index Libr.), 304–5.
[33] Complete Peerage, vii. 418.
[34] Cal. Close, 1318–23, 579.
[35] Ibid. 1413–19, 386; R. Somerville, Duchy of Lanc. i. 340.
[36] D.L. 42/23 f. 16.
[37] D.L. 42/21 f. 200; Somerville, op. cit. 340.
[38] D.L. 42/108 f. 46v.; Somerville, op. cit. 559.
[39] D.L. 1/120/C 3; Somerville, op. cit. 395, 632; Hoare, Mod. Wilts. Elstub and Everley, 3.
[40] See below.
[41] W.R.O. 651/1, notes from par. reg.

[42] C 66/2351 m. 16.
[43] Cal. S.P. Dom. 1635–6, 187, 230. For the Evelyn fam. see Burke, Land. Gent. (1952), 780.
[44] Cal. S.P. Dom. 1640–1, 328.
[45] Wilts. Q. Sess. Rec. ed. Cunnington, 210.
[46] C.P. 25(2)/608/1649 Mich.
[47] B.L. Add. MS. 36149, f. 18. For the fam. see Burke, Ext. & Dorm. Baronetcies (1838), 37.
[48] C.P. 25(2)/1445/5 Geo. III Mich.; Hoare, Mod. Wilts. Elstub and Everley, 7.
[49] See below.
[50] The descent of the Astleys is from Burke, Peerage (1949), 92–3.
[51] W.R.O. 175, Astley papers.
[52] Edwards, Everleigh (priv. print. 1967), 15.
[53] Ibid.   [54] Wilts. Cuttings, xiv. 83.
[55] Ex inf. Defence Land Agent, Durrington.
[56] Edwards, op. cit. 15.
[57] See plate facing p. 145.

Astleys' home at Elsham in 1890 and in 1917 was sold at Christies.[58]

Some sections of the brickwork of the north front of the house may survive from a 17th-century house with a central range and projecting wings. That house appears to have been converted to a double pile plan with main fronts of nine bays in the 18th century. Before 1773, and perhaps soon after Sir John Astley (d. 1771) acquired the manor in 1765, the house was greatly enlarged by the addition of balancing wings, each of seven bays and with a central pediment. That on the west, which may have incorporated an earlier range, contained service rooms, that on the east an orangery. Beyond and at right angles to the latter there are stables of similar date with a pedimented loggia to the garden on the otherwise blind west wall.

In 1882 a fire seriously damaged the central block of the house which was virtually reconstructed in 1882–3, probably from designs by John Birch. Additions on the west during the 19th century obscured the symmetry of the original layout and to a lesser extent there have been additions and alterations during the conversion of the house for laboratory use. There is an ice-house to the east of the stable block.

After selling the manor in 1649 Sir John Evelyn retained a property in Everleigh called Taylorshold which in 1658 he conveyed to Thomas Clark.[59] From Clark it passed to Richard Watson, D.D., who some time after 1672 conveyed it to Queens' College, Cambridge.[60] In 1734 Sir John Astley (d. 1771), wishing to acquire a base in Everleigh from which to hunt, bought a small estate at Kingston (Cambs.) in order to exchange it with the college for their land in Everleigh.[61] The exchange was effected by private Act.[62] By it Sir John gained land and outbuildings then called Lake's, but almost certainly to be identified as Lower House farm,[63] and an inn called the Rose and Crown which he proposed to renovate to provide the accommodation and stabling he desired.[64]

A farm of some 200 a. in Everleigh descended with the manor of Collingbourne Ducis.[65] In 1765, when it was called Everleigh or Noyes farm, it was bought by Sir John Astley and merged with Everleigh manor.[66]

ECONOMIC HISTORY. In 1212 Everleigh was valued at £23 10s. and, with the addition of its stock, at £32.[67] By the late 13th century, besides a capital messuage with its curtilage and dovecot, there were on the manor 524 a. of arable valued at £8 14s. 8d. and 80 a. of poor land worth 13s. 4d. There were 8 a. of meadow worth 24s., and pasture in several and in common worth 65s. 4d. Rents of free tenants were valued at 77s. a year, of customers and cottars at £4 1s., and labour services and customary payments were valued at £10 6s. 7d.[68] A fuller extent of 1361 gives 360 a. of arable, half of which could be sown every year, while the other half lay fallow and could be exploited in common by the tenants. The meadow was also pastured in common after haymaking. There was pasture for 3 draught beasts, 12 oxen, and 500 sheep.[69]

In 1552–3 East and West Everleigh each had a common arable field called respectively East and West field. A third arable field was called Middle field. There were at that date three free tenants on the manor. Two held pieces of arable in all three fields as well as a few closes of pasture; the third, besides a few closes of pasture, had arable in two of the three fields. There were sixteen copyholders with holdings mostly of 1 or 2 virgates, and three tenants at will. Amongst the lands of some of the copyholders was a holding called a workland which seems then to have measured 2½ a.[70] The freeholdings, which were quite small, may have been merged to form the first estate which Sir John Astley, Bt. (d. 1771), bought in Everleigh in 1736, later known as Lower House farm.

By 1662 two more arable fields are mentioned called Drove field and Cowpashe. By then East field had been subdivided into north, south, and middle divisions.[71] Consolidation of holdings was probably a slow process, achieved in the course of the 18th century by agreement. When in 1765 Sir John Astley bought Noyes farm, 218 a., he pointed out that the transaction would enable him to effect some consolidation and so introduce certain improvements. He remarked, however, that he had no intention of inclosing with hedges or fences, for such action was impracticable on the barren country of the downs.[72] An Act for inclosure was passed in 1816, but so far as is known no award followed, and it presumably ratified an existing state of affairs achieved over the years by agreement.[73] One such agreement, dated 1779, covering land in the south of the parish survives.[74]

In the mid 16th century the demesne farm had 9 yardlands of arable and three sheep downs, allowing the flock to be moved according to the season. Besides a down of 100 a. there were Lent down, c. 50 a., and Summer down, c. 60 a. The tenantry downs were Cowpas, 40 a., and Gore, 16 a. Holders of yardlands in East Everleigh were allowed to pasture 60 sheep, 4 working cattle, and 2 horses for every yardland held, while in West Everleigh the numbers permitted were 80 sheep, 4 working cattle, and 2 horses. Holders of worklands throughout the manor were allowed to pasture 10 sheep and 2 working cattle.[75] Besides the workland there was a holding on the manor called the Mondayland. Originally it was the holding of the Mondaymen, whose once-weekly labour services, chiefly for the demesne flock, are specified throughout the 15th century.[76] A green existed in the mid 16th century

[58] Burke, *Seats and Arms of Noblemen and Gentlemen* (1852), 113–15; W.R.O. 175, sale cat.
[59] Camb. Univ. Libr., Queens' Coll. Mun. 83.
[60] Ibid. [61] Ibid. 17/16/1–2.
[62] Act for Exchanging Lands, 9 Geo. II, c. 9 (Priv. Act).
[63] Hoare, *Mod. Wilts.* Elstub and Everley, 7. For Lakes see also W.R.O. 1392, terrier, 1672.
[64] Act for Exchanging Lands, 9 Geo. II, c. 9 (Priv. Act); Camb. Univ. Libr., Queens' Coll. Mun. 17/16/5; 17/16/7–8. [65] See p. 109.

[66] W.R.O. 9, sale of Noyes farm.
[67] *Rot. Litt. Claus.* (Rec. Com.), i. 130.
[68] *Wilts. Inq. p.m.* 1242–1326 (Index Libr.), 217–18.
[69] Ibid. 1327–77 (Index Libr.), 287–8.
[70] D.L. 42/108 f. 46v.
[71] Sar. Dioc. R.O., Glebe Terrier.
[72] W.R.O. 9, sale of Noyes farm; see above.
[73] 56 Geo. III, c. 68 (Private, not printed).
[74] W.R.O. 1392, 'Everleigh Award'.
[75] D.L. 42/108 f. 46v. [76] *V.C.H. Wilts.* iv. 29.

for which all the tenants using it were charged 2d. a year.[77] There was a windmill at East Everleigh which still stood in the early 19th century.[78]

In such a region large flocks of sheep were maintained throughout the Middle Ages. In 1212 a demesne flock of 533 sheep is mentioned.[79] In the 15th century, when Everleigh was part of the duchy of Lancaster's Wiltshire estate, the duchy's stock-keeper leased the demesne farm for some years.[80] Flocks of around 1,000 sheep then existed and it was usual for wool from Everleigh to be sent to Aldbourne, another duchy manor, for collection.[81] In 1598 there was a tenant flock of 120 sheep.[82] In 1803 the tenant farmer of Lower House farm kept a flock of 1,500 pure-bred Southdowns.[83] Cobbett, visiting Everleigh in 1826, witnessed flocks of several hundreds leaving the downs in the evenings for the folds.[84] There was still a flock of about 800 sheep in 1936 when the wool was sent to the Marlborough wool fair.[85]

In 1815 the largest farms in the parish were Lower House and West or Lower Everleigh farms. There was also a home farm, and 129 a. were attached to the Crown inn. William Pinkney was the tenant at Lower House where he remained for about 40 years.[86] After 1871 and until the sale of the Astley estate c. 1918 Lower House was farmed by Benjamin and Arthur Nuth and West Everleigh farm by a Mr. Strong.[87] After the sale they were farmed in partnership by Joseph Nicholls and W. F. Hazell.[88] In 1934 the two farms were separated and W. E. Cave farmed Lower House, while Hazell and his sons carried on at West Everleigh.[89] In 1975 Mr. W. E. Cave farmed Lower House and Mr. Richard Carter West Everleigh.[90]

As occurred in the rest of the region, there was much ploughing of the downland in the 18th and 19th centuries.[91] In 1783 the tenant of Lower farm was permitted to convert some downland to arable, for a limited period and on condition that he surrendered another piece of down to the lord of the manor.[92] In 1841 there were 1,678 a. of arable, 139 a. of meadow or pasture, and 1,166 a. of down.[93] In 1936 barley was the chief crop, as it had long been, and smaller acreages of oats and wheat were grown.[94] The acquisitions of land by the War Department in 1937 and 1954 put certain restrictions upon the land-use but the area of arable has remained roughly the same.[95]

Although well suited for sheep and corn farming, Everleigh's special renown until the 20th century was as sporting, particularly hunting, country. It was presumably no mere chance that Sir Ralph and Henry Sadler, both expert falconers, had connexions with the manor in the 16th century.[96] The exploitation of a great sporting estate, as it apparently was from very early times, presumably created a certain amount of employment. The leasing of the hare warren,[97] and later of the sporting rights over the whole estate were, moreover, important sources of income to the lords of the manor.

A forest of Everleigh is quite often mentioned in the Middle Ages, and within it Simon de Montfort had a park in 1234.[98] Gifts of deer to stock it were made by the king in 1244 and 1245.[99] There was a keeper for it in 1249,[1] no doubt then a working employee, but later the keepership became an office to be bestowed as a piece of patronage. In 1441 it was granted to William Collingbourne for life.[2] In 1460 Edward, earl of March (later Edward IV), was granted, among other offices, the keepership of the parks of Mere and Everleigh.[3] Sir Walter Hungerford was keeper in 1485.[4] In 1545 Sir William Herbert (created earl of Pembroke in 1551), steward of the duchy of Lancaster's lands in Wiltshire, was lieutenant of the forest and chase of Aldbourne and Everleigh.[5] The keepership was included in the grant of the manor to the duke of Somerset in 1547 and with the manor reverted to the duchy in 1552.[6] In 1559 Sir James Stumpe was keeper of the park.[7]

The park lay in the north-eastern part of the manor.[8] In the mid 16th century it covered 200 a. and was inclosed by 1½ mile of paling. The paling had come from Collingbourne Ducis, but since that manor had passed to the earl of Hertford wood was not available for repairs. There were 40 a. of parkland given over to rabbits. There was a coppice of 3 a. and many oaks 200 years old. A working keeper received 30s. 4d. a year, together with 2s. 8d. for his dog. There was a lodge for his dwelling.[9]

A rabbit warren was valued at 60s. in 1297.[10] The profits from it were leased with the demesne in 1496.[11] By the 15th century a hare warren had become a feature of the estate and was frequently leased separately from it.[12] In 1565–6 Sir Edward Rogers, comptroller of the queen's household, was the lessee.[13] The warren lay in the south-western part of the manor, as shown on a map of 1773.[14] In 1581 it extended 3 miles in all directions.[15] Besides frequent raids by poachers, the warren was often threatened by the creation of unauthorized rabbit warrens which were detrimental to the well-being and safety of the hares.[16] It was still a noteworthy feature in Aubrey's day,[17] but in 1695 the lord of the manor agreed to destroy his warren in return

[77] D.L. 42/108 f. 46v.　　[78] W.R.O. 1392, map.
[79] *Rot. Litt. Claus.* (Rec. Com.), i. 117–18.
[80] D.L. 29/684/11078; D.L. 29/685/11089.
[81] e.g. D.L. 29/683/11070.
[82] *Extents for Debts* (W.R.S. xxviii), pp. 104–5.
[83] *W.A.M.* xliii. 456.
[84] Cobbett, *Rural Rides*, ed. G. D. H. and Margaret Cole, i. 356–7.
[85] Wilts. Cuttings, xviii. 2.
[86] W.R.O. 651/10, terrier.
[87] *W.A.M.* xlii. 87; ex inf. Mr. W. E. Cave, Everleigh.
[88] Wilts. Cuttings, xiv. 83.
[89] Ibid.; ex inf. Mr. Cave.　　[90] Ex inf. Mr. Cave.
[91] There is reference to recent ploughing in Burke, *Seats and Arms of Noblemen and Gentlemen* (1852), 114.
[92] W.R.O. 1392, agreement, Astley and Gibbs.
[93] Ibid. Tithe Award.
[94] Wilts. Cuttings, xviii. 2.　　[95] Ex inf. Mr. Cave.

[96] See above.　　　　　　　[97] See below.
[98] *Cur. Reg. R.* xv. 256.
[99] *Close R.* 1242–7, 268, 288.
[1] *Crown Pleas, 1249* (W.R.S. xvi), p. 197.
[2] *W.N. & Q.* vii. 258.
[3] *Cal. Pat.* 1452–61, 632.　　[4] Ibid. 1485–9, 54.
[5] *L. & P. Hen. VIII*, xx. 182.　　[6] See p. 137.
[7] D.L. 42/23 f. 140v.　　[8] D.L. 1/120/C 3
[9] D.L. 44/R 5; D.L. 44/R 11; D.L. 42/108 f. 46v.; D.L. 42/21 f. 200.
[10] *Wilts. Inq. p.m.* 1242–1326 (Index Libr.), 217–18.
[11] D.L. 42/21 f. 200.
[12] e.g. D.L. 29/684/11078; D.L. 29/685/11089.
[13] D.L. 1/66/D 3.
[14] D.L. 1/120/C 3; *Andrews and Dury, Map* (W.R.S. viii), pl. 9.　　[15] D.L. 44/313.
[16] D.L. 1/66/D 3; D.L. 44/313.
[17] Aubrey, *Nat. Hist. Wilts.* ed. Britton, 59.

for small payments from tenants who grazed their animals on it.[18] The suitability of the terrain for breeding and hunting hares was emphasized in the 19th century by Cobbett's verdict that Everleigh was the most famous place in all England for coursing.[19]

Its high altitude has made Everleigh a good place for training racehorses. Horses were trained from stables attached to the Crown inn in the 19th century and from them came the winner of the Grand National in 1897. Other stables were built close to the village c. 1903.[20]

LOCAL GOVERNMENT. In 1249 Everleigh stood at the head of a small liberty belonging to the earls of Leicester who had some sort of prison there.[21] Collingbourne Ducis was the other main constituent of the liberty, although at times in the 14th century Compton, in Enford, and Haxton, in Fittleton, both like Everleigh and Collingbourne Ducis manors of the earls of Leicester, were said to belong to it.[22] The privilege of return of writs belonged to the liberty, but that was a franchise belonging to all the fees of the honor of Leicester.[23] It is not known whether the honor's other two Wiltshire fees, Chitterne and Ablington in Figheldean, ever formed part of the liberty of Everleigh.[24] By the 16th century the liberty had been merged in the hundred of Elstub.[25] The last mention found of it occurs in 1539.[26]

In 1766 a court leet and view of frankpledge for Everleigh, and a court baron were held. Meetings were held at the White Hart and the court made arrangements for perambulating the parish boundaries. After 1771 only the court baron was held. It ceased in 1841.[27] After the Poor Law Amendment Act of 1834 Everleigh became part of the Pewsey poor-law union.[28]

CHURCH. By 1228 the church of Everleigh had been granted to Wherwell Abbey (Hants).[29] A vicarage seems to have been ordained by 1291.[30] It is mentioned again in 1428.[31] No further reference to it has been found and at least since the 14th century, when records of presentations begin, the living has always been a rectory.[32] It was held in plurality with the united benefice of Manningford Abbots and Manningford Bruce from 1967.[33] In 1975 it

was united with the benefice of the Collingbournes to form the benefice of the Collingbournes and Everleigh.[34] The ecclesiastical parish was united with that of Collingbourne Ducis in 1977 to create a new parish called Collingbourne Ducis and Everleigh.[35]

Wherwell Abbey retained the advowson until the Dissolution and presentations to the rectory were made by the abbesses, except in 1361 when the king presented by voidance.[36] In 1544 the advowson was granted to Nicholas Bacon and Thomas Skipworth,[37] who probably sold it immediately, for in 1546 Sir Thomas Wriothesley, later earl of Southampton (d. 1550), presented.[38] The patronage did not pass to the earl's successor and between 1556 and 1660 the Crown presented.[39] In 1662, however, it was granted in fee to Wriothesley's descendant, namely Thomas Wriothesley, earl of Southampton (d. 1667).[40] Lord Southampton died without surviving male heirs and his honours became extinct.[41] The advowson of Everleigh passed to a relation, Wriothesley Baptist Noel, earl of Gainsborough (d. 1690), and from him to his daughter Elizabeth, wife of Henry Bentinck, earl of Portland (d. 1726).[42] Lord and Lady Portland presented in 1716 and conveyed the patronage for one turn to Henry Somerset, duke of Beaufort (d. 1745), who presented when the rectory fell vacant again in the same year.[43] Thereafter the dukes of Portland presented until 1805.[44] By 1812 the advowson had been purchased by Francis Dugdale Astley (d. 1818).[45] The lords of the manor continued as patrons until 1917. In 1931 presentation was by the Martyrs Memorial Trust.[46] In 1975 the patron was allotted the second of five turns.[47]

The church was valued at £8 and the vicarage at £5 6s. 8d. in 1291.[48] In 1535 the church was reckoned to be worth £19 a year.[49] In 1650 the annual value was given as £180.[50] In 1831 the average net income over the last three years had been £675.[51]

There were c. 18 a. of glebe belonging to the living. The arable lay in parcels throughout the fields of the parish and there was a small farmstead and some pasture adjoining the rectory-house.[52] When the church was rebuilt an exchange of land for glebe was agreed between the rector and Francis Dugdale Astley.[53] All tithes were payable to the rector and were commuted for a rent-charge of £700 in 1841.[54] A pension of £2 was due to the abbess of Wherwell annually from the church in 1291 and was

[18] W.R.O. 382/1, f. 142, bk. of transcripts.
[19] Cobbett, *Rural Rides*, ed. G. D. H. and Margaret Cole, i. 356.
[20] Edwards, *Everleigh* (priv. print. 1967), 28.
[21] *Crown Pleas, 1249* (W.R.S. xvi), p. 197, which is an earlier reference to the liberty than that in *V.C.H. Wilts.* v. 52.
[22] *V.C.H. Wilts.* iv. 299, 308.
[23] *Wilts. Inq. p.m. 1327–77* (Index Libr.), 15; S. Painter, *Eng. Feudal Barony*, 118.
[24] Fox, 'Honor of Leic.', *E.H.R.* liv. 402.
[25] See pp. 106–7.
[26] *L. & P. Hen. VIII*, xiv (1), p. 301.
[27] W.R.O. 679/2, ct. bk. There are some 18th- and 19th-cent. ct. rec. ibid. 1392.
[28] *V.C.H. Wilts.* v. 253.
[29] Dugdale, *Mon.* ii. 638.
[30] *Tax. Eccl.* (Rec. Com.), 189.
[31] *Feud. Aids*, v. 283.
[32] Phillipps, *Wilts. Inst.* (index in *W.A.M.* xxviii. 220).
[33] *V.C.H. Wilts.* x. 111, 117.

[34] Ex inf. Dioc. Registrar.
[35] *Lond. Gaz.* 18 Feb. 1977, p. 2319.
[36] *Cal. Pat. 1361–4*, 86.
[37] *L. & P. Hen. VIII*, xix (1), p. 371.
[38] Phillipps, *Wilts. Inst.* i. 212.
[39] Ibid. 218, 222; ii. 1, 23.
[40] *Cal. S.P. Dom. 1661–2*, 244.
[41] *Complete Peerage*, s.v. Southampton.
[42] Ibid. s.v. Gainsborough, Portland.
[43] Phillipps, *Wilts. Inst.* ii. 53, 54.
[44] Ibid. 67, 77, 84, 86, 96, 104.
[45] *W.A.M.* xli. 133.
[46] Edwards, *Everleigh* (priv. print. 1967), 29.
[47] Ex inf. Dioc. Registrar.
[48] *Tax. Eccl.* (Rec. Com.), 189.
[49] *Valor Eccl.* (Rec. Com.), ii. 149.
[50] *W.A.M.* xl. 297.
[51] *Rep. Com. Eccl. Revenues*, 832.
[52] Sar. Dioc. R.O., Glebe Terriers.
[53] W.R.O. 1392, papers concerning exchange.
[54] Ibid. Tithe Award.

still payable in 1535.[55] It was possibly transferred to the chapter of Salisbury after the Dissolution, for a pension of that amount due to it is mentioned twice in the mid 17th century.[56] There is a single reference to a pension of 4s. 6d. for the vicar of Collingbourne Kingston in 1535.[57]

In 1316 the rector of Everleigh was given charge of the rectory of Fittleton because of the non-residence of the incumbent there.[58] Many rectors held other preferments and may have been non-resident. John Jeffreys, presented in 1564, was also prebendary of Hurstbourne, and complained that for 5 years Richard of Inkpen illegally took the profits of Everleigh rectory.[59] John Barnstone, rector in 1598, was prebendary of Bishopstone in 1600 and a residentiary canon at Salisbury from 1634 until his death in 1645. He founded a Hebrew Lecture at Brasenose College, Oxford.[60] Christopher Tesdall, rector in 1646, was a canon of Chichester and of Wells, rector of Rollestone, and a member of the Assembly of Divines.[61] John Wallis instituted in 1716 was Laudian Professor of Arabic at Oxford from 1703 until 1738. His successor Abraham le Moine, the theological controversialist,[62] had been domestic chaplain to his patron, William, duke of Portland.[63] In 1783 the rector, Basil Cane, appears to have been serving the church of Cholderton as curate, while Dr. Samuel Starkey, who had a living in Cumberland, served Everleigh as curate and, it was thought, took its profits. Starkey succeeded Cane as rector in 1791.[64] In 1812 the rector, Daniel David Bergner, was non-resident.[65] Between 1830 and 1856 Everleigh and Manningford Abbots were held in plurality by Francis Bickley Astley, who lived at Manningford Abbots and employed a resident curate at Everleigh.[66] His successors served only Everleigh and lived in the rectory-house there until 1966. In that year the rector, Charles Frederick Smith, was appointed to the benefices of Manningford Abbots and Manningford Bruce and left the rectory-house in Everleigh, which had been rebuilt in 1960, to live in Manningford.[67]

In 1660 the rector, William Eastman, known as the 'tinker', allegedly his former calling, was ejected from the living.[68] In 1676 214 conformists were recorded in Everleigh.[69] In 1783 two services were held on Sundays and there were about twenty communicants in the parish. The rector complained, however, that some too frequently absented themselves from church.[70] In 1864 there were between 30 and 40 communicants and a congregation of around 130 was usual.[71]

By 1973 attendances had declined so severely and the church was so dilapidated that it was decided to ask the Redundant Churches Fund to accept responsibility. In the belief that it would be more convenient, communion services were held in a house in the village.[72] In 1974 the church was declared redundant, and in 1975 its care vested in the Redundant Churches Fund.[73]

The medieval church dedicated to St. Peter stood south-east of the manor-house. It had a squat tower and aisled nave with south porch, both built of chalk and flint. The small chancel was of worked flint and stone, finished with an elaborately carved parapet said to be ornamented with the arms of the see of Winchester.[74]

In 1674 the roof was very defective and repairs were proposed.[75] In 1711 the church was whitewashed and adorned with verses by John Gambol, a mason of Devizes.[76] In 1811 it was described as a miserable heap of rubbish held together inside by iron clamps and outside by brick buttresses and was considered by the Astleys to be inconveniently close to their home.[77]

At the cost of Francis Dugdale Astley a new church of *ST. PETER* was built c. 800 m. north-west of the old, roughly half-way between East and West Everleigh. The old church was then pulled down. The architect for the new church, opened in 1814, was John Morlidge.[78] The church is of Bath stone and has nave with south porch, chancel with south chapel, and west tower. It is in a mixture of late Gothic styles.

There are many memorials within it to the Astley family, the most striking being the large monument to Francis Dugdale Astley, the builder of the new church, buried there in 1818. A marble tablet commemorates Anthony Aylmer Astley, rector 1877–1917, the last member of the family to live in the village.[79] The glass in the east windows was given in 1873 by Sir John Dugdale Astley, Bt., to commemorate his parents. There are four hatchments of arms in the nave. Several memorials, mostly to former rectors, were brought from the old church. The church was restored in 1903 when the box-pews were converted into the existing ones. The 12th-century font from the old church was installed in 1911.[80]

There are six bells presented by Francis Dugdale Astley and cast by James Wells of Aldbourne. They were rehung in 1933.[81] In 1553 18 oz. silver were left for the parish and 4 oz. taken for the king.[82] There is also a flagon presented by William Sweatman in 1754 and a chalice given by Anne Astley in 1813.[83] The registers begin in 1598 and are complete.[84]

[55] *Tax. Eccl.* (Rec. Com.), 189; *Valor Eccl.* (Rec. Com.), ii. 149.
[56] *W.A.M.* xix. 187; xl. 298.
[57] *Valor Eccl.* (Rec. Com.), ii. 149.
[58] *Reg. Martival* (Cant. & York Soc.), ii. 158–9.
[59] Req. 2/227/23; *Fasti Eccl. Sar.* ed. W. H. Jones, ii. 396 (1558).
[60] Jones, op. cit. 365; *W.A.M.* xxxv. 148.
[61] *W.A.M.* xxxiv. 187.
[62] *D.N.B.*
[63] J. Foster, *Alumni Oxon. 1500–1714*, iv. 1562; Hoare, *Mod. Wilts.* Elstub and Everley, 12; *W.N. & Q.* i. 269.
[64] *Vis. Queries, 1783* (W.R.S. xxvii), pp. 66, 99.
[65] *W.A.M.* xli. 133.
[66] Edwards, *Everleigh* (priv. print. 1967), 24.
[67] Ibid.

[68] *Calamy Revised*, ed. A. G. Matthews, 177; Hoare, *Mod. Wilts.* Elstub and Everley, 11.
[69] *W.N. & Q.* i. 269.
[70] *Vis. Queries, 1783* (W.R.S. xxvii), p. 66.
[71] Sar. Dioc. R.O., Vis. Queries.
[72] *Wilts. Gaz.* 14 June 1973.
[73] Ex inf. Dioc. Registrar.
[74] W.R.O. 651/21, notes from par. reg.
[75] Sar. Dioc. R.O., Chwdns.' Pres. 1668.
[76] W.R.O. 651/21, par. reg.
[77] Ibid.   [78] Ibid.
[79] *W.A.M.* xxxix. 514–15.
[80] Edwards, *Everleigh* (priv. print. 1967), 23.
[81] Walters, *Wilts. Bells*, 83; Edwards, op. cit. 23.
[82] Nightingale, *Wilts. Plate*, 167–8.
[83] Edwards, op. cit. 23.
[84] W.R.O. 651.

NONCONFORMITY. There is little evidence of nonconformity in Everleigh, but in 1824 the house of James Watson was registered for religious worship by a group of dissenters.[85] The house of A. Jee was similarly registered in 1825, but there was no dissenter in the parish in 1851,[86] and no chapel has been built.

EDUCATION. In 1819 there was a school kept by a woman in the village for 22 children. The poor, it was said, wished for better means of educating their children.[87] There were two schools in 1833 educating between them 31 boys and girls. Both were financed partly by subscription and partly by the parents.[88] In 1844 Sir Francis Dugdale Astley, Bt., gave a site for a school to be conducted in conjunction with the National Society.[89] In 1906 it had accommodation for 100 children but average attendance was 44.[90] It acquired controlled status in 1947. In 1975 there were some eighteen children in the school.[91] The single-storeyed gabled schoolroom had a teacher's house added to it later in the 19th century.

CHARITIES FOR THE POOR. None known.

FITTLETON

UNLIKE its north and south neighbours, Fittleton does not lie across the Avon, but occupies the land east of the river only.[92] The opposite western side is the territory of Netheravon parish. Fittleton has, therefore, only a half share of the valley's alluvial soils and gravel.[93] The area of meadow land is consequently relatively small, although drainage of the marshy ground beside the river has remedied that to some extent. The area of chalk downland is, on the other hand, very large, for from the valley the parish stretches roughly in the shape of a pear up on to Salisbury Plain for over 6 km. In its widest east part it extends for more than 4 km. over the bare downland country where the light loamy soil covering the chalk is thickly strewn with flints.

The climb from the valley to the plain is fairly gentle except in the south-west corner of the parish where the slope forms an almost sheer cliff of chalk. In the north-west corner a steep sided coomb, made by a now dry tributary of the Avon, cuts into the plain and marks the beginning of the boundary between Fittleton and the appropriately named Coombe, a tithing of Enford. On the plain the land is undulating, reaching 171 m. on Weather hill and 187 m. on the slopes of Sidbury hill, in North Tidworth, and dipping gently in the shallow valleys made by the now dry Nine Mile river and its tributaries.

The parish, which measures 1,300 ha. (3,213 a.), is divided lengthways almost exactly in halves into the tithings of Fittleton in the north and Haxton in the south. The two settlements, which adjoin and make a single village, lie in a curve of the river where the terrace of valley gravel widens to provide a site above flood level. The activity of prehistoric man on the upland part of the parish is abundantly attested. Haxton down has a group of bowl-barrows and a long barrow is situated on the west side of Weather hill.[94] Several stretches of bank and ditch,

perhaps connected with near-by Sidbury camp in North Tidworth, run through the parish and one makes part of the boundary between Fittleton and Collingbourne Kingston.[95] A Romano-British settlement a little south of Beach's Barn was excavated in 1894.[96]

Fittleton is roughly 20 km. north of Salisbury, and the same distance south of Marlborough, and south-east of Devizes. Salisbury and Devizes were the main market centres in the 19th century.[97] The village is bypassed by the present north–south main road running down the west bank of the Avon. Roads forking from Haxton bridge, however, give easy access to it. Until c. 1847 the Avon was crossed at Haxton by a ford and a footbridge. An iron suspension bridge was then provided which was replaced in 1907 by the present brick bridge.[98] The road along the east side of the river was turnpiked from Amesbury as far as Fittleton in 1762.[99] The ancient Marlborough–Salisbury road, never turnpiked south of Everleigh, ran through the eastern part of the parish. Tracks leading towards it from the village were closed after the Army established its training areas on the plain. A road running east to Everleigh was, however, constructed partly by the Army and remained open for public use in 1976.[1]

Of the two tithings, Haxton, closer to the crossing of the Avon, was the larger and more prosperous in the Middle Ages. Fittleton was closely connected with Coombe in Enford from the 13th century to the 17th.[2] In 1334 the two were taxed together at 26s. 8d. Haxton, at the time part of the liberty of Everleigh, was taxed at 90s.[3] In 1377 Fittleton and Coombe together had 60 poll-tax payers, and Haxton 68.[4] Haxton was sometimes detached from Fittleton for taxation purposes even when the two shared a common lordship and after the liberty of Everleigh had become merged in the hundred of Elstub. In 1545 it was assessed with the parish of

[85] W.R.O., Return of Regns.
[86] H.O. 129/261/2/8.
[87] Educ. of Poor Digest, 1026.
[88] Educ. Enquiry Abstract, 1037.
[89] W.R.O. 651/20.
[90] Return of Non-Provided Schs. 206.
[91] Ex inf. Chief Education Officer, County Hall, Trowbridge.
[92] This article was written in 1976–7.
[93] Maps used include O.S. Maps 1/50,000, sheet 184 (1974 edn.); 1/25,000, 41/14 (1948 edn.), 41/15 (1951 edn.), 41/24 (1948 edn.), 41/25 (1948 edn.); 6″, Wilts. XLVII

(1889 and later edns.), XLVIII (1883 and later edns.); Geol. Surv. Map 1″, drift, sheet 282 (1959 edn.).
[94] V.C.H. Wilts. i (1), 140, 176.
[95] W.A.M. xxxviii. 235, 257.
[96] V.C.H. Wilts. i (1), 71.
[97] W.A.S. Libr., Revd. J. Wilkinson's par. hist. colls. no. 13.
[98] Ibid. no. 16; W.I. Scrapbk. (1956), penes Col. R. S. D. Maunsell, Fittleton Man.
[99] V.C.H. Wilts. iv. 257, 270.
[1] Ibid. 266.
[2] See p. 144.
[3] V.C.H. Wilts. iv. 299.
[4] Ibid. 308.

Ham at £4 18s. Fittleton alone was then rated at 46s. 8d.[5] In 1576 the two together paid £6 10s.[6]

Only twice in the 19th century did the Census enumerators return separate population figures for the two tithings.[7] In 1811 the population of Haxton was 139 and that of Fittleton 110. In 1841 Haxton had 161 people and Fittleton 175, but the larger number at Fittleton may be accounted for by the 15 people living in tents, perhaps casual agricultural workers. In 1871 the population of the parish was 394. It then declined until in 1911 it was 308. After the establishment of an airfield in 1913, the population rose and was 480 in 1921. It thereafter dropped and was 265 in 1971.[8]

The airfield was made in 1913 for No. 3 Squadron of the recently formed Royal Flying Corps.[9] It lies along the boundary between Fittleton and Figheldean with buildings in both parishes. Until the site was ready service personnel were housed in the former cavalry school at Netheravon, and perhaps for that reason the airfield has always been called Netheravon airfield. For a short while in 1914 it was used for training as an annexe of the Central Flying School at Upavon, but for most of the First World War it was an operational base. After the war it was again used for training and became No. 1 Flying Training School. In 1939 it was renamed No. 1 Service Flying Training School and became a centre for glider training. Between 1950 and 1952 the station was placed on a care and maintenance basis and certain specialist sections of the police force, including that concerned with dog handling, were trained there. In 1952 it became the depot for the R.A.F. police wing. In 1963 it was transferred to the War Department, and in 1976 was the headquarters of the Army Flying Corps.[10]

The villages of Haxton and Fittleton lie along a loop road branching from the Amesbury–Upavon road and along short extensions towards Haxton bridge and Figheldean. Within the loop lie the parks belonging to Fittleton Manor, in 1976 rough fields with some fine trees, but partly built over with council housing. The northern end of the loop road, or village street, may be the road called the 'Weende' in the 14th century, alongside which the lord of the manor had a grange with residential quarters.[11] The church, rectory-house, and manor-house stand close together at the northern end of the street. Lining the street are several houses and cottages of 17th- or 18th-century date. Some are thatched and the varied use of brick, flint, and chalk block, often in combination and in horizontal bands or chequer patterns, is a feature in the village. Here and there stand walls with exposed timber frames infilled with brick. Some of the houses bear dates, among them

no. 341 Haxton which has the dates 1671 and 1691, and no. 322 Lower Street, Haxton, 1774. The house almost opposite Fittleton Manor, called in 1976 the Green Vine, was formerly the Green Dragon inn.[12] With its chequered flint work, thatched roof, and brick and chalk walls it is a typical example of the building style of the village. Some walls of plastered cob survive along the street.

MANORS AND OTHER ESTATES. Vitel, thought to be a well-to-do thegn, held Fittleton in 1066.[13] Robert son of Gerald held it in 1086 and was succeeded by his nephew William de Roumare (created earl of Lincoln c. 1141).[14] William founded the cell, later priory, of Neufmarché (Seine Maritime), and it may have been he who endowed it with an estate in Fittleton.[15] William's grandson William de Roumare, earl of Lincoln, died without issue c. 1198 and *FITTLETON* was granted by the king to Hubert de Burgh (created earl of Kent in 1226, d. 1243), who held it in 1242 as of his honor of Camel (Som.).[16] Hubert's son John surrendered the honor with the lands attached to it to Edward I who granted the overlordship of Fittleton to his own son Edmund (d. 1330), created earl of Kent in 1321.[17] The overlordship passed with the earldom of Kent to John, earl of Kent (d. 1352), and was held by his widow Elizabeth until her death in 1411.[18] Thereupon the overlordship was divided between Joan, sister of John, earl of Kent (d. 1352), and Thomas Montagu, earl of Salisbury (d. 1428), husband of Eleanor, a grand-niece of that John.[19] No further reference to the divided overlordship has been found, and thereafter Fittleton was held in chief.

In 1086 Fittleton was held of Robert son of Gerald by Rainer.[20] There were apparently three estates held of the de Burghs, one by Baldwin de Ver, another by Simon of Coombe, and the third by the prior of Neufmarché.[21] After Hubert de Burgh's death Baldwin's land was granted by Henry III to Adam Cok to be held in chief at fee farm.[22] Adam granted it c. 1252 to Robert Pipard, husband of his daughter and heir Agnes.[23] By 1255 Robert had died and by 1275 Agnes had married Henry of Candover.[24] She died in 1275 without issue and her land in Fittleton was granted by the king to Henry of Candover for life.[25] Henry was dead in 1279 when the king granted the estate to Richard of Coombe at fee farm for a rent of £12.[26] The estate was reckoned to be a third of the manor. The rent had been reduced to £10 by 1467 and is last mentioned in 1484.[27]

Richard of Coombe already held land in Fittleton

[5] *Taxation Lists* (W.R.S. x), 3.   [6] Ibid. 123.
[7] Unless stated, figures from *V.C.H. Wilts.* iv. 348.
[8] *Census,* 1971.
[9] Unless stated, inf. from Air Hist. Branch, Lond.
[10] Ex inf. the incumbent, the Revd. J. E. Jackson, Netheravon Vicarage.
[11] *Cat. Anct. D.* iii, C 3073.
[12] Robert Finch, *Netheravon and Fittleton Guide* (1968), 18.   [13] *V.C.H. Wilts.* ii, pp. 67, 153.
[14] Ibid. p. 153; *Complete Peerage,* s.v. Lincoln.
[15] F. A. Cazel, Junr., 'Norman and Wessex Chart. of Roumare Fam.', *Early Medieval Miscellany for D. M. Stenton* (P.R.S. n.s. xxxvi), 78; see below.
[16] Cazel, op. cit. 78; *Bk. of Fees,* ii. 717.
[17] Cazel, op. cit. 78; *Cal. Inq. p.m.* vii, p. 231.

[18] *Complete Peerage,* s.v. Kent; *Cal. Inq. p.m.* x, p. 57; C 137/224 no. 35.
[19] C 139/66 no. 43; *Cal. Close,* 1409–13, 247–50.
[20] *V.C.H. Wilts.* ii, p. 153.
[21] *Bk. of Fees,* ii. 717; *Rot. Hund.* (Rec. Com.), ii (1), 258.
[22] *Cal. Pat.* 1232–47, 421; *Rot. Hund.* (Rec. Com.), ii (1), 230.
[23] *Cal. Chart. R.* 1226–57, 400.
[24] *Rot. Hund.* (Rec. Com.), ii (1), 230, 258; *Wilts. Inq. p.m.* 1242–1326 (Index Libr.), 123.
[25] *Wilts. Inq. p.m.* 1242–1326 (Index Libr.), 106; *Cal. Pat.* 1272–81, 135.
[26] *Cal. Chart. R.* 1257–1300, 221.
[27] *Cal. Pat.* 1467–77, 41; *Cal. Close,* 1476–85, 375.

A HISTORY OF WILTSHIRE

in 1275, perhaps that held by Simon of Coombe of
Hubert de Burgh in 1242.[28] The Richard of Coombe
who died c. 1293, besides the land of Henry of
Candover later sometimes called the manor of
King's Fee, held the estate in Fittleton, reckoned
at two-thirds of the manor, which the prior of
Neufmarché held of the honor of Camel in 1275.[29]
A fee farm rent of £8 was due to the prior. It was
still due in 1415–16,[30] but in the following year
was transferred to the priory of Sheen (Surr.),
which was founded in 1414 and endowed with the
temporalities of Neufmarché.[31]

Richard of Coombe was succeeded in both
estates by his son Simon who died c. 1300 and was
followed by a posthumous son Richard.[32] Richard
died c. 1329 and the two estates were delivered to
his widow Maud for their son Richard, then a
minor.[33] In 1352 Richard, then Sir Richard of
Coombe (d. 1361), enfeoffed Robert of Ramsbury,
his mother's second husband, with the estate held
in chief.[34] Some years later he granted the rest of
the manor to William Holbeach, citizen of London.[35]
Robert of Ramsbury died in 1362 and his son John
relinquished King's Fee to Holbeach and his wife
Maud.[36]

Holbeach died in 1367 and the combined estate
passed like the manor of Coombe in Enford to his
widow Maud.[37] By 1384 Maud had sold it to Robert
Dyneley and his wife Margaret.[38] Robert died in
1395 having settled Fittleton on Margaret.[39]
Margaret married secondly Sir Percival Sowdan,
who was probably dead by 1421,[40] and in 1427 she
and her son Robert Dyneley sold the manor to
William Darell.[41]

Fittleton then passed like Coombe in Enford in
the Darell family to Sir Edward Darell (d. 1549)
and then to his son William (d. 1589) who sold the
manor in two parts.[42] He sold the part once known
as King's Fee in 1558 to George Fettiplace. Fettiplace's grandson John, of Coln St. Aldwyn (Glos.),
sold it in 1650 to William Adlam who sold it in 1665
to William Beach.[43] It passed to Beach's grandson
Thomas Beach (d. 1753).

Darell sold the other part of the manor in 1588 to
William Stubbs.[44] From Stubbs it passed in 1599
to Thomas Jeay (d. 1623) who was rector of Fittleton.[45] Thomas was followed by his son, Sir
Thomas.[46] From Sir Thomas the land passed to
Mary, daughter of his brother Benjamin.[47] Mary
married Henry Edes (d. 1703), a canon of Chichester.[48]
They were followed by Henry's sister Mary, wife
of John Briggs, and John and Mary conveyed the

estate in 1721 to George Parker.[49] By 1734 it had
passed to Thomas Francis and his wife Mary who
in that year conveyed it to Thomas Beach.[50]

From Thomas Beach Fittleton passed to his son
William (d. 1790) and then like Cormayles manor
in Netheravon to Sir Michael Edward Hicks Beach,
Bt. (later Earl St. Aldwyn, d. 1916).[51] Sir Michael
sold it to the War Department in 1898.[52]

The manor-house was repurchased by Michael
Hugh Hicks Beach, son of Sir Michael (d. 1916), in
1901. Hicks Beach, by then Viscount Quenington,
was killed in battle, shortly before the death of his
father, leaving an infant son and heir. The manor-
house then had a succession of tenants until 1946
when Lady Victoria (d. 1963) and Lady Susan Hicks
Beach (d. 1965) went to live in it.[53] After the death
of the last the house was bought by Colonel R. S. D.
Maunsell, the owner in 1977.

The western side of the manor-house, in 1977
largely incorporated in the service wing, is an
L-shaped building which may date from the early
17th century. A new block was built on the east side
later in the same century, and the court formed
between the two blocks was built over in 1902 after
the house was acquired by M. H. Hicks Beach. The
later-17th-century block has a principal elevation of
five bays in banded and panelled brick with
mullioned and transomed windows and a coved
cornice. The interior is notable for the quality of
the fittings, which include a late-17th-century oak
staircase with twisted balusters, and for several
panelled rooms of various dates.

In 1294 Robert Mackrell granted the remainder
of a small estate in Fittleton and Coombe, then held
by Thomas Mackrell and his wife, to Nicholas of
Warwick and his wife Joan.[54] Soon afterwards Peter
the Chamberlain enlarged the holding of Nicholas
and Joan in Fittleton with a grant of more land.[55]
In 1324 William, son of Nicholas, conveyed an estate,
probably the same, to John of Hastings, Lord
Hastings (d. 1325).[56] John's son Laurence (d. 1348)
was created earl of Pembroke in 1339.[57] He granted
the land to Richard Field for life.[58] On Richard's
death in 1361 it reverted to Laurence's widow Agnes
(d. 1368), and from her it passed to her son John
Hastings, earl of Pembroke (d. 1375).[59] On the death
in 1389 of John's son John, earl of Pembroke, his
lands and earldom were taken into the king's hands.[60]
The Fittleton estate was at the time held of Robert
Dyneley, lord of the manor of Fittleton. Edward
Seymour, Viscount Beauchamp (later duke of
Somerset, d. 1552), held a small estate, perhaps the

[28] Rot. Hund. (Rec. Com.), ii (1), 258.
[29] Wilts. Inq. p.m. 1242–1326 (Index Libr.), 197; Rot. Hund. (Rec. Com.), ii (1), 258. Called King's Fee in 1394: Cat. Anct. D. i, C 777.
[30] S.C. 6/1249/21.
[31] S.C. 6/1249/22; Dugdale, Mon. vi (1), 29.
[32] Wilts. Inq. p.m. 1242–1326 (Index Libr.), 277–8.
[33] Ibid. 1327–77, 44–5; Cal. Fine R. 1327–37, 144.
[34] Cat. Anct. D. iii, C 3073; B.L. Harl. MS. 1623, f. 20.
[35] Cat. Anct. D. vi, C 6376; B.L. Harl. MS. 1623, f. 20.
[36] Wilts. Inq. p.m. 1327–77 (Index Libr.), 316; Cat. Anct. D. i, C 1676.
[37] Wilts. Inq. p.m. 1327–77 (Index Libr.), 342–3.
[38] Cal. Inq. p.m. xvi, p. 8; Cal. Pat. 1388–92, 145.
[39] C 136/83 no. 11.
[40] Phillipps, Wilts. Inst. i. 102. He was certainly dead in 1423: Cat. Anct. D. vi, C 6033.
[41] Cat. Anct. D. ii, C 2677.
[42] See p. 121; Williamstrip Mun. MTD/125/2.
[43] Williamstrip Mun. MTD/125/2.
[44] C.P. 25(2)/241/31 Eliz. I Trin.
[45] Wilts. Inq. p.m. 1625–49 (Index Libr.), 3; Phillipps, Wilts. Inst. i. 233.
[46] Wilts. Inq. p.m. 1625–49 (Index Libr.), 3.
[47] Williamstrip Mun. MTD/59/4a–5a.
[48] Le Neve, Fasti Eccl. Angl. ii. 76.
[49] Glos. R.O., D 2440, box 13, deeds, 1600–1848.
[50] Williamstrip Mun. MTD/125/2.
[51] See pp. 169–70.
[52] Ex inf. Defence Land Agent, Durrington.
[53] W.I. Scrapbk. (1956).
[54] Feet of F. 1272–1327 (W.R.S. i), p. 39.
[55] Ibid. p. 44.
[56] Ibid. p. 111.
[57] Complete Peerage, s.v. Hastings, Pembroke.
[58] V.C.H. Wilts. vii. 190, where date of d. is incorrect.
[59] Wilts. Inq. p.m. 1327–77 (Index Libr.), 329; Cal. Close, 1364–8, 27.
[60] Cal. Inq. p.m. xvi, pp. 343, 357.

STANDLYNCH

Trafalgar House, built in 1733, with wings added in 1766

EAST KNOYLE

Clouds House, built 1881–3, as reconstructed after a fire of 1889

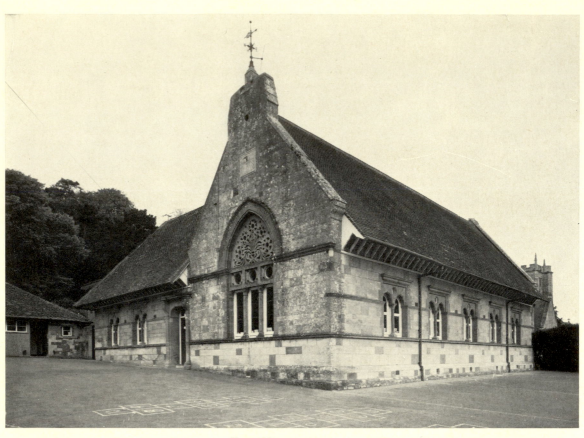

EAST KNOYLE SCHOOL
Built 1872–3

EVERLEIGH MANOR
The entrance hall, rebuilt 1882–3

same one, in Fittleton in 1536.[61] How he acquired it is not known. The estate amounted to fewer than 50 a., but seems to have had some special significance, for payments were made by Seymour for the upkeep of a house and farm there.[62] In 1536 it was leased to William Devenish, his wife Isabel, and Thomas their son for their lives.[63] A quit-rent was paid for the estate to Sir Edward Darell, lord of Fittleton manor.[64] Seymour's son, the earl of Hertford (d. 1621), was a free tenant of the manor at the end of the 16th century and was receiving a rent from his land there at his death.[65] The later descent of the estate has not been traced.

Besides the estates which became united under the Coombes, later called the manor of Fittleton, an estate was held in 1330 by Peter of Fosbury of the same overlord, Edmund, earl of Kent.[66] Peter was dead in 1373[67] and it has not been possible to trace his successors in the land. It was last mentioned in 1411 when the overlordship of Fittleton was divided between the heirs of John, earl of Kent (d. 1352), and that of Peter's land was allotted to Thomas, earl of Salisbury (d. 1428), and his wife Eleanor.[68]

Haxton is not mentioned in Domesday Book, but like Everleigh it was in 1172–3 in the hands of Robert, earl of Leicester (d. 1190).[69] With the rest of the Beaumont family's lands HAXTON formed part of the honor of Leicester in the 12th century,[70] and with the honor passed to Edmund, fourth son of Henry III, created earl of Lancaster in 1267.[71] It descended with the earldom, later dukedom, of Lancaster, and with the duchy of Lancaster was attached to the Crown on the accession of Henry IV.[72] The duchy's overlordship of Haxton is last heard of in 1461.[73]

In 1297 there were two estates in Haxton held of the honor of Leicester.[74] One was held by Amaury de St. Amand (d. 1285) and was merged with his land in Netheravon.[75] The other was held by John Fleming who granted it in 1303 to Stephen of Brigmerston.[76] Stephen acquired more land in Haxton from John le Lymbernere in 1310.[77] George Brigmerston, Stephen's son and heir, granted two-thirds of the manor in 1317 to Philip de la Beche for life with the reversion of the other third after the death of Stephen's widow.[78] Soon afterwards Philip's lands were forfeited to the Crown.[79] The Brigmerstons' interest in the manor then seems to have been lost, although in 1400 it was thought necessary for John Herriard, great-grandson of Stephen, to renounce all right to two-thirds of it.[80] By 1331 the lands had been restored to Philip de la Beche, who in that year settled them on himself for life with successive remainders to his heirs and to those of his brother John.[81] By 1338 Philip had been succeeded by his son Nicholas.[82] Nicholas died without issue in 1345,[83] and Haxton passed like the manor of Beaumys in Swallowfield (Berks.) to his brother Edmund de la Beche (d. 1364), archdeacon of Berkshire, for life, with reversion to Nicholas's heirs.[84] In 1364 the heirs were Andrew Sackville and Edmund Danvers, sons respectively of Joan and Alice who were daughters of John (d. 1328) the elder brother of Nicholas and Edmund, and John Duyn, grandson of Isabel FitzEllis who was a daughter of the elder John de la Beche.[85]

The descent of Haxton for about the following 30 years is obscure, but it seems that the thirds which passed to Andrew Sackville and Edmund Danvers were amalgamated,[86] and by 1394 had been acquired by Robert Dyneley and Margaret his wife, already lords of Fittleton.[87] The third which passed to John Duyn has not been traced, but it may have gone to Sir William Hankeford (d. 1423), lord of the manor of Netheravon with Haxton.[88] Margaret, after the death of Robert in 1395, married Sir Percival Sowdan and after his death she and her son Robert Dyneley exchanged Haxton in 1429 with William Darell and his wife Elizabeth for land elsewhere.[89]

Haxton then passed like Fittleton in the Darell family and in 1548 was held by Sir Edward Darell (d. 1549).[90] It was sold by William Darell (d. 1589) to Robert Reeve (d. 1609) who in 1585 settled it on his son Robert, then about to marry Alice Kettleby.[91] Robert died in 1626 and under the terms of a settlement was succeeded at Haxton by James Clark, then aged eight, son of his daughter Kettleby and her husband Thomas Clark.[92] James was followed by his brother Henry who died holding Haxton in 1712.[93] During the ownership of the two Clarks Haxton farm was much enlarged by various grants, including one in 1689 of Hart's living, described as a third of Haxton farm.[94] It may be that Hart's living represents the third which passed to John Duyn in 1364 and has not been certainly traced thereafter.

Haxton passed from Henry Clark to his cousin Mary Gladman who married Abraham Gapper. The Gappers were followed by their younger son Robert and he by his son William (d. 1811) who in 1803 sold it to John Perkins. By his will dated 1819 Perkins devised Haxton to his son John. The younger John died in 1846, unmarried and intestate, and the farm was bought from his four sisters by Sir Michael Hicks Beach, Bt. (d. 1854).[95] It was sold with Fittleton by Sir Michael's son in 1898 to the War Department.[96]

[61] Longleat Mun., rent roll, 1536, ff. 271v.–272v.
[62] Hist. MSS. Com. 58, *Bath*, iv, pp. 326–7, 329.
[63] Longleat Mun., rent roll, 1536, f. 271v.
[64] Ibid. f. 272v.; Williamstrip Mun. MCR/7.
[65] *Wilts. Inq. p.m.* 1625–49 (Index Libr.), 27.
[66] *Cal. Inq. p.m.* vii, p. 231.
[67] Ibid. xiii, p. 139.   [68] See above.
[69] *Pipe R.* 1173 (P.R.S. xix), 103; see above, p. 136.
[70] For an acct. of the formation of the honor see Levi Fox, 'Honor of Leic. 1066–1399', *E.H.R.* liv. 386–7.
[71] *Cal. Inq. p.m.* iii, p. 307; *Complete Peerage*, vii. 379.
[72] *Complete Peerage*, vii. 379.
[73] *Cal. Fine R.* 1461–71, 141.
[74] *Cal. Inq. p.m.* iii, p. 307.   [75] See p. 170.
[76] *Feet of F.* 1272–1327 (W.R.S. i), p. 47.
[77] Ibid. p. 78.   [78] *Cat. Anct. D.* ii, C 2504.
[79] *Rot. Parl.* i. 395.
[80] Hist. MSS. Com. 78, *Hastings*, i, p. 242.
[81] *Feet of F.* 1327–77 (W.R.S. xxix), p. 30.
[82] *V.C.H. Berks.* iv. 4.   [83] *Cal. Close*, 1343–5, 529.
[84] *V.C.H. Berks.* iii. 270.
[85] *Cal. Close*, 1364–8, 107; 1381–5, 68–9.
[86] Ibid. 1364–8, 208, 271.
[87] *Cat. Anct. D.* i, C 777.   [88] See below.
[89] *Cat. Anct. D.* ii, C 2625.
[90] E 301/58/65; see above.
[91] C 142/307 no. 37.
[92] *Wilts. Inq. p.m.* 1625–49 (Index Libr.), 36.
[93] Glos. R.O., D 2440, box 37, bdle. (1689)–1852; *Endowed Char. Wilts.* (S. Div.), 173.
[94] Glos. R.O., D 2440, box 37, bdle. (1689)–1852.
[95] Ibid.   [96] See above.

The main range of Haxton Manor was probably built in the later 17th century. It has a principal east front of five bays with walls of red brick with bands and panels of black brick. The north gable is decorated with a chequer of chalk block and flint. To the south there is an 18th-century addition of two bays and there are later additions on the south and west. A porch was added in the early 19th century and the interior was extensively refitted at various dates in that century, perhaps after the farm was acquired by the Hicks Beach family in 1846.

The endowments of the free chapel of Haxton, consisting largely of tithes from certain lands of Haxton farm, passed to the Crown at the Dissolution.[97] In 1606 that estate, sometimes called the *PORTIONARY*, was granted to Thomas Emmerson.[98] From Emmerson it was bought by Thomas Jeay (d. 1623), lord of Fittleton manor.[99] By his will Thomas devised the Portionary to one of his younger sons, Benjamin, from whom it passed, like Fittleton manor, to his daughter Mary.[1] The Portionary then followed the same descent as that manor. The tithes were commuted for a rent-charge of £64 16s. in 1840.[2]

ECONOMIC HISTORY. Fittleton, rated at 10 hides, had land for 12 ploughs in 1086. The demesne measured 5 hides and 1 virgate, and on it were 3 ploughs and 6 serfs. Apart from the demesne there were 6 villeins and 12 bordars with 3 ploughs. The area of meadow, 3 a., was small for an estate of 10 hides. The pasture measured 1 league by $\frac{1}{2}$ league. In 1066 and 1086 the estate was worth £12.[3]

Areas of common pasture on two downs are mentioned in 1278.[4] From 1279 until c. 1360 the two estates in Fittleton were treated as separate units.[5] In 1329 that known as King's Fee was estimated to have 161 a. of arable, a meadow, and pasture on Bull down for 300 sheep. There were four customary tenants who held 2½ virgates for a money rent and performed no labour service. There were also three cottars paying rent. The estate was valued at c. £10. The estate held of the prior of Neufmarché had at the same date 322 a. of arable, 2 a. of meadow, and pasture on 'Lyntedown' for 600 sheep. There were free tenants and four customary tenants paying rent and performing no labour service. There were also eight rent-paying cottars. On that estate, but apparently not then on the other, there was a capital messuage with a garden and a dovecot. At £23 it was the more highly valued of the two estates.[6] Later extents credit the King's Fee estate with 300 a. of arable, 2 a. of meadow, and 600 a. of pasture. A house is also mentioned.[7]

When Fittleton, with Haxton, and Coombe in Enford, passed to the Dyneleys in the late 14th century the distinction between the two estates in Fittleton disappeared and they were leased together as a single demesne farm.[8] Sheep farming predominated, as is to be expected in a parish with such a large proportion of downland. In 1307 a theft of 200 sheep from a single farm occurred.[9] In 1329 there was pasture on the two estates for a demesne flock of at least 900 sheep.[10] Deaths among the flock c. 1340 were said to have caused much hardship and the inability to pay tithe or tax.[11] In 1386–7 agistment was paid to the lord of the manor for 780 sheep in the fold of 'Northendeworth', and for 164 in the fold of Fittleton. The demesne flock numbered over 670 sheep. In the same year oats were bought to provide gruel for the farm servants, possibly a purchase made necessary by a dearth of home-grown crops.[12]

In 1550 there were three freeholders and eleven customary tenants of Fittleton manor.[13] The small freehold estate of Edward Seymour, later the Protector Somerset,[14] included 34 a. of arable, distributed in small parcels among nine fields, and pasture in common for 70 sheep. There was also pasture for six beasts.[15] The estate was administered with Seymour's other Wiltshire estates by his steward, and a bailiff was employed at Fittleton. Among the farm servants in 1536 were two carters, a shepherd, a smith, and a housekeeper.[16]

Early in the 18th century downland was being converted to arable, thereby reducing the number of sheep stints.[17] Field names occurring in the 17th and 18th centuries include Summer, Mileball, Warborough, Greenway, and Blissmore fields.[18] Detailed regulations for the husbandry of the common fields, and for rights of way to the downs and fields from the village, were made in the manor courts of the 17th and 18th centuries.[19] In 1735 the lord of the manor, Thomas Beach (d. 1753), was presented for driving his sheep along the wrong route.[20] By 1777 Fittleton, then all in the hands of William Beach (d. 1790), had been organized as two farms. Home farm, based in the village, had 726 a. Down farm, with buildings later known as Beach's Barn, had 702 a.[21] The total area of the manor, including 47 a. of glebe, was 1,477 a.[22] Fittleton was inclosed in 1796 when two allotments, totalling 678 a., were made to the lord of the manor, and one of 32 a. was made to the rector.[23]

In 1839 of the land within Fittleton tithing 832 a. were arable and 552 a. downland. There were 10 a. of wood and only 51 a. of meadow.[24] In 1846 Sir Michael Hicks Beach, Bt. (d. 1854), added Haxton farm, measuring some 970 a., to his estate and the three farms were thenceforth farmed under

[97] See pp. 148–9.
[98] C 66/1711 m. 11. Here, as in many other instances, the grant, although of the portion only, is said to be of the free chapel, which was often called the free chapel of Fittleton. [99] *W.A.M.* xi. 259–60.
[1] *Wilts. Inq. p.m.* 1625–49 (Index Libr.), 3, where Benjamin is incorrectly called Bartholomew; see above.
[2] W.R.O., Tithe Award.
[3] *V.C.H. Wilts.* ii, p. 153.
[4] *Cat. Anct. D.* iii, C 3625. [5] See above.
[6] *Wilts. Inq. p.m.* 1327–77 (Index Libr.), 44–5.
[7] Ibid. 228, 316. [8] S.C. 6/1249/20–2.
[9] *Cal. Pat.* 1301–7, 543.

[10] *Wilts. Inq. p.m.* 1327–77 (Index Libr.), 44–5.
[11] *Inq. Non.* (Rec. Com.), 170. [12] S.C. 6/1249/20.
[13] S.C. 12/1/35. [14] See above.
[15] Longleat Mun., rent roll, 1536, ff. 271v.–272v.
[16] Hist. MSS. Com. 58, *Bath*, iv, pp. 324, 327.
[17] Sar. Dioc. R.O., Glebe Terrier, 1705.
[18] Ibid. 1629; Williamstrip Mun. EMP/34.
[19] Williamstrip Mun. MCR/2/13; MCR/2/15; MCR/2/38.
[20] Ibid. MCR/2/38.
[21] Ibid. EMP/34; EMS/4/1.
[22] Ibid. EMS/4/1.
[23] W.R.O., Inclosure Award.
[24] Ibid. Tithe Award.

the Hicks Beach family by tenant farmers. Home farm and Beach's Barn farm were held by the same tenant. Many improvements were undertaken, including the building of new barns in the village and on the downs. Part of the down towards Sidbury hill was ploughed. Large flocks of Hampshire Downs were kept. An allotment system was introduced for the benefit of the poor.[25] After it was sold to the War Department in 1898[26] the land of the parish was farmed subject to certain restrictions.

Nothing is known of agriculture in Haxton until 1384 when for the first time it shared a common lordship with Fittleton.[27] Under Robert Dyneley (d. 1395) the demesne farm was leased, to a different tenant from that of Fittleton, for c. £11.[28] Certain land of Haxton farm lying in the common fields was subject to special tithe arrangements.[29] In the early 18th century there were some 57 a. of such land, lying in fairly large blocks bounded by linches. The rest of the arable land of the farm lay dispersed in smaller strips in the furlongs into which the fields were divided.[30] About 1800 the farm measured 908 a., including 492 a. on Great down and 64 a. on Little down. The tenantry down lay along the southern parish boundary. Besides the farmhouse, five houses or cottages and a blacksmith's shop went with the estate.[31] Haxton was inclosed in 1839 when John Perkins (d. 1846), lord of the manor, received an allotment of 224 a.[32] In that year 645 a. were arable, 992 a. downland, and 36 a. meadow.[33] Like Fittleton Haxton had but little meadow land.

In 1976 the land of the former Home farm in Fittleton was farmed by Mr. R. L. Spencer with his farm in Figheldean. Most of the Fittleton land was licensed only for grazing because of the requirements of the Army.[34] In the north-east part of the parish the land of the former Down farm or Beach's Barn farm was worked by Mr. W. E. Cave, of Lower House farm in Everleigh. Its use was likewise restricted. Haxton farm, farmed by Mr. J. Lamont, had some land across the river in Netheravon. Some of the lower ground could be used freely for pasture, but the higher land was farmed subject to military needs.

There was a mill paying 22s. 6d. in Fittleton in 1086.[35] A mill on the estate held of the prior of Neufmarché is mentioned in 1329.[36] In 1386, after the two estates in Fittleton had been merged, there was a mill on each. One was leased for £4, the other for 15s.[37] The two mills continue to be mentioned until 1417.[38] By 1352 there was a fishery in the mill-pond of

the King's Fee estate.[39] It occurs in records concerning that estate throughout the 14th century.[40] In 1416–17 it was leased.[41] Fish for sport were bred in tanks in the river at Haxton in 1976.[42]

LOCAL GOVERNMENT. In 1275 the earl of Lancaster claimed gallows and the assize of bread and of ale in Haxton as part of the honor of Leicester.[43] No record of a separate court for Haxton has been found and, when it shared a common lordship with Fittleton, Haxton's affairs were presumably dealt with in the courts of Fittleton. In the 16th century the court was sometimes called the court for Fittleton and Haxton.[44]

Henry of Candover (d. by 1279), to whom the king granted the estate in Fittleton later called King's Fee, held a court for his free tenants and exercised certain franchisal jurisdiction.[45] Margaret, relict of Robert Dyneley (d. 1395), and her husband Sir Percival Sowdan held combined views of frankpledge and manor courts for Fittleton and for Coombe in Enford.[46] After Fittleton had passed to the Darells in the earlier 15th century, the prior of St. Swithun's, Winchester, lord of Elstub hundred, accused William Darell of usurping his right to hold the view for Fittleton and Coombe.[47] The lords of the manor continued, however, to hold the view.[48]

From the mid 16th century to the mid 18th there is a substantial collection of court records.[49] Sometimes the courts are described as courts leet and baron, but more often as merely courts baron.[50] Business was confined to agrarian regulation, in which sphere the courts were very active in the earlier 18th century.[51] Under the Beaches the court was called a private court baron.[52]

Among the parish records are some overseers' accounts and notes for the period 1691–1835.[53] Fittleton became part of Pewsey poor-law union in 1835.[54]

CHURCH. Fittleton church was mentioned in 1291.[55] In 1953 the rectory was united with Netheravon vicarage. In 1973 Enford was added, and the benefice of Netheravon with Fittleton and Enford was created.[56]

The advowson of Fittleton followed closely, but not exactly, the descent of the manor. The first patron named was Simon of Coombe (d. c. 1300) who presented in 1297.[57] Richard of Casterton, the husband of Simon's relict Alice, presented James of Coombe in 1303, and in the same year Agnes of Coombe, possibly the relict of Richard of Coombe

[25] W.A.S. Libr., Wilkinson's colls. no. 13.
[26] See above.   [27] See above.
[28] S.C. 6/1249/20–2.   [29] See p. 148.
[30] Sar. Dioc. R.O., Glebe Terriers, 1705, 1718.
[31] Glos. R.O., D 2440, boxes 15, 37.
[32] W.R.O., Inclosure Award.
[33] Ibid. Tithe Award.
[34] All inf. in this para. from Defence Land Agent, Durrington.
[35] V.C.H. Wilts. ii, p. 153.
[36] Wilts. Inq. p.m. 1327–77 (Index Libr.), 45.
[37] S.C. 6/1249/20.   [38] S.C. 6/1249/21–2.
[39] Wilts. Inq. p.m. 1327–77 (Index Libr.), 228.
[40] Ibid. 316; Cat. Anct. D. i, C 1676; Cal. Pat. 1385–9, 43.
[41] S.C. 6/1249/22.

[42] For some acct. of the Min. of Defence fishery in the Avon between Fittleton and Netheravon see p. 175.
[43] Rot. Hund. (Rec. Com.), ii (1), 258.
[44] Williamstrip Mun. MCR/7.
[45] Wilts. Inq. p.m. 1242–1326 (Index Libr.), 162.
[46] S.C. 2/208/59.   [47] B.L. Harl. Roll CC. 23.
[48] S.C. 2/208/59 m. 12.
[49] N.R.A. List, Hicks Beach MSS., pt. ii.
[50] Williamstrip Mun. MCR/4b–d; MCR/4i.
[51] See above.
[52] Williamstrip Mun. MCR/2/41.
[53] In the ch.
[54] Poor Law Com. 2nd Rep. 560.
[55] Tax. Eccl. (Rec. Com.), 180.
[56] Ex inf. Dioc. Registrar.
[57] Phillipps, Wilts. Inst. i. 1.

(d. c. 1293) and Simon's mother, and her husband, Adam of Poulshot, presented John of Coombe. John, however, was not instituted.[58] In 1307 Richard of Abingdon, guardian of Simon's son Richard (d. c. 1329), presented John Hambledon. Hambledon may likewise not have been instituted for 2 years later, still during the minority of Richard, the dean of Arches presented him again.[59] In 1315 Agnes of Coombe, Richard's grandmother, presented James of Coombe but once more no institution followed.[60] Richard himself presented in 1322.[61] The king exercised the patronage during the minority of Richard's son Richard (d. 1361).[62] The advowson thenceforth followed the descent of the manor until 1721 except on the following occasions. In 1383 four citizens of London, feoffees for the settlement of the manor on Maud Holbeach, presented.[63] In 1401 William Hornby, feoffee for a settlement on Margaret Dyneley, presented.[64] In 1540 the king exercised the patronage during the minority of Sir Edward Darell (d. 1549).[65] Mary (d. 1598), second wife of that Sir Edward, presented in 1554 when she was the wife of Philip Maunsell.[66] Sir Henry Fortescue, then Mary's husband, presented in 1569; and, although the manor and advowson were sold in 1588, Mary retained her right to the patronage which in 1594 she conceded to Robert Jackson, clerk.[67] William Stubbs, purchaser of manor and advowson in 1588, conveyed both c. 1599 to Thomas Jeay (d. 1623) who was then the incumbent.[68] By his will Thomas devised the next turn to his son William, who apparently presented himself.[69] In 1637 Sir Thomas Jeay, William's eldest brother, conveyed the manor and the advowson to Benjamin (d. by c. 1654), a younger brother.[70] No presentation was made by Benjamin, but a John Jeay, perhaps his brother, presented in 1662.[71] From the Jeays the advowson passed like the manor to John Briggs who sold it in 1721 to Magdalen College, Oxford.[72] The college transferred the patronage to the bishop of Salisbury in 1947.[73] In 1973 the bishop, also patron of Netheravon, was allotted the second and third of three turns to present to the united benefice.[74]

The church was valued at £10 in 1291.[75] In 1535 it was reckoned to be worth nearly £23 net.[76] During the Interregnum a value of £180 was given.[77] The average net income for the three years ending 1831 was £444.[78] The rector had all tithes in Fittleton and Haxton except those which had been appropriated to endow the free chapel of Haxton.[79] When the tithes were commuted in 1840 the rector was awarded a rent-charge of £461.[80] A virgate of glebe belonged to the church in 1291.[81] In 1629 the glebe measured c. 45 a. and the rector had common of pasture for 80 sheep, 5 rother beasts, and 4 horses. [2] At inclosure the rector was allotted 32 a.[83] In 1898 the greater part of the glebe was sold to the War Department and permission was given for the demolition of the tithe barn.[84] The rectory-house was largely rebuilt in 1742 by Robert Merchant (d. 1773), the first Fellow of Magdalen College to be rector.[85] His initials and those of his wife appear above the main doorway. The service wing at the back incorporates part of an earlier house with 17th-century outer walls of brick and flint. The new block, to the east, has a central staircase hall with one room to each side. The walls are of brick with a stone plinth and the east elevation has rusticated stone quions and stone pilasters defining the central bays. The house was extended southwards by two bays by Thomas Philips, another Fellow of Magdalen, rector from 1842 to 1854.[86] At about the same time there was some refitting within the rest of the house. After the benefice was united with that of Netheravon in 1953 the house became a private residence; it has been renamed Fittleton House.

The prior of Neufmarché had a portion of 13s. 4d. from the church.[87] Upon the suppression of the alien priories in the 15th century, that portion and a fee farm rent from an estate in Fittleton[88] were granted to Sheen Priory (Surr.) founded in 1414.[89] The portion is last heard of in 1535, 4 years before the dissolution of Sheen.[90] There is mention in 1291 of a pension, not then being paid, to Walter, clerk (clericus) of one of the lords de Montfort.[91]

A free chapel in Haxton was endowed with the tithes of all corn and of two-thirds of the wool and lambs from lands of Haxton farm called the portionary lands, and with a barn and ½ a.[92] It was served by chaplains who were presented.[93] The advowson in the main followed the descent of Haxton manor. In 1323 and 1324 the king presented because of the forfeiture by Philip de la Beche.[94] In 1324 a presentation was also made by Richard of Coombe, lord of Fittleton manor.[95] Afterwards the advowson was restored to the Beches and in 1339 Nicholas de la Beche (d. 1345) was given licence to grant it to Sandleford Priory (Berks.) in exchange for land in that county.[96] There is no record of presentation by Sandleford, but the priory probably retained the advowson until 1378.[97] On the other hand, when Haxton manor was divided c. 1364 among the three

58 Phillipps, *Wilts. Inst.* i. 5.   59 Ibid. 8, 10.
60 *Reg. Martival* (Cant. & York Soc.), i. 22; Phillipps, *Wilts. Inst.* i. 13.
61 Phillipps, *Wilts. Inst.* i. 19.
62 Ibid. 22.   63 Ibid. 67.
64 Ibid. 87.   65 Ibid. 208.
66 Ibid. 216; *Cal. Pat.* 1547–8, 360–1.
67 Phillipps, *Wilts. Inst.* i. 224, 233.   68 Ibid.
69 Ibid. ii. 12; *W.A.M.* xix. 189.
70 C.P. 25(2)/510/13 Chas. I Mich.
71 Phillipps, *Wilts. Inst.* ii. 25.
72 W. D. Macray, *Reg. Magdalen Coll.* v. 7.
73 Ex inf. Dioc. Registrar.   74 Ibid.
75 *Tax. Eccl.* (Rec. Com.), 180.
76 *Valor Eccl.* (Rec. Com.), ii. 145.
77 *W.A.M.* xl. 299.
78 *Rep. Com. Eccl. Revenues*, 834–5.
79 See below.   80 W.R.O., Tithe Award.
81 *Inq. Non.* (Rec. Com.), 170.
82 Sar. Dioc. R.O., Glebe Terrier.

83 W.R.O., Inclosure Award.
84 Macray, *Reg. Magdalen Coll.* vii. 16, 17.
85 W.A.S. Libr., Wilkinson's colls. no. 50.
86 Finch, *Netheravon and Fittleton*, 17.
87 *Tax. Eccl.* (Rec. Com.), 180. He is frequently and incorrectly called abbot: *Reg. Martival* (Cant. & York Soc.), iii. 30.
88 See p. 144.
89 *V.C.H. Surr.* ii. 89, 92.
90 *Valor Eccl.* (Rec. Com.), ii. 52.
91 *Tax. Eccl.* (Rec. Com.), 180. For the de Montforts, earls of Leics., see *Complete Peerage*, vii. 537–47.
92 C 66/1711 m. 11.
93 Phillipps, *Wilts. Inst.* i. 21, 30, 100, 102, 111, 125, 171, 179.
94 Ibid. 21; see above.
95 *Reg. Martival* (Cant. & York Soc.), i. 295.
96 *Cal. Pat.* 1338–40, 243. For Sandleford see *V.C.H. Berks.* ii. 86.
97 Mun. St. Geo.'s Chap., Windsor, XV. 54, 164.

heirs of Nicholas de la Beche (d. 1345) the advowson was apparently likewise divided.[98] By 1411 two-thirds of it had been attached to the two-thirds of the manor which had passed to the Dyneleys,[99] and in 1411 and 1413 Sir Percival Sowdan, then the husband of Margaret Dyneley, presented.[1] Shortly afterwards Sir William Hankeford (d. 1423), lord of the manor of Netheravon with Haxton, claimed a right to present. His claim suggests that he had acquired the third of Haxton manor which cannot be traced after the division of c. 1364, and that a third of the advowson passed with it. Sir William was successful in extinguishing any right that the prior of Sandleford might still have had,[2] and his dispute with the Dyneleys was settled by an agreed stipulation that he should have every third turn.[3] Two-thirds of the advowson passed with Haxton manor to the Darells and Sir William Darell presented in 1434.[4] In 1487 Sir John Sapcotes (d. 1501) and his wife Elizabeth, relict of Fulk Bourchier, Lord FitzWarin (d. 1479), lord of Netheravon with Haxton, presented.[5] The next and last presentation was in 1497 by Sir Edward Darell (d. 1530), lord of Fittleton and Haxton manors.[6] The chapel appears to have fallen out of use at a very early date and no record of it serving any religious function survives. A house (domus) to which tithes valued at 40s. were attached, which was held by Robert de la Beche in 1341, may be a reference to all that then remained.[7] The so-called free chapel, then no more than a portion, was suppressed in 1548. Robert Eve, who may then have held Haxton farm, was lessee of the portion for which he paid £3 5s., to the lord of the manor although John Blyth, presented in 1497, was still said to be the incumbent.[8] Early in the 18th century the chapel's site was said to be in the Bury, a field south of the churchyard.[9]

Several patrons of Fittleton presented members of their own families to the living. There were at least two Coombes, two Dyneleys, and three Jeays.[10] The first incumbent to be named was in 1294 given royal protection to travel for a year. He was then also serving the church of Warlingham (Surr.).[11] In 1302 the rector was given leave to study in Oxford for two years on condition that he provided a substitute and made a payment of alms.[12] Leave of absence was given to John Hambledon in 1310 and 1311. He overstayed that leave, however, and in 1316 the rector of Everleigh was placed in charge of Fittleton. Hambledon, charged with immoral conduct, resigned.[13] William Bird, rector in 1511, and vicar of Bradford on Avon in 1535, was attainted in 1540 with Walter, Lord Hungerford (d. 1540), his friend and patron, on charges of

treason. He was replaced in both places by Thomas Morley, suffragan bishop of Marlborough.[14] William Jeay, who followed his father as rector in 1623, was accused of royalist activities and scandalous conduct and was removed from the living in 1648. For a time the rectory was held by Matthew Hind and Jeay was imprisoned. When Jeay died, however, in 1659 the family's connexion with the church was restored when William's brother Stephen was presented.[15] After 1721 several Fellows of Magdalen College were rectors. In 1783 Stephen Jenner, vice-president of the college and the brother of the discoverer of vaccination, held the benefice but employed a curate.[16] Another Fellow, John Parkinson, also held the benefices of Brocklesby and East Ravendale (both Lincs.) and in 1837 was licensed to be absent from Fittleton.[17]

Two sermons were endowed. 'The Revd. Mr. Jay', by will of c. 1693, directed that part of a bequest of £80 should pay for an annual sermon.[18] In 1803 the preacher received 6s. 8d.[19] In 1962 he was paid half that amount.[20] From the rent-charge imposed on Haxton farm by Henry Clark (d. 1712), 10s. was allotted for an annual sermon on the anniversary of Clark's baptism (8 December). The beneficiaries of Clark's other charities were required to attend.[21] The payment continued after Haxton farm was bought by the War Department in 1898.[22]

In 1783 two Sunday services were held, and there were about 20 or 30 communicants in the parish.[23] On Census Sunday in 1851 41 attended morning service and 86 that in the afternoon.[24] No significant change had taken place by 1864 when the congregation was said to remain constant.[25] One service was held every Sunday in 1976 when the rector had two other churches to serve.[26]

The church of *ALL SAINTS* is built of flint and rubble, mostly rendered, with dressings of ashlar, and has a chancel, aisled nave with south porch, and west tower. The 12th-century bowl of the font[27] is not notably older than the earliest identifiable part of the structure, which is the 13th-century chancel arch. The early-14th-century tower arch may indicate the original length of the nave, and the slightly later arcades, which extend further west, may be part of a never completed enlargement. Also in the 14th century the chancel was refenestrated and probably enlarged. New windows were inserted in the aisles in the 15th century and the nave roof was renewed in the 16th century. Some repairs were undertaken in 1841 and a new three-light window was inserted in the north aisle. No architect was employed and the work was

98 *Cal. Close*, 1364–8, 208.
1 Phillipps, *Wilts. Inst.* i. 100, 102.
3 B.L. Harl. MS. 1623, ff. 22v.–23.
4 Phillipps, *Wilts. Inst.* i. 125.
5 Ibid. 171.
7 *Inq. Non.* (Rec. Com.), 170.
8 E 301/58/65.
9 W.A.S. Libr., Wilkinson's colls. nos. 3, 46.
10 Phillipps, *Wilts. Inst.* i. 5, 13, 111, 121, 126, 233; ii. 12, 22.
11 *Cal. Pat.* 1292–1301, 121.
12 *Reg. Ghent* (Cant. & York Soc.), ii. 858.
13 *Reg. Martival* (Cant. & York Soc.), ii. 158–9; iii. 28, 55.
14 *V.C.H. Wilts.* vii. 25–6; Phillipps, *Wilts. Inst.* i. 208.
15 *Walker Revised*, ed. A. G. Matthews, 375; Phillipps,

99 See above.
2 Ibid. 111.

6 Ibid. 179.

Wilts. Inst. ii. 22, 25. For the relationship of Wm. and Steph. see *Wilts. Inq. p.m.* 1625–49 (Index Libr.), 4.
16 *Vis. Queries, 1783* (W.R.S. xxvii), pp. 102–3; J. R. Bloxham, *Reg. Magdalen Coll.* vi. 287.
17 P.C. 1/3966; Macray, *Reg. Magdalen Coll.* v. 114.
18 *Endowed Char. Wilts.* (S. Div.), 172; see below.
19 *Endowed Char. Wilts.* (S. Div.), 172.
20 Char. Com. file 204028.
21 *Endowed Char. Wilts.* (S. Div.), 173; see below.
22 Char. Com. file 204027.
23 *Vis. Queries, 1783* (W.R.S. xxvii), p. 103.
24 H.O. 129/261/1/2.
25 Sar. Dioc. R.O., Vis. Queries.
26 Ex inf. the incumbent, the Revd. J. E. Jackson, Netheravon Vicarage.
27 J. Buckler, water-colour in W.A.S. Libr., viii. 5 (1805).

done by a Devizes builder.[28] A grant towards the expense was made by Magdalen College. In 1857 two windows from the college chapel were given to the rector, Thomas Pearse,[29] and inserted in the west wall of the tower. Pearse, a Fellow of Magdalen, paid for the restoration of the nave in 1878. In 1903, with grants from the college and Pearse's widow, the chancel and the tower were restored by C. E. Ponting.[30] A memorial on the south wall of the chancel to Anne Jeay (d. 1612), wife of Thomas and mother of eleven children, begins 'The joy of Jeaye is gone from world's woe To heavenly Joy and happie rest'.

Edward VI's commissioners took 15 oz. of silver for the king and left a chalice of 9 oz. for the parish. The plate in 1976 included a silver gilt chalice with paten, hall-marked 1610, and a silver paten and flagon given in 1720 by Roger Kay (d. 1731), a parish benefactor and rector.[31] In 1553 there were three bells. In 1903 there were five. In that year a treble was added and (ii) and (iii) were recast. Bell (iii) was originally cast in 1679 by William Tosier of Salisbury, (iv) is dated 1603, (v) 1628, and (vi) 1660.[32] The registers begin in 1582 and are complete.[33]

ROMAN CATHOLICISM. A brick building in Figheldean, part of Netheravon Flying School, was converted into a Roman Catholic church c. 1934 and dedicated to St. Thomas More and St. John Fisher. In 1976 it was no longer connected with the service establishment, but was used by the civilian population of the surrounding area, and was served by a priest living in Amesbury.[34]

PROTESTANT NONCONFORMITY. There was no nonconformist in the parish in 1783.[35] In 1826 a room in the house of Roger Hitchcock in Haxton was registered for use by Particular Baptists.[36] There were said to be about 30 dissenters in the parish in 1864,[37] chiefly Baptists, but no nonconformist chapel has been built.

EDUCATION. Three bequests for education in Fittleton were made in the earlier 18th century. Henry Clark (d. 1712) directed that from the annual rent of £12 charged by his will upon his farm at Haxton, £5 should be spent on teaching ten poor children to read and write. He also allotted 10s. of it to buy books.[38] Soon afterwards Elizabeth Buckenham, widow of the rector John Buckenham (d. 1689), bequeathed £50 to be invested and the interest used to teach a few children to read.

Elizabeth's executors gave the money to 'Mr. Beach' in 1718, and annual payments were thenceforth made by the Beach family for teaching four or five girls.[39]

In 1722 the rector, Roger Kay, built a school in the village on land called Piper's Orchard. The building was to provide a house for a schoolmaster and a schoolroom for ten poor boys of the parish. The boys were to be members of the Church of England and were to stay at school until they were fourteen. They were to be chosen by Kay, and after his death by the two largest landowners in the parish and their heirs. The rector and churchwardens were to be governors. By his will, proved in 1731, Kay bequeathed £40 for the maintenance of the building. The main front of the school has five bays and is of brick with decorative panels and bands of knapped flint. It originally consisted of one large schoolroom, a parlour, back room, and three or four bedrooms.[40]

In 1819 there were fourteen children in the school which was said to have funds of about £80. The teacher was paid £7 a year. The poor of the parish were reputed to want more education for their children, provided that it did not interfere with their labour.[41] In 1833 the ten free places in the school were usually given to boys aged five or six who stayed at school for 3 or 4 years. The £5 10s. from the rent-charge on Haxton farm was paid regularly to the schoolmaster by the tenant of that farm.[42] In 1835 eighteen boys and eight girls had free places, and there were some fee paying children. The salaries of a master and mistress were raised by subscription.[43]

In 1843 a small schoolroom was added to the side of the original building at the expense of Sir Michael Hicks Beach, Bt. (d. 1854).[44] In 1859 there were about 50 pupils, some of whom were boarders.[45] The school was united with the National Society in 1870.[46] Two years later another schoolroom was added.[47]

In 1897 Sir Michael Hicks Beach (later Earl St. Aldwyn, d. 1916), representing his family who until then had held and administered the bequests of Elizabeth Buckenham and Roger Kay for the repair of the school, paid £50 and £40 respectively to the Charity Commissioners for investment. The interest on the two investments produced about £2 in 1901 and was used for the general expenses of the school.[48] The interest was the same in 1962.[49] The annual rent-charge of £5 was likewise used for the school's general expenses.[50] In 1906 the school had accommodation for 76 children and an average attendance of 43.[51]

In 1926 the school was reorganized as a junior school. Another classroom was added in 1934.[52] In 1964 Fittleton and Netheravon schools were

[28] W.A.S. Libr., Wilkinson's colls. nos. 17, 20; Macray, *Reg. Magdalen Coll.* vi. 18; J. Buckler, water-colour in W.A.S. Libr., v. 6 (1801).
[29] Macray, op. cit. vi. 46.
[30] *Devizes Gaz.* 22 Oct. 1903; Macray, op. cit. vii. 22.
[31] Nightingale, *Wilts. Plate,* 115–16; Finch, *Netheravon and Fittleton,* 13.
[32] Walters, *Wilts. Bells,* 87–8; Finch, op. cit. 15.
[33] In the ch.
[34] *V.C.H. Wilts.* iii. 97; ex inf. the Revd. J. E. Jackson.
[35] *Vis. Queries, 1783* (W.R.S. xxvii), pp. 102–3.
[36] W.R.O., Return of Regns.
[37] Sar. Dioc. R.O., Vis. Queries.
[38] *Endowed Char. Wilts.* (S. Div.), 173.

[39] Ibid. 174.
[40] Ibid. 176.
[41] *Educ. of Poor Digest,* 1027.
[42] *Endowed Char. Wilts.* (S. Div.), 173.
[43] *Educ. Enquiry Abstract,* 1037.
[44] W.A.S. Libr., Wilkinson's colls. no. 48.
[45] *Acct. of Wilts. Schs.* 24.
[46] *Return of Non-Provided Schs.* 23.
[47] H. R. Pink, *Fittleton Sch.* (Wilts. C.C. 1972).
[48] *Endowed Char. Wilts.* (S. Div.), 176.
[49] Char. Com. file 309399; 309382.
[50] *Endowed Char. Wilts.* (S. Div.), 175; Char. Com. file 204027.
[51] *Return of Non-Provided Schs.* 23.
[52] Pink, *Fittleton Sch.*

amalgamated so that the older children of both villages attended Fittleton school, and the infants went to Netheravon.[53] In 1976 there were 80 children at Fittleton and a mobile classroom was in use.[54]

CHARITIES FOR THE POOR. Besides endowing a sermon 'the Revd. Mr. Jeay', possibly Stephen Jeay,[55] is reputed to have given by his will dated 1693 about £80 for the poor of the parish.[56] The money was not invested and remained idle until 1803 when it was paid to Michael Hicks Beach (d. 1830). It was not invested then, but thenceforth the Hicks Beaches gave £4 annually to the poor. In 1897 Sir Michael Hicks Beach (later Earl St. Aldwyn, d. 1916) paid £80 to the Official Trustees for investment. In 1901 small sums of money were given to a number of poor persons. In 1962 Jeay's charity yielded about £1 15s. for distribution to the poor.[57]

Henry Clark (d. 1712) by his will charged his farm of Haxton with an annual rent of £12 for charitable purposes. Besides sums for education and a sermon[58] £2 was to be spent on the poor, and £4 put towards apprenticing a boy to a trade.[59] In 1833 and 1901 the £2 for the poor was distributed with the income from Jeay's bequest. The apprenticing fund was allowed to accumulate, and in 1829 and 1830 four boys were apprenticed with premiums of about £20 each. Premiums for apprenticeships were rare c. 1901, but when paid were usually for blacksmithing or bricklaying. By his will, proved in 1886, the rector, Thomas Pearse, bequeathed money in trust to help with the expenses of boys beginning work. By a Scheme of 1934 Pearse's and Clark's apprenticing charities were combined, and the interest allowed to accumulate so that in 1958 a grant of £30 was possible. In 1962 the two charities yielded roughly £4 each.[60]

HAM

THE parish,[61] in a secluded position away from main thoroughfares, is on the eastern boundary of Wiltshire.[62] Until that part of Shalbourne which abuts on the west was transferred from Berkshire to Wiltshire in 1894, Ham, with its southern neighbour Buttermere, formed a peninsular jutting eastwards into Berkshire.[63] Hungerford (Berks.), the nearest town, is 6 km. north-east. Ham comprises 669 ha. (1,652 a.).[64] The northern half of the parish is rectangular. The village stands in its north-west corner centred upon a small green. A few dwellings lie along the north side of Spray Road which leads eastwards from the village. South of Ham a few houses stand on either side of the secondary road to Fosbury, in Tidcombe and Fosbury. The southern portion of Ham consists of a tail of land projecting south-westwards from the rectangle. The parish is 3 km. broad on a line north of the village to the area in the north-east corner called Spray. There a scatter of houses and cottages stands along the south side of Spray Road. From north to south over Ham hill the parish is also 3 km. long.

A belt of Upper Greensand extends from the northern boundary of Ham southwards for c. 1.5 km.[65] The broad terrace so formed lies around the 152 m. contour line and is locally called the vale of Ham.[66] In 1976, as in former times, it was covered by woodland in the north-east corner at Spray.[67] Beyond the vale successive strata of Lower, Middle, and Upper Chalk outcrop on the broad open scarp of the downs, the site of the former open fields and still mostly under arable cultivation in 1976. The

chalk pit cut in the escarpment on the east side of the road to Fosbury may have been in use in the later 19th century.[68] On the crest of the downs, on Ham hill, a height of 256 m. is reached. The figure of a horse was cut out there by Charles Wright, owner of the Ham Spray estate from 1869 to 1879, but afterwards became overgrown.[69] There is a deposit of clay-with-flints in the south-east corner of the parish. South of Ham hill the Upper Chalk dips gently away across the tail of the parish, once occupied by old inclosures, to about 183 m. on the southern boundary.

Although the greensand vale was apparently not settled until Saxon times,[70] the uplands of Ham provide evidence of prehistoric and Roman activity. An ancient ridge way crosses the summit of the downs and forms that part of the parish boundary which runs from Ham hill eastwards to Inkpen (Berks.). Two primary cremations were found in a bowl-barrow near the eastern parish boundary north of that track. Another bowl-barrow on Ham hill may once have had a ditch.[71] The remains of a ditch running north-eastwards from Collingbourne Kingston are visible inside the south-western boundary.[72] Another ditch runs for a short distance on a north–south course on the west side of the road south of Ham hill.[73] Roman foundations were found near Inwood copse on the north-eastern parish boundary.[74] The East Wansdyke may have formed part of Ham's north-eastern boundary.[75]

In 1377 119 people were assessed for the poll tax.[76] The smallness of the population of Ham in

[53] See p. 181.
[54] Ex inf. Mr. H. R. Pink, Fittleton.
[55] See above.
[56] Unless stated inf. in this para. is from *Endowed Char. Wilts.* (S. Div.), 172–3.
[57] Char. Com. file 204028.   [58] See above.
[59] Inf. in this para. is from *Endowed Char. Wilts.* (S. Div.), 173, 175.
[60] Char. Com. file 309520; 204027.
[61] This article was written in 1976.
[62] The following maps have been used: O.S. Maps 1/50,000, sheet 174 (1974 edn.); 1/25,000, SU 36 (1961 edn.); 6″, Wilts. XXXVII (1877 edn.), XLIII (1877, 1882 edns.); 1/10,000, SU 36 SW. (1975 edn.).

[63] *V.C.H. Wilts.* v. 273.
[64] *Census*, 1961, 1971.
[65] This para. is based on Geol. Surv. Map. 1″, drift, sheet 267 (1957 edn.), sheet 283 (1959 edn.).
[66] *W.A.M.* xlii. 72.   [67] See pp. 155–6.
[68] O.S. Map 6″, Wilts. XXXVII (1877 edn.).
[69] *W.A.M.* xlii. 73.
[70] For the etymology of the name 'Ham' see *P.N. Wilts.* (E.P.N.S.), 348–9, 433.
[71] *V.C.H. Wilts.* i (1), 177.   [72] Ibid. 254.
[73] Ibid. 256.   [74] Ibid. 75.
[75] O. G. S. Crawford, 'E. End of Wansdyke', *W.A.M.* lv. 119 sqq.
[76] *V.C.H. Wilts.* iv. 309.

the Middle Ages and later is indicated by the insignificant amounts the parish contributed to various taxations, and by the fact that it was sometimes combined for assessment with other small areas. In 1524 it was assessed with Henley, in Buttermere, part of Kinwardstone hundred, and in 1545 with Haxton in Fittleton.[77] The population, when first officially enumerated in 1801, was 188.[78] Numbers rose to 195 in 1811 but dropped to 171 in 1821. Thereafter a steady increase took the population to 255 in 1871. There were only 199 people in the parish in 1881, but 241 in 1891. The population declined gradually to 160 in 1921. It rose to 179 in 1931 but afterwards declined once more.[79] In 1971 149 people lived in the parish.[80]

Most lanes which ran through Ham in the later 18th century and in the earlier 19th century, if not still in use as roads, could be traced as footpaths or tracks in 1976.[81] The secondary road which runs from the Hungerford–Andover road at Shalbourne eastwards through the village towards Inkpen on a course parallel to the ridge way may also be of considerable age. Its course east of Ham at Spray, called Spray Road in 1877, lay between greensand embankments, and it was overhung by numerous mature trees including many beeches. Such steep wooded banks also enclose the lane which winds south from Ham village. That part of the lane south of Ham hill was called Ashley drove in 1877. The courses of Field and Pills lanes, so named in 1877, which led respectively west to Shalbourne and east to Ham Spray House, could still be seen south of the village as tracks in 1976.[82]

Ham's site, enfolded in the downs and approached from east and south by sunken lanes often overhung by trees, emphasizes its seclusion and rural character. The centre of the village clusters round a triangular green formed from a small greensand outcrop formerly surmounted by trees. North of the green stands Ham Cross and to the north-west Dove's, formerly the Laurels, houses respectively of 17th- and 18th-century date. Huddling close to the roadside to the west and south-east of it are several large cottages with thatched roofs: they are mostly timber-framed with brick infilling and of 17th- and 18th-century date. The Crown and Anchor inn, so named in the 19th century and apparently of that date, is said to have been formed from two cottages. Another inn, the Cross Keys, stood inside the northern parish boundary beside the lane leading from the green to Shalbourne in the 19th century.[83] Its site was marked in 1976 by a modern house. At the green's south-west corner, south of the school, a formerly semicircular lane, Church Road, branches south-westwards down a slight incline.[84] At its western end the church stands on a rise in the

ground, and beyond it the Manor is screened by a well established yew hedge. The lane formerly rejoined the Ham–Fosbury road west of the drive to East Court but ceased at the Manor in 1976.[85]

Scattered settlement south of the village on either side of the Ham–Fosbury road includes a few cottages of similar type and date to those at the green, and some dwellings of 20th-century construction. Beyond them Manor Farm, originally a cottage of 17th-century date and converted to a farm-house in the 19th century, stands on the west side of the road. The few council houses south of Manor Farm date from the mid 20th century. On the opposite side of the road Copyhold Farm formerly lay east of a short drive. New Buildings, the only dwelling in the tail of the parish and of later-19th-century date, stands in a high and exposed position on open downland. The house was occupied as two cottages in 1976, as it was in the earlier 20th century.[86]

East of the green, beyond the two former rectory-houses, a few more substantial houses, concealed behind high embankments, and beyond them to the east some council houses, were built on the north side of Spray Road in the earlier 20th century. Further east, on the south side of the road, Acorn and Breach Cottages are of similar date. Ham Spray House stands south-east of them at the end of a long drive from Spray Road. Wan's Dyke End, which stands east of Ham Spray House in Captain's copse, is approached from Spray Road by a double drive. It is a large house built in 18th-century style by G. E. Huth in the 1920s.[87]

MANORS AND OTHER ESTATES. In 931 Athelstan granted his thegn Wulfgar 9 *cassati* at Ham.[88] Soon after Wulfgar devised the estate to his wife Aeffe for life with remainder to the Old Minster, Winchester.[89] By 1086 its profits had been assigned by the bishop to support the monks there.[90] The estate was confirmed to the convent by the bishop in 1284.[91] In 1300 the prior and convent were granted free warren in their demesne lands at Ham.[92] They retained the manor of *HAM*, the profits of which were assigned to the conventual chamberlain from at least the early 14th century, until the Dissolution.[93]

In 1541 the Crown granted the manor to the new cathedral chapter of Winchester, which remained owner until the 19th century.[94] The chapter forfeited the estate in 1649 when the parliamentary trustees granted the farm-house and demesne of c. 304 a. to Henry and Thomas Hunt of Ham, and the remainder of the land and the manorial rights to Hugh Whistler of Faccombe (Hants) and

[77] *V.C.H. Wilts.* iv. 299; *Taxation Lists* (W.R.S. x), 3, 122; E 179/197/152.
[78] Except where stated figures from *V.C.H. Wilts.* iv. 349.
[79] *Census*, 1961.   [80] Ibid. 1971.
[81] *Andrews and Dury, Map* (W.R.S. viii), pl. 12; W.R.O., Inclosure Award map; I.R. 30/38/130.
[82] O.S. Map 6″, Wilts. XXXVII (1877 edn.).
[83] Ibid.; *Kelly's Dir. Wilts.* (1855 and later edns.).
[84] O.S. Map 6″, Wilts. XXXVII (1877 edn.); Mun. D. & C. Winton., N.R.A. box 114, sale cat.
[85] O.S. Map 6″, Wilts. XXXVII (1877 edn.).
[86] Mun. D. & C. Winton., N.R.A. box 114, sale cat.
[87] *Kelly's Dir. Wilts.* (1923, 1927); O.S. Map 1/10,000,

SU 36 SW. (1975 edn.).
[88] Finberg, *Early Wessex Chart.* p. 82.
[89] Ibid. p. 85.
[90] *V.C.H. Wilts.* ii, p. 120.
[91] *Reg. Pontoise* (Cant. & York Soc.), ii. 436.
[92] *Cal. Chart. R.* 1300–26, i.
[93] *Cal. Papal Letters*, i. 21; *Rot. Hund.* (Rec. Com.), ii (1), 260; Katharine A. Hanna, 'Winch. Cath. Custumal' (Southampton Univ. Coll. M.A. thesis, 1954), 351; *Obedientiaries' R. St. Swithun's*, ed. G. W. Kitchin (Hants Rec. Soc.), 130, 363, 372, 375, 377; *Valor Eccl.* (Rec. Com.), vi, App. p. ix.
[94] *L. & P. Hen. VIII*, xvi, p. 417; W.R.O., Inclosure Award (1828).

another,[95] but it was restored. Until 1828 the estate contained some land in Buttermere. At that date the Buttermere land was exchanged with the owner of East Court farm, whose land it abutted, for land in Ham.[96] In 1839 the manorial estate comprised a leasehold demesne farm of 384 a., a copyhold of 51 a. (later called Copyhold farm), and a holding of 482 a. formed from numerous small copyholds in the east part of the parish.[97] The larger copyhold farm was enfranchised in favour of the tenant in 1847.[98] Its later descent is described below.

The remainder of the chapter's Ham estate became vested in the Ecclesiastical Commissioners in 1861. Six years later they regranted to the chapter as a permanent endowment 612 a., west of the Ham–Fosbury road, which included Ham Manor and its grounds, and Manor and Copyhold farms.[99] In 1914 the estate was sold by the Commissioners to S. W. Farmer (d. 1926), who already owned Dove's and East Court farms.[1] By 1928 S. R. Brown had acquired Farmer's Ham estate of 1,350 a. and in that year he offered it for sale in the following lots: Ham Manor and its grounds of 44 a., Manor farm (324 a.), Dove's (also called the Laurels) farm (267 a.), East Court (also called Canning's) farm (236 a.), and New Buildings farm (241 a.).[2] East Court farm was then bought by G. E. Huth, and in 1930 New Buildings farm was the property of A. D. and Catherine M. Hart.[3] Dove's farm was owned by F. Hill in 1939.[4] S. R. Brown apparently retained Ham Manor and Manor farm and was still lord in 1959.[5] In 1976 house and farm were in separate ownership.

By the later 16th century the Hunt family had established themselves as demesne farmers at Ham. John Hunt (d. 1590) devised his lease of the demesne to his wife Christian. On her death shortly afterwards the lease seems to have passed to one of the Hunts of Ashampstead (Berks.).[6] The Hunts remained lessees into the 18th century.[7] In 1780 John Hunt Watts (d. 1813) was farmer.[8] Another John Hunt Watts was lessee until his death in 1829 when Manor farm passed to his brother Francis R. Watts (d. 1867).[9] Henry D. Woodman was lessee in the later 19th century.[10]

Ham Manor originally comprised a timber-framed east–west range built in the 16th century, of the same length as the present south front. That house was enlarged in the later 17th century by the conversion of either end to a cross-wing. The south front has a central clock turret of uncertain date housing a 17th-century mechanism. Additions, mostly of brick, were made to the north in the 18th and 19th centuries.[11] The inside of the house was rearranged, and a new staircase introduced, c. 1800. Much 17th-century panelling was then reset in the entrance hall and on the first floor. An early-18th-century pigeon-house stands south-east of the house. North-west of the house are the remnants of a garden enclosed by formally arranged box and yew hedges of considerable age. A rectangular ornamental mound, possibly of 17th-century origin, stands in the west part of the garden.

In 1086 an estate of 2 hides, previously granted by a bishop of Winchester, was held of the bishop by William Scudet.[12] It is probably to be identified with that known from the 17th century as the manor of HAM or EAST COURT.[13] The overlordship of what was apparently that estate was held by William Marshal, earl of Pembroke (d. 1219), and descended like the manor of Hampstead Marshall (Berks.).[14] It is last mentioned in 1362 when it was held by Isabel, daughter of Edward III.[15]

What was probably William Scudet's land was held by John of Ham in 1249. In that year John granted 2 hides in Ham to Adam of Portland and his wife Isabel. Adam and Isabel in return conveyed a life interest in the capital messuage and half the estate to him for 10s. yearly.[16] In 1287 William of Ham held what seems to be the same property, which then included land at Spray and at Moordown in Buttermere. In that year he granted a life estate therein to Isabel of Ham.[17] Walter of Ham apparently held the estate in the early 14th century and before 1317 granted it to Richard Polhampton and his wife Margaret.[18] After Richard's death in 1317 the lands passed to his widow.[19] In 1320 Margaret seems to have reconveyed the entire estate to Walter of Ham. Walter retained about a third, but regranted two-thirds and the reversion of two small estates of 16 a. and 40 a. to Margaret (d. 1331) for life with remainder to her son Richard.[20]

The estate so acquired by Margaret was held in 1362 by Geoffrey Polhampton and his wife Christine.[21] Although its descent is thereafter obscure, it evidently remained in the Polhampton family until the later 17th century. John Polhampton (will proved 1619) devised his farm at Ham to his son John.[22] In 1668 another John Polhampton, perhaps the younger John's son, his wife Anne, and William

[95] C 54/3464 no. 30; C 54/3459 no. 17; J. Foster, *Alumni Oxon. 1500–1714*, iv. 1611.
[96] W.R.O., Inclosure Award; see below.
[97] I.R. 29/38/130; I.R. 30/38/130; O.S. Map 6", Wilts. XXXVII (1877 edn.).
[98] Mun. D. & C. Winton., copyhold enfranchisement letter-bk. 1845–53.
[99] *Lond. Gaz.* 23 Aug. 1867, pp. 4668, 4676–7; I.R. 29/38/130; I.R. 30/38/130.
[1] H.R.O., Eccl. Commrs. 326880; *W.A.M.* xliii. 494; see below.
[2] Mun. D. & C. Winton., N.R.A. box 114, sale cat.
[3] Ibid.; I.R. 29/38/130; I.R. 30/38/130.
[4] *Kelly's Dir. Wilts.* (1939).
[5] Wilts. Cuttings, xxi. 234.
[6] Req. 2/64/31; mon. in ch.
[7] Mun. D. & C. Winton., bk. of John Chase, f. 91 and v.; W.R.O. 334/4, deed, Hunt to Hunt, 1637; C 54/3464 no. 30; *Q. Sess. 1736* (W.R.S. xi), 138.
[8] W.R.O., Land Tax; 1022/1, burial reg. 1813–1955.
[9] Ibid. Land Tax; 1022/1, burial reg. 1813–1955; Mun.

D. & C. Winton., N.R.A. box 21, will of John H. Watts, dated 1829; I.R. 29/38/130; I.R. 30/38/130.
[10] *Kelly's Dir. Wilts.* (1875 and later edns.).
[11] The date 1727 on an external chimney-stack relates to the reconstitution of the NE. corner of the old ho.
[12] *V.C.H. Wilts.* ii, p. 120.
[13] C.P. 25(2)/372/19 Jas. I Mich.; C.P. 25(2)/744/16 & 17 Chas. II Hil.
[14] *Civil Pleas, 1249* (W.R.S. xxvi), p. 120; *Complete Peerage*, x. 358 sqq.; xii (1), 429; *V.C.H. Berks.* iv. 179–80; *Wilts. Inq. p.m. 1242–1326* (Index Libr.), 416–17.
[15] *Wilts. Inq. p.m. 1327–77* (Index Libr.), 317–18.
[16] C.P. 25(1)/251/15 no. 3.
[17] *Feet of F. 1272–1327* (W.R.S. i), p. 29.
[18] *Cat. Anct. D.* ii, C 2477.
[19] *Wilts. Inq. p.m. 1242–1326* (Index Libr.), 416–17.
[20] *Feet of F. 1272–1327* (W.R.S. i), p. 106; *V.C.H. Berks.* iv. 175.
[21] *Wilts. Inq. p.m. 1327–77* (Index Libr.), 317–18.
[22] W.R.O., Archd. Wilts. (will of John Polhampton).

and Adam Polhampton, conveyed the property to Ferdinand Gunter.[23] He may perhaps have been an assignee of Thomas Gunter, to whom the estate was mortgaged in 1666, and who seems to have been in possession by 1672.[24] Through Thomas's eldest daughter, Margaret, who married Thomas Brotherton, the estate passed to the Brotherton family.[25] William Browne Brotherton was owner from at least 1780 to the early 1820s.[26] In 1822 Thomas W. B. Brotherton was owner.[27] East Court Manor farm, or East Court farm, as it was called from the 19th century, was in the possession of Thomas Cowderoy in 1825 and he retained it until at least 1831.[28] In 1828 he added more land in Buttermere, formerly held by copy of Ham manor, to the farm by exchange.[29] The Revd. John Bushnell was owner of the farm, 279 a., in 1839.[30] By 1843 John Canning had acquired it.[31] It was as the property of H. D. Woodman, however, that it was sold to S. W. Farmer in 1908.[32] After 1914 it became part of the Ham manor estate.[33]

East Court, as the farm-house from which the estate was worked until the earlier 20th century was called in 1976, stands at the south-eastern corner of Ham village.[34] It comprises two 17th-century ranges which form an L-shaped plan. The earlier eastern wing is timber-framed. The later wing, which extends the south front, was apparently refronted in the 18th century. The entire house was considerably altered in the 19th century and was extended and refitted c. 1965.

The estate known variously as Ham Spray farm, Spray farm, or the Spray[35] originated in a copyhold farm built up in the north-east of the parish in the early 19th century,[36] and in 1847, when it comprised 482 a., enfranchised by Winchester chapter for its tenant William Woodman (d. 1862). Woodman was apparently succeeded there by H. D. Woodman (d. 1915).[37] Charles Wright bought the property in 1869. Ten years later his Ham Spray estate was offered for sale and apparently repurchased by H. D. Woodman.[38] In the earlier 20th century Ham Spray House, from which the estate was worked in the 19th century, and the farm were in separate ownership.[39] In 1976 the farm was owned by Mr. Gerald Boord.

Ham Spray House was bought in 1924 by Ralph Partridge (d. 1960) and the critic and biographer Lytton Strachey (d. 1932).[40] The original house of c. 1830 was a two-storeyed villa with a principal five-bay south front facing the downs.[41] It was considerably enlarged to the north and east in the

later 19th century. During Lytton Strachey's occupation much of the interior was redecorated by his friends, particularly Dora Carrington, the painter (Mrs. Ralph Partridge, d. 1932), and Boris Anrep, the mosaicist. Nothing of their work remained in 1976. Guy Elwes, who bought the house in 1961, added a westerly bay to the north-west drawing-room and replanned and redecorated the interior.

The farm called Dove's in the 19th century occupied some 77 a. in the north-west corner of the parish and may have originated in the estate held by John Clarke in the later 13th century or the early 14th.[42] Another John Clarke was a freeholder in 1525, and Richard Clarke held what was presumably the same land in 1578.[43] It is possibly to be identified with the estate held by Daniel Dove in 1672.[44] F. R. Watts (d. 1867) was owner in the earlier 19th century and worked the estate from Dove's Farmhouse, in 1976 called Ham Cross.[45] The farm was afterwards acquired by H. D. Woodman who sold in 1908 to S. W. Farmer.[46] After 1914 it became part of the Ham manor estate.[47]

Ham Cross, which stands north of the green, is probably of 17th-century origin. The house is partly timber-framed and originally comprised a main east–west range of three or four rooms with a short rear wing. An upstairs room retains 17th-century panelling. There are also several dividing walls of heavy framed oak panelling. During the 18th century the walls of the west end of the main range were rebuilt in flint with brick dressings. The east end of that range was completely rebuilt in the earlier 20th century, possibly after a fire.

ECONOMIC HISTORY. In 1066 the capital manor was assessed for geld on $10\frac{1}{2}$ hides and $\frac{1}{2}$ virgate and was worth £6. In 1086 there was land enough for 7 ploughs. The $5\frac{1}{2}$ demesne hides, to which 1 serf was attached, maintained 3 of those ploughs and were worth £9. Elsewhere on the estate there were 9 villeins and 10 *coscez* with 3 ploughs. There were 8 a. of meadow, pasture 3 furlongs long and 1 furlong broad, and woodland 6 furlongs long and 3 furlongs broad. The 2 hides William Scudet held of the capital manor, the later East Court farm, were worth £3 in 1086.[48] Of that estate, and of the other small freehold farm, Dove's, which emerged by the early 14th century,[49] little is known until the 19th century.

The manor was worth £16 in 1210, of which £4

[23] C.P. 25(2)/744/16 & 17 Chas. II Hil.; C.P. 25(2)/745/20 Chas. II Mich.
[24] W.R.O. 367/5, deed, Earles to Gunter, 1666; Mun. D. & C. Winton., N.R.A. box 84, ct. roll, 1672.
[25] *V.C.H. Berks.* iv. 464.
[26] W.R.O., Land Tax; Foster, *Alumni Oxon. 1715–1886*, i. 169; C.P. 25(2)/1447/23 Geo. III Trin.
[27] W.R.O., Land Tax; *Army List* (1822).
[28] W.R.O., Land Tax; 211/2/15/17; O.S. Map 6″, Wilts. XXXVII (1877 edn.).
[29] W.R.O., Inclosure Award; see above.
[30] I.R. 29/38/130; I.R. 30/38/130.
[31] W.R.O. 211/2/15/17.
[32] Mun. D. & C. Winton., N.R.A. box 114, sale cat.
[33] See above.
[34] W.R.O., Inclosure Award (1828); I.R. 29/38/130; I.R. 30/38/130; Mun. D. & C. Winton., N.R.A. box 114, sale cat.
[35] *Kelly's Dir. Wilts.* (1859 and later edns.).

[36] W.R.O., Inclosure Award; I.R. 29/38/130; I.R. 30/38/130.
[37] *Kelly's Dir. Wilts.* (1859, 1867); mon. to Wm. Woodman in churchyard; mon. to H. D. Woodman in ch.
[38] W.R.O. 374/130, sale cat.; *W.A.M.* xlii. 73.
[39] *Kelly's Dir. Wilts.* (1923).
[40] *D.N.B.*; M. Holroyd, *Lytton Strachey*, ii. 474–5, 718–19; ex inf. Mrs. Frances Partridge.
[41] That ho. was built between 1828 and 1839: W.R.O., Inclosure Award; I.R. 29/38/130; I.R. 30/38/130.
[42] O.S. Map 6″, Wilts. XXXVII (1877 edn.); W.R.O, Inclosure Award (1828); Hanna, 'Winch. Cath. Custumal', 46.   [43] Mun. D. & C. Winton., ct. rolls.
[44] Ibid. N.R.A. box 84, ct. roll.
[45] W.R.O., Inclosure Award; 1022/1, burial reg. 1813–1955; I.R. 29/38/130; I.R. 30/38/130.
[46] Mun. D. & C. Winton., N.R.A. box 114, sale cat.
[47] See above.
[48] *V.C.H. Wilts.* ii, p. 120.   [49] See above.

represented the assessed rents.[50] It was taxed at £13 14s. 8d. in 1291.[51] At least from the 14th century to the 17th the manorial revenues included a payment of £3 yearly from the lord of Buttermere.[52] In the early 14th century, and until the Dissolution, the profits of Ham manor belonged to the conventual chamberlain of St. Swithun's.[53] In the earlier 15th century he received £19 yearly from Ham, and £23 in the later 15th century and the earlier 16th.[54] With the chamberlain's Hampshire manors of Chilbolton and West Meon the manor formed part of an economic unit in which interchange of workers, stock, and produce was usual. Chilbolton tenants were apparently required to work in the woods at Ham, while certain Ham tenants were bound to drive stock to Chilbolton. Wool and cheeses were apparently sent direct to St. Swithun's.[55] The usual sheep-and-corn husbandry prevailed.[56] In addition Ham's abundant woodland yielded a considerable nut harvest.[57]

From at least the 16th century to the earlier 17th the manorial demesne, which lay mostly south of the manor-house and west of the Ham–Fosbury road, was let for 21-year terms at £7 6s. 8d. yearly. Edmund Polhampton was farmer in 1502 and Thomas Faller from at least 1545 to 1572.[58] The Hunts and their successors the Wattses were farmers from the later 16th century to the mid 19th.[59] In 1649 the farm comprised 302 a., of which 13 a. were inclosed meadow, 52 a. pasture, and 212 a. arable worth 3s. an acre.[60] In 1779, of the farm's overall area of 400 a., 120 a. were open field arable, 101 a. inclosed arable under the hill, and 54 a. inclosed arable on the hill.[61] At parliamentary inclosure in 1828 the demesne farmer was allotted 384 a. for his land, both in the open fields and old inclosures.[62]

In the early 14th century there were 7 virgaters, 12 ½-virgaters, 9 tenants with 10 cottage holdings, and 7 tenants who held messuages. Several tenants also held small plots of 'forripelond'. The virgaters each held 30 a. for which they owed rents of 5s. yearly and corn-rents. Besides the usual agricultural duties they gathered nuts and apples. The ½-virgaters each held 15 a. and owed half the virgaters' duties. They each had to provide two men to reap at autumn boon-work, and from them were chosen the woodward and hayward. The cottagers held 10 a. each for 2s. yearly. Their duties included threshing and reaping and their wives were bound to wash the sheep. From them were drawn the ploughman, shepherd, and swineherd. Those who held mes-

suages mostly held 5 a. each for 1s. yearly and the duties of driving animals to Chilbolton and of hoeing and reaping.[63] In 1649 there were 25 copyholders within the manor: 1 held 2 yardlands, 2 held 1½ yardland, and 8 held 1 yardland. Four holdings were apparently at Henley, in Buttermere, adjoining the south-east side of the parish. The total copyhold land of the manor was estimated to be 474 a., of which 14 a. were meadow and the rest, of which 5 a. were inclosed, arable. Of the 93 a. then said to be at Henley 79 a. were inclosed.[64] About 1687 24 copyholders held 541 a. within Ham manor. Only one copyhold, of c. 30 a., was then expressly described as at Henley.[65] That land was exchanged at inclosure in 1828 for land in Ham belonging to East Court farm.[66] The accumulation of copyhold estates in the hands of a few tenants seems to have taken place during the 18th century. In 1828 the most substantial of the six copyholders, who held 748 a. mostly in the east part of the parish, was John Hunt Watts, the demesne farmer, who had acquired fourteen copyhold estates totalling 681 a.[67] In 1839 the copyhold farm later known as Ham Spray was reckoned at 482 a. and tenanted by F. R. Watts.[68]

In the 16th century pasture was situated at Spray.[69] Then, and in the 17th century, tenants of the manor who held land at Henley had pasture rights on Ashley common, which probably lay at the extreme south end of the parish.[70] A common at Ham was inclosed in the mid 17th century.[71] The open fields of the parish extended from the southern outskirts of the village to the scarp of the downs. They were called East, West, Up, Little, and Pills fields in the later 17th century and in the earlier 19th Great, Little, and Pidget fields, and the Down.[72] By 1828 some 975 a. in the parish, which represented all the land in Ham except open field arable, had already been inclosed. When the open fields, 639 a., were inclosed, however, that land was re-allotted. Besides the allotments already mentioned, Thomas Cowderoy received 320 a. for East Court farm and F. R. Watts 77 a. for Dove's farm.[73]

Ham, abundantly wooded in the 11th century, in the 13th century was considered to lie within Savernake forest.[74] In the early 14th century tenants at Henley held Henley wood at will of the lord of Ham.[75] There were 22 a. of coppices on the demesne in 1649. The 423 trees, mostly oaks, were worth 10s. 6d. each, and the 800 saplings 2s. each. The total value of the demesne timber was then £209. The tenants were allowed timber from

[50] *Interdict Doc.* (Pipe R. Soc. N.S. xxxiv), 24.
[51] *Tax. Eccl.* (Rec. Com.), 192.
[52] Hanna, 'Winch. Cath. Custumal', 352; Mun. D. & C. Winton., acct. rolls, 1470, 1502, 1524; ibid. N.R.A. box 84, ct. roll, 1672.
[53] See p. 152.
[54] *Obedientiaries' R. St. Swithun's*, ed. Kitchin, 69, 372, 377; *Valor Eccl.* (Rec. Com.), vi, App. p. ix.
[55] Hanna, 'Winch. Cath. Custumal', pp. xlii–xliii, 341, 350.
[56] *Interdict Doc.* (Pipe R. Soc. N.S. xxxiv), 24; Mun. D. & C. Winton., acct. rolls, 1363, 1470.
[57] Hanna, 'Winch. Cath. Custumal', pp. xl, 343.
[58] Mun. D. & C. Winton., acct. roll, 1502; ibid. N.R.A. box 87, acct. rolls, 1545, 1554, 1557, 1572; survey of chap. man. 1649, f. 98; W.R.O., Inclosure Award (1828).
[59] See above.
[60] Mun. D. & C. Winton., survey of chap. man. ff. 97–8.

[61] Ibid. N.R.A. box 21, survey of man.
[62] W.R.O., Inclosure Award.
[63] Hanna, 'Winch. Cath. Custumal', 46, 341 sqq.
[64] Mun. D. & C. Winton., survey of chap. man. ff. 99–108.   [65] Ibid. estate bk. 7, ff. 1–26.
[66] See above.   [67] W.R.O., Inclosure Award.
[68] I.R. 29/38/130; I.R. 30/38/130.
[69] Mun. D. & C. Winton., ct. roll, 1578.
[70] Ibid.; survey of chap. man. 1649, ff. 108–9; Ashley coppice stood on the SW. par. boundary: W.R.O., Inclosure Award (1828).
[71] Florence R. Goodman, *Revd. Landlords and their Tenants* (Winch. priv. print. 1930), 48.
[72] Sar. Dioc. R.O., Glebe Terriers, 1677, 1684; W.R.O., Inclosure Award (1828).
[73] W.R.O., Inclosure Award.
[74] *V.C.H. Wilts.* iv. 418–19.
[75] Hanna, 'Winch. Cath. Custumal', 351.

Ashley common to repair their houses.[76] Ham coppices, 19 a., which comprised Thorney Down and Gibbs coppices and a coppice on the hill, and represented most of the demesne woods, were leased separately in 1779 and in the earlier 19th century.[77] In 1839 Ham contained 113 a. of woodland. The demesne farm's woodland, 60 a., lay in the south-west part of the parish and in the north-east part at Spray. The largest coppices were Spray Way, 24 a., Grubbed Mead, 9 a., and Inlands, 7 a. The Ham Spray estate then contained 34 a. including South Close coppice, 18 a., and Pidget and Gibbs coppices.[78] The area around Spray still bore a fairly thick cover of deciduous trees in 1976.

By 1867 H. D. Woodman had leased 499 a. of the manorial estate from the Ecclesiastical Commissioners and he worked it from Manor Farm.[79] He seems to have secured a lease of Ham manor and the 113 a. surrounding it some time afterwards.[80] S. W. Farmer (d. 1926), of the firm of Frank Stratton & Co., became tenant of much of Woodman's Ham Spray land and in 1909 farmed some 700 a. in the north and east parts of the parish as both owner and tenant.[81] It was probably he who varied the arable farming prevalent in the parish by the introduction of dairy herds.[82]

In 1976 mixed farming prevailed at Ham. There were then four farms in the parish: Manor, Dove's, Ham Spray, and East Court. Of those, Ham Spray and East Court were worked together by Mr. Gerald Boord in conjunction with land elsewhere in Wiltshire and Berkshire.

LOCAL GOVERNMENT. Records of courts of Ham manor survive from the 14th century to the 19th century.[83] Ham apparently owed suit at Kinwardstone hundred court until the 14th century at least.[84] During that time the business of the Ham courts was entirely manorial. In the 15th century, however, the prior of St. Swithun's, who by then seems to have detached Ham from Kinwardstone and to have included it in his own hundred of Elstub, over which he claimed extensive franchisal jurisdiction,[85] held view of frankpledge within Ham manor. The Ham courts, generally held once or twice yearly, were thenceforth called successively views of frankpledge, views of frankpledge and courts, and views of frankpledge, courts leet, and

courts. At them a tithingman made presentments and another tithingman was elected for the following year. The manorial aspect of the court's affairs was mostly limited to copyhold business and the regulation of agricultural matters.

Accounts of the overseers of the poor run from 1683 to 1797. Sums disbursed during that time rose from about £5 in 1683, to £45 in 1751, to £106 in the year ending 1794.[86] Ham was included in the Hungerford (Berks.) poor-law union in 1835.[87] Until 1883, when they were sold, there were two parish cottages in Ham.[88]

CHURCH. The bishop of Winchester confirmed the right of St. Swithun's Priory to present rectors to Ham church in 1172.[89] The priory, however, ceded its right to the bishop in 1284.[90] Thereafter the bishops of Winchester presented until the 19th century, except in 1319 when the king presented because the see was vacant, and in 1393 when, for an unknown reason, Robert Kymberle presented.[91] In 1869 the advowson was transferred to the bishop of Oxford, who presented rectors until 1933 when the rectory was united with that of Buttermere.[92] The bishop was then entitled to present alternately to the united benefice of Ham with Buttermere with Windsor chapter, patron of Buttermere.[93] The bishop of Oxford's turn was transferred to the bishop of Salisbury in 1953.[94] In 1956 Shalbourne vicarage was added to create the united benefice of Shalbourne and Ham. The bishop was to have the first turn of presentation and Windsor chapter, as patron of both Buttermere and Shalbourne, the second and third turns.[95]

The rectory was assessed for taxation at £6 13s. 4d. in 1291.[96] It was valued at £13 in 1535.[97] The living was let, generally for £20 yearly, in the later 16th century.[98] It was worth £70 yearly in 1650.[99] From 1829 to 1831 the yearly average net value was £457.[1]

The tithes of Ham apparently formed the sole rectorial endowment until the later 14th century. In 1363, however, Geoffrey Polhampton, owner of the estate later called East Court manor, and his wife Christine endowed the rector with 20 a. and some meadow land at Ham. Although expressly granted to support a chaplain to say mass daily in the church,[2] the land was afterwards regarded as

[76] Mun. D. & C. Winton., survey of chap. man. ff. 97–8, 108–9.
[77] Ibid. N.R.A. box 21, survey of man.; W.R.O., Inclosure Award; I.R. 29/38/130; I.R. 30/38/130.
[78] I.R. 29/38/130; I.R. 30/38/130.
[79] Lond. Gaz. 23 Aug. 1867, pp. 4668, 4676–7.
[80] Ibid.; Kelly's Dir. Wilts. (1875 and later edns.).
[81] Kelly's Dir. Wilts. (1903, 1907 edns.); I.R. 29/38/130; I.R. 30/38/130; W.A.M. xliii. 494; see above.
[82] W.A.M. xlv. 340; Mun. D. & C. Winton., N.R.A. box 114, sale cat. (1928).
[83] All inf. in this para., except where otherwise stated, is from Mun. D. & C. Winton., ct. rolls, 1377, 1388, 1390, 1428, 1431, 1434, 1436, 1441–2, 1470–1, 1525, 1558, 1578; ibid. N.R.A. box 84, ct. rolls, 1661–1700; N.R.A. box 110, ct. rolls, 1701–24; N.R.A. box 104, ct. rolls, 1734–6, 1740–2, 1744–60; N.R.A. box 101, ct. rolls, 1736–7; N.R.A. boxes 8–11, progress bks. 1760–1847; H.R.O., Eccl. Commrs. 59521–2, ct. bks. 1853–79.
[84] See p. 105.
[85] Ibid.; Rot. Hund. (Rec. Com.), ii (1), 230, 258.
[86] W.R.O. 626/1.

[87] Poor Law Com. 1st Rep. H.C. 500, p. 242 (1835), xxxv.
[88] H.R.O., Eccl. Commrs. 271464–5.
[89] Reg. Pontoise (Cant. & York Soc.), ii. 625.
[90] Ibid. 431.
[91] Phillipps, Wilts. Inst. (index in W.A.M. xxviii. 221); Cal. Pat. 1317–21, 407, 409; Clerical Guide (1822); Clergy List (1859).
[92] Lond. Gaz. 4 June 1852, pp. 1578, 1580; 15 Aug. 1933, pp. 5411–13; Handbk. Brit. Chronology (1961 edn.), ed. F. M. Powicke and E. B. Fryde, 259; Crockford (1896 and later edns.).
[93] Lond. Gaz. 15 Aug. 1933, pp. 5411–13; Crockford (1935).
[94] Ex inf. Dioc. Registrar.
[95] Lond. Gaz. 11 Sept. 1956, p. 5168; Crockford (1961–2).
[96] Tax. Eccl. (Rec. Com.), 189.
[97] Valor Eccl. (Rec. Com.), ii. 149.
[98] C 78/55 no. 5.   [99] W.A.M. xl. 298.
[1] Rep. Com. Eccl. Revenues, 834–5.
[2] Wilts. Inq. p.m. 1327–77 (Index Libr.), 317–18; Cal. Pat. 1361–4, 304.

glebe. It is to be identified as the glebe estate of a little over 20 a., which lay scattered in East, West, Up, Little, and Pills fields, described in the later 17th century.[3] By 1705 the rector no longer had land in Little field but had acquired 5 a. in the 'new' inclosure.[4] When the open fields were inclosed in 1828 the rector received an allotment of 20 a. north and south of the then Rectory.[5] In 1839 he was allotted a rent-charge of £435 to replace his tithes.[6]

In 1341 the rector had a house and garden.[7] The rectory-house mentioned in the later 17th century may have been that which in 1828 stood east of the village on the north side of Spray Road.[8] The central range and eastern cross-wing survive from the 17th-century house and originally had timber-framed walls which by the earlier 19th century had either been rebuilt in brick or encased with brick and mathematical tiling. In 1864 Charles S. Burder, rector from 1864 to c. 1900, replaced the west end of the house by a tall brick cross-wing built to designs by Waring & Blake of London.[9] The central range was later extended northwards by a block similar in design to that of the west end. That Rectory was apparently sold as a private dwelling, in 1976 called the Old Rectory, and replaced by a modern house east of it some time after 1933.[10] That, in 1976 called Field House, was in turn sold after 1956 when Ham with Buttermere was united with Shalbourne, where the incumbents of the united benefice have since lived.[11]

Many rectors, at least from the 16th century, probably did not live at Ham. Erasmus Webb, rector 1582–1614, held other preferments including a canonry of Windsor, and employed a curate at Ham.[12] His successor Nicholas Darell (d. 1629), rector 1614–18, was also a canon of Winchester.[13] Robert Newlin, president of Corpus Christi College, Oxford, was rector from 1643 until his death in 1688.[14] From 1660 he was also sinecure rector of Wroughton.[15] Ham rectory was sequestered in 1646 and Henry Newlin, reported a zealous preacher, intruded.[16] Richard Willowes and John Wilmer may also have served Ham before Robert Newlin's restoration in 1660.[17] At least during the second part of Newlin's incumbency curates performed his duties at Ham.[18] Curates, who apparently often lived outside the parish, assisted the rectors in the later 18th century and the earlier 19th century.[19] From 1829 to 1831 the assistant curate received £60

yearly.[20] In 1783 an assistant curate held morning and afternoon services at Ham each Sunday and celebrated Holy Communion four times yearly. The previous Easter about ten people had communicated.[21] On Census Sunday in 1851 129 people attended morning and 137 afternoon service.[22] Services were still held twice on Sundays in 1864.[23]

The church of *ALL SAINTS* is built of rubble and brick with ashlar dressings, and comprises chancel with south vestry, nave with west gallery and north porch, and a west tower.[24] Both nave and chancel appear to be of 13th-century construction, and are lit by single lancet windows and a two-light east window. That window was given a new head in the 19th century. The tower was added in the 14th century.[25] Windows of nave and chancel were reported broken in 1553.[26] The tower was reroofed and perhaps heightened c. 1611.[27] The extensive restoration which began c. 1733 and continued intermittently throughout the 18th century obscured many of the church's earlier features. The south chancel wall and most of that of the nave were rebuilt in 1733.[28] Other 18th-century alterations and additions probably included the removal of the chancel arch, and the renewal of the chancel's roof and of the tower's casing.[29] A west gallery lit by dormer windows to north and south was inserted. The south nave wall was again repaired, and two windows in 12th-century style inserted, in 1849.[30] At the same time the vestry was added and the north porch renewed. The 17th-century pulpit was lowered in 1871.[31] Other fittings include a 17th-century altar table and 18th-century altar rails. The church was restored in 1896–7 and again in 1970.[32]

John Hunt (d. 1590) and his wife are depicted on a monumental brass.[33] Richard Gillingham, rector 1688–1719,[34] is commemorated by a cartouche ornamented with a shield of arms and heads of *putti*. The churchyard, the north side of which is shaded by yews of considerable age, contains, amongst others, 18th- and 19th-century monuments to members of the Hunt and Watts families.

In 1828 the churchwardens and overseers were allotted c. ½ a. to the north-east of East Court when the open fields were inclosed. The £1 rent from Church Plot was used for church repairs. In 1905 it was paid to the church's expenses fund.[35] The charity was deemed lost in 1976.[36]

[3] Sar. Dioc. R.O., Glebe Terriers, 1677, 1684.
[4] Ibid. Glebe Terrier.
[5] W.R.O., Inclosure Award.
[6] I.R. 29/38/130.   [7] E 179/196/18B.
[8] Sar. Dioc. R.O., Glebe Terriers, 1677, 1684; W.R.O., Inclosure Award.
[9] Sar. Dioc. R.O., Mortgages, no. 162; Crockford (1896, 1907).
[10] Lond. Gaz. 15 Aug. 1933, pp. 5411–13.
[11] Ibid. 11 Sept. 1956, p. 5168.
[12] Phillipps, Wilts. Inst. i. 231; ii. 8; Foster, Alumni Oxon. 1500–1714, iv. 1588; Prob. 11/123 (P.C.C. 31 Lawe).
[13] Phillipps, op. cit. ii. 8–9; Foster, op. cit. i. 373.
[14] Foster, op. cit. iii. 1061.
[15] Ibid.; see below, p. 250.
[16] Walker Revised, ed. A. G. Matthews, 378; W.A.M. xix. 187.
[17] Walker Revised, ed. Matthews, 378; Calamy Revised, ed. A. G. Matthews, 535.
[18] Sar. Dioc. R.O., Chwdns.' Pres. 1674; Glebe Terriers, 1677, 1684.
[19] Vis. Queries, 1783 (W.R.S. xxvii), pp. 113–14; W.R.O. 508/2, burial reg. 1784–1812; 1022/1, burial reg.

1813–1955; W.A.M. xli. 133.
[20] Rep. Com. Eccl. Revenues, 834–5.
[21] Vis. Queries, 1783 (W.R.S. xxvii), pp. 113–14.
[22] H.O. 129/121/1/11.
[23] Sar. Dioc. R.O., Vis. Queries.
[24] A water-colour of 1806 by J. Buckler depicts the ch. from the NE.: W.A.S. Libr., vol. iv. 4.
[25] The date 1349 inside the tower was visible in 1923: All Saints Ch. (ch. guide).
[26] Sar. Dioc. R.O., Detecta Bk. 1550–3, f. 141.
[27] All Saints Ch. (ch. guide).
[28] Date on wall.
[29] The date 1787 is inscribed on the tower. The 18th-cent. additions may be seen on Buckler, water-colour in W.A.S. Libr., vol. iv. 4.
[30] The date 1849 is inscribed on the S. chancel wall.
[31] W.R.O. 1022/1, burial reg. 1813–1955.
[32] Mun. D. & C. Winton., chap. act bk. 1896–1914, pp. 18, 45; Wilts. Cuttings, xxiii. 328.
[33] See p. 153.
[34] Phillipps, Wilts. Inst. ii. 42, 55.
[35] Endowed Char. Wilts. (N. Div.), 497–8.
[36] Ex inf. the incumbent, the Revd. J. H. Torrens, Shalbourne Vicarage.

In 1553 the king's commissioners took 2 oz. of plate but left a chalice of 9 oz. That was probably replaced by the cup and paten-cover hall-marked 1576 which the parish retained in 1976. There were then also a paten of 1719 and a flagon hall-marked and inscribed 1868.[37]

In 1976 as in 1553 there was a ring of four bells: (i) founded in 1712 by William and Robert Cor; (ii), (iii), and (iv) founded in 1663 by William Purdue. The bell-frames were renewed in 1663.[38]

No registration of baptisms, burials, and marriages earlier than 1720 was extant in 1783. Baptisms and burials are recorded from 1720. Marriage registrations, which begin in 1722, appear to be lacking from 1744 to 1755.[39]

NONCONFORMITY. No evidence of dissent in the parish has been found.

EDUCATION. In 1808 children were taught at a 'petty' school in the parish.[40] A private school may have existed at Ham ten years later.[41] Twenty children, paid for by their parents, were taught at a daily school in 1833.[42] In 1858 30–40 children were taught by a mistress in a small schoolroom.[43] That school was chiefly supported by the rector.[44] On return day in 1871 24 boys and 37 girls, including a few from Buttermere, attended the school, which was by then connected with the National Society.[45] New school buildings, which incorporated a teacher's house, were provided in 1874 on the south-west side of the green.[46] In 1906 an average of 53 children had attended over the past year.[47] An average of just over 40 pupils attended until 1914 and thereafter numbers declined gradually to 25 in 1938.[48] Some 40 children from Ham and its neighbourhood were taught there in 1976 by two teachers.[49]

CHARITIES FOR THE POOR. John Hunt (d. 1719)[50] bequeathed £20 in trust, the interest to be distributed yearly among the poor of Ham. Doles in money or kind were apparently paid by the Hunt family in the 18th century but no payment seems to have been made after c. 1820. The charity was deemed lost in 1834.[51]

HAM SPRAY HOUSE

[37] Nightingale, *Wilts. Plate*, 168–9.
[38] Walters, *Wilts. Bells*, 94–5, 292, 301, 310.
[39] *Vis. Queries, 1783* (W.R.S. xxvii), pp. 113–14; W.R.O. 508/1–5; 1022/1; there are transcripts for 1606–9, 1620–3, 1628–35, 1666, 1698, 1711–26, 1749–52 in Sar. Dioc. R.O.
[40] Lambeth MS. 1732.
[41] *Educ. of Poor Digest*, 1027. While the private school may well have been at Ham, a school said to be supported there by a Mr. Russell has been misidentified. The vicar named in the return shows the school to have been that at Ilam (Staffs.): Foster, *Alumni Oxon. 1715–1886*, iii.

1132; *Educ. of Poor Digest*, 861.
[42] *Educ. Enquiry Abstract*, 1038.
[43] *Acct. of Wilts. Schs.* 25.
[44] *Kelly's Dir. Wilts.* (1855, 1859).
[45] *Returns relating to Elem. Educ.* 418–19.
[46] *Kelly's Dir. Wilts.* (1875, 1880); O.S. Map 6″, Wilts. XXXVII (1877 edn.).
[47] *Return of Non-Provided Schs.* 23.
[48] *Bd. of Educ., List 21* (H.M.S.O.).
[49] Ex inf. the Revd. J. H. Torrens.
[50] Sar. Dioc. R.O., Bp.'s Transcripts.
[51] *Endowed Char. Wilts.* (N. Div.), 496–7.

LITTLE HINTON

HINTON[52] was anciently part of an estate based on its westerly neighbour Wanborough and held by the monks of Winchester.[53] It had probably acquired its own name, 'the farm of the (monastic) community', by the 10th century, but is not found as a separate parish until the 12th century, or as a distinct estate until the 13th.[54] Earlscourt, a tongue of land intruding into Hinton from the north and extending as far south as West Hinton hamlet, also formed part of the estate based on Wanborough, but by 1086 had been detached from it.[55] It was afterwards part of Wanborough parish.[56] In 1277 arbitrators settled a boundary dispute between the prior of Winchester as lord of Hinton and the mesne lord of Earlscourt.[57] On either side of Earlscourt lay the tithings of East and West Hinton, into which the parish was divided from at least the earlier 14th century.[58]

From at least the 15th century the parish was often known as Little Hinton, perhaps to distinguish it from Broad Hinton some 14 km. south-west of it.[59] The alternative epithet 'Parva' was also used from the 17th century.[60] Both forms occurred in 1976.[61] Hinton was topographically similar to Wanborough, from which it was divided to the north-west by the river Lidd. It comprised a long narrow strip of land slanting from the river Cole, the northern parish boundary, in a south-easterly direction for 8 km. to Hinton downs. The parish was 2 km. broad along the Icknield Way which transected it a little south of the village and of West Hinton hamlet, c. 500 m. west of the village. In 1884 Earlscourt's incorporation in Little Hinton increased the area of the civil parish to 2,161 a. (874 ha.).[62] Hinton merged with Bishopstone, its eastern neighbour formerly in Ramsbury hundred, in 1934.[63]

The heavy clay soils of the northern third of Hinton, which lies around the 91 m. contour line, lie on Kimmeridge Clay near the Cole valley, a band of Lower Greensand on which Mount Pleasant and Hinton Marsh Farms are sited, and a wide bed of Gault which extends to West Hinton.[64] There is a flat featureless landscape of permanent pasture land relieved only by trees and the northwards flowing head-streams of the Cole which drain it. Hinton village and West Hinton hamlet stand on a terrace of Upper Greensand, the site of the former open arable fields, at about 122 m. South of them the terrace is superseded by the steeply rising chalk scarp of the downs. South-west of the village a wide semicircular coomb has been cut into the scarp face and in it the greensand is exposed. South-east of it a longer narrower coomb, Cowtail, marked part of the parish boundary.[65] Beyond the coombs the land rises steadily southwards to 253 m. on Charlbury hill, the natural outcrops of which resemble barrows.[66] A small deposit of clay-with-flints south of the ridge way near Fox hill is on land over 244 m. South of the ridge way the downs, the former sheep runs of the parish, slope gently away to under 198 m. at the south-eastern corner of the parish.

Although Hinton was crossed by three ancient thoroughfares and bounded on the south by a fourth,[67] little evidence of prehistoric activity has been found. A bowl-barrow on Hinton downs contained a primary cist cremation and an extended burial intruded in pagan Saxon times.[68] A Roman brooch was also found on the downs.[69]

Medieval taxation assessments indicate a small population: 71 people were assessed for the poll tax of 1377.[70] The parish's contribution to 16th-century taxes, in particular the benevolence of 1545 and the subsidy of 1576, were among the smaller ones made by the places in Elstub hundred.[71] The parish had 143 inhabitants in 1700.[72] The Census of 1801 recorded 239 people living in Hinton. That figure gradually increased until 1851 when the population numbered 354. Although numbers thereafter generally declined, slight increases were seen in 1891 and 1911. In 1931 208 people lived at Hinton.[73]

Hinton's main lines of communication with the surrounding countryside, including its northern boundary river, the Cole, all followed east–west routes. A few tracks, some to be seen as footpaths in 1976, provided a north–south link. The courses of all are mostly unchanged since the later 18th century.[74] Of the ancient roads which crossed the parish, the most northerly, the Rogues way, could be traced in 1976 as a bridleway running south of Hinton Marsh Farm towards Horpit in Wanborough.

[52] This article was written in 1976. Maps used include O.S. Maps 1/50,000, sheet 174 (1974 edn.); 1/25,000, SU 27 (1960 edn.), SU 28 (1960 edn.); 6″, Wilts. XVI (1887 edn.), SU 27 NE. (1960 edn.), SU 28 SE. (1960 edn.), SU 28 SW. (1960 edn.), SU 28 NW. (1960 edn.).
[53] V.C.H. Wilts. ix. 174, 176; see below, p. 160.
[54] P.N. Wilts. (E.P.N.S.), 286–7; Finberg, Early Wessex Chart. p. 74; Chartulary Winch. Cath. ed. A. W. Goodman, p. 19; Reg. Pontoise (Cant. & York Soc.), ii. 625.
[55] I.R. 30/38/143; T. R. Thomson, 'Early Bounds of Wanborough and Little Hinton', W.A.M. lvii. 203–11, and map facing p. 210; V.C.H. Wilts. ix. 176.
[56] V.C.H. Wilts. ix. 174 sqq.
[57] Chartulary Winch. Cath. ed. Goodman, p. 228, where the lord is called Ric. of Oaksey. He is probably identifiable with Ric. of Earlscourt (fl. 1275): V.C.H. Wilts. ix. 177.
[58] Mun. D. & C. Winton., ct. roll, 1334; survey of chap. man. 1649, ff. 126–39; ledger bk. XXXVI, pp. 55–68; W.R.O. 212B/3539; 212B/3541.
[59] Cal. Pat. 1467–77, 578, 589; Valor Eccl. (Rec. Com.), ii. 127; Sar. Dioc. R.O., Detecta Bk. 1550–3, ff. 31, 137. P.N. Wilts. (E.P.N.S.), 286–7, refers to 'Little Hynyngton'

in 1311. The man. mentioned then is clearly not Little Hinton: Cal. Pat. 1307–13, 342, and cf. descent given below.
[60] Sar. Dioc. R.O., Glebe Terriers and Chwdns.' Pres.; Andrews and Dury, Map (W.R.S. viii), pl. 15; Kelly's Dir. Wilts. (1848 and later edns.); Crockford (1896 and later edns.).
[61] Signs at E. and W. entrances to the former par. 'Parva' first occurs on O.S. Map 1/25,000, SU 28 SW. (1960 edn.).
[62] V.C.H. Wilts. iv. 350 n. j; Census, 1891.
[63] Census, 1931.
[64] Except where stated, this para. is based on Geol. Surv. Maps 1″, drift, sheets 34 (1857 edn.), 267 (1957 edn.), 253 (1971 edn.).
[65] Cowtail coomb is so called in 1773: Andrews and Dury, Map (W.R.S. viii), pl. 15.
[66] V.C.H. Wilts. i (1), 159.   [67] See below.
[68] V.C.H. Wilts. i (1), 159.   [69] Ibid. 42.
[70] Ibid. iv. 299, 310.
[71] Taxation Lists (W.R.S. x), 3, 123; E 179/197/152; E 179/198/259; E 179/198/336.
[72] W.R.O. 212B/7202A.   [73] V.C.H. Wilts. iv. 350.
[74] Andrews and Dury, Map (W.R.S. viii), pl. 15; I.R. 30/38/143.

Hinton village stands on the north side of the Icknield Way, in 1976 the secondary road from Bishopstone to Wanborough. The ridge way's course takes it across the summit of the chalk escarpment. The southern parish boundary marks the line of the Thieves way.[75] That stretch of the motorway linking Badbury in Chiseldon and Maidenhead (Berks.) was constructed across the south-west tip of the parish in 1971.[76]

The village, in East Hinton tithing, stands on the greensand some distance north of the spring line. It comprises a single lane which takes a rectangular course northwards from the Bishopstone–Wanborough road. Despite its position between Swindon, 8 km. north-west, and the motorway Hinton, enfolded by the downs, in 1976 remained secluded and rural, lacking much modern housing. The church, fronted by a miniature green, stands at the north-west corner of the village. The Manor, partly obscured by the church, lies in a slight depression north of it. Hinton coppice, which is situated some distance behind the house, is mentioned in 1841.[77] Several substantial farm-houses, once attached to copyhold farms within the manorial estate, cluster on either side of the lane. Two, which have thatched roofs and are partly timber-framed, are probably of 17th-century origin. Others are externally of late-18th- or early-19th-century date and have walls of chalk blocks, many apparently re-used, with brick dressings. A row of council houses was built south of Somerset Farmhouse at the south-west corner of the village in the 1950s. Of Hinton's outlying farmhouses, Mount Pleasant Farm and Hinton Marsh Farm to the north are respectively of earlier- and later-19th-century construction. Hill Manor, on the downs to the south, appears to have been built in the later 19th century.

The hamlet of West Hinton was in 1773 called West Town.[78] It comprises some larger houses, all formerly attached to copyholds within the manor, and a few cottages, all externally of the 18th and 19th centuries, strung out along either side of a semicircular lane which forms a loop north of the Bishopstone–Wanborough road. At the eastern junction of the lane and the road stands the former school which bears a date tablet inscribed 'CS 1821'.[79] The New Inn, possibly also later called the Harrow, stood in the later 18th century at the westwards bend of the lane through the hamlet.[80] West Hinton Farm, which stands further west on the south side of the lane, is of stone with a slated roof and bears the inscription 'L/IA 1727' on what appears to

be an easterly extension. The Grove, which stands back from the line of the road some metres directly north, was also once attached to a manorial copyhold[81] and is an elegant brick house of three bays dating from the earlier 19th century.

MANOR AND OTHER ESTATES. The bounds of the 20 hides, then described as at Wanborough and granted in 854 by Ethelwulf to the church of Winchester, show the estate to have occupied the area of the later parish of Little Hinton and to have included Earlscourt.[82] Although Hinton, which owed its name to the monks' ownership, seems to have acquired a separate identity by the 10th century, it apparently still formed part of a larger estate held by the Winchester community at Wanborough in the 11th.[83] By 1066 Earlscourt had become a lay fee, and by the 12th century land which formed the later manor of Wanborough had also passed into lay hands.[84] Thus the manor of HINTON, or, as it was called from at least the 17th century, LITTLE HINTON, alone remained the property of the monks of the Old Minster.[85] In 1284 it was confirmed to the convent of St. Swithun's.[86] In 1300 the convent received a grant of free warren there.[87] From at least the 14th century the profits of the estate were assigned to the hoarder of St. Swithun's.[88]

The estate passed to the Crown at the Dissolution but in 1541 was granted to the new cathedral chapter at Winchester, which thereafter held it until the 19th century.[89] The chapter's tenure was interrupted during the Interregnum when the parliamentary trustees sold to John Butler of Oxford.[90] In 1841 the manorial estate comprised 1,816 a. apportioned among numerous copyhold farms, of which the largest were West Hinton farm, 335 a., and others of 144 a. and 211 a., and leasehold farms of 522 a., the former demesne (later called Manor farm), 132 a., and 92 a., Hinton Marsh farm.[91]

In the later 19th century Winchester chapter and its successors the Ecclesiastical Commissioners, in whom the chapter property became vested in 1861, enfranchised much leasehold and copyhold land at Hinton.[92] Thus in 1847 West Hinton farm was enfranchised in favour of Thomas Brown.[93] As lessee of Manor farm John Brown acquired its reversion in 1853.[94] Both farms were bought, presumably from the Brown family, by Henry Tucker (d. 1875) in 1871.[95] In 1896 Tucker's Hinton estate, 929 a., which then included Manor, Hill, and West Hinton farms, was offered for sale in lots.[96] In

75 *W.A.M.* lvii, map facing p. 210; O.S. Maps 1/25,000, SU 27 (1960 edn.), SU 28 (1960 edn.).
76 *Birth of a Road*, comp. Wilts. Schs. M4 Motorway Project (Lond. 1973), 15; *Wilts. Gaz.* 21 Oct. 1971.
77 I.R. 29/38/143; I.R. 30/38/143.
78 *Andrews and Dury, Map* (W.R.S. viii), pl. 15.
79 See p. 164.
80 *Andrews and Dury, Map* (W.R.S. viii), pl. 15; W.A.S. Libr., ch. acct. bk.
81 I.R. 29/38/143; I.R. 30/38/143; W.A.S. Libr., sale cat. xii, no. 34.
82 Finberg, *Early Wessex Chart.* p. 74; Thomson, 'Wanborough and Little Hinton', *W.A.M.* lvii. 204 sqq.; see above.
83 Finberg, *Early Wessex Chart.* p. 74; *P.N. Wilts.* (E.P.N.S.), 286–7; *W.A.M.* lvii. 204.
84 *V.C.H. Wilts.* ix. 176.
85 *Chartulary Winch. Cath.* ed. Goodman, p. 19; *Bk. of Fees*, ii. 737; *Reg. Pontoise* (Cant. & York Soc.), ii. 436;

Valor Eccl. (Rec. Com.), vi, App. p. viii; C 54/3458 no. 12.
86 *Reg. Pontoise* (Cant. & York Soc.), ii. 436.
87 *Cal. Chart. R.* 1300–26, 1.
88 *Obedientiaries' R. St. Swithun's*, ed. G. W. Kitchin (Hants Rec. Soc.), 253, 282, 299; *Valor Eccl.* (Rec. Com.), vi, App. p. viii.
89 *Winch. Chap. Doc. 1541–7*, ed. G. W. Kitchin and F. T. Madge (Hants Rec. Soc.), 71–2; W.R.O. 212B/3539; 212B/3541; I.R. 29/38/143.
90 C 54/3458 no. 12.
91 I.R. 29/38/143; I.R. 30/38/143; W.A.S. Libr., sale cat. xii, no. 34.
92 *Lond. Gaz.* 16 Apr. 1861, pp. 1582 sqq.
93 W.A.S. Libr., sale cat. xii, no. 34; Mun. D. & C. Winton., copyhold enfranchisement letter-bk. 1845–53; chap. act bk. 1824–50, p. 398.
94 W.A.S. Libr., sale cat. xii, no. 34.
95 Ibid. iii, no. 5.
96 Ibid.

ENFORD
The church of All Saints in 1807

OVERTON
The church of St. Michael and All Angels in 1807

Stockton House, built *c.* 1599

Stockton Almshouse, founded in 1640

STOCKTON

1860 and 1863 the two unnamed copyhold farms mentioned above were enfranchised for Thomas Anger.[97]

Other land in Hinton was retained by Winchester chapter and the Ecclesiastical Commissioners in the later 19th century. Thus in 1853 the interest of the lessee in Hinton Marsh farm was purchased,[98] and in 1879 that of the tenants in the farm of 132 a. mentioned above was bought.[99] In 1883 the commissioners owned 243 a. at Hinton. In 1976 their property was represented by Little Hinton farm.[1]

Little Hinton Manor, to which only a small acreage was then attached, was owned in 1977 by Mr. and Mrs. M. C. Talbot-Ponsonby. It incorporates the farm-house of the tenants of the manorial estate, which appears to have been a low stone building of the 17th century. Additions were made to the east and in the earlier 19th century the house was heightened in brick. Its conversion to a gentleman's residence began in the late 19th century and continued in the 20th century, when some of the principal rooms were panelled with re-used material of the 17th and 18th centuries.

A few small estates at Hinton are mentioned in the 13th century, but it has not proved possible to trace them beyond that period. Before 1249 Walter, son of Adam of Bradley, granted Agnes, widow of Richard of Oaksey, 4½ virgates there. In 1249 Walter's brother Adam waived his claim to ¾ virgate there in favour of Agnes.[2]

In 1270 the prior of St. Swithun's, Winchester, confirmed to Herbert of Oaksey of West Hinton 2 virgates, formerly held of Winchester but afterwards freely for a yearly rent.[3]

Some land at Hinton was conveyed in 1279 by Agnes Marsh and her sisters Margery Quintyn, Amy del Molyn, and Maud de Barneville to Philip de Gay. In 1305 a Philip de Gay, perhaps the same, conveyed the lands to Adam de Bromesdon and his wife Agnes.[4]

Walter Jokyn of Hinton acquired 1 virgate at Hinton from John de Aldrington in 1281. In the same year Walter and his wife Isabel obtained 1 carucate of land there from John Jokyn.[5]

ECONOMIC HISTORY. From the 13th century until at least the 19th century the sheep-and-corn husbandry typical of the area prevailed on both the demesne and the tenantry lands of Hinton.

Some time before 1280 the whole manor was reported to have been farmed, although it may have been the demesne alone which was so let.[6] In 1445, however, the demesne was permanently at farm.[7] Throughout most of the 16th century the Walrond family were farmers at a rent of £12 6s. 8d. yearly.[8]

In 1624 William Keate became farmer at the same rent, and was succeeded by his daughter Elizabeth and her husband Francis Hungerford.[9] In 1649, during Hungerford's tenancy, the demesne farm's 386 a. comprised 240 a. of arable land, 44 a. of meadow, and 100 a. of down. There was also a coppice of 2 a. The farm's land in the common meadow was then worth 26s. 8d. the acre, its arable in the open fields 4s. 6d. the acre, and its downland 5s. the acre.[10] In 1791 of the farm's 471 a. about two-thirds were arable and a third pasture.[11] In 1820 Thomas Brown, a member of a well known Wiltshire farming family, was farmer at Manor farm, as it was later called, and he was succeeded there by John Brown.[12] The farm, then reckoned at 522 a. and situated north of Hinton village and in the south-eastern quarter of the parish, included 17 a. of water-meadows north and east of Hinton coppice in 1841.[13]

The remainder of the parish was given over to the tenantry lands. About 1280 26 virgaters, who held 27 estates, owed the usual agricultural services and money rents totalling £7. Of those 27 estates 14 were of 1 virgate, 8 of ½ hide, 3 of 3 virgates, 1 of 2 virgates, and 1 of ½ virgate. The nineteen cottagers, including the miller, all held a few acres in both open fields, for which they owed services and money rents totalling some £3.[14] In 1649 576 a. in West Hinton tithing were shared among twelve copyholders, of whom over half had farms of some 60 a. Since the demesne lands lay in East Hinton tithing the copyhold acreage there was much smaller, amounting to only 186 a. Of the seven copyholders there, only one had about 60 a. All shared a common down of 50 a. and a common marsh there.[15] After inclosures of 1659 and 1787[16] larger copyhold farms emerged. Thus in 1791 of the seventeen copyholders within the manor, George Lea had a farm of 241 a., John Anger one of 152 a., and John Wood one of 134 a.[17] In 1841 the following tenant farms could be distinguished: West Hinton farm, 335 a. formed from seven small copyhold estates and farmed by Thomas Brown; a farm of 211 a. formed from four copyholds; a leasehold farm of 132 a. worked by Elizabeth Gibbs; a farm of 144 a. comprising two copyholds and farmed by George Edwards; and Hinton Marsh farm, a leasehold of 92 a. farmed by Harry Chester.[18]

Flocks and wool yields on the demesne were substantial throughout the Middle Ages. Nothing, however, is known of the economy of the tenantry lands. In 1210 over 200 sheep of various types were accounted for on the demesne.[19] The demesne ewe and lamb flocks in 1248 were large and included 115 lambs sent from Winchester Priory's estate at Wroughton.[20] In 1273 537 sheep's and 144 lambs'

[97] H.R.O., Eccl. Commrs. 286905, 121592.
[98] Mun. D. & C. Winton., copyhold enfranchisement letter-bk. 1845–53; chap. act bk. 1876–96, p. 27.
[99] Sar. Dioc. R.O., Ch. Commrs., Bpric. 38, no. 10.
[1] Ex inf. Ch. Commrs.
[2] C.P. 25(1)/251/16 no. 90.
[3] Chartulary Winch. Cath. ed. Goodman, p. 235.
[4] Feet of F. 1272–1327 (W.R.S. i), pp. 11, 54.
[5] Ibid. pp. 18–19.
[6] Katharine A. Hanna, 'Winch. Cath. Custumal' (Southampton Univ. Coll. M.A. thesis, 1954), 618.
[7] Mun. D. & C. Winton., acct. roll.
[8] Ibid. N.R.A. box 87, acct. roll, 1557; bk. of John Chase, f. 90v.

[9] Ibid. survey of chap. man. 1649, ff. 126–39; Berks. Pedigrees (Harl. Soc. lvi), 231.
[10] Mun. D. & C. Winton., survey of chap. man., ff. 126–39.   [11] W.A.S. Libr., ch. acct. bk.
[12] W.R.O., Land Tax; I.R. 29/38/143; I.R. 30/38/143.
[13] I.R. 29/38/143; I.R. 30/38/143.
[14] Hanna, 'Winch. Cath. Custumal', pp. lviii and n. 3, 607–17.
[15] Mun. D. & C. Winton., survey of chap. man., ff. 126–39.   [16] See below.
[17] W.A.S. Libr., ch. acct. bk.
[18] I.R. 29/38/143; I.R. 30/38/143.
[19] Interdict Doc. (Pipe R. Soc. N.S. xxxiv), 25.
[20] Mun. D. & C. Winton., acct. roll.

fleeces were recorded at Hinton.[21] The heavy clay soils in the northern third of the parish supported herds of cows. Ten cows, as well as numerous calves, were accounted for on the demesne in 1210.[22] In 1273 38 winter and 173 summer cheeses were produced.[23] In the 14th century the hoarder of St. Swithun's, to whom the profits of the estate were allotted, received some £62 yearly from Hinton, an income which gradually declined throughout the later Middle Ages.[24]

The manorial estate contained an east and a west field in the later 13th century.[25] In 1638 there were two commons called the Marsh and Lambslade shared between the demesne farmer and the copyholders.[26] In 1659 the Down fields south of the village, the Reeve lands, the Marsh, East mead, and the open fields below the hill in West Hinton were inclosed by agreement between the demesne farmer and the tenants. As farmer, Francis Hungerford was allotted 115 a., and the eighteen copyholders a total of 523 a.[27] Some, at least, of the land in East Hinton was re-allotted in 1787 when the East and West fields there, which contained 410 a., were inclosed. The demesne farmer then received 248 a., and of the nine copyholders in the tithing, John Anger received 76 a., and John Woodward 49 a.[28] The open fields of West Hinton, the West, East, and North fields below Coombe, the West and East fields above Coombe, and New England, which contained a total of 450 a., were, with certain old inclosures, allotted by agreement in 1821. Six tenants in the tithing received allotments and the largest, 259 a., was made to Thomas Evans.[29]

Little re-arrangement of the farms within the manorial estate took place until the later 19th century. By 1896 the area of Manor farm had been reduced to 169 a. by the creation of a hill farm of 609 a. worked from Hill Manor. The area of West Hinton farm had by then been reduced to 20 a.[30] After 1879 the Ecclesiastical Commissioners' land in the parish formed a farm of over 200 a.[31]

In 1976 the land of Little Hinton was given over to mixed farming, with dairying predominant on the northerly low-lying clays. Little Hinton, Hinton Marsh, and Mount Pleasant farms were situated there. South of them were Church farm, owned by Charlbury Farms (Hinton) Ltd., and the large Hill Manor farm, owned by Mr. M. C. Wilson. Market-gardening was carried out on the Upper Greensand at the Water Garden Nurseries west of the former school. The Parva Stud, which occupied the stables of the former manor-house, was managed by Richard Pitman, the National Hunt jockey. Apart from those employed locally in agriculture, most inhabitants of Little Hinton then commuted daily to Swindon or further afield.

MILLS. A mill on Hinton's manorial demesne is mentioned in 1248 and is perhaps to be identified with the later Cuttle Mill.[32] It was repaired in 1273 and its house in 1280. In both years the miller received 5s.[33] In 1281 the mill was leased for 10 years at £1 4s. yearly.[34] Cuttle Mill, which may have stood near Hinton Marsh Farm on the north-east boundary stream of the parish, was leased by Winchester chapter to the Walrond family in the later 16th century. From c. 1583 a farm of 75 a., which included Clark's holding, was leased with it.[35] In the later 18th century mill and farm, then usually leased for 21-year terms, were tenanted by the Woodward family.[36] In 1845 John Tucker (d. 1856) was tenant and he was succeeded by his brother Thomas (d. 1868).[37] The mill is last expressly mentioned in 1859 but may have fallen into disuse long before.[38] In 1879 John Tucker's surviving devisees surrendered the property to Winchester chapter's successors, the Ecclesiastical Commissioners, in whom the reversion had become vested in 1861.[39]

A second mill in East Hinton attached to the manorial estate is mentioned in 1419 and is identifiable with Berry Mill.[40] It was then, and remained until the later 19th century, a copyhold of Hinton manor. Some 17 a. of land were attached to it. The mill was held in the 16th and 17th centuries by the Berry family and in the later 18th century and the earlier 19th by the Lea family.[41] It stood on the north-east boundary stream some distance southeast of Hinton Marsh Farm.[42] John Tucker became copyholder in 1845 and the mill thereafter passed like the Cuttle Mill estate and was absolutely surrendered to the Ecclesiastical Commissioners in 1879.[43] Although the precise sites of the mills are not known earthworks, including a leat and embankments, survive in the meadow south of Hinton Marsh Farm.

LOCAL GOVERNMENT. In 1281 the prior of St. Swithun, Winchester, claimed that Henry III had granted the priors view of frankpledge, assizes of bread and of ale, and gallows in Hinton manor.[44] The priors and their successors at Hinton, Winchester chapter, exercised both franchisal and

[21] Mun. D. & C. Winton., acct. roll.
[22] Interdict Doc. (Pipe R. Soc. N.S. xxxiv), 25.
[23] Mun. D. & C. Winton., acct. roll.
[24] Obedientiaries' R. St. Swithun's, ed. Kitchin, 253, 279, 293; Valor Eccl. (Rec. Com.), vi, App. p. viii.
[25] Mun. D. & C. Winton., acct. rolls, 1273, 1280.
[26] C 78/1920 no. 18.   [27] C 78/651 no. 9.
[28] W.R.O. 212B/3539; 212B/3541.
[29] Mun. D. & C. Winton., ledger bk. XXXVI, pp. 55–68.
[30] W.A.S. Libr., sale cat. iii, no. 5; xii, no. 34.
[31] See above.
[32] Mun. D. & C. Winton., acct. roll.
[33] Ibid. acct. rolls.   [34] Ibid. acct. roll.
[35] Ibid. ct. roll, 1419; bk. of John Chase, f. 90v.; W.R.O. 700/187, deeds, 1760–1832; Sar. Dioc. R.O., Ch. Commrs., Bpric. 42, abstr. of title no. 3. In 1773 'Bury' Mill was depicted on the site of Hinton Marsh Farm: Andrews and Dury, Map (W.R.S. viii), pl. 15. Berry Mill clearly stood SE. of that farm-ho., so the 'Bury' Mill of 1773 may possibly mark the site of Cuttle Mill: I.R. 29/38/143; I.R. 30/38/143.
[36] W.R.O. 700/187, deeds, 1760–1832.
[37] Sar. Dioc. R.O., Ch. Commrs., Bpric. 42, abstr. of title nos. 2, 3.
[38] Ibid. abstr. of title no. 3. The mill is not mentioned in 1839: I.R. 29/38/143; I.R. 30/38/143.
[39] Sar. Dioc. R.O., Ch. Commrs., Bpric. 42, abstr. of title no. 3; Bpric. 38, no. 10; Lond. Gaz. 16 Apr. 1861, pp. 1582 sqq.
[40] Mun. D. & C. Winton., ct. roll.
[41] Ibid. ct. rolls, 1516, 1527; survey of chap. man. 1649, ff. 126–39; estate bk. 1; W.R.O., Land Tax; Sar. Dioc. R.O., Ch. Commrs., Bpric. 42, abstr. of title no. 3.
[42] I.R. 29/38/143; I.R. 30/38/143.
[43] Sar. Dioc. R.O., Ch. Commrs., Bpric. 42, abstr. of title no. 3; Bpric. 38, nos. 7, 10, 13.
[44] Plac. de Quo Warr. (Rec. Com.), 806.

manorial jurisdiction at courts held half-yearly until the 17th century, and from then until 1847 yearly in early autumn.[45] From the 15th century until the 18th courts were called views of frankpledge with courts, but from the later 18th century the usual title was view of frankpledge, court leet, and court. The only non-tenurial business with which the courts dealt consistently was the election, until at least the earlier 18th century, of tithingmen for the tithings of East and West Hinton, into which the parish was apparently divided for administrative purposes from at least the earlier 14th century. Other matters dealt with, such as the repair of ruinous tenements, were manorial and mostly confined to copyhold business.

Overseers' records exist for the later 18th century and the earlier 19th.[46] In 1835 Little Hinton became part of Highworth and Swindon poor-law union.[47]

CHURCH. Although in 1172 the bishop of Winchester confirmed St. Swithun's Priory as patron of Hinton church, he had apparently regained the advowson by 1244.[48] In that year, as in 1280, the Crown presented a rector *sede vacante*.[49] In 1284 St. Swithun's relinquished its claim to the advowson in the bishop's favour.[50] The bishops thereafter presented rectors until the 19th century, except in 1565 when Roger Colley presented.[51] In 1869 the advowson was vested in the bishop of Gloucester and Bristol.[52] After the combined see was divided in 1897 the right to present was allotted to the bishop of Bristol, who remained patron in 1976.[53] In 1946 Hinton rectory was united with the vicarage of Bishopstone (formerly in Ramsbury hundred), also in the gift of the bishop of Bristol, and the united benefice of Bishopstone with Little Hinton was thus created.[54]

In 1284, in return for the priory's acknowledgement of his patronage rights, the bishop of Winchester allowed St. Swithun's to continue to take a pension of 40s. from Hinton church.[55] After the Dissolution the payment was transferred to Winchester chapter, which still received it in the early 19th century.[56]

The church was valued at £10 13s. 4d. for taxation purposes in 1291.[57] In 1535 it was worth £13 6s. 8d., a sum which represented the value of all the tithes arising from Hinton and of some land.[58] Its value

was £100 in 1650.[59] In 1659, when certain arable lands in the parish were inclosed, the rector's right to tithes in kind was replaced by composition payments totalling £110.[60] The glebe, first expressly mentioned in 1671, comprised 2 a. of meadow land on the north-eastern parish boundary.[61] In 1791 the rector's composition payments amounted to £224.[62] From 1829 to 1831 the net yearly value of the benefice averaged £444.[63] The rector's composition payments were replaced in 1841 by a rent-charge of £520.[64]

A rectory-house is mentioned in the later 17th century and in the 18th. In 1783 it was described as thatched, built of various materials, and containing thirteen rooms.[65] It was replaced in 1810 by a house built south of the church by Richard Pace of Lechlade (Glos.).[66] After the union of Hinton and Bishopstone the incumbent lived at Bishopstone, and Little Hinton Rectory was sold as a private dwelling.[67]

In 1556 the rector held two benefices.[68] Peter Nicholls, rector from 1635 to c. 1653, apparently preached every Sunday.[69] Rectors seem generally not to have resided in the 18th and the earlier 19th and to have delegated their duties to curates.[70] Thomas Coker, rector 1684–1741, probably did not live in the parish after 1696 when he was appointed to the prebend of Bishopstone.[71] Thomas Garnier (d. 1873), rector 1807–8 and later dean of Winchester, was also rector of Bishopstoke (Hants), where he apparently lived.[72] Nowes Lloyd, rector 1751–89, was also vicar of Hinton's neighbour Bishopstone and of Enbourne (Berks.).[73] His curate at both Bishopstone and Hinton apparently served Little Hinton most efficiently. Each Sunday in 1783 he held services, at which sermons were preached, alternately morning and afternoon with those at Bishopstone. Prayers were read at Little Hinton on certain weekday festivals and on state holidays. Holy Communion, celebrated four times a year, was received by 20–30 communicants.[74] In 1812 the curate held Sunday services alternately morning and afternoon with those at Wanborough, where he also served the cure. The Sacrament was then administered to an average of ten communicants at the four customary seasons.[75] On Census Sunday in 1851 100 people attended morning, and 113 afternoon service.[76]

[45] All inf. about cts. from Mun. D. & C. Winton., ct. rolls; ibid. N.R.A. box 84, 17th-cent. ct. rolls; N.R.A. boxes 104 and 110, 18th-cent. ct. rolls; N.R.A. boxes 8–11, 18th- and 19th-cent. progress bks.
[46] W.R.O. 1364/53–9.
[47] Poor Law Com. 2nd Rep. 559.
[48] Reg. Pontoise (Cant. & York Soc.), ii. 625; Cal. Pat. 1232–47, 421.
[49] Cal. Pat. 1232–47, 421; 1272–81, 398.
[50] Reg. Pontoise (Cant. & York Soc.), ii. 431.
[51] Phillipps, Wilts. Inst. (index in W.A.M. xxviii. 222); Clerical Guide (1822).
[52] Lond. Gaz. 4 June 1852, p. 1583; Handbk. Brit. Chronology (1961 edn.), ed. F. M. Powicke and E. B. Fryde, 259.
[53] Powicke and Fryde, op. cit. 209 n. 1; Clergy List (1905); Crockford (1907 and later edns.).
[54] Lond. Gaz. 27 Feb. 1940, p. 1164; Crockford (1940 and later edns.).
[55] Reg. Pontoise (Cant. & York Soc.), ii. 437.
[56] Tax. Eccl. (Rec. Com.), 190; Valor Eccl. (Rec. Com.), vi, App. p. viii; Sar. Dioc. R.O., Glebe Terrier, 1783; W.A.S. Libr., ch. acct. bk.   [57] Tax. Eccl. (Rec. Com.), 190.
[58] Valor Eccl. (Rec. Com.), ii. 127.

[59] W.A.M. xl. 300.
[60] C 78/651 no. 9; see above, p. 162.
[61] Sar. Dioc. R.O., Glebe Terriers, 1671, 1677, 1705, 1783; I.R. 29/38/143; I.R. 30/38/143.
[62] W.A.S. Libr., ch. acct. bk.
[63] Rep. Com. Eccl. Revenues, 836–7.
[64] I.R. 29/38/143.
[65] Sar. Dioc. R.O., Glebe Terriers, 1671, 1677, 1705, 1783.
[66] Colvin, Brit. Architects, 605; I.R. 29/38/143; I.R. 30/38/143.
[67] Lond. Gaz. 27 Feb. 1940, p. 1164.
[68] Sar. Dioc. R.O., Detecta Bk.
[69] W.A.M. xix. 189; Phillipps, Wilts. Inst. ii. 18; Prob. 11/230 (P.C.C. 289 Brent).
[70] Vis. Queries, 1783 (W.R.S. xxvii), pp. 122–3; W.A.S. Libr., ch. acct. bk.; W.A.M. xli. 136.
[71] Phillipps, Wilts. Inst. ii. 39, 44, 69.
[72] Ibid. 105–6; D.N.B.
[73] Phillipps, Wilts. Inst. ii. 74, 95; Vis. Queries, 1783 (W.R.S. xxvii), p. 122 and n. 6.
[74] Vis. Queries, 1783 (W.R.S. xxvii), pp. 122–3.
[75] W.A.M. xli. 136.
[76] H.O. 129/250/2/3.

The church of *ST. SWITHUN*[77] stands in the centre of the village. It is built of rubble with ashlar dressings and comprises chancel, aisled and clerestoried nave with south porch, and a west tower.[78] The nave is earlier than its arcades. Of those, which are of two bays with long spans, that to the south is of the later 12th century and that to the north of the earlier 13th century. East windows were inserted in both aisles, which are probably of their original dimensions, in the 13th century. The chancel arch was reconstructed in the earlier 13th century. The chancel itself, however, was rebuilt a century later and retains three contemporary windows and a priest's doorway. The base of the west tower is contemporary with the west nave wall. Its upper stages, surmounted by a tiled pyramidal roof, may have been rebuilt in the 14th century. The clerestory, lit by square-headed windows of three lights, was added in the early 16th century when the nave was reroofed. At the same time windows similar to those in the clerestory were inserted in the aisle walls, and a south porch was constructed. Some small repairs were made to the chancel in 1798 and 1802.[79] A thorough restoration, which included the construction of a north doorway and to which Winchester chapter as lord of the manor contributed £20, was carried out in 1860.[80]

The stem and base of the font are probably of the later 12th century. The bowl, on which various birds and animals are depicted, is possibly of later date. It was much restored *c.* 1860.[81] A three-decker pulpit, given by Martha Hinton in 1637, survived in a mutilated condition in 1976.[82] The royal arms dated 1789 hang above the tower arch on the west nave wall.

In 1553 the king's commissioners took 1½ oz. of plate but left the parish a chalice.[83] The church in 1891, and still in 1976, possessed, besides a later-16th-century chalice and paten cover, a flagon of 1634 and two patens of 1719, all inscribed as the gift of Thomas Coker, rector 1684–1741.[84]

As in 1553 there was a ring of three bells in 1976: (i) *c.* 1730, probably from the Aldbourne foundry and by John Cor; (ii) 1698, by Robert Cor; (iii) *c.* 1500, from the Bristol foundry.[85] The church retained its sanctus bell.[86] Registrations of baptisms begin in 1649, of burials in 1653, and of marriages in 1654, and all are complete.[87]

NONCONFORMITY. There was said to be no papist nor other dissenter in the parish in 1783.[88] A group of Methodists, probably Wesleyans, certified Charles Wilson's house at Little Hinton for worship in 1820.[89] The group evidently flourished for a while and by 1851 a Wesleyan Methodist chapel had been built. It was then reported to have been attended by an average congregation of twenty on Sunday afternoons over the past year.[90] The chapel's location is unknown and no more is heard of it. In 1829 Sarah Jones's house was certified by an unspecified group of protestants.[91]

In the early 20th century Evangelicals met for worship at Batt's Farmhouse. In 1911 the Country Towns Mission provided the group with a hall on the south side of the lane running north-west from the church. Services, attended by some ten people, were still held there on Sunday evenings in 1976.[92]

EDUCATION. In 1777 Thomas Coker, rector of Doynton (Glos.) and son of Thomas Coker, rector of Little Hinton 1684–1741, conveyed land at Shrivenham (Berks.) and a rent-charge of 30s. yearly from land at Purton in trust, the profits to provide a school at Little Hinton.[93] Coker regulated the conduct of the school and appointed the trustees. The rector, as one of the trustees, was to appoint a teacher who would receive half-yearly 12s. for each pupil. Numbers were limited to ten, although more children could be accepted if funds allowed. The rector was to have £1 yearly for administering the school, 10s. yearly was to be spent on books, and 10s. on a trustees' dinner every other year. In 1818 ten children were taught by a master and mistress. At another school twelve to twenty children were taught to read for 3d. weekly, but most left school as soon as possible to work on the land.[94]

By 1819 Coker's school had apparently lapsed for lack of a schoolroom. In that year timber from the trust lands was sold for £80 to raise funds to provide another. In 1821 Winchester chapter, as lord of Hinton, granted land for a school on the south side of the Bishopstone–Wanborough road west of the village, and a cottage was built on it.[95] At least twenty children were to be taught there and their teacher paid £10 yearly. Some 20–30 pupils attended in 1833.[96] In 1834 the children, who entered at four, were all taught reading and the girls also did needlework. A room of the cottage built in 1821 was then still used, but afterwards other accommodation was apparently rented. In 1839 the land at Shrivenham was sold to the G.W.R. and £755 invested. More land near that conveyed in 1821 was granted in 1846 by Winchester chapter which in 1848 gave £30 towards the enlargement of the cottage.[97]

[77] So dedicated in 1763: J. Ecton, *Thesaurus*, 401. An alternative dedication to St. Anne occurs in the later 19th and early 20th cents.: O.S. Map 6″, Wilts. XVI (1887 edn.); *Crockford* (1896); *Clergy List* (1905). It was noted in 1924 that the village feast day used to be 26 July, the feast of St. Anne. That date, it was suggested, would, according to the reckoning of time used before 1752, formerly have been St. Swithun's day: *W.A.M.* xlii. 590.
[78] Water-colour by J. Buckler, giving a SE. view, in W.A.S. Libr., vol. vii. 10 (1810).
[79] W.A.S. Libr., ch. acct. bk.
[80] Mun. D. & C. Winton., chap. act bk. 1850–76, p. 180. The church was reopened in 1861: Wilts. Cuttings, xvi. 176.　　[81] *W.A.M.* xxx. 197 and n. 1; liv. 21.
[82] Inscription in pulpit.　　[83] *W.A.M.* xii. 364.
[84] Nightingale, *Wilts. Plate*, 182.
[85] Walters, *Wilts. Bells*, 105.
[86] Sar. Dioc. R.O., Glebe Terrier, 1783.

[87] W.R.O. 1364/36–41.
[88] *Vis. Queries, 1783* (W.R.S. xxvii), pp. 122–3.
[89] Sar. Dioc. R.O., Certs. Dissenters' Meeting-Houses.
[90] H.O. 129/250/2/4.
[91] Sar. Dioc. R.O., Certs. Dissenters' Meeting-Houses.
[92] Ex inf. Mr. J. Williams, Somerset Farmhouse, Little Hinton.
[93] All inf. about Coker's char., unless otherwise stated, from *Endowed Char. Wilts.* (N. Div.), 569–73, where Thos. Coker was misidentified as vicar of Bishopstone in Ramsbury hund. Cf. *Vis. Queries, 1783* (W.R.S. xxvii), pp. 122–3; *V.C.H. Oxon.* vi. 24; J. Foster, *Alumni Oxon. 1715–1886*, i. 273; Phillipps, *Wilts. Inst.* ii. 39, 61, 69, 72, 91.　　[94] *Educ. of Poor Digest*, 1029.
[95] Date tablet on sch.
[96] *Educ. Enquiry Abstract*, 1039.
[97] Mun. D. & C. Winton., chap. act bk. 1824–50, pp. 377, 413; W.R.O. 1364/51.

John Brown (d. 1856), of Aldbourne, bequeathed £200 to be invested after his wife's death for the school's benefit.[98] Some 30–40 children, said to be well versed in religious knowledge, were taught at the school in 1859 by an uncertificated mistress and monitors.[99] On return day in 1871 21 boys and 13 girls attended the school, by then affiliated to the National Society.[1] In 1903 Coker's rent-charge was applied to a school at Bishopstone, formerly in Ramsbury hundred, but the remaining income, £20 10s., and £5 8s. from Brown's charity helped to maintain that at Little Hinton. Although Coker's rules were then generally disregarded, the rector of Little Hinton still received £1 yearly and 10s. was still put towards a trustees' dinner. In 1906 an average of 32 pupils had attended over the past year.[2] Average attendances remained steady until after the First World War but thereafter declined. An average of seventeen attended when the school was closed in 1927.[3] Hinton children thereafter attended Wanborough school, although a few attended that at Bishopstone in 1976.[4] After the school's closure its buildings served as a community centre and in 1976 were being converted for use as a village hall.[5]

The income from Coker's and Brown's bequests was between £27 and £50 in 1976 and known as the Little Hinton Educational Foundation. It was administered in accordance with a Scheme of 1929 which allotted a third to supporting a Sunday school at Hinton and the rest to general educational purposes.[6]

CHARITIES FOR THE POOR. Thomas Harding (d. 1721) bequeathed a rent-charge of 10s. arising from land at Wanborough to be paid each 20 September to the unrelieved poor of Little Hinton. In 1834 2s. doles were paid. The 10s. was administered with Batt's charity (see below) in 1903.[7]

Thomas Coker, rector 1684–1741, reputedly gave £6, and an unknown benefactor £14, c. 1742 for the poor. The money was deemed lost in 1903.[8]

Nathaniel Batt, by will proved 1793, bequeathed interest on stock to certain persons, and after the death of the survivor £10 each Easter Monday to the poor of Little Hinton who received no other relief. Any money which remained after distribution was to be paid to the parish clerk or to whomever cleaned the church. In 1847 Batt's surviving legatee transferred the stock to Winchester chapter as lord of Little Hinton manor. In 1903 the yearly income of £8 8s. was administered with the income from Harding's charity and used to buy coal, which was distributed in amounts of 7 cwt. to the unrelieved poor. In 1902 22 people received 7½ cwt. each.[9]

By will proved 1883 John Wilson bequeathed £150 to trustees, the income to be spent each Christmas on bread and coal for all the parish poor. In 1903 the yearly income of £3 6s. was spent on coal. In the previous year 21 coal tickets for 1½ cwt. and 3 for 9 cwt. had been given out.[10]

In 1936 Harding's, Batt's, and Wilson's charities were amalgamated. The joint yearly income was thereafter used to supply needy people living within the area of the former parish of Little Hinton with clothing, bedding, food, fuel, or other goods in kind, or with financial help. The income was about £12 yearly in 1973.[11]

NETHERAVON

NETHERAVON is mostly on the elevated and exposed eastern side of Salisbury Plain mid-way between Upavon and Amesbury.[12] The modern civil parish comprises a rectangular block of land which measures 6 km. from the western boundary across open downland to the Christchurch Avon and extends a little over 3 km. from north to south.[13] The ancient parish included West Chisenbury, a detached tithing 4 km. to the north separated from its parent by the western part of Enford, and had an overall area of 5,160 a. (2,088 ha.).[14] That area was reduced to 1,431 ha. (3,535 a.) when West Chisenbury, c. 1,624 a., was transferred to Enford in 1885.[15] West Chisenbury measured 6 km. from west to east and stretched from north to south for c. 1.5 km. Netheravon and West Chisenbury are topographically similar and in each case the Avon

formed the only natural boundary, the remaining ones running over the chalk uplands.[16] The village of Netheravon and the hamlet of West Chisenbury both lie under the lee of the plain beside the river. From the 13th century until the 19th West Chisenbury, named from the gravel terrace on which it is situated, was known interchangeably as West Chisenbury and Chisenbury de la Folly, a suffix taken from its 13th- and 14th-century lords the de la Folyes, to distinguish it from the Chisenbury in Enford on the east bank of the Avon.[17]

East of West Chisenbury Farm and south-east of Netheravon village the alluvium west of the Avon is 100–200 m. broad.[18] It marks the extent of the flood plain, which lies below the 91 m. contour line. It still bears a covering of lush grass and is the site of the water-meadows which until the early 20th

[98] All inf. about Brown's char., unless otherwise stated, from *Endowed Char. Wilts.* (N. Div.), 573.
[99] *Acct. of Wilts. Schs.* 27.
[1] *Returns relating to Elem. Educ.* 418–19.
[2] *Return of Non-Provided Schs.* 24.
[3] *Bd. of Educ., List 21* (H.M.S.O.).
[4] Ex inf. Chief Education Officer, County Hall, Trowbridge; the incumbent, the Revd. P. Slade, Bishopstone Vicarage.   [5] Ex inf. the Revd. P. Slade.
[6] Ibid.; Char. Com. rec.
[7] *Endowed Char. Wilts.* (N. Div.), 569, 572.
[8] Ibid. 571, 576; Phillipps, *Wilts. Inst.* ii. 39, 69; Foster, *Alumni Oxon. 1500–1714*, i. 299.
[9] *Endowed Char. Wilts.* (N. Div.), 574.

[10] Ibid. 575.   [11] Char. Com. file 234179.
[12] This article was written in 1974.
[13] Maps used include: O.S. Maps 1/50,000, sheet 184 (1974 edn.); 1/25,000, 41/14 (1948 edn.), 41/15 (1951 edn.), SU 04 (1958 edn.), 41/05 (1948 edn.); 6″, Wilts. XLVII (1889 and later edns.), LIV (1887 and later edns.), SU 04 NE. (1961 edn.), SU 14 NE. (1961 edn.), SU 14 NW. (1961 edn.), SU 14 NE. (1975 edn.).
[14] *Census*, 1881.   [15] Ibid. 1891.
[16] The boundaries of W. Chisenbury are shown on W.R.O., Inclosure Award map (1794–5).
[17] *P.N. Wilts.* (E.P.N.S.), 328.
[18] This para. is based on Geol. Surv. Map 1″, drift, sheet 282 (1959 edn.); Fry, *Land Utilisation Wilts.*

century were important to the economy of the area. River gravel succeeds the alluvium at both West Chisenbury and Netheravon. At Netheravon the gravel terrace extends westwards and northwards from the village along the floor of the shallow valley cut through the chalk of the plain by a now dry tributary of the Avon. Around that valley the Upper Chalk forms a wide U-shaped ridge over 122 m. high. At West Chisenbury the Lower Chalk outcrops west of the Upavon–Salisbury road and beyond it successive strata of Middle and Upper Chalk rise north-westwards to 163 m. on the northern boundary near Widdington Farm in Upavon. South-west of that point the Middle Chalk is exposed on the floor of the dry valley called Water Dean Bottom which lies below 107 m. Beyond that the Upper Chalk rises again to over 152 m. Until the earlier 20th century the area west of the Upavon–Salisbury road was occupied by large open arable fields which extended over the chalk for *c.* 2.5 km. in West Chisenbury and over 3 km. in Netheravon. The most westerly third of each tithing was rough downland for grazing. After the War Department bought Netheravon and West Chisenbury in 1898 farming on the downs, at least in Netheravon, probably continued much as before until 1922 when a machine gun school was established at Netheravon.[19] The land west of Wexland Farm has since been used as a firing range and is thus agriculturally of limited use.[20]

A long barrow, some bowl-barrows, a ditch, and two field systems of *c.* 65 ha. and 202 ha. severally provide evidence of prehistoric activity on Netheravon down.[21] A Roman villa stood on the southeastern slope of an outcrop of chalk above the river valley where Netheravon House now stands. Its bath and a tessellated pavement, which may have overlain another of earlier date, were uncovered in 1907. Coins of Constantine I and Claudius Gothicus were found on the site. Another piece of pavement was revealed in 1936.[22]

In 1334 Netheravon contributed 70*s.* to the fifteenth, a medium total for Elstub hundred as then constituted.[23] Netheravon had 111 poll-tax payers in 1377, the highest number in the hundred.[24] 'Chisenbury' at both dates was assessed separately, but whether both East Chisenbury and West Chisenbury were included, or East Chisenbury alone, is unknown.[25] Taxation assessments of the 16th century show Netheravon, then including West Chisenbury, to have been the most highly rated parish, after Enford and its tithings, in the enlarged hundred of Elstub and Everleigh.[26] When the first official Census was undertaken in 1801, the population of Netheravon, including West Chisenbury, was 479.[27] It had fallen by 1811 to 403, of whom 365 lived in Netheravon and 38 in West Chisenbury. Thereafter the population of the parish rose steadily, with two small fluctuations in 1841 and 1861, until 1881 when there were 582 inhabitants. The population of West Chisenbury, which had been transferred to Enford in 1885, was 47 in 1891.[28] The population of Netheravon, 505 in 1891, fell to 440 in 1901. The establishment of a cavalry school in 1904[29] accounted for the large increase in population to 741 by 1911.[30] The continued presence of the Army kept population figures over 700 until the 1930s. By 1951 numbers had risen to 1,032 and in 1971 1,107 people lived in the parish.[31]

At West Chisenbury an eastward loop of the Avon enclosed the hamlet on three sides. The river's course has determined the pattern of settlement in Netheravon and West Chisenbury and also the means of communication with the surrounding area. The road which runs the length of the Avon valley from Upavon through West Chisenbury and Netheravon to Amesbury probably originated in Saxon times.[32] Its route between two chalk masses made it one of the main thoroughfares linking the settlements of the Pewsey Vale with Salisbury. Its importance was increased after the closure of routes across the plain when the downland was acquired by the War Department in the late 19th century and later.[33] Both it and the high street at Netheravon, which branches east from it, were turnpiked in 1840.[34] The sharp V-shaped bend at West Chisenbury Farm was relegated to a double drive leading to the farm-house when the road was then rerouted on a more direct course to the west.[35]

West Chisenbury and Netheravon have been linked with the villages and hamlets east of the Avon by three bridges since at least the 18th century.[36] The footbridge between West and East Chisenbury was from 1848 to 1960 a suspension bridge.[37] At the north-eastern end of Netheravon High Street the road to Haxton in Fittleton is carried across the Avon by Haxton bridge, probably that known in the Middle Ages as 'little bridge'.[38] In 1773 a lane led south from High Street and ran south-eastwards round the church on a course marked in 1975 by the church drive and the footpath which continues from it through the grounds of Netheravon House towards the river, where there was a bridge.[39] By 1790 the lane had fallen into disuse and all that then remained was the stretch providing access to the church.[40] The lane was replaced in the 19th century by the road which in 1975 extended east from Kennel Row and ran across the Avon to Haxton. Of the roads which formerly led westwards over the plain, a few nearer the settlements were still used as farm tracks in 1975. The rest, however, were closed to the public after the War Department bought the land in the late 19th century.

The excellent sport, particularly coursing and hawking, to be had on the downs led the dukes of Beaufort to base a large sporting estate at Nether-

[19] See p. 177.
[20] O.S. Maps 6″, Wilts. XLVII. SW. (1901, 1926 edns.), LIV. NE. (1901, 1926 edns.), LIV. NW. (1901, 1926 edns.).
[21] *V.C.H. Wilts.* i (1), 142, 184, 205, 257, 277.
[22] Ibid. 90–1.   [23] Ibid. iv. 299.
[24] Ibid. 308.
[25] Ibid. 299, 308; and see above, p. 117.
[26] *Taxation Lists* (W.R.S. x), 4, 125.
[27] All population figures, unless otherwise stated, from *V.C.H. Wilts.* iv. 354.

[28] *Census*, 1891.   [29] See p. 177.
[30] *V.C.H. Wilts.* iv. 325.   [31] *Census*, 1971.
[32] *V.C.H. Wilts.* iv. 254.
[33] Ibid. 266.   [34] Ibid. 264.
[35] W.R.O., Inclosure Award map (1794–5).
[36] *Andrews and Dury, Map* (W.R.S. viii), pl. 8.
[37] See p. 118.
[38] *Public Works in Medieval Law*, ii (Selden Soc. xl), p. 235.
[39] *Andrews and Dury, Map* (W.R.S. viii), pl. 8.
[40] W.R.O., Inclosure Award map.

avon in the earlier 18th century. Under the management of the Hicks Beach family, the Beauforts' successors, the estate survived intact until the end of the 19th century.[41] The good trout fishing provided by the Avon, which north of Netheravon becomes a chalk stream, has, especially in the 20th century, also been exploited.[42] A friendly benefit society, popularly called the Top Hat club from the headgear worn by members, was founded at the Fox and Hounds inn in 1840. The rules stipulated that a feast should be held yearly on 29 May and imposed penalties for non-attendance.[43]

Evidence of 17th-century building is visible at either end of Netheravon village. Features of that date are apparent at its south-western corner in the cottage west of the Dog and Gun inn which housed the Sheppard family of blacksmiths in the 18th and 19th centuries.[44] Much building in and around the village took place in the 18th century. There was then settlement north of the church around a grid of lanes between the present church drive and the Upavon–Salisbury road. The lane to the chuch was then built up on either side with the prebendal house and the former Vicarage on the east. Then, as in 1975, settlement also extended west along Kennel Row, northwards along the winding high street, which was built up on either side, and into its northern extension Mill Road.[45] Building in that road, known in 1775 as Mill Row, was confined to the west side since the extensive buildings of Netheravon mill occupied the east side.[46]

Despite 19th- and 20th-century alterations and infilling, High Street retained much of its 18th-century character in 1975. Although many of the cottages, particularly at its southern end, have been altered to form middle class residences, some with thatched roofs and built of brick, chalk, and flint still provide typical examples of the local building style of the Avon valley. The line of the street is broken at various points on either side by the intrusion of a few larger dwellings set back behind gardens. Ivy Cottage, at the south-western end of the street, was formerly attached to Newton farm, and is a small 18th-century house of chequered brick. North of it farm buildings behind a cob wall mark the site of another house attached to the farm.[47] Another house, of similar date but more stylish in design, stands opposite. In the later 18th century it was the home of the Staples family, small freeholders in Netheravon.[48] Court Farm, which stood at the north-western end of High Street until it was burnt down in 1971, was a substantial 18th-century thatched house with later additions.[49] Its site lay derelict in 1975. The sites of other houses were marked in 1975 by high tiled cob walls. Such walls were evidently always a feature of the village and were noticed by Cobbett in the early 19th century.[50] Manor Farm, which stands partly enclosed by

walls at the south-western end of the village, cannot certainly be associated with any of the manors in Netheravon. The house, built early in the 18th century on a U-shaped plan, had its open court on the west filled in soon afterwards. In the early 19th century the interior was extensively refitted and the staircase was moved to the centre of the south front. Then, or soon afterwards, a semi-octagonal bay was added to the centre of the east front at ground floor level and various service quarters, recently demolished in 1975, were built to the north. A large aisled 18th-century barn stands north-west of the house. Wexland Farm was built on the downs c. 800 m. north-west of Manor Farm after 1789.[51] Originally L-shaped, it was refronted in the earlier 19th century and service rooms were added later.

Netheravon House, which stands south of the church, was built after 1734 as a hunting-box by Henry Somerset (afterwards Scudamore), duke of Beaufort (d. 1745).[52] The commanding position of the chalk bluff overlooking the Avon valley, on which it stands, and the discovery of a Roman villa near by indicate a house site of some antiquity. The duke probably built on the site either of the manor-house of Cormayles manor or of that of Netheravon with Haxton manor, but nothing is known of the building which the present house succeeded. The brick house had an asymmetrical double pile plan and a tiled roof with overhanging eaves. The three-storeyed entrance front, which faces southwards across the downs, extends across five bays and has a pedimented porch. The north elevation has an additional basement storey to accommodate the fall in the ground. The duke established a conifer plantation to the south of the house.[53] After 1791 an additional block, which housed a service staircase and one large room on each floor, was added in the centre of the north front from designs by Sir John Soane.[54] Possibly at the same time the overhanging eaves of the main house were replaced by a low parapet wall. The imposing symmetrical stable court, joined to the house by a roofed colonnade, was added to the north-west in the earlier 19th century. An 18th-century dovecot, still used as such in 1975, to the north of the stable range retains its original stone nesting-boxes. The house was often let as a gentleman's residence by the Hicks Beaches in the later 19th century.[55] Except for modern infilling in the north-west corner, it appeared little altered externally in 1975 but internally had been adapted for use as the Officers' Mess of the Support Weapons Wing of the School of Infantry at Netheravon.

The dampness of the marshy ground on which the houses between Kennel Row and the church stood may have led to their abandonment in the early 19th century, and, as in the case of the Vicarage which was rebuilt on the west side of

[41] See p. 177. [42] See p. 175.
[43] W.R.O. 52, doc. concerning friendly soc.; Wilts. Cuttings, xix. 221. [44] See p. 176.
[45] *Andrews and Dury, Map* (W.R.S. viii), pl. 8; W.R.O., Inclosure Award map (c. 1790).
[46] *Andrews and Dury, Map* (W.R.S. viii), pl. 8; W.R.O., Inclosure Award map; Glos. R.O., D 2440, box 37, cts. for Cormayles and Lambert man., 5 Dec. 1821.
[47] W.R.O., Inclosure Award; see below.
[48] W.R.O., Inclosure Award.
[49] Ex inf. Defence Land Agent, Durrington.

[50] W. Cobbett, *Rural Rides*, ed. G. D. H. and Margaret Cole, ii. 379.
[51] Williamstrip Mun. EMS/5, survey of New farm, 1789.
[52] Beaufort Estate Act, 13 Geo. III, c. 110 (Priv. Act); see below, p. 170, and plate facing p. 33.
[53] An oil-painting at Badminton Ho. (Glos.) depicting the duke with a hawking party shows both ho. and plantation.
[54] Williamstrip Mun. EM/BP/1/1–2; working drawings in Soane's Mus., Lond.
[55] Glos. R.O., D 2440, box 76; *Kelly's Dir. Wilts.* (1855 and later edns.).

High Street, their rebuilding elsewhere. In 1975 no trace of settlement remained near the church, which then stood solitary among the meadows across which it was approached through an avenue of elms. Cottages in Kennel Row, probably so called from the kennels of the dukes of Beaufort established there in the earlier 18th century, were replaced in the earlier 19th century by a terrace of brick cottages with sliding casements at first floor level. During the 19th century High Street took on the appearance it presented in 1975. Some cottages of earlier date, which retain their thatched roofs, were then cased in brick, and terraced cottages, larger tradesmen's houses, and a school were built.

The purchase of almost the entire parish of Netheravon by the War Department in 1898 has meant that 20th-century development has been mostly limited to housing for those associated with the various military establishments based at Netheravon House since 1904. Barracks and some associated houses, including a large red-brick villa for the Officer Commanding, have been built in its grounds, and some smaller villa-type residences for officers on the south side of Wexland Avenue. In the village development has been confined to the triangle of land between High Street and the Upavon–Salisbury road. A War Department estate was constructed there in the earlier 20th century and the Court Farm estate, on land formerly belonging to that farm, was built south of it. Cottages on the west side of Mill Road were replaced by council houses in the 1960s. Some new houses were being built in Kennel Row in 1975.

The growth of the parish in the earlier 20th century was accompanied by a corresponding increase in amenities. The village had a police station in 1903 and in 1923 a sub-branch of Lloyds Bank Ltd.[56] By 1926 the former mill buildings east of Mill Road had been converted to an electricity generating station.[57] The Netheravon sewage disposal works, and the cemetery opened c. 1952 by the Pewsey rural district council, are a little east of the parish boundary in Figheldean.[58]

In the late 18th century West Chisenbury was a hamlet straddling the Upavon–Salisbury road. West Chisenbury Farm stood on the east side of the road, a few cottages lay north of it, and one or two cottages were west of the road.[59] By 1975 the cottages on the west side had been replaced by West Chisenbury House. The only other dwellings in the hamlet in 1975 were terraced farm-workers' houses of 20th-century date which stood north of that house on the same side of the road.

MANORS AND OTHER ESTATES. Land at 'Nigravre', to be identified with the later manor of *NETHERAVON*, was held in 1066 by Harold and

in 1086 by William I. Five burgesses of Wilton were tenants of the estate in 1086.[60] The estate was granted to the Beaumont earls of Leicester and was thenceforth considered part of the honor of Leicester. It was temporarily resumed by the Crown in 1174 after the defeat and forfeiture of Robert, earl of Leicester (d. 1190), who had joined the rebellion of the king's sons a year earlier.[61] Robert's son Robert died without issue in 1204 and his Netheravon estate was partitioned with the rest of the honor of Leicester in 1206–7 between Simon de Montfort, earl of Leicester (d. 1218), and Saier de Quency, earl of Winchester, the son and husband respectively of Amice (d. 1215) and Margaret (d. 1235), the younger Robert's sisters and coheirs.[62]

The share of Margaret de Quency, countess of Winchester, passed on her death in 1235 to her son Roger (d. 1264). Roger's coheirs, his daughters Margaret or Margery de Ferrers, countess of Derby (d. c. 1281), Elizabeth or Isabel Comyn, countess of Buchan, and Helen or Ellen (d. c. 1296), wife of Sir Alan de la Zouche, in 1275 held a total of 3 knight's fees, 5 hides, and 1 virgate in Netheravon.[63] The lands were partitioned in 1277.[64] No further mention has been found of the Buchan and Zouche shares, but that allotted to Margaret or Margery, countess of Derby, passed to her grandson Sir John Ferrers, Lord Ferrers (d. 1312), who had livery of his lands in 1293.[65] His heir was his son John (d.s.p. c. 1324), a minor, whose lands at Netheravon were apparently in the keeping of the elder Hugh le Despenser.[66] It was presumably that estate which Despenser claimed had been plundered during his banishment in 1321.[67] Queen Isabel entered the lands after the Despensers' downfall in 1326 and in the following year she was granted the estate at Netheravon, then called a manor, for life.[68] After Isabel's defeat at Nottingham in 1330, Edward III granted the estate in the following year to Edward de Bohun.[69] At de Bohun's death in 1334 Netheravon passed to his widow Margaret (d. 1341) as dower.[70] Although in 1337 a grant of the reversion, repeated in 1340, was made to Hugh le Despenser (d.s.p. 1349), grandson of the elder Hugh, the estate, like the manor of Seend in Melksham, passed on Margaret's death to her husband's brother and heir Humphrey, earl of Hereford and Essex.[71] Humphrey died seised of the view of frankpledge of Netheravon in 1361 and was succeeded by his nephew Humphrey (d. 1373), who at his death held the view of frankpledge and the overlordship of a knight's fee in Netheravon.[72] That estate was assigned in 1384 to his younger daughter and coheir Mary, wife of Henry, earl of Derby (later Henry IV).[73] In 1414, with the rest of the Hereford inheritance, it was incorporated with the duchy of Lancaster.[74] Mary's purparty was detached from the duchy in 1421, however, and the lands reparti-

[56] *Kelly's Dir. Wilts.* (1903, 1923).
[57] O.S. Maps 6″, Wilts. XLVII. SE. (1901, 1926 edns.).
[58] Ex inf. the Revd. J. E. Jackson, Netheravon Vicarage.
[59] W.R.O., Inclosure Award map.
[60] *V.C.H. Wilts.* ii, p. 118.
[61] *Complete Peerage*, s.v. Leicester; *Pipe R.* 1174 (P.R.S. xxi), 34; Levi Fox, 'Honor of Leic. 1066–1399', *E.H.R.* liv. 389.
[62] Fox, 'Honor of Leic.', *E.H.R.* liv. 385–99; *Complete Peerage*, s.v. Leicester; Sanders, *Eng. Baronies*, 61.
[63] *Complete Peerage*, xii (2), 748 sqq.; *Rot. Hund.* (Rec. Com.), ii (1), 258.

[64] Hist. MSS. Com. 78, *Hastings*, i, pp. 323 sqq.
[65] *Complete Peerage*, v. 305 sqq.; iv. 197 sqq.
[66] Ibid. v. 305 sqq.; *Feud. Aids*, v. 202; E 142/33 m. 5.
[67] *Cal. Close*, 1318–23, 543.
[68] E 142/33 m. 5; *Cal. Pat.* 1327–30, 67.
[69] *Cal. Chart. R.* 1327–41, 200.
[70] *V.C.H. Wilts.* ix. 28–9; *Cal. Pat.* 1334–8, 461.
[71] *Cal. Pat.* 1334–8, 461, 518; *V.C.H. Wilts.* ix. 28–9; vii. 100.
[72] *Wilts. Inq. p.m.* 1327–77 (Index Libr.), 322, 371–2.
[73] *Cal. Close*, 1381–5, 511.
[74] R. Somerville, *Duchy of Lanc.* i. 177.

tioned.[75] The Netheravon estate was allotted to the king and again annexed to the duchy of Lancaster.[76]

The share allotted in 1206–7 to Amice, countess of Leicester, passed with the Leicester title until the death of her grandson Simon de Montfort at Evesham in 1265. Simon's lands were granted in that year by Henry III to his son Edmund (d. 1296), whom he created earl of Leicester and, shortly after, earl of Lancaster. The estate descended with the honor of Lancaster like Everleigh manor and passed to Henry, duke of Lancaster, who became king as Henry IV.[77]

By the mid 14th century the Hereford moiety had been subinfeudated. The estate so created was reckoned at a knight's fee worth £5 and was held in 1373 and 1384 by John Matham's heir.[78] The Leicester moiety may possibly be identified with the carucate held of that honor in 1324 and 1330 by Roger de Cormayles.[79] What is probably the same estate was held by another Roger de Cormayles in 1361 of Maud, elder daughter and coheir of Henry, duke of Lancaster (d. 1361).[80] No more is known of the mesne tenants of either estate until the early 16th century.

After the reunification of the moieties within the duchy of Lancaster the Crown apparently alienated the land while retaining certain franchisal and seignorial rights over it.[81] In 1505 Elizabeth Wallopp died seised of the land, then called Netheravon manor and reckoned at 300 a. Her estate apparently passed in turn to her three sisters and coheirs like the manor of Stoke Charity (Hants).[82] It came eventually to the youngest, Joan, wife of John Waller, and passed in the Waller family to Joan's great-grandson William Waller, who was in possession in the early 1570s.[83] In 1575 Waller conveyed 5 virgates at Netheravon to John Barnard (d. c. 1587).[84] In 1576 Barnard sold to his nephew Richard Legg.[85] Members of the Legg family, all called Richard, held the estate until 1693 when Richard Legg of Grateley (Hants) agreed to sell to Joseph Legg of Netheravon.[86] On Joseph Legg's death c. 1716 the lands passed to his widow Jane for life.[87] She had died by 1736 when their son Richard was in possession.[88] Charles Noel Somerset, duke of Beaufort (d. 1756), evidently acquired the estate c. 1755 and thereafter it descended like the manor of Netheravon Cormayles.[89]

In 1255 John de Cormayles and his wife Lettice held an estate in Netheravon.[90] What were apparently the same lands were held of the coheirs of Roger, earl of Winchester (d. 1264), by Edmund de Cormayles in 1275.[91] In 1277 the overlordship of the estate, then tenanted by Lettice de Cormayles, was allotted to one of the coheirs, Elizabeth Comyn, countess of Buchan.[92] No later mention of the overlordship has been found.

The estate is identifiable with the later manor of *CORMAYLES* or *WARDOUR'S*. By the early 15th century it had been acquired by John Levesham who died seised in 1418.[93] In 1419 the lands were committed to a royal keeper because of the minority of Agnes, John's granddaughter and heir.[94] By 1428 Agnes had married Thomas Temse and in 1436–7 they settled Cormayles manor on themselves and their heirs.[95] Thomas (d. 1475) survived Agnes and was succeeded by his grandson William Temse, a minor.[96] William's heir at his death in 1502 was his sister Joan, wife of Nicholas Wardour.[97] She was succeeded at her death in 1531 by her grandson William Wardour, who in 1541 settled his Netheravon estate on himself, his future wife Mary Bamfield, and their heirs.[98] Mary Wardour held the lands from her husband's death in 1563 until 1586, when her son Chidiock Wardour (d. c. 1611) recovered the manor, which by 1592 was also known as Wardour's.[99] Chidiock was succeeded by his son Edward (later Sir Edward) Wardour (d. 1646), and his grandson Edward Wardour.[1] That Edward was apparently still owner at the end of the 17th century.[2] At his death the manor passed, in accordance with a settlement of 1667, to his only child Anne, in possession by 1705. In 1711 she and her husband Arthur Savage sold the manor to William Lewis Le Grand.[3] He was succeeded in 1734 by his son Edward who immediately sold the manor to Henry, duke of Beaufort.[4]

The manor passed with the Beaufort title until at least 1773 when it was settled by Act of Parliament upon trust for sale.[5] William Beach (d. 1790) had bought the estate by 1780. He was succeeded by his daughter Henrietta Maria (d. 1837) and her husband Michael Hicks (d. 1830), who assumed the additional surname Beach in 1790. Henrietta Maria Hicks Beach was succeeded by her grandson Sir Michael Hicks Beach, Bt. (d. 1854), and great-

75 Ibid. 178 sqq.
76 Ibid. 178 sqq., 399.
77 Sanders, *Eng. Baronies*, 61; *Complete Peerage*, vii. 378 sqq.; *Pipe R.* 1218 (P.R.S. n.s. xxxix), 10; E 372/64–5; *Rot. Hund.* (Rec. Com.), ii (1), 258; Somerville, *Duchy of Lanc.* i. 31; *Cal. Close, 1360–4*, 208.
78 *Wilts. Inq. p.m. 1327–77* (Index Libr.), 322; *Cal. Close, 1381–5*, 511, 514.
79 *Feet of F. 1272–1327* (W.R.S. i), pp. 112–13; *Feud. Aids*, vi. 574.   80 *Cal. Close, 1360–4*, 208.
81 D.L. 30/127/1902–3; D.L. 41/3/10; E 317/Wilts. 37 m. 3.
82 C 1/387/67; *V.C.H. Hants*, iii. 448.
83 *V.C.H. Hants*, iii. 448; C.P. 25(2)/239/14 & 15 Eliz. I Mich. no. 683; C.P. 25(2)/260/17 Eliz. I Trin.
84 Badminton Mun. 110. 5. 2, deed, Waller to Barnard; Prob. 11/70 (P.C.C. 18 Spencer).
85 Badminton Mun. 110. 5. 2, deed, Barnard to Legg.
86 D.L. 42/115 ff. 56v. sqq.; Badminton Mun. 110. 5. 2, deeds.
87 Badminton Mun. 110. 5. 2, will of Joseph Legg.
88 Ibid.; *Q. Sess. 1736* (W.R.S. xi), 138.
89 *Complete Peerage*, ii. 54–5; Badminton Mun. 110. 5. 2, endorsement on deeds; see below.

90 *Ex. e Rot. Fin.* (Rec. Com.), ii. 208–9.
91 *Rot. Hund.* (Rec. Com.), ii (1), 258; for the overlordship see above.
92 Hist. MSS. Com. 78, *Hastings*, i, p. 329.
93 C 138/30 no. 7.
94 Ibid.; *Cal. Fine R. 1413–22*, 279.
95 *Feud. Aids*, v. 233; *Cal. Pat. 1436–41*, 26; C.P. 25(1)/257/63 no. 7.
96 C 142/216 no. 61; C 140/43 no. 11; C 140/51 no. 15; *Cal. Inq. p.m. Hen. VII*, i, p. 394.
97 *Cal. Inq. p.m. Hen. VII*, ii, p. 425.
98 C 142/54 no. 96; C 142/216 no. 61.
99 C 142/216 no. 61; Prob. 11/118 (P.C.C. 75 Wood); C 142/232 no. 43.
1 C.P. 25(2)/369/3 Jas. I Trin.; C.P. 25(2)/510/13 Chas. I Hil.; *Musgrave's Obituary* (Harl. Soc. xlix), vi. 204; C.P. 25(2)/761/18 & 19 Chas. II Hil.
2 C.P. 25(2)/887/2 Wm. & Mary Hil.
3 Williamstrip Mun. MTD/34/2.
4 *Musgrave's Obituary* (Harl. Soc. xlvii), iv. 41; *Reg. Adm. Middle Temple*, comp. H. A. C. Sturgess, i. 299; Williamstrip Mun. MTC/39; C.P. 43/605 m. 9.
5 *Complete Peerage*, s.v. Beaufort; Beaufort Estate Acts, 32 Geo. II, c. 23, 13 Geo. III, c. 110 (Priv. Acts).

grandson Sir Michael Edward Hicks Beach, Bt. (later Earl St. Aldwyn, d. 1916).[6] In 1898 Sir Michael, then Chancellor of the Exchequer, sold the manor to the War Department and in 1974 it belonged to the Ministry of Defence.[7]

It was on either the Cormayles estate or the manor of Netheravon with Haxton, bought in 1739, that Henry, duke of Beaufort (d. 1745), built the mansion known as Netheravon House.[8]

Before 1265 Hugh of Manby held an estate at Netheravon of Simon, earl of Leicester.[9] The overlordship of the estate, later called *ST. AMAND'S* manor or, more often, *NETHERAVON* manor, afterwards passed like the Leicester moiety of the capital manor to the earls (later dukes) of Lancaster. It is last mentioned in 1491.[10]

In 1275 the estate, in Netheravon and Haxton, was held by Amaury de St. Amand.[11] At his death in 1285 Amaury was succeeded by his son Guy, a minor, whose Netheravon lands were in the keeping of William Monterville in 1286.[12] Guy, who was dead in 1287, was succeeded by his brother Amaury, then a minor.[13] Amaury's successor on his death in 1310 was his brother John (d. before 25 Jan. 1330), at the time of whose death the Netheravon estate was held by Edmund Ilsley.[14] John's son Amaury, to whom Ilsley conveyed his interest in 1330, died seised of the estate in 1381 and was succeeded by his son Amaury, who in 1402 settled the estate, then first called a manor, on himself and his wife Eleanor for life.[15] After Amaury's death in 1402 Eleanor held the estate until her own death in 1426. It then reverted to Amaury's heir, his great-granddaughter by his first wife Ida, Elizabeth Braybroke, *suo jure* Baroness St. Amand (d. 1491), who married first William Beauchamp (d. 1457), and secondly Roger Tocotes (d. 1492).[16] On the attainder of Tocotes in 1484, the manor was granted by Richard III to William Miles. It was restored to Elizabeth and her husband a year later.[17] Elizabeth was succeeded by her son Richard Beauchamp, Lord St. Amand (d. 1508), who devised his lands to his wife Anne (d. 1511) with remainder to his illegitimate son Anthony St. Amand.[18] In 1524 Anthony and his wife Anne conveyed their Netheravon estate to Richard Lyster,[19] who sold to Sir John Brune in 1557.[20]

From Sir John (d. 1559), the estate passed to his son Henry (d. 1594), and grandson John (d. 1639).[21] Sir John Brune sold in 1626 to Sir Richard Grobham (d. 1629).[22] Sir Richard's eventual heir was apparently his sister Joan, wife of John Howe of Bishop's Lydeard (Som.).[23] The property passed from Joan to her son Sir John Howe, Bt., grandson Sir Richard Howe, Bt. (d. 1703), and great-grandson, another Sir Richard (d.s.p. 1730).[24] The estate then passed to Sir Richard's cousin John Howe (cr. Baron Chedworth 1741, d. 1742), and thereafter descended with the Chedworth title until the death of John, Lord Chedworth, in 1804.[25] It was offered for sale in 1807.[26] The lands were acquired by the Hicks Beach family in the following year and afterwards formed part of their Netheravon estate,[27] which then comprised c. 673 a. in Netheravon and c. 410 a. in Haxton.[28]

In 1275 Amaury de St. Amand (d. 1285) held an estate in Netheravon of the coheirs of Roger, earl of Winchester (d. 1264), to be identified with the estate later called the manor of *NETHERAVON* or *NETHERAVON* with *HAXTON*.[29] The overlordship of Amaury's lands was allotted to the eldest coheir Margaret or Margery, countess of Derby, in 1277 and thereafter followed the descent of her share of the capital manor.[30] Last mentioned in 1381, the overlordship was then held by Thomas, earl of Buckingham, in right of his wife Eleanor, elder coheir of Humphrey, earl of Hereford and Essex (d. 1373).[31]

The estate passed like St. Amand's manor to Amaury de St. Amand (d. 1381).[32] Sir William Hankeford (d. 1423) seems to have acquired it by 1412, when it also included a small amount of land at Haxton.[33] Sir William was succeeded by his grandson Richard Hankeford (d. 1431), from whom the land passed to his relict Anne, with whom he had held jointly.[34] Anne married secondly Sir Lewis John (d. 1442) and thirdly John Holand, duke of Exeter (d. 1447). On her death in 1457 the estate reverted to her first husband's heir, his grandson Fulk Bourchier, later Lord FitzWarin (d. 1479). Fulk settled it on his wife Elizabeth Dinham for life in 1466.[35] In 1507 their son John, Lord FitzWarin, confirmed his mother's life estate.[36] On the death in 1516 of Elizabeth, who married secondly Sir John

---

[6] W.R.O., Land Tax; Inclosure Award; for the Beach and Hicks Beach fams. see Burke, *Land. Gent.* (1846), i. 73; Burke, *Peerage* (1959), 1975; *Kelly's Dir. Wilts.* (1848 and later edns.).

[7] *Salisbury Plain (Property Purchased)*, H.C. 14, pp. 2–3 (1900), xlix. [8] See p. 167. [9] E 142/121.

[10] *Rot. Hund.* (Rec. Com.), ii (1), 258; *Cal. Inq. p.m.* vii, pp. 208–9; *Feud. Aids*, vi. 574; *Cal. Close, 1360–4*, 208; 1402–5, 28; *Cal. Inq. p.m. Hen. VII*, i, p. 313; see above.

[11] *Rot. Hund.* (Rec. Com.), ii (1), 258. This acct. of the St. Amands amplifies that given in *V.C.H. Wilts.* ix. 178 and corrects that in *V.C.H. Berks.* iv. 26 and, unless otherwise stated, is based on *Complete Peerage*.

[12] *Cal. Inq. p.m.* ii, p. 350; *Cal. Pat.* 1281–92, 221.

[13] *Cal. Close*, 1288–96, 62, 68; *Cal. Inq. p.m.* ii, p. 454.

[14] *Cal. Inq. p.m.* v, pp. 148–9; vii, pp. 208–9.

[15] *Feet of F. 1327–77* (W.R.S. xxix), p. 26; *Cal. Close, 1360–4*, 208; C.P. 25(1)/290/59 no. 50.

[16] C 137/37 no. 40; *Cal. Close, 1402–5*, 28; C.P. 25(1)/292/67 no. 142; C.P. 25(1)/292/69 no. 213.

[17] *Cal. Pat.* 1476–85, 392; *Complete Peerage*, xi. 302 and n. h.

[18] *Cal. Inq. p.m. Hen. VII*, i, pp. 304, 313; *Cal. Close*, 1500–9, pp. 346–8.

[19] C.P. 25(2)/46/319/15 Hen. VIII Hil. no. 14.

[20] C.P. 25(2)/81/694/3 & 4 Phil. & Mary East. no. 37.

[21] *V.C.H. Hants*, iii. 219; C 142/239 no. 112; C.P. 25(2)/508/2 Chas. I Trin.

[22] C.P. 25(2)/508/2 Chas. I Trin.; *Wilts. Inq. p.m.* 1625–49 (Index Libr.), 103–7.

[23] *V.C.H. Wilts.* vi. 42.

[24] *Wilts. Pedigrees* (Harl. Soc. cv, cvi), 75; Burke, *Ext. & Dorm. Baronetcies* (1844), 271; C.P. 25(2)/616/1652 Mich. no. 26; W.R.O. 130/61, deed, Howe, Thynne, 1704.

[25] *Complete Peerage*, iii. 156–7; C.P. 25(2)/1476/22 Geo. III East.; *W.A.M.* xlv. 468.

[26] W.R.O. 530, sale cat.

[27] Hoare, *Mod. Wilts.* Elstub and Everley, 28; Glos. R.O., D 2440/27, list of Wilts. deeds, 1850, no. 23; see above.

[28] Williamstrip Mun. MTA/4; for Haxton see below.

[29] *Rot. Hund.* (Rec. Com.), ii (1), 258.

[30] Hist. MSS. Com. 78, *Hastings*, i, p. 325; see above.

[31] *Cal. Inq. p.m.* xv, p. 234. [32] Ibid.; see above.

[33] *Feud. Aids*, vi. 537; C 139/12 no. 32; the following descent of the Hankeford and FitzWarin fams. is, unless otherwise stated, based on *Complete Peerage*, s.v. Fitz-Warin, Bath.

[34] C 139/12 no. 32; *Cal. Close*, 1422–9, 108; 1429–35, 87.

[35] C 139/170 no. 41; C.P. 25(1)/294/74 no. 35; *Cal. Close*, 1468–76, p. 253. [36] C.P. 25(1)/294/81 no. 147.

Sapcotes (d. 1501) and thirdly Sir Thomas Brandon (d. 1510), the estate reverted to John, Lord Fitz-Warin (created earl of Bath 1536, d. 1539). Thereafter it descended with the Bath title until the death of Henry, earl of Bath, in 1654.[37] Henry's widow Rachel (d. 1680) seems to have retained a life interest in some of the land,[38] but the estate itself passed to Henry's cousins and coheirs, the three daughters of Edward, earl of Bath (d. 1637). Those, each of whom inherited a third of the lands, were Elizabeth (d.s.p. 1670), later wife of Basil, earl of Denbigh, Dorothy, who married first Sir Thomas Grey, Lord Grey of Groby, and Anne (d. 1662), who married first James Cranfield, earl of Middlesex (d.s.p.m. 1651), and secondly Sir Chichester Wray (d. 1668).[39] Dorothy's heir, Thomas Grey, earl of Stamford (d. 1720), and Anne's heir, Sir Bourchier Wray, each held a moiety in 1677 and 1680 respectively.[40] Together they dealt by fine with the entire estate in 1685.[41] By 1698 Richard Kitson was owner and remained such in 1701.[42] John Gore was owner in 1710 and in 1722 Elizabeth and Mary Gore, presumably his daughters, seem to have held the estate jointly.[43] Mary afterwards married Henry Dawson and Elizabeth married John Toms; Dawson and Toms were described as lords in 1733.[44] In 1739 the estate, which then included two mills,[45] was held by Joseph Howe and his wife Elizabeth who in that year sold it to Henry, duke of Beaufort (d. 1745).[46] Thereafter it desended like Cormayles manor.[47]

In 1309 William de Burne conveyed land at Netheravon and the remainder of a rent of £10 12s. there to John de Angens for life.[48] Other members of the Angens family held land there in the mid 15th century.[49]

William de Angens in 1401–2 held a fee in Netheravon of the duchy of Lancaster, an overlordship last expressly mentioned in 1634.[50] The estate, later known as the manor of *NETHERAVON LAMBERT*, had apparently passed to Christine, wife of John Keynell, by 1482.[51] In that year Christine and John gave up the land to Edmund Lambert for a yearly rent out of it during Christine's life.[52] On Edmund's death in 1493 his son William succeeded.[53] When William died in 1504 the estate

passed as dower to his widow Alice, on whose death it reverted to William's heir and nephew, another William Lambert.[54] In 1556 William and his wife Elizabeth conveyed the estate to Thomas Golding, who in 1570 sold to Thomas Bushell.[55]

Thomas Bushell was succeeded by his son Thomas in 1591.[56] At his death in 1634 the younger Thomas's property in Netheravon included a virgate called Newton and another known as 'Sawcers', from its 14th-century tenants, as well as the manor. Margery, Thomas's widow, held the estate in dower.[57] Thomas's heir, his grandson John Bushell, was in possession in 1635.[58] By 1685 Samuel (later Sir Samuel) Eyre (d. 1698) had acquired the estate.[59] It descended in the Eyre family and in 1750 his grandson Robert (d. 1752) sold to Charles Noel, duke of Beaufort.[60] The estate afterwards descended like the manor of Cormayles.[61]

Until the mid 18th century an estate called *NEWTON* farm formed part of the demesne of the manor of Netheravon Lambert.[62] Henry, duke of Beaufort (d. 1803), apparently sold it as a separate farm to William Pinniger, who in turn sold it to Richard Compton (d. 1779).[63] Richard devised the farm to his brothers Daniel and James. On his death in 1780 Daniel's moiety passed to his son Daniel, while that of James (d. 1799) came to his son James. Shortly after his father's death the younger James sold his share to his cousin Daniel (will pr. 1817). The whole farm, 316 a., came eventually to Daniel's son James Townsend Compton, who in 1840 sold to Sir Michael Hicks Beach, Bt. Newton farm was thereafter part of the Hicks Beach estate in the parish.

Robert, earl of Leicester (d. 1190), confirmed gifts made to Lire Abbey (Eure) by his father and other ancestors.[64] Among them was evidently land at Netheravon, described as a manor and worth 50s. c. 1210.[65] The overlordship of the estate descended like the capital manor and was included in that moiety which passed to the coheirs of Roger, earl of Winchester (d. 1264).[66] It was allotted in 1277 to one of the coheirs, Elizabeth, countess of Buchan, and is not mentioned again.[67]

In 1275 the estate, reckoned at 3 virgates, was administered from Carisbrooke Priory (I.W.), a

[37] C.P. 25(2)/241/27 Eliz. I Trin.; C 142/407 no. 69; C 142/486 no. 140.
[38] Williamstrip Mun. MCR/13/5; *Complete Peerage*, ii. 19.
[39] C 142/486 no. 140; C.P. 25(2)/616/1652 Hil.; C.P. 25(2)/616/1652 Mich.; C.P. 25(2)/617/1655 Mich.; *Complete Peerage*, s.v. Bath, FitzWarin; G.E.C. *Baronetage*, ii. 41 sqq.
[40] G.E.C. *Baronetage*, ii. 41 sqq.; *Complete Peerage*, xii (1), 221 sqq.; C.P. 25(2)/762/28 & 29 Chas. II Hil.; C.P. 25(2)/763/32 Chas. II Mich.
[41] C.P. 25(2)/806/1 Jas. II East.
[42] Williamstrip Mun. MCR/13/1–4; MCR/13/6–7; MCR/13/9.
[43] Ibid. MCR/13/11–12.
[44] C.P. 25(2)/1079/13 Geo. I Trin.; Williamstrip Mun. MCR/13/14.   [45] See below.
[46] C.P. 25(2)/1233/12 Geo. II Hil. no. 797; C.P. 43/623 m. 3; *Complete Peerage*, ii. 54–5.
[47] See above.
[48] *Feet of F.* 1272–1327 (W.R.S. i), p. 123.
[49] *Wilts. Pedigrees* (Harl. Soc. cv, cvi), 27–8.
[50] *Feud. Aids*, vi. 632; *Wilts. Inq. p.m.* 1625–49 (Index Libr.), 344–5.
[51] So called in the earlier 17th cent.: Sar. Dioc. R.O., ct. bk. of chap. man.
[52] W.R.O. 283/221, deed, Hampton, Michell, Lambert, Keynell.   [53] *Cal. Inq. p.m. Hen. VII*, i, p. 404.
[54] Ibid. ii, pp. 502, 541; C 142/25 no. 4; C.P. 25(2)/81/694/2 & 3 Phil. & Mary East. no. 17.
[55] C.P. 25(2)/81/694/2 & 3 Phil. & Mary East. no. 17; C.P. 25(2)/239/12 & 13 Eliz. I Mich. pt. 1 no. 543.
[56] C 142/232 no. 43.
[57] *Wilts. Inq. p.m.* 1625–49 (Index Libr.), 344–5; *Feet of F.* 1327–77 (W.R.S. xxix), p. 103.
[58] *Wilts. Inq. p.m.* 1625–49 (Index Libr.), 344–5; Sar. Dioc. R.O., ct. bk. of chap. man.
[59] W.R.O. 51/20, deed, Mills, Eyre; C 78/1939 no. 5; for Eyre fam. see Burke, *Commoners* (1833–8), iii. 291–2.
[60] C.P. 25(2)/1234/23 Geo. II Hil. no. 623.
[61] See above.
[62] See above; W.R.O. 51/20, deed, Mill to Eyre, 1685; C 78/1939 no. 5; Glos. R.O., D 2440/13, deed, Gifford, Ludlow, Giles, 1703.
[63] *Complete Peerage*, ii. 54–5. The following descent is based on Glos. R.O., D 2440/27, abstr. of title of Sir M. H. Hicks Beach.
[64] G. W. Watson, 'Ancient Earls of Leics.', *Genealogist*, N.S. x. 13; see above.
[65] *Interdict Doc.* (Pipe R. Soc. N.S. xxxiv), 18, 29.
[66] *Rot. Hund.* (Rec. Com.), ii (1), 258.
[67] Hist. MSS. Com. 78, *Hastings*, i, p. 330.

dependency of Lire.[68] Wareham Priory (Dors.), another dependency of Lire, was entitled to take the 50s. rent from Netheravon in 1325.[69] In 1414 Henry V gave most land in England belonging to Lire to the Carthusian house he had founded at Sheen (Surr.),[70] and property at Netheravon belonging to Sheen is mentioned in the later 15th century.[71] No more is known of the estate.

An unnamed thegn held an estate of 2½ hides at Netheravon in 1086.[72] The estate may be that held by Sir William Longespée (d. 1257) at 'Sethehavene'. In 1270 William de Wyghebergh, who in that year succeeded his father Richard in the estate, held of Sir William's daughter and heir Margaret, countess of Lincoln and *suo jure* countess of Salisbury from 1261.[73] Margaret's daughter and heir Alice de Lacy, who married Thomas, earl of Lancaster (d. 1322), had livery of her mother's lands in 1311.[74] She conveyed land at Netheravon to the younger Hugh le Despenser in 1325.[75] After the downfall of the Despensers in 1326 the land seems to have passed eventually to the Montagu earls of Salisbury like the manors of Lake, in Wilsford, and Alton Barnes.[76] William de Montagu, earl of Salisbury, died in 1397 seised of an estate in Netheravon.[77] His nephew and heir John (executed 1400) was succeeded by his son Thomas (d. 1428), who had livery of the Netheravon estate in 1409.[78] The estate has not been traced further.

An estate of 1½ hide at Netheravon held in 1066 by Edwin had passed to Harvey of Wilton by 1086.[79] Harvey afterwards gave the land to St. Pancras's Priory, Lewes (Suss.), when he became a monk there. In the earlier 12th century Roger, bishop of Salisbury (d. 1139), acquired the estate by exchanging it with St. Pancras for land elsewhere.[80] Thereafter it apparently became part of the prebendal estate at Netheravon.[81]

In the early 12th century the profits of Netheravon church were taken to endow a prebend in Salisbury cathedral.[82] The alienation of the three estates which had formed the church's original endowment meant that its revenues were then much depleted. In order to remedy that deficiency Bishop Roger acquired the estate held by Harvey of Wilton in 1086. A century later Parnel, countess of Leicester (d. 1212), assigned to the church the great tithes from her dower lands at Netheravon, and exhorted her son's tenants there to do likewise.[83] The prebendal estate, assessed for taxation in 1291 at £20,[84] in 1613 consisted of 102 a. of land, all tithes of corn except those from the prebendal glebe, most hay tithes, and tithes of wool and lambs from West Chisenbury manor with two-thirds of those from Cormayles and St. Amand's manors and two other estates in Netheravon.[85] When Netheravon was inclosed in 1790 the prebendary was allotted a corn-rent to replace his tithes arising from Netheravon and 176 a. to replace his lands.[86] In 1796, when the open fields of West Chisenbury were inclosed, he was allotted a corn-rent to replace tithes.[87] The estate was held by the prebendaries until the mid 19th century, except for an interruption in the Interregnum after it was sold by the parliamentary trustees to Thomas Pile and Henry Dirdo in 1651.[88] Under the provisions of the Cathedrals and Ecclesiastical Commissioners Act of 1840, it passed to the Ecclesiastical Commissioners and became vested in them in 1846.[89] The sale of the property was authorized in 1856.[90] In 1860 the commissioners conveyed their reversionary right in the land and in the corn-rent from West Chisenbury to the lessee, Sir Michael Edward Hicks Beach, Bt. Thenceforth the 176 a. formed part of the Hicks Beach estate at Netheravon. In return Sir Michael surrendered his leasehold interest in the corn-rent from Netheravon to the commissioners.[91] That rent was converted into a tithe rent-charge in 1864 and most of it was given to augment the vicarage.[92] The balance of £94 was transferred to Salisbury chapter from 1895.[93]

Lessees of the prebendal estate, traceable from the 16th century, included Henry Brouncker, who obtained a 41-year term in 1535, and William Symonds, the brother of a prebendary, who in 1548 was granted a 90-year term from the expiry of Brouncker's lease.[94] Later lessees included Thomas Bushell (d. 1591) and his son Thomas (d. 1634), owners of Netheravon Lambert manor, Gabriel Pile (1649), and William Reeves (c. 1725).[95] After 1790, when William Beach was tenant,[96] leases passed in the Hicks Beach family like the manor of Netheravon Cormayles until the freehold was bought in 1860.[97]

In the 1550s the house attached to the estate, especially its 'hall', was dilapidated.[98] Its 'banqueting house' and seven bedchambers were mentioned in 1649.[99] That house apparently stood north of the church and although still standing in 1838 had been demolished by the later 19th century.[1] Another house, which formerly stood on the west side of the Upavon–Salisbury road at its junction with the lane leading to Manor Farm, was also considered part of

[68] *Rot. Hund.* (Rec. Com.), ii (1), 258; *V.C.H. Hants*, ii. 230–1.   [69] S.C. 6/1127/11 m. 2; *V.C.H. Dors.* ii. 121.
[70] *V.C.H. Dors.* ii. 122.
[71] B.L. Cott. MS. Otho B. xiv, f. 49.
[72] *V.C.H. Wilts.* ii, p. 118.
[73] *Wilts. Inq. p.m.* 1242–1326 (Index Libr.), 59; *Cal. Inq. p.m.* i, p. 244; *Complete Peerage*, xi. 384–5.
[74] *Complete Peerage*, xi. 384–5; R. Somerville, *Duchy of Lanc.* i. 21.
[75] *Feet of F.* 1272–1327 (W.R.S. i), p. 132; *Cal. Pat. 1324–7*, 102.
[76] See above; *V.C.H. Wilts.* vi. 214; x. 9.
[77] C 136/94/35/14; *Complete Peerage*, xi. 385 sqq.
[78] *Complete Peerage*, xi. 385 sqq.; *Cal. Close, 1405–9*, 458.   [79] *V.C.H. Wilts.* ii, pp. 75, 165.
[80] *Cal. Doc. France*, ed. Round, p. 511; *Reg. Regum Anglo-Norm.* iii, no. 450.
[81] See below.   [82] See p. 178.
[83] *V.C.H. Wilts.* iii. 3–4; *Sar. Chart. and Doc.* (Rolls Ser.), 53; *Complete Peerage*, vii. 532.

[84] *Tax. Eccl.* (Rec. Com.), 182.
[85] Sar. Dioc. R.O., dean of Sar., Glebe Terrier.
[86] W.R.O., Inclosure Award.
[87] Ibid.   [88] C 54/3606 no. 25.
[89] 3 & 4 Vic. c. 113; *Lond. Gaz.* 1 Aug. 1856, p. 2659; *Fasti Eccl. Sar.* ed. W. H. Jones, ii. 406.
[90] *Lond. Gaz.* 1 Aug. 1856, p. 2659.
[91] Ch. Commrs. file 10031.
[92] I.R. 29/38/202; see below, p. 179.
[93] *Lond. Gaz.* 30 June 1896, pp. 3775 sqq.
[94] *W.A.M.* xl. 302.
[95] Prob. 11/77 (P.C.C. 29 Sainberbe); *W.A.M.* xl. 300 sqq.; W.R.O. 415/280, deed, Reeves to Poore.
[96] W.R.O., Inclosure Award.
[97] Ch. Commrs., survey bk. Z 2 (Salisbury cath.), pp. 489 sqq.; see above.
[98] C 1/1333/8.   [99] *W.A.M.* xl. 301.
[1] W.R.O., Inclosure Award; Williamstrip Mun. EMS/5; O.S. Maps 6", Wilts. XLVII (1889 edn.), LIV (1887 edn.).

the prebendal estate.[2] It had been converted into three cottages by 1848.[3]

The hide of land at Netheravon, held in 1066 by Spirtes the priest and by Niel the physician in 1086, belonged to the church there. Durand of Gloucester was then Niel's tenant.[4] Niel is not mentioned again and the overlordship of the estate, to be identified with the later manor of *WEST CHISENBURY* or *CHISENBURY DE LA FOLLY*, descended like the capital manor of Chirton to Durand's heirs, the Bohun earls of Hereford and Essex. As part of the honor of Hereford it was annexed to the duchy of Lancaster in the early 15th century.[5] The overlordship is last expressly mentioned in 1524.[6]

Niel's estate had been subinfeudated by the 12th century. It was held by Roger de la Folye, whose grandson Roger de la Folye was in possession in 1201.[7] Richard de la Folye held the land in 1224.[8] It was perhaps the same Richard who held land at Chisenbury 'la Folye' in 1275.[9] Henry de la Folye tenanted 2 carucates and 6 a. of meadow and was entitled to a 40s. rent at West Chisenbury in 1313.[10] A Henry de la Folye, perhaps the same, in 1337 settled the estate on himself and his wife Isabel for lives with successive remainders to his son Adam and daughter Joan.[11] Adam apparently died without issue and the estate seems to have passed to Joan, probably to be identified with the first wife of John Breamore.[12] John, who had held jointly with Joan, died seised in 1361 and was succeeded by their daughter Avice.[13] From Avice the estate passed to her widower John Romsey who at his death in 1377 was succeeded by Avice's half-sister Joan Bayford, the daughter of John Breamore (d. 1361) and his second wife Margaret.[14] In 1392 Margaret, then wife of Philip Dauntsey, renounced her dower rights in the estate, then called a manor, in favour of her daughter.[15] Joan married secondly Thomas Chaplin and in 1401 they settled the property on themselves and on Joan's heirs.[16] Thus on Thomas's death in 1415 the manor was delivered to Joan's daughters by her first husband William Bayford, Joan, wife of Thomas Ringwood, and Clemence, wife of Richard Devereux.[17] It was apparently allotted to Clemence, whose second husband Robert Browning in 1428 held land formerly Henry de la Folye's.[18] The manor descended in the Browning family to Richard Browning (d. 1524).[19] He was succeeded in turn by

his son Richard (d. 1573), grandson Richard Browning (d. 1612), and great-grandson Anthony Browning (d. 1663).[20] From Anthony the estate passed to his younger son Edmund. Richard Browning, Edmund's son, was in possession in 1706 and in 1708 sold the estate to John Flower (will dated 1723). Flower's heir was apparently his nephew George Flower who was succeeded by his son George. William Beach bought the estate from the younger George Flower in 1776.[21] Thereafter it descended like the manor of Netheravon Cormayles to Sir Michael Edward Hicks Beach, Bt., who in 1861 sold the land, 1,011 a., to Welbore Ellis Agar, earl of Normanton.[22] The estate passed with the Normanton title until 1898 when Sidney, earl of Normanton, sold it to the War Department.[23] The land belonged to the Ministry of Defence in 1974.[24]

Before the Upavon–Salisbury road was diverted to the west in the earlier 19th century West Chisenbury Farm stood close beside it. The road's former course is marked by the farm drive. The house, which dates from the 18th century, was probably reduced in size in the mid 19th century when a large new farm-house, in 1975 known as West Chisenbury House, was built on the west side of the road. The old house, which is of two storeys with attics, includes work of several dates in the 18th and 19th centuries. Although mostly of brick and rubble construction, the building also incorporates earlier stonework.

In 1201 Roger de la Folye, mesne lord of the capital manor of West Chisenbury, conveyed to Peter Bacon an estate of $5\frac{1}{2}$ virgates in 'Chisenbury'.[25] The land continued to be held of the lords of the capital manor. Thus the estate, then called the manor of *CHISENBURY* or *CHISENBURY DE LA FOLLY*, was held in free socage of the Browning family in the early 17th century.[26] It formed part of a larger estate which included land in Whiteparish, Upavon, and Rushall.[27]

Adam Bacon and his wife Maud settled the estate in 1312 on John Bacon and Ellen, daughter of Laurence of Upavon.[28] Bacon continued to hold the land and in the later 16th century Nicholas Bacon (will pr. 1599) was seised.[29] He was apparently succeeded by his daughter Joan, wife of William Noyes.[30] Joan's heir at her death in 1622 was her son William Noyes who in 1624 sold the land to

[2] W.R.O., Inclosure Award (1790).
[3] Ch. Commrs., survey bk. Z 2 (Salisbury cath.), p. 507.
[4] *V.C.H. Wilts.* ii, pp. 157–8.
[5] Ibid. p. 108; x. 62; *Rot. Hund.* (Rec. Com.), ii (1), 258; *Wilts. Inq. p.m.* 1327–77 (Index Libr.), 276; C 138/16 no. 50; *Feud. Aids*, v. 233.
[6] C 142/44 no. 107.
[7] C.P. 25(1)/250/2 no. 12.
[8] *Cur. Reg. R.* xi, p. 532.
[9] *Rot. Hund.* (Rec. Com.), ii (1), 258.
[10] *Feet of F.* 1272–1327 (W.R.S. i), p. 84.
[11] *Feet of F.* 1327–77 (W.R.S. xxix), p. 48.
[12] *V.C.H. Hants*, iv. 571; *Wilts. Inq. p.m.* 1327–77 (Index Libr.), 399–400.
[13] *Wilts. Inq. p.m.* 1327–77 (Index Libr.), 276.
[14] Ibid. 399–400; *V.C.H. Hants*, iv. 571.
[15] C.P. 25(1)/289/56 no. 59; *V.C.H. Hants*, iv. 510.
[16] *V.C.H. Hants*, iv. 571; C.P. 25(1)/290/59 no. 44; *Cal. Fine R.* 1413–22, 140.
[17] *V.C.H. Hants*, iv. 571; C 138/16 no. 50; *Cal. Fine R.* 1413–22, 140.
[18] C.P. 25(1)/292/67 no. 15; *Feud. Aids*, v. 233.

[19] C 142/44 no. 107.
[20] Ibid.; *Herald and Gen.* iii. 519; *V.C.H. Hants*, iii. 48, 70; C.P. 25(2)/526/1 Chas. I East. no. 10; C.P. 25(2)/527/12 Chas. I Trin.; C.P. 25(2)/616/1652 Trin.
[21] All inf. from Glos. R.O., D 2440/37, sched. of deeds, 1861.
[22] See above; Glos. R.O., D 2440/37, deed, Hicks Beach to Normanton; for the Normantons see Burke, *Peerage* (1949), 1501.
[23] *Salisbury Plain* (*Property Purchased*), H.C. 14, pp. 2–3 (1900), xlix.
[24] Ex inf. Defence Land Agent, Durrington.
[25] C.P. 25(1)/250/2 no. 12; see above.
[26] *Wilts. Inq. p.m.* 1625–49 (Index Libr.), 124–6; see above.
[27] *V.C.H. Wilts.* x. 165; *Feet of F.* 1272–1327 (W.R.S. i), p. 81; C 3/257/35; *Wilts. Inq. p.m.* 1625–49 (Index Libr.), 124–6.
[28] *Feet of F.* 1272–1327 (W.R.S. i), p. 81.
[29] C 3/257/35; Prob. 11/94 (P.C.C. 90 Kidd).
[30] *V.C.H. Wilts.* x. 165; *Wilts. Inq. p.m.* 1625–49 (Index Libr.), 124–6.

William Rolfe.[31] Rolfe sold it in 1635 to John Merewether (will proved 1649).[32] In 1643 Merewether settled it on the marriage of his son John and Eleanor Adlam.[33] The younger John added another 81 a. in West Chisenbury to the estate in 1648.[34] Immediately after his death in 1680 his son John (will dated 1689) settled the enlarged estate on his marriage with Mary Bridges.[35] That John's son John sold the land to John Flower, owner of the capital manor of West Chisenbury, in 1720.[36]

Some time in the 13th century John de la Roches, probably a member of the Bromham family of that name, acquired a tenement in West Chisenbury and certain other rights there from Peter Lavington.[37] John had a son Gilbert who married Christine, one of the daughters and coheirs of John de la Folye. When John de la Folye's lands were partitioned in 1252, Gilbert and Christine were allotted ⅓ carucate and 2 virgates at Chisenbury, probably West Chisenbury, and at Coombe in Enford.[38] A sister of Christine, Margaret or Margery, wife of John Saucer, also held land in West Chisenbury since she conveyed 2 a. there to Gilbert.[39] In 1354 Isabel, daughter and coheir of John Saucer, and her husband Thomas de Gomeldon conveyed to John de la Roches of Bromham all the land in West Chisenbury which Isabel had inherited from her father.[40] In 1362 John de la Roches, perhaps the same, granted his West Chisenbury estate for 10 years to Adam Spenser.[41] Sir John de la Roches similarly granted the lands, for term of his life and 1 year after, to Richard Hendy of Haxton in 1379.[42] Sir John de la Roches and his wife William in 1399 settled the estate, then held for life by John Lupeyate and his wife Alice, on themselves and their heirs.[43] Although Sir John and William had a son Robert, their lands passed to their two daughters and coheirs. The West Chisenbury estate was allotted to Elizabeth, wife of Sir Walter Beauchamp, in 1411.[44] In 1439 Elizabeth, then a widow, granted the land to Thomas Forde and his wife Nichole for their lives.[45]

The estate passed like the manor of Roches in Bromham to Sir William Beauchamp (d. 1457), who married Elizabeth, suo jure Baroness St. Amand (d. 1491). After Sir William's death, Elizabeth held jointly with her second husband Sir Roger Tocotes (d. 1492). On Sir Roger's death the estate passed to Elizabeth's son Richard Beauchamp, Lord St. Amand, on those death without legitimate issue in

1508, it passed like Bromham Roches to his kinsman John Baynton.[46] The lands passed in the Baynton family to Andrew Baynton (d. 1563), who in 1555 conveyed them to Nicholas Snell.[47] In 1562 Nicholas (d. 1577) settled the estate on himself for life with remainder to his son Thomas (d. 1607) and Thomas's wife Elizabeth.[48] Thomas's heir was his son Richard (d. 1638), who was succeeded by his son John (d. 1658).[49] From John the estate passed to his son Charles Snell, who in 1683 conveyed it to Walter Ernle (d. 1721).[50] Walter's son, Sir Walter Ernle, Bt. (d. 1732), sold to John Flower in 1723 and the lands became merged in the capital manor of West Chisenbury.[51]

In 1227 the king confirmed the grant of a small estate in 'Chisenbury' by Richard de la Folye, mesne lord of the capital manor of West Chisenbury, to Maiden Bradley Priory.[52] The confirmation was repeated in 1270.[53] The house retained the land until its dissolution in 1536.[54]

A small amount of land at West Chisenbury belonged to the preceptory of Ansty, a house of the Knights Hospitallers, during the Middle Ages.[55]

In 1612 Matthew and William Browning conveyed an estate of 5½ yardlands in West Chisenbury to Giles Tooker.[56] On Tooker's death in 1623 the land seems to have passed under his will to his younger son William in tail male.[57] William's nephew, Sir Giles Tooker, Bt. (d.s.p. 1675), was in possession in 1670 and apparently sold at about that date to Edward Mason.[58] By will dated 1671 Mason devised the estate to his wife.[59] In 1683 his widow Edith held it, and on her death it passed, under the terms of a settlement of 1683, to her nephew William Jay.[60] In 1710 William conveyed the lands to his son William who immediately sold them to John Flower, owner of the capital manor of West Chisenbury.[61]

In 1612 Giles Spicer and his wife Alice held a small estate in West Chisenbury inherited by Alice from her paternal grandfather Thomas Jarvis.[62] Giles, then a widower, sold it in 1640 to Richard Adams (d. 1643) of Enford, who was succeeded by his brother Gabriel (will pr. 1661).[63] Another Gabriel Adams, presumably the elder Gabriel's son, sold in 1690 to William Sainsbury of Market Lavington.[64] William (will pr. 1691) was succeeded by Samuel Sainsbury, who in 1696 sold to Stephen Rutt.[65] Rutt in 1700 sold the lands, then called

[31] Wilts. Inq. p.m. 1625–49 (Index Libr.), 124–6; C.P. 25(2)/372/22 Jas. I Mich.
[32] C.P. 25(2)/510/11 Chas. I Trin.; Prob. 11/210 (P.C.C. 170 Fairfax). [33] Williamstrip Mun. MTD/55/7.
[34] Ibid. MTD/55/8.
[35] V.C.H. Wilts. vii. 212; Williamstrip Mun. MTD/55/10; MTD/55/12.
[36] Williamstrip Mun. MTD/55/15a–b; see above.
[37] V.C.H. Wilts. vii. 181; W.R.O. 212B/2982.
[38] W.R.O. 212B/2985; C.P. 25(1)/251/17 no. 14.
[39] C.P. 25(1)/251/17 no. 14; W.R.O. 212B/2988.
[40] W.R.O. 212B/2989.   [41] Ibid. 212B/2990.
[42] Ibid. 212B/2991.   [43] Cal. Close, 1396–9, 500.
[44] Ibid. 1409–13, 138.   [45] W.R.O. 212B/2992.
[46] V.C.H. Wilts. vii. 181; Complete Peerage, s.v. St. Amand; Cal. Close, 1485–1500, p. 161.
[47] C.P. 25(2)/46/324/38 Hen. VIII Trin. no. 30; C.P. 25(2)/81/693/1 & 2 Phil. & Mary East. no. 56; V.C.H. Wilts. viii. 242 n.
[48] C 142/179 no. 99; Prob. 11/59 (P.C.C. 17 Daughtry); W.A.M. iv, pedigree at pp. 44–5.
[49] W.A.M. iv, pedigree at pp. 44–5.

[50] Wilts. Pedigrees (Harl. Soc. cv, cvi), 184; C.P. 25(2)/747/34 & 35 Chas. II Hil.; Burke, Land. Gent. (1846), ii. 1526.
[51] Burke, Land. Gent. (1846), ii. 1526; C.P. 25(2)/1079/9 Geo. I East.; see above.
[52] Cal. Chart. R. 1226–57, 42; see above.
[53] Cal. Chart. R. 1257–1300, 152.
[54] V.C.H. Wilts. iii. 301.
[55] S.C. 6/7262/Hen. VIII m. 6d.
[56] Williamstrip Mun. MTD/56/1.
[57] Wilts. Inq. p.m. 1625–49 (Index Libr.), 38–41.
[58] Burke, Ext. & Dorm. Baronetcies (1844), 529; Williamstrip Mun. MTD/56/6.
[59] Williamstrip Mun. MTD/56/11.
[60] Ibid. MTD/56/12a–b.
[61] Ibid. MTD/56/13; MTD/56/16b; see above.
[62] C 2/Jas. I/S 21/7; Williamstrip Mun. MTD/54/1.
[63] Williamstrip Mun. MTD/54/3a; MTD/54/7; Prob. 11/303 (P.C.C. 15 May).
[64] Williamstrip Mun. MTD/54/12a–b.
[65] Prob. 11/405 (P.C.C. 123 Vere); Williamstrip Mun. MTD/54/13a–b.

Adams's, to Walter Ernle (d. 1721).[66] The estate apparently merged with the other owned by Ernle in West Chisenbury and afterwards became part of the capital manor.

ECONOMIC HISTORY. In the later 11th century Netheravon contained, besides the capital manor, two smaller estates attached to it. One, of 1½ hide, later formed the prebendal glebe.[67] In 1086 that estate had on it 1 plough, contained 4 a. of pasture, and was worth 30s. The second was held by a thegn in 1086, and, reckoned at 2½ hides, also had on it 1 plough.[68] The estate of 1 hide, which then belonged to Netheravon church, was in West Chisenbury.[69]

The capital manor of Netheravon was reckoned in 1086 at 20 hides, although the two estates then attached to it may have been included in that total. Two of those hides were worked in demesne by 46 serfs and 8 coliberts and had on them 6 ploughs. Elsewhere on the estate there were 16 ploughs, 30 villeins, and 40 bordars. There were 70 a. of meadow land and pasture 3 leagues by ½ league. The value of the manor increased from £40 in 1066 to £57 in 1086.[70]

By the earlier 13th century subinfeudation had resulted in the creation of at least seven lesser estates.[71] The few facts known about medieval agricultural practice both within them and on the capital manor itself indicate the usual sheep-and-corn husbandry. In 1212 the main manor was worth £6, of which £2 10s. represented the value of the stock. It supported 8 oxen and 150 sheep.[72] Lire Abbey's estate was farmed at 50s. yearly c. 1210.[73] Before 1265 an estate, probably to be identified as St. Amand's manor, was worth £2 16s. 7d. At least 28 a. of arable land were worth 6d. the acre; 1 a. of meadow land was worth 1s. An additional pasture was rented from Nicholas Trenchefoil, tenant of the mill estate, at 10s. 6d. yearly.[74]

In the earlier 18th century the dukes of Beaufort built up a compact sporting and agricultural estate in Netheravon, a process which began in 1734 with the purchase of Cormayles manor and ended c. 1755 with the acquisition of the capital manor. In 1768 the estate contained 21 rack-rent holdings which yielded a yearly rent of £709. The 895 a. which they occupied included 50 a. of meadow land, the remainder being arable. Together they supported 2,450 sheep and there were 95 cow leazes. Among the holdings there were three substantial farms: the largest, 508 a., the 'great farm', was tenanted by John Miles; another of 142 a. was occupied by William Sutton, who held another 30 a. at rack-rent; and one of 102 a. was farmed by Joseph Legg. Another 49 estates, all under 100 a., were held upon leases for lives. They occupied 413 a., of which 6 a. were meadow, and supported 924 sheep, and there

were 38 cow leazes.[75] There was apparently no significant rearrangement of the existing farming pattern by the Beauforts, who seem chiefly to have been interested in the sport the estate afforded.

The Hicks Beach family, successors of the Beauforts, maintained and exploited the game on the estate, and in the later 19th century often let the sporting rights.[76] The number of hares south-east of Netheravon House in an area later called the Hare field was remarked upon by Cobbett in the earlier 19th century.[77] A meeting of the National Coursing Club was held at Netheravon in 1841.[78] Fishing rights in the Avon, then known where it flowed through the tithing as Netheravon water, belonged in the 16th century to the sovereign as duke of Lancaster and lord of the capital manor.[79] In 1698 it was customary for the tenants of Netheravon with Haxton manor to fish as 'bankers' along a specified stretch of the river at certain times.[80] The fishing rights were acquired by the War Department in 1898. In the early 20th century the fishing was leased to the Officers' Fishing Association and in 1975 to the Services Dry Fly Fishing Association.[81] The fishery, which extended over some 10 km., stretched northwards to Coombe in Enford and southwards to a point a little north of Amesbury. The use of powdered chalk to cleanse the river bed and to combat pollution and to promote natural regeneration of stock by encouraging spawning on the gravel shallows was pioneered successfully at the fishery by Frank Sawyer, river-keeper for some 50 years. The process was afterwards adopted elsewhere in Great Britain and abroad. Despite its success, the popularity of the fishery, which is confined to grayling and trout, has necessitated some artificial rearing of stock and for that purpose five artificial lakes, stews, nursery ponds, and a hatchery have been constructed in the Avon between Netheravon and Fittleton.[82]

The area between the village and the downland track from Tilshead to Larkhill, in Durrington, was divided into two arable fields.[83] The westerly was known in the earlier 17th century as the Summer field and that nearest the village as the Home field. By that time subdivision had already occurred and both then contained South, North, and Middle fields.[84] Further divisions were afterwards made and in the later 18th century the Summer field also contained Outland South and Inland North fields, and the Home field the Inland South field.[85] The common meadows between the village and the river were named in 1790 as Broad, Landshare, Church, and Picked meads. Another, Corfe mead, lay separate from the rest north-west of High Street. The downland in the most westerly third of the tithing was divided into Outland down to the north and Inland down to the south.

By 1790 it seems that little or no arable or meadow

[66] Williamstrip Mun. MTD/54/14a–b; Burke, *Land. Gent.* (1846), ii. 1526.

[67] See p. 172.   [68] *V.C.H. Wilts.* ii, pp. 118, 165.

[69] See below.   [70] *V.C.H. Wilts.* ii, p. 118.

[71] See above.

[72] *Rot. Litt. Claus.* (Rec. Com.), i. 117–18, 130.

[73] *Interdict Doc.* (Pipe R. Soc. N.S. xxxiv), 29.

[74] E 142/121; see below.

[75] Badminton Mun. 110. 5. 1, survey.

[76] Glos. R.O., D 2440, box 76, letting of Netheravon Ho. 1850–61.

[77] Cobbett, *Rural Rides*, ed. G. D. H. and Margaret Cole, ii. 110–11, 379.   [78] *V.C.H. Wilts.* iv. 383.

[79] D.L. 30/127/1902 ff. 1–2; *W.A.M.* vi. 194–5.

[80] Williamstrip Mun. MCR/13/1–3.

[81] Ex inf. Defence Land Agent, Durrington; *V.C.H. Wilts.* iv. 364, 366.

[82] Ex inf. Brig. E. N. Oldrey, Figheldean, to whom thanks are due.

[83] W.R.O., Inclosure Award (1790).

[84] Sar. Dioc. R.O., dean of Sar., Glebe Terrier, 1613; *W.A.M.* xl. 300 sqq.   [85] W.R.O., Inclosure Award.

land had been inclosed. In that year 3,300 a. were apportioned. William Beach, who then owned the main manor and the manors of Cormayles or Wardour's, Lambert, and Netheravon with Haxton, was allotted 2,144 a. for his demesne lands. It is impossible to distinguish the farms which were included in that total. For St. Amand's manor, Lord Chedworth, under whom William Beach was lessee, received an allotment of 673 a. For the prebendal estate the prebendary of Netheravon was allotted 176 a., and Daniel and James Compton were allotted 165 a. and 160 a. respectively for their lands.[86]

About 1790 the arable, c. 1,252 a., amounted to less than the down pasture, c. 1,624 a. Meadow land totalled 214 a., much of which was presumably floated. The importance of the water meadows in providing early bite for sheep and pasture for cattle after mowing led the inclosure commissioners to make provision for the annual election of a water-man in 1790. That officer was to be chosen yearly at Michaelmas and paid by the owners of water-meadows to distribute the water fairly.[87] Such meadows were still a distinctive feature of both the village's economy and topography in 1826, when they were noticed by Cobbett, and in 1855, when they covered 50 a.[88]

What little woodland there was in Netheravon in the 18th and 19th centuries seems to have been planted for sporting purposes. By 1790 some 3 a., including Black Ball and Robin Hood's plantations, had been established as coverts west of the village.[89] More planting was carried out in 1973 on downland attached to Manor farm by the Department of the Environment, which then administered the defence lands of the plain.[90]

The Hicks Beaches, owners of Netheravon by 1780, altered the pattern of land tenure. The process apparently began before parliamentary inclosure in 1790 since New (later Wexland) farm, 886 a., was in existence in 1789.[91] The creation of new farms and the consolidation of existing ones accelerated after parliamentary inclosure and the process was probably complete in 1838. It was facilitated because in the early 19th century the Hicks Beach family held, chiefly as freeholders, but in a few cases as lessees, nearly all the land in the tithing. In 1838 there were, besides eleven small freeholds, five substantial farms in Netheravon. Of those, four stretched from east to west to include meadow, arable, and down pasture. The largest, the 'great farm', was estimated at 1,188 a., and included the estate bought from the Chedworth trustees in 1808. It occupied most land south of the downland track called Warminster way and was worked from the house later called Manor Farm. The second largest, Wexland farm, was worked with land belonging to Court farm. Estimated at 912 a., the lands lay across the tithing north of Warminster way. The prebendal

glebe, in the same area and reckoned at 176 a., was also worked from Wexland Farm. Court farm, 228 a., and Newton farm, 317 a., both lay in the north part of the tithing. The fifth farm, Newfoundland, 408 a., comprised Outland down in the north-west corner of Netheravon.[92] When the same farms were surveyed in 1855 the area of 'old' arable which they contained jointly was similar to that in the late 18th century. Additionally in 1855 there were 622 a. of down arable. Of the 50 a. of water-meadows 30 a. belonged to the 'great farm'. Another 77 a. of dry meadows lay near the village. Newton and Court farms, whose lands were around the village, then had no down arable, but Newfoundland farm was made up solely of arable and pasture on the downs.[93]

Of the usual rural trades which flourished at Netheravon in the 19th century, the blacksmith's business carried on by the Sheppard family prospered from at least 1779 until the early 20th century. The house from which the Sheppards worked may be identified as that opposite the Dog and Gun inn. A decayed blacksmith's forge could still be seen behind the house in 1974.[94] The Buckland family made edge-tools in the village from at least 1848 until the end of the 19th century.[95] There was a brewhouse attached to the Fox and Hounds inn c. 1852.[96] By 1880 Thomas W. Hussey (d. 1910) had established a brewing and malting business there which was continued by his son A. E. Hussey for a few years.[97]

The hide held by Niel the physician and attached to the church of Netheravon in 1086 is to be identified with the manor of West Chisenbury. There was then land enough for 1 plough. The 3 bordars on the estate had between them ½ plough. Meadow land amounted to 6 a. and the pasture measured 4 by 2 furlongs. Its value in 1066 and 1086 was £3.[98]

By the 13th century the size of the capital manor had been reduced by the creation of at least three other estates.[99] It was worth overall £5 3s. 4d. in 1361. It was then extended at 3 carucates, each of which contained 80 a. worth 3d. the acre. There were in addition 12 a. of meadow land worth 2s. the acre. On the common pastures 6 working cattle, 20 oxen, and 400 sheep could graze.[1] During the 18th century all the estates in West Chisenbury were reunited with the capital manor, and also became part of the Beach estate at Netheravon. In 1782 West Chisenbury was worked as a single farm by James Gibbs.[2] About 1805 Gibbs was succeeded by Henry Jenner, members of whose family were farmers at West Chisenbury until at least the later 19th century.[3]

The tithing had c. 1,012 a. in 1796, of which a total of 966 a. was allotted at parliamentary inclosure in that year to Michael Hicks Beach as lord. Of that total, 518 a. represented the former open arable and 447 a. the downland. There were

86 W.R.O., Inclosure Award. 87 Ibid.
88 Cobbett, *Rural Rides*, ed. G. D. H. and Margaret Cole, ii. 364; Williamstrip Mun. EMS/5, survey.
89 W.R.O., Inclosure Award.
90 Ex inf. Mrs. A. S. Burgess, Manor Farm.
91 Williamstrip Mun. EMS/5, surveys, 1789, 1838.
92 W.R.O., Inclosure Award; Williamstrip Mun. EMS/5, survey.
93 Williamstrip Mun. EMS/5, survey.
94 Ex inf. Mr. J. A. Reeves, Royal Com. Hist. Monuments (Eng.), Salisbury; W.R.O., Inclosure Award. The

Sheppards' acct. bks. from 1779 were preserved at the ho. in 1974.
95 *Kelly's Dir. Wilts.* (1848 and later edns.).
96 Glos. R.O., D 2440, box 37, abstr. of title.
97 *Kelly's Dir. Wilts.* (1880 and later edns.).
98 *V.C.H. Wilts.* ii, p. 157.   99 See above.
1 *Wilts. Inq. p.m.* 1327–77 (Index Libr.), 276.
2 H.R.O., Normanton Mun., box 3, bdle. 104, agreement, Beach and Gibbs.
3 W.R.O., Land Tax; *Kelly's Dir. Wilts.* (1848 and later edns.).

two downs, West Chisenbury down, 347 a., and, occupying the most westerly triangle of land in the tithing, Lavington Way down, 100 a.[4] The estate, then known as Chisenbury farm, 1,053 a., was arranged in much the same way in 1861. There was then a water-meadow of *c.* 5 a. by the Avon north-east of the hamlet.[5]

The expansion of the Hicks Beach estate in Netheravon was arrested by the agricultural depression of the later 19th century. Rents on the estate fell 40 per cent from the mid 1870s to the 1890s.[6] The decline in arable and sheep farming at that time resulted in large tracts of rough pasture on Salisbury Plain falling out of use. It was decided to turn the plain over to military use and estates around its perimeter were bought up. Among the first acquired by the War Department were the Netheravon estate, bought from Sir Michael Hicks Beach, Bt., then Chancellor of the Exchequer, and the West Chisenbury estate, bought from the earl of Normanton.[7] The extremely favourable price obtained by Sir Michael at a time of diminishing returns on land gave rise to much adverse comment both locally and nationally.[8] Since then both Netheravon and West Chisenbury have been entirely in state ownership, and the arable and rough pasture occupying the western half of each have been used for military training since at least the 1920s. The lands were administered in 1975 by the Department of the Environment.

In 1904 the War Department set up a cavalry training centre with indoor riding-school and stabling in the grounds of Netheravon House, which itself was used as the officers' mess.[9] During the First World War the school closed and the house was occupied by convalescent Canadian troops. Although the cavalry school re-opened in 1919, it closed in 1922 and was amalgamated with the Royal Artillery Riding Establishment at Weedon (Northants.). In 1922 the Machine Gun School moved to Netheravon from Seaford (Suss.), and occupied the outbuildings of the cavalry school as instructional rooms and Netheravon House as an officers' mess. In 1974 the school, then called Support Weapons Wing and operated as a branch of the School of Infantry at Warminster, taught instructors to use various weapons and other defensive equipment. There was a permanent instructional and administrative staff of *c.* 100 at Netheravon in 1974, mostly accommodated on an army estate south of Netheravon House.

The growth of the village after the establishment of an army camp in the early 20th century was reflected in the numerous small businesses in High Street in 1975. They included butcher's, grocer's,

clock repairer's, and hairdresser's shops. The former brewery buildings on the east side of the street were then occupied by a firm of electrical contractors, E. J. Wordsell & Son, and those of the former mill were in industrial use.[10] In 1975, however, despite the presence of the Army, the parish's economy was still predominantly agricultural. The incorporation of the downland west of the village in the firing ranges of Salisbury Plain severely limited its use for practical farming purposes, but much was still leased to local farmers in 1975 and used for grazing. The two largest farms in Netheravon were then devoted to mixed farming. Wexland farm, leased to Bennett Bros., contained some 1,000 a. which could be farmed subject to certain restrictions.[11] Manor farm comprised some 200 a. of unrestricted land in the south-west part of Netheravon and was tenanted by A. S. Burgess.[12] In 1975 West Chisenbury farm was held by A. M. Baxter and given over to mixed farming. It contained much land which could be used only for grazing.[13]

MILLS. In 1086 three mills on the royal estate at Netheravon were worth together 30s.[14] By 1185 one had been granted to the Templars, probably by Robert, earl of Leicester (d. 1190), lord of the capital manor. It was attached to their estate at Inglewood, in Kintbury (Berks.), and leased to a clerical tenant for ½ mark.[15] No more is known of it.

A second mill was apparently allotted to Amice, countess of Leicester, in 1206–7 and *c.* 1265 was held of Amice's grandson Simon, earl of Leicester, by Hugh of Manby. It was then worth only 12d. because it was in bad repair.[16] It is not mentioned again.

The third mill apparently passed with that moiety of the capital manor allotted in 1206–7 to Saier, earl of Winchester, and his wife Margaret.[17] In the 13th century William Trenchefoil held the mill of an earl of Winchester, either Saier (d. 1219), or his son Roger (d. 1264).[18] Although no mill was then expressly mentioned, what was clearly the same estate was held by Nicholas Trenchefoil of the coheirs of Roger, earl of Winchester, in 1277. It was then worth yearly £10.[19] A water-mill and 100 a. of land at Netheravon were held by John Trenchefoil in 1384.[20] In 1393 Felice, John's widow, conveyed the mill, 6 a. of land, and some meadow to William Hankeford. Thereafter the mill estate descended like the manor of Netheravon with Haxton, passed with it into the Hicks Beach estate at Netheravon in the later 18th century, and in 1898 became War Department property.[21] It belonged to the Ministry of Defence in 1975.

The mill and its buildings were always leased out and were tenanted for most of the 19th century by the Bray family.[22] The mill stood on the west bank

[4] W.R.O., Inclosure Award.
[5] H.R.O., Normanton Mun., box 3, bdle. 105a, plan; Glos. R.O., D 2440, box 37, val.
[6] V.C.H. Wilts. iv. 105.
[7] Salisbury Plain (Property Purchased), H.C. 14, pp. 2–3 (1900), xlix.
[8] W.A.M. xxx. 359.
[9] Inf. in this para. supplied by Maj. E. W. Leask, Support Weapons Wing, Sch. of Infantry, Netheravon.
[10] See below.
[11] Ex inf. Mrs. Bennett, Wexland Farm.
[12] Ex inf. Mrs. A. S. Burgess, Manor Farm.
[13] Local information.   [14] V.C.H. Wilts. ii, p. 118.
[15] Rec. Templars in Eng. in 12th Cent. ed. Beatrice A.

Lees, p. 52 and n.
[16] E 142/121; see above, p. 169.
[17] Hist. MSS. Com. 78, Hastings, i, p. 342; see above, p. 168.
[18] Hist. MSS. Com. 78, Hastings, i, p. 342; Sanders, Eng. Baronies, 61.
[19] Hist. MSS. Com. 78, Hastings, i, pp. 324, 327, 329.
[20] Public Works in Medieval Law, ii (Selden Soc. xl), p. 235.
[21] C.P. 25(1)/256/57 no. 10; C.P. 25(2)/1233/12 Geo. II Hil. no. 797; see above.
[22] Williamstrip Mun. MCR/13/5; EMA/35/15; Glos. R.O., D 2440, box 68, rent accts. 1806–61 (acct. for 1830); Kelly's Dir. Wilts. (1848 and later edns.).

of the Avon north-west of Haxton bridge.[23] From at least the later 16th century the building was described as containing two water-mills.[24] Milling continued in 1911 but seems to have ceased soon after.[25] An electricity generating station had been set up in the former mill buildings by 1926.[26] In 1975 the large building, a red-brick structure of 19th-century date, was occupied by a plastics firm, C.D.M. of Durrington.[27] The former mill-house, which stands south-west of it, is principally of earlier-19th-century date but retains part of an early-18th-century building at its eastern end.

LOCAL GOVERNMENT. In 1275 Edmund, earl of Lancaster, who held a moiety of the capital manor of Netheravon, claimed to have gallows there and to hold assizes of bread and of ale.[28] No mention was then made of franchisal jurisdiction attached to the moiety held by the coheirs of Roger, earl of Winchester. In the later 14th century and the earlier 15th, however, whoever held that moiety was entitled to hold view of frankpledge, worth 6s. 8d. yearly.[29] After the reunification of the moieties within the duchy of Lancaster in the earlier 15th century, the duchy alienated the estate but retained both franchisal and seignorial jurisdiction. Records of courts, designated views of frankpledge, survive for 1542, 1543, 1545, and 1548. At the courts tithingmen and constables were elected and the presentments of the tithing jury and of the manorial homage received.[30] In 1597 the Crown granted Netheravon all liberties and franchises to which duchy tenants were entitled.[31] In 1652 the court there, then called a court leet, could try all actions under 40s. between duchy tenants.[32]

In the 17th century courts baron for the manors of Netheravon Lambert and Netheravon with Haxton were also held, sometimes twice, but more often once, yearly. Records of courts for Lambert manor survive for 1635–6, 1644, and 1740, while those for Netheravon with Haxton cover 1698–1701, 1710, 1722, and 1733. Both courts met chiefly to deal with copyhold business. Sometimes manorial customs were recited, as at the court for Netheravon with Haxton manor held in 1698. Particular nuisances were also dealt with, as in 1740 when Henry, duke of Beaufort, was presented by the homage of Netheravon Lambert for illegally building a kennel within the manor.[33] There seems to have been a brief attempt by Michael Hicks Beach to revive the Netheravon courts in the 1820s. A joint

court baron for Lambert and Cormayles manors was held in 1821.[34] Perhaps in an attempt to revive the franchisal jurisdiction to which the lords of the capital manor had earlier been entitled, views of frankpledge and courts baron were held for the manor of Netheravon with Haxton in 1821, 1827, and 1829.[35] Tithingmen were appointed at the views and manorial officials at the courts baron, but little other business was transacted.[36] No record of courts for the West Chisenbury manors is known to exist.

Minutes of meetings between 1846 and 1922 show the vestry dealing with the usual business. In 1848 it was concerned to assist certain parishioners to emigrate to Australia.[37] Netheravon and West Chisenbury became part of Pewsey poor-law union in 1835.[38]

CHURCH. The church at Netheravon was held in 1066 by Spirtes the priest and in 1086 by Niel the physician.[39] Its endowments then comprised three substantial estates identifiable with the later manors of East Chisenbury in Enford, West Chisenbury, and Stratton St. Margaret.[40] The size and the value, £32, of the endowment suggest the existence at Netheravon of a religious community, either regular or secular, before the reign of Edward the Confessor. The community, however, was presumably no longer there in 1066.[41] Probably in the later 11th century the three estates became lay fees.[42] The church apparently reverted to the king and in the early 12th century Henry I granted it to Salisbury chapter.[43] Thenceforth its profits were appropriated to endow a prebend in the cathedral. The peculiar jurisdiction exercised by the prebendaries enabled them to hold visitations and to deal with all ecclesiastical matters, administrative and judicial, within the parish until such powers were abolished in 1846.[44] The prebendaries presented vicars to serve the cure until the 19th century. A vicarage had been ordained by 1316, when a vicar is first mentioned. So far as is known, the prebendaries delegated their right of patronage only twice, in 1568 when John Linch presented, and in 1587 when Hugh Powell did so.[45] The advowson was transferred to the bishop of Salisbury under an Act of 1840.[46] From 1931 the vicarage was held in plurality with the rectory of Fittleton.[47] Vicarage and rectory, which from 1947 was also in the gift of the bishop, were united in 1953.[48] The vicarage of Enford was added in 1973 and the united benefice of Netheravon with Fittleton and Enford was created. The first

[23] Williamstrip Mun. EMP/1; W.R.O., Inclosure Award (1790).
[24] C.P. 25(2)/241/27 Eliz. I Trin.; Williamstrip Mun. EMA/35/15; EMP/1.
[25] Kelly's Dir. Wilts. (1911, 1923).
[26] Local information; O.S. Map 6", Wilts. XLVII. SE. (1901 edn.), XLVII. SE. (1926 edn.); Kelly's Dir. Wilts. (1931, 1939). [27] Local information.
[28] Rot. Hund. (Rec. Com.), ii (1), 258.
[29] Wilts. Inq. p.m. 1327–77 (Index Libr.), 322; D.L. 42/18 p. 49.
[30] D.L. 30/127/1902 ff. 1–3, 35; D.L. 30/127/1903 m. 2d.
[31] D.L. 41/3/10.
[32] E 317/Wilts. 37 m. 3.
[33] Sar. Dioc. R.O., ct. bk. of chap. man.; Williamstrip Mun. MCR/2/42; MCR/13/1–4; MCR/13/6–7; MCR/13 9–12; MCR/13/14.
[34] Glos. R.O., D 2440, box 37, ct. rec. 5 Dec. 1821.
[35] Ibid. 6 Dec. 1821.
[36] Ibid. 5, 6 Dec. 1821.
[37] Vestry mins. penes the Revd. J. E. Jackson, Netheravon Vicarage.
[38] Poor Law Com. 2nd Rep. 560.
[39] V.C.H. Wilts. ii, pp. 31, 118.
[40] Ibid. pp. 118, 157.
[41] Ibid. p. 31. [42] See pp. 124, 173.
[43] Reg. St. Osmund (Rolls Ser.), i. 201; V.C.H. Wilts. iii. 159.
[44] Ct. and vis. papers, presentments, and vis. returns, 16th–19th cent., are in Sar. Dioc. R.O.; Fasti Eccl. Sar. ed. W. H. Jones, i. 52.
[45] Reg. Martival (Cant. & York Soc.), ii. 79; Sar. Dioc. Regy., Dean's Inst. Reg. 1549–1846, ff. 12, 18v., 27v., 60v., 73v., 74v., 92, 93v., 98, 112v., 121, 156v., 158, 189v.
[46] 3 & 4 Vic. c. 113.
[47] Crockford (1935 and later edns.).
[48] Lond. Gaz. 30 Oct. 1953, p. 5776; ex inf. Dioc. Registrar.

turn of presentation was then allotted to Christ's Hospital, Horsham (Suss.), patron of Enford, and the second and third turns to the bishop.[49]

In 1535 the vicarage was worth £13 6s. 8d.[50] No more is known of its value until the earlier 19th century when, from 1829 to 1831, it was worth yearly an average of £101 net.[51] That sum represented the value of the tithes and a yearly payment of £20 by the prebendaries of Netheravon, later continued by the Ecclesiastical Commissioners.[52] Augmentations of £400 and £100, given as one benefaction by the then vicar of Netheravon and the trustees of a Mrs. Pyncombe respectively, and another of £200 from Queen Anne's Bounty, were made in 1838.[53] The Ecclesiastical Commissioners granted £30 yearly in 1848.[54] That sum and the payments of £20 were withdrawn in 1865 when the Ecclesiastical Commissioners transferred to the vicar the yearly sum of £268, which represented most of the prebendal tithe rent-charge due to them from Netheravon.[55]

The vicar took all tithes from the prebendal glebe and all tithes of wool, lambs, and hay in the parish except those to which the prebendary was entitled.[56] In the early 17th century the vicar of Upavon took a third of the wool tithes from a farm in West Chisenbury but no further mention of the payment is made.[57] In 1790 the vicar was allotted a corn-rent of £66 to replace his tithes from Netheravon and in 1796 one of £15 in place of those from West Chisenbury.[58]

A small close of meadow by the Avon constituted the vicarial glebe.[59] In 1846 it was exchanged with Sir Michael Hicks Beach, Bt., for 1 a. called Oram's near the Vicarage.[60] The vicar in 1861 acquired another 3 a. west of the Vicarage which the Ecclesiastical Commissioners had bought from Sir Michael Edward Hicks Beach, Bt., a year earlier.[61]

The vicarage-house, first mentioned in 1613, was burned down c. 1694. Until the late 18th century the Vicarage stood some distance north of the church.[62] In 1793, because of its unfit state, it was exchanged for a newly rebuilt house on the west side of High Street.[63] A new Vicarage was built on the same site c. 1838.[64]

A chapel of ease at West Chisenbury is mentioned in 1405. It was dedicated to St. John the Baptist and among its possessions were a silver chalice and a bell It was no longer standing c. 1535.[65]

John Ring, vicar 1610–61, subscribed to the *Concurrent Testimony* of 1648 and in 1650 was reported to preach every Sunday.[66] The fact that Richard Lewis, vicar 1685–1725, celebrated Holy Communion in the chancel, and not in the nave, and that he excluded certain parishioners from receiving it, led some people in Netheravon to complain to the dean of Salisbury in 1688. The parishioners also objected to the unreasonable and aggressive manner in which he collected his tithes.[67] Curates assisted the vicars in the later 17th century and in the 18th century, in the period 1829–31, and in 1864.[68] Among them was Sydney Smith (d. 1845), curate in the later 1790s.[69] During his short stay he attempted to improve the condition of the poor and established a Sunday school which still flourished in the earlier 19th century.[70] He had little contact with the parish, the dullness of which he loathed, after Michael Hicks Beach (d. 1830), lord of the manor, appointed him travelling tutor to his eldest son. Later one of the founders of the *Edinburgh Review*, Smith afterwards moved to London, where he acquired a reputation as a man of letters.

The distance of some 4 km. between West Chisenbury and the parish church led to the infrequent attendance of those living in that hamlet. A suggestion of c. 1650 that the tithing should be annexed to Enford for ecclesiastical purposes came to nothing.[71] During 1850–1 an average congregation of 150 people attended morning services and 200 those on Sunday afternoons.[72] Services with either the celebration of Holy Communion or a sermon were held on Sunday mornings in 1864. Afternoon services always included a sermon. Weekday services were said to be poorly attended. About 80 people in the parish were said to be regular communicants.[73]

The church of *ALL SAINTS* stands at the southern end of the village. It has a chancel with north vestry and south porch, aisled and clerestoried nave, and west tower.

A church stood at Netheravon on the site of the present church in the earlier 11th century.[74] It was cruciform and comprised a small chancel or apse where the present nave stands, *porticus* to the north

---

[49] Ex inf. Dioc. Registrar.
[50] *Valor Eccl.* (Rec. Com.), ii. 145.
[51] *Rep. Com. Eccl. Revenues*, 842–3.
[52] Ch. Commrs., survey bk. Z 2 (Salisbury cath.), pp. 489 sqq.; *Lond. Gaz.* 7 Feb. 1865, pp. 570 sqq.
[53] C. Hodgson, *Queen Anne's Bounty* (1845 edn.), pp. ccxxv, cccxxxvi.
[54] *Lond. Gaz.* 1 Sept. 1848, pp. 3221 sqq.
[55] Ibid. 7 Feb. 1865, pp. 570 sqq.; see above, p. 172.
[56] Sar. Dioc. R.O., dean of Sar., Glebe Terrier, 1613; W.R.O., Inclosure Award; see above, p. 172.
[57] Sar. Dioc. R.O., dean of Sar., Glebe Terrier, 1613; *V.C.H. Wilts.* x. 171.
[58] W.R.O., Inclosure Awards.
[59] Sar. Dioc. R.O., dean of Sar., Glebe Terrier, 1613; W.R.O., Inclosure Award (1790).
[60] Glos. R.O., D 2440/13, deed, Blandy, Lear, and others, 1846.
[61] Ch. Commrs., survey bk. Z 2 (Salisbury cath.), p. 673; file 10031; *Lond. Gaz.* 16 Apr. 1861, pp. 1601–2.
[62] Sar. Dioc. R.O., dean of Sar., Glebe Terrier, 1613; Chwdns.' Pres. 1694; W.R.O., Inclosure Award.
[63] Sar. Dioc. R.O., Netheravon prebend, deeds, dean of Sar. and Dyke; W.R.O., Inclosure Award.
[64] Sar. Dioc. R.O., dean of Sar., Mortgages; Ch.

Commrs., survey bk. Z 2 (Salisbury cath.), p. 513.
[65] Sar. Dioc. Regy., Reg. Dean Chaundler, ff. 48–9, 76; W.A.M. x. 268.
[66] Sar. Dioc. Regy., Dean's Inst. Reg. ff. 27v., 60v.; *Calamy Revised*, ed. A. G. Matthews, 557; W.A.M. xl. 299.
[67] Sar. Dioc. Regy., Dean's Inst. Reg. ff. 74v., 92; W.A.M. xlv. 84–6. Lewis was imprisoned at Fisherton Anger c. 1694: Sar. Dioc. R.O., dean of Sar., Chwdns.' Pres. 1694.
[68] W.A.M. xlv. 479; Sar. Dioc. R.O., Netheravon prebend, vis. and ct. rec. 1738–99; *Rep. Com. Eccl. Revenues*, 842–3; Sar. Dioc. R.O., Vis. Queries, 1864.
[69] All inf. about Sydney Smith from *D.N.B.*; *Dict. Eng. Ch. Hist.* ed. S. L. Ollard, G. Crosse, M. F. Bond (1948 edn.), 574.
[70] Lambeth MS. 1732; *Educ. of Poor Digest*, 1033; *Educ. Enquiry Abstract*, 1043.
[71] Sar. Dioc. R.O., dean of Sar., Chwdns.' Pres. later 1560s; Netheravon prebend, vis. and ct. rec. 1626–39; W.A.M. xl. 299.   [72] H.O. 129/261/1/1.
[73] Sar. Dioc. R.O., Vis Queries.
[74] Unless otherwise stated, the following description is based on W.A.M. xlvii. 606–7; Pevsner, *Wilts.* (2nd edn.), 353–4.

and south of the central tower, and nave to the west. The positions of the *porticus* are indicated by fragments of masonry on the west wall of the tower and by blocked round-headed doorways in its north and south walls. A doorway surviving in the middle stage of the north wall of the tower shows that there was a room above that *porticus*. That building was ruinous in 1086 and the roof in danger of collapse.[75] Part of it may have remained in use until the 13th century when a new aisled and clerestoried nave, of four bays, and a chancel were built to the east of the old tower. That tower and its western arch, with roughly sculptured beasts depicted on the capitals, were retained, a new upper stage added, and an arch inserted in the east wall. The church thus attained its present size and shape. A two-light window was inserted at the west end of the south aisle in the 14th century. The corresponding window in the north aisle is a modern copy. With the exception of their west walls, the nave aisles were rebuilt in the 15th century. Each was entered by a door sheltered by a porch with tiled roof in the second bay from the west.[76] From the mid 16th century both nave and chancel were frequently reported out of repair.[77] Simon Symonds, prebendary 1534–51, was accused of allowing his brother William, to whom he had leased the prebendal estate, to remove the lead from the chancel roof.[78] The chancel may then have been reroofed with the tiles which covered it in 1803.[79] About 1600 the lead of the nave roof and tiles of the aisle porches apparently needed renewing.[80] Cresting and pinnacles were added to the tower in 1626.[81] Repair of the south aisle, at least during the 17th century, was the responsibility of the owners of Cormayles or Wardour's manor, or of their lessees.[82] It was perhaps during the restoration of the church undertaken in 1839, or shortly afterwards, that the aisle porches were removed and the doorways replaced by copies of the other aisle windows.[83] The south aisle may then have been extended eastwards and its porch re-sited at the eastern end to provide separate access to the chancel from near-by Netheravon House. The low ceiled leaden roof of the nave, so depicted in 1803, was replaced in 1888 during C. E. Ponting's restoration by a tiled one of steeper pitch. The 13th-century chancel arch was then replaced by a new one of freestone.[84]

In 1833 William Gill and John Herne were reported to have conveyed 4 a. of arable in the open fields of Netheravon to trustees in 1668, for the use of the parish church.[85] At inclosure in 1790 the churchwardens were allotted some 7 a. called the Landshare allotment in the north part of Netheravon.[86] The income of £6 13s. 4d. was used to pay

for church repairs in 1833. The War Department bought the land in 1900 and some £338 was invested by the Official Trustee of Charitable Funds. The following year the income was still used for church purposes. It was afterwards incorporated in the general church account and in 1974 was still used to pay for repairs.[87]

In 1553 the king's commissioners left a chalice weighing 10 oz. Elizabeth (d. 1799), widow of Charles Noel, duke of Beaufort, in 1759 gave the church a chalice, paten, flagon, and alms-dish made by Magdalene Feline. A small chalice and paten dated 1923 were given by A. E. Hussey. The parish retained those pieces in 1974.[88] Netheravon had three bells and a sanctus bell in 1553. There was a ring of six in 1974. The fourth, cast by John Wallis, is dated 1585. Wallis also made the treble (ii in 1974) dated 1609 and the tenor dated 1588. A. E. Hussey had both recast in 1911 by Taylor of Loughborough (Leics.) in memory of his father T. W. Hussey. A new treble made by the same firm was then added, also in memory of T. W. Hussey, and the whole peal rehung. The third and fifth bells are of 17th-century date.[89]

Registrations of baptisms begin in 1582 but are lacking from 1594 to 1611. Records of baptisms resume, and those of marriages and burials begin, in 1611 and thereafter are complete.[90]

ROMAN CATHOLICISM. The Browning family, established at West Chisenbury from the 15th century, seems consistently to have resisted the religious changes of the 16th century.[91] Thomas Browning and his wife were presented for not receiving the Sacrament at the parish church in 1597.[92] Anthony Browning, lord of West Chisenbury manor from 1612 until his death in 1663, maintained the family's recusant tradition.[93] The Roman Catholic church in Figheldean was set up partly to serve Netheravon.[94]

PROTESTANT NONCONFORMITY. Thomas Bushell (d. 1634), lord of the manor of Netheravon Lambert, apparently held conventicles at his house in the 1590s which were attended by John Davies and two others.[95] In 1597 a Mr. Lapthorne expounded the scriptures there. He also claimed from the pulpit in Netheravon church that salvation was possible only through prayer and preaching. Thomas Bushell himself asserted that the then vicar's unwillingness to preach made him an unsuitable minister.[96] Dissent appears to have continued and in 1672

[75] *V.C.H. Wilts.* ii, p. 118.
[76] The N. porch is shown in a water-colour by J. Buckler: W.A.S. Libr., vol. v. 6 (1803).
[77] Sar. Dioc. R.O., Netheravon prebend, vis. and ct. rec.
[78] C 1/1333/8; Le Neve, *Fasti, 1300–1541, Salisbury*, 73.
[79] Buckler, water-colour in W.A.S. Libr., vol. v. 6.
[80] Sar. Dioc. R.O., Netheravon prebend, vis. and ct. rec. 1595–1623.   [81] *W.A.M.* xxxi. 356.
[82] Sar. Dioc. R.O., Netheravon prebend, vis. and ct. rec. 1595–1623, 1664–83, 1684–9.
[83] Wilts. Cuttings, i. 227; chwdns.' accts. 1744–1874 *penes* the Revd. J. E. Jackson, Netheravon Vicarage.
[84] Buckler, water-colour in W.A.S. Libr., vol. v. 6 (1803); Wilts. Cuttings, iii. 130.
[85] Unless otherwise stated, all inf. from *Endowed Char. Wilts.* (S. Div.), 341–2.

[86] W.R.O., Inclosure Award.
[87] Ex inf. the Revd. J. E. Jackson.
[88] Nightingale, *Wilts. Plate*, 116; *Complete Peerage*, ii. 54–5; ex inf. the Revd. J. E. Jackson.
[89] Walters, *Wilts. Bells*, 142; ex inf. the Revd. J. E. Jackson.
[90] The reg. are recorded on microfilm in W.R.O.; transcripts for 1579–87, 1600–3, 1606–9 are in Sar. Dioc. R.O.
[91] See above; *V.C.H. Hants.* iii. 48.
[92] Sar. Dioc. R.O., Netheravon prebend, vis. and ct. rec. 1595–1623.
[93] *W.N. & Q.* viii. 343; *Cal. Cttee. for Money*, ii. 1154.
[94] See p. 150.
[95] Sar. Dioc. R.O., dean of Sar., Chwdns.' Pres. 1590s.
[96] Ibid. Netheravon prebend, vis. and ct. rec. 1595–1623.

presbyterians were licensed to worship at Richard Hearne's house in Netheravon.[97]

A Baptist cause seems to have been established at Netheravon in the early 19th century.[98] The group probably occupied a house certified for worship in 1816.[99] A chapel for the same congregation, then called Particular Baptists, was built at Netheravon in 1820. Stephen Offer was pastor there from 1824 until his death in 1854.[1] On Census Sunday in 1851 the Old Chapel, as it was then called, was attended by congregations of 80, 113, and 33 in the morning, afternoon, and evening respectively.[2] The chapel, which was approached by a passage at the north-east end of High Street, was burnt down in 1946. A vestry was rebuilt and services held there.[3] The graveyard was all that remained to mark the site in 1974.

A building at Netheravon was certified for Methodist worship in 1820.[4] Primitive Methodists had a chapel there in 1839.[5] They built a new one in 1847 south-west of the Particular Baptist chapel.[6] On Census Sunday in 1851 21 people attended morning, 39 afternoon, and 65 evening service there.[7] Services were held in the chapel on Sunday evenings in 1974.[8]

EDUCATION. Katharine and Margaret Greene were reported to keep a school at Netheravon without licence in 1632.[9] An old woman taught a few children in the parish in 1808.[10] About 1818 the inhabitants were said to be prepared to have their children taught provided that schooling did not interrupt their daily work.[11] By 1833 eight boys and ten girls, paid for by their parents, were taught in a school at Netheravon. Another recently established school, supported by Mrs. Hicks Beach (d. 1837), was then attended by six boys and twenty girls.[12]

A new school, with one classroom, was built c. 1846 on the east side of High Street. Although it was largely supported by subscriptions, children who attended made small weekly payments in 1848.[13] A mistress taught the 30 boys and girls and 40–50 infants who attended in 1858.[14] On return day in 1871 18 boys and 31 girls were present at the school, by that time affiliated to the National Society.[15] An average of 79 children attended in 1906,[16] and in 1911 90 children and infants attended during the year. Numbers dropped slightly during the First World War but rose again afterwards. The school was reorganized in 1926 as a senior mixed school, and in the following year an average of 119 children attended. The average attendance figure was 124 in 1938.[17]

A further reorganization took place in 1964 when the school was amalgamated with that at Fittleton 800 m. away.[18] All the juniors from both parishes thenceforth attended the Fittleton school. All the infants, including those from the army camp at Netheravon, attended that in Netheravon High Street and were taught by two full-time teachers helped occasionally by staff from Fittleton.[19]

CHARITIES FOR THE POOR. None known.

OVERTON

OVERTON[20] was made up of two separate triangles of land and contained approximately 7,000 a. (2,834 ha.).[21] The main triangle stood 6 km. west of Marlborough.[22] It comprised the chapelry of Fyfield and the tithings of East Overton, which contained the parish church, Lockeridge, Shaw, and West Overton. A detached portion of West Overton tithing, Overton Heath, lay in the south-east corner of the triangle. The triangle measured 8 km. from its apex north of New Totterdown in Fyfield to its southern boundary south of Wansdyke and was crossed from east to west by the river Kennet and the London–Bath road. The settlement in West and East Overton, called West Overton village from the later 18th century,[23] and that in Lockeridge are all immediately south of the river. Further east the village of Fyfield lies mainly north of the river with some settlement to its east on the north side of the London–Bath road. The base of the triangle a little south of Wansdyke measured some 5 km. The southern and eastern sides of the triangle followed no physical feature. The eastern boundary between Fyfield and Clatford, in Preshute, was revised by the inclosure commissioners in 1819.[24] To the west an ancient ridge way, which follows the western summits of the Marlborough Downs, separated the triangle from Winterbourne Monkton, Avebury, and East Kennett.

[97] Cal. S.P. Dom. 1672, 299.
[98] W.A.M. xxviii. 152; registrations of births are extant 1814–37: R.G. 4/2241.
[99] Sar. Dioc. R.O., Certs. Dissenters' Meeting-Houses.
[1] V.C.H. Wilts. iii. 139; R. W. Oliver, Strict Bapt. Chapels Eng. (Strict Bapt. Hist. Soc.), v. 20–1.
[2] H.O. 129/261/1/2.
[3] R. W. Oliver, op. cit. 20–1; O.S. Maps 6″, Wilts. XLVII (1889 edn.), LIV (1887 edn.).
[4] Sar. Dioc. R.O., Certs. Dissenters' Meeting-Houses.
[5] Ibid.
[6] H.O. 129/261/1/3; date tablet on chapel.
[7] H.O. 129/261/1/3.
[8] Ex inf. the Revd. J. E. Jackson.
[9] Sar. Dioc. R.O., Netheravon prebend, vis. and ct. rec. 1626–39.
[10] Lambeth MS. 1732.
[11] Educ. of Poor Digest, 1033.
[12] Educ. Enquiry Abstract, 1043.

[13] Ch. Commrs., survey bk. Z 2 (Salisbury cath.), p. 514.
[14] Acct. of Wilts. Schs. 35.
[15] Returns relating to Elem. Educ. 426–7.
[16] Return of Non-Provided Schs. 26.
[17] Bd. of Educ., List 21 (H.M.S.O.).
[18] Ex inf. Chief Education Officer, County Hall, Trowbridge.
[19] Ex inf. the Revd. J. E. Jackson.
[20] This article was written in 1977.
[21] Census, 1881; New Coll., Oxf., Mun. 4970, Alton Priors tithe award (1848).
[22] The following maps have been used: O.S. Maps 6″, Wilts. XXVIII (1889 edn.), XXXV (1889 edn.), SU 16 SW. (1961 edn.), SU 16 NW. (1961 edn.), SU 16 NE. (1961 edn.), SU 17 SW. (1960 edn.); 1/25,000, SU 16 (1961 edn.), SU 17 (1960 edn.); 1/50,000, sheet 173 (1974 edn.).
[23] Andrews and Dury, Map (W.R.S. viii), pl. 11.
[24] W.R.O., Inclosure Award.

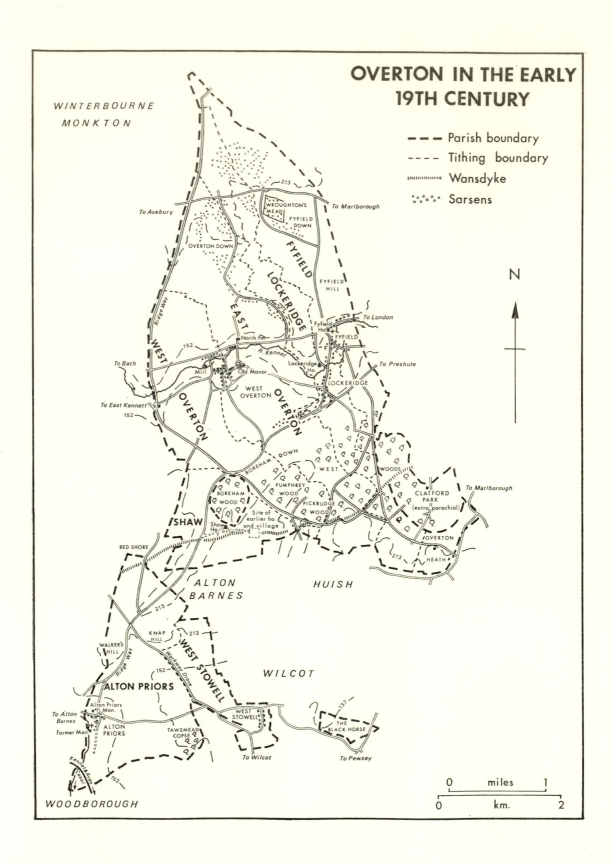

OVERTON IN THE EARLY
19TH CENTURY

- - - Parish boundary
- - - Tithing boundary
||||||||| Wansdyke
°°°°° Sarsens

N

WINTERBOURNE
MONKTON

To Avebury

WROUGHTON'S
MEAD
FYFIELD
DOWN

OVERTON DOWN

213

To Marlborough

FYFIELD

FYFIELD
HILL

LOCKERIDGE

EAST

Ridge Way

152

North Fm.

To Bath

Mill

Old Manor

R. Kennet

Fyfield
Ho.

FYFIELD

To London

Lockeridge
Ho.

LOCKERIDGE

To Preshute

WEST

OVERTON

To East Kennett

152

WEST
OVERTON

OVERTON

BOREHAM DOWN

WEST

WOODS

PUMPHREY
WOOD

CLATFORD
PARK
(extra parochial)

To Marlborough

BOREHAM
WOOD

PICKRUDGE
WOOD

SHAW

Site of
earlier ho.
and village

Shaw
Ho.

OVERTON
HEATH

213

RED SHORE

ALTON
BARNES

HUISH

213

WALKER'S
HILL

KNAP
HILL

213

Ridge Way

WEST STOWELL

WILCOT

152

Workway Drove

ALTON PRIORS

152

Alton Priors
Man.

To Alton
Barnes

ALTON
PRIORS

Former Man.

WEST
STOWELL

TAWSMEAD
COPSE

137

THE
BLACK HORSE

Kennet Avon Canal

152

To Wilcot

To Pewsey

WOODBOROUGH

0   miles   1

0   km.   2

182

The second triangle, 6 km. south-west of West Overton church, comprised the chapelry of Alton Priors and was separated from the first by that part of Shaw which was in Alton Barnes. It was separated on the south-west from Alton Barnes by an ancient track which ran southwards from Walker's hill to the two Altons and south of them by the stream, from which those settlements derived their name, flowing south from Broad Well spring to join the Christchurch Avon. The chapelry contained Alton Priors tithing, West Stowell tithing, which formed a spur-like projection east of Alton Priors, and a small detached rectangle, the Black Horse, 1.5 km. east of West Stowell and geographically in Wilcot. Alton Priors village was ranged along the south-west boundary with Alton Barnes while the hamlet of West Stowell clustered in the north-east corner of the spur. Alton Priors took its suffix from its ownership by the priory of St. Swithun, Winchester. For a short time in the later 16th century, when the Crown held the manor there, the village was called Queen's Alton.[25] It is 11 km. south-west from Marlborough. From its northern boundary south of Furze hill in East Kennett the chapelry measured a little over 3 km. to its southern boundary north of Woodborough hill in Woodborough, and about the same distance from west to east on a line with the lane linking Alton Priors village with the hamlet of West Stowell.

Shaw township originally constituted a diamond-shaped wedge between Overton and Alton Barnes. Shaw village, which straddled the Wansdyke 3 km. south of West Overton village, was apparently deserted in the earlier 15th century.[26] It may have been then that the township was divided into two triangles, of which the northern was attached to Overton as a tithing and the southern to Alton Barnes. It is likely, however, that the boundary between them was not finally fixed until Shaw down, common to both Shaws, was inclosed in 1674.[27] Since the church was in that part allotted to Alton Barnes, most aspects of Shaw's history have been treated elsewhere.[28]

It is probable that Overton Heath and Clatford Park, which both lay on the western fringe of Savernake forest, were originally part of an estate at Rainscombe, in North Newnton, given in 934 to the abbey of Wilton.[29] In the earlier 18th century, and probably much earlier, the portion then called the land at Savernake park, and later Overton Heath, was considered part of West Overton manor and township, also a former Wilton property.[30] Since it had once lain within the forest the land remained tithe-free and was therefore deemed an extra-parochial place in the 19th century.[31] The crescent shaped area north of Overton Heath, also tithe-free, was called Clatford Park from the 16th century and

remained unattached to any parish. It was bounded on the north by the Wansdyke. Its southern boundary may have been established when the land was imparked. Both Overton Heath and Clatford Park were deemed civil parishes in the later 19th century.[32]

In the earlier 19th century the tithings of West Overton, East Overton, and Lockeridge, in one of which Shaw tithing was probably then included, were a poor-law parish of 1,719 ha. (4,248 a.) called West Overton.[33] The chapelries of Alton Priors and Fyfield then each relieved their own poor.[34] That apparently led the Census enumerators of 1841 to class Fyfield, with its medieval chapel, incorrectly as an ancient parish.[35] All three became civil parishes in the later 19th century and as such are dealt with separately below.

In 1885 the detached fragment of Alton Priors called the Black Horse, reckoned to contain some 75 a. (30 ha.), was transferred to Wilcot, and Shaw in Alton Barnes to Alton Priors.[36] The area of Alton Priors was thereafter 1,909 a. (773 ha.).[37] The two small civil parishes of Clatford Park, 310 a. (125 ha.), and Overton Heath, 124 a. (50 ha.), were merged in 1895 and called the civil parish of Clatford Park.[38] That in the following year became part of the civil parish of Fyfield, increasing Fyfield's area from 1,121 a. (454 ha.) to 629 ha. (1,555 a.)[39] In 1934 Alton Priors and Alton Barnes were merged to form the civil parish of Alton.[40]

WEST OVERTON. The civil parish comprises two exposed chalk masses transected by the alluvium and associated gravel terraces of the Kennet valley. The two areas in most respects mirror one another.[41] Around the northern apex, which stands at about 254 m., and at the south end, slightly lower-lying around the 213 m. contour, the Upper Chalk is overlain by clay-with-flints. The south-eastern deposits support extensive woodland called Pumphrey wood and West Woods.[42] On Overton down the Upper Chalk, particularly around Down and Pickledean barns, is strewn with hard siliceous sandstones called sarsen stones, or, from their resemblance at a distance to a flock of sheep, grey wethers. Similar scatters occur west of Lockeridge House on the chalk beyond the south bank of the Kennet and in Lockeridge dene.[43] Those in Pickledean and Lockeridge dene have been under the protection of the National Trust since the early 20th century.[44] From Overton down the land slopes gently downwards to the south for 4 km. across the Upper and Middle Chalk of the dip slope of the Marlborough Downs. That area was the site of the open fields and was still mostly arable in 1977. Similarly in the south part of the parish the land inclines from 223 m. on Boreham down northwards

[25] P.N. Wilts. (E.P.N.S.), 317; S.R.O., DD/WHb 663.
[26] V.C.H. Wilts. x. 10.
[27] S.R.O., DD/WHb 2049.
[28] V.C.H. Wilts. x. 8, 10 sqq.
[29] Ibid. 126; iv. 418–19; Arch. Jnl. lxxvi. 190–1.
[30] Survey of Lands of Wm., First Earl of Pembroke, ed. C. R. Straton (Roxburghe Club, 1909), i. 147, 287; Wilton Ho. Mun., W. Overton survey, 1706. Overton Heath is correctly identified in 1889 but most later O.S. maps locate it incorrectly: W.A.M. liii. 310 n. 29.
[31] Wilton Ho. Mun., W. Overton survey, c. 1794; V.C.H. Wilts. iv. 355.

[32] W.N. & Q. ii. 350; Census, 1891.
[33] Poor Law Com. 2nd Rep. 559; Census, 1891.
[34] Poor Law Com. 2nd Rep. 559–60.
[35] V.C.H. Wilts. iv. 349.
[36] Ibid. 339 n. o; x. 190.   [37] Census, 1891.
[38] V.C.H. Wilts. iv. 334; Endowed Char. Wilts. (N. Div.), 484.
[39] Endowed Char. Wilts. (N. Div.), 484; Census, 1901–71.
[40] V.C.H. Wilts. iv. 339; x. 8.
[41] This para. is based on Geol. Surv. Map 1″, drift, sheet 266 (1964 edn.).   [42] See p. 198.
[43] See plate facing p. 208.   [44] W.A.M. lxiii. 83.

for over 3 km. across the chalk, in 1977 largely arable, to the valley cut out by the Kennet below 152 m. South of the river the alluvium bears a cover of rich pasture land, once the site of extensive water-meadows. Beyond it to the south gravel deposits provide the terrace 1 km. wide on which the village of West Overton grew up. Both north and south of the river the chalk strata have been breached by head-streams, their beds long since dry, which gouged out valleys, or deans, at right angles to the Kennet. The courses of those valleys at Pickledean, Lockeridge dene, and Hursley bottom are mostly characterized by gravel deposits. It was in Lockeridge dene that the hamlet of Lockeridge, which lies nearly 2 km. east of West Overton but at about the same height, grew up on an exposed tongue of Middle Chalk.

West Overton tithing, which lies on the periphery of an area of considerable prehistoric settlement, has been the scene of human activity from Neolithic times.[45] Numerous barrows of various types, some of which have associated inhumations and crema-tions, as well as artefacts of the Neolithic Period and the Bronze Age, have been found.[46] A group of seven bowl-barrows on Overton hill and another four near North Farm have given rise locally to the names Sevenbarrow hill and Four Hill fields.[47] An ancient ditch extends across Overton down from Ave-bury.[48] The chalk uplands north and west of North Farm seem to have been particularly favoured as a settlement site from the Iron Age. North-west of the farm-house an Iron-Age enclosure of some 2 ha. is surrounded by a bank and ditch.[49] There are Romano-British settlement sites north of the Bell inn, in the coomb near Down barn, and further north on Overton down. Both the Down barn and Overton down areas contain numerous hut sites which possibly represent the villages of *coloni* at-tached to larger estates. The Overton down settle-ment, which is of the later 3rd or earlier 4th century, is associated with an earlier field system to the south-west.[50] Also on Overton down are the remains of some funerary monuments of Roman date which have occasionally been mistaken for bowl-barrows. Their mounds, which may originally have been drum-shaped with ditches and fences around, contained cremations and, so far as is known, are unique in the British Isles.[51] A field system, possibly of Romano-British date, extends into West Overton from Avebury and Winterbourne Monkton.[52] A contemporary field system extends over 8 ha. west of Boreham wood and another of early-Iron-Age date over 44 ha. on Boreham down.[53] The Wansdyke crosses West Overton south of Shaw House and continues eastwards through West Woods.[54]

Although the settlements in the civil parish of West Overton were in different hundreds for administra-tive purposes, several medieval taxation assessments show that together they represented a fairly prosperous unit.[55] There were 37 poll-tax payers in West Overton, 41 in Lockeridge, and 63 in East Overton tithings in 1377.[56] In the later 16th century and the earlier 17th East Overton and West Overton, which for taxation purposes may then have included Lockeridge, contained several inhabitants prosperous enough to be assessed at large sums.[57] In 1801 there were 172 people living in East Overton,[58] the same number in West Overton, and 194 in Lockeridge. The total number living in the three townships had increased to 563 in 1811 and to 734 by 1821. The emigration of a Lockeridge farmer and some of his men to Australia in 1830 may have accounted for the slight decrease in population to 718 by 1831.[59] Numbers had increased to 791 by 1841 but there-after in general showed a decline. The decrease in the population of East and West Overton townships noted in 1871 had apparently occurred because houses there had been demolished, while Locke-ridge's population had increased slightly because new houses had been built.[60] Thereafter numbers declined until in 1931 there were 454 people living in the civil parish. In 1971 there were 478 people living in West Overton.[61]

Most roads and lanes which served West Overton in the later 18th century were either still in use or could be traced as tracks in 1977.[62] Of the numerous ancient thoroughfares which cross the downs north of the Kennet one, later than the field system which it crosses, led from the eastern entrance of Avebury eastwards across Overton down, where it branched out into numerous tracks, to Marlborough. It probably continued in use until fairly recent times.[63] An ancient ridge way runs along the western parish boundary.[64] The course of the Roman road from Mildenhall to Bath may be traced a short distance north of the London–Bath road west of North Farm.[65] The London–Bath road itself was turn-piked in 1743.[66] Much of its traffic had, however, been diverted to the motorway 12 km. to the north by 1977. Within West Overton village only two changes of any significance have taken place in the network of lanes. The first was the building *c.* 1819 of New Road on the north side of a tract of open arable, probably at the time of parliamentary inclosure.[67] The second was the incorporation into the churchyard, probably *c.* 1877, of the eastern end of the lane running south of the Old Manor.[68] The lane north of the Kennet linking Lockeridge with Fyfield was a footpath in 1977.[69] Another lane, no trace of which remained in 1977, led north-westwards from it in the later 18th century to join

[45] The arch. of the area has been discussed by P. J. Fowler and others, 'Arch. of Fyfield and Overton Downs', *W.A.M.* lviii. 98 sqq., 342 sqq.; lxii. 16 sqq.
[46] *V.C.H. Wilts.* i (1), 120, 145, 153, 195–6, 211, 214, 230, 233, 237, 241.
[47] Ibid. 195–6.   [48] Ibid. 251.
[49] Ibid. 120; *W.A.M.* lviii. 101.
[50] *V.C.H. Wilts.* i (1), 121, 273; i (2), 444–5; *W.A.M.* lviii. 101.
[51] *V.C.H. Wilts.* i (1), 195–6; *W.A.M.* lix. 68–9, 76–7.
[52] *V.C.H. Wilts.* i (1), 273.
[53] Ibid. 278.   [54] Ibid. i (2), 479.
[55] Ibid. iv. 299, 301; see above, p. 105.
[56] *V.C.H. Wilts.* iv. 310.
[57] *Taxation Lists* (W.R.S. x), 4, 23, 104, 123; E 179/
198/329; E 179/198/334; E 179/199/370; E 179/199/398; E 179/199/400.
[58] Population figures, unless otherwise stated, from *V.C.H. Wilts.* iv. 355.
[59] Ibid. 84.   [60] Ibid. 324.
[61] *Census,* 1971.
[62] *Andrews and Dury, Map* (W.R.S. viii), pls. 11–12.
[63] *W.A.M.* lviii. 106 sqq.
[64] Ibid. 107.   [65] Ibid. 106 sqq.
[66] *V.C.H. Wilts.* iv. 258; *L.J.* xxvi. 241.
[67] W.R.O., Inclosure Award map (1815–16); 778/2.
[68] *Andrews and Dury, Map* (W.R.S. viii), pl. 11; W.R.O. 778/2; Wilts. Cuttings, i. 203; O.S. Map 6″, Wilts. XXVIII (1889 edn.).
[69] *Andrews and Dury, Map* (W.R.S. viii), pl. 11.

the lane running northwards past Lockeridge House to the London–Bath road.[70]

Where it flows in wide meanders eastwards through West Overton the Kennet is no more than a sluggish stream except after heavy rain. Since water is extracted from near-by chalk strata to supply Swindon and Marlborough its bed is often dry in the low-water season from June to December.[71] By the later 18th century the river had been bridged east of the mill in West Overton tithing and in East Overton tithing south of the George inn. There may also have been a footbridge carrying a lane across the river mid-way between those bridges on the tithing boundary between East and West Overton.[72] The George bridge, which took its name from the near-by inn, was rebuilt, and the road it carried widened, c. 1929.[73] South of Lockeridge House the river appears to have been crossed by a ford in the later 18th century.[74] A bridge seems to have been built by 1816.[75]

Although the London–Bath road crossed the parish, the nearness of Marlborough discouraged the establishment of inns in West Overton. The George, first mentioned in 1736, stood on the south side of the main road west of the lane leading into the eastern end of Overton village.[76] No mention of it after 1827 has been found.[77] The New Inn, first mentioned in 1819, changed its name c. 1823 to the Bell.[78] That inn, which was enlarged at various dates in the 19th century, stands further west on the south side of the main road at its junction with the lane leading to West Overton Farm. By 1906 Lockeridge had two inns. The Masons' Arms, once apparently called the New Found Out, stood near the green at the south-west end of the hamlet's main street. It closed c. 1956.[79] That later called the Who'd 'a Thought It stands further north on the west side of the road.[80]

In the earlier 20th century there were two bands in West Overton, the Overton Mission Band based at the Primitive Methodist chapel in West Overton, and the Lockeridge Prize Band. They were amalgamated c. 1934 to form the Kennet Vale Silver Band which still flourished in 1977.[81]

The village of West Overton lies entirely south of the Kennet and is approached by two lanes running south from the London–Bath road. West Overton Farm stands at the village's western entrance whence the main street runs almost imperceptibly uphill towards the church, which stands on a knoll with the Old Manor and the former Vicarage (now called Overton House) to the west. Most of the older houses are on the wide gravel terrace close to the street and to another road, parallel to the street, which runs along the southern side of the valley floor. South Farm, the most substantial of them, has a long south range with sarsen walls which is probably of the 17th century. That range was

partly rebuilt in brick c. 1800 and a north wing added at its eastern end to provide a new symmetrical entrance front. New windows were inserted in that front in the later 19th century. Houses which lay on the north bank of the Kennet east of the lane leading from the New Inn (later the Bell) in the later 18th century and the earlier 19th had disappeared by the later 19th century.[82] Earthworks south of the church suggest that settlement may once have spread further up the hill in that area. Sarsen, used both as squared ashlar and rubble, red brick, and timber-framing, all occur as walling materials. The use of timber-framing, of 17th- or early-18th-century date, seems to have been replaced in the later 18th century and the 19th by that of brick and sarsen.[83] In 1977, however, the village was mostly one of small closes of council houses of the 1950s and of more recent private developments. Southfield, beyond South Farm, was being developed by G. B. Thorner (Homes) Ltd. in 1977.

North Farm, the only substantial house in West Overton to stand north of the London–Bath road, was begun in 1801.[84] Of red brick, it has a square main block with a three-bay south front and a service wing to the rear. To the north-east a large farmyard with central stockyard is surrounded on three sides by farm buildings of various dates from the early 19th century.[85] The modern buildings on the east have replaced an aisled barn which had a thatched roof. Two outlying stockyards on the downs beyond North Farm, Pickledean barn, and beyond it to the north-west, Down barn, were called respectively Old and New barns in 1773.[86] They were reconstructed in the 19th century and have enclosing walls of squared sarsen stone.

The hamlet of Lockeridge lies along the bottom of a small valley running south-westwards from the Kennet towards Boreham down. At least three of the houses have outer walls of timber-framing, perhaps of the 17th century, which was by 1977 much replaced by brick. Dene (formerly Glebe) Farm, which stands on the west side of the street south of its junction with the lane running from Manton, in Preshute, to West Overton, has a long later-17th-century range of coursed sarsen blocks with mullioned and transomed windows and a thatched roof. A secondary wing was added on the west in the earlier 19th century. Most of the other older houses appear to be of later-18th- or earlier-19th-century origin. Lockeridge Dene House was converted from cottages in the earlier 20th century.[87] At Lockeridge, as at West Overton, red brick or sarsen rubble are the usual walling materials and many of the roofs are still thatched. Where the street turns south-west into Lockeridge dene there is a small green around which in the later 18th century were several cottages. The green formerly extended over the sarsen field bought in 1907 by the National Trust.[88]

[70] Ibid.   [71] V.C.H. Wilts. iv. 364.
[72] Andrews and Dury, Map (W.R.S. viii), pl. 11.
[73] Ch. Commrs. file 57305, letter, 6 July 1929.
[74] Andrews and Dury, Map (W.R.S. viii), pl. 11.
[75] W.R.O., Inclosure Award map.
[76] Q. Sess. 1736 (W.R.S. xi), p. 66; Andrews and Dury, Map (W.R.S. viii), pl. 11.
[77] W.R.O. 778/2; Alehousekeepers' Recognizances, 1822–7.
[78] Ibid. 778/2; Alehousekeepers' Recognizances, 1822–7.
[79] Ibid. 106, sale cat., Meux N. Wilts. estates; Wilts. Cuttings, xxi. 393; Kelly's Dir. Wilts. (1923 and later edns.).

[80] W.R.O. 106, sale cat. Meux N. Wilts. estates; Kelly's Dir. Wilts. (1931); Wilts. Cuttings, xxi. 393.
[81] Ex inf. Mrs. K. M. Johnson, Fyfield, and Mr. J. Watts, Lockeridge.
[82] Andrews and Dury, Map (W.R.S. viii), pl. 11; W.R.O. 778/2; O.S. Map 6", Wilts. XXVIII (1889 edn.).
[83] The use of squared sarsen stones is said to date from c. 1850: W.A.M. lxiii. 87.
[84] W.R.O. 1079/3.   [85] See plate facing p. 209.
[86] Andrews and Dury, Map (W.R.S. viii), pl. 11.
[87] Local information.
[88] Andrews and Dury, Map (W.R.S. viii), pl. 11.

Much of the later-19th-century building was at the north end of the hamlet where there are estate cottages, a school, and the Who'd 'a Thought It inn. All were built, probably at the expense of the Meux family, in the style associated with C. E. Ponting, an architect and agent for the Meux estates.[89] Lockeridge House is separated from the rest of the hamlet by the flood-plain of the Kennet. A few houses are scattered along the road from Lockeridge to West Overton. The most notable are Lockeridge Cottage of c. 1800, the former home of C. E. Ponting, and the later-19th-century building formerly used as the Meux estate office.[90] There are some modern private houses along the lane leading east from the green.

That part of the former village of Shaw which lies within West Overton consists of a hollow way with embanked areas, presumably the sites of houses, on each side. The village street ran north-westwards towards the Wansdyke and close to their junction was the original site of the house and buildings of Shaw manor.

FYFIELD. The civil parish has similar geological features to those of West Overton.[91] North and south of the Kennet's alluvial plain and gravel terraces are extensive chalk masses overlain at their extremities by clay-with-flints.[92] Near New Totterdown on Fyfield down the clay-with-flints lies at c. 259 m. and is thickly littered with sarsen stones. In 1644 the area was 'a place so full of a grey pebble stone of great bigness as is not usually seen', where 'they lie so thick as you may go upon them all the way'.[93] The site formed part of the Nature Conservancy area on Fyfield down in 1977. Between Fyfield down and Fyfield hill the uplands are broken by a dry valley, part of Clatford bottom, which lies below 168 m. South of Fyfield hill the village of Fyfield lies on the gravel terrace at c. 137 m. in the Kennet valley, clustering in a wide meander of the river on its north bank. As in West Overton the riverside settlement was sandwiched between the arable of the chalk uplands north and south of the Kennet. In the south part of the parish Clatford Park Farm, lying at c. 200 m., and the road by which it is approached from Clatford, are on the gravel deposits of another dry valley cut through the Upper Chalk by a head-stream of the Kennet. On either side of that road deposits of clay-with-flints coat the Upper Chalk and lie between 213 m. and 229 m. Those west of Clatford Park Farm are thickly wooded.

Two bowl-barrows at Totterdown and a bell-barrow on Fyfield down attest activity in Fyfield in early prehistoric times.[94] As in West Overton the downs north of the Kennet were the site of settlement of a more permanent nature in early-Iron-Age and Romano-British times. A field system of 121 ha. on Fyfield down, which extends westwards

into West Overton and eastwards into Preshute, has yielded material of both periods. Some of its field boundaries are marked with sarsen stones and within it are ditches and ponds which may be contemporary.[95] The remains of a Roman pavement were found south of Fyfield village in the early 19th century.[96] Within Wroughton mead on Fyfield down there was a farmstead from at least the later 12th century until c. 1300. It consisted of three small inclosures within a larger inclosure and its buildings included a long-house which could accommodate both men and beasts.[97]

In 1334 Fyfield, then called Little Fyfield, was assessed for taxation with East Overton.[98] The chapelry had 22 poll-tax payers in 1377.[99] At least eight of its inhabitants were able to contribute to the benevolence of 1545.[1] Until 1831 the population was possibly enumerated with that of East Overton or Lockeridge. Numbers were first returned separately in 1841, when 150 people lived in Fyfield.[2] There were 200 people in 1861, and thereafter the population fell gradually until 1891 when there were 152 inhabitants. Because of the transference in 1896 to Fyfield of the civil parish of Clatford or Clatford Park, which included the former extra-parochial place at Overton Heath, numbers had risen to 178 by 1901.[3] The population had declined to 143 by 1931 and stood at 134 in 1971.[4]

The population of Clatford Park rose from 15 in 1841 to 25 in 1881. Just before it was merged in Fyfield, Clatford Park in 1891 had thirteen inhabitants. In 1841 25 people lived at Overton Heath. Numbers there fluctuated little over the next 40 years but rose from 24 in 1881 to 34 in 1891.[5]

The track from Avebury which enters Fyfield from West Overton and crosses the field system on Fyfield down is of ancient origin.[6] The London–Bath road, turnpiked in 1743, crosses Fyfield as well as West Overton. It is carried a short distance north of the Kennet's flood-plain on a ridge of Middle Chalk.[7] The courses of most lanes which ran through Fyfield in the later 18th century and the earlier 19th, if not still in use, could in 1977 be traced as footpaths. Such a footpath, part of which formed the village's main street in 1773, leaves the lane running from the London–Bath road towards the Kennet and leads southwards to Lockeridge House. There was no trace in 1977, however, of the small lanes which once led northwards from that lane. The lane which runs south-east from the London–Bath road towards the Kennet, over which it has been carried by a bridge since the later 18th century, formerly split south of the river into two lanes.[8]

The church and Fyfield House stand south of the London–Bath road on slightly higher ground at what was originally the northern end of the village. Until the later 19th century settlement lay close to the river along the lane which ran southwards from

[89] Kelly's Dir. Wilts. (1875, 1885). The cottages, however, bear the initials of a member of the Rebbeck fam., tenants of the Meux estate at Lockeridge in the later 19th cent.
[90] Kelly's Dir. Wilts. (1875, 1885); O.S. Map 6″, Wilts. SU 16 NW. (1961 edn.). [91] See above.
[92] This para. is based on Geol. Surv. Map 1″, drift, sheet 266 (1964 edn.).
[93] Diary of the Marches of the Royal Army (Camd. Soc. [1st ser], lxxiv), 151.
[94] V.C.H. Wilts. i (1), 176, 209. [95] Ibid. 276.

[96] Ibid. 72. [97] W.A.M. lviii. 109–15.
[98] V.C.H. Wilts. iv. 299; see above.
[99] V.C.H. Wilts. iv. 310.
[1] Taxation Lists (W.R.S. x), 4.
[2] Population figures, except where otherwise stated, from V.C.H. Wilts. iv. 349. [3] See above.
[4] Census, 1961, 1971. [5] V.C.H. Wilts. iv. 345, 355.
[6] W.A.M. lviii. 107; see above.
[7] V.C.H. Wilts. iv. 258.
[8] Andrews and Dury, Map (W.R.S. viii), pls. 11–12; W.R.O., Inclosure Award map (1815–16).

the London–Bath road.[9] That site was subject to frequent flooding and, after numerous cottages there were burned down c. 1860, was abandoned in favour of one higher up the valley along the main road, where there was already settlement including the Fighting Cocks inn, first mentioned in 1811.[10] Many cottages, particularly those on the south side, the inn, and the Congregational chapel were demolished when the road was widened in the later 1930s.[11] In the earlier 20th century council houses were built near the western boundary of the civil parish immediately south of the London–Bath road on a site, part of which was once glebe land, called Priestacre.[12] Most of the inhabitants of Fyfield lived there in 1977. A few private houses have been built south of the village near the bridge over the Kennet at various dates since the First World War. Beyond them sewage disposal works to serve the area upstream were opened in 1973.[13]

Overton Heath and Clatford Park, which are on the eastern fringe of extensive woodland, contained little settlement in 1773 as in 1977. Clatford Park contained only a farm-house at both dates.[14] Apart from Park Farm, which stands beside the lane to Clatford, Overton Heath contains on its eastern boundary a former Wesleyan Methodist chapel and one or two houses. Other houses were built on the west side of the road to Wilcot between 1802 and 1862 but had disappeared by 1889.[15] Further south on that side of the road Yew Tree Cottage stands on the site of the house, burned down some time in the 19th century, in 1773 called the Dog House and in 1788 the Old Dog.[16]

ALTON PRIORS. The former chapelry lies almost entirely on the elongated chalk bluff which bounds the Vale of Pewsey to the north.[17] The northern tip stands on the Upper Chalk between the 244 m. and 259 m. contours. About 500 m. south of it, a little north of New Town, the Upper is succeeded by the Middle Chalk which is divided into twin summits, Walker's hill[18] to the west and Knap hill to the east. Both hills stand at 260 m. and, with the uplands to the north, have always provided pasture. The open Lower Chalk terrace, mainly under arable cultivation in 1977 as formerly, lies south of them between the 137 m. and 168 m. contours and extends for some 2 km. to the chapelry's former southern boundary. The village of Alton Priors lies in the south-west corner of the former chapelry at c. 136 m. on a narrow strip of Upper Greensand facing its westerly neighbour, Alton Barnes, across

withy fringed streams. The hamlet of West Stowell also stands on Upper Greensand at about the same height. The detached rectangle of land to the east once called the Black Horse lies at c. 137 m.

Numerous barrows of various types, with associated primary cremations and later intrusive burials, show the uplands north of Alton Priors to have been settled from the Neolithic Period[19] when a causewayed camp which belonged to the Windmill Hill culture was constructed on Knap hill.[20] The site was refortified with a plateau enclosure in the early Iron Age and apparently remained in use in Roman times.[21] Another two enclosures lie west and north-west of New Town.[22] Of the four ditches in Alton Priors, that extending south-west from Knap hill is called locally the Devil's trackway.[23] Traces of a building of Romano-British date have been found in a field called Stanchester at West Stowell.[24] Walker's hill, below which an ancient ridge way runs on a north–south course, was of strategic importance in Pagan-Saxon times. It was probably to prevent incursions from the north along such a route early in that period that the Wansdyke, which crosses the northernmost tip of the former chapelry, was constructed, leaving a pass for the ridge way at Red Shore.[25] The Neolithic long barrow on Walker's hill, called Adam's Grave, may be identified with *Wodnesbeorg*, or Woden's Barrow, the site of battles in 592 and 715.[26]

In 1334 Alton Priors and 'Stowell', which possibly included not only West Stowell tithing but also East Stowell in Wilcot, was, apart from Westwood and Wroughton, the most highly rated unit in Elstub hundred as then constituted.[27] It seems likely that inhabitants of both West Stowell and Alton Priors were numbered among the 114 poll-tax payers accounted for at 'Stowell' in Swanborough hundred in 1377.[28] Various taxation assessments of the later 16th century and earlier 17th century show Alton Priors and West Stowell to have contained several inhabitants of sufficient substance to be assessed.[29] In 1801 178 people lived in Alton Priors and West Stowell.[30] Numbers had declined to 161 by 1911 but thereafter increased, and in 1841, of the chapelry's 251 inhabitants, 194 lived at Alton and 57 at Stowell. The population was 253 in 1851 but had declined to 207 by 1861. There was an increase to 221 in 1871 but the population again declined and stood at 178 in 1891. By 1901 numbers had increased to 217 but thereafter declined. In 1931, the last date at which figures are available, 172 people lived at Alton Priors and West Stowell.

[9] *Andrews and Dury, Map* (W.R.S. viii), pl. 11.
[10] Ibid.; Wilts. Cuttings, xxi. 398; B.L. Map Libr., map of Fyfield man. (1811); *Kelly's Dir. Wilts.* (1848 and later edns.).
[11] 'Ch. Guide' (TS. in ch.).
[12] W.R.O., Inclosure Award (1815–16).
[13] Ex inf. Public Relations Officer, Kennet District Council.
[14] *Andrews and Dury, Map* (W.R.S. viii), pl. 12.
[15] W.R.O., W. Overton Inclosure Award map (1802); B.L. Map Libr., map of W. Overton tithing (1862); O.S. Map 6″, Wilts. XXXV (1889 edn.).
[16] *Andrews and Dury, Map* (W.R.S. viii), pl. 12; W.R.O. 754/26, deeds, 1788–1824.
[17] This para. is based on Geol. Surv. Map 1″, drift, sheet 266 (1964 edn.).
[18] The origin of the name is uncertain. It is considered, probably incorrectly, to derive from Clement Walker: *P.N. Wilts.* (E.P.N.S.), 318, where Walker is said to have

died in 1801. He died in 1681 having married Mary, sister of Sir John Button (d. 1712): Aubrey, *Topog. Coll.* ed. Jackson, 43. The Button fam. appear to have been succeeded as lessees of Alton Priors man. in 1651 and it is therefore unlikely that Walker ever had any connexion with the estate either as owner or lessee: see below, p. 193.
[19] *V.C.H. Wilts.* i (1), 147, 149, 206, 227, 231, 244–5.
[20] Ibid. 26; i (2), 293, 296. The site is fully described by Graham Connah and others, 'Excavations at Knap Hill, 1961', *W.A.M.* lx. 1 sqq.
[21] *V.C.H. Wilts.* i (1), 26–7, 261.   [22] Ibid. 261.
[23] Ibid. 250.   [24] *W.A.M.* lxv. 207.
[25] *V.C.H. Wilts.* i (2), 478–9.
[26] Ibid. i (1), 137; i (2), 478.
[27] Ibid. iv. 299.
[28] Ibid. 310.
[29] *Taxation Lists* (W.R.S. x), 124; E 179/198/329; E 179/199/370; E 179/199/398.
[30] Population figures from *V.C.H. Wilts.* iv. 339, 355.

The ridge way which forms the western boundary of West Overton continues on a southerly route inside the western boundary of Alton Priors. Entering Alton Priors at Red Shore through the gap in the Wansdyke it formed part of the road linking the Altons with Woodborough which was turnpiked in 1840.[31] The track formerly called Workway drove, which marked part of the boundary between Alton Priors and West Stowell tithings,[32] once provided a more direct link between the hamlet of West Stowell and that road at Knap hill.[33] Those sections of the ridge way which were not turnpiked could, like the courses of most other later-18th-century and 19th-century roads in Alton and Stowell, be traced as footpaths in 1977.[34] The Kennet & Avon canal, constructed across the south-west angle of the chapelry in 1807, was opened in 1810.[35]

The Manor stands on the north side of the lane leading to West Stowell, but apart from some more modern housing east of that house, settlement in Alton Priors in 1977, as in the later 18th century, was mainly south of the lane. The mid-19th-century house which stands opposite the Manor is surrounded by an earlier walled garden and probably replaced an earlier house. In 1977, however, most of the houses clustered, as they did in 1773, close together along a lane running southwards from the Manor towards the church.[36] At least one incorporates some 17th-century work but the remaining older houses appear to have been rebuilt in the earlier 19th century. Some houses of more recent construction flank the lane's southern end. The village may formerly have extended west of the lane into the field north of the church where there are still earthworks.[37] There was apparently little settlement there by 1773 when the church and the original manor-house, in 1977 much reduced in size and called the Priory, stood, as in 1977, isolated beside the streams separating the two Altons.

Settlement in West Stowell lies, as in 1773, in the easterly spur of the tithing and is confined to the eastern branch of a triangular lane which runs north of the lane from Alton Priors to Wilcot.[38] Apart from a few farm buildings, the hamlet included in 1977 West Stowell House on the east side of the lane and a chapel opposite on the west.

MANORS AND OTHER ESTATES. In 939 Athelstan granted a nun, Wulfswyth, 15 *mansae* at Overton.[39] That estate is to be identified with the 15 hides at Overton, later called the manor of *OVERTON* or, from the later 16th century, *EAST OVERTON*, which both in 1066 and in 1086 belonged to the bishop of Winchester.[40] By 1086 the estate had been assigned by the bishop for the support of the monks of the Old Minster.[41] The prior and convent of St. Swithun's received a grant of free warren within their demesne lands at East Overton in 1300, and held the estate until the Dissolution, when it passed to the Crown.[42]

In 1541 Winchester chapter received a royal grant of the manor, which it reconveyed to the Crown in 1547.[43] In the same year the Crown granted East Overton to Sir William Herbert (created earl of Pembroke in 1551) and it descended with that title to Philip, earl of Pembroke and Montgomery (d. 1683), who sold it in 1682 to William Clarke (d. 1688).[44] Clarke devised the manor in trust for his son John, who in 1720 sold it to a director of the South Sea Co., Francis Hawes. Hawes's property, including East Overton, was confiscated by parliamentary trustees when the South Sea Bubble burst shortly after and was sold by them in 1726 to the trustees of John Churchill, duke of Marlborough (d. 1722). From the duke's eldest daughter Henrietta Godolphin, countess of Godolphin and *suo jure* duchess of Marlborough, the manor passed to her nephew Charles Spencer, duke of Marlborough (d. 1758), and thereafter descended with the title to John Spencer-Churchill, duke of Marlborough (d. 1883), who sold it in 1866 to R. C. Long (d. 1869).[45] In 1870 under Long's will his brothers F. S. and W. Long sold it to the trustees of Sir Henry Meux, Bt. (d. 1883). By that date the much augmented estate included South Overton and North Overton farms, representing East Overton manor, and Fyfield, Lockeridge, Glebe, and Clatford Park farms. There was also West Woods, 718 a. Sir Henry was succeeded by his son Sir Henry Bruce Meux, Bt. (d. 1900), whose widow sold most of the estate in 1906 to Alexander Taylor of Manton House in Preshute.[46] Taylor afterwards sold the estate to the Olympia Agricultural Co. Ltd., whose chairman was Joseph Watson (created Baron Manton and d. 1922).[47] The company's farm manager, Frank Swanton, bought North, South, and Fyfield farms in 1925. After Swanton's death in 1971 his sons R. G. F. and R. Swanton farmed in partnership as F. Swanton & Sons. In 1977 Mr. R. G. F. Swanton farmed Fyfield and South farms, 880 a., and Mr. R. Swanton North farm, 700 a.[48]

Some land on Overton and Fyfield downs, 800 a., was retained by the Olympia Agricultural Co. Ltd., however, and in 1977 was owned by Mr. J. V. Bloomfield as part of his estate at Manton.[49] West Woods, 1,008 a., sold by the Olympia Agricultural

---

[31] *V.C.H. Wilts.* i (2), 478; iv. 264.
[32] New Coll., Oxf., Mun. 4970, deed, Best and Mackintosh to New Coll., 1912, and attached map.
[33] *Andrews and Dury, Map* (W.R.S. viii), pl. 11; *P.N. Wilts.* (E.P.N.S.), 318; O.S. Map 6", Wilts. XXXV (1889 edn.).
[34] *Andrews and Dury, Map* (W.R.S. viii), pl. 11.
[35] *V.C.H. Wilts.* iv. 273.
[36] *Andrews and Dury, Map* (W.R.S. viii), pl. 11.
[37] *W.A.M.* lxviii. 138.
[38] *Andrews and Dury, Map* (W.R.S. viii), pl. 11.
[39] Finberg, *Early Wessex Chart.* p. 85.
[40] *V.C.H. Wilts.* ii, p. 120; *Rot. Hund.* (Rec. Com.), ii (1), 269; *Cal. Pat.* 1547–8, 172; *First Pembroke Survey*, ed. Straton, i. 251.
[41] *V.C.H. Wilts.* ii, p. 120.
[42] *Cal. Chart. R.* 1300–26, 1; *Feud. Aids*, v. 202; *Valor Eccl.* (Rec. Com.), vi, App. p. vii.

[43] *L. & P. Hen. VIII*, xvi, p. 417; *Cal. Pat.* 1547–8, 172.
[44] *Cal. Pat.* 1547–8, 172; *Complete Peerage*, x. 405 sqq.; C 142/264 no. 181; *Wilts. Inq. p.m.* 1625–49 (Index Libr.), 97–101; W.R.O. 212B/5208.
[45] W.R.O. 212B/5208; Basil Williams, *Whig Supremacy, 1714–60*, 176–8; *Cobbett's Parl. Hist.* vii. 693; *Complete Peerage*, s.v. Marlborough; Blenheim Mun. E/P/90, mid-19th-cent. survey; E/A/14, rental, 1862–5; E/A/15, rental, 1866–70; abstr. of title to Old Man., Overton, *penes* Sir Maur. Dorman.
[46] Abstr. of title *penes* Sir Maur. Dorman; W.R.O. 106, sale cat.; *Kelly's Dir. Wilts.* (1907).
[47] *Kelly's Dir. Wilts.* (1907 and later edns.); Burke, *Peerage* (1949), 1330.
[48] Ex inf. Messrs. R. G. F. and R. Swanton.
[49] Ex inf. Mr. J. V. Bloomfield, Manton Ho.

Co. Ltd. in 1928, was acquired in 1931 by the Forestry Commission, owner in 1977.[50]

Before the rearrangement of East Overton manor into North and South farms, it is probable that the estate was farmed from the Old Manor. That house stands west of the church. Its west range is a small house of the earlier 17th century which has walls partly of sarsen rubble, with ovolo-moulded windows, and partly timber-framed. A later wing, which may have been a parish reading room, was incorporated on the east and remodelled in the later 19th century. The whole house was remodelled in the later 20th century when one room in the west range was filled with panelling brought from a house in Stafford.[51] Sir Maurice Dorman was owner in 1977.

In 972 King Edgar granted Alflaed 10 *mansae*, then said to be at 'Kennett' but clearly identifiable with the later manor of *OVERTON* or *WEST OVERTON*.[52] In 1066 the estate belonged to Wilton Abbey and at the Dissolution passed to the Crown.[53]

The manor was granted in tail male to Sir William Herbert (created earl of Pembroke 1551, d. 1570) and his wife Anne in 1544.[54] The estate, which included a detached part at Overton Heath abutting the south-east corner of the ancient parish, thereafter descended with the Pembroke title.[55] In 1917 Reginald, earl of Pembroke and Montgomery, sold West Overton farm, 665 a., to J. H. E. Poole, 257 a. including Pickrudge and Pumphrey woods to F. Spearman, and Park farm, 116 a. at Overton Heath, to F. W. Harvey.[56] The woodland, 180 a., bought by Spearman was sold in 1940 by the administrator of the estate of G. Spearman to the Forestry Commission, owner in 1977.[57] West Overton farm, 705 a., was owned in 1977 by Mereacre Ltd.[58]

The site of the manor's original farm-house is unknown but may have been opposite West Overton Farm.[59] West Overton Farm, called Overton House in the later 19th century and the earlier 20th,[60] is a square red-brick house of *c.* 1825 with a contemporary walled garden to the north and large farmyard to the south.

The 2 hides at Lockeridge held in 1066 by Elmar had passed to Durand of Gloucester by 1086.[61] Durand's estate descended to his grand-nephew Miles of Gloucester (created earl of Hereford in 1141, d. 1143).[62] Between 1141 and 1143 Miles

granted the lands, the later manor of *LOCKE-RIDGE*, to the Templars.[63] In 1567 and 1719 Lockeridge was considered to be a free tenancy of East Overton manor.[64]

After the suppression of the order of Templars in 1308, the estate passed, with other Temple property, to the Knights Hospitallers.[65] Thenceforth the estate was administered from the preceptory at Sandford (Oxon.) until the Dissolution, when it passed to the Crown.[66]

In 1543 Richard Andrews was granted the manor by the Crown and immediately conveyed it to Christopher Dismore (d. 1564) and his wife Joan or Jane.[67] After her husband's death Jane, who married secondly Edward Passion, held Lockeridge for life.[68] In 1577 John Dismore, on whom his cousin Christopher had settled the reversion of the manor, sold the reversion to Henry, earl of Pembroke, who was in actual possession of Lockeridge at his death in 1601.[69]

The manor passed like that of East Overton to Philip, earl of Pembroke and Montgomery (d. 1683), who sold it in 1680 to Edmund Naish. Naish sold it in 1683 to Thomas Cholwell (will proved 1694), who devised Lockeridge to Richard Kent.[71] In 1717, after Kent's death, his trustees conveyed the manor to his daughter Hester (d. 1739) and her husband John Chetwynd.[72] John Chetwynd, who became 2nd Viscount Chetwynd in 1736, sold it in 1756 to Charles, duke of Marlborough (d. 1758).[73] The manor afterwards descended again like that of East Overton.

In 1086 Durand of Gloucester held freely of the church of Winchester 2 hides, all but 1 virgate, which in 1066 had apparently been held of the church by lease.[74] The land passed like Lockeridge manor to Miles, earl of Hereford, and descended to Miles's eldest daughter and coheir, Margaret, wife of Humphrey de Bohun, as part of the honor of Hereford. The estate continued to pass with the honor and in 1243 was still deemed to be held of the bishop of Winchester.[75] After the death in 1373 of Humphrey de Bohun, earl of Hereford and Essex, it was allotted in 1384 to his younger daughter and coheir Mary, wife of Henry, earl of Derby (later Henry IV).[76] The estate is last mentioned as part of the honor of Hereford in 1402.[77]

Richard Quintin held the lands, then reckoned at 1 knight's fee, of Humphrey de Bohun, earl of

[50] Ex inf. Chief Forester, Savernake Forest Office, Marlborough.   [51] Ex inf. Sir Maur. Dorman.
[52] Finberg, *Early Wessex Chart.* p. 98; *V.C.H. Wilts.* ii, p. 91. The estate is called W. Overton in 1275: *Rot. Hund.* (Rec. Com.), ii (1), 269. Overton Abbess was an alternative in the earlier 16th cent.: *P.N. Wilts.* (E.P.N.S.), 305.
[53] *V.C.H. Wilts.* ii, p. 129; *Feud. Aids*, v. 205; *Valor Eccl.* (Rec. Com.), ii. 110.
[54] *L. & P. Hen. VIII*, xix (1), p. 38; for the earls of Pembroke and Montgomery see *Complete Peerage*, x. 405 sqq.
[55] C 142/264 no. 181; *Wilts. Inq. p.m.* 1625–49 (Index Libr.), 97–101; Wilton Ho. Mun., survey, *c.* 1794; W.R.O., Inclosure Award (1802).
[56] W.A.S. Libr., sale cat. x, no. 17; Wilton Ho. Mun., farm audit bk. ii. 121–9.
[57] Ex inf. Chief Forester, Savernake Forest Office.
[58] Ex inf. Mr. T. E. Trigg, W. Overton Farm.
[59] *First Pembroke Survey*, ed. Straton, i. 141; W.R.O., Inclosure Award (1802).
[60] O.S. Map 6", Wilts. XXVIII (1889 edn.); W.R.O. 106, sale cat. Meux N. Wilts. estates (1906).

[61] *V.C.H. Wilts.* ii, p. 148.
[62] Ibid. p. 104; x. 62; *Complete Peerage*, vi. 451 and n. g.
[63] *Rec. Templars in Eng. in 12th Cent.* ed. Beatrice A. Lees, p. 207; C 1/1123/28.
[64] *First Pembroke Survey*, ed. Straton, i. 251–2; H.R.O. 7M54/227.   [65] *V.C.H. Wilts.* iii. 328.
[66] Ibid.; S.C. 6/Hen. VIII/3996.
[67] *L. & P. Hen. VIII*, xviii (1), pp. 535–6, 539; C 142/140 no. 197.
[68] C.P. 40/1351 Carte rot. 34.
[69] Ibid.; C 142/264 no. 181.
[70] Blenheim Mun., Wilts. deeds, Pembroke to Naish.
[71] Ibid. Naish to Cholwell; Prob. 11/418 (P.C.C. 5 Box, will of Thomas Cholwell).
[72] Blenheim Mun., Wilts. deeds; *Complete Peerage*, iii. 188.
[73] Blenheim Mun., Wilts. deeds, sched. of Clatford man. deeds, 1716–56; *Complete Peerage*, iii. 188; viii. 499–500.
[74] *V.C.H. Wilts.* ii, p. 120.
[75] *Complete Peerage*, vi. 457 sqq.; *Bk. of Fees*, ii. 748.
[76] *Cal. Inq. p.m.* xiii, pp. 130, 139; *Cal. Close*, 1381–5, 514–15.   [77] *Feud. Aids*, vi. 632.

Hereford and Essex, in 1243.[78] A Richard Quintin still held that fee in 1275.[79] What is probably the same estate was held in 1316 by John of Berwick.[80] In 1327 John of Berwick, perhaps the same, settled lands at Lockeridge, Shaw, East Kennett, and West Kennett, in Avebury, on himself for life with reversion to John of Fosbury and his wife Alice.[81] In the later 14th century the lands were held by Peter of Fosbury's heir.[82] William Sparshot held them in 1412.[83]

The estate apparently passed like an estate at Woodborough to Richard Benger (d. 1529), whose heir was his sister Anne, wife of Thomas Smith.[84] Anne and her husband were still seised of it in 1551.[85] In 1559, however, Anne, then a widow, settled an estate which included land at Lockeridge on herself for life, with reversion to Ralph Henslowe (d. 1578) and his wife Clare.[86] Ralph's son Thomas sold the estate in 1594 to Thomas Smith.[87] The Smith family held the land until the earlier 18th century, when Richard Smith of West Kennett sold the Lockeridge estate in moieties.[88]

A portion was sold in 1713 to William Andrews who in 1726 settled it on the marriage of his son William and Elizabeth Franklin. William and Elizabeth sold it in 1768 to George, duke of Marlborough.[89]

The other portion, which seems to have comprised no more than a few acres, was sold in 1723 by Richard Smith and his son Thomas to George Brown. In 1757 George conveyed it to his son George, who sold it in 1763 to George, duke of Marlborough.[90] Both moieties thereafter passed like the manor of East Overton.

In the earlier 12th century 2 hides at Lockeridge, the provenance of which is unknown, were held by Walter de Beauchamp (d. 1131). The estate passed to Walter's son William (d. 1170), who between 1155 and 1169 granted it to the Templars.[91] It was presumably merged with their manor of Lockeridge, as was another hide there granted by Robert of Ewias in the earlier 12th century.[92]

The Macy family held a small estate at Lockeridge in the earlier 13th century.[93] In 1281 William Macy granted 60 a. of land there to the priory of St. Margaret, Marlborough.[94] The priory's estate at Lockeridge was augmented c. 1294 by 40 a., held of the honor of Hereford, which Philip Francis granted

to it.[95] The priory held the manor of *LOCKE-RIDGE* or, as it was later called, *UPPER LOCKERIDGE* until the Dissolution.[96]

In 1539 the manor was granted to Anne of Cleves as jointure.[97] Edward Seymour, earl of Hertford (created duke of Somerset in 1547, executed in 1552), received a grant of it in 1542.[98] In 1550, however, Thomas Goddard (d. 1550) was in possession.[99] In 1582 his son Thomas sold the manor to Richard Wroth.[1] In 1588, however, Richard Browne was seised of it. After his death Bariscourt farm, as the estate was then also called, was held for life by his widow Katharine Muffett.[2] The land descended in the Browne family to Richard Browne, who, with his wife Jane, sold it in 1688 to Sir Thomas Fowle (will proved 1693).[3] Under Sir Thomas's will the estate passed to his nephew Thomas Fowle, and on the nephew's death to another nephew, Robert Fowle (d. 1705), who devised it to his kinsman the Revd. John Fowle (d. 1710).[4] By 1737 Peter Delme (d. 1770) had acquired the estate, and he sold it in 1759 to George, duke of Marlborough.[5] The manor thereafter descended with that of East Overton.

Immediately after he had bought the estate, the duke of Marlborough leased Lockeridge House and some adjoining meadows to Peter Delme.[6] The house was thereafter always let as a gentleman's residence until offered for sale as part of the Meux estate at Overton in 1906.[7] It was occupied in the late 19th century and the earlier 20th by H. R. Giffard, who later bought the freehold.[8]

Lockeridge House was built c. 1700 and has a double pile plan with principal fronts to the north and south of five bays. Two small additions were made on the west in the early 18th century and another on the south in the early 19th century, when new windows and a porch were added to the east front. Most of the 18th-century rooms retain original panelling and fittings. To the north-west there is a small stable court and to the north part of an entrance court with early-18th-century gate-piers and walls. Other 18th-century walls remain around the gardens to the south.

An estate comprising 2 hides and 1½ virgate at Shaw was held in 1066 by Cudulf. By 1086 it had passed to Robert son of Gerald and was held of him by a tenant Hugh.[9] It is to be identified with the later manor of *SHAW*.[10] It passed like the manor

[78] *Bk. of Fees*, ii. 748.
[79] *Rot. Hund.* (Rec. Com.), ii (1), 269.
[80] *Feud. Aids*, v. 205.
[81] *Feet of F. 1327–77* (W.R.S. xxix), p. 15.
[82] *Cal. Inq. p.m.* xiii, pp. 130, 139; *Cal. Close, 1381–5*, 514–15.
[83] *Feud. Aids*, vi. 534.   [84] *V.C.H. Wilts.* x. 218.
[85] C.P. 25(2)/65/532 no. 70.
[86] C.P. 25(2)/239/1 Eliz. I Trin. no. 24; *V.C.H. Hants*, iii. 346.   [87] C.P. 25(2)/242/36 Eliz. I Trin.
[88] *Wilts. Inq. p.m.* 1625–49 (Index Libr.), 183; W.R.O. 568/7, deeds, 1690, 1712.
[89] W.R.O. 212B/5212, ff. 3–4.
[90] Ibid. f. 5; Blenheim Mun., Wilts. deeds, Smith to Brown; Brown to Brown.
[91] *Rec. Templars in Eng.* ed. Lees, p. 208; Sanders, *Eng. Baronies*, 75–6.
[92] Lees, op. cit. pp. 208–9.
[93] *Civil Pleas, 1249* (W.R.S. xxvi), p. 101.
[94] *Feet of F. 1272–1327* (W.R.S. i), p. 15.
[95] *Wilts. Inq. p.m.* 1242–1326 (Index Libr.), 203–4.
[96] *Feud. Aids*, vi. 531; *Valor Eccl.* (Rec. Com.), ii. 148; C.P. 25(2)/744/15 Chas. II Trin.
[97] *L. & P. Hen. VIII*, xiv (2), p. 154.

[98] Ibid. xvii, p. 322; *Complete Peerage*, vi. 504.
[99] C 142/94 no. 93.
[1] Ibid.; C.P. 25(2)/260/24 & 25 Eliz. I Mich.
[2] Sar. Dioc. R.O., Overton Glebe Terrier, 1588; Req. 2/303/72.
[3] *Cal. Cttee. for Compounding*, iii. 2386; C.P. 25(2)/744/13 Chas. II Mich.; C.P. 25(2)/744/15 Chas. II Trin.; Blenheim Mun., Wilts. deeds, final concord, Fowle and Browne; will of Sir Thomas Fowle.
[4] Blenheim Mun., Wilts. deeds, wills of Sir Thomas, Robert, and John Fowle.
[5] Ibid. Delme to Delme, 1737; sale partics.; deed, Delme to Marlborough trustees.
[6] Ibid. plan of ho.
[7] Ibid. letters concerning Lockeridge Ho., Shipton to Walker, 1791–2; *Kelly's Dir. Wilts.* (1848 and later edns.); W.R.O. 106, sale cat.
[8] *Kelly's Dir. Wilts.* (1898 and later edns.); W.R.O. 106, sale cat.
[9] *V.C.H. Wilts.* ii, pp. 153–4.
[10] R. R. Darlington identified the estate with Shaw farm, in Chute: ibid. The overlordship shows it to be Shaw in Selkley hund. The estate is first called a man. in 1395: S.R.O., DD/WHb 2026.

of Fittleton to Hubert de Burgh, earl of Kent (d. 1243).[11]

In 1243 Simon le Dun held the estate of the earl of Kent, and Henry le Dun held it of Simon.[12] Henry le Dun the younger was in possession in the later 13th century.[13] In 1316, however, John of Hartington held Shaw.[14] In 1327 Walter of Hartington held it and was still lord in 1333.[15] In 1386 Robert Devenish, who had apparently acquired the lands from John Wylye and Robert of Etchilhampton, granted the estate to Joan, widow of Robert Blake of Quemerford, and her son John.[16] John Blake was in possession in 1395.[17] Robert Blake held Shaw in 1428.[18] The manor descended in the Blake family to Thomas Blake, who in 1575 sold Shaw farm to William Button (d. 1591) of Alton Priors.[19]

William Button was succeeded at Shaw by his son Ambrose, who in 1595–6 sold the farm to his younger brother William (d. 1599).[20] William's son, Sir William Button, Bt. (d. 1655), in 1648 settled it on himself for life, with remainder to his second son Sir Robert Button (d. 1678).[21] It thereafter passed like the manor of Lyneham to John Walker (d. 1758), whose son John sold it to George, duke of Marlborough, in 1770.[22] The duke sold it c. 1801 to John Stratton, still owner c. 1815.[23] In the early 1840s, however, William Brough owned Shaw farm, 481 a.[24] The farm afterwards changed hands frequently.[25] It was bought in 1921 by Frank Stratton (d. 1941), whose grandson Mr. C. A. Cutforth was owner in 1977.[26]

The manor-house at Shaw mentioned in 1648 and 1660 stood at the junction of the street of the former village of Shaw with the Wansdyke. It may have survived into the 19th century and the last of its out-buildings, a barn, was demolished c. 1970.[27] Soon after 1800 that house was replaced by a new one some 400 m. west.[28] The red-brick house,[29] which is approached from the south-west by a short avenue of beeches, has a principal south front of three bays and stands amid walled gardens. The stable block of 1909 east of the house was built by Spencer Compton, the then owner.[30]

The part of Boreham wood claimed by Thomas of Kennett when the wood was put out of Savernake forest in 1225 may possibly be identified with the estate at Shaw held by the same Thomas or a namesake in 1243.[31] The estate was then apparently held of the bishop of Winchester.[32] A Thomas of Kennett still had land at Shaw in 1265.[33] What may be the same estate was settled by John of Berwick on Gilbert of Stubbington and his wife Margery and on Margery's heirs in 1299.[34]

The estate's later descent is unknown. It may possibly be represented either by land at Shaw sold in 1511 by John Ernle to John Button and his wife Edith,[35] or by another estate there, which included land at East Kennett, owned by the Weston family in the 16th century and sold in 1586–7 by Richard Weston and his wife Margaret to William Button.[36] Both were merged with the manor of Shaw.

The priory of St. Swithun, Winchester, appropriated Overton church and its chapels in 1291.[37] The rectory estate, which consisted of tithes alone, passed with East Overton manor until 1553.[38] In that year William, earl of Pembroke, conveyed the tithes from Alton Priors chapelry to the Crown.[39] The Pembrokes later recovered that portion, however, and the reunited rectory descended with East Overton manor to Philip, earl of Pembroke and Montgomery (d. 1683).[40]

In 1680 the earl sold the tithes of Alton Priors chapelry with Alton Priors manor to Samuel Brewster and Nicholas Fownes in moieties. After the moieties were reunited in 1714 the great tithes of Alton tithing were deemed to be merged.[41] In 1812 those of West Stowell tithing were sold by the lord of Alton manor to William Hitchcock, owner of West Stowell farm.[42] In 1848 rent-charges of £250 and £100 respectively were allotted to the owners of the Alton Priors and West Stowell estates. Since the tithes were already considered to be merged, however, the sums so allotted were not apportioned.[43]

In 1682 Philip, earl of Pembroke and Montgomery, while retaining the demesne tithes of West Overton manor, sold some of the great tithes arising from the tenantry lands there, with all the impropriated tithes arising from East Overton, Fyfield, and Lockeridge, to William Clarke with East Overton manor. Those tithes, thereafter deemed to be the impropriated rectory of Overton, descended like East Overton manor.[44] In 1802 the tithes from the tenantry lands of West Overton manor were re-allotted between the duke of Marlborough as impropriator and the earl of Pembroke and

[11] *Bk. of Fees*, ii. 748; see above, p. 143.
[12] *Bk. of Fees*, ii. 748.
[13] S.R.O., DD/WHb 2022–3.   [14] *W.A.M.* xii. 19.
[15] S.R.O., DD/WHb 2024; *Feet of F.* 1327–77 (W.R.S. xxix), p. 38.   [16] S.R.O., DD/WHb 2025.
[17] Ibid. DD/WHb 2026.   [18] *Feud. Aids*, v. 269.
[19] S.R.O., DD/WHb 2144; DD/WHb 2027–8; DD/WHb 2036; *Wilts. Pedigrees* (Harl. Soc. cv, cvi), 21–2; *V.C.H. Wilts.* ix. 94.
[20] *Wilts. Pedigrees* (Harl. Soc. cv, cvi), 33; *Extents for Debts* (W.R.S. xxviii), pp. 102–3; B.L. Add. Ch. 40086; *V.C.H. Wilts.* ix. 94.
[21] S.R.O., DD/WHb 686; DD/WHb 2045–6; Blenheim Mun., Wilts. deeds, abstr. of title, 1799.
[22] *V.C.H. Wilts.* ix. 94; Blenheim Mun., Wilts. deeds, abstr. of title, 1799.
[23] Blenheim Mun., Wilts. deeds, letter, Hughes to Brooks, 1801; W.R.O., Land Tax; Inclosure Award.
[24] I.R. 29/38/235; I.R. 30/38/235; *Kelly's Dir. Wilts.* (1848).
[25] W.A.S. Libr., sale cat. xvii, no. 44; xvii, no. 45; list of title deeds *penes* Mr. C. A. Cutforth, Shaw Farm.
[26] List of title deeds *penes* Mr. Cutforth; *W.A.M.* xlix. 375–6.

[27] S.R.O., DD/WHb 686; DD/WHb 2045–8; B.L. Map Libr., map of Shaw farm; *Andrews and Dury, Map* (W.R.S. viii), pl. 11; W.R.O., Inclosure Award map; O.S. Map 6″, Wilts. XXXV (1889 edn.); ex inf. Mr. Cutforth.
[28] The ho. first appears on a map c. 1815: W.R.O., Inclosure Award map.
[29] A brick on the E. wall bears the scratched inscription 'I.S. 1810'.
[30] List of title deeds *penes* Mr. Cutforth.
[31] *V.C.H. Wilts.* iv. 418; *Bk. of Fees*, ii. 748.
[32] *Bk. of Fees*, ii. 748.   [33] *Close R.* 1264–8, 123.
[34] *Feet of F.* 1272–1327 (W.R.S. i), p. 45.
[35] S.R.O., DD/WHb 2029; DD/WHb 2031.
[36] Ibid. DD/WHb 2037–9; DD/WHb 2052.
[37] See p. 199.
[38] *L. & P. Hen. VIII*, xvi, p. 417; *Cal. Pat.* 1547–8, 172.
[39] *Cal. Pat.* 1553, 177.
[40] C 66/1684 m. 8; C.P. 25(2)/387/20 Jas. I Trin.
[41] W.R.O. 492/38, abstr. of title, 1680–1810.
[42] W.R.O. 473/64, sale cat.
[43] New Coll., Oxf., Mun. 4970, tithe award; declaration of J. T. Parker, 1848.
[44] W.R.O. 212B/5208; Wilton Ho. Mun., W. Overton survey, c. 1794.

Montgomery as lord of the manor.[45] The duke of Marlborough was allotted 512 a. in the open fields of East Overton, Fyfield, and Lockeridge to replace his impropriated tithes there in 1821.[46]

By 1840 the owner of Shaw farm had in some way acquired the great tithes of his estate. They were thereafter considered to be merged.[47]

In 1066 the bishop of Winchester held an estate of 5 hides at Fyfield. At an unknown date it was assigned to the sacrist of the cathedral church and in 1066 was held of the bishop by a monk, Alsi. In 1086, however, Edward held it of the bishop.[48] In 1243 the prior of St. Swithun's claimed the manor of *FYFIELD*, which was finally confirmed to him by the bishop in 1284.[49] The prior and convent received a grant of free warren in their demesne there in 1300.[50] Thereafter the estate, like East Overton manor, was held by St. Swithun's until the Dissolution, when it passed to the Crown.[51]

In 1547 the Crown granted the manor, with East Overton, to Sir William Herbert, later earl of Pembroke, and it thereafter passed with the title to Philip, earl of Pembroke and Montgomery (d. 1683).[52] Thomas Fowle had acquired it by 1697 and it afterwards descended in the Fowle family to the Revd. F. C. Fowle (d. 1840).[53] It was presumably he who offered the estate for sale in 1812.[54] It was bought by John Goodman, in possession by 1815.[55] The manor was later bought by R. C. Long, described as lord in 1867,[56] and thereafter descended again like East Overton manor.[57]

The east front of Fyfield House, from which the estate was farmed until c. 1975,[58] was probably added c. 1820 to an earlier house which was demolished and rebuilt in the later 19th century to provide secondary rooms and a service wing. West of the house are barns and extensive stabling of 19th-century date, of which the larger part to the west was built in 1872.[59]

It is possible that the small estate called *CLAT-FORD PARK* in the later 16th century may have originated in land at Rainscombe granted in 934 by Athelstan to Wilton Abbey.[60] The land may have passed after the Dissolution with other Wilton estates in the area to Sir William Herbert.

Before 1597, however, the ground called Clatford Park, then apparently lately inclosed, belonged to Sir Thomas Wroughton (d. 1597), who had bought it from Robert and Thomas Wroth.[61] Shortly before his death Sir Thomas sold it to Sir Robert Wroth (d. 1606), who devised the park to his younger sons John, Henry, and Thomas.[62] In 1618 John and Henry Wroth confirmed the park to Richard Goddard, who may have acquired it some years earlier.[63] It may have been that Richard Goddard who disparked the land c. 1631.[64] By 1717 Clatford Park seems to have been acquired by John Chetwynd, later Viscount Chetwynd, owner of Lockeridge manor.[65] It was sold with Lockeridge in 1756 to the duke of Marlborough. Clatford Park thereafter descended like East Overton manor until 1906 when, reckoned at 182 a. and called Clatford Park Home farm, it was offered for sale as part of the Meux estate.[66] It was acquired at some date by the Forestry Commission, who sold the farm to E. N. and N. S. Baker in 1956.[67] Clatford Park Farm, a brick house of c. 1800 which may have replaced an earlier one,[68] and the surrounding land were owned in 1977 by Mr. C. Morgan-Smith.

Between 871 and 899 Ceolwen, widow of Osmod, granted the reversion of 15 hides at Alton, which she had inherited from her husband, to the church of Winchester for its refectory.[69] By the 11th century Winchester's Alton estate also included the later manor of Patney.[70] In 1086 the estate, reckoned at 20 hides, was among those which had been allotted by the bishop for the support of the monks of the Old Minster.[71]

Between 1047 and 1052 Bishop Stigand and the monks of Winchester leased 2 hides and 1 virgate at Alton to Wulfric for two lives.[72] The estate was afterwards held by Wulfward Belgisone, and between 1078 and 1085 the bishop, at William I's instigation, granted the same land to William Scudet for life.[73] It was restored to the convent in 1108.[74]

In 1284 the estate, by then separate from Patney, was finally confirmed to St. Swithun's by the bishop.[75] It comprised the land of the tithings of Alton and West Stowell. The convent received a grant of free warren within the demesne of the manor of *ALTON PRIORS*, or *ALTON PRIORS AND STOWELL*, as it was later known, in 1300.[76] St. Swithun's held the estate until the Dissolution, when it passed to the Crown.[77]

[45] W.R.O., W. Overton Inclosure Award.
[46] Ibid. E. Overton, Lockeridge, Fyfield Inclosure Award.   [47] I.R. 29/38/235.
[48] *V.C.H. Wilts.* ii, pp. 120, 201.
[49] *Bk. of Fees*, ii. 748; *Reg. Pontoise* (Cant. & York Soc.), ii. 436.
[50] *Cal. Chart. R.* 1300–26, 1.
[51] *Feud. Aids*, v. 205; *Valor Eccl.* (Rec. Com.), vi, App. p. vii.
[52] *Cal. Pat.* 1547–8, 172; Wards 7/12 f. 51; C 142/264 no. 181; *Wilts. Inq. p.m.* 1625–49 (Index Libr.), 97–101; Wilton Ho. Mun., ct. roll, 1677.
[53] W.R.O. 57/1, deed, Brettland and Fowle to Beasley, 1697; deed, Fowle to Dymer, 1709; 57/2, deed, Fowle to trustee, 1763; J. Foster, *Alumni Oxon. 1715–1886*, ii, p. 485; B.L. Map Libr., map of Fyfield man. (1811).
[54] W.R.O. 57/4, sale partics.
[55] Ibid. Inclosure Award (1821) and map (1815–16).
[56] *Kelly's Dir. Wilts.* (1867).
[57] W.R.O. 106, sale cat. Meux N. Wilts. estates, 1906.
[58] Ex inf. Mr. R. G. F. Swanton.
[59] By Sir Henry Meux, Bt. (d. 1883), whose initials and the date appear on the external N. wall.
[60] *V.C.H. Wilts.* x. 126, 128; *Arch. Jnl.* lxxvi. 190–1.

[61] *W.N. & Q.* ii. 350; C 142/249 no. 81; Prob. 11/91 (P.C.C. 36 Lewyn, will of Thomas Wroughton); *V.C.H. Glos.* xi. 168.
[62] C 142/294 no. 87.
[63] C 2/Jas. I/G 17/66; C.P. 25(2)/371/16 Jas. I Trin.
[64] W.R.O. 754/22, deed, Goddard to Pyke, 1631.
[65] C.P. 25(2)/1077/3 Geo. I East.; W.R.O. 212B/5201.
[66] W.R.O. 106, sale cat.
[67] Ex inf. Chief Forester, Savernake Forest Office, Marlborough.
[68] *Andrews and Dury, Map* (W.R.S. viii), pl. 12.
[69] Finberg, *Early Wessex Chart.* p. 77.
[70] *V.C.H. Wilts.* ii, pp. 85, 120.
[71] Ibid. p. 120.
[72] Finberg, *Early Wessex Chart.* p. 105.
[73] J. H. Round, *King's Serjeants*, 10.
[74] *Reg. Regum Anglo-Norm.* ii, no. 884.
[75] *Reg. Pontoise* (Cant. & York Soc.), ii. 436.
[76] Mun. D. & C. Winton., ct. roll, 1295–6; *Cal. Chart. R.* 1300–26, 1; *Cal. Pat.* 1553, 177; W.R.O. 492/38, abstr. of title, 1680–1810. The suffix 'Priors' occurs in 1199: *Pipe R.* 1199 (P.R.S. n.s. x), 177.
[77] *Feud. Aids*, v. 271; S.C. 6/Hen. VIII/3343 mm. 45 sqq.

In 1541 Alton was granted to Winchester chapter, who returned it to the Crown in 1547.[78] In that year Sir William Herbert, later earl of Pembroke, received a royal grant of it, but he returned it to the Crown in 1553.[79] The manor was later restored to the Herbert family, earls of Pembroke, however, and in 1630 William, earl of Pembroke, died seised of Alton and Stowell.[80] The manor descended with the title to Philip, earl of Pembroke and Montgomery (d. 1683), who in 1680 sold it in moieties while retaining the manorial rights.[81]

In 1681 Nicholas Fownes sold the moiety which he had bought to John Smith the elder (d. 1691) of Alton Priors. Samuel Brewster, who bought the other moiety, settled it on his son Samuel in 1692. In 1708 the younger Samuel mortgaged the moiety to George Noble, whose interest therein was declared absolute in the same year. Noble sold it in 1714 to the elder John Smith's son John (d. 1726), and thus the moieties were reunited.[82] The manorial rights apparently passed like Patney manor to Sir William Pynsent (d. 1719), who conveyed them in 1717 to John Smith.[83]

John Smith was succeeded in 1726 by his son John.[84] That John died in 1742 having devised the manor to his daughters Dilarevere, Priscilla, and Elizabeth in turn. Dilarevere, wife of Michael Smith, died without issue in 1769, and her sister Priscilla, wife of Michael Ewen, also died childless. Their sister Elizabeth, wife of James Burrough, succeeded, and in 1778 she sold Alton Priors to her son Michael (d. 1831).[85]

In 1812 Michael Burrough sold Alton Priors to Thomas Caldecott (d. 1833). Caldecott was succeeded by his nephew, the Revd. J. T. Parker, who sold the manor in 1849 to J. G. Simpkins. In the following year Simpkins sold it to Head Pottinger Best (d. 1887). Best settled it on his daughter Rosamond, wife of W. L. Stucley, who predeceased her father in 1877. Her husband, created a baronet, held the manor for his lifetime. On his death in 1911 it reverted to Rosamond's half-brother, Marmaduke Head Best (d. 1912), whose widow and another sold the Alton estate, 1,100 a., in 1912 to New College, Oxford, owner in 1977.[86]

The Button family were lessees of the demesne, and probably resident at Alton, from the later 15th century. John Button (d. 1491), his son John (d. 1524), grandson William (d. 1547), and great-grandson William (d. 1591), were all tenants.[87] Thereafter the lease passed like Lyneham manor to Sir William Button (d. 1655).[88] In 1651 John Smith

became lessee.[89] It may have been the same John Smith (d. 1691), who acquired the freehold of a moiety of the estate in 1681.[90]

The Priory, as it was called in 1977, probably represents a wing of the manor-house of c. 1700 built of brick with stone dressings.[91] It incorporates some timber-framed walling and the reset head of a fire-place of the later 16th century. The house was reduced in size c. 1810 and the surviving part divided into cottages, which were reunited and restored c. 1970.[92] South-east of the house fragments of the 18th- and 19th-century walls of a formal garden remain.

Soon after 1810 a new manor-house was built on the north side of the lane from West Stowell to Alton Barnes. Although Alton Priors Manor incorporates some features of a house of c. 1815, it is the product of an extensive reconstruction in the mid 19th century. There are extensions to the north.

In 1680 Philip, earl of Pembroke and Montgomery, sold seven copyholds totalling 4 yardlands at Alton Priors to Daniel Hodges (d. 1689).[93] The land passed in the Hodges family from Daniel to his son Edward (d. 1738), and grandsons George (d.s.p. 1739) and Edward Hodges (d. 1769). The daughters of Edward the grandson, Hannah, wife of James Beezely, and Anne, wife of Nicholas Symmonds, succeeded as tenants in common. In 1771 Nicholas Symmonds bought Hannah's moiety and in 1783 sold the reunited estate to Michael Burrough. The estate thus merged with Alton Priors manor.

In 1680 the earl also sold 3 yardlands at Alton Priors to John Stiffe. In 1691 John's widow and devisee, Mary, conveyed the land to their daughter Mary and her husband Ebenezer Cawdron. The Cawdrons sold it in 1698 to William Stretch of Alton Priors. The land passed in the Stretch family to another William who sold it in 1783 to Michael Burrough, lord of Alton Priors.[94]

It seems possible that the land at West Stowell which formed part of Alton Priors manor was also sold c. 1680. In 1780 the West Stowell estate was owned by John Hitchcock and it passed in the Hitchcock family until at least the earlier 19th century.[95] Elizabeth Clark was owner in 1848.[96] F. A. Cave was owner in 1912.[97] Sir Eric Phipps acquired the estate c. 1930. His widow sold the farm and West Stowell House separately in the early 1950s to the Hosier Estate Co. and Pewsey rural district council respectively. The Hosier Estate Co. sold the farm to Sir Philip Dunn, Bt., in the late 1960s.

[78] L. & P. Hen. VIII, xvi, p. 417; Cal. Pat. 1547–8, 25.
[79] Cal. Pat. 1547–8, 172; 1553, 177; Complete Peerage, s.v. Pembroke.
[80] S.R.O., DD/WHb 692; Wilts. Inq. p.m. 1625–49 (Index Libr.), 97.
[81] Wilton Ho. Mun., ct. recs. 1670, 1676–8; Complete Peerage, s.v. Pembroke; W.R.O. 492/38, abstr. of title, 1680–1810.
[82] W.R.O. 492/38, abstr. of title, 1680–1810; Wilts. Cuttings, xvi. 52–3.
[83] C.P. 25(2)/889/9 Wm. III Mich.; W.R.O. 490/471, abstr. of title, 1674–c. 1763.
[84] Wilts. Cuttings, xvi. 52–3.
[85] Ibid.; W.R.O. 496/5; 492/38, abstr. of title, 1680–1810; Land Tax.
[86] New Coll., Oxf., Mun. 4970, conveyance and mortgage, 1849; abstr. of title of M. H. Best; deed, Best and Mackintosh to New Coll., 1912; ex inf. Mr. A. G. Stratton, Alton Priors. For the Best and Stucley fams. see

Burke, Land. Gent. (1906), i. 118; Burke, Peerage (1931), 2260–1.
[87] S.R.O., DD/WHb 8–9; DD/WHb 660; DD/WHb 663; DD/WHb 2029; I. H. Jeayes, 'Cat. Button-Walker-Heneage Mun.' (TS. ibid.), p. 27; Coll. Topog. et Gen. v. 390.
[88] S.R.O., DD/WHb 692; Wilton Ho. Mun., receivers' acct. roll, 1633; V.C.H. Wilts. ix. 94; Jeayes, op. cit. p. 28; New Coll., Oxf., Mun. 1302, chancery bill, 1660.
[89] New Coll., Oxf., Mun. 1302, chancery bill, 1660.
[90] W.R.O. 492/38, abstr. of title, 1680–1810.
[91] Andrews and Dury, Map (W.R.S. viii), pl. 11.
[92] Wilts. Cuttings, xvi. 53; W.R.O. 503/3, deed, Caldecott to Miller (1827); ex inf. Mr. Stratton.
[93] All inf. from W.R.O. 492/38, abstr. of title, 1680–1810.
[94] Ibid.   [95] Ibid. Land Tax.
[96] New Coll., Oxf., Mun. 4970, tithe award.
[97] Ibid. 4970, deed, Best and Mackintosh to New Coll., 1912, and attached map.

Sir Philip's daughter, the Hon. Mrs. Jacob Rothschild, was owner in 1977.[98]

West Stowell House, a square red-brick house of the earlier 19th century with fronts of three bays, was much remodelled and enlarged to the designs of Guy Aylmer for Sir Eric Phipps c. 1930.[99] After it was acquired by the local authority it was used by Pewsey hospital as a school until 1971.[1] In 1977 the house and its out-buildings were being remodelled as eight separate dwellings.

ECONOMIC HISTORY. During the Middle Ages Overton contained, besides the Winchester manors of East Overton, Fyfield, and Alton Priors, economically independent estates at Lockeridge, West Overton, and Shaw. East Overton and Alton Priors, while part of the inter-manorial structure of the estates of St. Swithun's Priory in Wiltshire and Hampshire, remained separate economic units. Fyfield manor, however, seems to have been administered as part of East Overton manor for economic purposes by the later 13th century, although with separate open fields. What is known of the economy of the most substantial of the Lockeridge estates, which was held by the Templars, and of the economies of West Overton, a Wilton property, and Shaw, is mentioned below.

In 1066 East Overton was assessed for geld at 15 hides. In 1086 the estate contained land enough for 7 ploughs. The 8½ demesne hides supported 2 ploughs and those held in villeinage 5 ploughs. The demesne's value had increased from £6 in 1066 to £8. There were 15 a. of meadow and the pasture was 8 furlongs in length and 4 furlongs broad.[2]

In 1066 the bishop of Winchester's Fyfield estate was assessed for geld at 5 hides. In 1086 there was land enough for 3 ploughs. There were 2 ploughs and 1 serf on the 3 demesne hides. Elsewhere on the estate there were 3 villeins and 9 bordars with 2 ploughs. There were 3 a. of meadow, 30 a. of pasture, and woodland 3 furlongs long by 1 broad. In 1066 and 1086 the value of the estate was £5.[3]

In 1210 East Overton and Fyfield, still economically independent, were valued at £16 and £8 respectively.[4] In 1309 the manors were interdependent and their joint income was £116.[5] During the 16th century the two estates were valued at £52 yearly, a sum which included the worth of the rectorial tithes of both.[6]

By the later 13th century it is possible that Fyfield's demesne was worked with that of East Overton, which was then in hand.[7] The demesne of East Overton, leased to farmers from at least the 16th century, certainly included a considerable acreage at Fyfield in 1567.[8] Some 291 a. at Fyfield

were still included in the East Overton demesne, 755 a., in 1728, although the owners of the two manors were then different.[9]

Of the tenancies within the combined manors of East Overton and Fyfield in the later 13th century only one, of ½ virgate held by a cottar, may be located with certainty and it was at Fyfield. Eleven holdings of 1 virgate, reckoned at 20 a. each, were then held for the usual agricultural services and small money rents. The virgater who acted as woodward was excused certain of the usual duties but was instead bound to carry the lot and crop of the manorial timber to the lord's court. There were also thirteen holdings of ½ virgate. Their tenants owed services similar to those of the virgaters and half their money rent. The ½-virgater, or cottar, who acted as shepherd paid no rent. The chief task of the cottar at Fyfield, whose holding was probably at Wroughton's mead, was to look after two of the lord's plough-teams at the ox-yard there.[10]

In 1567 the demesne farmer leased an additional 3 yardlands. At that date both East Overton and Fyfield contained several small copyhold farms. At East Overton there were 4 holdings of 2 yardlands, 4 of 1½ yardland, 1 of 1 yardland, and 2 of ½ yardland. At Fyfield there were 1 of 2 yardlands, 5 of 1½ yardland, and 2 of 1 yardland.[11] By 1724 the number of East Overton leaseholders had increased to ten, and the largest leasehold farm contained 100 a. Of the nine copyhold farms at East Overton the largest contained 113 a.[12]

In 1210 the demesne flock at East Overton numbered 300, and at Fyfield 100 sheep.[13] The chalk uplands continued to support large numbers of sheep throughout the Middle Ages. In 1299 the combined manor of East Overton and Fyfield supported a flock of 717 ewes, 400 hoggasters, and 322 lambs.[14] They were folded in three sheepcots, one south of the Kennet at Audley's Cottages in Fyfield and two north of the river at Hackpen and at 'Raddon' or Wroughton's mead in Fyfield.[15] There was much interchange of stock, particularly of lambs and hoggasters, between the Overton flock and those of some of the Hampshire manors of St. Swithun's Priory such as Barton, Hurstbourne Priors, and Mapledurham, in Buriton.[16] In 1567 at both East Overton and Fyfield sheep were stinted at 100 to the yardland.[17]

The open fields of East Overton and those of Fyfield occupied the wide chalk terraces north and south of the Kennet. In 1567 East Overton's fields were named as South, East, and North fields, and Fyfield's as North, South, and Rylands fields.[18] In the Overton fields at least, subdivision had taken place by the early 18th century, and in 1728 there were North, Yonder, South, Vicar's, Coneys, Long,

[98] Ex inf. Mr. J. Wallis, Humberts, Pewsey.

[99] Ex inf. Mrs. Bonar Sykes, Conock Man., Devizes.

[1] Wilts. Gaz. 24 Dec. 1975.

[2] V.C.H. Wilts. ii, pp. 120–1. [3] Ibid. p. 120.

[4] Interdict Doc. (Pipe R. Soc. N.S. xxxiv), 17.

[5] Mun. D. & C. Winton., acct. roll, 1309.

[6] Valor Eccl. (Rec. Com.), vi, App. p. vii; Winch. Chap. Doc. 1541–7, ed. G. W. Kitchin and F. T. Madge (Hants Rec. Soc.), 95; First Pembroke Survey, ed. Straton, i. 260.

[7] Katharine A. Hanna, 'Winch. Cath. Custumal' (Southampton Univ. Coll. M.A. thesis, 1954), pp. lvi–lvii, 465–6.

[8] First Pembroke Survey, ed. Straton, i. 257 sqq.

[9] Blenheim Mun., Wilts. deeds, E. Overton survey.

[10] Hanna, 'Winch. Cath. Custumal', pp. lvi–lvii, 458 sqq. Foundations which may represent the ox-yard buildings were excavated c. 1960: W.A.M. lviii. 109 sqq.

[11] First Pembroke Survey, ed. Straton, i. 251 sqq.

[12] Blenheim Mun., Wilts. deeds, survey.

[13] Interdict Doc. (Pipe R. Soc. N.S. xxxiv), 24–5.

[14] Mun. D. & C. Winton., acct. roll, 1299.

[15] W.A.M. lviii. 114.

[16] Joan G. Greatrex, 'Admin. Winch. Cath. Priory temp. Beaufort' (Ottawa Univ. Ph.D. thesis, 1972), App. I. E, pp. xxxv, xxxvii–xxxix, xli–xlii.

[17] First Pembroke Survey, ed. Straton, i. 252 sqq.

[18] Ibid.

Bittam, Hatch Yatt, White Barrow, and Pound fields.[19]

In 1567 there was a common meadow in East Overton called Broad mead and another in Fyfield called Berry mead. At the same date the common pastures of East Overton, called Prior's Ball, Full Ridge, and Hursley, were estimated at 100 a. and used by the manorial tenants all the year. The tenantry sheep downs were on Broad, 34 a., and Little, 8 a., downs. Fyfield then contained a sheep down of 130 a. called North down. 'Atleys' or Audley's down, 80 a., at Fyfield, south of the village, was common to the tenants there during spring, summer, and autumn, but after 11 November the farmer of East Overton was entitled to it.[20] In 1728 East Overton manor contained Hackpen and 'Roddon' downs, 276 a., Hursley down, 26 a., and a tenantry down of 101 a.[21]

In 1719 some lands in the open fields and common meadows of East Overton and Fyfield were inclosed, and in some cases exchanged, by agreement between the lord of East Overton, his tenants there, the freeholders and leaseholders of Lockeridge tithing, the lord of Fyfield manor, and others.[22] At parliamentary inclosure in 1821 the lord of East Overton was allotted some 800 a. in East Overton tithing and some 500 a. in Fyfield chapelry for the manor of East Overton. Within Fyfield manor, administered separately from East Overton from at least 1697 and perhaps much reduced in size by that date, the lord was allotted 218 a. At the same date arrangements were made to pay the owner of the mill in the neighbouring tithing of West Overton £27 yearly for turning water out of the mill dam to irrigate the water-meadows of East Overton, partitioned into 7 'stems' on either side of the Kennet, from December to the beginning of April and again from the beginning of May until the end of June.[23]

Much reorganization of the farms in East Overton and Fyfield took place before parliamentary inclosure. In 1812 Fyfield manor comprised three farms, two, of 338 a. and 27 a., containing land on either side of the Bath road, and one of 112 a. representing the remnant of the former demesne.[24] The division of the manorial estate at East Overton into North and South farms on either side of the London–Bath road probably occurred c. 1800.[25] In 1856 North farm at East Overton and Fyfield farm were worked together but by 1906 North, 958 a., and South, 451 a., farms at Overton and Fyfield farm, 573 a., had been let to three different tenants.[26]

In the later 19th century and the early 20th both Overton and Fyfield downs were exploited, as part of the Meux estates in north Wiltshire, for sporting purposes. Both areas provided training courses for such notable racehorse trainers as Alexander Taylor

and his son Alexander.[27] A large rabbit warren of some 536 a., established on Fyfield down by 1880, was managed as a game warren until c. 1910, when Alexander Taylor the younger killed c. 14,000 rabbits to make the downland gallops safer.[28]

In 1066 Wilton Abbey's West Overton estate was assessed for geld at 10 hides. In 1086 7 hides and ½ virgate were in demesne. There was land enough for 4 ploughs. On the demesne there were 2 ploughs and 2 serfs. Elsewhere on the estate were the remaining 2 ploughs and 3 villeins and 8 bordars. There were 5 a. of meadow, 20 a. of pasture, and 20 a. of woodland. The whole estate was worth £5 in 1086.[29]

Nothing is known of the estate's economy later in the Middle Ages. In 1535 the manor was worth £21, of which £9 represented the rents of free and customary tenants and £12 the farm of the demesne.[30]

The demesne in 1567 contained 168 a. of arable and 7 a. of meadow and supported a large flock.[31] The Kingman family were farmers in the earlier 17th century and the Cooke family for most of the 18th century.[32] Edward Pumphrey became tenant in 1784 and his family held West Overton farm, reckoned at 232 a. in 1794, well into the 19th century.[33]

In 1567 the estate contained, besides 3 freeholders and 1 cottager, 11 customary tenants who paid yearly rents totalling £7: 2 copyholders held 2 yardlands each, 4 held 1½ yardland, 3 held 1 yardland, and 2 held ½ yardland.[34] There was the same number of customary holdings in 1631.[35] In 1706 there were 24 manorial tenants, of whom the most substantial held no more than 30 a. Three of their holdings included land at Overton Heath.[36] About 1794, of the seventeen tenants holding some 560 a., most held about 30 a. each, but a few worked farms of 50–100 a.[37]

West Overton's arable fields, on the chalk soils north and south of the settlement, were named in 1631 as North, West or Little, and South fields.[38] Some subdivision had apparently taken place by c. 1794 when the arable lands north of the London–Bath road were named as Upper, Middle, and Lower fields and those to the south as Ditch Hedge, Double Hedge, and Windmill fields.[39] In 1631 common meadow lay in South and Little meads and in Northside and Southside meadows.[40] There were two downs, a cow down of 100 a. and Allens down, 40 a., within the manor in 1567. The farmer and the tenants then had herbage and pasture rights in a common of 30 a. called Common woods. Another common, of 40 a., called the Heath or Abbess Wood and abutting the south-east corner of

[19] Blenheim Mun., Wilts. deeds, survey.
[20] *First Pembroke Survey*, ed. Straton, i. 252 sqq.; B.L. Map Libr., map of Fyfield man. (1811); W.R.O. 57/4.
[21] Blenheim Mun., Wilts. deeds, survey.
[22] H.R.O. 7M54/227.
[23] W.R.O., Inclosure Award and map.
[24] Ibid. 57/4, sale partic.
[25] North Farm was built c. 1801.
[26] Blenheim Mun. E/P/90, mid-19th-cent. survey; W.R.O. 106, sale cat. Meux N. Wilts. estates.
[27] *V.C.H. Wilts.* iv. 382; Blenheim Mun. E/P/90, mid-19th-cent. survey; W.R.O. 106, sale cat. Meux N. Wilts. estates.
[28] W.R.O. 106, sale cat. Meux N. Wilts. estates. The

warren is described by N. E. King and J. Sheail, 'Old Rabbit Warren on Fyfield Down', *W.A.M.* lxv. 1 sqq.
[29] *V.C.H. Wilts.* ii, p. 129.
[30] *Valor Eccl.* (Rec. Com.), ii. 110.
[31] *First Pembroke Survey*, ed. Straton, i. 141–2.
[32] Wilton Ho. Mun., surveys, 1631, 1706.
[33] Ibid. survey, c. 1794; deeds, Pembroke to Pumphrey, 1806, 1818; *Kelly's Dir. Wilts.* (1848 and later edns.).
[34] *First Pembroke Survey*, ed. Straton, i. 140 sqq.
[35] Wilton Ho. Mun., survey, 1631.
[36] Ibid. survey, 1706.
[37] Ibid. survey, c. 1794.
[38] Ibid. survey, 1631.
[39] Ibid. survey, c. 1794.   [40] Ibid. survey, 1631.

the parish, was shared with the tenants of North Newnton and its tithing Hilcott, which were also owned by the Pembrokes.[41] The manorial pasture was reckoned at 177 a. c. 1794 and called Cow and Tenantry downs, Mill ham, and Church ditch.[42]

In 1802 551 a. in the open fields and common meadows and pastures of West Overton were inclosed at the expense of the earl of Pembroke and Montgomery. The demesne farmer, whose land had been augmented by several copyholds by that date, was allotted 131 a., and the earl's other tenants a total of 385 a.[43] Immediately afterwards rents within the estate rose from £655 to £916, making available the capital necessary for improvement.[44] By 1818 the West Overton estate contained two consolidated farms, the former demesne, then called West Overton farm, 330 a., and another, probably to be identified with the later Park farm at Overton Heath, which was reckoned at 200 a., of which 10 a. were water-meadows by the Kennet.[45]

In 1066 the estate later called Lockeridge manor paid geld for 2 hides and was worth £2. In 1086 1 hide was held in demesne. The estate then supported 1 plough and contained 1 villein, 2 bordars, and 1 serf. There were 1 a. of meadow, 12 a. of pasture, and 6 a. of woodland. The value of the estate had fallen to 30s. by 1086.[46]

That estate, acquired by the Templars between 1141 and 1143, was augmented in the later 12th century by another 3 hides at Lockeridge.[47] The lands were thenceforth administered from Rockley, in Ogbourne St. Andrew.[48] By 1185, however, only that land given by William de Beauchamp seems to have been held by tenants: 2 were cottagers, and of the remaining 9, 2 held 10 a. each for 6s. yearly, and 7 held 5 a. each for 3s. yearly. Besides boon-work, all owed certain renders in kind which had apparently been introduced by the Templars. An assart and 4 a. were then held in common.[49] In 1338 receipts from the estate totalled £20, a sum which included £7 representing rents, works, and customary payments. Outgoings amounted to £7, making a profit of £13 to be sent to the preceptory at Sandford (Oxon.), from which the estate was then administered.[50]

By 1768 the duke of Marlborough had acquired the manors of Lockeridge and Upper Lockeridge. He also owned the land, deemed part of the Overton estate of the monks of Winchester, held in 1086 by Durand of Gloucester.[51] That estate, reckoned at 2 hides all but ½ virgate, was worth £1 in 1066 and 1086.[52] When the open fields and common pastures of Lockeridge were inclosed in 1821 the duke of Marlborough as lord was allotted 300 a. there.[53]

By the mid 19th century most of the land in Lockeridge tithing north of the Kennet had been included in North farm at Overton. What remained of Lockeridge farm, 177 a., was south of the river. It then included the allotment at Lockeridge made in 1821 to replace vicarial tithes and glebe, which was leased from the vicar.[54] The composite farm so formed was worked in the later 19th century by members of the Rebbeck family.[55] By 1906, however, the former glebe, by then like Lockeridge the freehold property of Lady Meux, was worked separately and known as Glebe farm.[56]

In 1066 Shaw paid geld for 2 hides and 1½ virgate and was worth 20s. In 1086 the estate contained land enough for 1 plough and supported 1 villein and 2 serfs. There were 30 a. of pasture and woodland 1 league long by 1 furlong broad. In 1086 its value had increased to £2.[57]

By the 14th century it is likely that the lands of the part of Shaw in Overton had been consolidated as one farm.[58] It contained a very small arable acreage and was probably exploited as a sheep-rearing hill farm.[59] Under the ownership of the Button family Shaw was worked in conjunction with their West Tockenham estate in Lyneham. In the 1670s the Shaw flock numbered some 600 sheep. Much of the stock was transferred each summer to West Tockenham for fattening on the lusher pastures there.[60]

The owner of Shaw farm was accustomed to pasture over 1,000 sheep on Shaw down, where in the mid 17th century he inter-commoned with the tenant of Alton Barnes.[61] When Shaw down was inclosed in 1674 and apportioned between the owners of Shaw in Overton and Alton Barnes, Sir Robert Button as lord of Shaw in Overton was allotted certain woods and 150 a. south of Wansdyke.[62] That apportionment was repeated in 1680.[63] When Skilling heath, another near-by common shared with neighbouring estates, was inclosed in 1693, the owner of Shaw farm received some 5 a.[64] By 1834 the farm's arable acreage had greatly increased, possibly through the clearance of woodland, and, of its 425 a., 112 a. represented arable land in Boreham and Rowdown fields and 66 a. arable land in South field.[65] From 1907 to 1918 the farm was worked by Arthur Stratton in conjunction with the farm at Alton Priors, and it was at Shaw that Stratton established a pioneer school for Land Women.[66]

In 1066 a composite estate based on Alton Priors paid geld for 20 hides, 5 of which represented the later manor of Patney. Of those 20 hides, then worth £24, 6 hides and 1 virgate were in demesne in 1086. There were then 4 ploughs and 8 serfs on the demesne, and elsewhere on the estate 8 ploughs and 27 villeins and 15 coscez. There were 100 a. of

41 *First Pembroke Survey*, ed. Straton, i. 141 sqq.
42 Wilton Ho. Mun., survey, c. 1794.
43 W.R.O., Inclosure Award.
44 *V.C.H. Wilts.* iv. 90.
45 Wilton Ho. Mun., deeds, Pembroke to Pumphrey; Pembroke to Cooke.
46 *V.C.H. Wilts.* ii, p. 148.   47 See pp. 189–90.
48 *Rec. Templars in Eng.* ed. Lees, p. 53.
49 Ibid. pp. 53, 57.
50 *Knights Hospitallers in Eng.* (Camd. Soc. [1st ser.], lxv), 187.   51 *V.C.H. Wilts.* ii, p. 120.
52 Ibid.
53 W.R.O., Inclosure Award.

54 Blenheim Mun. E/P/90, mid-19th-cent. survey; see below.
55 *Kelly's Dir. Wilts.* (1867 and later edns.).
56 W.R.O. 106, sale cat.
57 *V.C.H. Wilts.* ii, pp. 153–4.
58 *Feet of F.* 1327–77 (W.R.S. xxix), p. 38.
59 Ibid.; *Extents for Debts* (W.R.S. xxviii), pp. 102–3.
60 S.R.O., DD/WHb 3114; *V.C.H. Wilts.* ix. 98.
61 *Woodward's Notes* (W.R.S. xiii), 85.
62 S.R.O., DD/WHb 2049.
63 Ibid. DD/WHb 2050.   64 Ibid. DD/WHb 691.
65 W.A.S. Libr., sale cat. ix, no. 42.
66 *Kelly's Dir. Wilts.* (1907); *W.A.M.* xl. 278–9.

meadow, pasture 6 furlongs long by 4 broad, and woodland 7 furlongs long by 2 broad. The estate of 3 hides held as an under-tenancy in 1086, which comprised land at both Alton Priors and Patney, then contained land enough for 2 ploughs and was valued separately at £5.[67]

In 1210 Alton Priors manor, by then separate from Patney, was worth £32, of which £8 represented assessed rents.[68] The estate's profits were possibly allotted at an early date to the almoner of St. Swithun's, Winchester.[69] By 1334, however, the profits seem to have been paid directly to the prior's treasury at Winchester.[70] In the earlier and mid 16th century the estate was worth £34, a value which included the appropriated tithes of Alton Priors chapelry.[71]

Alton Priors demesne, except 15 a. in West Stowell and 8 a. in Alton Priors, probably remained in hand and was administered by a bailiff appointed by St. Swithun's Priory until the 15th century. The demesne had been divided into Great and Little farms by 1774, but in 1827 was again in single occupation and called Alton farm.[72]

In the later 13th century assessed rents from the manor totalled £8. The largest customary holding was then that of ½ hide in West Stowell tithing held for 8s. rent and labour services including autumn boon-work. Also in that tithing were fifteen holdings of 1 virgate for which half the rent and services of the ½ hide were owed. Each virgater was additionally entitled to 1 a. of demesne land. In Alton Priors tithing there were eight holdings of 1 virgate, the tenants of which owed the same yearly rent as the West Stowell tenants and the usual agricultural duties, and three of ½ virgate held for half the rent and services of the virgaters. Another twelve holdings of ½ virgate were held by cottars for rents of 3s. yearly and an obligation to perform the humbler agricultural tasks and certain weekly work. One of the cottars acted as ploughman and the cottars' wives milked the ewes or carried wool. Some 8 a. of demesne were let to them for 2s. yearly.[73] In 1595 of the seven Alton Priors copyholders, who paid a yearly rent of £6, the three most substantial held 4½, 3, and 2½ yardlands respectively. In West Stowell of the four copyholders, who paid £3 yearly, two held 3 yardlands each and two held 2 yardlands each.[74]

Like East Overton, Alton Priors played its part in the inter-manorial economy of the estates of St. Swithun's Priory. In 1210 there were 32 oxen and 250 sheep within the estate.[75] Of the 464 ewes

maintained there in 1261, 100 were sent to Overton, and of the 380 lambs raised there, 121 were sent to the same estate after shearing. In the same year 193 qr. of wheat were accounted for, as well as varying quantities of barley, oats, and dredge which were sent to Enford and Overton.[76] In 1299 138 cheeses had been produced over the past year.[77] Similar numbers of sheep and quantities of wheat, oats, and barley continued to be maintained and produced within the manor in the 14th century.[78] During the 14th and 15th centuries stock continued to be sent from Alton to other priory manors in Wiltshire and Hampshire and to be received from them in turn.[79]

There appear to have been two open fields on the manor in the 13th century.[80] They were later named as North and South fields.[81] In the later 16th century, however, those fields appear to have been exclusive to Alton Priors while West Stowell had its own East and West fields.[82] It is likely that the subdivision, the later emergence of West Stowell as a separate farm, and the acquisition by the lord of Alton Priors of two small freeholds within the manor in 1783, made formal inclosure unnecessary.[83]

Since the manor was almost entirely on chalk soils, it relied for meadow land and hay on another priory manor, Patney, with which it had been associated in the early Middle Ages. Hay was brought to Alton from Patney in the 14th century, and in the mid 16th century certain meadows in Patney were usually leased with Alton Priors manor.[84]

Manor farm at Alton Priors was tenanted in the later 19th century by Arthur Stratton (d. 1918), who established there a business for contracting agricultural machinery, the largest in Wiltshire for cultivating, threshing, hauling, and cutting. Shortly before the First World War the firm's work force at times of greatest demand was 24 men and during the same time the cultivating tackle let out increased from three to five sets.[85]

It is likely that in the 12th and 13th centuries the entire parish lay within Savernake forest.[86] Woodland seems to have been most plentiful within the tithings of West Overton, Shaw, and Lockeridge.[87] Boreham wood in Shaw, although put out of the forest in 1225, became part of it again a year or so later. It was still part of the forest in 1842, but was afterwards acquired by an owner of Shaw farm.[88] In 1543 Lockeridge manor contained 29 a. of woodland.[89] Tawsmead copse was part of Alton Priors manor in 1552 and in 1977.[90] The woodland of East Overton in 1567 comprised Little wood, 16 a.

[67] V.C.H. Wilts. ii, p. 120.
[68] Interdict Doc. (Pipe R. Soc. N.S. xxxiv), 24.
[69] Mun. D. & C. Winton., acct. roll, 1299.
[70] Obedientiaries' R. St. Swithun's, ed. G. W. Kitchin (Hants Rec. Soc.), 120.
[71] Valor Eccl. (Rec. Com.), vi, App. p. vii; Winch. Chap. Doc. 1541–7, ed. Kitchin and Madge, 95; E 318/1862 m. 32.
[72] W.R.O. 473/340, poor-rate, 1774; 503/3, deed, Caldecott to Miller (1827).
[73] Hanna, 'Winch. Cath. Custumal', pp. lvii, 486 sqq.
[74] S.R.O., DD/WHb 676.
[75] Interdict Doc. (Pipe R. Soc. N.S. xxxiv), 24.
[76] Mun. D. & C. Winton., acct. roll, 1261.
[77] Ibid. acct. roll, 1299.
[78] Ibid. acct. rolls, 1312, 1373, 1395.
[79] Greatrex, 'Admin. Winch. Cath.', App. 1. E, pp. xxxvii–xxxviii, xlii.
[80] Hanna, 'Winch. Cath. Custumal', 490.
[81] Mun. D. & C. Winton., acct. rolls, 1261, 1299, 1309, 1312, 1395.
[82] S.R.O., DD/WHb 677.   [83] See p. 193.
[84] Mun. D. & C. Winton., acct. roll, 1309; First Pembroke Survey, ed. Straton, i. 248–9.
[85] W.R.O. 853/41, correspondence, Stratton and others; W.A.M. xl. 278–9.
[86] V.C.H. Wilts. iv. 418.
[87] A fact attested in the case of Shaw by the etymology of the name: P.N. Wilts. (E.P.N.S.), 307; B.L. Map Libr., map of Shaw farm (1734); W.R.O., East Overton, Lockeridge, and Fyfield Inclosure Award map (1815–16).
[88] V.C.H. Wilts. iv. 418; I.R. 30/38/235; ex inf. Mr. C. A. Cutforth, Shaw Farm. Boreham wood was wrongly considered part of Savernake c. 1950: V.C.H. Wilts. iv. 451.   [89] C 66/724 m. 12.
[90] S.R.O., DD/WHb 660; ex inf. Mr. A. G. Stratton, Alton Priors. Tawsmead copse was wrongly considered to be part of Savernake c. 1950: V.C.H. Wilts. iv. 451.

planted with oaks, and Wools grove, 40 a., then both fairly recently established. At the same date Fyfield contained Fyfield wood, 40 a., and Audley's coppice, 8 a. The woods of West Overton, which included Wykeham Hasset, 4 a., Allen's coppice, 27 a., and Chichangles coppice (later Pumphrey wood), 25 a., were then considered dissafforested lands of Savernake.[91] After the Lockeridge estates and East Overton manor were acquired by the dukes of Marlborough in the 18th century, their woodland, augmented in the later 19th century by a considerable acreage in Fyfield, was husbanded for sporting as well as economic purposes.[92] In 1906 West Woods, as the woodland of the enlarged estate was then called, comprised 718 a. of oak, fir, and larch.[93] The woods suffered depredation by timber merchants before their acquisition in 1931 by the Forestry Commission, which thenceforth worked them from Savernake Forest. The land in East Overton, Lockeridge, and Fyfield was replanted mainly with beech in the 1930s and that in West Overton similarly replanted in the 1950s.[94]

The huge boulders, or sarsen stones, which littered the Kennet valley and Overton and Fyfield downs were used as building material locally from earliest times until the 20th century.[95] Their systematic exploitation began in the 19th century when improving farmers began to clear them from the arable fields. In the mid 19th century the Free and Cartwright families established themselves as stone-masons in the parish. Both firms, which employed local labour, also functioned as coal merchants, transporting sarsen stones to Honey Street wharf in Woodborough and carting coal back to Overton. Sarsen was used chiefly for tram-sets and kerbing, but was replaced by concrete in the earlier 20th century. Shortly before the industry finished in 1939, four waggon-loads of sarsen blocks were used to repair Windsor Castle. The main areas worked were on the downs north of the river. Some protection was offered to the Pickledean and Lockeridge dene areas in 1907 when 12 a. in Pickledean and 8 a. in Lockeridge dene were bought by the National Trust.[96] The sarsens on Fyfield down are within the 610 a. there declared a Nature Conservancy area in 1956.[97]

In 1977 North farm, 700 a., although a distinct unit from South and Fyfield farms, 880 a., was worked in conjunction with them by the partnership of F. Swanton & Sons. Fyfield and South farms, then under grass, supported dairy cows and young female stock, while North farm was given over to cereal production and the rearing of beef and pigs.[98] Some 200 a. on Fyfield down were then used as gallops for the training of horses, mostly for flat

racing, by Mr. J. V. Bloomfield of Manton House in Preshute.[99] West Overton farm, 705 a., was then mainly under arable cultivation with 228 a. under winter wheat and 118 a. spring barley. It was farmed in conjunction with land in Beechingstoke and Patney.[1] Within Alton Priors farm, 1,000 a. including Tawsmead farm, there were 600 a. of arable under a rotation of corn, kale, and grass, 100 a. of permanent pasture on which a dairy herd was maintained, and 300 a. of downland grazing for beef cattle.[2] West Stowell farm then contained 344 a. devoted to mixed farming.[3] Shaw farm in 1977 had, besides its pasture lands on which a dairy herd of 110 cows was maintained, 460 a. of arable mostly devoted to barley and wheat.[4]

MILLS. In 1086 a mill attached to the abbess of Wilton's estate at Overton paid 10s. yearly.[5] Richard Cuffe (d. 1504) held a water-mill and some land freely within West Overton manor and paid a yearly rent of £1 2s. to Wilton Abbey. His heir was his daughter Maud, wife of John True.[6] A John True held the same mill and land in 1567.[7] By 1631 the mill estate was held by Robert Smith.[8] Before 1730 William Smith of Salisbury sold to Stowell Smith of Overton (will proved 1731) a farm at Overton to which a water-mill and a windmill were attached.[9] The estate eventually passed to Stowell Smith's nephew Thomas Smith (will proved 1763), who devised it to his kinswoman Hannah Martyn. She, who died c. 1804, devised the lands on trust for her granddaughter Thermuthis Ashe.[10] Thermuthis and her trustees sold them in 1806 to Richard Matthews of East Kennett.[11] Edward Pumphrey was owner of West Overton water-mill in 1821.[12]

The water-mill seems to have fallen into disuse by the mid 19th century. It stood beside the Kennet north of West Overton Farm. Most of the associated leats had been filled in but some stone-work remained in 1977. The site of the windmill, which stood in Windmill field about 1.5 km. south-west of Overton village,[13] was not recognizable in 1977.

Lockeridge manor contained a windmill in 1564.[14] No more is heard of it.

There were two mills worth 12s. 6d. within Winchester's Alton estate in 1086, presumably one at Alton Priors and one at Patney.[15] Alton Priors mill stood on the stream dividing the two Altons and was apparently demolished c. 1650.[16]

LOCAL GOVERNMENT. The prior of St. Swithun's, Winchester, withdrew his manors of East Overton and Fyfield from Selkley hundred and

[91] First Pembroke Survey, ed. Straton, i. 147, 262, 264.
[92] Blenheim Mun. E/P/90, mid-19th-cent. survey.
[93] W.R.O. 106, sale cat.
[94] Ex inf. Chief Forester, Savernake Forest Office, Marlborough.
[95] Inf. in this para., except where stated, from N. E. King, 'Kennet Valley Sarsen Ind.', W.A.M. lxiii. 83 sqq.
[96] W.A.M. xxxv. 497.
[97] Wilts. Cuttings, xx. 101.
[98] Ex inf. Mr. and Mrs. R. Swanton, North Farm, Overton, and Mr. R. G. F. Swanton, Fyfield.
[99] Ex inf. Mr. Bloomfield.
[1] Ex inf. Mr. T. E. Trigg, West Overton Farm.
[2] Ex inf. Mr. Stratton.
[3] Ex inf. Mr. J. Wallis, Humberts, Pewsey.

[4] Ex inf. Mr. Cutforth.
[5] V.C.H. Wilts. ii, p. 129.
[6] Cal. Inq. p.m. Hen. VII, ii, pp. 614–15.
[7] First Pembroke Survey, ed. Straton, i. 141.
[8] Wilton Ho. Mun., survey, ii, f. 3.
[9] Ibid. survey, 1706; W.R.O. 1366/19, abstr. of title, 1806.
[10] W.R.O. 1366/19, abstr. of title, 1806; Land Tax.
[11] Ibid. 1366/19, abstr. of title, 1806.
[12] Ibid. East Overton, Lockeridge, and Fyfield Inclosure Award.   [13] W.A.M. xlii. 62.
[14] C.P. 40/1219 Carte rot. 52.
[15] V.C.H. Wilts. ii, p. 120.
[16] Hanna, 'Winch. Cath. Custumal', 490; V.C.H. Wilts. x. 10, 12.

included them in his own hundred of Elstub in the earlier 13th century. Alton Priors had been withdrawn from Swanborough hundred and included in Elstub by 1281.[17] It was at Alton that the prior held the courts for the Kennet valley portion of Elstub hundred, which comprised the tithings of Alton, West Stowell, East Overton, and Fyfield and the near-by manor of Patney. At the courts, held twice yearly, the prior exercised franchisal and manorial jurisdiction from at least 1281.[18] His franchisal rights included infangthief and outfangthief, return of writs, view of frankpledge, which he claimed to hold, in Alton at least, by grant of Henry III, and pleas of vee de naam.[19] He accordingly claimed right of gallows within East Overton manor in 1234 and 1275 and within Alton in 1275.[20] In 1255 he claimed to hear pleas of vee de naam at Alton, and in 1281 to hold assizes of bread and of ale there by virtue of the grant of the view.[21]

The tithings of Lockeridge, West Overton, and Shaw owed suit at the courts of Selkley hundred.[22] No medieval manorial record for those manors is known to survive.

Records of courts for West Overton, East Overton, Alton Priors and West Stowell, and Lockeridge, all Pembroke properties c. 1600, show the courts to have been held locally, sometimes on the same day, once or twice yearly. All, except the West Overton courts, in which no franchisal jurisdiction seems to have been exercised, were usually called views of frankpledge and courts. The business of the views was transacted and recorded separately from that of the courts. The main business of the views was to appoint tithingmen and of the courts to regulate agricultural practice and to appoint haywards. Records of courts for East Overton and Fyfield, at which each tithingman and homage presented separately, survive for 1559, 1566–7, 1632–5, 1666–7, 1670, and 1676.[23] West Overton court records are extant for 1559, 1566–7, 1632–5, 1667, 1670, 1675–6, 1678, 1688, and 1724–1822,[24] and those of the Lockeridge views and courts for 1632–3, 1666–7, and 1676–8.[25] The Alton views and courts, at which the tithingmen and homages of Alton and West Stowell presented separately, are recorded for 1544–6, for 1564–5 and 1567 when the tenant William Button held them, and for 1666–7, 1670, and 1676–8.[26]

The chapelries of Alton Priors and Fyfield both relieved their own poor.[27] Alton and Stowell

became part of Pewsey poor-law union in 1835.[28] In the same year Fyfield and the poor-law parish of West Overton, which included East Overton, West Overton, Shaw, and Lockeridge tithings, were included in Marlborough union.[29]

A church book for Overton, 1810–77, records church rates 1811–70, churchwardens' accounts 1810–77, and a few vestry minutes for the earlier 19th century.[30] A vestry minute book for Fyfield chapelry, 1849–1922, records rates levied for chapel repairs and the appointments of churchwardens, overseers of the poor, and way-wardens.[31]

CHURCHES. In the 12th century there were churches at East Overton, Fyfield, and Alton Priors. Between 1142 and 1171 Henry, bishop of Winchester, and Jocelin, bishop of Salisbury, together granted Alton church to the hospital of St. Cross near Winchester.[32] A later-12th-century confirmation of the grant stipulated that suitable provision be made for a vicar to serve it.[33] In the late 12th or the 13th century the hospital restored Alton to the bishop of Winchester in return for a yearly pension therefrom. That pension was reckoned at £2 in 1337 and in the 1540s,[34] but by the early 19th century, and still in 1977, £3 4s. was paid yearly to the hospital out of Alton Priors.[35] In 1291 another pension, of £1 3s. 4d., was paid from Overton church to the deacon in the abbey church at Wilton.[36] In 1284 St. Swithun's Priory gave up any right to the advowson of Overton, to which Fyfield was then already attached as a parochial chapel with rights of baptism and burial, and to that of Alton in favour of the bishop in return for his acknowledgement of its lordship over manors including Fyfield and Alton.[37] By 1290, when the advowson of Overton was regranted by the bishop to the convent, Alton church had also been annexed as a parochial chapel.[38] St. Swithun's appropriated Overton church with its dependent chapels in 1291.[39] Vicars were afterwards appointed to serve the cure and a vicarage was ordained probably by 1308.[40] The benefice was called the vicarage of Overton until the earlier 18th century but was afterwards referred to as that of Overton with Fyfield and Alton Priors.[41] The priors presented vicars until the Dissolution.[42]

A grant of tithes from his lands at Lockeridge by Walter of Gloucester to the church of St. Owen at

[17] Plac. de Quo Warr. (Rec. Com.), 806; see above, p. 105.
[18] Mun. D. & C. Winton., 13th- and 14th-cent. ct. rolls.
[19] Rot. Hund. (Rec. Com.), ii (1), 230; Plac. de Quo Warr. (Rec. Com.), 806.
[20] Cur. Reg. R. xv, pp. 276–7; Rot. Hund. (Rec. Com.), ii (1), 270, 274–5.
[21] Rot. Hund. (Rec. Com.), ii (1), 234; Plac. de Quo Warr. (Rec. Com.), 806.
[22] D.L. 30/127 no. 1908.
[23] B.L. Add. Ch. 24440–1; Wilton Ho. Mun., 17th-cent. ct. rec.
[24] B.L. Add. Ch. 24440–1; Wilton Ho. Mun., 17th-, 18th-, and 19th-cent. ct. rec.
[25] Wilton Ho. Mun., 17th-cent. ct. rec.
[26] Mun. D. & C. Winton., ct. rolls, 1544–5; S.R.O., DD/WHb 659; DD/WHb 663; Wilton Ho. Mun., 17th-cent. ct. rec.
[27] W.R.O. 473/340, Alton Priors poor-rate (1774); 1079/52.
[28] Poor Law Com. 2nd Rep. 560.
[29] Ibid. 559.
[30] Ch. bk. penes the Revd. P. J. Harrison, Overton Vicarage.
[31] W.R.O. 1079/52.
[32] B.L. Harl. MS. 1616, f. 12.   [33] Ibid. f. 2v.
[34] Obedientiaries' R. St. Swithun's, ed. Kitchin, 247; Winch. Chap. Doc. 1541–7, ed. Kitchin and Madge, 95.
[35] W.R.O. 473/64, sale cat. (1812); 503/3, deed, Caldecott to Miller (1827); 374/128, no. 64; New Coll., Oxf., Mun. 4970, deed, Best and Mackintosh to New Coll. (1912); ex inf. Land Agent, New Coll.
[36] V.C.H. Wilts. iii. 236.
[37] Reg. Pontoise (Cant. & York Soc.), ii. 431; Phillimore, Eccl. Law, ii. 1453–4.
[38] Reg. Pontoise (Cant. & York Soc.), i. 39.
[39] Sar. Chart. and Doc. (Rolls Ser.), 366.
[40] Mun. D. & C. Winton., ct. roll, 1308–9; Phillipps, Wilts. Inst. i. 22; although the original ordination has not been found, its terms survive: Sar. Dioc. R.O., Glebe Terrier, 1588.
[41] Phillipps, Wilts. Inst. (index in W.A.M. xxviii. 227); Clerical Guide (1822); Clergy List (1859); Crockford (1896 and later edns.).
[42] Phillipps, Wilts. Inst. (index in W.A.M. xxviii. 227).

Gloucester before 1129 may suggest the existence of a proprietary church there.[43] The tithes passed to the priory of Llanthony in Gloucester when Walter's son Miles (d. 1143) conveyed St. Owen's church and its possessions to the newly established house in 1137.[44] Miles's son Roger, earl of Hereford (d. 1155), confirmed the grant of tithes to Llanthony.[45] Since no more is known of any payment of tithes from Lockeridge to Llanthony it is likely that they were afterwards paid to the church of Overton.

In 1541 the Crown granted the advowson to the newly formed Winchester chapter and it afterwards descended like the manor of East Overton.[46] The lords presented, except in 1545 when Richard Paulet, to whom Winchester chapter had granted a turn, presented and in 1623 and 1624 when John Hayes and Robert Vaisey, to whom William, earl of Pembroke, had granted consecutive turns, did so respectively.[47] The chapelry of Alton Priors, including West Stowell tithing, was detached from the vicarage and united with the rectory of Alton Barnes in 1913. West Stowell was detached from Alton Barnes and annexed to the ecclesiastical parish of Wilcot in 1928.[48] In 1929 the benefice of East Kennett was united with the vicarage of Overton with Fyfield and the patronage of Overton transferred from the Olympia Agricultural Co. Ltd. to the bishop of Salisbury, patron of East Kennett. The united benefice was called Overton and Fyfield with East Kennett.[49] In 1975 that benefice was united with three others, Avebury with Winterbourne Monkton and Berwick Bassett, Broad Hinton, and Winterbourne Bassett, to form the benefice of Upper Kennet. A team ministry was formed consisting of a rector at Avebury and two vicars at Overton and Broad Hinton. The rector was to be collated by the bishop of Salisbury and the two vicars chosen by the bishop and rector together. Rector and vicars were all to serve for terms of seven years.[50]

In 1291 the church, including Fyfield chapelry, was assessed for taxation at £13 6s. 8d. Alton Priors was assessed separately at £6 13s. 4d.[51] The vicarage was worth £20 in 1535.[52] The vicar then received a pension of £1 18s. 9d. from the appropriated rectory.[53] The owners of the rectory estate continued to pay it after the Dissolution and it is last mentioned in 1725, when it was paid by the lord of East Overton manor.[54] From 1829 to 1831 the benefice had an average yearly net value of £319.[55]

The vicar, probably in the later 13th century or the earlier 14th, was allotted all the small tithes

from Overton and its chapelries except those arising from the lands of St. Swithun's Priory. The prior of St. Margaret, Marlborough, was then expressly allowed to take the small tithes from his manor of Upper Lockeridge in return for a 3s. payment yearly to the vicar.[56] That modus continued to be paid in the later 18th century.[57] The lords of West Overton manor also apparently took the small tithes from their demesne.[58] By 1812 the small tithes of Alton Priors had been commuted for £5 7s. 4d. a year, and £5 6s. a year replaced those from West Stowell.[59] When the open fields of the tithings of East Overton, Fyfield, and Lockeridge were inclosed in 1821 the vicar was allotted 200 a. in place of tithes.[60] He received a rent-charge of £31 to replace those arising from Shaw tithing in 1840.[61]

The vicarial glebe, presumably allotted at the same time as the tithes, comprised some 64 a. of which 46 a. were in the open fields of East Overton and 18 a. in those of Fyfield.[62] The vicar received 40 a., mostly in East Overton tithing, to replace that estate when the open fields were inclosed in 1821.[63] With the 200 a. in place of tithes a glebe farm of 240 a. was formed. It was worked from the farm-house called Dene Farm in 1977. The estate was sold by the vicar to the trustees of Sir Henry Meux in 1883.[64] The money raised was in the same year used to buy estates at Beckenham (Kent) and Battersea (Surr.).[65]

The vicarage-house at Overton, first mentioned in 1588, stood west of the church.[66] The house was rebuilt in the early 19th century, incorporating older walling, and enlarged later in the century. The incumbent of the united benefice of Overton with Fyfield and East Kennett lived there after 1929. The Vicarage was sold in 1939 and was afterwards called Overton (later West Overton) House.[67] A new house for the united benefice was built on the south-eastern outskirts of West Overton village.[68]

In the later 16th century there were also houses belonging to the benefice at Fyfield and Alton Priors. That at Alton is not mentioned again. The vicar was ordered to rebuild that at Fyfield in 1686 but no more is heard of it.[69]

At an unknown date 2 a. of land in Lockeridge field were given to maintain a lamp in the church at Fyfield. The land was let for 6s. yearly in 1548.[70] The Crown granted the 2 a. to Thomas Gratwicke and Anselm Lambe in 1557 and they immediately reconveyed them to Christopher Dismore, lord of Lockeridge manor.[71]

Among the more notable non-resident incumbents

[43] C 115/K 1/6679 f. 21; *V.C.H. Wilts.* x. 69.
[44] C 115/K 1/6679 f. 21v.; *V.C.H. Wilts.* x. 69.
[45] C 115/K 1/6679 f. 23v.; *Complete Peerage*, vi. 454–5.
[46] *L. & P. Hen. VIII*, xvi, p. 417.
[47] Phillipps, *Wilts. Inst.* (index in *W.A.M.* xxviii. 227).
[48] *V.C.H. Wilts.* x. 12.
[49] *Lond. Gaz.* 10 May 1929, pp. 3114–17; *Crockford* (1935).
[50] Ex inf. Mr. R. A. Read, Sar. Dioc. Regy.
[51] *Tax. Eccl.* (Rec. Com.), 189.
[52] *Valor Eccl.* (Rec. Com.), ii. 131.
[53] Ibid. vi, App. p. vii.
[54] *Winch. Chap. Doc. 1541–7*, ed. Kitchin and Madge, 95; Sar. Dioc. R.O., Glebe Terriers, 1588, 1608, 1671, 1705; W.A.S. Libr., sale cat. xxviii, no. 105.
[55] *Rep. Com. Eccl. Revenues*, 844–5.
[56] Sar. Dioc. R.O., Glebe Terrier, 1588.
[57] Ibid.; Blenheim Mun., Wilts. deeds, partic. of man. (1758).
[58] Sar. Dioc. R.O., Glebe Terrier, 1588; Wilton Ho.

Mun., survey, c. 1794.
[59] W.R.O. 473/64, sale cat.; W.A.S. Libr., notebk. for Overton vicarage, p. 3. In 1912 £6 5s. was payable from Alton Priors: New Coll., Oxf., Mun. 4970, deed, Best and Mackintosh to New Coll.
[60] W.R.O., Inclosure Award.   [61] I.R. 29/38/235.
[62] Sar. Dioc. R.O., Overton Glebe Terriers, 1588, 1608, 1671, 1705; Fyfield Glebe Terriers, c. 1608, 1704.
[63] W.R.O., Inclosure Award.
[64] Ch. Commrs., copy deeds (new ser.), vol. 237, no. 22748.   [65] Ex inf. Mr. Read.
[66] Sar. Dioc. R.O., Glebe Terriers, 1588, 1671, 1705; Vis. Queries, 1864; *Rep. Com. Eccl. Revenues*, 844–5.
[67] Ex inf. the Revd. P. J. Harrison, Overton Vicarage.
[68] W.R.O. 1079/60, copy deed and map.
[69] Sar. Dioc. R.O., Overton Glebe Terrier, 1588; Fyfield Glebe Terrier, c. 1608; Chwdns.' Pres. 1686.
[70] E 301/58 no. 127.
[71] *Cal. Pat. 1557–8*, 134; C.P. 40/1175 Carte rot. 11.

of Overton were William Fauntleroy and John Moore. Fauntleroy, vicar 1496–1511, and later vicar of Enford, held many more lucrative preferments.[72] Moore (d. 1805), vicar 1759–73, was tutor to the younger sons of his patron, the duke of Marlborough. While vicar, Moore was also rector of Liddington, a prebendary of Durham, and dean of Canterbury. He later became successively bishop of Bangor and archbishop of Canterbury.[73]

It seems probable that chaplains served Alton Priors and Fyfield churches in the Middle Ages. One at Fyfield is mentioned in 1281.[74] Curates were employed at each in the 1550s.[75] A reader served Fyfield church in 1584 but it was unknown whether he was licensed to do so.[76] A neighbouring incumbent served Alton Priors in 1585. In the same year the vicar's son officiated at Fyfield but whether he had episcopal licence to do so was unknown.[77] A sequestered royalist, John Gregson, served Alton Priors between 1650 and 1652 but by 1656 he had been ousted by the puritan rector of Alton Barnes.[78] The two Altons were once more briefly united from 1829 to 1833 when Augustus Hare, rector of Alton Barnes, unofficially served the chapelry.[79] In 1851 the same assistant curate, who lived at Lockeridge, served both Overton and Fyfield.[80] Curates seem always to have assisted the vicars in the later 19th and earlier 20th centuries.[81]

In 1851 it was reckoned that over the past year an average congregation of 250 had attended morning and 410 afternoon services at Overton.[82] At Fyfield over the same period morning congregations had averaged 150 and evening ones 250.[83] On Sundays in 1864 morning and afternoon services with sermons were held alternately at Overton and Fyfield. Weekday prayers were said, presumably at Overton, during Lent and Eastertide. Holy Communion, attended by an average of twelve communicants, was celebrated at the great festivals and on the first Sunday in each month.[84] Alton Priors church then seems to have been served separately but no details of its life have been found.

The parish church of ST. MICHAEL AND ALL ANGELS is built of flint and sarsen with ashlar dressings and has a chancel with north organ chamber and south vestry, a nave with north aisle and south porch, and a west tower.[85] It was built in a mixture of gothic styles between 1877 and 1883 to designs by C. E. Ponting and replaced the medieval church which had become dilapidated. The earlier church had a chancel, nave with south porch and west tower and, although the later building follows its plan except for the aisle and a lengthened chancel, appears to have been generally lower in height.[86] The chancel arch of the earlier church, which is reset between the present aisle and

organ chamber, is of 14th-century date, and three nave windows, much restored and reset in the south wall, are of the 15th century. The small plain tower appears to have been of later-medieval construction but apparently bore the date 1697.

The church of ST. NICHOLAS, Fyfield, is mostly built of ashlar and rubble and has a chancel, nave with north aisle and south porch, and a west tower. The nave was rebuilt during a restoration of 1849 by C. H. Gabriel but its predecessor may have been of 12th-century origin.[87] The chancel, which has lancets and a decorated corbel table, was built in the earlier 13th century and the tower of ashlar was added in the later 15th when the nave was given new windows, heightened, and reroofed. When the nave was rebuilt that roof was reset but the windows were replaced by lower ones in a simple 14th-century style and the north aisle with a two-bay arcade was added. The timber-framed south porch, which was probably post-medieval, was also rebuilt and the chancel reroofed and provided with a new east wall with three lancets where there had formerly been only one small window. The church has a circular 12th-century font which is decorated with interlacing arcading, but most other fittings are of the 19th century.

The church of ALL SAINTS, Alton Priors, is built of freestone, rubble, and red brick and has a chancel, nave, and west tower.[88] The chancel arch survives from the 12th-century church. The nave was rebuilt and widened towards the south in the 14th century. The tower, which is similar in design to that at Fyfield, was added in the later 15th century or the earlier 16th, and at about that time the chancel appears to have been reconstructed and a rood-stair put into the north wall of the nave. In 1491 John Button bequeathed lead to roof part of the church.[89] The nave roof was renewed in the later 18th century and the chancel roof is probably of similar date. The chancel walls were refaced in brick in the earlier 19th century and the nave walls restored later in that century. Further restoration of the whole building was undertaken c. 1960 and c. 1976.[90] On the north side of the chancel a tomb-chest surmounted by a monumental brass commemorates William Button (d. 1591). The church was declared redundant in 1973 and in 1977 was in the care of the Redundant Churches Fund.[91]

The king's commissioners took 8½ oz. of plate from Overton church in 1553 but left a chalice. Fyfield then apparently had no plate but 1 oz. was taken for the king from Alton Priors. In 1977 Overton's plate comprised a silver chalice, paten, and flagon in medieval style given at the church's rebuilding in 1878. Fyfield in 1977 had a chalice and paten hall-marked 1732, a cup given in 1733, and

[72] A.B. Emden, *Biog. Reg. Univ. Oxf. to 1500*, ii. 671.
[73] Phillipps, *Wilts. Inst.* ii. 78, 86; *V.C.H. Wilts.* ix. 72.
[74] Mun. D. & C. Winton., ct. roll, 1281.
[75] Sar. Dioc. R.O., Detecta Bk. 1550–3, ff. 27v., 29, 144, 146v.
[76] Ibid. Detecta Bk. 1584, f. 18v.
[77] Ibid. Detecta Bk. 1585, f. 26 and v.
[78] *Walker Revised*, ed. A. G. Matthews, 373; *Calamy Revised*, ed. A. G. Matthews, 534.
[79] *V.C.H. Wilts.* x. 13.
[80] H.O. 129/255/1/33; H.O. 129/255/1/35.
[81] Sar. Dioc. R.O., Vis. Queries, 1864; *Clergy List* (1859, 1915); *Crockford* (1896 and later edns.).
[82] H.O. 129/255/1/35.   [83] H.O. 129/255/1/33.

[84] Sar. Dioc. R.O., Vis. Queries.
[85] Except where otherwise stated, this description is based on *Ch. Guide* (priv. print.).
[86] J. Buckler, water-colour in W.A.S. Libr., vol. iv. 43 (1807); see plate facing p. 160.
[87] *W.A.M.* liv. 201; J. Buckler, water-colour in W.A.S. Libr., vol. iv. 36 (1807).
[88] J. Buckler, water-colour in W.A.S. Libr., vol. iv. 25 (1807).
[89] S.R.O., DD/WHb 8–9.
[90] Wilts. Cuttings, xxi. 193; ex inf. Mr. T. Ingram-Hill, Alton Priors.
[91] *Lond. Gaz.* 18 Dec. 1973, p. 15039; ex inf. Mr. Ingram-Hill.

an alms-dish hall-marked 1781 and given in 1833.[92] Alton's plate then comprised a cup and paten hall-marked 1577 and 1638 respectively.[93]

Overton church had three bells in 1553. In 1977 there was a ring of six: (i), (ii), (iii) are by Gillett & Co., Croydon, 1883; (iv), of the earlier 16th century, is by H. Jefferies of Bristol; (v), 1683, by Roger (II) Purdue and recast in 1883 by Gillett & Co.; (vi), 1606, by John Wallis.[94] There were three bells at Fyfield in 1553 and two in 1977: (i), c. 1540, is attributed to Thomas Jefferies of Bristol; (ii) is dated 1629.[95] Alton church retained its three bells in 1977: (i), (ii), 1709, are by William and Robert Cor; (iii), 1736, is by William Cockey of Frome (Som.).[96]

Those baptisms, marriages, and burials performed at Overton and Fyfield are recorded in the same register from 1682 to 1731. Thereafter the two churches kept separate registers, which are complete.[97] Alton Priors apparently kept a separate register: entries of baptisms and burials begin in 1664 and are complete. Marriage registrations, which start in 1702, appear to be lacking from 1753 to 1758 but are otherwise complete.[98]

ROMAN CATHOLICISM. A chapel of ease, dedicated to the Holy Family, was established at West Stowell by Lady (Frances) Phipps in 1934.[99] It was served from Devizes but ceased to be used regularly when a church was opened at Pewsey in 1964. In 1977 services were held infrequently at the chapel, then still owned by Lady Phipps.[1]

PROTESTANT NONCONFORMITY. A group at Fyfield, including Richard Kingsman and his family, was presented for not attending Fyfield church in 1662 and 1674.[2] Some of those presented may have been among the five nonconformists recorded in Overton parish in 1676.[3]

Independents certified a house at Fyfield in 1797.[4] No more is known of that meeting. Dissenters met at Fyfield again in the later 19th century. Their chapel was closed in 1895.[5] A Congregational chapel, which apparently stood near the Fighting Cocks inn at Fyfield, was demolished in the 1930s.[6]

Independency flourished in West Overton and what was possibly one group certified houses there in 1825, 1827, and 1849.[7] In 1851 the Overton meeting was served by a lay preacher and over the

past year an average of 40 people had attended afternoon services and 35 those held in the evening.[8]

Thomas James's house at Lockeridge was certified by Independents in 1849.[9] The group still met in 1851 when it was estimated that over the past year an average of 30 people had attended both afternoon and evening services.[10]

Wesleyan Methodists certified two houses at Lockeridge in 1817, another at Overton in 1819, and one at Alton Priors in 1836.[11] The group at Alton flourished,[12] and in the 20th century met in a small chapel south-east of Alton Priors Manor until c. 1947. In 1977 the building was used as a garage.[13] Wesleyans certified a new building at Overton Heath in 1846.[14] In 1851 that chapel was served by a minister from Marlborough. During the past year an average of 110 people had attended afternoon, and 40 evening, services there.[15] The chapel, described as at 'Park', was still used in 1894 but had closed by 1935.[16] The building was used as a store in 1977.

Methodists, designated 'independent', certified a house at Fyfield in 1821.[17] In 1851 what is clearly the same group, then described as Primitive Methodists, still flourished and over the past year an average of 13 people had attended morning, and 51 afternoon, services in a cottage at Fyfield.[18] On Census Sunday that year some 58 Primitive Methodists attended afternoon service in a house at Lockeridge.[19]

Primitive Methodists built a chapel at the western end of Overton village in 1901.[20] When it closed in 1966 its members attended the chapel at Lockeridge mentioned below.[21]

Two evangelists from the Christian Brethren established at Regent Place, Swindon, started a mission in a cottage in Lockeridge dene c. 1906. A new chapel was later built in Lockeridge village. The brethren, who were 'open', held regular Sunday services there in 1977.[22]

EDUCATION. In 1808 labourers' children were taught in a school at Overton supported by the duke of Marlborough. Other children, paid for by their parents, attended two small day-schools elsewhere in the parish.[23] Some 30 children were taught in 1818 at a day-school supported by subscriptions and contributions from the parish rates. The master who kept the school was paid £30 yearly.[24] The parish

[92] Nightingale, *Wilts. Plate*, 150–1; ex inf. the Revd. P. J. Harrison.
[93] Nightingale, *Wilts. Plate*, 151; ex inf. Mr. Ingram-Hill.
[94] Walters, *Wilts. Bells*, 155, 293; ex inf. the Revd. P. J. Harrison.
[95] Walters, *Wilts. Bells*, 91–2; ex inf. the Revd. P. J. Harrison.
[96] Walters, *Wilts. Bells*, 11, 310; ex inf. Mr. Ingram-Hill.
[97] W.R.O. 1079/1–11; 1079/42–5. Transcripts for Overton 1605–10, 1615, 1621–3, 1635–6, 1665–79, and for Fyfield 1605–10, 1621–2, 1635, 1666–78 are in Sar. Dioc. R.O.
[98] W.R.O. 496/5–6. Transcripts for 1605, 1619–23, 1633, 1666–80, c. 1699 are in Sar. Dioc. R.O.
[99] *V.C.H. Wilts.* iii. 97; ex inf. Mrs. Bonar Sykes, Conock Man., Devizes.
[1] Ex inf. Mrs. Sykes; *Cath. Dir.* (1977).
[2] Sar. Dioc. R.O., Chwdns.' Pres.
[3] *W.N. & Q.* iii. 536.   [4] *W.A.M.* lxi. 65.

[5] G.R.O. Worship Reg. no. 7715.
[6] Ex inf. Mrs. K. M. Johnson, Fyfield; 'Ch. Guide' (TS. in ch.).
[7] Sar. Dioc. R.O., Certs. Dissenters' Meeting-Houses.
[8] H.O. 129/255/1/36.
[9] Sar. Dioc. R.O., Certs. Dissenters' Meeting-Houses.
[10] H.O. 129/255/1/37.
[11] Sar. Dioc. R.O., Certs. Dissenters' Meeting-Houses.
[12] O.S. Map 6", Wilts. XXXV (1889 edn.).
[13] Ex inf. Mr. A. G. Stratton, Alton Priors.
[14] Sar. Dioc. R.O., Certs. Dissenters' Meeting-Houses.
[15] H.O. 129/255/1/39.
[16] W.R.O., Clerk's Files, no. 56; G.R.O. Worship Reg. nos. 3819, 47479.
[17] Sar. Dioc. R.O., Certs. Dissenters' Meeting-Houses.
[18] H.O. 129/255/1/34.   [19] H.O. 129/255/1/38.
[20] *Kelly's Dir. Wilts.* (1907).
[21] Wilts. Cuttings, xxiii. 8.
[22] *V.C.H. Wilts.* ix. 158; ex inf. Mrs. Johnson and Mr. J. Watts, Lockeridge.
[23] Lambeth MS. 1732.   [24] *Educ. of Poor Digest*, 1034.

contained four schools in 1833. One, begun in 1823 and supported partly by the incumbent and partly by parental contributions, was attended by twenty children. At the others, all begun after 1828, 26 children, paid for by their parents, were taught.[25] Children from Alton Priors in 1833 attended a school in Alton Barnes, and continued to do so thereafter.[26] In 1858 30 infants were taught by an old woman in a cottage kitchen at Overton. At a 'tidy and business-like' school in Fyfield between 60 and 70 children from Fyfield and Lockeridge were taught in 1859 by a trained mistress.[27]

About 1872 a school, affiliated to the National Society, was built at Lockeridge to the design of C. E. Ponting to serve West Overton, Fyfield, and Lockeridge.[28] In 1906 that school had been attended over the past year by an average of 117 pupils.[29] Thereafter average attendance gradually declined and was 66 in 1938.[30] In 1977 the school was attended by 42 children, who nearly all came from West Overton, Lockeridge, and Fyfield.[31]

CHARITIES FOR THE POOR. In 1704 Robert Fowler of Lockeridge gave £20, the interest to be distributed yearly amongst the unrelieved poor of the parish. Interest was usually allowed to accumu-late in the earlier 19th century and £3 was distributed triennially in small money doles. Income was 12s. yearly in the 1860s. In 1902 accumulated interest of £8 was apportioned in sums of £2 and £6 respectively between a coal and clothing club and a fund for the sick and needy. The yearly income was 6s. or 7s. in 1905 and then deemed applicable only to the civil parish of West Overton.[32] In the 1960s the yearly income of under £1 was allowed to accumulate and in 1969 there was a balance of £10.[33]

At an unknown date Mary Tasker of Fyfield gave £20, the interest to be distributed yearly amongst the unrelieved poor of Fyfield tithing. In the earlier 19th century interest was allowed to accumulate and then distributed in small money doles. The yearly interest of 12s. was distributed in fuel in the 1860s. In 1895 accumulated interest totalling £4 was used to buy coal for distribution at Christmas. In the earlier 20th century the annual income of 6s. or 7s. was similarly allowed to accumulate until there were sufficient funds to provide coal for all the poor of Fyfield.[34] In 1965 the charity had an income of under £1.[35]

In the 1970s the funds of both charities were allowed to accumulate and at Christmas 1976 doles of 50p were distributed to twenty people in the parishes of West Overton and Fyfield.[36]

PATNEY

PATNEY[37] lies at the western end of the Vale of Pewsey 7 km. south-east of Devizes.[38] The south-eastwards flowing head-streams of the Christ-church Avon, from which the parish's name derives, enclose a featureless and exposed islet of 358 ha. (884 a.) at the southern end of Cannings marsh.[39] The parish is roughly oval with a narrow triangular north-west extension. It measures a little over 2 km. from the northern point of the triangle to the southern boundary stream, and some 2.5 km. from west to east on a line north of the village, which is in the south of the parish.

The low-lying alluvial soils which border the boundary streams mostly extend no more than a few metres across lush withy fringed banks.[40] Two larger deposits of alluvium occur west and north-east of the village. That to the west was once the site of one of the parish's larger common meadows, while that to the north-east provided most of its pasture land. Apart from the alluvium, which lies around or below the 107 m. contour, and a small rise of Lower Chalk, which reaches 121 m. north of the village, Patney is characterized by a wide belt of Upper Greensand. The land rises almost imper-ceptibly north-eastwards. Formerly the site of the open arable fields, the greensand was partly pasture in 1976.

Very little evidence of prehistoric or Roman settlement has been found in the parish. Patney's assessments for medieval taxes appear small. There were 90 poll-tax payers in 1377.[41] Somewhat larger contributions to later-16th- and earlier-17th-century taxations were made by the several copyholders among whom the manor was then apportioned.[42] The Census of 1801 recorded 130 people at Patney.[43] The population thereafter rose steadily to 196 in 1841. It declined slightly in the two following decades because some families moved elsewhere,[44] rose from 106 to 127 between 1891 and 1901, but by 1921 had fallen to 85. It grew to 133 in 1951 and in 1971 135 people lived in the parish.[45]

In 1773 the roads which linked Patney with its north-west, east, and south neighbours entered the parish over Hail, Limber Stone, and Weir bridges.[46] The last two were still in use in 1976 and carried secondary roads. The road carried by Hail bridge,

[25] Educ. Enquiry Abstract, 1044.
[26] Ibid. 1027; Acct. of Wilts. Schs. 3; Kelly's Dir. Wilts. (1885 and later edns.); V.C.H. Wilts. x. 13.
[27] Acct. of Wilts. Schs. 36.
[28] W.R.O. 782/81, plans; Return of Non-Provided Schs. 30; Kelly's Dir. Wilts. (1875).
[29] Return of Non-Provided Schs. 30.
[30] Bd. of Educ., List 21 (H.M.S.O.).
[31] Ex inf. the head-teacher.
[32] Endowed Char. Wilts. (N. Div.), 808–10.
[33] Char. Com. file 242274.
[34] Endowed Char. Wilts. (N. Div.), 483–4.
[35] Char. Com. file 239612.
[36] Ex inf. the Revd. P. J. Harrison, Overton Vicarage.
[37] This article was written in 1976.
[38] The following maps have been used: O.S. Maps 6″, Wilts. XL (1888 edn.), XLI (1889 edn.), SU 05 NE. (1961 edn.), SU 06 SE. (1961 edn.); 1/25,000, SU 05 (1958 edn.); 1/50,000, sheet 173 (1974 edn.).
[39] Census, 1961, 1971; P.N. Wilts. (E.P.N.S.), 314.
[40] This para. is based on Geol. Surv. Map 1″, drift, sheet 282 (1959 edn.).
[41] V.C.H. Wilts. iv. 299, 310.
[42] Taxation Lists (W.R.S. x), 125; E 179/198/284; E 179/199/370; E 179/259/22; see below.
[43] All population figures, unless otherwise stated, from V.C.H. Wilts. iv. 355.
[44] Ibid. 322, 355.
[45] Census, 1961, 1971.
[46] Andrews and Dury, Map (W.R.S. viii), pl. 11.

however, was no more than a track in 1976. In the later 18th century a lane, in 1976 to be seen as a track south of the church, led westwards from the road junction at the southern end of the village to the mill and then on to Wedhampton in Urchfont.[47] In the earlier 19th century a semicircular track at the junction of the greensand and alluvium ran from Limber Stone bridge south-eastwards to Church Mill, in Chirton.[48] The track leading north to Stanton mill (later Stanton Dairy), in Stanton St. Bernard, probably ceased to be used when the Berks. & Hants Extension Railway was constructed through the centre of Patney and opened in 1862.[49] At the same time the secondary road leading north to All Cannings was diverted over a bridge. A station, Patney & Chirton Junction, was built west of the bridge and an extension from it to Westbury was constructed and opened by the G.W.R. in 1900.[50] The station was closed in 1966 and its buildings demolished, but in 1976 the line through Patney to Westbury was still part of a main westerly rail route.[51] The plan of the village is as it was in the later 18th century.[52] Settlement is centred on the T-junction, formerly cross-road, east of the church with the schoolroom, in 1976 a store, and the former Rectory to the south, and the mill to the west beyond the church. It extends northwards and north-eastwards from the junction along two lanes. The older cottages stand along both sides of the north-easterly lane and include at least one timber-framed house of the 17th century. Opposite Manor Farm, which in 1976 marked the limit of settlement on the north side of the lane, Home Farm, formerly called Queen Anne's Cottage, may possibly have been attached to the small estate held in the 18th century by the earls of Abingdon.[53] It is a later-17th- or earlier-18th-century brick house with stone dressings. The north-west entrance front, in 1976 much altered, originally had five bays of mullioned and transomed windows. Apart from two brick cottages built on glebe land south of the church by Henry Weaver of Devizes in 1875,[54] later building in Patney, both council and private, has taken place at the northern end of the lane leading to All Cannings but has not extended north of the railway line.

MANOR AND OTHER ESTATES. In 963 King Edgar made 5 *mansae* at Patney bookland for himself.[55] That estate is to be identified with the later manor of *PATNEY*.[56] By the mid 11th century it was among the possessions of the bishop of

Winchester and the monks of the Old Minster.[57] Possibly then, and certainly in 1086, it formed part of a larger estate based on Alton Priors, in Overton, the profits of which the community at Winchester received for its support.[58]

In the mid 11th century Bishop Stigand and the monks of the Old Minster leased 3 virgates at Patney to Wulfric in the same way as they did land at Alton Priors.[59] The estate so created was later held by Wulfward Belgisone and afterwards by William Scudet.[60] It was restored to St. Swithun's Priory in 1108.[61]

In 1284 the bishop of Winchester confirmed Patney, by then separate from Alton, to the convent.[62] In 1300 the house received a grant of free warren within the demesnes of Patney manor.[63] At the Dissolution the estate passed to the Crown.[64]

In 1541 the manor was granted by the Crown to the new cathedral chapter at Winchester.[65] In 1547 the chapter ceded the manor to the Crown which immediately granted it to Sir William Herbert (created earl of Pembroke in 1551, d. 1570).[66] It descended with the Pembroke title to Philip, earl of Pembroke and Montgomery (d. 1683),[67] who, shortly before he died, mortgaged it to William Pynsent (created a baronet in 1687, d. 1719).[68] Pynsent acquired the manor in 1692. It was confirmed to him in 1697 by Lord Pembroke's daughter and heir Charlotte and her husband John Jeffreys, Lord Jeffreys.[69]

Patney thereafter descended like the Pynsent estate at Urchfont to William Pitt (created earl of Chatham in 1766), who in 1767 sold it to William Bouverie, earl of Radnor (d. 1776).[70] It descended with the Radnor title until 1919 when Jacob, earl of Radnor, sold the estate, 590 a., to H. H. Pickford.[71] In 1974 Manor farm, 607 a., was owned by English Farms Ltd. and in 1976, when it was reckoned at 542 a., by Mereacre Ltd.[72]

Manor Farm, which has a principal south-west front of six bays, incorporates some sections of 17th-century timber-framed walling. The original 17th-century house was enlarged in brick and given stone window-frames c. 1700. In the earlier 19th century it was extended to the north-east, reroofed, and remodelled internally, and the south-west front was rendered. To that date, too, belongs the garden at the rear, which is enclosed by high brick thatched walls which incorporate a gazebo to the north-east.

In the earlier 13th century St. Swithun's Priory held an estate of some 16 a.[73] What may possibly be

47 *Andrews and Dury, Map* (W.R.S. viii), pl. 11.
48 W.R.O. 490/1057, early-19th-cent. survey.
49 *V.C.H. Wilts.* iv. 286–7; x. 151–2.
50 Ibid. iv. 289.   51 Ibid. x. 61.
52 *Andrews and Dury, Map* (W.R.S. viii), pl. 11.
53 See below.
54 Sar. Dioc. R.O., Mortgages, no. 230.
55 Finberg, *Early Wessex Chart.* p. 95.
56 First so called in 1243: *Reg. Pontoise* (Cant. & York Soc.), ii. 618.
57 Finberg, *Early Wessex Chart.* p. 105.
58 *V.C.H. Wilts.* ii, pp. 85, 120; see above, p. 192.
59 *V.C.H. Wilts.* ii, p. 83.
60 J. H. Round, *King's Serjeants*, 10; *V.C.H. Wilts.* ii, p. 120.
61 *Reg. Regum Anglo-Norm.* ii, no. 884.
62 *Reg. Pontoise* (Cant. & York Soc.), ii. 436.
63 *Cal. Chart. R.* 1300–26, 1.
64 *Valor Eccl.* (Rec. Com.), vi, App. p. vii.
65 *L. & P. Hen. VIII*, xvi, p. 417.
66 *Cal. Pat.* 1547–8, 25, 172; for the earls of Pembroke see *Complete Peerage*, x. 405 sqq.
67 Wards 7/12 f. 51; *Cal. Pat.* 1572–5, p. 394; C.P. 25(2)/387/20 Jas. I Trin.; C.P. 25(2)/527/11 Chas. I Mich.; W.R.O. 490/471, abstr. of title, 1674–c. 1763.
68 W.R.O. 490/471, abstr. of title; G.E.C. *Baronetage*, iv. 145–6; C 78/1846 no. 5.
69 W.R.O. 490/471, abstr. of title; *Complete Peerage*, vii. 84–5.
70 *V.C.H. Wilts.* x. 178; G.E.C. *Baronetage*, iv. 145–6; W.R.O. 490/76, deeds, Taylor to Romney; for the earls of Radnor see *Complete Peerage*, x. 717 sqq.
71 W.A.S. Libr., sale cat. xiii, no. 29; Wilts. Cuttings, xiv. 120.
72 *Daily Telegraph*, 18 May 1974; ex inf. Mr. T. E. Trigg, W. Overton Farm, W. Overton.
73 Katharine A. Hanna, 'Winch. Cath. Custumal' (Southampton Univ. Coll. M.A. thesis, 1954), 366.

the same land was held of the priory by the Eyre family in the earlier 14th century.[74] John Eyre was succeeded in it *c.* 1329 by an idiot son John.[75] Keepers thereafter administered the estate.[76] The younger John was still living in 1336.[77]

It was perhaps the same land which John Dauntsey (d. 1559) held at Patney in 1558. John was succeeded in the estate, 35 a., by his son John (later Sir John) Dauntsey.[78] At Sir John's death in 1630 the land passed, in accordance with a settlement made in 1628, to his granddaughter Elizabeth and her husband Sir John Danvers (d. 1655).[79] It apparently descended in the same way as the manors of Lavington Rector in Market Lavington and Westbury Seymour in Westbury to the earls of Abingdon.[80] It was owned in 1710 by Montagu Bertie, earl of Abingdon, and thereafter descended with the Abingdon title to Willoughby, earl of Abingdon, who sold it in 1764 to Robert Amor.[81] After Amor's death in 1771 or 1772 his Patney lands passed successively to his sons Robert (d. 1781 or 1782), and William (d. 1783), and then to his daughter Sarah. In 1787 they were settled on Sarah's marriage with William Tinker, who apparently still owned them in the earlier 19th century.[82] They were bought in 1828 by an earl of Radnor, possibly William Pleydell-Bouverie (d. 1869), and were thereafter merged in the manor.[83]

ECONOMIC HISTORY. In the 11th century Patney was included in the Winchester community's Alton Priors estate.[84] In 1210 the Patney estate, then separate from Alton, was stocked with 8 oxen and 50 sheep and was worth £11.[58] In the earlier 13th century the almoner of St. Swithun's received the profits of 3 virgates at Patney, perhaps the land leased T.R.E. to Wulfric. Another tenant held ½ hide for 6s. 8d. and certain ploughing services; 3 more ½-hiders each paid 10s. yearly and owed labour services; 13 virgaters including the miller, who held, apart from the mill, 1 virgate and some arable and meadow land for money rents only, paid 5s. yearly and owed half the duties of the ½-hiders; 3 ½-virgaters each paid 2s. 6d. yearly and owed half the virgaters' services; 3 more tenants each held a few acres for money rents and certain sowing, reaping, and hay-making duties; and another 2 held crofts for small money rents.[86] The almoner's

right to the profits of the 3 virgates was not afterwards mentioned and in the 14th century the revenue of the entire manor was apparently paid direct to the prior's treasury.[87]

Patney was valued for taxation at £22 in 1291 and was worth £29 in 1535.[88] In the Middle Ages it was part of the inter-manorial economy of the estate of St. Swithun's Priory. Yearly interchange of grain and stock took place chiefly with East Overton and Alton Priors manors but sometimes with Stockton and Wroughton as well.[89] In 1267 oxen and ewes from Patney were sent to Wroughton, and ewes and lambs to Alton Priors. Of the 197 doves hatched at Patney in that year most were sent to Devizes Castle to provide food for the falcons kept there. The rest were sent to Alton. In the same year Patney produced 157 cheeses.[90]

In the later 16th century the manor seems to have been apportioned among eleven customary tenants who paid a total rent of £27 and between them held 519 a. of arable land and 101 a. of meadow. Of those tenants, four held farms of over 50 a.[91] In 1773 Patney was estimated at 894 a. of which 62 a. were in three small freeholds, 25 a. were in hand, 223 a. in four leaseholds, and 421 a. in nine copyholds. Of the leaseholds, two were held by George Lewis and made a farm of some 130 a. Three of the copyholds were held by Robert Amor the younger as a farm of 160 a.[92]

The east and west open arable fields, first mentioned in the 13th century, had been subdivided by the 18th.[93] In 1773 open arable was in the Clay field in the north part of the parish, in Puckland and Little fields respectively west and east of the lane leading from Chirton through the village to All Cannings, and in the Sand field which occupied the south-east corner of the parish.[94] The arable was surrounded by a narrow belt of meadow land and pasture.[95] In 1567 the meadow was reckoned at some 139 a. and in 1773 at 90 a.[96] The largest common meadow, West mead, was in Patney's south-west corner.[97] From the 13th century at the latest to the 17th century certain meadows within the manor were farmed. In 1248 a total rent of £2 was received from them.[98] What were possibly the same meadows were farmed by John Foster for £2 13s. 4d. in the earlier 16th century and afterwards by William Button (d. 1547) and his son William (d. 1591).[99] Both before and after the Dissolution certain landowners and tenants in other

[74] *Cal. Pat.* 1327–30, 365; *Wilts. Inq. p.m.* 1242–1326 (Index Libr.), 72.   [75] *Cal. Pat.* 1327–30, 365.
[76] Ibid.; *Cal. Fine R.* 1327–37, 244.
[77] *Cal. Fine R.* 1327–37, 479.
[78] B.L. Add. Ch. 24440; *Wilts. Pedigrees* (Harl. Soc. cv, cvi), 43–5.
[79] *Wilts. Pedigrees* (Harl. Soc. cv, cvi), 43–5; *Wilts. Inq. p.m.* 1625–49 (Index Libr.), 118–20.
[80] *V.C.H. Wilts.* viii. 150; x. 88.
[81] W.R.O. 335/182, ct. bk. 1665–1819, f. 14; 490/474, abstr. of title of Wm. Tinker; for Abingdon see *Complete Peerage*, i. 45 sqq.
[82] W.R.O. 490/474, abstr. of title of Tinker.
[83] Ibid. label on bdle.; W.A.S. Libr., survey of Radnor estates, earlier-19th-cent., p. 254; *Complete Peerage*, s.v. Radnor; see above.   [84] See above.
[85] *Interdict Doc.* (Pipe R. Soc. N.S. xxxiv), 24.
[86] Hanna, 'Winch. Cath. Custumal', pp. lvi, 366 sqq.
[87] *Obedientiaries' R. St. Swithun's*, ed. G. W. Kitchin (Hants Rec. Soc.), 226, 245.

[88] *Tax. Eccl.* (Rec. Com.), 185; *Valor Eccl.* (Rec. Com.), vi, App. p. vii.
[89] Mun. D. & C. Winton., acct. rolls, 1248, 1267, 1271, 1312.
[90] Ibid. acct. roll, 1267.
[91] *Survey of Lands of Wm., First Earl of Pembroke*, ed. C. R. Straton (Roxburghe Club), i. 243 sqq.
[92] W.R.O. 490/1057, survey.
[93] Mun. D. & C. Winton., acct. rolls, 1267, 1271; W.R.O. 490/1057, survey, 1773.
[94] W.R.O. 490/1057, surveys, 1773, early-19th-cent.
[95] Ibid. survey, early-19th-cent.
[96] *First Pembroke Survey*, ed. Straton, i. 243 sqq.; W.R.O. 490/1057, survey, 1773.
[97] W.R.O. 490/1057, survey, early-19th-cent.
[98] Mun. D. & C. Winton., acct. roll, 1248.
[99] Florence R. Goodman, *Revd. Landlords and their Tenants* (Winch. priv. print. 1930), 79; Mun. D. & C. Winton., acct. roll, 1541; *First Pembroke Survey*, ed. Straton, i. 248–9; *V.C.H. Wilts.* viii. 66, 70.

parishes, notably Enford and Chirton, were entitled to hay from Patney's meadows to augment their own meagre resources.[1]

By 1773 some 88 a. of meadow, 128 a. of pasture, and 58 a. of arable land in the parish had already been inclosed.[2] It seems possible, however, that those lands were re-allotted at parliamentary inclosure in 1780. The earl of Radnor then received 101 a.; the rector was allotted 127 a.; 7 small freeholders between them received 46 a.; 3 leaseholders received 87 a.; and 9 copyholders tenanting eleven estates were allotted 177 a. The rector's allotment became Rectory farm, and in the earl of Radnor's allotment the nucleus of Manor farm may be seen. Two of the farms mentioned in 1773 were consolidated. That held by Robert Amor after inclosure comprised 73 a. of freehold and copyhold land, while the other, leased to George Lewis, was estimated at 65 a.[3]

Manor farm which emerged after 1780 also included the water-mill and some former copyholds. It was let in 1783 to Edward Bouverie (d. 1810) but soon after seems to have been tenanted by Thomas Powys (later Baron Lilford, d. 1800).[4] The farm was augmented in 1828 by freehold land once Robert Amor's, and in 1828 and 1829 by two small copyholds.[5] By 1830 Stephen Akerman was tenant of both Manor and Rectory farms.[6]

In the earlier 20th century the Radnor estate at Patney, probably by then divided into Manor, 216 a., and Home, 256 a., farms, was let to Frank Stratton & Co. The company remained tenant until the farms were sold in 1919.[7] The farms were later merged and in 1976 Manor farm measured 542 a., of which some 230 a. were permanent pasture or under grass and 289 a. were given over to arable farming. Manor farm was then worked in conjunction with Manor farm, Beechingstoke.[8]

MILL. Of the two mills within the bishop of Winchester's Alton Priors estate in 1086, one may possibly have been at Patney.[9] In the early 13th century John the miller, a substantial customary tenant of St. Swithun's Priory, held a water-mill and 3 a. of land within Patney manor for 10s. yearly.[10] William Gilbert held the mill by copy in the later 16th century.[11] From the later 18th century, however, it was apparently leased with Manor farm.[12] It was offered for sale with that farm in 1919.[13]

Patney mill stood west of the church.[14] Its brick base, apparently of the 19th century, was visible in 1976. Its wheel was driven by water from a leat constructed from Patney's western boundary stream. The leat flowed some distance south-west of the mill and water was conveyed from it to the mill by a timber aqueduct.

LOCAL GOVERNMENT. In the mid 13th century the prior of St. Swithun's, Winchester, exercised franchisal jurisdiction within his hundred of Elstub, to which he transferred Patney from Studfold hundred c. 1248.[15] He apparently had a prison at Patney in 1249.[16]

Until the Dissolution Patney apparently owed suit at the courts, at which both franchisal and manorial jurisdiction was exercised, held by St. Swithun's at Alton Priors.[17] Although the lords of Patney continued to be entitled to view of frankpledge, courts held in the later 16th century seem to have dealt with purely manorial business. Those courts were sometimes held at Stanton St. Bernard once or twice yearly with those for North Newnton and Stanton, both also Pembroke properties. Business for each manor was recorded separately. From the 17th century, however, courts appear to have been held separately at Patney. Views, at which a tithing-man was elected, and manorial courts, which dealt with copyhold business and small agricultural matters, were then held on the same day but their business was recorded separately. From c. 1694, however, the business of the two courts was recorded together.[18]

In the mid 1830s an average sum of some £85 yearly was spent on the poor of Patney. In 1835 the parish became part of Devizes poor-law union.[19]

CHURCH. In the 12th century the advowson of Patney church belonged to the prior and monks of St. Swithun's, Winchester. Their right to present rectors was apparently challenged in the early 12th century by William Giffard, bishop of Winchester, but he seems to have restored the advowson to St. Swithun's c. 1124.[20] The priory's right to present was confirmed by the bishop in 1172.[21] In the early 13th century, however, the advowson was held by the bishops, to whom the convent finally ceded their right in 1284.[22] The bishops presented rectors until the mid 19th century, except in 1280 when the king presented sede vacante, in 1573 when the lord of Patney manor, Henry, earl of Pembroke, did so, and in 1639 when for an unknown reason the

[1] C 142/257 no. 72; W.R.O. 490/1057, survey, 1773; V.C.H. Wilts. x. 63.

[2] W.R.O. 490/1057, survey.

[3] Ibid. Inclosure Award.

[4] First Pembroke Survey, ed. Straton, i. 243 sqq.; W.R.O. 490/477, lease, Radnor to Bouverie; 490/705, survey, 1784; Land Tax; Burke, Peerage (1959), 1858; Complete Peerage, vii. 657–8; see below.

[5] W.A.S. Libr., survey, earlier-19th-cent.; see above.

[6] W.R.O., Land Tax.

[7] W.A.S. Libr., sale cat. xiii, no. 29.

[8] Ex inf. Mr. T. E. Trigg, W. Overton Farm, W. Overton; V.C.H. Wilts. x. 15.

[9] V.C.H. Wilts. ii, p. 120.

[10] Hanna, 'Winch. Cath. Custumal', 367. John may be the John the miller mentioned at Patney in 1210: Interdict Doc. (Pipe R. Soc. N.S. xxxiv), 24.

[11] B.L. Add. Ch. 24440; First Pembroke Survey, ed. Straton, i. 246.

[12] W.R.O. 335/184, survey, 18th-cent.; 490/705, survey, 1784; 490/477, lease, Radnor to Antrobus (1814).

[13] W.A.S. Libr., sale cat. xiii, no. 29.

[14] O.S. Map 6", Wilts. XL (1888 edn.).

[15] Rot. Hund. (Rec. Com.), ii (1), 230, 235; V.C.H. Wilts. x. 4; see above, p. 105.

[16] Crown Pleas, 1249 (W.R.S. xvi), p. 229.

[17] Mun. D. & C. Winton., ct. rolls, 13th–14th cent., 1545; see above, p. 199.

[18] First Pembroke Survey, ed. Straton, i. 249; B.L. Add. Ch. 24440–1; Wilton Ho. Mun., ct. bk. 1633–4; ct. rolls, 1666–7, 1670, 1676–8; box 25, no. 455; W.R.O. 335/182, ct. bk. 1665–1819.

[19] Poor Law Com. 2nd Rep. 559.

[20] Reg. Pontoise (Cant. & York Soc.), ii. 621.

[21] Ibid. 625.

[22] Ibid. 431; Cal. Pat. 1232–47, 271; Handbk. Brit. Chronology (1961 edn.), ed. F. M. Powicke and E. B. Fryde, 258.

king presented.[23] In 1869 the right to present was transferred to the bishop of Oxford, and in 1953 to the bishop of Salisbury.[24] The rectory was held in plurality with the united benefice of Chirton with Marden from 1951, and united with it in 1963.[25] In 1976 the united benefice of Charlton with North Newnton and Wilsford was dismembered and Charlton and Wilsford added to the united benefice of Chirton with Marden and Patney. The patronage of the new united benefice of Chirton, Marden, Patney, Charlton, and Wilsford was thereafter to be exercised in a series of five turns. The first and fifth were assigned to the bishop of Salisbury as patron of Chirton, Marden, and Patney, the second and fourth to Christ Church chapter, Oxford, as patron of Charlton, and the third to St. Nicholas's Hospital, Salisbury, as patron of Wilsford.[26]

The church was valued at £5 in 1291.[27] Its worth in 1535 was £19.[28] Those sums represented the value of all the tithes of Patney, of the tithe of Bellartsham in All Cannings, and of some 15 a. of glebe in the commons and open fields of Patney.[29] In 1705 the miller was paying 3s. 4d. yearly in place of tithes.[30] At inclosure in 1780 the rector was allotted 15 a. to replace his glebe and 112 a. in place of tithes.[31] The estate so formed was afterwards called Rectory farm. The net yearly income of the benefice from 1829 to 1831 averaged £225.[32] In 1928 the farm, 143 a., was let to H. W. H. Snook (d. 1975).[33] His son, Mr. D. Snook, was tenant in 1977.[34]

A rectory-house is mentioned in 1341, 1608, and 1705.[35] Although that standing c. 1829 was considered habitable, it was demolished and replaced, apparently on the same site south of the church, by a house designed and built in 1833 by William Dyer of Alton (Hants).[36] Its northerly red-brick extension is of the later 19th century. The Rectory was let as a farm-house to the tenant of Rectory farm c. 1949.[37]

Of the rectors who served Patney, many, because of preferments and interests elsewhere, did not reside. John of Ilsley, rector 1307–18, frequently obtained leave of absence to study between 1308 and 1312. In 1309 a deputy was appointed to serve the cure. John later became a royal clerk and afterwards served as a baron (1332–4) and as chancellor (1334–41) of the Exchequer.[38] Thomas

Romsey, rector from 1401 to c. 1405, was also headmaster of Winchester College.[39] Robert Parker, rector 1591–3, was afterwards forced to live abroad because of his extreme puritan views.[40] Geoffrey Bigge, rector from 1593 to c. 1631, was also master of St. Thomas's Hospital, Salisbury.[41] Among the many preferments of James Wedderburn, rector 1631–9, was the bishopric of Dunblane, to which he was elected in 1636.[42] Wedderburn's successor Samuel Marsh (d. 1657) had been ejected by 1647.[43] By that date a puritan, John Massey, who subscribed to the 1648 *Concurrent Testimony*, had been intruded.[44] An assistant curate of puritan sympathies served Patney in 1641.[45] In 1783 the rector of Woodborough acted as curate because the incumbent lived at Britford, where he was vicar.[46] A curate assisted the rector in 1818,[47] and from 1949 to 1951 the incumbent of the united benefice of Chirton with Marden was curate-in-charge of Patney.[48]

In 1783 services with sermons were held alternately morning and evening each Sunday. None was held on weekdays. Holy Communion, then attended by some six communicants, was celebrated at Christmas, Easter, and Whitsun.[49] On Census Sunday in 1851 65 people attended morning service and 70 that held in the afternoon.[50] Two Sunday services, attended on average by about 30 people in the morning and 45 in the afternoon, were held in 1864. The Sacrament was administered to some eight communicants on the Sunday after Christmas, Easter day, and Whit Sunday.[51]

The church of *ST. SWITHUN* stands west of the village. It is built of rubble with freestone dressings and comprises chancel and nave with north vestry, south porch, and central bellcot. The later-13th-century church was lit by windows consisting of grouped cusped lancets.[52] Its chancel was reported out of repair in 1662.[53] In the period 1876–8 the church was partly rebuilt and was thoroughly restored as an exact copy of the original by Henry Weaver of Devizes.[54] Weaver also removed the west gallery, added the north vestry, and largely refitted the church,[55] which in 1976, however, retained a 12th-century font, 14th-century piscena, and earlier-17th-century pulpit.

In 1553 15 oz. of plate were taken for the king's use and a chalice of 10 oz. was left for the parish.

[23] *Cal. Pat.* 1272–81, 405; Phillipps, *Wilts. Inst.* (index in *W.A.M.* xxviii. 227).
[24] *Lond. Gaz.* 4 June 1852, p. 1580; *Handbk. Brit. Chronology* (1961 edn.), ed. Powicke and Fryde, 259; ex inf. Dioc. Registrar.
[25] *V.C.H. Wilts.* x. 69.   [26] Ex inf. Dioc. Registrar.
[27] *Tax. Eccl.* (Rec. Com.), 180.
[28] *Valor Eccl.* (Rec. Com.), ii. 146.
[29] *Inq. Non.* (Rec. Com.), 171; *First Pembroke Survey*, ed. Straton, i. 243; Sar. Dioc. R.O., Glebe Terriers, 1608, 1705.   [30] Sar. Dioc. R.O., Glebe Terrier.
[31] W.R.O., Inclosure Award.
[32] *Rep. Com. Eccl. Revenues*, 844–5.
[33] W.R.O. 509/7, deed, Bloomfield to Snook; ex inf. the incumbent, the Revd. C. Bryant, Chirton Vicarage.
[34] Ex inf. the Revd. C. Bryant.
[35] *Inq. Non.* (Rec. Com.), 171; Sar. Dioc. R.O., Glebe Terriers.
[36] *Rep. Com. Eccl. Revenues*, 844–5; Sar. Dioc. R.O., Mortgages, no. 70; Pigot, *Nat. Com. Dir.* (1830), 405; Pigot, *Dir. Hants* (1844), 6.
[37] Ex inf. the Revd. C. Bryant.
[38] *Reg. Ghent* (Cant. & York Soc.), ii. 886, 888, 901, 911; A. B. Emden, *Biog. Reg. Univ. Oxf. to 1500*, ii. 933–4.

[39] Phillipps, *Wilts. Inst.* i. 88, 93; Emden, op. cit. iii. 1588.
[40] Phillipps, *Wilts. Inst.* 232–3; *D.N.B.* which is corrected by *V.C.H. Wilts.* x. 152–3.
[41] Phillipps, *Wilts. Inst.* i. 233; ii. 16; J. Foster, *Alumni Oxon. 1500–1714*, i. 122.
[42] Phillipps, *Wilts. Inst.* ii. 16, 20; J. and J. A. Venn, *Alumni Cantab.* i (4), 357.
[43] *Walker Revised*, ed. A. G. Matthews, 377.
[44] *Calamy Revised*, ed. A. G. Matthews, 343.
[45] *Walker Revised*, ed. Matthews, 369.
[46] *Vis. Queries, 1783* (W.R.S. xxvii), p. 173; *V.C.H. Wilts.* x. 223.
[47] *Educ. of Poor Digest*, 1034.
[48] *Crockford* (1951–2).
[49] *Vis. Queries, 1783* (W.R.S. xxvii), p. 173.
[50] H.O. 129/256/1/7.
[51] Sar. Dioc. R.O., Vis. Queries.
[52] J. Buckler, water-colour in W.A.S. Libr., vol. x. 12 (1807).
[53] Sar. Dioc. R.O., Chwdns.' Pres.
[54] W.R.O. 509/10, faculty, 8 July 1876; Wilts. Cuttings, xvi. 326.
[55] W.R.O. 509/10, faculty, 8 July 1876.

In 1976 the plate comprised a chalice of 1706, paten of 1722, and flagon of 1766, all presented in 1839 by a Miss Lewis of Wedhampton, in Urchfont.[56] The church had two bells in 1553 and in the 20th century: (i) is by W. and R. Cor (fl. 1694–1724); (ii) is of c. 1500 and was possibly cast in Dorset.[57]

Registrations of baptisms and burials are extant from 1592, and of marriages from 1594. Burials are lacking for 1765–73.[58]

NONCONFORMITY. There was a nonconformist at Patney in 1676.[59] Independents certified a house there in 1799.[60] In 1830 Thomas Wells's house was certified for worship;[61] the group which met there was probably attached to the New Baptist chapel at Devizes.[62]

EDUCATION. There was a boarding- and day-school for some 40 children in the parish in 1808.[63]

A woman taught about six poor children in 1818.[64] In 1858 about twenty children were taught by a mistress in a small schoolroom. Reading and writing were then apparently better taught at Patney than at other schools near by.[65] That school flourished and by 1871 was connected with the National Society. On return day in that year six boys and eleven girls attended.[66] The school stood south-west of the road junction at the centre of the village.[67] An average of 28 boys and girls attended during the year 1906–7. Average attendance remained fairly steady until the end of the First World War. In 1922, however, there had been an average attendance of only fourteen children over the past year, and in 1924 the school was closed.[68] Patney children afterwards attended Chirton school 1 km. away.[69] In 1976 the former schoolroom was used as a store.

CHARITIES FOR THE POOR. None for the parish is known.

ROLLESTONE

ROLLESTONE, 8 km. west of Amesbury, probably appears in Domesday Book as Winterbourne and the form Winterbourne Rollestone was occasionally used in the 13th century and the early 14th.[70] In 1242–3 Rollestone was the name of both the parish and the mesne tenant of the manor,[71] and the family may have given its name to lands earlier associated with Winterbourne Stoke, which bounds Rollestone to the south and west. The long narrow parish extended 4.5 km. north-east from the river Till, broadening from 800 m. wide in the river valley to 1.6 km. on its eastern boundary with Durrington and Figheldean.[72] The boundary of the ancient parish bore little relation to the physical landscape of the downs, but in the south-west it followed the course or valley of the river and north of the village turned north-east along a dry tributary valley. Two detached portions of Shrewton on the banks of the Till south of Rollestone were attributed to the parish in 1812 but that seems to have been a cartographical error.[73] In 1878 the parish measured 870 a. (359.5 ha.).[74] The south-west boundary was straightened in 1885 when 4 a. of water-meadow were transferred from Shrewton to Rollestone.[75] In 1934 Rollestone was included with Maddington in the parish of Shrewton.[76]

Only the Till valley and its dry tributary lie below 91 m., and the highest point in the parish is 129 m. in the north-east corner at its junction with Shrewton and Figheldean. Upper Chalk outcrops over the whole parish, covered by gravel in the valleys.[77] The downs have provided grazing for sheep and cattle, and between that pasture and a strip of meadow on the banks of the river lay the arable lands of the parish. The only woodland was a small clump of trees north of the Shrewton–Durrington road.[78]

The main Salisbury–Devizes road, turnpiked in the early 1760s, crossed the down parallel to and inside the eastern boundary of the parish. When firing ranges were established in the area of Larkhill in Durrington in the early 20th century, the road was closed north of the Bustard Hotel in Shrewton. The Warminster–Amesbury road, which passes close to the village of Rollestone, rising sharply out of the valley near the church, became part of the main route between Devizes and Salisbury.[79] The Shrewton–Durrington road, which crosses the old Salisbury–Devizes road on Rollestone down, remained open to the public. The tracks which in the late 18th century led from the Warminster–Amesbury road south and south-east towards the

[56] Nightingale, Wilts. Plate, 117; ex inf. the Revd. C. Bryant.
[57] Walters, Wilts. Bells, 155–6, 308–10; ex inf. the Revd. C. Bryant.
[58] W.R.O. 509/1–4. The deficiencies in burial regns. are remedied by transcripts in Sar. Dioc. R.O. The marriage reg. has been printed: Wilts. Par. Reg. (Mar.), ed. W. P. W. Phillimore and J. Sadler, vi. 93–9.
[59] W.N. & Q. iii. 536.   [60] W.A.M. lxi. 65.
[61] W.R.O., Certs. Dissenters' Meeting-Houses.
[62] Ibid. The cert. was signed by J. S. Bunce, pastor of the chapel 1830–46: V.C.H. Wilts. x. 296.
[63] Lambeth MS. 1732.
[64] Educ. of Poor Digest, 1034.
[65] Acct. of Wilts. Schs. 36.
[66] Returns relating to Elem. Educ. 422–3.
[67] O.S. Map 6″, Wilts. XL (1888 edn.).
[68] Bd. of Educ., List 21 (H.M.S.O.).
[69] V.C.H. Wilts. x. 71.
[70] Ibid. ii, p. 162 and n.; Feet of F. 1272–1327 (W.R.S. i), pp. 40, 116.
[71] Bk. of Fees, ii. 731.
[72] This article was written in 1978. Maps used include O.S. Maps 1″, sheet 14 (1817 edn.); 1/25,000, SU 04 (1958 edn.), SU 14 (1958 edn.); 6″, Wilts. LIII (1889 edn.), LIV (1887 edn.).
[73] W.R.O., Winterbourne Stoke Inclosure Award.
[74] O.S. Map 6″, Wilts. LIV (1887 edn.).
[75] W.R.O., Tithe Award; O.S. Map 6″, Wilts. LIII (1889 edn.); W.A.S. Libr., sale cat. vi, no. 7.
[76] V.C.H. Wilts. iv. 357 n.
[77] Geol. Surv. Map 1″, drift, sheet 282 (1967 edn.).
[78] W.R.O., Tithe Award; Air 2/359.
[79] V.C.H. Wilts. iv. 266, 270.

OVERTON

Sarsen stones in Lockeridge dene

STOCKTON

Street scene in 1934

OVERTON: 19TH-CENTURY STOCKYARD AT NORTH FARM

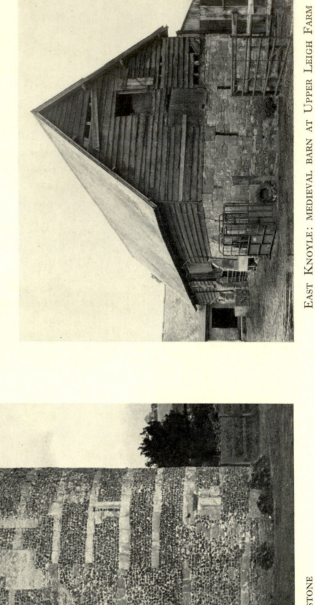

EAST KNOYLE: MEDIEVAL BARN AT UPPER LEIGH FARM

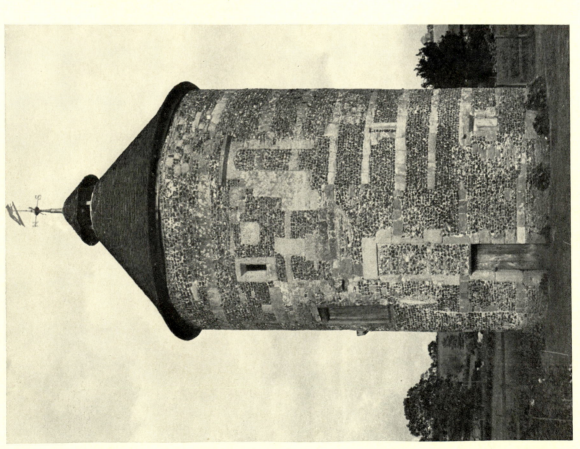

BISHOPSTONE
Corner tower, fomerly part of Faulston House

church and Winterbourne Stoke and north-east to Middle Farm were still marked on maps in 1957,[80] but there was little trace of them in 1978.

On the downland 30 barrows of different types have been identified. There are two principal groups, at the junction of the Shrewton–Durrington road with the north-west boundary of the parish and east of Middle Farm on the north-east boundary. Other barrows are scattered between those groups.[81]

In 1428 there were fewer than ten householders in the parish and the settlement was of much the same size in 1901 when there were only eight inhabited houses.[82] During the 19th century the population grew from 34 in 1801 to 52 in 1861, but by 1891 it had fallen to 28. The establishment of an R.A.F. station on the down in the early 20th century greatly increased the population. Between 1911 and 1921 the total rose from 41 to 152, including military personnel, and in 1931, the last year for which separate figures for Rollestone are available, it stood at 189.[83]

Neither the existence of the R.A.F. station nor the diversion of the Salisbury–Devizes road affected the size or location of the village. It is on the valley gravel in the western corner of the parish, separated from Shrewton by an unmade road leading from the main road towards the river. The church and the Old Rectory stand slightly apart from the rest of the village, on higher ground to the south-east. Most of the buildings lie beside the unmade road south-west of Rollestone Manor, which stands at the junction of that road with the main road. Since the Second World War the village of Shrewton has extended along the Warminster–Amesbury road to the former boundary and in 1978 Rollestone, like Elston, in Orcheston St. George, and Maddington, both north of Shrewton, formed part of the larger settlement. In the early 19th century there were farm buildings on the down east and west of the Salisbury–Devizes road.[84] By 1877 the buildings west of the road had become known as Middle Farm.[85] A single-storey farm-house was built in the 20th century. Rollestone Bake Farm, east of the road, was first mentioned by name in 1899.[86] It was part of the property purchased for the Army in 1902 and then consisted of cottages and outbuildings. In 1978 a late-19th-century barn and a stockyard were still used.

Much of the downland in the north-east part of the parish has been used by the Army or Air Force since the early 20th century. In 1926 there were firing ranges near the boundary with Figheldean,[87] and the area east of the old Salisbury–Devizes road and north of the Shrewton–Durrington road has since been used by the Royal School of Artillery at Larkhill. The Royal Flying Corps took possession of over 50 a. west of the old Salisbury–Devizes road opposite Rollestone Bake Farm under an emergency land hiring agreement in 1916. The station established there, No. 1 Balloon School, provided instruction in the use of kite balloons for the British Expeditionary Force.[88] The R.A.F. School of Balloon Training, as it was called in 1920, was the only one in England between 1926 and 1935 and was run in co-operation with the Royal Artillery and the Royal Navy.[89] Known in 1929 as Larkhill Kite Balloon Station and in 1932 as the R.A.F. Balloon Centre, it was renamed No. 2 Balloon Training Unit in 1936 when balloon stations were established elsewhere. In 1939 it was replaced by the R.A.F. Anti-Gas School which remained at Rollestone until 1945. There was then a landing ground, approximately 1.3 km. by 400 m., south-east of the track from the village to Middle Farm. The staff was reduced to a care and maintenance party in 1945 and the R.A.F. withdrew from the camp in 1946.[90] In 1978 Rollestone Camp was used by the Salisbury Plain (Training) Camp Staff.[91]

MANOR AND OTHER ESTATE. In 1066 and 1086 Cudulf held lands then said to be in Winterbourne which have been identified as those of the later manor of *ROLLESTONE*.[92] Roger de Quency, earl of Winchester (d. 1264), had an estate in Rollestone in 1242–3.[93] In 1275 it was held by his three daughters and coheirs and when the inheritance was divided in 1277 was allotted to Elizabeth or Isabel, wife of Alexander Comyn, earl of Buchan.[94] Rollestone was not afterwards named among the Buchan estates and in 1344 the manor was held by Humphrey de Bohun, earl of Hereford and Essex (d. 1361).[95] It is not clear how the earl acquired the manor: it may have passed with Netheravon manor in the portion of Margaret or Margery de Ferrers, countess of Derby, daughter of Roger de Quency.[96] Although not expressly mentioned among the Hereford estates acquired by Henry, earl of Derby, in 1384 or at the repartitioning of the Bohun inheritance in 1421,[97] the manor was, like Netheravon, held by the king as part of the duchy of Lancaster in 1428.[98]

The first of several intermediate tenants in 1242–3 was Ernis de Neville (d. 1257), who was succeeded by his son Gilbert (d. 1294), and grandson John Neville (d. 1334).[99] John's son Gilbert held of the earl of Hereford in 1344, the last occasion on which the family is known to have held land in Rollestone.[1]

The tenant of the manor in demesne in 1242–3 was Nicholas of Rollestone.[2] By 1275 his son William had inherited,[3] and in 1294 Joan and Christine,

[80] *Andrews and Dury, Map* (W.R.S. viii), pl. 8; O.S. Map 1″, sheet 167 (1960 edn.).
[81] *V.C.H. Wilts.* i (1), 190–1, 211, 219.
[82] Ibid. iv. 314; *Endowed Char. Wilts.* (S. Div.), 364.
[83] *V.C.H. Wilts.* iv. 356–7.
[84] O.S. Map 1″, sheet 14 (1817 edn.); W.R.O., Tithe Award.
[85] W.R.O., Tithe Award; O.S. Map 6″, Wilts. LIV (1887 edn.).
[86] O.S. Map 6″, Wilts. LIV. NW. (1901 edn.).
[87] Ibid. LIV. NW. (1926 edn.).
[88] Ex inf. Air Hist. Branch, Lond.
[89] Ibid.; *Air Force List* (1926–35 edns.); Air 2/359.
[90] Ex inf. Air Hist. Branch, Lond.; Air 28/666.
[91] Ex inf. Defence Land Agent, Durrington.

[92] *V.C.H. Wilts.* ii, pp. 127 and n., 162 and n., 179.
[93] *Bk. of Fees*, ii. 731; *Complete Peerage*, xii (2), 751–4.
[94] *Rot. Hund.* (Rec. Com.), ii (1), 254; Hist. MSS. Com. 78, *Hastings*, i, p. 330.
[95] *Year Bk.* 18 Edw. III (Rolls Ser.), 126–7.
[96] See p. 168.
[97] *Cal. Close*, 1381–5, 511; R. Somerville, *Duchy of Lanc.* i. 180–1, 339.
[98] *Feud. Aids*, v. 243.
[99] *Bk. of Fees*, ii. 731; *Cal. Inq. p.m.* i, p. 101; iii, p. 114; vii, p. 428.
[1] *Year Bk.* 18 Edw. III (Rolls Ser.), 126–7.
[2] *Bk. of Fees*, ii. 731.
[3] C.P. 25(1)/252/22 no. 41; *Rot. Hund.* (Rec. Com.), ii (1), 254.

daughters of Walter of Rollestone, conveyed lands in Rollestone to a trustee.[4] A holding in Rollestone was confirmed by Nicholas Lambard in 1325 to another Nicholas of Rollestone and Catherine his wife.[5] Their son Henry, rector of Orcheston St. Mary, perhaps disposed of the holding as he did the family's possessions at Eastcott in Urchfont in 1363.[6] In 1369 the manor was granted by John Littlecote to Henry Fleming and his wife Joan for the term of her life with reversion to Michael Skilling and Alice his wife and their heirs.[7] It descended with the manor of Shoddesden in Kimpton (Hants) to the Skillings' grandson John Skilling,[8] whose daughter Elizabeth, wife of John Wynnard, conveyed it to John Wydeslade and William Estecote in 1465.[9] The estate was later forfeited, for a reason that is not known, and in 1483 or 1484 a royal grant of the manor, said to have been held by Thomas Milbourne, was made to John Cawmfield.[10] In 1508 it was settled on a relative of Elizabeth Wynnard, John Skilling (d. 1526) of Draycot Fitz Payne in Wilcot.[11] John was succeeded by his son Walter, then a minor.[12] At his marriage in 1556 the manor was settled on Walter's son William.[13] In 1566 the Skillings sold it to Giles Estcourt, recorder of Salisbury and M.P. for the city between 1563 and 1587.[14]

Estcourt (d. 1587) was succeeded by his son Sir Edward (d. 1608) and grandson Sir Giles Estcourt (created a baronet in 1627, d. 1668). The manor passed in turn to each of Sir Giles's surviving children, none of whom left issue: to Giles (d. 1675), William (d. 1684), Amy (d. 1696) wife of Alexander Haddon, and Anne (d. 1704).[15] Anne devised Rollestone to a cousin, Edmund Estcourt, with remainder to Walter Estcourt of Shipton Moyne (Glos.), also her cousin and perhaps Edmund's elder brother.[16] Although Edmund lived until 1717 the manor was immediately on Anne's death occupied by Walter, either as tenant or in his own right.[17] On Walter's death in 1726 Rollestone passed with Shipton Moyne to his cousins Thomas Estcourt (d. 1746) and Edmund Estcourt (d. 1758) in turn. Edmund devised his entire estate to a kinsman, another Thomas Estcourt,[18] who sold the manor in 1791 to Nathaniel Dance, later Sir Nathaniel Holland (d. 1811), the portrait-painter and foundation member of the Royal Academy.[19] By the will of Nathaniel's widow Harriett (d. 1825) it passed to her nephew Robert Brudenell, earl of Cardigan.[20]

In 1827 Lord Cardigan sold the manor, which then included nearly the whole parish, to the Revd. Samuel Heathcote.[21] In 1847 it passed to Heathcote's

son William in trust for William's children. At William's death in 1882 it was divided between his son Samuel and four daughters or their heirs.[22] Samuel occupied the manor until his death in 1886, holding a fifth in his own right, a fifth by a conveyance of 1883 from his sister Catherine, and a third of a fifth by another conveyance of that year from George William Heathcote, son of his sister Eliza.[23] He held the rest of the estate on lease from George William's siblings, from his sister Maria Wyndham, and from the children of his sister Sophia Walsh.[24] After Samuel's death mismanagement of the estate led to a suit in Chancery to secure the portions of Sophia's children Henry and Sophia Walsh.[25] The court ordered the sale of the manor in 1902. The Secretary of State for War purchased 265 a. of downland east of the Salisbury–Devizes road,[26] and the remainder was sold to T. W. Pratt.[27] In 1931 and 1932 the Air Ministry bought a further 57 a. of downland from Pratt.[28] The Ministry of Defence still held 130 ha. (321 a.) in 1978. What remained of the manor was acquired in 1932 by G. R. Smith. After Smith's death in 1972 Middle farm was sold and the rest of the estate, c. 300 a., passed to his widow Mrs. Janetta R. Smith. Middle farm was sold again in 1978.[29]

Rollestone Manor was built in the later 18th century. The 16th-century structural timbers and panelling which have been re-used in the house may have been taken from its predecessor which appears to have been completely demolished. The new house was of stone and flint but was given a new entrance front of red brick early in the 19th century. It was extended westwards in 1839.[30] The farm buildings are of the 19th century and include a timber-framed barn and a weatherboarded granary.

Services from tenants in Rollestone belonged to the manor of Norton Bavant granted as part of the estate of Roger Bavant to the prioress of Dartford (Kent) in 1362.[31] At the Dissolution 2 virgates in Rollestone and Maddington passed from the priory to the Crown.[32] The later descent of the holding has not been traced.

ECONOMIC HISTORY. In 1084 Cudulf's demesne lands were assessed at 5½ hides and ½ virgate.[33] In 1086 his whole estate of 6 hides was worth £3 and included land for 3 ploughs, 4 a. of meadow, and ½ league of pasture. There were 2 ploughs on the demesne and 1 held by 5 serfs, 1 villein, and 2 bordars.[34]

In the late 16th century Giles Estcourt and his

---

[4] *Feet of F. 1272–1327* (W.R.S. i), p. 40.
[5] Ibid. p. 116; *Year Bk.* 18 Edw. III (Rolls Ser.), 126–7.
[6] *V.C.H. Wilts.* x. 178–9.
[7] *Feet of F. 1327–77* (W.R.S. xxix), p. 134.
[8] *V.C.H. Hants*, iv. 374; *V.C.H. Wilts.* x. 35; *Feud. Aids*, v. 243. [9] C.P. 25(1)/296/74 no. 26.
[10] B.L. Harl. MS. 433, ff. 58, 173.
[11] W.A.S. Libr., Simpson MS. 19; *V.C.H. Hants*, iii. 445; C 142/44 no. 130.
[12] C 142/44 no. 130. [13] C 3/310/23.
[14] C.P. 25(2)/239/8 & 9 Eliz. I Mich. no. 345; *W.N. & Q.* v. 325.
[15] *W.N. & Q.* v. 325–8; G.E.C. *Baronetage*, ii. 10–11; W.A.S. Libr., Manley MS. M. 23.
[16] Prob. 11/479 (P.C.C. 251 Ash).
[17] Prob. 11/560 (P.C.C. 192 Whitfield); Glos. R.O., D 1571/R 48.

[18] *V.C.H. Glos.* xi. 251; W.A.S. Libr., Manley MS. M. 23.
[19] W.R.O. 451/494; *D.N.B.*; G.E.C. *Baronetage*, v. 333–4.
[20] W.R.O. 451/494. [21] Ibid.
[22] Prob. 11/2048 i. 37; E. D. Heathcote, *Fams. of Heathcote* (Winch. 1899). [23] J 4/5192/2779.
[24] W.R.O. 1042/5; J 4/5002/3170. [25] J 4/4803/4190.
[26] J 15/2591/873; J 4/6441/1443.
[27] J 15/2618/1291.
[28] Ex inf. Defence Land Agent, Durrington.
[29] Ex inf. Mrs. Smith, Rollestone Man.
[30] Date on bldg.
[31] *Cal. Close, 1360–4*, 383; *1389–92*, 241; *V.C.H. Kent*, iii. 181.
[32] S.C. 6/Hen. VIII/1757 m. 28.
[33] *V.C.H. Wilts.* ii, p. 179. [34] Ibid. p. 162.

tenants claimed rights to common grazing for their cattle on Net down and certain meadows in Shrewton.[35] The size of the tenants' holdings is not known, but they were presumably small since in the early 18th century the demesne was the one substantial farm in the parish.[36] In 1827 the few cottagers in the village and other tenants from Shrewton and Maddington held only 12 a. between them.[37] Because of the accumulation of land into a single farm, no inclosure award was necessary to end common cultivation in the greater part of the parish.

Throughout the 18th century and in the early 19th Rollestone farm was worked by tenants, although rarely by the same family for more than a generation.[38] No lease has been found of a date later than 1833 and by 1882 the Heathcotes occupied the farm themselves.[39] In 1838 it measured 820 a. including 458 a. of arable and 362 a. of pasture and watered meadow. Most of the pasture was on the down east of the Salisbury–Devizes road, except for a few strips of glebe near the north-west boundary and 4 a. beside Rollestone Manor.[40] The area of arable may have been increased later by burn-baking the down pasture, as the name of Rollestone Bake Farm implies.[41] In 1894 Rollestone Bake and Middle Farms were additional farmsteads from which Rollestone farm was worked.[42] In 1902 both had barns and cottages and there were also stables at Middle Farm.[43] Shortly before the Royal Flying Corps took possession of the site of Rollestone Camp in 1916 the area had been inclosed for wintering cattle.[44] In 1978 Middle farm consisted of 190 a. of downland. Rollestone Manor farm was worked by a tenant from the yards adjacent to the manor-house.[45]

LOCAL GOVERNMENT. No record has been found of a private view of frankpledge for Rollestone or of the manor court. There is similarly no evidence of parish government before Rollestone joined Amesbury poor-law union in 1835.[46]

CHURCH. A church at Rollestone, mentioned in 1291,[47] was apparently built in the earlier 13th century. The prior of the order of St. John of Jerusalem in England presented to the rectory at least from 1302 until the advowson passed to the Crown at the Dissolution.[48] The only known exception was in 1471 when the bishop collated by lapse.[49] In 1923 the rectory was united with the adjacent living to form the benefice of Shrewton with Maddington and Rollestone. The right of presentation at every third turn was retained by the Crown,[50] and in 1958 the Crown became sole patron after an exchange with the bishop of Salisbury.[51] The three parishes were united in 1970,[52] and in 1972 the name of the living was changed to Shrewton.[53]

The rectory had an annual value of £4 6s. 8d. in 1291, one of only two livings in the deanery of Wylye with revenues of less than £5.[54] The assessments of £7 18s. in 1535 and £40 in 1650 were still low by comparison with other benefices of the deanery and hundred.[55] By the 19th century, however, the rector's income was relatively good, in view of the size of the parish. Between 1829 and 1831 he received an average of £150 a year.[56] Most of that came from tithes, which were due to the rector from the whole parish.[57] Payment in kind had ceased by the early 19th century and in 1839 a yearly rent-charge was substituted for the tithes, then valued at £170.[58] In 1341 the 6 a. of glebe were worth 6s. 8d. a year.[59] In 1838 the glebe, c. 5 a., included arable and pasture scattered about the western part of the parish.[60] A rectory-house was built in the late 17th century and probably replaced in the 18th. In 1835 and 1864 the house was described as unfit for residence.[61] From 1877 to 1922 it was probably occupied by the rector but since 1923 the incumbent of the united benefice has lived at Shrewton.[62] The small 18th-century rectory-house of flint and stone was sold in 1944 and later extended to the north.[63]

Few rectors resided at Rollestone. In 1303 Andrew of Tothale, rector 1301–14, was licensed to study at Oxford for 2 years.[64] There is evidence that the living was farmed and a curate employed in the mid and late 16th century. In 1556 a proprietor, a term which presumably indicated a lessee of the rectory estate, was ordered with the parishioners to replace furnishings in the church, and in 1584 the lack of quarterly sermons was blamed on Giles Estcourt, lord of the manor and probably also a lessee.[65] In 1644 James White, who held a second parish and a prebend at Salisbury, was sequestered from the rectory.[66] He was replaced by George Hadfield, a presbyterian, who was said to have preached twice every Sunday at Rollestone.[67] In 1674 the minister was described as very careful in the performance of his duties,[68] but pluralism and non-residence again became usual until the late 19th century. Only two absentee rectors are known to

[35] C 3/61/9.
[36] Glos. R.O., D 1571/A 2, pp. 155–7, 194–5.
[37] W.R.O. 451/493–4.
[38] Glos. R.O., D 1571/A 1, pp. 6, 54–9, 208; D 1571/A 2, pp. 133–40; D 1571/E 252; D 1571/L 40.
[39] H.R.O. 27M54/18; J 4/5002/3170.
[40] W.R.O. 451/494; Tithe Award.
[41] P.N. Wilts. (E.P.N.S.), 450.
[42] J 4/4803/4190.
[43] W.A.S. Libr., sale cat. vi, no. 7.
[44] Air 2/359.
[45] Ex inf. Mrs. Smith.
[46] Poor Law Com. 2nd Rep. 558.
[47] Tax. Eccl. (Rec. Com.), 181.
[48] Phillipps, Wilts. Inst. (index in W.A.M. xxviii. 228).
[49] Phillipps, Wilts. Inst. i. 161.
[50] Lond. Gaz. 2 Feb. 1923, pp. 782–3.
[51] Ibid. 31 Jan. 1958, p. 687.
[52] Ibid. 4 June 1970, p. 6218.

[53] Ibid. 10 Feb. 1972, p. 1695.
[54] Tax. Eccl. (Rec. Com.), 181.
[55] Valor Eccl. (Rec. Com.), ii. 104; W.A.M. xl. 300.
[56] Rep. Com. Eccl. Revenues, 844.
[57] W.R.O., Tithe Award.
[58] Sar. Dioc. R.O., Pet. for Faculties, bdle. 2, no. 25; W.R.O., Tithe Award.
[59] Inq. Non. (Rec. Com.), 178.
[60] W.R.O., Tithe Award.
[61] W.A.M. l. 273–4; Rep. Com. Eccl. Revenues, 844; Sar. Dioc. R.O., Vis. Queries, 1864.
[62] W.A.M. xlii. 87; J 4/5192/2779; Lond. Gaz. 2 Feb. 1923, pp. 782–3.
[63] Ex inf. Mrs. D. McCulloch, Rollestone Old Rectory.
[64] Reg. Ghent (Cant. & York Soc.), ii. 860.
[65] Sar. Dioc. R.O., Detecta Bk. 1556; 1584.
[66] Walker Revised, ed. A. G. Matthews, 382.
[67] W.A.M. xl. 300.
[68] Sar. Dioc. R.O., Chwdns.' Pres.

have employed curates. White did so in 1639, and in 1864, when the rector was vicar of Andover and a Fellow of Winchester College, his curate was also non-resident.[69]

From the later 18th century Holy Communion was celebrated four times a year, a practice which continued into the 20th century.[70] In 1783 attendance at the Sunday service, held alternately in the morning and the afternoon, was unreliable and the children failed to attend for catechism.[71] In 1851 the congregation was said to be three times the population of the parish.[72] A more cautious estimate of 1864 suggested that average attendance was between 40 and 150, depending on the weather and the presence of worshippers from other parishes.[73]

The church of *ST. ANDREW*, whose dedication cannot be traced before the mid 19th century,[74] is faced with flint and stone and has a chancel and nave with south porch. Reset lancet windows in the chancel indicate that it was built in the earlier 13th century and the small nave may be of the same date. The font is also early-13th-century. Later windows in the nave are to the west, probably 14th-century, to the north, 15th-century, and to the south, early-16th-century. The nave was reroofed in the 16th century and of the 17th-century fittings the communion table and font cover remain. In 1845 the chancel and chancel arch were apparently rebuilt, much of the nave refaced, and the porch added.[75]

There is one bell of c. 1860.[76] In 1553 2 oz. of plate were confiscated for the king's use.[77] A chalice and cover of 1576 were still held by the church in 1978, but nothing was then known of a paten of 1694 which was said in 1891 to belong to the parish.[78] The registers begin in 1654 but do not cover the years 1714–1812.[79]

NONCONFORMITY.
In 1669 a considerable number of dissenters met at Rollestone under the leadership of John Read of Porton, in Idmiston, one of several Baptist teachers in the area.[80] Nothing more is known of that conventicle and there was no further report of nonconformity in the parish.

EDUCATION.
There is no evidence of a school in the parish. Children from Rollestone attended schools in Shrewton and Maddington in 1858 and in Shrewton in 1870.[81] In 1978 the children still attended Shrewton school.[82]

CHARITY FOR THE POOR.
By will proved 1704 Anne Estcourt gave an annual rent-charge of £30 from property in Long Newnton (now Glos.), Rollestone, and Shrewton to apprentice six poor boys from those parishes each year. In 1827 the purchasers of Rollestone manor were exempted from payment of the rent-charge which continued to be borne by the Estcourt estate. The donor left no instruction for the management of the charity and the provisions were not given effect until 1711. In that year the Commissioners for Charitable Uses decreed that the rent-charge and the arrears should be divided equally between the three parishes, an arrangement very favourable to the small population of Rollestone. The trustees appointed for each parish were to buy land with the arrears. No purchase was made by the Rollestone trustees and in 1791 the rent-charge of £10 was said to be insufficient for two apprenticeships a year.[83] The charity was rarely used in the early 19th century. After 1833 the accumulated surplus was reinvested to provide one apprenticeship each year. There was a scarcity of candidates from Rollestone and by 1900 most of those who benefited came from Shrewton, although there is no evidence that the restriction to Rollestone was formally abolished. In 1871 the trustees contributed £200 towards the enlargement of Shrewton school but permission for a further donation of £50 was refused by the Charity Commissioners in 1904.[84] The apprenticing charities of Shrewton and Rollestone were combined by a Scheme of 1910. Money not spent on apprenticeships was thereafter used to help boys attending Dauntsey's agricultural school. A further Scheme of 1919 allowed contributions to any form of training for poor children of the two parishes. In 1963 the yearly income of the combined charities was £80.[85]

STOCKTON

THE parish of Stockton, in the Wylye valley 18 km. WNW. of Salisbury and 13 km. ESE. of Warminster, measured 2,122 a. (859 ha.).[86] It is on the south side of the Wylye, running back from the river to the downs as a rectangle 4 km. from north to south and 2.5 km. from east to west. A number of parishes in the Wylye valley, including Stockton's near neighbours Boyton, Fisherton de la Mere, and Wylye, contained more than a single village and were divided into several townships or tithings.[87] Stockton almost became such a parish: it contained two sets of commonable fields based on separate

[69] *Subscription Bk. 1620–40* (W.R.S. xxxii), pp. 40, 82; Sar. Dioc. R.O., Vis. Queries, 1864.
[70] *Vis. Queries, 1783* (W.R.S. xxvii), pp. 184–5; Sar. Dioc. R.O., Vis. Queries, 1864; W.R.O. 1336/76.
[71] *Vis. Queries, 1783* (W.R.S. xxvii), pp. 184–5.
[72] H.O. 129/262/1/6/7.
[73] Sar. Dioc. R.O., Vis. Queries.
[74] H.O. 129/262/1/6/7.
[75] J. M. J. Fletcher and A. S. Robins, *Guide to the Chs. of Shrewton, Maddington and Rollestone* (priv. print. 1943).
[76] Walters, *Wilts. Bells*, 164.
[77] *W.A.M.* xiii. 364.
[78] Nightingale, *Wilts. Plate*, 72; ex inf. the incumbent, the Revd. A. G. Miles, Shrewton Vicarage.
[79] Transcripts for 1608 and 1624–38 are in Sar. Dioc.
R.O. The marriage reg. has been printed: *Wilts. Par. Reg. (Mar.)*, ed. W. P. W. Phillimore and J. Sadler, vi. 149–52.
[80] G. L. Turner, *Original Rec.* i. 121, 222; *V.C.H. Wilts.* iii. 112.
[81] *Acct. of Wilts. Schs.* 38; *Returns relating to Elem. Educ.* 426–7.   [82] Ex inf. the Revd. A. G. Miles.
[83] Glos. R.O., D 1571/R 48; *Endowed Char. Wilts.* (S. Div.), 628–34.
[84] *Endowed Char. Wilts.* (S. Div.), 363–4.
[85] Char. Com. file 50911.
[86] This article was written in 1978. Maps used include O.S. Maps 1″, sheet 14 (1817 edn.), sheet 167 (1960 edn.); 1/50,000, sheet 184 (1974 edn.); 1/25,000, ST 93 (1958 edn.); 6″, Wilts. LVIII (1889 edn.), LIX (1889 edn.).
[87] e.g. *V.C.H. Wilts.* iv. 341, 348, 361.

definable settlements.[88] Its division, however, was never institutionalized. Its settlements, called the east end and the west end of Stockton, were never differently named nor deemed separate in administration or government. The transfer of Bapton from Fisherton de la Mere in 1934 increased Stockton to 1,334 ha. (3,296 a.).[89]

The boundaries of Stockton were defined and recorded in 901 in terms which suggest that they were afterwards little changed.[90] To the north the Wylye separates it from Codford St. Mary, and to the south Grim's ditch separates it from Fonthill Bishop and Chilmark on the watershed of Wylye and Nadder. To the west the boundary with Sherrington follows a coomb, but to the east that with Bapton was drawn straight. The geology and relief of the parish are typical of the Wylye valley.[91] Near the river alluvium and gravel, and on the downs clay-with-flints, have been deposited on the otherwise outcropping chalk. The land slopes in ridges and dry valleys from the watershed, 207 m. near the boundary with Fonthill Bishop, to the Wylye, below 76 m. The pattern of land-use has also been typical, with meadow land on the alluvium, pasture and arable land on the gravel, arable land on the nearer and rough pasture on the further chalk, and Stockton wood on the clay-with-flints. In the 18th century the clay-with-flints west of Stockton wood was apparently ploughed,[92] and in the 20th century there has been afforestation on the downs.[93]

Stockton downs have been crossed by three main routes. The Roman road from Old Salisbury to the Mendips, which was possibly a ridge way in origin, passed through Stockton wood.[94] A downland road from Warminster to Wilton via Teffont Magna and Dinton passed between Stockton wood and an Iron-Age settlement called Stockton earthworks. Its crossing of Grim's ditch marked the south-east corner of the parish.[95] It was presumably ancient and was apparently well used in the later 18th century and the early 19th,[96] but it was not turnpiked and was superseded by other routes. The Amesbury–Mere road crosses the south-east corner of the parish. It was turnpiked between Amesbury and Willoughby Hedge in West Knoyle under an Act of 1762 and has become part of the main London–Exeter road.[97] Stockton is on the road linking Sherrington, Wylye, and the other villages on the south bank of the Wylye, which was turnpiked between Little Langford and Boyton as a branch of the road from Amesbury to Willoughby Hedge.[98] That road has never been so well used as the Warminster–Wilton road north of the Wylye, with which Stockton is linked by the bridge at Codford St. Mary. From Stockton village a road ran south past Conygar barn across the downs to

Chilmark.[99] It has never been made up and was no more than a track in 1978. The Wilts., Somerset & Weymouth railway line, which was built by the G.W.R. across the parish a little south of the village, was opened between Warminster and Salisbury in 1856.[1] Wylye and Codford were the nearest stations, both closed in 1955.[2]

There are a few barrows in Stockton but archaeological discoveries have been most numerous at Stockton earthworks, a settlement site of some 100 a. which has twice been excavated.[3] The settlement, one of several on the downs between the Wylye and the Nadder, lasted from the late pre-Roman Iron Age to the late Roman Period. It was a farming village but may have been additionally a posting station and even a minor market. It declined after 370.[4] The later settlement was on lower land. The charter which described its lands in 901 did not mention Stockton or a village,[5] and it is likely that the village of Stockton, first mentioned in 1086,[6] originated after and perhaps as a result of that early-10th-century charter. It was founded like so many other villages on the gravel shelf near the Wylye.[7] Among those villages Stockton was of slightly above average wealth in the early 14th century, and there were 140 poll-tax payers in 1377, again above average for the Wylye valley.[8] Stockton's assessments appear high because they included what might elsewhere have been reckoned two villages.[9] In the 16th and 17th centuries taxation assessments were possibly about average.[10] In 1801 and 1811 the population was 224. It had risen to 307 by 1841 but thereafter declined almost without interruption to 177 in 1931. The population of the enlarged parish was 268 in 1951, 214 in 1971.[11]

Settlement in Stockton village apparently began at the east end, where a nucleated village a short distance south of the Sherrington–Wylye road was clustered around the church, demesne farm-house, and rectory-house. Settlement at the west end, which was presumably later, was along the road as a street village. The two could be distinguished c. 1627 when the tenements in the west end were listed,[12] and until the mid 20th century there was a short space between them. The original and different patterns of settlement at the two ends can still be discerned but both have been modified. The east end spread westwards along the Sherrington–Wylye road, and buildings which presumably originated as small tenant farmsteads have given that end too the appearance of a street village. The lane to the church and Long Hall has never been made up and, perhaps c. 1900, was gated. There is in it a range of much altered 17th-century thatched cottages and, at its junction with the street, the school and an 18th-century house on which a

[88] See below.
[89] V.C.H. Wilts. viii. 34; Census, 1971.
[90] Eng. Hist. Doc. c. 500–1042, ed. Dorothy Whitelock, pp. 499–500.
[91] Geol. Surv. Map 1″, drift, sheet 298 (1950 edn.).
[92] W.R.O., Inclosure Award; see below.
[93] Ex inf. Mr. J. M. Stratton, Stockton Man.
[94] V.C.H. Wilts. i (1), map viii; i (2), 458; Arch. Jnl. lxxv. 101.
[95] W.R.O., Inclosure Award map.
[96] Ibid.; Andrews and Dury, Map (W.R.S. viii), pls. 4–5.
[97] V.C.H. Wilts. iv. 261–2, 265.
[98] Ibid. 257, 262.
[99] W.R.O., Inclosure Award map.

[1] V.C.H. Wilts. iv. 284.
[2] Ex inf. P.R. Dept., British Rail, W.R.
[3] V.C.H. Wilts. i (1), 108–9, 143, 191.
[4] Ibid. i (2), 429, 458, 460.
[5] Eng. Hist. Doc. c. 500–1042, ed. Whitelock, pp. 499–500.   [6] P.N. Wilts. (E.P.N.S.), 230.
[7] Geol. Surv. Map 1″, drift, sheet 298 (1950 edn.).
[8] V.C.H. Wilts. iv. 299, 307.
[9] See above.
[10] Taxation Lists (W.R.S. x), 3 (where the assessment of Thomas Topp is apparently misprinted), 124; E 179/199/370; E 179/199/398.
[11] V.C.H. Wilts. iv. 358; Census, 1971.
[12] B.L. Add. Ch. 24745.

late-15th-century stone mantelpiece from a house in Codford has been incorporated in the porch.[13] Near that house is the stump of the village cross which was moved from the west end *c.* 1604.[14] In the 18th century two substantial houses were built further east, a two-storey farm-house of chequered stone and flint bearing the date 1740 and the new rectory-house. The farm-house, which became Glebe Farm, was given an attic storey in 1864.[15] The farm buildings north-east of it are of the 19th and 20th centuries. A few of the cottages and small houses at the east end standing in 1815 have been demolished but most remain.[16] The 17th-century origins of the majority are apparent, and there are more of the 18th century there than at the west end. There has been very little building since 1815. The erection of three large buildings away from the street has given settlement at the west end a slightly more dispersed appearance than it perhaps had originally. Stockton Manor (formerly Manor Farm) was built south of the street, apparently in the Middle Ages, on arable land at the boundary between the east and west end fields.[17] In the 1590s Stockton House was built nearer the river on common pasture land north-west of the street.[18] Much of the land around it was later imparked and the direct road from Codford bridge to the village was closed. In the mid 19th century farm buildings called New (later Dairy) Farm were erected west of the village on higher land south of the Sherrington–Wylye road.[19] Most of the cottages in the street, including the Carrier's Arms built in the early 19th century when it was called the New Inn,[20] are on the north side.[21] They include a gardener's cottage of the 19th century at the entrance to Stockton park, a range of thatched cottages built in 1962, and several cottages apparently of 17th-century origin. On the south side are two 17th-century farm-houses, one dated 1693, the other restored in 1966.[22] The space between the east and west ends on the north side of the street was filled in 1948 when ten council houses were built.[23] Two more were built later. A downland farmstead where two houses were being built in 1831[24] was occupied in the 19th century, but apart from that there has been no settlement outside the village.

MANORS AND OTHER ESTATES. An estate by the Wylye, known to be that later called the manor of *STOCKTON*,[25] was forfeited in the late 9th century by the ealdorman Wulfhere and his wife when he deserted his lord and king, probably at the time of the Danish invasion. King Edward the Elder granted the land to Athelwulf in 901 when it was settled on Deorswith, apparently on her marriage to Athelwulf.[26] In 946 or 947 it was devised by Athelwold to clothe the canons of the Old Minster at Winchester.[27] Stockton passed with the see as one of the manors held by the bishops to support the monks of St. Swithun's,[28] was confirmed to the prior and monks by the pope in 1205,[29] and in 1284 was quitclaimed to the prior and convent by Bishop Pontoise as part of the composition between them.[30] Free warren was granted in 1300.[31] After the Dissolution the manor was among the estates with which in 1541 the dean and chapter of Winchester were endowed,[32] but in 1547 it was granted to Edward VI who immediately granted it to Sir William Herbert (created earl of Pembroke in 1551).[33] In 1585 Pembroke's son Henry, earl of Pembroke, sold it to John Topp, a citizen and merchant tailor of London.[34] Topp (fl. 1524, d. 1596) was a younger son of Thomas Topp (d. 1560) and grandson of Thomas Archbold alias Topp (fl. 1544), both of whom were yeomen holding in Stockton by copy and lease. John belonged to the first of three generations of the family in each of which two brothers were called John.[35] In 1595 he settled the manor and other land in Stockton which he had bought before 1585[36] on his nephew John, elder son John of John's elder brother John Topp (d. 1573) of Stockton.[37] The nephew John, sheriff of Wiltshire 1630–1, was succeeded in 1632 by his elder son John (d. 1640) whose heir was his brother John (d. 1660). John's heir was his brother Edward (d. 1665) who was succeeded by his son John (d. 1675), that John's son Edward (d. 1740), and Edward's son John (d.s.p. 1745).[38] The last John Topp's heirs were his sisters Susan, wife of Robert Everard, and Christiana, wife of Richard Lansdown. The Everards had a daughter Susan, wife of Robert Everard Balch, and in 1749 the Balches held the manor except for Lower farm.[39] In 1772 Balch sold it to Henry Biggs (d. 1800) whose heir was his son Harry (d. 1856).[40] Lower farm, sold by Lansdown to John Pinchard *c.* 1755, had passed *c.* 1760 to Pinchard's son William Wansborough Pinchard (d. 1815). William was succeeded by his son John and grandson William Price Pinchard who in 1841 sold the farm to Harry Biggs.[41] Biggs was succeeded by his son Henry Godolphin Biggs (d. 1877) and he by his nephew Maj.-Gen. Arthur Godolphin Yeatman who took the additional name Biggs in 1878. Yeatman-Biggs (d. 1898) was succeeded by his brother Huyshe Wolcott Yeatman (Yeatman-Biggs from 1898, d. 1922), bishop successively of Southwark, Worcester, and Coventry, who in 1898 bought Glebe farm.[42] In 1921 Bishop Yeatman-Biggs sold the manor to the Hon. Violet Frances Skeffington-Smyth (d. 1930) who in 1927 sold it to Oswald

13 *W.A.M.* xii. 204–5.   14 B.L. Add. Ch. 24745.
15 W.R.O. 401/2, f. 64.   16 Ibid. Inclosure Award map.
17 See below.   18 See below.
19 W.R.O., Inclosure Award map; O.S. Map 6″, Wilts. LVIII (1889 edn.).   20 W.R.O. 906/S 184.
21 See plate facing p. 208.   22 Dates on bldgs.
23 W.R.O. 401/2, f. 88.   24 Ibid. 384/6.
25 *Reg. Pontoise* (Cant. & York Soc.), ii. 610.
26 *Eng. Hist. Doc. c. 500–1042*, ed. Whitelock, pp. 499–500.
27 Finberg, *Early Wessex Chart.* p. 88.
28 *V.C.H. Wilts.* ii, p. 121.
29 *Cal. Papal Reg.* i. 21.
30 *Reg. Pontoise* (Cant. & York Soc.), ii. 436.
31 *Cal. Chart. R.* 1300–26, 1.

32 *L. & P. Hen. VIII*, xvi, p. 417.
33 *Cal. Pat.* 1547–8, 25, 172.
34 W.R.O. 212B/6262.
35 Hoare, *Mod. Wilts.* Heytesbury, 242; *W.A.M.* xxvi. 270–7; W.R.O. 130/44, deed, Gifford to Topp; 649/6, lease, Stantor to Topp.   36 See below.
37 W.R.O. 529/105, deed, Topp to Davyes.
38 *Wilts. Inq. p.m.* 1625–49 (Index Libr.), 144–7, 425–7; Hoare, *Mod. Wilts.* Heytesbury, 242; *W.A.M.* xii. 199.
39 Hoare, *Mod. Wilts.* Heytesbury, 242; *W.A.M.* xii. 106, 204; C.P. 25(2)/1234/23 Geo. II Hil.
40 Cf. W.R.O. 203/8; 906/S.C. 36, ct. held 30 Oct. 1772. For the Biggses see Burke, *Land. Gent.* (1952), 176.
41 W.R.O. 401/1, ff. 90, 130.
42 See p. 220.

Toynbee Falk.[43] In 1934 Falk sold it to the Hon. Michael Simon Scott (d. 1938).[44] In 1950 Scott's widow sold it to Mr. J. M. Stratton who owned the land in 1978.[45] Glebe farm passed in 1922 to Bishop Yeatman-Biggs's son William Huyshe Yeatman-Biggs at whose death in 1952 it passed to his grandson Mr. N. H. Yeatman-Biggs, the owner in 1978.[46]

A new farm-house called Lower Farm in the 17th century and now Long Hall was built on the manor in the Middle Ages. Two smoke-blackened trusses in the roof of the main east–west range of Long Hall are those of the medieval house. In the 16th century a massive chimney stack and a first floor were built in the hall and in the 17th century balancing wings were added to the south side of the range at the east and west ends. Surviving 17th-century fittings include the staircase in the eastern wing and some stone fire-places. In the later 18th century the north front was refaced, presumably for a Pinchard. It is of red brick with stone dressings and a central doorway beneath a Venetian window which lights a refitted first floor drawing-room with a moulded plaster ceiling. In 1900 new doorways were made in the inner faces of the south wings and short wings were added on the east and west sides.[47] In 1902 the house was leased to Henry Martin Foster-Vesey-FitzGerald (d. 1924).[48] It has since been the home of the Yeatman-Biggses. In 1923 more extensive kitchen and service quarters were added on the south and west of the west wing which had most of its floors and walls removed to form a new dining-room and picture gallery.[49]

In the late 1590s John Topp (d. 1632) built Stockton House on land of his estate called Gifford's in the then open west marsh.[50] The house passed with the manor of Stockton. It has walls of banded flint and sarsen and the plan is that of a simple rectangle, four bays by three.[51] It is, however, not certain that all the rectangle was at first, as now, built over, or whether there was originally an open central court built over in the early 19th century. The original entrance was through a three-storey porch set near the centre of the west front and into the south end of a north-west hall. The original decoration of all but one of the rooms on the ground floor has been destroyed but there are two richly moulded ceilings on the first floor and some panelling, most notably in the drawing-room.[52] There, as elsewhere in the house, the panelling appears structurally later than the ceiling and may even have been reset from another room or house. In 1802 Jeffry Wyatt designed a new staircase and redecorated several small rooms in the centre of the east side of the house.[53] He may also have made the south doorway. The sills of some of the windows in the south and west fronts have been lowered. Between 1877 and 1882 extensive restora-

tions and additions were carried out under Edmund and E. B. Ferrey for Maj.-Gen. A. G. Yeatman-Biggs.[54] The hall was decorated in the Jacobean style and an arcaded opening was made from it into the staircase hall. Additions were made on the north side of the house and continued as a two-storeyed service wing which projected some distance beyond the east front. When O. T. Falk owned the house most of the Ferreys' decorations were removed and several antique fittings, including an early-16th-century fire-place in the hall, were introduced. After 1945 all the late-19th-century additions except the water-tower and the east wing were removed. Extensive restoration work, notably on the staircase hall and the landing, has recently been done. Close to the north-west corner of the house is a mid-17th-century building which was formerly a chapel,[55] and beyond it there is a range of 17th-century stables.

Free tenure in lands assessed at 5 hides and 2½ hides was created between 1066 and 1086. The lands were then held respectively by Richer and Anschitil from whom their descents cannot be traced.[56]

In 1215 a fee of Walter de Vernon in Stockton was forfeited and ordered to be given to the bishop of Winchester because of Walter's opposition to King John, but it was presumably restored.[57] The land seems to have been Robert Vernon's in 1270 and to have passed to his son John.[58] It possibly passed in the Vernon family with land in Horningsham and, by the marriage of Isabel daughter of Richard Vernon (fl. 1333) to Peter Stantor, directly to members of the Stantor family,[59] but there is no proof of that. In 1419 a holding which had possibly been Vernon's was settled on Walter Tornay who held it in 1428, and in 1462 John Tornay apparently held it.[60] In 1479, however, land in Stockton, later reputed a manor called *STOCKTON STANTOR*,[61] belonged to Alexander Stantor who died seised of it in 1504.[62] Alexander's heir was his son Peter whose grandson Thomas Stantor held the land in 1544.[63] In 1591 Thomas's son Roger died seised of it and in 1592 Roger's son Alexander sold it to Jerome Potticary.[64] By his will Potticary (d. 1596) gave his elder son Christopher the option to buy the land for the very low sum of £200 from his younger son Jerome, to whom he devised it, within 3 years of his death or their majorities. Christopher paid and Jerome released the land to him in 1615.[65] In the early 17th century John Topp (d. 1632) and Christopher Potticary disputed the lordship of the common and waste lands at the west end of Stockton, on which Topp had built Stockton House and which had afterwards been inclosed. By successfully claiming rent in respect of Potticary's land Topp denied that land's status of manor and Potticary's claim to the lordship. The two men only 'little by

[43] W.R.O. 401/2, f. 95v.
[44] Wilts. Cuttings, xxi. 114.
[45] Ex inf. Mr. Stratton, Stockton Man.
[46] Ex inf. Mr. Yeatman-Biggs, Long Hall, Stockton.
[47] W.R.O. 401/2, f. 55v.
[48] Ibid. 153/1, lease, Southwark to FitzGerald.
[49] Ibid. 401/2, f. 55v.
[50] B.L. Add. Ch. 24745; see below.
[51] See plate facing p. 161.   [52] See *frontispiece*.
[53] *Country Life*, 21 Oct. 1905.
[54] *Builder*, 12 Aug. 1882.   [55] W.R.O. 906/S 163.
[56] *V.C.H. Wilts.* ii, p. 121.
[57] *Rot. Litt. Claus.* i. 242.

[58] C.P. 25(1)/252/22 no. 15; *Year Bk.* 18 & 19 Edw. III (Rolls Ser.), p. 293 n.
[59] Hoare, *Mod. Wilts.* Heytesbury, 47–8. A fuller acct. of the Vernons and Stantors is reserved for a later vol.
[60] W.R.O. 906/S 13; *Feud. Aids*, v. 242; B.L. Add. Ch. 26784.
[61] e.g. C 2/Jas. I/S 18/30.
[62] B.L. Add. Ch. 24876; *Cal. Inq. p.m. Hen. VII*, ii, pp. 453–4.
[63] W.R.O. 649/6, lease, Stantor to Topp; Hoare, *Mod. Wilts.* Heytesbury, 48.
[64] C 142/232 no. 38; C.P. 25(2)/242/34 Eliz. I Trin.
[65] W.R.O. 130/44, deed, Potticary to Potticary.

little grew good friends'.[66] In 1649 Potticary (d. 1650)[67] sold the estate to John Topp (d. 1660), and the lands were merged with Stockton manor.[68] A house stood on the reputed manor south of the village at the west end. In 1544 Thomas Stantor leased some of the lands to Thomas Archbold alias Topp on the condition that Topp should build a new hall-house on the site of a predecessor.[69] The condition was apparently met, and part of Topp's house was possibly the timber-framed range, jettied to the north, which was demolished in the 19th century.[70] The remainder of Topp's house was presumably demolished when in 1618, soon after he had acquired full seisin of the land, Christopher Potticary added a stone block containing principal rooms to the east.[71] In 1832 the interior of the block was altered to provide a new staircase hall.[72] In 1968 Mr. J. M. Stratton added a new building containing kitchen and service rooms to the south-west with Chilmark stone re-used from Tisbury workhouse.[73] The house was called Stockton Manor in 1978. To the north is a cruck-framed building formerly used as a barn and to the west of that a large 17th-century thatched barn with a later extension to the north.

In 1249 John de Thyny was overlord of land in Stockton[74] which apparently passed to John Vernon (fl. 1272). John Vernon granted the services due to him from it to John Tornay who was succeeded by his son John, his grandson John Tornay, and that John's son Walter (fl. 1344).[75] In 1249 and under John Vernon the tenant in demesne was Thomas Andrew,[76] possibly a descendant of Robert son of Andrew who held land in Stockton in 1199 and 1224.[77] Thomas was succeeded by his son Richard who granted much of the land freely to John Petefyn (fl. 1290) and his wife Joan.[78] That land was Alice Petefyn's in 1344.[79] In 1349 it was settled on her and her husband Richard Farley who already held an estate in Stockton.[80] Alice and Richard were apparently childless but the land seems to have descended in the Farley family, presumably through the heirs of Richard's younger brother Richard,[81] to John Farley (fl. 1416–17) and his son John on whom it was settled in 1439–40.[82] The estate was apparently held by a succession of John Farleys, by Thomas Farley in 1533–4,[83] and in 1555 by John Farley of Stratford sub Castle whose relict Elizabeth,

then wife of Richard Ockeden, held it in 1565.[84] It was afterwards acquired by a Topp and in 1619 *FARLEY'S* belonged to John Topp (d. 1632).[85] It was merged with Stockton manor.

In 1290 Walter Scudamore entered on a freely held estate,[86] in the 16th century called *GIFFORD'S*. Its previous owners are not known but it was possibly the knight's fee held by Sir Henry de Stawell in the 1260s and formerly by Robert Gifford, to whom Scudamore may have been related.[87] In 1293 Scudamore sought to replevy the land which had been taken into the king's hand for his default in a plea of Mabel, relict of his uncle Peter Scudamore who presumably held the land before him.[88] Walter Scudamore held it in 1294,[89] and the estate passed in the Scudamore family like the manor of Upton Scudamore to Thomas Reynes who in 1416 sold it to John Osborne.[90] It passed in the Osborne family, members of which held land at Boreham in Warminster.[91] John's son John died before 1446.[92] The land passed to Alice Osborne, presumably the son's widow, who was succeeded c. 1466 by her son Robert Osborne.[93] By 1492 it had descended to Robert's son Gregory (d. before 1518), and it passed, as did Boreham, to Thomas Gifford who was a grandson of Elizabeth, sister of a John Osborne, and Edward Gifford.[94] Thomas's father Maurice was a feoffee of Gregory Osborne in 1492.[95] Thomas held the land until his death between 1566 and 1577.[96] In 1582 his son John sold it to John Topp (d. 1596), and Gifford's was in 1585 merged with Stockton manor.[97] John Topp (d. 1632) built Stockton House on what had been Gifford's.[98]

In 1194 Ernold de Genuges held a free tenement.[99] In 1236 Thomas of Bapton and Cecily de Genuges conveyed an estate, possibly the same one, to Thomas le Porter.[1] It apparently passed in the Porter family. Thomas and Andrew Porter held land freely in 1282,[2] and Richard Porter of Sparsholt apparently held it before 1294.[3] In 1309 Andrew Porter of Sparsholt conveyed it to John Pedeleure,[4] possibly in trust since Porters continued to live and hold land in Stockton.[5] In 1392 Edward Porter succeeded Thomas Porter in the land.[6] In 1458 John Greenfields held freely an estate called Porter's,[7] which possibly passed to John Cockerell who settled an estate later called *EYRE'S* on himself and his wife Joan in 1493.[8] After Cockerell's

[66] B.L. Add. Ch. 24745 which summarizes, incapsulates, and enlarges upon proceedings in Chancery, the ct. of Requests, and other cts.
[67] *W.A.M.* xii. 203.
[68] W.R.O. 529/105, deed, Howe to Topp.
[69] Ibid. 649/6, lease, Stantor to Topp.
[70] Photograph in ibid. 401/1, facing f. 84v.
[71] Date on bldg. [72] *W.A.M.* xii. 203.
[73] Ex inf. Mr. Stratton.
[74] *Civil Pleas, 1249* (W.R.S. xxvi), p. 98.
[75] *Year Bk.* 18 & 19 Edw. III (Rolls Ser.), pp. 293–7.
[76] *Civil Pleas, 1249* (W.R.S. xxvi), p. 98; *Year Bk.* 18 & 19 Edw. III (Rolls Ser.), p. 293 n.
[77] *Feet of F.* 1198–9 (Pipe R. Soc. xxiv), pp. 134–5; *Cur. Reg. R.* xi, p. 321.
[78] *Year Bk.* 18 & 19 Edw. III (Rolls Ser.), p. 295 n.; Mun. D. & C. Winton., ct. roll, 1290–1.
[79] *Year Bk.* 18 & 19 Edw. III (Rolls Ser.), p. 293 and n.
[80] B.L. Add. Ch. 24745; W.R.O. 906/S 4–5.
[81] W.R.O. 906/S 9–10.
[82] B.L. Add. Ch. 24745.
[83] Ibid.; 24380 (1486); 24383 (1518).
[84] W.R.O. 906/S 23–4. [85] C 2/Jas. I/T 7/19.
[86] Mun. D. & C. Winton., ct. roll, 1290–1.

[87] *Reg. Pontoise* (Cant. & York Soc.), ii. 390; Hoare, *Mod. Wilts.* Heytesbury, 238.
[88] *Cal. Close,* 1288–96, 327.
[89] *Feet of F.* 1272–1327 (W.R.S. i), p. 39.
[90] *V.C.H. Wilts.* viii. 81; B.L. Add. Ch. 24874.
[91] *V.C.H. Wilts.* viii. 103.
[92] W.R.O. 906/S.C. 11, ct. held 7 Oct. 1446.
[93] Ibid. 906/S.C. 13, ct. held 16 Apr. 1466.
[94] B.L. Add. Ch. 24381; 24383; W.R.O. 906/S 17; *V.C.H. Wilts.* viii. 103.
[95] W.R.O. 906/S 17.
[96] *Survey of Lands of Wm., First Earl of Pembroke,* ed. C. R. Straton (Roxburghe Club, 1909), i. 207; W.R.O. 130/44, deed, Gifford to Topp.
[97] W.R.O. 130/44, deed, Gifford to Topp; see above.
[98] B.L. Add. Ch. 24745.
[99] *Cur. Reg. R.* 1194–5 (Pipe R. Soc. xiv), 74.
[1] C.P. 25(1)/250 no. 85.
[2] Mun. D. & C. Winton., ct. roll, 1281–2.
[3] *Chartulary Winch. Cath.* ed. A. W. Goodman, p. 101.
[4] *Feet of F.* 1272–1327 (W.R.S. i), p. 75.
[5] e.g. *Inq. Non.* (Rec. Com.), 171.
[6] W.R.O. 108/13.
[7] B.L. Add. Ch. 24369. [8] W.R.O. 906/S 18–19.

death his land passed, apparently before 1514, to Robert Eyre, the husband of Cockerell's relative and heir Elizabeth.[9] Cockerell's executor conveyed it to Eyre in 1528–9.[10] Eyre's land passed to his son William and after William's death to John Cooke of Ringwood (Hants).[11] In 1586 Cooke sold it to Jerome Potticary and from 1592 Eyre's passed with the reputed manor of Stockton Stantor.[12]

ECONOMIC HISTORY. Prehistoric stock husbandry and agriculture on the downs are indicated by the evidence of enclosures near the site of the settlement at Stockton earthworks and of the extensive field system north and east of it.[13] In 901 Stockton was reckoned as 10 hides, in 946 or 947 as 12 hides, and in 1066 again as 10 hides.[14] In 1086 it contained the demesne lands of the bishop of Winchester, 3½ hides, the lands of his 4 villeins and 6 bordars, and the lands of his 2 free tenants, highly rated at 7½ hides. Each class of land had on it 2 ploughs. The demesne was worth over £5, the tenants' lands £4. There were 10 a. of meadow, pasture 5 furlongs by 2 furlongs, and 40 a. of woodland.[15] Later there were at Stockton two separate units of common husbandry, each with its own arable fields, meadows, and pastures. That in the eastern half of the parish was the demesne and customarily held lands of Stockton manor, worked from the settlement at the east end, and that in the western half was the freeholders' land, worked from the settlement at the west end.[16] The two were separated by the drove leading to the down past the present Stockton Manor.[17] In 1566 the east end contained some 23 yardlands, c. 1627 the west end some 24 yardlands; the two ends some 1,150 a. and 950 a. respectively in 1815.[18] The separate development of the two units cannot be precisely dated. It is, however, possible that the grant of extensive land to be held freely, made by the bishop between 1066 and 1086,[19] either laid the foundation of or reflected the existence of the division, and likely that, although not unequivocally mentioned in documents earlier than the 16th century, the two economic units of the manor were separate throughout the Middle Ages.

The demesne and customary land at the east end included some 450 a. of arable land c. 1810.[20] That was worked in two fields in the 13th century,[21] in four in the 16th century and later.[22] South of it there were also some 450 a. of common down c. 1810.[23] In the 13th century, when great areas were said to be ploughed,[24] there was perhaps more arable land and less pasture, and in the later Middle Ages perhaps less arable land and more pasture since in the 17th and 18th centuries, when sheep stints were reduced,[25] pasture was possibly going under the plough. In 1566 there were nominally over 500 a. of arable land. The area of down, which included a cow down, was clearly under-estimated at 200 a. There was a common meadow, Broad mead, c. 15 a., and a common pasture, East marsh, 3½ a., for the tenants who also had certain feeding rights in the demesne Oxen marsh, c. 2 a.[26]

In 1248 a nominal 260 a. were sown on the demesne,[27] a figure rather below average for the 13th century, and in 1316 a nominal 292 a. were sown.[28] The demesne land was scattered about the fields but, at least in the 16th century, was largely in complete furlongs.[29] By then Conygar close, 2 a., had been inclosed.[30] In the Middle Ages labour services seem to have been largely sufficient to cultivate the demesne.[31] They were supplemented or replaced by wage labour in the 13th century but remained the basis of demesne cultivation in the 14th.[32] The arable land, meadows, and lowland pastures of the prior and convent of St. Swithun's demesne had been leased by 1396.[33] In 1248 over 400 demesne wethers were kept on the common downs,[34] and throughout the 13th century totals over 300 were normal. In the later 13th century a ewe flock of c. 50 was kept for the prior and convent,[35] but afterwards the wether flock was usually supplied from their breeding flocks at Enford and Alton Priors.[36] The flock was not leased with the land, and wool continued to be supplied from Stockton to St. Swithun's until c. 1484 when the flock was leased. By then, however, it had been reduced from over 400 in the early 15th century to between 150 and 200.[37] In 1566 the demesne farm measured some 250 a. with feeding for 690 sheep. The farmer shared his 4 a. in Broad mead and 3 a. called Black mead north of the Wylye with the farmer of Fonthill Bishop manor.[38]

In the later 13th century there were some 4 virgaters, 12 ½-virgaters, and 7 other customary tenants. They owed low money rents and labour services based on harvest work for the virgaters, work 3 days a week and additionally in certain seasons for the ½-virgaters, and daily harvest work

[9] Ibid. 906/S.C. 18, ct. held 19 May 1514; C 1/405/13.
[10] W.N. & Q. ii. 562.
[11] C 146/8600; C 2/Eliz. I/C 16/25.
[12] W.R.O. 130/44, covenant, Cooke with Potticary; see above.
[13] V.C.H. Wilts. i (1), 269, 278; i (2), 429.
[14] Finberg, Early Wessex Chart. pp. 79, 88; V.C.H. Wilts. ii, p. 121.
[15] V.C.H. Wilts. ii, p. 121.
[16] Cf. First Pembroke Survey, ed. Straton, i. 207–15; B.L. Add. Ch. 24745; Sar. Dioc. R.O., Glebe Terriers, late 16th cent., 1608.
[17] Cf. W.R.O. 153/1, map, 1640; Inclosure Award map.
[18] First Pembroke Survey, ed. Straton, i. 208–13; B.L. Add. Ch. 24745; W.R.O., Inclosure Award.
[19] V.C.H. Wilts. ii, p. 121.
[20] W.R.O., Inclosure Award map.
[21] e.g. Mun. D. & C. Winton., acct. roll, 1280.
[22] First Pembroke Survey, ed. Straton, i. 208–9; W.R.O. 906/S 143.
[23] W.R.O., Inclosure Award map.

[24] Katharine A. Hanna, 'Winch. Cath. Custumal' (Southampton Univ. Coll. M.A. thesis, 1954), 474; Mun. D. & C. Winton., acct. roll, 1282.
[25] e.g. W.R.O. 906/S.C. 25, ct. held 9 Oct. 1616; 212B/6263, ct. held 24 May 1704.
[26] First Pembroke Survey, ed. Straton, i. 208–15.
[27] Mun. D. & C. Winton., acct. roll, 1248.
[28] e.g. ibid. acct. roll, 1316.
[29] Ibid.; First Pembroke Survey, ed. Straton, i. 208–9.
[30] First Pembroke Survey, ed. Straton, i. 208.
[31] Hanna, 'Winch. Cath. Custumal', 468–74.
[32] e.g. Mun. D. & C. Winton., acct. rolls, 1280, 1316.
[33] Joan G. Greatrex, 'Admin. Winch. Cath. Priory temp. Beaufort' (Ottawa Univ. Ph.D. thesis, 1972), 98–9.
[34] Mun. D. & C. Winton., acct. roll, 1248.
[35] e.g. ibid. acct. rolls, 1267, 1280, 1282.
[36] e.g. ibid. acct. rolls, 1309, 1316; Greatrex, 'Admin. Winch. Cath.', 170.
[37] B.L. Add. Ch. 24395–420.
[38] First Pembroke Survey, ed. Straton, i. 208–9.

and a day a week at other times for the remainder. When works were performed there were large allowances of produce and food.[39] Personal servitude, which was still occasionally noticed in the 16th century,[40] perhaps survived longer at Stockton than was usual elsewhere. In 1566 twelve copyholders shared some 12 yardlands, each of which was reckoned to contain a nominal 24 a. of arable land, a small close, rights in the common meadow and marsh, and feeding for 60 sheep and stints for other animals. They held a nominal 274 a. of arable land and rights for 690 sheep.[41]

By the early 18th century some 9 a. of upland pasture had been inclosed, allotted in at least ten several pieces, and converted to arable, and part of Stockton wood had apparently been made a cow down, 28 a.[42] The demesne had by then been split into at least two, Lower farm and a farm worked from a house called Luxous.[43] It was later reunited as Lower farm by William Wansborough Pinchard who apparently occupied and added to his farm some land he held by lease.[44] About 1765 most of the remaining east end lands of Stockton manor were held by lease. The pattern seems to have remained one of small- or medium-sized holdings worked from farmsteads in the street.[45] The largest known is that of John Barnes, 69 a. with feeding rights in 1759.[46] Until the later 18th century husbandry remained genuinely in common, the frequent changes in its rules and practices being constantly recorded by the manor court.[47] By the time that the Stockton Inclosure Act was passed in 1809, however, the Biggses had kept in hand or bought nearly all the leaseholds.[48] After inclosure, which was apparently in 1810 although an award was not made until 1815,[49] the east end was split almost entirely into two several farms. John Pinchard's (Lower), some 195 a. of his own and some 70 a. held by lease from Harry Biggs, was worked from Long Hall; the rector's (Glebe), some 650 a. allotted to replace glebe in the west end and tithes, was worked from a farmstead north of the Sherrington–Wylye road given by Biggs in exchange for land.[50]

The freeholders' land at the west end c. 1810 included some 400 a. of arable in which the usual strip cultivation prevailed,[51] a roughly similar area of down, an apparently common meadow, and a common marsh.[52] It was earlier divided among some five principal estates of which only Stantor's is known to have included land held by customary tenants.[53] Stantor's and Farley's were each assessed at 5 yardlands c. 1627,[54] Gifford's at 4 in 1353 and

c. 1627,[55] Eyre's at 7 in 1566 and c. 1627,[56] and the glebe at 2 in 1341 and c. 1627.[57] None seems to have included land or feeding rights in the east end beyond very limited use of Broad mead.[58]

In the mid 16th century Topps took most of the lands on long leases, Eyre's before c. 1540,[59] 2½ yardlands of Stantor's in 1544 and ½ yardland later,[60] Gifford's in 1563,[61] and Farley's in 1565.[62] A lawsuit between a Thomas Topp and William Eyre over the use of Eyre's chief messuage c. 1545, and a lease in reversion by Eyre in 1559 expressly prohibiting assignment to Topp and his kinsmen, suggest that they could be difficult tenants.[63] About 1600 all the freeholds apart from the glebe belonged to John Topp (d. 1632) and Christopher Potticary.[64] Topp's were apparently merged into a single farm but, until lives ended and leases expired, Potticary had several tenants including Topp. Apparently by agreement between Topp, Potticary, and the rector the common marsh, on which Topp had built Stockton House, was divided and inclosed c. 1602.[65] The marsh was apparently a wide strip of land, perhaps 50 a., running from north-west to south-east between the Wylye and the old road to Codford St. Mary.[66] After inclosure parts of it were possibly irrigated for Topp by John Knight who irrigated Wylye meadows in 1632, lived at Stockton, and whose presumed relative William Knight held a close at the west end.[67] Topp's newly built weir on the Wylye was mentioned in 1633.[68] When it was mapped in 1640 the west end arable land included some 50 a. north of the Sherrington–Wylye road of which some 5 a. near Stockton House were in a new close.[69] There were then three fields in which the pattern of strips remained with only a few furlongs undivided.[70] By 1671 a fourth field had been created. To judge from the rector's stint feeding on the down was roughly at the rate of 40 sheep to a yardland in summer, 30 in winter.[71]

Topp's, possibly worked from buildings near Stockton House, and Potticary's, worked from the buildings later called Manor Farm (now Stockton Manor), apparently remained separate farms.[72] In the 18th century, however, the two were merged as Upper farm, worked from Manor Farm, and common husbandry was virtually eliminated.[73] By 1736 an area of down had been burn-baked, presumably the c. 60 a. on the clay-with-flints in the extreme south part of the parish called the Beaks in 1815.[74] It was divided between Edward Topp and the rector who was allotted 4 a. of arable land and 3 a. of furze.[75] The rector's arable land remained in scattered strips, but at least from 1789 they were

[39] Hanna, 'Winch. Cath. Custumal', 468–74.
[40] e.g. Mun. D. & C. Winton., ledger bk. II, f. 64v.
[41] First Pembroke Survey, ed. Straton, i. 210–15.
[42] W.R.O. 906/S 71; 212B/6263, ct. held 24 May 1704; cf. Inclosure Award map.   [43] Ibid. 906/S 97.
[44] Ibid. Land Tax.   [45] Ibid. 906/S 153.
[46] Ibid. 906/S 143.   [47] e.g. ibid. 906/S.C. 36.
[48] Ibid. Inclosure Award; cf. 906/S 186; 906/S 188–9; 906/S 191.   [49] Ibid. 906/S 193; 906/S.C. 46.
[50] Ibid. Inclosure Award.   [51] Ibid.; 906/S 11.
[52] Ibid. Inclosure Award; Hanna, 'Winch. Cath. Custumal', 474; B.L. Add. Ch. 26784; 24745.
[53] C 3/176/23.   [54] B.L. Add. Ch. 24745.
[55] Ibid.; 24394.
[56] First Pembroke Survey, ed. Straton, i. 207; B.L. Add. Ch. 24745.
[57] Inq. Non. (Rec. Com.), 171; B.L. Add. Ch. 24745.

[58] First Pembroke Survey, ed. Straton, i. 215.
[59] C 1/1118/53–6.
[60] W.R.O. 649/6, lease, Stantor to Topp; 906/S 27.
[61] B.L. Add. Ch. 24878.
[62] W.R.O. 906/S 24.
[63] C 1/1118/53–6; C 146/8600.
[64] See above.   [65] B.L. Add. Ch. 24745.
[66] Cf. ibid.; W.R.O., Inclosure Award map.
[67] Pembroke Man. 1631–2 (W.R.S. ix), p. 138; Sar. Dioc. R.O., Glebe Terrier, 1608.
[68] Wilts. Inq. p.m. 1625–49 (Index Libr.), 145.
[69] W.R.O. 153/1.
[70] Ibid.; Sar. Dioc. R.O., Glebe Terrier, 1608.
[71] Sar. Dioc. R.O., Glebe Terrier.
[72] W.R.O. 906/S 49.   [73] Ibid. 906/S.C. 41/1.
[74] Ibid. 906/S 101; Inclosure Award map.
[75] Sar. Dioc. R.O., Glebe Terrier, 1783.

leased to Henry Biggs and were presumably part of Upper farm.[76] The rector's commonable and inclosed lands in the west end were all allotted to and exchanged with Harry Biggs at inclosure when Upper became a several farm of c. 925 a. including some 60 a. of east end land.[77]

In the 19th century some 300 a. of woodland and park were kept in hand by the lords of the manor.[78] Manor (formerly Upper) farm, 952 a. in 1841,[79] was held by Thomas Chandler, whose patented liquid-manure drill was being manufactured by the firm of Reeves in 1848.[80] Lower remained a separate farm until c. 1870 when it was added to Manor;[81] the farm buildings at Long Hall were subsequently given up. For a short time in the late 19th century Glebe was possibly united to Manor,[82] but it has otherwise remained a separate mixed farm of some 650 a.[83] In the mid 19th century New (later Dairy) Farm was built as a new dairy for Manor farm, 1,120 a. in 1925.[84] Manor farm has since taken in much of the park-land around Stockton House, and in 1978 its c. 1,450 a. were worked by its owner with lands in Codford St. Mary and Chitterne as an extensive mixed farm.[85]

There were 40 a. of woodland in 1086.[86] In 1566 there were four coppices of hazels and small oaks, 56 a., presumably Stockton wood on the east end down,[87] which in 1613 John Topp (d. 1632) accused his tenant of Lower farm of misusing.[88] In 1815 there were in addition some 30 a. of woodland on the downs.[89] In the 20th century the woodland on the downs has been increased to some 250 a., including the former cow down, whose uses included sport and some commercial exploitation.[90]

The Topp and Potticary families both included clothiers. Richard (d. c. 1570), Jerome (d. 1596), and Christopher Potticary (d. 1650) were all described as clothiers.[91] Their business was presumably the manufacturing of cloth. Christopher was a prominent clothier who in 1611 sold broadcloths in London and in 1621 was charged with roving cloth outside a corporate town.[92] Later he favoured say-dyed cloths and c. 1627 was said to have £2,000 stock.[93] Although several Stockton weavers were named in the late 16th century and the 17th,[94] it is not clear how much of the Potticarys' manufacturing was at Stockton. John Topp (d. 1596), who bought Stockton manor, and another John Topp were London clothiers.[95] There is, however, no evidence that they practised their trade at Stockton.

There was a mill worth 10s. at Stockton in 1086.[96]

LOCAL GOVERNMENT. By 1248 the prior and convent of St. Swithun's had begun to hold a biannual private view of frankpledge and to enforce the assize of ale for Stockton.[97] The prior's liberty to do so by prescription was recorded in 1255,[98] and in the mid 13th century courts were held at Martin-mas and Hock-tide as was usual on the estates of both see and priory of Winchester.[99] Jurisdiction over the whole parish was claimed,[1] and only in the 17th century, when Christopher Potticary required his tenants in the west end to refuse to attend court or serve as tithingman, was the claim challenged, and then unsuccessfully.[2] Records of the courts held from the 13th century to the 19th survive in unusual number.[3] They reveal, however, little unusual in the procedure and business of the courts. In the Middle Ages the normal business of the manor, pleas between tenants, payment of the incidents of personal servitude, and, especially when it was in hand, trespasses on the demesne, was recorded with the biannual view. Offences under leet jurisdiction were presented by the tithingman whose presentments were verified and sometimes supplemented by a jury of freemen from c. 1335. There was a constable in 1339.[4] Many affrays and breaches of the assize of ale were presented in the 14th century, but the number declined in the 15th so that in the 1490s the courts transacted comparatively little business. By then, however, public nuisances, proscribed games, and butchers' and bakers' offences were being occasionally dealt with. The courts were busier in the 16th and 17th centuries. Presentments in the view by the homage began to be recorded in the 1470s and in the 16th century the increasing numbers of public nuisances and breaches of manorial custom were presented by the free jurors. The tithingman was restricted to increasingly infrequent presentments of affrays and breaches of the assizes. In the 17th century the courts, or at least their recorded transactions, were split into a view of frankpledge proceeding on the presentments of a 'jury for the king' and a court baron held the same day and proceeding on the present-ments of the homage. The jurors presented failures to repair roads, footpaths, and ditches and, for example, in 1629 listed those who had failed to obey an order of the parish overseers to repair.[5] The homage dealt with manorial business such as holdings needing repair and unlicensed sub-letting, and presented the customs of the manor and deaths of tenants. The two courts merged in the 18th century and became annual. The homage presented and in the later 18th century their presentment of the customs became almost the only business. That ceased at inclosure and the last court was held c. 1838.

There are overseers' accounts for the period 1661–1763.[6] They record expenditure of £9 9s. 6d. in 1660, a sum slightly below average for the period

76 Ibid.; W.R.O. 153/1, lease, Good to Biggs.
77 W.R.O., Inclosure Award.   78 Ibid. 93/4 (1855).
79 Ibid. 906/S 210.   80 V.C.H. Wilts. iv. 193 n.
81 W.R.O. 93/5.   82 Ibid. 185, rate bk.
83 e.g. ibid.; local information.
84 W.R.O., Inclosure Award map; O.S. Map 6", Wilts. LVIII (1889 edn.); W.A.S. Libr., sale cat. xix, no. 1.
85 Ex inf. Mr. J. M. Stratton, Stockton Man.
86 V.C.H. Wilts. ii, p. 121.
87 First Pembroke Survey, ed. Straton, i. 215.
88 Early-Stuart Tradesmen (W.R.S. xv), p. 74.
89 W.R.O., Inclosure Award.
90 Ex inf. Mr. Stratton.
91 W.N. & Q. iv. 108, 112; v. 411; mon. in ch.

92 Early-Stuart Tradesmen (W.R.S. xv), pp. 63, 99.
93 V.C.H. Wilts. iv. 154; B.L. Add. Ch. 24745.
94 Wilts. Par. Reg. (Mar.), ed. W. P. W. Phillimore and J. Sadler, iii. 90–2.   95 W.A.M. xxiv. 285–6.
96 V.C.H. Wilts. ii, p. 121.
97 Mun. D. & C. Winton., acct. roll, 1248.
98 Rot. Hund. (Rec. Com.), ii (1), 233.
99 Mun. D. & C. Winton., acct. roll, 1267.
1 e.g. First Pembroke Survey, ed. Straton, i. 215.
2 B.L. Add. Ch. 24745.
3 The remainder of this para. is based on ct. rec. in B.L.; Winch. cath. libr.; W.R.O.
4 W.R.O. 108/1.
5 B.L. Add. Ch. 24392.   6 W.R.O. 203/7.

1660–1700. Expenditure was over £20 a year in the period 1714–16 but otherwise averaged some £15 a year from 1700 to 1750. The old, the sick, and the young were relieved mainly by the provision of food, clothing, and fuel and of money to pay rent and to keep children. After 1750 regular doles were more often given and average expenditure roughly doubled in the period 1750–62. The parish joined Warminster poor-law union in 1835 when average expenditure on its poor was £105.[7] There are road surveyors' accounts for 1837–50 and various later records.[8]

CHURCH. A priest mentioned c. 1130[9] possibly served a church at Stockton, but the earliest firm evidence of the church is later. Before 1172 Jocelin de Bohun, bishop of Salisbury, at the request of Henry de Blois, bishop of Winchester, and Walter, the prior in England of the order of St. John of Jerusalem, granted the church to the hospital of St. Cross near Winchester, founded by Bishop Blois and committed to the care of the prior. The church was among the hospital's possessions confirmed by Richard I in 1189.[10] Hubert Walter, bishop of Salisbury 1189–93, confirmed Jocelin's grant but required that a vicar should be provided for.[11] It is unlikely that a vicarage was ordained. Possibly after one of the late-12th-century disputes over the hospital between the bishop of Winchester and the prior of St. John's, the hospital apparently surrendered the church to the bishop of Winchester for a yearly pension from it of £5, then a large proportion of its value.[12] It seems likely that the bishop appointed a rector since the advowson later passed with the see of Winchester. The king presented sede vacante in 1238.[13] The bishop's right of patronage was confirmed in 1284.[14] Presentations were made by bishops of Winchester except that in 1472 the bishop of Salisbury collated by lapse.[15] In 1852 the advowson was transferred to the see of Oxford and in 1885 by exchange to the dean and chapter of Salisbury.[16] In 1929 Bapton was transferred to Stockton parish from Fisherton de la Mere parish,[17] a transfer recommended by the parliamentary commissioners in 1650.[18] The rectory was united with the benefice of Wylye with Fisherton de la Mere in 1957. That united benefice was dissolved in 1973 when a new benefice of Codford St. Peter with St. Mary, Upton Lovell and Stockton was created. The dean and chapter of Salisbury had the right to alternate presentation from 1957 to 1973 and to a presentation third in turn after 1973.[19]

The living was valued at £6 13s. 4d. in 1291, at £18 net in 1535, and at £115 net in 1650, valuations which suggest rather more than average income.[20] Under the inclosure award of 1815 the rector was allotted 623 a. in place of tithes and received by exchange a farmstead.[21] The living, with a net yearly income averaging £493 in the period 1829–31, was not poor in the 19th century.[22] The pension to St. Cross was still paid in the mid 19th century.[23] Glebe farm was sold in 1898.[24]

In 1341 the rector was possibly entitled to all the tithes of the whole parish.[25] The prior and convent of St. Swithun's later claimed freedom from tithes for the sheep on their demesne and moduses for the tithes of their hay and wood. About 1510 the rector denied the convent's claim which in respect of the sheep was then limited to the stock of 200 nominally leased to the farmer.[26] The exemption and moduses apparently continued. The lord of the manor claimed them in 1566,[27] and in the late 16th century and in 1671 they were recorded in terriers of the glebe.[28] In the early 18th century, however, when other tithes were paid in kind, the rector claimed tithe of the 200 sheep and tithe in kind from the former demesne meadows, both of which were then part of Lower farm. There was a decree in the rector's favour but Edward Topp refused to allow his tenant of Lower farm to pay more than the modus and the dispute was protracted.[29] In 1783 the moduses of 3d. for the hay of Lower farm and of 3s. 4d. for the eastern woods were paid. The rector was then entitled to the remaining tithes in kind, presumably including those of all the sheep on Lower farm.[30]

In the 13th century the glebe was reckoned as ½ hide, at Stockton equivalent to 2 virgates.[31] In the later 16th century and in 1608 it was estimated at 50–55 a., most of it at the west end, to which feeding rights for 2 virgates were attached. In 1783 it measured 51 a., again with feeding rights.[32] After inclosure Glebe farm was some 625 a.[33] In 1591 eight trees were granted for Stockton rectory-house, possibly being rebuilt by the then new rector.[34] The house adjoined the churchyard to the east.[35] In 1772 a malt-house attached to it, some service rooms, and a cottage on the glebe called 'the vicarage-house' were pulled down.[36] In 1783 the house consisted of five rooms on the ground floor and four on the first floor, and several extensions carried the range southwards.[37] A new house was built east of the old between 1790 and 1792 to designs of Anthony Sarjeant of Wimborne Minster (Dors.).[38] It has a principal front of five bays in red

[7] Poor Law Com. 2nd Rep. 560.
[8] W.R.O. 93/1–13; 185; 203/9–10.
[9] Reg. St. Osmund (Rolls Ser.), i. 349.
[10] B.L. Harl. MS. 1616, ff. 10v.–12; V.C.H. Hants, ii. 193–4.   [11] B.L. Harl. MS. 1616, f. 2v.
[12] Ibid. ff. 36–37v.; V.C.H. Hants, ii. 194; see below.
[13] Cal. Pat. 1232–47, 229.
[14] Reg. Pontoise (Cant. & York Soc.), ii. 420, 431.
[15] Phillipps, Wilts. Inst. (index in W.A.M. xxviii. 230).
[16] Lond. Gaz. 4 June 1852, p. 1580; 2 Jan. 1885, pp. 15–16.   [17] Ibid. 20 Dec. 1929, pp. 8281–2.
[18] V.C.H. Wilts. viii. 44.
[19] Lond. Gaz. 1 Nov. 1957, pp. 6321–2; 16 Nov. 1973, p. 13643.
[20] Tax. Eccl. (Rec. Com.), 181; Valor Eccl. (Rec. Com.), ii. 103; W.A.M. xl. 299.
[21] W.R.O., Inclosure Award; see above, p. 218.
[22] Rep. Com. Eccl. Revenues, 848–9.
[23] W.A.S. Libr., W. H. Jones, par. hist. notes.
[24] Wilts. Cuttings, xii. 201.
[25] Inq. Non. (Rec. Com.), 171.
[26] Mun. D. & C. Winton., ledger bk. II, ff. 46, 77v.
[27] First Pembroke Survey, ed. Straton, i. 209.
[28] Sar. Dioc. R.O., Glebe Terriers.
[29] E 126/18 f. 532 and v.; E 134/4 Anne Trin./5; E 134/5 & 6 Anne Hil./5; W.R.O. 906/S 67–70.
[30] Sar. Dioc. R.O., Glebe Terrier.
[31] Hanna, 'Winch. Cath. Custumal', 468, 474.
[32] Sar. Dioc. R.O., Glebe Terriers.
[33] W.R.O., Inclosure Award; 93/4.
[34] E 178/3100; see below.   [35] W.R.O. 628 (1742).
[36] Sar. Dioc. R.O., Faculties, iii, p. 193.
[37] Ibid. Glebe Terrier.
[38] Ibid. Mortgages, no. 2.

brick and a service wing to the south. There were additions and alterations at various times in the 19th century. The house was sold c. 1957.[39]

In 1393 the income from the benefice was sequestrated because the rector Nicholas Salisbury was non-resident. Salisbury claimed that he was licensed to be absent but in 1394 resigned on an exchange.[40] John Wykeham, a relative of his patron, was presented in 1395 before he had taken sub-deacon's orders.[41] James Blakedon, bishop of Achonry and suffragan in Salisbury and Bath and Wells dioceses, was presented in 1447.[42] John Terry, rector 1590–1625, was the author of anti-Roman tracts.[43] His successor was a pluralist, Christopher Green, who was assisted by a curate in 1631 and 1641.[44] Green was expelled and Samuel Wright was admitted in 1646.[45] Wright, who sub-scribed to the *Concurrent Testimony* of 1648, in 1650 preached twice on Sundays and expounded once a week.[46] In 1662 it was said that much had been done to restore the Anglican order.[47] Edward Innes, rector 1772–89, was rector of Devizes and lived there.[48] In 1783 his curate, who was probably also curate of Codford St. Mary and Fisherton de la Mere, held services twice on Sundays and celebrated Holy Communion four times a year. He catechized children in Lent and expounded scripture to them.[49] On Census Sunday in 1851 services were attended by congregations of 60 in the morning and 100 in the afternoon.[50] In 1864 there were still two Sunday services and communion was administered to 35–40 communicants some six times in the year.[51] A surpliced choir was formed by Robert White Fiske, rector from 1883.[52] In 1901 Holy Communion was celebrated every Sunday and twice at the great festivals and on the first Sunday in every month, there were three other Sunday services including a children's service at which there was catechizing, and there were daily services.[53]

The church of *ST. JOHN THE BAPTIST*, so called in 1560,[54] is built of ashlar and has a chancel with north vestry, aisled and clerestoried nave with north porch, and west tower. The two-bay nave arcades are of the late 12th century. The tower and the west window of the north aisle were built in the early 13th century, perhaps in the last stage in the same phase of construction as the arcades. The chancel was apparently enlarged in the 13th century and nothing in it seems to be older than that. In the earlier 14th century both aisles appear to have been widened and the south aisle was rebuilt. The division between the nave and chancel was apparently

moved several feet eastwards. An arched opening was then made through the wall east of the arcade and rather later a similar opening was made to the north aisle. The upper stage of the tower was possibly reconstructed about the same time. The clerestory and the porch were added in the 15th century and the wall between chancel and nave, which formerly had brackets for a rood beam on its west face,[55] was possibly built about the same time. The east end of the north aisle appears to have been partly rebuilt in the 17th century when the large Topp monument was placed there. The roof of the south aisle is of 1662–4, that of the nave, reconstructed in 1757,[56] was essentially of the 15th century until renewed in 1958.[57] The chancel was partly rebuilt in 1840, the eastern end of the north aisle was again rebuilt in 1842 when a vaulted ceiling was removed,[58] and the south aisle was restored in 1844.[59] In 1879 there was a general restoration to designs of Edmund and E. B. Ferrey.[60] The west gallery, which had existed in 1730,[61] was removed and the vestry built. In 1910 an elaborate oak rood-screen, designed by Bodley and Garner, was erected by Bishop Yeatman-Biggs.[62]

There were three bells in 1553.[63] In 1660 they were cast into four by John Lott of Warminster. Bell (iii) was recast by the younger John Lott in 1683,[64] and the tenor was later replaced by a bell founded at Salisbury in the period 1380–1420.[65] Those four bells were still hanging in the church in 1978.[66]

In 1553 2 oz. of plate were taken for the king and a chalice of 8 oz. left. Two flagons, one hall-marked 1634, were given in 1640 by John Topp (d. 1640) who devised £20 to ornament the communion table. A new chalice and paten hall-marked 1681 were given by another John Topp, presumably either him who died in 1675 or him who died in 1745. In 1843 the rector Roger Frampton St. Barbe gave an alms-dish and c. 1890 there was also an old pewter alms-basin.[67] The church retains the Topp donations.[68]

The registers date from 1589.[69] The earliest entries are transcriptions made by the schoolmaster Thomas Crockford who was vicar of Fisherton de la Mere from 1613, and until the late 1620s kept Stockton registers as elaborately as he did those of Fisherton and Wylye.[70]

NONCONFORMITY. A parishioner said in 1674 to have been excommunicated for refusing to attend

[39] *Lond. Gaz.* 1 Nov. 1957, pp. 6321–2.
[40] *V.C.H. Wilts.* iii. 24; Phillipps, *Wilts. Inst.* i. 80.
[41] Phillipps, *Wilts. Inst.* i. 81; *Reg. Wykeham* (Hants Rec. Soc.), 339; A. B. Emden, *Biog. Reg. Univ. Oxf. to 1500*, iii. 2110–11.
[42] Phillipps, *Wilts. Inst.* i. 138; Emden, op. cit. i. 197–8.
[43] *D.N.B.*
[44] *Walker Revised*, ed. A. G. Matthews, 373; *Cal. S.P. Dom. 1631–3*, 63; *W.N. & Q.* vii. 499.
[45] *Walker Revised*, ed. Matthews, 373.
[46] *W.A.M.* xl. 299; *Calamy Revised*, ed. A. G. Matthews, 558. [47] *V.C.H. Wilts.* iii. 44.
[48] Phillipps, *Wilts. Inst.* ii. 85, 95; *Vis. Queries, 1783* (W.R.S. xxvii), p. 204 n.
[49] *Vis. Queries, 1783* (W.R.S. xxvii), pp. 204–5.
[50] H.O. 129/260/3/9/11.
[51] Sar. Dioc. R.O., Vis. Queries.
[52] *V.C.H. Wilts.* iii. 78. [53] Wilts. Tracts, 96, no. 1.
[54] *W.A.M.* xxvi. 270. [55] Ibid. xxvii. 254.
[56] W.R.O. 203/7, chwdns.' accts.
[57] H. J. S. Banks, *Ch. of St. John the Baptist at Stockton* (Wilton, priv. print. 1976).
[58] *W.A.M.* xii. 117; xxvii. 252, 253.
[59] Ibid. xii. 111; W.R.O. 203/8.
[60] Sar. Dioc. R.O., Pet. for Faculties, bdle. 27, no. 5.
[61] W.R.O. 203/7, chwdns.' accts.
[62] Sar. Dioc. R.O., Pet. for Faculties, bdle. 42, no. 32; plaque in ch. [63] Walters, *Wilts. Bells*, 206.
[64] Ibid.; W.R.O. 203/7, chwdns.' accts.
[65] Walters, *Wilts. Bells*, 206.
[66] Ex inf. the incumbent, the Revd. A. B. Elkins, Codford Rectory. [67] Nightingale, *Wilts. Plate*, 75–7.
[68] Ex inf. the Revd. A. B. Elkins.
[69] W.R.O. 203/1–6. The marriage reg. has been printed: *Wilts. Par. Reg. (Mar.)*, ed. Phillimore and Sadler, iii. 89–100.
[70] *W.N. & Q.* vii. 575; *W.A.M.* xxxviii. 139; *V.C.H. Wilts.* viii. 45.

church had presumably conformed or left the parish by 1676 when there was said to be no nonconformist.[71] In the later 18th century and the early 19th there were a few dissenters, and in 1812 a house was licensed for meetings.[72] There was a small school for dissenters' children in 1859 and there were three families of Independents in 1864,[73] but no nonconformist chapel has been built in the parish.

EDUCATION. A concern for education perhaps unusual for the period manifested itself in 1387 and 1391 when bondmen were amerced for keeping their sons at school, probably in Salisbury,[74] and in 1410 when a John Schoolmaster, apparently of Stockton, was mentioned.[75] A school was held in the early 17th century by that scholarly Latinist Thomas Crockford, vicar of Fisherton de la Mere from 1613. Crockford claimed to have held the school for 14 years from 1602 and to have lived for 5 or 6 of those years with the rector.[76] No later schoolmaster is known.

In 1808 there were three schools each for some eight young children.[77] In 1818 there were two schools and the number of children being educated had risen to 34.[78] In 1833 the education of more than half the children was paid for by the wives of the rector and the lord of the manor.[79] In 1859 a mistress taught 25–30 children in two rooms of a cottage, a school thought to be a good example of its type. The second school was then for some ten children of dissenters.[80] In 1861 and 1862 a shop and 17th-century cottage near the church were converted to a school and school-house.[81] Boys were taught until they were eight or nine, girls until they were ten, and there was a well attended winter evening-school for boys.[82] The average attendance at school in 1900–1 was 59.[83] It was 62 in 1906 but thereafter declined gradually to 18 in 1938.[84] The school was closed in 1971.[85]

CHARITIES FOR THE POOR. By will John Topp (d. 1640) gave £1,000 for charitable use in Wiltshire or Oxford University to benefit the poor, preference being given to his kinsmen and afterwards to Wiltshiremen and especially to those of Stockton and Codford St. Mary.[86] In 1641 Topp's trustees decided to build an alms-house in Stockton and in 1648 declared the trusts of the charity and bought land.[87] The precise dates at which the house was built and opened are not clear but, the decision to build having been taken, it seems unlikely that the capital would have been used to buy land before the building was erected, and likely that in the period

1641–8 the trustees built the house and prepared to purchase the land to endow it. The deed of constitution was enrolled in 1658.[88] Stockton alms-house was presumably occupied by then. It stands south of the street and west of the church on land given by John Topp (d. 1660) and Edward Topp (d. 1665),[89] and was built round three sides of an enclosed courtyard to house six alms-people in separate pairs of rooms. Its accommodation was increased to eight by the addition of north and south wings in 1714.[90]

The trustees became the board of governors, one of whom was to be warden and to receive the charity's income.[91] In 1668 the office of warden was replaced by that of a salaried steward. Apparently in the early 19th century the steward's duties were restricted to the management of the house and a receiver was appointed. Apart from the alms-house and its orchard the charity's endowment was Spearywell farm in Mottisfont (Hants), 154 a. in 1831, and a yearly rent-charge of £4 from a close in Stockton given in 1658 by John Topp (d. 1660) to pay the steward. The annual rent from the farm was £45 in 1674,[92] £55 in 1779, £120 in 1831. Accumulated income was invested in stock which in 1833 amounted to £1,150 yielding annually £34 10s. The stock was then reduced by £350 to pay for repairs, and in 1849 Spearywell farm was sold and Green farm in Upton Scudamore bought. Green farm, 68 a., was later found to be encumbered with a mortgage of a previous owner. Partly because of the proceedings in Chancery which that discovery led to and partly because of the need to repair, the charity's income became insufficient in the mid 19th century. In 1877 it was proposed to sell the farm. There was a campaign to prevent that and only the farm-house and 4 a. were sold.[93] The proceeds of the sale were invested, and in 1902 the income from the farm was £60 and from the investments £34. The farm was later sold and the proceeds invested.[94]

In 1668 the governors framed articles for the management of the house.[95] The founder's preferences in the choice of inmates were observed. There is no evidence that a kinsman was housed and at least in the late 17th century and the early 18th beneficiaries were drawn from beyond Stockton and Codford.[96] Benefit was limited to those aged over 60 or impotent who were unmarried, respectable, and poor. The six inmates, eight from 1714, were each given fuel, a cloak each year, and a weekly allowance. They shared equally the orchard or the income from it. The allowance gradually increased from 2s. c. 1668 to 4s. 6d. in 1833 when allowances, fuel, and cloaks totalled some £135 a year. A resident nurse was also employed then.[97]

[71] Sar. Dioc. R.O., Chwdns.' Pres.; *W.N. & Q.* iii. 537.
[72] *W.N. & Q.* ii. 567; *Vis. Queries, 1783* (W.R.S. xxvii), p. 204; Sar. Dioc. R.O., Return of Cert. Places.
[73] *Acct. of Wilts. Schs.* 42; Sar. Dioc. R.O., Vis. Queries.
[74] W.R.O. 108/11; B.L. Add. Ch. 24350.
[75] W.R.O. 906/S 11.
[76] Ibid. 522/1; *V.C.H. Wilts.* viii. 45.
[77] Lambeth MS. 1732.
[78] *Educ. of Poor Digest,* 1038.
[79] *Educ. Enquiry Abstract,* 1048.
[80] *Acct. of Wilts. Schs.* 42.
[81] W.R.O. 401/1, f. 156v.
[82] Sar. Dioc. R.O., Vis. Queries, 1864.
[83] Wilts. Tracts, 96, no. 1.
[84] *Bd. of Educ., List 21* (H.M.S.O.).

[85] Ex inf. Chief Education Officer, County Hall, Trowbridge.
[86] *Endowed Char. Wilts.* (S. Div.), 664.
[87] W.R.O. 384/3; 384/1.
[88] Ibid. 384/3.   [89] Ibid. 384/1.
[90] *W.A.M.* xii. 205, 207; see plate facing p. 161.
[91] Except where stated inf. in this para. is from *Endowed Char. Wilts.* (S. Div.), 664–9.
[92] Sar. Dioc. R.O., Chwdns.' Pres.
[93] J. Baron, *Reasons against Alienation of Property of Stockton Almshouse in Upton Scudamore* (priv. print. 1877).
[94] Local information.
[95] *Endowed Char. Wilts.* (S. Div.), 667.
[96] W.R.O. 384/3.
[97] *Endowed Char. Wilts.* (S. Div.), 664–8.

In the 19th century the need to spend proportionately more on the alms-house and less on its inmates is exemplified by the expensive repairs made in 1833, the later closing of two of the dwellings to save money, and the raising of new funds.[98] By a deed of 1896 Marguerite Augusta Dodd of Stockton House gave £1,300, yielding £41 a year, raised by herself and her friends to increase the endowment. New articles broadly similar to those of 1668, but including provision for a resident nurse, were made in 1897. In 1900 the charity's income was £145 of which some £112 was spent on the residents' subsistence,[99] and by will proved 1921 and under a Scheme of that year Emilie Gay gave £750 to increase the allowances.[1] In the mid 20th century, however, the failure of the charity's income to match the rising cost of repairs and the lessening need to support the inmates have caused the governors to concentrate more on providing housing than subsistence. In 1960 income was £280 of which £135

was given to the inmates. By a Scheme of 1977, however, special funds were established for routine maintenance and extraordinary repairs and were to receive £720 a year. Allowances were discontinued and the trustees were enabled to demand from the alms-people weekly contributions of £5 towards running costs and further contributions towards fuel. Marriage no longer disqualified.[2]

By their wills proved 1910 and 1921 John Thomas Gay and Emilie Gay founded nursing charities consolidated by a Scheme of 1922 into Gays' Nursing Charity. The capital of respectively £444 and £511 was invested for the nursing needs first of Stockton and afterwards of the area served by the Wylye Valley Nursing Association. By a Scheme of 1950 the income was assigned to the special needs of the sick in those areas, including the supply of special medicines, domestic help, and money for convalescence. The income was £24 in 1962.[3] In 1978 the charity was still managed under the terms of the 1950 Scheme.[4]

WESTWOOD

WESTWOOD is 2.5 km. south-west of Bradford on Avon and 4 km. north-west of Trowbridge.[5] On the south-west and west it adjoins Somerset, and, since 1974, the new county of Avon.[6] Westwood was a chapelry of Bradford but, because it relieved its own poor and dealt with other civil matters, it was deemed a poor-law, and later a civil, parish in the 19th century. It achieved full parochial status in 1876 when it was constituted an ecclesiastical parish.[7] The chapelry was roughly oval with a jagged eastern boundary. It stretched 2.5 km. from west to east and 1.5 km. from north to south, and included five small settlements, Lower Westwood near the centre, Upper Westwood and Avoncliff to the north, Lye Green to the north-east, and Iford, which was partly in Somerset, to the south-west. The parish was enlarged in 1882 when a small detached part of the civil parish of Wingfield with Rowley, which was already geographically in Westwood between Upper Westwood and Lye Green, was added, and in 1885 when several detached parts of the civil parish of Great Bradford, which were also within Westwood and included one near Lye Green, were transferred to it. The total of 19 a. so added increased the area from 813 a. to 832 a.[8] That area was increased in 1934 to 387 ha. (957 a.). The additional 125 a., which included Elms Cross, were transferred from the civil parishes of Bradford on Avon and Bradford Without and comprised a tongue of land 1 km. long by 200 m. broad east of Westwood bounded by Westwood Road to the south-west, Wid brook to the south-east, and Rowden Lane to the north-east.[9]

Westwood is in the angle formed by the north-

wards flowing river Frome, which forms the parish and county boundary south of Iford, and the westwards flowing Bristol Avon, which forms the northern parish boundary.[10] North of Iford the boundary skirts Staples hill on an arbitrary course east of the Frome. The parish is on the limestone plateau of 'Cotswold' Wiltshire and inclines from north-west to south-east. The parish as constituted before 1934 stood entirely on strata of the Great Oolite series. The highest point, 99 m., occurs west of the settlement at Upper Westwood which, like that at Lye Green, is on a wide band of Forest Marble. In the north-west part of the parish a band of Great Oolite Limestone, a tongue of which intrudes north-westwards between Shrub down and Avoncliff wood, curves in a semi-circle from Avoncliff to Iford. The hamlet of Iford stands beneath the plateau scarp on the east bank of the Frome at 61 m. The Fuller's Earth, which underlies the Oolite strata near Iford and Avoncliff, provided, with the ample water-power yielded by the Frome and Avon, the foundations upon which the cloth industry of the area thrived from the Middle Ages. Sections of the lower ragstone deposits, upon which the Fuller's Earth rests, occur at Upper Westwood and have been extensively quarried. Although the clay soils of the limestone plateau were under arable cultivation until the 19th century, in 1978 they were more suitably under grass for the most part and given over to dairying. On the north, south, and west of the plateau slippage of the Fuller's Earth, which in places carried with it scatters of lower ragstones, caused the land to fall away sharply to the valleys of the Frome and Avon. It was

[98] Ibid. 667, 671; Baron, *Reasons against Alienation*; *W.A.M.* xii. 207.
[99] *Endowed Char. Wilts.* (S. Div.), 670–2.
[1] Char. Com. file 205021.
[2] Ibid.
[3] Ibid. 204773.
[4] Ex inf. Mr. Frank Sykes, Stockton.
[5] This article was written in 1978.
[6] The following maps have been used: O.S. Maps 6″, Wilts. XXXII (1889 edn.), XXXVIII (1890 edn.), ST 75 NE. (1961 edn.), ST 85 NW. (1961 edn.), ST 86 SW.

(1961 edn.); 1/10,000, ST 85 NW. (1974 edn.), ST 86 SW. (1977 edn.); 1/25,000, ST 75 (1958 edn.), 31/85 (1950 edn.), 31/86 (1948 edn.); 1/50,000, sheet 173 (1974 edn.); Sta. Cha. 8/169/21.
[7] *Lond. Gaz.* 1 Dec. 1876, pp. 6676 sqq.; *Census*, 1881, 1891. [8] *Census*, 1881, 1891; I.R. 30/38/276.
[9] *Census*, 1921, 1931.
[10] This para. is based on Geol. Surv. Map 1″, solid and drift, sheet 281 (1965 edn.); Fry, *Land Utilisation Wilts.* 151, 158–9, 171, 208–9; *W.A.M.* vi. 3–4; xi. 321.

presumably from the thick cover of woodland, which formerly overlay much of the chapelry and in 1978 still distinguished the cliff formed by the slippage of the Fuller's Earth, that the settlements of Upper and Lower Westwood were named.[11] Avoncliff, which derives its name from the steep north face of the landslip itself,[12] stands on a limestone outcrop. North of it the alluvial soils of the flood plain of the Avon, which are lush meadow land, lie around the 30 m. contour. The Hinton Charterhouse fault is marked by the course of the lane from Iford to Lower Westwood, whence it continues north-eastwards across the parish.

Some prehistoric activity is attested by a few artefacts of the Neolithic Period and Bronze Age found in the north-west corner of Westwood. Pieces of wall-plaster, roof slabs, flue tiles, much pottery, and an inhumation found in the same area show it to have been settled in Roman times.[13]

About 45 poll-tax payers in the chapelry were assessed in 1377.[14] Other medieval taxation assessments show Westwood to have ranked among the more prosperous fiscal units in Bradford hundred. In 1545, when Westwood was part of Elstub hundred, the contribution which the chapelry made to the benevolence was second in the hundred only to that of Enford.[15] Later assessments show Westwood to have remained one of the more highly rated units in Elstub hundred.[16] In 1801 446 people lived in the chapelry.[17] The decline to 390 in 1831 was attributed to the absence of a large family and to the fact that people had left the area for lack of employment there.[18] The opening of the Bradford union workhouse at Avoncliff in 1835 accounted for the steep rise by 1841 to 631, of whom 220 were lodged in the workhouse.[19] In 1851 249 of the 605 people in the chapelry were workhouse inmates.[20] Thereafter the population increased from 469 in 1861 to 543 in 1871, an increase attributed to the return of several families to the area.[21] It fell to 516 in 1881 and, although it had risen to 540 by 1891, had declined steadily to 468 by 1921. There was afterwards a steady rise which accelerated during and after the Second World War when some light industry was introduced to the parish, and in 1951 915 people lived there. There was a temporary decrease to 771 in 1961 but numbers had risen to 961 by 1971.[22]

All the roads and tracks which served the chapelry in 1773 were still in use in 1978.[23] The road running westwards through Lower Westwood to Iford was turnpiked in 1752.[24] The short stretch of road linking it with the Bradford–Frome road was turnpiked later.[25] In 1838 the course of a footpath from Upper Westwood to the workhouse at Avoncliff

was set out.[26] The Kennet & Avon canal had been constructed south of the Avon inside the north-eastern boundary of the chapelry by 1804.[27] It was carried northwards out of the chapelry across the Avon valley by a triple-arched aqueduct designed by John Rennie.[28] After its opening in 1810 the canal carried coal from the Somerset coal-field to wharves such as that at Avoncliff for distribution by road.[29] By 1903 the porous nature of the local rag-stone, from which the aqueduct was partly built, had led to leakage. Traffic had almost ceased by the Second World War and in 1954 the Westwood section of the canal was drained. The canal bed was blocked by two landslips in 1970.[30] Work on clearing it, partly financed by the Kennet & Avon Canal Trust, was in progress in 1978.[31] The parish was served by that section of the Wilts., Somerset & Weymouth Railway constructed from Bradford along the north side of the Avon valley and opened in 1857. There was a station on the north bank of the river opposite the hamlet of Avoncliff called Avoncliff Halt.[32]

The ancient centre of the village of Lower Westwood is in the angle of the lanes from Iford and Farleigh Hungerford, in Norton St. Philip (Som.). There stands the church with Westwood Manor set back from the lane to the north-west, the Vicarage due west, and the Old Vicarage south-west. In 1773 scattered settlement flanked the lane to Iford and then, as in 1978, the eastern limit of the village did not extend much beyond the New Inn.[33] So named by 1822, the inn is of 19th-century construction but contains a later-16th-century fire-place introduced from elsewhere.[34] The cottages which cluster close to the roadside west of the inn are externally of the later 18th century or the 19th but incorporate earlier features such as stone mullioned windows of the 17th century or the early 18th. Of the former copyhold farm-houses which stood along that lane, the Old Malthouse (formerly the Limes), at the junction of the lanes to Iford and Upper Westwood, is a later-18th-century house with additions on the west.[35] On the south side of the lane to Iford a school was built in 1841 and on the north side a Baptist chapel and Sunday school somewhat later.[36] Early in the Second World War 94 bungalows and other buildings were erected by the War Department north of the lane to house people employed at Upper Westwood by the Enfield Motor Cycle Co. After the war some houses were built by the council which c. 1960 acquired the bungalows. The sewage works constructed by the War Department south-east of Iford to serve the bungalow estate were integrated c. 1962 with a new system for the entire parish, and a pumping station was built near Cuffley Lane. In the later 1960s the

[11] P.N. Wilts. (E.P.N.S.), 122.
[12] Ibid. The name was often used in corrupt forms in the 18th cent. and the earlier 19th, e.g. Ancliff, Anckliffe, Anckley or Hanckley: Andrews and Dury, Map (W.R.S. viii), pl. 10; W.R.O. 445/1; 445/8; 687/24; 847/10.
[13] V.C.H. Wilts. i (1), 121.
[14] Ibid. iv. 306.
[15] E 179/197/155; Taxation Lists (W.R.S. x), 4.
[16] Taxation Lists (W.R.S. x), 122; E 179/198/259; E 179/198/297; E 179/199/370.
[17] Except where stated otherwise, population figures are from V.C.H. Wilts. iv. 360.
[18] Ibid. 318.   [19] Ibid. 320.   [20] Ibid. 321.
[21] Ibid. 325.   [22] Census, 1961, 1971.
[23] Andrews and Dury, Map (W.R.S. viii), pl. 10.

[24] V.C.H. Wilts. iv. 257, 259, 268; L.J. xxvii. 704; Andrews and Dury, Map (W.R.S. viii), pl. 10.
[25] V.C.H. Wilts. iv. 257.
[26] W.R.O. 847/10.   [27] V.C.H. Wilts. iv. 273.
[28] W.A.M. xi. 321; see plate facing this page.
[29] V.C.H. Wilts. iv. 273-4.
[30] Wilts. Cuttings, xxiii. 359.
[31] Ex inf. Mr. T. E. Scrase, British Waterways Board.
[32] V.C.H. Wilts. iv. 283-4.
[33] Andrews and Dury, Map (W.R.S. viii), pl. 10.
[34] W.R.O., Alehousekeepers' Reg.
[35] Mun. D. & C. Winton., estate bk. 22A, survey, 1792; H.R.O. 11M59/8082; I.R. 29/38/276; I.R. 30/38/276; O.S. Map 6″, Wilts. XXXVIII (1890 edn.).
[36] See below.

Aqueduct at Avoncliff

Old Court at Avoncliff

WESTWOOD

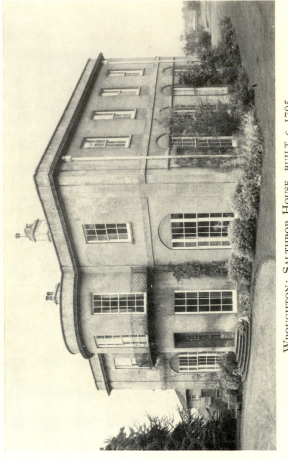

WROUGHTON: SALTHROP HOUSE, BUILT *c.* 1795

EVERLEIGH

The Crown, built from the early 18th century

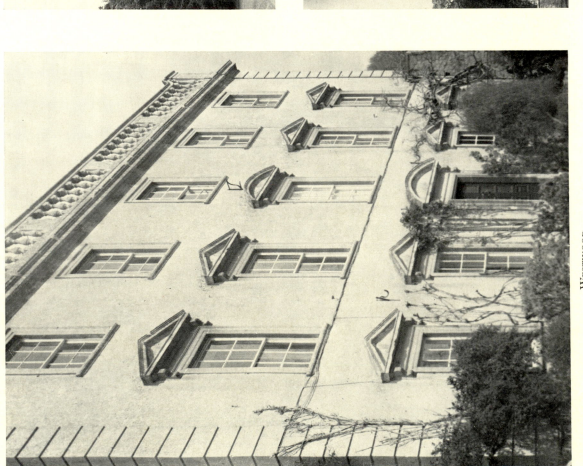

WESTWOOD

Iford Manor, the west front built in the mid 18th century

bungalows were replaced by a new council estate centred on Boswell Road, Tynyngs Way, and Hebden Road.[37] Private estates flanked the council development in 1978.

The hamlet of Upper Westwood is strung out along either side of a lane on the crest of the limestone ridge overlooking the Avon valley, settlement being restricted to the north side in the 18th century.[38] Houses of that date, as well as some of the 19th and 20th centuries, stood there in 1978, when a modern private housing development occupied part of the south side of the lane. Of two former copyhold farm-houses, Upper Westwood Farm stands at the eastern entrance to the hamlet. That called the Well House in 1890 is further west along the north side of the lane,[39] from which it is set back behind a tall stone wall pierced by a central gateway which has panelled stone gate-posts with ball finials and wrought-iron gates. In 1978 it comprised a central later-17th-century block, flanked by small gabled wings built in the style of the earlier 17th century, and was occupied as two houses called Greenhill House and Westhill. The eastern wing represents part of a house of the later 16th century or the earlier 17th incorporated into the new house built on the west as a gentleman's residence by the tenant, Zachary Walter, c. 1680.[40] That house has a principal south entrance front of five bays in the classical style. The range is one room deep with a staircase wing projecting northwards. When the owner, E. H. J. Leslie, restored the house c. 1913 he built a balancing wing on the west.[41] In the later 18th century the house had a wooded garden on the south side of the road.[42] The trees were apparently felled in the later 19th century,[43] and Leslie laid out the gardens in a formal manner.[44] The former stable block north-east of the garden, of the later 18th century, had by 1978 been converted to a dwelling called the Long House.

There had apparently been some settlement at Lye Green on the north side of the lane from Upper Westwood to Bradford by the later 18th century.[45] Lye Green Farm, until the later 19th century attached to a small copyhold within Westwood manor,[46] and near-by cottages appear to be externally of 19th- and 20th-century construction.

The former mill and its associated buildings in 1773, as in 1978, marked the eastern limit of the settlement at Avoncliff.[47] The 17th-century Cross Guns inn, so named by 1822, is the oldest building in the terrace which stretches westwards to the lane to Upper Westwood. It may be identifiable with the public house called the Carpenters' Arms which

was converted from a house in the later 18th century.[48] Most of the houses which complete the terrace are externally of the later 18th century and the 19th. The settlement may have grown somewhat in the later 18th century when cloth began to be manufactured at the mill and again c. 1800 when the Kennet & Avon canal was constructed immediately north. West of the lane to Upper Westwood are the substantial 19th-century houses of Bath stone called Avon Villa and Avon Cottage, and the Old Court, the former Bradford union workhouse.[49] That building, probably erected shortly after 1792, comprised seventeen industrial dwellings which formed terraces round three sides of a square.[50] Apart from the central house in the south range, which was of three bays, the houses were one bay wide and three storeys high. The windows on the uppermost floors were originally of double width and lit workrooms. When bought by the Bradford guardians in 1835 the internal walls were removed from the smaller houses to form wards and workrooms for women on the east and for men on the west. The central house was occupied by the workhouse master and at the rear a large new block was added to accommodate a kitchen, dining-room, and chapel.[51] A gate-house was built, possibly at the same time, on the north side of the square.

After the few remaining inmates had been transferred to Warminster workhouse in 1917 the Bradford guardians let the empty building to the British Red Cross Society as a hospital.[52] They sold it in 1923 to Walter Morres, who converted it to a hotel called the Old Court.[53] Part of the east wing was then demolished to open up the central court and the gate-house was pulled down. In the 1950s work, still in progress in 1978, was begun to convert the building into flats and small houses.[54] A schoolroom built at the southern end of the workhouse garden in the later 19th century was demolished in the later 20th century.[55] South-west of the former workhouse a small stone vaulted building has a central chimney which serves two external fire-places. It is divided into four compartments which may have been used as punishment cells for workhouse inmates. The original purpose of the building, in the later 18th century and the early 19th, was probably to serve as a drying-house for wool.

The hamlet of Iford, which straddles the county boundary, is on either side of the road up Iford hill. Its nucleus is Iford Manor which stands in the angle formed by the road and the river Frome. The associated buildings north of Iford Manor and Iford Mill on the west bank of the Frome were in

[37] Ex inf. Mr. G. G. Mumford, Surveyor, W. Wilts. district council.
[38] *Andrews and Dury, Map* (W.R.S. viii), pl. 10.
[39] O.S. Map 6″, Wilts. XXXVIII (1890 edn.).
[40] Mun. D. & C. Winton., box 84, ct. roll, 26 Aug. 1680; box 87, ct. roll, 26 Nov. 1685; estate bk. 3, ff. 75v.–76.
[41] Ex inf. Mrs. N. G. Marlow, the occupier in 1978.
[42] *Andrews and Dury, Map* (W.R.S. viii), pl. 10; Mun. D. & C. Winton., estate bk. 22A, survey, 1792; H.R.O. 11M59/8082.
[43] H.R.O., Eccl. Commrs. 59616; 11M59/8083; O.S. Map 6″, Wilts. XXXVIII (1890 edn.).
[44] Ex inf. Mrs. Marlow.
[45] *Andrews and Dury, Map* (W.R.S. viii), pl. 10.
[46] Mun. D. & C. Winton., estate bk. 22A, survey, 1792; H.R.O. 11M59/8082–3; Eccl. Commrs. 59616; Ch. Commrs. survey bk. DD 3 (Winch. chap.), pp. 557–663.
[47] *Andrews and Dury, Map* (W.R.S. viii), pl. 10.
[48] W.R.O. 415/275, abstr. of title, 1787–1807; Alehouse-keepers' Reg.
[49] O.S. Map 6″, Wilts. XXXVIII (1890 edn.); Mun. D. & C. Winton., box 114, sale cat. and map, 1911.
[50] See p. 231 and plate facing p. 224. The architectural evidence makes it improbable that, as suggested in *V.C.H. Wilts.* iv. 157, the houses were built for Dutch immigrants in the later 17th cent.
[51] W.R.O., poor-law union rec., plans of workhouse; M.H. 12/13668.
[52] W.R.O., poor-law union rec., union min. bk. 1916–21, pp. 124–6.
[53] Ibid. poor-law union rec., union min. bk. 1921–5, pp. 129, 135; *Kelly's Dir. Wilts.* (1927).
[54] Ex inf. Mr. A. L. Dunsdon, Old Court.
[55] I.R. 30/38/276; maps listed above, p. 223, n. 6.

Somerset and afterwards Avon, as was Iford bridge which carried the lane from Iford westwards over the Frome.[56] Although of ancient origin, the bridge, which is built of stone and has a single arch, is apparently of 18th-century construction.[57] The stone figure of Britannia was placed on the southern parapet of the bridge by H. A. Peto in the early 20th century.[58]

MANORS AND OTHER ESTATES. An estate to be identified with the later manor of *WEST-WOOD* may have been held by Sealemudda before 983.[59] In 983 King Ethelred granted his thegn Alfnoth 2½ *mansae* at Westwood.[60] In 987, however, Ethelred granted what may be the same estate, then comprising 3 *mansae* and some common land at Farleigh Hungerford, to his huntsman Leofwine.[61] The estate may afterwards have been taken in hand again and possibly included in the grant of Bradford minster and its property made by Ethelred to Shaftesbury Abbey in 1001.[62] In the following year, however, Westwood was apparently again in hand and was assigned by Ethelred to his queen, Emma, in dower. The estate was afterwards confirmed to her by her second husband, King Cnut, and by their son Harthacnut.[63] After Harthacnut's death Emma gave Westwood to the church of Winchester in his memory c. 1043.[64]

In 1086 Westwood was among the lands of the bishop of Winchester assigned for the support of the monks of the cathedral church.[65] The bishop confirmed the manor to the prior of St. Swithun's in 1284 as part of a composition between them.[66] In the 13th century some, at least, of the profits of Westwood may have been paid to the hoarder, who gave up his claim to them in favour of the prior in 1337.[67] St. Swithun's received a grant of free warren in its demesne lands in 1300, and held the manor until the Dissolution when it passed to the Crown.[68]

In 1541 the Crown granted Westwood to the newly established cathedral chapter at Winchester.[69] In 1650 parliamentary trustees sold the manor, including the franchisal rights, to Edward Woodford and Westwood Manor and the demesne farm to Elizabeth Bampfield and Henry Foster.[70] The entire estate was afterwards restored to the chapter, which retained it until 1861. In that year the manor was transferred to the Ecclesiastical Commissioners.[71]

The Commissioners sold their reversionary interest in the estate, 333 a., to their tenant, G. C. Tugwell, in 1864.[72] In 1911 the estate, enlarged to 536 a. by the acquisition of the Joyce estate at Upper Westwood, was sold in lots.[73] The manor-house and some land became the property of E. G. Lister (d. 1956). He gave the National Trust protective covenants over Westwood Manor in 1943 and finally devised it with an endowment to the Trust, owner in 1978.[74]

The manor, or parts of it, were apparently leased in the earlier 13th century. Gilbert de Bolebec had some interest in an estate at Westwood in 1235.[75] In 1243 James de Bolebec held probably the manor itself.[76] Between 1261 and 1265 another Bolebec, possibly Jordan, regranted the convent land in Westwood held at fee farm.[77] Between 1265 and 1276 the manor was granted at fee farm to Henry de Montfort whose brother and successor at Westwood, Nicholas, surrendered the estate to St. Swithun's between 1276 and 1286.[78] In the later 13th century the manor was leased in moieties of which one was held by Robert Waspray and afterwards by his widow.[79] John Waspray also held of St. Swithun's an estate, called a manor, which he apparently returned to the convent in 1313–14.[80]

Thereafter the manor remained in hand until the later 14th century when the demesne alone was leased.[81] Henry Culverhouse, farmer in 1434, was succeeded c. 1469 by Thomas Culverhouse, who was at Westwood until at least 1485.[82] Thomas Horton (d. 1530) was the farmer in 1518. He was succeeded by his widow Mary (will proved 1543), nephew Thomas Horton (d. 1549), Thomas's widow Margery (will proved 1564), and Thomas's son Edward (d. 1603).[83] The last Horton lessee was Edward's grand-nephew Toby Horton, who sold his unexpired term c. 1616 to his brother-in-law John Farewell (d. 1642), whose widow Melior (d. 1675) succeeded him at Westwood.[84] John Wallis, who became lessee in 1675, was possibly a kinsman of the Farewells.[85] In the 18th century lessees,

---

[56] The acct. of Iford in this article relates to the entire hamlet.
[57] The bridge is mentioned in the 17th cent.: W.R.O. 473/54, Iford man. ct. papers, 1680–3, 1686.
[58] Pevsner, *Wilts.* (2nd edn.), 276.
[59] Finberg, *Early Wessex Chart.* p. 100. The man. is first so described in 1243: *Reg. Pontoise* (Cant. & York Soc.), ii. 618.
[60] Finberg, *Early Wessex Chart.* p. 100.
[61] Ibid. p. 101.
[62] Ibid. p. 103; *V.C.H. Wilts.* ii, p. 95; vii. 13.
[63] *Annales Monastici* (Rolls Ser.), ii. 18.
[64] Ibid.; Finberg, *Early Wessex Chart.* p. 105; *Reg. Pontoise* (Cant. & York Soc.), ii. 609.
[65] *V.C.H. Wilts.* ii, p. 120.
[66] *Chartulary Winch. Cath.* ed. A. W. Goodman, pp. 19–20; *Reg. Pontoise* (Cant. & York Soc.), ii. 436, 618.
[67] Katharine A. Hanna, 'Winch. Cath. Custumal' (Southampton Univ. Coll. M.A. thesis, 1954), 427 and n. 2.
[68] *Cal. Chart. R.* 1300–26, 1; *Feud. Aids,* v. 210, 246; *Valor Eccl.* (Rec. Com.), vi, App. p. vii.
[69] C 66/709 m. 10.
[70] C 54/3460 no. 12; C 54/3461 no. 27.
[71] I.R. 29/38/276; I.R. 30/38/276; *Lond. Gaz.* 16 Apr. 1861, pp. 1582 sqq.; 25 Mar. 1862, pp. 1611 sqq.
[72] Ch. Commrs., copy deeds, lxi, no. 5054.
[73] Mun. D. & C. Winton., box 114, sale cat.; see below.
[74] *Wilts. Cuttings,* xvii. 24; Country Life Ltd. for Nat. Trust, *Westwood Man.* (1962), 21–2.
[75] *Cat. Anct. D.* iii, D 220.
[76] *Bk. of Fees,* ii. 741.
[77] *Chartulary Winch. Cath.* ed. Goodman, p. 237; *V.C.H. Hants,* ii. 115; *Cal. Pat.* 1313–17, 626.
[78] *Chartulary Winch. Cath.* ed. Goodman, p. 113; *V.C.H. Hants,* ii. 115; *Complete Peerage,* ix. 130–2.
[79] Hanna, 'Winch. Cath. Custumal', 427, 433.
[80] Ibid. 437 sqq.; *Cal. Pat.* 1307–13, 326; *Abbrev. Rot. Orig.* (Rec. Com.), i. 180; Mun. D. & C. Winton., bk. of John Chase, f. 86v.
[81] Mun. D. & C. Winton., 14th- and 15th-cent. acct. rolls.
[82] Ibid. acct. rolls, 1434–85.
[83] Ibid. acct. rolls, 1518–19, 1528, 1534, 1537; box 87, acct. rolls, 1554, 1564, 1567, 1569, 1572; ledger bk. II, f. 29.; *W.A.M.* v, pedigree at pp. 316–17; Prob. 11/30 (P.C.C. 1 Pynnyng); *W.N. & Q.* iv. 165, 169; *W.A.M.* xli. 245–6.
[84] *W.A.M.* v, pedigree at pp. 316–17; C 2/Jas. I/F 12/35; C 2/Jas. I/F 10/69; *Westwood Man.* 15; Mun. D. & C. Winton., ledger bk. XI, f. 6; survey of chap. man. 1649, ff. 198 sqq.; Sar. Dioc. R.O., bp.'s transcripts.
[85] Mun. D. & C. Winton., ledger bk. XVIII, f. 60v.; *Westwood Man.* 19.

including the Tugwell family who acquired a lease in the second half of that century, probably sub-let the estate. The Tugwells remained lessees until 1864 when G. C. Tugwell bought the freehold.[86]

Westwood Manor, which comprises two old ranges set at right angles in an L-shape, was formerly much larger and H-shaped.[87] The north hall range, which lies east–west, originally formed the cross-wing of the H. In 1480 Thomas Culverhouse built a new house, the building accounts for which have been interpreted as relating to that surviving hall range on the basis of its length, although the range contains no visibly 15th-century feature.[88] The main doorway and an internal doorway are probably of the early 16th century and most of the fittings were introduced in the earlier 17th century by John Farewell, who inserted the upper floor, renewed the roof, and added the porch and turret stair. To the south-west the adjacent rooms of the west range, which in 1978 housed the dining-room with a bedroom above, probably date from the earlier 16th century. They appear to be of later date than the southern part of the range. The surviving part of the original west range, which may be of the later 15th century or the earlier 16th, retains its original roof, part of which is painted. That range originally had three rooms on the first floor which appear to have been lodgings with separate entrances before John Farewell refurbished them as bedrooms in the earlier 17th century. The windows and doorways have been much altered and the first floor oriel window on the eastern elevation was probably inserted in the early 16th century.

An eastwards extension of the north range and a short east range survived until the later 19th century.[89] They probably housed kitchens and service rooms.[90] There is also structural evidence of a former range or room extending northwards from the west end of the north range.

After acquiring the Manor in 1911 E. G. Lister carried out an extensive restoration, imported some panelling and other features,[91] and added a short kitchen wing on the west side of the west range. He also laid out the gardens and rebuilt the surrounding walls, including the gateway to the forecourt in early-17th-century style.[92] A large barn south-east of the house has walls of the 15th century

or the 16th. The roof has been renewed, possibly in the 19th century.

In the mid 14th century William of Iford held freely of Westwood manor a small estate in Iford and its neighbourhood, to be identified with the later manor of *IFORD*, which afterwards passed to his brother Master Nicholas of Iford.[93] With the permission of the prior of St. Swithun's, Winchester, Nicholas's feoffees granted the estate, then reckoned 2 carucates, to the Carthusian priory of Hinton (Som.) c. 1374.[94] The priory held the estate, with 4 a. in Westwood acquired in 1412,[95] until the Dissolution, when it passed to the Crown.

In 1543 the Crown granted the estate, which by then straddled the county boundary and included land in both Wiltshire and Somerset, to Sir John Williams and Anthony Stringer.[96] They sold it immediately to Thomas Horton, members of whose family had formerly been tenants.[97] On Thomas Horton's death in 1549 the estate, in accordance with his will, passed successively to his wife Margery (d. 1564) and son William.[98] On William's death in 1584 the lands passed in turn to his son William and grandson Toby.[99]

Toby Horton and his wife Barbara sold Iford in 1625 to Sir Edward Hungerford (d.s.p. 1648), from whom the manor, like Upavon manor, passed to his widow Margaret (d. 1673).[1] At her death the estate reverted to Sir Edward's nephew Sir Edward Hungerford (d. 1711), who sold it in 1687 to Henry Baynton (d. 1691) of Spye Park in Bromham.[2] Baynton devised it on trust for sale and in 1700 his trustees sold Iford to William Chanler.[3]

William Chanler (will proved 1710) devised the estate to his wife Eleanor during their son Samuel's minority.[4] Eleanor regained it, however, when Samuel (will proved 1733) devised Iford to her in fee.[5] Eleanor Chanler (will proved 1743) devised most of the estate, comprising Iford manor and Shute's farm, to her cousin John Halliday. Halliday, by will dated 1749, in turn devised his Iford lands to his son Simon, who sold them in 1764 to Charles Dingley.[6] Dingley's daughter Susannah and her husband John Smith Meggott sold them in 1773 to John Turner, who sold them in 1777 to John Gaisford.[7] Gaisford (d. 1810) was succeeded by his son the Revd. Thomas Gaisford (d. 1855), later dean

[86] Mun. D. & C. Winton., ledger bk. XXI, f. 149; XXII, ff. 75v., 124v.; XXIII, ff. 54, 112; XXV, f. 12; XXVI, f. 42; XXVII, f. 11; XXVIII, f. 24; XXIX, f. 41v.; W.R.O. 847/1; Land Tax; I.R. 29/38/276; I.R. 30/38/276; *Kelly's Dir. Wilts.* (1848 and later edns.).

[87] The bldg. hist. given here differs significantly from those in *Country Life*, 14, 21 Aug. 1926 and *Westwood Man.*

[88] Mun. D. & C. Winton., acct. roll, 1480; see above.

[89] See plate facing p. 32. The E. wing was demolished c. 1860: *W.A.M.* xliv. 485.

[90] It has been suggested that the kitchen built in 1511 was sited there: Mun. D. & C. Winton., acct. roll, 1511; *Westwood Man.* 8.

[91] The series of royal portraits in the room at the E. end of the N. range was brought from Keevil Man. and the panelling in the dining-room from a ho. in Bristol: *Westwood Man.* 21.

[92] The original gateway was painted by J. Buckler, water-colour in W.A.S. Libr., vol. v. 38 (1808).

[93] *Feet of F.* 1327–77 (W.R.S. xxix), pp. 109–10; Mun. D. & C. Winton., ct. roll, 1359; ledger bk. I, f. 2v. The man. is first so called in 1610: *W.A.M.* xli. 249.

[94] Mun. D. & C. Winton., ledger bk. I, f. 2v.; *Cal. Pat.* 1361–4, 223; 1374–7, 31.

[95] C 143/444 no. 12.

[96] *Valor Eccl.* (Rec. Com.), i. 156; *L. & P. Hen. VIII*, xviii, p. 131; E 318/1227 m. 20.

[97] *L. & P. Hen. VIII*, xviii, p. 285; S.C. 6/Hen. VIII/ 3144 m. 44; E 318/1227 m. 20.

[98] *W.N. & Q.* iv. 169; C.P. 40/1156 Carte rot. 20; *W.A.M.* v, pedigree at pp. 316–17 where Margery is wrongly called Margaret. For her name cf. Prob. 11/47 (P.C.C. 31 Stevenson).

[99] C 142/205 no. 186; *W.A.M.* xli. 249; v, pedigree at pp. 316–17; C 2/Jas. I/H 31/17.

[1] C.P. 25(2)/526/1 Chas. I Trin.; *Complete Peerage*, vi. 626 n. c; B.L. Add. Ch. 40131; *V.C.H. Wilts.* x. 163.

[2] *V.C.H. Wilts.* x. 163; B.L. Add. Ch. 40131; W.R.O. 445/1; Burke, *Ext. & Dorm. Baronetcies* (1844), 453. The following descent amplifies, and at certain points corrects, that given for the man. of Rowley alias Wittenham, in Wingfield, in *V.C.H. Wilts.* vii. 72.

[3] W.R.O. 445/1.

[4] Ibid. 445/119.

[5] Ibid. 445/8; 687/24, abstr. of title to Avoncliff mills.

[6] Ibid. 445/12; 445/45; 445/121. A mill, or mills, at Avoncliff was devised separately: see below. For Shute's farm, see below.

[7] W.R.O. 445/17–23.

of Christ Church, Oxford, and grandson Thomas Gaisford (d. 1898).[8]

In 1858 Thomas Gaisford sold the Iford estate, then reckoned at 170 a. of which some 72 a. were in Westwood, to William W. Rooke (d. 1864), who devised it for life to his wife Julia (d. 1896).[9] Rooke's trustees sold it in 1899 to Sarah M. Crossley, who sold it in 1903 to her brother H. A. Peto (d. 1933).[10] Peto, who had apparently occupied Iford Manor since 1899, was succeeded by his nephew J. M. Peto (later Sir Michael Peto, Bt., d. 1971).[11] During Sir Michael's lifetime, however, the Iford estate passed to his daughter Serena, Lady Matheson, who in 1965 sold it to Miss Elizabeth Cartwright, the owner in 1978.[12]

Iford Manor was so called c. 1900 but until then had been called Iford House.[13] Traces of a house built on the site in the later 16th century survive in the lower parts of the south range and may in their turn incorporate features from a later-15th-century house. Most of the 16th-century house, however, was probably demolished when a principal range, which faces west across the Frome valley, was constructed to the north in the 17th century. In the mid 18th century the west entrance front was heightened to three storeys and given an imposing five-bay façade of ashlar with a stone cornice and balustraded parapet.[14] At the same date a spacious staircase was inserted in the angle between the south and west ranges. An extension somewhat lower than the west range was built to the north in the later 18th century or the earlier 19th. An extension to the south, which may have been of similar date, was demolished c. 1900 by H. A. Peto who replaced it with a loggia and added a conservatory on the east.[15] J. M. Peto much enlarged the service range on the east side of the main block.[16]

The interior of the house retains some 17th-century features and much 18th-century panelling. The rooms along the south front were remodelled by H. A. Peto to incorporate antique carved woodwork and panel paintings mostly of European origin.[17]

The stables north-west of the house are probably of the later 18th century but have been much remodelled. They were occupied in 1978 as cottages and a flat. The gardens, surrounded by woodland, are ranged in terraces up the hillside to the south and east of the house. They were created in an Italianate style by H. A. Peto to display much antique carved stonework and sculpture which he had collected in Europe.

A small copyhold farm, in 1672 held by William Shute, formed part of Iford manor.[18] In 1791 John Gaisford sold Shute's farm in moieties to John Moggeridge and Thomas Joyce (will proved 1817), both Bradford clothiers.[19] Moggeridge's moiety is not mentioned again and may have been acquired by Joyce. In 1843 Maria Joyce held what were probably the reunited moieties which then amounted to 59 a.[20] Besides Shute's farm Maria Joyce held copyholds totalling some 100 a. from Winchester chapter, including that farmed from the house called Upper Westwood Farm in the later 19th century.[21] The copyhold land was enfranchised for Caroline Joyce in 1867.[22] By 1911, however, the farm, then called Upper Westwood farm, was part of the main Westwood estate.[23]

The building which existed on the site of Upper Westwood Farm in the later 16th century or the earlier 17th was mostly replaced in the later 17th century by a house with a symmetrical south front of five bays. A porch incorporating 17th-century stonework was, despite a later date on the cresting,[24] probably added to the central bay of that wing c. 1800. A low gabled wing to the east was retained from the original house as service quarters.

In the earlier 18th century the Wickham family had an estate at Iford which stretched over the county boundary southwards into Farleigh Hungerford and westwards into Freshford (Som.). Elizabeth Wickham and her son John sold it in 1721 to George Houghton, a clothier.[25] In 1728 Houghton (will proved 1760) settled the property on his marriage with Anne Webb, who succeeded him at Iford.[26] From Anne Houghton (will proved 1782) the small estate passed to her nephew Samuel Webb (will proved 1797), who devised it to his wife Anne for life with remainder to his kinsman Edward Webb.[27] Edward Webb sold the reversion to Benjamin Browne.[28] On Anne Webb's death Browne entered and by will proved 1822 devised the land to trustees who sold it in 1822 to the Revd. Thomas Gaisford.[29] It was thereafter merged with the main Iford estate.[30]

George Houghton may have built the large house which was attached to the estate and in 1773 stood on the east bank of the river Frome.[31] Anne Houghton apparently left the house immediately after her husband's death.[32] By the early 19th century it had apparently been pulled down,[33] and by 1858 its site had been used as a kitchen garden for Iford House.[34] It was still cultivated as a garden in 1978, when fragments of the demolished house,

[8] Land. Gent. (1906), i. 644; I.R. 29/38/276; I.R. 30/38/276; D.N.B.; W.R.O. 445/24.
[9] W.R.O. 445/24; 840/8/1.
[10] Ibid. 840/8/1; 840/9. For the Peto fam. see Burke, Peerage (1959), 1777–8; mon. to H. A. Peto in ch.
[11] Who's Who, 1975, 2475.
[12] Daily Telegraph, 14 Aug. 1965.
[13] W.R.O. 473/54, ct. papers, 29 Mar. 1686; C.P. 43/775 rot. 159; Kelly's Dir. Wilts. (1855 and later edns.).
[14] See plate facing p. 225.
[15] Iford Man. and Gardens (Trowbridge, priv. print. 1959), 5, penes Miss Cartwright, Iford Mill.
[16] Ibid.; H. A. Peto's alterations to, and innovations in, both ho. and gardens are more fully described in Country Life, 26 Aug. 1922; 2 Sept. 1922.
[17] The wooden figure sculpture is described in Country Life, 17 Dec. 1927.
[18] W.R.O. 473/54, later-17th-cent. survey; 445/45; 445/121.

[19] Ibid. 445/106; Mun. D. & C. Winton., N.R.A. box 26, copy will of Thomas Joyce; see below.
[20] I.R. 29/38/276; I.R. 30/38/276.
[21] H.R.O., Eccl. Commrs. 59616; 11M59/8083; O.S. Map 6″, Wilts. XXXVIII (1890 edn.).
[22] Ch. Commrs. file 31341.
[23] Mun. D. & C. Winton., box 114, sale cat.; see above.
[24] The last two figures of the date were illegible in 1978.
[25] W.R.O. 445/69–70. No evidence has been found to attest the property's connexion with the cloth ind.
[26] Ibid. 445/69–71.
[27] Ibid. 445/72–3; 445/75.
[28] Ibid. 445/75.
[29] Ibid.; 445/78.
[30] Ibid. 445/81; see above.
[31] Andrews and Dury, Map (W.R.S. viii), pl. 10; W.R.O. 445/78; 445/81.
[32] W.R.O. 445/72.
[33] Ibid. 445/75.
[34] Ibid. 445/81.

such as stone window-frames, could be seen incorporated in the northern side of its surrounding wall.

ECONOMIC HISTORY. In 1066 the land that later became Westwood and Iford manors was assessed for geld at 3 hides. It was worth £6 but only £4 in 1086. That decline in value is possibly reflected in the fact that although the estate could support 5 ploughs in 1066, there were only 4 in 1086. There were 3 ploughs and 3 serfs on the 2 demesne hides, 1 plough and 6 villeins and 4 bordars on the remaining hide. There were 6 a. of meadow and woodland 2 furlongs by 1 furlong.[35]

In the early 14th century the overall value of Westwood manor was some £20, a sum which included assessed rents of £7, and a rent of 7½ sticks of eels from the tenant of that moiety of the mill which formed part of John Waspray's estate. Robert Waspray's share of the manor was then farmed at £3 10s. yearly, and John Waspray's at £3 but was apparently worth £6 upon improvement.[36] In 1649 Westwood manor as then constituted was worth £177, again upon improvement.[37]

The entire manor of Westwood was let at farm during the 13th century and the early 14th.[38] It was only for a brief period after c. 1314 that it functioned within the inter-manorial economy of the estates of St. Swithun's Priory. In 1314 oxen were sold to the reeve of Enford, and in 1324 122 sheep were sent from Westwood to Enford after shearing.[39] The demesne was farmed from at least 1365. The farm, then £7 yearly, gradually fell over the next century and by 1469 had become fixed at £5, a sum that remained constant until at least the 18th century.[40]

Probably in the early 14th century there were 124 a. of arable in demesne scattered throughout the open fields. There was a pasture for between twelve and sixteen oxen, 13 a. of meadow of which 3 a. were apparently mown every other year, and pasture for 250 second-year sheep. That portion of the estate held by John Waspray contained 89 a., of which 60 a. were arable, and pasture for 100 second-year sheep.[41] In 1649 the demesne farm contained 192 a. Of that there were 37 a. of meadow, 30 a. of pasture in inclosures, and 33 a. of 'down' pasture. Of the 67 a. of arable, 30 a. were in open fields and 37 a. inclosed.[42] The farm, which extended to most parts of the chapelry, was worked from Westwood Manor and reckoned at 337 a. in 1792, an acreage which remained more or less constant until the farm was offered for sale in lots in the early 20th century.[43]

The arable and pasture mostly seem to have been inclosed by the mid 17th century.[44] In 1847, when the arable was reckoned at 413 a., the largest parcels were in Great down south of Avoncliff wood, in fields and furlongs east of the lane from Upper to Lower Westwood, and in Westwood and Iford fields in the south-west corner of the chapelry. Pasture, 242 a., was on Shrub down in the west part of the chapelry, in Elm Hayes north-east, in Cow leaze south, in Hay grove and New leaze south-west, and in Further and Hither Bustings east of Lower Westwood.[45]

There were 11 free tenants within that part of Westwood manor held by Robert Waspray in the later 13th century or the early 14th: 1 held 1 virgate, 3, including the tenant who held a moiety of the mill, ½ virgate each, and the remaining 7 no more than a few acres each. Of the 9 unfree tenants 2 held ½ virgate each for 3s. 4d. yearly, and 7, who held a few acres each, similarly paid money rents.[46] Two more lists of tenants, possibly of similar date, perhaps refer to the remaining moiety of the manor. The first, which is certainly to be identified with John Waspray's portion of Westwood, records 6 free tenants and 6 villeins of whom 2 held ½ virgate each and 4 were cottars. The second list records 14 free tenants, of whom 2 held 1 virgate each, 2, including the tenant who held the remaining moiety of the mill, ½ virgate, and the rest a few acres each. The duties of the 3 unfree tenants within that portion of the manor were confined to mowing, haymaking, hoeing, and hurdle-making.[47]

Early inclosure assisted the emergence of fairly compact copyhold farms which occupied an area roughly in the centre of the chapelry between Upper and Lower Westwood.[48] In 1649, of the sixteen copyholds totalling some 190 a. within Westwood manor, nine were small farms of between 10 a. and 40 a.[49] Osmund Gibbs's copyhold, which contained a quarry, is identifiable with the later Greenhill farm, reckoned at 34 a. in 1692.[50] Zachary Walter, the tenant from 1680 to 1685, built Greenhill House on it.[51] G. C. Tugwell, the lessee of the manorial demesne, acquired the copyhold, 50 a., between 1843 and 1847, and it was enfranchised for him in 1850.[52] Although after 1864 it formed part of the Tugwells' freehold estate at Westwood, Greenhill farm retained its identity and in 1911 was a dairy farm of 61 a.[53] William Hayward's copyhold, which also included a quarry, was reckoned at 40 a. in 1649.[54] The land is possibly that to which Thomas Joyce was admitted in 1815.[55] The Joyce family's copyhold estate, worked from the house called Upper Westwood Farm from the later 19th century,

[35] V.C.H. Wilts. ii, p. 120; see above.
[36] Hanna, 'Winch. Cath. Custumal', pp. lvi, lix, 427 sqq.
[37] Mun. D. & C. Winton., survey of chap. man. f. 208.
[38] See above.
[39] Mun. D. & C. Winton., acct. rolls, 1314, 1324.
[40] Ibid. acct. rolls, 14th–16th cent.; box 87, acct. rolls, 16th-cent.; ledger bk. XI, ff. 6, 105; XV, f. 68; XXIII, ff. 54, 112.
[41] Hanna, 'Winch. Cath. Custumal', pp. lvi, lix, 430–3, 438–9.
[42] Mun. D. & C. Winton., survey of chap. man. ff. 198 sqq.
[43] Ibid. estate bk. 22A, survey, 1792; H.R.O., Eccl. Commrs. 59616; 11M59/8082–3; Ch. Commrs., survey bk. DD 3 (Winch. chap.), pp. 557–663.
[44] Mun. D. & C. Winton., survey of chap. man. f. 206.

[45] H.R.O., Eccl. Commrs. 59616; 11M59/8083.
[46] Hanna, 'Winch. Cath. Custumal', 433–5.
[47] Ibid. 436–9.
[48] Mun. D. & C. Winton., estate bk. 22A, survey, 1792; H.R.O. 11M59/8082.
[49] Mun. D. & C. Winton., survey of chap. man. ff. 198 sqq.
[50] Ibid. estate bk. 3, ff. 75v.–76.
[51] Ibid.; box 84, ct. roll, 26 Aug. 1680; box 87, ct. roll, 26 Nov. 1685; see above, p. 225.
[52] I.R. 29/38/276; I.R. 30/38/276; H.R.O., Eccl. Commrs. 59616; 11M59/8083; Mun. D. & C. Winton., list of enfranchisements, f. 3v.; see above.
[53] Mun. D. & C. Winton., box 114, sale cat.
[54] Ibid. survey of chap. man. ff. 202 sqq.
[55] H.R.O., Eccl. Commrs. 59512.

was enlarged by the addition of more copyhold land during the 19th century, and by 1847 contained, besides the quarry north-west of the farm-house, 100 a. The land, farmed with the freehold Shute's farm, 59 a., was enfranchised in 1867.[56] Upper Westwood farm, 112 a., was devoted to dairying in 1911.[57] In 1792 18 tenants held 234 a. as copyhold of the manor, 43 held 239 a. in 1847, and 29 held 160 a. in 1862. The reversions were sold by the Ecclesiastical Commissioners between 1864 and 1873.[58]

Westwood, once thickly wooded, was included within the Wiltshire portion of Selwood forest until the early 14th century. From that time Avoncliff wood, 35–40 a., formed part of the manorial demesne.[59] Addy (by 1890 Becky Addy) wood was partly in the hands of freeholders and partly of three copyholders in the 19th century.[60] Both Avoncliff, 54 a., and Becky Addy, 36 a., woods were part of the Westwood Manor estate in 1911.[61]

In the 15th century two quarries, one described as in Mandeville's grove and the other held by the Doggett family, were let at 2s. and 4s. respectively.[62] That in Mandeville's grove had been leased with the demesne by 1482, as apparently had the other by the earlier 16th century.[63] They were somewhere on the Bath Oolite which extends north-east to south-west across the chapelry. Both had ceased to be used by 1649.[64] Of the two quarries then worked, one was part of the copyhold later called Upper Westwood farm.[65] It was in woodland some distance north-west of the farm-house and was still worked in 1862 when the copyholder, who paid £3 yearly to the Ecclesiastical Commissioners, sub-let.[66]

William Godwin was a quarry-master at Westwood in the later 19th century and the firm of Godwin Bros. still existed there in 1903.[67] Another firm, Randell, Saunders & Co. Ltd., became part of Bath Stone Firms Ltd. in 1887.[68] The Bath & Portland Group Ltd. still owned the quarries west of the lane from Lower to Upper Westwood in 1978. Stone was transported from Upper Westwood to the canal wharf at Avoncliff by means of a tramway in the later 19th century and the earlier 20th.[69] The quarries, which then, as in 1978, were entered north-west of Upper Westwood Farm, were taken over in 1939 by the Ministry of Supply. In 1941 the Enfield (later Royal Enfield) Motor Cycle Co. of Redditch (Worcs.) moved there and cleared the underground workings to make factory accommodation. During the Second World War fire-control instruments were made there for the Directorate of Instrument Production and afterwards parts for

motor-cycles. About 1969 the firm, then called Enfield Precision Engineers and owned by the firm of E. & H. P. Smith, vacated the quarries, which extended some considerable distance underground on either side of the lane from Upper to Lower Westwood. The easterly part was leased from the Bath & Portland Group Ltd. by Darlington Mushrooms of Bradford on Avon and mushrooms were grown there from 1934 to 1959. Although the firm was still lessee in 1978, mushrooms were then no longer produced. In 1978 only a small area of the quarries south of Upper Westwood Farm was worked intermittently for the Bath & Portland Group Ltd. Part was then let to a local engineering firm, Willett & Wilkins. Other surface buildings were also let separately.[70]

Iford manor was worth £8 a year in the mid 16th century. Of that sum £4 represented assessed rents from Iford and £2 those from Westwood. Three tenants in Westwood and one in Freshford were then attached to the estate.[71] The manor apparently had no open field of its own and shared in those of Westwood.[72]

The position of the estate at the confluence of the Frome and Avon, which provided ample water-power, and its proximity to supplies of Fuller's Earth gave it an importance incommensurable with its size. In 1700 it contained, besides mills at Iford and Avoncliff,[73] some 100 a., some of which lay on the western bank of the Frome in Somerset but most around Iford House and in the north-west corner of Westwood chapelry.[74] It was reduced in size by the loss in 1743 of Avoncliff mills and in 1791 of Shute's farm, 42 a., the only copyhold of any size, which occupied the land between Iford and Avoncliff and included a freestone quarry.[75] Iford mill was sub-let and the remaining 45 a. became, and remained in the 20th century, a gentleman's estate.[76]

Apart from the small industrial concerns at Upper Westwood, the parish was entirely devoted to agriculture in 1978. On the numerous small farms, none of which was owner-occupied,[77] dairying predominated. Most inhabitants then worked outside Westwood in Bristol, Bath, or Trowbridge.

MILLS. In 1086 a mill which paid 10s. was attached to the estate held by the church of Winchester at Westwood.[78] It probably stood on the Avon. In the later 13th century a moiety of the mill and ½ virgate were held freely by Reynold of Cliff for 6s. yearly, and a moiety and another ½ virgate by Henry of

[56] H.R.O., Eccl. Commrs. 59516; 11M59/8083.
[57] Mun. D. & C. Winton., sale cat.
[58] Ibid. estate bk. 22A, survey, 1792; H.R.O., Eccl. Commrs. 59616; 11M59/8082–3; Ch. Commrs., survey bk. DD 3 (Winch. chap.), pp. 557–663.
[59] V.C.H. Wilts. iv. 415; Hanna, 'Winch. Cath. Custumal', 432–3; H.R.O., Eccl. Commrs. 59597, pp. 1–2; I.R. 29/38/276; I.R. 30/38/276; Ch. Commrs., survey bk. DD 3 (Winch. chap.), p. 573.
[60] I.R. 29/38/276; I.R. 30/38/276; O.S. Map 6″, Wilts. XXXVIII (1890 edn.).
[61] Mun. D. & C. Winton., box 114, sale cat.
[62] Ibid. acct. rolls, 1405 and later years in the 15th cent.
[63] Ibid. acct. rolls, 1482, 1484–5, 1491–2, 1499; ledger bk. II, f. 29; Winch. Chap. Doc. 1541–7, ed. G. W. Kitchin and F. T. Madge (Hants Rec. Soc.), 96.
[64] Mun. D. & C. Winton., survey of chap. man. f. 206.
[65] Ibid.; see above.

[66] H.R.O., Eccl. Commrs. 59616; 11M59/8083; Ch. Commrs., survey bk. DD 3 (Winch. chap.), p. 659.
[67] Kelly's Dir. Wilts. (1848 and later edns.).
[68] Ibid. (1885 and later edns.); ex inf. Mr. G. P. P. Hart, Secretary, Bath & Portland Group Ltd., Bath.
[69] O.S. Map 6″, Wilts. XXXVIII (1890 edn.); Mun. D. & C. Winton., box 114, sale cat. map (1911).
[70] Ex inf. Mr. Hart; Mr. K. G. M. Pointing, Darlington Mushrooms, Bradford on Avon; the Revd. S. E. W. Guy Westwood Vicarage.
[71] Valor Eccl. (Rec. Com.), i. 156–7; E 318/1227 m. 20.
[72] W.R.O. 473/54, later-17th-cent. survey; see above.
[73] See below.
[74] W.R.O. 445/1; I.R. 29/38/276; I.R. 30/38/276.
[75] W.R.O. 445/106.
[76] I.R. 29/38/276; I.R. 30/38/276; W.R.O. 840/8/1.
[77] Ex inf. the Revd. S. E. W. Guy.
[78] V.C.H. Wilts. ii, p. 120.

Cliff who paid yearly to St. Swithun's Priory 12s. and 7½ sticks of eels and owed suit of court at Westwood manor.[79] No more is known of either moiety.

Nicholas of Iford conveyed a mill as part of an estate at Iford to Hinton Priory in the later 14th century. The mill thereafter descended with the manor of Iford and was still part of the estate in 1978.[80]

The position of Iford mill in an area endowed with the necessary natural resources for cloth making presumably attracted John Horton (will proved 1497) to become tenant there in the later 15th century. While most of the Iford estate lay in Wiltshire, the mill stood just within the parish of Hinton Charterhouse in Somerset. It may have been John Horton who converted the mill for fulling purposes and established a cloth manufacturing business there.[81] It was due, however, to the acumen of his son Thomas (d. 1530), one of the most successful clothiers of his time, that the business flourished.[82] When Thomas's nephew Thomas acquired the freehold from the Crown in 1543 the mill-house contained four fulling stocks.[83] The last Horton to own Iford, Toby, took no active part in the manufacture of woollen cloth there, as far as is known, and soon after acquiring the mill let the two fulling stocks at the eastern end of the mill-house to John Yerbury (will dated 1614) and his sons John and William. The Yerbury family's tenancy presumably ended in 1615 when the survivor, John the younger, became a lunatic.[84] In 1650 the Bradford clothier Paul Methuen was tenant of the same two stocks, and from 1687 the Trowbridge clothier William Brewer, said to be the leading manufacturer of medleys in England, and his son William (will dated 1709) were tenants.[85] The younger William's widow assigned the lease to Thomas Harding, whose family leased the mill and all four of its stocks until 1749.[86] The entire mill was let to Samuel Perkins in 1767 and to Thomas Perkins in 1787.[87] It was still used for fulling in 1839 when Sarah Perkins was tenant.[88]

The main range of Iford mill retains some 16th- or earlier-17th-century features including a wind-braced roof.[89] The four stocks which the mill formerly contained seem to have been disposed in sets of two, each set driven by a separate water-wheel, at the east and west ends.[90] The mill, which incorporated the mill-house, was extended westwards in the later 17th century. There were presumably in the 16th century, as in the 17th and 18th centuries, associated industrial buildings near

by including a clay-house, dye-house, and drying-room. Iford House itself contained a room used as a beating-loft.[91] Male & Marchant of Freshford reconstructed and refitted the mill c. 1965 as a house for Miss Elizabeth Cartwright[92] who lived there in 1978.

A mill or mills at Avoncliff formed part of Iford manor in the later 17th century. Avoncliff mills, as the property was then known, and some meadow land were sold in 1700 with the manor by Henry Baynton's trustees to William Chanler.[93] By will proved 1743 Chanler's widow Eleanor devised the mills to Margaret, wife of Gabriel Goldney.[94] Margaret Goldney was still owner in 1762 but in the following year the property was bought by Richard Stratton, a fuller.[95] Stratton sold it in 1767 to Edward Hall, who in 1768 sold it to Joseph H. Saunders.[96] Saunders sold it in 1781 to John Yerbury of Bradford.[97] Yerbury (will proved 1825) devised the property to his sons Francis and John as tenants in common.[98] In 1853 Francis sold his moiety to John (d. 1858).[99] In 1860 J. A. Wheeler was owner and so remained until 1878.[1] The mill was owned by George Harman c. 1885 but by the end of the century was the property of William Selwyn, whose firm still operated it in 1939.[2]

The conversion from grist- to fulling-mill in the 18th century may have been a gradual one. In 1731 a dye-house was attached to the grist-mill, and 10 years later a cloth-worker occupied a near-by cottage. The process was complete in 1763 when, besides the dye-house, there was a stove. Stove and dye-house, however, had been converted to two dwellings by 1781.[3] In the late 18th century and the early 19th the mill was let on a series of short tenancies in some of which the elder John Yerbury, as owner, apparently had some interest. The cloth manufacturing business of John Moggeridge, Yerbury's son-in-law, and Moggeridge's partner Thomas Joyce, who became tenants in 1790, extended beyond Avoncliff to near-by areas.[4] It was presumably they who further mechanized the cloth making process at Avoncliff by installing machinery driven by water-power, as far as is known the first instance in the area, c. 1791. It was perhaps to provide both housing and workshops that the U-shaped building called Avoncliff or 'Ankley' Square was built on the south bank of the Avon after 1792 on land bought by Moggeridge and Joyce in 1791.[5] In 1798 Avoncliff mill itself was no longer connected with Moggeridge's and Joyce's cloth making business, but the 'houses' at Avoncliff were still the property of Thomas Joyce c. 1814.[6] Another tenant installed

[79] Hanna, 'Winch. Cath. Custumal', 427 sqq., 434, 436.
[80] Mun. D. & C. Winton., ledger bk. I, f. 2v.; Cal. Pat. 1374-7, 31.
[81] W.N. & Q. iv. 170.
[82] V.C.H. Wilts. iv. 141-2.
[83] E 318/1227 m. 20.
[84] Wilts. Inq. p.m. 1625-49 (Index Libr.), 160-1.
[85] W.R.O. 445/53; V.C.H. Wilts. vii. 43, 138.
[86] W.R.O. 445/53-5.
[87] Ibid. 445/56-7.
[88] K. H. Rogers, Wilts. & Som. Woollen Mills, 193.
[89] Local tradition considers the roof to have been brought from the ch. of Wittenham with Rowley (in Wingfield) in the 16th cent.: V.C.H. Wilts. vii. 75.
[90] E 318/1227 m. 20; W.R.O. 445/53-5.
[91] W.R.O. 445/53; Rogers, Wilts. & Som. Woollen Mills, 192-3, where a full acct. of Iford mill is given.
[92] Wilts. Tracts, 171, no. 22.
[93] W.R.O. 687/24, abstr. of title.
[94] Ibid. 445/121; 687/24, abstr. of title.

[95] Ibid. 687/24, abstr. of title; deed, Stratton to Miles, 1766.
[96] Ibid. deed, Stratton to Hall; deed, Hall to Saunders.
[97] Ibid. deed, Saunders to Yerbury.
[98] Prob. 11/1694 (P.C.C. 50 St. Albans).
[99] W.R.O. 687/27, deed, Yerbury to Yerbury; fam. settlement, 1875.
[1] Except where stated otherwise, the remaining inf. about the mill is from Rogers, Wilts. & Som. Woollen Mills, 164-5, where a comprehensive acct. is given.
[2] Kelly's Dir. Wilts. (1885 and later edns.).
[3] W.R.O. 687/24, abstr. of title.
[4] Rogers, op. cit. 157, 164, 194, 196.
[5] Ibid. 32; H.R.O. 11M59/8082.
[6] W.R.O. 847/10. The bldgs. were sold to Bradford guardians as a workhouse in 1835: see above, p. 225, where a description of the bldgs. is given.

dressing and brushing machinery in the mill in 1804.[7] From 1860 and still in 1939 the owners of the mill manufactured flock there.[8]

In 1811 Avoncliff mill had four floors and two wheels, one of which drove four pairs of stocks and the other the machinery. By 1878 a collection of factory buildings had grown up around the mill on the south bank of the river at Avoncliff on the east side of the lane leading to Upper Westwood. Besides the main four-storeyed mill, to which power was supplied by a turbine wheel, perhaps the horizontal turbine wheel extant in 1978, there were also a south mill, a tearing and willying shop of two floors, and a three-storeyed hot-air stove. By 1978 the main mill, then called the Old Mill or Weavers' Mill, had, although still displaying features of 18th-century date, been much reduced in size and height and converted to a private dwelling. The south mill was then also a dwelling, but the other buildings, including a tall brick and stone chimney, were ruinous.

LOCAL GOVERNMENT. In the 13th century the prior of St. Swithun's claimed, by virtue of various royal grants, to be quit of suit of shire and hundred at the court of Bradford hundred, in which Westwood was then included.[9] Attempts were apparently made to compel the prior to attend the sheriff's tourns at Bradford in the early 14th century.[10] Records of courts held twice yearly at Westwood show the attempts to have been unsuccessful. At those courts the prior held view of frankpledge as well as exercising manorial jurisdiction, but, as far as is known, claimed no other franchise.[11] The attendance of the prior's men at the Bradford tourn was successfully enforced in 1439 but from the later 15th century the prior seems to have exercised unchallenged his right to hold the view at Westwood.[12]

From the 15th century to the 18th courts were called views of frankpledge and courts and during the 19th usually views of frankpledge, courts leet, and courts of the manor.[13] During the 17th and 18th centuries courts were generally held once a year in late summer or autumn, and in the 19th once a year or every other year in the early summer. The last known was held in 1863. At a view in 1540 Westwood tithing, which comprised Westwood and Iford manors and was conterminous with the chapelry, was enjoined to repair roads at Upper and Lower Westwood,[14] but from the 17th century business

there was mostly formal, such as the election of a tithingman for the following year. Business at the manorial courts was concerned with the regulation of small agricultural matters, the presentments of nuisances, and copyhold surrenders and admittances.

Records of courts for Iford manor survive for various years in the later 17th century.[15] The courts were held once or twice yearly in spring and autumn. In 1676 and 1677 the rails round the mill and its pond were ordered to be repaired, and in the 1680s the owner of Iford House was yearly enjoined to repair the road between Iford bridge and mill.

Westwood chapelry apparently relieved its own poor by the early 19th century.[16] Churchwardens' accounts for 1798–1869 and vestry minutes for 1802–72, entered in the same book, show Westwood to have pursued a vigorous policy in dealing with paupers.[17] The instigator and chief exponent of that policy was John Spackman, tenant farmer at Manor farm, who as a result incurred much enmity among local labourers and paupers.[18] A board of health consisting of six parishioners, appointed in 1831 to take precautionary measures against cholera, convened a sub-committee which reported that Westwood was generally in a clean and healthy state.

In 1835 Spackman was instrumental in setting up Bradford poor-law union in which Westwood was included in the same year.[19] Spackman, too, was probably responsible for the selection as a workhouse and subsequent purchase of the building in the north of Westwood called Avoncliff Square.[20] Declining numbers of inmates in the early 20th century resulted in those remaining being transferred to Warminster workhouse in 1917. The empty building was sold in 1923.[21]

CHURCH. The royal grant of 1001 to Shaftesbury Abbey of a large estate centred on Bradford probably included land to be identified with the later manor of Westwood. Although Westwood was alienated in the following year, it remained dependent ecclesiastically on the church of Bradford as a parochial chapelry with rights of baptism, marriage, and burial until the later 19th century.[22] The rectors and, after 1349, the vicars of Bradford appointed chaplains and, later, assistant curates nominated either to Bradford, or to Bradford and Westwood, or to Westwood and one or more of Bradford's other chapelries.[23] Because the vicars took the great tithes of the chapelry after 1349 they were sometimes called

[7] V.C.H. Wilts. iv. 169.
[8] Kelly's Dir. Wilts. (1867 and later edns.).
[9] Chartulary Winch. Cath. ed. Goodman, pp. 97, 226; Plac. de Quo Warr. (Rec. Com.), 806.
[10] Chartulary Winch. Cath. ed. Goodman, p. 226; Abbrev. Plac. (Rec. Com.), 338.
[11] Mun. D. & C. Winton., ct. rolls, 1313–14, 1321–2, 1327, 1359–60.
[12] W.A.M. xiii. 118; Mun. D. & C. Winton., ct. rolls, 1443–4, 1517–19, 1540; W.R.O. 906/S.C. 14, Westwood ct. 1477.
[13] This para. is based on Mun. D. & C. Winton., box 84, 16th- and 17th-cent. ct. rolls; ibid. N.R.A. boxes VIII–XI, progress bks. 1731–1847; W.A.M. xli. 239–41; H.R.O., Eccl. Commrs. 59501; 59512; 59516; 59519–59522.
[14] Mun. D. & C. Winton., ct. roll, 1540.
[15] This para. is based on W.R.O. 118/128, copy of ct. roll, 1657; 118/92, copy of ct. roll, 1658; 473/54, ct. papers, 1675–7, 1680–3, 1686.

[16] Poor Law Com. 1st Rep. H.C. 500, p. 243 (1835), xxxv.
[17] This para. is based on W.R.O. 847/10.
[18] Wilts. Tracts, 163, no. 13; I.R. 29/38/276.
[19] M.H. 12/13668; Poor Law Com. 1st Rep. (1835), App. D, p. 243.
[20] M.H. 12/13668; see above, pp. 225, 231.
[21] W.R.O., poor-law union rec., union min. bk. 1916–21, pp. 124–6; 1921–5, pp. 129, 135.
[22] Ibid. 847/1–6; V.C.H. Wilts. vii. 23 sqq.
[23] V.C.H. Wilts. vii. 23 sqq.; W.N. & Q. viii. 74 sqq.; iv. 165; Phillipps, Wilts. Inst. (index in W.A.M. xxviii. 214); Valor Eccl. (Rec. Com.), ii. 145; Sar. Dioc. R.O., Detecta Bk. 1550–3, f. 19v.; Detecta Bk. 1584, f. 43; Detecta Bk. 1585, f. 21; Bradford Glebe Terrier, 1704; bp.'s transcripts, 17th–19th cent.; curates' nominations, 1786–1829; Vis. Queries, 1864; W.R.O. 335/173, deed, Chapman to Reynolds (1771); 77/7, curates' licences, 1858–9, 1861, 1872; Rep. Com. Eccl. Revenues, 824–5; H.O. 129/258/1/7; Clergy List (1859); Lond. Gaz. 1 Dec. 1876, p. 6676.

rectors of Westwood.[24] The chapelry is expressly mentioned in 1299 when John Waspray, who held Westwood manor at farm, presented a chaplain to the ordinary for institution.[25] By what right he did so is unknown, and his presentee was apparently not instituted. Since he restored the 'advowson of the church' of Westwood with the manor to St. Swithun's Priory in 1313–14, the presentation may possibly represent an attempt by the convent, as lord of Westwood, to create an independent benefice there.[26]

In 1876 Westwood was detached from the vicarage of Bradford and constituted a separate ecclesiastical parish and a perpetual curacy in the gift of Bristol chapter.[27] Under the Act of 1868, however, the living was at once deemed a vicarage and its incumbent styled a vicar.[28] In 1975, with the benefices of Holy Trinity and Christ Church, both in Bradford, Monkton Farleigh with South Wraxall, and Winsley, the vicarage became part of Bradford group ministry.[29]

When a vicarage was ordained at Bradford in 1349 the entire profits of the chapelry of Westwood were assigned to the vicar. They then included all the tithes of the chapelry and perhaps the 18 a. of glebe mentioned in 1704.[30] The value of the chapelry was always included in that of Bradford vicarage.[31] In 1771, however, the chapelry property was let to a layman separately from that of the vicarage at £54 yearly.[32] In 1843 the tithes of Westwood were commuted for a rent-charge of £190. A rent-charge of £1 8s. was allotted to the incumbent of Farleigh Hungerford for the tithes from 4 a., apparently originally part of Farleigh, to which he was entitled in Westwood.[33] When the chapelry became a parish in 1876 the rent-charge and the glebe lands were allotted to the incumbent of the new benefice.[34] In the following year the Ecclesiastical Commissioners provided an additional yearly endowment of £125.[35] The vicar of Westwood still had some 18 a. of glebe in 1978.[36]

Possibly in 1349, and certainly in 1704, there was a glebe-house attached to the chapelry.[37] In 1843 it was described as a cottage and stood south-west of the church.[38] Its unsuitability led the vicar of Bradford to remark in 1864 that, if better accommodation could be provided at Westwood, an assistant curate might be persuaded to live there.[39] In 1870 it was proposed that the cottage be refurbished but in 1877–8, with £1,500 granted by the Ecclesiastical Commissioners, a new house for the vicarage was

built south-west of the church by Voisey & Wills of Bristol.[40] That house was sold in 1965 and replaced by another immediately east where the vicar lived in 1978.[41]

Few assistant curates, at least from the later 17th century, seem to have remained long. The curacy of Caleb Bevan, who apparently lived at Westwood, was unusual in lasting from 1622 to 1668.[42] From the late 19th century, at least, the vicars of Westwood frequently served as chaplains to the Bradford union workhouse at Avoncliff.[43] On Census Sunday in 1851 there was only one Sunday service. Over the past year, however, an average congregation of 70 had attended morning, and 100 afternoon, services.[44] The difficulty the vicar of Bradford encountered in persuading assistant curates to live at Westwood in the 1860s apparently did not result in spiritual torpor within the chapelry. Services with sermons were held at the church twice on Sundays in 1864 and were attended by an average congregation of 80 in the mornings and 100 in the afternoons. Congregations were similarly large at services held on Christmas day and Good Friday. Holy Communion, then celebrated at Christmas, Easter, and Whitsun and in every other month, was received by an average of fifteen communicants.[45]

The church of *ST. MARY THE VIRGIN*, so called in the later 19th century but in the early 14th dedicated to All Saints,[46] is built of ashlar rubble and has a chancel, nave with short north aisle, and west tower.[47] A window, reset piscina, and a doorway in the chancel are all of the 13th century. The narrow three-bay nave perhaps retains 12th- or 13th-century proportions, and masonry of early character survives in the lower part of the north wall. It has no doorway either to north or south. A lancet window in the north wall of the chancel was blocked when the church was enlarged in the later 15th century by the addition of a north aisle entered through a two-bay arcade. That aisle served as a chapel and a squint was inserted to provide a view of the high altar. The coloured decoration on the aisle walls was obliterated during a 19th-century restoration. It may have been at the same time that the west half of the aisle ceiling, which was of carved oak, was replaced by one of lath and plaster. A plain wooden ceiling to match the original east half was put up in 1968.[48] It has been suggested that the 15th-century glass in the chancel windows was moved there from those of the north aisle.[49] The

[24] W.R.O. 906/S.C. 14, Westwood ct. 1477; Phillipps, *Wilts. Inst.* i. 163, 168; I.R. 29/38/276.
[25] *Reg. Ghent* (Cant. & York Soc.), ii. 601 and n. 1; see above, p. 226.
[26] *Reg. Ghent* (Cant. & York Soc.), ii. 601; Mun. D. & C. Winton., bk. of John Chase, f. 86v.
[27] *Lond. Gaz.* 1 Dec. 1876, pp. 6676 sqq.
[28] Incumbents Act, 1868, 31 & 32 Vic. c. 117, s. 2.
[29] Ch. Commrs. file N.B. 34/371.
[30] *W.N. & Q.* viii. 74 sqq.; Sar. Dioc. R.O., Bradford Glebe Terrier.
[31] *Valor Eccl.* (Rec. Com.), ii. 145; *Rep. Com. Eccl. Revenues*, 824–5.
[32] W.R.O. 335/173, deed, Chapman to Reynolds.
[33] I.R. 29/38/276. The date of the transfer of the 4 a. to Westwood is unknown: *V.C.H. Wilts.* vii. 75.
[34] *Lond. Gaz.* 1 Dec. 1876, pp. 6676 sqq.
[35] Ibid. 16 Feb. 1877, p. 759.
[36] Ex inf. Ch. Commrs.; the Revd. S. E. W. Guy, Westwood Vicarage.   [37] *W.N. & Q.* viii. 77.
[38] I.R. 29/38/276; I.R. 30/38/276.

[39] Sar. Dioc. R.O., Vis. Queries.
[40] Ibid. Mortgages, no. 192; *Lond. Gaz.* 16 Feb. 1877, p. 759; Ch. Commrs. file 54844, pt. 1/2.
[41] Ex inf. Ch. Commrs.
[42] Sar. Dioc. R.O., bp.'s transcripts, 17th–19th cent.; curates' nominations, 1786–1829; Vis. Queries, 1864; W.R.O. 77/7, curates' licences, 1858–9, 1861, 1872.
[43] *Crockford* (1896 and later edns.); *Clergy List* (1915).
[44] H.O. 129/258/1/7.
[45] Sar. Dioc. R.O., Vis. Queries.
[46] Ibid.; *Crockford* (1907 and later edns.); Mun. D. & C. Winton., bk. of John Chase, f. 86v. The original dedication had apparently been lost by the 16th cent.: J. Ecton, *Thesaurus*, 395.
[47] J. Buckler, water-colour in W.A.S. Libr., vol. v. 38 (1808).
[48] Guide in ch. In the 19th cent. W. H. Jones noted that the initials 'T.H.', representing either Thomas Horton (d. 1530) or his nephew and namesake (d. 1549), were visible on the ceiling: ibid.
[49] Wilts. Tracts, 130, no. 24.

south nave wall was probably rebuilt when the tower was constructed by Thomas Horton (d. 1530).[50] The tower, elaborately designed with panelled faces and embattled parapets, has an octagonal stair turret with a dome at the south-east corner. The ornamental plasterwork of the nave ceiling may date from 1786. The south wall of the chancel was rebuilt c. 1840. An extensive restoration, during which the west gallery erected c. 1696 was dismantled and the chapel repewed, was undertaken by W. H. Jones, vicar of Bradford 1851–84 and a noted antiquary, and the church was reopened in 1856.[51]

The font is of the early 13th century and has an elaborate 16th-century cover, suspended from an iron bracket, which imitates the cupola on the stair turret of the tower. Above the font on the west wall of the nave is a carved stone devil of the early 16th century, known as the 'old lad of Westwood' and 'the Westwood imp', beneath which is inscribed 'Resist me and I will flee'. The pulpit, dated 1607, is said to have been brought from Norton St. Philip.[52] The 17th-century screen probably served originally as the communion rail. A large oval plaque by T. King of Bath on the south nave wall commemorates Richard Cox (d. 1789).

The plate was lost in the earlier 19th century and by 1891 had been replaced by a chalice, paten, and flagon of plated metal.[53] In 1978 Westwood had, besides a modern set of plate, an antique chalice and paten given by Sir Michael Peto, Bt.[54] The church had four bells in 1553. In the earlier 20th century, as in 1978, there was still a ring of four: (i), 1677, is by John (II) Lott of Warminster; (ii) and (iii) are by Henry Jefferies (fl. mid 16th cent.) of Bristol; (iv), possibly of the later 15th century, was cast at Bristol. All were recast between 1884 and 1886 by Llewellins & James of Bristol.[55] Registrations of baptisms are extant from 1666, but are lacking from 1697 to 1726; those of burials are entered from 1669 and are complete; and marriage entries survive from 1672, but are lacking from 1685 to 1727.[56]

ROMAN CATHOLICISM. A chapel of ease, served from Trowbridge, was founded at Westwood in 1940 and was attended by Irish workers building the factory in the quarry at Upper Westwood. It closed c. 1942 after the work was finished.[57]

PROTESTANT NONCONFORMITY. Baptists registered a house at Westwood in 1814.[58] What was probably the same group certified another house there in 1817.[59] The meeting flourished and a chapel at Lower Westwood was opened in 1865.[60] It was connected with the Particular Baptist meeting at Back (now Church) Street, Trowbridge, later called Emmanuel chapel, of which the Westwood attenders were considered members.[61] A room for a Sunday school was built north-west of the chapel and opened in 1885.[62] Some fifteen people attended the chapel c. 1890 when there was also a flourishing Sunday school.[63] The chapel was still affiliated to Emmanuel chapel, Trowbridge, in 1950.[64] In 1978 the chapel was used as a studio and the schoolroom as a store.

A Wesleyan Methodist group at Upper Westwood originated c. 1840. Early meetings were held at the farm-house, in 1978 called Greenhill House, where the group's deacon, John Tanner, lived.[65] In 1851 an average of 20 people in the afternoons, and 60 in the evenings, had attended meetings there over the past year.[66] The group opened a chapel at the western end of the hamlet in 1862.[67] It was closed before 1971[68] and by 1978 had been converted to a private dwelling.

EDUCATION. The only school in Westwood chapelry in the early 19th century was a Sunday school.[69] In 1841, however, a day-school was built on the south side of the lane leading from Lower Westwood to Iford.[70] In 1859 a mistress taught 30 boys and girls at the school, which was affiliated to the National Society and supported mainly by subscriptions. Some ten or fifteen children from the chapelry then attended a school run by dissenters at Freshford.[71] On return day in 1871 thirteen boys and twelve girls attended the Westwood school.[72] The workhouse children attended a school in the workhouse grounds in the later 19th century.[73] In 1908 an average of 92 pupils, a much increased number which may have resulted from the closure of the workhouse school, had attended the National school over the past year. Average attendance remained fairly steady until 1913 but afterwards showed a gradual decrease until c. 1930. Thereafter figures dwindled rapidly and in 1938 only an average of 27 children had attended during the past year.[74]

The school proved inadequate for the increased numbers resulting from Westwood's growth after the Second World War and was closed in 1976. It was replaced in that year by Westwood with Iford County Primary School at the north end of Boswell

[50] The initials 'T.H.' appear in the spandrels of the W. doorway.
[51] Guide in ch.; Florence R. Goodman, *Revd. Landlords and their Tenants* (Winch. priv. print. 1930), 89; Wilts. Tracts, 163, no. 13; *Clergy List* (1859, 1892); W.R.O. 847/10.
[52] Guide in ch.
[53] The plate was reputedly pawned by an earlier-19th-cent. par. clerk and proved untraceable at his death: W.R.O. 847/2; 847/10; Nightingale, *Wilts. Plate*, 131.
[54] Ex inf. the Revd. S. E. W. Guy.
[55] Walters, *Wilts. Bells*, 231, 266, 268–9, 304, 322; ex inf. the Revd. S. E. W. Guy.
[56] W.R.O. 847/1–6. The deficiencies of the fragmentary 1st reg. (847/1) are in part remedied by entries from it copied into the 2nd (847/2), and by transcripts in Sar. Dioc. R.O.
[57] *V.C.H. Wilts.* iii. 97; ex inf. the Revd. S. E. W. Guy.
[58] W.R.O., Return of Regns.; W. Doel, *Twenty Golden Candlesticks!*, 156.
[59] Sar. Dioc. R.O., Certs. Dissenters' Meeting-Houses.
[60] Doel, op. cit. 157; date on chapel.
[61] Doel, op. cit. 156–7; *V.C.H. Wilts.* iii. 138 and n. 54; vii. 159.
[62] Doel, op. cit. 157; date on sch.
[63] Doel, op. cit. 158.
[64] *V.C.H. Wilts.* vii. 160.
[65] Doel, op. cit. 156; I.R. 29/38/276; I.R. 30/38/276; H.O. 129/258/1/8; and see above, p. 225.
[66] H.O. 129/258/1/8.
[67] G.R.O. Worship Reg. no. 15271.
[68] Ibid.
[69] *Educ. of Poor Digest*, 1040; *Educ. Enquiry Abstract*, 1051.
[70] Mun. D. & C. Winton., chap. act bk. 1824–50, p. 299; date tablet on sch.
[71] *Acct. of Wilts. Schs.* 9; Mun. D. & C. Winton., chap. act bk. 1850–76, p. 53.
[72] *Returns relating to Elem. Educ.* 424–5.
[73] See p. 225.
[74] *Bd. of Educ., List 21* (H.M.S.O.).

Road where 120 children from Westwood and the surrounding area were taught in 1978.[75]

CHARITIES FOR THE POOR. None for the chapelry is known.

WROUGHTON

WROUGHTON, covering 2,813 ha. (6,950 a.), bounds upon Swindon to the north.[76] As a result of Swindon's boundary extensions Wroughton lost 148 a. (60 ha.) to the municipal borough in 1928 and 36 a. (15 ha.) in 1934.[77] Wroughton's southern boundary, 9 km. distant, is on the Marlborough Downs, and is formed by the trackway known as Smeathe's ridge which passes through the middle of Barbury Castle to meet the ridge way west of it.[78] A more or less straight road formerly running from Swindon up to Smeathe's ridge and Barbury down makes the eastern boundary. The western boundary also follows the straight course of an ancient road leading to the downs and known in the 14th century as Salthrop way.[79] After c. 4 km., however, the boundary leaves that road to take an irregular course which has the effect of excluding the Basset Down estate in Lydiard Tregoze and, since 1934, of including 19 a. called Can Court fields until then in Lydiard Tregoze.[80] From Can Court fields the boundary turns eastwards and then southwards to join the ridge way.

Until the boundary changes of 1928 and 1934 the north-east corner of the parish lay on the lower slopes of Swindon hill, the geology of which has been discussed elsewhere.[81] The rest of the parish is divided between Kimmeridge Clay in the north half and Lower Chalk in the south half.[82] A belt of Gault separates the two and provided the site for the early settlement of Wroughton. South of the Gault an outcrop of Upper Greensand forms an escarpment, the first of the two stages by which the land climbs to the outcrops of Middle and Upper Chalk around the 259 m. contour on Barbury down.

The greensand escarpment, which runs right across the parish, provides from the top a commanding view of the flat clay lands of the Thames valley. At Quidhampton and Salthrop in the west part of the parish it is well wooded, and in the east part two wooded coombs, Coombe bottom and Markham bottom, cut deeply into it. The church, Vicarage, and former rectory-house (now Wroughton House) stand together on a promontory almost at the top of the escarpment, apart from and overlooking the village below. Traces of a bank and ditch southwest of the church show that the site, a natural vantage-point, was once enclosed by earthworks.[83] Also on the promontory is the pasture called the

Ivory, a name commemorating the Lovels of Ivry-la-Bataille (Eure), lords of Elcombe from the 12th century to the 15th.[84] From the escarpment the ground rises more gently for about 3 km. before making the second stage of the ascent to 259 m. and the great Iron-Age camp of Barbury Castle, one of a string of camps which crown the northern edge of the Marlborough Downs.[85] Seven bowl-barrows lie near the camp, and some rectangular earthworks north of it are of Roman date.[86]

Two battles have been fought within Wroughton. The first was in 556 when the West Saxons led by Cynric and Ceawlin defeated the Britons near Barbury Castle.[87] Although it is marked on Ordnance Survey maps north-west of the camp, the exact site cannot be proved.[88] The second was the battle of Ellendune in 825 when Egbert, king of Wessex, defeated the Mercian king, Beornwulf, in what has been described as 'one of the most decisive battles of Anglo-Saxon history'.[89] Again the site is debatable, but the suggestion that it was on the downs above Markham bottom seems reasonable. The stream which runs through that coomb might then be the stream said by chroniclers to run red with blood.[90]

The parish was divided into five tithings. Elcombe, Overtown, Salthrop, and Westlecott all lay in Blackgrove (later Kingsbridge) hundred. Blagrove Farm in the north-west corner of the parish represents the meeting-place of that hundred.[91] The prior of St. Swithun's, Winchester, held an estate in the fifth tithing, Wroughton, which was therefore in the prior's hundred of Elstub. It is not known how exactly the tithing of Wroughton represents the prior's estate, which was called Ellendune in 1086. Attempts have been made to trace the bounds of Ellendune as given in 956.[92] Probably included in the tithing, 'Wervetone', identified as Lower Wroughton, was a separate estate in 1086 although later the site of the prior's manor-house.[93]

In the 13th century the name used for the prior's manor was not Ellendune but Wroughton, but the fact that the manor undoubtedly included Ellendune is shown by the phrase, used in 1270, 'Elendone quod est Worftone'.[94] Land in Ellendune was given at an early date to the parish church. The connexion between Ellendune and the church, which was usually called Ellendune church until the 19th century,[95] suggests that the name Ellendune may

[75] Ex inf. Chief Education Officer, County Hall, Trowbridge.
[76] This article was written in 1976–7.
[77] Census, 1961, pt. i, Table 4; pt. ii, Table B.
[78] Among maps used are O.S. Maps 1/50,000, sheet 173 (1974 edn.); 1/25,000, SU 17 (1960 edn.), SU 18 (1959 edn.); 1/2,500, Wilts. XV, XXII (1886 edn.).
[79] Cal. Pat. 1350–4, 148.
[80] V.C.H. Wilts. ix. 75, for a fuller acct. of that stretch of boundary.
[81] W. J. Arkell, 'Geol. Map of Swindon', W.A.M. lii. 195–212.
[82] Geol. Surv. Map 1″, drift, sheet 266 (1925 edn.); solid and drift, sheet 252 (1974 edn.).
[83] W.A.M. xxxviii. 374; V.C.H. Wilts. i (1), 271.

[84] W.R.O. 700/282; see below.
[85] V.C.H. Wilts. i (1), 94, 268; i (2), 469.
[86] Ibid. i (1), 204; W.A.M. xxxviii. 374.
[87] F. M. Stenton, Anglo-Saxon Eng. 28 and n. 2; A.-S. Chron. ed. Dorothy Whitelock (1961), 12.
[88] e.g. O.S. Map 1/50,000, sheet 173 (1974 edn.). See also W.A.M. liii. 399.
[89] Stenton, Anglo-Saxon Eng. 231.
[90] W.A.M. lvi. 270–1; Hen. of Huntingdon, Hist. Anglorum (Rolls Ser.), 132.
[91] V.C.H. Wilts. ix. 3, 5.
[92] Arch. Jnl. lxxv. 183–7; lxxvii. 54–5; W.A.M. lvi. 265–6.   [93] See below.
[94] Reg. Pontoise (Cant. & York Soc.), ii. 609; see below, p. 238.   [95] W.A.M. xxxvii. 400.

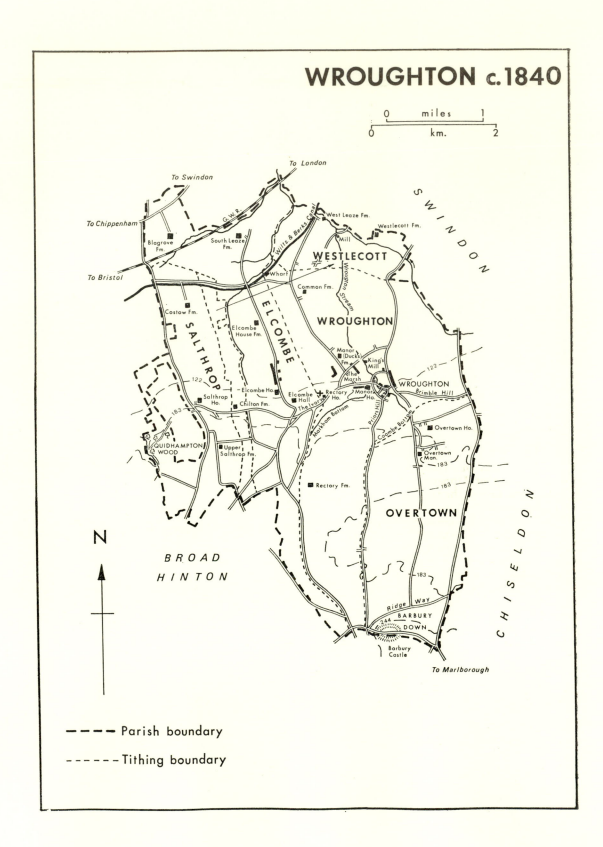

WROUGHTON c.1840

- - - - Parish boundary
- - - - - Tithing boundary

at some time have been expressly applied to the upland part of the parish where the church stands. The name, thought to mean elder tree down, supports the suggestion, while the name Wroughton, meaning farm on the river Worfe, an early name for the Wroughton stream, presumably refers to the lower part of the parish.[96] The presence of six mills in Ellendune in 1086, however, suggests that it also embraced the lower part of the parish. It seems that lowland estates were taken from the larger estate called Ellendune,[97] which encompassed a settlement and the church, and with their farmsteads were called Wroughton, and that they gave their name to the tithing and to all the estates and settlements in it. Although in 1086 Ellendune was only one of six estates within the parish, its name, taking many forms,[98] was long used for the entire parish. In 1324, for example, Quidhampton was said to lie 'in parochia de Elydon'.[99] Wroughton began to take over as the parish name towards the end of the 15th century. The form Wroughton alias Elyndon was then frequently used.[1]

Although Wroughton was the largest of the tithings and contained within it the parish church and the main settlement, Elcombe and Overtown were once fairly populous. In 1334 when Wroughton's contribution to the fifteenth was 106s., Elcombe and Overtown contributed 72s. and 70s. respectively, Westlecott paid 33s. and Salthrop 19s.[2] In 1377 Wroughton had 160 poll-tax payers, Elcombe 86, Overtown 63, and Salthrop 27.[3] To the benevolence of 1545 only the contributions of Wroughton, £3 18s. 8d., and Salthrop and Westlecott, both 33s. 4d., are known.[4] To the subsidy of 1576 Wroughton contributed £7 10s. and Elcombe £3 1s. 8d.[5] Only in 1841, when 220 labourers working on the G.W.R. line were included in the count, were the populations of the tithings given separately by the census enumerators. Wroughton then had a population of 1,445, Elcombe 348, Overtown 78, Salthrop 56, and Westlecott 36.[6]

Much of the population made up the labour force required to work the numerous farms in all the tithings and was dispersed. At Elcombe, however, which had a chapel until the 15th century,[7] there was a small settlement. In the earlier 17th century Elcombe street, as it was then called, leading north from Elcombe Hall to Elcombe common, was lined with cottages on either side.[8] In 1977 few of those remained and Elcombe consisted mainly of three or four scattered farms.

It has been suggested that a small settlement at Quidhampton (sometimes pronounced 'Quidding-ton'),[9] lying below the ridge in Salthrop tithing, was destroyed by a landslide in the 19th century.[10] Reference to a chapel in the 16th century gives weight to the suggestion that there was a hamlet at Quidhampton,[11] and a substantial farm-house in the area, perhaps the remains of Quidhampton manor-house, was destroyed by a landslide c. 1822.[12] At Overtown, which lies entirely on the chalk upland part of the parish, faint traces of earthworks in the park-land south of Overtown House may indicate another small settlement.[13] The tithing of Westlecott, in two portions, contained no hamlet. Chilton Farm lies in the southern portion. The history of the northern portion, in which lies Westlecott Farm, has been closely connected with that of Swindon within which much of it lay after 1934.[14]

The road which formed the western boundary of the parish led southwards towards Avebury and the Kennet valley by a route avoiding the highest land of the Marlborough Downs. It now diverges from its old route south of Salthrop House and winds south-eastwards to join the road from Wroughton to Beckhampton, in Avebury. From Salthrop a road ran eastwards across the parish to the church and was known in 1616 as Churchway.[15] The eastern boundary road climbed to the crest of Barbury down and continued across the downs to Marlborough. It originally entered Wroughton from the north on a direct course from Swindon up Ladder hill. By the later 18th century, when the road was turnpiked, that northern section had been abandoned, and to reach Swindon the road had been diverted westwards down Brimble hill.[16] It began to lose its position as a main road to Marlborough after 1819 when the road through Badbury, in Chiseldon, was turnpiked.[17] In 1866 it was still in use as a road to Marlborough,[18] but in 1977 it led only as far as Barbury Camp country park, established c. 1975, and thereafter became a rough track. Another road leading to the downs made the boundary between the tithings of Wroughton and Overtown. In 1977 it, too, ended on the downs. A small stretch of the main road from Swindon to Chippenham crosses the north-west corner of the parish, and was presumably one of the roads said in 1633 to impede farming in the region.[19] Apart from that the only main road through the parish in 1977 was that from Swindon, which passed through the village as High Street, and left it up Church Hill for Beckhampton. It was turnpiked in the later 18th century.[20] A bridge to carry it over the motor-way from London to South Wales was built in 1971.[21]

The Wilts. & Berks. canal was cut across the parish in 1804 with a wharf where coal was the chief commodity handled.[22] Traffic ceased in 1906 and in 1962 the canal was filled in.[23] The section of the G.W.R. line from London to Bristol was completed across the parish in 1840.[24] The line between Swindon and Marlborough, opened in 1881 and closed in 1961, skirted the parish in the north.[25]

A reservoir for Swindon Water Company's

[96] P.N. Wilts. (E.P.N.S.), 278.   [97] See below.
[98] P.N. Wilts. (E.P.N.S.), 278.
[99] W.A.M. xxxvi. 94.
[1] e.g. Phillipps, Wilts. Inst. i. 177, 184, 201.
[2] V.C.H. Wilts. iv. 297, 299.
[3] Ibid. 306, 309.
[4] Taxation Lists (W.R.S. x), 20, 21.
[5] Ibid. 105, 123.   [6] V.C.H. Wilts. iv. 361.
[7] See p. 250.   [8] W.R.O. 631/1/1/3.
[9] Ex inf. Mr. N. M. Arnold-Forster, Salthrop Ho.
[10] W.N. & Q. i. 311.   [11] See p. 250.
[12] W.N. & Q. i. 311.

[13] Ex inf. Mr. D. J. Bonney, Royal Com. Hist. Monuments (Eng.), Salisbury.
[14] V.C.H. Wilts. ix. 116, 127.   [15] W.R.O. 631/1/1/3.
[16] V.C.H. Wilts. iv. 257; Andrews and Dury, Map (W.R.S. viii), pl. 15.   [17] V.C.H. Wilts. iv. 263.
[18] O.S. Map 1/2,500, Wilts. XXII. 12 (1886 edn.).
[19] Charterhouse Mun. M.R. 5/150.
[20] V.C.H. Wilts. iv. 257.
[21] Evening Advertiser, 31 Mar. 1971.
[22] V.C.H. Wilts. iv. 273.
[23] Ibid. 277; Evening Advertiser, 6 Dec. 1962.
[24] V.C.H. Wilts. iv. 282.   [25] Ibid. 289; ix. 6.

waterworks was constructed on the site of Bedford's mill at the foot of Coombe bottom in 1866. The stream coming from the coomb was thereby dammed.[26] The reservoir was abandoned in 1971 when the works were no longer in use.[27]

In 1937 a large area of downland in the south part of the parish was acquired for the R.A.F. as an airfield, and hangars, workshops, and other accommodation for an aircraft supply and servicing depot were built.[28] No. 15 Maintenance Unit was established there in 1940. From 1941 to 1946 No. 76 Maintenance Unit (Packing Depot) was also at Wroughton. In 1972 the R.A.F. establishment was closed and the airfield and buildings were transferred to the Royal Navy. In 1941 more land in Overtown was taken for an R.A.F. hospital. The hospital was opened with accommodation for 56 patients, but has since been much enlarged. During the war it was used as a casualty clearing station. In 1967 it was renamed Princess Alexandra's R.A.F. hospital and was recognized as a teaching hospital with over 300 beds.

The old village of Wroughton lay at the foot of the greensand escarpment where two streams coming from the chalk, head-streams of the river Ray, met to flow northwards as Wroughton stream. At the same point three roads from the downs converge, and round the rough circle formed by their meeting and along the narrow lanes connecting them the earliest village was sited c. 400 m. from the church. The manor-house of the Winchester cathedral manor,[29] demolished in 1961, stood in the middle of the village at the foot of Prior's hill, with a large rectangular moat, presumably on the site of its medieval predecessor, beside it. Two of the parish's eight mills, with their substantial mill-houses, stood within the village where the network of narrow lanes is closely built up with cottages and small houses mostly of 18th- and 19th-century origin. The road leading from the village to the church, in 1977 called High Street, was probably built up early. In 1773 it was lined with houses on both sides.[30] A fire destroyed many of the thatched houses in the street in 1896.[31] A few remain. During the 18th century many cottages were built on the common and around the Marsh, an area north of High Street where Markham Road and Wharf Road ran in 1977.[32]

In 1801 the population of the parish was 1,100 and by the middle of the 19th century 1,645.[33] The building of the canal and wharf early in that century had led to a little development along Wharf Road. In the second half of the century New Swindon rose as an industrial centre but, apart from some housing near the boundary with Old Swindon in an area now called North Wroughton, and the building of a few large houses, such as Wroughton Hall,[34]

in the middle of the village, Wroughton showed little sign of growth. Alfred Williams, writing c. 1913, remarked that the agricultural workers lived in the old cob and thatch cottages in the village, while those working in Swindon lived lower down in houses of brick and tile.[35]

In 1901 the population was 2,448. The first large development of council housing occurred in 1921 when Perry's Lane was built up.[36] At about the same time vacant sites within the village were used for small private houses. The boundary changes of 1928 and 1934 made little difference to Wroughton's population as only 30 people were transferred to Swindon. In 1951 the population was 4,085. By 1961 it had risen to 5,108[37] and the 1960s were the period of Wroughton's great expansion. Coventry farm, Manor (formerly Duck's) farm, and part of Berkeley farm, north of the old village, were developed as private estates. Houses were built on the site of the manor-house and in 1973 its moat was planted as a small public garden. Council development took place along Wharf Road and associated roads to its west.[38] By 1971 the population had risen by over 3,000 to 8,263.[39] In 1973 Wroughton was provided with a new shopping centre built in the grounds of the former Wroughton Hall and on land east of it. A new library and a community centre were part of the same complex. Apart from the expansion of Wroughton village and housing for service personnel on the downs, there has been little building elsewhere in the parish in the 20th century. In 1975 Thamesdown Borough Council purchased all the land in Wroughton north of the railway line for housing development which had been begun by 1977.[40]

MANORS AND OTHER ESTATES. A charter of King Ethelwulf of 844 granting 30 hides at Ellendune to the church of Malmesbury is thought to contain much spurious material, and there is no evidence to confirm that Ellendune belonged to Malmesbury.[41] In 956 King Edwy granted 30 hides in the same place to his thegn Elfheah.[42] By his will of 968 × 972 Elfheah gave the land back to the king.[43] In 1086 the bishop of Winchester held those 30 hides which had been assigned for the support of the monks of the cathedral priory.[44]

The manor held by the bishops for the monks was called, not Ellendune, but *WROUGHTON*.[45] In the early 13th century the prior was receiving the profits of the manor,[46] and in 1242–3 he was said to hold the township of Wroughton in chief.[47] Disputes between the prior and the bishop made necessary a papal confirmation of the priory's right to administer its own estates,[48] and in 1284, when

[26] *V.C.H. Wilts.* ix. 135; see below, p. 248.
[27] Scrapbk. (containing a collection of cuttings) compiled by Ernest Cripps. Thanks are due to Mrs. Cripps, 107 Perry's Lane, Wroughton, for making the scrapbk. available.
[28] Inf. in this para. supplied by Air Hist. Branch, Lond.
[29] See below.
[30] *Andrews and Dury, Map* (W.R.S. viii), pl. 14.
[31] Cripps, Scrapbk.
[32] Mun. D. & C. Winton., estate bk. XVIII, f. 26v.; *Andrews and Dury, Map* (W.R.S. viii), pl. 14.
[33] Unless otherwise stated population figures are from *V.C.H. Wilts.* iv. 361.

[34] Cripps, Scrapbk.
[35] A. Williams, *Villages of the White Horse*, 60.
[36] Ex inf. Mrs. Cripps.   [37] *Census*, 1961.
[38] Cripps, Scrapbk.; *Guide to Wroughton* (1973 edn.).
[39] *Census*, 1971.
[40] Ex inf. Legal Dept., Thamesdown Boro. Council.
[41] Finberg, *Early Wessex Chart.* pp. 73, 200.
[42] Ibid. pp. 92, 200.   [43] Ibid. p. 98.
[44] *V.C.H. Wilts.* ii, p. 120.
[45] See above.
[46] *Interdict Doc.* (Pipe R. Soc. N.S. xxxiv), 17.
[47] *Bk. of Fees*, ii. 737.
[48] *V.C.H. Hants*, ii. 109; *Cal. Papal Reg.* i. 201.

the disputes were ended, the bishop surrendered to the prior all his rights within Wroughton manor except those of warren and chase.[49]

At the Dissolution Wroughton was granted to the newly formed chapter of Winchester cathedral.[50] Upon the commutation of chapter estates in 1861 it passed to the Ecclesiastical Commissioners. The manor then comprised 1,140 a. The manor-house and 615 a., including 99 a. of copyhold land, were sold by the commissioners in 1864 to William Wyndham Codrington (d. 1905) whose ancestors had been lessees of the demesne land since 1813.[51] The remaining copyhold lands were enfranchised.

W. W. Codrington bought the land of the rectory estate, of which he was lessee, shortly after he bought Wroughton manor,[52] and the two estates were merged. Codrington was succeeded by his son William Frederick (d.s.p. 1947), who in 1911 sold Hackpen farm, part of Wroughton manor, to John Dixon of Chiseldon.[53] In 1919 Codrington sold Wroughton House with some land to his cousin Claude Alexander Codrington (d. 1955).[54] Rectory farm was sold in 1920 to E. Manners, who sold it in 1937 as part of the site for Wroughton airfield. Wharf and Common farms, parts of the manor, were sold in 1919 to the county council as part of its smallholdings scheme. In 1977 they still belonged to the council.[55]

In the early 17th century the chief messuage and the demesne lands of the manor were leased to Giles Franklyn.[56] In 1631 one Chadwell was lessee, perhaps the Edmund Chadwell who was lessee in 1649.[57] Chadwell was followed as lessee by Gabriel Stert.[58] In 1771 the lessee was Hill Haggard and in 1785 Arthur Evans.[59] Evans was succeeded in 1792 by his widow Catherine who in 1813 was followed as lessee by Mary Codrington.[60] Mary's son William (d. 1842) and grandson W. W. Codrington succeeded her as lessees.[61]

Expenditure on repairs in the 15th century suggests that the prior of Winchester had a large house in Wroughton. A great gate giving entrance to a courtyard and a large barn are mentioned in 1488.[62] In 1649 the house had a hall, a parlour, and seven chambers as well as various smaller rooms and many outhouses. It had a dovecot, fishpond, and large moat.[63] When sold in 1916 it was described as gabled, with stone tiled roofs, and with much interior panelling, and it had recently been restored.[64] It was demolished in the 1960s.[65]

In 1086 an estate of 10 hides at Wroughton was held by Alfred, a king's thegn. In 1066 two other Englishmen, Bricnod and Alwin, had held it.[66] The estate, which cannot be located positively, perhaps lay in Lower Wroughton.[67] It may have been detached from the bishop of Winchester's demesne at an early date,[68] but seems to have been reunited with the manor.

Godric held 1½ hide of the bishop of Winchester's demesne in Ellendune in 1066. Free tenure of the land was created after the Conquest and an unnamed knight held it in 1086.[69] It was probably the land which Walter Daundely held of the bishop in 1242–3.[70]

In 1275, when it was held by Robert Daundely, it was said to be in Lower Wroughton,[71] and it was later called the manor of *LOWER WROUGH-TON*.[72] By the 1280s Robert had been followed by another Walter Daundely. The bishop then relinquished all claim to Wroughton manor to the prior of St. Swithun's, and Daundely's land, while still said to be held of the bishop, was expressly said to lie within the prior's manor.[73] Although the descent of Lower Wroughton is not thereafter clear, the Daundelys' heirs were the Bayntons and it was presumably by inheritance that the manor was held by Nicholas Baynton in 1401.[74] John Baynton, Nicholas's grandson, held it of the prior of St. Swithun's in 1428.[75] It passed with the Baynton's manor in Overwroughton until the attainder of Sir Robert Baynton in 1471, [76] but never seems to have been restored to a Baynton. It may afterwards have been merged in Wroughton manor.

The estate in Wroughton held by sinecure rectors consisted of the great and some of the lesser tithes of the parish.[77] A landed estate was mentioned in 1249.[78] Under inclosure awards of 1796 and 1797 the rector received land in place of tithes.[79] The remaining tithes were converted into a rent-charge of £570 in 1843.[80] After the abolition of the sinecure rectory in 1840 the estate, consisting of over 600 a. and the rent-charge, passed to the Ecclesiastical Commissioners.[81] In 1869 the commissioners sold the land, Rectory farm, to William Wyndham Codrington (d. 1905), already the lessee.[82] It was merged with Wroughton manor as the Codrington estate.

The rectory estate was leased to Giles Franklyn

[49] *Reg. Pontoise* (Cant. & York Soc.), ii. 436.
[50] *L. & P. Hen. VIII,* xvi, p. 417.
[51] W.A.S. Libr. (M 18), letter to Canon F. H. Manley from Eccl. Commrs., 9 Dec. 1921; *Lond. Gaz.* 16 Apr. 1861, pp. 1582 sqq.; see below.
[52] See below.
[53] Wilts. Cuttings, xiii. 226.
[54] Inf. about sales and the fam. is from Miss N. E. Codrington, Wroughton Ho., to whom thanks are due for much help. A genealogy of the fam. is in Burke, *Land. Gent.* (1952), 483–4.
[55] Ex inf. Lands and Val. Dept., County Hall, Trowbridge.
[56] Mun. D. & C. Winton., N.R.A. box 88.
[57] Ibid. estate bk. I; survey of chap. man. 1649, f. 170.
[58] C 54/3508 m. 24.
[59] Mun. D. & C. Winton., ledger bk. XXXI, ff. 31, 288.
[60] Ibid. ledger bk. XXXII, f. 313; ledger bk. XXXIV, f. 487.
[61] Ibid. ledger bk. XXXVII, f. 109; W.A.S. Libr. (M 18), letter of 9 Dec. 1921.
[62] Mun. D. & C. Winton., acct. rolls, 1419, 1480, 1488.
[63] Ibid. survey of chap. man. f. 168.

[64] Wilts. Cuttings, xvi. 331.
[65] Ex inf. Miss Codrington.
[66] *V.C.H. Wilts.* ii, p. 162.
[67] *W.A.M.* lvi. 265.
[68] For some discussion of lands belonging to the king's thegns see *V.C.H. Wilts.* ii, p. 82.
[69] Ibid. pp. 79, 120.
[70] *Bk. of Fees,* ii. 735.
[71] *Rot. Hund.* (Rec. Com.), ii (1), 243.
[72] *Cat. Anct. D.* iv, A 10413.
[73] *Reg. Pontoise* (Cant. & York Soc.), ii. 387.
[74] *V.C.H. Hants,* iv. 185; *Cat. Anct. D.* iv, A 10413.
[75] *Feud. Aids,* v. 279.   [76] See p. 243.
[77] *Inq. Non.* (Rec. Com.), 162; W.A.S. Libr. (M 18), letter to Canon F. H. Manley from Eccl. Commrs., 22 June 1921.
[78] *Civil Pleas, 1249* (W.R.S. xxvi), p. 35; see below, p. 245.
[79] W.R.O., Inclosure Awards.
[80] Ibid. Tithe Award.
[81] W.A.S. Libr. (M 18), letter to Canon F. H. Manley from Eccl. Commrs., 29 Sept. 1921.
[82] *W.A.M.* xli. 477.

early in the 17th century and continued to be leased to the Franklyn family at least until 1782.[83] By 1786 Sarah Franklyn had been succeeded as lessee by William Codrington (d. 1802).[84] Thereafter Codringtons remained lessees until 1869.

The rectory-house, immediately east of the church, has been renamed Wroughton House. In 1671 it was described as an old mansion-house.[85] It may have been largely rebuilt soon afterwards for the main block of the present house dates from c. 1700 and has an elevation of five bays with north and south entrances. Later in the 18th century, perhaps when William Codrington became lessee, extensive additions were made to the east and north-east, mainly to provide service rooms.[86] Further small additions were made beyond them in the earlier 19th century. In all the new work the external details of the old house were reproduced. At the same time the principal rooms were remodelled and refitted. In 1977 the service wings were being converted into two houses.

Elcombe was among the estates which had belonged to Earl Aubrey de Couci but which he had forfeited some years before 1086.[87] Many of those estates had belonged before the Conquest to an Englishman, Harding. By 1130 they had passed to Robert, earl of Leicester (d. 1168).[88]

In 1206–7 the honor of Leicester was divided between the sisters of Robert, earl of Leicester (d.s.p. 1204). Two virtually new honors resulted from that partition, those of Leicester and of Winchester.[89] The overlordship of *ELCOMBE* was at different times ascribed to both. In 1242–3 it was said to belong to Simon de Montfort, earl of Leicester, and in 1361 was considered to have passed with other Leicester lands to Henry, duke of Lancaster.[90] When last heard of in 1467 the overlordship was said to belong to the duchy of Lancaster.[91] Between 1264 and 1362, however, it was sometimes said to belong to the heirs of Roger de Quency, earl of Winchester (d. 1264), son of Saier de Quency, earl of Winchester (d. 1219), to whom some of the Leicester lands had passed at the partition of 1206–7.[92]

In 1167–8 Elcombe was held of Robert, earl of Leicester, by William Lovel or d'Ivry.[93] William, whose family came from Ivry-la-Bataille (Eure), had married Robert's sister Maud.[94] By 1170 William had been succeeded by his son Waleran d'Ivry.[95] Waleran was succeeded before 1177 by his brother William Lovel (d. 1213).[96] William was followed by a son John (d. by 1252) and a grandson Sir John

Lovel (d. 1287).[97] His great-grandson John Lovel became Lord Lovel, on whose death in 1310 Elcombe passed as dower to his widow Joan (d. 1348).[98] Lord Lovel was succeeded by a son John (d. 1314) and a grandson John (d. 1347).[99] John (d. 1347) was succeeded by his son John who died a minor and unmarried in 1361 to be succeeded by his brother John.[1] That John, Lord Lovel, died in 1408 holding Elcombe jointly with his wife Maud to whom the manor was delivered.[2] After Maud's death in 1423 Elcombe passed to her grandson William, Lord Lovel, and from father to son in the Lovel family to Francis, Lord Lovel.[3] Francis, created Viscount Lovel in 1483 by Richard III, with whom he was in high favour, was attainted in 1485 and afterwards disappeared, having presumably been killed at the battle of Stoke in 1487.[4]

Between 1485 and 1499 the profits of the manor were taken by Sir John Cheyne (created Lord Cheyne in 1487, d. 1499).[5] They were taken by the king from 1499 to 1512 when the manor, with other lands formerly Viscount Lovel's, was granted to William Compton (knighted in 1513) and his wife Werburgh, formerly wife of Sir Francis Cheyne.[6] Sir William Compton was succeeded in 1528 by his son Peter, and Peter in 1544 by his son Henry, later Lord Compton. Henry died in 1589 and his son William, Lord Compton (d. 1630), sold Elcombe in 1605 to Thomas Sutton (d. 1611).[7] Sutton was the founder of the London Charterhouse and Elcombe was one of the manors with which he endowed his foundation. It remained part of the Charterhouse estate until 1919 when it was sold to the Wiltshire county council to provide smallholdings for discharged soldiers.[8] Elcombe Hall was sold in 1924 to Mrs. I. D. Taylor, and in 1977 was the home of Dr. W. L. Calnan. Land in the south part of the estate was sold in 1922 and more in the north part in 1973 and 1975, but in 1977 the county council still owned nearly 2,000 a. in Elcombe.[9]

Elcombe Hall was built in the earlier 19th century on the site of an older house of which nothing remains above ground. In 1616 a house of about the same size stood on the site.[10]

In 1066 Salthrop belonged to Ulwin. In 1086 it was held in chief by Humphrey Lisle.[11] It passed with the rest of Humphrey's fief, which included Castle Combe, to the Dunstanvilles and in 1242–3 was held by Walter de Dunstanville (d. 1269).[12] The manor of *SALTHROP* descended with the barony of Castle Combe and was conveyed with it in 1309 by William de Montfort, son of Parnel de Dunstanville

[83] Mun. D. & C. Winton., N.R.A. box 88.
[84] W.R.O., Land Tax (Five Tithings in Kingsbridge hund.).
[85] Sar. Dioc. R.O., Glebe Terrier.
[86] *W.A.M.* xli. 459.
[87] *V.C.H. Wilts.* ii, pp. 98, 134.
[88] *V.C.H. Leics.* i. 290–1.
[89] Levi Fox, 'Honor of Leic. 1066–1399', *E.H.R.* liv. 391.
[90] *Bk. of Fees*, ii. 730; *Wilts. Inq. p.m.* 1327–77 (Index Libr.), 289.
[91] C 142/487 no. 20.
[92] Hist. MSS. Com. 78, *Hastings*, i, p. 325; *Wilts. Inq. p.m.* 1242–1326 (Index Libr.), 168, 378; 1327–77, 177, 309.   [93] *Pipe R.* 1168 (P.R.S. xii), 168.
[94] *Complete Peerage*, viii. 211.
[95] *Pipe R.* 1170 (P.R.S. xv), 63.

[96] Ibid. 1177 (P.R.S. xxvi), 101.
[97] *Complete Peerage*, viii. 214–15.
[98] Ibid. 217; *Feud. Aids*, v. 207.
[99] *Complete Peerage*, viii. 217–18.
[1] *Wilts. Inq. p.m.* 1327–77 (Index Libr.), 309–10.
[2] *Cal. Close*, 1405–9, 414–15; *Complete Peerage*.
[3] *Complete Peerage*, viii. 221–3.
[4] Ibid. 225.
[5] E 149/968 no. 7; *Complete Peerage*, s.v. Cheyne.
[6] *Cal. Chart. R.* 1427–1516, 280–1.
[7] C.P. 25(2)/369/3 Jas. I Mich. For Sutton see *D.N.B.*
[8] *V.C.H. Wilts.* ix. 81.
[9] Ex inf. Lands and Val. Dept.
[10] W.R.O. 631/1/1/3.
[11] *V.C.H. Wilts.* ii, p. 144.
[12] G. Poulett Scrope, *Castle Combe* (priv. print. 1852), 15; *Bk. of Fees*, ii. 726.

and Robert de Montfort, to Bartholomew of Badlesmere, Lord Badlesmere.[13] It was probably among those Castle Combe estates which passed after the execution of Badlesmere in 1322 to the Despensers.[14] It was certainly restored, after the elder Hugh le Despenser's death in 1326, to Badlesmere's widow Margaret as dower in 1331.[15] It passed to Margaret's son Giles, Lord Badlesmere (d.s.p. 1338), and to her daughter Margaret (d. 1344), wife of John Tybotot, Lord Tybotot (d. 1367).[16] The last reference to the overlordship occurs in 1370 when it was held by Robert, Lord Tybotot (d. 1372).[17]

As part of the barony of Castle Combe Salthrop, reckoned a single fee, was held in 1242–3 by Geoffrey Bluet.[18] In 1275 the fee was said to be divided between Robert Bluet and the abbot of Stanley, most of whose land, however, lay in the neighbouring parish of Lydiard Tregoze.[19] In 1281 Salthrop was settled on Peter Bluet and his wife Lucy.[20] In 1311 it was settled on Peter and Lucy for life with remainder to William Everard and his wife Beatrice.[21] Peter was dead in 1329 but Lucy lived until 1337.[22] She was succeeded by William Everard.[23] William died in 1343.[24] His son, Sir Edmund Everard, died in 1370 holding the manor jointly with his wife Felice and leaving as heirs his sisters, Elizabeth, wife of Robert of London, and Margaret, widow of Thomas of Ramsbury.[25] It is possible that Margaret left no issue, for in 1380 Salthrop was settled on Robert and Elizabeth.[26] They left no issue and their estates were evidently divided; some manors passed by a sister of Robert to the Calston family and thence to the Darells of Littlecote in Ramsbury, but others, including Salthrop, passed in a way which is not clear to the Lovel family.[27] Salthrop was held by John, Lord Lovel, jointly with his wife Maud at the time of his death in 1408.[28] Thereafter it followed the same descent as Elcombe manor and the Charterhouse was endowed with it in the early 17th century.[29]

In 1739 Thomas Bennet, whose ancestors had been lessees of Salthrop from at least 1616, exchanged the manor with the governors of the Charterhouse for his manor of Costow.[30] Bennet's heir was his daughter Martha (d. 1787) who married Peter Legh (d. 1754). Their daughter Elizabeth married Anthony James Keck, and secondly William Bathhurst Pye who took the name Bennet.[31] Elizabeth's daughter Elizabeth Keck married Thomas Calley (d. 1836) of Burderop in Chiseldon, thereby bringing Salthrop into the Calley family.[32] Thomas's son, John James Calley (d. 1854), sold the manor to Arthur Wellesley, duke of Wellington (d. 1852), whose son Arthur, duke of Wellington, sold it in 1861 to M. H. N. Story-Maskelyne (d. 1911).[33] In 1976 it was owned by Mr. N. M. Arnold-Forster, a direct descendant of Story-Maskelyne.[34]

Salthrop House occupies a site where there was a large house in the earlier 17th century.[35] The present house has an ashlar faced main block of c. 1795 in the style of James Wyatt.[36] The entrance front to the west is of three bays with a central bow, whilst the north and east fronts are of four and five bays respectively. The house has a principal room at each corner and a curved central staircase below an oval skylight. Most of the original fittings survive. In the later 19th century a grey-brick service wing was added to the north.

Although not named in Domesday Book, the lands on which the manors of Quidhampton and Costow were based were probably included in Humphrey Lisle's Salthrop and Overwroughton holdings in 1086.[37] They passed with those holdings to the barony of Castle Combe.[38]

The overlordship of QUIDHAMPTON passed with the rest of the Castle Combe lands to Bartholomew, Lord Badlesmere.[39] After the death without issue of Giles, Lord Badlesmere, in 1338 Quidhampton formed part of the dower of his widow Elizabeth.[40] Later, on the partition of his lands among his sisters in 1341, it was allotted to the eldest sister Margery, wife of William de Ros, Lord Ros of Helmsley (d. 1343).[41] There is no later reference to a lord of Castle Combe as overlord. In 1472 the manor was said to be held of the prior of Bradenstoke,[42] and, probably erroneously, in 1506 of the abbess of Wilton, and in 1616 of William Herbert, earl of Pembroke, who was successor to the abbess's estates.[43]

Quidhampton was named as a separate estate in the later 13th century when it was held by Richard of Highway. Richard gave some part of it in 1269 to Stanley Abbey, reserving for himself the hall, ox-house, and western part of the court.[44] Richard's son William acquired more land in Quidhampton in 1304 when he conveyed all his land there to his son Richard.[45] In 1324 the estate passed from Richard of Highway to John Goudhyne who granted it in 1337 to Robert Russell.[46] Robert was dead in 1364, and in 1412 Thomas Russell held what was then called Quidhampton manor.[47] Thomas was

[13] Poulett Scrope, op. cit. pedigree facing p. 18.
[14] Ibid. 62. [15] Cal. Close, 1330–3, 234.
[16] Wilts. Inq. p.m. 1327–77 (Index Libr.), 133–4; Cal. Close, 1339–41, 283.
[17] Wilts. Inq. p.m. 1327–77 (Index Libr.), 358; Poulett Scrope, Castle Combe, pedigree facing p. 54.
[18] Bk. of Fees, ii. 726.
[19] Rot. Hund. (Rec. Com.), ii (1), 243; V.C.H. Wilts. ix. 80–1. [20] Feet of F. 1272–1327 (W.R.S. i), p. 13.
[21] Ibid. p. 80.
[22] Cal. Inq. p.m. vii, p. 96; viii, p. 56.
[23] Wilts. Inq. p.m. 1327–77 (Index Libr.), 133–4.
[24] Cal. Inq. p.m. viii, p. 288.
[25] Wilts. Inq. p.m. 1327–77 (Index Libr.), 358.
[26] C.P. 25(1)/289/52 no. 45.
[27] W.A.S. Libr., Story-Maskelyne MSS. file N.
[28] Cal. Close, 1405–9, 422; 1419–22, 107.
[29] See above.
[30] Wilts. Tracts, 102, no. 13; Charterhouse Mun. M.R. 5/149; see below.

[31] Aubrey, Topog. Coll. ed. Jackson, 368; W.R.O. 212B/7386.
[32] Aubrey, op. cit. 335. For the Calleys see V.C.H. Wilts. ix. 10.
[33] Aubrey, op. cit. 335. For the Story-Maskelyne fam. see W.A.M. xxxix. 419.
[34] For the relationship see V.C.H. Wilts. ix. 82.
[35] W.R.O. 631/1/1/3.
[36] See plate facing p. 225.
[37] V.C.H. Wilts. ii, p. 144.
[38] See above.
[39] Poulett Scrope, Castle Combe, 262.
[40] Cal. Close, 1339–41, 280.
[41] Wilts. Inq. p.m. 1327–77 (Index Libr.), 325.
[42] W.A.M. xxxvi. 103.
[43] C 142/20 no. 9; C 142/370 no. 77.
[44] W.A.M. xxxvi. 90–1.
[45] Ibid. 92–3. [46] Ibid. 94–6, 100.
[47] Wilts. Inq. p.m. 1327–77 (Index Libr.), 325; Feud. Aids, vi. 537.

followed by John Russell, but in 1473 the lordship of the Russells came to an end. In a way no longer understood John Collingbourne made good a claim to be John Russell's heir.[48] His successor, William Collingbourne, was attained and executed for his support of Henry Tudor.[49] After Bosworth, however, his lands were restored to his heirs,[50] and in 1489 Quidhampton was held by his daughter Margaret and her husband George Chaddington.[51] George and Margaret sold the manor in 1502 to Sir Bartholomew Reed (d. 1506), an alderman and goldsmith of London.[52] Reed settled Quidhampton on his wife Elizabeth for life with remainder to his nephew William Reed.[53] By 1543 William Reed had been succeeded by John Reed and in 1582 a John Reed sold the manor to Thomas Crane.[54] In 1596 Crane devised it to his daughter Sarah.[55] Sarah married William Brocket and in 1603 they sold the manor to Richard Spenser (d. 1616),[56] members of whose family had been lessees since 1543.[57] Spenser was succeeded by his son John,[58] who died in 1628 having settled the estate on his wife Ann for life.[59] His son John, a minor in 1628, sold it in 1648 to Sir Thomas Bennet (d. 1670).[60] Quidhampton thereafter passed with Costow manor and from 1739 with Salthrop manor.[61]

The lands on which the manor of *COSTOW* was based, probably part of the Overwroughton and Salthrop holdings of Humphrey Lisle in 1086, passed to the Dunstanvilles, lords of Castle Combe.[62] Walter de Dunstanville (d. 1269) held land in Costow which he granted to Stanley Abbey.[63] On the partition of the Castle Combe estates among the heirs of Giles, Lord Badlesmere, the overlordship of Costow was awarded to his sister Maud, wife of John de Vere, earl of Oxford (d. 1360).[64] It passed to John's son Thomas, earl of Oxford (d. 1371),[65] but was apparently forfeited by his grandson Robert de Vere, earl of Oxford (d.s.p. 1392), who was found guilty of treason and deprived of all honours and estates.[66] It was held by Thomas Beauchamp, earl of Warwick (d. 1401), at the time of his death but no later reference to it has been found.[67]

Costow was referred to by name in 1182 when a grant of 1 hide there by Roger son of Geoffrey to Bradenstoke Priory received papal confirmation.[68] Whether this land was part of the Dunstanville estate is not known. The grant was again confirmed by bull in 1184.[69] Bradenstoke still had land there in 1231 when a tenement was disputed by the prior and the abbot of Stanley.[70] Costow was not afterwards named as a Bradenstoke estate, and the priory either lost it or it was merged in the adjoining

estate of Chaddington in Lydiard Tregoze which also belonged to Bradenstoke.[71]

Besides the land granted by Walter de Dunstanville, Stanley Abbey was granted land in Costow by John son of Peter, a grant confirmed in 1227.[72] Stanley retained the estate called Costow until the Dissolution when, with some of the abbey's estates in Lydiard Tregoze, it was granted to Edward Seymour, Viscount Beauchamp (from 1537 earl of Hertford, from 1546 duke of Somerset, the Lord Protector, d. 1552).[73] It passed to Somerset's son, Edward Seymour, earl of Hertford (d. 1621), who sold it in 1608 to Sir John Bennet (d. by 1627).[74] Sir John settled the farm on his son William in 1621 and William devised it in 1635 to his brother Sir Thomas Bennet.[75] Sir Thomas (d. 1670) was succeeded by his son Thomas (d. 1703).[76] In 1739 Costow was exchanged for Salthrop manor by Thomas Bennet, probably the son of Thomas (d. 1703).[77] Upon that exchange Costow farm became part of the Elcombe estate of the Charterhouse.[78]

A small estate in Costow called Cockharis was held in 1539 by Michael Quintin who leased it to John Sadler.[79] In 1560 Quintin sold it to John's widow Agnes and son Thomas.[80] Anthony Sadler, Thomas's son, sold the estate in 1597 to William Bennet (d. 1608).[81] At the same time Anthony and his brother William assigned to Bennet their lease of Costow farm.[82] From 1608 the Cockharis estate and Costow farm were held by Sir John Bennet, William's brother, and they descended together.[83]

Costow Farm appears to have stood further north in the earlier 17th century.[84] The present substantial brick house is of the late 18th century or the early 19th.

Overwroughton was held in 1086 by Humphrey Lisle and of him by Robert. In 1066 it had been held by Alnod.[85] Like Salthrop it became part of the barony of Castle Combe and the overlordship of the two estates followed the same descent.[86]

A knight's fee in *OVERWROUGHTON* was granted early in the 12th century to Tewkesbury Abbey by Adelize, wife of Robert de Dunstanville, and probably heir of Humphrey Lisle.[87] It was confirmed to the abbey by Walter de Dunstanville, probably him who died in 1195.[88] Tewkesbury retained a manor in Overwroughton until the Dissolution.[89]

In 1540 the site of the abbey's manor and lands called Turneys and Uffcott were granted to William Richmond alias Webb (d. 1579).[90] In 1546 William

[48] *W.A.M.* ii. 284.
[49] He is said to have composed the verse 'The Rat, the Cat and Lovel our dog, rule all England under the Hog': R. Fabyan, *Chron.* 672.
[50] *Cal. Pat.* 1563–6, p. 482; Aubrey, *Topog. Coll.* ed. Jackson, 248 n.
[51] *W.A.M.* xxxvi. 106.
[52] Ibid. 106–8.
[53] C 142/20 no. 9.
[54] *W.A.M.* xxxvi. 112.
[55] Ibid. 114–15.
[56] Ibid. 121.
[57] Ibid. 112–24.
[58] C 142/370 no. 77.
[59] *Wilts. Inq. p.m.* 1625–49 (Index Libr.), 80–1.
[60] *W.A.M.* xxxvi. 225–7.
[61] See below and above.
[62] See above.
[63] *W.A.M.* ii. 278.
[64] *Cal. Close,* 1341–3, 150.
[65] *Wilts. Inq. p.m.* 1327–77 (Index Libr.), 365–6.
[66] *Complete Peerage,* x. 231.
[67] C 137/169 no. 58.
[68] B.L. Stowe MS. 925, f. 31.
[69] Ibid. f. 32.
[70] *Pat. R.* 1225–32, 509.
[71] *V.C.H. Wilts.* ix. 82.
[72] *Cal. Chart. R.* 1226–57, 38.
[73] *L. & P. Hen. VIII,* x, p. 526.
[74] *W.A.M.* xxxvi. 267–72.
[75] Ibid. 270–80; *D.N.B.*
[76] *W.A.M.* xxxv. 465–6; *D.N.B.*
[77] See above.
[78] See above.
[79] *W.A.M.* xxxvi. 235.
[80] Ibid. 236–8.
[81] Ibid. 238–9.
[82] Ibid. 244–5.
[83] Ibid. 254, 267–72.
[84] W.R.O. 631/1/1/3.
[85] *V.C.H. Wilts.* ii, p. 144.
[86] See above.
[87] Poulett Scrope, *Castle Combe,* 26–8.
[88] Dugdale, *Mon.* ii. 68, 74; *V.C.H. Glos.* ii. 65.
[89] *V.C.H. Glos.* ii. 65.
[90] *L. & P. Hen. VIII,* xv, p. 341.

conveyed the same estate to Sir George Baynham.[91] Sir George died in 1546, leaving a son and heir Christopher, then a minor.[92] In 1554 Christopher Baynham conveyed half the manor with half of Turneys and Uffcott to Thomas Sadler. The remainder he sold in equal portions to William and John Sadler, Thomas's brothers.[93] In 1584 there was some repartition of the property among the Sadlers, the exact outcome of which is unknown. In 1611 Robert Sadler, perhaps Thomas's grandson, and his wife Grace conveyed his share to a John Sadler.[94] In 1627 an estate described as the capital messuage, farm, and premises of Overtown, then replacing the earlier name of Overwroughton, was conveyed by a John Sadler of Overtown and his wife Susan and a William Sadler and his wife Joan to William Calley (knighted 1629, d. 1641) of Burderop.[95] That conveyance, however, does not seem to have included all the estate that had been granted to William Richmond alias Webb at the Dissolution. In 1631 Oliver Richmond Webb (d. 1635), William's great-grandson, sold 172 a., said to be parcel of the farm, to Sir William Calley.[96] From Sir William Overtown House and farm passed in the Calley family in the same way as Burderop to Joan Marion Calley.[97] She died unmarried in 1973 and was succeeded by her kinsman Sir Henry Langton (since 1974 Sir Henry Calley).

A house of the earlier 17th century is represented by the south-eastern corner of the present Overtown House. It had a short east range with a central entrance and a longer wing to the west. Late in the 17th century a west range was added and a new staircase was placed in the west end of the old house. The open court formed by the three ranges was built over in the 18th century, partly to house a new main stair. About 1800 low projecting wings of red brick were added to each end of the east front. In the earlier 19th century the west range was extensively remodelled, both inside and out. The house was completely reroofed in 1976–7.

The earl of Gloucester held a fee in Overwroughton in 1275.[98] Only one other reference to the Gloucester overlordship has been found: in 1428 John Baynton was said to hold lands in Overwroughton, sometimes called *ROCHES* manor, of the honor of Gloucester.[99] Baynton's estate, however, was held of several lords and there was probably confusion about the overlordship.

In 1331 John Turney settled an estate, called the manor of Overwroughton, on himself for life with remainder to Gilbert of Berwick.[1] A John Turney

still held land in Overwroughton in 1336, it was said of the abbots of Hyde and Tewkesbury.[2] Gilbert had possibly succeeded to the Turney estate by 1353,[3] and in 1356 he was said to hold Overwroughton manor of the prior of Farleigh.[4] In 1359 what was presumably another estate, also called Overwroughton manor, was conveyed to him by Sir John FitzPayne and Joan his wife.[5]

When Gilbert of Berwick died in 1361 his estate in Wroughton was said to be held of the priory of Newent (Glos.), an alien priory of the Norman abbey of Cormeilles, which had land probably near Barbury Castle.[6] The estate passed to his daughter Agnes and her husband John de la Roches and to his grandson Sir John de la Roches.[7] Sir John settled it in 1399 on himself, his wife William, and their son.[8] He died in 1401[9] and William in 1410 when, reckoned as half Overwroughton manor and called Roches manor, the estate was held of Tewkesbury Abbey.[10] At William's death the Rocheses' heirs were Sir John's daughter, Elizabeth, wife of Walter Beauchamp (d. 1430), and John Baynton, son of Elizabeth's sister Joan.[11] In 1412 Walter Beauchamp held the Overwroughton manor,[12] but by 1428 John Baynton (d. 1465) had come of age and the estate had passed to him.[13] Sir John held Lower Wroughton manor as well as the Rocheses' half of Overwroughton manor.[14] The two estates passed like Faulston manor in Bishopstone at least until 1485.[15] In 1536 land in Wroughton was acquired by Sir Edward Baynton, Sir Robert's grandson, along with lands formerly belonging to Stanley Abbey.[16] Sir Edward's manor in Overwroughton was probably smaller than the earlier Roches manor and at his death in 1545 was said to be held of Chiseldon manor.[17] In 1547 Sir Edward's son Andrew conveyed the manor to William Sharington.[18] Sharington was attainted soon afterwards, and although most of his lands were restored in 1550 his Overwroughton manor was apparently not among them.[19] What happened to it is not clear but it was perhaps acquired by William Richmond alias Webb after he had conveyed c. 1546 most of the Overwroughton manor which had belonged to Tewkesbury Abbey.

When Richmond alias Webb died in 1579 he held an estate in Overwroughton which was described as a manor and could have been Roches since in 1635 it was said to be held of Chiseldon manor.[20] From him the Overwroughton manor passed to his son Thomas,[21] from Thomas (d. before 1564) to his son Edmund (d. 1621),[22] and from Edmund to his son Oliver (d.s.p. 1635). Oliver settled the manor on his

[91] Ibid. xxi (1), p. 150.　　[92] C 142/75 no. 92.
[93] W.R.O. 374/591, abstr. of title.
[94] Ibid. Pedigrees of the Sadlers of Wroughton by N. Story-Maskelyne are in W.A.S. Libr., K/6/4.
[95] W.R.O. 374/591, abstr. of title.
[96] Ibid. For Webb pedigree see *Misc. Gen. et Herald.* 5th ser. vii. 41–5.
[97] *V.C.H. Wilts.* ix. 10.
[98] *Rot. Hund.* (Rec. Com.), ii (1), 243.
[99] See below.
[1] *Feet of F.* 1327–77 (W.R.S. xxix), pp. 32–3. The abbot of Hyde cannot be explained, unless he was confused with the prior of St. Swithun's, Winchester, who held Wroughton man.
[2] *Wilts. Inq. p.m.* 1327–77 (Index Libr.), 119–20.
[3] *Cal. Pat.* 1350–4, 485.
[4] *Wilts. Inq. p.m.* 1327–77 (Index Libr.), 245.
[5] *Feet of F.* 1327–77 (W.R.S. xxix), 116.

[6] *Wilts. Inq. p.m.* 1327–77 (Index Libr.), 279. The lands of the priory passed to Fotheringhay Coll., Northants., and the coll. had lands at Barbury Castle in the 16th cent.
[7] The elder John Roches was probably dead in 1376: *Cal. Pat.* 1374–7, 390.
[8] *Cal. Close,* 1396–9, 500.
[9] C 137/164 no. 41.　　[10] C 137/225 no. 38.
[11] Ibid. For the relationship of John and Eliz. see *Complete Peerage,* xi. 303 n. g.
[12] *Feud. Aids,* vi. 530.　　[13] Ibid. v. 278.
[14] C 140/494 no. 30; see above.　　[15] See p. 8.
[16] *L. & P. Hen. VIII,* x, p. 526.
[17] C 142/72 no. 109.　　[18] *W.N. & Q.* iii. 373.
[19] *Cal. Pat.* 1549–51, 188–9.
[20] C 142/187 no. 118; *Wilts. Inq. p.m.* 1625–49 (Index Libr.), 437.
[21] C 142/187 no. 118.　　[22] C 142/389 no. 97.

nephew Edward Richmond Webb (d. 1645).[23] It passed to Edward's great-grandson, Borlase Richmond Webb (d. 1737),[24] who sold it in 1733 to Peter Delmé. Delmé sold it in 1779 to George Boughey.[25] In 1795, after Boughey's death, the estate, called Overtown farm, was sold to the tenant Thomas Washbourne.[26] It remained in the Washbourne family at least until 1859.[27] By 1870 it had been bought by a Mr. Kemble and in 1882 Henry Kemble, probably his son, owned it.[28] Several owners followed. In 1919 it was bought by F. T. White who in 1920 added Parslo's and Mudgell farms to his estate.[29] In 1977 the farm, known as Overtown Manor, belonged to his grandson Mr. J. F. F. White.

Overtown Manor is an L-shaped house of the early 17th century. It was extended to the east, probably in 1693 when the north front was re-organized as seven bays with a central entrance. There was an extensive renewal of the fittings soon after 1800 when the entrance was moved to the west front. In 1879, when the Kembles lived in the house, the south wing was demolished and rebuilt to a larger scale to provide new principal rooms.

Thomas Sadler owned land in Overwroughton in 1699.[30] By 1780 he had been succeeded by William Sadler.[31] William conveyed the estate, then called the manor of Overwroughton, to William Powell Bendery in 1787.[32] Bendery had been succeeded by 1819 by a member of the Brook family.[33] In 1843 the estate belonged to Samuel Brook.[34] In 1859 it belonged to Edwin Parslo and was known as Parslo's farm.[35] In 1937 most of its land was sold to make Wroughton airfield.

In 1086 one Harold held an estate of 5 hides in WESTLECOTT of Hugh the Ass. In 1066 it had been held by Levric.[36] In the 13th century there were two holdings in Westlecott. In 1224–5 John son of Simon was at variance with Geoffrey Bluet and Alice his wife over half the manor.[37] John is to be identified with John of Fifhide who in 1228 renounced his right in half the manor to Geoffrey, who was to hold it of Alan Basset. Basset was apparently overlord in the right of his wife Aline,[38] and the overlordship descended like Wootton Bassett manor until at least 1336.[39]

Geoffrey Bluet still held the moiety in 1242–3.[40] In 1281, like Salthrop manor, it was settled on Peter Bluet and his wife Lucy,[41] and from that date the two estates passed in the same way.[42] In 1370 land said to be in Chilton formed part of the Westlecott estate and in the 15th century Chilton, which was

sometimes described as a manor, appears as the name for that moiety of Westlecott.[43] That connexion between Westlecott and Chilton presumably accounts for the fact that Chilton farm was a detached part of Westlecott tithing in the 19th century.[44]

The other moiety of Westlecott manor was held in 1242–3 by Amfelice Pilk.[45] In 1262 it was held by Roger, son of William Lof.[46] Roger sold the estate to Katharine, relict of John Lovel, who granted it to Lacock Abbey.[47] Her brother Philip Basset (d. 1271) released the nuns from service due to his manor of Wootton Bassett.[48] Westlecott was held by the abbey until the Dissolution.[49] In 1540 it was granted to the lessee, John Goddard,[50] whose son Thomas (d. 1598) bought Swindon manor. Westlecott descended like Swindon,[51] and Westlecott farm remained part of the Goddard estate in 1977.[52]

The manor-house, which in 1977 stood in Westlecott Road in the suburbs of Swindon, was enlarged and remodelled in 1926. The main doorway and the south-facing walls are, however, probably of the later 16th century. A stone, possibly not in situ, on the south front bears the initials of Thomas Goddard and the date 1589. The Goddards may have lived in the house before moving to the manor-house in Swindon.[53] The house was a private nursing-home for a time in the 1960s, but in 1977 was in private occupation.[54]

ECONOMIC HISTORY. The largest estate in Wroughton in 1086 was that of 30 hides held by the bishop of Winchester for the benefit of the monks of St. Swithun's. The demesne was assessed at 15 hides and on it there were 3 serfs and 4 ploughs. Beyond the demesne there were 25 villeins and 14 bordars with 7 ploughs. There were 60 a. of meadow, and pasture ½ league long by 3 furlongs broad. There were 20 a. of wood. The estate had appreciated from £14 in 1066 to £18. In Lower Wroughton the estate assessed at 10 hides held by a king's thegn had land for 4 ploughs, supported 5 serfs, 3 villeins, and 3 bordars, and in 1086 was worth £5. There was 1 plough on the estate assessed at 1½ hide.[55]

In the 13th century the prior of St. Swithun's manor probably included all those lands except the 1½ hide and a small estate taken to endow Wroughton church. In 1210 the manor, valued at £25, was the fourth most valuable among the priory's Wiltshire estates. Assized rents amounted to £13. The stock included 22 oxen, 100 sheep, and 16 pigs. Two

23 Wilts. Inq. p.m. 1625–49 (Index Libr.), 437.
24 Misc. Gen. et Herald. 5th ser. vii. 44–5.
25 W.R.O. 130/31b, deed to produce title deeds.
26 W.A.S. Libr., sale cat. ix, no. 32; W.R.O., Land Tax (Five Tithings in Kingsbridge hund.).
27 Kelly's Dir. Wilts. (1859).
28 Note by F. T. White penes Mr. J. F. F. White, Overtown Man.; W.R.O. 856/3, deed of apportionment.
29 Note by F. T. White penes Mr. White.
30 Charterhouse Mun. M.R. 5/209.
31 W.R.O., Land Tax (Five Tithings in Kingsbridge hund.).
32 C.P. 25(2)/1447/28 Geo. III Trin.
33 W.R.O., Land Tax (Five Tithings in Kingsbridge hund.).
34 Ibid. Tithe Award.
35 Kelly's Dir. Wilts. (1859).
36 V.C.H. Wilts. ii, p. 156.
37 E 372/69 m. 7d.   38 C.P. 25(1)/250/8 no. 3.
39 Wilts. Inq. p.m. 1327–77 (Index Libr.), 117; V.C.H. Wilts. ix. 190.
40 Bk. of Fees, ii. 731.
41 Feet of F. 1272–1327 (W.R.S. i), p. 13.
42 See above.
43 Wilts. Inq. p.m. 1327–77 (Index Libr.), 358; Cal. Close, 1419–22, 107.   44 See p. 237.
45 Bk. of Fees, ii. 731.   46 Cat. Anct. D. iv, A 8976.
47 Lacock Abbey Mun., Older Chartulary, f. 33.
48 Ibid. ff. 32v.–33; Wards 2/94C/5; Wards 2/94B/8; Cal. Chart. R. 1300–26, 272.
49 S.C. 6/Hen. VIII/3985 m. 30.
50 L. & P. Hen. VIII, xv, p. 296.
51 V.C.H. Wilts. ix. 120.
52 Ex inf. Messrs. Townsend, solicitors, 42 Cricklade Street, Swindon.
53 V.C.H. Wilts. ix. 120.
54 Thamesdown Public Libr., cutting L 911 (728).
55 V.C.H. Wilts. ii, pp. 120, 162.

bailiffs (*custodes*) were in charge.[56] Slightly later there were nine customary tenants, including four millers, nearly all of them with holdings of ½ hide. All paid small rents and owed much labour service, for which they received allowances of food and drink. Most of their arable land was divided between two fields. Some seventeen virgaters held land likewise distributed, and owed smaller amounts of rent and service. They were allowed to use the marsh for their sheep after Lammas, and could keep their flocks on their own land for the rest of the year. There were about eighteen cottars holding a few acres each in the two fields, and paying small rents or performing labour services. From that group were drawn farm servants such as ploughmen, shepherds, and cowmen.[57]

By 1387 the priory had leased the demesne, and had probably been doing so for some time.[58] The manor continued to be supervised by the prior's officers who visited regularly to audit accounts and hold courts.[59] In 1541 Wroughton, rated at about £31, was the second most highly valued of the dean and chapter of Winchester's Wiltshire estates. The demesne was leased for £10 13s. 4d., but the farmer was allowed 10s. for collecting rents due to St. Swithun's, and 6s. 8d. for a livery gown ('pro toga sua').[60] The 6s. 8d. was still being allowed in 1649.[61]

Because the manor extended over the whole length of the parish it contained a good balance of soils.[62] Sheep-and-corn husbandry could be undertaken in the southern half, and pasture farming on the heavier land in the northern half. In 1649 the demesne farm had four pieces of inclosed pasture, 78 a. in the Lammas meadow, and 300 a. of arable in the common fields.[63] Later evidence shows one field to have been high on the downs at Hackpen,[64] and another, called West field, at the bottom of Market hill.[65] In 1649 there were 20 a. of sheep down for the demesne flock, 70 a. of grazing for cattle, and 30 a. for horses. At that time there were two freeholders and some nineteen copyholds.[66]

In 1794 the chapter agreed to inclose at the request of William Codrington, the lessee of the rectory estate which then included land scattered throughout the common fields of Wroughton tithing.[67] The award was made in 1796. Much of the land in the 37 allotments was awarded to the rector,[68] and 392 a. were awarded to the lessee of the manor. Field names included Great and Little Upper fields, West, Market Hill, and Ladder Hill fields.[69]

In 1861 Wroughton manor included the manor farm, c. 516 a., and 624 a. of copyhold land. The 615 a. bought by W. W. Codrington in 1864 were

merged with Rectory farm.[70] Most of the remaining land was divided between four or five farms.[71] The Codrington estate was broken up and sold at sales of 1907, 1911, and 1919.[72] A large part of the downland was lost to agriculture when the airfield was established in 1937, but Hackpen farm, worked by F. J. Horton & Sons in 1977, continued.[73] Two farms and part of another were sold for building land in the 1960s,[74] but in 1977 Common, Wharf, Berkeley, Artis, Wood, and Cowleze were still small working farms.[75]

The rectory estate consisted of tithes and land.[76] In 1249 the rector, perhaps occupying his own lands, admitted ploughing one of his meadows and so depriving a tenant of his pasture rights. The rector was ordered to restore the land to pasture.[77] About 1291 the estate was valued at £33.[78] In 1341 it included 2 carucates of arable land and some meadow land and pasture. The rents and services of the tenants were valued at 10s.[79] In 1535 the estate was worth c. £38 gross.[80] Early in the 17th century the land, 117 a., consisted chiefly of arable, lying scattered in the Upper and Hackpen fields of Wroughton tithing. There was also a plot of marsh in East field, a few dispersed acres of meadow, and 4 a. of inclosed pasture.[81] Later in the 17th century, when the total area was reckoned at 148 a., there was a little more inclosed pasture. The arable was divided between the Lower field, where a quarter was left fallow each year, and the poorer land of the Upper field, where half was left fallow.[82] By the Wroughton inclosure award of 1796 the rector was allotted over 550 a. to replace tithes and glebe, and by the Elcombe inclosure award of 1797 was allotted c. 124 a. in place of tithes.[83] Most of the land formed Rectory farm in Wroughton tithing and became part of the Codrington estate in 1869.[84] Rectory farm was in 1920 a downland farm of some 450 a., mostly pasture and grazing land.[85] Since 1937 its land has been covered by the airfield.

Elcombe, at 27 hides, was the second most highly assessed estate in Wroughton in 1086. There were only 5 ploughs although there was land for 8; the demesne of 24 hides was worked by 6 serfs with 2 ploughs, and the remaining land supported 3 villeins and 14 bordars with 3 ploughs. There were 60 a. each of pasture and meadow and 20 a. of wood. The value of the estate had fallen from £27 in 1066 to £24 in 1086.[86]

In 1172–3 the sheriff rendered account for 68s. rent from Elcombe with 40s. for the farm of the

[56] *Interdict Doc.* (Pipe R. Soc. N.S. xxxiv), 17, 25.
[57] Katharine A. Hanna, 'Winch. Cath. Custumal' (Southampton Univ. Coll. M.A. thesis, 1954), pp. lvii, 475–85.
[58] Mun. D. & C. Winton., ct. roll, 1387.
[59] Joan G. Greatrex, 'Admin. Winch. Cath. Priory temp. Beaufort' (Ottawa Univ. Ph.D. thesis, 1972), 95–6.
[60] *Winch. Chap. Doc. 1541–7*, ed. G. W. Kitchin and F. T. Madge (Hants Rec. Soc.), 77, 84.
[61] Mun. D. & C. Winton., survey of chap. man. f. 240.
[62] Ibid. f. 185, where the bounds of the man. are given.
[63] Ibid. f. 169.
[64] Ibid. estate bk. XVIII, f. 26v.
[65] H.R.O., Eccl. Commrs. 58591.
[66] Mun. D. & C. Winton., survey of chap. man. f. 169.
[67] Ibid. chap. act bk. 1776–1803, f. 266.
[68] See below.
[69] W.R.O., Inclosure Award.

[70] See above and below.
[71] W.A.S. Libr. (M 18), letter to Canon F. H. Manley from Eccl. Commrs. 9 Dec. 1921.
[72] Ibid. sale cat. vi, no. 47; Wilts. Cuttings, xiii. 226; ex inf. Miss N. E. Codrington, Wroughton Ho.
[73] Ex inf. Miss Codrington.   [74] See above.
[75] Local information.   [76] See p. 239.
[77] *Civil Pleas, 1249* (W.R.S. xxvi), p. 35, where 'Ellesden' has been wrongly identified as Elston.
[78] *Tax. Eccl.* (Rec. Com.), 190.
[79] *Inq. Non.* (Rec. Com.), 162.
[80] *Valor Eccl.* (Rec. Com.), ii. 128.
[81] W.R.O. 529/91.
[82] Sar. Dioc. R.O., Glebe Terriers.
[83] W.R.O., Inclosure Awards.   [84] See p. 239.
[85] Wilts. Cuttings, xiii. 226; ex inf. Miss Codrington.
[86] *V.C.H. Wilts.* ii, p. 134.

manor at Michaelmas. Stock worth £6 4s. was sold.[87] In 1287 the manor was said to comprise 140 a. of arable land, 16 a. of meadow land, common pasture for 50 oxen, and an inclosed pasture at Blagrove. The 32 customary tenants held 13 virgates and their works and dues were valued at £9 6s.[88] The area of the manor referred to in the 14th century was inexplicably variable.[89] The greatest area of arable land, 350 a., was mentioned in 1348.[90] Of 80 a. of inclosed pasture in 1362, 40 a. lay among the thorns.[91] In 1310 there were two free tenants, holding 1 virgate and ½ virgate, and 27 customary tenants.[92] In 1362 there were twenty bond tenants and a free tenant.[93]

In the 13th century the Lovels had a fishpond at Elcombe which the constable of Marlborough Castle was twice ordered to stock with bream.[94] They also had a park which, after Francis Lovel's attainder in 1485, was granted for life to a member of the royal household.[95] The park, which included a rabbit warren,[96] lay east of Elcombe street and was divided into an upper and a lower park.[97] It was later merged in Elcombe farm as pasture.[98]

In the later Middle Ages Elcombe was the centre of an estate which included Salthrop manor and lands at Uffcott in Broad Hinton and at Mannington in Lydiard Tregoze.[99] By the mid 16th century the Wroughton part of the estate included, besides the demesne farm of Elcombe, two large farms, Salthrop and Chilton.[1] In 1633 the estate comprised about fourteen farms. The demesne farm measured 251 a., and there was a farm of 129 a. called Elcombe Street farm. Chilton farm, 209 a., had all its arable land consolidated on the downland. On the clay in the north part of the tithing Blagrove farm had been divided into north, west, and east farms, but the pasture of those farms was considered to be the worst on the manor because of its wetness. Farms called South Leaze and West Leaze on the clay west of Blagrove were, on the other hand, reckoned to be excellent pasture farms. West Leaze was formerly called Westcott and was one of the farms of Westlecott manor which became part of the Elcombe estate in the 15th century.[2] The common pastures of the Elcombe estate were Elcombe Horse hay, Elcombe marsh, Mare leys, Black croft, and a green called Elcombe Street green. The common down was on Markham Down hills.[3] Throughout the 17th century many of the farms were leased to members of the Sadler family, sometimes one member of the family working more than one farm.[4] There were some eighteen copyholders occupying 685 a.[5]

An inclosure award for Elcombe was made in 1797 when some 1,296 a. were inclosed, including the lands in Uffcott but not those in Lydiard Tregoze.[6] By 1832 many of the farms on the Elcombe estate had been amalgamated. The demesne farm was then known as Upper farm, and Lower farm presumably represented Elcombe Street farm. North and West Blagrove farms were worked together with land in Lydiard Tregoze. South Leaze and East Blagrove farms were worked together.[7] The closeness of the railway and the nature of the land encouraged a great expansion of dairy farming on all the farms in the late 19th century.[8] In 1919 the Elcombe estate was broken up when it was sold to the county council for smallholdings.[9] In 1977 five or six farms were working mainly as dairy and pasture farms.

In 1086 Salthrop was assessed at 10 hides of which 8 were in demesne. On the demesne there were 3 serfs and 2 ploughs and elsewhere on the estate there were 9 bordars and 1 plough. There were 20 a. of meadow and 30 a. of pasture. The value of the estate had fallen to £4 from £5 in 1066.[10]

From the early 15th century Salthrop was one of the largest farms on the Elcombe estate.[11] In 1616 Salthrop farm measured 326 a. and its arable and meadow lands, above and below the escarpment, lay intermingled with those of Costow farm, which was not part of the Elcombe estate, and with those of Studley farm in Lydiard Tregoze. The common land of Salthrop was shared between Salthrop and Costow farms.[12] The land of Salthrop was inclosed and allotted in 1739 and Salthrop and Costow farms were exchanged.[13] In 1846 Upper Salthrop farm and Quidhampton farm, both downland farms, measured 595 a. and were worked together.[14] By 1977 they had been amalgamated and with land in Lydiard Tregoze formed Salthrop farm, 500 a.[15]

In 1086 the estate which later passed to Tewkesbury Abbey was rated at 10 hides, 2 of which were held by a 'Frenchman'. It had land for 4 ploughs. There were 2 ploughs on the demesne of 5½ hides and 6 villeins and 9 bordars also had 2 ploughs. There were 30 a. of pasture and 2 a. of wood. The value of the estate was £5 and had been in 1066.[16] About 1210 Tewkesbury Abbey's Overwroughton estate was valued at £10. Among the farm stock were 16 oxen, 27 ewes, 20 hoggets, and 15 lambs. Rents of assize totalled £4 13s. 6d. A hayward, carter, and dairyman were among the farm servants.[17] Shortly before the Dissolution the farm was leased for £11 14s. 8d.[18] The farm which the Calleys acquired in the 17th century measured 479 a. in the

[87] *Pipe R.* 1173 (P.R.S. xix), 103–4.
[88] *Wilts. Inq. p.m.* 1242–1326 (Index Libr.), 168–9.
[89] Ibid. 378; 1327–77 (Index Libr.), 177, 309.
[90] Ibid. 1327–77 (Index Libr.), 177.
[91] Ibid. 309.
[92] Ibid. 1242–1326 (Index Libr.), 378.
[93] Ibid. 1327–77 (Index Libr.), 309.
[94] *Close R.* 1261–4, 7, 321.
[95] *L. & P. Hen. VIII*, i (1), p. 465.
[96] Charterhouse Mun. M.R. 5/147.
[97] Ibid. M.R. 5/169; W.R.O. 700/282.
[98] Charterhouse Mun. M.R. 5/167.
[99] *Wilts. Inq. p.m.* 1327–77 (Index Libr.), 309; *V.C.H. Wilts.* ix. 81, 84.
[1] Charterhouse Mun. M.R. 5/147.
[2] Ibid. M.R. 5/149; M.R. 5/150.

[3] Ibid. M.R. 5/150; W.R.O. 631/1/1/4.
[4] e.g. Charterhouse Mun. M.R. 5/147; M.R. 5/149; M.R. 5/150.
[5] Ibid. M.R. 5/150.
[6] W.R.O., Inclosure Award.
[7] Charterhouse Mun., rental, 1832.
[8] *V.C.H. Wilts.* iv. 100.
[9] Ibid. ix. 81.
[10] Ibid. ii, p. 144.
[11] See above.
[12] W.R.O. 621/1/1/4; Charterhouse Mun. M.R. 5/149.
[13] Charterhouse Mun., Elcombe correspondence; *W.A.M.* xxxvii. 413.
[14] W.R.O., Tithe Award and map.
[15] Ex inf. Mr. N. M. Arnold-Forster, Salthrop Ho.
[16] *V.C.H. Wilts.* ii, p. 144.
[17] *Interdict Doc.* (Pipe R. Soc. N.S. xxxiv), 27, 31.
[18] *Valor Eccl.* (Rec. Com.), ii. 475.

19th century and had land at Hackpen mead and Hackpen field. In 1853 it had 410 a. of arable land, chiefly for wheat but also bearing crops of beans, peas, clover, and vetches. It was then well cultivated and considered to be a remarkably compact farm, apart from the land at Hackpen.[19]

The farm held by the Richmond Webbs from the 16th century to the 17th, represented by Overtown Manor farm in 1977, measured nearly 600 a. in the later 18th century.[20] Part of Parslo's and Mudgell farms were added to it in 1920, but in 1937 much downland was taken for the airfield.[21] In 1977 Overtown Manor farm, c. 1,000 a., comprised the greater part of the land available for agriculture in Overtown tithing. Overtown House farm lost land to the airfield and had some 120 a. in 1977.[22]

In 1086 Westlecott was assessed at 5 hides of which 4 were demesne. There was land for 4 ploughs. The demesne supported 1 serf and 1½ plough. There were additionally 3 villeins and 6 bordars with ½ plough. There were 25 a. of meadow and 30 a. of pasture. In 1066 and in 1086 it was worth £2.[23]

Of the two parts into which the manor had divided by the 13th century[24] one, containing Chilton and Westcott (later West Leaze) farms, became part of the Elcombe estate in the 15th century.[25] The other, in the north-east corner of the parish, contained the farm still called Westlecott in the 20th century. It was one of the first farms near Swindon to be acquired by the Goddards and, as their estate there expanded, Westlecott farm was involved in the agrarian arrangements of other farms.[26] It lay on the southern and lower slopes of Swindon hill and in the 17th century measured c. 166 a., mostly pasture and meadow land. Among the pastures were Cliff pasture and Bushey leaze.[27] Such arable as it had perhaps lay in West Swindon field, a large arable field of the adjoining Goddard manor of West Swindon, within which was a field called Westlecott.[28] Arable belonging to Westlecott was said to lie in Swindon in 1836.[29]

Until the airfield was built over part of the gallops in 1937 there were several training stables for racehorses in Wroughton.[30] Tom Leader of Fairwater House in the High Street trained the winner of the Derby in 1874.[31] Horses from the same stables, trained by E. A. Craddock, also won a number of important races. In 1906 the Hon. Aubrey Hastings took over the Barcelona stables in the Pitchens from which he trained several Grand National winners. He was followed in 1929 by Ivor Anthony whose horses maintained a high record of successes. In 1977 horses were bred and trained at Overtown House and Overtown Manor.[32]

The only large manufacturing industry in Wroughton is the firm of R. A. Lister & Co. Ltd. After the Second World War the firm, which was based in Dursley (Glos.), bought the workshops built for the Admiralty during the war. There they established their subsidiary, Marine Mountings Ltd., manufacturing small internal combustion engines. In 1952 about 350 people were employed.[33] In 1963 the firm became part of the Hawker Siddeley Diesel Group, but continued in business as R. A. Lister & Co. Ltd. At about the same time it began making diesel cylinders for civil engineering, agricultural, and marine uses. The works were later much enlarged and in 1977 about 750 people were employed.[34]

A small business making agricultural implements was opened in 1891 in the High Street by H. H. Barrett. From there it moved to Moormead Road where wooden wheels for waggons were made and later trailers for tractors. In 1977 the business was in the same premises, somewhat enlarged, under the management of Mr. Eric Barrett, and employed about 40 people.[35]

MILLS. There were eight mills on the Domesday estates in Wroughton. Those of Overwroughton and Westlecott each had one, paying 15d. and 5s. respectively, and Ellendune had six, paying together 42s. 6d.[36] In the earlier 19th century there were still seven mills along the stream which rose in Coombe bottom, joined another in the village, and flowed north to Swindon.

All the mills have had many different names, usually taken from those of their owners or occupiers. A mill owned by three generations of the Freeman family was known as Freeman's mill in 1572.[37] There were two mills on the dean and chapter of Winchester's manor in 1649. One, occupied by Richard Franklyn, was a grist-mill with 11½ a. attached. The other, described as an overshot grist-mill, was occupied by Richard Sadler with 38 a.[38] Sadler had been accused in 1647 of raising the level of the water passing through his mill to the detriment of the mill above his on the stream.[39]

In the later 18th century and the earlier 19th the Seymour family worked the mill in Perry's Lane later called King's mill.[40] It was equipped with a steam-engine in 1860, but soon afterwards ceased working.[41] In 1977 the mill, of brick with a tiled roof and bearing a date-stone 'J.S. 1771', was occupied as a private house. Considerable 19th-century alterations are evident. In 1820 Thomas Fielden Woodham was milling at the mill later called Woodham's on the east side of Bakers Road. He was succeeded in 1829 by Philip Pavey, and Pavey in 1845 by John Edwards.[42] Woodham's, in 1977 a brick and rubble

[19] W.R.O. 374/186.
[20] W.A.S. Libr., sale cat. ix, no. 32; see above.
[21] See above.
[22] Ex inf. Sir Hen. Calley, Overtown Ho.
[23] V.C.H. Wilts. ii, p. 156.
[24] See above.
[25] See above.
[26] V.C.H. Wilts. ix. 120–4, 125–6.
[27] Thamesdown Public Libr., Goddard MS. 957.
[28] V.C.H. Wilts. ix. 125; Thamesdown Public Libr., Goddard MSS. 230, 267.
[29] Thamesdown Public Libr., Goddard MS. 583.
[30] Guide to Wroughton (1973 edn.), 23–4.
[31] W.A.M. xlvi. 132.

[32] Guide to Wroughton (1973 edn.), 23–4.
[33] For a fuller acct. of the early hist. of the firm see V.C.H. Wilts. iv. 205.
[34] Ex inf. Deputy General Works Manager, R. A. Lister & Co., Ltd.
[35] E. Cripps, Scrapbk.; ex inf. Mrs. Cripps, Wroughton.
[36] V.C.H. Wilts. ii, pp. 120, 144, 156.
[37] Req. 2/205/47.
[38] Mun. D. & C. Winton., survey of chap. man. ff. 235, 236.
[39] Wilts. Q. Sess. Rec. ed. Cunnington, 184.
[40] Mun. D. & C. Winton., estate bk. XVIII, f. 9v.
[41] Cripps, Scrapbk.
[42] Mun. D. & C. Winton., estate bk. XVIII, f. 24v.

building of the 19th century, was the largest mill in the parish. When offered for sale in 1864 it was a three-storey flour-mill with three pairs of stones driven by a steam-engine. It also had an overshot water-wheel and stones for bone and seed milling.[43] Soon after 1864, however, it ceased working as a mill. It was converted into a private house in 1967.[44] Detached and to the east is a substantial early-19th-century mill-house. Between 1816 and 1845 Thomas Bedford and his son Thomas worked a mill in Overtown dell at the foot of Coombe bottom.[45] Called Bedford's mill, it was bought in 1866 by the Swindon Water Company as the site of a reservoir.[46] At the same time the company purchased the water rights of King's and Woodham's mills and of a mill, sometimes called Green's, south of Green's Lane, which were all deprived of a sufficient volume of water by the damming of the stream for the reservoir.[47] North of King's mill and lower on the stream were two more mills. One near Coventry Farm was converted to steam in 1854, and another north of that has sometimes been called Lower mill. Both ceased working in the later 19th century. Coventry mill was demolished in 1940.[48]

The mill in Westlecott was leased with its tolls by Thomas Goddard (d. 1704) to a Swindon baker in 1687.[49] In 1791 a mill, perhaps the same one, then recently occupied by George Wayte and called Wayte's mill, was let by Ambrose Goddard (d. 1815) to Henry Cook, a Swindon carpenter and mill-wright.[50] Like the other mills it ceased working in the later 19th century.

There was a windmill on Elcombe manor in 1287 and it was still there in 1348.[51] It may have stood for much longer, but it has not been traced.

LOCAL GOVERNMENT. Records of the courts of Wroughton manor survive from the later 13th century to the 18th.[52] By the later 13th century the prior of St. Swithun's had withdrawn his suit from Blackgrove hundred court and thereafter Wroughton tithing was transferred to his hundred of Elstub, while the other four tithings, Elcombe, Overtown, Salthrop, and Westlecott, remained in Blackgrove (later Kingsbridge hundred).[53] From c. 1274 the prior had full franchisal jurisdiction within Wroughton tithing, and the manor courts, which were held twice a year, were also called views of frankpledge and courts leet. From the mid 15th century to the mid 16th separate presentments were made by the hayward, an ale-taster, and the chief tithingman. The hayward and ale-taster presented faults relevant to their spheres of authority. Among offences brought before the court by the chief tithingman were overcharging by butchers or sellers of fish,

and the imposing of excessive tolls by millers.[54] At later courts business came to be almost entirely confined to copyhold and agrarian matters.[55]

Sir John Lovel (d. 1287) claimed full franchisal jurisdiction for Elcombe, basing his claim upon the overlordship of the honor of Leicester.[56] Elcombe may thereafter have been withdrawn from the hundred court, and the tithing was not present at the tourns held for Kingsbridge hundred in 1439, 1502, and 1511.[57] Manor court rolls survive for Elcombe and its members from the 16th century to the 18th.[58] The court was given various names, but was usually called a view of frankpledge and court baron. Occasionally the two were held separately. From the 17th century the chief business of the court was the appointment of officers, including a constable, two tithingmen, and two surveyors of the wastes and fields. The court dealt with such matters as the relegation of sheep to certain fields and the ringing of pigs. In the 18th century the obligation to serve as tithingmen was attached to certain farms.

Lacock Abbey was released from service due to the manor of Wootton Bassett for their estate in Westlecott by Philip Basset (d. 1271), and in 1299 Hugh le Despenser made a further release of the same service.[59] There is no record to show whether Westlecott was represented in any court other than the hundred court in the Middle Ages. After the mid 16th century it was presumably dealt with in the courts held by the Goddards for their other estates in the neighbourhood.[60] That part of Westlecott which was merged in the Elcombe estate was represented at the Elcombe courts.[61] The only record found of courts held for Overtown is a fragment of a court book of the mid 16th century for the manor held by the Bayntons.[62]

Among the parish records are accounts of church-wardens, 1649–1898, overseers, 1649–1828, and surveyors, 1715–67, and vestry minutes 1785–1904.[63] In 1692 and throughout the 18th century allowances for the poor were fixed in advance every month by the vestry.[64] In the 17th century there were three or four overseers, the office being filled by the occupiers of certain farms.[65] In the 18th century the parish was organized for taxation and most administrative purposes by two sides known as the Elcombe side and the Wroughton side.[66] In 1633 three cottages in Elcombe street were used for the poor.[67] By 1798, when there were 35 residents, a row of cottages off Markham Road served as a workhouse for the parish.[68] In 1803 the workhouse was farmed out for a year at the rate of 1s. 9d. per inmate per week.[69] In 1795 payments to the poor both within and without the workhouse were increased because of the high price of wheat. Two

43 W.R.O. 137/125/91.
44 Cripps, Scrapbk.
45 Mun. D. & C. Winton., estate bk. XVIII, f. 17v.; W.I. Scrapbk.
46 W.I. Scrapbk.; and see above, pp. 237–8.
47 W.I. Scrapbk.; Williams, *Villages of the White Horse*, 47.
48 O.S. Map 1/2,500, Wilts. XV. 12 (1886 edn.); Cripps, Scrapbk.
49 Thamesdown Public Libr., Goddard MS. 566.
50 W.R.O. 529/79.
51 *Wilts. Inq. p.m.* 1242–1326 (Index Libr.), 168–9; 1327–77 (Index Libr.), 177.
52 Mun. D. & C. Winton., ct. rec.

53 *V.C.H. Wilts.* ix. 3–4.
54 Mun. D. & C. Winton., ct. rolls, 1489, 1506, 1507.
55 e.g. ibid. ct. roll, 1578; ibid. N.R.A. boxes 108, 110.
56 *Rot. Hund.* (Rec. Com.), ii (1), 244.
57 *V.C.H. Wilts.* ix. 5.
58 Charterhouse Mun. M.R. 5/1–17, on which the rest of this para. is based.
59 *V.C.H. Wilts.* iii. 307; *Cat. Anct. D.* vi, A 9357.
60 *V.C.H. Wilts.* ix. 133.   61 See above.
62 W.R.O. 84/35.   63 All in ibid. 551.
64 Ibid. 551/77.
66 Ibid.   67 Charterhouse Mun. M.R. 5/150.
68 W.R.O. 551/99; 551/114.
69 Ibid. 551/35.
65 Ibid. 551/35.

more cottages were built in 1800, bringing to five the total used for the poor. In 1815 the vestry appointed a manager of the workhouse who was also to act as vestry clerk and assistant to the overseers.[70] The cottages were sold in 1847 and the money put towards the building of the union workhouse.[71] Estimates for building a smallpox house were received in 1792 and a pest-house was built.[72] Wroughton became part of the Highworth and Swindon poor-law union in 1835.[73]

CHURCH. A church wall is mentioned in the bounds of Ellendune appended to the charter of 956.[74] Since that church, of which no trace remains, was almost certainly on the boundary between Ellendune and Elcombe, it may have been on the site of the present church which stands on or very close to that boundary. By 1107 the bishop of Winchester had assigned the church to the precentor of St. Swithun's Priory for making books ('ad libros faciendos').[75] Although the estate called Ellendune came to be called Wroughton, the church was long known as Ellendune church.[76] About 1124 it was among the churches which the bishop acknowledged that he had wrongfully appropriated.[77] It was confirmed to the precentor c. 1150 when it provided an endowment for repairing the organs as well as for writing books.[78] In 1243 the prior obtained papal confirmation of his right to the church.[79] In 1284, however, as part of the composition between them, the prior surrendered all claim to the church to the bishop, except for an annual pension from it, perhaps a recognition of the earlier endowment for the precentor.[80] The church was not appropriated by the bishop and the benefice was a sinecure rectory until such benefices were abolished under the Cathedrals and Ecclesiastical Commissioners Act of 1840.[81]

It is not known whether the prior presented to the church. In 1172 the bishop confirmed the priory's patronage of churches, including Wroughton,[82] but the bishop regained the advowson, if he had ever lost it, and a presentation by the king in 1250 was made sede vacante.[83] The king may have attempted to gain the advowson soon afterwards[84] but in 1284 surrendered all claim to the bishop.[85] Thereafter, with a few exceptions, presentations of rectors were by the bishops of Winchester or, sede vacante, by the king. An exception occurred in 1493 when the bishop of Salisbury presented during a vacancy at Winchester.[86] In 1530 the archbishop of York

presented with the bishop of Winchester.[87] The bishop conceded the patronage twice, in 1551 when three persons, one a mercer and citizen of London, presented, and in 1610 when Nicholas Longford presented.[88] The last presentation of a rector was in 1825 and on the death of the rector then presented the rectory estate passed to the Ecclesiastical Commissioners.[89]

It is not known when the rectors began presenting vicars to serve the church, but by c. 1291 a vicarage had been endowed.[90] The first known presentation was in 1316, but the vicar then presented was replacing an earlier one.[91] Thereafter the rectors presented vicars except in 1389, 1491, and 1778 when the bishop of Salisbury presented, apparently by lapse.[92] During the sequestration of the rectory in 1649 an incumbent was appointed by the Wiltshire Committee for Scandalous Ministers and endowed with all the assets of the rectory.[93] After the Restoration rectors presented vicars until the sinecure rectory was abolished.[94] The advowson of the vicarage then passed to the bishop of Winchester, but it was transferred in 1852 to the bishop of Gloucester and Bristol in whose diocese Wroughton had been since 1836. In 1897 the advowson passed to the bishop of the new diocese of Bristol.[95]

The vicarage was worth £4 c. 1291.[96] In 1535 it was valued at roughly £12, including an annual pension of 13s. 4d. from St. Swithun's Priory.[97] By 1671 the value had risen to £80 and the vicar was receiving £45 a year charged upon the rectory and paid by the rector's lessee.[98] That payment was abolished in 1876 when the Ecclesiastical Commissioners gave to the vicarage £265 of the rent-charge which they received in respect of the rectory estate.[99] In 1828 the vicarage had received two augmentations of £200 from Queen Anne's Bounty, and the then vicar gave £400.[1] In 1829–31 the average gross annual income was £160.[2] In 1851 the annual income was £178.[3]

By 1843 the payment of all vicarial tithe had been extinguished either by allotments of land under the inclosure awards, or by the substitution of prescriptive annual payments. Most of the dean and chapter of Winchester's land was tithe free. In 1843 the vicar was awarded a rent-charge of £22 for payments still due.[4]

The vicarage glebe was small. In 1671 there was 1 a. of pasture adjoining the churchyard and a vicarage-house.[5] The glebe was enlarged by allotments of 29 a. and 18 a. in place of tithes under the inclosure awards of 1796 and 1797.[6] The Ecclesiastical

[70] Ibid.
[71] Ibid. 551/111.
[72] Ibid. 551/35. For its site see 551/114.
[73] Poor Law Com. 2nd Rep. 559.
[74] Cart. Sax. ed. Birch, iii, p. 127. Thanks are due to Mr. J. McN. Dodgson, Univ. Coll., Lond., for help with interpreting the relevant parts of the chart.
[75] Chartulary Winch. Cath. ed. A. W. Goodman, 5.
[76] See p. 235.
[77] Reg. Pontoise (Cant. & York Soc.), 620–2.
[78] Chartulary Winch. Cath. ed. Goodman, 6.
[79] Dugdale, Mon. i. 211.
[80] Reg. Pontoise (Cant. & York Soc.), ii. 431.
[81] 3 & 4 Vic. c. 113.
[82] Reg. Pontoise (Cant. & York Soc.), ii. 624.
[83] Cal. Pat. 1247–58, 82.
[84] Reg. Pontoise (Cant. & York Soc.), ii. 609.
[85] Cal. Chart. R. 1267–1300, 273.
[86] Phillipps, Wilts. Inst. i. 175.
[87] Ibid. 201.
[88] Ibid. 215; ii. 6.

[89] W.A.M. xli. 468.
[90] Tax. Eccl. (Rec. Com.), 190.
[91] Phillipps, Wilts. Inst. i. 21.
[92] Ibid. 74, 175; ii. 89.
[93] Mun. D. & C. Winton., survey of chap. man. f. 185.
[94] See above.
[95] W.A.M. xli. 457–8.
[96] Tax. Eccl. (Rec. Com.), 190.
[97] Valor Eccl. (Rec. Com.), ii. 128; vi, App. p. vi.
[98] Sar. Dioc. R.O., Glebe Terrier.
[99] W.A.S. Libr. (M 18), letter to Canon F. H. Manley from Eccl. Commrs., 9 Dec. 1921.
[1] C. Hodgson, Queen Anne's Bounty (1845 edn.), pp. ccix, cccxxxvi.
[2] Rep. Com. Eccl. Revenues, 854–5.
[3] H.O. 129/250/2/14.
[4] W.R.O., Tithe Award.
[5] Sar. Dioc. R.O., Glebe Terrier.
[6] W.R.O., Wroughton and Elcombe Inclosure Awards.

Commissioners added a small piece of ground in 1897.[7] The vicarage-house was considered old in 1787, although not unsuited to such a meagre living.[8] The house, which was of stone, ran north–south. It was extended to the east in brick in 1727,[9] and refronted to the west in the 19th century. It was replaced as the vicarage-house in 1968 by a smaller one built near by and came to be called Ivery House.[10]

The pension of £5 awarded to St. Swithun's Priory out of the church in 1284 is mentioned in 1291 and 1539, and after the Dissolution passed to Winchester chapter.[11] In 1127 tithe due to the church from land in Elcombe was given as a portion to the priory of Minster Lovell (Oxon.), a cell of the abbey of St. Mary of Briaco at Ivry (Eure) of which the Lovels of Elcombe were benefactors.[12] The prior of Minster Lovell received £2 from Elcombe in 1291. When Minster Lovell was suppressed as an alien house in the 15th century, the land was transferred to Eton College, founded in 1440. As Bryan's acre, or sometimes Eton College piece, the land was leased by the college until 1797 when it was possibly sold to the lessee.[13]

A chapel or chantry of Elcombe existed in 1308.[14] Priests to serve it were presented by the Lovels, one of whom was presumably its founder. Between 1349 and 1363 three presentations were made by the king while he had the wardships of John, Lord Lovel (d. 1361), and his son John (d. 1408).[15] The chapel was once said to be in the parish church, but it is generally believed to have stood some way away, perhaps in a field opposite Elcombe Farm. Stones from it are thought to have been used in the building of the school near the church.[16] In 1419 it was said to be dedicated to St. Mary.[17] No reference to it after 1448 has been found.[18] A single reference has been found to a chapel of St. Anne at Quidhampton in 1589.[19]

The rector mentioned in 1249 perhaps resided in the parish.[20] Few, if any, later rectors resided and they were almost invariably pluralists, holding prebends or other dignities elsewhere.[21] Although the profits of the rectory were not taken, as might have been expected, to endow a prebend, one rector, Francis Morley (d. 1696), styled himself prebendary of Elingdon alias Wroughton in Winchester cathedral.[22]

Pluralism and non-residence were fairly rare among the vicars until the 19th century.[23] John Honyland, presented in 1439, was also rector of Hornblotton (Som.). About 1440 he was accused of breaking into Wroughton church and stealing a book,

some vestments, candles, and other goods belonging to his parishioners.[24] Several 19th-century vicars held other benefices and lived away from the parish where they employed curates. James Merest, vicar 1783–1827, was curate of Wortham and rector of Brandon and of Wangford (all three in Suff.). After 1812 he also kept a school in Diss (Norf.). His curate at Wroughton also served the churches of Broad Hinton and Berwick Bassett.[25]

In 1783 Merest's curate held two services on Sundays in the summer and one in winter. Holy Communion was celebrated four times a year. There were then between 20 and 35 communicants in the parish. Many were said to absent themselves from church.[26] In 1812 the average number of communicants was 50 and a sermon was preached on Sunday afternoons by subscription.[27] On Census Sunday in 1851 200 people were in church in the morning and 300 in the afternoon.[28] A small iron mission church, dedicated to St. Andrew, was built at North Wroughton in 1935. It was served by the vicar of the parish church. It was closed in 1969.[29]

The church of *ST. JOHN THE BAPTIST AND ST. HELEN* is built of dressed sarsen stone and has a chancel with north chapel and organ chamber, an aisled and clerestoried nave with south porch, and a west tower.[30] It was extensively restored in the mid 19th century when some of its medieval features as well as many later fittings were removed.[31]

The north and south doorways of the nave are both of the 12th century and although reset may originally have led into an aisled nave whose north arcade appears to have survived until the 19th-century restoration. In the 14th century the chancel was rebuilt, presumably on a larger scale than its predecessor, and the first two bays of the south arcade were also rebuilt. The western bay of that arcade is of the 15th century and probably the result of a delayed rebuilding of the 12th-century original. In the 15th century the tower, porch, and north chapel and vestry were added and the outer walls of both aisles were rebuilt. That work probably coincided with the building of the clerestory and a new nave roof.

Until the 19th century the interior of the church contained a notable collection of pews and galleries. In addition to the box-pews which filled the nave and aisles, there was a private pew in the north chapel and another, in the form of a gallery, at the west end of the chancel. At the west end of the nave there were two superimposed galleries, the upper one presumably for a choir or church band. Apart from the north arcade, which was rebuilt in a 14th-

[7] *W.A.M.* xli. 478.
[8] Sar. Dioc. R.O., Archd. Wilts., Vis.
[9] Date-stone on ho.
[10] Wilts. Cuttings, xxiii. 208; E. Cripps, Scrapbk.
[11] *Tax. Eccl.* (Rec. Com.), 190; *Valor Eccl.* (Rec. Com.), ii. 128; Mun. D. & C. Winton., estate bk. IX, pensions list.   [12] *W.A.M.* xxxvii. 413–16.
[13] Ibid.; Charterhouse Mun. M.R. 5/204; W.R.O., Inclosure Award.
[14] Phillipps, *Wilts. Inst.* i. 8.
[15] Ibid. 48, 52, 56; *Cal. Pat. 1361–4*, 318; *Complete Peerage*, viii. 207–25.
[16] *Cal. Pat. 1358–61*, 512; *W.A.M.* xli. 459–60.
[17] Phillipps, *Wilts. Inst.* i. 108.
[18] Ibid. 139.   [19] C 66/1324 m. 15.
[20] *Civil Pleas, 1249* (W.R.S. xxvi), p. 35, where 'Ellesden' has been wrongly identified.

[21] For the rectors see *W.A.M.* xli. 460–8.
[22] Phillipps, *Wilts. Inst.* ii. 66.
[23] List in *W.A.M.* xli. 468–72.
[24] *Cal. Pat. 1441–6*, 264.
[25] *W.A.M.* xli. 471–2; *Vis. Queries, 1783* (W.R.S. xxvii), p. 97.
[26] *Vis. Queries, 1783* (W.R.S. xxvii), p. 97.
[27] *W.A.M.* xli. 138.   [28] H.O. 129/250/2/14.
[29] Par. ch. council mins. *penes* the Revd. R. G. Wolsey, Wroughton Vicarage.
[30] A detailed description is in *W.A.M.* xxxviii. 415–25, corrected ibid. 642–3.
[31] A model made by one Lloyd in 1839 (in 1977 in Wroughton Ho.) and water-colours by J. Buckler in W.A.S. Libr., vol. vii. 8; vol. viii. 28, 33, 58, 65 (all four 1810), show some of the features removed in 1846; see plate facing p. 96.

century style, the other structural losses of the 19th century were the chapel and vestry on the north side of the chancel and several windows, most notably those in the south aisle which had square heads and were rebuilt in 14th-century style.

Besides the font in use in 1977 there was in the church the bowl of another of the early 14th century. The pulpit was given by H. W. M. Light, vicar 1840–75. The royal arms in the south aisle are dated 1817. The bellcot at the east end of the nave roof came from the Lawn, the former Goddard family home in Swindon, in 1966 to replace an earlier one.[32]

The king's commissioners took 16 oz. of plate in 1553 but left a chalice of 16 oz. with a paten. In 1977 the plate included a cup and paten with hall-marks of 1576, a flagon of 1710, a paten given in 1719, and some alms-dishes given in 1851.[33]

There are six bells: (i), 1660, is by William Purdue of Salisbury; (ii), 1622, and (iii), 1596, are by John Wallis of Salisbury; (iv), 1784, is by Robert Wells of Aldbourne; (v), 1624, is by John Danton of Salisbury; and (vi), 1955, is by Mears and Stainbank of Whitechapel.[34]

Registers of baptisms begin in 1653 and of marriages and burials in 1654. All are complete.[35]

ROMAN CATHOLICISM. A small community of Presentation Sisters living in Wroughton taught at the Groundwell Road school in Swindon in the early 1960s. In 1964 they left Wroughton to live in Swindon. A community of the Sisters of the Holy Spirit then moved to Wroughton from where they did missionary work in Swindon and the neighbourhood.[36] They lived in Barcelona House until the convent of the Holy Spirit was built for them in the Pitchens c. 1970.[37] St. Joseph's church in Devizes Road was dedicated in 1954 and was served from Swindon until the early 1970s when it became the church of its own parish.[38]

PROTESTANT NONCONFORMITY. There was a dissenter, probably a Baptist or a Quaker, in the parish in 1676.[39] In 1683 there was none.[40] Licence for a village station for Baptists was granted in 1782. No permanent Baptist congregation resulted, although a mission was established for a time c. 1886.[41]

In the 19th century five houses were licensed as dissenters' meeting-places: those of Thomas Pickett in 1818 and of William Pickett in 1829, that of Frederick Newport in 1833, that of George Gibbs in 1850, and that of Robert Hiles at Elcombe in 1836.[42] Of those meetings only those led by the Picketts and Gibbs are known to have established themselves for any length of time. In 1851 William Pickett led a group of Calvinistic dissenters which

on Census Sunday in that year met with a congregation of around twenty. It had no meeting-house, but assembled in the kitchen of a private house, and it has not been possible to link the congregation with any of the later chapels.[43] The group of Primitive Methodists meeting under the leadership of George Gibbs in 1850 was still worshipping in a private house in 1851 when on Census Sunday attendance in the afternoon was 80 and in the evening 70.[44] The house may have been that at Lower Wroughton known to have been used by Primitive Methodists. It was later demolished and in 1976 its site was covered by the buildings of the Roman Catholic convent.[45]

A Primitive Methodist chapel was built in the High Street in 1853, perhaps for Gibbs's congregation. Another chapel was built in 1880 and is still in use as a Methodist church.[46]

A Wesleyan Methodist chapel was built in Devizes Road in 1823. On Census Sunday in 1851 attendance was 150 in the morning and 165 in the evening.[47] The chapel had been unused for many years when demolished in the early 1970s to make way for the Community Centre.[48]

EDUCATION. In 1743 Thomas Bennet of Salthrop charged Quidhampton farm with an annual payment of £40 to found schools in Wroughton and Broad Hinton.[49] The Wroughton school was intended for poor children between the ages of five and sixteen born in the parish. In 1787 the number of pupils was limited to 36. By 1808 others had been admitted and the schoolmaster's original salary of £20 a year was augmented by subscription.[50] A few children were paid for by their parents. In 1818 the school was united with the National Society and had about 200 pupils.[51] The rent-charge was extinguished in 1902 by an investment of £1,650 by the owner of Quidhampton farm. The interest was then used for promoting religious instruction and for general school purposes. The annual income in 1962 was £26.[52]

The school stood in the garden of the rectory-house. It had a room above for girls and one below, traditionally called the 'abbey kitchen', for boys. It was in poor condition in 1859. In 1866 it was replaced by a new school built near by. That school was for boys. A school for girls was built soon afterwards just off High Street.[53] In 1908 the girls' school had an average attendance of 114, the boys' of 140.[54] In the late 1920s the boys' school became a senior mixed school and the girls' a junior mixed school with accommodation in 1932 for 148 and 156 respectively.[55]

In 1948 the schools were so overcrowded that the senior children were moved to a secondary modern school opened as a temporary measure in a hutted camp built during the war in Burderop Park in Chiseldon.[56] They remained there until 1967 when

[32] Mark Child, *Visitor's Guide* (in ch. in 1976).
[33] Nightingale, *Wilts. Plate*, 192; Child, *Guide*.
[34] Walters, *Wilts. Bells*, 244; Child, *Guide*.
[35] W.R.O. 551.   [36] *V.C.H. Wilts.* ix. 151.
[37] E. Cripps, *Scrapbk.*
[38] Local information.
[39] *W.N. & Q.* iii. 535; *V.C.H. Wilts.* iii. 115.
[40] Sar. Dioc. R.O., Chwdns.' Pres.
[41] *V.C.H. Wilts.* iii. 137 n. 37; ix. 157.
[42] W.R.O., Certs. Dissenters' Meeting-Houses.
[43] H.O. 129/250/2/15.   [44] Ibid.
[45] *Guide to Wroughton* (1973 edn.), 21.
[46] Ibid.   [47] H.O. 129/250/2/17.
[48] *Guide to Wroughton* (1973 edn.), 21.
[49] Except where stated information about this sch. is from *Endowed Char. Wilts.* (N. Div.), 1041, 1043–4.
[50] Lambeth MS. 1732.   [51] *Educ. of Poor Digest*, 1042.
[52] Char. Com. file 309341.
[53] *Kelly's Dir. Wilts.* (1903).
[54] *Bd. of Educ., List 21, 1908* (H.M.S.O.), 508.
[55] Ibid. *1932* (H.M.S.O.), 412.
[56] *V.C.H. Wilts.* v. 355; ix. 23.

they moved to the county junior and comprehensive schools newly built in Inverary Road.[57] In 1976 the junior school had about 600 pupils and the comprehensive, which was known as the Ridgeway School and drew children from a wide area, about 1,150.[58] The old school near the church was opened as a diocesan youth centre called Legge House in 1968.[59]

An elementary school for infants was opened in Lower Wroughton in 1877 and average attendance in 1903 was 135.[60] It was closed in 1929 when average attendance was about 90, and the infants were moved to their own buildings on the site of the girls' school off the High Street.[61] The school, with much enlarged accommodation, remained there in 1976 when about 420 children attended it.[62]

A church school was opened for children living on the Salthrop side of the parish in 1864.[63] Average attendance was 32 in 1908 and 18 in 1938.[64] The school was closed in 1966.[65]

CHARITIES FOR THE POOR. Thomas Bennet of Salthrop[66] charged a farm in Broad Hinton with £300 for the benefit of the Wroughton poor. In 1834 £10 10s. was paid by the owner of the farm and was distributed among the twenty most deserving of the second poor. Another charge of £200 was imposed upon the same farm by Elizabeth Bennet, Thomas's sister, to help girls entering domestic service. In 1834 £7 was distributed from Elizabeth's benefaction. In 1903 60 applicants received 10s. 6d. each from Thomas Bennet's charity and 12 applicants received 10s. each from Elizabeth Bennet's.[67]

Thomas Sutton (d. 1611), founder of the London Charterhouse and lord of Elcombe manor, with three other persons bequeathed small sums to provide an apprenticing charity for Wroughton boys. In 1834 the bequests were in the form of a rent-charge on a house and land in Wroughton and produced about £10 a year. The money was allowed to accumulate until it was possible to pay premiums of £15. In the 1890s several boys were apprenticed. In 1902 the charity had about £11 in hand.[68]

The Bennet and Sutton charities were combined by a Scheme in 1969. Thereafter the money was to be used to help needy young people entering a trade or profession.[69]

[57] V.C.H. Wilts. ix. 23; E. Cripps, Scrapbk.
[58] Ex inf. Deputy Headmaster, Ridgeway Sch.
[59] Cripps, Scrapbk.
[60] Kelly's Dir. Wilts. (1903).
[61] Bd. of Educ., List 21, 1932 (H.M.S.O.), 412.
[62] Ex inf. Deputy Headmaster, Ridgeway Sch.
[63] Return of Non-Provided Schs. 41.

[64] Bd. of Educ., List 21, 1908 (H.M.S.O.), 508 1938 (H.M.S.O.), 426.
[65] Ex inf. Deputy Headmaster, Ridgeway Sch.
[66] Probably Thomas Bennet (fl. 1739): see p. 242.
[67] Endowed Char. Wilts. (N. Div.), 1042, 1043.
[68] Ibid. 1042, 1046.
[69] Char. Com. file 254590.

INDEX

An italic page-number refers to a map or an illustration on that or the facing page.

The following are among the abbreviations used: adv., advowson; agric., agriculture; Alex., Alexander; Alf., Alfred; And., Andrew; Ant., Anthony; abp., archbishop; archit., architecture; Bart., Bartholomew; Benj., Benjamin; bp., bishop; Brit., British; bro., brother; cast., castle; cath., cathedral; Cath., Catherine; cent., century; chant., chantry; chap., chapel; char., charity; Chas., Charles; Chris., Christopher; ch., church; coll., college; cttee., committee; ctss., countess; ct., court; cust., customary; Dan., Daniel; dau., daughter; d., died; dom., domestic; dchss., duchess; Edm., Edmund; Edw., Edward; Eliz., Elizabeth; fam., family; f., father; fl., flourished; Fred., Frederick; Geof., Geoffrey; Geo., George; Gilb., Gilbert; grds., grandson; Hen., Henry; Herb., Herbert; hosp., hospital; ho., house; Humph., Humphrey; hund., hundred; inc., inclosure; ind., industry; Jas., James; Jos., Joseph; Kath., Katharine, Katherine; man., manor; Marg., Margaret; mkt., market; m., married; Mat., Matthew; Maur., Maurice; Mic., Michael; Min., Ministry; Nat., Nathaniel; Nic., Nicholas; nonconf., nonconformity; n, note; par., parish; parl., parliamentary; Phil., Philip; pop., population; prehist., prehistoric; prot., protestant; rly., railway; Reg., Reginald; rem., remains; rep., representation; Ric., Richard; riv., river; Rob., Robert; Rog., Roger; Rom., Roman, Romano; Sam., Samuel; sch., school; Sim., Simon; sis., sister; s., son; sta., station; Steph., Stephen; Thos., Thomas; vct., viscount; Wal., Walter; w., wife; Wm., William.

Abarrow, Ric., 54
Abergavenny, marquess of, see Larnach-Nevill
Abingdon, Ric. of, 148
Abingdon, earls of, 204–5; and see Bertie
Ablington (in Figheldean), 106, 140
Achonry (Sligo), bp. of, see Blakedon
Adams:
  Gabriel (d. c. 1661), 174
  Gabriel (fl. 1690), 174
  (alias Coleman), John, 134
  Ric., 174
Adlam:
  Eleanor, m. John Merewether, 174
  Wm., 144
Aeffe, m. Wulfgar, 152
Agar:
  Sidney, earl of Normanton, 173, 177
  Welbore Ellis, earl of Normanton, 122–3, 173
agricultural implement making, 43, 112, 247
agricultural machinery contracting, 197
Ailesbury:
  earldom, 109, 113
  earls of, see Bruce; Brudenell-Bruce
  marquesses of, 109; and see Brudenell-Bruce
Aileva (fl. 1066), 85
Air Ministry, 210
Aitchison, G., 97
Akerman:
  Steph., 206
  Wm., 123, 128, 131
Aldbourne, 96, 115, 139, 141, 164–5, 251
  forest and chase, 139
Alderbury, 58, 76–7, 89
  poor-law union, 27, 45, 68
  and see Ivychurch; Whaddon
Aldrington, John de, 161
ale-tasters, 16, 44, 248
Alexander, Francis, 137
Alfgar (fl. 986), 6
Alflaed (fl. 972), 189
Alfnoth (fl. 983), 226
Alfred (fl. 1086), 239
Alfric (fl. 957), 6
Alfsige (fl. 947), 6
Allen, Jos., 115
alms-house, see Stockton
Alnod (fl. 1066), 242
Alsi (fl. 1066), 192
Alt, J. H., vicar of Enford, 134
Alton, 183
Alton (Hants), 207
Alton (in Figheldean), 117
Alton, Queen's, see Alton Priors

Alton Barnes, 172, 183, 196, 200–1, 203
  rector, see Hare, Augustus
  and see Shaw
Alton Priors (in Overton), 9, 105, 107, 183, 187–8, 191, 193, 198–200, 203–5, 217
  agric., 196–7
  boundaries, 183
  Broad Well spring, 183
  ch., 188, 199–202
  cts., 107, 199, 206
  curate, 201
  cust. tenants, 197
  dom. archit., 188
  farms, 196–8
  glebe-ho., 200
  Knap hill, 187–8
  man., 183, 187 n, 191–4, 197, 199, 205–6
  man.-ho., 188, 193
  mill, 198
  place-name, 183
  pop., 187
  prehist. rem., 187
  Priory, the, 188, 193
  prot. nonconf., 202
  'Queen's Alton', 183
  Red Shore, 187–8
  roads, 188
  Rom.-Brit. rem., 187
  tithes, 191, 197, 200
  Walker's hill, 183, 187
  woodland, 197
Alward (fl. 1086), 69
Alwi son of Turber, 69
Alwin (fl. 1066), 239
Ames, Jas., 103
Amesbury, 117 n, 150
  hund., 106, 117
  poor-law union, 211
  priory, 124
Amice, ctss. of Leicester, m. 1 Sim. de Montfort, 2 Wm. des Barres, 136–7, 168–9, 177
Amor:
  Rob. (d. 1771–2), 205
  Rob. (d. 1781–2), 205–6
  Sarah, m. Wm. Tinker, 205
  Wm., 205
Amport (Hants), see Sarson
Andely, see Daundely
Anderson, N. J. M., 60
Andover (Hants), 118, 129, 212
Andrew, Rob. s. of, see Robert
Andrew:
  Ric., 216
  Thos., 216
Andrews:
  Edw., 111
  Eliz., see Franklin

Hen., and his w. Mary, 137
Sir Mat., 99
Ric., 189
Wm., 190
Wm., s. of Wm., 190
Angens:
  John de, 171
  Wm. de, 171
  fam., 171
Anger:
  John, 161–2
  Thos., 161
Angoulême, Isabel of, see Isabel
animals (less common), see dog-breeding; foxes, silver
Anne (of Cleves), queen of Hen. VIII, 190
Anrep, Boris, 154
Anschitil (fl. 1086), 215
Ansdell, L. C., 9
Ansgot (fl. 1086), 31
Ansty, 174
Antell:
  Josiah, 9
  Percy, 9
  Thos., 9
Anthony, Ivor, 247
Antrobus:
  Sir Edm. (d. 1870), 119, 134
  Sir Edm. (d. 1899), 119
apples, 155
ApRice, Thos., 11
Archbold (alias Topp), Thos., 214, 216
Archer:
  Lady Eliz., w. of Hen., 33
  Hen., 33
Arches (ct. of), dean of, 148
architects and designers, see Aitchison; Aylmer; Birch; Blomfield; Blore; Blow; Bodley & Garner; Brandon, David; Bridgeman, Chas.; Butterfield; Caröe; Carpenter, R. H.; Cipriani; Dawber; Dyer; Ferrey, E. B. and Edm.; Gabriel; Gover; Ingelow; King, Thos. (d. 1804); Lowder; Male & Marchant; Morlidge; Morris; Osmond; Overton, Sam.; Pace; Peniston; Ponting; Pugin; Rennie; Revett; Sarjeant, Ant.; Scott, Sir Gilb.; Soane; Street; Voisey & Wills; Ward & Hughes; Waring & Blake; Weaver; Webb, Phil.; Wood; Wren, Chris., rector of East Knoyle; Wyatt, Jas., Jeffry, and T. H.
Army Flying Corps, see Fittleton: R.A.F. sta.
Arnold-Forster, N. M., 241

Dunn, *see* Dun
Dunstanville:
  Adelize, w. of Rob. de, 242
  Parnel de, m. Rob. de Montfort, 240
  Rob. de, 242
  Wal. de (d. 1195), 242
  Wal. de (d. 1269), 240, 242
  fam., 240, 242
Dunworth hundred, 1
Duppa, Brian, bp. of Winchester, 86
Durham, cath. ch., prebendary of, *see* Moore, John
Durrington, 178; *and see* Larkhill
Dursley (Glos.), 247
Duyn, *see* Dun
Dyer, Wm., 207
Dyneley:
  Marg., w. of Rob., m. 2 Sir Percival Sowdan, 106, 121, 144–5, 147–9
  Rob. (d. 1395), 121, 144–5, 147
  Rob. (fl. 1427), 144–5
  fam., 146, 149
Dyper, Wm., 110

Earle, John, rector and vicar of Bishopstone, bp. of Worcester and of Salisbury, 17–18
Earlscourt, Ric. of, *see* Oaksey
Earlscourt (in Wanborough), 159–60
Eastcott (in Urchfont), 210
Eastleigh (Hants), 112
Eastman:
  Alice, w. of Wal., 64
  Cecily, 64
  John (fl. 1523–60), 64
  John (fl. 1592), 64
  Mary, w. of Moses, 65
  Moses, 65
  Thos., 65
  Wal. (two of the name), 64
  Wm., rector of Everleigh, 141
  fam., 56, 64
'Ebbesborne' (regional name), 3, 6; *and see* Bishopstone (in Downton hund.)
Ebbesborne Wake, 3
Ebble, riv., 3, 15, 19, 63
Ecclesiastical Commissioners, 29, 40, 49, 58, 78, 86–7, 122, 124, 126, 153, 156, 160–2, 172, 179, 226, 230, 233, 239, 249–50; *and see* Church Commissioners
Eden, Sir John, 95
Edendon, Wm., bp. of Winchester, 47; *and see* Edington
Edes:
  Hen., canon of Chichester, 144
  Mary, w. of Hen., *see* Jeay
  Mary, m. John Briggs, 144
Edgar, King, 6, 189, 204
edge-tools manufacture, 40, 42, 176
Edington, Thos. of, rector of Downton, 47; *and see* Edendon
Edmund, earl of Kent, 143, 145
Edmund, earl of Lancaster and of Leicester, 120, 124, 126, 137, 145, 147, 169, 178
Edred, King, 6, 28
Edward the Elder, King, 6, 27, 214
Edward I, 46, 59, 143
Edward III, 153, 168
Edward IV, *see* Plantagenet
Edward VI, 6, 28, 85, 214
Edward (fl. 1086, a thegn), 76
Edward (fl. 1086, tenant of the bp. of Winchester), 192
Edwards:
  Geo., 161
  John, 247
Edwin (fl. 1066), 172
Edwy, King, 6, 238
eel fishery, 40–1
Egbert, King, 235

Elcombe (in Wroughton), 105, 235, 237, 248–50
  agric., 245–6
  chap., 237, 250
  ct., 248
  cust. tenants, 246
  Elcombe Hall, 240
  farms, 246, 248
  inc., 239, 245–6, 249
  man., 235, 240–2, 246–8, 252
  mill, 248
  park, 246
  pop., 237
  prot. nonconf., 251
  tithes, 250
Eleanor (of Provence), queen of Hen. III, 124
electricity generating, 40, 71, 178
Elfheah (fl. 956), 238
Eling (Hants), *see* Paultons; Wade
Eliott, *see* Elliott
Elizabeth I, 37, 47, 73, 86, 95
Elizabeth, w. of John, earl of Kent, 143
Ellendune, *see* Wroughton
Elliott (Eliott):
  John (fl. 1557), 9
  John (fl. 1721), 34
  Nic., 34
  Thos., 34
Elmar (fl. 1066), 189
Elms Cross, *see* Westwood
Elsham (Lincs.), 137–8
Elston (in Orcheston St. George), 209
Elstub and Everleigh hundred, *104*, **105–7**, 117–18, 129, 135, 140, 142, 147, 156, 159, 166, 187, 199, 206, 224, 235, 248; *and see* Everleigh: liberty
Elwes, Guy, 154
Emma, queen of King Ethelred, queen of King Cnut, 226
Emmerson, Thos., 146
Enbourne (Berks.), vicar of, *see* Lloyd
Enfield (later Royal Enfield) Motor Cycle Co. (later Enfield Precision Engineers), 230
Enford, John, vicar of Enford, 131
Enford, 105–7, **115–34**, *116*, 165–6, 174, 179, 197, 206, 217, 229
  advs., 130
  agric., 117, 126–8
  boundaries, 115
  bridges, 118
  chant., 131, 134
  chant.-ho., 131
  chars., 131, 134
  Chisenbury, East, *q.v.*
  ch., 118, 124, 130–4, *160*, 179
  common meadows, 117
  Compton, *q.v.*
  Coombe, *q.v.*
  cts., 107, 129–30
  curates, 132
  cust. tenants, 126–7, 129
  dom. archit., 118
  farm, 126–8
  field systems, 117
  Fifield, *q.v.*
  glebe, 119, 124, 131
  inc., 127, 131
  Littlecott, *q.v.*
  Longstreet, *q.v.*
  man., 106–7, 119–32, 134
  man.-ho., 118–19
  mill, *see* Littlecott: mill
  New Town, 117
    dom. archit., 118
    pop., 117
  poor-relief, 130
  pop., 117
  prehist. rem., 117
  prot. nonconf., 133–4
  rectors, 130–1, 133
  rectory, 124, 130
  roads, 117–18

Rom.-Brit. rem., 117, 135
schs., 134
tithes, 124, 130–1
vicarage, 130–1, 147, 178
vicarage-ho., 118, 131
vicars, 124, 130–3; *and see* Alt; Boyer; Cooke, Wm.; Culpeper, Hen.; Enford, John; Fauntleroy; Jacob, Thos.; Jeay, Thos.; Prince; Westley
Water Dean Bottom, 117, 119, 121
'Engenold' (fl. 1086), 53
'Engenulf' (fl. 1086), 53
English Farms Ltd., 204
Environment, Department of the, 128, 176–7
Ernle:
  Ant., 87
  Eliz., m. Rob. Titherley, 88
  John, 191
  Marg., w. of Ant., m. 2 Hen. Milbourne, 3 Rog. Yorke, 87–8
  Wal. (d. 1721), 174–5
  Sir Wal. (d. 1732), 174
Essex, earls of, *see* Bohun; Capell
Estcourt:
  Amy, m. Alex. Haddon, 210
  Anne, 210, 212
  Edm. (fl. 1566), 60
  Edm. (d. 1717), 210
  Edm. (d. 1758), 210
  Sir Edw., 210
  Giles (d. 1587), recorder of, and M.P. for, Salisbury, 60, 210–11
  Sir Giles (d. 1668), 210
  Giles (d. 1675), 210
  Thos., f. of Edm. (fl. 1566), 60
  Thos., s. of Edm. (fl. 1566), 60
  Thos., grds. of Edm. (fl. 1566), 60
  Thos. (d. 1746), 210
  Thos. (fl. 1758), 210
  Wal., 210
  Wm., 210
  fam., 212
Estcourt (firm), 88
Estecote, Wm., 210
estreats, 43
Etchilhampton, Rob. of, 191
Ethelred, King, 6, 28, 226
Ethelwulf, King, 238
Ethelwulf (fl. 854), 160
Eton (Bucks.), coll., 124, 250
Evangelicals, 164
Evans:
  Arthur, 239
  Cath., w. of Arthur, 239
  Jas., 102
  John, chaplain of Hindon, 102
  Thos., 162
Eve, Rob., 149
Evelyn:
  Geo., 137
  Sir John, 137–8
Everard:
  Beatrice, w. of Wm., 241
  Sir Edm., 241
  Eliz., m. Rob. of London, 241
  Felice, w. of Sir Edm., 241
  Marg., m. Thos. of Ramsbury, 241
  Rob., 214
  Susan, w. of Rob., *see* Topp
  Susan, m. Rob. Everard Balch, 214
  Wm., 241
Everett:
  Jos. Hague, 110
  Mr., 110
Everleigh, 32, 105–7, 110, **135–42**
  adv., 140
  agric., 138–9
  boundaries, 135–6
  chase, 139
  ch., 135–6, 140–1
  common meadows, 138
  cts., 106, 140
  curates, 141
  cust. tenants, 138

A HISTORY OF WILTSHIRE

Lawrence, John, *see* Uffenham
Le Grand:
Edw., 169
Wm. Lewis, 169
Lea:
Geo., 161
fam., 162
and see Legh; Leigh; Ley; Lye
Leader, Tom, 247
Lear:
Francis, rector of Bishopstone, archdeacon of Salisbury, 17
Thos., vicar of Downton, 48
leather trades, 41–3, 101
Lechlade (Glos.), 163
Leeds, duke of, *see* Godolphin, John Francis
leet jurisdiction (courts leet), 15, 43, 130, 147, 156, 163, 178, 219, 232, 248
Legg:
Jane, w. of Jos., 169
Jos. (d. *c.* 1716), 169
Jos. (fl. 1768), 175
Ric. (fl. 1576), 169
Ric. (fl. 1693), of Grateley, 169
Ric. (fl. 1736), 169
Ric. (fl. 1576–1693, others), 169
fam., 169
Legh:
Eliz., m. 1 Ant. Jas. Keck, 2 Wm. Bathhurst Pye, 241
Martha, *see* Bennet
Peter, 241
and see Lea; Leigh; Ley; Lye
Leicester:
ctss. of, *see* Amice
earldom, 109, 136–7, 168–9
earls of, 106, 120, 126, 140; *and see* Beaumont, Rob. de; Edmund; Montfort; Robert (three of the name)
honor, 108, 120, 124, 126, 137, 140, 145, 147, 168–9, 240, 248
Leicestershire, 120; *and see* Loughborough
Leigh:
Sir John, *see* Lye
R. C., 34
and see Lea; Legh; Ley; Lye
Leland, John, 24
Leofing (fl. 1066), 69
Leofwine (fl. 987), 226
Leslie, E. H. J., 225
Lestrange:
Joan, *see* Ingham
Sir Rog., Lord Strange, 60
Levesham, John, 169
Levric (fl. 1066), 244
Lewes (Suss.), priory, 172
Lewis:
Anne, 74
Chris., 74
Geo., 205–6
Ric., vicar of Netheravon, 179
Miss, 208
Ley:
Hen., earl of Marlborough, 120
Jas., earl of Marlborough, 120
and see Lea; Legh; Leigh; Lye
liberties (franchises), 1, 15, 106–7, 129–30, 147, 156, 162–3, 169, 178, 199, 206, 226, 248; *and see* assize of bread and ale; blindhouse; estreats; felons' chattels; frankpledge; free fishing; free warren; gallows; infangthief; leet jurisdiction; outfangthief; pillory; prisons; suit; stallage; stocks; tumbril; vee de naam; writs
libraries, 27, 238; *and see* reading rooms
Lichfield (Staffs.), cath. ch., prebend in, 46
dbury camp, *see* Chisenbury, East

Lidd, riv., 159
Liddington, rector of, *see* Moore, John
Light, H. W. M., vicar of Wroughton, 251
Lilford, Baron, *see* Powys
lime-making, 42
Linch, *see* Lynch
Lincoln:
ctsses. of, *see* Lacy; Longespée
earls of, *see* Roumare
Lincoln, cath. ch.:
canon, *see* Fauntleroy
prebend, 48
Lincolnshire, *see* Brocklesby; Elsham; Ravendale, East
Lindley (Yorks. W.R.), 33
Linford:
Joan, *see* Woodfalls
Thos., 33
Lingiur:
Alice, m. Wm. de la Falaise, 69
Phil., 69
liquid-manure drill manufacture, 219
Lire (Eure, France), abbey, 171–2, 175
Lisle:
Humph., 240–2
Joan, w. of John, ? m. 2 Geof. Rookley, 9
John de, 9
Lister (Lyster):
E. G., 226–7
F. V., 125, 129
R. A., & Co. Ltd., 247
Ric., 170
Littlecote, John, 210
Littlecote (in Ramsbury), 241
Littlecott:
Alice, m. Rob. Thornborough, 122
John of, 124
Ralph, 121–2
Sim. (fl. after 1484), 122
Sim. of (fl. 1333), 121
Sim. of (fl. 1360, another), 121
Littlecott (in Enford), 105, 107, 117, 126, 129–30, 134
agric., 128
dom. archit., 118
farms, 122–3, 128, 131
glebe, 131
inc., 124, 128, 131
Littlecott Farm, 122
Littlecott Ho., 118
Lower Farm, 123
man., 121–4
mill, 126, 128–9, 131
pop., 117
tithes, 124, 131
Llanthony, *see* Gloucester
Llewellins & James, 234
Lloyd, Nowes, rector of Little Hinton, vicar of Bishopstone, vicar of Enbourne, 163
Lloyds Bank Ltd., 168
Lock:
Rob., 87
Susanna, w. of Rob., 87
Lockeridge (in Overton), 105, 181, 183–4, 192, 194–5, 198–201, 203, 208
agric., 196
bridge, 185
ch., 200
ct., 199
cust. tenants, 196
dom. archit., 185–6
farms, 188, 190, 196
glebe, 196
inc., 196, 200
inns, 185–6
Lockeridge Ho., 186, 190
man., 189–90, 192, 194, 196–8, 200
pop., 184, 186
prot. nonconf., 202
roads, 184–5

sch., 186, 203
tithes, 191–2, 196, 199–200
windmill, 198
woodland, 197–8
Lodden, riv., 82
Lof:
Rog., 244
Wm., 244
London:
Eliz., *see* Everard
Rob. of, 241
London, 15–16, 49, 98, 157, 179, 219
aldermen, *see* Barker, Wm.; Chaplin, Sir Francis; Reed, Sir Bart.
bp., *see* Lowth, Rob.
cath. ch. of St. Paul, prebend in, 48
Charterhouse, 240–2, 252
governors, 241
citizens, 148, 249; *and see* Holbeach, Wm.; Topp, John (d. 1596)
City, 137
hosp. of St. Kath. by the Tower, 124–5, 127, 130–1
and see Christ's Hospital; National Portrait Gallery; Royal Academy
London General Assembly, 96
Long:
Edw., 126
F. S., 188
Gifford, 126
Hen., 110
Joan, w. of Thos., 126
Mary, *see* Lye
R. C. (d. 1869), 188, 192
Ric. (fl. late 17th cent.), 110
Thos., 125
W. (fl. 1870), 188
Wm. (d. by 1524), 7
Wm. (fl. 1656), 110
Long Close (in Downton), *see* Wick
Longespée:
Marg., ctss. of Salisbury, m. Hen. de Lacy, earl of Lincoln, 172
Sir Wm., 172
Longford, Nic., 249
Longford (in Britford), 73
Longford Castle, 30–1, 65; *and see* Longford estate
park, 62–3
water-meadows, 66
Longford estate, 28, 32, 38, 41, 54–5, 57–8, 63–6, 70–1, 73–4
Longstreet (in Enford), 105, 107, 117, 126, 129–30, 133
agric., 128
Baden Farm, 123
bridge, 118
dom. archit., 118
farms, 118, 122–3, 128, 134
'Fyfhyde' (Fifield), 'Langefyfyde' (Long Fifield), 117
glebe, 131
Grange, the, 123
inc., 128, 131
inn, 118
Longstreet Ho., 122
man., 122–3
pop., 117
sch., 134
tithes, 124, 131
water-meadow, 128
Lonsdale, V. O., 74
Loosehanger (in Downton), *see* Redlynch
Loretta, w. of Rob., earl of Leicester, 136
Lott:
John, 133, 221
John, s. of John, 221, 234
Loughborough (Leics.), 133, 180
Lousley, John, *see* Lansley
Lovel:
Francis (d. ? 1487), Vct. Lovel, 240, 246

270